DATE DUE

DEMCO 38-297

Fundamental accounting principles

THE WILLARD J. GRAHAM SERIES IN ACCOUNTING

Consulting Editor
ROBERT N. ANTHONY
Harvard University

Fundamental accounting principles

WILLIAM W. PYLE

KERMIT D. LARSON
The University of Texas at Austin

Ninth edition

RICHARD D. IRWIN, INC.
Homewood, Illinois   60430

IRWIN-DORSEY LIMITED
Georgetown, Ontario   L7G 4B3

1981

© RICHARD D. IRWIN, INC., 1955, 1959, 1963, 1966, 1969, 1972, 1975, 1978, and 1981

ISBN 0-256-02386-7
Library of Congress Catalog Card No. 80–81156

Printed in the United States of America

4 5 6 7 8 9 0 K 8 7 6 5 4 3 2 1

LEARNING SYSTEMS COMPANY—
a division of Richard D. Irwin, Inc.—has developed a
PROGRAMMED LEARNING AID
to accompany texts in this subject area.
Copies can be purchased through your bookstore
or by writing PLAIDS,
1818 Ridge Road, Homewood, Illinois 60430.

Dedication

During the past year, the accounting community lost a distinguished colleague and widely cherished friend. Dr. John Arch White died on May 9, 1980, after devoting his professional life to students, faculty associates, and his University. His contributions to accounting included but extended far beyond his co-authorship of several previous editions of this book. For example, he served as Accounting Department Chairman and Dean of the College of Business Administration at The University of Texas, and as President of the American Accounting Association. His life was a rare combination of leadership and personal warmth. We are privileged to join the many thousands of his students and accounting friends in this dedication to him.

Preface

■ *Fundamental Accounting Principles* is intended for use in the first, year-long, accounting course at the college and university level. Both financial and managerial accounting topics are covered, so that the course will be useful to students in their personal affairs, in their varied areas of educational specialty and, for those who so choose, in their subsequent careers in accountancy. The text is focused on the concepts and principles which guide the development of accounting information. It shows the student how accounting data are accumulated and how the resulting reports and statements can be effectively used in decision making. Thus, a solid foundation is built for later courses in business as well as accounting. In writing *Fundamental Accounting Principles,* we have assumed that the student's previous business contacts, vocabulary, and understanding of business practices are limited. Consequently, all new terms, business practices, and accounting principles are fully explained when first introduced.

Highlights of the Ninth Edition and its supplementary materials

1. The book continues to be organized into 28 chapters, which allows complete coverage in a concentrated, year-long, accounting course or selective coverage in a more moderately paced course.
2. Primary reliance in the early chapters continues to be on the easily understood single proprietorship. However, the Ninth Edition also begins in the first chapter to build the vocabulary and knowledge

necessary for an understanding of corporations and their accounting. Consequently, by the time chapters are devoted exclusively to corporation accounting, students are comfortable with this form of business organization.

3. As in the previous edition, important accounting concepts and principles are integrated into the topical discussions rather than being placed in an isolated separate chapter. As a result, students are able to see the practical importance of each concept or principle immediately upon learning its definition and conceptual significance.

4. Both the conceptual significance of each accounting principle and the procedures used in its application are presented. Thus, both the *why* and the *how to apply* of each principle are explained.

5. In response to requests by adopters, the coverage of corporate bonds payable has been combined with stock investments and is presented in Chapter 17.

6. The chapter on current and long-term liabilities has been rewritten to include coverage of present values in the body of the chapter. The chapter also has been expanded to cover liabilities from leasing, a very important topic in today's business world.

7. A concise but expanded explanation and illustration of reversing entries is present in Chapter 8. This was facilitated by a revised and simpler presentation of notes receivable.

8. Previous adopters should note that the method of treating inventories on a work sheet has been changed to appear as adjusting entries rather than as closing entries. While this change is not of conceptual importance, the new method is easily presented to students and was adopted in response to the many, many requests from adopters.

9. The questions, exercises, and problems at the end of each chapter have been thoroughly revised, and provide an expanded range of assignment material, both in terms of length of assignment and degree of difficulty. The alternative set of problems allows variability in assignments from semester to semester, or planned repetition of selected problem types. In addition, one to three *provocative problems* are provided and may be used to help students analyze the material in a somewhat more complex or uncertain context as would be true in the real world.

10. As in the previous edition, learning objectives stated in terms of specific activities the student should master are enumerated at the beginning of each chapter. These objectives are also reviewed in the *study guides* for the Ninth Edition. A glossary of new words and terms is presented at the end of each chapter; and the study guides have been expanded to include a comprehensive review of the glossary.

11. An example of corporate financial statements, including footnotes, is presented in an appendix at the end of the book. The financial

statements show the real-world applicability of many of the principles discussed. They also suggest to the student the relevance of further study in accounting.

12. Several chapters have been updated to reflect new pronouncements and recent events. The latest relevant pronouncements of authoritative bodies such as the Financial Accounting Standards Board and the Securities and Exchange Commission are presented and footnoted throughout the book.

13. Chapter 28 on income taxes has been completely updated and now reflects new tax rates on corporations and individuals, new exclusion rules on interest and dividend income, deletion of the alternative tax on capital gains for individuals, new long-term capital gains deductions, and other tax law developments.

14. Numerous sections have been revised or reorganized to improve readability and teaching effectiveness. These include expansions and revisions in the variety of supplementary materials as well as changes in the text.

The supplementary materials for the Ninth Edition include:

Working papers   Separate booklets of working papers for solutions to the problems and alternate problems are provided for Chapters 1–14 and Chapters 14–28. To eliminate much of the tedious "busy work" in completing assigned problems, account titles and beginning account balances are provided in the working papers. Also, account titles and, where possible, account balances are entered on the work sheet forms. Note that Chapter 14 is included in both booklets to increase flexibility in course design.

Study guides   The study guides and solutions for the Ninth Edition have been approximately doubled in length, so that separate booklets are now available for Chapters 1–14 and Chapters 14–28. Learning objectives, an outline of major points, and a variety of self-testing questions and short problems with answers are included for each chapter.

Practice sets   Three practice sets are available for use with *Fundamental Accounting Principles*. The first is designed to illustrate accounting for a small merchandising business organized as a corporation. It uses columnar journals and may be assigned after the completion of Chapter 8. An alternative single proprietorship set has similar objectives but includes a variety of business papers to be used in analyzing transactions. A third practice set pertains to a manufacturing company and may be assigned after coverage of Chapter 22.

Achievement tests   Revised achievement tests are available in bulk to adopters. Ten tests plus two final examinations make up a series, and three alternative series are available.

Additional examination materials   The booklet of additional examination and quiz material has been revised and expanded. Included in the booklet are solutions to the examination questions in the booklet and solutions to the achievement tests. A large number of objective questions are available to adopters for use in computer-gradable examinations.

Solutions Manual Complete solutions to all of the questions, exercises, and problems in the text are provided in the *Solutions Manual*. The estimated time required by an average student to complete each problem is included.

Transparencies The set of transparencies of the solutions to problems and alternative problems has been expanded to include the exercises following each chapter. Additionally, the illustrative transparencies for use in teaching have once again been expanded.

Check figures This list of key figures gives students an indication of possible errors in their solutions to the problems and alternate problems. The check figures are available in quantity from the publisher.

We are indebted to a large number of people for their comments, criticisms, and varied contributions to the Ninth Edition. Among those we wish to acknowledge are: Robert Arogeti, Deloitte Haskins & Sells; William J. Coffey, Pace University; Al A. Evans, Evangel College; Anna Fowler, the University of Texas at Austin; Esther Grant, Hillsborough Community College; Carl High, New York City Community College; Ralph P. Knost, University of Cincinnati; James E. Lane, Indiana State University; Marie Celeste Lierman, Ernst & Whinney; Earl Monical, University of Wisconsin, River Falls; Bernard Newman, Pace University; Robert H. Nilsen, Milwaukee Area Community College; Katherine Olson, Spokane Falls Community College; Robert L. Pease, Penn Valley Community College; H. Michael Ryan, Jr., Essex Community College; Daniel Short, The University of Texas at Austin; Frank F. Silloway, Essex Community College; Jeffrey Slater, North Shore Community College; Marvin J. Slovacek, San Antonio College; Anita Sweeney, Ernst & Whinney; Charles E. Thompson, Jr., El Camino College; and Bill Wells, Tulsa Junior College.

William W. Pyle
Kermit D. Larson

Contents

PART ONE
Introduction

1

Accounting, an introduction to its concepts

After studying Chapter 1, you should be able to:

☐ Tell the function of accounting and the nature and purpose of the information it provides.

☐ List the main fields of accounting and tell the kinds of work carried on in each field.

☐ List the accounting concepts and principles introduced and tell the effect of each on accounting records and statements.

☐ Describe the purpose of a balance sheet and of an income statement and tell the kinds of information presented in each.

☐ Recognize and be able to indicate the effects of transactions on the elements of an accounting equation.

☐ Prepare simple financial statements.

☐ Tell in each case the extent of the responsibility of a business owner for the debts of a business organized as a single proprietorship, a partnership, or a corporation.

☐ Define or explain the words and phrases listed in the chapter Glossary.

Accounting, an introduction to its concepts

■ Accounting is a service activity. Its function is to provide quantitative information about economic entities. The information is primarily financial in nature and is intended to be useful in making economic decisions.[1] If the entity for which the information is provided is a business, for example, the information is used by its management in answering questions such as: What are the resources of the business? What debts does it owe? Does it have earnings? Are expenses too large in relation to sales? Is too little or too much merchandise being kept? Are amounts owed by customers being collected rapidly? Will the business be able to meet its own debts as they mature? Should the plant be expanded? Should a new product be introduced? Should selling prices be increased?

In addition, grantors of credit such as banks, wholesale houses, and manufacturers use accounting information in answering such questions as: Are the customer's earning prospects good? What is his debt-paying ability? Has he paid his debts promptly in the past? Should he be granted additional credit?[2] Likewise, governmental units use accounting information in regulating businesses and collecting taxes, labor

---

[1] Accounting Principles Board, "Basic Concepts and Accounting Principles Underlying Financial Statements of Business Enterprises," *APB Statement No. 4* (New York: AICPA, October 1970), par. 9. Copyright (1970) by the American Institute of CPAs.

[2] Obviously, women as well as men are customers—and students and accountants. In this discussion as in others not referring to a specific person, the pronouns *he, his,* and *him* are used in their generic sense and should be understood to include both men and women.

unions use it in negotiating working conditions and wage agreements, and investors make wide use of accounting data in investment decisions.

WHY STUDY ACCOUNTING

Information for use in answering questions like the ones listed is conveyed in accounting reports. If a person is to use these reports effectively, he or she must have some understanding of how their data were gathered and the figures put together. He or she must appreciate the limitations of the data and the extent to which portions are based on estimates rather than precise measurements, and must understand accounting terms and concepts. Needless to say, these understandings are gained in a study of accounting.

Another reason to study accounting is to make it one's lifework. A career in accounting can be very interesting and highly rewarding.

ACCOUNTANCY AS A PROFESSION

Over the past half century accountancy as a profession has attained a stature comparable with that of law or medicine. All states license *certified public accountants* or *CPAs* just as they license doctors and lawyers. The licensing helps ensure a high standard of professional service. Only individuals who have passed a rigorous examination of their accounting and related knowledge, met other education and experience requirements, and have received a license may designate themselves as certified public accountants.

The requirements for the CPA certificate or license vary with the states. In general an applicant must be a citizen, 21 years of age, of unquestioned moral character, and a college graduate with a major concentration in accounting. Also the applicant must pass a rigorous three-day examination in accounting theory, accounting practice, auditing, and business law. The three-day examination is uniform in all states and is given on the same days in all states. It is prepared by the American Institute of Certified Public Accountants (AICPA) which is the national professional organization of CPAs. In addition to the examination, many states require an applicant to have one or more years of work experience in the office of a CPA or the equivalent before the certificate is granted. However, some states do not require the work experience and some states permit the applicant to substitute one or more years of experience for the college level education requirement. On this score the AICPA's Committee on Education and Experience Requirements for CPAs expressed the opinion that at least five years of college study are necessary to obtain the body of knowledge needed to be a CPA. For those meeting this standard, it recommends that no previous work experience should be required.[3] However, it will be several years before all states accept this recommendation. In the meantime, interested students can learn the requirements of any state in which they are interested by writing to its state board of accountancy.

THE WORK OF AN ACCOUNTANT

Accountants are commonly employed in three main fields: (1) in public accounting, (2) in private accounting, or (3) in government.

Public accounting

Public accountants are individuals who offer their professional services and those of their employees to the public for a fee, in much the same manner as a lawyer or a consulting engineer.

Auditing   The principal service offered by a public accountant is auditing. Banks commonly require an *audit* of the financial statements of a company applying for a sizable loan, with the audit being performed by a CPA who is not an employee of the audited concern but an independent professional person working for a fee. Companies whose securities are offered for sale to the public generally must also have such an audit before the securities may be sold. Thereafter additional audits must be made periodically if the securities are to continue being traded.

The purpose of an audit is to lend credibility to a company's financial statements. In making the audit, the auditor carefully examines the company's statements and the accounting records from which they were prepared. In the examination, the auditor makes sure the statements fairly reflect the company's financial position and operating results and were prepared in accordance with generally accepted accounting principles from records kept in accordance with such principles. Banks, investors, and others rely on the information in a company's financial statements in making loans, granting credit, and in buying and selling securities. They depend on the auditor to verify the dependability of the information the statements contain.

Management advisory services   In addition to auditing, accountants commonly offer *management advisory services*. An accountant gains from an audit an intimate knowledge of the audited company's accounting procedures and its financial position. He or she is thus in an excellent position to offer constructive suggestions for improving the procedures and strengthening the position. Clients expect these suggestions as a useful audit by-product. They also commonly engage

---

[3] *Report of the Committee on Education and Experience Requirements for CPAs* (New York: AICPA, 1969), p. 11. Copyright (1969) by the American Institute of CPAs.

certified public accountants to conduct additional investigations for the purpose of determining ways in which their operations may be improved. Such investigations and the suggestions growing from them are known as management advisory services.

Management advisory services include the design, installation, and improvement of a client's general accounting system and any related information system it may have for determining and controlling costs. They also include the application of machine methods to these systems, plus advice in financial planning, budgeting, forecasting, and inventory control. In fact, they include all phases of information systems and related matters.

Tax services   In this day of increasing complexity in income and other tax laws and continued high tax rates, few important business decisions are made without consideration being given to their tax effect. A certified public accountant, through training and experience, is well qualified to render important service in this area. The service includes not only the preparation and filing of tax returns but also advice as to how transactions may be completed so as to incur the smallest tax.

Private accounting

When an accountant is employed by a single enterprise, he or she is said to be in private accounting. A small business may employ only one accountant or it may depend upon the services of a public accountant and employ none. A large business, on the other hand, may have more than a hundred employees in its accounting department. They commonly work under the supervision of a chief accounting officer, commonly called the *controller*, who is often a CPA. The title, controller, results from the fact that one of the chief uses of accounting data is to control the operations of a business.

The one accountant of the small business and the accounting department of a large concern do a variety of work, including general accounting, cost accounting, budgeting, and internal auditing.

General accounting   *General accounting* has to do primarily with recording transactions and preparing financial and other reports for the use of management, owners, creditors, and governmental agencies. The private accountant may design or help the public accountant design the system used in recording the transactions. He or she will also supervise the clerical or data processing staff in recording the transactions and preparing the reports.

Cost accounting   The phase of accounting that has to do with collecting, determining, and controlling costs, particularly costs of producing a given product or service, is called *cost accounting*. A knowledge of costs and controlling costs is vital to good management. Therefore, a large company may have a number of accountants engaged in this activity.

Budgeting Planning business activities before they occur is called *budgeting*. The objective of budgeting is to provide management with an intelligent plan for future operations. Then after the budget plan has been put into effect, it provides summaries and reports that can be used to compare actual accomplishments with the plan. Many large companies have a number of people who devote all their time to this phase of accounting.

Internal auditing In addition to an annual audit by a firm of certified public accountants, many companies maintain a staff of internal auditors. The internal auditors constantly check the records prepared and maintained in each department or company branch. It is their responsibility to make sure that established accounting procedures and management directives are being followed throughout the company.

Governmental accounting

Furnishing governmental services is a vast and complicated operation in which accounting is just as indispensable as in business. Elected and appointed officials must rely on data accumulated by means of accounting if they are to complete effectively their administrative duties. Accountants are responsible for the accumulation of these data. Accountants also check and audit the millions of income, payroll, and sales tax returns that accompany the tax payments upon which governmental units depend. And finally, federal and state agencies, such as the Interstate Commerce Commission, Securities and Exchange Commission, and so on, use accountants in many capacities in their regulation of business.

ACCOUNTING AND BOOKKEEPING

Many people confuse *accounting* and *bookkeeping* and look upon them as one and the same. In effect they identify the whole with one of its parts. Actually, bookkeeping is only part of accounting, the record-making part. To keep books is to record transactions, and a bookkeeper is one who records transactions. The work is often routine and primarily clerical in nature. The work of an accountant goes far beyond this, as a rereading of the previous section will show.

ACCOUNTING STATEMENTS

Accounting statements are the end product of the accounting process, but a good place to begin the study of accounting. They are used to convey a concise picture of the profitability and financial position of a business. The two most important are the income statement and the balance sheet.

The income statement

A company's *income statement* (see Illustration 1–1) is perhaps more important than its balance sheet. It shows whether or not the business achieved or failed to achieve its primary objective—earning a "profit" or net income. A *net income* is earned when revenues exceed expenses, but a *net loss* is incurred if the expenses exceed the revenues. An income statement is prepared by listing the revenues earned during the period, listing the expenses incurred in earning the revenues, and subtracting the expenses from the revenues to determine if a net income or a net loss was incurred.

Coast Realty
Income Statement for Year Ended December 31, 19—

Revenues:		
Commissions earned	$31,450	
Property management fees	1,200	
Total revenues		$32,650
Operating expenses:		
Salaries expense	$ 7,800	
Rent expense	2,400	
Utilities expense	315	
Telephone expense	560	
Advertising expense	2,310	
Total operating expenses		13,385
Net income		$19,265

Illustration 1–1

Revenues are inflows of cash or other properties received in exchange for goods or services provided to customers. Rents, dividends, and interest earned are also revenues. Coast Realty of Illustration 1–1 had revenue inflows from services which totaled $32,650.

Expenses are goods and services consumed in operating a business or other economic unit. Coast Realty consumed the services of its employees (salaries expense), the services of a telephone company, and so on.

The heading of an income statement tells the name of the business for which it is prepared and the time period covered by the statement. Both bits of information are important. However, the time covered is extremely significant, since the items on the statement must be interpreted in relation to the period of time. For example, the item "Commissions earned, $31,450" on the income statement of Illustration 1–1 has little significance until it is known that the amount represents one year's commissions and not the commissions of a week or a month.

The balance sheet

The purpose of a *balance sheet* is to show the financial position of a business on a specific date. It is often called a *position statement.* Financial position is shown by listing the *assets* of the business, its *liabilities* or debts, and the *equity of the owner or owners.* The name of the business and the date are given in the balance sheet heading. It is understood that the item amounts shown are as of the close of business on that date.

Before a business manager, investor, or other person can make effective judgments based on balance sheet information, he or she must gain several concepts and understandings. To illustrate, assume that on August 3, Joan Ball began a new business, called World Travel Agency. During the day she completed these transactions in the name of the business:

Aug. 3   Invested $18,000 of her personal savings in the business.
    3   Paid $15,000 of the agency's cash for a small office building and the land on which it was built (cost of the building, $10,000, and cost of the land, $5,000).
    3   Purchased on *credit* from Office Equipment Company office equipment costing $2,000. (Purchased on credit means purchased with a promise to pay at a later date.)

A balance sheet reflecting the effects of these transactions appears in Illustration 1–2. It shows that after completing the transactions the agency has four assets, a $2,000 debt, and that its owner has an $18,000 equity in the business.

World Travel Agency
Balance Sheet, August 3, 19—

Assets		Liabilities	
Cash	$ 3,000	Accounts payable	$ 2,000
Office equipment	2,000		
Building	10,000		
Land	5,000	*Owner's Equity*	
		Joan Ball, capital	18,000
Total assets	$20,000	Total equities	$20,000

Illustration 1–2

Observe that the two sides of the balance sheet are equal. This is where it gets its name. Its two sides must always be equal because one side shows the resources of the business and the other shows who supplied the resources. For example, World Travel Agency has $20,000 of resources (assets) of which $18,000 were supplied by its owner and $2,000 by its creditors. (*Creditors* are individuals and organizations to whom the business owes debts.)

ASSETS, LIABILITIES, AND OWNER'S EQUITY

The assets of a business are, in general, the properties or economic resources owned by the business. They include cash, amounts owed to the business by its customers for goods and services sold to them on credit (called *accounts receivable*), merchandise held for sale by the business, supplies, equipment, buildings, and land. Assets may also include such intangible rights as those granted by a patent or copyright.

The liabilities of a business are its debts. They include amounts owed to creditors for goods and services bought on credit (called *accounts payable*), salaries and wages owed employees, taxes payable, notes payable, and mortgages payable.

When a business is owned by one person, the owner's interest or equity in the assets of the business is shown on a balance sheet by listing the person's name, followed by the word "capital," and then the amount of the equity. The use of the word "capital" comes from the idea that the owner has furnished the business with resources or "capital" equal to the amount of the equity.

Liabilities are also sometimes called *equities*. An equity is a right, claim, or interest; and a liability represents a claim or right to be paid. The law recognizes this right. If a business fails to pay its creditors, the law gives the creditors the right to force the sale of the assets of the business to secure money to meet creditor claims. Furthermore, if the assets are sold, the creditors are paid first, with any remainder going to the business owner. Obviously, then, by law creditor claims take precedence over those of a business owner.

Since creditor claims take precedence over those of an owner, an owner's equity in a business is always a residual amount. Creditors recognize this. When they examine the balance sheet of a business, they are always interested in the share of its assets furnished by creditors and the share furnished by its owner or owners. The creditors recognize that if the business must be liquidated and its assets sold, the shrinkage in converting the assets into cash must exceed the equity of the owner or owners before the creditors will lose.

GENERALLY ACCEPTED ACCOUNTING PRINCIPLES

An understanding of financial statement information requires a knowledge of the generally accepted accounting principles that govern the accumulation and presentation of the data appearing on such statements. A common definition of the word "principle" is: "A broad general law or rule adopted or professed as a guide to action; a settled ground or basis of conduct or practice. . . ." Consequently, generally accepted accounting principles may be described as broad rules adopted by the accounting profession as guides in measuring, recording, and reporting the financial affairs and activities of a business. They consist of a number of concepts, principles, and procedures which are first discussed at the points shown in the following list. They also are referred to again and again throughout this text in order to increase your understanding of the information conveyed by accounting data.

	First introduced	
	Chapter	Page
Generally accepted concepts:		
1. Business entity concept	1	13
2. Continuing-concern concept...........	1	14
3. Stable-dollar concept.................	1	15
4. Time-period concept	3	75
Generally accepted principles:		
1. Cost principle	1	13
2. Objectivity principle	1	14
3. Realization principle	1	20
4. Matching principle	3	84
5. Full-disclosure principle	8	282
6. Materiality principle	8	294
7. Consistency principle.................	9	313
8. Conservatism principle	9	317
Generally accepted procedures:		
These specify the ways data are processed and reported and are described and discussed throughout the text.		

SOURCE OF ACCOUNTING PRINCIPLES

Generally accepted accounting principles are not natural laws in the sense of the laws of physics and chemistry. They are man-made rules that depend for their authority upon their general acceptance by the accounting profession. They have evolved from the experience and thinking of members of the accounting profession, aided by such groups as the American Institute of Certified Public Accountants, the Financial Accounting Standards Board, the American Accounting Association, and the Securities and Exchange Commission.

The American Institute of Certified Public Accountants (AICPA) has long been influential in describing and defining generally accepted accounting principles. During the years from 1939 to 1959 it published a series of *Accounting Research Bulletins* which were recognized as expressions of generally accepted accounting principles. In 1959 it established an 18-member Accounting Principles Board (APB) composed of practicing accountants, educators, and representatives of industry, and gave the board authority to issue opinions that were to be regarded by members of the AICPA as authoritative expressions of generally accepted accounting principles. During the years 1962 through 1973 the Board issued 31 such opinions. Added importance was given to these opinions beginning in 1964 when the AICPA ruled that its members must disclose in footnotes to published financial statements of the companies they audit any departure from generally accepted accounting principles as set forth in the *Opinions of the Accounting Principles Board.*

In 1973, after 11 years of activity, the Accounting Principles Board was terminated. Its place was taken by a seven-member Financial Accounting Standards Board (FASB). The seven members serve full time, receive salaries, and must resign from accounting firms and other employment. They must have a knowledge of accounting, finance, and business, but are not required to be CPAs. This differs from the Accounting Principles Board, all members of which were CPAs, who served part time, without pay, and continued their affiliations with accounting firms and other employment. The FASB issues *Statements of Financial Accounting Standards* which like the *Opinions of the Accounting Principles Board* must be considered as authoritative expressions of generally accepted accounting principles. Both the *Statements* and *Opinions* are referred to again and again throughout this text.

The American Accounting Association, an organization with strong academic ties, has also been influential in describing and defining generally accepted accounting principles. It has sponsored a number of research studies and has published many articles dealing with accounting principles. However, its influence has not been as great as the AICPA, since it has no power to impose its views on the accounting profession but must depend upon the prestige of its authors and the logic of their arguments.

The Securities and Exchange Commission (SEC) plays a prominent role in financial reporting. The SEC is an independent quasi-judicial agency of the federal government. It was established to administer the provisions of various securities and exchange acts dealing with the distribution and sale of securities. Such securities, to be sold, must be registered with the SEC. This requires the filing of audited financial statements prepared in accordance with the rules of the SEC. Furthermore, the information contained in the statements must be kept current by filing additional audited annual reports. The SEC does not appraise the registered securities. However, it attempts to safeguard investors by requiring that all material facts affecting the worth of the securities be made public and that no important information be withheld. Its rules carry over into the annual reports of large companies and have contributed to the usefulness of these reports. In a real sense, the SEC should be viewed as the dominant authority in respect to the establishment of accounting principles. However, it has relied on the accounting profession, particularly the AICPA and the FASB, to determine and enforce accepted accounting principles. At the same time it has pressured the accounting profession to reduce the number of acceptable accounting procedures.

UNDERSTANDING ACCOUNTING PRINCIPLES

Your authors believe that an understanding of *accounting principles* is best conveyed with examples illustrating the application of each principle. The examples must be such that a student can understand at his or her level of experience. Consequently, three *accounting concepts* and two accounting principles are introduced here. Discussions of the others are delayed until later in the text when meaningful examples of their application can be developed.

Business entity concept

Under the *business entity concept*, for accounting purposes, every business is conceived to be and is treated as a separate entity, separate and distinct from its owner or owners and from every other business. Businesses are so conceived and treated because, insofar as a specific business is concerned, the purpose of accounting is to record its transactions and periodically report its financial position and profitability. Consequently, the records and reports of a business should not include either the transactions or assets of another business or the personal assets and transactions of its owner or owners. To include either distorts the financial position and profitability of the business. For example, the personally owned automobile of a business owner should not be included among the assets of the owner's business. Likewise, its gas, oil, and repairs should not be treated as an expense of the business, for to do so distorts the reported financial position and profitability of the business.

Cost principle

In addition to the *business entity concept,* an accounting principle called the *cost principle* should be borne in mind when reading financial statements. Under this principle all goods and services purchased are recorded at cost and appear on the statements at cost. For example, if a business pays $50,000 for land to be used in carrying on its operations, the purchase should be recorded at $50,000. It makes no difference if the owner and several competent outside appraisers thought the land "worth" at least $60,000. It cost $50,000 and should appear on the balance sheet at that amount. Furthermore, if five years later, due to booming real estate prices, the land's market value has doubled, this makes no difference either. The land cost $50,000 and should continue to appear on the balance sheet at $50,000 even though its estimated market value is twice that.

In applying the *cost principle,* costs are measured on a cash or cash-equivalent basis. If the consideration given for an asset or service is cash, cost is measured at the entire cash outlay made to secure the asset or service. If the consideration is something other than cash, cost is measured at the cash-equivalent value of the consideration given or the cash-equivalent value of the thing received, whichever is more clearly evident.[4]

Why are assets and services recorded at cost and why are the balance sheet amounts for the assets not changed from time to time to reflect changing market values? The *objectivity principle* and the *continuing-concern concept* supply answers to these questions.

Objectivity principle

The *objectivity principle* supplies the reason transactions are recorded at cost, since it requires that transaction amounts be objectively established. Whims and fancies plus, for example, something like an opinion of management that an asset is "worth more than it cost" have no place in accounting. To be fully useful, accounting information must be based on objective data. As a rule, costs are objective, since they normally are established by buyers and sellers, both striking the best possible bargains for themselves.

Continuing-concern concept

Balance sheet amounts for assets used in carrying on the operations of a business are not changed from time to time to reflect changing market values. A balance sheet is prepared under the assumption that the business for which it is prepared will continue in operation, and as a continuing or going concern the assets used in carrying on its operations are not for sale. In fact, they cannot be sold without disrupting the business. Therefore, since the assets are for use in the business and are not for sale, their current market values are not particularly relevant and need not be shown. Also, without a sale, their current market values usually cannot be objectively established, as is required by the *objectivity principle.*

The *continuing-concern or going-concern concept* applies in most situations. However, if a business is about to be sold or liquidated, the *continuing-concern concept* and the *cost and objectivity principles* do not apply in the preparation of its statements. In such cases amounts other than costs, such as estimated market values, become more useful and informative.

---

[4] APB, "Accounting for Nonmonetary Transactions," *APB Opinion No. 29* (New York: AICPA, 1973), par. 18. Copyright (1970) by the American Institute of CPAs.

The stable-dollar concept

In our country accounting transactions are measured, recorded, and reported in terms of dollars. In the measuring, recording, and reporting process the dollar has been treated as a stable unit of measure, like a gallon, an acre, or a mile. However, unfortunately the dollar, like other currencies, is not a stable unit of measure. When the general price level (the average of all prices) changes, the value of money (its purchasing power) also changes. For example, during the past ten years the general price level has approximately doubled, which means that over these years the purchasing power of the dollar has declined from 100 cents to approximately 50 cents.

Nevertheless, although the instability of the dollar is recognized, accountants in their reports continue to add and subtract items acquired in different years with dollars of different sizes. In effect they ignore changes in the size of the measuring unit. For example, assume a company purchased land some years ago for $10,000 and sold it today for $20,000. If during this period the purchasing power of the dollar declined from 100 cents to 50 cents, it can be said that the company is no better off for having purchased the land for $10,000 and sold it for $20,000 because the $20,000 will buy no more goods and services today than the $10,000 at the time of the purchase. Yet, using the dollar to measure both transactions, the accountant reports a $10,000 gain from the purchase and sale.

The instability of the dollar as a unit of measure is recognized. Therefore, the question is should the amounts shown on financial statements be adjusted for changes in the purchasing power of the dollar. Techniques have been devised to convert the historical dollars of statement amounts into dollars of current purchasing power. Such statements are called *price-level-adjusted statements*. Also, by consulting catalogs and securing current prices from manufacturers and wholesalers, it is possible to determine replacement costs for various assets owned. As a result, such costs could be used in preparing financial statements. However, financial statements showing current replacement costs and also price-level-adjusted statements require subjective judgments in their preparation. Consequently, most accountants are of the opinion that the traditional statements based on the *stable-dollar concept* are best for general publication and use. Nevertheless, they also recognize that the information conveyed by traditional statements can be made more useful if accompanied by replacement cost and/or price-level-adjusted information. This is discussed in Chapter 20.

From the discussions of the *cost principle*, the *continuing-concern concept*, and *stable-dollar concept*, it should be recognized that in most instances a balance sheet does not show the amounts at which the listed assets can be sold or replaced. Nor does it show the "worth" of the business for which it was prepared, since some of the listed assets may be salable for much more or much less than the dollar amounts at which they are shown.

BUSINESS ORGANIZATIONS

Accounting is applicable to all economic entities such as business concerns, schools, churches, fraternities, and so on. However, this text will focus on accounting for business concerns organized as single proprietorships, partnerships, and corporations.

Single proprietorships

An unincorporated business owned by one person is called a *single proprietorship*. Small retail stores and service enterprises are commonly operated as single proprietorships. There are no legal requirements to be met in starting a single proprietorship business. Furthermore, single proprietorships are the most numerous of all business concerns.

In accounting for a single proprietorship, the *business entity concept* is applied and the business is treated as a separate entity, separate and distinct from its owner. However, insofar as the debts of the business are concerned, no such legal distinction is made. The owner of a single proprietorship business is personally responsible for its debts. As a result, if the assets of such a business are not sufficient to pay its debts, the personal assets of the proprietor may be taken to satisfy the claims of the business creditors.

Partnerships

When a business is owned by two or more people as partners, it is called a *partnership*. Like a single proprietorship, there are no special legal requirements to be met in starting a partnership business. All that is required is for two or more people to enter into an agreement to operate a business as partners. The agreement becomes a contract and may be either oral or written, but to avoid disagreements, a written contract is preferred.

For accounting purposes a partnership business is treated as a separate entity, separate and distinct from its owners. However, just as with a single proprietorship, insofar as the debts of the business are concerned no such legal distinction is made. A partner is personally responsible for all the debts of the partnership, both his or her own share and the shares of any partners who are unable to pay. Furthermore, the personal assets of a partner may be taken to satisfy all the debts of a partnership if other partners cannot pay.

Corporations

A business incorporated under the laws of a state or the federal government is called a *corporation.* Unlike a single proprietorship or partnership, a corporation is a separate legal entity, separate and distinct from its owners. The owners are called *stockholders* or *shareholders* because their ownership is evidenced by shares of the corporation's *capital stock* which may be sold and transferred from one shareholder to another without affecting the operation of the corporation.

Separate legal entity is the most important characteristic of a corporation. It makes a corporation responsible for its own acts and its own debts and relieves its stockholders of liability for either. It enables a corporation to buy, own, and sell property in its own name, to sue and be sued in its own name, and to enter into contracts for which it is solely responsible. In short, separate legal entity enables a corporation to conduct its business affairs as a legal person with all the rights, duties, and responsibilities of a person. However, unlike a person, it must act through agents.

A corporation is created by securing a charter from one of the 50 states or the federal government. The requirements for obtaining a charter vary, but in general call for filing an application with the proper governmental official and paying certain fees and taxes. If the application complies with the law and all fees and taxes have been paid, the charter is granted and the corporation comes into existence. At that point the corporation's organizers and perhaps others buy the corporation's stock and become stockholders. Then, as stockholders they meet and elect a board of directors. The board then meets, appoints the corporation's president and other officers, and makes them responsible for managing the corporation's business affairs.

Lack of stockholder liability and the ease with which stock may be sold and transferred have enabled corporations to multiply, grow, and become the dominant form of business organization in our country. Nevertheless, because of its simplicity, it is best to begin the study of accounting with a single proprietorship.

THE BALANCE SHEET EQUATION

As previously stated, a balance sheet is so called because its two sides must always balance. The sum of the assets shown on the balance sheet must equal liabilities plus the equity of the owner or owners of the business. This equality may be expressed in equation form for a single proprietorship business as follows:

$$\text{Assets} = \text{Liabilities} + \text{Owner's equity}$$

When balance sheet equality is expressed in equation form, the resulting equation is called the *balance sheet equation.* It is also known as the *accounting equation,* since all double-entry accounting is based on it. And, like any mathematical equation, its elements may be transposed and the equation expressed:

$$\text{Assets } - \text{ Liabilities } = \text{ Owner's equity}$$

The equation in this form illustrates the residual nature of the owner's equity. An owner's claims are secondary to the creditors' claims.

EFFECTS OF TRANSACTIONS ON THE ACCOUNTING EQUATION

A *business transaction* is an exchange of goods or services, and business transactions affect the elements of the accounting equation. However, regardless of what transactions a business completes, its accounting equation always remains in balance. Also, its assets always equal the combined claims of its creditors and its owner or owners. This may be demonstrated with the transactions of the law practice of Larry Owen, a single proprietorship business, which follows.

On July 1 Larry Owen began a new law practice by investing $2,500 of his personal cash, which he deposited in a bank account opened in the name of the business, Larry Owen, Attorney. After the investment, the one asset of the new business and the equity of Owen in the business are shown in the following equation:

$$\text{Assets } = \text{ Owner's equity}$$

Cash, $2,500   Larry Owen, capital, $2,500

Observe that after its first transaction the new business has one asset, cash, $2,500. Therefore, since it has no liabilities, the equity of Owen in the business is $2,500.

To continue the illustration, after the investment, (2) Owen used $600 of the business cash to pay the rent for three months in advance on suitable office space and (3) $1,200 to buy office equipment. These transactions were exchanges of cash for other assets. Their effects on the accounting equation are shown in color in Illustration 1–3. Observe that the equation remains in balance after each transaction.

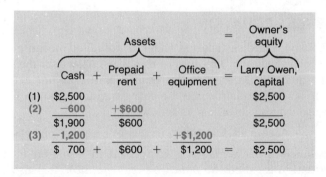

	Cash	+	Prepaid rent	+	Office equipment	=	Larry Owen, capital
(1)	$2,500						$2,500
(2)	−600		+$600				
	$1,900		$600				$2,500
(3)	−1,200				+$1,200		
	$ 700	+	$600	+	$1,200	=	$2,500

Illustration 1–3

Continuing the illustration, assume that Owen needed office supplies and additional equipment in the law office. However, he felt he should conserve the cash of the law practice. Consequently, he purchased on credit from Alpha Company office equipment costing $300 and office supplies that cost $60. The effects of this transaction (4) are shown in Illustration 1–4. Note that the assets were increased by the purchase. However, Owen's equity did not change because Alpha Company acquired a claim against the assets equal to the increase in the assets. The claim or amount owed Alpha Company is called an account payable.

	Cash +	Prepaid rent +	Office supplies +	Office equipment	= Accounts payable +	Larry Owen, capital
			Assets		= Liabilities +	Owner's equity
(1)	$2,500					$2,500
(2)	−600	+600				
	$1,900	$600				$2,500
(3)	−1,200			+$1,200		
	$ 700	$600		$1,200		$2,500
(4)			+$60	+300	+$360	
	$ 700 +	$600 +	$60 +	$1,500 =	$360 +	$2,500

Illustration 1–4

A primary objective of a business is to increase the equity of its owner or owners by earning a profit or a net income. Owen's law practice will accomplish this objective by providing legal services to its clients on a fee basis. Of course, the practice will earn a net income only if legal fees earned are greater than the expenses incurred in earning the fees. Legal fees earned and expenses incurred affect the elements of an accounting equation. To illustrate their effects, assume that on July 12 Larry Owen completed legal work for a client (transaction 5) and immediately collected $400 in cash for the services rendered. Also, the same day (transaction 6) he paid the salary of the office secretary for the first two weeks of July, a $250 expense of the business. The effects of these transactions are shown in Illustration 1–5.

Observe first the effects of the legal fee. The $400 fee is a revenue, an inflow of assets from the sale of services. Note that the revenue not only increased the asset cash but also caused a $400 increase in Owen's equity. Owen's equity increased because total assets increased without an increase in liabilities.

Next observe the effects of paying the secretary's $250 salary, an expense. Note that the effects are opposite those of a revenue. Expenses

		Assets			= Liabilities +	Owner's equity
Cash +	Prepaid rent +	Office supplies +	Office equipment	=	Accounts payable +	Larry Owen, capital
(1) $2,500						$2,500
(2) −600	+$600					
$1,900	$600					$2,500
(3) −1,200			+$1,200			
$ 700	$600		$1,200			$2,500
(4)		+$60	+300		+$360	
$ 700	$600	$60	$1,500		$360	$2,500
(5) +400						+400
$1,100	$600	$60	$1,500		$360	$2,900
(6) −250						−250
$ 850 +	$600 +	$60 +	$1,500	=	$360 +	$2,650

Illustration 1–5

are goods and services consumed in the operation of a business. In this instance the business consumed the secretary's services. When the services were paid for, both the assets and Owen's equity in the business decreased. Owen's equity decreased because cash decreased without an increase in other assets or a decrease in liabilities.

Now note this about earning a net income. A business earns a net income when its revenues exceed its expenses, and the income increases both net assets and the equity of the owner or owners. (*Net assets* are the excess of assets over liabilities.) Net assets increase because more assets flow into the business from revenues than are consumed and flow out for expenses. The equity of the owner or owners increases because net assets increase. A net loss has opposite effects.

To simplify the material and emphasize the actual effects of revenues and expenses on owner's equity, in this first chapter revenues are added directly to and expenses are deducted from the owner's capital. However, this is not done in actual practice. In actual practice revenues and expenses are first accumulated in separate categories. They are then combined, and their combined effect, the net income or loss, is added to or deducted from owner's capital. A further discussion of this is deferred to later chapters.

REALIZATION PRINCIPLE

In transaction 5 the revenue inflow was in the form of cash. However, revenue inflows are not always in cash because of the *realization principle* (also called the *recognition principle*), which governs the recognition of revenue. This principle (1) defines a revenue as an inflow of assets (not necessarily cash) in exchange for goods or services. (2) It requires that the revenue be recognized (entered in the accounting records as revenue) at the time, but not before, it is earned (which generally is at the time title to goods sold is transfered or services are rendered). (3) It also requires that the amount of revenue recognized be measured by the cash received plus the cash equivalent (fair value) of any other asset or assets received.

To demonstrate the recognition of a revenue inflow in a form other than cash, assume that (transaction 7) Larry Owen completed legal work for a client and sent the client a $750 bill for the services rendered. Also assume that ten days later the client paid in full (transaction 8) for the services rendered. The effects of the two transactions are shown in Illustration 1–6.

Observe in transaction 7 that the asset flowing into the business was the right to collect $750 from the client, an account receivable. Compare transactions 5 and 7 and note that they differ only as to the type of asset received. Next observe that the receipt of cash (ten days after the services were rendered) is nothing more than an exchange of assets, cash for the right to collect from the client. Also note that the receipt of cash did not affect Owen's equity because the revenue was recognized in accordance with the *realization principle* and Owen's equity was increased upon completion of the services rendered.

As a final transaction assume that on July 30 Larry Owen paid Alpha

	Cash +	Accounts receivable +	Prepaid rent +	Office supplies +	Office equipment	= Accounts payable +	Larry Owen, capital
(1)	$2,500						$2,500
(2)	−600		+$600				
	$1,900		$600				$2,500
(3)	−1,200				+$1,200		
	$ 700		$600		$1,200		$2,500
(4)				+$60	+300	+$360	
	$ 700		$600	$60	$1,500	$360	$2,500
(5)	+400						+400
	$1,100		$600	$60	$1,500	$360	$2,900
(6)	−250						−250
	$ 850		$600	$60	$1,500	$360	$2,650
(7)		+750					+750
	$ 850	$750	$600	$60	$1,500	$360	$3,400
(8)	+750	−750					
	$1,600 +	0 +	$600 +	$60 +	$1,500 =	$360 +	$3,400

Assets = Liabilities + Owner's equity

Illustration 1–6

	Cash	+	Accounts receivable	+	Prepaid rent	+	Office supplies	+	Office equipment	=	Accounts payable	+	Larry Owen, capital
			Assets							= Liabilities +			Owner's equity	
(1)	$2,500												$2,500	
(2)	−600				+$600									
	$1,900				$600								$2,500	
(3)	−1,200								+$1,200					
	$ 700				$600				$1,200				$2,500	
(4)							+$60		+300		+$360			
	$ 700				$600		$60		$1,500		$360		$2,500	
(5)	+400												+400	
	$1,100				$600		$60		$1,500		$360		$2,900	
(6)	−250												−250	
	$ 850				$600		$60		$1,500		$360		$2,650	
(7)			+$750										+750	
	$ 850		$750		$600		$60		$1,500		$360		$3,400	
(8)	+750		−750											
	$1,600		0		$600		$60		$1,500		$360		$3,400	
(9)	−100										−100			
	$1,500	+			$600	+	$60	+	$1,500	=	$260	+	$3,400	

Illustration 1–7

Company $100 of the $360 owed for the equipment and supplies purchased in transaction 4. This transaction reduced in equal amounts both assets and liabilities, and its effects are shown in Illustration 1–7.

IMPORTANT TRANSACTION EFFECTS

Look again at Illustration 1–7 and observe that every transaction affected at least two items in the equation; and in each case, after the effects were entered in the columns, the equation remained in balance. The accounting system you are beginning to study is called a *double-entry system*. It is based on the fact that every transaction affects two or more items in an accounting equation such as that in Illustration 1–7 and requires a "double entry" or, in other words, entries in two or more places. Also, the fact that the equation remained in balance after each transaction is important, for this is a proof of the accuracy with which the transactions were recorded.

BASES OF REVENUE RECOGNITION

Returning to the discussion of revenue recognition, the Accounting Principles Board ruled that revenue is realized and in most cases should be recognized in the accounting records upon the completion of a sale or when services have been performed and are billable.[5] This is known as the *sales basis of revenue recognition*. Under it a sale is considered to be completed when assets such as cash or the right to collect cash within a short period of time are received in exchange for goods sold or services rendered. Theoretically, revenue is earned throughout the entire performance of a service or throughout the whole process of securing goods for sale, taking a customer's order, and delivering the goods.[6] Yet, until all steps are completed and there is a right to collect the sale price, the requirements of the *objectivity principle* are not fulfilled and revenue is not recognized.

An exception to the required use of the sales basis is made for installment sales when payments are to be made over a relatively long period of time and there is considerable doubt as to the amounts that ultimately will be collected. For such sales, when collection of the full sale price is in doubt, revenue may be recognized as it is collected in cash.[7] This is known as the *cash basis of revenue recognition*.

A second exception to the required use of the sales basis applies to construction firms. Large construction jobs often take two or more years to complete. Consequently, if a construction firm has only a few jobs in process at any time and it recognizes revenue on a sales basis (upon the completion of each job), it may have a year in which no jobs are completed and no revenue is recognized even though the year is one of heavy activity. As a result, construction firms may and do recognize revenue on a *percentage-of-completion basis*. Under this basis, for example, if a firm has incurred 40% of the estimated cost to complete a job, it may recognize 40% of the job's contract price as revenue.

Space does not permit a full discussion of the cash basis and the percentage-of-completion basis of revenue recognition. This must be reserved for a more advanced text.

GLOSSARY

Accounting. The art of recording, classifying, reporting, and interpreting the financial data of an organization.

Accounting concept. An abstract idea that serves as a basis in the interpretation of accounting information.

Accounting equation. An expression in dollar amounts of the equivalency of the assets and equities of an enterprise, usually stated

---

[5] APB, "Omnibus Opinion—1966," *APB Opinion No. 10* (New York: AICPA, December 1966), par. 12. Copyright (1970) by the American Institute of CPAs.

[6] *APB Statement No. 4*, par. 149.

[7] *APB Opinion No. 10*, par. 12.

Assets = Liabilities + Owner's equity. Also called a *balance sheet equation.*

Accounting principle. A broad rule adopted by the accounting profession as a guide in measuring, recording, and reporting the financial affairs and activities of a business.

Account payable. A debt owed to a creditor for goods or services purchased on credit.

Account receivable. An amount receivable from a debtor for goods or services sold on credit.

AICPA. American Institute of Certified Public Accountants, the professional association of certified public accountants in the United States.

APB. Accounting Principles Board, a committee of the AICPA that was responsible for formulating accounting principles.

Asset. A property or economic resource owned by an individual or enterprise.

Audit. A critical exploratory review by a public accountant of the business methods and accounting records of an enterprise, made to enable the accountant to express an opinion as to whether the financial statements of the enterprise fairly reflect its financial position and operating results.

Balance sheet. A financial report showing the assets, liabilities, and owner equity of an enterprise on a specific date. Also called a *position statement.*

Balance sheet equation. Another name for the *accounting equation.*

Bookkeeping. The record-making phase of accounting.

Budgeting. The phase of accounting dealing with planning the activities of an enterprise and comparing its actual accomplishments with the plan.

Business entity concept. The idea that a business is separate and distinct from its owner or owners and from every other business.

Business transaction. An exchange of goods, services, money, and/ or the right to collect money.

Capital stock. Ownership equity in a corporation resulting from the sale of shares of the corporation's stock to its stockholders.

Continuing-concern concept. The idea that a business is a going concern that will continue to operate, using its assets to carry on its operations and, with the exception of merchandise, not offering the assets for sale.

Controller. The chief accounting officer of a large business.

Corporation. A business incorporated under the laws of a state or other jurisdiction.

Cost accounting. The phase of accounting that deals with collecting and controlling the costs of producing a given product or service.

Cost principle. The accounting rule that requires assets and services plus any resulting liabilities to be taken into the accounting records at cost.

CPA. Certified public accountant, an accountant who has met legal requirements as to age, education, experience, residence, and moral character and is licensed to practice public accounting.

Creditor. A person or enterprise to whom a debt is owed.

Debtor. A person or enterprise that owes a debt.

Equity. A right, claim, or interest in property.

Expense. Goods or services consumed in operating an enterprise.

FASB. Financial Accounting Standards Board, the seven-member board which replaced the Accounting Principles Board and has the authority to formulate rules governing the practice of accounting.

General accounting. That phase of accounting dealing primarily with recording transactions and preparing financial statements.

Going-concern concept. Another name for the *continuing-concern concept.*

Income statement. A financial statement showing revenues earned by a business, the expenses incurred in earning the revenues, and the resulting net income or net loss.

Internal auditing. A continuing examination of the records and procedures of a business by its own internal audit staff to determine if established procedures and management directives are being followed.

Liability. A debt owed.

Management advisory services. The phase of public accounting dealing with the design, installation, and improvement of a client's accounting system, plus advice on planning, budgeting, forecasting, and all other phases of accounting.

Net assets. Assets minus liabilities.

Net income. The excess of revenues over expenses.

Net loss. The excess of expenses over revenues.

Objectivity principle. The accounting rule requiring that wherever possible the amounts used in recording transactions be based on objective evidence rather than on subjective judgments.

Owner's equity. The equity of the owner (or owners) of a business in the assets of the business.

Partnership. A business owned by two or more people as partners.

Position statement. Another name for the *balance sheet.*

Price-level-adjusted statements. Financial statements showing item amounts adjusted for changes in the purchasing power of money.

Realization principle. The accounting rule that defines a revenue as an inflow of assets, not necessarily cash, in exchange for goods or services and requires the revenue to be recognized at the time, but not before, it is earned.

Recognition principle. Another name for the *realization principle*.

Revenue. An inflow of assets, not necessarily cash, in exchange for goods and services sold.

Sharehold. A person or enterprise owning a share or shares of stock in a corporation. Also called a *stockholder*.

Single proprietorship. A business owned by one individual.

Stable-dollar concept. The idea that the purchasing power of the unit of measure used in accounting, the dollar, does not change.

Stockholder. Another name for a *shareholder*.

Tax services. The phase of public accounting dealing with the preparation of tax returns and with advice as to how transactions may be completed in a way as to incur the smallest tax liability.

QUESTIONS FOR CLASS DISCUSSION

1. What is the nature of accounting and what is its function?
2. How does a business executive use accounting information?
3. Why do the states license certified public accountants?
4. What is the purpose of an audit? What do certified public accountants do when they make an audit?
5. A public accountant may provide management advisory services. Of what does this consist?
6. What do the tax services of a public accountant include beyond preparing tax returns?
7. Differentiate between accounting and bookkeeping.
8. What does an income statement show?
9. As the word is used in accounting, what is a revenue? An expense?
10. Why is the period of time covered by an income statement of extreme significance?
11. What does a balance sheet show?
12. Define (a) asset, (b) liability, (c) equity, and (d) owner's equity.
13. Why is a business treated as a separate entity for accounting purposes?
14. What is required by the cost principle? Why is such a principle necessary?
15. Why are not balance sheet amounts for the assets of a business changed from time to time to reflect changes in market values?
16. A business shows office stationery on its balance sheet at its $50 cost, although the stationery can be sold for not more than $0.25 as scrap paper. What accounting principle and concept justify this?
17. In accounting, transactions are measured, recorded, and reported in terms of dollars and the dollar is assumed to be a stable unit of measure. Is the dollar a stable unit of measure?

18. What are generally accepted accounting principles?
19. Why are the *Statements* of the Financial Accounting Standards Board and the *Opinions* of the Accounting Principles Board of importance to accounting students?
20. How does separate legal entity affect the responsibility of a corporation's stockholders for the debts of the corporation? Does this responsibility or lack of responsibility for the debts of the business apply to the owner or owners of a single proprietorship or partnership business?
21. What is the balance sheet equation? What is its importance to accounting students?
22. Is it possible for a transaction to increase or decrease a single liability without affecting any other asset, liability, or owner's equity item?
23. In accounting, what does the realization principle require?

CLASS EXERCISES

Exercise 1–1

On May 31 of the current year the balance sheet of Hillside Shop, a single proprietorship, showed the following:

Cash	1,500
Other assets	30,000
Accounts payable	15,000
Jack Hill, capital	16,500

On that date Jack Hill sold the "Other assets" for $20,000 in preparation for ending and liquidating the business of Hillside Shop.

Required:
1. Prepare a balance sheet for the shop as it would appear immediately after the sale of the assets.
2. Tell how the shop's cash should be distributed in ending the business and why.

Exercise 1–2

Determine the missing amount on each of the following lines:

	Assets	=	Liabilities	+	Owner's equity
a.	$32,600		$8,400		?
b.	28,800		?		$16,500
c.	?		7,200		12,500

Exercise 1–3

Describe a transaction that will—

a. Increase an asset and decrease an asset.
b. Increase an asset and increase a liability.

c. Decrease an asset and decrease a liability.
d. Increase an asset and increase owner's equity.
e. Decrease an asset and decrease owner's equity.

Exercise 1–4

A business had the following assets and liabilities at the beginning and at the end of a year:

	Assets	Liabilities
Beginning of the year	$65,000	$20,000
End of the year	70,000	10,000

Determine the net income or net loss of the business during the year under each of the following unrelated assumptions:

a. The owner of the business made no additional investments in the business and no withdrawals of assets from the business during the year.
b. The owner made no additional investments in the business during the year but had withdrawn $1,500 per month to pay personal living expenses.
c. During the year the owner had made no withdrawals but had made a $20,000 additional investment in the business.
d. The owner had withdrawn $1,000 from the business each month to pay personal living expenses and near the year-end had invested an additional $10,000 in the business.

Exercise 1–5

Jane Ball began the practice of dentistry and during a short period completed these transactions:

a. Invested $3,000 in cash and dental equipment having a $2,000 fair value in a dental practice.
b. Paid the rent on suitable office space for two months in advance, $1,200.
c. Purchased additional dental equipment for cash, $500.
d. Completed dental work for a patient and immediately collected $100 cash for the work.
e. Completed dental work for a patient on credit, $600.
f. Purchased additional dental equipment on credit, $400.
g. Paid the dental assistant's wages, $300.
h. Collected $200 of the amount owed by the patient of transaction (e).
i. Paid for the equipment purchased in transaction (f).

Required:

Arrange the following asset, liability, and owner's equity titles in an equation form like Illustration 1–7: Cash; Accounts Receivable; Prepaid Rent; Dental Equipment; Accounts Payable; and Jane Ball, Capital. Then show by additions and subtractions the effects of the transactions on the elements of the equation. Show new totals after each transaction.

Exercise 1–6

On October 1 of the current year Ted Lee began the practice of law, and on October 31 his records showed the following asset, liability, and owner's equity items including revenues earned and expenses. From the information prepare an income statement for the month and a month-end balance sheet like Illustration 1–2. Head the statements Ted Lee, Attorney. (The October 31, $2,500 amount for Lee's capital is the amount of his capital after it was increased and decreased by the October revenues and expenses shown.)

Cash	$ 600	Ted Lee, capital	$2,500
Accounts receivable	200	Legal fees earned	1,200
Prepaid rent	300	Rent expense	300
Law library	1,500	Salaries expense	400
Accounts payable	100	Telephone expense	50

PROBLEMS

Problem 1–1

Sue Davis began the practice of dentistry and during a short period completed the following transactions:

a. Sold for $18,765 a personal investment in General Electric stock, which she had inherited, and deposited $18,000 of the proceeds in a bank account opened in the name of the practice.
b. Purchased for $50,000 a small building to be used as an office. She paid $15,000 in cash and signed a mortgage contract promising to pay the balance over a period of years.
c. Took dental equipment, which she had purchased in college, from home for use in the practice. The equipment has a $500 fair value.
d. Purchased dental supplies for cash, $400.
e. Purchased dental equipment on credit, $6,000.
f. Completed dental work for a patient and immediately collected $150 for the work done.
g. Paid the local newspaper $25 for a small notice of the opening of the practice.
h. Completed $135 of dental work for a patient, for which the patient paid $35 in cash and promised to pay the balance within a few days.
i. Made a $500 installment payment on the equipment purchased on credit in transaction (e).
j. The patient of transaction (h) paid $50 of the amount he owed.
k. Paid the dental assistant's wages, $300.
l. Sue Davis withdrew $200 from the bank account of the dental practice to pay personal living expenses.

Required:
1. Arrange the following asset, liability, and owner's equity titles in an equation like Illustration 1–7: Cash; Accounts Receivable; Dental Supplies; Dental

Equipment; Building; Accounts Payable; Mortgage Payable; and Sue Davis, Capital.

2. Show by additions and subtractions, as in Illustration 1–7, the effects of each transaction on the elements of the equation. Show new totals after each transaction.

Problem 1–2

Ned Hall, a young lawyer, began the practice of law and completed these transactions during August of the current year:

Aug. 1 Transferred $3,000 from his personal savings account to a checking account opened in the name of the law practice, Ned Hall, Attorney.

1 Rented the furnished office of a lawyer who was retiring, and paid cash for three months' rent in advance, $900.

1 Purchased the law library of the retiring lawyer for $2,000, paying $500 in cash and agreeing to pay the balance within one year.

3 Purchased office supplies for cash, $50.

8 Completed legal work for a client and immediately collected $150 in cash for the work done.

9 Purchased law books on credit, $300.

14 Completed legal work for Guaranty Bank on credit, $600.

18 Purchased office supplies on credit, $25.

19 Paid for the law books purchased on August 9.

22 Completed legal work for Apex Realty on credit, $750.

24 Received $600 from Guaranty Bank for the work completed on August 14.

31 Paid the office secretary's salary, $800.

31 Paid the monthly utility bills, $80.

31 Recognized that one month's rent on the office had expired and become an expense. (Reduce the prepaid rent and the owner's equity.)

31 Took an inventory of unused office supplies and determined that $25 of supplies had been used and had become an expense.

Required:

1. Arrange the following asset, liability, and owner's equity titles in an equation like Illustration 1–7: Cash; Accounts Receivable; Prepaid Rent; Office Supplies; Law Library; Accounts Payable; and Ned Hall, Capital.

2. Show by additions and subtractions the effects of each transaction on the items of the equation. Show new totals after each transaction.

3. Prepare for the law practice an August 31 balance sheet like Illustration 1–2.

4. Analyze the increases and decreases in the last column of the equation and prepare an August income statement for the practice.

Problem 1–3

The records of June Cole's accounting practice show the following assets and liabilities as of the ends of 1980 and 1981:

| | December 31 | |
	1980	1981
Cash	$1,100	$ 600
Accounts receivable	3,800	5,300
Prepaid rent	500	
Office supplies............	200	100
Prepaid insurance	400	500
Office equipment	4,200	4,800
Land		15,000
Building		35,000
Accounts payable	500	600
Note payable		2,500
Mortgage payable		40,000

During the last week of December 1981, Ms. Cole purchased in the name of the accounting practice, June Cole, CPA, a small office building and moved the practice from rented quarters to the new building. The building and the land it occupied cost $50,000. The practice paid $10,000 in cash and assumed a mortgage liability for the balance. Ms. Cole had to invest an additional $6,000 in the practice to enable it to pay the $10,000. The practice earned a satisfactory net income during 1981, which enabled Ms. Cole to withdraw $1,500 per month from the business to pay her personal living expenses.

Required:

1. Prepare balance sheets for the practice as of the ends of 1980 and 1981.
2. Calculate the amount of net income earned by the practice during 1981.

Problem 1–4

Gary Blake graduated from college in June of the current year with a degree in architecture and on July 1 began the practice of his profession by investing $3,000 in cash in the business. He then completed these additional transactions:

July 1   Rented the furnished office and equipment of an architect who was retiring, paying $1,500 cash for three months' rent in advance.

1   Purchased drafting supplies for cash, $65.

2   Purchased insurance protection for one year in advance for cash by paying the premiums on two policies, $360.

4   Completed architectural work for a client and immediately collected $150 cash for the work done.

8   Completed architectural work for Valley Realty on credit, $750.

15   Paid the salary of the draftsman, $400.

18   Received payment in full for the work completed for Valley Realty on July 8.

19   Completed architectural work for Western Contractors on credit, $450.

20   Purchased additional drafting supplies on credit, $25.

23   Completed architectural work for Dale West on credit, $500.

27   Purchased additional drafting supplies on credit, $40.

July 29   Received payment in full from Western Contractors for the work completed on July 19.

30   Paid for the drafting supplies purchased on July 20.

31   Paid the July telephone bill, $25.

31   Paid the July utilities expense, $35.

31   Paid the salary of the draftsman, $400.

31   Recognized that one month's office rent had expired and become an expense. (Reduce the prepaid rent and owner's equity to record the expense.)

31   Recognized that one month's prepaid insurance, $30, had expired.

31   Took an inventory of drafting supplies and determined that $60 of drafting supplies had been used and had become an expense.

Required:

1. Arrange the following asset, liability, and owner's equity titles in an equation like Illustration 1–7: Cash; Accounts Receivable; Prepaid Rent; Prepaid Insurance; Drafting Supplies; Accounts Payable; and Gary Blake, Capital.

2. Show the effects of the transactions on the elements of the equation by recording increases and decreases in the appropriate columns. Indicate an increase with a + and a decrease with a − before the amount. *Do not determine new totals for the items of the equation after each transaction.*

3. After recording the last transaction, determine and insert on the next line the final total for each item of the equation and determine if the equation is in balance.

4. Prepare a July 31 balance sheet for the practice like the one in Illustration 1–2. Head the statement Gary Blake, Architect.

5. Analyze the items in the last column of the equation and prepare a July income statement for the practice.

ALTERNATE PROBLEMS

Problem 1–1A

Sue Davis began the practice of dentistry and during a short period completed these transactions:

a. Sold a personal investment in IBM stock that she had inherited for $19,250 and deposited $19,000 of the proceeds in a bank account opened in the name of the practice.

b. Purchased the office building and dental equipment of a dentist who was retiring. The building had a $48,000 fair value, and the equipment had a $12,000 fair value. Paid the retiring dentist $15,000 in cash and signed a mortgage contract promising to pay the balance over a period of years.

c. Purchased dental supplies for cash, $350.

d. Purchased additional dental equipment on credit, $500.

e. Completed dental work for a patient and immediately collected $100 for the work done.

f. Paid the local newspaper $50 for a small notice of the opening of the practice.

g. Completed dental work for a patient on credit, $350.

h. Made a $250 installment payment on the equipment purchased in transaction (d).

i. Completed $300 of dental work for a patient. The patient paid $150 cash and promised to pay the balance within a short period.

j. The patient of transaction (g) paid in full for her dental work.

k. Paid the dental assistant's wages, $400.

l. Sue David withdrew $250 from the bank account of the practice to pay personal expenses.

Required:

1. Arrange the following asset, liability, and owner's equity titles in an equation like Illustration 1–7: Cash; Accounts Receivable; Dental Supplies; Dental Equipment; Building; Accounts Payable; Mortgage Payable; and Sue Davis, Capital.

2. Show by additions and subtractions, as in Illustration 1–7, the effects of each transaction on the elements of the equation. Show new totals after each transaction.

Problem 1–2A

Ned Hall began the practice of law and completed these transactions during October of the current year:

Oct. 2 Sold a personal investment in Xerox stock for $2,650 and deposited $2,500 of the proceeds in a bank account opened in the name of the law practice, Ned Hall, Attorney.

2 Rented the furnished office of a lawyer who was retiring, and paid cash for two months' rent in advance, $550.

2 Moved from home to the law office law books acquired in college. (In other words, invested the books in the practice.) The books had a $500 fair value.

4 Purchased office supplies for cash, $65.

6 Purchased additional law books on credit, $600.

8 Completed legal work for a client and immediately collected $125 in cash for the work done.

12 Completed legal work for Valley Bank on credit, $650.

16 Made a $200 installment payment on the law books purchased on October 6.

21 Completed legal work for Vista Realty on credit, $550.

22 Received $650 from Valley Bank for the work completed on October 12.

31 Paid the salary of the office secretary, $700.

31 Paid the October telephone bill, $25.

31 Recognized that one month's rent on the office had expired and become an expense. (Reduce the prepaid rent and the owner's equity.)

31 Took an inventory of unused office supplies and determined that $30 of supplies had been used and had become an expense.

Required:

1. Arrange the following asset, liability, and owner's equity titles in an equation like Illustration 1–7: Cash; Accounts Receivable; Prepaid Rent; Office Supplies; Law Library; Accounts Payable; and Ned Hall, Capital.
2. Show by additions and subtractions the effects of each transaction on the items of the equation. Show new totals after each transaction.
3. Prepare an October 31 balance sheet for the law practice like the one in Illustration 1–2.
4. Analyze the increases and decreases in the last column of the equation and prepare an October income statement for the practice.

Problem 1–3A

The records of Teresa Juarez's dental practice show the following assets and liabilities as of the ends of 1980 and 1981:

	December 31	
	1980	*1981*
Cash	$1,400	$ 500
Accounts receivable	3,200	3,600
Prepaid rent	600	
Office supplies............	300	200
Prepaid insurance	500	800
Office equipment	8,700	9,100
Land		20,000
Building		65,000
Accounts payable	300	800
Note payable		5,000
Mortgage payable		60,000

During the last week of December 1981, Dr. Juarez purchased in the name of the dental practice, Teresa Juarez, DDS, a small office building and moved her practice from rented quarters to the new building. The building and the land it occupies cost $85,000. The practice paid $25,000 in cash and assumed a mortgage liability for the balance. Dr. Juarez had to borrow $5,000 in the name of the practice, signing a $5,000 note payable, and invest an additional $15,000 in the practice to enable it to pay the $25,000. The practice earned a satisfactory net income during 1981, which enabled Dr. Juarez to withdraw $1,500 per month from the practice to pay her personal living expenses.

Required:

1. Prepare balance sheets for the practice as of the ends of 1980 and 1981.
2. Prepare a calculation to show the amount of net income earned by the practice during 1981.

Problem 1–4A

Gary Blake received his degree in architecture in June of the current year and on July 1 began the practice of his profession by investing $2,500 in cash in the practice. He then completed these additional transactions:

July 1 Rented the office and equipment of an architect who was retiring, paying $1,200 cash for three months' rent in advance.

1 Purchased insurance protection for one year by paying the premium on two policies, $300.

2 Purchased drafting supplies for cash, $75.

5 Completed a short architectural assignment for a client and immediately collected $100 cash for the work done.

8 Purchased additional drafting supplies on credit, $35.

10 Completed architectural work for Ajax Contractors on credit, $650.

15 Paid the salary of the draftsman, $350.

18 Paid for the drafting supplies purchased on July 8.

20 Received payment in full from Ajax Contractors for the work completed on July 10.

23 Completed architectural work for Valley Realtors on credit, $450.

26 Purchased additional drafting supplies on credit, $40.

30 Completed additional architectural work for Ajax Contractors on credit, $500.

31 Paid the salary of the draftsman, $350.

31 Paid the July telephone bill, $20.

31 Paid the July electric bill, $65.

31 Recognized that one month's office rent had expired and become an expense. (Reduce the prepaid rent and the owner's equity to record the expense.)

31 Recognized that one month's prepaid insurance, $25, had expired.

31 Took an inventory of the unused drafting supplies and determined that supplies costing $60 had been used and had become an expense.

Required:

1. Arrange the following asset, liability, and owner's equity titles in an equation like Illustration 1–7: Cash; Accounts Receivable; Prepaid Rent; Prepaid Insurance; Drafting Supplies; Accounts Payable; and Gary Blake, Capital.
2. Show the effects of the transactions on the elements of the equation by recording increases and decreases in the appropriate columns. Indicate an increase with a + and a decrease with a − before the amount. *Do not determine new totals for the items after each transaction.*
3. After recording the last transaction, determine and enter on the next line the final total for each item and determine if the equation is in balance.
4. Prepare a July 31 balance sheet for the practice like the one in Illustration 1–2. Head the statement Gary Blake, Architect.
5. Analyze the items in the last column of the equation and prepare a July income statement for the practice.

PROVOCATIVE PROBLEMS

Provocative problem 1–1
Annual homecoming

Jerry Marsh invested $500 in a short-term enterprise, the sale of soft drinks during the annual homecoming celebration in his small town. He paid the town $100 for the exclusive right to sell soft drinks in the town park, the center of the celebration, and constructed a stand from which to make his sales, at a cost of $45 for lumber and crepe paper, none of which had any value at the end of the celebration. He bought ice for which he paid $40 and purchased soft drinks costing $500. At that point he had only $315 in cash and could not pay in full for the drinks, but since his credit rating was good, the soft drink company accepted $300 in cash and the promise that he would pay the balance the day after the celebration. During the celebration he collected $925 in cash from sales and at the end of the day paid $20 each to two boys hired to help with the sales. He also had soft drinks left over that cost $35 and could be returned to the soft drink company. Assemble the information in a manner that will enable you to prepare a balance sheet like that in Illustration 1–2 for Jerry Marsh as of the end of the celebration and an income statement showing the results of the day's operations.

Provocative problem 1–2
Speedway Service

Bob Hill ran out of money during his sophomore year in college and had to go to work. He could not find a satisfactory job; and since he owned a Honda motorcycle having an $1,800 fair value, he decided to go into business for himself. Consequently, he began Speedway Service with no assets other than the motorcycle. He kept no accounting records; and now, at the year-end, he has engaged you to determine the net income earned by the service during its first partial year of 45 weeks. You find that the service has a year-end bank balance of $800 plus $25 of undeposited cash, and local stores owe the service $150 for delivering packages during the past month. The service still owns the Honda, but from use it has depreciated $300 during the past 45 weeks. In addition, the service has a new delivery truck that cost $6,200 and has depreciated $500 since its purchase, and on which the service still owes the finance company $3,500. When the truck was purchased, Bob Hill borrowed $1,000 from his father to help make the down payment. The loan was made to the delivery service, was interest free, and has not been repaid. Finally, since the service has been profitable from the beginning, Bob Hill has withdrawn $100 of its earnings each week for personal expenses.

Determine the net income earned by the service during the 45 weeks of its operations. Present figures to prove your answer.

PART TWO
Processing accounting data

After studying Chapter 2, you should be able to:

☐ Explain the mechanics of double-entry accounting and tell why transactions are recorded with equal debits and credits.

☐ State the rules of debit and credit and apply the rules in recording transactions.

☐ Tell the normal balance of any asset, liability, or owner's equity account.

☐ Record transactions in a General Journal, post to the ledger accounts, and prepare a trial balance to test the accuracy of the recording and posting.

☐ Define or explain the words and phrases listed in the chapter Glossary.

2

Recording transactions

■ Transactions are the raw material of the accounting process. The process consists of identifying transactions, recording them, and summarizing their effects on periodic reports for the use of management and other decision makers.

Some years ago almost all concerns used pen and ink in recording transactions. However, today only small concerns use this method, concerns small enough that their bookkeeping can be done by one person working as bookkeeper a part of his or her day. Larger, modern concerns use electric bookkeeping machines, computers, punched cards, and magnetic tape in recording transactions.

Nevertheless, most students begin their study of accounting by learning a double-entry accounting system based on pen and ink. There are several reasons for this. First, since accounting reports evolved from and are based on double entry, the effective use of these reports requires some understanding of the system. Second, there is little lost motion from learning the system, since almost everything about it is applicable to machine methods. Primarily the machines replace pen and ink as the recording medium, taking the drudgery out of the recording process. And last, for the student who will start, manage, or own a small business, one small enough to use a pen-and-ink system, the system applies as it is taught.

BUSINESS PAPERS

Business papers provide evidence of transactions completed and are the basis for accounting entries to record the transactions. For example, when goods are sold on credit, two or more copies of an invoice or sales ticket are prepared. One copy is enclosed with the goods or is delivered to the customer. The other is sent to the accounting department where it becomes the basis for an entry to record the sale. Also, when goods are sold for cash, the sales are commonly "rung up" on a cash register that prints the amount of each sale on a paper tape locked inside the register. At the end of the day, when the proper key is depressed, the register prints on the tape the total cash sales for the day. The tape is then removed and becomes the basis for an entry to record the sales. Also, when an established business purchases assets, it normally buys on credit and receives an invoice that becomes the basis for an entry to record the purchase. Likewise, when the invoice is paid, a check is issued and the check or a carbon copy becomes the basis for an entry to record the payment. Obviously then, business papers are the starting point in the accounting process. Furthermore, verifiable business papers, particularly those originating outside the business, are also objective evidence of transactions completed and the amounts at which they should be recorded, as required by the *objectivity principle.*

ACCOUNTS

A concern with an accounting system based on pen and ink or electric bookkeeping machines uses *accounts* in recording its transactions. A number of accounts are normally required, with a separate account being used for summarizing the increases and decreases in each asset, liability, and owner's equity item appearing on the balance sheet and each revenue and expense appearing on the income statement.

In its most simple form an account looks like the letter "T," is called a *T-account,* and appears as follows:

(Place for the Name of the Item Recorded in This Account)	
(Left side)	(Right side)

Note that the "T" gives the account a left side, a right side, and a place for the name of the item, the increases and decreases of which are recorded therein.

When a T-account is used in recording increases and decreases in an item, the increases are placed on one side of the account and the decreases on the other. For example, if the increases and decreases in the cash of Larry Owen's law practice of the previous chapter are recorded in a T-account, they appear as follows:

Cash			
Investment	2,500	Prepayment of rent	600
Legal fee earned	400	Equipment purchase	1,200
Collection of account		Salary payment	250
receivable	750	Payment on account	
		payable	100

The reason for putting the increases on one side and the decreases on the other is that this makes it easy to add the increases and then add the decreases. The sum of the decreases may then be subtracted from the sum of the increases to learn how much of the item recorded in the account the company has, owns, or owes. For example, the increases in the cash of the Owen law practice were:

Investment	$2,500
Legal fee earned	400
Collection of an account receivable ..	750
Sum of the increases	$3,650

And the decreases were:

Prepayment of office rent	$ 600
Equipment purchase	1,200
Salary payment	250
Payment on account payable ..	100
Sum of the decreases ..	$2,150

And when the sum of the decreases is subtracted from the sum of the increases,

Sum of the increases	$3,650
Sum of the decreases...........	2,150
Balance of cash remaining ..	$1,500

the subtraction shows the law practice has $1,500 of cash remaining.

Balance of an account

When the increases and decreases recorded in an account are separately added and the sum of the decreases is subtracted from the sum of the increases, the procedure is called determining the *account bal-*

ance. The balance of an account is the difference between its increases and decreases. It is also the amount of the item recorded in the account that the company has, owns, or owes at the time the balance is determined.

ACCOUNTS COMMONLY USED

A business uses a number of accounts in recording its transactions. However, the specific accounts used vary from one concern to another, depending upon the assets owned, the debts owed, and the information to be secured from the accounting records. Nevertheless, although the specific accounts vary, the accounts discussed on the following pages are common.

Asset accounts

If useful records of a concern's assets are to be kept, an individual account is needed for each kind of asset owned. Some of the more common assets for which accounts are maintained are as follows:

Cash   Increases and decreases in cash are recorded in an account called Cash. The cash of a business consists of money or any medium of exchange that a bank will accept at face value for deposit. It includes coins, currency, checks, and postal and bank money orders. The balance of the Cash account shows both the cash on hand in the store or office and that on deposit in the bank.

Notes receivable   A formal written promise to pay a definite sum of money at a fixed future date is called a *promissory note.* When amounts due from others are evidenced by promissory notes, the notes are known as notes receivable and are recorded in a Notes Receivable account.

Accounts receivable   Goods and services are commonly sold to customers on the basis of oral or implied promises of future payment. Such sales are known as sales on credit or sales on account; and the oral or implied promises to pay are known as accounts receivable. Accounts receivable are increased by sales on credit and are decreased by customer payments. Since it is necessary to know the amount currently owed by each customer, a separate record must be kept of each customer's purchases and payments. However, a discussion of this separate record is deferred until Chapter 6, and for the present all increases and decreases in accounts receivable are recorded in a single account called Accounts Receivable.

Prepaid insurance   Fire, liability, and other types of insurance protection are normally paid for in advance. The amount paid is called a premium and may give protection from loss for from one to five years. As a result, a large portion of each premium is an asset for a considerable time after payment. When insurance premiums are paid, the asset "prepaid insurance" is increased by the amount paid. The increase is normally recorded in an account called Prepaid Insurance. Day by day, insurance premiums expire. Consequently, at intervals the insurance that has expired is calculated and the balance of the Prepaid Insurance account is reduced accordingly.

Office supplies   Stamps, stationery, paper, pencils, and like items are known as office supplies. They are assets when purchased, and continue to be assets until consumed. As they are consumed, the amounts consumed become expenses. Increases and decreases in the asset "office supplies" are commonly recorded in an account called Office Supplies.

Store supplies   Wrapping paper, cartons, bags, string, and similar items used by a store are known as store supplies. Increases and decreases in store supplies are recorded in an account of that name.

Other prepaid expenses   Prepaid expenses are items that are assets at the time of purchase but become expenses as they are consumed or used. Prepaid insurance, office supplies, and store supplies are examples. Other examples are prepaid rent, prepaid taxes, and prepaid wages. Each is accounted for in a separate account.

Equipment   Increases and decreases in such things as typewriters, desks, chairs, and office machines are commonly recorded in an account called Office Equipment. Likewise, changes in the amount of counters, showcases, cash registers, and like items used by a store are recorded in an account called Store Equipment.

Buildings   A building used by a business in carrying on its operations may be a store, garage, warehouse, or factory. However, regardless of use, an account called Buildings is commonly employed in recording the increases and decreases in the buildings owned by a business and used in carrying on its operations.

Land   An account called Land is commonly used in recording increases and decreases in the land owned by a business. Land and the buildings placed upon it are inseparable in physical fact. Nevertheless, it is usually desirable to account for land and its buildings in separate accounts because buildings depreciate and wear out but land does not.

Liability accounts

Most companies do not have as many liability accounts as asset accounts; however, the following are common:

Notes payable   Increases and decreases in amounts owed because of promissory notes given to creditors are accounted for in an account called Notes Payable.

Accounts payable   An account payable is an amount owed to a creditor. Accounts payable result from the purchase of merchandise, supplies, equipment, and services on credit. Since it is necessary to know the amount owed each creditor, an individual record must be kept of the purchases from and the payments to each. However, a discussion of this individual record is deferred until Chapter 6, and for the present all increases and decreases in accounts payable are recorded in a single Accounts Payable account.

Unearned revenues   The *realization principle* requires that revenue be earned before it is recognized as revenue. Therefore, when a company collects for its products or services before delivery, the amounts collected are unearned revenue. An unearned revenue is a liability that will be extinguished by delivering the product or service paid for in advance. Subscriptions collected in advance by a magazine publisher, rent collected in advance by a landlord, and legal fees collected in advance by a lawyer are examples. Upon receipt, the amounts collected are recorded in liability accounts such as Unearned Subscriptions. Unearned Rent, and Unearned Legal Fees. When earned by delivery, the amounts earned are transferred to the revenue accounts, Subscriptions Earned, Rent Earned, and Legal Fees Earned.

Other short-term payables   Wages payable, taxes payable, and interest payable are illustrations of other short-term liabilities for which individual accounts must be kept.

Mortgage payable   A *mortgage payable* is a long-term debt for which the creditor has a secured prior claim against some one or more of the debtor's assets. The mortgage gives the creditor the right to force the sale of the mortgaged assets through a foreclosure if the mortgage debt is not paid when due. An account called Mortgage Payable is commonly used in recording the increases and decreases in the amount owed on a mortgage.

Owner's equity accounts

Several kinds of transactions affect the equity of a business owner. In a single proprietorship these include the investment of the owner, his or her withdrawals of cash or other assets for personal use, revenues earned, and expenses incurred. In the previous chapter all such transactions were entered in a column under the name of the owner. This simplified the material of the chapter but made it necessary to analyze the items entered in the column in order to prepare an income statement. Fortunately such an analysis is not necessary. All that is required to avoid it is a number of accounts, a separate one for each owner's equity item appearing on the balance sheet and a separate one for each revenue and expense on the income statement. Then as each transaction affecting owner's equity is completed, it is recorded in the proper account. Among the accounts required are the following:

Capital account   When a person invests in a business of his or her own, the investment is recorded in an account carrying the owner's name and the word "Capital." For example, an account called Larry Owen, Capital is used in recording the investment of Larry Owen in his law practice. In addition to the original investment, the *capital account* is used for any permanent additional increases or decreases in owner's equity.

Withdrawals account　　Usually a person invests in a business to earn income. However, income is earned over a period of time, say a year. Often during this period the business owner must withdraw a portion of the earnings to pay living expenses or for other personal uses. These withdrawals reduce both assets and owner's equity. To record them, an account carrying the name of the business owner and the word "Withdrawals" is used. For example, an account called Larry Owen, Withdrawals is used to record the withdrawals of cash by Larry Owen from his law practice. The *withdrawals account* is also known as the *personal account* or *drawing account.*

An owner of a small unincorporated business often withdraws a fixed amount each week or month for personal living expenses, and often thinks of these withdrawals as a salary. However, in a legal sense they are not a salary because the owner of an unincorporated business cannot enter into a legally binding contract with himself to hire himself and pay himself a salary. Consequently, in law and custom it is recognized that such withdrawals are neither a salary nor an expense of the business but are withdrawals in anticipation of earnings.

Revenue and expense accounts　　When an income statement is prepared, it is necessary to know the amount of each kind of revenue earned and each kind of expense incurred during the period covered by the statement. To accumulate this information, a number of revenue and expense accounts are needed. However, all concerns do not have the same revenues and expenses. Consequently, it is impossible to list all revenue and expense accounts to be encountered. Nevertheless, Revenue from Repairs, Commissions Earned, Legal Fees Earned, Rent Earned, and Interest Earned are common examples of revenue accounts. And Advertising Expense, Store Supplies Expense, Office Salaries Expense, Office Supplies Expense, Rent Expense, Utilities Expense, and Insurance Expense are common examples of expense accounts. It should be noted that the kind of revenue or expense recorded in each above-mentioned account is evident from its title. This is generally true of such accounts.

Real and nominal accounts

To add to your vocabulary, it may be said here that balance sheet accounts are commonly called *real accounts.* Presumably this is because the items recorded in these accounts exist in objective form. Likewise, income statement accounts are called *nominal accounts* because items recorded in these accounts exist in name only.

THE LEDGER

A business may use from two dozen to several thousand accounts in recording its transactions. Each account is placed on a separate page in a bound or loose-leaf book, or on a separate card in a tray of cards. If the accounts are kept in a book, the book is called a *ledger*. If they are kept on cards in a file tray, the tray of cards is a ledger. Actually, as used in accounting, the word "ledger" means a group of accounts.

DEBIT AND CREDIT

As previously stated, a T-account has a left side and a right side. However, in accounting the left side is called the *debit* side, abbreviated "Dr."; and the right side is called the *credit* side, abbreviated "Cr." Furthermore, when amounts are entered on the left side of an account, they are called *debits*, and the account is said to be *debited*. When amounts are entered on the right side, they are called *credits*, and the account is said to be *credited*. The difference between the total debits and the total credits recorded in an account is the *balance of the account*. The balance may be either a *debit balance* or a *credit balance*. It is a debit balance when the sum of the debits exceeds the sum of the credits and a credit balance when the sum of the credits exceeds the sum of the debits. An account is said to be *in balance* when its debits and credits are equal.

The words "to debit" and "to credit" should not be confused with "to increase" and "to decrease." To debit means simply to enter an amount on the left side of an account. To credit means to enter an amount on the right side. Either may be an increase or a decrease. This may readily be seen by examining the way in which the investment of Larry Owen is recorded in his Cash and capital accounts which follow:

Cash		Larry Owen, Capital	
Investment 2,500			Investment 2,500

When Owen invested $2,500 in his law practice, both the business cash and Owen's equity were increased. Observe in the accounts that the increase in cash is recorded on the left or debit side of the Cash account, while the increase in owner's equity is recorded on the right or credit side. The transaction is recorded in this manner because of the mechanics of *double-entry accounting*.

MECHANICS OF DOUBLE-ENTRY ACCOUNTING

The mechanics of double-entry accounting are such that every transaction affects and is recorded in two or more accounts with equal debits and credits. Transactions are so recorded because equal debits and credits offer a means of proving the recording accuracy. The proof is, if every transaction is recorded with equal debits and credits, then the debits in the ledger must equal the credits.

The person who first devised double-entry accounting based the system on the accounting equation, $A = L + OE$. He assigned the recording of increases in assets to the debit sides of asset accounts. He then recognized that equal debits and credits were possible only if increases in liabilities and owner's equity were recorded on the opposite or credit sides of liability and owner's equity accounts. In other words, he recognized that if increases in assets were to be recorded as debits, then increases and decreases in all accounts would have to be recorded as follows:

Assets		=	Liabilities		+	Owner's equity	
Debit for increases	Credit for decreases		Debit for decreases	Credit for increases		Debit for decreases	Credit for increases

From the T-accounts it is possible to formulate rules for recording transactions under a double-entry system. The rules are:

1. Increases in assets are debited to asset accounts; consequently, decreases must be credited.
2. Increases in liability and owner's equity items are credited to liability and owner's equity accounts; consequently, decreases must be debited.

At this stage, beginning students will find it helpful to memorize these rules. They should also note that in a single proprietorship there are four kinds of owner's equity accounts: (1) the capital account, (2) the withdrawals account, (3) revenue accounts, and (4) expense accounts. Furthermore, for transactions affecting these accounts, students should observe these additional points:

1. The original investment of the owner of a business plus any more or less permanent changes in the investment are recorded in the capital account.
2. Withdrawals of assets for personal use, including cash to pay personal expenses, decrease owner's equity and are debited to the owner's withdrawals account.

3. Revenues increase owner's equity and are credited in each case to a revenue account that shows the kind of revenue earned.
4. Expenses decrease owner's equity and are debited in each case to an expense account that shows the kind of expense incurred.

TRANSACTIONS ILLUSTRATING THE RULES OF DEBIT AND CREDIT

The following transactions of Larry Owen's law practice illustrate the application of debit and credit rules. They also show how transactions are recorded in the accounts. The number preceding each transaction is used throughout the illustration to identify the transaction in the accounts. Note that most of the transactions are the same ones used in Chapter 1 to illustrate the effects of transactions on the accounting equation.

To record a transaction, it must be analyzed to determine what items are increased and decreased. The rules of debit and credit are then applied to determine the debit and credit effects of the increases or decreases. An analysis of each of the following transactions is given in order to demonstrate the process.

1. On July 1 Larry Owen invested $2,500 in a new law practice.

	Cash		
(1)	2,500		

	Larry Owen, Capital	
		(1)	2,500

Analysis of the transaction: The transaction increased the cash of the practice and at the same time it increased the equity of Owen in the business. Increases in assets are debited, and increases in owner's equity are credited. Consequently, to record the transaction, Cash should be debited and Larry Owen, Capital should be credited for $2,500.

2. Paid the office rent for three months in advance, $600.

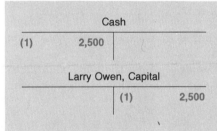

	Cash		
(1)	2,500	(2)	600

	Prepaid Rent		
(2)	600		

Analysis of the transaction: The asset prepaid rent, the right to occupy the office for three months, is increased; and the asset cash is decreased. Increases in assets are debited, and decreases are credited. Therefore, to record the transaction, debit Prepaid Rent and credit Cash for $600.

3. Purchased office equipment for cash, $1,200.

	Cash		
(1)	2,500	(2)	600
		(3)	1,200

Office Equipment	
(3)	1,200

Analysis of the transaction: The asset office equipment is increased, and the asset cash is decreased. Debit Office Equipment and credit Cash for $1,200.

4. Purchased on credit from Alpha Company office supplies, $60, and office equipment, $300.

Office Supplies	
(4)	60

Office Equipment	
(3)	1,200
(4)	300

Accounts Payable	
(4)	360

Analysis of the transaction: This transaction increased the assets office equipment and office supplies, but it also created a liability. Increases in assets are debits, and increases in liabilities are credits; therefore, debit Office Supplies for $60 and Office Equipment for $300 and credit Accounts Payable for $360.

5. Completed legal work for a client and immediately collected a $400 fee.

	Cash		
(1)	2,500	(2)	600
(5)	400	(3)	1,200

Legal Fees Earned	
(5)	400

Analysis of the transaction: This revenue transaction increased both assets and owner's equity. Increases in assets are debits, and increases in owner's equity are credits. Therefore, Cash is debited; and in order to show the nature of the increase in owner's equity and at the same time accumulate information for the income statement, the revenue account Legal Fees Earned is credited.

6. Paid the secretary's salary for the first two weeks of July, $250.

	Cash		
(1)	2,500	(2)	600
(5)	400	(3)	1,200
		(6)	250

Office Salaries Expense	
(6)	250

Analysis of the transaction: The secretary's salary is an expense that decreased both assets and owner's equity. Debit Office Salaries Expense to decrease owner's equity and also to accumulate information for the income statement, and credit Cash to record the decrease in cash.

7. Signed a contract with Coast Realty to do its legal work on a fixed-fee basis for $100 per month. Received the fee for the first month and a half in advance, $150.

Cash			
(1)	2,500	(2)	600
(5)	400	(3)	1,200
(7)	150	(6)	250

Unearned Legal Fees			
		(7)	150

Analysis of the transaction: The $150 inflow increased cash, but the inflow is not a revenue until earned. Its acceptance before being earned created a liability, the obligation to do the client's legal work for the next month and a half. Consequently, debit Cash to record the increase in cash and credit Unearned Legal Fees to record the liability increase.

8. Completed legal work for a client on credit and billed the client $750 for the services rendered.

Accounts Receivable		
(8)	750	

Legal Fees Earned			
		(5)	400
		(8)	750

Analysis of the transaction: Completion of this revenue transaction gave the law practice the right to collect $750 from the client, and thus increased assets and owner's equity. Consequently, debit Accounts Receivable for the increase in assets and credit Legal Fees Earned to increase owner's equity and at the same time accumulate information for the income statement.

9. Paid the secretary's salary for the second two weeks of the month.

Cash			
(1)	2,500	(2)	600
(5)	400	(3)	1,200
(7)	150	(6)	250
		(9)	250

Office Salaries Expense		
(6)	250	
(9)	250	

Analysis of the transaction: An expense that decreased assets and owner's equity. Debit Office Salaries Expense to accumulate information for the income statement and credit Cash.

10. Larry Owen withdrew $200 from the law practice to pay personal expenses.

	Cash		
(1)	2,500	(2)	600
(5)	400	(3)	1,200
(7)	150	(6)	250
		(9)	250
		(10)	200

Larry Owen, Withdrawals			
(10)	200		

Analysis of the transaction: This transaction reduced in equal amounts both assets and owner's equity. Cash is credited to record the asset reduction; and the Larry Owen, Withdrawals account is debited for the reduction in owner's equity.

11. The client paid the $750 legal fee billed in transaction 8.

	Cash		
(1)	2,500	(2)	600
(5)	400	(3)	1,200
(7)	150	(6)	250
(11)	750	(9)	250
		(10)	200

Accounts Receivable			
(8)	750	(11)	750

Analysis of the transaction: One asset was increased, and the other decreased. Debit Cash to record the increase in cash, and credit Accounts Receivable to record the decrease in the account receivable, or the decrease in the right to collect from the client.

12. Paid Alpha Company $100 of the $360 owed for the items purchased on credit in transaction 4.

	Cash		
(1)	2,500	(2)	600
(5)	400	(3)	1,200
(7)	150	(6)	250
(11)	750	(9)	250
		(10)	200
		(12)	100

Accounts Payable			
(12)	100	(4)	360

Analysis of the transaction: Payments to creditors decrease in like amounts both assets and liabilities. Decreases in liabilities are debited, and decreases in assets are credited. Debit Accounts Payable and credit Cash.

13. Paid the July telephone bill, $30.
14. Paid the July electric bill, $35.

	Cash		
(1)	2,500	(2)	600
(5)	400	(3)	1,200
(7)	150	(6)	250
(11)	750	(9)	250
		(10)	200
		(12)	100
		(13)	30
		(14)	35

Analysis of the transactions: These expense transactions are alike in that each decreased cash; they differ in each case as to the kind of expense involved. Consequently, in recording them, Cash is credited; and to accumulate information for the income statement, a different expense account, one showing the nature of the expense in each case, is debited.

Telephone Expense	
(13)	30

Heating and Lighting Expense	
(14)	35

THE ACCOUNTS AND THE EQUATION

In Illustration 2–1 the transactions of the Owen law practice are shown in the accounts, with the accounts brought together and classified under the elements of an accounting equation.

Assets			=	**Liabilities**			+	**Owner's equity**		
Cash				Accounts Payable				Larry Owen, Capital		
(1)	2,500	(2)	600	(12)	100	(4)	360		(1)	2,500
(5)	400	(3)	1,200							
(7)	150	(6)	250	Unearned Legal Fees				Larry Owen, Withdrawals		
(11)	750	(9)	250			(7)	150	(10)	200	
		(10)	200							
		(12)	100					Legal Fees Earned		
		(13)	30						(5)	400
		(14)	35						(8)	750
Accounts Receivable								Office Salaries Expense		
(8)	750	(11)	750					(6)	250	
								(9)	250	
Prepaid Rent								Telephone Expense		
(2)	600							(13)	30	
Office Supplies								Heating and Lighting Expense		
(4)	60							(14)	35	
Office Equipment										
(3)	1,200									
(4)	300									

Illustration 2–1

PREPARING A TRIAL BALANCE

As previously stated, in a double-entry accounting system every transaction is recorded with equal debits and credits so that the equality of the debits and credits may be tested as a proof of the recording accuracy. This equality is tested at intervals by preparing a *trial balance*. A trial balance is prepared by (1) determining the balance of each account in the ledger; (2) listing the accounts having balances, with the debit balances in one column and the credit balances in another (as in Illustration 2–2); (3) adding the debit balances; (4) adding the credit balances; and then (5) comparing the sum of the debit balances with the sum of the credit balances.

Larry Owen, Attorney
Trial Balance, July 31, 19—

Cash	$1,135	
Prepaid rent	600	
Office supplies	60	
Office equipment	1,500	
Accounts payable		$ 260
Unearned legal fees		150
Larry Owen, capital		2,500
Larry Owen, withdrawals	200	
Legal fees earned		1,150
Office salaries expense	500	
Telephone expense	30	
Heating and lighting expense	35	
Totals	$4,060	$4,060

Illustration 2–2

The illustrated trial balance was prepared from the accounts in Illustration 2–1. Note that its column totals are equal, or in other words, the trial balance is in balance. When a trial balance is in balance, debits equal credits in the ledger and it is assumed that no errors were made in recording transactions.

THE PROOF OFFERED BY A TRIAL BALANCE

If when a trial balance is prepared it does not balance, an error or errors have been made. The error or errors may have been either in recording transactions, in determining the account balances, in copying the balances on the trial balance, or in adding the columns of the trial balance. On the other hand, if a trial balance balances, it is assumed that no errors have been made. However, a trial balance that balances is not absolute proof of accuracy. Errors may have been made that did not affect the equality of its columns. For example, an error in which a correct debit amount is debited to the wrong account or a correct credit amount is credited to the wrong account will not cause a trial balance to be out of balance. Likewise, an error in which a wrong amount is both debited and credited to the right accounts will not cause a trial balance to be out of balance. Consequently, a trial balance in balance is only presumptive proof of recording accuracy.

STANDARD ACCOUNT FORM

T-accounts like the ones shown thus far are commonly used in textbook illustrations and also in accounting classes for blackboard demonstrations. In both cases their use eliminates details and permits the student to concentrate on ideas. However, although widely used in textbooks and in teaching, T-accounts are not used in business for recording transactions. In recording transactions, accounts like the one in Illustration 2–3 are generally used. (Note the year in the date column of the illustrated account. Throughout the remainder of this text, years will be designated 198A, 198B, 198C, and so forth. In all such situations, 198A is the earliest year, 198B is the succeeding year, and so on through the series.)

Cash					ACCOUNT NO. 1
DATE	EXPLANATION	POST REF.	DEBIT	CREDIT	BALANCE
198A July 1		G1	2 500 00		2 500 00
1		G1		600 00	1 900 00
3		G1		1 200 00	700 00
12		G1	400 00		1 100 00

Illustration 2–3

The account of Illustration 2–3 is called a *balance column account.* It differs from a T-account in that it has columns for specific information about each debit and credit entered in the account. Also, its Debit and Credit columns are placed side by side and it has a third or Balance column. In this Balance column the account's new balance is entered each time the account is debited or credited. As a result, the last amount in the column is the account's current balance. For example, on July 1 the illustrated account was debited for the $2,500 investment of Larry Owen, which caused it to have a $2,500 debit balance. It was then credited for $600, and its new $1,900 balance was entered. On July 3 it was credited again for $1,200, which reduced its balance to

$700. Then on July 12 it was debited for $400 and its balance was increased to $1,100.

When a balance column account like that of Illustration 2–3 is used, the heading of the Balance column does not tell whether the balance is a debit balance or a credit balance. However, this does not create a problem because an account is assumed to have its normal kind of balance, unless the contrary is indicated. Furthermore, an accountant is expected to know the normal balance of any account. Fortunately this too is not difficult because the balance of an account normally results from recording in it a larger sum of increases than decreases. Consequently, if increases are recorded as debits, the account normally has a debit balance. Likewise, if increases are recorded as credits, the account normally has a credit balance. Or, increases are recorded in an account in each of the following classifications as shown, and its normal balance is:

Account classification	Increases are recorded as—	And the normal balance is—
Asset	Debits	Debit
Contra asset*	Credits......	Credit
Liability.................	Credits......	Credit
Owner's equity:		
Capital	Credits......	Credit
Withdrawals	Debits	Debit
Revenue	Credits......	Credit
Expense	Debits	Debit
* Explained in the next chapter.		

When an unusual transaction causes an account to have a balance opposite from its normal kind of balance, this opposite from normal kind of balance is indicated in the account by entering it in red or entering it in black and encircling the amount. Also when a debit or credit entered in an account causes the account to have no balance, some bookkeepers place a -0- in the Balance column on the line of the entered amount. Other bookkeepers and bookkeeping machines write 0.00 in the column to indicate the account does not have a balance.

NEED FOR A JOURNAL

It is possible to record transactions by entering debits and credits directly in the accounts, as was done earlier in this chapter. However, when this is done and an error is made, the error is difficult to locate, because even with a transaction having only one debit and one credit, the debit is entered on one ledger page or card and the credit on another, and there is nothing to link the two together.

Consequently, to link together the debits and credits of each transaction and to provide in one place a complete record of each transaction, it is the universal practice in pen-and-ink systems to record all transactions in a *journal*. The debit and credit information about each transaction is then copied from the journal to the ledger accounts. These procedures are important when errors are made, since the journal record makes it possible to trace the debits and credits into the accounts and to see that they are equal and properly recorded.

The process of recording transactions in a journal is called journalizing transactions. Also, since transactions are first recorded in a journal and their debit and credit information is then copied from the journal to the ledger, a journal is called a *book of original entry* and a ledger a *book of final entry*.

THE GENERAL JOURNAL

The simplest and most flexible type of journal is a *General Journal*. For each transaction it provides places for recording (1) the transaction date, (2) the names of the accounts involved, and (3) an explanation of the transaction. It also provides a place for (4) the account numbers of the accounts to which the transaction's debit and credit information is copied and (5) the transaction's debit and credit effect on the accounts named. A standard ruling for a general journal page with two of the transactions of the Owen law practice recorded therein is shown in Illustration 2–4.

The first entry in Illustration 2–4 records the purchase of supplies and equipment on credit, and three accounts are involved. When a transaction involves three or more accounts and is recorded with a general journal entry, a compound entry is required. A *compound journal entry* is one involving three or more accounts. The second entry records a legal fee earned.

GENERAL JOURNAL   PAGE *1*

DATE		ACCOUNT TITLES AND EXPLANATION	POST. REF.	DEBIT	CREDIT
1984 July	5	Office Supplies		60 00	
		Office Equipment		300 00	
		Accounts Payable			360 00
		Purchased supplies and equipment on credit.			
	12	Cash		400 00	
		Legal Fees Earned			400 00
		Collected a legal fee.			

Illustration 2–4

RECORDING TRANSACTIONS IN A GENERAL JOURNAL

To record transactions in a General Journal:

1. The year is written in small figures at the top of the first column.
2. The month is written on the first line in the first column. The year and the month are not repeated except at the top of a new page or at the beginning of a new month or year.
3. The day of each transaction is written in the second column on the first line of the transaction.
4. The names of the accounts to be debited and credited and an explanation of the transaction are written in the Account Titles and Explanation column. The name of the account debited is written first, beginning at the left margin of the column. The name of the account credited is written on the following line, indented about one inch. The explanation is placed on the next line, indented about a half inch from the left margin. The explanation should be short but sufficient to explain the transaction and set it apart from every other transaction.
5. The debit amount is written in the Debit column opposite the name of the account to be debited. The credit amount is written in the Credit column opposite the account to be credited.
6. A single line is skipped between each journal entry to set the entries apart.

At the time transactions are recorded in the General Journal, nothing is entered in the *Posting Reference (Post. Ref.) column*. However, when the debits and credits are copied from the journal to the ledger, the account numbers of the ledger accounts to which the debits and credits are copied are entered in this column. The Posting Reference column is sometimes called the *Folio column*.

POSTING TRANSACTION INFORMATION

The process of copying journal entry information from the journal to the ledger is called *posting*. Normally, near the end of a day all transactions recorded in the journal that day are posted. In the posting procedure, journal debits are copied and become ledger account debits and journal credits are copied and become ledger account credits.

The posting procedures for a journal entry are shown in Illustration 2–5 on the next page, and they may be described as follows. To post a journal entry:

For the debit:

1. Find in the ledger the account named in the debit of the entry.
2. Enter in the account the date of the entry as shown in the journal, the *journal page number* from which the entry is being posted,

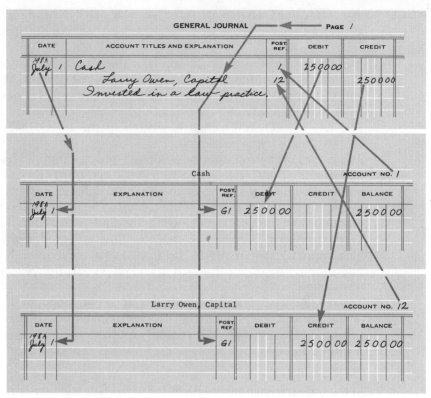

Illustration 2–5

and in the Debit column the debit amount. Note the letter "G" preceding the journal page number in the Posting Reference column of the account. The letter indicates that the amount was posted from the General Journal. Other journals are introduced in Chapter 6, and each is identified by a letter.

3. Determine the effect of the debit on the account balance and enter the new balance.
4. Enter in the Posting Reference column of the journal the account number of the account to which the amount was posted.

For the credit:

Repeat the foregoing steps, with the exception that the credit amount is entered in the Credit column and has a credit effect on the account balance.

Observe that the last step (Step 4) in the posting procedure for either the debit or the credit of an entry is to insert the account number in the Posting Reference column of the journal. Inserting the account number in this column serves two purposes: (1) The account number in the journal and the journal page number in the account act as a cross-reference when it is desired to trace an amount from one record to the other. And, (2) writing the account number in the journal as a last step in posting indicates that posting is completed. If posting is interrupted, the bookkeeper, by examining the journal's Posting Reference column, can easily see where posting stopped.

LOCATING ERRORS

When a trial balance does not balance, an error or errors are indicated. To locate the error or errors, check the journalizing, posting, and trial balance preparation steps in their reverse order. First check the addition of the columns in the trial balance to see that no error in addition was made. Then check to see that the account balances were correctly copied from the ledger. Then recalculate the account balances. If at this stage the error or errors have not been found, check the posting and then the original journalizing of the transactions.

CORRECTING ERRORS

When an error is discovered in either the journal or the ledger, it must be corrected. Such an error is never erased, for this seems to indicate an effort to conceal something. However, the method of correction will vary with the nature of the error and the stage in the accounting procedures at which it is discovered.

If an error is discovered in a journal entry before the error is posted, it may be corrected by ruling a single line through the incorrect amount or account name and writing in above the correct amount or account name. Likewise, a posted error or an error in posting in which only the amount is wrong may be corrected in the same manner. However, when a posted error involves a wrong account, it is considered best to correct the error with a correcting journal entry. For example, the following journal entry to record the purchase of office supplies was made and posted:

Oct.	14	Office Furniture and Fixtures	15.00	
		Cash		15.00
		To record the purchase of office supplies.		

Obviously, the debit of the entry is to the wrong account; consequently, the following entry is needed to correct the error:

Oct.	17	Office Supplies	15.00	
		Office Furniture and Fixtures		15.00
		To correct the entry of October 14 in which		
		the Office Furniture and Fixtures account was		
		debited in error for the purchase of office		
		supplies.		

The debit of the second entry correctly records the purchase of supplies, and the credit cancels the error of the first entry. Note the full explanation of the correcting entry. Such an explanation should always be full and complete so that anyone can see exactly what has occurred.

BOOKKEEPING TECHNIQUES

Commas and decimal points in dollar amounts

When amounts are entered in a journal or a ledger, commas to indicate thousands of dollars and decimal points to separate dollars and cents are not necessary. The ruled lines accomplish this. However, when statements are prepared on unruled paper, the decimal points and commas are necessary.

Dollar signs

Dollar signs are not used in journals or ledgers but are required on financial reports prepared on unruled paper. On such reports, a dollar sign is placed (1) before the first amount in each column of figures and (2) before the first amount appearing after a ruled line that indicates an addition or a subtraction. Examine Illustration 3–5, page 90, for examples of the use of dollar signs on a financial report.

Omission of zeros in the cents columns

When an amount to be entered in a ledger or a journal is an amount of dollars and no cents, some bookkeepers will use a dash in the cents column in the place of two zeros to indicate that there are no cents. They feel that the dash is easier and more quickly made than the two zeros. This is a matter of choice in journal and ledger entries. However, on financial reports the two zeros are preferred because they are neater in appearance.

Often in this text, where space is limited, exact dollar amounts are used in order to save space. Obviously, in such cases, neither zeros nor dashes are used to show that there are no cents involved.

GLOSSARY

Account. An accounting device used in recording and summarizing the increases and decreases in a revenue, an expense, asset, liability, or owner's equity item.

Account balance. The difference between the increases and decreases recorded in an account.

Account number. An identifying number assigned to an account.

Balance column account. An account having a column for entering the new account balance after each debit or credit is posted to the account.

Book of final entry. A ledger to which amounts are posted.

Book of original entry. A journal in which transactions are first recorded.

Business paper. A sales ticket, invoice, check, or other document arising in and evidence of the completion of a transaction.

Capital account. An account used to record the more or less permanent changes in the equity of an owner in his or her business.

Compound journal entry. A journal entry having more than one debit or more than one credit.

Credit. The right-hand side of a T-account.

Debit. The left-hand side of a T-account.

Double-entry accounting. An accounting system in which each transaction affects and is recorded in two or more accounts with equal debits and credits.

Drawing account. Another name for the *withdrawals account.*

Folio column. Another name for the *Posting Reference column.*

General Journal. A book of original entry in which any type of transaction can be recorded.

Journal. A book of original entry in which transactions are first recorded and from which transaction amounts are posted to the ledger accounts.

Journal page number. A posting reference number entered in the Posting Reference column of each account to which an amount is posted and which shows the page of the journal from which the amount was posted.

Ledger. A group of accounts used by a business in recording its transactions.

Mortgage payable. A debt, usually long term, that is secured by a special claim against one or more assets of the debtor.

Nominal accounts. The income statement accounts.

Normal balance of an account. The usual kind of balance, either debit or credit, that a given account has and which is a debit balance if increases are recorded in the account as debits and a credit balance if increases are recorded as credits.

Personal account. Another name for the *withdrawals account.*

Posting. Transcribing the debit and credit amounts from a journal to the ledger accounts.

Posting Reference (Post. Ref.) column. A column in a journal and in each account for entering posting reference numbers. Also called a *folio column.*

Posting reference numbers. Journal page numbers and ledger account numbers used as a cross-reference between amounts entered in a journal and posted to the ledger accounts.

Promissory note. An unconditional written promise to pay a definite sum of money on demand or at a fixed or determinable future date.

Real accounts. The balance sheet accounts.

T-account. An abbreviated account form, two or more of which are used in illustrating the debits and credits required in recording a transaction.

Trial balance. A list of accounts having balances in the ledger, the debit or credit balance of each account, the total of the debit balances, and the total of the credit balances.

Withdrawals account. The account used to record the withdrawals from a business by its owner of cash or other assets intended for personal use. Also known as *personal account* or *drawing account.*

QUESTIONS FOR CLASS DISCUSSION

1. What is an account? What is a ledger?
2. What determines the number of accounts a business will use?
3. What are the meanings of the following words and terms: (a) debit, (b) to debit, (c) credit, and (d) to credit?
4. Does debit always mean increase and credit always mean decrease?
5. A transaction is to be entered in the accounts. How do you determine the accounts in which amounts are to be entered? How do you determine whether a particular account is to be debited or credited?
6. Why is a double-entry accounting system so called?
7. Give the rules of debit and credit for (a) asset accounts and (b) for liability and owner's equity accounts.
8. Why are the rules of debit and credit the same for both liability and owner's equity accounts?
9. List the steps in the preparation of a trial balance.
10. Why is a trial balance prepared?
11. Why is a trial balance considered to be only presumptive proof of recording accuracy? What types of errors are not revealed by a trial balance?

12. What determines whether the normal balance of an account is a debit or a credit balance?

13. Can transaction debits and credits be recorded directly in the ledger accounts? What is gained by first recording transactions in a journal and then posting to the accounts?

14. In recording transactions in a journal, which is written first, the debit or the credit? How far is the name of the account credited indented? How far is the explanation indented?

15. What is a compound entry?

16. Are dollar signs used in journal entries? In the accounts?

17. If decimal points are not used in journal entries to separate dollars from cents, what accomplishes this purpose?

18. Define or describe each of the following:

a. Journal.
b. Ledger.
c. Book of original entry.
d. Book of final entry.
e. Folio column.
f. Posting.
g. Posting Reference column.
h. Posting reference numbers.

19. Entering in the Posting Reference column of the journal the account number to which an amount was posted is the last step in posting the amount. What is gained by making this the last step?

CLASS EXERCISES

Exercise 2–1

Prepare the following columnar form. Then (1) indicate the treatment for increases and decreases by entering the words "debited" and "credited" in the proper columns. (2) Indicate the normal balance of each kind of account by entering the word "debit" or "credit" in the last column of the form.

Kind of Account	Increases	Decreases	Normal Balance
Asset			
Liability			
Owner's capital			
Owner's withdrawals			
Revenue			
Expense			

Exercise 2–2

Place the following T-accounts on a sheet of notebook paper: Cash; Accounts Receivable; Office Supplies; Office Equipment; Accounts Payable; Carl Wells, Capital; Revenue from Services; and Utilities Expense. Then record these transactions by entering debits and credits directly in the accounts. Use the transaction letters to identify amounts in the accounts.

a. Carl Wells began a service business, called Quick Service, by investing $1,000 in the business.
b. Purchased office supplies for cash, $50.
c. Purchased office equipment on credit, $300.
d. Earned revenue by rendering services for a customer for cash, $100.
e. Paid for the office equipment purchased in transaction (c).
f. Earned revenue by rendering services for a customer on credit, $200.
g. Paid the monthly utility bills, $25.
h. Collected $150 of the amount owed by the customer of transaction (f).

Exercise 2–3

After recording the transactions of Exercise 2–2, prepare a trial balance for Quick Service. Use the current date.

Exercise 2–4

Prepare a form on notebook paper with the following three column headings: (1) Error, (2) Amount Out of Balance, and (3) Column Having Larger Total. Then for each of the following errors: (1) list the error by letter in the first column, (2) tell the amount it will cause the trial balance to be out of balance in the second column, and (3) tell in the third column which trial balance column will have the larger total as a result of the error. If the error does not affect the trial balance, write "none" in each of the last two columns.

a. A $70 debit to Office Supplies was debited to Office Equipment.
b. A $90 credit to Office Equipment was credited to Sales.
c. A $60 credit to Sales was credited to the Sales account twice.
d. A $40 debit to Office Supplies was posted as a $45 debit.
e. A $35 debit to Office Supplies was not posted.
f. A $11 credit to Sales was posted as a $110 credit.

Exercise 2–5

A trial balance did not balance. In looking for the error, the bookkeeper discovered that a transaction for the purchase of a calculator on credit for $350 had been recorded with a $350 debit to Office Equipment and a $350 debit to Accounts Payable. Answer each of the following questions, giving the dollar amount of the misstatement, if any.

a. Was the balance of the Office Equipment account overstated, understated, or correctly stated in the trial balance?
b. Was the balance of the Accounts Payable account overstated, understated, or correctly stated in the trial balance?
c. Was the debit column total of the trial balance overstated, understated, or correctly stated?
d. Was the credit column total of the trial balance overstated, understated, or correctly stated?

e. If the credit column total of the trial balance was $96,000 before the error was corrected, what was the total of the debit column?

Exercise 2–6

A careless bookkeeper prepared the following trial balance which does not balance, and you have been asked to prepare a corrected trial balance. In examining the records of the concern you discover the following: (1) The debits to the Cash account total $13,200, and the credits total $10,750. (2) A $75 receipt of cash from a customer in payment of the customer's account was not posted to Accounts Receivable. (3) A $25 purchase of shop supplies on credit was entered in the journal but was not posted to any account. (4) Two digits in the balance of the Revenue from Services account, as shown on the trial balance of the bookkeeper, were transposed in copying the balance from the ledger to the trial balance. The correct amount is $12,100.

RED ROCK COMPANY
Trial Balance, September 30, 19—

Cash	$ 2,550	
Accounts receivable		$ 3,175
Shop supplies	300	
Shop equipment	1,500	
Accounts payable	550	
Wages payable	50	
Joe Sims, capital	3,175	
Joe Sims, withdrawals	7,200	
Revenue from services		11,200
Rent expense		1,200
Advertising expense	125	
Totals	$15,450	$15,575

PROBLEMS

Problem 2–1

Mary Hall began a new real estate agency called Phoenix Realty, and during a short period completed these transactions:

a. Began business by investing the following assets at their fair values: cash, $3,500; office equipment, $1,500; automobile, $3,000; land, $15,000; and building, $45,000. Security Bank holds a $30,000 mortgage on the land and building.
b. Purchased office supplies, $50, and office equipment, $175, on credit.
c. Collected a $3,500 commission from the sale of property for a client.
d. Purchased additional office equipment on credit, $150.
e. Paid cash for advertising that had appeared in the local paper, $75.
f. Traded the company automobile and $4,500 in cash for a new automobile.
g. Paid the office secretary's salary, $350.
h. Paid for the supplies and equipment purchased in transaction (b).

i. Completed a real estate appraisal for a client on credit, $200.
j. Paid for the equipment purchased in transaction *(d)*.
k. The client of transaction *(i)* paid $100 of the amount the client owed.
l. Paid the secretary's salary, $350.
m. Paid $125 cash for newspaper advertising that had appeared.
n. Mary Hall withdrew $500 from the business to pay personal expenses.

Required:

1. Open the following T-accounts: Cash; Accounts Receivable; Office Supplies; Office Equipment; Automobile; Land; Building; Accounts Payable; Mortgage Payable; Mary Hall, Capital; Mary Hall, Withdrawals; Commissions Earned; Appraisal Fees Earned; Office Salaries Expense; and Advertising Expense.
2. Record the transactions by entering debits and credits directly in the accounts. Use the transaction letters to identify each debit and credit amount.
3. Prepare a trial balance using the current date.

Problem 2–2

Susan Kent began a public accounting practice and completed these tranactions during October of the current year:

Oct. 1 Invested $3,500 cash in a public accounting practice begun this day.
      1 Paid cash for three months' office rent in advance, $900.
      2 Purchased office supplies, $60, and office equipment, $2,100, on credit.
      3 Paid the premium on two insurance policies, $375.
      8 Completed accounting work for Mary Hall and collected $150 cash therefor.
    13 Completed accounting work for Valley Bank on credit, $350.
    15 Purchased additional office supplies on credit, $25.
    23 Received $350 from Valley Bank for the work completed on October 13.
    25 Made a $250 installment payment on the supplies and equipment purchased on October 2.
    30 Susan Kent wrote a $45 check on the bank account of the accounting practice to pay the electric bill of her personal residence.
    31 Completed accounting work for Evans Company on credit, $300.
    31 Paid the monthly utility bills of the accounting office, $30.

Required:

1. Open the following accounts: Cash; Accounts Receivable; Prepaid Rent; Prepaid Insurance; Office Supplies; Office Equipment; Accounts Payable; Susan Kent, Capital; Susan Kent, Withdrawals; Accounting Revenue; and Utilities Expense. Number the accounts beginning with 1.
2. Prepare general journal entries to record the transactions, post to the accounts, and prepare a trial balance. Head the trial balance Susan Kent, CPA.

Problem 2–3

Fred Oaks began a new business called A–1 Dirt Digger, and during a short period completed these transactions:

   a. Began business by investing $18,000 in cash and office equipment having a $500 fair value.

   b. Purchased for $10,000 land to be used as an office site and for parking equipment. Paid $3,000 in cash and signed a promissory note for the balance.

   c. Purchased excavating equipment costing $22,500. Paid $7,500 in cash and signed promissory notes for the balance.

   d. Paid $5,000 cash for the erection of a quonset-type office building.

   e. Paid the premiums on several insurance policies, $875.

   f. Completed an excavating job and collected $825 cash in payment therefor.

   g. Completed $1,200 of excavating work for Tri-City Contractors on credit.

   h. Paid the wages of the equipment operator, $750.

   i. Paid $225 cash for repairs to excavating equipment.

   j. Received $1,200 from Tri-City Contractors for the work of transaction (*g*).

   k. Completed $650 of excavating work for Ralph Sims on credit.

   l. Recorded as an account payable a bill for rent of a special machine used on the Ralph Sims job, $75.

   m. Purchased additional excavating equipment on credit, $850.

   n. Fred Oaks withdrew $50 from the business for personal use.

   o. Paid the wages of the equipment operator, $1,000.

   p. Paid the account payable resulting from renting the machine of transaction (*l*).

   q. Paid for gas and oil consumed by the excavating equipment, $175.

Required:

1. Open the following T-accounts: Cash; Accounts Receivable; Prepaid Insurance; Office Equipment; Excavating Equipment; Building; Land; Notes Payable; Accounts Payable; Fred Oaks, Capital; Fred Oaks, Withdrawals; Excavating Revenue; Equipment Repairs Expense; Wages Expense; Equipment Rentals Expense; and Gas and Oil Expense.
2. Record the transactions by entering debits and credits directly in the T-accounts. Use the transaction letters to identify amounts in the accounts.
3. Prepare a trial balance using the current date.

Problem 2–4

Ann Evans began the practice of architecture and completed these transactions during October of the current year:

Oct. 2 Opened a bank account in the name of the practice, Ann Evans, Architect, and deposited $2,500 therein.

      2 Rented suitable office space and paid two months' rent in advance, $600.

      3 Purchased $3,800 of office and drafting equipment under an agreement calling for a $500 down payment and the balance in monthly installments. Paid the down payment.

      3 Purchased drafting supplies for cash, $250.

      9 Delivered a set of building plans to a contractor and collected $500 in full payment therefor.

     10 Paid the premiums on fire and liability insurance policies, $525.

Oct. 11   Purchased additional drafting supplies, $40, and drafting equipment, $100, on credit.

16   Completed and delivered a set of plans to Lakeside Developers on credit, $900.

16   Paid the salary of the draftsman, $500.

22   Received $900 from Lakeside Developers for the plans delivered on October 16.

22   Paid for the supplies and equipment purchased on October 11.

26   Completed additional architectural work for Lakeside Developers on credit, $250.

28   Paid $125 cash for blueprinting expense.

30   Ann Evans withdraw $500 cash for personal expenses.

31   Paid the monthly utility bills, $65.

31   Paid the salary of the draftsman, $500.

Required:

1. Open the following accounts, numbering them beginning with 1: Cash; Accounts Receivable; Prepaid Rent; Drafting Supplies; Prepaid Insurance; Office and Drafting Equipment; Accounts Payable; Ann Evans, Capital; Ann Evans, Withdrawals; Architectural Fees Earned; Salaries Expense; Blueprinting Expense; and Utilities Expense.
2. Prepare general journal entries to record the transactions, post to the accounts, and prepare a trial balance.

Problem 2–5

Ned Lake graduated from college with a law degree in June of the current year, and during July he completed these transactions:

July 1   Began the practice of law by investing $2,000 in cash and law books acquired in college and having a $600 fair value.

1   Rented the furnished office of a lawyer who was retiring due to illness, and paid two months' rent in advance, $800.

1   Paid the premium on a liability insurance policy giving one year's protection, $480.

2   Purchased office supplies on credit, $40.

8   Completed legal work for a client and immediately collected $200 cash for the work.

12   Paid for the office supplies purchased on July 2.

15   Completed legal work for Evans Realty on credit, $650.

22   Completed legal work for Security Bank on credit, $500.

25   Received $650 from Evans Realty for the work completed on July 15.

27   Ned Lake wrote a $25 check on the bank account of the legal practice to pay his home telephone bill, $25.

29   Purchased additional office supplies on credit, $30.

31   Paid the July telephone bill of the office, $35.

31   Paid the salary of the office secretary, $600.

31   Recognized that one month's rent on the office had expired and had become an expense. (Make a general journal entry to transfer the

amount of the expense from the asset account to the Rent Expense account.)

July 31   Recognized that one month's insurance had expired and become an expense.

    31   Took an inventory of the unused office supplies and determined that supplies costing $25 had been used and had become an expense.

Required:

1. Open the following accounts, numbering them beginning with 1: Cash; Accounts Receivable; Prepaid Rent; Prepaid Insurance; Office Supplies; Law Library; Accounts Payable; Ned Lake, Capital; Ned Lake, Withdrawals; Legal Fees Earned; Rent Expense; Salaries Expense; Telephone Expense; Insurance Expense; and Office Supplies Expense.
2. Prepare general journal entries to record the transactions, post to the accounts, and prepare a trial balance headed Ned Lake, Attorney.
3. Analyze the trial balance and prepare a July 31 balance sheet and a July income statement for the practice. (The $2,600 trial balance amount of capital for Ned Lake is his July 1 beginning-of-the-month capital. To determine the July 31 balance sheet amount of his capital, remember that the net income increased his equity and the withdrawal decreased it. Show his ending equity as in Illustration 1–2.)

ALTERNATE PROBLEMS

Problem 2–1A

Mary Hall began business as a real estate agent. She called her agency Red Rock Realty, and during a short period completed these transactions:

a. Invested $12,000 in cash and office equipment having a $2,500 fair value in the agency.
b. Purchased land valued at $18,000 and a small office building valued at $32,000, paying $10,000 cash and signing a mortgage contract to pay the balance over a period of years.
c. Purchased office supplies on credit, $75.
d. Took her personal automobile, which had a $5,500 fair value, for exclusive use in the business.
e. Purchased additional office equipment on credit, $400.
f. Paid the office secretary's salary, $300.
g. Collected a $2,500 commission from the sale of property for a client.
h. Paid cash for newspaper advertising that had appeared, $65.
i. Paid for the supplies purchased in transaction (c).
j. Gave a typewriter carried in the accounting records at $110 and $650 cash for a new typewriter.
k. Completed a real estate appraisal for a client on credit, $150.
l. Paid the secretary's salary, $300.
m. Received payment in full for the appraisal of transaction (k).
n. Mary Hall withdrew $250 from the business to pay personal living expenses.

Required:

1. Open the following T-accounts: Cash; Accounts Receivable; Office Supplies; Office Equipment; Automobile; Land; Building; Accounts Payable; Mortgage Payable; Mary Hall, Capital; Mary Hall, Withdrawals; Commissions Earned; Appraisal Fees Earned; Office Salaries Expense; and Advertising Expense.
2. Record the transactions by entering debits and credits directly in the accounts. Use the transaction letters to identify each debit and credit amount.
3. Prepare a trial balance using the current date.

Problem 2–2A

Susan Kent, CPA, completed the following transactions during August of the current year:

Aug. 2 Began a public accounting practices by investing $2,000 in cash and office equipment having a $3,500 fair value.
   2 Purchased on credit office supplies, $50, and office equipment, $250.
   2 Paid two months' rent in advance on suitable office space, $700.
   5 Completed accounting work for a client and immediately collected $100 cash therefor.
   9 Completed accounting work for Valley Bank on credit, $500.
  11 Paid for the items purchased on credit on August 2.
  12 Paid the premium on an insurance policy, $525.
  19 Received $500 from Valley Bank for the work completed on August 9.
  25 Susan Kent withdrew $200 from the practice for personal expenses.
  29 Completed accounting work for Dennis Realty on credit, $350.
  30 Purchased additional office supplies on credit, $35.
  31 Paid the August utility bills, $85.

Required:

1. Open the following accounts: Cash; Accounts Receivable; Prepaid Rent; Prepaid Insurance; Office Supplies; Office Equipment; Accounts Payable; Susan Kent, Capital; Susan Kent, Withdrawals; Accounting Revenue; and Utilities Expense. Number the accounts beginning with 1.
2. Prepare general journal entries to record the transactions, post to the accounts, and prepare a trial balance. Head the trial balance Susan Kent, CPA.

Problem 2–3A

Fred Oaks began business as an excavating contractor and during a short period completed these transactions:

a. Began business under the firm name of Dirt Mover by investing cash, $12,500; office equipment, $650; and excavating equipment, $28,500.
b. Purchased land for use as an office site and for parking equipment. Paid $2,500 cash and signed a $5,000 promissory note for the balance of the $7,500 total cost.

c. Purchased for cash a small prefabricated building and moved it onto the land for use as an office, $5,000.
d. Paid the premiums on two insurance policies, $550.
e. Completed an excavating job and collected $800 cash in payment therefor.
f. Purchased additional excavating equipment costing $5,000. Gave $1,000 in cash and signed a promissory note for the balance.
g. Completed excavating work for Western Contractors on credit, $1,100.
h. Purchased additional excavating equipment on credit, $350.
i. Completed an excavating job for Barry Fox on credit, $725.
j. Received and recorded as an account payable a bill for rent on a special machine used on the Barry Fox job, $100.
k. Received $1,100 from Western Contractors for the work of transaction (g).
l. Paid the wages of the equipment operator, $600.
m. Paid for the equipment purchased in transaction (h).
n. Paid $150 cash for repairs to excavating equipment.
o. Fred Oaks wrote a check on the bank account of the business for repairs to his personal automobile, $60. (The car is not used for business purposes.)
p. Paid the wages of the equipment operator, $600.
q. Paid for gas and oil consumed by the excavating equipment, $125.

Required:

1. Open the following T-accounts: Cash; Accounts Receivable; Prepaid Insurance; Office Equipment; Excavating Equipment; Building; Land; Notes Payable; Accounts Payable; Fred Oaks, Capital; Fred Oaks, Withdrawals; Excavating Revenue; Equipment Repairs Expense; Wages Expense; Equipment Rentals Expense; and Gas and Oil Expense.
2. Record the transactions by entering debits and credits directly in the accounts, and prepare a trial balance. (Use the transaction letter to identify each amount in the accounts. Use the current date for the trial balance.)

Problem 2–4A

Ann Evans completed these transactions during October of the current year:

Oct. 1 Began the practice of architecture by investing cash, $2,000; drafting supplies, $125; and office and drafting equipment, $3,450.
    1 Paid two months' rent in advance on suitable office space, $800.
    2 Purchased drafting equipment, $325, and drafting supplies, $35, on credit.
    2 Paid the premium on an insurance policy taken out in the name of the practice, $475.
    8 Delivered a set of plans to a contractor and collected $300 in full payment therefor.
   15 Completed and delivered a set of plans to Phoenix Contractors on credit, $600.
   15 Paid the draftsman's salary, $450.
   17 Paid for the equipment and supplies purchased on October 2.
   18 Purchased drafting supplies on credit, $45.

Oct. 24 Received payment in full from Phoenix Contractors for the plans delivered on October 15.

26 Ann Evans withdrew $75 from the practice for personal expenses.

28 Paid for the supplies purchased on October 18.

30 Completed architectural work for Sears Realty on credit, $350.

31 Paid the draftsman's salary, $450.

31 Paid the October utility bills, $65.

31 Paid the blueprinting expense for October, $55.

Required:

1. Open the following accounts, numbering them beginning with 1: Cash; Accounts Receivable; Prepaid Rent; Drafting Supplies; Prepaid Insurance; Office and Drafting Equipment; Accounts Payable; Ann Evans, Capital; Ann Evans, Withdrawals; Architectural Fees Earned; Salaries Expense; Blueprinting Expense; and Utilities Expense.
2. Prepare general journal entries to record the transactions, post to the accounts, and prepare a trial balance. Use as the name of the business Ann Evans, Architect.

PROVOCATIVE PROBLEMS

Provocative problem 2–1
Lake Pleasant

Jed Monroe has just completed the first summer's operation of a concession on Lake Pleasant at which he rents boats and sells hamburgers, soft drinks, and candy. He began the summer's operation with $2,500 in cash and a five-year lease on a boat dock and small concession building on the lake. The lease calls for a $1,000 annual rental, although the concession is open only from May 15 to September 15. On opening day Jed paid the first year's rent in advance and also purchased four boats at $300 each, paying cash. He estimated the boats would have a five-year life, after which he could sell them for $50 each.

During the summer he purchased food, soft drinks, and candy costing $4,175, all of which was paid for by summer's end, excepting food costing $150 which was purchased during the last week's operations. He also paid electric bills, $165, and wages of a part-time helper, $800; and he withdrew $200 of the earnings of the concession each week for 16 weeks for personal expenses.

He took in $1,450 in boat rentals during the summer and sold $9,650 of food and drinks, all of which was collected in cash, except $125 he had not collected from Hill Company for food and drinks for an employees' party.

When he closed for the summer, he was able to return to the soft drink company several cases of soft drinks for which he received a $40 cash refund. However, he had to take home for consumption by his family a number of candy bars and some hamburger and buns which cost $15 and could have been sold for $45.

Prepare an income statement showing the results of the summer's operations and a September 15 balance sheet. Head the statements Lake Pleasant

Concession. Determine Jed Monroe's ending equity by subtracting the liability from the assets. Then prepare a different calculation to prove the amount of the equity. (T-accounts will be helpful in organizing the data.)

Provocative problem 2–2
Valley Glass Service

Ed Cook began a window cleaning service by depositing $500 in a bank account opened in the name of the business, Valley Glass Service. He then made a $250 down payment and signed a promissory note payable to purchase a secondhand truck priced at $800; and he spent $150 for detergents, sponges, and other supplies to be used in the business. He also paid $50 for newspaper advertising through which he gained a number of customers who together agreed to pay him approximately $250 per week for his services.

After six months, on June 30, 19—, Ed's records showed that he had collected $5,800 in cash from customers for services and that other customers owed him $300 for washing their windows. He had bought additional supplies for cash, $350, which brought the total supplies purchased during the six months to $500; however, supplies that had cost $100 were on hand unused at the period end. He spent $275 for gas and oil used in the truck and through payments had reduced the balance owed on the truck to $250; but through use the truck had worn out and depreciated an amount equal to one fourth of its cost. Also, he had withdrawn sufficient cash from the business each week to pay his personal living expenses.

Under the assumption the business had a total of $400 of cash at the period end, determine the amount of cash Ed had withdrawn from the business. Prepare an income statement for the six months and a balance sheet as of the period end. Determine Ed Cook's end-of-the-period equity by subtracting the balance owed on the note payable from the total of the assets. Then prepare a calculation to prove in another way the amount of the ending equity. (T-accounts will be useful in organizing the data.)

After studying Chapter 3, you should be able to:

☐ Explain why the life of a business is divided into accounting periods of equal length and why the accounts of a business must be adjusted at the end of each accounting period.

☐ Prepare adjusting entries for prepaid expenses, accrued expenses, unearned revenues, accrued revenues, and depreciation.

☐ Prepare entries to dispose of accrued revenue and expense items in the new accounting period.

☐ Explain the difference between the cash and accrual bases of accounting.

☐ Explain the importance of comparability in the financial statements of a business, period after period; and tell how the realization principle and the matching principle contribute to comparability.

☐ Define each asset and liability classification appearing on a balance sheet, classify balance sheet items, and prepare a classified balance sheet.

☐ Define or explain the words and phrases listed in the chapter Glossary.

3

Adjusting the accounts and preparing the statements

■ The life of a business often spans many years, and its activities go on without interruption over the years. However, taxes based on annual income must be paid governmental units, and the owners and managers of a business must have periodic reports on its financial progress. Consequently, a *time-period concept* of the life of a business is required in accounting for its activities. This concept results in a division of the life of a business into time periods of equal length, called *accounting periods*. Accounting periods may be a month, three months, or a year in length. However, *annual accounting periods*, periods one year in length, are the norm.

An accounting period of any 12 consecutive months is known as a *fiscal year*. A fiscal year may coincide with the calendar year and end on December 31 or it may follow the *natural business year*. When accounting periods follow the natural business year, they end when inventories are at their lowest point and business activities are at their lowest ebb. For example, in department stores the natural business year begins on February 1, after the Christmas and January sales, and ends the following January 31. Consequently, the annual accounting periods of department stores commonly begin on February 1 and end the following January 31.

NEED FOR ADJUSTMENTS AT THE END OF AN ACCOUNTING PERIOD

As a rule, at the end of an accounting period, after all transactions are recorded, several of the accounts in a concern's ledger do not show proper end-of-the-period balances for preparing the statements. This is true even though all transactions were correctly recorded. The balances are incorrect for statement purposes, not through error but because of the expiration of costs brought about by the passage of time. For example, the second item on the trial balance of Owen's law practice, as prepared in Chapter 2 and reproduced again as Illustration 3–1, is "Prepaid rent, $600." This $600 represents the rent for three months paid in advance on July 1. However, by July 31, $600 is not the balance sheet amount for this asset because one month's rent, or $200, has expired and become an expense and only $400 remains as an asset. Likewise, a portion of the office supplies as represented by the $60 debit balance in the Office Supplies account has been used, and the office equipment has begun to wear out and depreciate. Obviously, then, the balances of the Prepaid Rent, Office Supplies, and Office Equipment accounts as they appear on the trial balance do not reflect the proper amounts for preparing the July 31 statements. The balance of each and the balances of the Office Salaries Expense and Legal Fees Earned accounts must be *adjusted* before they will show proper amounts for the July 31 statements.

Larry Owen, Attorney
Trial Balance, July 31, 19—

Cash	$1,135	
Prepaid rent	600	
Office supplies	60	
Office equipment	1,500	
Accounts payable		$ 260
Unearned legal fees		150
Larry Owen, capital		2,500
Larry Owen, withdrawals	200	
Legal fees earned		1,150
Office salaries expense	500	
Telephone expense	30	
Heating and lighting expense	35	
Totals	$4,060	$4,060

Illustration 3–1

ADJUSTING THE ACCOUNTS

Prepaid expenses

As the name implies, a *prepaid expense* is an expense that has been paid for in advance of its use. At the time of payment an asset is acquired that will be used or consumed, and as it is used or consumed, it becomes an expense. For example:

On July 1 the Owen law practice paid three months' rent in advance and obtained the right to occupy a rented office for the following three months. On July 1 this right was an asset valued at its $600 cost. However, day by day the agency occupied the office, and each day a portion of the prepaid rent expired and became an expense. On July 31 one month's rent, valued at one third of $600, or $200, had expired. Consequently, if the agency's July 31 accounts are to reflect proper asset and expense amounts, the following adjusting entry is required:

July	31	Rent Expense	200.00	
		Prepaid Rent		200.00
		To record the expired rent.		

Posting the adjusting entry has the following effect on the accounts:

Prepaid Rent				Rent Expense	
July 1	600	July 31	200	July 31	200

After the entry is posted, the Prepaid Rent account with a $400 balance and the Rent Expense account with a $200 balance show proper statement amounts.

To continue, early in July, the Owen law practice purchased some office supplies and placed them in the office for use. Each day the secretary used a portion. The amount used or consumed each day was an expense that daily reduced the supplies on hand. However, the daily reductions were not recognized in the accounts because day-by-day information as to amounts used and remaining was not needed. Also, bookkeeping labor could be saved if only a single amount, the total of all supplies used during the month, was recorded.

Consequently, if on July 31 the accounts are to reflect proper statement amounts, it is necessary to record the amount of office supplies used during the month. However, to do this, it is first necessary to learn the amount used. To learn the amount used, it is necessary to count or inventory the unused supplies remaining and to deduct their cost from the cost of the supplies purchased. If, for example, $45 of unused supplies remain, then $15 ($60 − $45 = $15) of supplies have been used and have become an expense. The following entry is required to record this:

July	31	Office Supplies Expense	15.00	
		Office Supplies		15.00
		To record the supplies used.		

The effect of the adjusting entry on the accounts is:

Office Supplies				Office Supplies Expense	
July 5	60	July 31	15	July 31	15

Often, unlike in the two previous examples, items that are prepaid expenses at the time of purchase are both bought and fully consumed within a single accounting period. For example, a company pays its rent in advance on the first day of each month. Each month the amount paid results in a prepaid expense that is entirely consumed before the month's end and before the end of the accounting period. In such cases, it is best to ignore the fact that an asset results from each prepayment, because an adjustment can be avoided if each prepayment is originally recorded as an expense.

Other prepaid expenses that are handled in the same manner as prepaid rent and office supplies are prepaid insurance, store supplies, and factory supplies.

Depreciation

An item of equipment used in carrying on the operations of a business in effect represents a "quantity of usefulness." Also, since the equipment will eventually wear out and be discarded, the cost of its "quantity of usefulness" must be charged off as an expense over the useful life of the equipment. This is accomplished by recording *depreciation.*

Depreciation is an *expense* just like the expiration of prepaid rent. For example, if a company purchases a machine for $4,500 that it expects to use for four years, after which it expects to receive $500 for the machine as a trade-in allowance on a new machine, the company has purchased a $4,000 quantity of usefulness ($4,500 − $500 = $4,000). Furthermore, this quantity of usefulness expires or the machine depreciates at the rate of $1,000 per year [$4,500 − $500) ÷ 4 years = $1,000]. Actually, when depreciation is compared to the expiration of a prepaid expense, the primary difference is that since it is often impossible to predict exactly how long an item of equipment will be used or how much will be received for it at the end of its useful life, the amount it depreciates each accounting period is only an estimate.

Estimating and apportioning depreciation can be simple, as in the foregoing example, or it can become complex. A discussion of more complex situations is unnecessary at this point and is deferred to Chapter 10. However, to illustrate the recording of depreciation, assume that on July 31 the Owen law practice estimated its office equipment had depreciated $20 during the month. The depreciation reduced the assets and increased expenses, and the following adjusting entry is required:

July	31	Depreciation Expense, Office Equipment	20.00	
		Accumulated Depreciation,		
		Office Equipment.		20.00
		To record the July depreciation.		

The effect of the entry on the accounts is:

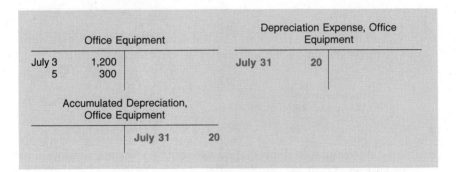

After the entry is posted, the Office Equipment account and its related Accumulated Depreciation, Office Equipment account together show the July 31 balance sheet amounts for this asset. The Depreciation Expense, Office Equipment account shows the amount of depreciation expense that should appear on the July income statement.

In most cases a decrease in an asset is recorded with a credit to the account in which the asset is recorded. However, note in the illustrated accounts that this procedure is not followed in recording depreciation. Rather, depreciation is recorded in a *contra account*, the Accumulated Depreciation, Office Equipment account. (A contra account is an account the balance of which is subtracted from the balance of an associate account to show a more proper amount for the item recorded in the associated account.)

There are two good reasons for using contra accounts in recording depreciation. First, although based on objective evidence whenever possible, at its best depreciation is only an estimate. Second, the use of contra accounts better preserves the facts in the lives of items of equipment. For example, in this case the Office Equipment account preserves a record of the equipment's cost, and the Accumulated Depreciation, Office Equipment account shows its depreciation to date.

A better understanding of the second reason for using contra accounts, along with an appreciation of why the word "accumulated" is used in the account name, can be gained when it is pointed out that depreciation is recorded at the end of each accounting period in a depreciating asset's life. As a result, at the end of the third month in the life of the law practice's office equipment, the Office Equipment and its related accumulated depreciation account will look like this:

Office Equipment		Accumulated Depreciation, Office Equipment	
July 3 1,200		July 31 20	
5 300		Aug. 31 20	
		Sept. 30 20	

And the equipment's cost and three months' *accumulated depreciation* will be shown on its September 30 balance sheet thus:

Office equipment	$1,500	
Less accumulated depreciation	60	$1,440

Accumulated depreciation accounts are sometimes found in ledgers and on statements under titles such as "Allowance for Depreciation, Store Equipment" or the totally unacceptable caption, "Reserve for Depreciation, Office Equipment." However, more appropriate terminology is "Accumulated Depreciation, Store Equipment" and "Accumulated Depreciation, Office Equipment." The "Accumulated" terminology is better because it is more descriptive of the depreciation procedure.

Accrued expenses

Most expenses are recorded during an accounting period at the time they are paid. However, when a period ends there may be expenses that have been incurred but have not been paid and recorded because payment is not due. These unpaid and unrecorded expenses for which payment is not due are called *accrued expenses.* Earned but unpaid wages are a common example. To illustrate:

The Owen law practice has a part-time secretary who is paid $25 per day or $125 per week for a week that begins on Monday and ends on Friday. The secretary's wages are due and payable every two weeks on Friday; and during July they were paid on the 12th and 26th and recorded as follows:

Cash		Office Salaries Expense	
July 12	250	July 12	250
26	250	26	250

If the calendar for July appears as illustrated and the secretary worked on July 29, 30, and 31, then at the close of business on Wednesday, July 31, the secretary has earned three days' wages that are not paid and recorded because payment is not due. However, this $75 of earned but unpaid wages is just as much a part of the July expenses as the $500 of wages that have been paid. Furthermore, on July 31, the unpaid wages are a liability. Consequently, if the accounts are to show the correct amount of wages for July and all liabilities owed on July 31, then an adjusting entry like the following must be made:

JULY						
S	M	T	W	T	F	S
		1	2	3	4	5	6
7	8	9	10	11	12	13
14	15	16	17	18	19	20
21	22	23	24	25	26	27
28	29	30	31			

July	31	Office Salaries Expense	75.00	
		Salaries Payable		75.00
		To record the earned but unpaid wages.		

The effect of the entry on the accounts is:

Office Salaries Expense		Salaries Payable	
July 12	250		
26	250	July 31	75
31	75		

Unearned revenues

An *unearned revenue* results when payment is received for goods or services in advance of their delivery. For instance, on July 15 Larry Owen entered into an agreement with Coast Realty to do its legal work on a fixed-fee basis for $100 per month. On that date Owen received $150 in advance for services during the remainder of July and the month of August. The fee was recorded with this entry:

July	15	Cash	150.00	
		Unearned Legal Fees		150.00
		Received a legal fee in advance.		

Acceptance of the fee in advance increased the cash of the law practice and created a liability, the obligation to do Coast Realty's legal work for the next month and a half. However, by July 31 the law practice has discharged $50 of the liability and earned that much income, which according to the *realization principle* should appear on the July income statement. Consequently, on July 31 the following entry is required:

July	31	Unearned Legal Fees	50.00	
		Legal Fees Earned		50.00
		To record legal fees earned.		

Posting the entry has this effect on the accounts:

Unearned Legal Fees				Legal Fees Earned		
July 31	50	July 15	150		July 12	400
					19	750
					31	50

The effect of the entry is to transfer the $50 earned portion of the fee from the liability account to the revenue account. It reduces the liability and records as a revenue the $50 that has been earned.

Accrued revenues

An *accrued revenue* is a revenue that has been earned but has not been collected because payment is not due. For example, assume that on July 15 Larry Owen also entered into an agreement with Guaranty Bank to do its legal work on a fixed-fee basis for $150 per month to be paid monthly. Under this assumption, by July 31 the law practice has earned half of a month's fee, $75, which according to the *realization principle* should appear on its July income statement. Therefore the following entry is required:

July	31	Accounts Receivable	75.00	
		Legal Fees Earned		75.00
		To record legal fees earned.		

Posting the entry has this effect on the accounts:

Accounts Receivable				Legal Fees Earned	
July 19	750	July 29	750	July 12	400
31	75			19	750
				31	50
				31	75

THE ADJUSTED TRIAL BALANCE

A trial balance prepared before adjustments is known as an *unadjusted trial balance,* or simply a trial balance. One prepared after adjustments is known as an *adjusted trial balance.* A July 31 adjusted trial balance for the law practice appears in Illustration 3–2.

Larry Owen, Attorney
Adjusted Trial Balance, July 31, 19—

Cash	$1,135	
Accounts receivable........................	75	
Prepaid rent	400	
Office supplies	45	
Office equipment	1,500	
Accumulated depreciation, office equipment....		$ 20
Accounts payable...........................		260
Salaries payable...........................		75
Unearned legal fees		100
Larry Owen, capital		2,500
Larry Owen, withdrawals....................	200	
Legal fees earned		1,275
Office salaries expense.....................	575	
Telephone expense	30	
Heating and lighting expense................	35	
Rent expense	200	
Office supplies expense	15	
Depreciation expense, office equipment	20	
Totals	$4,230	$4,230

Illustration 3–2

PREPARING STATEMENTS FROM THE ADJUSTED TRIAL BALANCE

An adjusted trial balance shows proper balance sheet and income statement amounts. Consequently, it may be used in preparing the statements. When it is so used, the revenue and expense items are arranged into an income statement, as in Illustration 3–3. Likewise, the asset, liability, and owner's equity items are arranged into a balance sheet as in Illustration 3–4.

When the statements are prepared, the income statement is normally prepared first because the net income, as calculated on the income statement, is needed in completing the balance sheet's owner's equity section. Observe in Illustration 3–4 how the net income is combined with the withdrawals and the excess is added to Owen's July 1 capital. The income increased Owen's equity, and the withdrawals reduced it. Consequently, when the excess of the income over the withdrawals is added to the beginning equity, the result is the ending equity.

THE ADJUSTMENT PROCESS

The *adjustment process* described in this chapter arises from recognition that the operation of a business results in a continuous stream of transactions. Some of the transactions affect several accounting periods. And, the objective of the process is to allocate to each period that portion of a transaction's effects applicable to the period. For example, if a revenue is earned over several accounting periods, the adjustment process apportions and credits to each period its fair share. Likewise, if an expense benefits several periods, the adjustment process charges a fair share to each benefited period.

The adjustment process is based on two accounting principles, the *realization principle* and the *matching principle*. The *realization principle* requires that revenue be assigned to the accounting period in which it is earned, rather than to the period it is collected in cash. The *matching principle* requires that revenues and expenses be matched. As for matching revenues and expenses, it is recognized that a business incurs expenses in order to earn revenues. Consequently, it is only proper that expenses be matched with (deducted on the income statement from) the revenues they helped to produce.

The basic purpose behind the adjustment process, the *realization principle,* and the *matching principle* is to make the information on accounting statements comparable from period to period. For example, the Owen law practice paid its rent for three months in advance on July 1 and debited the $600 payment to Prepaid Rent. Then at the end of July it transferred $200 of this amount to its Rent Expense account and the $200 appeared on its July income statement as the

Larry Owen, Attorney
Adjusted Trial Balance, July 31, 19—

Cash	$1,135	
Accounts receivable	75	
Prepaid rent	400	
Office supplies	45	
Office equipment	1,500	
Accumulated depreciation, office equipment		$ 20
Accounts payable		260
Salaries payable		75
Unearned legal fees		100
Larry Owen, capital		2,500
Larry Owen, withdrawals	200	
Legal fees earned		1,275
Office salaries expense	575	
Telephone expense	30	
Heating and lighting expense	35	
Rent expense	200	
Office supplies expense	15	
Depreciation expense, office equipment	20	
Totals	$4,230	$4,230

Larry Owen, Attorney
Income Statement for Month Ended July 31, 19—

Revenue:		
Legal fees earned		$1,275
Operating expenses:		
Office salaries expense	$575	
Telephone expense	30	
Heating and lighting expense	35	
Rent expense	200	
Office supplies expense	15	
Depreciation expense, office equipment	20	
Total operating expense		875
Net income		$ 400

Illustration 3–3

PREPARING THE BALANCE SHEET
FROM THE ADJUSTED TRIAL BALANCE

Larry Owen, Attorney
Adjusted Trial Balance, July 31, 19—

Cash	$1,135	
Accounts receivable	75	
Prepaid rent	400	
Office supplies	45	
Office equipment	1,500	
Accumulated depreciation, office equipment		$ 20
Accounts payable		260
Salaries payable		75
Unearned legal fees		100
Larry Owen, capital		2,500
Larry Owen, withdrawals	200	
Legal fees earned		1,275
Office salaries expense	575	
Telephone expense	30	
Heating and lighting expense	35	
Rent expense	200	
Office supplies expense	15	
Depreciation expense, office equipment	20	
Totals	$4,230	$4,230

Larry Owen, Attorney
Balance Sheet, July 31, 19—

Assets

Current assets:			
Cash	$1,135		
Accounts receivable	75		
Prepaid rent	400		
Office supplies	45		
Total current assets			$1,655
Plant and equipment:			
Office equipment	$1,500		
Less accumulated depreciation	20		
Total plant and equipment			1,480
Total assets			$3,135

Liabilities

Current liabilities:		
Accounts payable	$ 260	
Salaries payable	75	
Unearned legal fees	100	
Total liabilities		$ 435

Owner's Equity

Larry Owen, capital, July 1, 19—			$2,500
July net income	$400		
Less withdrawals	200		
Excess of income over withdrawals			200
Larry Owen, capital, July 31, 19—			2,700
Total liabilities and owner's equity			$3,135

July net income
from the July
income statement

Illustration 3–4

July rent expense. At the end of August it will transfer another $200 to rent expense, and at the end of September it will transfer the third $200. As a result, the amounts shown for rent expense on its July, August, and September income statements will be comparable.

An unsatisfactory alternate procedure would be to debit the entire $600 to Rent Expense at the time of payment and permit the entire amount to appear on the July income statement as rent expense for July. However, if this were done, the July income statement would show $600 of rent expense and the August and September statements would show none. Thus the income statements of the three months would not be comparable. In addition, the July net income would be understated $400 and the net incomes of August and September would be overstated $200 each. As a result, a person seeing only the fluctuations in net income might draw an incorrect conclusion.

ARRANGEMENT OF THE ACCOUNTS IN THE LEDGER

Normally the accounts of a business are classified and logically arranged in its ledger. This serves two purposes: (1) it aids in locating any account and (2) it aids in preparing the statements. Obviously, statements can be prepared with the least difficulty if accounts are arranged in the ledger in the order of their statement appearance. This causes the accounts to appear on the adjusted trial balance in their statement order, which aids in rearranging the adjusted trial balance items into a balance sheet and an income statement. Consequently, the balance sheet accounts beginning with Cash and ending with the owner's equity accounts appear first in the ledger. These are followed by the revenue and expense accounts in the order of their income statement appearance.

DISPOSING OF ACCRUED ITEMS

Accrued expenses

Several pages back the July 29, 30, and 31 accrued wages of the secretary were recorded as follows:

July	31	Office Salaries Expense	75.00	
		Salaries Payable		75.00
		To record the earned but unpaid wages.		

When these wages are paid on Friday, August 9, the following entry is required:

Aug.	9	Salaries Payable	75.00	
		Office Salaries Expense	175.00	
		Cash		250.00
		Paid two weeks' wages.		

The first debit in the August 9 entry cancels the liability for the three days' wages accrued on July 31. The second debit records the wages of August's first seven working days as an expense of the August accounting period. The credit records the amount paid the secretary.

Accrued revenues

On July 15 Larry Owen entered into an agreement to do the legal work of Guaranty Bank on a fixed-fee basis for $150 per month. On July 31 the following entry was made to record one-half month's revenue earned under this contract:

July	31	Accounts Receivable	75.00	
		Legal Fees Earned		75.00
		To record legal fees earned.		

And when payment of the first month's fee is received on August 15, the following entry will be made:

Aug.	15	Cash	150.00	
		Accounts Receivable		75.00
		Legal Fees Earned		75.00
		Received legal fees earned.		

The first credit in the August 15 entry records the collection of the fee accrued at the end of July. The second credit records as revenue the fee earned during the first half of August.

CASH AND ACCRUAL BASES OF ACCOUNTING

For income tax purposes an individual or a business in which inventories are not a factor may report income on either a *cash basis* or an *accrual basis.* Under the cash basis no adjustments are made for prepaid, unearned, and accrued items. Revenues are reported as being earned in the accounting period in which they are received in cash.

Expenses are deducted from revenues in the accounting period in which cash is disbursed in their payment. As a result, under the cash basis, net income is the difference between revenue receipts and expense disbursements. Under the accrual basis, on the other hand, adjustments are made for accrued and deferred (prepaid and unearned) items. Under this basis revenues are credited to the period in which earned, expenses are matched with revenues, and no consideration is given to when cash is received and disbursed. As a result, net income is the difference between revenues earned and the expenses incurred in earning the revenues.

The cash basis of accounting is satisfactory for individuals and a few concerns in which accrued and deferred items are not important. However, it is not satisfactory for most concerns since it results in accounting reports that are not comparable from period to period. Consequently, most businesses keep their records on an accrual basis.

CLASSIFICATION OF BALANCE SHEET ITEMS

The balance sheets in the first two chapters were simple ones, and no attempt was made to classify the items. However, a balance sheet becomes more useful when its assets and liabilities are classified into significant groups, because a reader of a *classified balance sheet* can better judge the adequacy of the different kinds of assets used in the business. The reader can also better estimate the probable availability of funds to meet the various liabilities as they become due.

Accountants are not in full agreement as to the best way in which to classify balance sheet items. As a result, they are classified in several ways. A common way classifies assets into (1) current assets, (2) long-term investments, (3) plant and equipment, and (4) intangible assets. It classifies liabilities into (1) current liabilities and (2) long-term liabilities.

Of the four asset classifications listed, only two, current assets and plant and equipment, appear on the balance sheet of Valley Store, Illustration 3–5 on the next page. The store is small and has no long-term investments and intangible assets.

Current assets

Current assets are primarily those to which current creditors (current liabilities) may look for payment. As presently defined, current assets consist of cash and assets that are reasonably expected to be realized in cash or be sold or consumed within one year or within one *operating cycle of the business,* whichever is longer. The accounts and notes receivable of Illustration 3–5 are expected to be realized in cash. The merchandise (merchandise inventory) is expected to be sold either

Valley Store
Balance Sheet, December 31, 198A

Assets

Current assets:

Cash	$ 1,050	
Notes receivable	300	
Accounts receivable	3,961	
Merchandise inventory	10,248	
Prepaid insurance	109	
Office supplies	46	
Stores supplies	145	
Total current assets		$15,859

Plant and equipment:

Office equipment	$ 1,500		
Less accumulated depreciation	300	$ 1,200	
Store equipment	$ 3,200		
Less accumulated depreciation	800	2,400	
Buildings	$25,000		
Less accumulated depreciation	7,400	17,600	
Land		4,200	
Total plant and equipment			25,400
Total assets			$41,259

Liabilities

Current liabilities:

Notes payable	$ 3,000	
Accounts payable	2,715	
Wages payable	112	
Mortgage payable (current portion)	1,200	
Total current liabilities		$ 7,027

Long-term liabilities:

First mortgage payable, secured by a mortgage on land and buildings		8,800
Total liabilities		$15,827

Owner's Equity

Samuel Jackson, capital, January 1, 198A		$23,721
Net income for the year	$19,711	
Less withdrawals	18,000	
Excess of income over withdrawals		1,711
Samuel Jackson, capital, December 31, 198A		25,432
Total liabilities and owner's equity		$41,259

Illustration 3–5

for cash or accounts receivable that will be realized in cash. The prepaid insurance and supplies are to be consumed.

The operating cycle of a business is the average period of time between its acquisition of merchandise or raw materials and the realization of cash from the sale of the merchandise or the sale of the products manufactured from the raw materials. In many concerns this interval is less than one year, and as a result these concerns use a one-year period in classifying current assets. However, due to an aging process or other cause, some concerns have an operating cycle longer than one year. For example, distilleries must age some products for several years before the products are ready for sale. Consequently, in such concerns inventories of raw materials, manufacturing supplies, and products being processed for sale are classified as current assets, although the products made from the inventories will not be ready for sale for more than a year.

Such things as prepaid insurance, office supplies, and store supplies are called *prepaid expenses.* Until consumed they are classified as current assets. An AICPA committee said: "Prepaid expenses are not current assets in the sense that they will be converted into cash but in the sense that, if not paid in advance, they would require the use of current assets during the operating cycle."[1] This means that if the prepaid expense items were not already owned, current assets would be required for their purchase during the operating cycle.

The prepaid expenses of a business, as a total, are seldom a major item on its balance sheet. As a result, instead of listing them individually, as in Illustration 3–5, they are commonly totaled and only the total is shown under the caption "Prepaid expenses."

Long-term investments

The second balance sheet classification is long-term investments. Stocks, bonds, and promissory notes that will be held for more than one year or one cycle appear under this classification. Also, such things as land held for future expansion but not now being used in the business operations appear here.

Plant and equipment

Plant assets are relatively long-lived assets of a tangible nature that are held for use in the production or sale of other assets or services. Examples are items of equipment, buildings, and land. The key words in the definition are "long-lived" and "held for use in the production or sale of other assets or services." Land held for future expansion is not a plant asset. It is not being used to produce or sell other assets, goods, or services.

The words "Plant and equipment" are commonly used as a balance sheet caption. More complete captions are "Property, plant, and equipment" and "Land, buildings, and equipment." However, all three cap-

---

[1] Committee on Accounting Procedure, "Accounting Research Bulletin No. 43," *Accounting Research and Terminology Bulletins, Final Edition* (New York: AICPA, 1961), p. 20. Copyright (1961) by the American Institute of CPAs.

tions are long and unwieldy. As a result, items of plant and equipment will be called plant assets in this book.

The order in which plant assets are listed within the balance sheet classification is not uniform. However, they are often listed from the ones of least permanent nature to those of most permanent nature.

Intangible assets

Intangible assets are assets having no physical nature. Their value is derived from the rights conferred upon their owner by possession. Goodwill, patents, and trademarks are examples.

Current liabilities

Current liabilities are debts or other obligations that must be paid or liquidated within one year or one operating cycle, using presently listed current assets. Common current liabilities are notes payable, accounts payable, wages payable, taxes payable, interest payable, and unearned revenues. Also, that portion of a long-term debt due within one year or one operating cycle, for example, the $1,200 portion of the mortgage debt shown in Illustration 3–5, is a current liability. The order of their listing within the classification is not uniform. Often notes payable are listed first because notes receivable are listed first after cash in the current asset section.

Unearned revenues are classified as current liabilities because current assets will normally be required in their liquidation. For example, payments for future delivery of merchandise will be earned and the obligation for delivery will be liquidated by delivering merchandise, a current asset.

Long-term liabilities

The second main liability classification is long-term liabilities. Liabilities that are not due and payable for a comparatively long period, usually more than one year, are listed under this classification. Common long-term liability items are mortgages payable, bonds payable, and notes payable due more than a year after the balance sheet date.

OWNER'S EQUITY ON THE BALANCE SHEET

Single proprietorship

The equity of the owner of a single proprietorship business may be shown on a balance sheet as follows:

Owner's Equity

James Gibbs, capital, January 1, 198A		$23,152
Net income for the year	$10,953	
Withdrawals	12,000	
Excess of withdrawals over income		(1,047)
James Gibbs, capital, December 31, 198A		$22,105

The withdrawals of James Gibbs exceeded his net income, and in the equity section the excess is enclosed in parentheses to indicate that it is a negative or subtracted amount. Negative amounts are commonly shown in this way on financial statements.

The illustrated equity section shows the increases and decreases in owner's equity resulting from earnings and withdrawals. Some accountants prefer to put these details on a supplementary schedule attached to the balance sheet and called a *statement of owner's equity*. When this is done, owner's equity is shown on the balance sheet as follows:

Owner's Equity

James Gibbs, capital (see schedule attached)...... $22,105

Partnerships

Changes in partnership equities resulting from earnings and withdrawals are commonly shown in a statement of partners' equities. Then, only the amount of each partner's equity and the total of the equities as of the statement date are shown on the balance sheet, as follows:

Partners' Equities

John Reed, capital	$16,534	
Robert Burns, capital	18,506	
Total equities of the partners		$35,040

Corporations

Corporations are regulated by state corporation laws. These laws require that a distinction be made between amounts invested in a corporation by its stockholders and the increase or decrease in stockholders' equity due to earnings, losses, and dividends. Consequently, stockholders' equity is commonly shown on a corporation balance sheet as follows:

Stockholders' Equity

Common stock	$500,000	
Retained earnings	64,450	
Total stockholders' equity ...		$564,450

If a corporation issues only one kind of stock (others are discussed later), it is called *common stock*. The $500,000 amount shown here for this item is the amount originally invested in this corporation by its stockholders through the purchase of the corporation's stock. The $64,450 of *retained earnings* represents the increase in the stockholders' equity resulting from earnings that exceeded any losses and any *dividends* paid to the stockholders. (A dividend is a distribution of assets made by a corporation to its stockholders. A dividend of cash reduces corporation assets and the equity of its stockholders in the same way a withdrawal reduces assets and owner's equity in a single proprietorship.)

ARRANGEMENT OF BALANCE SHEET ITEMS

The balance sheet of Illustration 1–2 in the first chapter, with the liabilities and owner's equity placed to the right of the assets, is called an *account form balance sheet*. Such an arrangement emphasizes that assets equal liabilities plus owner's equity. Account form balance sheets are often reproduced on a double page with the assets on the left-hand page and the liabilities and owner's equity on the right-hand page.

The balance sheet of Illustration 3–5 is called a *report form balance sheet*. Its items are arranged vertically and better fit a single page. Both forms are commonly used, and neither is preferred.

CLASSIFICATION OF INCOME STATEMENT ITEMS

An income statement, like a balance sheet, is more useful with its items classified. However, the classifications used depend upon the type of business for which the statement is prepared and the nature of its costs and expenses; consequently, a discussion of this is deferred to Chapter 5, after more income statement items are introduced.

GLOSSARY

Account form balance sheet. A balance sheet with the assets on the left and the liability and owner's equity items on the right.

Accounting period. The time interval over which the transactions of a business are recorded and at the end of which its financial statements are prepared.

Accrual basis of accounting. The accounting basis in which revenues are assigned to the accounting period in which earned regardless of whether or not received in cash and expenses incurred in earning the revenues are deducted from the revenues regardless of whether or not cash has been disbursed in their payment.

Accrued expense. An expense which has been incurred during an accounting period but which has not been paid and recorded because payment is not due.

Accrued revenue. A revenue that has been earned during an accounting period but has not been received and recorded because payment is not due.

Accumulated depreciation. The cumulative amount of depreciation recorded against an asset or group of assets during the entire period of time the asset or assets have been owned.

Adjusted trial balance. A trial balance showing account balances brought up to date by recording appropriate adjusting entries.

Adjusting entries. Journal entries made to assign revenues to the period in which earned and to match revenues and expenses.

Adjustment process. The end-of-the-period process of recording appropriate adjusting entries to assign revenues to the period in which earned and to match revenues and expenses.

Cash basis of accounting. The accounting basis in which revenues are reported as being earned in the accounting period received in cash and expenses are deducted from revenues in the accounting period in which cash is disbursed in their payment.

Classified balance sheet. A balance sheet with assets and liabilities classified into significant groups.

Common stock. The name given to a corporation's stock when it issues only one kind or class of stock.

Contra account. An account the balance of which is subtracted from the balance of an associated account to show a more proper amount for the item recorded in the associated account.

Current asset. Cash or an asset that may reasonably be expected to be realized in cash or be consumed within one year or one operating cycle of the business, whichever is longer.

Current liability. A debt or other obligation that must be paid or liquidated within one year or one operating cycle, and the payment or liquidation of which will require the use of presently classified current assets.

Depreciation. The expiration of a plant asset's "quantity of usefulness."

Depreciation expense. The expense resulting from the expiration of a plant asset's "quantity of usefulness."

Dividend. A distribution of cash or other assets made by a corporation to its stockholders.

Fiscal year. A period of any 12 consecutive months used as an accounting period.

Intangible asset. An asset having no physical existence but having value because of the rights conferred as a result of its ownership and possession.

Matching principle. The accounting rule that all expenses incurred in earning a revenue be deducted from the revenue in determining net income.

Natural business year. Any 12 consecutive months used by a business as an accounting period, at the end of which the activities of the business are at their lowest point.

Operating cycle of a business. The average period of time between the acquisition of merchandise or materials by a business and the realization of cash from the sale of the merchandise or product manufactured from the materials.

Plant and equipment. Tangible assets having relatively long lives that are used in the production or sale of other assets or services.

Prepaid expense. An asset that will be consumed in the operation of a business, and as it is consumed it will become an expense.

Report form balance sheet. A balance sheet prepared on one page, at the top of which the assets are listed, followed down the page by the liabilities and owner's equity.

Retained earnings. Stockholders' equity in a corporation resulting from earnings in excess of losses and dividends declared.

Time-period concept. The idea that the life of a business is divisible into time periods of equal length.

Unadjusted trial balance. A trial balance prepared after transactions are recorded but before any adjustments are made.

Unearned revenue. Payment received in advance for goods or services to be delivered at a later date.

QUESTIONS FOR CLASS DISCUSSION

1. Why are the balances of some of a concern's accounts normally incorrect for statement purposes at the end of an accounting period even though all transactions were correctly recorded?
2. Other than to make the accounts show proper statement amounts, what is the basic purpose behind the end-of-the-period adjustment process?
3. A prepaid expense is an asset at the time of its purchase or prepayment. When is it best to ignore this and record the prepayment as an expense? Why?
4. What is a contra account? Give an example.
5. What contra account is used in recording depreciation? Why is such an account used?

6. What is an accrued expense? Give an example.
7. How does an unearned revenue arise? Give an example of an unearned revenue.
8. What is the balance sheet classification of an unearned revenue?
9. What is an accrued revenue? Give an example.
10. When the statements are prepared from an adjusted trial balance, why should the income statement be prepared first?
11. The adjustment process results from recognizing that some transactions affect several accounting periods. What is the objective of the process?
12. When are a concern's revenues and expenses matched?
13. Why should the income statements of a concern be comparable from period to period?
14. What is the usual order in which accounts are arranged in the ledger?
15. Differentiate between the cash and the accrual bases of accounting?
16. What is a classified balance sheet?
17. What are the characteristics of a current asset? What are the characteristics of an asset classified as plant and equipment?
18. What are current liabilities? Long-term liabilities?
19. The equity section of a corporation balance sheet shows two items, common stock and retained earnings. What does the sum of the items represent? How did each item arise?

CLASS EXERCISES

Exercise 3–1

A company has two shop employees who together earn a total of $100 per day for a five-day week that begins on Monday and ends on Friday. They were paid for the week ended Friday, December 26, and both worked full days on Monday, Tuesday, and Wednesday, December 29, 30, and 31. January 1 of the next year was an unpaid holiday and none of the employees worked, but all worked a full day on Friday, January 2. Give in general journal form the year-end adjusting entry to record the accrued wages and the entry to pay the employees on January 2.

Exercise 3–2

Give in general journal form the year-end adjusting entry for each of the following situations:

a. The Shop Supplies account had a $225 debit balance on January 1; $340 of supplies were purchased during the year; and a year-end inventory showed $120 of unconsumed supplies on hand.
b. The Prepaid Insurance account had a $765 debit balance at the end of the accounting period before adjustment for expired insurance. An examination of insurance policies showed $410 of insurance expired.
c. The Prepaid Insurance account had an $880 debit balance at the end of the accounting period before adjustment for expired insurance. An examination of insurance policies showed $315 of unexpired insurance.

d. Depreciation on shop equipment was estimated at $625 for the accounting period.

e. Three months' property taxes, estimated at $320, have accrued but are unrecorded at the accounting period end.

Exercise 3–3

Assume that the required adjustments of Exercise 3–2 were not made at the end of the accounting period and tell for each adjustment the effect of its omission on the income statement and balance sheet prepared at that time.

Exercise 3–4

Determine the amounts indicated by the question marks in the columns below. The amounts in each column constitute a separate problem.

	(a)	(b)	(c)	(d)
Supplies on hand on January 1	$235	$140	$375	?
Supplies purchased during the year	450	530	?	$630
Supplies remaining at the year-end	165	?	215	240
Supplies consumed during the year	?	480	670	560

Exercise 3–5

A company paid the $900 premium on a three-year insurance policy on June 1, 198A.

a. How many dollars of the premium should appear on the 198A income statement as an expense?

b. How many dollars of the premium should appear on the December 31, 198A, balance sheet as an asset?

c. Under the assumption that the Prepaid Insurance account was debited in recording the premium payment, give the December 31, 198A, adjusting entry to record the expired insurance.

d. Under the assumption that the bookkeeper incorrectly debited the Insurance Expense account for $900 in recording the premium payment, give the December 31, 198A, adjusting entry. (Hint: Did the bookkeeper's error change the answers to questions [a] and [b] of this exercise?)

Exercise 3–6

a. A tenant rented space in a building on November 1 at $300 per month, paying six months' rent in advance. The building owner credited Unearned Rent to record the $1,800 received. Give the year-end adjusting entry of the building owner.

b. Another tenant rented space in the building at $400 per month on October 1. The tenant paid the rent on the first day of October and again on the first day of November; but by December 31 the December rent had not yet been paid. Give the required adjusting entry of the building owner.

c. Assume the foregoing tenant paid the rent for December and January on January 2 of the new year. Give the entry to record the receipt of the $800.

PROBLEMS

Problem 3–1

The following information for adjustments was available on December 31, the end of a yearly accounting period. Prepare an adjusting journal entry for each unit of information.

a. The Store Supplies account had a $125 debit balance at the beginning of the year, $560 of supplies were purchased during the year, and an inventory of unused store supplies at the year-end totaled $135.
b. An examination of insurance policies showed three policies, as follows:

Policy	Date of purchase	Life of policy	Cost
1....	October 1 of previous year	3 years	$720
2....	April 1 of current year	2 years	480
3....	August 1 of current year	1 year	180

Prepaid Insurance was debited for the cost of each policy at the time of its purchase. Expired insurance was correctly recorded at the end of the previous year.
c. The company's two office employees earn $40 per day and $50 per day, respectively. They are paid each Friday for a five-day workweek that begins on Monday. This year December 31 falls on Tuesday, and the employees both worked on Monday and Tuesday.
d. The company owns a building that it completed and occupied for the first time on June 1 of the current year. The building cost $288,000, has an estimated 40-year life, and is not expected to have any salvage value at the end of that time.
e. The company occupies most of the space in its building but it also rents space to two tenants. One tenant rented a small amount of space on September 1 at $120 per month. The tenant paid the rent on the first day of each month September through November, and the amounts paid were credited to Rent Earned. However, the tenant has not paid the rent for December, although on several occasions the tenant said the rent would be paid the next day. (f) The second tenant agreed on November 1 to rent a small amount of space at $150 per month, and on that date paid three months' rent in advance. The amount paid was credited to the Unearned Rent account.

Problem 3–2

A trial balance of the ledger of Rockhill Realty at the end of its annual accounting period carried these items:

ROCKHILL REALTY
Trial Balance, December 31, 19—

Cash	$ 2,940	
Prepaid insurance	815	
Office supplies	290	
Office equipment	3,250	
Accumulated depreciation, office equipment		$ 920
Automobile	6,780	
Accumulated depreciation, automobile		1,150
Accounts payable		225
Unearned management fees		420
Alice Hall, capital		6,745
Alice Hall, withdrawals	15,600	
Sales commissions earned		34,210
Office salaries expense	10,300	
Advertising expense	830	
Rent expense	2,400	
Telephone expense	465	
Totals	$43,670	$43,670

Required:

1. Open the accounts of the trial balance plus these additional ones: Accounts Receivable; Office Salaries Payable; Management Fees Earned; Insurance Expense; Office Supplies Expense; Depreciation Expense, Office Equipment; and Depreciation Expense, Automobile. Enter the trial balance amounts in the accounts.
2. Use the following information to prepare and post adjusting journal entries:
   a. An examination of insurance policies showed $585 of expired insurance.
   b. An inventory showed $75 of unused office supplies on hand.
   c. The year's depreciation on office equipment was estimated at $325 and (d) on the automobile at $1,100.
   e. and (f) Rockhill Realty offers property management services and has two contracts with clients. In the first contract (e) it is agreed to manage an office building beginning on November 1. The contract called for a $140 monthly fee, and the client paid the fees for the first three months in advance at the time the contract was signed. The amount paid was credited to the Unearned Management Fees account. In the second contract (f) it agreed to manage an apartment building for a $100 monthly fee payable at the end of each quarter. The contract was signed on October 15, and two and a half months' fees have accrued.
   g. The one office employee is paid weekly, and on December 31 three days' wages at $40 per day have accrued.
3. After posting the adjusting entries, prepare an adjusted trial balance, an income statement, and a classified balance sheet.

Problem 3–3

A trial balance of the ledger of Phoenix Moving and Storage Service carried these items:

PHOENIX MOVING AND STORAGE SERVICE
Trial Balance, December 31, 19—

Cash	$ 1,240	
Accounts receivable	590	
Prepaid insurance	1,580	
Office supplies	220	
Office equipment	2,650	
Accumulated depreciation, office equipment		$ 680
Trucks	24,200	
Accumulated depreciation, trucks		8,540
Buildings	68,000	
Accumulated depreciation, buildings		8,600
Land	7,500	
Unearned storage fees		730
Mortgage payable		37,500
Ted Lee, capital		35,290
Ted Lee, withdrawals	13,000	
Revenue from moving services		56,860
Storage fees earned		3,770
Office salaries expense	8,580	
Movers' wage expense	18,730	
Gas, oil, and repairs expense	2,680	
Mortgage interest expense	3,000	
Totals	$151,970	$151,970

Required:

1. Open the accounts of the trial balance plus these additional ones: Wages Payable; Insurance Expense; Office Supplies Expense; Depreciation Expense, Office Equipment; Depreciation Expense, Trucks; and Depreciation Expense, Buildings. Enter the trial balance amounts in the accounts.

2. Use this information to prepare and post adjusting journal entries:
   a. An examination of insurance policies showed $1,270 of expired insurance.
   b. An inventory of office supplies showed $60 of unused supplies on hand.
   c. Estimated depreciation on office equipment, $240; *(d)* trucks, $3,000; and *(e)* buildings, $2,400.
   f. The company credits the storage fees of customers who pay in advance to the Unearned Storage Fees account. Of the $730 credited to this account during the year, $420 had been earned by the year-end.
   g. Accrued storage fees earned but unrecorded in the accounts and uncollected at the year-end totaled $160.
   h. There were $540 of accrued movers' wages at the year-end.

3. After posting the adjusting journal entries, prepare an adjusted trial balance, an income statement, and a classified balance sheet. A $2,500 installment on the mortgage is due within one year.

Problem 3–4

After all its transactions had been recorded at the end of its annual accounting period, a trial balance of the ledger of RV Trailer Park carried these items:

RV TRAILER PARK
Trial Balance, December 31, 19—

Cash	$ 3,540	
Prepaid insurance	825	
Office supplies	260	
Office equipment	1,450	
Accumulated depreciation, office equipment		$ 420
Buildings and improvements	72,000	
Accumulated depreciation, buildings		
and improvements		8,350
Land	85,000	
Unearned rent		480
Mortgage payable		108,000
Jane Wells, capital		35,635
Jane Wells, withdrawals	10,500	
Rent earned		39,865
Wages expense	8,120	
Utilities expense	525	
Property taxes expense	2,115	
Interest expense	8,415	
Totals	$192,750	$192,750

Required:

1. Open the accounts of the trial balance plus these additional ones: Accounts Receivable; Wages Payable; Property Taxes Payable; Interest Payable; Insurance Expense; Office Supplies Expense; Depreciation Expense, Office Equipment; and Depreciation Expense, Buildings and Improvements.
2. Use the following information to prepare and to post adjusting journal entries:

   a. An examination of insurance policies showed $650 of insurance expired.
   b. An office supplies inventory showed $110 of unused supplies on hand.
   c. Estimated depreciation of office equipment, $125; and (d) on the buildings and improvements, $2,450.
   e. RV Trailer Park follows the practice of crediting the Unearned Rent account for rents paid in advance by tenants, and an examination revealed that $360 of the balance of this account had been earned by year-end.
   f. A tenant is a month in arrears on rent payments, and this $75 of accrued revenue was unrecorded at the time the trial balance was prepared.
   g. The one employee works a five-day week at $30 per day. The employee was paid last week but has worked two days this week for which no pay was received.
   h. Three months' property taxes expense, totaling $700, has accrued but is unrecorded.
   i. One month's interest on the mortgage, $765, has accrued but is unrecorded.

3. After posting the adjusting journal entries, prepare an adjusted trial balance, an income statement, and a classified balance sheet. A $3,000 installment on the mortgage is due within one year.

Problem 3–5

The 198A and 198B balance sheets of a company showed the following asset and liability amounts at the end of each year:

	December 31	
	198A	198B
Prepaid insurance	$600	$300
Interest payable	400	100
Unearned property management fees	200	500

The concern's records showed the following amounts of cash disbursed and received for these items during 198B:

Cash disbursed to pay insurance premiums	$1,600
Cash disbursed to pay interest	1,200
Cash received for managing property	2,300

Required:

Present calculations to show the amounts to be reported on the 198B income statements for (a) insurance expense, (b) interest expense, and (c) property management fees earned.

ALTERNATE PROBLEMS

Problem 3–1A

The following information for adjustments was available on December 31, the end of an annual accounting period. Prepare an adjusting journal entry for each unit of information.

a. The Office Supplies account showed the following items:

Office Supplies

Jan. 1	Balance	85
Feb. 9	Purchase	140
Oct. 4	Purchase	65

The year-end office supplies inventory showed $75 of unused supplies on hand.

b. The Prepaid Insurance account showed these items:

Prepaid Insurance

Jan. 1	Balance	280
June 1		540
Aug. 1		720

The January 1 balance represents the unexpired premium on a one-year policy purchased on June 1 of the previous year. The June 1 debit resulted from paying the premium on a one-year policy, and the August 1 debit represents the cost of a three-year policy.

c. The company's three office employees earn $24, $32, and $40 per day, respectively. They are paid each Friday for a five-day workweek that begins on Monday. They were paid last week and have worked Monday, Tuesday, and Wednesday, December 29, 30, and 31, this week.

d. The company owns and occupies a building that was completed and occupied for the first time on March 1 of the current year. Previously the company had rented quarters. The building cost $360,000, has an estimated 40-year useful life, and is not expected to have any salvage value at the end of its life.

e. The company rents portions of the space in its building to two tenants. One tenant agreed beginning on September 1 to rent a small amount of space at $125 per month, and on that date the tenant paid six months' rent in advance. The $750 payment was credited to the Unearned Rent account.

f. The other tenant pays $150 rent per month on the space occupied by the tenant. During the months May through November the tenant paid the rent each month on the first day of the month, and the amounts paid were credited to Rent Earned. However, recently the tenant experienced financial difficulties and has not as yet paid the rent for the month of December.

Problem 3–2A

A trial balance of the ledger of Hillside Realty at the end of its annual accounting period carried these items:

HILLSIDE REALTY
Trial Balance, December 31, 19—

Cash	$ 2,940	
Prepaid insurance	815	
Office supplies	290	
Office equipment	3,250	
Accumulated depreciation, office equipment		$ 920
Automobile	6,780	
Accumulated depreciation, automobile		1,150
Accounts payable		225
Unearned management fees		420
Alice Hall, capital		6,745
Alice Hall, withdrawals	15,600	
Sales commissions earned		34,210
Office salaries expense	10,300	
Advertising expense	830	
Rent expense	2,400	
Telephone expense	465	
Totals	$43,670	$43,670

Required:

1. Open the accounts of the trial balance plus these additional ones: Accounts Receivable; Office Salaries Payable; Management Fees Earned; Insurance Expense; Office Supplies Expense; Depreciation Expense, Office Equipment; and Depreciation Expense, Automobile. Enter the trial balance amounts in the accounts.

2. Use the following information to prepare and post adjusting journal entries:

   a. An examination of insurance policies showed $210 of unexpired insurance.

   b. An office supplies inventory showed $120 of unused supplies on hand.

   c. Depreciation for the year on the office equipment was estimated at $400, and *(d)* it was estimated at $1,150 on the automobile.

   e. The company offers property management services and has two clients under contract. It agreed to manage an apartment building for the first client for a $60 monthly fee payable at the end of each quarter. The contract with this client was signed on November 1, and two months' fees have accrued.

   f. For the second client it agreed to manage an office building for a $70 monthly fee. The contract with this client was signed on October 15, and at that time the client paid six months' fees in advance, which were credited on receipt to the Unearned Management Fees account.

   g. The office secretary is paid weekly, and on December 31 four days' wages at $40 per day have accrued.

   h. The December telephone bill, $45, arrived in the mail on December 31. It has not been recorded or paid.

3. After posting the adjusting entries, prepare an adjusted trial balance, an income statement, and a classified balance sheet.

Problem 3-3A

At the end of its annual accounting period Carefree Moving and Storage Service prepared the following trial balance:

CAREFREE MOVING AND STORAGE SERVICE
Trial Balance, December 31, 19—

Cash	$ 1,240	
Accounts receivable	590	
Prepaid insurance	1,580	
Office supplies	220	
Office equipment	2,650	
Accumulated depreciation, office equipment		$ 680
Trucks	24,200	
Accumulated depreciation, trucks		8,540
Buildings	68,000	
Accumulated depreciation, buildings		8,600
Land	7,500	
Unearned storage fees		730
Mortgage payable		37,500
Ted Lee, capital		35,290
Ted Lee, withdrawals	13,000	
Revenue from moving services		56,860
Storage fees earned		3,770
Office salaries expense	8,580	
Movers' wages expense	18,730	
Gas, oil, and repairs expense	2,680	
Mortgage interest expense	3,000	
Totals	$151,970	$151,970

Required:

1. Open the accounts of the trial balance plus these additional ones: Wages Payable; Insurance Expense; Office Supplies Expense; Depreciation Expense, Office Equipment; Depreciation Expense, Trucks; and Depreciation Expense, Buildings. Enter the trial balance amounts in the accounts.
2. Use this information to prepare and post adjusting journal entries:
   a. An examination of insurance policies showed that $1,310 of insurance had expired.
   b. An inventory of office supplies showed $40 of unused supplies on hand.
   c. Estimated depreciation on office equipment, $285; *(d)* trucks, $4,200; and *(e)* buildings, $2,800.
   f. The company credits the storage fees of customers who pay in advance to the Unearned Storage Fees account. Of the $730 credited to this account during the year, $380 had been earned by the year-end.
   g. Accrued storage fees earned but unrecorded in the accounts and uncollected at the year-end totaled $130.
   h. There were $490 of earned but unpaid movers' wages at the year-end.
3. After posting the adjusting journal entries, prepare an adjusted trial balance, an income statement, and a classified balance sheet. A $3,500 installment on the mortgage is due within one year.

Problem 3–4A

An inexperienced bookkeeper prepared the first of the following income statements but forgot to adjust the accounts before its preparation. However, the oversight was discovered, and the second correct statement was prepared. Analyze the two statements and prepare the adjusting journal entries that were made between their preparation. Assume that one fourth of the additional property management fees resulted from recognizing accrued management fees and three fourths resulted from previously recorded unearned fees that were earned by the time the statements were prepared. (You will need only general journal paper for the solution of this problem. You may use the paper provided for Problems 3–4 or 3–4A or for any other unassigned problem.)

ACTION REALTY
Income Statement for Year Ended December 31, 19—

Revenues:

Commissions earned		$31,540
Property management fees earned		2,235
Total revenues		$33,775
Operating expenses:		
Rent expense	$3,025	
Salaries expense	8,280	
Advertising expense	1,315	
Utilities expense	675	
Telephone expense	545	
Gas, oil, and repairs expense	925	
Total operating expenses		14,765
Net income		$19,010

ACTION REALTY
Income Statement for Year Ended December 31, 19—

Revenues:

Commissions earned		$31,540
Property management fees earned		2,875
Total revenues		$34,415

Operating expenses:

Rent expense	$3,300	
Salaries expense	8,345	
Advertising expense	1,380	
Utilities expense	675	
Telephone expense	545	
Gas, oil, and repairs expense	940	
Office supplies expense	215	
Insurance expense	985	
Depreciation expense, office equipment	420	
Depreciation expense, automobile	1,210	
Taxes expense	185	
Total operating expenses		18,200
Net income		$16,215

Problem 3–5A

Robert Snell, a lawyer, has always kept his accounting records on a cash basis; and at the end of 198B he prepared the following cash basis income statement:

ROBERT SNELL, ATTORNEY
Income Statement for Year Ended December 31, 198B

Revenues	$46,400
Expenses	22,300
Net income	$24,100

In preparing the income statement, the following amounts of accrued and deferred items were ignored at the ends of 198A and 198B:

	End of	
	198A	198B
Prepaid expenses	$1,215	$ 840
Accrued expenses	2,240	1,925
Unearned revenues	1,370	1,535
Accrued revenues	1,860	1,490

Required:

Assume that the 198A prepaid and unearned items became expenses or were earned in 198B, the ignored 198A accrued items were either received in cash or were paid in 198B, and prepare a condensed 198B accrual basis income statement for Robert Snell. Attach to your income statement calculations showing how you arrived at each income statement amount.

PROVOCATIVE PROBLEMS

Provocative problem 3–1
Andy Handy

On January 2 of this year Andy Handy began a small business he calls Handy Repair Shop. He has kept no formal accounting records, but he does file any unpaid invoices for things purchased by impaling them on a nail in the wall over his workbench. He has kept a good check stub record of the year's receipts and payments, which shows the following:

	Receipts	Payments
Investment	$ 3,000	
Shop equipment		$ 2,000
Repair parts and supplies		3,220
Rent expense		1,950
Insurance premiums		470
Newpaper advertising		250
Utilities		340
Helper's wages		6,180
Andy Handy for personal uses		13,900
Revenue from repairs	26,890	
Subtotals	$29,890	$28,310
Cash balance, December 31, 19—		1,580
Totals.........................	$29,890	$29,890

Andy wants to know how much his business actually earned during its first year, and he would like for you to prepare an accrual basis income statement and a year-end classified balance sheet. You learn that the shop equipment has an estimated ten-year life, after which it will be worthless. There is a $275 unpaid invoice on the nail over Andy's workbench for supplies received, and an inventory shows $330 of unused supplies on hand. The shop space rents for $150 per month on a five-year lease. The lease contract requires payment for the first and last months' rents in advance, which were paid. The insurance premiums paid for two policies taken out on January 2. The first is a one-year policy that cost $110, and the second is a two-year policy that cost $360. There are $60 of accrued wages payable to the helper, and customers owe the shop $415 for services they have received.

Provocative problem 3–2
Dale's TV Service

Dale West began a new business on January 2 of this year. He calls the business Dale's TV Service, and he has asked you for help in determining the results of its first year's operations and its year-end financial position. He feels that the business has done a lot of work, but the bank has begun to dishonor its checks, its creditors are dunning the business and it is unable to pay, and he just cannot understand why.

You find the service's accounting records, such as they are, have been kept by Dale West's wife, who has had no formal training in record keeping. However she has prepared the following statement of cash receipts and disbursements for your inspection:

DALE'S TV SERVICE
Cash Receipts and Disbursements
For Year Ended December 31, 19—

Receipts:

Investment	$ 5,000	
Received from customers for services	34,490	$39,490

Disbursements:

Rent expense	$ 2,600	
Repair equipment purchased	4,200	
Service truck expense	6,975	
Wages expense	19,240	
Insurance expense	890	
Repair parts and supplies...............	5,650	39,555
Bank overdraft		$ (65)

There were no errors in the statement and you learn these additional facts:

1. The lease contract for the shop space runs for five years and requires rent payments of $200 per month, with the first and last months' rent to be paid in advance. All required payments were made on time.
2. The repair equipment purchased has an estimated six-year life, after which it will be valueless. It has been used for the full year.
3. The service truck expense consists of $6,100 paid for the truck on January 2, plus $875 paid for gas, oil, and repairs to the truck. Mr. West expects to use the truck four years, after which he thinks he will get $2,100 for it as a trade-in on a new truck.
4. The wages expense consists of $6,240 paid the service's one employee since he was hired on June 1 plus $250 per week withdrawn by Mr. West for personal living expenses. In addition, $100 is owed the one employee on December 31 for wages earned since the employee's last payday.
5. The $890 of insurance expense resulted from paying the premiums on two insurance policies on January 2. One policy cost $170 and gave protection for one year, and the other policy cost $720 for two years' protection.
6. In addition to the $5,650 of repair parts and supplies paid for during the year, creditors are dunning the business for $515 for parts and supplies purchased and delivered, but not paid for. Also, an inventory shows there are $985 of unused parts and supplies on hand.
7. Mr. West reports that the business does most of its work for cash, but customers do owe $450 for repair work done on credit.

Prepare an income statement showing the results of the first year's operations of the business and a classified balance sheet showing its financial position as of the year-end.

After studying Chapter 4, you should be able to:

☐ Explain why a work sheet is prepared and be able to prepare a work sheet for a service-type business.

☐ Explain why it is necessary to close the revenue and expense accounts at the end of each accounting period.

☐ Prepare entries to close the temporary accounts of a service business and prepare a post-closing trial balance to test the accuracy of the end-of-the-period adjusting and closing procedures.

☐ Explain the nature of the retained earnings item on corporation balance sheets.

☐ Explain why a corporation with a deficit cannot pay a legal dividend.

☐ Prepare entries to close the Income Summary account of a corporation and to record the declaration and payment of a dividend.

☐ List the steps in the accounting cycle in the order in which they are completed.

☐ Define or explain the words and phrases listed in the chapter Glossary.

The work sheet and closing the accounts of proprietorships, partnerships, and corporations

■ As an aid in their work, accountants prepare numerous memoranda, analyses, and informal papers that serve as a basis for the formal reports given to the management or to their clients. These analyses and memoranda are called *working papers* and are invaluable tools of the accountant. The work sheet described in this chapter is such a working paper. It is prepared solely for the accountant's use. It is not given to the owner or manager of the business for which it is prepared but is retained by the accountant. Normally it is prepared with a pencil, which makes changes and corrections easy as its preparation progresses.

WORK SHEET IN THE ACCOUNTING PROCEDURES

In the accounting procedures described in the previous chapter, at the end of an accounting period, as soon as all transactions were recorded, recall that adjusting entries were entered in the journal and posted to the accounts. Then an adjusted trial balance was prepared and used in making an income statement and balance sheet. For a very small business these are satisfactory procedures. However, if a company has more than a very few accounts and adjustments, errors in adjusting the accounts and in preparing the statements are less apt to be made if an additional step is inserted in the procedures. The additional step is the preparation of a *work sheet*. A work sheet is a tool of accountants upon which they (1) achieve the effect of adjusting the accounts before entering the adjustments in the accounts, (2) sort the adjusted account balances into columns according to whether the accounts are used in preparing the income statement or balance sheet, and (3) calculate and prove the mathematical accuracy of the net income. Then after the work sheet is completed, (4) accountants use the work sheet in preparing the income statement and balance sheet and in preparing adjusting journal entries.

PREPARING A WORK SHEET

The Owen law practice of previous chapters does not have sufficient accounts or adjustments to warrant the preparation of a work sheet. Nevertheless, since its accounts and adjustments are familiar, they are used here to illustrate the procedures involved.

During July the Owen law practice completed a number of transactions. On July 31, after these transactions were recorded but *before any adjusting entries were prepared and posted,* a trial balance of its ledger appeared as in Illustration 4–1.

Larry Owen, Attorney		
Trial Balance, July 31, 19—		
Cash	$1,135	
Prepaid rent	600	
Office supplies	60	
Office equipment	1,500	
Accounts payable		$ 260
Unearned legal fees		150
Larry Owen, capital		2,500
Larry Owen, withdrawals	200	
Legal fees earned		1,150
Office salaries expense	500	
Telephone expense	30	
Heating and lighting expense	35	
Totals	$4,060	$4,060

Illustration 4–1

Notice that the trial balance is an *unadjusted trial balance.* The accounts have not been adjusted for expired rent, supplies consumed, depreciation, and so forth. Nevertheless, this unadjusted trial balance is the starting point in preparing the work sheet for the law practice. The work sheet is shown in Illustration 4–2.

Note that the work sheet has five pairs of money columns and that the first pair is labeled "Trial Balance." In this first pair of columns is copied the unadjusted trial balance of the law practice. Often when a work sheet is prepared, the trial balance is prepared for the first time in its first two money columns.

The second pair of work sheet columns is labeled "Adjustments."

Larry Owen, Attorney
Work Sheet for Month Ended July 31, 19--

ACCOUNT TITLES	TRIAL BALANCE DR.	TRIAL BALANCE CR.	ADJUSTMENTS DR.	ADJUSTMENTS CR.	ADJUSTED TRIAL BALANCE DR.	ADJUSTED TRIAL BALANCE CR.	INCOME STATEMENT DR.	INCOME STATEMENT CR.	BALANCE SHEET DR.	BALANCE SHEET CR.
Cash	1,135 00				1,135 00				1,135 00	
Prepaid rent	600 00			(a)200 00	400 00				400 00	
Office supplies	60 00			(b) 15 00	45 00				45 00	
Office equipment	1,500 00				1,500 00				1,500 00	
Accounts payable		260 00				260 00				260 00
Unearned legal fees		150 00	(e) 50 00			100 00				100 00
Larry Owen, capital		2,500 00				2,500 00				2,500 00
Larry Owen, withdrawals	200 00				200 00				200 00	
Legal fees earned		1,150 00		(e)125 00		1,275 00		1,275 00		
Office salaries expense	500 00		(d) 75 00		575 00		575 00			
Telephone expense	30 00				30 00		30 00			
Heating & lighting expense	35 00				35 00		35 00			
	4,060 00	4,060 00								
Rent expense			(a)200 00		200 00		200 00			
Office supplies expense			(b) 15 00		15 00		15 00			
Depr. expense, office equip.			(c) 20 00		20 00		20 00			
Accum. depr., office equip.				(c) 20 00		20 00				20 00
Salaries payable				(d) 75 00		75 00				75 00
Accounts receivable			(e) 75 00		75 00				75 00	
			435 00	435 00	4,230 00	4,230 00	875 00	1,275 00	3,355 00	2,955 00
Net income							400 00			400 00
							1,275 00	1,275 00	3,355 00	3,355 00

Illustration 4-2

The adjustments are entered in these columns. Note they are, with one exception, the same adjustments for which adjusting journal entries were prepared and posted in the previous chapter. The one exception is the last one, *(e)*, in which the two adjustments affecting the Legal Fees Earned account are combined into one compound adjustment. They were combined because both result in credits to the same account.

Note that the adjustments on the illustrated work sheet are keyed together with letters. When a work sheet is prepared, after it is completed, the adjusting entries still have to be entered in the journal and posted to the ledger. At that time the key letters help identify each adjustment's related debits and credits. Explanations of the adjustments on the illustrated work sheet are as follows:

Adjustment (a): To adjust for the rent expired.
Adjustment (b): To adjust for the office supplies consumed.
Adjustment (c): To adjust for depreciation of the office equipment.
Adjustment (d): To adjust for the accrued secretary's salary.
Adjustment (e): To adjust for unearned and accrued revenue.

Each adjustment on the illustrated work sheet required that one or two additional account names be written in below the original trial balance. These accounts did not have balances when the trial balance was prepared. Consequently, they were not listed in the trial balance. Often, when a work sheet is prepared, the effects of the adjustments are anticipated and any additional accounts required are provided without amounts in the body of the trial balance.

When a work sheet is prepared, after the adjustments are entered in the Adjustments columns, the columns are totaled to prove the equality of the adjustments.

The third set of work sheet columns is labeled "Adjusted Trial Balance." In preparing a work sheet, each amount in the Trial Balance columns is combined with its adjustment in the Adjustments columns, if any, and is entered in the Adjusted Trial Balance columns. For example, in Illustration 4–2 the Prepaid Rent account has a $600 debit balance in the Trial Balance columns. This $600 debit is combined with the $200 credit in the Adjustments columns to give Prepaid Rent a $400 debit in the Adjusted Trial Balance columns. Rent Expense has no balance in the Trial Balance columns, but it has a $200 debit in the Adjustment columns. Therefore, no balance combined with a $200 debit gives Rent Expense a $200 debit in the Adjusted Trial Balance columns. Cash, Office Equipment, and several other accounts have trial balance amounts but no adjustments. As a result, their trial balance amounts are carried unchanged into the Adjusted Trial Balance columns. Notice that the result of combining the amounts in the Trial Balance columns with the amounts in the Adjustments columns is an adjusted trial balance in the Adjusted Trial Balance columns.

After the combined amounts are carried to the Adjusted Trial Balance columns, the Adjusted Trial Balance columns are added to prove their equality. Then, the amounts in these columns are sorted to the proper Balance Sheet or Income Statement columns according to the statement on which they will appear. This is an easy task that requires only two decisions: (1) is the item to be sorted a debit or a credit and (2) on which statement does it appear. As to the first decision, an adjusted trial balance debit amount must be sorted to either the Income Statement debit column or the Balance Sheet debit column. Likewise, a credit amount must go into either the Income Statement credit or Balance Sheet credit column. In other words, debits remain debits and credits remain credits in the sorting process. As to the second decision, it is only necessary in the sorting process to remember that revenues and expenses appear on the income statement and assets, liabilities, and owner's equity items go on the balance sheet.

After the amounts are sorted to the proper columns, the columns are totaled. At this point, the difference between the totals of the Income Statement columns is the net income or loss. The difference is the net income or loss because revenues are entered in the credit column and expenses in the debit column. If the credit column total exceeds the debit column total, the difference is a net income. If the debit column total exceeds the credit column total, the difference is a net loss. In the illustrated work sheet, the credit column total exceeds the debit column total, and the result is a $400 net income.

After the net income is determined in the Income Statement columns, it is added to the total of the Balance Sheet credit column. The reason for this is that with the exception of the balance of the capital account, the amounts appearing in the Balance Sheet columns are "end-of-the-period" amounts. Therefore, it is necessary to add the net income to the Balance Sheet credit column total to make the Balance Sheet columns equal. Also, adding the income to this column has the effect of adding it to the capital account.

Had there been a loss, it would have been necessary to add the loss to the debit column. This is because losses decrease owner's equity, and adding the loss to the debit column has the effect of subtracting it from the capital account.

Balancing the Balance Sheet columns by adding the net income or loss is a proof of the accuracy with which the work sheet was prepared. When the income or loss is added in the Balance Sheet columns and the addition makes these columns equal, it is assumed that no errors were made in preparing the work sheet. However, if the addition does not make the columns equal, it is proof that an error or errors were made. The error or errors may have been either mathematical or an amount may have been sorted to a wrong column.

Although balancing the Balance Sheet columns with the net income or loss is a proof of the accuracy with which a work sheet was prepared, it is not an absolute proof. These columns will balance even when errors have been made if the errors are of a certain type. For example, an expense amount carried into the Balance Sheet debit column or an asset amount carried into the debit column of the income statement section will cause both of these columns to have incorrect totals. Likewise, the net income will be incorrect. However, when such an error is made, the Balance Sheet columns will balance, but with the incorrect amount of income. Therefore, when a work sheet is prepared, care must be exercised in sorting the adjusted trial balance amounts into the correct Income Statement or Balance Sheet columns.

WORK SHEET AND THE FINANCIAL STATEMENTS

As previously stated, the work sheet is a tool of the accountant and is not for management's use or publication. However, as soon as it is completed, the accountant uses it in preparing the income statement and balance sheet that are given to management. To do this the accountant rearranges the items in the work sheet's Income Statement columns into a formal income statement and rearranges the items in the Balance Sheet columns into a formal balance sheet.

WORK SHEET AND ADJUSTING ENTRIES

Entering the adjustments in the Adjustments columns of a work sheet does not get these adjustments into the ledger accounts. Consequently, after the work sheet and statements are completed, adjusting entries like the ones described in the previous chapter must still be entered in the General Journal and posted. The work sheet makes this easy, however, because its Adjustments columns provide the information for these entries. All that is needed is an entry for each adjustment appearing in the columns.

As for the adjusting entries for the illustrated work sheet, they are the same as the entries in the previous chapter, with the exception of the entry for adjustment (e). Here a compound entry having a $50 debit to Unearned Legal Fees, a $75 debit to Accounts Receivable, and a $125 credit to Legal Fees Earned is used.

CLOSING ENTRIES

After the work sheet and statements are completed, in addition to adjusting entries, it is also necessary to prepare and post *closing entries*. Closing entries clear and close the revenue and expense accounts. The accounts are cleared in the sense that their balances are transferred to another account. They are closed in the sense that they have zero balances after closing entries are posted.

WHY CLOSING ENTRIES ARE MADE

The revenue and expense accounts are cleared and closed at the end of each accounting period by transferring their balances to a summary account, called *Income Summary*. Their summarized amount, which is the net income or loss, is then transferred in a single proprietorship to the owner's capital account. These transfers are necessary because—

a. Revenues actually increase owner's equity and expenses decrease it.

b. However, throughout an accounting period these increases and decreases are accumulated in revenue and expense accounts rather than in the owner's capital account.

c. As a result, closing entries are necessary at the end of each accounting period to transfer the net effect of these increases and decreases out of the revenue and expense accounts and on to the owner's capital account.

In addition, closing entries also cause the revenue and expense accounts to begin each new accounting period with zero balances. This too is necessary because—

a. An income statement reports the revenues and expenses incurred during *one* accounting period and is prepared from information recorded in the revenue and expense accounts.

b. Consequently, these accounts must begin each new accounting period with zero balances if their end-of-the-period balances are to reflect just *one* period's revenues and expenses.

CLOSING ENTRIES ILLUSTRATED

At the end of July, after its adjusting entries were posted but before its accounts were cleared and closed, the owner's equity accounts of Owen's law practice had the balances shown in Illustration 4–3. (An account's Balance column heading as a rule does not tell the nature of an account's balance. However, in Illustration 4–3 and in the illustrations immediately following, the nature of each account's balance is shown as an aid to the student.)

Observe in Illustration 4–3 that Owen's capital account shows only its $2,500 July 1 balance. This is not the amount of Owen's equity on July 31. Closing entries are required to make this account show the July 31 equity.

Note also the third account in Illustration 4–3, the Income Summary account. This account is used only at the end of the accounting period in summarizing and clearing the revenue and expense accounts.

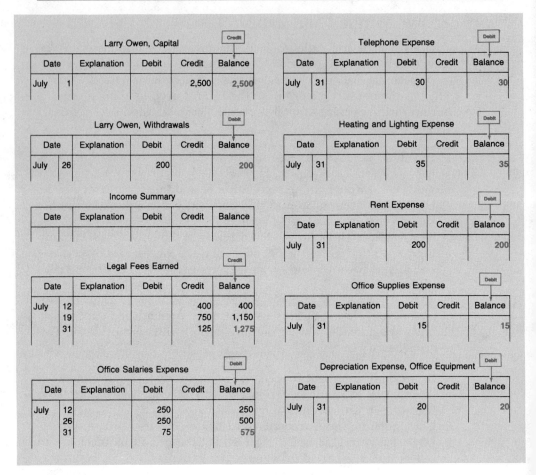

Illustration 4–3

Closing revenue accounts

Before closing entries are posted, revenue accounts have credit balances. Consequently, to clear and close a revenue account an entry debiting the account and crediting Income Summary is required.

The Owen law practice has only one revenue account, and the entry to close and clear it is:

July	31	Legal Fees Earned	1,275.00	
		Income Summary		1,275.00
		To clear and close the revenue account.		

Posting the entry has this effect on the accounts:

Legal Fees Earned				Credit		Income Summary				Credit
Date	Explanation	Debit	Credit	Balance	Date	Explanation	Debit	Credit	Balance
July 12			400	400	July 31			1,275	1,275
19			750	1,150					
31			125	1,275					
31		1,275		–0–					

Note that the entry clears the revenue account by transferring its balance as a credit to the Income Summary account. It also causes the revenue account to begin the new accounting period with a zero balance.

Closing expense accounts

Before closing entries are posted, expense accounts have debit balances. Consequently, to clear and close a concern's expense accounts, a compound entry debiting the Income Summary account and crediting each individual expense account is required. The Owen law practice has six expense accounts, and the compound entry to clear and close them is:

July	31	Income Summary	875.00	
		Office Salaries Expense..................		575.00
		Telephone Expense		30.00
		Heating and Lighting Expense		35.00
		Rent Expense		200.00
		Office Supplies Expense		15.00
		Depreciation Expense, Office Equipment ...		20.00
		To close and clear the expense accounts.		

Posting the entry has the effect shown in Illustration 4–4. Turn to Illustration 4–4 on the next page and observe that the entry clears the expense accounts of their balances by transferring the balances in a total as a debit to the Income Summary account. It also causes the expense accounts to begin the new period with zero balances.

Closing the Income Summary account

After a concern's revenue and expense accounts are cleared and their balances transferred to the *Income Summary account,* the balance

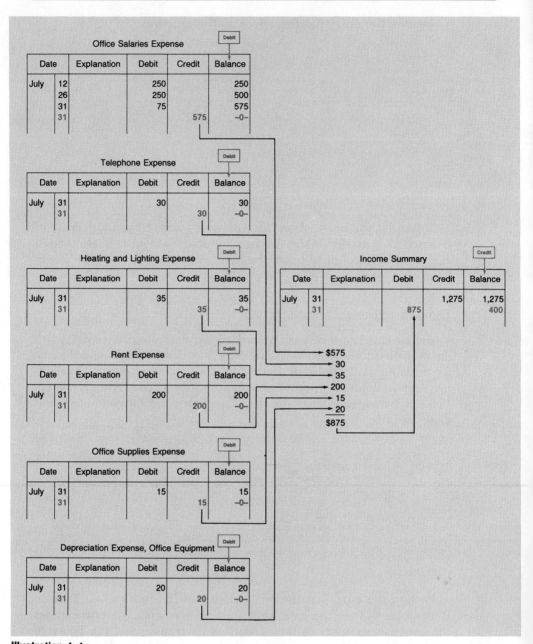

Illustration 4–4

of the Income Summary account is equal to the net income or loss. When revenues exceed expenses, there is a net income and the Income Summary account has a credit balance. On the other hand, when expenses exceed revenues, there is a loss and the account has a debit balance. But, regardless of the nature of its balance, the Income Summary account is cleared and its balance, the amount of net income or loss, is transferred to the capital account.

The Owen law practice earned $400 during July. Consequently, after its revenue and expense accounts are cleared, its Income Summary account has a $400 credit balance. This balance is transferred to the Larry Owen, Capital account with an entry like this:

July	31	Income Summary	400.00	
		Larry Owen, Capital		400.00
		To clear and close the Income Summary account.		

Posting this entry has the following effect on the accounts:

Income Summary (Credit)

Date		Explanation	Debit	Credit	Balance
July	31			1,275	1,275
	31		875		400
	31		400		–0–

Larry Owen, Capital (Credit)

Date		Explanation	Debit	Credit	Balance
July	1			2,500	2,500
	31			400	2,900

Observe that the entry clears the Income Summary account, transferring its balance, the amount of the net income in this case, to the capital account.

Closing the withdrawals account

At the end of an accounting period the withdrawals account shows the owner's withdrawals. The account is closed, and its debit balance is transferred to the capital account with an entry like this:

July	31	Larry Owen, Capital	200.00	
		Larry Owen, Withdrawals		200.00
		To close and clear the withdrawals account.		

Posting the entry has this effect on the accounts:

	Larry Owen, Withdrawals			Debit			Larry Owen, Capital			Credit
Date	Explanation	Debit	Credit	Balance	Date	Explanation	Debit	Credit	Balance
July 26		200		200	July 1			2,500	2,500
31			200	-0-	31			400	2,900
					31		200		2,700

After the entry closing the withdrawals account is posted, observe that the two reasons for making closing entries are accomplished: (1) All revenue and expense accounts have zero balances. And (2) the net effect of the period's revenue, expense, and withdrawal transactions on the owner's equity is shown in the capital account.

Temporary accounts

Revenue and expense accounts plus the Income Summary and withdrawals accounts are often called *temporary accounts* because in a sense the items recorded in these accounts are only temporarily recorded therein. At the end of each accounting period, through closing entries their debit and credit effects are transferred out and on to other accounts.

THE ACCOUNTS AFTER CLOSING

At this stage, after both adjusting and closing entries have been posted, the Owen law practice accounts appear as in Illustration 4–5. Observe in the illustration that the asset, liability, and the owner's

		Cash				ACCOUNT NO. 1	
DATE	EXPLANATION	POST. REF.	DEBIT		CREDIT		BALANCE
198A July 1		G1	2 5 0 0 00				2 5 0 0 00
1		G1			6 0 0 00		1 9 0 0 00
3		G1			1 2 0 0 00		7 0 0 00
12		G1	4 0 0 00				1 1 0 0 00
12		G1			2 5 0 00		8 5 0 00
15		G1	1 5 0 00				1 0 0 0 00
26		G2			2 5 0 00		7 5 0 00
26		G2			2 0 0 00		5 5 0 00
29		G2	7 5 0 00				1 3 0 0 00
30		G2			1 0 0 00		1 2 0 0 00
31		G2			3 0 00		1 1 7 0 00
31		G2			3 5 00		1 1 3 5 00

Illustration 4–5

Accounts Receivable   ACCOUNT NO. 2

DATE	EXPLANATION	POST. REF.	DEBIT	CREDIT	BALANCE
198A July 19		G2	7 5 0 00		7 5 0 00
29		G2		7 5 0 00	– 0 –
31		G3	7 5 00		7 5 00

Prepaid Rent   ACCOUNT NO. 3

DATE	EXPLANATION	POST. REF.	DEBIT	CREDIT	BALANCE
198A July 1		G1	6 0 0 00		6 0 0 00
31		G3		2 0 0 00	4 0 0 00

Office Supplies   ACCOUNT NO. 4

DATE	EXPLANATION	POST. REF.	DEBIT	CREDIT	BALANCE
198A July 5		G1	6 0 00		6 0 00
31		G3		1 5 00	4 5 00

Office Equipment   ACCOUNT NO. 5

DATE	EXPLANATION	POST. REF.	DEBIT	CREDIT	BALANCE
198A July 3		G1	1 2 0 0 00		1 2 0 0 00
5		G1	3 0 0 00		1 5 0 0 00

Accumulated Depreciation, Office Equipment   ACCOUNT NO. 6

DATE	EXPLANATION	POST. REF.	DEBIT	CREDIT	BALANCE
198A July 31		G3		2 0 00	2 0 00

Accounts Payable   ACCOUNT NO. 7

DATE	EXPLANATION	POST. REF.	DEBIT	CREDIT	BALANCE
198A July 5		G1		3 6 0 00	3 6 0 00
30		G2	1 0 0 00		2 6 0 00

Illustration 4–5 *(continued)*

Salaries Payable   ACCOUNT NO.   8

DATE	EXPLANATION	POST. REF.	DEBIT	CREDIT	BALANCE
198A July 31		G3		7 5 00	7 5 00

Unearned Legal Fees   ACCOUNT NO.   9

DATE	EXPLANATION	POST. REF.	DEBIT	CREDIT	BALANCE
198A July 15		G1		1 5 0 00	1 5 0 00
31		G3	5 0 00		1 0 0 00

Larry Owen, Capital   ACCOUNT NO. 10

DATE	EXPLANATION	POST. REF.	DEBIT	CREDIT	BALANCE
198A July 1		G1		2 5 0 0 00	2 5 0 0 00
31		G3		4 0 0 00	2 9 0 0 00
31		G3	2 0 0 00		2 7 0 0 00

Larry Owen, Withdrawals   ACCOUNT NO. 11

DATE	EXPLANATION	POST. REF.	DEBIT	CREDIT	BALANCE
198A July 26		G2	2 0 0 00		2 0 0 00
31		G3		2 0 0 00	- 0 -

Income Summary   ACCOUNT NO. 12

DATE	EXPLANATION	POST. REF.	DEBIT	CREDIT	BALANCE
198A July 31		G3		1 2 7 5 00	1 2 7 5 00
31		G3	8 7 5 00		4 0 0 00
31		G3	4 0 0 00		- 0 -

Illustration 4–5 *(continued)*

Legal Fees Earned   ACCOUNT NO. 13

DATE	EXPLANATION	POST. REF.	DEBIT	CREDIT	BALANCE
198A July 12		G1		4 0 0 00	4 0 0 00
19		G2		7 5 0 00	1 1 5 0 00
31		G3		1 2 5 00	1 2 7 5 00
31		G3	1 2 7 5 00		- 0 -

Office Salaries Expense   ACCOUNT NO. 14

DATE	EXPLANATION	POST. REF.	DEBIT	CREDIT	BALANCE
198A July 12		G1	2 5 0 00		2 5 0 00
26		G2	2 5 0 00		5 0 0 00
31		G3	7 5 00		5 7 5 00
31		G3		5 7 5 00	- 0 -

Telephone Expense   ACCOUNT NO. 15

DATE	EXPLANATION	POST. REF.	DEBIT	CREDIT	BALANCE
198A July 31		G2	3 0 00		3 0 00
31		G3		3 0 00	- 0 -

Heating and Lighting Expense   ACCOUNT NO. 16

DATE	EXPLANATION	POST. REF.	DEBIT	CREDIT	BALANCE
198A July 31		G2	3 5 00		3 5 00
31		G3		3 5 00	- 0 -

Rent Expense   ACCOUNT NO. 17

DATE	EXPLANATION	POST. REF.	DEBIT	CREDIT	BALANCE
198A July 31		G3	2 0 0 00		2 0 0 00
31		G3		2 0 0 00	- 0 -

Illustration 4–5 *(continued)*

Office Supplies Expense		ACCOUNT NO. 18			
DATE	EXPLANATION	POST. REF.	DEBIT	CREDIT	BALANCE
198A July 31		G3	1 5 00		1 5 00
31		G3		1 5 00	- 0 -

Depreciation Expense, Office Equipment		ACCOUNT NO. 19			
DATE	EXPLANATION	POST. REF.	DEBIT	CREDIT	BALANCE
198A July 31		G3	2 0 00		2 0 00
31		G3		2 0 00	- 0 -

Illustration 4–5 (concluded)

capital accounts show their end-of-the-period balances. Observe also that the revenue and expense accounts have zero balances and are ready for recording the new accounting period's revenues and expenses.

THE POST-CLOSING TRIAL BALANCE

It is easy to make errors in adjusting and closing the accounts. Consequently, after all adjusting and closing entries are posted, a new trial balance is prepared to retest the equality of the accounts. This new, after-closing trial balance is called a *post-closing trial balance,* and for Owen's law practice appears as in Illustration 4–6.

Larry Owen, Attorney
Post-Closing Trial Balance, July 31, 19—

Cash	$1,135	
Accounts receivable	75	
Prepaid rent	400	
Office supplies	45	
Office equipment	1,500	
Accumulated depreciation, office equipment		$ 20
Accounts payable		260
Salaries payable		75
Unearned legal fees		100
Larry Owen, capital		2,700
Totals	$3,155	$3,155

Illustration 4–6

Compare Illustration 4–6 with the accounts having balances in Illustration 4–5. Note that only asset, liability, and the owner's capital accounts have balances in Illustration 4–5. Note also that these are the only accounts that appear on the post-closing trial balance. The revenue and expense accounts have been cleared and have zero balances at this point.

ACCOUNTING FOR PARTNERSHIPS AND CORPORATIONS

Partnership accounting

Accounting for a partnership is like accounting for a single proprietorship except for transactions directly affecting the partners' capital and withdrawal accounts. For these transactions there must be a capital account and a withdrawals account for each partner. Also, the Income Summary account is closed with a compound entry that allocates to each partner his or her share of the income or loss.

Corporation accounting

A corporation's accounting also differs from that of a single proprietorship for transactions affecting the accounts that show the equity of the corporation's stockholders in the assets of the corporation. The differences result because accounting principles require a corporation to distinguish between stockholders' equity resulting from amounts invested in the corporation by its stockholders and stockholders' equity resulting from earnings. This distinction is also important because in most states a corporation cannot pay a legal dividend unless it has stockholders' equity resulting from earnings. In making the distinction, two kinds of stockholder equity accounts are kept: (1) *contributed capital accounts* and (2) *retained earnings accounts.* Amounts invested in a corporation by its stockholders are shown in a contributed capital account such as the Common Stock account. Stockholders' equity resulting from earnings is shown in a retained earnings account.

To demonstrate corporation accounting, assume that five persons secured a charter for a new corporation. Each invested $10,000 in the corporation by buying 1,000 shares of its $10 par value common stock. The corporation's entry to record their investments is:

Jan.	5	Cash	50,000.00	
		Common Stock		50,000.00
		Sold and issued 5,000 shares of $10 par value common stock.		

If during its first year the corporation earned $8,000, the entry to close its Income Summary account is:

Dec.	31	Income Summary	8,000.00	
		Retained Earnings		8,000.00
		To close the Income Summary account.		

If these were the only entries affecting the stockholders' equity during the first year, the corporation's year-end balance sheet will show the equity as follows:

Stockholders' Equity

Common stock, $10 par value, 5,000 shares authorized		
and outstanding	$50,000	
Retained earnings	8,000	
Total stockholders' equity		$58,000

Since a corporation is a separate legal entity, the names of its stockholders are of little or no interest to a balance sheet reader and are not shown in the equity section. However, in this case the section does show that the corporation's stockholders have a $58,000 equity in its assets, $50,000 of which resulted from their purchase of the corporation's stock and $8,000 from earnings. As to the equity from earnings, $8,000 more assets flowed into the corporation from revenues than flowed out for expenses. This not only increased the assets but also increased the stockholders' equity in the assets by $8,000.

Many beginning students have difficulty understanding the nature of the retained earnings item in the equity section of a corporation balance sheet. They would perhaps have less difficulty if the item were labeled "Stockholders' equity resulting from earnings." However, the retained earnings caption is common. Therefore, upon seeing it a student must recognize that it represents nothing more than stockholders' equity resulting from earnings. Furthermore, it does not represent a specific amount of cash or any other asset, since these are shown in the asset section of the balance sheet.

To continue, assume that on January 10 of the corporation's second year its board of directors met and by vote declared a $1 per share dividend payable on February 1 to the January 25 *stockholders of record* (stockholders according to the corporation's records). The entries to record the declaration and payment are as follows:

Jan.	10	Retained Earnings	5,000.00	
		Common Dividend Payable		5,000.00
		Declared a $1 per share dividend.		
Feb.	1	Common Dividend Payable	5,000.00	
		Cash		5,000.00
		Paid the dividend declared on January 10.		

Note in the two entries that the dividend declaration and payment together reduced corporation assets and stockholders' equity just as a withdrawal of cash by the owner of a single proprietorship reduces assets and the owner's equity.

A cash dividend is normally paid by mailing checks to the stockholders. Also, as in this case, three dates are normally involved in a dividend declaration and payment: (1) the *date of declaration,* (2) the *date of record,* and (3) the *date of payment.* Since stockholders may sell their stock to new investors at will, the three dates give new stockholders an opportunity to have their ownership entered in the corporation's records in time to receive the dividend. Otherwise it would go to the old stockholders.

A dividend must be formally voted by a corporation's board of directors. Furthermore, courts have generally held that the board is the final judge of when if at all a dividend should be paid. Consequently, stockholders have no right to a dividend until declared. However, as soon as a cash dividend is declared, it becomes a liability of the corporation, normally a current liability, and must be paid. Furthermore, stockholders have the right to sue and force payment of a cash dividend once it is declared.

If during its second year the corporation of this illustration suffered a $7,000 net loss, the entry to close its Income Summary account is:

Dec.	31	Retained Earnings	7,000.00	
		Income Summary		7,000.00
		To close the Income Summary account.		

Posting the entry has the effect shown on the third line of the following Retained Earnings account.

Retained Earnings

Date		Explanation	Post. Ref.	Debit	Credit	Balance
198A Dec.	31	Net income	G4		8,000.00	8,000.00
198B Jan.	10	Dividend declaration	G5	5,000.00		3,000.00
Dec.	31	Net loss	G9	7,000.00		4,000.00

After the entry was posted, due to the dividend and the net loss, the Retained Earnings account has a $4,000 debit balance. A debit balance in a Retained Earnings account indicates a negative amount of retained earnings, and a corporation with a negative amount of retained earnings is said to have a *deficit*. A deficit may be shown on a corporation's balance sheet as follows:

Stockholders' Equity	
Common stock, $10 par value, 5,000 shares authorized and outstanding	$50,000
Deduct retained earnings deficit	(4,000)
Total stockholders' equity	$46,000

In most states it is illegal for a corporation with a deficit to pay a cash dividend. Such dividends are made illegal because as a separate legal entity a corporation is responsible for its own debts. Consequently, if its creditors are to be paid, they must be paid from the corporation's assets. Therefore, making a dividend illegal when there is a deficit helps prevent a corporation in financial difficulties from paying out all of its assets in dividends and leaving nothing for payment of its creditors.

THE ACCOUNTING CYCLE

Each accounting period in the life of a business is a recurring *accounting cycle*, beginning with transactions recorded in a journal and ending with a post-closing trial balance. All steps in the cycle have now been discussed. A knowledge of accounting requires that each step be understood and its relation to the others seen. The steps in the order of their occurrence are as follows:

1. *Journalizing* .... Analyzing and recording transactions in a journal.
2. *Posting* .... Copying the debits and credits of journal entries into the ledger accounts.
3. *Preparing a trial balance* ..... Summarizing the ledger accounts and testing the recording accuracy.
4. *Preparing a work sheet* .... Gaining the effects of the adjustments before entering the adjustments in the accounts. Then sorting the account balances into the balance sheet and income statement columns and finally determining and proving the income or loss.
5. *Preparing the statements* .... Rearranging the work sheet information into a balance sheet and an income statement.

6. *Adjusting the ledger*
   accounts .... Preparing adjusting journal entries from information in the Adjustments columns of the work sheet and posting the entries in order to bring the account balances up to date.

7. *Closing the temporary*
   accounts .... Preparing and posting entries to close the temporary accounts and transfer the net income or loss to the capital account or accounts in a single proprietorship or partnership and to the Retained Earnings account in a corporation.

8. *Preparing a post-closing*
   trial balance .... Proving the accuracy of the adjusting and closing procedures.

GLOSSARY

Accounting cycle. The accounting steps that recur each accounting period in the life of a business and which begin with the recording of transactions and proceed through posting the recorded amounts, preparing a trial balance, preparing a work sheet, preparing the financial statements, preparing and posting adjusting and closing entries, and preparing a post-closing trial balance.

Closing entries. Entries made to close and clear the revenue and expense accounts and to transfer the amount of the net income or loss to a capital account or accounts or to the Retained Earnings account.

Closing procedures. The preparation and posting of closing entries and the preparation of the post-closing trial balance.

Contributed capital. Stockholders' equity in a corporation resulting among other ways from amounts invested in the corporation by its stockholders.

Date of declaration. Date on which a dividend is declared.

Date of payment. Date for the payment of a dividend.

Date of record. Date on which the stockholders who are to receive a dividend is determined.

Deficit. A negative amount of retained earnings.

Income Summary account. The account used in the closing procedures to summarize the amounts of revenues and expenses, and from which the amount of the net income or loss is transferred to the owner's capital account in a single proprietorship, the partners' capital accounts in a partnership, or the Retained Earnings account in a corporation.

Post-closing trial balance. A trial balance prepared after closing entries are posted.

Stockholders of record. A corporation's stockholders according to its records.

Temporary accounts. The revenue, expense, Income Summary, and withdrawals accounts.

Working papers. The memoranda, analyses, and other informal papers prepared by accountants and used as a basis for the more formal reports given to clients.

Work sheet. A working paper used by an accountant to bring together in an orderly manner the information used in preparing the financial statements and adjusting entries.

QUESTIONS FOR CLASS DISCUSSION

1. A work sheet is a tool accountants use to accomplish three tasks. What are these tasks?
2. Is it possible to complete the statements and adjust and close the accounts without preparing a work sheet? What is gained by preparing a work sheet?
3. At what stage in the accounting process is a work sheet prepared?
4. From where are the amounts that are entered in the Trial Balance columns of a work sheet obtained?
5. Why are the adjustments in the Adjustments columns of a work sheet keyed together with letters?
6. What is the result of combining the amounts in the Trial Balance columns with the amounts in the Adjustments columns of a work sheet?
7. Why must care be exercised in sorting the items in the Adjusted Trial Balance columns to the proper Income Statement or Balance Sheet columns?
8. In extending the items in the Adjusted Trial Balance columns of a work sheet, what would be the effect on the net income of extending (a) an expense into the Balance Sheet debit column, (b) a liability into the Income Statement credit column, and (c) a revenue into the Balance Sheet debit column? Would each of these errors be automatically detected on the work sheet? Which would be automatically detected? Why?
9. Why are revenue and expense accounts called temporary accounts?
10. What two purposes are accomplished by recording closing entries?
11. What accounts are affected by closing entries? What accounts are not affected?
12. Explain the difference between adjusting and closing entries.
13. What is the purpose of the Income Summary account?
14. Why is a post-closing trial balance prepared?
15. An accounting student listed the item, "Depreciation expense, building, $1,800," on a post-closing trial balance. What did this indicate?

16. What two kinds of accounts are used in accounting for stockholders' equity in a corporation?
17. Explain how the retained earnings item found on corporation balance sheets arises.
18. What three dates are normally involved in the declaration and payment of a cash dividend?
19. Explain why the payment of a cash dividend by a corporation with a deficit is made illegal.

CLASS EXERCISES

Exercise 4–1

The balances of the following alphabetically arranged accounts appeared in the Adjusted Trial Balance columns of a work sheet. Copy the account numbers in a column on a sheet of note paper and beside each number indicate by letter the income statement or balance sheet column to which the account's balance would be sorted in completing the work sheet. Use the letter *a* to indicate the Income Statement debit column, *b* to indicate the Income Statement credit column, *c* to indicate the Balance Sheet debit column, and *d* to indicate the Balance Sheet credit column.

1. Accounts Payable.
2. Accounts Receivable.
3. Accumulated Depreciation, Repair Equipment.
4. Advertising Expense.
5. Cash.
6. Ed Lee, Capital.
7. Ed Lee, Withdrawals.
8. Prepaid Insurance.
9. Rent Expense.
10. Repair Equipment.
11. Repair Supplies.
12. Revenue from Repairs.
13. Wages Expense.

Exercise 4–2

The following item amounts are from the Adjustments columns of a work sheet. From the information prepare adjusting journal entries. Use December 31 as the date.

	Adjustments			
	Debit		Credit	
Prepaid insurance			(a)	850
Office supplies			(b)	215
Accumulated depreciation, office equipment			(c)	540
Accumulated depreciation, delivery equipment ..			(d)	3,345
Office salaries expense	(e)	50		
Truck drivers' wages	(e)	280		
Insurance expense, office equipment	(a)	85		
Insurance expense, delivery equipment	(a)	765		
Office supplies expense	(b)	215		
Depreciation expense, office equipment	(c)	540		
Depreciation expense, delivery equipment	(d)	3,345		
Salaries and wages payable			(e)	330
Totals		5,280		5,280

Exercise 4–3

Copy the following T-accounts and their end-of-the-period balances on a sheet of note paper. Below the accounts prepare entries to close the accounts. Post to the T-accounts.

Dale Nash, Capital		Rent Expense	
	Dec. 31 12,500	Dec. 31 2,400	

Dale Nash, Withdrawals		Salaries Expense	
Dec. 31 15,600		Dec. 31 10,200	

Income Summary		Insurance Expense	
		Dec. 31 800	

Commissions Earned		Depreciation Expense, Equipment	
	Dec. 31 32,600	Dec. 31 500	

Exercise 4–4

Following is a list of trial balance accounts and their balances. All are normal balances. To save your time, the balances are in one- and two-digit numbers; however, to increase your skill in sorting adjusted trial balance amounts to the proper work sheet columns, the accounts are listed in alphabetical order.

TRIAL BALANCE ACCOUNTS AND BALANCES

Accounts payable	$2	Rent expense	$ 2
Accounts receivable	3	Revenue from repairs	18
Accumulated depreciation, shop equipment	2	Robert Ross, capital	11
Cash	5	Robert Ross, withdrawals	2
Notes payable	1	Shop equipment	7
Prepaid insurance	3	Shop supplies	4
		Wages expense	8

Required:

1. Prepare a work sheet form on notebook paper and enter the trial balance accounts and amounts on the work sheet in their alphabetical order.
2. Complete the work sheet using the following information:
   a. Estimated depreciation of shop equipment, $1.
   b. Expired insurance, $1.
   c. Unused shop supplies per inventory, $1.
   d. Earned but unpaid wages, $2.

Exercise 4–5

1. On a sheet of note paper open the following T-accounts: Cash, Accounts Receivable, Equipment, Notes Payable, Common Stock, Retained Earnings, Income Summary, Revenue from Services, and Operating Expenses.

2. Record directly in the T-accounts these transactions of a corporation:
   a. Sold and issued $10,000 of common stock for cash.
   b. Purchased $9,000 of equipment for cash.
   c. Sold and delivered $25,000 of services on credit.
   d. Collected $22,000 of accounts receivable.
   e. Paid $20,000 of operating expenses.
   f. Purchased $5,000 of additional equipment, giving $3,000 in cash and a $2,000 promissory note.
   g. Closed the Revenue from Services, Operating Expenses, and Income Summary accounts.
3. Answer these questions:
   a. Does the corporation have retained earnings?
   b. Does it have any cash?
   c. If the corporation has retained earnings, why does it not also have cash?
   d. Can the corporation declare a legal cash dividend?
   e. Can it pay the dividend?
   f. In terms of assets, what does the balance of the Notes Payable account represent?
   g. In terms of assets, what does the balance of the Common Stock account represent?
   h. In terms of assets, what does the balance of the Retained Earnings account represent?

PROBLEMS

Problem 4–1

Walter Jenkins, Paul Kern, and Ned Lang began a business on January 8, 198A, in which each man invested $25,000. During 198A the business lost $6,000, and during 198B it earned a $27,000 net income. On January 3, 198C, the three men agreed to pay out to themselves $15,000 of the accumulated earnings of the business, and on January 8 the $15,000 was paid out.

Required:

1. Under the assumption that the business is a partnership in which the partners share losses and gains equally, give the entries to record the investments and to close the Income Summary account at the end of 198A and again at the end of 198B. Under the further assumption that the partners shared equally in the $15,000 of earnings paid out, give the entry to record the withdrawals.
2. Under the assumption that the business is organized as a corporation and that each man invested in the corporation by buying 2,500 shares of its $10 par value common stock, give the entries to *(a)* record the investments, *(b)* close the Income Summary account at the end of 198A and again at the end of 198B, and *(c)* to record the declaration and payment of the $2 per share dividend. (Ignore corporation income taxes and assume that the three men are the corporation's board of directors.)

Problem 4-2

A trial balance of the ledger of Quick Repair Shop carried these amounts at the end of its annual accounting period:

QUICK REPAIR SHOP
Trial Balance, December 31, 19—

Cash	$ 1,125	
Prepaid insurance	415	
Repair supplies	1,550	
Repair equipment	4,220	
Accumulated depreciation, repair equipment		$ 1,120
Accounts payable		250
Perry Winkle, capital		3,665
Perry Winkle, withdrawals	12,000	
Revenue from repairs		23,475
Wages expense	7,775	
Rent expense	1,200	
Advertising expense	225	
Totals	$28,510	$28,510

Required:

1. Enter the trial balance amounts in the Trial Balance columns of a work sheet and complete the work sheet using the following information:
   a. Expired insurance, $265.
   b. A repair supplies inventory showed $380 of unused supplies on hand.
   c. Estimated depreciation on repair equipment, $650.
   d. Wages earned by the one employee but unpaid and unrecorded, $25.
2. From the work sheet prepare an income statement and a classified balance sheet.
3. Prepare adjusting journal entries and compound closing entries.

Problem 4-3
(Covers two accounting cycles)

On October 2 Mary Nash opened a real estate office she called Mary Nash Realty, and during October she completed these transactions:

Oct. 2 Invested $2,500 in cash and an automobile having a $7,200 fair value in the real estate agency.
      2 Rented furnished office space and paid one month's rent, $325.
      3 Purchased office supplies for cash, $135.
     10 Sold a building lot and collected a $1,250 commission.
     15 Paid the biweekly salary of the office secretary, $350.
     16 Paid the premium on a one-year insurance policy, $480.
     29 Paid the biweekly salary of the office secretary, $350.
     31 Paid the October telephone bill, $55.
     31 Paid for gas and oil used in the agency car during October, $65.

Required work for October:

1. Open the following accounts: Cash; Prepaid Insurance; Office Supplies; Automobile; Accumulated Depreciation, Automobile; Salaries Payable; Mary Nash, Capital; Mary Nash, Withdrawals; Income Summary; Commissions Earned; Rent Expense; Salaries Expense; Gas, Oil, and Repairs Expense; Telephone Expense; Insurance Expense; Office Supplies Expense; and Depreciation Expense, Automobile.
2. Prepare and post journal entries to record the transactions.
3. Prepare a trial balance in the Trial Balance columns of a work sheet form and complete the work sheet using the following information.
   a. One half of a month's insurance has expired.
   b. An inventory shows $110 of unused office supplies remaining.
   c. Estimated depreciation on the automobile, $100.
   d. Accrued but unpaid salary of the secretary, $70.
4. Prepare an October income statement and an October 31 classified balance sheet.
5. Prepare and post adjusting and closing journal entries.
6. Prepare a post-closing trial balance.

During November the real estate agency completed these transactions:

Nov. 1   Paid the November rent on the office space, $325.
     3   Purchased additional office supplies for cash, $25.
  12   Paid the biweekly salary of the office secretary, $350.
  14   Sold a house and collected a $4,200 commission.
  16   Withdrew $1,500 from the business to pay personal living expenses.
  26   Paid the biweekly salary of the office secretary, $350.
  30   Paid for gas and oil used in the agency car during November, $60.
  30   Paid the November telephone bill, $35.

Required work for November:

1. Prepare and post journal entries to record the transactions.
2. Prepare a trial balance in the Trial Balance columns of a work sheet form and complete the work sheet using the following information:
   a. One month's insurance has expired.
   b. An inventory of office supplies shows $115 of unused supplies remaining.
   c. Estimated depreciation on the automobile, $100.
   d. Accrued but unpaid secretary's salary, $140.
3. Prepare a November income statement and a November 30 classified balance sheet.
4. Prepare and post adjusting and closing journal entries.
5. Prepare a post-closing trial balance.

Problem 4–4

The ledger accounts of Leisure Alleys showing account balances as of the end of its annual accounting period appear in the booklet of working papers that accompanies this text and a trial balance of the ledger is reproduced on a work sheet form provided there. The trial balance has these items:

LEISURE ALLEYS

Trial Balance, December 31, 19—

Cash	$ 1,575	
Bowling supplies	2,420	
Prepaid insurance	575	
Bowling equipment	36,565	
Accumulated depreciation, bowling equipment		$ 9,640
Mortgage payable		10,000
Walter Hall, capital		14,025
Walter Hall, withdrawals	9,000	
Bowling revenue		35,500
Salaries expense	13,655	
Advertising expense	750	
Equipment repairs expense	420	
Rent expense	2,400	
Utilities expense	1,135	
Taxes expense	220	
Interest expense	450	
Totals	$69,165	$69,165

Required:

1. If the working papers are being used, complete the work sheet provided there for the solution of this problem, using the information that follows. If the working papers are not being used, enter the trial balance on a work sheet form and complete the work sheet.

    a. Bowling supplies inventory, $590.

    b. Expired insurance, $445.

    c. Estimated depreciation of bowling equipment, $3,875.

    d. Salaries earned but unpaid and unrecorded, $315.

    e. The lease contract on the building calls for an annual rental equal to 10% of the annual bowling revenue, with $200 payable each month on the first day of the month. The $200 was paid each month and debited to the Rent Expense account.

    f. Personal property taxes on the bowling equipment amounting to $85 have accrued but are unrecorded and unpaid.

    g. The mortgage debt was incurred on September 1, and interest on the debt is at the rate of 9% annually or $75 per month. The mortgage contract calls for the payment of $225 interest each three months in advance. Interest payments of $225 each were made on September 1 and December 1. The first payment on the mortgage principal is not due until two years after the date on which the debt was incurred.

2. Prepare an income statement and a classified balance sheet.
3. Prepare adjusting and closing journal entries.
4. Post the adjusting and closing entries and prepare a post-closing trial balance. (If the working papers are not being used, omit this last requirement.)

Problem 4–5

The accounts of A–1 Delivery Service showing balances as of the end of its annual accounting period appear in the booklet of working papers that accompanies this text, and a trial balance of the accounts is reproduced on a work sheet form provided there. The trial balance carries these items:

A–1 DELIVERY SERVICE
Trial Balance, December 31, 19—

Cash	$ 2,225	
Accounts receivable	470	
Prepaid insurance	1,275	
Office supplies	245	
Office equipment	2,460	
Accumulated depreciation, office equipment		$ 470
Delivery equipment	12,790	
Accumulated depreciation, delivery equipment ..		3,150
Accounts payable		290
Unearned delivery service revenue		450
Carl Bush, capital		9,855
Carl Bush, withdrawals	13,000	
Delivery service revenue		46,555
Office rent expense	600	
Telephone expense	245	
Office salaries expense	8,060	
Truck drivers' wages expense	16,320	
Gas, oil, and repairs expense	2,180	
Garage rent expense	900	
Totals	$60,770	$60,770

Required:

1. If the working papers are being used, complete the work sheet provided for the solution of this problem, using the following information. If the working papers are not being used, enter the trial balance on a work sheet form and complete the work sheet.

    a. Insurance expired on office equipment, $75; and on the delivery equipment, $915.

    b. An inventory showed $115 of unused office supplies on hand.

    c. Estimated depreciation on office equipment, $180; and (d) on delivery equipment, $2,345.

    e. Three stores entered into contracts with the delivery service in which they agreed to pay a fixed fee for having packaged delivered. Two of the stores made advance payments on their contracts, and the amounts were credited to Unearned Delivery Service Revenue. An examination of the contracts shows $325 of the $450 paid in advance was earned by the accounting period end. The contract of the third store provides for a $150 monthly fee to be paid at the end of each month's service. It was signed on December 15, and a half month's revenue has accrued but is unrecorded.

    f. Office salaries, $70, and truck drivers' wages, $280, have accrued.

2. Prepare an income statement and a classified balance sheet.

3. Prepare adjusting and closing entries.

4. Post the adjusting and closing entries to the accounts and prepare a post-closing trial balance. (Omit this requirement if the working papers are not being used.)

ALTERNATE PROBLEMS

Problem 4–1A

On January 5, 198A, Fred Gage, Dale Hall, and Carl Russ began a business in which Fred Gage invested $15,000, Dale Hall invested $30,000, and Carl Russ invested $45,000. During 198A the business lost $6,000, and during 198B it earned a $30,000 net income. On January 4, 198C, the three men agreed to pay out to themselves $18,000 of the accumulated earnings of the business, and on January 12 the $18,000 was paid out.

Required:

1. Under the assumption the business is a partnership in which the partners share losses and gains in proportion to their investments, give the entries to record the investments and to close the Income Summary account at the end of 198A and again at the end of 198B. Under the further assumption that the partners paid out the $18,000 of accumulated earnings in proportion to their investments, give the entry to record the withdrawals.
2. Under the alternate assumption that the business is organized as a corporation and that the men invested in the corporation by buying its $10 par value common stock, with Fred Gage buying 1,500 shares, Dale Hall buying 3,000 shares, and Carl Russ buying 4,500 shares, give the entries to (a) record the investments, (b) close the Income Summary account at the end of 198A and again at the end of 198B, and (c) to record the declaration and payment of the $2 per share dividend. (Ignore corporation income taxes and assume the three men are the corporation's board of directors.)

Problem 4–2A

At the end of its annual accounting period a trial balance of the ledger of Sparkling Janitorial Service carried the items that follow.

Required:

1. Enter the trial balance amounts on a work sheet form and complete the work sheet using the following information:
   a. Expired insurance, $625.
   b. An inventory of cleaning supplies showed $135 of unused cleaning supplies on hand.
   c. The cleaning service rents garage and equipment storage space. At the beginning of the year three months' rent was prepaid as shown by the debit balance of the Prepaid Rent account. Rents for the months April through November were paid on the first day of each month and debited to the Rent Expense account. The December rent was unpaid on the trial balance date.
   d. Estimated depreciation on cleaning equipment, $375; and (e) on the trucks, $1,500.
   f. On November 20 the janitorial service contracted and began cleaning the office of Western Realty for $90 per month. The realty company

SPARKLING JANITORIAL SERVICE
Trial Balance, December 31, 19—

Cash	$ 835	
Accounts receivable	180	
Prepaid insurance	765	
Cleaning supplies	840	
Prepaid rent	225	
Cleaning equipment	2,830	
Accumulated depreciation, cleaning equipment		$ 1,220
Trucks	8,690	
Accumulated depreciation, trucks		3,610
Accounts payable		135
Unearned janitorial revenue		180
Timothy Watts, capital		6,870
Timothy Watts, withdrawals	10,400	
Janitorial revenue		28,730
Wages expense	14,700	
Rent expense	600	
Gas, oil, and repairs expense	680	
Totals	$40,745	$40,745

paid in advance for two months' service, and the amount paid was credited to Unearned Janitorial Revenue. The janitorial service also entered into a contract and began cleaning the office of Valley Insurance Agency on December 15. By the month's end a half month's revenue, $40, had been earned on this contract but was unrecorded.

g. Employees' wages amounting to $120 had accrued but were unrecorded on the trial balance date.

2. From the work sheet prepared an income statement and a classified balance sheet.

3. Prepare adjusting and closing entries for the janitorial service.

Problem 4–3A
(Covers two accounting cycles)

On July 1 of the current year Mary Nash opened a new real estate office called Mary Nash Realty, and during the month she completed these transactions:

July 1 Invested $1,500 in cash and an automobile having a $6,500 fair value.
2 Rented a furnished office and paid one month's rent, $350.
2 Paid the premium on a one-year insurance policy, $420.
3 Purchased office supplies for cash, $125.
12 Sold a house and collected a $3,850 commission.
15 Paid the biweekly salary of the office secretary, $300.
29 Paid the biweekly salary of the office secretary, $300.
31 Paid the July telephone bill, $50.
31 Paid the gas and oil used in the agency car during July, $60.

Required work for July:

1. Open the following accounts: Cash; Prepaid Insurance; Office Supplies; Automobile; Accumulated Depreciation, Automobile; Salaries Payable; Mary Nash, Capital; Mary Nash, Withdrawals; Income Summary; Commissions Earned; Rent Expense; Salaries Expense; Gas, Oil, and Repairs Expense; Telephone Expense; Insurance Expense; Office Supplies Expense; and Depreciation Expense, Automobile.
2. Prepare and post journal entries to record the July transactions.
3. Prepare a trial balance in the Trial Balance columns of a work sheet form and complete the work sheet using the following information:
   a. One month's insurance has expired.
   b. An inventory shows $95 of unused office supplies remaining.
   c. Estimated depreciation on the automobile, $100.
   d. Accrued but unpaid salary of the secretary, $60.
4. Prepare a July income statement and a July 31 classified balance sheet.
5. Prepare and post adjusting and closing journal entries.
6. Prepare a post-closing trial balance.

During August the real estate agency completed these transactions:

Aug. 1 Paid the August rent on the office space, $350.
     12 Paid the biweekly salary of the office secretary, $300.
     14 Purchased additional office supplies for cash, $35.
     17 Sold a building lot and collected a $1,200 commission.
     26 Paid the biweekly salary of the office secretary, $300.
     31 Paid for gas and oil used in the agency car, $55.
     31 Paid the August telephone bill, $45.
     31 Mary Nash withdrew $1,000 from the business to pay personal expenses.

Required work for August:

1. Prepare and post journal entries to record the August transactions.
2. Prepare a trial balance in the Trial Balance columns of a work sheet and complete the work sheet using the following information:
   a. One month's insurance has expired.
   b. An inventory shows $105 of unused office supplies remaining.
   c. Estimated depreciation on the automobile, $100.
   d. Accrued but unpaid salary of the secretary, $120.
3. Prepare an August income statement and an August 31 classified balance sheet.
4. Prepare and post adjusting and closing journal entries.
5. Prepare a post-closing trial balance.

Problem 4–4A

The ledger of Leisure Alleys showing account balances as of the end of its annual accounting period appears in the booklet of working papers that accompanies this text and a trial balance of the ledger is reproduced on a work sheet form provided there. The trial balance carries these items:

LEISURE ALLEYS
Trial Balance, December 31, 19—

Cash	$ 1,575	
Bowling supplies	2,420	
Prepaid insurance	575	
Bowling equipment	36,565	
Accumulated depreciation, bowling equipment		$ 9,640
Mortgage payable		10,000
Walter Hall, capital		14,025
Walter Hall, withdrawals	9,000	
Bowling revenue		35,500
Salaries expense	13,655	
Advertising expense	750	
Equipment repairs expense	420	
Rent expense	2,400	
Utilities expense	1,135	
Taxes expense	220	
Interest expense	450	
Totals	$69,165	$69,165

Required:

1. If the working papers are being used, complete the work sheet provided there for the solution of this problem, using the information that follows. If the working papers are not being used, enter the trial balance on a work sheet form and complete the work sheet.
   a. Bowling supplies inventory, $225.
   b. Expired insurance, $530.
   c. Estimated depreciation of bowling equipment, $3,850.
   d. Salaries accrued but unrecorded and unpaid on December 31, $240.
   e. The lease contract on the building calls for an annual rental equal to 8% of the annual bowling revenue, with $200 payable monthly on the first day of each month. The $200 was paid each month and debited to the Rent Expense account.
   f. On December 31 personal property taxes of $115 have accrued on the bowling equipment but are unrecorded and unpaid.
   g. The mortgage liability was incurred on May 1 of the current year, and interest on the debt is at the rate of 9% annually or $75 per month. The mortgage contract calls for annual payments of $1,000 on the anniversary date of the mortgage to reduce the amount of the debt. It also calls for quarterly interest payments of $225 each at the end of each quarter. Quarterly payments were made on July 31 and October 31.
2. Prepare an income statement and a classified balance sheet.
3. Prepare adjusting and closing entries.
4. Post the adjusting and closing entries and prepare a post-closing trial balance. (If the working papers are not being used, omit this last requirement.)

Problem 4–5A

The accounts of A–1 Delivery Service showing balances as of the end of its annual accounting period appear in the booklet of working papers that accompany this text, and a trial balance of the accounts is reproduced on a work sheet form provided there. The trial balance has these items:

A–1 DELIVERY SERVICE
Trial Balance, December 31, 19—

Cash	$ 2,225	
Accounts receivable	470	
Prepaid insurance	1,275	
Office supplies	245	
Office equipment	2,460	
Accumulated depreciation, office equipment		$ 470
Delivery equipment	12,790	
Accumulated depreciation, delivery equipment		3,150
Accounts payable		290
Unearned delivery service revenue		450
Carl Bush, capital		9,855
Carl Bush, withdrawals	13,000	
Delivery service revenue		46,555
Office rent expense	600	
Telephone expense	245	
Office salaries expense	8,060	
Truck drivers' wages expense	16,320	
Gas, oil, and repairs expense	2,180	
Garage rent expense	900	
Totals	$60,770	$60,770

Required:

1. If the working papers are being used, complete the work sheet provided there for the solution of this problem, using the information that follows. If the working papers are not being used, enter the trial balance on a work sheet form and complete the work sheet.

   a. Insurance expired on office equipment, $90; and on delivery equipment, $975.

   b. An inventory showed $125 of unused office supplies on hand.

   c. Estimated depreciation on office equipment, $215; and (d) on delivery equipment, $2,420.

   e. Three stores entered into contracts with the delivery service in which they agreed to pay a fixed fee for having packages delivered. Two of the stores made advance payments on their contracts, and the amounts were credited to Unearned Delivery Service Revenue. An examination of their contracts shows that $280 of the $450 paid in advance was earned by the accounting period end. The contract of the third store provides for a $150 monthly fee to be paid at the end of each month's service. It was signed on December 10, and two thirds of a month's revenue has accrued but is unrecorded.

   f. A $30 December telephone bill and a $55 bill for repairs to one of the delivery trucks arrived in the mail on December 31. Neither bill was paid nor recorded on the trial balance date.

g. Office salaries, $50, and truck drivers' wages, $170, have accrued but are unpaid and unrecorded.

2. Prepare an income statement and a classified balance sheet.
3. Prepare adjusting and closing entries.
4. Post the adjusting and closing entries to the accounts and prepare a post-closing trial balance. (If the working papers are not being used, omit this requirement.)

PROVOCATIVE PROBLEMS

Provocative problem 4–1
Susan Bell, Attorney

During the first year-end closing of the accounts of Susan Bell's law practice the office secretary and bookkeeper was in an accident and is in the hospital in a coma. Ms. Bell is certain the secretary prepared a work sheet, income statement, and balance sheet, but she has only the income statement and cannot find either the work sheet or balance sheet. She does have a trial balance of the accounts of the law practice, and she wants you to prepare adjusting and closing entries from the following trial balance and income statement. She also wants you to prepare a classified balance sheet. She says she has no legal work in process on which fees have accrued, and that the $600 of unearned fees on the trial balance represents a retainer fee paid by Security Bank. The bank retained Susan Bell on November 15 to do its legal work, agreeing to pay her $300 per month for her service.

SUSAN BELL, ATTORNEY
Trial Balance, December 31, 19—

Cash	$ 1,250	
Legal fees receivable	1,500	
Office supplies	400	
Prepaid insurance	625	
Furniture and equipment	5,500	
Accounts payable		$ 200
Unearned legal fees		600
Susan Bell, capital		7,500
Susan Bell, withdrawals	15,000	
Legal fees earned		29,800
Rent expense	4,550	
Office salaries expense	9,025	
Telephone expense	250	
Totals	$38,100	$38,100

SUSAN BELL, ATTORNEY
Income Statement for Year Ended December 31, 19—

Revenue:
Legal fees earned $30,250

Operating expenses:
Rent expense $4,200
Office salaries expense   9,100
Telephone expense   295
Accrued property taxes expense   125
Office supplies expense   275
Insurance expense   425
Depreciation expense, furniture and equipment   700
Total operating expenses   15,120
Net income $15,130

Provocative problem 4–2
Majestic Dry Cleaners

During his second year in college, Gregory Moss, as the only heir, inherited Majestic Dry Cleaners, a cash-and-carry dry cleaning business, upon the death of his father. He immediately dropped out of school and took over management of the business. At the time he took over, Greg recognized he knew little about accounting, but he reasoned that if the business cash increased, the business was doing OK. Therefore, he was pleased as he watched the balance of the concern's cash grow from $2,630 when he took over at the beginning of the year to $7,455 at the year-end. Furthermore, at the year-end he reasoned that since he had withdrawn $16,500 from the business to buy a new car and pay personal living expenses, the business had earned $21,325 during the year. He arrived at the $21,325 by adding the $4,825 increase in cash to the $16,500 he had withdrawn from the business, and he was shocked when he received the following income statement and learned the business had earned less than the amounts withdrawn.

MAJESTIC DRY CLEANERS
Income Statement for Year Ended December 31, 19—

Cleaning revenue earned $51,690

Operating expenses:
Salaries and wages expense $28,450
Cleaning supplies expense   840
Insurance expense   960
Depreciation expense, cleaning equipment   1,500
Depreciation expense, building   3,600
Property taxes expense   825
Total operating expenses   36,175
Net income $15,515

After mulling the statement over for several days, he has asked you to explain how in a year in which the cash increased $4,825 and he had withdrawn

$16,500, the business could have earned only $15,515. In examining the accounts of the business you note that accrued salaries and wages payable at the beginning of the year were $145, but had increased to $385 at the year's end. Also, the balance of the Cleaning Supplies account had decreased $160 between the beginning and the end of the year and the balance of the Prepaid Insurance account had decreased $310. However, except for the changes in these accounts, the change in cash, and the changes in the balances of the accumulated depreciation accounts, there were no other changes in the balances of the company's asset and liability accounts between the beginning and the end of the year. Back your explanation with a calculation accounting for the increase in cash.

After studying Chapter 5, you should be able to:

☐ Explain the nature of each item entering into the calculation of cost of goods sold and be able to calculate cost of goods sold and gross profit from sales.

☐ Prepare a work sheet and the financial statements for a merchandising business organized as a corporation and using a periodic inventory system.

☐ Prepare adjusting and closing entries for a merchandising business organized as a corporation.

☐ Define or explain the words and phrases listed in the chapter Glossary.

Accounting for a merchandising concern organized as a corporation

■ The accounting records and reports of the Owen law practice, as described in previous chapters, are those of a service enterprise. Other service enterprises are laundries, taxicab companies, barber and beauty shops, theaters, and golf courses. Each performs a service for a commission or fee, and the net income of each is the difference between fees or commissions earned and operating expenses.

A merchandising concern, on the other hand, whether a wholesaler or retailer, earns revenue by selling goods or merchandise. In such a concern a net income results when revenue from sales exceeds the cost of the goods sold plus operating expenses, as illustrated below:

XYZ Store
Condensed Income Statement

Revenue from sales	$100,000
Less cost of goods sold	60,000
Gross profit from sales	$ 40,000
Less operating expenses	25,000
Net income	$15,000

The store of the illustrated income statement sold for $100,000 goods that cost $60,000. It thereby earned a $40,000 gross profit from sales. From this it subtracted $25,000 of operating expenses to show a $15,000 net income.

Gross profit from sales, as shown on the illustrated income statement, is the "profit" before operating expenses are deducted. Accounting for the factors that enter into its calculation differentiates the accounting of a merchandising concern from that of a service enterprise.

Gross profit from sales is determined by subtracting cost of goods sold from the revenue resulting from their sale. However, before the subtraction can be made, both revenue from sales and cost of goods sold must be determined.

REVENUE FROM SALES

Revenue from sales consists of gross proceeds from merchandise sales less returns, allowances, and discounts. It may be reported on an income statement as follows:

Kona Sales, Incorporated
Income Statement for Year Ended December 31, 198B

Revenue from sales:		
Gross sales		$306,200
Less: Sales returns and allowances	$1,900	
Sales discounts	4,300	6,200
Net sales		$300,000

Gross sales

The gross sales item on the partial income statement is the total cash and credit sales made by the company during the year. Cash sales were "rung up" on a cash register as each sale was completed. At the end of each day the register total showed the amount of that day's cash sales, which was recorded with an entry like this:

Nov.	3	Cash	1,205.00	
		Sales		1,205.00
		To record the day's cash sales.		

In addition, an entry like this was used to record credit sales:

Nov.	3	Accounts Receivable	45.00	
		Sales		45.00
		Sold merchandise on credit.		

Sales returns and allowances

In most stores a customer is permitted to return any unsatisfactory merchandise purchased. Or the customer is sometimes allowed to keep the unsatisfactory goods and is given an allowance or an amount off its sales price. Either way, returns and allowances result from dissatisfied customers. Consequently, it is important for management to know the amount of such returns and allowances and their relation to sales. This information is supplied by the Sales Returns and Allowances account when each return or allowance is recorded as follows:

Nov.	4	Sales Returns and Allowances................	20.00	
		Accounts Receivable (or Cash)		20.00
		Customer returned unsatisfactory merchandise.		

Sales discounts

When goods are sold on credit, the terms of payment are always made definite so there will be no misunderstanding as to the amount and time of payment. The *credit terms* normally appear on the invoice or sales ticket and are part of the sales agreement. Exact terms granted usually depend upon the custom of the trade. In some trades it is customary for invoices to become due and payable ten days after the end of the month *(EOM)* in which the sale occurred. Invoices in these trades carry terms, "n/10 EOM." In other trades invoices become due and payable 30 days after the invoice date and carry terms of "n/30." This means that the net amount of the invoice is due 30 days after the invoice date.

When credit periods are long, creditors usually grant discounts, called *cash discounts,* for early payments. This reduces the amount invested in accounts receivable and tends to decrease losses from uncollectible accounts. When discounts for early payment are granted, they are made part of the credit terms and appear on the invoice as, for example, "Terms: 2/10, n/60." Terms of 2/10, n/60 means that the *credit period* is 60 days but that the debtor may deduct 2% from the invoice amount if payment is made within 10 days after the invoice date. The ten-day period is known as the *discount period.*

Since at the time of a sale it is not known if the customer will pay within the discount period and take advantage of a cash discount, normally sales discounts are not recorded until the customer pays. For example, on November 12, Kona Sales, Incorporated, sold $100 of merchandise to a customer on credit, term 2/10, n/60, and recorded the sale as follows:

Nov.	12	Accounts Receivable	100.00	
		Sales		100.00
		Sold merchandise, terms 2/10, n/60.		

At the time of the sale the customer could choose either to receive credit for paying the full $100 by paying $98 any time before November 22, or to wait 60 days, until January 11, and pay the full $100. If the customer elected to pay by November 22 and take advantage of the cash discount, Kona Sales, Incorporated, would record the receipt of the $98 as follows:

Nov.	22	Cash	98.00	
		Sales Discounts	2.00	
		Accounts Receivable		100.00
		Received payment for the November 12 sale less the discount.		

Sales discounts are accumulated in the Sales Discounts account until the end of an accounting period. Their total is then deducted from gross sales in determining revenue from sales. This is logical. A sales discount is an "amount off" the regular price of goods that is granted for early payment. As a result, it reduces revenue from sales.

COST OF GOODS SOLD

An automobile dealer or an appliance store make a limited number of sales each day. Consequently, they can easily refer to their records at the time of each sale and record the cost of the car or appliance sold. A drugstore, on the other hand, would find this difficult. For instance, if a drugstore sells a customer a tube of toothpaste, a box of aspirin, and a magazine, it can easily record with a cash register the sale of these items at marked selling prices. However, it would be difficult to maintain records that would enable it to also "look up" and record as "cost of goods sold" the costs of the items sold. As a result, stores such as drug, grocery, and others selling a volume of low-priced items make no effort to record the cost of the goods sold at the time of each sale. Rather, they wait until the end of an accounting period, take a physical inventory, and from the inventory and their accounting records determine at that time the cost of all goods sold during the period.

The end-of-the-period inventories taken by drug, grocery, or like stores in order to learn the cost of the goods they have sold are called *periodic inventories.* Also, the system used by such stores in accounting for cost of goods sold is known as a *periodic inventory system.* Such a system is described and discussed in this chapter. The system used by a car or appliance dealer to record the cost of each car or appliance sold depends on a *perpetual inventory record* of cars or appliances in stock. As a result, it is known as a *perpetual inventory system of accounting for goods on hand and sold.* It is discussed in Chapter 9.

COST OF GOODS SOLD, PERIODIC INVENTORY SYSTEM

As previously said, a store using a periodic inventory system makes no effort to determine and record the cost of items sold as they are sold. Rather, it waits until the end of an accounting period and determines at one time the cost of all the goods sold during the period. And to do this, it must have information as to (1) the cost of the merchandise it had on hand at the beginning of the period, (2) the cost of the merchandise purchased during the period, and (3) the cost of the unsold goods on hand at the period end. With this information a store can, for example, determine the cost of the goods it sold during a period as follows:

Cost of goods on hand at beginning of period	$ 19,000
Cost of goods purchased during the period	232,000
Goods available for sale during the period	$251,000
Unsold goods on hand at the period end	21,000
Cost of goods sold during the period	$230,000

The store of the calculation had $19,000 of merchandise at the beginning of the accounting period. During the period it purchased additional merchandise costing $232,000. Consequently, it had available and could have sold $251,000 of merchandise. However, $21,000 of this merchandise was on hand unsold at the period end. Therefore, the cost of the goods it sold during the period was $230,000.

The information needed in calculating cost of goods sold is accumulated as follows:

Merchandise inventories

The merchandise on hand at the beginning of an accounting period is called the *beginning inventory* and that on hand at the end is the *ending inventory.* Furthermore, since accounting periods follow one after another, the ending inventory of one period always becomes the beginning inventory of the next.

When a periodic inventory system is in use, the ending inventory is determined by (1) counting the items on the shelves in the store and in the stockroom, (2) multiplying the count for each kind of goods by its cost, and (3) adding the costs of the different kinds.

After the cost of the ending inventory is determined in this manner, it is subtracted from the cost of the goods available for sale to determine cost of goods sold. Also, by means of an adjusting entry the ending inventory is posted to an account called Merchandise Inventory. It remains there throughout the succeeding accounting period as a record of the inventory at the end of the period ended and the beginning of the succeeding period.

It should be emphasized at this point that, other than to correct errors, entries are made in the Merchandise Inventory account only at the end of each accounting period. Furthermore, since some goods are soon sold and other goods purchased, the account does not long show the dollar amount of goods on hand. Rather, as soon as goods are sold or purchased, its balance becomes a historical record of the dollar amount of goods that were on hand at the end of the last period and the beginning of the new period.

Cost of merchandise purchased

Cost of merchandise purchased is determined by subtracting from purchases any discounts, returns, and allowances and then adding any freight charges on the goods purchased. However, before examining this calculation it is best to see how the amounts involved are accumulated.

Under a periodic inventory system, when merchandise is bought for resale, its cost is debited to an account called Purchases, as follows:

Nov.	5	Purchases.	1,000.00	
		Accounts Payable		1,000.00
		Purchased merchandise on credit, invoice dated November 2, terms 2/10, n/30.		

The Purchases account has as its sole purpose the accumulation of the cost of all merchandise bought for resale during an accounting period. The account does not at any time show whether the merchandise is on hand or has been disposed of through sale or other means.

If a credit purchase is subject to a cash discount, payment within the discount period results in a credit to Purchases Discounts, as in the following entry:

Nov.	12	Accounts Payable	1,000.00	
		Purchases Discounts		20.00
		Cash		980.00
		Paid for the purchase of November 5 less the discount.		

When *purchases discounts* are involved, it is important that every invoice on which there is a discount be paid within the discount period, so that no discounts are lost. On the other hand, good cash management requires that no invoice be paid until the last day of its discount period. Consequently, to accomplish these objectives, every invoice must be filed in such a way that it automatically comes to the attention of the person responsible for its payment on the last day of its discount period. A simple way to do this is to provide a file with 31 folders, one for each day in a month. Then after an invoice is recorded, it is placed in the file folder of the last day of its discount period. For example, if the last day of an invoice's discount period is November 12, it is filed in folder number 12. Then on November 12 this invoice together with any other invoices in the same folder, are removed and paid or refiled for payment without a discount on a later date.

Sometimes merchandise received from suppliers is not acceptable and must be returned. Or, if kept, it is kept only because the supplier grants an allowance or reduction in its price. When merchandise is returned, purchasers "get their money back"; but from a managerial point of view more is involved. Buying merchandise, receiving and inspecting it, deciding that the merchandise is unsatisfactory, and returning it is a costly procedure that should be held to a minimum. The first step in holding it to a minimum is to know the amount of returns and allowances. To make this information available, returns and allowances on purchases are commonly recorded in an account called Purchases Returns and Allowances, as follows:

Nov.	14	Accounts Payable	65.00	
		Purchases Returns and Allowances		65.00
		Returned defective merchandise.		

When an invoice is subject to a cash discount and a portion of its goods is returned before the invoice is paid, the discount applies to just the goods kept. For example, if $500 of merchandise is purchased and $100 of the goods are returned before the invoice is paid, any discount applies only to the $400 of goods kept.

Sometimes a manufacturer or wholesaler pays transportation costs on merchandise it sells. The total cost of the goods to the purchaser then is the amount paid the manufacturer or wholesaler. Other times the purchaser must pay transportation costs *(freight-in)*. When this occurs, such charges are a proper addition to the cost of the goods purchased and may be recorded with a debit to the Purchases account. However, more complete information is obtained if such costs are debited to an account called Freight-In, as follows:

Nov.	24	Freight-In	22.00	
		Cash		22.00
		Paid express charges on merchandise pur-		
		chased.		

When transportation charges are involved, it is important that the buyer and seller understand which party is responsible for the charges. Normally, in quoting a price, the seller makes this clear by quoting a price of, say $400, *FOB* factory. FOB factory means free on board or loaded on board the means of transportation at the factory free of loading charges. The buyer then pays transportation costs from there. Likewise FOB destination means the seller will pay transportation costs to the destination of the goods.

Sometimes, when terms are FOB factory, the seller will prepay the transportation costs as a service to the buyer. In such a case, if a cash discount is involved, the discount does not apply to the transportation charges.

When a classified income statement is prepared, the balances of the Purchases, Purchases Returns and Allowances, Purchases Discounts, and Freight-In accounts are combined on it as follows to show the cost of the merchandise purchased during the period:

Purchases		$235,800	
Less: Purchases returns and allowances	$1,200		
Purchases discounts	4,100	5,300	
Net purchases		$230,500	
Add freight-in.............................		1,500	
Cost of goods purchased			$232,000

Cost of goods sold

The last item in the foregoing calculation is the cost of the merchandise purchased during the accounting period. It is combined with the beginning and ending inventories to arrive at cost of goods sold as follows:

Cost of goods sold:			
Merchandise inventory, January 1, 198B			$ 19,000
Purchases		$235,800	
Less: Purchases returns and allowances	$1,200		
Purchases discounts	4,100	5,300	
Net purchases		$230,500	
Add freight-in		1,500	
Cost of goods purchased			232,000
Goods available for sale			$251,000
Merchandise inventory, December 31, 198B			21,000
Cost of goods sold			$230,000

Inventory losses

Under a periodic inventory system the cost of any merchandise lost through shrinkage, spoilage, or shoplifting is automatically included in cost of goods sold. For example, assume a store lost $500 of merchandise to shoplifters during a year. This caused its year-end inventory to be $500 less than it otherwise would have been, since these goods were not available for inclusion in the year-end count. Therefore, since the year-end inventory was $500 smaller because of the loss, the cost of the goods the store sold was $500 greater.

Many stores are troubled with shoplifting. Although under a periodic inventory system such losses are automatically included in cost of goods sold, it is often important to know their extent. Consequently, a way to estimate shoplifting losses is described in Chapter 9.

INCOME STATEMENT OF A MERCHANDISING CONCERN

A classified income statement for a merchandising concern has (1) a revenue section, (2) a cost of goods sold section, and (3) an operating expenses section. The first two sections have been discussed, but note in Illustration 5–1 on the next page how they are brought together to show gross profit from sales.

Observe also in Illustration 5–1 how operating expenses are classified as either "Selling expenses" or "General and administrative expenses." *Selling expenses* include expenses of storing and preparing goods for sale, promoting sales, actually making sales, and delivering goods to customers. *General and administrative expenses* include the general office, accounting, personnel, and credit and collection expenses.

Sometimes an expenditure should be divided or prorated part to selling expenses and part to general and administrative expenses. Kona Sales, Incorporated, divided the rent on its store building in this manner, as an examination of Illustration 5–1 will reveal. However, it did not prorate its insurance expense because the amount involved was so small the company felt the extra exactness did not warrant the extra work.

The last item subtracted in Illustration 5–1 is income taxes expense. This income statement was prepared for Kona Sales, Incorporated, a corporation. Of the three kinds of business organizations, corporations alone are subject to the payment of state and federal income taxes. Often on a corporation income statement, as in Illustration 5–1, the operating expenses are subtracted from gross profit from sales to arrive at income from operations, after which income taxes are deducted to arrive at net income.

Kona Sales, Incorporated
Income Statement for Year Ended December 31, 198B

Revenue from sales:			
Gross sales			$306,200
Less: Sales returns and allowances		$ 1,900	
Sales discounts		4,300	6,200
Net sales			$300,000
Cost of goods sold:			
Merchandise inventory, January 1, 198B		$ 19,000	
Purchases	$235,800		
Less: Purchases returns and allowances	$1,200		
Purchase discounts	4,100	5,300	
Net purchases		$230,500	
Add freight-in		1,500	
Cost of goods purchased		232,000	
Goods available for sale		$251,000	
Merchandise inventory, December 31, 198B		21,000	
Cost of goods sold			230,000
Gross profit from sales			$ 70,000
Operating expenses:			
Selling expenses:			
Sales salaries expense	$ 18,500		
Rent expense, selling space	8,100		
Advertising expense	700		
Store supplies expense	400		
Depreciation expense, store equipment	3,000		
Total selling expenses		$ 30,700	
General and administrative expenses:			
Office salaries expense	$ 25,200		
Rent expense, office space	900		
Insurance expense	600		
Office supplies expense	200		
Depreciation expense, office equipment	700		
Total general and administrative expenses		27,600	
Total operating expenses			58,300
Income from operations			$ 11,700
Less income taxes expense			2,300
Net income			$ 9,400

Illustration 5–1

WORK SHEET OF A MERCHANDISING CONCERN

A concern selling merchandise, like a service-type company, uses a work sheet in bringing together the end-of-the-period information needed in preparing its income statement, balance sheet, and adjusting entries. Such a work sheet, that of Kona Sales, Incorporated, is shown in Illustration 5–2 on pages 160 and 161.

Illustration 5–2 differs from the work sheet in the previous chapter in several ways, the first of which is that it was prepared for a corporation. This is indicated by the word "Incorporated" in the company name. It is also indicated by the appearance on the work sheet of the Common Stock and Retained Earnings accounts. Note on lines 13 and 14 how the balances of these two accounts are carried unchanged from the Trial Balance credit column into the Balance Sheet credit column.

Illustration 5–2 also differs in that it does not have any Adjusted Trial Balance columns. The experienced accountant commonly omits these columns from a work sheet in order to reduce the time and effort required in its preparation. He or she enters the adjustments in the Adjustments columns, combines the adjustments with the trial balance amounts, and sorts the combined amounts directly to the proper Income Statement or Balance Sheet columns in a single operation. In other words, the experienced accountant simply omits the adjusted trial balance in preparing a work sheet.

The remaining similarities and differences of Illustration 5–2 are best described column by column.

Account Titles column

Several accounts that do not have trial balance amounts are listed in the Account Titles column, with each being listed in the order of its appearance on the financial statements. These accounts receive debits and credits in making the adjustments. Entering their names on the work sheet in statement order at the time the work sheet is begun makes later preparation of the statements somewhat easier. If required account names are anticipated and listed without balances, as in Illustration 5–2, but later it is discovered that a name not listed is needed, it may be entered below the trial balance totals as was done in Chapter 4.

Trial Balance columns

The amounts in the Trial Balance columns of Illustration 5–2 are the unadjusted account balances of Kona Sales, Incorporated, as of the end of its annual accounting period. They were taken from the company's ledger after all transactions were recorded but before any end-of-the-period adjustments were made.

KONA SALES, INCORPORATED

Work Sheet for Year Ended December 31, 198B

	ACCOUNT TITLES	TRIAL BALANCE Dr.	TRIAL BALANCE Cr.	ADJUSTMENTS Dr.	ADJUSTMENTS Cr.	INCOME STATEMENT Dr.	INCOME STATEMENT Cr.	BALANCE SHEET Dr.	BALANCE SHEET Cr.
1	Cash	820000						820000	
2	Accounts receivable	1120000						1120000	
3	Merchandise inventory	1900000		(b)2100000	(a)1900000			2100000	
4	Prepaid insurance	90000			(c)60000			30000	
5	Store supplies	60000			(d)40000			20000	
6	Office supplies	30000			(e)20000			10000	
7	Store equipment	2910000						2910000	
8	Accumulated depreciation, store equipment		250000		(f)300000				550000
9	Office equipment	440000						440000	
10	Accumulated depreciation, office equipment		60000		(g)70000				130000
11	Accounts payable		360000						360000
12	Income taxes payable				(h)10000				10000
13	Common stock		5000000						5000000
14	Retained earnings		460000						460000
15	Income summary			(a)1900000	(b)2100000	1900000	2100000		
16	Sales		30620000				30620000		
17	Sales returns and allowances	190000				190000			
18	Sales discounts	430000				430000			
19	Purchases	23580000				23580000			
20	Purchases returns and allowances		120000				120000		
21	Purchases discounts		410000				410000		
22	Freight-in	150000				150000			
23	Sales salaries expense	1850000				1850000			

#	Account							
24	Rent expense, selling space	810000			810000			
25	Advertising expense	70000			70000			
26	Store supplies expense		(d)40000		40000			
27	Depreciation expense, store equipment		(f)300000		300000			
28	Office salaries expense	2520000			2520000			
29	Rent expense, office space	90000			90000			
30	Insurance expense		(c)60000		60000			
31	Office supplies expense		(e)20000		20000			
32	Depreciation expense, office equipment		(g)70000		70000			
33	Income taxes expense	220000	(h)10000		230000			
34		37280000	4500000	4500000	32310000	33250000	7450000	6510000
35	Net income				940000			940000
36					33250000	33250000	7450000	7450000
37								
38								
39								
40								
41								
42								
43								
44								
45								
46								
47								
48								
49								

Illustration 5-2

Note the $19,000 inventory amount appearing in the Trial Balance debit column on line 3. This is the amount of inventory the company had on January 1, at the beginning of the accounting period. The $19,000 was debited to the Merchandise Inventory account at the end of the previous period and remained in the account as its balance throughout the current accounting period.

Adjustments columns

Of the adjustments appearing on the illustrated work sheet, only those for inventories and for income taxes are new.

Inventory adjustments   The company of Illustration 5–2 determined that it had a $21,000 ending inventory by counting its items of unsold merchandise. It then made adjustments *(a)* and *(b)* on its work sheet, the effects of which are shown in T-accounts in Illustration 5–3. Observe that adjustment *(a)* removes the amount of the beginning inventory from the inventory account and charges (debits) it to Income Summary. Adjustment *(b)* then enters the amount of the ending inventory in the inventory account. (After the work sheet and statements are completed, the effects shown in Illustration 5–3 are obtained in the accounts by preparing and posting two adjusting entries.)

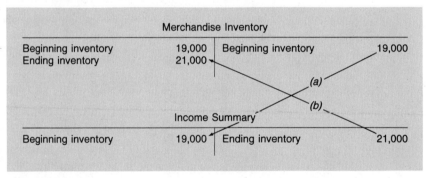

Illustration 5–3

Look again at the work sheet and observe that combining the amounts on line 3 results in the extension of the $21,000 ending inventory amount into the Balance Sheet debit column. This is as it should be. The company has a $21,000 ending inventory, and it should appear on the balance sheet as an asset of that amount.

Next observe on line 15 that both the $19,000 beginning inventory amount and the $21,000 ending inventory amount are extended from the Adjustments columns into the Income Statement columns. The beginning inventory is extended as a debit, and the ending inventory as a credit. Observe too that the balances of the Purchases, Purchases

Returns and Allowances, Purchases Discounts, and Freight-In accounts are also extended into the Income Statement columns in the same debit and credit positions they occupy in the Trial Balance columns. These six items, which are emphasized in color in the Income Statement columns, are the items that enter into the calculation of cost of goods sold. Note in the following calculation that the sum of the three debit items minus the sum of the three credit items equals the $230,000 cost of goods sold amount shown in Illustration 5–1.

Debits	Credits
$ 19,000	$21,000
235,800	1,200
1,500	4,100
$256,300	$26,300
(26,300)	
$230,000	

Therefore, extending the six amounts into the Income Statement columns in effect extends cost of goods sold into these columns.

Income tax adjustment   As previously explained, a business organized as a corporation is subject to the payment of state and federal income taxes. As to the federal tax, near the beginning of each year a corporation must estimate the amount of income it expects to earn during the year. It must then pay in advance in installments an estimated tax on this income. The advance payments are debited to the Income Taxes Expense account as each installment is paid. Consequently, a corporation that expects to earn a profit normally reaches the end of the year with a debit balance in its Income Taxes Expense account. However, since the balance is an estimate and usually less than the full amount of the tax, an adjustment like that on lines 12 and 33 normally must be made to reflect the additional tax owed.

COMPLETING THE WORK SHEET

After all adjustments are entered on a work sheet like that of Illustration 5–2 and totaled, the amounts in the Trial Balance columns are combined with the amounts in the Adjustments columns and sorted to the proper Income Statement and Balance Sheet columns. In sorting each amount, two decisions are required: (1) Is the amount a debit or a credit and (2) on which statement does it appear? As to the first decision, debit amounts must be sorted to a debit column and credit amounts must go into a credit column. As to the second decision, revenue, cost of goods sold, and expense items go on the income statement. Asset, liability, and stockholders' (owners') equity items go on the balance sheet. After the amounts are sorted to the proper columns, the work sheet is completed in the manner described in the previous chapter.

PREPARING THE STATEMENTS

After the work sheet is completed, the items in its Income Statement columns are arranged into a formal income statement. The items in its Balance Sheet columns are then arranged into a formal balance sheet. A classified income statement prepared from information in the Income Statement columns of Illustration 5–2 is shown in Illustration 5–1. The balance sheet appears in Illustration 5–4. Observe that since none of the company's prepaid items are material in amount, they are totaled and shown as a single item on the balance sheet. The $14,000 retained earnings amount on the balance sheet is the sum of the $4,600 of retained earnings appearing on line 14 of the work sheet plus the company's $9,400 net income.

Kona Sales, Incorporated
Balance Sheet, December 31, 198B

Assets

Current assets:			
Cash		$ 8,200	
Accounts receivable		11,200	
Merchandise inventory		21,000	
Prepaid expenses.............................		600	
Total current assets			$41,000
Plant and equipment:			
Store equipment..............................	$29,100		
Less accumulated depreciation	5,500	$23,600	
Office equipment	$ 4,400		
Less accumulated depreciation	1,300	3,100	
Total plant and equipment			26,700
Total assets.......................			$67,700

Liabilities

Current liabilities:			
Accounts payable.............................		$ 3,600	
Income taxes payable		100	
Total current liabilities			$ 3,700

Stockholders' Equity

Common stock, $5 par value, 10,000			
shares authorized and outstanding..............		$50,000	
Retained earnings		14,000	
Total stockholders' equity....................			64,000
Total liabilities and stockholders' equity ..			$67,700

Illustration 5–4

RETAINED EARNINGS STATEMENT

In addition to an income statement and a balance sheet, a third financial statement called a *retained earnings statement* is commonly prepared for a corporation. It reports the changes that have occurred in the corporation's retained earnings during the period and accounts for the difference between the retained earnings reported on balance sheets of successive accounting periods.

The retained earnings statement of Kona Sales, Incorporated, appears in Illustration 5–5. It shows that the company began the year with $8,600 of retained earnings, which is also the amount of retained earnings it reported on its previous year's balance sheet. Its retained earnings were reduced by the declaration of $4,000 of dividends and increased by the $9,400 net income to the $14,000 reported on its year-end balance sheet. Information as to the beginning retained earnings and the dividends declared were taken from the company's Retained Earnings account.

Kona Sales, Incorporated
Retained Earnings Statement
For Year Ended December 31, 198B

Retained earnings, January 1, 198B	$ 8,600
Add 198B net income	9,400
Total	$18,000
Deduct dividends declared	4,000
Retained earnings, December 31, 198B ..	$14,000

Illustration 5–5

ADJUSTING AND CLOSING ENTRIES

In a merchandising concern, as in a service-type business, after the work sheet and statements are completed, adjusting and closing entries must be prepared and posted. The entries for Kona Sales, Incorporated, are shown in Illustration 5–6. They differ from previously illustrated adjusting and closing entries in that an explanation for each entry is not given. Individual explanations may be given, but are unnecessary. The words "Adjusting entries" before the first adjusting entry and "Closing entries" before the first closing entry are sufficient to explain the entries.

The effects of adjusting and closing entries on the accounts were illustrated in Chapters 3 and 4. However, since the inventory adjustments, as well as the closing entries, affect the Income Summary account of Kona Sales, Incorporated, the account is reproduced as Illustra-

DATE	ACCOUNT TITLES AND EXPLANATION	POST. REF.	DEBIT	CREDIT
198B	Adjusting entries:			
Dec. 31	Income Summary	313	19 000 00	
	Merchandise Inventory	113		19 000 00
31	Merchandise Inventory	113	21 000 00	
	Income Summary	313		21 000 00
31	Insurance Expense	653	600 00	
	Prepaid Insurance	115		600 00
31	Store Supplies Expense	614	400 00	
	Store Supplies	116		400 00
Dec. 31	Office Supplies Expense	651	200 00	
	Office Supplies	117		200 00
31	Depreciation Expense, Store Equipment	615	3 000 00	
	Accumulated Depr., Store Equipment	132		3 000 00
31	Depreciation Expense, Office Equipment	655	700 00	
	Accumulated Depr., Office Equipment	134		700 00
31	Income Taxes Expense	711	100 00	
	Income Taxes Payable	213		100 00
	Closing entries:			
31	Sales	411	306 200 00	
	Purchases Returns and Allowances	512	1 200 00	
	Purchases Discounts	513	4 100 00	
	Income Summary	313		311 500 00
31	Income Summary	313	304 100 00	
	Sales Returns and Allowances	412		1 900 00
	Sales Discounts	413		4 300 00
	Purchases	511		235 800 00
	Freight-In	514		1 500 00
	Sales Salaries Expense	611		18 500 00
	Rent Expense, Selling Space	612		8 100 00
	Advertising Expense	613		700 00
	Store Supplies Expense	614		400 00
	Depreciation Expense, Store Equip.	615		3 000 00
	Office Salaries Expense	651		25 200 00
	Rent Expense, Office Space	652		900 00
	Insurance Expense	653		600 00
	Office Supplies Expense	654		200 00
	Depreciation Expense, Office Equip.	655		700 00
	Income Taxes Expense	711		2 300 00
31	Income Summary	313	9 400 00	
	Retained Earnings	312		9 400 00

Illustration 5–6

Income Summary					Account No. 313
Date	Explanation	Post. Ref.	Debit	Credit	Balance
198B					
Dec. 31	Beginning inventory	G23	19,000		19,000
31	Ending inventory	G23		21,000	2,000
31	Sales, etc.	G23		311,500	313,500
31	Expenses, etc.	G23	304,100		9,400
31	Net income	G23	9,400		–0–

Illustration 5–7

tion 5–7. To aid understanding, each amount in the account is identified. However, such identifications are not required in the posting procedure. The nature of the account's balance after the second entry is determined by examining the relative sizes of the two inventory amounts.

Illustration 5–8 shows the company's Retained Earnings account after the last closing entry was posted. The company earned $8,600

Retained Earnings					Account No. 312
Date	Explanation	Post. Ref.	Debit	Credit	Balance
198A					
Dec. 31	198A net income	G10		8,600	8,600
198B					
Oct. 15	Dividend declared	G20	4,000		4,600
Dec. 31	198B net income	G23		9,400	14,000

Illustration 5–8

during 198A, its first year in business, and it began 198B with that amount of retained earnings. It declared a $4,000 dividend in October and earned a $9,400 net income. The account is reproduced here so that its information may be compared with that in the company's retained earnings statement, Illustration 5–5.

INCOME STATEMENT FORMS

The income statement in Illustration 5–1 is called a classified income statement because its items are classified into significant groups. It is also a *multiple-step income statement* because cost of goods sold and the expenses are subtracted in steps to arrive at net income. Another income statement form, the *single-step form,* is shown in Illustration 5–9. This form is commonly used for published statements. Also, although it need not be, its information is commonly condensed as shown. Note how cost of goods sold and the expenses are added together in the illustration and are subtracted in "one step" from net sales to arrive at net income, thus the name of the form.

Kona Sales, Incorporated		
Income Statement for Year Ended December 31, 198B		
Revenue from sales.........................		$300,000
Expenses:		
Cost of goods sold........................	$230,000	
Selling expenses	30,700	
General and administrative expenses	27,600	
Income taxes expense	2,300	
Total expenses		290,600
Net income		$ 9,400

Illustration 5–9

COMBINED INCOME AND RETAINED EARNINGS STATEMENT

Many companies combine their income and retained earnings statements into a single statement. Such a statement may be prepared in either single-step or multiple-step form. A single-step statement is shown in Illustration 5–10.

Kona Sales, Incorporated		
Statement of Income and Retained Earnings		
For Year Ended December 31, 198B		
Revenue for sales		$300,000
Expenses:		
Cost of goods sold	$230,000	
Selling expenses	30,700	
General and administrative expenses	27,600	
Income taxes expense	2,300	
Total expenses		290,600
Net income		$ 9,400
Add retained earnings, January 1, 198B......		8,600
Total		$ 18,000
Deduct dividends declared		4,000
Retained earnings, December 31, 198B........		$ 14,000

Illustration 5–10

STATEMENT OF CHANGES IN FINANCIAL POSITION

In addition to the retained earnings statement, another very important financial statement commonly prepared for a corporation is the *statement of changes in financial position.* It shows where the concern secured funds and where it applied or used the funds, such as in the purchase of plant assets or the payment of dividends. A discussion of this statement is deferred until Chapter 18, after further discussion of corporation accounting.

BUSINESS PRACTICES

Taking an ending inventory

As previously stated, when a periodic inventory system is in use, the dollar amount of the ending inventory is determined by counting the items of unsold merchandise remaining in the store, multiplying the count for each kind by its cost, and adding the costs for all the kinds. In making the count, items are less apt to be counted twice or omitted from the count if prenumbered *inventory tickets* like the one in Illustration 5–11 are used. Before beginning the inventory, a sufficient number of the tickets, at least one for each kind of product on hand, is issued to each department in the store. Next a clerk counts the quantity of each product and from the count and the price tag attached to the merchandise fills in the information on the inventory ticket and attaches it to the counted items. After the count is com-

INVENTORY

TICKET no._____ *786*_____

Item

Quantity counted	
Sales price	$
Cost price	$
Purchase date	

Counted by_____

Checked by_____

Illustration 5–11

pleted, each department is examined for uncounted items. At this stage, inventory tickets are attached to all counted items. Consequently, any products without tickets attached are uncounted. After all items are counted and tickets attached, the tickets are removed and sent to the accounting department for completion of the inventory. To ensure that no ticket is lost or left attached to merchandise, all the prenumbered tickets issued are accounted for when the tickets arrive in the accounting department.

In the accounting department, the information on the tickets is copied on inventory summary sheets. The sheets are then completed by multiplying the number of units of each product by its unit cost. This gives the dollar amount of each product on hand, and the total for all products is the amount of the inventory.

Debit and credit memoranda

Merchandise purchased that does not meet specifications on delivery, goods received in damaged condition, goods received that were not ordered, goods received short of the amount ordered and billed, and invoice errors are matters for adjustment between the buyer and seller. In some cases the buyer can make the adjustment, and in others the adjustment is a subject for negotiation between the buyer and the seller. When there are invoice errors or when goods are received that were not ordered, the purchasing firm may make the adjustment. If it does, it must notify the seller of its action. It commonly does this by sending a *debit memorandum* or a *credit memorandum.*

A debit memorandum is a business form on which are spaces for the name and address of the concern to which it is directed and the printed words, "WE DEBIT YOUR ACCOUNT," followed by space for typing in the reason for the debit. A credit memorandum carries the words, "WE CREDIT YOUR ACCOUNT." To illustrate the use of a debit memorandum, assume a buyer of merchandise discovers an invoice error that reduces the invoice total by $10. For such an error the buyer notifies the seller with a debit memorandum reading: "WE DEBIT YOUR ACCOUNT to correct a $10 error on your November 17 invoice." A debit memorandum is sent because the correction reduces an account payable of the buyer, and to reduce an account payable requires a debit. In recording the purchase, the buyer normally marks the correction on the invoice and attaches a copy of the debit memorandum to show that the seller has been notified. The buyer then debits Purchases and credits Accounts Payable for the corrected amount.

Some adjustments, such as damaged merchandise or merchandise that does not meet specifications, normally require negotiations between the buyer and the seller. In such cases the buyer may debit Purchases for the full invoice amount and enter into negotiations with the seller for a return or a price adjustment. If the seller agrees to the return or adjustment, the seller notifies the buyer with a credit memorandum. A credit memorandum is used because the return or adjustment reduces an account receivable on the books of the seller, and to reduce an account receivable requires a credit.

From this discussion it can be seen that a debit or a credit memorandum may originate with either party to a transaction. The memorandum gets its name from the action of the originator. If the originator debits, the originator sends a debit memorandum. If the originator credits, a credit memorandum is sent.

Trade discounts

A *trade discount* is a deduction (often as much as 40% or more) from a *list* (or catalog) *price* that is used in determining the actual price of the goods to which it applies. Trade discounts are commonly used by manufacturers and wholesalers to avoid republication of catalogs when selling prices change. If selling prices change, catalog prices can be adjusted by merely issuing a new list of discounts to be applied to the catalog prices. Such discounts are discussed here primarily to distinguish them from the cash discounts described earlier in this chapter.

Trade discounts are not entered in the accounts by either party to a sale. For example, if a manufacturer sells on credit an item listed in its catalog at $100, less a 40% trade discount, it will record the sale as follows:

Dec.	10	Accounts Receivable	60.00	
		Sales		60.00
		Sold merchandise on credit.		

The buyer will also enter the purchase in the records at $60. Also, if a cash discount is involved, it applies only to the amount of the purchase, $60.

Code numbers as a means of identifying accounts

The account numbering scheme used in the chapters before this has been a simple one in which the accounts have been numbered consecutively. Such a scheme is satisfactory in a small business. However, in a larger more complicated accounting system, account numbers commonly become code numbers. The *account code numbers* not only identify accounts but also tell their statement classifications.

For example, in one numbering system three-digit numbers with each digit having a significant meaning are used. In this system the first digit in each account number tells the major balance sheet or income statement classification of the account to which it is assigned. For example, account numbers with first digits of 1, numbers 111 to 199, are assigned to asset accounts. Liability accounts are then assigned numbers with the first digits of 2, numbers 211 to 299. When this system is used, main balance sheet and income statement account classifications may be assigned the following numbers:

111 to 199 are assigned to asset accounts.
211 to 299 are assigned to liability accounts.
311 to 399 are assigned to owner's equity accounts.
411 to 499 are assigned to sales or revenue accounts.
511 to 599 are assigned to cost of goods sold accounts.
611 to 699 are assigned to operating expense accounts.
711 to 799 are assigned to other revenue and expense accounts.

In the system under discussion, the second and third digits further classify an account. For example, the second digits under each of the following main classifications indicate the subclassification shown:

111 to 199. Asset accounts
    111 to 119. Current asset accounts (second digits of 1)
    121 to 129. Long-term investment accounts (second digits of 2)
    131 to 139. Plant asset accounts (second digits of 3)
    141 to 149. Intangible asset accounts (second digits of 4)

211 to 299. Liability accounts
    211 to 219. Current liability accounts (second digits of 1)
    221 to 229. Long-term liability accounts (second digits of 2)

611 to 699. Operating expense accounts
    611 to 629. Selling expense accounts (second digits of 1 and 2)
    631 to 649. Delivery expense accounts (second digits of 3 and 4)
    651 to 669. General administrative expense accounts (second digits of 5 and 6)

The third digit in each number further classifies the account. For example, in the system under discussion, all selling expense accounts, which have account numbers with first digits of 6 and second digits of 1 and 2, are further classified as follows:

611 to 699. Operating expense accounts
    611 to 629. Selling expense accounts
        611. Sales salaries expense (third digit of 1)
        613. Advertising expense (third digit of 3)
        615. Depreciation expense, store equipment (third digit of 5)

GLOSSARY

Account code number. An identifying number assigned to an account and used as the account's posting reference number.

Cash discount. A deduction from the invoice price of goods allowed if payment is made within a specified period of time.

Credit memorandum. A memorandum sent to notify its recipient that the business sending the memorandum has in its records credited the account of the recipient.

Credit period. The agreed period of time for which credit is granted and at the end of which payment is expected.

Credit terms. The agreed terms upon which credit is granted in the sale of goods or services.

Debit memorandum. A memorandum sent to notify its recipient that the business sending the memorandum has in its records debited the account of the recipient.

Discount period. The period of time in which a cash discount may be taken.

EOM. An abbreviation meaning "end of month."

Freight-in. Transportation charges on merchandise purchased for resale.

FOB. The abbreviation for "free on board," which is used to denote that goods purchased are placed on board the means of transportation at a specified geographic point free of any loading and transportation charges to that point.

General and administrative expenses. The general office, accounting, personnel, and credit and collection expenses.

Gross profit from sales. Net sales minus cost of goods sold.

Inventory ticket. A form attached to counted items in the process of taking an inventory.

List price. The catalog or other listed price from which a trade discount is deducted in arriving at the invoice price for goods.

Merchandise inventory. The unsold merchandise on hand at a given time.

Multiple-step income statement. An income statement on which cost of goods sold and the expenses are subtracted in steps to arrive at net income.

Periodic inventory system. An inventory system in which periodically, at the end of each accounting period, the cost of the unsold goods on hand is determined by counting units of each product on hand, multiplying the count for each product by its cost, and adding costs of the various products.

Perpetual inventory system. An inventory system in which an individual record is kept for each product of the units on hand at the beginning, the units purchased, the units sold, and the new balance after each purchase or sale.

Purchases discounts. Discounts taken on merchandise purchased for resale.

Retained earnings statement. A statement which reports changes in a corporation's retained earnings during an accounting period.

Sales discounts. Discounts given on sales of merchandise.

Selling expenses. The expenses of preparing and storing goods for sale, promoting sales, making sales, and if a separate delivery department is not maintained, the expenses of delivering goods to customers.

Single-step income statement. An income statement on which cost of goods sold and the expenses are added together and subtracted in one step from revenue to arrive at net income.

Trade discount. The discount that may be deducted from a catalog list price to determine the invoice price of goods.

QUESTIONS FOR CLASS DISCUSSION

1. What is gross profit from sales?
2. May a concern earn a gross profit on its sales and still suffer a loss? How?
3. Why should a concern be interested in the amount of its sales returns and allowances?
4. Since sales returns and allowances are subtracted from sales on the income statement, why not save the effort of this subtraction by debiting all such returns and allowances directly to the Sales account?
5. What is a cash discount? If terms are 2/10, n/60, what is the length of the credit period? What is the length of the discount period?
6. How and when is cost of goods sold determined in a store using a periodic inventory system?
7. Which of the following are debited to the Purchases account of a grocery store: (a) the purchase of a cash register, (b) the purchase of a refrigerated display case, (c) the purchase of advertising space in a newspaper, and (d) the purchase of a case of tomato soup?
8. If a concern may return for full credit all unsatisfactory merchandise purchased, why should it be interested in controlling the amount of its returns?
9. When applied to transportation terms, what do the letters FOB mean? What does FOB destination mean?
10. At the end of an accounting period, which inventory, the beginning inventory or the ending, appears on the trial balance?
11. What is shown on a retained earnings statement? What is the purpose of the statement?

12. How does a single-step income statement differ from a multiple-step income statement?

13. What is gained by using inventory tickets in taking a physical inventory?

14. During a year a company purchased merchandise costing $220,000. What was the company's cost of goods sold if there were (a) no beginning or ending inventories? (b) a beginning inventory of $28,000 and no ending inventory? (c) a $25,000 beginning inventory and a $30,000 ending inventory? and (d) no beginning inventory and a $15,000 ending inventory?

15. In counting the merchandise on hand at the end of an accounting period, a clerk failed to count, and consequently omitted from the inventory, all the merchandise on one shelf. If the cost of the merchandise on the shelf was $100, what was the effect of the omission on (a) the balance sheet and (b) the income statement?

16. Suppose that the omission of the $100 from the inventory (Question 15) was not discovered. What would be the effect on the balance sheet and income statement prepared at the end of the next accounting period?

17. Distinguish between cash discounts and trade discounts. Is the amount of a trade discount on merchandise purchased credited to the Purchases Discounts account?

18. When a debit memorandum is issued, who debits, the originator of the memorandum or the company receiving it?

19. When a three-digit account numbering system like the one described in this chapter is in use, which digit of an account's number is the most significant?

CLASS EXERCISES

Exercise 5–1

Rock Shop purchased merchandise having a $1,000 invoice price, terms 2/10, n/60, from Hill Company and paid for the merchandise within the discount period. (a) Give without dates the journal entry made by Rock Shop to record the purchase and payment and (b) give without dates the entries made by Hill Company to record the sale and collection. (c) If Rock Shop borrowed sufficient money at 9% interest on the last day of the discount period in order to pay the invoice, how much did it save by borrowing to take advantage of the discount?

Exercise 5–2

The following items, with expenses condensed to conserve space, appeared in the Income Statement columns of a work sheet prepared for Campus Shop, Incorporated, as of December 31, 198B, the end of its annual accounting period. From the information prepare a 198B income statement for the shop.

| | Income Statement | |
	Debit	Credit
Income summary	18,000	20,000
Sales		100,000
Sales returns and allowances	500	
Sales discounts	800	
Purchases	60,000	
Purchases returns and allowances		300
Purchases discounts		1,200
Freight-in	200	
Selling expenses	15,000	
General and administrative expenses	7,000	
Income taxes expense	4,000	
	105,500	121,500
Net income	16,000	
	121,500	121,500

Exercise 5-3

Rule a balance-column Merchandise inventory account on note paper, and under the date, December 31, 198A, enter the $18,000 beginning inventory of Exercise 5-2 as its balance. Then prepare (a) the adjusting entry that removes the beginning inventory from the inventory account and charges it to Income Summary and (b) the adjusting entry that enters the ending inventory in the inventory account. Post the entries to the Merchandise Inventory account.

Exercise 5-4

Prepare entries to close the revenue, expense, and Income Summary accounts of Campus Shop, Incorporated, as they appear in Exercise 5-2.

Exercise 5-5

Copy the following tabulation and fill in the missing amounts. Indicate a loss by placing a minus sign before the amount. Each horizontal row of figures is a separate problem situation.

Sales	Begin-ning In-ventory	Pur-chases	Ending In-ventory	Cost of Goods Sold	Gross Profit	Ex-penses	Net Income or Loss
80,000	50,000	40,000	?	65,000	?	20,000	?
95,000	35,000	?	45,000	50,000	?	25,000	20,000
120,000	50,000	?	40,000	?	55,000	35,000	20,000
?	40,000	70,000	35,000	?	40,000	35,000	?
110,000	40,000	65,000	?	60,000	?	25,000	?
70,000	30,000	?	35,000	40,000	?	?	10,000
?	40,000	50,000	30,000	?	40,000	?	-5,000
80,000	?	50,000	35,000	?	30,000	?	10,000

Exercise 5–6

The following trial balance was taken from the ledger of Alpha, Incorporated, at the end of its annual accounting period. (To simplify the problem and to save time, the account balances are in numbers of not more than two digits.)

Required:

Prepare a work sheet form having no Adjusted Trial Balance columns on note paper and copy the trial balance on the work sheet. Then complete the work sheet using the following information:

a. Ending merchandise inventory, $6.
b. Ending store supplies inventory, $1.
c. Estimated depreciation of store equipment, $1.
d. Accrued sales salaries payable, $2.

ALPHA, INCORPORATED
Trial Balance, December 31, 19—

Cash	$ 3	
Accounts receivable	2	
Merchandise inventory	5	
Store supplies	4	
Store equipment	9	
Accumulated depreciation, store equipment		$ 2
Accounts payable		2
Salaries payable		—
Common stock, $1 par value		10
Retained earnings		6
Income summary	—	—
Sales		31
Sales returns	1	
Purchases	12	
Purchases discounts		1
Freight-in	1	
Salaries expense	6	
Rent expense	7	
Advertising expense	2	
Depreciation expense, store equipment	—	
Store supplies expense	—	
Totals	$52	$52

PROBLEMS

Problem 5–1

Prepare general journal entries to record the following transactions:

Nov. 1 Purchased merchandise on credit, terms 2/10, n/30, $800.
   1 Paid $35 cash for freight charges on the merchandise shipment of the previous transaction.

Nov. 4 Sold merchandise on credit, terms 2/10, 1/15, n/60, $500.
      7 Purchased on credit a new typewriter for office use, $550.
      9 Purchased merchandise on credit, terms 2/10, n/60, $580.
     11 Received a $30 credit memorandum for merchandise purchased on November 9 and returned for credit.
     13 Sold merchandise for cash, $65.
     15 Purchased office supplies on credit, $75.
     16 Received a credit memorandum for unsatisfactory office supplies purchased on November 15 and returned for credit, $15.
     17 Sold merchandise on credit, terms 2/10, 1/15, n/60, $540.
     18 Issued a $40 credit memorandum to the customer of November 17 who returned a portion of the merchandise purchased.
     19 Paid for the merchandise purchased on November 9, less the return and the discount.
     19 The customer who purchased merchandise on November 4 paid for the purchase of that date less the applicable discount.
     27 Received payment for the merchandise sold on November 17, less the return and applicable discount.
     30 Paid for the merchandise purchased on November 1.

Problem 5–2

Valley Sales, Inc., began the year with $23,450 of retained earnings, and during the year it declared and paid $20,000 of dividends on its outstanding common stock. At the year-end the Income Statement columns of its work sheet carried the following amounts:

	Income Statement	
	Debit	Credit
Income summary	21,310	22,460
Sales		215,280
Sales returns and allowances	1,120	
Purchases	144,530	
Purchases returns and allowances		470
Purchases discounts		2,280
Freight-in	890	
Sales salaries expense	18,780	
Rent expense, selling space	10,800	
Advertising expense	880	
Store supplies expense	550	
Depreciation expense, store equipment	1,410	
Office salaries expense	10,200	
Rent expense, office space	1,200	
Telephone expense	435	
Office supplies expense	115	
Insurance expense	850	
Depreciaiton expense, office equipment	420	
Income taxes expense	4,500	
	217,990	240,490
Net income	22,500	
	240,490	240,490

Required:

1. Under the assumption that the annual accounting period of Valley Sales, Inc., ends on December 31, prepare a classified, multiple-step income statement for the concern, showing the expenses and the items entering into cost of goods sold in detail.
2. Prepare a retained earnings statement for the concern.
3. Prepare for the concern a single-step, combined income and retained earnings statement with the items condensed as is commonly done on published financial statements.

Problem 5–3

Hobby Shop, Inc., began the current year with $16,585 of retained earnings, declared and paid $12,000 of dividends, and at the year-end the following trial balance was taken from its ledger:

HOBBY SHOP, INC.
Trial Balance, December 31, 19—

Cash	$ 3,350	
Merchandise inventory	20,760	
Store supplies	575	
Office supplies	180	
Prepaid insurance	935	
Store equipment	22,410	
Accumulated depreciation, store equipment		$ 3,120
Office equipment	5,210	
Accumulated depreciation, office equipment		1,130
Accounts payable		895
Income taxes payable	—	
Common stock, $10 par value		20,000
Retained earnings		4,585
Income summary	—	—
Sales		181,240
Sales returns and allowances	510	
Purchases	112,650	
Purchases discounts		1,830
Freight-in	670	
Sales salaries expense	19,410	
Rent expense, selling space	8,100	
Store supplies expense	—	
Depreciation expense, store equipment	—	
Office salaries expense	12,540	
Rent expense, office space	900	
Office supplies expense	—	
Insurance expense	—	
Depreciaiton expense, office equipment	—	
Income taxes expense	4,600	
Totals	$212,800	$212,800

Required:

1. Copy the trial balance on an eight-column work sheet form and complete the work sheet using the following information:

   a. Ending merchandise inventory, $21,115.

   b. Store supplies inventory, $135; and office supplies inventory, $50.

   c. Expired insurance, $780.

   d. Estimated depreciation on store equipment, $1,515; and on office equipment, $510.

   e. Additional federal income taxes expense, $320.

2. Prepare a multiple-step classified income statement showing expenses and the items entering into the calculation of cost of goods sold in detail.

3. Prepare a retained earnings statement.

4. In addition to the foregoing, prepare a single-step combined income and retained earnings statement with the items condensed as is commonly done in published statements.

Problem 5–4

(If the working papers that accompany this text are not being used, omit this problem.)

The unfinished eight-column work sheet of Eastgate Shop, Incorporated, is reproduced in the booklet of working papers.

Required:

1. Complete the work sheet by combining the trial balance amounts with the adjustments and sorting the items to the proper Income Statement and Balance Sheet columns.

2. Prepare an income statement for the company showing the details of cost of goods sold and the expenses. Also prepare a balance sheet and a retained earnings statement. The company began the year with $19,425 of retained earnings, and it declared and paid $16,000 of dividends during the year.

3. In addition to the foregoing statements, prepare a combined income and retained earnings statement with the items condensed as is common in published statements.

4. Prepare adjusting and closing entries for Eastgate Shop, Incorporated.

Problem 5–5

The following trial balance was taken from the ledger of Western Sales, Inc., at the end of its annual accounting period.

Required:

1. Enter the trial balance on an eight-column work sheet form and complete the work sheet using the following information:

   a. Ending merchandise inventory, $25,115.

   b. Store supplies inventory, $180; and office supplies inventory, $110.

   c. Expired insurance, $1,020.

   d. Estimated depreciation of store equipment, $3,240; and of office equipment, $730.

      e. Accrued sales salaries payable, $210; and accrued office salaries payable, $160.

      f. Additional income taxes expense, $325.

2. From the work sheet prepare a multiple-step income statement showing the details of cost of goods sold and the expenses. Also prepare a balance sheet and a retained earnings statement. The company began the year with $17,565 of retained earnings, and it declared and paid $12,000 of dividends during the year.

3. In addition to the foregoing statements, prepare a combined income and retained earnings statement on which the items are condensed and the expenses are subtracted in a single step.

4. Prepare adjusting and closing entries for the company.

WESTERN SALES, INC.

Trial Balance, December 31, 19—

Cash	$ 5,120	
Accounts receivable	6,985	
Merchandise inventory	23,980	
Store supplies	695	
Office supplies	325	
Prepaid insurance	1,410	
Store equipment	27,770	
Accumulated depreciation, store equipment		$ 3,165
Office equipment	5,980	
Accumulated depreciation, office equipment		690
Accounts payable		1,395
Salaries payable		—
Income taxes payable		—
Common stock, $10 par value		30,000
Retained earnings		5,565
Income summary	—	—
Sales		320,255
Sales returns and allowances	2,910	
Purchases	223,675	
Purchases returns and allowances		875
Purchases discounts		3,140
Freight-in	3,270	
Sales salaries expense	27,210	
Rent expense, selling space	9,720	
Advertising expense	3,190	
Store supplies expense	—	
Depreciation expense, store equipment	—	
Office salaries expense	14,820	
Rent expense, office space	1,080	
Telephone expense	545	
Insurance expense	—	
Office supplies expense	—	
Depreciation expense, office equipment	—	
Income taxes expense	6,400	
Totals	$365,085	$365,085

ALTERNATE PROBLEMS

Problem 5–1A

Prepare general journal entries to record the following transactions:

Nov. 1 Purchased merchandise on credit, terms 1/10, n/30, $700.
    4 Sold merchandise for cash, $55.
    7 Purchased office equipment on credit, $300.
    8 Purchased merchandise on credit, terms 2/10, n/60, $645.
    8 Paid $30 cash for freight charges on the merchandise shipment of the previous transaction.
   11 Received a $45 credit memorandum for merchandise purchased on November 8 and returned for credit.
   12 Sold merchandise on credit, terms 2/10, 1/15, n/60, $500.
   15 Purchased office supplies on credit, $85.
   16 Sold merchandise on credit, terms 2/10, 1/15, n/60, $675.
   17 Received a credit memorandum for unsatisfactory office supplies purchased on November 15 and returned, $20.
   18 Issued a $25 credit memorandum to the customer who purchased merchandise on November 16 and returned a portion for credit.
   18 Paid for the merchandise purchased on November 8, less the return and the discount.
   26 Received payment for the merchandise sold on November 16, less the return and applicable discount.
   27 The customer of November 12 paid for the purchase of that date, less the applicable discount.
   30 Paid for the merchandise purchased on November 1.

Problem 5–2A

Red Rock Sales, Inc., began the year with $41,235 of retained earnings, and during the year declared and paid $20,000 of dividends on its outstanding common stock. At the year-end the following items appeared in the Income Statement columns of a work sheet covering its annual accounting period:

Required:

1. Prepare a classified, multiple-step income statement for the company, showing the expenses and the items entering into cost of goods sold in detail.
2. Prepare a retained earnings statement for the company.
3. Prepare for the company a single-step, combined income and retained earnings statement with the items condensed as is commonly done in published financial statements.

	Income statement	
	Debit	Credit
Income summary	31,445	29,340
Sales		393,750
Sales returns and allowances	1,550	
Sales discounts	4,310	
Purchases	279,125	
Purchases returns and allowances		1,175
Purchases discounts		4,580
Freight-in	2,335	
Sales salaries expense	31,315	
Rent expense, selling space	12,960	
Advertising expense	2,915	
Store supplies expense	610	
Depreciation expense, store equipment	3,560	
Office salaries expense	15,340	
Rent expense, office space	1,440	
Telephone expense	645	
Insurance expense	1,215	
Office supplies expense	280	
Depreciation expense, office equipment	965	
Income tax expense	8,045	
	398,055	428,845
Net income	30,790	
	428,845	428,845

Problem 5–3A

Universal Sales, Inc., began the current year with $24,045 of retained earnings, declared and paid $20,000 of dividends during the year, and prepared the following trial balance of its ledger at the year-end.

Required:

1. Copy the trial balance on an eight-column work sheet form and complete the work sheet using the following information:
   a. Ending merchandise inventory, $24,745.
   b. Store supplies inventory, $175; and office supplies inventory, $115.
   c. Expired insurance, $965.
   d. Estimated depreciation on store equipment, $2,965; and on office equipment, $825.
   e. Additional federal income taxes expense, $810.
2. Prepare a multiple-step classified income statement showing in detail the items entering into cost of goods sold and the expenses.
3. Prepare a retained earnings statement.
4. In addition to the foregoing statements, prepare a combined income and retained earnings statement in single-step form with the items condensed as is commonly done in published statements.

UNIVERSAL SALES, INC.
Trial Balance, December 31, 19—

Cash	$ 4,345	
Merchandise inventory	26,560	
Store supplies...............................	915	
Office supplies	310	
Prepaid insurance	1,295	
Store equipment	28,950	
Accumulated depreciation, store equipment		$ 3,170
Office equipment	7,440	
Accumulated depreciation, office equipment....		985
Accounts payable		2,135
Income taxes payable		—
Common stock, $10 par value		25,000
Retained earnings		4,045
Income summary	—	—
Sales		295,310
Sales returns and allowances	615	
Purchases	198,285	
Purchases discounts		1,820
Freight-in	2,610	
Sales salaries expense	27,560	
Rent expense, selling space	11,200	
Store supplies expense	—	
Depreciation expense, store equipment	—	
Office salaries expense	15,380	
Rent expense, office space	1,200	
Office supplies expense	—	
Insurance expense	—	
Depreciation expense, office equipment	—	
Income taxes expense	5,800	
Totals	$332,465	$332,465

Problem 5–5A

Apex Sales, Inc., began the current year with $13,855 of retained earnings, declared and paid $10,000 of dividends during the year, and prepared the following trial balance of its ledger at the year-end:

Required:

1. Enter the trial balance on an eight-column work sheet form and complete the work sheet using the following information:
   a. Ending merchandise inventory, $33,110.
   b. Store supplies inventory, $220; and office supplies inventory, $130.
   c. Expired insurance, $1,150.
   d. Estimated depreciation on store equipment, $3,840; and on office equipment, $885.

APEX SALES, INC.

Trial Balance, December 31, 19—

Cash	$ 6,345	
Accounts receivable	10,220	
Merchandise inventory	31,315	
Store supplies	885	
Office supplies	340	
Prepaid insurance	1,570	
Store equipment	32,320	
Accumulated depreciation, store equipment		$ 4,215
Office equipment	7,980	
Accumulated depreciation, office equipment		1,035
Accounts payable		1,240
Salaries payable		—
Income taxes payable		—
Common stock, $10 par value		50,000
Retained earnings		3,855
Income summary	—	—
Sales		347,885
Sales returns and allowances	2,610	
Purchases	242,450	
Purchases returns and allowances		1,095
Purchases discounts		3,535
Freight-in	3,920	
Sales salaries expense	31,315	
Rent expense, selling space	10,500	
Advertising expense	4,310	
Store supplies expense	—	
Depreciation expense, store equipment	—	
Office salaries expense	18,635	
Rent expense, office space	1,500	
Telephone expense	645	
Office supplies expense	—	
Insurance expense	—	
Depreciation expense, office equipment	—	
Income taxes expense	6,000	
Totals	$412,860	$412,860

    e. Accrued sales salaries payable, $265; and accrued office salaries payable, $180.

    f. Additional income taxes expense, $590.

2. From the work sheet prepare a multiple-step income statement showing the details of cost of goods sold and the expenses. Also prepare a balance sheet and a retained earnings statement.

3. In addition to the foregoing statements, prepare a combined income and retained earnings statement in single-step form with the items condensed as is commonly done on published statements.

4. Prepare adjusting and closing entries for the company.

PROVOCATIVE PROBLEMS

Provocative problem 5–1
Larkin Paint Store

Elmer Larkin retired from farming last year, sold his equipment, paid off his debts, and placed the remaining cash in a savings account. However, he soon became restless, and six months ago he opened a retail paint store in his small rural community. At that time there was no such store in the community, and it appeared that the venture would be profitable.

He began business by transferring $35,000 from his savings account to a checking account opened in the store's name. He immediately bought for cash store equipment costing $6,000, which he expected to use ten years, after which it would be worn out and valueless, and a stock of merchandise costing $20,000. He paid six months' rent in advance on the store building, $2,400.

He estimated that like stores in neighboring communities marked their goods for sale at prices 35% above cost. In other words, an item costing $10 was marked for sale at $13.50. In order to get his store off to a good start, he decided to mark his goods for sale at 30% above cost, and because of his low overhead, he thought this would still leave a net income of 10% on sales.

Since he was in a rural farming community, Mr. Larkin granted liberal credit terms, telling his credit-worthy customers to pay "when the crops are in." His suppliers granted Mr. Larkin the normal 30-day credit period on his purchases.

Today, October 1, six months after opening the store, Mr. Larkin has come to you for advice. He thinks business has been excellent. He has paid his suppliers for all purchases when due and owes only for purchases, $9,000, made during the last 30 days and for which payment is not due. He has replaced his original inventory three times during the last six months, and an income statement he has prepared shows $85,500 of sales, a $25,500 gross profit, and an $8,900 net income, which is a little better than he anticipated. He says he has a full stock of merchandise which cost $20,000 and his customers owe him $26,200. In addition to the rent paid in advance, he has paid all of his other expenses, $14,200, with cash.

Nevertheless, Mr. Larkin doubts the validity of his gross profit and net income figures, since he started business with $35,000 in cash and now has only $700 in the bank and owes $9,000 for merchandise purchased on credit.

Did Mr. Larkin actually meet his profit expectations? If so, explain to him the apparent paradox of adequate income and a declining cash balance. Back your explanation with a statement accounting for the October 1 cash balance, a six months' income statement, and a September 30 balance sheet.

Provocative problem 5–2
Jed's Feed Store

Jed Reed opened a feed store, Jed's Feed Store, on January 4 of the current year by investing $2,500 in cash and a $7,500 inventory of merchandise. During the year he paid out in cash $28,000 to purchase additional merchandise and

$9,600 for operating expenses. He also withdrew $12,000 in cash from the business for personal use, and at the year-end he prepared the following balance sheet:

JED'S FEED STORE
Balance Sheet, December 31, 19—

Assets		Equities	
Cash	$ 2,000	Accounts payable (for	
Accounts receivable	6,200	merchandise)	$ 6,500
Merchandise inventory	9,000	Jed Reed, capital	10,700
Total assets	$17,200	Total equities	$17,200

Based on the information given, prepare an income statement showing the results of the first year's operations of the business. Support your income statement with schedules showing your calculations of net income, cost of goods sold, and sales.

After studying Chapter 6, you should be able to:

☐ Explain how columnar journals save posting labor.

☐ Tell the kind of transaction recorded in each columnar journal described.

☐ Explain how a controlling account and its subsidiary ledger operate and give the rule for posting to a subsidiary ledger and its controlling account.

☐ Record transactions in and post from the columnar journals described.

☐ Tell how the accuracy of the account balances in the Accounts Receivable and Accounts Payable Ledgers is proved and be able to make such a proof.

☐ Describe how data is processed in a large business.

☐ Define or explain the words and phrases listed in the chapter Glossary.

Accounting systems

■ An *accounting system* consists of the business papers, records, and reports plus the procedures that are used in recording transactions and reporting their effects. Operation of an accounting system begins with the preparation of a business paper, such as an invoice or check, and includes the capture of the data entered on this paper and its flow through the recording, classifying, summarizing, and reporting steps of the system. Actually an accounting system is a data processing system, and it is now time to introduce more efficient ways of processing data.

REDUCING WRITING AND POSTING LABOR

The General Journal used thus far is a flexible journal in which it is possible to record any transaction. However, each debit and credit entered in such a journal must be individually posted. Consequently, using a General Journal to record all the transactions of a business results in too much writing and too much labor in posting the individual debits and credits.

One way to reduce the writing and the posting labor is to divide the transactions of a business into groups of like transactions and to provide a separate *special journal* for recording the transactions in each group. For example, if the transactions of a merchandising business are examined, the majority fall into four groups. They are sales on credit, purchases on credit, cash receipts, and cash disbursements. If a special journal is provided for each group, the journals are:

189

1. A Sales Journal for recording credit sales.
2. A Purchases Journal for recording credit purchases.
3. A Cash Receipts Journal for recording cash receipts.
4. A Cash Disbursements Journal for recording cash payments.

In addition, a General Journal must be provided for the few miscellaneous transactions that cannot be recorded in the special journals and also for adjusting, closing, and correcting entries.

Special journals require less writing in recording transactions than does a General Journal, as the following illustrations will show. In addition, they save posting labor by providing special columns for accumulating the debits and credits of like transactions. The amounts entered in the special columns are then posted as column totals rather than as individual amounts. For example, if credit sales for, say a month, are recorded in a Sales Journal like the one at the top of Illustration 6–1, posting labor is saved by waiting until the end of the month, totaling the sales recorded in the journal, and debiting Accounts Receivable and crediting Sales for the total.

Only seven sales are recorded in the illustrated journal. However, if the seven sales are assumed to represent 700 sales, a better appreciation is gained of the posting labor saved by the one debit to Accounts Receivable and the one credit to Sales, rather than 700 debits and 700 credits.

The special journal of Illustration 6–1 is also called a *columnar journal* because it has columns for recording the date, the customer's name, invoice number, and the amount of each charge sale. Only charge sales can be recorded in it, and they are recorded daily with the information about each sale being placed on a separate line. Normally the information is taken from a copy of the sales ticket or invoice prepared at the time of the sale. However, before discussing the journal further, the subject of *subsidiary ledgers* must be introduced.

SUBSIDIARY LEDGERS

The Accounts Receivable account used thus far does not readily tell how much each customer bought and paid for or how much each customer owes. As a result, a business selling on credit must maintain additional accounts receivable, one for each customer, to provide this information. These individual customer accounts are in addition to the Accounts Receivable account used thus far. They are normally kept in a book or file tray, called a *subsidiary ledger,* that is separate and distinct from the book or tray containing the financial statement accounts. Also, to distinguish the two, the book or tray containing the customer accounts is called the *Accounts Receivable Ledger,* while the one containing the financial statement accounts is known as the *General Ledger.*

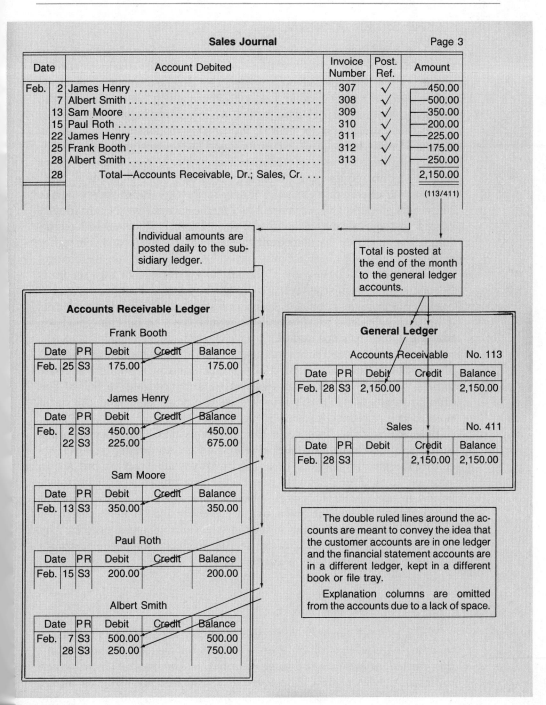

Sales Journal   Page 3

Date		Account Debited	Invoice Number	Post. Ref.	Amount
Feb.	2	James Henry	307	✓	450.00
	7	Albert Smith	308	✓	500.00
	13	Sam Moore	309	✓	350.00
	15	Paul Roth	310	✓	200.00
	22	James Henry	311	✓	225.00
	25	Frank Booth	312	✓	175.00
	28	Albert Smith	313	✓	250.00
	28	Total—Accounts Receivable, Dr.; Sales, Cr. ...			2,150.00
					(113/411)

Individual amounts are posted daily to the subsidiary ledger.

Total is posted at the end of the month to the general ledger accounts.

Accounts Receivable Ledger

Frank Booth

Date		PR	Debit	Credit	Balance
Feb.	25	S3	175.00		175.00

James Henry

Date		PR	Debit	Credit	Balance
Feb.	2	S3	450.00		450.00
	22	S3	225.00		675.00

Sam Moore

Date		PR	Debit	Credit	Balance
Feb.	13	S3	350.00		350.00

Paul Roth

Date		PR	Debit	Credit	Balance
Feb.	15	S3	200.00		200.00

Albert Smith

Date		PR	Debit	Credit	Balance
Feb.	7	S3	500.00		500.00
	28	S3	250.00		750.00

General Ledger

Accounts Receivable   No. 113

Date		PR	Debit	Credit	Balance
Feb.	28	S3	2,150.00		2,150.00

Sales   No. 411

Date		PR	Debit	Credit	Balance
Feb.	28	S3		2,150.00	2,150.00

The double ruled lines around the accounts are meant to convey the idea that the customer accounts are in one ledger and the financial statement accounts are in a different ledger, kept in a different book or file tray.

Explanation columns are omitted from the accounts due to a lack of space.

Illustration 6–1

POSTING THE SALES JOURNAL

When customer accounts are placed in a subsidiary ledger, a Sales Journal is posted as in Illustration 6–1. The individual sales recorded in the journal are posted each day to the proper customer accounts in the Accounts Receivable Ledger. These daily postings keep the customer accounts up to date, which is important in granting credit. When a customer asks for credit, the person responsible for granting it should know the amount currently owed by the customer. The source of this information is the customer's account. If the account is not up to date, an incorrect decision may be made.

Note the check marks in the journal's Posting Reference column. They indicate that the sales recorded in the journal were individually posted to the customer accounts in the Accounts Receivable Ledger. Check marks rather than account numbers are used because customer accounts commonly are not numbered. Rather, as an aid in locating individual accounts, they are alphabetically arranged in the Accounts Receivable Ledger. New accounts are then added in their proper alphabetical positions as required. Consequently, numbering the accounts is impractical, since many numbers would have to be changed each time new accounts are added.

In addition to the daily postings to customer accounts, at the end of the month the Sales Journal's Amount column is totaled and the total is debited to Accounts Receivable and credited to Sales. The credit records the month's revenue from charge sales, and the debit records the resulting increase in accounts receivable.

Before going on, note again that the individual customer accounts in the subsidiary Accounts Receivable Ledger do not replace the Accounts Receivable account described in previous chapters but are in addition to it. The Accounts Receivable account must still be maintained in the General Ledger where it serves three functions. (1) It shows the total amount owed by all customers. (2) It helps keep the General Ledger a balancing ledger in which debits equal credits. And (3) it offers a means of proving the accuracy of the total of the customer accounts in the subsidiary ledger.

IDENTIFYING POSTED AMOUNTS

When several journals are posted to ledger accounts, it is necessary to indicate in the Posting Reference column before each posted amount the journal as well as the page number of the journal from which the amount was posted. The journal is indicated by using its initial. Thus, items posted from the Cash Disbursements Journal carry the initial "D" before their journal page numbers in the Posting Reference columns. Likewise, items from the Cash Receipts Journal carry the letter "R." Those from the Sales Journal carry the initial "S." Items from the Purchases Journal carry the initial "P," and from the General Journal, the letter "G."

CONTROLLING ACCOUNTS

When a company maintains an Accounts Receivable account in its General Ledger and puts its customer accounts in a subsidiary ledger, the Accounts Receivable account is said to control the subsidiary ledger and is called a *controlling account*. The extent of the control is that after all posting is completed, if no errors were made, the sum of the customer account balances in the subsidiary ledger will equal the balance of the controlling account in the General Ledger. This equality is also a proof of the total of the customer account balances.

CASH RECEIPTS JOURNAL

A Cash Receipts Journal designed to save labor through posting column totals must be a multicolumn journal. A multicolumn journal is necessary because cash receipts differ as to sources and, consequently, as to the accounts credited when cash is received from different sources. For example, if the cash receipts of a store are classified as to sources, they normally fall into three groups: (1) cash from charge customers in payment of their accounts, (2) cash from cash sales, and (3) cash from miscellaneous sources. Note in Illustration 6–2 on the next page how a special column is provided for the credits resulting when cash is received from each of these sources.

Cash from charge customers

When a Cash Receipts Journal like Illustration 6–2 is used in recording cash received from a customer in payment of the customer's account, the customer's name is entered in the journal's Account Credited column. The amount credited to the customer's account is entered in the Accounts Receivable Credit column, and the debits to Sales Discounts and Cash are entered in the journal's last two columns.

Give close attention to the Accounts Receivable credit column. Observe that (1) only credits to customer accounts are entered in this column. (2) The individual credits are posted daily to the customer accounts in the subsidiary Accounts Receivable Ledger. And (3) the column total is posted at the month end to the credit of the Accounts Receivable controlling account. This is the normal recording and posting procedure when controlling accounts and subsidiary ledgers are used. When such accounts and ledgers are used, transactions are normally entered in a journal column. The individual amounts are then posted to the subsidiary ledger accounts, and the column total is posted to the controlling account.

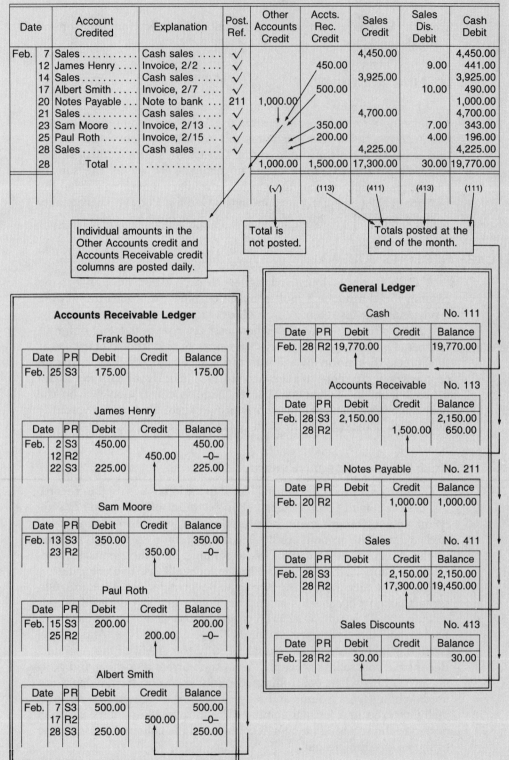

Illustration 6–2

Cash sales

Cash sales are commonly "rung up" on one or more cash registers, and their total is recorded by means of a journal entry at the end of the day. When such sales are recorded in a Cash Receipts Journal like that of Illustration 6–2, the debits to Cash are entered in the Cash debit column and a special column headed "Sales Credit" is provided for the credits to Sales. By entering each day's cash sales in this column, the cash sales of a month may be posted at the month's end in a single amount, the column total. (Although cash sales are normally recorded daily from the cash register readings, the cash sales of Illustration 6–2 are recorded only once each week in order to shorten the illustration.)

At the time daily cash sales are recorded in the Cash Receipts Journal, some bookkeepers, as in Illustration 6–2, place a check mark in the Posting Reference column to indicate that no amount is individually posted from that line of the journal. Other bookkeepers use a double check ($\sqrt{}\sqrt{}$) to distinguish amounts not posted from amounts posted to customer accounts.

Miscellaneous receipts of cash

Most cash receipts are from customer collections and cash sales. However, cash is occasionally received from other sources such as, for example, the sale for cash of an unneeded asset, or a promissory note is given to a bank in order to borrow money. For miscellaneous receipts such as these, the Other Accounts credit column is provided. In an average company, the items entered in this column are few and are posted to a variety of general ledger accounts. As a result, postings are less apt to be omitted if these items are also posted daily.

The Cash Receipts Journal's Posting Reference column is used only for daily postings from the Other Accounts and Accounts Receivable columns. The account numbers appearing in the column indicate items posted to general ledger accounts. The check marks indicate either that an item like a day's cash sales was not posted or that an item was posted to the subsidiary Accounts Receivable Ledger.

Month-end postings

The amounts in the Accounts Receivable, Sales, Sales Discounts, and Cash columns of the Cash Receipts Journal are posted as column totals at the end of the month. However, the equality of the debits and credits in the journal is proved by *crossfooting* or cross adding the column totals before they are posted. To *foot* a column of figures is to add it. To crossfoot the Cash Receipts Journal, the debit column totals are added together. The credit column totals are then added together and the two sums are compared for equality. For Illustration 6–2 the two sums appear as follows:

Debit columns		Credit columns	
Sales discounts debit	$ 30.00	Other accounts credit	$ 1,000.00
Cash debit	19,770.00	Accounts receivable credit	1,500.00
		Sales credit	17,300.00
Total	$19,800.00	Total	$19,800.00

And since the sums are equal, the debits in the journal are assumed to equal the credits.

After the debit and credit equality is proved by crossfooting, the totals of the last four columns are posted as indicated in each column heading. As for the Other Accounts column, since the individual items in this column are posted daily, the column total is not posted. Note in Illustration 6–2 the check mark below the Other Accounts column. The check mark indicates that the column total was not posted. The account numbers of the accounts to which the remaining column totals were posted are indicated in parentheses below each column.

Posting items daily from the Other Accounts column with a delayed posting of the offsetting items in the Cash column (total) causes the General Ledger to be out of balance throughout the month. However, this is of no consequence because, before the trial balance is prepared, the offsetting amounts reach the General Ledger in posting the Cash column total.

POSTING RULE

Posting to a subsidiary ledger and its controlling account from two journals has been demonstrated, and a rule to cover all such postings can now be given. The rule is: *In posting to a subsidiary ledger and its controlling account, the controlling account must be debited periodically for an amount or amounts equal to the sum of the debits to the subsidiary ledger and it must be credited periodically for an amount or amounts equal to the sum of the credits to the subsidiary ledger.*

CREDITOR ACCOUNTS

As with accounts receivable, the Accounts Payable account used thus far does not show how much is owed each creditor. As a result, to secure this information, an individual account, one for each creditor, must be maintained. These creditor accounts are commonly kept in an *Accounts Payable Ledger* that is controlled by an Accounts Payable controlling account in the General Ledger. Also, the controlling account, subsidiary ledger, and columnar journal techniques demonstrated thus far with accounts receivable apply to the creditor accounts. The only difference is that a Purchases Journal and a Cash Disbursements Journal are used in recording most of the transactions affecting these accounts.

PURCHASES JOURNAL

A Purchases Journal having one money column may be used to record purchases of merchandise on credit. However, a multicolumn journal in which purchases of both merchandise and supplies can be recorded is commonly preferred. Such a journal may have the columns shown in Illustration 6–3. In the illustrated journal the invoice date and terms together indicate the date on which payment for each purchase is due. The Accounts Payable credit column is used to record the amounts credited to each creditor's account. These amounts are posted daily to the individual creditor accounts in the Accounts Payable Ledger. The column total is posted to the Accounts Payable controlling account at the end of the month. The items purchased are recorded in the debit columns and are posted in the column totals at the end of the month.

THE CASH DISBURSEMENTS JOURNAL AND ITS POSTING

The Cash Disbursements Journal, like the Cash Receipts Journal, has columns that make it possible to post repetitive debits and credits in column totals. The repetitive debits and credits of cash payments are debits to the Accounts Payable controlling account and credits to both Purchases Discounts and Cash. In most companies the purchase of merchandise for cash is not common. Therefore, a Purchases column is not needed and a cash purchase is recorded as on line 2 of Illustration 6–4.

Observe that the illustrated journal has a column headed "Check No." To gain control over cash disbursements, all such disbursements, except petty cash disbursements, should be made by check. (Petty cash disbursements are discussed in the next chapter.) The checks should be prenumbered by the printer and should be entered in the journal in numerical order with each check's number in the "Check No." column. This makes it possible to scan the numbers in the column for omitted checks. When a Cash Disbursements Journal has a column for check numbers, it is often called a *Check Register*.

A Cash Disbursements Journal or Check Register like Illustration 6–4 is posted as follows. The individual amounts in the Other Accounts column are posted daily to the debit of the general ledger accounts named. The individual amounts in the Accounts Payable column are posted daily to the subsidiary Accounts Payable Ledger to the debit

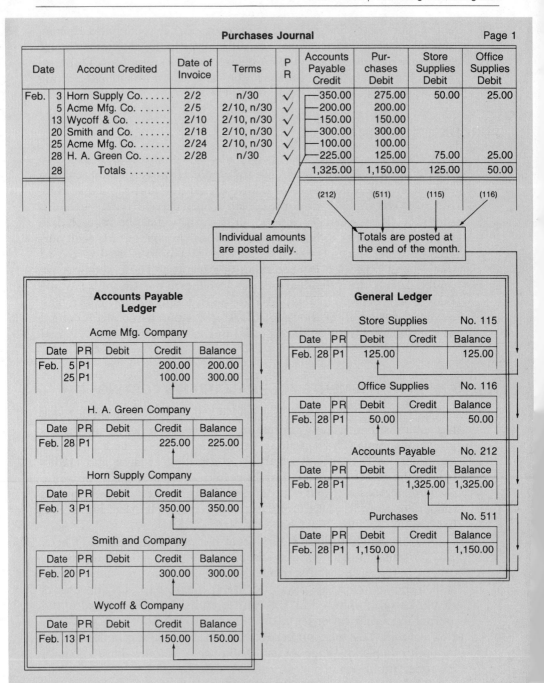

Illustration 6–3

Cash Disbursements Journal   **Page 2**

Date	Ch. No.	Payee	Account Debited	P R	Other Accounts Debit	Accts. Pay. Debit	Pur. Disc. Credit	Cash Credit
Feb. 3	105	L. & N. Railroad ..	Freight-In	514	15.00			15.00
12	106	East Sales Co.	Purchases	511	25.00			25.00
15	107	Acme Mfg. Co. ...	Acme Mfg. Co. ...	√		200.00	4.00	196.00
15	108	Jerry Hale	Salaries Expense .	611	250.00			250.00
20	109	Wycoff & Co.	Wycoff & Co.	√		150.00	3.00	147.00
28	110	Smith and Co.....	Smith and Co.....	√		300.00	6.00	294.00
28		Totals			290.00	650.00	13.00	927.00
					(√)	(212)	(513)	(111)

Individual amounts in the Other Accounts debit column and Accounts Payable debit column are posted daily.

Totals posted at the end of the month.

Accounts Payable Ledger

Acme Mfg. Company

Date	PR	Debit	Credit	Balance
Feb. 5	P1		200.00	200.00
15	D2	200.00		–0–
25	P1		100.00	100.00

H. A. Green Company

Date	PR	Debit	Credit	Balance
Feb. 28	P1		225.00	225.00

Horn Supply Company

Date	PR	Debit	Credit	Balance
Feb. 3	P1		350.00	350.00

Smith and Company

Date	PR	Debit	Credit	Balance
Feb. 20	P1		300.00	300.00
28	D2	300.00		–0–

Wycoff & Company

Date	PR	Debit	Credit	Balance
Feb. 13	P1		150.00	150.00
20	D2	150.00		–0–

General Ledger

Cash   No. 111

Date	PR	Debit	Credit	Balance
Feb. 28	R2	19,770.00		19,770.00
28	D2		927.00	18,843.00

Accounts Payable   No. 212

Date	PR	Debit	Credit	Balance
Feb. 28	P1		1,325.00	1,325.00
28	D2	650.00		675.00

Purchases   No. 511

Date	PR	Debit	Credit	Balance
Feb. 12	D2	25.00		25.00
26	P1	1,150.00		1,175.00

Purchases Discounts   No. 513

Date	PR	Debit	Credit	Balance
Feb. 28	D2		13.00	13.00

Freight-In   No. 514

Date	PR	Debit	Credit	Balance
Feb. 3	D2	15.00		15.00

Salaries Expense   No. 611

Date	PR	Debit	Credit	Balance
Feb. 15	D2	250.00		250.00

Illustration 6–4

of the creditors named. At the end of the month, after the column totals are crossfooted to prove their equality, the Accounts Payable column total is posted to the debit of the Accounts Payable controlling account. The Purchases Discounts column total is credited to the Purchases Discounts account, and the Cash column total is credited to the Cash account. Since the items in the Other Accounts column are posted individually, the column total is not posted.

PROVING THE LEDGERS

Periodically, after all posting is completed, the General Ledger and the subsidiary ledgers are proved. The General Ledger is normally proved first by preparing a trial balance. If the trial balance balances, the accounts in the General Ledger, including the controlling accounts, are assumed to be correct. The subsidiary ledgers are then proved, commonly by preparing schedules of accounts receivable and accounts payable. A *schedule of accounts payable,* for example, is prepared by listing with their balances the accounts in the Accounts Payable Ledger having balances. The balances are totaled; and if the total is equal to the balance of the Accounts Payable controlling account, the accounts in the Accounts Payable Ledger are assumed to be correct. Illustration 6–5 shows a schedule of the creditor accounts having balances in the Accounts Payable Ledger of Illustration 6–4. Note that the schedule total is equal to the balance of the Accounts Payable controlling account in the General Ledger of Illustration 6–4. A *schedule of accounts receivable* is prepared in the same way as a schedule of accounts payable. Also, if its total is equal to the balance of the Accounts Receivable controlling account, the accounts in the Accounts Receivable Ledger are also assumed to be correct.

Hawaiian Sales Company	
Schedule of Accounts Payable, December 31, 19—	
Acme Mfg. Company	$100.00
H. A. Green Company	225.00
Horn Supply Company	350.00
Total accounts payable	$675.00

Illustration 6–5

Instead of a formal schedule to prove the accounts in a subsidiary ledger, an adding machine list may be used. For example, the balances of the accounts in the Accounts Payable Ledger may be proved by listing on an adding machine the balance of each account in the ledger, totaling the list, and comparing the total with the balance of the Accounts Payable controlling account. A similar list may be used to prove the accounts in the Accounts Receivable Ledger.

SALES TAXES

Many cities and states require retailers to collect sales taxes from their customers and periodically remit these taxes to the city or state treasurer. When a columnar Sales Journal is used, a record of taxes collected can be obtained by adding special columns in the journal as shown in Illustration 6–6.

In posting the journal, the individual amounts in the Accounts Receivable column are posted daily to customer accounts in the Accounts Receivable Ledger and the column total is posted at the end of the month to the Accounts Receivable controlling account. The individual amounts in the Sales Taxes Payable and Sales columns are not posted. However, at the end of the month the total of the Sales Taxes Payable column is credited to the Sales Taxes Payable account and the total of the Sales column is credited to Sales.

Sales Journal

Date	Account Debited	Invoice Number	P R	Accounts Receivable Debit	Sales Taxes Payable Credit	Sales Credit
Dec. 1	D. R. Horn	7-1698		103.00	3.00	100.00

Illustration 6–6

A concern making cash sales upon which sales taxes are collected may add a special Sales Taxes Payable column in its Cash Receipts Journal.

SALES INVOICES AS A SALES JOURNAL

To save labor, many companies do not enter charge sales in a Sales Journal. These companies post each sales invoice total directly to the customer's account in a subsidiary Accounts Receivable Ledger. Copies of the invoices are then bound in numerical order in a binder. At the end of the month, all the invoices of that month are totaled and a general journal entry is made debiting Accounts Receivable and crediting Sales for the total. In effect, the bound invoice copies act as a Sales Journal. Such a procedure is known as direct posting of sales invoices.

SALES RETURNS

A company having only a few sales returns may record them in a General Journal with an entry like the following:

Oct.	17	Sales Returns and Allowances	412	17.50	
		Accounts Receivable—George Ball ..	113/√		17.50
		Returned defective merchandise.			

The debit of the entry is posted to the Sales Returns and Allowances account. The credit is posted to both the Accounts Receivable controlling account and to the customer's account. Note the account number and the check, 113/√, in the Posting Reference column on the credit line. This indicates that both the Accounts Receivable controlling account in the General Ledger and the George Ball account in the Accounts Receivable Ledger were credited for $17.50. Both were credited because the balance of the controlling account in the General Ledger will not equal the sum of the customer account balances in the subsidiary ledger unless both are credited.

Companies having sufficient sales returns can save posting labor by recording them in a special Sales Returns and Allowances Journal like that of Illustration 6–7. Note that this is in keeping with the generally recognized idea that a company can design and use a special journal for any group of like transactions in which there are within the group sufficient transactions to warrant the journal. When a Sales Returns and Allowances Journal is used to record returns, the amounts entered in the journal are posted daily to the credit of each affected customer account. At the end of the month the journal total is debited to Sales Returns and Allowances and credited to Accounts Receivable.

Sales Returns and Allowances Journal

Date		Account Credited	Explanation	Credit Memo No.	P R	Amount
Oct.	7	Robert Moore	Defective mdse	203	√	10.00
	14	James Warren	Defective mdse	204	√	12.00
	18	T. M. Jones	Not ordered	205	√	6.00
	23	Sam Smith	Defective mdse	206	√	18.00
	31	Sales Returns and Allow., Dr.; Accounts Rec., Cr.				46.00
						412/113

Illustration 6–7

GENERAL JOURNAL ENTRIES

When columnar journals like the ones described are used, a General Journal must be provided for adjusting, closing, and correcting entries and for a few transactions that cannot be recorded in the special journals. Among these transactions, if a Sales Returns and Allowances Journal is not provided, are sales returns, purchases returns, and purchases of plant assets. Illustrative entries for the last two kinds of transactions follow:

Oct.	8	Accounts Payable—Medford Company ...	212/✓	32.00	
		Purchases Returns and Allowances ..	512		32.00
		Returned defective merchandise.			
	11	Office Equipment	133	685.00	
		Accounts Payable—ABC Supply Co. .	212/✓		685.00
		Purchased a typewriter.			

MACHINE METHODS

Pen-and-ink records like the ones described thus far are used by many small concerns. However, even very small concerns also use adding machines, desk calculators, and multicopy forms to save time and effort in processing accounting data. Likewise, small concerns having sufficient transactions may use electronic bookkeeping machines. Illustration 6–8 shows such a machine.

The illustrated machine has a typewriter-like keyboard and the keyboard of a ten-key calculator. It also has seven function keys that direct the machine's operation, instructing it to calculate, tabulate, and/or print out stored data. It handles accounting for sales, cash receipts,

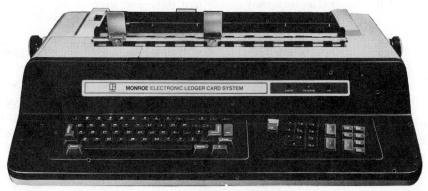

Courtesy Monroe, The Calculator Co., A Division of Litton Industries

Illustration 6–8

purchases, cash payments, payroll, and other transactions, as well as posting to the General Ledger. No attempt will be made here to describe the machine's operation in each of these applications. However, when used in accounting for credit sales, for example, it makes the entry in the Sales Journal for each sale, posts to the customer's account, updates the account balance, enters the sale on the customer's month-end statement, and updates the statement. At the same time it accumulates the Sales Journal total for the month-end debit to Accounts Receivable and credit to Sales. Furthermore, it does all of this in one operation from one entry into the machine of the proper data. And, it is just as proficient in handling other kinds of transactions.

Bookkeeping machines like the one shown speed the processing of accounting data. They also reduce transposition errors by printing the same information on several different records in one operation. However, the speed of operation and the amount of work such a machine can do efficiently are limited. Consequently, as a business grows it will at some point turn to automated data processing.

AUTOMATED DATA PROCESSING

Automated data processing is the processing of data without human intervention through the use of a *computer,* with a computer being a complex electronic machine that is capable of—

1. Accepting and storing data.
2. Performing arithmetic operations on the data.
3. Comparing units of the data and making yes-or-no decisions.
4. Sorting and rearranging the data and preparing reports therefrom.

Computers vary in size and in the speed with which they process data. They range from small machines similar to Illustration 6–9 to machines that with their peripheral equipment occupy a large room. Illustration 6–10 shows a large computer and its peripheral equipment. Peripheral equipment consists of data preparation equipment, input and output machines, and machines containing stored data on reels of magnetic tapes or on magnetic disks.

Data are entered into a computer by means of an electric typewriter, previously prepared punched cards, reels of magnetic tape, and in other ways, some of which are described later. Inside the computer each alphabetical letter or numerical digit of data becomes a combination of electrical or magnetic states that a computer can manipulate with the speed of light. Consequently, if of sufficient size, a computer can do millions of additions, subtractions, multiplications, and divisions per second, all without computer error in a predetermined sequence according to instructions stored in the machine.

For this discussion an understanding of what goes on inside a computer is not required. It is only necessary to recognize that a computer is a machine that can do nothing without a previously prepared set

Courtesy of Burroughs Corporation

Illustration 6–9

of instructions, called a *program*, being entered and stored in the computer. However, with a properly prepared program, a computer will accept data, store and process the data, and produce the processed results, often in seconds, in the form of a report displayed on a TV-like screen, or typed out on an electric typewriter at the rate of approximately ten characters per second, or printed by a line printer at upwards to 2,000 lines per minute.

The program

A computer program is a set of coded instructions specifying each operation a computer is to perform. It is entered into the machine

Design Model

Courtesy of International Business Machines Corporation

Illustration 6–10

by means of punched cards or magnetic tape before the processing of a batch of data is begun. It may contain from a few to several thousand detailed instructions like the following from a program for processing customers' orders for merchandise.

Program Instructions for Processing Customers' Orders

1. For the first item on the customer's order, compare the quantity ordered with the quantity on hand as shown by inventory data stored in the computer.

    a. If the quantity ordered is not on hand:

    (1) Prepare a back order notifying the customer that the goods are not available but will be shipped as soon as a new supply is received.

    (2) Go to the next item on the customer's order.

    b. If the quantity on hand is greater than the amount ordered:

    (1) Deduct the amount ordered from the amount on hand.

    (2) Prepare instructions to ship the goods.

    (3) Compare the amount of the item remaining after filling the customer's order with the reorder point for the item.

(a) If the amount remaining is greater than the reorder point:
    1. Go to the next item on the customer's order.
(b) If the amount remaining is less than the reorder point:
    1. Compute the amount to be purchased and prepare documents for the purchase.
    2. Go to the next item on the customer's order.

In addition to these instructions, a program for processing customer orders would also have instructions for preparing the invoices, recording the sales, and updating the customer accounts. However, the foregoing instructions are sufficient to show the ability of a computer to make yes-or-no decisions.

Yes-or-no decisions

The ability to compare numbers and make yes-or-no decisions makes it possible for a computer to process data containing exceptions, such as in the processing of customers' orders. However, it should be observed that the computer does not really make decisions. It only makes a comparison in each case. It then processes the data one way or another, depending upon the result of the comparison. Also, for a computer to do this, a person called a programmer must first design a program for the computer to follow. In designing the program, the programmer must determine in advance what exceptions can occur. He or she must then devise a set of yes-or-no questions that will isolate each exception. The programmer must then tell the computer how to process each exception. Finally, after all this, the computer can follow through the program's maze of decisions and alternate instructions, rapidly and accurately. However, if it encounters an exception not anticipated in the program, it is helpless and can only process the exception incorrectly or stop.

The ability to accept and store a program and then to race through its maze of yes-or-no decisions and alternate instructions is what distinguishes a computer from an electronic bookkeeping machine. To appreciate this, some electronic bookkeeping machines can do an addition, a multiplication, or a division at the speed of a computer. Yet with all this speed, their operating rates are relative slow, since they must depend on a person to push their function keys to tell them what to do.

Inputting data

Computers operate either *off line* or *on line*. In off-line operation the program and the basic data for a job, say the program for processing customers' orders and the required inventory data, are removed from the computer after a day's orders are processed. The program for a new job and a new set of data are then entered and the new job is processed. This is called batch processing and may result in customers' orders being processed daily, the payroll being run each week, financial statements being prepared monthly, and the processing of other jobs on a time-available basis. Because transactions are processed in batches, off-line operation is usually less expensive than on-line operation and is used when an immediate processing or an immediate computer response is not required. Also, off-line processing may be used in operating the computer at night with on-line operation during the day.

In on-line processing a single program is kept in the computer along with its required data. Input devices then enter new data into the computer on a continuous basis. For example, in some large department stores the cash registers are connected to and enter information directly into the store's computer. In addition to cash sales, the registers are used as follows in recording charge sales. After the customer selects merchandise for purchase, the salesperson uses the customer's plastic credit card to print the customer's name on a blank sales ticket. He or she then places the sales ticket in the Forms Printer of the cash register and records the sale in the same way as a cash sale. The register prints all pertinent information on the sales ticket and totals it. Then in order to finalize the sale, controls within the register require that the salesperson depress the proper register keys to record the customer's account number. By this final act the salesperson, in effect, posts the sale to the customer's account. He or she does not actually post to the account. Rather, from the information entered with the cash register's keys, the store's computer will update the customer's account and produce the customer's month-end statement, ready for mailing without further bookkeeping labor.

Another example of on-line operation is found in supermarkets, where each item of merchandise is imprinted with a machine-readable price tag similar to Illustration 6–11. At one of the store's checkout stands, each item of merchandise selected by a customer is passed over an optical scanner in the counter top or an optical scanner in a wand is passed over each item's price tag. This actuates the cash register and eliminates the need for handkeying information into the register. It also transmits the sales information to a computer which updates the store's inventory records and prepares orders to a central warehouse to restock any item in low supply. Also, at closing time the computer prints out detailed summaries of the day's sales and item inventories. It thus provides management with up-to-the-minute information that could not otherwise be obtained.

Illustration 6–11

Other examples of on-line operations are found in banks and in factories. However, all have the same results; they reduce human labor, create more accurate records, and provide management with both better and more up-to-date reports. Furthermore, when there are sufficient transactions, they do the work at less cost per transaction.

Time sharing

Computer service companies provide computer service to many concerns on a time-sharing basis, using computers that are capable of working on many jobs simultaneously. In providing such service, the computer service company installs an input-output device on the premises of a subscriber to its service. The input-output device is connected to the service company's computer through wires leased from the phone company. The subscriber uses the input-output device to input data into the service company's computer. It is held in storage there until processing time is available, usually within a few seconds. The computer then processes the data and transmits the results to the subscriber. For this service the subscriber pays a monthly fee plus a charge for the computer time used.

Through *time sharing* a growing number of concerns are using computers, even very small businesses. For example, a dentist or a physician practicing alone is a very small business. Yet an increasing number of such dentists and physicians are having their accounts receivable and customer billing done by computer service companies. And, in the future more companies will make use of computers through time sharing and otherwise. Consequently, today's accounting student must learn about computers and their operation.

GLOSSARY

Accounting system. The business papers, records, reports, and procedures used by a business in recording transactions and reporting their effects.

Accounts Payable Ledger. A subsidiary ledger having an account for each creditor.

Accounts Receivable Ledger. A subsidiary ledger having an account for each customer.

Automated data processing. The processing of data without human intervention.

Check Register. A book of original entry for recording payments by check.

Columnar journal. A book of original entry having columns for entering specific data about each transaction of a group of like transactions.

Computer. A complex electronic machine used to process data and prepare reports.

Controlling account. A general ledger account that controls the accounts in a subsidiary ledger.

Crossfoot. To add the column totals of a journal or a report.

Foot. To add a column of figures.

General Ledger. A ledger containing the financial statement accounts of a business.

Off-line processing of data. Processing data in batches with a new program and a new set of data being placed in the computer for each batch.

On-line processing of data. Processing data of one kind on a continuous basis using input devices such as cash registers or optical scanners to enter new data.

Program. A set of computer instructions for processing data.

Schedule of accounts payable. A list of creditor account balances with the total.

Schedule of accounts receivable. A list of customer account balances with the total.

Special journal. A columnar book of original entry for recording one kind of transaction.

Subsidiary ledger. A group of accounts other than general ledger accounts which show the details underlying the balance of a controlling account in the General Ledger.

Time sharing. The sharing of computer processing time.

QUESTIONS FOR CLASS DISCUSSION

1. How does a columnar journal save posting labor?
2. Why should sales to and receipts of cash from charge customers be recorded and posted daily?
3. What functions are served by the Accounts Receivable controlling account?
4. Both credits to customer accounts and credits to miscellaneous accounts are individually posted from a Cash Receipts Journal like that of Illustration 6–2. Why not put both kinds of credits in the same column and thus save journal space?
5. How is a multicolumn journal crossfooted? Why is such a journal crossfooted?
6. How is the equality of a controlling account and its subsidiary ledger accounts maintained?
7. Describe how copies of a company's sales invoices may be used as a Sales Journal.
8. When a general journal entry is used to record a returned charge sale, the credit of the entry must be posted twice. Does this cause the trial balance to be out of balance? Why or why not?
9. How does one tell from which journal a particular amount in a ledger account was posted?
10. How is a schedule of accounts payable prepared? How is it used to prove

the balances of the creditor accounts in the Accounts Payable Ledger? What may be substituted for a formal schedule?

11. After all posting is completed, the balance of the Accounts Receivable controlling account does not agree with the sum of the balances in the Accounts Receivable Ledger. If the trial balance is in balance, where is the error apt to be?

CLASS EXERCISES

Exercise 6–1

A company uses a Sales Journal, a Purchases Journal, a Cash Receipts Journal, a Cash Disbursements Journal, and a General Journal like the ones illustrated in this chapter. List the following transactions by letter, and opposite each letter write the name of the journal in which the transaction should be recorded.

a. Sale of merchandise on credit.
b. Purchase of office supplies on credit.
c. Purchase of merchandise on credit.
d. Purchase of office equipment on credit.
e. Sale of unneeded office equipment on credit.
f. Return of a charge sale.
g. Return of a cash sale, a check was issued.
h. Return of a credit purchase.
i. Payment of a creditor.
j. Adjusting entries.
k. Closing entries.

Exercise 6–2

At the end of November Rex Company's Sales Journal showed the following credit sales:

SALES JOURNAL

Date		Account Debited	Invoice Number	P R	Amount
Nov.	3	Dale Hall	123		250.00
	8	John Mohr	124		100.00
	19	Gary Roth	125		225.00
	26	Dale Hall	126		300.00
	30	Total			875.00

The company's General Journal carried this entry:

Nov.	22	Sales Returns and Allowances		25.00	
		Accounts Receivable—Gary Roth			25.00
		Customer returned merchandise.			

Required:

1. On a sheet of notebook paper open a subsidiary Accounts Receivable Ledger having a T-account for each of Dale Hall, John Mohr, and Gary Roth. Post the sales journal entries to the customer accounts and also post the portion of the general journal entry that affects a customer's account.
2. Open a General Ledger having an Accounts Receivable controlling account, a Sales account, and a Sales Returns and Allowances account. Post the portions of the sales journal and general journal entries that affect these accounts.
3. Prove the subsidiary ledger accounts with a schedule of accounts receivable.

Exercise 6–3

Harbor Company, a company that posts its sales invoices directly and then binds the invoices to make them into a Sales Journal, had the following sales during October:

Oct. 3	Robert Hall	$ 500
6	Carl Fetter	300
11	Taylor Gordon	700
18	Carl Fetter	200
21	Taylor Gordon	800
27	Walter Scott	400
	Total	$2,900

Required:

1. On a sheet of notebook paper open a subsidiary Accounts Receivable Ledger having a T-account for each customer with an invoice bound in the Sales Journal. Post the invoices to the subsidiary ledger.
2. Give the general journal entry to record the end-of-the-month total of the Sales Journal.
3. Open an Accounts Receivable controlling account and a Sales account and post the general journal entry.
4. Prove the subsidiary Accounts Receivable Ledger with a schedule of accounts receivable.

Exercise 6–4

A company that records credit sales in a Sales Journal and records sales returns in its General Journal made the following errors. List each error by letter, and opposite each letter tell when the error will be discovered:

a. Recorded a $15 credit sale in the Sales Journal as a $150 sale.
b. Correctly recorded a $10 sale in the Sales Journal but posted it to the customer's account as a $100 sale.
c. Posted a sales return recorded in the General Journal to the Sales Returns and Allowances account and also to the Accounts Receivable account but did not post to the customer's account.
d. Made an addition error in determining the balance of a customer's account.
e. Posted a sales return to the Accounts Receivable account and to the customer's account but did not post to the Sales Returns and Allowances account.
f. Made an addition error in totaling the Amount column in the Sales Journal.

Exercise 6–5

Following are a merchandising concern's condensed journals, the column headings of which are incomplete in that they do not tell whether the columns are debit or credit columns.

SALES JOURNAL

Account	Amount
Customer A............	1,200
Customer B............	1,400
Customer C	1,600
Total	4,200

PURCHASES JOURNAL

Account	Amount
Company One	1,000
Company Two	1,500
Company Three.........	2,000
Total	4,500

GENERAL JOURNAL

.....	...	Sales Returns and Allowances	400	
		Accounts Receivable—Customer B		400
		Customer returned merchandise.		
	...	Accounts Payable—Company Three	200	
		Purchases Returns and Allowances		200
		Returned defective merchandise.		

CASH RECEIPTS JOURNAL

Account	Other Accounts	Accounts Receivable	Sales	Sales Discounts	Cash
Customer A	.....	1,200	.....	24	1,176
Customer B	.....	500	.....	10	490
Sales	.....	.....	1,250	...	1,250
Notes Payable	5,000	.....	.....	...	5,000
Customer C	.....	800	.....	16	784
Sales	.....	.....	1,150	...	1,150
Totals	5,000	2,500	2,400	50	9,850

CASH DISBURSEMENTS JOURNAL

Account	Other Accounts	Accounts Payable	Purchases Discounts	Cash
Company Two	.....	750	15	735
Salaries Expense	650	.....	...	650
Company Three	.....	1,000	20	980
Salaries Expense	650	.....	...	650
Totals	1,300	1,750	35	3,015

Required:

1. Prepare T-accounts on a sheet of notebook paper for the following general ledger and subsidiary ledger accounts. Separate the accounts of each ledger into a group.

General Ledger accounts	Accounts Receivable Ledger accounts
Cash	Customer A
Accounts Receivable	Customer B
Notes Payable	Customer C
Accounts Payable	
Sales	Accounts Payable Ledger accounts
Sales Returns and Allowances	Company One
Sales Discounts	Company Two
Purchases	Company Three
Purchases Returns and Allowances	
Purchases Discounts	
Salaries Expense	

2. Without referring to illustrations showing complete column headings, post the journal amounts to the proper T-accounts.

PROBLEMS

Problem 6–1

(If the working papers that accompany this text are not being used, omit this problem.)

It is June 21 and you have just taken over the accounting work of Murphy Company, a concern operating with annual accounting periods that end each May 31. The previous accountant journalized the company's transactions through June 19 and posted all items which required posting as individual amounts, as an examination of the journals and ledgers in the booklet of working papers will reveal.

Murphy Company completed these transactions beginning on June 21:

June 21 Sold merchandise on credit to Roy Ness, Invoice No. 716, $625. (Terms of all credit sales, 2/10, n/60.)

22 Issued a credit memorandum to John Long for defective merchandise sold on June 18 and returned for credit, $15.

23 Purchased on credit from Lee Supply Company merchandise, $585; store supplies, $60; and office supplies, $25. Invoice dated this day, terms n/10 EOM.

25 Received a credit memorandum from Pace Company for merchandise received on June 18 and returned for credit, $75.

25 Received a credit memorandum from Lee Supply Company for store supplies received on June 23 and returned for credit, $35.

26 Issued Check No. 723 to Pace Company in payment of its June 16 invoice, less the return and the discount.

26 Received $735 from Alan Hall in full of the June 16 sale.

27 Issued Check No. 724 to Clark Company in payment of its June 17 invoice, less the discount.

June 27   Sold merchandise on credit to Ted Reed, Invoice No. 717, $815.

     27   Sold a local church group a roll of wrapping paper (store supplies) for cash at cost, $20.

     28   Received $539 from John Long in payment of the June 18 sale, less the return and discount.

     28   Purchased store equipment from Lee Supply Company on credit, invoice dated June 28, terms n/10 EOM, $450.

     29   Received merchandise and an invoice dated June 27, terms 2/10, n/60, from Acme Company, $445.

     30   Douglas Murphy, the owner of Murphy Company, used Check No. 725 to withdraw $400 cash from the business for personal use.

     30   Issued Check No. 726 to Gary Beal, the company's only sales employee, in payment of his salary for the last half of June plus some overtime, $350.

     30   Issued Check No. 727 to Northern Company to pay the June electric bill, $130.

     30   Cash sales for the last half of the month, $3,240. (Such sales are usually recorded daily but are recorded only twice in this problem in order to reduce the repetitive transactions.)

Required:

1. Record the transaction in the journals provided.
2. Post to the customer and creditor accounts and also post any amounts that should be posted as individual amounts to general ledger accounts. (Normally these amounts are posted daily, but they are posted only once in this problem in order to simplify it.)
3. Foot and crossfoot the journals and make the month-end postings.
4. Prepare a June 30 trial balance and prove the subsidiary ledgers with schedules of accounts receivable and accounts payable.

Problem 6–2

Hilltop Sales completed these transactions during February of the current year:

Feb. 1   Sold merchandise on credit to Tom Moss, Invoice No. 617, $750. (The terms of all credit sales are 2/10, n/60.)

     2   Received merchandise and an invoice dated January 30, terms 2/10, n/60, from Case Company, $1,685.

     3   Purchased office equipment from Office Outfitters, invoice dated February 3, terms n/10 EOM, $585.

     4   Sold merchandise on credit to John Rice, Invoice No. 618, $1,350.

     5   Purchased on credit from New Company merchandise, $1,595; store supplies, $65; and office supplies, $30. Invoice dated February 4, terms n/10 EOM.

     6   Received a credit memorandum from Case Company for unsatisfactory merchandise received on February 2 and returned for credit, $135.

     7   Received a credit memorandum from Office Outfitters for office equipment received on February 3 and returned for credit, $60.

     7   Cash sales for the first week of February, $1,445.

     7   *Post to the customer and creditor accounts and also post any amounts*

that should be posted as individual amounts to the general ledger accounts. (Normally such items are posted daily; but to shorten the problem, you are asked to post them only once each week.)

Feb. 9 Sent Case Company Check No. 312 in payment of its invoice of January 30, less the return and discount.

11 Sold merchandise on credit to Fred Able, Invoice No. 619, $1,710.

11 Received a check from Tom Moss in payment of the sale of February 1, less the discount.

13 Received a check from John Rice in payment of the sale of February 4, less the discount.

14 Received merchandise and an invoice dated February 11, terms 2/10, n/60, from Taylor Company, $1,700.

14 Issued Check No. 313, payable to Payroll, in payment of the sales salaries for the first half of the month, $815. Cashed the check and paid the employees.

14 Cash sales for the week ended February 14, $1,395.

14 *Post to the customer and creditor accounts and also post any amounts that should be posted as individual amounts to the general ledger accounts.*

16 Issued a $160 credit memorandum to Fred Able for defective merchandise sold on February 11 and returned.

17 Received merchandise and an invoice dated February 14, terms 2/10, n/60, from Taylor Company, $1,450.

18 Purchased on credit from New Company merchandise, $370; store supplies, $45; and office supplies, $20. Invoice dated February 17, terms n/10 EOM.

18 Sold merchandise on credit to Tom Moss, Invoice No. 620, $650.

21 Received a check from Fred Able in payment of the sale of February 11, less the return and discount.

21 Sent Taylor Company Check No. 314 in payment of its invoice of February 11, less the discount.

21 Cash sales for the week ended February 21, $1,425.

21 *Post to the customer and creditor accounts and also post any amounts that should be posted as individual amounts to the general ledger accounts.*

24 Sent Taylor Company Check No. 315 in payment of its invoice of February 14, less the discount.

25 Borrowed $4,000 by giving Valley National Bank a 60-day, 9% promissory note payable.

26 Sold merchandise on credit to Fred Able, Invoice No. 621, $915.

27 Sold merchandise on credit to John Rice, Invoice No. 622, $1,085.

28 Issued Check No. 316 to *The Gazette* for advertising expense, $375.

28 Issued Check No. 317 payable to Payroll for sales salaries, $815. Cashed the check and paid the employees.

28 Received a check from Tom Moss in payment of the February 18 sale, less the discount.

28 Cash sales for the last week of the month, $1,345.

28 *Post to the customer and creditor accounts and also post any amounts that should be posted as individual amounts to the general ledger accounts.*

Feb. 28 *Make the month-end postings from the journals.*

Required:

1. Open the following general ledger accounts: Cash, Accounts Receivable, Store Supplies, Office Supplies, Office Equipment, Notes Payable, Accounts Payable, Sales, Sales Returns and Allowances, Sales Discounts, Purchases, Purchases Returns and Allowances, Purchases Discounts, Advertising Expense, and Sales Salaries Expense.
2. Open the following accounts receivable ledger accounts: Fred Able, Tom Moss, and John Rice.
3. Open the following accounts payable ledger accounts: Case Company, New Company, Office Outfitters, and Taylor Company.
4. Prepare a Sales Journal, a Purchases Journal, a Cash Receipts Journal, a Cash Disbursements Journal, and a General Journal similar to the ones illustrated in this chapter.
5. Enter the transactions in the journals and post when instructed to do so.
6. Prepare a trial balance and prove the subsidiary ledgers with schedules of accounts receivable and payable.

Problem 6–3

Valley Sales completed these transactions during November:

Nov. 1 Purchased merchandise on credit from Grady Company, invoice dated October 29, terms 2/10, n/60, $2,100.

2 Issued Check No. 915 to *Daily Clarion* for advertising expense, $115.

2 Sold merchandise on credit to A. J. Allen, Invoice No. 821, $825. The terms of all credit sales are 2/10, n/60.

3 Sold merchandise on credit to Paul Eddy, Invoice No. 822, $750.

5 Purchased on credit from Hale Company merchandise, $85; store supplies, $60; and office supplies, $40. Invoice dated November 4, terms n/10 EOM.

8 Received a $20 credit memorandum from Hale Company for unsatisfactory store supplies received on November 5 and returned for credit.

8 Issued Check No. 916 to Grady Company in payment of its October 29 invoice, less the discount.

9 Issued a $75 credit memorandum to A. J. Allen for defective merchandise sold on November 2 and returned for credit.

10 Sold merchandise on credit to David Case, Invoice No. 823, $950.

11 Purchased store equipment on credit from Boden Company, invoice dated November 8, terms n/10 EOM, $465.

12 Received payment from A. J. Allen for the November 2 sale, less the return and discount.

13 Received payment from Paul Eddy for the November 3 sale, less the discount.

14 Sold merchandise on credit to A. J. Allen, Invoice No. 824, $650.

15 Issued Check No. 917, payable to Payroll, in payment of sales salaries for the first half of the month, $850. Cashed the check and paid the employees.

Nov. 15 Cash sales for the first half of the month, $2,445. (Cash sales are usually recorded daily from the cash register readings; however, they are recorded only twice during the month in this problem in order to shorten the problem.)

15 *Make the individual postings from the journals. (Normally such items are posted daily; but since they are so few in number in this problem, you are asked to post them on only two occasions.)*

18 Purchased merchandise on credit from Flint Company, invoice dated November 15, terms 2/10, n/60, $1,350.

19 Sold store supplies at cost for cash, $15.

20 Received payment from David Case for the November 10 sale less the discount.

21 Purchased on credit from Boden Company merchandise, $425; store supplies, $55; and office supplies, $30. Invoice dated November 19, terms n/10 EOM.

22 Purchased merchandise on credit from Grady Company, invoice dated November 19, terms 2/10, n/60, $1,050.

23 Received a $150 credit memorandum from Flint Company for defective merchandise purchased on November 18 and returned.

24 Received payment from A. J. Allen for the November 14 sale, less the discount.

25 Issued Check No. 918 to Flint Company in payment of its November 15 invoice, less the return and discount.

27 Sold merchandise on credit to Paul Eddy, Invoice No. 825, $735.

28 Borrowed $5,000 from Security Bank by giving a note payable.

29 Issued Check No. 919 to Grady Company in payment of its November 19 invoice, less the discount.

30 Sold merchandise on credit to David Case, Invoice No. 826, $515.

30 Issued Check No. 920, payable to Payroll, in payment of the sales salaries for the last half of the month, $850.

30 Cash sales for the last half of the month were $2,685.

30 *Make the individual postings from the journals.*

30 *Foot and crossfoot the journals and make the month-end postings.*

Required:

1. Open the following general ledger accounts: Cash, Accounts Receivable, Store Supplies, Office Supplies, Store Equipment, Notes Payable, Accounts Payable, Sales, Sales Returns and Allowances, Sales Discounts, Purchases, Purchases Returns and Allowances, Purchases Discounts, Advertising Expense, and Sales Salaries Expense.

2. Open these subsidiary accounts receivable ledger accounts: A. J. Allen, David Case, and Paul Eddy.

3. Open these accounts payable ledger accounts: Bodon Company, Flint Company, Grady Company, and Hale Company.

4. Prepare a General Journal, a Sales Journal, a Purchases Journal, a Cash Receipts Journal, and a Cash Disbursements Journal like the ones illustrated in this chapter.

5. Enter the transactions in the journals and post when instructed to do so.

6. Prepare a trial balance and prove the subsidiary ledgers by preparing schedules of accounts receivable and accounts payable.

Problem 6-4

CASH DISBURSEMENTS, PURCHASES, AND PURCHASES RETURNS JOURNAL

Sales Salaries Expense	Office Salaries Expense	Purchases	Accounts Payable	Other Accounts	Date	Account Titles and Explanations	P R	Other Accounts	Accounts Payable	Pur. Discounts	Cash
					Nov.						
		875.00			2	Ball Company			875.00		
		1,450.00			4	Dallas Company			1,450.00		
			125.00		5	Ball Company—Purchases Returns		125.00			
			750.00		8	Ball Company				15.00	735.00
				145.00	10	Store Supplies—AAA Suppliers			145.00		
		2,400.00			11	Cole Company			2,400.00		
			1,450.00		12	Dallas Company				29.00	1,421.00
925.00	450.00				15	First half of month's salaries					1,375.00
			2,400.00		17	Cole Company				48.00	2,352.00
				100.00	23	Advertising Expenses					100.00
		565.00		85.00	25	Store Supplies—Ball Company			650.00		
			35.00		28	Ball Company—Store Supplies		35.00			
925.00	450.00				30	Last half month's salaries					1,375.00
1,850.00	900.00	5,290.00	4,760.00	330.00	30	Totals		160.00	5,520.00	92.00	7,358.00

Problem 6–4

On page 219 is a columnar journal of Different Company, a journal unlike any described in your text. However, the posting principles described in this chapter apply to the journal. Consequently, the journal is designed to test your understanding of these principles.

Required:

1. Open a General Ledger having T-accounts for Cash, Store Supplies, Accounts Payable, Purchases, Purchases Returns and Allowances, Purchases Discounts, Sales Salaries Expense, Advertising Expense, and Office Salaries Expense.
2. Open an Accounts Payable Ledger having these accounts: AAA Suppliers, Ball Company, Cole Company, and Dallas Company.
3. Post the columnar journal, prepare a trial balance of the General Ledger, and prove the subsidiary ledger by preparing a schedule of accounts payable. (The Cash account will have a credit balance in the trial balance.)

ALTERNATE PROBLEMS

Problem 6–1A

(If the working papers that accompany this text are not being used, omit this problem.)

It is June 21 and you have just taken over the accounting work of Zest Company, a concern operating with annual accounting periods that end each May 31. The previous accountant journalized the company's transactions through June 19 and posted all items which required posting as individual amounts, as an examination of the journals and ledgers in the booklet of working papers will reveal.

Zest Company completed these transactions beginning on June 21:

June 21   Purchased on credit from Lee Supply Company merchandise, $615; store supplies, $75; and office supplies, $40. Invoice dated June 21, terms n/10 EOM.

     22   Received a $25 credit memorandum from Pace Company for merchandise received on June 18 and returned for credit.

     23   Received a credit memorandum from Lee Supply Company for office supplies received on June 21 and returned for credit, $15.

     24   Sold merchandise on credit to Alan Hall, Invoice No. 716, $585. (Terms of all credit sales are 2/10, n/60.)

     25   Issued a credit memorandum to John Long for defective merchandise sold on June 18 and returned for credit, $65.

     25   Purchased store equipment on credit from Lee Supply Company, invoice dated June 24, terms n/10 EOM, $545.

     26   Issued Check No. 723 to Pace Company in payment of its June 16 invoice, less the return and the discount.

June 26 Received $735 from Alan Hall in full payment of the June 16 sale.

27 Issued Check No. 724 to Clark Company in payment of its June 17 invoice, less the discount.

27 Sold merchandise on credit to Roy Ness, Invoice No. 717, $735.

27 Sold a local Boy Scout troop a roll of wrapping paper (store supplies) for cash at cost, $15.

28 Received $490 from John Long in payment of the June 18 sale, less the return and the discount.

29 Received merchandise and an invoice dated June 26, terms 2/10, n/60, from Clark Company, $655.

29 Douglas Murphy, the owner of Zest Company, used Check No. 725 to withdraw $500 cash from the business for personal use.

30 Issued Check No. 726 to Gary Beal, the company's only sales employee, in payment of his salary for the last half of June, $300.

30 Issued Check No. 727 to Public Service Company to pay the June electric bill, $165.

30 Cash sales for the last half of the month, $2,985. (Such sales are usually recorded daily but are recorded only twice in this problem in order to reduce repetitive transactions.)

Required:

1. Record the transactions in the journals provided.
2. Post to the customer and creditor accounts and also post any amounts that should be posted as individual amounts to the general ledger accounts. (Normally these amounts are posted daily, but they are posted only once in this problem in order to simplify it.)
3. Foot and crossfoot the journals and make the month-end postings.
4. Prepare a June 30 trial balance and prove the subsidiary ledgers with schedules of accounts receivable and accounts payable.

Problem 6–2A

Sierra Company completed these transactions during February of the current year:

Feb. 2 Received merchandise and an invoice dated January 31, terms 2/10, n/60, from Case Company, $3,100.

3 Sold merchandise on credit to Fred Able, $950. (Terms of all credit sales are 2/10, n/60. Number sales invoices beginning with 758.)

4 Sold merchandise on credit to John Rice, $1,400.

6 Purchased office equipment on credit from Office Outfitters, invoice dated February 2, terms n/10 EOM, $650.

7 Cash sales for the week ended February 7, $1,200.

7 *Post to customer and creditor accounts and also post any amounts that should be posted as individual amounts to the general ledger accounts. (Normally such items are posted daily; but to simplify the problem, you are asked to post them only once each week.)*

Feb. 9   Sold unneeded office equipment at cost for cash, $140.

9   Issued Check No. 522 to *The Daily News* for advertising, $185.

10   Sold merchandise on credit to Tom Moss, $800.

10   Purchased on credit from Taylor Company merchandise, $1,675; store supplies, $110; and office supplies, $65. Invoice dated February 6, terms n/10 EOM.

10   Sent Check No. 523 to Case Company in full of the invoice of January 31, less the discount.

13   Received a check from John Rice in full payment of the sale of February 4, less the discount.

13   Received a check from Fred Able in full payment of the sale of February 3, less the discount.

14   Cash sales for the week ended February 14, $1,450.

14   *Post to the customer and creditor accounts and also post any amounts that should be posted as individual amounts to the general ledger accounts.*

15   Sold merchandise on credit to Tom Moss, $900.

15   Issued Check No. 524, payable to Payroll, in payment of the sales salaries for the first half of the month, $600. Cashed the check and paid the employees.

17   Issued a credit memorandum to Tom Moss for defective merchandise purchased on February 15 and returned, $150.

18   Received a credit memorandum for defective office equipment purchased on February 6 and returned, $50.

18   Sold merchandise on credit to Fred Able, $1,300.

18   Received merchandise and an invoice dated February 15, terms 2/10, n/30, from New Company, $3,500.

20   Received a check from Tom Moss in full of the sale of February 10, less the discount.

21   Cash sales for the week ended February 21, $1,550.

21   *Post to the customer and creditor accounts and also post any amounts that should be posted as individual amounts to the general ledger accounts.*

22   Purchased on credit from Taylor Company merchandise, $1,170; store supplies, $45; and office supplies, $35. Invoice dated February 18, terms n/10 EOM.

22   Received merchandise and an invoice dated February 18, terms 2/10, n/60, from Case Company, $2,350.

23   Received a credit memorandum from New Company, $350. The merchandise covered by the memorandum did not meet specifications and had been returned.

24   Received a check from Tom Moss in full of the sale of February 15, less the return and the discount.

24   Sent New Company Check No. 525 in full of the invoice of February 15, less the return and the discount.

25   Sold merchandise on credit to John Rice, $1,175.

27   Borrowed $5,000 from the United States National Bank by giving a 60-day, 9% note payable.

Feb. 28 Sent Case Company Check No. 526 in full of the invoice of February 18, less the discount.

  28 Issued Check No. 527 payable to Payroll for sales salaries, $600. Cashed the check and paid the employees.

  28 Cash sales for the week ended February 28, $1,225.

  28 *Post to customer and creditor accounts and also post any amounts that should be posted as individual amounts to the general ledger accounts.*

  28 *Crossfoot the journals and make the month-end postings.*

Required:

1. Open the following general ledger accounts: Cash, Accounts Receivable, Store Supplies, Office Supplies, Office Equipment, Notes Payable, Accounts Payable, Sales, Sales Returns and Allowances, Sales Discounts, Purchases, Purchases Returns and Allowances, Purchases Discounts, Advertising Expense, and Sales Salaries Expense.
2. Open the following accounts receivable ledger accounts: Fred Able, Tom Moss, and John Rice.
3. Open the following accounts payable ledger accounts: Case Company, New Company, Office Outfitters, and Taylor Company.
4. Prepare a Sales Journal, Purchases Journal, Cash Receipts Journal, Cash Disbursements Journal, and General Journal similar to the ones illustrated in this chapter. Enter the transactions in the journals and post when instructed to do so.
5. Prepare a trial balance of the General Ledger and prove the subsidiary ledgers with schedules of accounts receivable and accounts payable.

Problem 6–3A

Speedy Sales completed these transactions during November:

Nov. 2 Sold merchandise on credit to Paul Eddy, Invoice No. 933, $700. (The terms of all credit sales are 2/10, n/60.)

  3 Purchased merchandise on credit from Hale Company, invoice dated October 31, terms 2/10, n/60, $1,385.

  5 Purchased store equipment on credit from Grady Company, invoice dated November 2, terms n/10 EOM, $435.

  6 Purchased on credit from Bodon Company merchandise, $80; store supplies, $55; and office supplies, $30. Invoice dated November 4, terms n/10 EOM.

  6 Borrowed $2,000 from Central Bank by giving a note payable.

  7 Received an $85 credit memorandum from Hale Company for merchandise received on November 3 and returned.

  10 Received a $40 credit memorandum from Bodon Company for unsatisfactory store supplies purchased on November 6 and returned.

  10 Issued Check No. 989 to Hale Company in payment of its October 31 invoice, less the return and discount.

Nov. 12 Sold merchandise on credit to David Case, Invoice No. 934, $785.

12 Received payment from Paul Eddy for the November 2 sale, less the discount.

13 Purchased merchandise on credit from Flint Company, invoice dated November 11, terms 2/10, n/60, $1,750.

15 Issued Check No. 990, payable to Payroll, for sales salaries for the first half of the month, $925. Cashed the check and paid the employees.

15 Cash sales for the first half of the month were $2,655. (Cash sales are usually recorded daily from the cash register readings; however, they are recorded only twice in this problem in order to shorten the problem.)

15 *Make the individual postings from the journals. (Normally such items are posted daily; but since they are so few in number in this problem, you are asked to post them on only two occasions.)*

16 Issued a $35 credit memorandum to David Case for defective merchandise sold on November 12 and returned for credit.

17 Purchased merchandise on credit from Flint Company, invoice dated November 14, terms 2/10, n/60, $1,500.

18 Sold merchandise to Paul Eddy on credit, Invoice No. 935, $650.

18 Purchased on credit from Bodon Company merchandise, $210; store supplies, $45; and office supplies, $25. Invoice dated November 15, terms n/10 EOM.

21 Issued Check No. 991 to Flint Company in payment of its November 11 invoice, less the discount.

21 Sold store supplies at cost for cash, $10.

22 Received payment from David Case for the November 12 sale, less the return and the discount.

24 Issued Check No. 992 to Flint Company in payment of its November 14 invoice, less the discount.

25 Sold merchandise on credit to David Case, Invoice No. 936, $885.

26 Sold merchandise on credit to A. J. Allen, Invoice No. 937, $745.

28 Issued Check No. 993 to *Daily Sun* for advertising expense, $295.

28 Received payment from Paul Eddy for the November 18 sale, less the discount.

30 Issued Check No. 994, payable to Payroll, in payment of the sales salaries for the last half of the month, $925. Cashed the check and paid the employees.

30 Cash sales for the last half of the month were $2,310.

30 *Make the individual postings from the journals.*

30 *Foot and crossfoot the journals and make the month-end postings.*

Required:

1. Open the following general ledger accounts: Cash, Accounts Receivable, Store Supplies, Office Supplies, Store Equipment, Notes Payable, Accounts Payable, Sales, Sales Returns and Allowances, Sales Discounts, Purchases, Purchases Returns and Allowances, Purchases Discounts, Advertising Expense, and Sales Salaries Expense.

2. Open the following accounts receivable ledger accounts: A. J. Allen, David Case, and Paul Eddy.
3. Open the following accounts payable ledger accounts: Bodon Company, Flint Company, Grady Company, and Hale Company.
4. Prepare a Sales Journal, a Purchases Journal, a Cash Receipts Journal, a Cash Disbursements Journal, and a General Journal like the ones illustrated in this chapter.
5. Enter the transactions in the journals and post when instructed to do so.
6. Prove the general ledger accounts with a trial balance and prove the subsidiary ledgers with schedules of accounts receivable and accounts payable.

DELTA SALES—A MINIPRACTICE SET

(If the working papers that accompany this text are not being used, omit this minipractice set.)

Assume it is Monday, February 2, the first business day of the month, and you have just been hired as accountant by Delta Sales, a company that operates with monthly accounting periods. All of the concern's accounting work has been completed through the end of January, its ledgers show January 31 balances, and you are ready to begin work by recording the following transactions:

Feb. 2   Issued Check No. 257 to Valley Realty in payment of the February rent, $800. (Use two lines in recording the transaction and charge 10% of the rent to Rent Expense, Office Space and the balance to Rent Expense, Selling Space.)

2   Received a $185 credit memorandum from Reliable Company for merchandise received on January 29 and returned for credit.

3   Sold merchandise to Owl Electric Company, Invoice No. 732, $1,250. (The terms of all credit sales are 2/10, n/60.)

4   Issued an $80 credit memorandum to Morgan and Son for defective merchandise sold on January 30 and returned for credit.

5   Purchased on credit from Fine Supply Company merchandise, $1,765; store supplies, $75; and office supplies, $45. Invoice dated February 3, terms n/10 EOM.

6   Issued Check No. 258 to Reliable Company in payment for the $1,435 of merchandise received on January 29, less the return and a 2% discount.

7   Sold a roll of wrapping paper (store supplies) to a local church group for cash, $20.

9   Received payment from Morgan and Son for the sale of January 30, less the return and the discount.

10   Purchased office equipment on credit from Fine Supply Company, invoice dated February 9, terms n/10 EOM, $535.

12   Received merchandise and an invoice dated February 9, terms 2/10, n/60, from Good Company, $3,250.

13   Received payment from Owl Electric Company for the sale of February 3, less the discount.

Feb. 14   Issued Check No. 259, payable to Payroll, in payment of the sales salaries for the first half of the month, $470, and office salaries, $350. Cashed the check and paid the employees.

14   Cash sales for the first half of the month, $4,875. (Such sales are usually recorded daily but are recorded only twice in this problem in order to reduce the number of repetitive transactions.)

14   *Post to customer and creditor accounts and also post any amounts that should be posted as individual amounts to the general ledger accounts. (Normally such items are posted daily; but to simplify the problem, you are asked to post only at the end of each two weeks in this problem.)*

16   Received a $60 credit memorandum from Fine Supply Company for defective office equipment received on February 10 and returned for credit.

16   Sold merchandise on credit to Stern Brothers, Invoice No. 733, $1,750.

17   Received merchandise and an invoice dated February 14, terms 2/10, n/60, from Quick Company, $2,750.

19   Issued Check No. 260 to Good Company in payment of its February 9 invoice, less the discount.

20   Sold merchandise on credit to Morgan and Son, Invoice No. 734, $1,745.

21   Sold merchandise on credit to Bush Construction Company, Invoice No. 735, $1,185.

23   Purchased on credit from Fine Supply Company merchandise, $1,840; store supplies, $65; and office supplies, $20. Invoice dated February 20, terms n/10 EOM.

24   Issued Check No. 261 to Quick Company in payment of its February 14 invoice, less the discount.

25   Received merchandise and an invoice dated February 22, terms 2/10, n/60, from Good Company, $1,565.

26   Received payment from Stern Brothers for the sale of February 16, less the discount.

27   Dale Nash, the owner of Delta Sales, used Check No. 262 to withdraw $750 from the business for personal use.

28   Issued Check No. 263 to Public Service Company in payment of the February electric bill, $180.

28   Issued Check No. 264, payable to Payroll, for sales salaries, $470; and office salaries, $350. Cashed the check and paid the employees.

28   Cash sales for the last half of the month were $5,115.

28   *Post to the customer and creditor accounts and also post any amounts that should be posted as individual amounts to the general ledger accounts.*

28   *Foot and crossfoot the journals and make the month-end postings.*

Required:

1. Enter the transactions in the journals and post when instructed to do so.
2. Prepare a trial balance in the Trial Balance columns of an eight-column work sheet and complete the work sheet using the following information:

     a. Ending merchandise inventory, $20,935.

     b. Expired insurance, $95.

     c. Ending store supplies inventory, $195; and ending office supplies inventory, $90.

     d. Estimated depreciation of store equipment, $125; and estimated depreciation of office equipment, $35.

3. Prepare a multiple-step, classified February income statement and a February 28 classified balance sheet.

4. Prepare and post adjusting and closing entries.

5. Prepare a post-closing trial balance and prove the subsidiary ledgers with schedules of accounts receivable and payable.

PART THREE
Accounting for assets

After studying Chapter 7, you should be able to:

☐ Explain why internal control procedures are needed in a large concern and state the broad principles of internal control.

☐ Describe internal control procedures to protect cash from cash sales, cash received through the mail, and cash disbursements.

☐ Tell how a petty cash fund operates and be able to make entries in a Petty Cash Record and the entries required to reimburse a petty cash fund.

☐ Explain why the bank balance of cash and the book balance of cash are reconciled and be able to prepare such a reconciliation.

☐ Tell how recording invoices at net amounts helps to gain control over cash discounts taken and be able to account for invoices recorded at net amounts.

☐ Define or explain the words and phrases listed in the chapter Glossary.

Accounting for cash

■ Cash has universal usefulness, small bulk for high value, and no convenient identification marks by which ownership may be established. Consequently, in accounting for cash, the procedures for protecting it from fraud and theft are very important. They are called *internal control procedures.* Internal control procedures apply to all assets owned by a business and to all phases of its operations.

INTERNAL CONTROL

In a small business the owner-manager commonly controls the entire operation through personal supervision and direct participation in the activities of the business. For example, he or she commonly buys all the assets, goods, and services bought by the business. Such a manager also hires and closely supervises all employees, negotiates all contracts, and signs all checks. As a result, in signing checks, for example, he or she knows from personal contact and observation that the assets, goods, and services for which the checks are in payment were received by the business. However, as a business grows it becomes increasingly difficult to maintain this personal contact. Therefore, at some point it becomes necessary for the manager to delegate responsibilities and rely on internal control procedures rather than personal contact in controlling the operations of the business. In a properly designed system the procedures encourage adherence to prescribed managerial policies. They also promote operational efficiencies; protect the business assets from waste, fraud, and theft; and ensure accurate and reliable accounting data.

Internal control procedures vary from company to company, depending on such factors as the nature of the business and its size. However, some broad principles of internal control are discussed below.[1]

Responsibilities should be clearly established

Good internal control necessitates that responsibilities be clearly established and for a given task, one person be made responsible. When responsibility is shared and something goes wrong, it is difficult to determine who was at fault. For example, when two salesclerks share the same cash drawer and there is a shortage, it is normally impossible to tell which clerk is at fault. Each will tend to blame the other. Neither can prove that he or she is not responsible. In such a situation each clerk should be assigned a separate cash drawer or one of the clerks should be given responsibility for making all change.

Adequate records should be maintained

Good records provide a means of control by placing responsibility for the care and protection of assets. Poor records invite laxity and often theft. When a company has poor accounting control over its assets, dishonest employees soon become aware of this and are quick to take advantage.

Assets should be insured and employees bonded

Assets should be covered by adequate casualty insurance, and employees who handle cash and negotiable assets should be bonded. Bonding provides a means for recovery if a loss occurs. It also tends to prevent losses, since a bonded employee is less apt to take assets if the employee knows a bonding company must be dealt with when the shortage is revealed.

Record keeping and custody should be separated

A fundamental principle of internal control requires that the person who has access to or is responsible for an asset should not maintain the accounting record for that asset. When this principle is observed, the custodian of an asset, knowing that a record of the asset is being

---

[1] For a discussion that continues to offer an unusually balanced analysis of the principles of internal control, see AICPA, *Internal Control* (New York, 1949). Copyright (1949) by the American Institute of CPAs.

kept by another person, is not apt to either misappropriate the asset or waste it; and the record keeper, who does not have access to the asset, has no reason to falsify the record. Furthermore, if the asset is to be misappropriated and the theft concealed in the records, collusion is necessary.

Responsibility for related transactions should be divided

Responsibility for a divisible transaction or a series of related transactions should be divided between individuals or departments in such a manner that the work of one acts as a check on that of another. This does not mean there should be duplication of work. Each employee or department should perform an unduplicated portion. For example, responsibility for placing orders, receiving the merchandise, and paying the vendors should not be given to one individual or department. To do so is to invite laxity in checking the quality and quantity of goods received and carelessness in verifying the validity and accuracy of invoices. It also invites the purchase of goods for an employee's personal use and the payment of fictitious invoices.

Mechanical devices should be used whenever practicable

Cash registers, check protectors, time clocks, and mechanical counters are examples of control devices that should be used whenever practicable. A cash register with a lock-in tape makes a record of each cash sale. A check protector by perforating the amount of a check into its face makes it very difficult to change the amount. A time clock registers the exact time an employee arrived on the job and when the employee departed.

INTERNAL CONTROL FOR CASH

A good system of internal control for cash should provide adequate procedures for protecting both cash receipts and cash disbursements. In the procedures, three basic principles should always be observed. First, there should be a separation of duties so that the people responsible for handling cash and for its custody are not the same people who keep the cash records. Second, all cash receipts should be deposited in the bank, intact, each day. Third, all payments should be made by check. The one exception to the last principle is that small disbursements may be made in cash from a petty cash fund. Petty cash funds are discussed later in this chapter.

The reason for the first principle is that a division of duties necessitates collusion between two or more people if cash is to be embezzled and the theft concealed in the accounting records. The second, requiring that all receipts be deposited intact each day, prevents an employee from making personal use of the money for a few days before depositing it. And, requiring that all receipts be deposited intact and all payments be made by check provides in the records of the bank a separate and external record of all cash transactions that may be used to prove the company's own records.

The exact procedures used to achieve control over cash vary from company to company. They depend upon such things as company size, number of employees, cash sources, and so on. Consequently, the following procedures are only illustrative of some that are in use.

Cash from cash sales

Cash sales should be rung up on a cash register at the time of each sale. To help ensure that correct amounts are rung up, each register should be so placed that customers can see the amounts rung up. Also, the clerks should be required to ring up each sale before wrapping the merchandise. Finally, each cash register should have a locked-in tape on which the amount of each sale and total sales are printed by the register.

Good cash control, as previously stated, requires a separation of custody for cash from record keeping for cash. For cash sales this separation begins with the cash register. The salesclerk who has access to the cash in the register should not have access to its locked-in tape. At the end of each day the salesclerk is usually required to count the cash in the register and to turn the cash and its count over to an employee in the cashier's office. The employee in the cashier's office, like the salesclerk, has access to the cash and should not have access to the register tape or other accounting records. A third employee, commonly from the accounting department, removes the tape from the register. He or she compares its total with the cash turned over to the cashier's office and uses the tape's information as a basis for the entry recording cash sales. This employee who has access to the register tape does not have access to the cash and therefore cannot take any. Likewise, since the salesclerk and the employee from the cashier's office do not have access to the cash register tape, they cannot take cash without the shortage being revealed.

Cash received through the mail

Control of cash coming in through the mail begins with a mail clerk who opens the mail and makes a list in triplicate of the money received. The list should give each sender's name, the purpose for which the money was sent, and the amount. One copy of the list is sent to the cashier with the money. The second copy goes to the bookkeeper. The third copy is kept by the mail clerk. The cashier deposits the money in the bank, and the bookkeeper records the amounts received in the accounting records. Then, if the bank balance is reconciled (discussed later) by a fourth person, errors or fraud by the mail clerk, the cashier, or bookkeeper will be detected. They will be detected because the cash deposited and the records of three people must agree. Furthermore, fraud is impossible, unless there is collusion. The mail clerk must report all receipts or customers will question their account balances. The cashier must deposit all receipts because the bank balance must agree with the bookkeeper's cash balance. The bookkeeper and the person reconciling the bank balance do not have access to cash and, therefore, have no opportunity to withhold any.

Cash disbursements

It is important to gain control over cash from sales and cash received through the mail. However, most large embezzlements have not involved cash receipts but have been accomplished through the payment of fictitious invoices. Consequently, procedures for controlling cash disbursements are equally as important and sometimes more important than those for cash receipts.

To gain control over cash disbursements, all disbursements should be made by check, excepting those from petty cash. If authority to sign checks is delegated to some person other than the business owner, that person should not have access to the accounting records. This helps prevent a fraudulent disbursement being made and concealed in the accounting records.

In a small business the owner-manager usually signs checks and normally knows from personal contact that the items for which the checks pay were received by the business. However, this is impossible in a large business. In a large business internal control procedures must be substituted for personal contact. The procedures tell the person who signs checks that the obligations for which the checks pay are proper obligations, properly incurred, and should be paid. Often these procedures take the form of a *voucher system.*

THE VOUCHER SYSTEM AND CONTROL

A voucher system helps gain control over cash disbursements as follows: (1) It permits only designated departments and individuals to incur obligations that will result in cash disbursements. (2) It establishes procedures for incurring such obligations and for their verification, approval, and recording. (3) It permits checks to be issued only in payment of properly verified, approved, and recorded obligations. Finally (4), it requires that every obligation be recorded at the time it is incurred and every purchase be treated as an independent transaction, complete in itself. It requires this even though a number of purchases may be made from the same company during a month or other billing period.

When a voucher system is in use, control over cash disbursements begins with the incurrence of obligations that will result in cash disbursements. Only specified departments and individuals are authorized to incur such obligations, and the kind each may incur is limited. For example, in a large store only the purchasing department may incur obligations by purchasing merchandise. However, to gain control, the purchasing-receiving-and-paying procedures are divided among several departments. They are the departments requesting that merchandise be purchased, the purchasing department, the receiving department, and the accounting department. To coordinate and control the responsibilities of these departments, business papers are used. A list of the papers follows, and an explanation of each will show how a large concern may gain control over cash disbursements resulting from the purchase of merchandise.

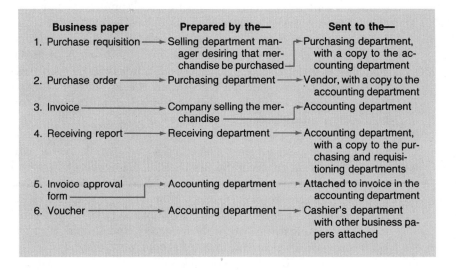

Business paper	Prepared by the—	Sent to the—
1. Purchase requisition	Selling department manager desiring that merchandise be purchased	Purchasing department, with a copy to the accounting department
2. Purchase order	Purchasing department	Vendor, with a copy to the accounting department
3. Invoice	Company selling the merchandise	Accounting department
4. Receiving report	Receiving department	Accounting department, with a copy to the purchasing and requisitioning departments
5. Invoice approval form	Accounting department	Attached to invoice in the accounting department
6. Voucher	Accounting department	Cashier's department with other business papers attached

Purchase requisition

The department managers in a large store cannot be permitted to place orders directly with supply sources. If each manager were permitted to deal directly with wholesalers and manufacturers, the amount of merchandise purchased and the resulting liabilities could not be controlled. Therefore, to gain control over purchases and resulting liabilities, department managers are commonly required to place all orders through the purchasing department. In such cases the function of the several department managers in the purchasing procedure is to inform the purchasing department of their needs. Each manager performs this function by preparing in triplicate and signing a business paper called a *purchase requisition.* On the requisition the manager lists the merchandise needs of his or her department. The original and a duplicate copy of the purchase requisition are sent to the purchasing department. The third copy is retained by the requisitioning department as a check on the purchasing department.

Purchase order

A *purchase order* is a business form used by the purchasing department in placing an order with a manufacturer or wholesaler. It authorizes the supplier to ship the merchandise ordered and takes the place of a typewritten letter placing the order. On receipt of a purchase requisition from a selling department, the purchasing department prepares four or more copies of the purchase order. The copies are distributed as follows:

Copy 1, the original copy, is sent to the supplier as a request to purchase and as authority to ship the merchandise listed.

Copy 2, with a copy of the purchase requisition attached, is sent to the accounting department where it will ultimately be used in approving the invoice of the purchase for payment.

Copy 3 is sent to the department issuing the requisition to acknowledge the requisition and tell the action taken.

Copy 4 is retained on file by the purchasing department.

Invoice

An *invoice* is an itemized statement of goods bought and sold. It is prepared by the seller or *vendor,* and to the seller it is a sales invoice. However, when the same invoice is received by the buyer or *vendee,* it becomes a purchase invoice to the buyer. Upon receipt of a purchase order, the manufacturer or wholesaler receiving the order ships the ordered merchandise to the buyer and mails a copy of the invoice covering the shipment. The goods are delivered to the buyer's receiving department. The invoice is sent directly to the buyer's accounting department.

Receiving report

Most large companies maintain a special department assigned the duty of receiving all merchandise or other assets purchased. As each shipment is received, counted, and checked, the receiving department prepares four or more copies of a *receiving report.* On this report are listed the quantity, description, and condition of the items received. The original copy is sent to the accounting department. The second copy is sent to the department that requisitioned the merchandise. The third copy is sent to the purchasing department. The fourth copy is retained on file in the receiving department. The copies sent to the purchasing and requisitioning departments act as notification of the arrival of the goods.

Invoice approval form

When the receiving report arrives in the accounting department, it has in its possession copies of the—

1. Requisition listing the items that were to be ordered.
2. Purchase order that lists the merchandise actually ordered.
3. Invoice showing quantity, description, unit price, and total of the goods shipped by the seller.
4. Receiving report that lists quantity and condition of the items received.

With the information of these papers, the accounting department is in position to approve the invoice for entry on the books and ultimate payment. In approving the invoice, the accounting department checks and compares the information on all the papers. To facilitate the checking procedure and to ensure that no step is omitted, an *invoice approval form* is commonly used. This may be a separate business paper that is attached to the invoice, or the information shown in Illustration 7–1 may be stamped directly on the invoice with a rubber stamp.

As each step in the checking procedure is completed, the clerk

INVOICE APPROVAL FORM

Purchase Order Number _____

Requisition Check _____

Purchase Order Check _____

Receiving Report Check _____

Invoice Check

    Price Approval _____

    Calculations _____

    Terms _____

Approved for Payment:

    _____

Illustration 7–1

making the check initials the invoice approval form. Initials in each space on the form indicate the following:

1. Requisition Check . . . . The items on the invoice agree with the requisition and were requisitioned.
2. Purchase Order Check . . . . The items on the invoice agree with the purchase order and were ordered.
3. Receiving Report Check . . . . . The items on the invoice agree with the receiving report and were received.
4. Invoice Check:
   Price Approval . . . . The invoice prices are the agreed prices.
   Calculations . . . . The invoice has no mathematical errors.
   Terms . . . . The terms are the agreed terms.

The voucher

When a voucher system is in use, after the invoice is checked and approved, a *voucher* is prepared. A voucher is a business paper on which a transaction is summarized, its correctness certified, and its recording and payment approved. Vouchers vary somewhat from company to company. However, in general they are so designed that the invoice, bill, or other documents from which they are prepared are attached to and folded inside the voucher. This makes for ease in filing. The inside of a voucher is shown in Illustration 7–2, and the outside in Illustration 7–3. The preparation of a voucher is a simple task requiring only that a clerk enter the required information in the proper blank spaces on a voucher form. The information is taken from the invoice and its supporting documents. After the voucher is completed, the invoice and its supporting documents are attached to and folded inside the voucher. The voucher is then sent to the desk of the chief clerk or auditor who makes an additional check, approves the accounting distribution (the accounts to be debited), and approves the voucher for recording.

After being approved and recorded, a voucher is filed until its due date, when it is sent to the office of the company cashier or other disbursing officer for payment. Here the person responsible for issuing checks depends upon the approved voucher and its signed supporting documents to verify that the obligation is a proper obligation, properly incurred, and should be paid. For example, the purchase requisition and purchase order attached to the voucher confirm that the purchase

Voucher No. ___767___

VALLEY SUPPLY COMPANY
Eugene, Oregon

Date ___Oct. 1, 19--___
Pay to ___A.B. Seay Wholesale Company___
City ___Salem___   State ___Oregon___

For the following: (attach all invoices and supporting papers)

Date of Invoice	Terms	Invoice Number and Other Details	Amount
Sept. 30,19--	2/10,n/60	Invoice No. C-11756 Less Discount Net Amount Payable	800.00 16.00 784.00

Payment Approved

W. O. Neal
Auditor

Illustration 7–2
Inside of a voucher

was authorized. The receiving report shows that the items were received, and the invoice approval form verifies that the invoice was checked for errors. As a result, there is little chance for fraud, unless all the documents were stolen and the signatures forged, or there was collusion.

THE VOUCHER SYSTEM AND EXPENSES

Under a voucher system, to gain control over disbursements, every obligation that will result in a cash disbursement must be approved for payment and recorded as a liability at the time it is incurred. This includes all expenses. As a result, for example, when the monthly telephone bill is received, it is verified and any long-distance calls are approved. A voucher is then prepared, and the telephone bill is attached to and folded inside the voucher. The voucher is then recorded, and a check is issued in its payment, or the voucher is filed for payment at a later date.

Voucher No. _767_

ACCOUNTING DISTRIBUTION

Account Debited	Amount
Purchases	800.00
Freight-In	
Store Supplies	
Office Supplies	
Sales Salaries	

Due Date ___October 6, 19--___

Pay to ___A.B. Seay Wholesale Co.___
City ___Salem___
State ___Oregon___

Total Vouch. Pay.Cr.	800.00

Summary of Charges:
Total Charges _____ 800.00
Discount _____ 16.00
Net Payment _____ 784.00

Record of Payment:
Paid _____
Check No. _____

Illustration 7–3
Outside of a voucher

Requiring that an expense be approved for payment and recorded as an expense and a liability at the time it is incurred helps ensure that every expense payment is approved when information for its approval is available. Often invoices, bills, and statements for such things as equipment repairs are received weeks after the work is done. If no record of the repairs exists, it is difficult at that time to determine whether the invoice or bill is a correct statement of the amount owed. Also, if no records exist, it is possible for a dishonest employee to arrange with an outsider for more than one payment of an obligation, for payment of excessive amounts, and for payment for goods and services not received, all with kickbacks to the dishonest employee.

RECORDING VOUCHERS

Normally a company large enough to use a voucher system will use bookkeeping machines or punched cards, magnetic tape, and a computer in recording its transactions. Consequently, for this reason and also because the primary purpose of this discussion is to describe the control techniques of a voucher system, a pen-and-ink system of recording vouchers is not described here. However, such a system is described in the Appendix at the end of this chapter.

THE PETTY CASH FUND

A basic principle in controlling cash disbursements is that all such disbursements be made by check. However, an exception to this rule is made for petty cash disbursements. Every business must make many small payments for items such as postage, express charges, telegrams, and small items of supplies. If each such payment is made by check, many checks for immaterial amounts are written. This is both time consuming and expensive. Therefore, to avoid writing checks for small amounts, a petty cash fund is established, and such payments are made from this fund.

When a petty cash fund is established, an estimate is made of the total small payments likely to be disbursed during a short period, usually not more than a month. A check is drawn and debited to the Petty Cash account for an amount slightly in excess of this estimate. The check is cashed and the money is turned over to a member of the office staff who is designated *petty cashier* and who is responsible for the petty cash and for making payments therefrom.

The petty cashier usually keeps the petty cash in a locked box in the office safe. As each disbursement is made, a *petty cash receipt,* Illustration 7–4, is signed by the person receiving payment. The receipt is entered in the *Petty Cash Record* (Illustration 7–6) and then placed with the remaining money in the petty cashbox. Under this system, the petty cashbox should always contain paid petty cash receipts and money equal to the amount of the fund.

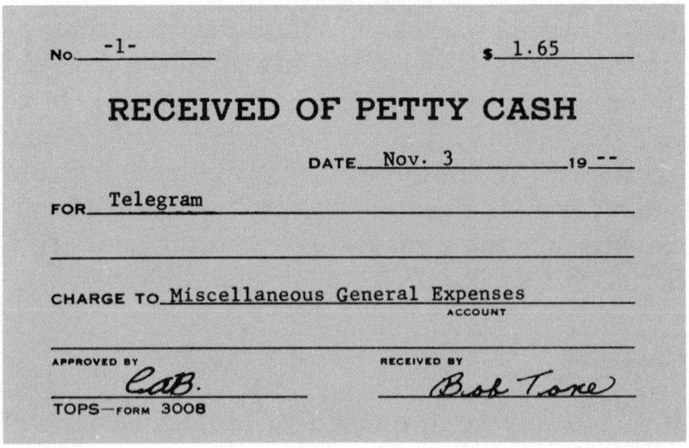

No. -1- $ 1.65

RECEIVED OF PETTY CASH

DATE Nov. 3 19 --

FOR Telegram

CHARGE TO Miscellaneous General Expenses
ACCOUNT

APPROVED BY CaB. RECEIVED BY Bob Tone

TOPS—FORM 3008

Courtesy Tops Business Forms

Illustration 7–4

Each disbursement reduces the money and increases the sum of the receipts in the petty cashbox. When the money is nearly exhausted, the fund is reimbursed. To reimburse the fund, the petty cashier presents the receipts for petty cash payments to the company cashier who retains the receipts and gives the petty cashier a check for their sum. When this check is cashed and the proceeds returned to the petty cashbox, the money in the box is restored to its original amount and the fund is ready to begin anew the cycle of its operations.

PETTY CASH FUND ILLUSTRATED

To avoid writing numerous checks for small amounts, a company established a petty cash fund, designating one of its office clerks, Ned Fox, petty cashier. A check for $35 was drawn, cashed, and the proceeds turned over to this clerk. The entry to record the check is shown in Illustration 7–5. The effect of the entry was to transfer $35 from the regular Cash account to the Petty Cash account.

Cash Disbursements Journal

Date	Ch. No.	Payee	Account Debited	P R	Other Accts. Debit	Cash Credit
Nov. 1	58	Ned Fox, Petty Cashier	Petty Cash...........		35.00	35.00

Illustration 7–5

The Petty Cash account is debited when the fund is established. It is not debited or credited again unless the size of the fund is changed. If the fund is exhausted and reimbursements occur too often, the fund should be increased. This results in an additional debit to the Petty Cash account and a credit to the regular Cash account for the amount of the increase. If the fund is too large, part of its cash should be returned to general cash.

During the first month of the illustrated fund's operation, the following petty cash payments were made:

Nov. 3	Telegram	$ 1.65
7	Purchased paper clips	0.50
12	Express on purchases	3.75
18	Postage on sale	3.80
19	Food for employee working overtime......	3.60
20	Purchased postage stamps	10.00
21	Express on purchases	2.80
27	Repair of typewriter	7.50
	Total	$33.60

Petty Cash Record

Date	Explanation	Re-ceipt No.	Receipts	Payments	Distribution of Payments			Miscellaneous Payments	
					Postage	Freight-In	Misc. General Expense	Account	Amount
Nov. 1	Established fund (Ch. No. 58)		35.00						
3	Telegram	1		1.65			1.65		
7	Purchased paper clips	2		.50				Office supplies	.50
12	Express on purchases	3		3.75		3.75			
18	Postage on sale	4		3.80				Delivery expense	3.80
19	Overtime meals	5		3.60			3.60		
20	Purchased postage stamps	6		10.00	10.00				
21	Express on purchases	7		2.80		2.80			
27	Repair of typewriter	8		7.50			7.50		
27	Totals		35.00	33.60	10.00	6.55	12.75		4.30
27	Balance			1.40					
	Totals		35.00	35.00					
Nov. 27	Balance		1.40						
27	Replenished fund (Ch. No. 106)		33.60						

Illustration 7-6

As each amount was disbursed, a petty cash receipt was signed by the person receiving payment. Each receipt was then recorded in the Petty Cash Record and placed in the petty cashbox. The Petty Cash Record with the paid receipts entered is shown in Illustration 7–6.

The Petty Cash Record is a supplementary record and not a book of original entry. A book of original entry is a journal or register from which postings are made. A supplementary record is one in which information is summarized but not posted. Rather, the summarized information is used as a basis for an entry in a regular journal or register, which is posted.

To continue the illustration, on November 27, after the last of the listed payments was made, only $1.40 in money remained in the fund. The petty cashier recognized that this would probably not cover another payment, so he gave his $33.60 of paid petty cash receipts to the company cashier in exchange for a $33.60 check to replenish the fund. On receiving the check, he ruled and balanced his Petty Cash Record (see Illustration 7–6) and entered the amount of the replenishing check. He then cashed the check and was ready to begin anew payments from the fund.

The reimbursing check was recorded in the Cash Disbursements Journal with the second entry of Illustration 7–7. Information for this entry was secured from a summarization of the entries in the Petty Cash Record. Its debits are to accounts affected by payments from the fund. Note that such an entry is necessary to get debits into the accounts for amounts paid from a petty cash fund. Consequently, petty cash must be reimbursed at the end of each accounting period, as well as at any time the money in the fund is low. If the fund is not reimbursed at the end of each accounting period, the asset petty cash is overstated and the expenses and assets of the petty cash payments are understated on the financial statements.

Cash Disbursements Journal

Date	Ch. No.	Payee	Account Debited	P R	Other Accts. Debit	Cash Credit
Nov. 1	58	Ned Fox, Petty Cashier	Petty Cash............		35.00	35.00
Nov. 27	106	Ned Fox, Petty Cashier	Postage		10.00	
			Freight-In		6.55	
			Misc. Gen. Expenses ..		12.75	
			Office Supplies		.50	
			Delivery Expense		3.80	33.60

Illustration 7–7

Many companies use a Petty Cash Record like the one described here. Other companies are of the opinion that such a record is unnecessary. In the latter, when the petty cash fund is reimbursed, the petty cashier sorts the paid petty cash receipts into groups according to the expense or other accounts to be debited in recording payments from the fund. Each group is then totaled, and a summary of the totals is used in making the reimbursing entry.

Occasionally, at the time of a petty cash expenditure a petty cashier will forget to secure a receipt and by the time the fund is reimbursed will have forgotten the expenditure. This causes the fund to be short. If at reimbursement time the petty cash fund is short and no errors or omitted entries can be found, the shortage is entered in the Petty Cash Record as a payment in the Miscellaneous Payments column. It is then recorded as an expense in the reimbursing entry with a debit to the Cash Over and Short account discussed in the next section.

CASH OVER AND SHORT

Regardless of care exercised in making change, customers are sometimes given too much change or are shortchanged. As a result, at the end of a day the actual cash from a cash register is commonly not equal to the cash sales "rung up" on the register. When this occurs and, for example, actual cash as counted is $557 but the register shows cash sales of $556, the entry in general journal form to record sales and the overage is:

Nov.	23	Cash	557.00	
		Cash Over and Short		1.00
		Sales		556.00
		Day's cash sales and overage.		

If, on the other hand, cash is short, the entry in general journal form to record sales and the shortage is:

Nov.	24	Cash	621.00	
		Cash Over and Short	4.00	
		Sales		625.00
		Day's cash sales and shortage.		

Over a period of time cash overages should about equal cash shortages. However, customers are more prone to report instances in which they are given too little change. Therefore, amounts of cash short are apt to be greater than amounts of cash over. Consequently, the *Cash Over and Short account* normally reaches the end of the accounting period with a debit balance. When it does so, the balance represents an expense. The expense may appear on the income statement as a separate item in the general and administrative expense section. Or if the amount is small, it may be combined with other miscellaneous expenses and appear as part of the item, miscellaneous expenses. When Cash Over and Short reaches the end of the period with a credit balance, the balance represents revenue and normally appears on the income statement as part of the item, miscellaneous revenues.

RECONCILING THE BANK BALANCE

Once each month banks furnish each commercial depositor a bank statement which shows (1) the balance of the depositor's account at the beginning of the month; (2) checks and any other amounts deducted from the account; (3) deposits and any other amounts added to the account; and (4) the account balance at the end of the month, according to the records of the bank. A bank statement is shown in Illustration 7–8.

MERCHANT'S NATIONAL BANK
Eugene, Oregon

STATEMENT OF ACCOUNT

BALANCE BROUGHT FORWARD		STATEMENT OF BALANCE		CHECKS RETURNED
Date	Balance	Date	Balance	
9/30/ --	1,578.00	10/31/ --	2,050.00	8

Valley Company .
10th and Pine Sts.
Eugene, Oregon

CHECKS IN DETAIL				DEPOSITS		DATE		BALANCE	
DM	3 00					10	1	1575	00
	55 00	200	00			10	2	1520	00
	120 00			240	00	10	5	1200	00
		75	00	150	00	10	6	1440	00
	25 00			180	00	10	10	1490	00
		50	00			10	18	1670	00
	10 00	135	00	100	00	10	23	1610	00
		DM 20	00			10	25	1575	00
				CM 495	00	10	28	1555	00
						10	30	2050	00

If no error is reported within ten days this account will be considered correct.

Illustration 7–8

Banks commonly mail a depositor's bank statement. Included in the envelope with the statement are the depositor's *canceled checks* and any debit or credit memoranda that have affected the account. The checks returned are the ones the bank has paid during the month. They are called canceled checks because they are canceled by stamping or punching to show that they have been paid. During any month, in addition to the checks the depositor has drawn, the bank may deduct from the depositor's account amounts for service charges, items deposited that are uncollectible, and for errors. The bank notifies the depositor of each such deduction with a debit memorandum. A copy of the memorandum is always included with the monthly statement. The bank may also add amounts to the depositor's account for errors and for amounts collected for the depositor. A credit memorandum is used to notify of any additions.

If all receipts are deposited intact and all payments, other than petty cash payments, are made by check, the bank statement becomes a device for proving the depositor's cash records. The proof normally begins with the preparation of a *reconciliation of the bank balance.*

Need for reconciling the bank balance

Normally, when the bank statement arrives, the balance of cash as shown by the statement does not agree with the balance shown by the depositor's accounting records. Consequently, in order to prove the accuracy of both the depositor's records and those of the bank, it is necessary to *reconcile* and account for any differences between the two balances.

Numerous things may cause the bank statement balance to differ from the depositor's book balance of cash. Some are the following:

1. *Outstanding checks.* These are checks that have been drawn by the depositor and deducted on the depositor's records but have not reached the bank for payment and deduction.
2. *Unrecorded deposits.* Concerns often make deposits at the end of each business day, after the bank has closed. These deposits are made in the bank's night depository and are not recorded by the bank until the next business day. Consequently, if a deposit is placed in the night depository the last day of the month, it does not appear on the bank statement for that month.
3. *Charges for service and uncollectible items.* A bank often deducts amounts from a depositor's account for services rendered and for items deposited that it is unable to collect. Insufficient funds checks are the most common of the latter. The bank notifies the depositor of each such deduction with a debit memorandum. If the item is material in amount, the memorandum is mailed to the depositor on the day of the deduction. Furthermore, in a well-managed com-

pany, each such deduction is recorded on the day the memorandum is received. However, occasionally there are unrecorded amounts near the end of the month.

4. *Collections.* Banks often act as collecting agents for their depositors, collecting for a small fee promissory notes and other items. When an item such as a promissory note is collected, the bank usually adds the proceeds to the depositor's account. It then sends a credit memorandum as notification of the transaction. As soon as the memorandum is received, it should be recorded. Occasionally, there are unrecorded amounts near the end of the month.

5. *Errors.* Regardless of care and systems of internal control for automatic error detection, both the bank and the depositor make errors that affect the bank balance. Occasionally, these errors are not discovered until the balance is reconciled.

Steps in reconciling the bank balance

The steps in reconciling the bank balance are the following:

1. Compare the deposits listed on the bank statement with deposits shown in the accounting records. Note any discrepancies and discover which is correct. List any errors or unrecorded items.

2. When canceled checks are returned by the bank, they are in a stack in the order of their listing on the bank statement. While the checks are in this order, compare each with its bank statement listing. Note any discrepancies or errors.

3. Rearrange the returned checks in numerical order, the order in which they were written. Secure the previous month's reconciliation and determine if any checks outstanding at the end of the previous month are still outstanding. If there are any, list them. Also, see that any deposits that were unrecorded by the bank at the end of the previous month have been recorded.

4. Insert among the canceled checks any bank memoranda according to their dates. Compare each check with its entry in the accounting records. Note for correction any discrepancies, and list any unpaid checks or unrecorded memoranda.

5. Prepare a reconciliation of the bank statement balance with the book balance of cash. Such a reconciliation is shown in Illustration 7–9.

6. Determine if any debits or credits appearing on the bank statement are unrecorded in the books of account. Make journal entries to record them.

ILLUSTRATION OF A BANK RECONCILIATION

To illustrate a bank reconciliation, assume that Valley Company found the following when it attempted to reconcile its bank balance of October 31. The bank balance as shown by the bank statement was $2,050, and the cash balance according to the accounting records was $1,373. Check No. 124 for $150 and Check No. 126 for $200 were outstanding and unpaid by the bank. A $145 deposit, placed in the bank's night depository after banking hours on October 31, was unrecorded by the bank. Among the returned checks was a credit memorandum showing the bank had collected a note receivable for the company on October 30, crediting the proceeds, $500 less a $5 collection fee, to the company account. Also returned with the bank statement was a $3 debit memorandum for checks printed by the bank and a NSF (not sufficient funds) check for $20. This check had been received from a customer, Frank Jones, on October 25, and had been included in that day's deposit. The collection of the note, the return of the NSF check, and the check printing charge were unrecorded on the company books. The statement reconciling these amounts is shown in Illustration 7–9.

Valley Company
Bank Reconciliation as of October 31, 19—

Book balance of cash		$1,373	Bank statement balance		$2,050
Add:			Add:		
Proceeds of note less			Deposit of 10/31		145
collection fee...........		495			$2,195
		$1,868			
Deduct:			Deduct:		
NSF check of Frank Jones ...	$20		Outstanding checks:		
Check printing charge	3	23	No. 124	$150	
			No. 126	200	350
Reconciled balance		$1,845	Reconciled balance		$1,845

Illustration 7–9

A bank reconciliation helps locate any errors made by either the bank or the depositor. It discloses any items which have been entered on the company books but have not come to the bank's attention. Also, it discloses items that should be recorded on the company books but are unrecorded on the date of the reconciliation. For example, in the reconciliation illustrated, the reconciled cash balance, $1,845, is the true cash balance. However, at the time the reconciliation is completed, Valley Company's accounting records show a $1,373 book balance. Consequently, entries must be made to adjust the book balance, increasing it to the true cash balance. This requires three entries. The first in general journal form is:

Nov.	2	Cash	495.00	
		Collection Expense	5.00	
		Notes Receivable		500.00
		To record the proceeds and collection		
		charge of a note collected by the bank.		

This entry is self-explanatory. The bank collected a note receivable, deducted a collection fee, and deposited the difference to the Valley Company account. The entry increases the amount of cash on the books, records the collection expense, and reduces notes receivable.

The second entry is:

Nov.	2	Accounts Receivable—Frank Jones	20.00	
		Cash		20.00
		To charge back the NSF check received		
		from Frank Jones.		

This entry records the NSF check returned as uncollectible. The check was received from Jones in payment of his account and was deposited as cash. The bank, unable to collect the check, deducted $20 from the Valley Company account. This made it necessary for the company to reverse the entry made when the check was received. After recording the returned check, the company will endeavor to collect the $20 from Jones. If after all legal means of collection have been exhausted and the company is still unable to collect, the amount will be written off as a bad debt. (Bad debts are discussed in the next chapter.)

The third entry debits the check printing charge to Miscellaneous General Expenses and in general journal form is:

Nov.	2	Miscellaneous General Expenses	3.00	
		Cash		3.00
		Check printing charge.		

OTHER INTERNAL CONTROL PROCEDURES

Internal control procedures apply to every phase of a company's operations from purchases through sales, cash receipts, cash disbursements, and the control of plant assets. Many of these procedures are discussed in later chapters. However, the way in which a company can gain control over purchases discounts can be discussed here where there is time and space for problems illustrating the technique.

Recall that thus far the following entries in general journal form have been used in recording the receipt and payment of an invoice for merchandise purchased.

Oct.	2	Purchases	1,000.00	
		Accounts Payable		1,000.00
		Purchased merchandise, terms 2/10, n/60.		
	12	Accounts Payable	1,000.00	
		Purchases Discounts		20.00
		Cash		980.00
		Paid the invoice of October 2.		

The invoice of these entries was recorded at its *gross*, $1,000, amount. This is the way in which invoices are recorded in many companies. However, well-managed companies follow the practice of taking all offered cash discounts. In many of these companies invoices are recorded at their *net*, after discount amounts. To illustrate, a company that records invoices at net amounts purchased merchandise having a $1,000 invoice price, terms 2/10, n/60. On receipt of the goods, it deducted the offered $20 discount from the gross invoice amount and recorded the purchase with this entry:

Oct.	2	Purchases	980.00	
		Accounts Payable		980.00
		Purchased merchandise on credit.		

If the invoice for this purchase is paid within the discount period (all invoices should be so paid), the cash disbursements entry to record the payment has a debit to Accounts Payable and a credit to Cash for $980. However, if payment is not made within the discount period and the discount is *lost*, an entry like the following must be made in the General Journal either before or when the invoice is paid:

Dec.	1	Discounts Lost.............................	20.00	
		Accounts Payable		20.00
		To record the discount lost.		

A check for the full $1,000 invoice amount is then drawn, recorded, and mailed to the creditor.

Advantage of the net method

When invoices are recorded at gross amounts, the amount of discounts taken is deducted from the balance of the Purchases account on the income statement to arrive at the cost of merchandise purchased. However, when invoices are recorded at gross amounts, if through oversight or carelessness discounts are lost, the amount of discounts lost does not appear in any account or on the income statement and may not come to the attention of management. On the other hand, when purchases are recorded at net amounts, the amount of discounts taken does not appear on the income statement. However, the amount of discounts lost is called to management's attention through the appearance on the income statement of the expense account, Discounts Lost, as in the condensed income statement of Illustration 7–10.

XYZ Company
Income Statement for Year Ended December 31, 19—

Sales	$100,000
Cost of goods sold	60,000
Gross profit from sales	$ 40,000
Operating expenses	28,000
Income from operations	$ 12,000
Other revenues and expenses:	
Discounts lost	(150)
Net income	$ 11,850

Illustration 7–10

Of the two methods, recording invoices at their net amounts probably supplies management with the more valuable information, the amount of discounts lost through oversight, carelessness, or other cause. It also gives management better control over the work of the people responsible for taking cash discounts. If discounts are lost, someone must explain why. As a result, few discounts are lost through carelessness.

APPENDIX

RECORDING VOUCHERS, PEN-AND-INK SYSTEM

When a voucher system is in use, an account called Vouchers Payable replaces the Accounts Payable account described in previous chapters. And, for every transaction that will result in a cash disbursement, a voucher is prepared and credited to this account. For example, when merchandise is purchased, the voucher covering the transaction is recorded with a debit to Purchases and a credit to Vouchers Payable. Likewise, when a plant asset is purchased or an expense is incurred, the voucher of the transaction is recorded with a debit to the proper plant asset or expense account and a credit to Vouchers Payable.

In a pen-and-ink system, vouchers are recorded in a *Voucher Register* similar to Illustration 7A–1. Such a register has a Vouchers Payable credit column and a number of debit columns. The exact debit columns vary from company to company, but merchandising concerns always provide a Purchases debit column. Also, as long as space is available, special debit columns are provided for transactions that occur frequently. In addition, an Other Accounts debit column is provided for transactions that do not occur often.

In recording vouchers in a register like that of Illustration 7A–1, all information about each voucher, other than information about its payment, is entered as soon as the voucher is approved for recording. The information as to payment date and the number of the paying check is entered later as each voucher is paid.

In posting a Voucher Register like that in Illustration 7A–1, the columns are first totaled and crossfooted to prove their equality. The Vouchers Payable column total is then credited to the Vouchers Payable account. The totals of the Purchases, Freight-In, Sales Salaries

Page 32								Voucher
Date 19—	Voucher No.	Payee	When and How Paid		Vouchers Payable Credit	Purchases Debit	Freight-In Debit	
			Date	Check No.				
Oct. 1	767	A. B. Seay Co.	10/6	733	800.00	800.00		1
1	768	Daily Sentinel	10/9	744	53.00			2
2	769	Seaboard Supply Co.	10/12	747	235.00	155.00	10.00	3
6	770	George Smith	10/6	734	85.00			4
6	771	Frank Jones	10/6	735	95.00			5
6	772	George Roth	10/6	736	95.00			6
30	998	First National Bank	10/30	972	505.00			33
								34
30	999	Pacific Telephone Co.	10/30	973	18.00			35
31	1000	Tarbell Wholesale Co.			235.00	235.00		36
31	1001	Office Equipment Co.	10/31	974	195.00			37
31		Totals			5,079.00	2,435.00	156.00	38
					(213)	(511)	(514)	39
								40
								41

Illustration 7A–1

Expense, Advertising Expense, Delivery Expense, and Office Salaries Expense are debited to these accounts. None of the individual amounts in these columns are posted. However, the individual amounts in the Other Accounts column are posted as individual amounts and the column total is not posted.

THE UNPAID VOUCHERS FILE

When a voucher system is in use, some vouchers are paid as soon as they are recorded. Others must be filed until payment is due. As an aid in taking cash discounts, vouchers for which payment is not due are generally filed in an unpaid vouchers file under the dates on which they are to be paid.

The file of unpaid vouchers takes the place of a subsidiary Accounts Payable Ledger. Actually, the file is a subsidiary ledger of amounts owed creditors. Likewise, the Vouchers Payable account is in effect a controlling account controlling the unpaid vouchers file. Consequently, after posting is completed at the end of a month, the balance of the Vouchers Payable account should equal the sum of the unpaid vouchers in the unpaid vouchers file. This is verified each month by preparing a schedule or an adding machine list of the unpaid vouchers in the file and comparing its total with the balance of the Vouchers

Register							Page 32
Sales Salaries Expense Debit	Adver- tising Expense Debit	Delivery Expense Debit	Office Salaries Expense Debit	Other Accounts Debit			
				Account Name	Post. Ref.	Amount Debit	
1							
2	53.00						
3				Store Supplies	117	70.00	
4			85.00				
5	95.00						
6	95.00						
33				Notes Payable	211	500.00	
34				Interest Expense	721	5.00	
35				Telephone Expense	655	18.00	
36							
37				Office Equipment	134	195.00	
38	740.00	115.00	358.00	340.00			935.00
39	(611)	(612)	(615)	(651)		(√)	
40							
41							

Payable account. In addition the unpaid vouchers in the file are compared with the unpaid vouchers shown in the Voucher Register's record of payments column. The number of each paying check and the payment date are entered in the Voucher Register's payments column as each voucher is paid. Consequently, the vouchers in the register without check numbers and payment dates should be the same as those in the unpaid vouchers file.

THE VOUCHER SYSTEM CHECK REGISTER

In a pen-and-ink voucher system, checks drawn in payment of vouchers are recorded in a simplified Check Register. It is simplified because under a voucher system no obligation is paid until a voucher covering the payment is prepared and recorded. Likewise, no check is drawn except in payment of a specific voucher. Consequently, all checks drawn result in debits to Vouchers Payable and credits to Cash, unless a discount must be recorded. Then there are credits to both Purchases Discounts and to Cash. Such a register is shown in Illustration 7A–2. Note that it has columns for debits to Vouchers Payable and credits to Purchases Discounts and to Cash. In posting, all amounts entered in these columns are posted in the column totals.

A Check Register like that shown in Illustration 7A–2 is used when vouchers are recorded at gross amounts because a column must be provided for the discounts taken when the vouchers are paid. However, when vouchers are recorded at net amounts, such a column is not

Check Register						
Date 19—	Payee	Voucher No.	Check No.	Vouchers Payable Debit	Purchases Discounts Credit	Cash Credit
Oct. 1	C. B. & Y. RR. Co.	765	728	14.00		14.00
3	Frank Mills	766	729	73.00		73.00
3	Ajax Wholesale Co.	753	730	250.00	5.00	245.00
4	Normal Supply Co.	747	731	100.00	2.00	98.00
5	Office Supply Co.	763	732	43.00		43.00
6	A. B. Seay Co.	767	733	800.00	16.00	784.00
6	George Smith	770	734	85.00		85.00
6	Frank Jones	771	735	95.00		95.00
30	First National Bank	998	972	505.00		505.00
30	Pacific Telephone Co.	999	973	18.00		18.00
31	Office Equipment Co.	1001	974	195.00		195.00
31	Totals			6,468,00	28.00	6,440.00
				(213)	(512)	(111)

Illustration 7A–2

needed because discounts are deducted before vouchers are recorded, rather than when they are paid. Consequently, when vouchers are recorded at net amounts, the Check Register used needs only one money column. The column is commonly headed "Vouchers Payable, Debit; Cash, Credit." At the end of a month its total is debited to Vouchers Payable and credited to Cash.

When invoices are recorded at net amounts and a discount is lost through error or oversight, the general journal entry to record the discount lost has a debit to Discounts Lost and a credit to Vouchers Payable.

PURCHASES RETURNS

Occasionally an item must be returned after the voucher recording its purchase has been prepared and entered in the Voucher Register. In such cases the return may be recorded with a general journal entry similar to the following:

Nov.	5	Vouchers Payable	15.00	
		Purchases Returns and Allowances		15.00
		Returned defective merchandise.		

In addition to the entry, the amount of the return is deducted on the voucher and the credit memorandum and other documents verifying the return are attached to the voucher. Then, when the voucher is paid, a check is drawn for its corrected amount.

GLOSSARY

Bank reconciliation. An analysis explaining the difference between an enterprise's book balance of cash and its bank statement balance.

Canceled checks. Checks paid by the bank and canceled by punching or stamping.

Cash Over and Short account. An account in which are recorded cash overages and cash shortages arising from making change.

Discounts lost. Cash discounts offered but not taken.

Gross method of recording invoices. Recording invoices at the full amount of the sale price without deducting offered cash discounts.

Internal controls system. The methods and procedures adopted by a business to control its operations and protest its assets from waste, fraud, and theft.

Invoice. A document listing items sold, together with prices, the customer's name, and the terms of sale.

Invoice approval form. A document used in checking an invoice and approving it for recording and payment.

Net method of recording invoices. Recording invoices at the full amount of the sale price less offered cash discounts.

Outstanding checks. Checks that have been written, recorded, and sent or given to payees but have not been received by the bank, paid, and returned.

Purchase order. A business form used in placing an order for the purchase of goods from a vendor.

Purchase requisition. A business form used within a business to ask the purchasing department of the business to buy needed items.

Receiving report. A form used within a business to notify the proper persons of the receipt of goods ordered and of the quantities and condition of the goods.

Reconcile. To account for the difference between two amounts

Vendee. The purchaser of something.

Vendor. The individual or enterprise selling something.

Voucher. A business paper used in summarizing a transaction and approving it for recording and payment.

Voucher Register. A book of original entry in which approved vouchers are recorded.

Voucher system. An accounting system used to control the incurrence and payment of obligations requiring the disbursement of cash.

QUESTIONS FOR CLASS DISCUSSION

1. Internal control procedures are important in every business, but at what stage in the development of a business do they become critical?
2. Name some of the broad principles of internal control.
3. Why should the person who keeps the record of an asset be a different person from the one responsible for custody of the asset?
4. Why should responsibility for a sequence of related transactions be divided among different departments or individuals?
5. In a small business it is sometimes impossible to separate the functions of record keeping and asset custody, and it is sometimes impossible to divide responsibilities for related transactions. What should be substituted for these control procedures?
6. What is meant by the phrase "all receipts should be deposited intact"? Why should all receipts be deposited intact on the day of receipt?
7. Why should a company's bookkeeper not be given responsibility for receiving cash for the company nor the responsibility for signing checks or making cash disbursements in any other way?

8. In purchasing merchandise in a large store, why are the department managers not permitted to deal directly with the sources of supply?

9. What are the duties of the selling department managers in the purchasing procedures of a large store?

10. Tell *(a)* who prepares, *(b)* who receives, and *(c)* the purpose of each of the following business papers:

   a. Purchase requisition.   *d.* Receiving report.

   b. Purchase order.   *e.* Invoice approval form.

   c. Invoice.   *f.* Voucher.

11. Do all companies need a voucher system? At what approximate point in a company's growth would you recommend the installation of such a system?

12. When a disbursing officer issues a check in a large business, he or she usually cannot know from personal contact that the assets, goods, or services for which the check pays were received by the business or that the purchase was properly authorized. However, if the company has an internal control system, the officer can depend on the system. Exactly what documents does the officer depend on to tell that the purchase was authorized and properly made and the goods were actually received?

13. Why are some cash payments made from a petty cash fund? Why are not all payments made by check?

14. What is a petty cash receipt? When a petty cash receipt is prepared, who signs it?

15. Explain how a petty cash fund operates.

16. Why must a petty cash fund be reimbursed at the end of each accounting period?

17. What are two results of reimbursing the petty cash fund?

18. What is a bank statement? What kind of information appears on a bank statement?

19. What is the meaning of the phrase "to reconcile"?

20. Why are the bank statement balance of cash and the depositor's book balance of cash reconciled?

21. What valuable information becomes readily available to management when invoices are recorded at net amounts? Is this information readily available when invoices are recorded at gross amounts?

CLASS EXERCISES

Exercise 7–1

A company established a $25 petty cash fund on July 5. Two weeks later, on July 19, there were in the fund $1.75 in cash and receipts for these expenditures: postage, $7.50; freight-in, $6.75; miscellaneous general expenses, $4; and office supplies, $5. Give in general journal form *(a)* the entry to establish the fund and *(b)* the entry to reimburse it. *(c)* Make the alternate assumption that since the fund was exhausted so quickly, it was not only reimbursed on July 19 but increased in size to $50, and give the entry to reimburse and increase the fund size.

Exercise 7–2

A company established a $50 petty cash fund on October 2, and on November 30 there were in the fund $22 in cash and receipts for the following expenditures: freight-in, $11; miscellaneous general expenses, $8; and office supplies, $6.50. The petty cashier could not account for the $2.50 shortage in the fund. Give in general journal form (a) the entry to establish the fund and (b) the November 30 entry to reimburse the fund and reduce it to $25.

Exercise 7–3

Western Shop deposits all receipts intact each day and makes all payments by check; and on November 30, after all posting was completed, its Cash account had a $1,420 debit balance; but its November 30 bank statement showed only $1,295 on deposit in the bank on that day. Prepare a bank reconciliation for Western Shop, using the following information:

a. Outstanding checks, $150.
b. The November 30 cash receipts, $315, were placed in the bank's night depository after banking hours on that date and were unrecorded by the bank.
c. Included with the November canceled checks returned by the bank was an unrecorded $5 debit memorandum for bank services.
c. Check No. 815 for store supplies was correctly drawn for $127 and paid by the bank, but it was erroneously recorded as though it were for $172.

Exercise 7–4

Prepare in general journal form any entries that Western Shop should make as a result of preparing the bank reconciliation of Exercise 7–3.

Exercise 7–5

Olive Company incurred $14,000 of operating expenses in August, a month in which it had $50,000 of sales. The company began August with a $26,000 merchandise inventory and ended the month with a $28,000 inventory. During the month it purchased merchandise having a $32,000 invoice price, all of which was subject to a 2% discount for prompt payment. The company took advantage of the discounts on $27,000 of purchases; but through an error in filing, it did not earn and could not take the discount on a $5,000 invoice paid on August 29.

Required:

1. Prepare an August income statement for the company under the assumption it records invoices at gross amounts.
2. Prepare a second income statement for the company under the assumption it records invoices at net amounts.

PROBLEMS

Problem 7–1

The following petty cash transactions were completed during November of the current year:

Nov. 1 Drew Check No. 543 payable to Ted Hall, Petty Cashier, to establish a $35 petty cash fund. Appointed Ted petty cashier and delivered the check and Petty Cash Record to him.

  5 Purchased postage stamps with petty cash funds, $7.50.

  8 Paid $6.50 COD delivery charges on merchandise purchased for resale.

  9 Paid $4.50 for minor repairs to an office machine.

  12 Gave Mrs. Walter Nash, wife of the owner of the business, $5 for cab fare.

  19 Paid $1.75 for a telegram.

  23 Paid $3.50 COD delivery charges on merchandise purchased for resale.

  26 Purchased office supplies with petty cash, $3.25.

  26 Drew Check No. 614 to reimburse the petty cash fund for expenditures and a $1 shortage.

Required:

Record the transactions in a Petty Cash Record and a Cash Disbursements Journal like the ones illustrated in this chapter. Balance and rule the Petty Cash Record before entering the replenishing check. Skip one line between entries in the Cash Disbursements Journal.

Problem 7–2

A company completed these petty cash transactions:

Oct. 4 Drew Check No. 214 to establish a $25 petty cash fund. Appointed June Cole, one of the office secretaries, petty cashier. Delivered the check and the Petty Cash Record to Ms. Cole.

  5 Paid $5 to have the office windows washed.

  8 Purchased postage stamps, $7.50.

  10 Paid $4.50 COD charges for the delivery of merchandise purchased for resale.

  11 Purchased carbon paper and paper clips, $6.25.

  11 Drew Check No. 235 to reimburse the petty cash fund, and because it had been exhausted so quickly, made the check sufficiently large to increase its size to $50.

  12 Joe Keller, the owner of the business, signed a petty cash receipt and took $1 from petty cash for coffee money.

  14 Paid $6.50 for minor repairs to an office typewriter.

  17 Paid $7.25 COD delivery charges on merchandise purchased for resale.

  23 Purchased postage stamps, $7.50.

Oct. 26 Paid $7.50 to Quick Printer for advertising circulars.

27 Paid a high school boy $5 to deliver the advertising circulars to prospective customers.

Nov. 3 Paid City Delivery Service $4.50 to deliver merchandise to a customer.

7 Paid $6 COD delivery charges on merchandise purchased for resale.

9 Drew Check No. 250 to reimburse the petty cash fund. There was $4.25 in cash in the fund and the petty cashier could not account for the shortage.

Required:

Record the transactions in a Petty Cash Record and, where required, in a Cash Disbursements Journal. Balance and rule the Petty Cash Record at the time of each reimbursement. Skip a line between each entry in the Cash Disbursements Journal.

Problem 7–3

Hillside Shop follows the practice of depositing all receipts intact and making payments by check. After all posting was completed, the balance of its Cash account on October 31 was $2,104.75. However, its bank statement of that date showed a $2,220.25 ending balance. The following information was available to reconcile the two amounts:

a. The September bank reconciliation showed two checks outstanding on September 30, No. 761 for $76.25 and No. 763 for $89.65. Check No. 763 was returned with the October bank statement, but Check No. 761 was not.

b. In comparing the October canceled checks with the entries in the accounting records, it was found that Check No. 799 was correctly drawn for $547 in payment for a new cash register. However, in recording this check the amount was transposed and it was recorded as though it were for $574.

c. It was also found that Checks No. 842 for $35.75 and No. 847 for $103.25, both written and recorded on October 28, were not among the canceled checks returned.

d. Two debit memoranda and a credit memorandum were included with the returned checks. None of the memoranda had been recorded at the time of the reconciliation. The first debit memorandum had a $65 NSF check written by a customer, Jay Neal, attached and had been used by the customer in paying his account. The second debit memorandum was a $3.25 memorandum for service charges. The credit memorandum was for $247 and represented the proceeds less a $3 collection fee from a $250 noninterest-bearing note collected for Hillside Shop by the bank.

e. The October 31 cash receipts, $305.50, had been placed in the bank's night depository after banking hours on that date; and, consequently, did not appear on the bank statement as a deposit.

Required:

1. Prepare an October 31 bank reconciliation for Hillside Shop.
2. Prepare general journal entries to record the information of the reconciliation.

Problem 7–4

Bluelake Company reconciled its bank balance on October 31 with two checks, No. 818 for $136 and No. 820 for $210, outstanding. The following information was available for the November 30 reconciliation:

		Bluelake Company 12 West 1st Street	Statement of account with FIRST NATIONAL BANK	
Date		Checks and Other Debits	Deposits	Balance
Nov.	1	Balance brought forward		2,215.00
	2	210.00	295.00	2,300.00
	3	175.00	244.00	2,369.00
	5	240.00	178.00	2,307.00
	9	562.00	270.00	2,015.00
	12	84.00 97.00		1,834.00
	14	42.00	127.00	1,919.00
	18	135.00	255.00	2,039.00
	21		365.00	2,404.00
	28	334.00	125.00	2,195.00
	29		245.00	2,440.00
	30	125.00 NSF 4.00 SC	497.00 CM	2,808.00

Code: CM Credit memorandum   NSF Not sufficient funds check
DM Debit memorandum   SC Service charge

Cash Receipts

Date		Cash Debit
Nov.	1	295.00
	2	244.00
	4	178.00
	7	270.00
	12	127.00
	17	255.00
	20	365.00
	26	125.00
	28	245.00
	30	285.00
		2,389.00

Cash Disbursements

Check No.	Cash Credit
821	175.00
822	240.00
823	84.00
824	42.00
825	562.00
826	97.00
827	124.00
828	185.00
829	334.00
830	105.00
	1,948.00

From the General Ledger
Cash

Date		Explanation	P R	Debit	Credit	Balance
Oct.	31	Balance	✓			1,869.00
Nov.	30		R8	2,389.00		4,258.00
	30		D9		1,948.00	2,310.00

Check No. 828 was correctly drawn for $135 in payment for store equipment; however, the bookkeeper misread its amount and recorded it as though it were for $185. The bank paid and deducted the correct $135 amount.

The NSF check was received from a customer, Roy Hall, in payment of his account. The credit memorandum resulted from a $500 noninterest-bearing note collected for Bluelake Company by the bank. The bank deducted a $3 fee for collecting the note. None of the memoranda, including the $4 for bank services, had been recorded.

Required:

1. Prepare a November 30 bank reconciliation for Bluelake Company.
2. Prepare in general journal form the entries required to bring the company's book balance for cash into agreement with the reconciled balance.

Problem 7–5

On November 30 the credit balance in the Sales account of Hurron Company showed it had sold $41,300 of merchandise during the month. The company had begun November with a $50,000 merchandise inventory and it ended the month with a $40,000 inventory, and it had $14,250 of operating expenses during the month. It had also recorded these transactions:

Nov. 1 Received merchandise purchased at a $3,000 invoice price, invoice dated October 29, terms 2/10, n/30.

5 Received merchandise purchased at a $5,000 invoice price, invoice dated November 3, terms 2/10, n/30.

7 Received a $500 credit memorandum (invoice price) for merchandise received on November 1 and returned for credit.

13 Paid the $5,000 invoice received on November 5, less the discount.

15 Received merchandise purchased at a $7,500 invoice price, invoice dated November 12, terms 2/10, n/30.

22 Paid the $7,500 invoice received on November 15, less the discount.

28 Paid the invoice received on November 1 and to which a $500 credit memorandum was attached. The invoice had been refiled in error, after the credit memorandum was attached on November 7, for payment on this date, the last day of its credit period.

Required:

1. Assume that Hurron Company records invoices at gross amounts and *(a)* prepare general journal entries to record the transactions. *(b)* Prepare a November income statement for the company.
2. Assume that the company records invoices at net amounts and *(a)* prepare a second set of journal entries to record the transactions. *(b)* Prepare a second income statement for the company under this assumption.

Problem 7–6

(This problem is based on information in the Appendix to this chapter.)

Kenton Company completed these transactions affecting vouchers payable:

Oct. 2 Prepared Voucher No. 817 payable to Driftwood Company for merchandise having a $1,250 invoice price, invoice dated September 29, terms FOB destination, 2/10, n/30.

Oct. 5   Prepared Voucher No. 818 payable to Surfside Company for merchandise having a $950 invoice price, invoice dated October 3, terms FOB Surfside Company's factory, 2/10, n/60. The vendor had prepaid the freight charges, $40, adding the amount to the invoice and bringing its total to $990.

   7   Received a credit memorandum for merchandise having a $250 invoice price. The merchandise was received on October 2, Voucher No. 817, and returned for credit.

   10   Prepared Voucher No. 819 to Office Supply Company for the purchase of office equipment having a $300 invoice price, terms n/10 EOM.

   13   Issued Check No. 817 in payment of the invoice of Voucher No. 818, less the discount.

   15   Prepared Voucher No. 820 payable to Payroll for sales salaries, $400, and office salaries, $200. Issued Check No. 818 in payment of the voucher. Cashed the check and paid the employees.

   21   Prepared Voucher No. 821 payable to Valley Sales for office supplies having a $150 invoice price, terms n/10 EOM.

   23   Prepared Voucher No. 822 payable to Beachside Company for merchandise having a $750 invoice price, invoice dated October 22, terms FOB the vendor's warehouse, 2/10, n/60. The vendor had prepaid the freight charges, $30, adding the amount to the invoice and bringing its total to $780.

   29   Discovered that Voucher No. 817 had been filed in error for payment on the last day of its credit period rather than the last day of its discount period, causing the discount to be lost. Issued Check No. 819 in payment of the voucher, less the return.

   30   Prepared Voucher No. 823 payable to *The Daily Gazette* for advertising, $150. Issued Check No. 820 in payment of the voucher.

   31   Prepared Voucher No. 824 payable to Payroll for sales salaries, $400, and office salaries, $200. Issued Check No. 821 in payment of the voucher. Cashed the check and paid the employees.

Required:

1. Prepare a Voucher Register, a Check Register, and a General Journal and record the transactions under the assumption Kenton Company records invoices at gross amounts.

2. Prepare a Vouchers Payable account and post those entry portions that affect the account.

3. Prove the balance of the Vouchers Payable account by preparing a schedule of unpaid vouchers.

Problem 7–7

(This problem is based on information in the Appendix of this chapter.)

1. Under the assumption that Kenton Company of Problem 7–6 records vouchers at net amounts, prepare a Voucher Register, a Check Register, and a General Journal and record the transactions of Problem 7–6 applying these special instructions in recording the October 29 transaction:

Oct. 29   Discovered that Voucher No. 817 had been filed in error for payment on the last day of its credit period rather than the last day of its discount period. Made a general journal entry to record the discount lost and issued Check No. 819 in payment of the voucher as adjusted for the return and the discount lost.

2. Prepare a Vouchers Payable account and post those entry portions that affect the account.

3. Prove the balance of the Vouchers Payable account by preparing a schedule of unpaid vouchers.

ALTERNATE PROBLEMS

Problem 7–1A

Robert West established a petty cash fund for his single proprietorship business and appointed Joe Marsh, a clerk in the office, petty cashier. The following petty cash transactions were then completed:

Oct. 2   Drew a $50 check, No. 165, payable to Joe Marsh, petty cashier, and delivered the check and Petty Cash Record to Joe.

   5   Paid $4.25 COD delivery charges on merchandise purchased for resale.

   6   Purchased postage stamps with petty cash, $15.

   8   Gave Mrs. West, wife of the business owner, $5 from petty cash for cab fare.

   10   Purchased carbon paper for office use, $4.50.

   13   Paid a service station attendant $3.50 upon delivery to the office of Mr. West's personal car, which the attendant had washed.

   15   Paid $5.50 COD delivery charges on merchandise purchased for resale.

   21   Paid $5 for minor repairs to an office typewriter.

   22   Paid City Delivery Service $3 to deliver merchandise sold to a customer.

   28   Paid City Delivery Service $2.50 to deliver merchandise sold to a customer.

   31   Drew Check No. 221 to reimburse the petty cash fund. There was $1 in cash in the fund and the petty cashier could not account for the shortage.

Required:

Record the transactions in a Petty Cash Record and, where required, in a Cash Disbursements Journal. Balance the Petty Cash Record before entering the replenishing check. Skip a line between entries in the Cash Disbursements Journal.

Problem 7–2A

Hilltop Sales completed these petty cash transactions:

Nov. 25   Drew Check No. 345 to establish a $25 petty cash fund, and appointed Jane Cory, the office secretary, petty cashier. Delivered the check and the Petty Cash Record to Ms. Cory.

Nov. 27 Paid $4.25 COD delivery charges on merchandise purchased for resale.
    29 Purchased carbon paper and other office supplies with petty cash, $6.
    30 Purchased postage stamps with petty cash, $7.50.
Dec. 3 Paid $5 to have the office windows washed.
     3 Drew Check No. 352 to reimburse the petty cash fund; and because the fund was so rapidly exhausted, made the check sufficiently large to increase the size of the fund to $50.
     6 Paid Speedy Delivery Service $3.50 to deliver merchandise sold to a customer.
     9 Paid the driver of Delux Cleaner's delivery truck $2.50 upon the delivery of cleaning Mr. Dale Mohr, owner of Hilltop Sales, had dropped off at the cleaners.
    14 Purchased postage stamps with petty cash, $7.50.
    17 Paid $4 COD delivery charges on merchandise purchased for resale.
    20 Gave Mrs. Mohr, wife of the business owner, $10 for cab fare and other personal expenses.
    22 Paid Speedy Delivery Service $3.25 to deliver merchandise sold to a customer.
    27 Paid $6.75 for minor repairs to an office typewriter.
    30 Paid $5.50 COD delivery charges on merchandise purchased for resale.
    31 Drew Check No. 380 to reimburse the petty cash fund at the end of the accounting period. There was $6.25 in cash in the fund, and the petty cashier could not account for the shortage.

Required:

Record the transactions in a Petty Cash Record and, where required, in a Cash Disbursements Journal. Balance the Petty Cash Record at the time of each reimbursement. Skip a line between entries in the Cash Disbursements Journal.

Problem 7–3A

Western Store's October 31 bank statement showed $1,735.75 on deposit on the last day of the month. The store follows the practice of depositing all receipts intact and paying all obligations with checks; and after posting was completed on the last day of October, its Cash account showed a $1,577 balance. The following information was available to reconcile the two amounts:

a. Checks No. 810 for $102.50 and No. 812 for $87.25 were outstanding on the September 30 bank reconciliation. Check No. 812 was returned with the October checks, but Check No. 810 was not.
b. In comparing the October canceled checks with the entries in the accounting records, it was found that Check No. 848 was correctly drawn for $142 in payment for several items of office supplies but had been recorded as though it were for $124. Also, Check No. 885 for $71.25 and Check No. 886 for $32.50, both drawn on October 31, were not among the canceled checks returned.
c. A debit memorandum with a $105.50 NSF check received from a customer,

Dale Green, on October 27 and deposited was among the canceled checks returned.

d. Also among the canceled checks was a $4.75 debit memorandum for bank services.

e. A credit memorandum enclosed with the bank statement indicated the bank had collected a $500 noninterest-bearing note for Western Store, deducted a $3.50 collection fee, and credited the remainder to the store's account. None of the memoranda enclosed with the canceled checks had been recorded.

f. The October 31 cash receipts of the store, $415.75, were placed in the bank's night depository after banking hours on October 31 and, consequently, did not appear on the bank statement as a deposit.

Required:

1. Prepare an October 31 bank reconciliation for Western Store.
2. Prepare in general journal form the entries the store would have to make to adjust its book balance of cash to the reconciled balance.

Problem 7–4A

South Company reconciled its bank balance on September 30 with two checks. No. 710 for $165 and No. 711 for $240, outstanding. The following information was available for the company's October 31 bank reconciliation:

		South Company 10 East 1st Street		*Statement of account with* THE SECURITY BANK	
Date		Checks and Other Debits		Deposits	Balance
Oct.	1	Balance brought forward			2,143.00
	2	240.00			1,903.00
	3	205.00		315.00	2,013.00
	5	175.00		295.00	2,133.00
	6	310.00			1,823.00
	12	190.00		425.00	2,058.00
	15	135.00	255.00	235.00	1,903.00
	22	260.00		535.00	2,178.00
	28	210.00	280.00	115.00	1,803.00
	30			550.00	2,353.00
	31	115.00 NSF	3.00 SC	396.00 CM	2,631.00
Code:		CM Credit memorandum DM Debit Memorandum		NSF Not sufficient funds check SC Service charge	

The NSF check returned was received from Earl Black in payment of his account. The credit memorandum resulted from a $400 noninterest-bearing note, less a $4 collection fee, which the bank had collected for South Company. None of the memoranda enclosed with the bank statement had been recorded.

Check No. 714 was correctly drawn for $190 in payment for office equipment. The bookkeeper had carelessly read the amount and had recorded the

Cash Receipts			Cash Disbursements		
Date		Cash Debit	Check No.		Cash Credit
Oct.	2	315.00	712		205.00
	4	295.00	713		310.00
	11	425.00	714		100.00
	14	235.00	715		175.00
	20	535.00	716		85.00
	27	115.00	717		135.00
	29	550.00	718		260.00
	31	220.00	719		280.00
		2,690.00	720		255.00
			721		210.00
			722		105.00
					2,120.00

From the General Ledger

Cash

Date	Explanation	P R	Debit	Credit	Balance
Sept. 30	Balance	✓			1,738.00
Oct. 31		R9	2,690.00		4,428.00
31		D8		2,120.00	2,308.00

check as though it were for $100. The bank had paid and deducted the correct $190 amount.

Required:

1. Prepare an October 31 bank reconciliation for South Company.
2. Prepare in general journal form the entries required to bring the company's book balance of cash into agreement with the reconciled balance.

Problem 7–5A

The October 31 credit balance in the Sales account of Northern Company showed it had sold $46,800 of merchandise during the month. The company began October with a $55,000 merchandise inventory and ended the month with a $43,000 inventory, and it had incurred $17,000 of operating expenses during the month. It had also recorded these transactions:

Oct. 2 Received merchandise purchased at a $6,500 invoice price, invoice dated September 30, terms 2/10, n/30.

6 Received a $1,000 credit memorandum (invoice price) for merchandise received on October 2 and returned for credit.

10 Received merchandise purchased at a $2,500 invoice price, invoice dated October 7, terms 2/10, n/30.

Oct. 14   Received merchandise purchased at a $7,500 invoice price, invoice dated October 12, terms 2/10, n/30.

  17   Paid for the merchandise received on October 10, less the discount.

  22   Paid for the merchandise received on October 14, less the discount.

  30   The invoice received on October 2 had been refiled in error, after the credit memorandum was attached, for payment on this, the last day of its credit period, causing the discount to be lost. Paid the invoice.

Required:

1. Assume the company records invoices at gross amounts and *(a)* prepare general journal entries to record the transactions. *(b)* Prepare an October income statement for the company.
2. Assume the company records invoices at net amounts and *(a)* prepare a second set of journal entries to record the transactions. *(b)* Prepare a second income statement for the company under this assumption.

Problem 7-6A

(This problem is based on information in the Appendix to this chapter.)

Huron Company completed these transactions affecting vouchers payable:

Nov. 1   Prepared Voucher No. 810 payable to Oak Company for merchandise having a $1,500 invoice price, invoice dated October 30, terms FOB the vendor's warehouse, 2/10, n/30. The vendor had prepaid the freight charges, $50, adding the amount to the invoice and bringing its total to $1,550.

  4   Prepare Voucher No. 811 payable to Office Outfitters for the purchase of office equipment having a $250 invoice price, terms n/10 EOM.

  6   Received a credit memorandum for merchandise having a $500 invoice price. The merchandise was received on November 1, Voucher No. 810, and returned for credit.

  9   Prepared Voucher No. 812 payable to Kenton Company for merchandise having a $750 invoice price, invoice dated November 7, terms FOB Kenton Company's warehouse, 2/10, n/30.

  9   Prepared Voucher No. 813 payable to Western Truck Lines for freight charges on the shipment of Voucher No. 812, $50. Issued Check No. 810 in payment of the voucher.

  14   Prepared Voucher No. 814 payable to Dale Sales Company for the purchase of office supplies having a $35 invoice price, terms n/10 EOM.

  17   Issued Check No. 811 in payment of the invoice of Voucher No. 812, less the discount.

  24   Prepared Voucher No. 815 payable to Driftwood Company for merchandise having an $850 invoice price, invoice dated November 22, terms FOB the vendor's factory, 2/10, n/60. The vendor had prepaid the freight charges, $45, adding the amount to the invoice and bringing it's total to $895.

Nov. 29   Discovered that Voucher No. 810 had been filed in error for payment
          on this date rather than the last day of its discount period, causing
          the discount to be lost. Issued Check No. 812 in payment of the
          voucher, less the return.

    30   Prepared Voucher No. 816 payable to *The Morning Star* for advertis-
          ing, $80. Issued Check No. 813 in payment of the voucher.

    30   Prepared Voucher No. 817 payable to Payroll for sales salaries, $800,
          and office salaries, $425. Issued Check No. 814 in payment of the
          voucher. Cashed the check and paid the employees.

Required:

1. Prepare a Voucher Register, a Check Register, and a General Journal and
   record the transactions under the assumption Huron Company records invoices at gross amounts.
2. Prepare a Vouchers Payable account and post those entry portions that
   affect the account.
3. Prove the balance of the Vouchers Payable account by preparing a schedule
   of unpaid vouchers.

Problem 7–7A

(This problem is based on information in the Appendix of this chapter.)

1. Under the assumption that Huron Company of Problem 7–6A records
   vouchers at net amounts, prepare a Voucher Register, a Check Register,
   and a General Journal and record the transactions of Problem 7–6A, applying
   these special instructions in recording the November 29 transaction:

   Nov. 29   Discovered that Voucher No. 810 had been filed in error for pay-
             ment on the last day of its credit period rather than the last day
             of its discount period. Made a general journal entry to record
             the discount lost and issued Check No. 812 in payment of the
             voucher less the return and discount lost.

2. Prepare a Vouchers Payable account and post the entry portions that affect
   the account.
3. Prove the balance of the Vouchers Payable account by preparing a schedule
   of unpaid vouchers.

PROVOCATIVE PROBLEMS

Provocative problem 7–1
Vagabond Trailer Company

Vagabond Trailer Company, a manufacturer of travel trailers, began operations in a very small way 15 years ago and has since grown rapidly in size.
Last year its sales were in excess of $5 million. However, its purchasing proce-
dures have not kept pace with its growth. When a plant supervisor or department head needs raw materials, plant assets, or supplies, he or she tells the
purchasing department manager by phone or in person. The purchasing department manager prepares a purchase order in duplicate, sends one copy

to the company selling the goods, and keeps the other copy in the files. When the invoice arrives, it is sent directly to the purchasing department; and when the goods arrive, receiving department personnel count and inspect the items and prepare one copy of a receiving report which is sent to the purchasing department. The purchasing department manager attaches the receiving report and the retained copy of the purchase order to the invoice; and if all is in order, stamps the invoice "approved for payment" and signs his name. The invoice and its attached documents are then sent to the accounting department where a voucher is prepared, the invoice and its supporting documents are attached, and the voucher is recorded. On its due date the voucher and its supporting documents are sent to the office of the company treasurer where a check in payment of the voucher is prepared and mailed. The voucher is then stamped "paid," the number of the paying check is entered on it, and the paid voucher is returned to the accounting department for an entry to record its payment.

Do the present procedures of Vagabond Trailer Company make it fairly easy for someone in the company to institute the payment of fictitious invoices by the company? If so, who is this person and what would the person have to do to receive payment for a fictitious invoice. What changes should be made in the company's purchasing procedures, and why should each change be made?

Provocative problem 7–2
Cinema East

Ted Gage owns and operates Cinema East, acting as both manager and projectionist. The theater has not been too profitable of late; and this morning at breakfast, while discussing ways to cut costs, his wife suggested that he discharge the theater's doorman whose job is to collect and destroy the tickets sold by the cashier, and that he permit the cashier to collect an admission from each patron without issuing a ticket. This, Mrs. Gage pointed out, would result in a double savings, the wages of the doorman and, also, since there would be no one to take up tickets, rolls of prenumbered tickets would not have to be purchased. Mr. Gage said he could not do this unless Mrs. Gage would take over the cashier's job.

Discuss the wife's suggestion and her husband's counter proposal from an internal control point of view. You may assume the cashier is a college student and that cashiers change frequently, since the job interferes with dating.

Provocate problem 7–3
Old bookkeeper

The bookkeeper at Todd's Department Store will retire next week after more than 40 years with the store, having been hired by the father of the store's present owner. He has always been a very dependable employee, and as a result has been given more and more responsibilities over the years. Actually, for the past 15 years he has "run" the store's office, keeping books, verifying invoices, and issuing checks in their payment, which in the absence of the store's owner, Jack Todd, he could sign. In addition, at the end of each day the store's salesclerks turn over their daily cash receipts to the old bookkeeper, who after counting the money and comparing the amounts with the cash register tapes, which he is responsible for removing from the cash registers, makes the journal entry to record cash sales and then deposits the money in the bank. He also reconciles the bank balance each month with his book balance of cash.

Mr. Todd, the store's owner, realizes he cannot expect a new bookkeeper to accomplish as much in a day as the old bookkeeper; and since the store is not large enough to warrant more than one office employee, he recognizes he must take over some of the old bookkeeper's duties when he retires. Mr. Todd already places all orders for merchandise and supplies and closely supervises all employees and does not want to add more to his duties than necessary.

Discuss the situation described here from an internal control point of view, setting forth which of the old bookkeeper's tasks should be taken over by Mr. Todd and which can be assigned to the new bookkeeper with safety.

After studying Chapter 8, you should be able to:

☐ Calculate interest on promissory notes and the discount on notes receivable discounted.

☐ Prepare entries to record the receipt of a promissory note and its payment or dishonor.

☐ Prepare entries to record the discounting of a note receivable and its payment by the maker or its dishonor.

☐ Prepare reversing entries and explain the advantage of making such entries.

☐ Prepare entries accounting for bad debts both by the allowance method and the direct write-off method.

☐ Explain the full-disclosure principle and the materiality principle.

☐ Define or explain the words and phrases listed in the chapter Glossary.

Notes and accounts receivable

■ Companies selling merchandise on the installment plan commonly take promissory notes from their customers. Likewise when the credit period is long, as in the sale of farm machinery, promissory notes are often required. Also, creditors frequently ask for promissory notes from customers who are granted additional time in which to pay their past-due accounts. In these situations creditors prefer notes to accounts receivable because the notes may be readily turned into cash before becoming due by discounting (selling) them to a bank. Likewise, notes are preferred because if a lawsuit is needed to collect, a note represents written acknowledgment by the debtor of both the debt and its amount. Also, notes are preferred because they generally earn interest.

PROMISSORY NOTES

A promissory note is an unconditional promise in writing to pay on demand or at a fixed or determinable future date a definite sum of money. In the note shown in Illustration 8–1, Hugo Brown promises to pay Frank Black or his order a definite sum of money at a fixed future date. Hugo Brown is the *maker* of the note. Frank Black is the *payee*. To Hugo Brown the illustrated note is a *note payable*, a liability. To Frank Black the same note is a *note receivable*, an asset.

The illustrated Hugo Brown note bears interest at 8%. Interest is a charge for the use of money. To a borrower, interest is an expense. To a lender, it is a revenue. A note may be interest bearing or it may be noninterest bearing. If a note bears interest, the rate or the amount of interest must be stated on the note.

275

$ 1,000.00   Eugene, Oregon   March 9, 19--

_____Thirty days_____after date_____I_____promise to pay to

the order of_____Frank Black_____

One thousand and no/100--dollars

for value received with interest at_____8%_____

payable at_First National Bank of Eugene, Oregon_____

_____Hugo Brown_____

Illustration 8–1

CALCULATING INTEREST

Unless otherwise stated, the rate of interest on a note is the rate charged for the use of the principal for one year. The formula for calculating interest is:

$$\begin{array}{c}\text{Prinicipal}\\\text{of the}\\\text{note}\end{array} \times \begin{array}{c}\text{Annual}\\\text{rate of}\\\text{interest}\end{array} \times \begin{array}{c}\text{Time of the}\\\text{note expressed}\\\text{in years}\end{array} = \text{Interest}$$

For example, interest on a $1,000, 8%, one-year note is calculated:

$$\$1,000 \times \frac{8}{100} \times 1 = \$80$$

Most note transactions involve a period less than a full year, and this period is usually expressed in days. When the time of a note is expressed in days, the actual number of days elapsing, not including the day of the note's date but including the day on which it falls due, are counted. For example, a 90-day note, dated July 10, is due on October 8. This October 8 due date, called the *maturity date*, is calculated as follows:

Number of days in July	31
Minus the date of the note	10
Gives the number of days the note runs in July	21
Add the number of days in August	31
Add the number of days in September	30
Total through September 30	82
Days in October needed to equal the time of the note, 90 days, also the maturity date of the note—October	8
Total time the note runs in days	90

Occasionally, the time of a note is expressed in months. In such cases, the note matures and is payable in the month of its maturity on the same day of the month as its date. For example, a note dated July 10 and payable three months after date is payable on October 10.

In calculating interest, it was once almost the universal practice to treat a year as having just 360 days. This simplified most interest calculations. However, the practice is no longer so common. Nevertheless, to simplify the calculation of interest in assigned problems and to be consistent in the illustrations and problems, the practice is continued in this text. It makes the interest calculation on a 90-day, 8%, $1,000 note as follows:

$$\text{Principal} \times \text{Rate} \times \frac{\text{Exact days}}{360} = \text{Interest}$$

or

$$\$1,000 \times \frac{8}{100} \times \frac{90}{360} = \text{Interest}$$

or

$$\cancel{\$1,000} \times \frac{\cancel{8}^{2}}{\cancel{100}} \times \frac{\cancel{90}}{\cancel{360}_{4}} = \$20$$

RECORDING THE RECEIPT OF A NOTE

Notes receivable are recorded in a single Notes Receivable account. Each note may be identified in the account by writing the name of the maker in the Explanation column on the line of the entry recording its receipt or payment. Only one account is needed because the individual notes are on hand. Consequently, the maker, rate of interest, due date, and other information may be learned by examining each note.

A note received at the time of a sale is recorded as follows:

Dec.	5	Notes Receivable	650.00	
		Sales		650.00
		Sold merchandise, terms six-month, 9% note.		

When a note is taken in granting a time extension on a past-due account receivable, the creditor usually attempts to collect part of the past-due account in cash. This reduces the debt and requires the acceptance of a note for a smaller amount. For example, Symplex Company agrees to accept $232 in cash and a $500, 60-day, 9% note from Joseph Cook in settlement of his $732 past-due account. When

Symplex receives the cash and note, the following entry in general journal form is made:

Oct.	5	Cash	232.00	
		Notes Receivable	500.00	
		Accounts Receivable—Joseph Cook		732.00
		Received cash and a note in settlement of an account.		

Observe that this entry changes the form of $500 of the debt from an account receivable to a note receivable.

When Cook pays the note, this entry in general journal form is made:

Dec.	4	Cash	507.50	
		Notes Receivable		500.00
		Interest Earned		7.50
		Collected the Joseph Cook note.		

Look again at the last two entries. If Symplex Company uses columnar journals, the entry of December 4 would be recorded in its Cash Receipts Journal. Two lines would be required, one for the credit to Interest Earned and a second for the credit to Notes Receivable. Likewise, the October 5 transaction would be recorded with two entries, one in the Cash Receipts Journal for the money received and a second entry in the General Journal for the note. Nevertheless, to simplify the illustrations, general journal entries are shown here and will be used through the remainder of this text. However, the student should realize that the entries would be made in a Cash Receipts Journal or other appropriate journal if in use.

DISHONORED NOTES RECEIVABLE

Occasionally, the maker of a note either cannot or will not pay the note at maturity. When a note's maker refuses to pay at maturity, the note is said to be *dishonored*. Dishonor does not relieve the maker of the obligation to pay. Furthermore, every legal means should be made to collect. However, collection may require lengthy legal proceedings.

The balance of the Notes Receivable account should show only the amount of notes that have not matured. Consequently, when a note is dishonored, its amount should be removed from the Notes Receivable account and charged back to the account of its maker. To illustrate, Simplex Company holds an $800, 9%, 60-day note of George Jones.

At maturity, Jones dishonors the note. To remove the dishonored note from its Notes Receivable account, the company makes the following entry:

Oct.	14	Accounts Receivable—George Jones	812.00	
		Interest Earned		12.00
		Notes Receivable		800.00
		To charge the account of George Jones for his dishonored note.		

Charging a dishonored note back to the account of its maker serves two purposes. It removes the amount of the note from the Notes Receivable account, leaving in the account only notes that have not matured. It also records the dishonored note in the maker's account. The second purpose is important. If in the future the maker of the dishonored note again applies for credit, his or her account will show all past dealings, including the dishonored note.

Observe in the entry that the Interest Earned account is credited for interest earned even though it was not collected. The reason for this is that Jones owes both the principal and the interest. Consequently, his account should reflect the full amount owed on the date of the entry.

DISCOUNTING NOTES RECEIVABLE

As previously stated, a note receivable is preferred to an account receivable because the note can be turned into cash before maturity by discounting (selling) it to a bank. In *discounting a note receivable,* the owner endorses and delivers the note to the bank in exchange for cash. The bank holds the note to maturity and then collects its maturity value from the maker. To illustrate, assume that on May 28 Symplex Company received a $1,200, 60-day, 8% note dated May 27 from John Owen. It held the note until June 2 and then discounted it at its bank at 9%. Since the maturity date of this note is July 26, the bank must wait 54 days after discounting the note to collect from Owen. These 54 days are called the *discount period* and are calculated as follows:

Time of the note in days		60
Less time held by Symplex Company:		
Number of days in May	31	
Less the date of the note	27	
Days held in May	4	
Days held in June	2	
Total days held		6
Discount period in days		54

At the end of the discount period the bank expects to collect the *maturity value* of this note from Owen. Therefore, as is customary, it bases its discount on the maturity value of the note, which is calculated as follows:

Principal of the note	$1,200
Interest on $1,200 for 60 days at 8%	16
Maturity value	$1,216

In this case the bank's discount rate, or the rate of interest it charges for lending money, is 9%. Consequencly, in discounting the note, it will deduct 54 days' interest at 9% from the note's maturity value and will give Symplex Company the remainder. The remainder is called the *proceeds of the note*. The amount of interest deducted is known as *bank discount*. The bank discount and the proceeds are calculated as follows:

Maturity value of the note	$1,216.00
Less interest on $1,216 for 54 days at 9%	16.42
Proceeds	$1,199.58

Observe in this case that the proceeds, $1,199.58, are $0.42 less than the $1,200 principal amount of the note. Consequently, Symplex will make this entry in recording the discount transaction:

June	2	Cash	1,199.58	
		Interest Expense	.42	
		Notes Receivable		1,200.00
		Discounted the John Owen note for 54 days at 9%.		

In recording the transaction, Symplex in effect offsets the $16 of interest it would have earned by holding the note to maturity against the $16.42 discount charged by the bank and records only the difference, the $0.42 excess of expense.

In the situation just described the principal of the discounted note exceeded the proceeds. However, in many cases the proceeds exceed the principal. When this happens, the difference is credited to Interest Earned. For example, suppose that instead of discounting the John Owen note on June 2, Symplex held the note and discounted it on June 26. If the note is discounted on June 26 at 9%, the discount period is 30 days, the discount is $9.12, and the proceeds of the note are $1,206.88, calculated as follows:

Maturity value of the note	$1,216.00
Less interest on $1,216 at 9% for 30 days	9.12
Proceeds	$1,206.88

And since the proceeds exceed the principal, the transaction is recorded as follows:

June	26	Cash	1,206.88	
		Interest Earned		6.88
		Notes Receivable		1,200.00
		Discounted the John Owen note for 30 days at 9%.		

Contingent liability

A person or company discounting a note is ordinarily required to endorse the note because an endorsement, unless it is restricted, makes the endorser contingently liable for payment of the note.[1] The *contingent liability* depends upon the note's dishonor by its maker. If the maker pays, the endorser has no liability. However, if the maker defaults, the endorser's contingent liability becomes an actual liability and the endorser must pay the note for the maker.

A contingent liability, since it can become an actual liability, may affect the credit standing of the person or concern contingently liable. Consequently, a discounted note should be shown as such in the Notes Receivable account. Also, if a balance sheet is prepared before the discounted note's maturity date, the contingent liability should be indicated on the balance sheet. For example, if in addition to the John Owen note, Symplex Company holds $500 of other notes receivable, the record of the discounted John Owen note may appear in its Notes Receivable account as follows:

Notes Receivable						
Date		Explanation	Post. Ref.	Debit	Credit	Balance
May	28	John Owen note	G6	1,200.00		1,200.00
June	7	Earl Hill note	G6	500.00		1,700.00
	26	Discounted the J. Owen note	G7		1,200.00	500.00

---

[1] A restricted endorsement is one in which the endorser states in writing that he or she will not be liable for payment.

The contingent liability resulting from discounted notes receivable is commonly shown on a balance sheet by means of a footnote. If Symplex Company follows this practice, it will show the $500 of notes it has not discounted and the contingent liability resulting from discounting the John Owen note on its June 30 balance sheet as follows:

Current assets:
Cash .... $ 5,315
Notes receivable (Footnote 2) 500
Accounts receivable 21,475

Footnote 2: Symplex Company is contingently liable for $1,200 of notes receivable discounted.

Full-disclosure principle

The balance sheet disclosure of contingent liabilities is required under the *full-disclosure principle.* Under this principle it is held that financial statements and their accompanying footnotes should disclose fully and completely all relevant data of a material nature relating to the financial position of the company for which they are prepared. This does not necessarily mean that the information should be detailed, for details can at times obscure. It simply means that all information necessary to an appreciation of the company's position be reported in a readily understandable manner and that nothing of a significant nature be withheld. For example, any of the following would be considered relevant and should be disclosed.

Contingent liabilities   In addition to discounted notes, a company that is contingently liable due to possible additional tax assessments, pending lawsuits, or product guarantees should disclose this on its statements.

Long-term commitments under a contract   If the company has signed a long-term lease requiring a material annual payment, this should be disclosed even though the liability does not appear in the accounts. Also, if the company has pledged certain of its assets as security for a loan, this should be revealed.

Accounting methods used   Whenever there are several acceptable accounting methods that may be followed, a company should report in each case the method used, especially when a choice of methods can materially affect reported net income. For example, a company should report by means of footnotes accompanying its statements the inventory method or methods used, depreciation methods, method of recognizing revenue under long-term construction contracts, and the like.[2]

---
[2] APB, "Disclosure of Accounting Policies," *APB Opinion No. 22* (New York: AICPA, April 1972), pars. 12 and 13. Copyright (1972), by the American Institute of CPAs.

DISHONOR OF A DISCOUNTED NOTE

A bank always tries to collect a discounted note directly from the maker. If it is able to do so, the one who discounted it will not hear from the bank and will need to do nothing more in regard to the note. However, according to law, if a discounted note is dishonored, the bank must before the end of the next business day notify each endorser of the note if it is to hold the endorsers liable on the note. To notify the endorsers, the bank will normally protest the dishonored note. To protest a note, the bank prepares and mails before the end of the next business day a *notice of protest* to each endorser. A notice of protest is a statement, usually attested by a notary public, that says the note was duly presented to the maker for payment and payment was refused. The cost of protesting a note is called a *protest fee,* and the bank will look to the one who discounted the note for payment of both the note's maturity value and the protest fee.

For example, suppose that instead of paying the $1,200 note previously illustrated, John Owen dishonored it. In such a situation the bank would notify Symplex Company immediately of the dishonor by mailing a notice of protest and a letter asking payment of the note's maturity value plus the protest fee. If the protest fee is, say $5, Symplex must pay the bank $1,221; and in recording the payment, Symplex will charge the $1,221 to the account of John Owen, as follows:

July	27	Accounts Receivable—John Owen	1,221.00	
		Cash		1,221.00
		To charge the account of Owen for the maturity value of his dishonored note plus the protest fee.		

Of course, upon receipt of the $1,221, the bank will deliver to Symplex the dishonored note. Symplex Company will then make every legal effort to collect from Owen, not only the maturity value of the note and protest fee but also interest on both from the date of dishonor until the date of final settlement. However, it may not be able to collect, and after exhausting every legal means to do so, it may have to write the account off as a bad debt. Normally in such cases no additional interest is taken onto the books before the write-off.

Although dishonored notes commonly have to be written off as bad debts, some are also eventually paid by their makers. For example, if 30 days after dishonor, John Owen pays the maturity value of his dishonored note, the protest fee, and interest at 8% on both for 30 days beyond maturity, he will pay the following:

Maturity value	$1,216.00
Protest fee	5.00
Interest on $1,221 at 8% for 30 days	8.14
Total	$1,229.14

And Symplex will record receipt of his money as follows:

Aug.	25	Cash	1,229.14	
		Interest Earned		8.14
		Accounts Receivable—John Owen		1,221.00
		Dishonored note and protest fee collected with interest.		

END-OF-THE-PERIOD ADJUSTMENTS

If any notes receivable are outstanding at the accounting period end, their accrued interest should be calculated and recorded. For example, on December 11 a company accepted a $3,000, 60-day, 9% note from a customer in granting an extension on a past-due account. If the company's accounting period ends on December 31, by then $15 interest has accrued on this note and should be recorded with this adjusting entry:

Dec.	31	Interest Receivable	15.00	
		Interest Earned		15.00
		To record accrued interest on a note receivable.		

The adjusting entry causes the interest earned to appear on the income statement of the period in which it was earned. It also causes the interest receivable to appear on the balance sheet as a current asset.

Collecting interest previously accrued

When the note is collected, the transaction may be recorded as follows:

Feb.	9	Cash	3,045.00	
		Interest Earned		30.00
		Interest Receivable		15.00
		Notes Receivable		3,000.00
		Received payment of a note and its interest.		

The entry's credit to Interest Receivable records collection of the interest accrued at the end of the previous period.

REVERSING ENTRIES

To correctly record a transaction like that of the February 9 entry just shown, a bookkeeper must remember the accrued interest recorded at the end of the previous year and divide the amount of interest received between the Interest Earned and Interest Receivable accounts. Many bookkeepers find this difficult, and they avoid "the need to remember" by preparing and posting entries to reverse any end-of-the-period adjustments of accrued items. These *reversing entries* are made after the adjusting and closing entries are posted and are normally dated the first day of the new accounting period.

To demonstrate reversing entries, assume that a company accepted a $4,000, 9%, 60-day note dated December 19, 12 days before the end of its annual accounting period. Sixty days interest on this note is $60, and by December 31 $12 of the $60 has been earned. Consequently, the company's bookkeeper should make the following adjusting and closing entries to record the accrued interest on the note and to close the Interest Earned account.

Dec.	31	Interest Receivable	12.00	
		Interest Earned		12.00
		To record the accrued interest.		
	31	Interest Earned	12.00	
		Income Summary		12.00
		To close the Interest Earned account.		

In addition to the adjusting and closing entries, if the bookkeeper chooses to make reversing entries, he or she will make the following entry to reverse the accrued interest adjusting entry:

Jan.	1	Interest Earned	12.00	
		Interest Receivable		12.00
		To reverse the accrued interest adjusting entry.		

Observe that the reversing entry is debit for credit and credit for debit the reverse of the adjusting entry it reverses. After the adjusting, closing, and reversing entries are posted, the Interest Receivable and Interest Earned accounts appear as follows:

Interest Receivable						Interest Earned				
Date	Explanation	Dr.	Cr.	Bal.		Date	Explanation	Dr.	Cr.	Bal.
Dec. 31	Adjusting	12		12		Dec. 31	Adjusting		12	12
Jan. 1	Reversing		12	-0-		31	Closing	12		-0-
						Jan. 1	Reversing	12		⑫

Notice that the reversing entry cancels the $12 of interest appearing in the Interest Receivable account. It also causes the accrued interest to appear in the Interest Earned account as a $12 debit. (Remember that an encircled balance means a balance opposite from normal.) Consequently, due to the reversing entry, when the note and interest are paid on February 17, the bookkeeper can record the transaction with this entry:

Feb.	17	Cash	4,060.00	
		Interest Earned		60.00
		Notes Receivable		4,000.00
		Received payment of a note and interest.		

The entry's $60 credit to Interest Earned includes both the $12 of interest earned during the previous period and the $48 of interest earned during the current period. However, when the entry is posted, because of the previously posted reversing entry, the balance of the Interest Earned account shows only the $48 of interest applicable to the current period, as follows:

Interest Earned				
Date	Explanation	Dr.	Cr.	Bal.
Dec. 31	Adjusting		12	12
31	Closing	12		-0-
Jan. 1	Reversing	12		⑫
Feb. 17	Payment		60	48

Reversing entries are applicable to all accrued items, such as accrued interest earned, accrued interest expense, accrued taxes, and accrued salaries and wages. Nevertheless, they are not required, but are a matter of convenience that enable a bookkeeper to forget an accrued item once its adjusting entry has been reversed.

BAD DEBTS

When goods and services are sold on credit, there are almost always a few customers who do not pay. The accounts of such customers are called *bad debts* and are a loss and an expense of selling on credit.

It might be asked: Why do merchants sell on credit if bad debts result? The answer is, of course, that they sell on credit in order to increase sales and profits. They are willing to take a reasonable loss from bad debts in order to increase sales and profits. Therefore, bad debt losses are an expense of selling on credit, an expense incurred in order to increase sales. Consequently, if the requirements of the *matching principle* are met, bad debt losses must be matched against the sales they helped produce.

MATCHING BAD DEBT LOSSES WITH SALES

A bad debt loss results from an error in judgment, an error in granting credit and making a sale to a customer who will not pay. Therefore, a bad debt loss is incurred at the moment credit is granted and a sale is made to such a customer. Of course the merchant making such a sale does not know at the time of the sale that a loss has been incurred. Actually, the merchant normally will not be sure of the loss for as much as a year or more, after every means of collecting has been exhausted. Nevertheless, final recognition a year or so later does not change the time of the loss. The loss occurred at the moment of the sale.

It is recognized that a bad debt loss occurs at the moment of a sale to a customer who will not pay. It is also recognized that a merchant cannot be sure the customer will not pay until a year or more after the sale. Consequently, if bad debt losses are matched with the sales they helped produce, they must be matched on an estimated basis. The *allowance method of accounting for bad debts* does just that.

ALLOWANCE METHOD OF ACCOUNTING FOR BAD DEBTS

Under the allowance method of accounting for bad debts, an estimate is made at the end of each accounting period of the total bad debts that are expected to result from the period's sales. An allowance is then provided for the loss. This has two advantages: (1) the estimated loss is charged to the period in which the revenue is recognized; and (2) the accounts receivable appear on the balance sheet at their estimated realizable value, a more informative balance sheet amount.

Estimating bad debts

In making the year-end estimate of bad debts that are expected to result from the year's sales, companies commonly assume that "history will repeat." For example, over the past several years Alpha Company has experienced bad debt losses equal to one half of 1% of its charge sales. During the past year its charge sales were $300,000. Consequently, if history repeats, Alpha Company can expect $1,500 of bad debt losses to result from the year's sales ($300,000 × 0.005 = $1,500).

Recording the estimated bad debts loss

Under the allowance method of accounting for bad debts, the estimated bad debts loss is recorded at the end of each accounting period with a work sheet adjustment and an adjusting entry. For example, Alpha Company will record its $1,500 estimated bad debts loss with a work sheet adjustment and an adjusting entry like the following:

Dec.	31	Bad debts Expense	1,500.00	
		Allowance for Doubtful Accounts		1,500.00
		To record the estimated bad debts.		

The debit of this entry causes the estimated bad debts loss to appear on the income statement of the year in which the sales were made. As a result, the estimated $1,500 expense of selling on credit is matched with the $300,000 of revenue it helped to produce.

Bad debt losses normally appear on the income statement as an administrative expense rather than as a selling expense because granting credit is usually not a responsibility of the sales department. Therefore, since the sales department is not responsible for granting credit, it should not be held responsible for bad debt losses. The sales department is usually not given responsibility for granting credit because it is feared the sales department would at times be swayed in its judgment of a credit risk by its desire to make a sale.

Bad debts in the accounts

If at the time its bad debts adjusting entry is posted, Alpha Company has $20,000 of accounts receivable, its Accounts Receivable and Allowance for Doubtful Accounts accounts will show these balances:

Accounts Receivable		Allowance for Doubtful Accounts	
Dec. 31 20,000			Dec. 31 1,500

The bad debts adjusting entry reduces the accounts receivable to their estimated realizable value. However, note that the credit of the entry is to the contra account, Allowance for Doubtful Accounts. It is necessary to credit the contra account because at the time of the adjusting entry it is not known for certain which customers will fail to pay. (The total loss from bad debts can be estimated from past experience. However, the exact customers who will not pay cannot be known until every means of collecting from each has been exhausted.) Consequently, since the bad accounts are not identifiable at the time of the adjusting entry, they cannot be removed from the subsidiary Accounts Receivable Ledger. As a result, the Allowance for Doubtful Accounts account must be credited instead of the controlling account. The allowance account must be credited because to credit the controlling account without removing the bad accounts from the subsidiary ledger would cause the controlling account balance to differ from the sum of the balances in the subsidiary ledger.

Allowance for doubtful accounts on the balance sheet

When the balance sheet is prepared, the *allowance for doubtful accounts* is subtracted thereon from the accounts receivable to show the amount that is expected to be realized from the accounts, as follows:

Current assets:		
Cash....................................		$11,300
Accounts receivable	$20,000	
Less allowance for doubtful accounts	(1,500)	18,500
Merchandise inventory		67,200
Prepaid expense		1,100
Total current assets		$98,100

Writing off a bad debt

When an allowance for doubtful accounts is provided, accounts deemed uncollectible are written off against this allowance. For example, after spending a year trying to collect, Alpha Company finally concluded the $100 account of George Vale was uncollectible and made the following entry to write it off:

Jan.	23	Allowance for Doubtful Accounts	100.00	
		Accounts Receivable—George Vale		100.00
		To write off an uncollectible account.		

Posting the credit of the entry to the Accounts Receivable account removes the amount of the bad debt from the controlling account. Posting it to the George Vale account removes the amount of the bad debt from the subsidiary ledger. Posting the entry has this effect on the general ledger accounts:

Accounts Receivable				Allowance for Doubtful Accounts			
Dec. 31	20,000	Jan. 23	100	Jan. 23	100	Dec. 31	1,500

Two points should be observed in the entry and accounts. First, although bad debts are an expense of selling on credit, the allowance account rather than an expense account is debited in the write-off. The allowance account is debited because the expense was recorded at the end of the period in which the sale occurred. At that time, the loss was foreseen, and the expense was recorded in the estimated bad debts adjusting entry.

Second, although the write-off removed the amount of the account receivable from the ledgers, it did not affect the estimated realizable amount of Alpha Company's accounts receivable, as the following tabulation shows:

	Before write-off	After write-off
Accounts receivable	$20,000	$19,900
Less allowance for doubtful accounts	1,500	1,400
Estimated realizable accounts receivable	$18,500	$18,500

Bad debts written off seldom equal the allowance provided

The uncollectible accounts from a given year's sales seldom, if ever, exactly equal the allowance provided for their loss. If accounts written off are less than the allowance provided, the allowance account reaches the end of the year with a credit balance. On the other hand, if accounts written off exceed the allowance provided, the allowance account reaches the period end with a debit balance, which is then eliminated with the new bad debts adjusting entry. In either case no harm is done if the allowance provided is approximately equal to the bad debts written off and is neither continually excessive nor insufficient.

Often when the addition to the allowance for doubtful accounts is based on a percentage of sales, the passage of several accounting periods is required before it becomes apparent the percentage is either too large or too small. In such cases when it becomes apparent the percentage is incorrect, a change in the percentage should be made.

BAD DEBT RECOVERIES

Frequently errors in judgment are made and accounts written off as uncollectible are later sometimes collected in full or in part. If an account is written off as uncollectible and later the customer pays part or all of the amount previously written off, the payment should be shown in the customer's account for future credit action. It should be shown because when a customer fails to pay and his or her account is written off, the customer's credit standing is impaired. Later when the customer pays, the payment helps restore the credit standing. When an account previously written off as a bad debt is collected, two entries are made. The first reinstates the customer's account and has the effect of reversing the original write-off. The second entry records the collection of the reinstated account.

For example, assume that George Vale, whose account was previously written off, pays in full on August 15. The entries in general journal form to record the bad debt recovery are:

Aug.	15	Accounts Receivable—George Vale	100.00	
		Allowance for Doubtful Accounts		100.00
		To reinstate the account of George Vale written off on January 23.		
	15	Cash	100.00	
		Accounts Receivable—George Vale		100.00
		In full of account.		

In this case George Vale paid the entire amount previously written off. Sometimes after an account is written off the customer will pay a portion of the amount owed. The question then arises, should the entire balance of the account be returned to accounts receivable or just the amount paid? The answer is a matter of judgment. If it is thought the customer will pay in full, the entire amount owed should be returned. However, only the amount paid should be returned if it is thought that no more will be collected.

AGEING ACCOUNTS RECEIVABLE

In estimating bad debt losses, many companies *age their accounts receivable*. This consists of preparing a schedule of accounts receivable with their balances entered in columns according to age, as in Illustration 8–2. After such a schedule is prepared, executives of the sales

Schedule of Accounts Receivable by Age					
Customer's Name	Not Due	1 to 30 Days Past Due	31 to 60 Days Past Due	61 to 90 Days Past Due	Over 90 Days Past Due
Charles Abbot	45.00				
Frank Allen	53.00				
George Arden			14.00		
Paul Baum					27.00

Illustration 8–2

and credit departments examine each account listed and by judgment decide which are probably uncollectible. Normally, most of the accounts on the schedule are current and not past due. These are examined for possible losses but receive less scrutiny than past-due accounts. The older accounts are more apt to prove uncollectible. These receive the greatest attention. After decisions are made as to which accounts are probably uncollectible, the allowance account is adjusted to provide for them.

To illustrate this adjustment, assume that a company ages its accounts receivable and estimates that accounts totaling $1,950 are probably uncollectible. Assume further that the company has a $250 credit balance in its allowance account. Under these assumptions the company will make the following adjusting entry to increase the balance of the allowance account to the amount needed to provide for the estimated uncollectible accounts:

Dec.	31	Bad Debts Expense	1,700.00	
		Allowance for Doubtful Accounts		1,700.00
		To increase the allowance for doubtful accounts to $1,950.		

The $1,700 credit of the entry increases the balance of the allowance account to the $1,950 needed to provide for the estimated bad debts. If it had been assumed that the allowance account had a $150 debit balance before adjustment, rather than the assumed $250 credit balance, it would have been necessary to increase the entry amounts to $2,100 ($150 + $1,950) in order to bring the account balance up to the required amount.

Aging accounts receivable and increasing the allowance for doubtful accounts to an amount sufficient to provide for the accounts deemed uncollectible normally provides a better balance sheet figure than does the percent of sales method, a figure closer to realizable value. However, the aging method may not as closely match revenues and expenses as the percent of sales method.

DIRECT WRITE-OFF OF BAD DEBTS

The allowance method of accounting for bad debts better fulfills the requirements of the *matching principle.* Consequently, it is the method that should be used in most cases. However, under certain circumstances another method, called the *direct write-off method,* may be used. Under this method, when it is decided that an account is uncollectible, it is written off directly to Bad Debts Expense with an entry like this:

Nov.	23	Bad Debts Expense	52.50	
		Accounts Receivable—Dale Hall		52.50
		To write off the uncollectible account.		

The debit of the entry charges the bad debt loss directly to the current year's Bad Debts Expense account. The credit removes the balance of the account from the subsidiary ledger and controlling account.

If an account previously written off directly to Bad Debts Expense is later collected in full, the following entries are used to record the recovery:

Mar.	11	Accounts Receivable—Dale Hall	52.50	
		Bad Debts Expense		52.50
		To reinstate the account of Dale Hall previously written off.		
	11	Cash	52.50	
		Accounts Receivable—Dale Hall		52.50
		In full of account.		

Sometimes a bad debt previously written off directly to the Bad Debts Expense account is recovered in the year following the write-off. If at that time the Bad Debts Expense account has no balance from other write-offs and no write-offs are expected, the credit of the entry recording the recovery can be to a revenue account called Bad Debt Recoveries.

Direct write-off mismatches revenues and expenses

The direct write-off method commonly mismatches revenues and expenses. The mismatch results because the revenue from a bad debt sale appears on the income statement of one year while the expense of the loss is deducted on the income statement of the following or a later year. Nevertheless, it may still be used in situations where its use does not materially affect reported net income. For example, it may be used in a concern where bad debt losses are immaterial in relation to total sales and net income. In such a concern, the use of direct write-off comes under the accounting *principle of materiality*.

The principle of materiality

Under the *principle of materiality* it is held that a strict adherence to any accounting principle, in this case the *matching principle,* is not required when adherence is relatively difficult or expensive and the lack of adherence does not materially affect reported net income. Or in other words, failure to adhere is permissible when the failure does not produce an error or misstatement sufficiently large as to influence a financial statement reader's judgment of a given situation.

GLOSSARY

Aging accounts receivable. Preparing a schedule listing accounts receivable by the number of days each account has been unpaid.

Allowance for doubtful accounts. The estimated amount of accounts receivable that will prove uncollectible.

Allowance method of accounting for bad debts. The accounting procedure whereby an estimate is made at the end of each accounting period of the portion of the period's credit sales that will prove uncollectible, and an entry is made to charge this estimated amount to an expense account and to an allowance account against which actual uncollectible accounts can be written off.

Bad debt. An uncollectible account receivable.

Bank discount. The amount of interest a bank deducts in lending money.

Contingent liability. A potential liability that may become an actual liability if certain events occur.

Direct write-off method of accounting for bad debts. The accounting procedure whereby uncollectible accounts are written off directly to an expense account.

Discount period of a note. The number of days for which a note is discounted.

Discounting a note receivable. Selling a note receivable to a bank or other concern.

Dishonoring a note. Refusing to pay a promissory note on its due date.

Full-disclosure principle. The accounting rule requiring that financial statements and their accompanying notes disclose all information of a material nature relating to the financial position and operating results of the company for which the statements are prepared.

Maker of a note. One who signs a note and promises to pay it at maturity.

Materiality principle. The accounting rule that a strict adherence to any accounting principle is not required when adherence is relatively difficult or expensive and lack of adherence will not materially affect reported net income.

Maturity date of a note. The date on which a note and any interest are due and payable.

Maturity value of a note. Principal of the note plus any interest due on the note's maturity date.

Notes receivable discounted. The amount of notes receivable that have been discounted or sold.

Notice of protest. A document that gives notice that a promissory note was presented for payment on its due date and payment was refused.

Payee of a note. The one to whom a promissory note is made payable.

Proceeds of a discounted note. The maturity value of a note minus any interest deducted because of its being discounted before maturity.

Protest fee. The fee charged for preparing and issuing a notice of protest.

Reversing entry. An entry that reverses the adjusting entry for an accrued item.

QUESTIONS FOR CLASS DISCUSSION

1. Why does a business prefer a note receivable to an account receivable?
2. Define:
   - *a.* Promissory note.
   - *b.* Payee of a note.
   - *c.* Maturity date.
   - *d.* Dishonored note.
   - *e.* Notice of protest.
   - *f.* Discount period of a note.
   - *g.* Maker of a note.
   - *h.* Principal of a note.
   - *i.* Maturity value.
   - *j.* Contingent liability.
3. What are the due dates of the following notes: *(a)* a 90-day note dated June 10, *(b)* a 60-day note dated May 13, and *(c)* a 90-day note dated November 12?

4. Distinguish between bank discount and cash discount.
5. What does the full-disclosure principle require in a company's accounting statements?
6. At what point in the selling-collecting procedures of a company does a bad debt loss occur?
7. In estimating bad debt losses it is commonly assumed that "history will repeat." How is this assumption used in estimating bad debt losses?
8. A company had $484,000 of charge sales in a year. How many dollars of bad debt losses may the company expect to experience from these sales if its past bad debt losses have averaged one fourth of 1% of charge sales?
9. What is a contra account? Why are estimated bad debt losses credited to a contra account rather than to the Accounts Receivable controlling account?
10. Classify the following accounts: (a) Accounts Receivable, (b) Allowance for Doubtful Accounts, and (c) Bad Debts Expense.
11. Explain why writing off a bad debt against the allowance account does not reduce the estimated realizable amount of a company's accounts receivable.
12. Why does the direct write-off method of accounting for bad debts commonly fail in matching revenues and expenses?
13. What is the essence of the accounting principle of materiality?

CLASS EXERCISES

Exercise 8-1

Prepare general journal entries to record these transactions:

Mar. 11   Accepted a $900, 60-day, 8% note dated this day from Carl Lee in granting a time extension on his past-due account.

May 10   Carl Lee dishonored his note when presented for payment.

Dec. 31   After exhausting all legal means of collecting, wrote off the account of Carl Lee against the allowance for doubtful accounts.

Exercise 8-2

Prepare general journal entries to record these transactions:

June 3   Sold merchandise to Fred Gage, $1,500, terms 2/10, n/60.

Aug. 15   Received $300 in cash and a $1,200, 60-day, 8% note dated August 12 in granting a time extension on the amount due from Fred Gage.

18   Discounted the Fred Gage note at the bank at 9%.

Oct. 16   Since notice protesting the Fred Gage note had not been received, assumed that Fred Gage had paid the note.

Exercise 8-3

Prepare general journal entries to record these transactions:

Aug. 5   Accepted a $1,000, 60-day, 9% note dated August 3 from Earl Ball in granting a time extension on his past-due account.

Aug. 27 Discounted the Earl Ball note at the bank at 10%.
Oct.   3 Received notice protesting the Earl Ball note. Paid the bank the
          maturity value of the note plus a $5 protest fee.
Nov.   1 Received payment from Earl Ball of the maturity value of his dishon-
          ored note, the protest fee, and interest at 9% on both for 30 days
          beyond maturity.

Exercise 8–4

On August 2 Mesa Sales sold Ted Hall merchandise having a $2,000 catalog
list price, less a 25% trade discount, 2/10, n/60. Hall was unable to pay and
was granted a time extension on receipt of his 60-day, 8% note for the amount
of the debt, dated October 10. Mesa Sales held the note until November 9,
when it discounted it at its bank at 9%. The note was not protested. Answer
these questions:

a. How many dollars of trade discount were granted on the sale?
b. How many dollars of cash discount could Hall have earned?
c. What was the maturity date of the note?
d. How many days were in the discount period?
e. How much bank discount was deducted by the bank?
f. What were the proceeds of the discounted note?

Exercise 8–5

Northland Sales accepted a $3,000, 9%, 60-day note dated December 11,
20 days before the end of its annual accounting period, in granting a time
extension on the past-due account of Lee Best.

Required:

1. Give in general journal form the entries made by Northland Sales *(a)* to
   record receipt of the note, *(b)* to record the accrued interest on the note
   on December 31, *(c)* to close the Income Summary account, *(d)* to reverse
   the accrued interest adjusting entry, and *(e)* to record payment of the note
   and interest on February 9.
2. Open balance column accounts for Interest Receivable and Interest Earned
   and post the portions of the foregoing entries that affect these accounts.

Exercise 8–6

On December 31, 198A, a company estimated it would lose as bad debts
an amount equal to one fourth of 1% of its $724,000 of 198A charge sales,
and it provided an addition to its allowance for doubtful accounts equal to
that amount. On the following March 27 it decided the $285 account of Arno
Fall was uncollectible and wrote it off as a bad debt. On July 7 Arno Fall
unexpectedly paid the amount previously written off. Give the required entries
in general journal form to record these transactions.

Exercise 8–7

At the end of each year a company ages its accounts receivable and increases its allowance for doubtful accounts by an amount sufficient to provide for the estimated uncollectible accounts. At the end of last year it estimated it would not be able to collect $2,450 of its total accounts receivable. *(a)* Give the entry to increase the allowance account under the assumption it had a $125 credit balance before the adjustment. *(b)* Give the entry under the assumption the allowance account had a $150 debit balance before the adjustment.

PROBLEMS

Problem 8–1

Prepare entries in general journal form to record these transactions:

Jan.   4   Sold merchandise to Ted Fall, terms $445 in cash and an $800, 60-day, 9% note dated this day.

Mar.   5   Received payment from Ted Fall of the maturity value of his $800 note.

      12   Accepted a $1,500, 60-day, 8% note dated March 10 in granting a time extension on the past-due account of Allen Moss.

      16   Discounted the Allen Moss note at the bank at 9%.

May 10   Received notice protesting the Allen Moss note. Paid the bank the maturity value of the note plus a $5 protest fee.

July   8   Received payment from Allen Moss of the maturity value of his dishonored note plus the protest fee and interest on both for 60 days beyond maturity at 8%.

      14   Accepted $350 in cash and a $1,200, 90-day, 8% note dated July 13 in granting a time extension on the past-due account of Joel Nash.

Sept. 11   Discounted the Joel Nash note at the bank at 9%.

Oct. 15   Since notice protesting the Joel Nash note had not been received, assumed it paid.

      16   Accepted an $800, 60-day, 9% note dated October 15 from Ned Green in granting a time extension on his past-due account.

Nov. 8   Discounted the Ned Green note at the bank at 10%.

Dec. 14   Received notice protesting the Ned Green note. Paid the bank the maturity value of the note plus a $4 protest fee.

      31   Wrote off as uncollectible the account of Ned Green against the allowance for doubtful accounts.

Problem 8–2

Prepare general journal entries to record these transactions:

Dec. 16   Accepted a $1,200, 60-day, 8% note dated this day in granting a time extension on the past-due account of Paul Roth.

Dec. 31   Made an adjusting entry to record the accrued interest on the Paul Roth note.

  31   Made an adjusting entry to increase the allowance for doubtful accounts by an amount equal to one third of 1% of the year's $828,000 of charge sales.

Jan. 1   Made an entry to reverse the accrued interest adjusting entry of December 31.

Feb. 14   Received payment from Paul Roth of the maturity value of his note.

Mar. 3   Accepted a $900, 8%, 60-day note dated March 2 in granting a time extension on the past-due account of Dale Parr.

Apr. 1   Discounted the Dale Parr note at the bank at 9%.

May 2   Received notice protesting the Dale Parr note. Paid the bank the maturity value of the note plus a $5 protest fee.

  5   Accepted $225 in cash and a $1,500, 60-day, 8% note dated May 3 in granting a time extension on the past-due account of Carl Lane.

  18   Discounted the Carl Lane note at the bank at 10%.

July 3   Received notice protesting the Carl Lane note. Paid the bank the maturity value of the note and a $5 protest fee.

Aug. 7   Received payment from Carl Lane of the maturity value of his dishonored note plus the protest fee and interest on both for 36 days beyond maturity at 8%.

  10   Accepted an $800, 60-day, 9% note dated this day in granting a time extension on the past-due account of Fred Hall.

Oct. 9   Fred Hall dishonored his note when presented for payment.

Dec. 28   Decided the accounts of Dale Parr and Fred Hall were uncollectible and wrote them off as bad debts.

Problem 8–3

Prepare general journal entries to record these transactions:

Dec. 21   Accepted an $1,800, 60-day, 8% note dated this day in granting a time extension on the past-due account of Lee Byrd.

  31   Made an adjusting entry to record the accrued interest on the Lee Byrd Note.

  31   Closed the Interest Earned account.

Jan. 1   Reversed the accrued interest adjusting entry of December 31.

  30   Discounted the Lee Byrd note at the bank at 9%.

Feb. 20   Received notice protesting the Lee Byrd note. Paid the bank the maturity value of the note plus a $5 protest fee.

Mar. 3   Accepted a $1,400, 9%, 60-day note dated this day from Walter Dent in granting a time extension on his past-due account.

  27   Discounted the Walter Dent note at the bank at 10%.

May 5   Since notice protesting the Walter Dent note had not been received, assumed it paid.

June 8   Accepted a $1,600, 9%, 60-day note dated this day from Ned Fox in granting a time extension on his past-due account.

Aug. 7   Received payment in full of the maturity value of the Ned Fox note.

  10   Accepted a $2,400, 8%, 60-day note dated August 9 from Ted Bush in granting a time extension on his past-due account.

Sept. 11   Discounted the Ted Bush note at the bank at 10%.
Oct.   9   Received notice protesting the Ted Bush note. Paid the bank the
            maturity value of the note plus a $4 protest fee.
Nov.   7   Received payment from Ted Bush of the maturity value of his dishon-
            ored note, the protest fee, and interest at 8% on both for 30 days
            beyond maturity.
Dec. 27   Wrote off the Lee Byrd account against the allowance for doubtful
            accounts.

Problem 8–4

Prepare general journal entries to record these transactions:

Dec. 19   Accepted $435 in cash and a $2,100, 60-day, 8% note dated this
            day in granting a time extension on the past-due account of Ned
            Ross.
       31   Made an adjusting entry to record the accrued interest on the Ned
            Ross note. (The accountant of the company does not make reversing
            entries.)
Jan. 18   Discounted the Ned Ross note at the bank at 9%.
Feb. 18   Received notice protesting the Ned Ross note. Paid the bank the
            maturity value of the note plus a $5 protest fee.
Mar. 19   Received payment from Ned Ross of the maturity value of his dishon-
            ored note, the protest fee, and interest on both for 30 days beyond
            maturity at 8%.
       21   Sold Dale Otis merchandise, terms $315 cash and a $1,200, 90-day,
            9% note dated this day.
June 19   Dale Otis dishonored his note when presented for payment.
       23   Accepted an $800, 60-day, 9% note dated June 22 from Lee Moss
            in granting a time extension on his past-due account.
Aug. 21   Lee Moss paid the maturity value of his 60-day note.
       24   Accepted $245 in cash and a $600, 60-day, 9% note dated this day
            from Carl Fry in granting a time extension on his past-due account.
Oct. 23   Carl Fry dishonored his note when presented for payment.
Dec. 15   Learned of the bankruptcy of Dale Otis and wrote off his account
            and the account of Carl Fry against the allowance for doubtful ac-
            counts.

Problem 8–5

A company completed these transactions during a 15-month period:

Oct.   8   Sold merchandise to Fred Best, $1,445, terms 2/10, n/60.
Dec. 16   Accepted $245 in cash and a $1,200, 60-day, 8% note dated this
            day in granting Fred Best a time extension on his past-due account.
       31   Made an adjusting entry to record the accrued interest on the Fred
            Best note.
       31   An examination showed a $135 credit balance in the Allowance for
            Doubtful Accounts account. Provided an addition to the allowance
            equal to one fourth of 1% of the year's $976,000 of charge sales.
       31   Closed the Interest Earned and Bad Debts Expense accounts.

Jan.   1   Reversed the accrued interest adjusting entry of December 31.
Feb. 14   Received payment of the maturity value of the Fred Best note.
      15   Learned of the bankruptcy of Joe Nash and made a claim on his receiver in bankruptcy for the $160 owed by Mr. Nash for merchandise purchased.
Apr. 14   After making every effort to collect, decided the $375 account of Lee Wolf was uncollectible and wrote it off as a bad debt.
July 17   Lee Wolf walked into the store and paid $150 of the amount written off on April 14. He said his financial position had improved and he expected to pay the balance of his account within a short period.
Oct. 15   Received $185 from Joe Nash's receiver in bankruptcy. A letter accompanying the payment stated that no more would be paid. Made an entry to record receipt of the cash and to write off the balance of Nash's account.
Dec. 18   Made a compound entry to write off the accounts of Earl Barker, $640; Jerry Davis, $585; and Lee Hall, $890.
      31   Provided an addition to the allowance for doubtful accounts equal to one fourth of 1% of the year's $964,000 of charge sales.
      31   Closed the Bad Debts Expense and Interest Earned accounts.

Required:

1. Open Interest Receivable, Allowance for Doubtful Accounts, Interest Earned, and Bad Debts Expense accounts. Enter the $135 credit balance in the Allowance for Doubtful Accounts account and prepare general journal entries to record the transactions. Post those portions of the entries that affect the four accounts opened.
2. Prepare an alternate bad debts adjusting entry for the second December 31 of the problem under the assumption that rather than providing an addition to the allowance account equal to one fourth of 1% of charge sales, the company aged its accounts, estimated that $2,100 of accounts were probably uncollectible, and increased its allowance to provide for them.

ALTERNATE PROBLEMS

Problem 8–1A

Prepare general journal entries to record these transactions:

Jan.   5   Accepted $300 cash and a $1,000, 60-day, 9% note dated this day in granting a time extension on the past-due account of Carl Rust.
Mar. 6   Received payment of the maturity value of the Carl Rust note.
      10   Accepted a $2,400, 9%, 60-day note dated this day in granting a time extension on the past-due account of Ted Lee.
      16   Discounted the Ted Lee note at the bank at 10%.
May 12   Since notice protesting the Ted Lee note had not been received, assumed it paid.
      15   Accepted $315 in cash and an $1,800, 9%, 60-day note dated this day in granting Fred Lane a time extension on his past-due account.

June 4   Discounted the Fred Lane note at the bank at 10%.

July 15   Received notice protesting the Fred Lane note. Paid the bank the maturity value of the note plus a $5 protest fee.

Aug. 13   Received payment from Fred Lane of the maturity value of his dishonored note, the protest fee, and interest at 9% on both for 30 days beyond maturity.

16   Accepted a $600, 90-day, 9% note dated August 15 in granting Gary Marsh a time extension on his past-due account.

Nov. 13   Gary Marsh dishonored his note when presented for payment.

Dec. 23   Decided the Gary Marsh note was uncollectible and wrote off its maturity value against the allowance for doubtful accounts.

Problem 8–2A

Prepare general journal entries to record these transactions:

Dec. 13   Accepted an $1,800, 60-day, 8% note dated this day in granting Earl Larr a time extension on his past-due account.

31   Made an adjusting entry to record the accrued interest on the Earl Larr note.

31   Closed the Interest Earned account.

Jan. 1   Reversed the accrued interest adjusting entry of December 31.

Feb. 11   Received payment of the maturity value of the Earl Larr note.

14   Accepted a $1,400, 30-day, 9% note dated this day in granting a time extension on the past-due account of Ted Hall.

Mar. 16   Ted Hall dishonored his 30-day note when presented for payment.

Apr. 5   Accepted a $1,200, 90-day, 9% note dated April 3 in granting Carl Jacks a time extension on his past-due account.

9   Discounted the Carl Jacks note at the bank at 10%.

July 5   Since notice protesting the Carl Jacks note had not been received, assumed it was paid.

7   Accepted an $800, 60-day, 9% note dated this day from Larry Moss in granting a time extension on his past-due account.

31   Discounted the Larry Moss note at the bank at 10%.

Sept. 6   Received notice protesting the Larry Moss note. Paid the bank the maturity value of the note plus a $4 protest fee.

Oct. 5   Received payment from Larry Moss of the maturity value of his dishonored note, the protest fee, and interest on both for 30 days beyond maturity at 9%.

Dec. 28   Decided the account of Ted Hall was uncollectible and wrote it off against the allowance for doubtful accounts.

Problem 8–3A

Prepare general journal entries to record these transactions:

Dec. 7   Accepted $225 in cash and a $2,400, 60-day, 8% note dated this day in granting Ned Ross a time extension on his past-due account.

31   Made an adjusting entry to record the accrued interest on the Ned Ross note. (The bookkeeper does not make reversing entries.)

Dec. 31   Made an adjusting entry to increase the allowance for doubtful accounts by an amount equal to one third of 1% of the year's $858,000 of charge sales.

Jan. 18   Discounted the Ned Ross note at the bank at 10%.

Feb. 9   Since notice protesting the Ned Ross note had not been received, assumed it was paid.

    12   Accepted a $2,000, 60-day, 9% note from John Ellis in granting a time extension on his past-due account. The note was dated February 10.

Apr. 11   Received payment of the maturity value of the John Ellis note.

    15   Decided the $435 account of Walter Sears was uncollectible and wrote it off against the allowance for doubtful accounts.

    22   Accepted an $1,800, 60-day, 9% note dated this day in granting Harold Jones an extension on his past-due account.

May 4   Discounted the Harold Jones note at the bank at 10%.

June 22   Received notice protesting the Harold Jones note. Paid the bank the note's maturity value plus a $5 protest fee.

July 6   Walter Sears paid $135 of the amount written off on April 15. In a letter accompanying the payment he said his finances had improved and he expected to pay the balance owed within a short time.

    21   Received payment from Harold Jones of the maturity value of his dishonored note, the protest fee, and interest on both for 30 days beyond maturity at 9%.

Problem 8–4A

Prepare general journal entries to record these transactions:

Dec. 21   Accepted $365 in cash and a $2,800, 60-day, 9% note dated this day in granting Jerry Neal a time extension on his past-due account.

    31   Made an adjusting entry to record the accrued interest on the Jerry Neal note.

    31   Made an adjusting entry to increase the allowance for doubtful accounts by an amount equal to one fourth of 1% of the year's $840,000 of charge sales.

    31   Closed the Bad Debts Expense and Interest Earned accounts.

Jan. 1   Reversed the accrued interest adjusting entry of December 31.

Feb. 1   Discounted the Jerry Neal note at the bank at 10%.

    20   Received notice protesting the Jerry Neal note. Paid the bank the note's maturity value plus a $6 protest fee.

Mar. 21   Received payment from Jerry Neal of the maturity value of his dishonored note, the protest fee, and interest on both for 30 days beyond maturity at 9%.

    24   Accepted a $2,400, 90-day, 9% note dated this day in granting a time extension on the past-due account of Fred Ball.

    30   Discounted the Fred Ball note at the bank at 10%.

June 27   Since notice protesting the Fred Ball note had not been received, assumed it paid.

Aug. 7   Accepted an $1,800, 8%, 60-day note dated this day in granting a time extension on the past-due account of Joel Kane.

Aug. 31 Discounted the Joel Kane note at the bank at 10%.

Oct. 7 Received notice protesting the Joel Kane note. Paid the bank the maturity value of the note plus a $5 protest fee.

Dec. 28 Decided the Joel Kane account was uncollectible and wrote it off against the allowance for doubtful accounts.

Problem 8–5A

A company completed these transactions:

Dec. 7 Accepted a $2,800, 9%, 60-day note dated this day and $475 in cash in granting a time extension on the past-due account of Larry Vale.

31 Aged the accounts receivable and estimated that $2,110 would prove uncollectible. Examined the Allowance for Doubtful Accounts account and determined that it had a $140 debit balance. Made an adjusting entry to provide for the estimated bad debts.

31 Made an adjusting entry to record the accrued interest on the Larry Vale note.

31 Closed the Bad Debts Expense and Interest Earned accounts.

Jan. 1 Reversed the accrued interest adjusting entry.

Feb. 5 Received payment of the maturity value of the Larry Vale note.

11 Learned that Earl Hill had gone out of business, leaving no assets to attach. Wrote off his $285 account as a bad debt.

Mar. 10 Learned of the bankruptcy of Joel Kane and made a claim on his receiver in bankruptcy for the $410 owed by Mr. Kane for merchandise purchased on credit.

May 15 Accepted $265 in cash and a $1,200, 9%, 60-day note dated this day in granting a time extension on the past-due account of Ted Rust.

June 14 Discounted the Ted Rust note at the bank at 10%.

July 15 Received notice protesting the Ted Rust note. Paid the bank the maturity value of the note plus a $5 protest fee.

Aug. 12 Earl Hill paid $100 of the amount written off on February 11. In a letter accompanying the payment he stated that his finances had improved and he expected to pay the balance owed within a short time.

Oct. 3 Received $85 from the receiver in bankruptcy of Joel Kane. A letter accompanying the payment said that no more would be paid. Recorded receipt of the $85 and wrote off the balance owed as a bad debt.

3 Decided the account of Ted Rust was uncollectible and wrote it off as a bad debt.

Dec. 22 Made a compound entry to write off the accounts of James Wells, $215, and Robert Neal, $185, as uncollectible.

31 Aged the accounts receivable and estimated that $2,300 would prove uncollectible. Made an adjusting entry to provide for the estimated bad debts.

31 Closed the Bad Debts Expense and Interest Earned accounts.

Required:

1. Open Interest Receivable, Allowance for Doubtful Accounts, Interest Earned, and Interest Expense accounts. Enter the $140 debit balance in the Allowance for Doubtful Accounts account.
2. Prepare general journal entries to record the transactions and post those portions of the entries that affect the accounts opened.

PROVOCATIVE PROBLEMS

Provocative problem 8–1
Red Rock Sales

When his auditor arrived early in January to begin the annual audit, Robert Hamilton, the owner of Red Rock Sales, asked that special attention be given the accounts receivable. Two things caused this request: (1) During the previous week Mr. Hamilton had encountered Ed Barr, a former customer, on the street and had asked him about his account which had recently been written off as uncollectible. Mr. Barr had indignantly replied that he had paid his $305 account in full, and he later produced canceled checks endorsed by Red Rock Sales to prove it. (2) The income statement prepared for the quarter ended the previous December 31 showed an unusually large volume of sales returns. The bookkeeper who had prepared the statement had resigned at the end of the first week in January. He had worked for Red Rock Sales only since October 1, after having been hired on the basis of out-of-town letters of reference. While on the job, in addition to doing all the record keeping, he had acted as cashier, receiving and depositing the cash from both cash sales and that received through the mail.

In the course of her investigation, the auditor prepared from the company's records the following analysis of the accounts receivable for the period October 1 through December 31:

	Ames	Barr	Cole	Doak	Eble	Finn	Glen
Balance, October 1	$ 315	$ 140	$ 285	$ 260	$ 140	$ 510	$ 445
Sales	580	165	560	–0–	725	385	520
Totals	$ 895	$ 305	$ 845	$ 260	$ 865	$ 895	$ 965
Collections	(480)	–0–	(525)	–0–	(445)	(385)	(585)
Returns	(95)	(65)	(30)	–0–	(110)	(80)	(15)
Bad debts written off ...	–0–	(240)	–0–	(260)	–0–	–0–	–0–
Balance, December 31 ..	$ 320	–0–	$ 290	–0–	$ 310	$ 430	$ 365

The auditor communicated with all charge customers and learned that although their account balances as of December 31 agreed with the amounts shown in Red Rock Company's records, the individual transactions did not. They reported credit purchases totaling $3,410 during the three-month period and $95 of returns for which credit had been granted. Correspondence with Mr. Doak, the customer whose $260 account had been written off, revealed that he had become bankrupt and his creditor claims had been settled by his receiver in bankruptcy at $0.25 on the dollar. The checks had been mailed by the receiver on November 8, and all had been paid and returned by the bank, properly endorsed by the recipients.

Under the assumption the late bookkeeper had embezzled cash from the company, determine the total amount he took and attempted to conceal with false accounts receivable entries. Account for the deficiency by listing the concealment methods used and the amount he attempted to conceal with each method. Also outline an internal control system that will help protect the company's cash from future embezzlement. Assume the company is small and can have only one office employee who must do all the bookkeeping.

Provocative problem 8–2
Jewels Unlimited

Jewels Unlimited, a jewelry store, has been in operation for five years. Three years ago Ted Hall, the store's owner, liberalized the store's credit policy in an effort to increase sales. Sales have increased, but Ted is now concerned with the effects of the more liberal credit policy. Bad debts written off (the store used the direct write-off method) have increased materially during the past two years, and now Ted wonders if the sales increase justifies the substantial bad debt losses which he is certain have resulted from the more liberal credit policy.

The following tabulation shows the store's operating results and bad debt losses. On the tabulation's last line bad debt losses are reclassified by years in which the sales that resulted in the losses were made. Consequently, the $2,790 of fifth-year losses includes $1,710 of estimated bad debts in present accounts receivable.

	1st year	2d year	3d year	4th year	5th year
Credit sales	$100,000	$110,000	$150,000	$180,000	$200,000
Cost of goods sold	49,900	55,100	75,300	89,800	99,700
Gross profit on credit sales	$ 50,100	$ 54,900	$ 74,700	$ 90,200	$100,300
Expenses other than bad debts . .	30,300	33,100	44,900	54,400	59,800
Income before bad debts	$ 19,800	$ 21,800	$ 29,800	$ 35,800	$ 40,500
Bad debts written off	100	520	700	2,350	2,300
Net income from credit sales	$ 19,700	$ 21,280	$ 29,100	$ 33,450	$ 38,200
Bad debts by year of sales	$ 360	$ 410	$ 1,960	$ 2,160	$ 2,790

Prepare a schedule showing in columns by years the following: income before bad debts, bad debts incurred, and net income from credit sales. Then below the net income figures show for each year bad debts written off as a percentage of sales followed on the next line by bad debts incurred as a percentage of sales. Also prepare a report to Mr. Hall answering his concern about the new credit policy and recommending any changes you consider desirable in his accounting for bad debts.

After studying Chapter 9, you should be able to:

☐ Calculate the cost of an inventory based on *(a)* specific invoice prices, *(b)* weighted-average cost, *(c)* Fifo, and *(d)* Lifo.

☐ Explain the income tax effect of the use of Lifo.

☐ Tell what is required by the accounting principle of consistency and why the application of this principle is important.

☐ Tell what is required of a concern when it changes its accounting procedures.

☐ Tell what is required by the accounting principle of conservatism.

☐ Explain the effect of an inventory error on the income statements of the current and succeeding years.

☐ Tell how a perpetual inventory system operates.

☐ Estimate an inventory by the retail method and by the gross profit method.

☐ Define or explain the words and phrases listed in the chapter Glossary.

Inventories and cost of goods sold

■ A merchandising business earns revenue by selling merchandise. For such a concern the phrase *merchandise inventory* is used to describe the aggregate of the items of tangible personal property it holds for sale. As a rule the items are sold within a year or one cycle. Consequently, the inventory is a current asset, usually the largest current asset on a merchandising concern's balance sheet.

MATCHING MERCHANDISE COSTS WITH REVENUES

An AICPA committee said: "A major objective of accounting for inventories is the proper determination of income through the process of matching appropriate costs against revenues."[1] The matching process referred to is one with which the student is already familiar. For inventories, it consists of determining how much of the cost of the goods that were for sale during a period should be deducted from the period's revenue and how much should be carried forward as inventory to be matched against a future period's revenue.

In separating cost of goods available for sale into its components of cost of goods sold and cost of goods not sold, the key problem is that of assigning a cost to the goods not sold or to the ending inventory. However, it should be borne in mind that the procedures for assigning

---

[1] Committee on Accounting Procedures, "Accounting Research Bulletin No. 43," *Accounting Research and Terminology Bulletins, Final Edition* (New York: AICPA, 1961), p. 28. Copyright (1961) by the American Institute of CPAs.

a cost to the ending inventory are also the means of determining cost of goods sold. For whatever portion of the cost of goods for sale is assigned to the ending inventory, the remainder goes into cost of goods sold.

ASSIGNING A COST TO THE ENDING INVENTORY

Assigning a cost to the ending inventory normally involves two problems: (1) determining the quantity of each product on hand and (2) pricing the products.

The quantity of unsold merchandise on hand at the end of an accounting period is usually determined by a physical inventory. Physical inventories and the way in which such inventories are taken were discussed in Chapter 5. Consequently, it is only necessary to repeat that in a physical inventory the unsold merchandise is counted to determine the units of each product on hand.

After an inventory is counted, the units are priced. Generally, inventories are priced at cost. However, a departure from cost is sometimes necessary when goods have been damaged or have deteriorated. Likewise, a departure from cost is sometimes necessary when replacement costs are less than the amounts paid for the items when they were purchased.[2] These points are discussed later in this chapter.

ACCOUNTING FOR AN INVENTORY AT COST

Pricing an inventory at cost is not difficult when costs remain fixed. However, when identical items were purchased during a period at different costs, a problem arises as to which costs apply to the ending inventory and which apply to the goods sold. There are four commonly used ways of assigning costs to goods in the ending inventory and to goods sold. They are (1) specific invoice prices; (2) weighted-average cost; (3) first-in, first-out; and (4) last-in; first-out. Each is a *generally accepted accounting procedure.*

To illustrate the four, assume that a company has on hand at the end of an accounting period 12 units of Article X. Also, assume that the company began the year and purchased Article X during the year as follows:

Jan. 1	Beginning inventory	......	10 units @ $100	=	$1,000
Mar. 13	Purchased	....	15 units @ $108	=	1,620
Aug. 17	Purchased	....	20 units @ $120	=	2,400
Nov. 10	Purchased	....	10 units @ $125	=	1,250
	Total	....	55 units		$6,270

---

[2] APB, "Basic Concepts and Accounting Principles Underlying Financial Statements of Business Enterprises," *APB Statement No. 4* (New York: AICPA, October 1970), par. 183. Copyright (1970) by the American Institute of CPAs.

Specific invoice prices

When it is possible to identify each item in an inventory with a specific purchase and its invoice, *specific invoice prices* may be used to assign costs. For example, assume that 6 of the 12 unsold units of Article X were from the November purchase and 6 were from the August purchase. Under this assumption, costs are assigned to the inventory and goods sold by means of specific invoice prices as follows:

Total cost of 55 units available for sale		$6,270
Less ending inventory priced by means of specific invoices:		
6 units from the November purchase at $125 each	$750	
6 units from the August purchase at $120 each	720	
12 units in ending inventory		1,470
Cost of goods sold		$4,800

Weighted average

Under this method prices for the units in the beginning inventory and in each purchase are weighted by the number of units in the beginning inventory and in each purchase and are averaged to find the *weighted-average cost* per unit as follows:

10 units @ $100	=	$1,000
15 units @ $108	=	1,620
20 units @ $120	=	2,400
10 units @ $125	=	1,250
55		$6,270

$6,270 ÷ 55 = $114, weighted-average cost per unit

After the weighted-average cost per unit is determined, this average is used to assign costs to the inventory and the units sold as follows:

Total cost of 55 units available for sale	$6,270
Less ending inventory priced on a weighted-average	
cost basis: 12 units at $114 each	1,368
Cost of goods sold	$4,902

First-in, first-out

In a merchandising business clerks are instructed to sell the oldest merchandise first. Consequently, when this instruction is followed, merchandise tends to flow out on a first-in, first-out basis. When first-in, first-out is applied in pricing an inventory, it is assumed that costs follow this pattern. As a result, the cost of the last items received are assigned to the ending inventory and the remaining costs are assigned to goods sold. When first-in, first-out, or *Fifo* as it is often called from its first letters, is used, costs are assigned to the inventory and goods sold as follows:

Total cost of 55 units available for sale		$6,270
Less ending inventory priced on a basis of Fifo:		
10 units from the November purchase at $125 each	$1,250	
2 units from the August purchase at $120 each	240	
12 units in the ending inventory		1,490
Cost of goods sold		$4,780

Last-in, first-out

Under this method of inventory pricing, commonly called *Lifo*, the costs of the last goods received are matched with revenue from sales. The theoretical justification for this is that a going concern must at all times keep a certain amount of goods in stock. Consequently, when goods are sold, replacements are purchased. Thus it is a sale that causes the replacement of goods. If costs and revenues are then matched, replacement costs should be matched with the sales that induced the acquisitions.

Under Lifo, costs are assigned to the 12 remaining units of Article X and to the goods sold as follows:

Total cost of 55 units available for sale		$6,270
Less ending inventory priced on a basis of Lifo:		
10 units in the beginning inventory at $100 each	$1,000	
2 units from the first purchase at $108 each	216	
12 units in the ending inventory		1,216
Cost of goods sold		$5,054

Notice that this method of matching costs and revenue results in the final inventory being priced at the cost of the oldest 12 units.

Tax effect of Lifo

During periods of rising prices Lifo offers a tax advantage to its users. This advantage arises because when compared with other methods the application of Lifo results in assigning greatest amounts of costs to goods sold. This in turn results in the smallest reported net incomes and income taxes.

The use of Lifo is not limited to concerns in which goods are actually sold on a last-in, first-out basis. A concern may choose Lifo even though it actually sells goods on a first-in, first-out basis, or on an indiscriminate basis.

Comparison of methods

In a stable market where prices remain unchanged, the inventory pricing method is of little importance. For when prices are unchanged over a period of time, all methods give the same cost figures. However, in a changing market where prices are rising or falling, each method may give a different result. This may be seen by comparing the costs of the units in the ending inventory and the units of Article X sold as calculated by the several methods discussed. These costs are as follows:

	Ending inventory	Cost of units sold
Based on specific invoice prices.....	$1,470	$4,800
Based on weighted average	1,368	4,902
Based on Fifo....................	1,490	4,780
Based on Lifo	1,216	5,054

Each of the four pricing methods is recognized as a generally accepted accounting procedure, and arguments can be advanced for the use of each. Specific invoice prices exactly match costs and revenues. However, this method is of practical use only for relatively high-priced items of which only a few units are kept in stock and sold. Weighted-average costs tend to smooth out price fluctuations. Fifo causes the last costs incurred to be assigned to the ending inventory. It thus provides an inventory valuation for the balance sheet that most closely approximates the current replacement costs. Lifo causes last costs incurred to be assigned to cost of goods sold. Therefore, it results in a better matching of current costs with revenues. However, the method used commonly affects the amounts of reported ending inventory, cost of goods sold, and net income. Consequently, the *full-disclosure principle* requires that a company show in its statements by means of footnotes or other manner the pricing method used.[3]

THE PRINCIPLE OF CONSISTENCY

Look again at the table of costs for Article X. Note that a company can change its reported net income for an accounting period simply by changing its inventory pricing method. However, the change would

---

[3] APB, "Disclosure of Accounting Policies," *APB Opinion No. 22* (New York: AICPA, April 1972), pars. 12 and 13. Copyright (1972) by the American Institute of CPAs.

violate the accounting *principle of consistency.* Furthermore, it would make a comparison of the company's inventory and income with previous periods more or less meaningless.

As with inventory pricing, more than one generally accepted method or procedure has been derived in accounting practice to account for an item or an activity. In each case one method may be considered better for one enterprise, while another may be considered more satisfactory for a concern operating under different circumstances. Nevertheless, the *principle of consistency* requires a persistent application by a company of any selected accounting method or procedure, period after period. As a result, a reader of a company's financial statements may assume that in keeping its records and in preparing its statements the company used the same procedures used in previous years. Only on the basis of this assumption can meaningful comparisons be made of the data in a company's statements year after year.

CHANGING ACCOUNTING PROCEDURES

In achieving comparability, the *principle of consistency* does not require that a method or procedure once chosen can never be changed. Rather, if a company decides that a different acceptable method or procedure from the one in use will better serve its needs, a change may be made. However, when such a change is made, the *full-disclosure principle* requires that the nature of the change, justification for the change, and the effect of the change on net income be disclosed in notes accompanying the statements.[4]

ITEMS INCLUDED ON AN INVENTORY

A concern's inventory should include all goods owned by the business and held for sale, regardless of where the goods may be located at the time of the inventory. In the application of this rule, there are generally no problems with respect to most items. For most items all that is required is to see that they are counted, that nothing is omitted, and that nothing is counted more than once. However, goods in transit, goods sold but not delivered, goods on consignment, and obsolete and damaged goods do require special attention.

When goods are in transit on the inventory date, the purchase should be recorded and the goods should appear on the purchaser's inventory if ownership has passed to the purchaser. Generally, if the buyer is responsible for paying the freight charges, ownership passes as soon as the goods are loaded aboard the means of transportation. Likewise,

---

[4] APB, "Accounting Changes," *APB Opinion No. 20* (New York: AICPA, July 1971), par. 17. Copyright (1971) by the American Institute of CPAs.

if the seller is to pay the freight charges, ownership passes when the goods arrive at their destination.

Goods on consignment are goods shipped by their owner (known as the *consignor*) to another person or firm (called the *consignee*) who is to sell the goods for the owner. Consigned goods belong to the consignor and should appear on the consignor's inventory.

Damaged goods and goods that have deteriorated or become obsolete should not be placed on the inventory if they are not salable. If such goods are salable but at a reduced price, they should be placed on the inventory at a conservative estimate of their realizable value (sale price less the cost of making the sale). This causes the accounting period in which the goods were damaged, deteriorated, or became obsolete to suffer the resultant loss.

Elements of inventory cost

As applied to inventories, cost means the sum of the applicable expenditures and charges directly or indirectly incurred in bringing an article to its existing condition and location.[5] Therefore, the cost of an inventory item includes the invoice price, less the discount, plus any additional incidental costs necessary to put the goods into place and condition for sale. The additional incidental costs include import duties, transportation, storage, insurance, and any other applicable costs, such as those incurred during an aging process.

If incurred, any of the foregoing enter into the cost of an inventory. However, in pricing an inventory, most concerns do not take into consideration the incidental costs of acquiring merchandise. They price the inventory on the basis of invoice prices only, and treat all incidental costs as expenses of the period in which incurred.

Although not correct in theory, treating incidental costs as expenses of the period in which incurred is commonly permissible and often best. In theory a share of each incidental cost should be assigned to every unit purchased. This causes a portion of each to be carried forward in the inventory to be matched against the revenue of the period in which the inventory is sold. However, the expense of computing costs on such a precise basis usually outweighs any benefit from the extra accuracy. Consequently, when possible, most concerns take advantage of the *principle of materiality* and treat such costs as expenses of the period in which incurred.

COST OR MARKET, THE LOWER

Over the years the traditional rule for pricing inventory items has been *the lower of cost or market.* "Cost" is the price that was paid

---

[5] *Accounting Research and Terminology Bulletins, Final Edition,* p. 28.

for an item when it was purchased. "Market" is the price that would have to be paid to purchase or replace the item on the inventory date. The use of this rule gained its wide acceptance because it placed an inventory on the balance sheet at a conservative figure, the lower of what the inventory cost or its replacement cost on the balance sheet date.

The argument advanced to support the use of lower of cost or market was that if the replacement cost of an inventory item had declined, then its selling price would probably have to be reduced. Since this might result in a loss, the loss should be anticipated and taken in the year of the price decline. It was a good argument. However, selling prices do not always exactly and quickly follow cost prices. As a result, the application of the rule often resulted in misstating net income in the year of a price decline and again in the succeeding year. For example, suppose that a firm purchased merchandise costing $1,000, marked it up to a $1,500 selling price, and sold one half of the goods. The gross profit on the goods sold would be calculated as follows:

Sales	$750
Cost of goods sold	500
Gross profit on sales	$250

However, if the $500 replacement cost of the unsold goods declined to $450 on the inventory date, an income statement based upon the traditional application of cost or market would show the following:

Sales		$750
Cost of goods sold:		
Purchases.................	$1,000	
Less ending inventory	450	550
Gross profit on sales		$200

The $450 would be a conservative balance sheet figure for the unsold goods. However, if these goods were sold at their full price early in the following year, the $450 inventory figure would have the erroneous effect of deferring $50 of income to the second year's income statement as follows:

Sales	$750
Cost of goods sold:	
Beginning inventory	450
Gross profit on sales	$300

Merchants are prone to be slow in marking down goods; they normally try to sell merchandise at its full price if possible. Consequently, the illustrated situation is not uncommon. For this reason the lower of cost or market rule has been modified as follows for situations in which replacement costs are below actual costs.[6]

1. Goods should be placed on an inventory at cost, even though replacement cost is lower, if there has not been and there is not expected to be a decline in selling price.
2. Goods should at times be placed on an inventory at a price below cost but above replacement cost. For example, suppose the cost of an item that is normally bought for $20 and sold for $30 declines from $20 to $16, and its selling price declines from $30 to $27. The normal profit margin on this item is one third of its selling price. If this normal margin is applied to $27, the item should be placed on the inventory at two thirds of $27, or at $18. This is below cost but above replacement cost.
3. At times, goods should be placed on an inventory at a price below replacement cost. For example, assume that the goods described in the preceding paragraph can only be sold for $18.50 and that the disposal costs are estimated at $3. In this case the goods should be placed on the inventory at $15.50, a price below their replacement cost of $16.

PRINCIPLE OF CONSERVATISM

Decisions based on estimates and opinions as to future events affect financial statements. Financial statements are also affected by the selection of accounting procedures. The *principle of conservatism* holds that accountants should be conservative in their estimates and opinions and in their selection of procedures, choosing those that neither unduly understate nor overstate the situation.

Something called balance sheet conservatism was once considered the "first" principle of accounting. Its objective was to place every item on the balance sheet at a conservative figure. This in itself was commendable. However, it was often carried too far and resulted not only in the misstatement of asset values but also in unconservative income statements. For example, when prices are falling, the blind application of the lower of cost or market to inventories may result in a conservative balance sheet figure for inventories. It may also result in an improper deferring of net income and in inaccurate income statements. Consequently, accountants recognize that balance sheet conservatism does not outweigh other factors. They favor practices that result in a fair statement of net income period after period.

---

[6] Ibid., pp. 30 and 31.

INVENTORY ERRORS

An error in determining the end-of-the-period inventory will cause misstatements in cost of goods sold, gross profit, net income, current assets, and owner's equity. Also, the ending inventory of one period is the beginning inventory of the next. Therefore, the error will carry forward and cause misstatements in the succeeding period's cost of goods sold, gross profit, and net income. Furthermore, since the amount involved in an inventory is often large, the misstatements can be material without being readily apparent.

To illustrate the effects of an inventory error, assume that in each of the years 198A, 198B, and 198C a company had $100,000 in sales. If the company maintained a $20,000 inventory throughout the period and made $60,000 in purchases in each of the years, its cost of goods sold each year was $60,000 and its annual gross profits were $40,000. However, assume the company incorrectly calculated its December 31, 198A, inventory at $18,000 rather than $20,000. The error would have the effects shown in Illustration 9–1.

Observe in Illustration 9–1 that the $2,000 understatement of the December 31, 198A, inventory caused a $2,000 overstatement in 198A cost of goods sold and a $2,000 understatement in gross profit and net income. Also, since the ending inventory of 198A became the beginning inventory of 198B, the error caused an understatement in the 198B cost of goods sold and a $2,000 overstatement in gross profit and net income. However, by 198C the error had no effect.

In Illustration 9–1 the December 31, 198A, inventory is understated. Had it been overstated, it would have caused opposite results—the 198A net income would have been overstated and the 198B income understated.

It has been argued that an inventory mistake is not too serious, since the error it causes in reported net income the first year is exactly offset by an opposite error in the second. However, such reasoning is unsound. It fails to consider that management, creditors, and owners

	198A		198B		198C	
Sales		$100,000		$100,000		$100,000
Cost of goods sold:						
Beginning inventory	$20,000		$18,000*		$20,000	
Purchases	60,000		60,000		60,000	
Goods for sale	$80,000		$78,000		$80,000	
Ending inventory	18,000*		20,000		20,000	
Cost of goods sold		62,000		58,000		60,000
Gross profit		$ 38,000		$ 42,000		$ 40,000

* Should have been $20,000.

Illustration 9–1

base many important decisions on fluctuations in reported net income. Consequently, such mistakes should be avoided.

PERPETUAL INVENTORIES

Concerns selling a limited number of products of relatively high value often keep perpetual or book inventories. Also, concerns that use computers in processing their accounting data commonly keep such records. Furthermore, the essential information provided is the same whether accumulated by computer or with pen and ink.

A perpetual or book inventory based on pen and ink makes use of a subsidiary record card for each product in stock. On these individual cards, the number of units received is recorded as units are received and the number of units sold is recorded as units are sold. Then, after each receipt or sale, the balance remaining is recorded. (An inventory record card for Product Z is shown in Illustration 9–2.) At any time, each perpetual inventory card tells the balance on hand of any one product; and the total of all cards is the amount of the inventory.

The January 10 sale on the card of Illustration 9–2 indicates that the inventory of this card is kept on a first-in, first-out basis, since the sale is recorded as being from the oldest units in stock. Perpetual inventories may also be kept on a last-in, first-out basis. When this is done, each sale is recorded as being from the last units received, until these are exhausted, then sales are from the next to last, and so on.

When a concern keeps perpetual inventory records, it normally

Item _Product Z_   Location in stock room _Bin 8_

Maximum _25_   Minimum _5_

Date	Received			Sold			Balance		
	Units	Cost	Total	Units	Cost	Total	Units	Cost	Balance
1/1							10	10.00	100.00
1/5				5	10.00	50.00	5	10.00	50.00
1/8	20	10.50	210.00				5	10.00	
							20	10.50	260.00
1/10				3	10.00	30.00	2	10.00	
							20	10.50	230.00

Illustration 9–2

also makes a once-a-year physical count of each kind of goods in stock in order to check the accuracy of its book inventory records.

Perpetual inventories not only tell the amount of inventory on hand at any time but they also aid in controlling the total amount invested in inventory. Each perpetual inventory card may have on it the maximum and minimum amounts of that item that should be kept in stock. By keeping the amount of each item within these limits, an oversupply or an undersupply of inventory is avoided.

PERPETUAL INVENTORY SYSTEMS

Under a *perpetual inventory system,* cost of goods sold during a period, as well as the ending inventory, may be determined from the accounting records. Under such a system an account called Merchandise is used in the place of the Purchases and Merchandise Inventory accounts. It is a controlling account that controls the numerous perpetual inventory cards described in previous paragraphs.

When merchandise is purchased by a concern using a perpetual inventory system, the acquisition is recorded as follows:

Jan.	8	Merchandise	210.00	
		Accounts Payable—Blue Company		210.00
		Purchased merchandise on credit.		

In addition to the entry debiting the purchase to the Merchandise account, entries are also made on the proper perpetual inventory cards in the Received columns to show the kinds of merchandise bought. (See Illustration 9–2.)

When a sale is made, since the inventory cards show the cost of each item sold, it is possible to record both the sale and the cost of the goods sold. For example, if goods that according to the inventory cards cost $30 are sold for $50, cost of goods sold and the sale may be recorded as follows:

Jan.	10	Accounts Receivable—George Black	50.00	
		Cost of Goods Sold	30.00	
		Sales		50.00
		Merchandise		30.00
		Sold merchandise on credit.		

In addition to the credit in this entry to the Merchandise account for the cost of the goods sold, the costs of the items sold are also deducted in the Sold columns of the proper inventory cards.

Note the debit to the Cost of Goods Sold account in the entry just given. If this account is debited at the time of each sale for the cost of the goods sold, the debit balance of the account will show at the end of the accounting period the cost of all goods sold during the period.

Note also the debit and the credit to the Merchandise account as they appear in the two entries just given. If this account is debited for the cost of merchandise purchased and credited for the cost of merchandise sold, at the end of an accounting period its debit balance will show the cost of the unsold goods on hand, the ending inventory.

ESTIMATED INVENTORIES

Retail method

Good management requires that income statements be prepared more often than once each year, and inventory information is necessary in their preparation. However, taking a physical inventory in a retail store is both time consuming and expensive. Consequently, many retailers use the so-called *retail inventory method* to estimate inventories for monthly or quarterly statements. These monthly or quarterly statements are called *interim statements*, since they are prepared in between the regular year-end statements.

Estimating an ending inventory by the retail method   When the retail method is used to estimate an inventory, a store's records must show the amount of inventory it had at the beginning of the period both *at cost* and *at retail*. At cost for an inventory means just that, while "at retail" means the dollar amount of the inventory at the marked selling prices of the inventory items.

In addition to the beginning inventory, the records must also show the amount of goods purchased during the period both at cost and at retail plus the net sales at retail. The last item is easy; it is the balance of the Sales account less returns and discounts. Then, with this information the interim inventory is estimated as follows: (Step 1) The amount of goods that were for sale during the period both at cost and at retail is first computed. Next (Step 2), "at cost" is divided by "at retail" to obtain a cost ratio. Then (Step 3), sales (at retail) are deducted from goods for sale (at retail) to arrive at the ending inventory (at retail). And finally (Step 4), the ending inventory at retail is multiplied by the cost ratio to reduce it to a cost basis. These calculations are shown in Illustration 9–3 on the next page.

This is the essence of Illustration 9–3: (1) The store had $100,000 of goods (at marked selling prices) for sale during the period. (2) These goods cost 60% of the $100,000 total amount at which they were marked for sale. (3) The store's records (its Sales account) showed that

		At cost	At retail
(Step 1)	Goods available for sale:		
	Beginning inventory	$20,500	$ 34,500
	Net purchases	39,500	65,500
	Goods available for sale...................	$60,000	$100,000
(Step 2)	Cost ratio: $60,000 ÷ $100,000 = 60%		
(Step 3)	Deduct sales at retail		70,000
	Ending inventory at retail		$ 30,000
(Step 4)	Ending inventory at cost ($30,000 × 60%)	$18,000	

Illustration 9–3

$70,000 of these goods were sold, leaving $30,000 of merchandise unsold and presumably in the ending inventory. Therefore, (4) since cost
in this store is 60% of retail, the estimated cost of this ending inventory
is $18,000.

An ending inventory calculated as in Illustration 9–3 is an estimate
arrived at by deducting sales (goods sold) from goods for sale. Inventories estimated in this manner are satisfactory for interim statements,
but for year-end statements, or at least once each year, a store should
take a physical inventory.

Using the retail method to reduce a physical inventory to cost   Items
for sale in a store normally have price tickets attached that show selling
prices. Consequently, when a store takes a physical inventory, it commonly takes the inventory at the marked selling prices of the inventoried items. It then reduces the dollar total of this inventory to a cost
basis by applying its cost ratio. It does this because the selling prices
are readily available and the application of the cost ratio eliminates
the need to look up the invoice price of each inventoried item.

For example, assume that the store of Illustration 9–3, in addition
to estimating its inventory by the retail method, also takes a physical
inventory at the marked selling prices of the inventoried goods. Assume
further that the total of this physical inventory is $29,600. Under these
assumptions the store may arrive at a cost basis for this inventory,
without having to look up the cost of each inventoried item, simply
by applying its cost ratio to the $29,600 inventory total as follows:

$$\$29,600 \times 60\% = \$17,760$$

The $17,760 cost figure for this store's ending physical inventory
is a satisfactory figure for year-end statement purposes. It is also acceptable to the Internal Revenue Service for tax purposes.

Inventory shortage   An inventory determined as in Illustration 9–
3 is an estimate of the amount of goods that should be on hand. However, since it is arrived at by deducting sales from goods for sale, it
does not reveal any actual shortages due to breakage, loss, or theft.
Nevertheless, the amount of such shortages may be determined by

first estimating an inventory as in Illustration 9–3 and then taking a physical inventory at marked selling prices.

For example, by means of the Illustration 9–3 calculations, it was estimated the store of this discussion had a $30,000 ending inventory at retail. However, in the previous section it was assumed that this same store took a physical inventory and had only $29,600 of merchandise on hand. Therefore, if this store should have had $30,000 of goods in its ending inventory as determined in Illustration 9–3, but had only $29,600 when it took a physical inventory, it must have had a $400 inventory shortage at retail or a $240 shortage at cost ($400 × 60% = $240).

Markups and markdowns   The calculation of a cost ratio is often not as simple as that shown in Illustration 9–3. It is not simple because many stores not only have a *normal markup* (often called a *markon*) that they apply to items purchased for sale but also make *additional markups* and *markdowns*. A normal markup or markon is the normal amount or percentage that is applied to the cost of an item to arrive at its selling price. For example, if a store's normal markup is 50% on cost and it applies this markup to an item that cost $10, it will mark the item for sale at $15. Normal markups appear in the calculation of a store's cost ratio as the difference between net purchases at cost and at retail.

Additional markups are markups made in addition to normal markups. Stores commonly give goods of outstanding style or quality such additional markups because they can get a higher than normal price for such goods. They also commonly mark down for a clearance sale any slow-moving merchandise.

When a store using the retail inventory method makes additional markups and markdowns, it must keep a record of them. It then uses the information in calculating its cost ratio and in estimating an interim inventory as in Illustration 9–4.

	At cost	At retail
Goods available for sale:		
Beginning inventory	$18,000	$27,800
Net purchases	34,000	50,700
Additional markups		1,500
Goods available for sale	$52,000	$80,000
Cost ratio: $52,000 ÷ $80,000 = 65%		
Sales at retail.................................		$54,000
Markdowns		2,000
Total sales and markdowns		$56,000
Ending inventory at retail ($80,000 less $56,000)		$24,000
Ending inventory at cost ($24,000 × 65%).........	$15,600	

Illustration 9–4

Observe in Illustration 9–4 that the store's $80,000 of goods for sale at retail were reduced $54,000 by sales and $2,000 by markdowns, a total of $56,000. (To understand the markdowns, visualize this effect of a markdown. The store had an item for sale during the period at $25. The item did not sell, and to move it the manager marked its price down from $25 to $20. By this act the amount of goods for sale in the store at retail was reduced by $5. Likewise, by a number of such markdowns during the year goods for sale at retail in the store of Illustration 9–4 were reduced $2,000.) Now back to the calculations of Illustration 9–4. The store's $80,000 of goods for sale were reduced $54,000 by sales and $2,000 by markdowns, leaving an estimated $24,000 ending inventory at retail. Therefore, since "cost" is 65% of "retail," the ending inventory at "cost" is $15,600.

Observe in Illustration 9–4 that markups enter into the calculation of the cost ratio but markdowns do not. It has long been customary in using the retail inventory method to add additional markups but to ignore markdowns in computing the percentage relation between goods for sale at cost and at retail. The justification for this was and is that a more conservative figure for the ending inventory results, a figure that approaches "cost of market, the lower." A further discussion of this phase of the retail inventory method is reserved for a more advanced text.

Gross profit method

Often retail price information about beginning inventory, purchases, and markups is not kept. In such cases the retail inventory method cannot be used. However, if a company knows its normal gross profit margin or rate; has information at cost in regard to its beginning inventory, net purchases, and freight-in; and knows the amount of its sales and sales returns, the company can estimate its ending inventory by the *gross profit method*.

For example, on March 27, the inventory of a company was totally destroyed by a fire. The company's average gross profit rate during the past five years has been 30% of net sales. And on the date of the fire the company's accounts showed the following balances:

Sales	$31,500
Sales returns	1,500
Inventory, January 1, 19—....	12,000
Net purchases	20,000
Freight-in	500

With this information the gross profit method may be used to estimate the company's inventory loss for insurance purposes. The first step in applying the method is to recognize that whatever portion of each dollar of net sales was gross profit, the remaining portion was cost of goods sold. Consequently, if the company's gross profit rate averaged 30%, then 30% of each dollar of net sales was gross profit and 70% was cost of goods sold. The 70% is used in estimating the inventory and inventory loss as in Illustration 9–5.

Goods available for sale:		
Inventory, January 1, 19—		$12,000
Net purchases	$20,000	
Add freight-in	500	20,500
Goods available for sale		$32,500
Less estimated cost of goods sold:		
Sales	$31,500	
Less sales returns	(1,500)	
Net sales	$30,000	
Estimated cost of goods sold (70% × $30,000)		(21,000)
Estimated March 27 inventory and inventory loss		$11,500

Illustration 9–5

To understand Illustration 9–5, recall that in a normal situation an ending inventory is subtracted from goods for sale to determine cost of goods sold. Then observe in Illustration 9–5 that the opposite subtraction is made. Estimated cost of goods sold is subtracted from goods for sale to arrive at the estimated ending inventory.

In addition to its use in insurance cases, as in this illustration, the gross profit method is also commonly used by accountants in checking on the probable accuracy of a physical inventory taken and priced in the normal way.

GLOSSARY

Conservatism principle. The rule that accountants should be conservative in their estimates and opinions and in their selection of procedures.

Consignee. One to whom something is consigned or shipped.

Consignor. One who consigns or ships something to another person or enterprise.

Consistency principle. The accounting rule requiring a persistent application of a selected accounting method or procedure, period after period.

Fifo inventory pricing. The pricing of an inventory under the assumption that the first items received were the first items sold.

Gross profit inventory method. A procedure for estimating an ending inventory in which an estimated cost of goods sold based on past gross profit rates is subtracted from the cost of goods available for sale to arrive at an estimated ending inventory.

Interim statements. Financial statements prepared in between the regular annual statements.

Inventory cost ratio. The ratio of goods available for sale at cost to goods available for sale at retail prices.

Lifo inventory pricing. The pricing of an inventory under the assumption that the last items received were the first items sold.

Lower-of-cost-or-market pricing of an inventory. The pricing of inventory at the lower of what each item actually cost or what it would cost to replace each item on the inventory date.

Markdown. A reduction in the marked selling price of an item.

Markon. The normal percentage of its cost that is added to the cost of an item to arrive at its selling price.

Markup. An addition to the normal markon given to an item.

Normal markup. A phrase meaning the same as markon.

Periodic inventory system. An inventory system in which inventories and cost of goods sold are based on periodic physical inventories.

Perpetual inventory system. An inventory system in which inventories and cost of goods sold are based on book inventory records.

Retail inventory method. A method for estimating an ending inventory based on the ratio of the cost of goods for sale at cost and cost of goods for sale at marked selling prices.

Specific invoice inventory pricing. The pricing of an inventory where each inventory item can be associated with a specific invoice and be priced accordingly.

Weighted-average cost inventory pricing. An inventory pricing system in which the units in the beginning inventory of a product and in each purchase of the product are weighted by the number of units in the beginning inventory and in each purchase to determine a weighted-average cost per unit of the product, and after which this weighted-average cost is used to price the ending inventory of the product.

QUESTIONS FOR CLASS DISCUSSION

1. It has been said that cost of goods sold and ending inventory are opposite sides of the same coin. What is meant by this?
2. Give the meanings of the following when applied to inventory:
   - *a.* First-in, first-out.
   - *b.* Fifo.
   - *c.* Last-in, first-out.
   - *d.* Lifo.
   - *e.* Cost.
   - *f.* Market.

g. Cost or market, the lower. i. Physical inventory.

h. Perpetual inventory. j. Book inventory.

3. If prices are rising, will the Lifo or the Fifo method of inventory valuation result in the higher gross profit?
4. May a company change its inventory pricing method at will?
5. What is required by the accounting principle of consistency?
6. If a company changes one of its accounting procedures, what is required of it under the full-disclosure principle?
7. Of what does the cost of an inventory item consist?
8. Why are incidental costs commonly ignored in pricing an inventory? Under what accounting principle is this permitted?
9. What is meant when it is said that inventory errors "correct themselves"?
10. If inventory errors "correct themselves," why be concerned when such errors are made?
11. What is required of an accountant under the principle of conservatism?
12. Give the meanings of the following when applied in the retail method of estimating an inventory: (a) at cost, (b) at retail, (c) cost ratio, (d) normal markup, (e) markon, (f) additional markup, and (g) markdown.

CLASS EXERCISES

Exercise 9–1

A company began a year and purchased Article A as follows:

Jan.	1	Beginning inventory	100 units @ 53¢	=	$ 53
Jan.	5	Purchased	300 units @ 51¢	=	153
May 21		Purchased	200 units @ 55¢	=	110
Oct.	3	Purchased	200 units @ 56¢	=	112
Dec.	7	Purchased	200 units @ 61¢	=	122
		Total	1,000		$550

Required:

Under the assumption the ending inventory of Article A consisted of 100 units from each of the last three purchases, a total of 300 units, determine the share of the cost of the units for sale that should be assigned to the ending inventory and the share that should be assigned to goods sold under each of the following additional assumptions: (a) costs are assigned on the basis of specific invoice prices, (b) costs are assigned on a weighted-average cost basis, (c) costs are assigned on the basis of Fifo, and (d) costs are assigned on the basis of Lifo.

Exercise 9–2

A company had $500,000 of sales during each of three consecutive years, and it purchased merchandise costing $300,000 during each of the years. It also maintained a $40,000 inventory throughout the three-year period. However, it made an error that caused the December 31, end-of-year-one, inventory to appear on its statements at $42,000, rather than the correct $40,000.

Required:

1. State the actual amount of the company's gross profit in each of the years.
2. Prepare a comparative income statement like the one illustrated in this chapter to show the effect of the error on the company's cost of goods sold and gross profit for each of Year 1, Year 2, and Year 3.

Exercise 9–3

During an accounting period a company sold $153,000 of merchandise at marked retail prices. At the period end the following information was available from its records:

	At cost	At retail
Beginning inventory	$30,000	$ 49,000
Net purchases	90,000	147,000
Additional markups		4,000
Markdowns		2,000

Use the retail method to estimate the store's ending inventory.

Exercise 9–4

Assume that in addition to estimating its ending inventory by the retail method, the store of Exercise 9–3 also took a physical inventory at marked selling prices that totaled $44,000. Determine the store's inventory shrinkage from breakage, theft, or other cause at retail and at cost.

Exercise 9–5

A company had a $25,000 inventory at cost on January 1 of the current year. During the year's first three months it bought merchandise costing $68,000, returned $1,000 of the merchandise, and paid freight charges on purchases totaling $3,000. During the past several years the company's gross profit rate has averaged 35%. Assume the company had $100,000 of sales during the three months and use the gross profit method to estimate its March 31 inventory.

PROBLEMS

Problem 9–1

Zeal Company began last year and purchased Article Z as follows:

January 1 inventory	1,000 units @ $6.10 per unit
Purchases:	
February 5	2,000 units @ $6.00 per unit
June 3	3,000 units @ $6.30 per unit
September 14	3,000 units @ $6.40 per unit
December 3	1,000 units @ $6.60 per unit

Required:

Under the assumption the company incurred $20,000 of selling and administrative expenses last year in selling 8,500 units of the product at $10 per unit, prepare a comparative income statement for the company showing in adjacent columns the net income earned from the sale of the product under the assumptions the company priced its ending inventory on the basis of *(a)* Fifo, *(b)* Lifo, and *(c)* weighted-average cost.

Problem 9–2

A company began an accounting period and made successive purchases of one of its products as follows:

Jan.   1   Beginning inventory ..... 200 units @ $75 per unit
Feb. 12   Purchased .... 300 units @ $90 per unit
Apr. 21   Purchased .... 400 units @ $100 per unit
June 14   Purchased .... 400 units @ $95 per unit
Aug. 30   Purchased .... 400 units @ $95 per unit
Nov. 27   Purchased .... 300 units @ $105 per unit

Required:

1. Prepare a calculation to show the number and total cost of the units for sale during the period.
2. Under the assumption the company had 400 units of the product in its end-of-the-year inventory, prepare calculations to show the portions of the total cost of the units for sale during the period that should be assigned to the ending inventory and to the units sold *(a)* first on a Fifo basis, *(b)* then on a Lifo basis, and *(c)* finally on a weighted-average cost basis.

Problem 9–3

A company that keeps perpetual inventory records completed the following transactions involving one of its products:

Dec.   1   Beginning inventory: 12 units costing $6.25 each.
     3   Received ten units costing $6.50 each.
     8   Sold five units.
    12   Sold eight units.
    18   Received ten units costing $7 each.
    22   Sold six units.
    30   Sold eight units.

Required:

1. Under the assumption the company keeps its records on a first-in, first-out basis, record the transactions on a perpetual inventory record card. Use two or more lines to show units on hand at each price or units sold when units costing different amounts are on hand or sold.
2. Record the transactions on a second card under the assumption the company keeps its records on a last-in, first-out basis.
3. Under the assumption that the last sale was to Carl Berg at $11 per unit,

prepare a general journal entry to record the sale and cost of goods sold on a last-in, first-out basis.

Problem 9–4

Sport Shop takes a year-end physical inventory at marked selling prices and reduces the total to a cost basis for year-end statement purposes. It also uses the retail method to estimate the dollar amount of inventory it should have at the end of a year, and by comparison determines any inventory shortages due to shoplifting or other cause. At the end of the current year the following information was available to make the calculations:

	At cost	At retail
Sales		$220,960
Sales returns		1,745
January 1 inventory	$ 21,630	32,950
Purchases	146,400	219,735
Purchases returns	980	1,470
Additional markups		5,785
Markdowns		1,285
December 31 year-end physical inventory.....		35,800

Required:

1. Prepare a calculation to estimate the dollar amount of the store's year-end inventory, using the retail method.
2. Prepare a calculation showing the amount of inventory shortage at cost and at retail.

Problem 9–5

Rockhill Company's records provide the following December 31, year-end information:

	At cost	At retail
January 1, beginning inventory	$ 24,510	$ 39,215
Purchases	194,460	310,340
Purchases returns	1,970	3,100
Additional markups		3,545
Markdowns		1,450
Sales		308,270
Sales returns		1,220
Year-end physical inventory		39,750

Required:

1. Use the retail method to estimate the company's year-end inventory at cost.
2. Prepare a schedule showing the company's inventory shortage at retail and at cost.

Problem 9–6

On May 20 of the current year Country Store burned and everything excepting the accounting records, which were kept in a fireproof vault, was destroyed.

The store's owner has asked you to prepare an estimate of the dollar amount of inventory in the store on the night of the fire, so an insurance claim can be filed. The following information is available:

1. The store's accounts were closed on the previous December 31.
2. The store has earned an average 32% gross profit on sales for a number of years.
3. After all posting was completed, the store's accounts showed these May 20 balances:

Merchandise inventory (January 1 balance).....	$ 42,850
Sales	188,950
Sales returns	2,450
Purchases	123,900
Purchases returns	1,250
Freight-in	2,730

Required:

Prepare an estimate of the store's inventory at the time of the fire.

Problem 9–7

Olive Company wants a June 30, midyear estimate of its inventory. During the past five years its gross profit rate has averaged 34%. The following information is available from its records for the first half of the year:

January 1, beginning inventory ...	$ 48,450
Purchases	198,370
Purchases returns	1,150
Freight-in	2,710
Sales	308,900
Sales returns	2,400

Required:

Use the gross profit method to prepare an estimate of the company's June 30 inventory.

ALTERNATE PROBLEMS

Problem 9–1A

Glendon Company sold 880 units of its Product X last year at $50 per unit. It began the year and purchased the product as follows:

January 1 inventory	100 units at $28 per unit
Purchases:	
February 12	100 units at $30 per unit
April 30	400 units at $32 per unit
August 3	300 units at $33 per unit
December 15	100 units at $35 per unit

Required:

Under the assumption the company's selling and administrative expenses were $10 per unit sold, prepare a comparative income statement for the company showing in adjacent columns the net income earned from the sale of the product with the ending inventory priced on the basis of *(a)* Fifo, *(b)* Lifo, and *(c)* weighted-average cost.

Problem 9–2A

A concern began an accounting period with 200 units of a product that cost $40 each, and it made successive purchases of the product as follows:

Jan. 10   500 units @ $50 each
Apr. 27   600 units @ $55 each
Aug. 22   300 units @ $60 each
Oct. 15   400 units @ $55 each

Required:

1. Prepare a calculation showing the number and total cost of the units for sale during the period.
2. Under the assumption the company had 500 units of the product in its December 31 end-of-the-period periodic inventory, prepare calculations to show the portions of the total cost of the units for sale during the period that should be assigned to the ending inventory and to the units sold *(a)* first on a Fifo basis, *(b)* then on a Lifo basis, and *(c)* finally on a weighted-average cost basis.

Problem 9–3A

A company's inventory records for one of its products showed the following transactions:

Jan. 1   Beginning inventory: 15 units costing $35 each.
     10   Purchased 10 units at $40 each.
     16   Sold five units.
     18   Sold eight units.
     20   Purchased 10 units at $45 each.
     25   Sold 14 units.

Required:

1. Assume the company keeps its records on a Fifo basis and enter the transactions on a perpetual inventory record card. Use two or more lines to show units on hand at each price or units sold when units costing different amounts are on hand or sold.
2. Assume the company keeps its records on a Lifo basis and record the transactions on a second record card.
3. Assume the last sale was on credit to Lee Barr for $900 and prepare an entry in general journal form to record the sale and cost of goods sold on a Fifo basis.

Problem 9–4A

A specialty shop has the following information from its records and from a year-end physical inventory at marked selling prices:

	At cost	At retail
January 1, beginning inventory.....	$ 23,980	$ 33,440
Purchases	166,290	232,920
Purchases returns	2,110	3,190
Additional markups		5,630
Markdowns......................		2,180
Sales...........................		235,450
Sales returns		1,230

The shop reduces its year-end physical inventory taken at marked selling prices to a cost basis by an application of the retail inventory method. However, the shop always estimates its year-end inventory by the retail method and by comparison determines the amount of inventory shortage, if any.

Required:

1. Prepare a calculation to estimate the shop's year-end inventory at cost.
2. Under the assumption the shop's year-end physical inventory at marked selling prices totaled $31,300, prepare a calculation showing the amount of its inventory shortage at cost and at retail.

Problem 9–5A

Berg Company's records provide the following information for the year ended last December 31:

	At cost	At retail
Sales		$321,250
Sales returns		2,440
January 1 inventory	$ 31,940	46,290
Purchases......................	218,240	316,420
Purchases returns	2,320	3,390
Additional markups................		5,180
Markdowns		3,940
December 31 physical inventory.......		40,250

Required:

1. Use the retail method to prepare a calculation estimating Berg Company's year-end inventory at cost.
2. Prepare a calculation showing the amount of its inventory shortage at cost and at retail.

Problem 9–6A

Valley Auto Parts suffered a disastrous fire during the night of April 5, and everything excepting the accounting records, which were in a fireproof vault, was destroyed. As an insurance adjuster, you have been called upon to determine the store's inventory loss. The following information is available from the store's accounting records:

Merchandise inventory on January 1	$ 33,150
Purchases, January 1 through April 5	92,215
Purchases returns for the same period	410
Freight on purchases for the period	1,285
Sales, January 1 through April 5	138,975
Sales returns and allowances	475
Average gross profit margin past five years ..	34%

Required:

Use the gross profit method to prepare a statement estimating the store's inventory loss.

Problem 9–7A

Cornelia, the owner and manager of Cornelia's Fur Salon, opened her shop on Monday morning, April 9, and discovered that thieves had broken in over the weekend and made off with the shop's entire inventory. Fortunately it was near the end of the season and the inventory was low. Nevertheless, as an insurance adjuster, you have been called upon to determine the loss. The following information is available from the shop's accounting records, which were closed the previous December 31.

Merchandise inventory, January 1	$ 75,410
Purchases	92,850
Purchases returns	1,730
Freight-in	880
Sales	178,480
Sales returns	2,230
Average gross profit rate for past four years ..	38%

Required:

Prepare a calculation estimating the shop's inventory loss.

PROVOCATIVE PROBLEMS

Provocative problem 9–1
Fashion Footwear, Ltd.

Fashion Footwear, Ltd., suffered extensive damage from water and smoke and a small amount of fire damage on the night of October 12. The store carried adequate insurance, and next morning the insurance company's claims agent arrived to inspect the damage. After completing a survey, the agent agreed with Dale Eble, the store's owner, that the inventory could be sold to a company specializing in fire sales for about one fifth of its cost. The agent offered Mr. Eble $20,000 in full settlement for the damage to the inventory. He suggested that Mr. Eble accept the offer and said he had authority to deliver at once a check for the amount of the damage. He pointed out that a prompt settlement would provide funds to replace the inventory in time for the store to participate in the Christmas shopping season.

Mr. Eble felt the loss might exceed $20,000 but he recognized that a time-consuming physical count and inspection of each item in the inventory would be necessary to establish the loss more precisely; and he was reluctant to take the time for the inventory, since he was anxious to get back into business before the Christmas rush, the season making the largest contribution to his annual profit. Yet he was also unwilling to take a substantial loss on the insurance settlement; so he asked for and received a 24-hour period in which to consider the insurance company offer, and he immediately went to his records for the following information:

	At cost	At retail
a. January 1 inventory	$ 23,480	$ 37,100
Purchases, January 1 through October 12 ...	181,900	288,700
Net sales, January 1 through October 12		282,200

b. On March 1 the remaining inventory of winter footwear was marked down from $12,000 to $9,600, and placed on sale in the annual end-of-the-winter-season sale. Three fourths of the shoes were sold; the markdown on the remainder was canceled, and the shoes were returned to their regular retail price. (A markdown cancellation is subtracted from a markdown, and a markup cancellation is subtracted from a markup.)

c. In June a special line of imported Italian shoes proved popular, and 60 high-styled pairs were marked up from their normal $40 retail price to $45 per pair. Forty pairs were sold at this higher price, and on August 1 the markup on the remaining 20 pairs was canceled and they were returned to their regular $40 per pair price.

d. Between January 1 and October 12 markdowns totaling $1,500 were taken on several odd lots of shoes.

Recommend whether or not you think Mr. Eble should accept the insurance company's offer. Back your recommendation with figures.

Provocative problem 9–2
Barr's Home Store

Barr's Home Store has been in business for five years, during which it has earned a 35% average annual gross profit on sales. However, night before last, on May 5, it suffered a disastrous fire that destroyed its entire inventory; and Ed Barr, the store's owner, has filed a $56,000 inventory loss claim with the store's insurance company. When asked on what he based his claim, he replied that during the day before the fire he had marked every item in the store down 20% in preparation for the annual summer clearance sale, and during the marking-down process he had also taken an inventory of the merchandise in the store. Furthermore, he said, "It's a big loss, but every cloud has a silver lining because I am giving you fellows (the insurance company) the benefit of the 20% markdown in filing this claim."

When it was explained to Mr. Barr that he had to back his loss claim with more than his word as to the amount of the loss, he produced the following information from his pre-sale inventory and his accounting records, which fortunately were in a fireproof vault and were not destroyed in the fire.

a. The store's accounts were closed on December 31, of last year.
b. After all posting was completed, the accounts showed these May 5 balances:

Sales	$189,860
Sales returns	4,760
Purchases.....................................	119,800
Purchases returns	1,450
Freight-in	3,140
Merchandise inventory (January 1, balance)	44,370

c. Mr. Barr's pre-fire inventory totaled $70,000 at pre-markdown prices.

Required:

1. Prepare a calculation showing the estimated amount of Mr. Barr's inventory loss.
2. Present figures showing how Mr. Barr arrived at the amount of his loss claim.
3. Present figures based on the amount of Mr. Barr's pre-fire inventory figure, $70,000, to substantiate the inventory estimate arrived at in Required 1 above.

☐ Tell what is included in the cost of a plant asset.

☐ Calculate depreciation by the *(a)* straight-line, *(b)* units-of-production, *(c)* declining-balance, and *(d)* sum-of-the-years'-digits methods.

☐ Explain how accelerated depreciation defers income taxes.

☐ Explain how the original cost of a plant asset is recovered through the sale of the asset's product or service.

☐ Explain why income tax expenses shown in financial statements may differ from taxes actually payable.

☐ Define or explain the words and phrases listed in the Glossary.

Plant and equipment

■ Assets used in the production or sale of other assets or services and that have a useful life longer than one accounting period are called *plant and equipment* or *fixed assets*. The phrase "fixed assets" has been used for many years in referring to items of plant and equipment. It was once commonly used as a balance sheet caption. However, as a caption it is rapidly disappearing from published balance sheets. It is being replaced by the more descriptive "plant and equipment" or the more complete "property, plant, and equipment."

Use in the production or sale of other assets or services is the characteristic that distinguishes a plant asset from an item of merchandise or an investment. An office or factory machine held for sale by a dealer is merchandise to the dealer. Likewise, land purchased and held for future expansion but presently unused is classified as a long-term investment. Neither is a plant asset until put to use in the production or sale of other assets or services. However, standby equipment for use in case of a breakdown or for use during peak periods of production is a plant asset. Also, when equipment is removed from service and held for sale, it ceases to be a plant asset.

A productive or service life longer than one accounting period distinguishes an item of plant and equipment from an item of supplies. An item of supplies may be consumed in a single accounting period. If consumed, its cost is charged to the period of consumption. The productive life of a plant asset, on the other hand, is longer than one period. It contributes to production for several periods. Therefore, as a result of the *matching principle,* its cost must be allocated to these periods in a systematic and rational manner.[1]

COST OF A PLANT ASSET

Cost is the basis for recording the acquisition of a plant asset. The cost of a plant asset includes all normal and reasonable expenditures necessary to get the asset in place and ready to use. For example, the cost of a factory machine includes its invoice price, less any discount for cash, plus freight, unpacking, and assembling costs. Cost also includes any special concrete base or foundation, electrical or power connections, and adjustments needed to place the machine in operation. In short, the cost of a plant asset includes all normal, necessary, and reasonable costs incurred in getting the asset in place and ready to produce.

A cost must be normal and reasonable as well as necessary if it is to be properly included in the cost of a plant asset. For example, if a machine is damaged by being dropped in unpacking, repairs should not be added to its cost. They should be charged to an expense account. Likewise, a fine paid for moving a heavy machine on city streets without proper permits is not part of the cost of the machine. However, if secured, the cost of the permits would be.

After being purchased but before being put to use, a plant asset must sometimes be repaired or remodeled before it meets the needs of the purchaser. In such a case the repairing or remodeling expenditures are part of its cost and should be charged to the asset account. Furthermore, depreciation charges should not begin until the asset is put in use.

When a plant asset is constructed by a concern for its own use, cost includes material and labor costs plus a reasonable amount of overhead or indirect expenses such as heat, lights, power, and depreciation on the machinery used in constructing the asset. Cost also includes architectural and design fees, building permits, and insurance during construction. Needless to say, insurance on the same asset after it has been placed in production is an expense.

When land is purchased for a building site, its cost includes the amount paid for the land plus any real estate commissions. It also includes escrow and legal fees, fees for examining and insuring the title, and any accrued property taxes paid by the purchaser, as well as expenditures for surveying, clearing, grading, draining, and landscaping. All are part of the cost of the land. Furthermore, any assessments incurred at the time of purchase or later for such things as

---

[1] APB, "Basic Concepts and Accounting Principles Underlying Financial Statements of Business Enterprises," *APB Statement No. 4* (New York: AICPA, October 1970), par. 159. Copyright (1970) by the American Institute of CPAs.

the installation of streets, sewers, and sidewalks should be debited to the Land account since they add a more or less permanent value to the land.

Land purchased as a building site sometimes has an old building that must be removed. In such cases the entire purchase price, including the amount paid for the to-be-removed building, should be charged to the Land account. Also, the cost of removing the old building, less any amounts recovered through the sale of salvaged materials, should be charged to this account.

Land used as a building site is assumed to have an unlimited life and is therefore not subject to depreciation. However, buildings and land improvements such as driveways, parking lots, fences, and lighting systems are subject to depreciation. Consequently, land, building, and land improvement costs should not be recorded in the same account. At least two accounts should be used, one for land and a second for buildings and land improvements. However, three accounts, one for land, a second for buildings, and a third for land improvements, would be better.

Often land, buildings, and equipment are purchased together for one lump sum. When this occurs, the purchase price must be apportioned among the assets on some fair basis, since some of the assets depreciate and some do not. A fair basis may be tax-assessed values or appraised values. For example, assume that land independently appraised at $30,000 and a building appraised at $70,000 are purchased together for $90,000. The cost may be apportioned on the basis of appraised values as follows:

	Appraised value	Percent of total	Apportioned cost
Land	$ 30,000	30	$27,000
Building	70,000	70	63,000
Totals ...	$100,000	100	$90,000

NATURE OF DEPRECIATION

When a plant asset is purchased, in effect a quantity of usefulness that will contribute to production throughout the service life of the asset is acquired. However, since the life of any plant asset (other than land) is limited, this quantity of usefulness is also limited and will in effect be consumed by the end of the asset's service life. Consequently, depreciation, as the term is used in accounting, is nothing more than the expiration of a plant asset's quantity of usefulness, and the recording of depreciation is a process of allocating and charging the cost of this usefulness to the accounting periods that benefit from the asset's use.

For example, when a company purchases an automobile to be used by one of its salespeople, it in effect purchases a quantity of usefulness, a quantity of transportation for the salesperson. The cost of this quantity of usefulness is the cost of the car less whatever will be received for it when sold or traded in at the end of its service life. And, recording depreciation on the car is a process of allocating the cost of this usefulness to the accounting periods that benefit from the car's use. Note that it is not the recording of physical deterioration nor recording the decline in the car's market value.

The foregoing is in line with the pronouncements of the AICPA's Committee on Accounting Procedure which described depreciation as follows:

> The cost of a productive facility is one of the costs of the services it renders during its useful economic life. Generally accepted accounting principles require that this cost be spread over the expected useful life of the facility in such a way as to allocate it as equitably as possible to the periods during which services are obtained from the use of the facility. This procedure is known as depreciation accounting, a system of accounting which aims to distribute the cost or other basic value of tangible capital assets, less salvage (if any), over the estimated useful life of the unit . . . in a systematic and rational manner. It is a process of allocation, not of valuation.[2]

SERVICE LIFE OF A PLANT ASSET

The *service life* of a plant asset is the period of time it will be used in producing or selling other assets or services. This may not be the same as the asset's potential life. For example, typewriters have a potential six- or eight-year life. However, if a company finds that it is wise to trade its old typewriters on new ones every three years, in this company typewriters have a three-year service life. Furthermore, in this business the cost of new typewriters less their trade-in value should be charged to depreciation expense over this three-year period.

Predicting a plant asset's service life is sometimes difficult because several factors are often involved. Wear and tear and the action of the elements determine the useful life of some assets. However, two additional factors, *inadequacy* and *obsolescence,* often need be considered. When a business acquires plant assets, it should acquire assets of a size and capacity to take care of its foreseeable needs. However, a business often grows more rapidly than anticipated. In such cases the capacity of the plant assets may become too small for the productive demands of the business long before they wear out. When this happens,

---

[2] Committee on Accounting Procedure, "Accounting Research Bulletin No. 43," *Accounting Research and Terminology Bulletins, Final Edition* (New York: AICPA, 1961), p. 76. Copyright (1961) by the American Institute of CPAs.

inadequacy is said to have taken place. Inadequacy cannot easily be predicted. Obsolescence, like inadequacy, is also difficult to foretell because the exact occurrence of new inventions and improvements normally cannot be predicted. Yet new inventions and improvements often cause an asset to become obsolete and make it wise to discard the obsolete asset long before it wears out.

A company that has previously used a particular type of asset may estimate the service life of a new asset of like kind from past experience. A company without previous experience with a particular asset must depend upon the experience of others or upon engineering studies and judgment. The Internal Revenue Service publishes information giving estimated service lives for hundreds of new assets. Many business executives refer to this information in estimating the life of a new asset.

SALVAGE VALUE

When a plant asset has a *salvage value,* the cost of its quantity of usefulness is the asset's cost minus its salvage value. The salvage value of a plant asset is the portion of its cost that is recovered at the end of its service life. Some assets such as typewriters, trucks, and automobiles are traded in on similar new assets at the end of their service lives. The salvage values of such assets are their trade-in values. Other assets may have no trade-in value and little or no salvage value. For example, at the end of its service life, some machinery can be sold only as scrap metal.

When the disposal of a plant asset involves certain costs, as in the wrecking of a building, the salvage value is the net amount realized from the sale of the asset. The net amount realized is the amount received for the asset less its disposal cost. Often in the case of a machine the cost to remove the machine will equal the amount that can be realized from its sale. In such a case the machine has no salvage value.

ALLOCATING DEPRECIATION

Many methods of allocating a plant asset's total depreciation to the several accounting periods in its service life have been suggested and are used. Four of the more common are the *straight-line method,* the *units-of-production method,* the *declining-balance method,* and the *sum-of-the-years'-digits method.* Each is acceptable and falls within the realm of *generally accepted accounting principles.*

Straight-line method

When the straight-line method is used, the cost of the asset minus its estimated salvage value is divided by the estimated number of accounting periods in the asset's service life. The result is the estimated amount the asset depreciates each period. For example, if a machine costs $550, has an estimated service life of five years, and an estimated $50 salvage value, its depreciation per year by the straight-line method is $100 and is calculated as follows:

$$\frac{\text{Cost} - \text{Salvage}}{\text{Service life in years}} = \frac{\$550 - \$50}{5} = \$100$$

Note that the straight-line method allocates an equal share of an asset's total depreciation to each accounting period in its life.

Units-of-production method

The purpose of recording depreciation is to charge each accounting period in which an asset is used with a fair share of its depreciation. The straight-line method charges an equal share to each period; and when plant assets are used about the same amount in each accounting period, this method rather fairly allocates total depreciation. However, in some lines of business the use of certain plant assets varies greatly from accounting period to accounting period. For example, a contractor may use a particular piece of construction equipment for a month and then not use it again for many months. For such an asset, since use and contribution to revenue may not be uniform from period to period, it is argued that the *units-of-production method* better meets the requirements of the *matching principle* than does the straight-line method.

When the units-of-production method is used in allocating depreciation, the cost of an asset minus its estimated salvage value is divided by the estimated units of product it will produce during its entire service life. This division gives depreciation per unit of product. Then the amount the asset is depreciated in any one accounting period is determined by multiplying the units of product produced in that period by depreciation per unit. Units of product may be expressed as units of product or in any other unit of measure such as hours of use or miles driven. For example, a truck costing $6,000 is estimated to have a $2,000 salvage value. If it is also estimated that during the truck's service life it will be driven 50,000 miles, the depreciation per mile, or the depreciation per unit of product, is $0.08 and is calculated as follows:

$$\frac{\text{Cost} - \text{Salvage value}}{\text{Estimated units of production}} = \frac{\text{Depreciation per}}{\text{unit of product}}$$

or

$$\frac{\$6,000 - \$2,000}{50,000 \text{ miles}} = \$0.08 \text{ per mile}$$

If these estimates are used and the truck is driven 20,000 miles during its first year, depreciation for the first year is $1,600. This is 20,000 miles at $0.08 per mile. If the truck is driven 15,000 miles in the second year, depreciation for the second year is 15,000 times $0.08, or $1,200.

Declining-balance method

The *Internal Revenue Code* permits depreciation methods for tax purposes which result in higher depreciation charges during the early years of a plant asset's life. These methods are also used in preparing financial reports to investors. The declining-balance method is one of these. Under this method, depreciation of up to twice the straight-line rate, without considering salvage value, may be applied each year to the declining book value of a new plant asset having an estimated life of three years or more. If this method is followed and twice the straight-line rate is used, depreciation on an asset is determined by (1) calculating a straight-line depreciation rate for the asset. Next, (2) doubling this rate. Then, (3) at the end of each year in the asset's life, this doubled rate is applied to the asset's remaining *book value*. (The book value of a plant asset is its cost less accumulated depreciation; it is the value shown for the asset on the books.)

If this method is used to charge depreciation on a $10,000 new asset that has an estimated five-year life and no salvage value, these steps are followed: (Step 1) A straight-line depreciation rate is calculated by dividing 100% by five (years) to determine the straight-line annual depreciation rate of 20%. Next (Step 2) this rate is doubled; and then (Step 3) annual depreciation charges are calculated as in the following table:

Year	Annual depreciation calculation	Annual depreciation expense	Remaining book value
1st year.........	40% of $10,000	$4,000.00	$6,000.00
2d year	40% of 6,000	2,400.00	3,600.00
3d year	40% of 3,600	1,440.00	2,160.00
4th year	40% of 2,160	864.00	1,296.00
5th year	40% of 1,296	518.40	777.60

Under the declining-balance method the book value of a plant asset never reaches zero. Consequently, when the asset is sold, exchanged, or scrapped, any remaining book value is used in determining the gain or loss on the disposal. However, if an asset has a salvage value, the asset may not be depreciated beyond its salvage value. For example, if instead of no salvage value the foregoing $10,000 asset has an estimated $1,000 salvage value, depreciation for its fifth year is limited to $296. This is the amount required to reduce the asset's book value to its salvage value.

Declining-balance depreciation results in what is called *accelerated depreciation* or higher depreciation charges in the early years of a plant asset's life. The sum-of-the-years'-digits method has a like result.

Sum-of-the-years'-digits method

Under the *sum-of-the-years'-digits method* the years in an asset's service life are added. Their sum then becomes the denominator of a series of fractions used in allocating total depreciation to the periods in the asset's service life. The numerators of the fractions are the years in the asset's life in their reverse order. For example, assume this method is used in allocating depreciation on a machine costing $7,000, having an estimated five-year life and an estimated $1,000 salvage value. The sum-of-the-years' digits in the asset's life are:

$$1 + 2 + 3 + 4 + 5 = 15$$

and annual depreciation charges are calculated as follows:

Year	Annual depreciation calculation	Annual depreciation expense
1st year	$5/15$ of $6,000	$2,000
2d year	$4/15$ of 6,000	1,600
3d year	$3/15$ of 6,000	1,200
4th year	$2/15$ of 6,000	800
5th year	$1/15$ of 6,000	400
Total depreciation		$6,000

When a plant asset has a long life, the sum-of-the-years' digits in its life may be calculated by using the formula: $SYD = n[(n + 1)/2]$. For example, sum-of-the-years' digits for a five-year life is: $5\left(\dfrac{5 + 1}{2}\right) = 15$.

Accelerated depreciation methods are advocated by many accountants who claim that their use results in a more equitable "use charge" for long-lived plant assets than other methods. These accountants point out, for example, that as assets grow older, repairs and maintenance increase. Therefore, when smaller amounts of depreciation are added to increasing repair costs, a more equitable total expense charge to match against revenue results. Also, they point out that as an asset grows older, in some instances its ability to produce revenue is reduced. For example, rentals from an apartment building are normally higher in the earlier years of its life but will decline as the building becomes less attractive. In such cases many accountants argue that the requirements of the *matching principle* are better met with heavier depreciation charges in the earlier years and lighter charges in the later years of the asset's life.

The foregoing are theoretical reasons for the use of accelerated depreciation methods. However, a tax reason rather than theoretical arguments is probably more responsible for their use. The tax reason is that accelerated depreciation normally results in *deferring income taxes* from the early years in a plant asset's life until its later years. Taxes are deferred because accelerated depreciation causes larger amounts of depreciation to be charged to the early years. This results in smaller amounts of income and income taxes in these years. However, the taxes are only deferred because smaller amounts of depreciation in later years result in larger amounts of income and taxes in these years. Nevertheless, through accelerated depreciation a company does have the "interest-free" use of the deferred tax dollars until the later years of a plant asset's life.

DEPRECIATION FOR PARTIAL YEARS

Plant assets are normally bought when needed and are sold or discarded when they are no longer usable or needed. And, the purchases and sales are not necessarily made at either the beginning or end of an accounting period. Because of this, depreciation must often be calculated for partial years. For example, a machine costing $4,500 and having an estimated five-year service life and a $500 estimated salvage value was purchased on October 8, 198A. If the yearly accounting period ends on December 31, depreciation for three months must be recorded on this machine on that date. Three months are three twelfths of a year. Consequently, the three months' depreciation is calculated:

$$\frac{\$4,500 - \$500}{5} \times \frac{3}{12} = \$200$$

In this illustration, depreciation is calculated for a full three months, even though the asset was purchased on October 8. Depreciation is an estimate. Therefore, calculation to the nearest full month is usually sufficiently accurate. This means that depreciation is usually calculated for a full month on assets purchased before the 15th of the month. Likewise, depreciation for the month in which an asset is purchased is normally disregarded if the asset is purchased after the middle of the month.

The entry to record depreciation for three months on the machine purchased on October 8 is:

Dec.	31	Depreciation Expense, Machinery	200.00	
		Accumulated Depreciation, Machinery		200.00
		To record depreciation for three months.		

On December 31, 198B, and at the end of each of the following three years, a journal entry to record a full year's depreciation on this machine is required. The entry is:

Dec.	31	Depreciation Expense, Machinery	800.00	
		Accumulated Depreciation, Machinery		800.00
		To record depreciation for one year.		

After the December 31, 198E, depreciation entry is recorded, the accounts showing the history of this machine appear as follows:

Machinery		Accumulated Depreciation, Machinery	
Oct. 8, '8A 4,500		Dec. 31, '8A 200	
		Dec. 31, '8B 800	
		Dec. 31, '8C 800	
		Dec. 31, '8D 800	
		Dec. 31, '8E 800	

If this machine is disposed of during 198F, two entries must be made to record the disposal. The first records 198F depreciation to the date of disposal, and the second records the actual disposal. For example, assume that the machine is sold for $700 on June 24, 198F. To record the disposal, depreciation for six months (depreciation to the nearest full month) must first be recorded. The entry for this is:

June	24	Depreciation Expense, Machinery	400.00	
		Accumulated Depreciation, Machinery		400.00
		To record depreciation for one-half year.		

After making the entry to record depreciation to the date of sale, a second entry to record the actual sale is made. This entry is:

June	24	Cash	700.00	
		Accumulated Depreciation, Machinery	3,800.00	
		Machinery		4,500.00
		To record the sale of a machine at book value.		

In this instance the machine was sold for its book value. Plant assets are commonly sold for either more or less than book value, and cases illustrating this are described in the next chapter.

APPORTIONING ACCELERATED DEPRECIATION

When accelerated depreciation is used and accounting periods do not coincide with the years in an asset's life, depreciation must be apportioned between periods if it is to be properly charged. For example, the machine for which sum-of-the-years'-digits depreciation is calculated on page 346 is to be depreciated $2,000 during its first year, $1,600 during its second year, and so on for its five-year life. If this machine is placed in use on April 1 and the annual accounting periods of its owner end on December 31, the machine will be in use for three fourths of a year during the first accounting period in its life. Consequently, this period should be charged with $1,500 depreciation ($2,000 × ¾ = $1,500). Likewise, the second accounting period should be charged with $1,700 depreciation [(¼ × $2,000) + (¾ × $1,600) = $1,700], and like calculations should be used for the remaining periods in the asset's life.

DEPRECIATION ON THE BALANCE SHEET

In presenting information about the plant assets of a business, the *full-disclosure principle* requires that both the cost of such assets and their accumulated depreciation be shown in the statements by major classes. Also, a general description of the depreciation method or methods used must be given in a balance sheet footnote or other manner.[3] To comply, the plant assets of a concern may be shown on its balance sheet or in a schedule accompanying the balance sheet as follows:

---

[3] Accounting Principles Board, "Omnibus Opinion—1967," *APB Opinion No. 12* (New York: AICPA, December 1967), par. 5. Copyright (1970) by the American Institute of CPAs.

	Cost	Accumulated depreciation	Book value	
Plant assets:				
Store equipment	$ 12,400	$1,500	$10,900	
Office equipment	3,600	450	3,150	
Building	72,300	7,800	64,500	
Land	15,000		15,000	
Totals	$103,300	$9,750		$93,550

When plant assets are thus shown and the depreciation methods described, a much better understanding can be gained by a balance sheet reader than if only information as to undepreciated cost is given. For example, $50,000 of assets with $40,000 of accumulated depreciation are quite different from $10,000 of new assets. Yet the net undepreciated cost is the same in both cases. Likewise, the picture is different if the $40,000 of accumulated depreciation resulted from accelerated depreciation rather than straight-line depreciation.

BALANCE SHEET PLANT ASSET VALUES

From the discussion thus far students should recognize that the recording of depreciation is not primarily a valuing process. Rather it is a process of allocating the costs of plant assets to the several accounting periods that benefit from their use. Furthermore, they should recognize that because the recording of depreciation is an allocating process rather than a valuing process, balance sheets show for plant assets undepreciated costs rather than market values.

The fact that balance sheets show undepreciated costs rather than market values seems to disturb many beginning accounting students. It should not. When a balance sheet is prepared, normally the company for which it is prepared has no intention of selling its plant assets. Consequently, the market values of these assets may be of little significance. The student should recognize that when a balance sheet is prepared, it is under the assumption the company for which it is prepared is a going concern that will continue in business long enough to recover the original costs of its plant assets through the sale of its products.

The assumption that a company is a going concern that will continue in business long enough to recover its plant asset costs through the sale of its products is known in accounting as the *continuing- or going-concern concept.* It provides the justification for carrying plant assets on the balance sheet at cost less accumulated depreciation, in other words at the share of their cost applicable to future periods. It is also the justification for carrying at cost such things as stationery imprinted with the company name, though salable only as scrap paper. In all such instances the intention is to use the assets in carrying on the business operations. They are not for sale, so it is pointless to place them on the balance sheet at market or realizable values, whether these values are greater or less than book values.

Uninformed financial statement readers sometimes mistakenly think that the accumulated depreciation shown on a balance sheet represents funds accumulated to buy new assets when present assets must be replaced. However, an informed reader recognizes that accumulated depreciation represents that portion of an asset's cost that has been charged off to depreciation expense during its life. Such a reader also knows that accumulated depreciation accounts are contra accounts having credit balances that cannot be used to buy anything. Furthermore, an informed reader knows that if a concern has cash with which to buy assets, it is shown on the balance sheet as a current asset "Cash."

RECOVERING THE COSTS OF PLANT ASSETS

A company that earns a profit or breaks even (neither earns a profit nor suffers a loss) eventually recovers the original cost of its plant assets through the sale of its products. This is best explained with a condensed income statement like that of Illustration 10–1 which shows that Even Steven Company broke even during the year of the illustrated income statement. However, in breaking even it also recovered $5,000 of the cost of its plant assets through the sale of its products. It recovered the $5,000 because of the $100,000 that flowed into the company from sales only $95,000 flowed out to pay for goods sold, rent, and salaries. No funds flowed out for depreciation expense. As a result, the company recovered this $5,000 portion of the cost of its plant assets through the sale of its products. Furthermore, if the company remains in business for the life of its plant assets, either breaking even or earning a profit, it will recover their entire cost in this manner.

At this point students commonly ask, "Where is the recovered $5,000?" The answer is that the company may have the $5,000 in the bank. However, the funds may also have been spent to increase

---

Even Steven Company
Income Statement for Year Ended December 31, 19—

Sales		$100,000
Cost of goods sold	$60,000	
Rent expense	10,000	
Salaries expense	25,000	
Depreciation expense	5,000	
Total		100,000
Net income		$ 0

Illustration 10–1

merchandise inventory, to buy additional equipment, to pay off a debt, or they may have been withdrawn by the business owner. In short, the funds may still be in the bank or they may have been used for any purpose for which a business uses funds, and only an examination of its balance sheets as of the beginning and end of the year will show this.

ACCELERATED DEPRECIATION AND INCOME TAXES

The primary objective in preparing an income statement for a business is to show the results of its operations, measured in accordance with generally accepted accounting principles. However, income measured in accordance with generally accepted accounting principles is not always the same as income subject to state and federal income taxes. They may differ because a taxpayer is permitted by law in some cases to use one accounting method or procedure for tax purposes and a different method or procedure for its accounting records and financial statements. For example, a business may choose straight-line depreciation for its accounting records because it best reflects periodic net income. However, at the same time it may use accelerated depreciation in preparing its tax returns because accelerated depreciation defers the recognition of income subject to income taxes and thus postpones the payment of income taxes.

Nevertheless, when a corporation elects one accounting procedure for tax purposes and a different procedure for its accounting records and financial statements, a problem arises as to how much income tax expense should be deducted each year on its published income statement. If the tax actually incurred is deducted, reported net income may vary from year to year due to the postponement and later payment of taxes. Consequently, since a corporation's stockholders may be misled by these variations, the APB ruled that income taxes should be allocated so that distortions caused by differences between tax accounting procedures and financial accounting procedures are avoided.[4]

TAXES AND THE DISTORTION OF NET INCOME

To appreciate the problem involved here, assume that a corporation has installed a $100,000 machine, the product of which will produce a half million dollars of revenue in each of the succeeding four years and $80,000 of income before depreciation and taxes. Assume further that the company must pay income taxes at a 50%[5] rate (round number

---

[4] APB, "Accounting for Income Taxes," *APB Opinion No. 11* (New York: AICPA, 1967). Copyright (1967) by the American Institute of CPAs.

[5] At this writing federal income tax may take as much as 46% of a corporation's before-tax income, and when state income tax is added, the combined rate may reach 50% or more.

assumed for easy calculation) and that it plans to use straight-line depreciation in its records but the declining-balance method for tax purposes. If the machine has a four-year life and an $8,000 salvage value, annual depreciation calculated by each method will be as follows:

Year	Straight line	Declining balance
1	$23,000	$50,000
2	23,000	25,000
3	23,000	12,500
4	23,000	4,500
Totals	$92,000	$92,000

And since the company has elected *declining-balance depreciation* for tax purposes, it will be liable for $15,000 of income tax on the first year's income, $27,500 on the second, $33,750 on the third, and $37,750 on the fourth. The calculation of these taxes is shown in Illustration 10–2.

Annual income taxes	Year 1	Year 2	Year 3	Year 4	Total
Income before depreciation and income taxes	$80,000	$80,000	$80,000	$80,000	$320,000
Depreciation for tax purposes (declining balance)	50,000	25,000	12,500	4,500	92,000
Taxable income	$30,000	$55,000	$67,500	$75,500	$228,000
Annual income taxes (50% of taxable income)	$15,000	$27,500	$33,750	$37,750	$114,000

Illustration 10–2

Furthermore, if the company were to deduct its actual tax liability each year in arriving at income to be reported to its stockholders, it would report the amounts shown in Illustration 10–3.

Observe in Illustrations 10–2 and 10–3 that total depreciation, $92,000, is the same whether calculated by the straight-line or the declining-balance method. Also note that the total tax liability for the four years, $114,000, is the same in each case. Then note the distortion of the final income figures in Illustration 10–3 due to the postponement of taxes.

If this company should report successive annual income figures of $42,000, $29,500, $23,250, and then $19,250, some of its stockholders might be misled as to the company's earnings trend. Consequently,

Income after deducting actual tax liabilities	Year 1	Year 2	Year 3	Year 4	Total
Income before depreciation and income taxes	$80,000	$80,000	$80,000	$80,000	$320,000
Depreciation per books (straight line)	23,000	23,000	23,000	23,000	92,000
Income before taxes	$57,000	$57,000	$57,000	$57,000	$228,000
Income taxes (actual liability of each year)	15,000	27,500	33,750	37,750	114,000
Remaining income	$42,000	$29,500	$23,250	$19,250	$114,000

Illustration 10–3

in cases such as this the APB ruled that income taxes should be allocated so that the distortion caused by the postponement of taxes is removed from the income statement. In essence, *APB Opinion No. 11* requires that—

When a procedure used in the accounting records and an alternative procedure used for tax purposes differ in respect to their timing of expense recognition or revenue recognition, the tax expense deducted on the income statement should not be the actual tax incurred, but the amount that would have resulted if the procedure used in the records had also been used in calculating the tax.

If the foregoing is applied in this case, the corporation will report to its stockholders in each of the four years the amounts of income shown in Illustration 10–4.

In examining Illustration 10–4, recall that the company's tax liabilities are actually $15,000 in the first year, $27,500 in the second, $33,750 in the third, and $37,750 in the fourth, a total of $114,000. Then observe that when this $114,000 liability is allocated evenly over the four years,

Net income that should be reported to stockholders	Year 1	Year 2	Year 3	Year 4	Total
Income before depreciation and income taxes	$80,000	$80,000	$80,000	$80,000	$320,000
Depreciation per books (straight line)	23,000	23,000	23,000	23,000	92,000
Income before taxes	$57,000	$57,000	$57,000	$57,000	$228,000
Income taxes (amounts based on straight-line depreciation)	28,500	28,500	28,500	28,500	114,000
Net income	$28,500	$28,500	$28,500	$28,500	$114,000

Illustration 10–4

the distortion of the annual net incomes due to the postponement of taxes is removed from the income statements.

ENTRIES FOR THE ALLOCATION OF TAXES

When income taxes are allocated as in Illustration 10–4, the tax liability of each year and the deferred taxes are recorded with an adjusting entry. The adjusting entries for the four years of Illustration 10–4 and the entries in general journal form for the payment of the taxes (without explanations) are as follows:[6]

Year 1	Income Taxes Expense	28,500.00	
	Income Taxes Payable		15,000.00
	Deferred Income Taxes		13,500.00
Year 1	Income Taxes Payable	15,000.00	
	Cash		15,000.00
Year 2	Income Taxes Expense	28,500.00	
	Income Taxes Payable		27,500.00
	Deferred Income Taxes		1,000.00
Year 2	Income Taxes Payable	27,500.00	
	Cash		27,500.00
Year 3	Income Taxes Expense	28,500.00	
	Deferred Income Taxes	5,250.00	
	Income Taxes Payable		33,750.00
Year 3	Income Taxes Payable	33,750.00	
	Cash		33,750.00
Year 4	Income Taxes Expense	28,500.00	
	Deferred Income Taxes	9,250.00	
	Income Taxes Payable		37,750.00
Year 4	Income Taxes Payable	37,750.00	
	Cash		37,750.00

In the entries the $28,500 debited to Income Taxes Expense each year is the amount that is deducted on the income statement in reporting annual net income. Also, the amount credited to Income Taxes Payable each year is the actual tax liability of that year.

Observe in the entries that since the actual tax liability in each of the first two years is less than the amount debited to Income Taxes Expense, the difference is credited to Deferred Income Taxes. Then note that in the last two years, since the actual liability each year is

---

[6] To simplify the illustration, it is assumed here that the entire year's tax liability is paid at one time. However, as previously explained, corporations are usually required to pay estimated taxes on a quarterly basis.

greater than the debit to Income Taxes Expense, the difference is debited to Deferred Income Taxes. Now observe in the following illustration of the company's Deferred Income Taxes account that the debits and credits exactly balance each other out over the four-year period:

	Deferred Income Taxes			
Year	Explanation	Debit	Credit	Balance
1			13,500.00	13,500.00
2			1,000.00	14,500.00
3		5,250.00		9,250.00
4		9,250.00		–0–

CONTROL OF PLANT ASSETS

Good internal control for plant assets requires specific identification of each plant asset and formal records. It also requires periodic inventories in which each plant asset carried in the records is identified and its continued existence and use are verified. For identification purposes, each plant asset is commonly assigned a serial number at the time it is acquired. The serial number is stamped, etched, or affixed to the asset with a small decal not easily removed or altered. The exact kind of records kept depends upon the size of the business and the number of its plant assets. They range from handwritten records to punched cards and computer tapes. However, regardless of their nature, all provide the same basic information contained in the handwritten records which follow.

In keeping plant asset records, concerns normally divide their plant assets into functional groups and provide in their General Ledger separate asset and accumulated depreciation accounts for each group. For example, a store will normally provide an Office Equipment account and an Accumulated Depreciation, Office Equipment account. It will also provide a Store Equipment account and an Accumulated Depreciation, Store Equipment account. In short, the store will normally provide in its General Ledger a separate plant asset account and a separate accumulated depreciation account for each functional group of plant assets it owns. Furthermore, each plant asset account and its related accumulated depreciation account is normally a controlling account controlling detailed subsidiary records. For example, the Office Equipment account and the Accumulated Depreciation, Office Equipment account control a subsidiary ledger having a separate record for each individual item of office equipment. Likewise, the Store Equipment account and its related Accumulated Depreciation, Store Equipment account become controlling accounts controlling a subsidiary store equipment ledger. In a handwritten system these subsidiary records are kept on plant asset record cards.

To illustrate handwritten plant asset records, assume that a concern's office equipment consists of just one desk and a chair. The general ledger record of these assets is maintained in the Office Equipment controlling account and the Accumulated Depreciation, Office Equipment controlling account. Since in this case there are only two assets, only two subsidiary record cards are needed. The general ledger and subsidiary ledger record of these assets appear as in Illustration 10–5.

Observe at the top of the cards the plant asset numbers assigned to these two items of office equipment. In each case the assigned number consists of the number of the Office Equipment account, 132, followed by the asset's number. As previously stated, these numbers are stenciled on or otherwise attached to the items of office equipment as a means of identification and to increase control over the items. The remaining information on the record cards is more or less self-

Plant Asset No. 132-1

SUBSIDIARY PLANT ASSET AND DEPRECIATION RECORD

Item _Office chair_   General Ledger Account _Office Equipment_
Description _Office chair_
Mfg. Serial No. _____   Purchased from _Office Equipment Co._
Where Located _Office_
Person Responsible for the Asset _Office Manager_
Estimated Life _12 years_ Estimated Salvage Value _$4.00_
Depreciation per Year _$6.00_ per Month _$0.50_

Date	Explanation	PR	Asset Record Dr.	Cr.	Bal.	Depreciation Record Dr.	Cr.	Bal.
July 2, 198A		G1	76.00		76.00			
Dec. 31, 198A		G23					3.00	3.00
Dec. 31, 198B		G42					6.00	9.00
Dec. 31, 198C		G65					6.00	15.00

Final Disposition of the Asset _____

Illustration 10–5

Plant Asset
No. *132-2*

SUBSIDIARY PLANT ASSET AND DEPRECIATION RECORD

General Ledger
Item *Desk*   Account *Office Equipment*
Description *Office desk*

Purchased
Mfg. Serial No.   from *Office Equipment Co.*
Where Located *Office*
Person Responsible for the Asset *Office Manager*
Estimated Life *12 years*   Estimated Salvage Value *$25.00*
Depreciation per Year *$36.00* per Month *$3.00*

Date	Explanation	P R	Asset Record			Depreciation Record		
			Dr.	Cr.	Bal.	Dr.	Cr.	Bal.
July 2, 198A		G1	457.00		457.00			
Dec. 31, 198A		G23					18.00	18.00
Dec. 31, 198B		G42					36.00	54.00
Dec. 31, 198C		G65					36.00	90.00

Final Disposition of the Asset _____

Office Equipment   ACCOUNT NO. 132

DATE	EXPLANATION	POST. REF.	DEBIT	CREDIT	BALANCE
198A July 2	Desk and chair	G1	5 3 3 00		5 3 3 00

Accumulated Depreciation, Office Equipment   ACCOUNT NO. 132A

DATE	EXPLANATION	POST. REF.	DEBIT	CREDIT	BALANCE
198A Dec. 31		G23		2 1 00	2 1 00
198B Dec. 31		G42		4 2 00	6 3 00
198C Dec. 31		G65		4 2 00	1 0 5 00

Illustration 10–5 *(concluded)*

evident. Note how the balance of the general ledger account, Office Equipment, is equal to the sum of the balances in the asset record section of the two subsidiary ledger cards. The general ledger account controls this section of the subsidiary ledger. Observe also how the Accumulated Depreciation, Office Equipment account controls the depreciation record section of the cards. The disposition section at the bottom of the card is used to record the final disposal of the asset. When the asset is discarded, sold, or exchanged, a notation telling of the final disposition is entered here. The card is then removed from the subsidiary ledger and filed for future reference.

PLANT ASSETS OF LOW COST

Individual plant asset records are expensive to keep. Consequently, many concerns establish a minimum, say $50 or a $100, and do not keep such records for assets costing less than the minimum. Rather, they charge the cost of such assets directly to an expense account at the time of purchase. Furthermore, if about the same amount is expended for such assets each year, this is acceptable under the *materiality principle.*

GLOSSARY

Accelerated depreciation. Any depreciation method resulting in greater amounts of depreciation expense in the early years of a plant asset's life and lesser amounts in later years.

Book value. The carrying amount for an item in the accounting records. When applied to a plant asset, it is the cost of the asset minus its accumulated depreciation.

Declining-balance depreciation. A depreciation method in which up to twice the straight-line rate of depreciation, without considering salvage value, is applied to the remaining book value of a plant asset to arrive at the asset's annual depreciation charge.

Deferred income tax. Amounts of income tax the incurrence of which is delayed or put off until later years due to accelerated depreciation or other cause.

Fixed asset. A plant asset.

Inadequacy. The situation where a plant asset does not produce enough product to meet current needs.

Internal Revenue Code. The codification of the numerous revenue acts passed by Congress.

Obsolescence. The situation where because of new inventions and improvements, an old plant asset can no longer produce its product on a competitive basis.

Office Equipment Ledger. A subsidiary ledger having a record card for each item of office equipment owned.

Salvage value. The share of a plant asset's cost recovered at the end of its service life through a sale or as a trade-in allowance on a new asset.

Service life. The period of time a plant asset is used in the production and sale of other assets or services.

Store Equipment Ledger. A subsidiary ledger having a record card for each item of store equipment owned.

Straight-line depreciation. A depreciation method that allocates an equal share of the total estimated amount a plant asset will be depreciated during its service life to each accounting period in that life.

Sum-of-the-years'-digits depreciation. A depreciation method that allocates depreciation to each year in a plant asset's life on a fractional basis. The denominator of the fractions used is the sum-of-the-years' digits in the estimated service life of the asset, and the numerators are the years' digits in reverse order.

Units-of-production depreciation. A depreciation method that allocates depreciation on a plant asset based on the relation of the units of product produced by the asset during a given period to the total units the asset is expected to produce during its entire life.

QUESTIONS FOR CLASS DISCUSSION

1. What are the characteristics of an asset classified as a plant asset?
2. What is the balance sheet classification of land held for future expansion? Why is such land not classified as a plant asset?
3. What in general is included in the cost of a plant asset?
4. A company asked for bids from several machine shops for the construction of a special machine. The lowest bid was $12,500. The company decided to build the machine for itself and did so at a total cash outlay of $10,000. It then recorded the machine's construction with a debit to Machinery for $12,500, a credit to Cash for $10,000, and a credit to Gain on the Construction of Machinery for $2,500. Was this a proper entry? Discuss.
5. As used in accounting, what is the meaning of the term "depreciation"?
6. Is it possible to keep a plant asset in such an excellent state of repair that recording depreciation is unnecessary?
7. A company has just purchased a machine that has a potential life of 15 years. However, the company's management believes that the development of a more efficient machine will make it necessary to replace the machine in eight years. What period of useful life should be used in calculating depreciation on this machine?

8. A building estimated to have a useful life of 30 years was completed at a cost of $85,000. It was estimated that at the end of the building's life it would be wrecked at a cost of $1,000 and that materials salvaged from the wrecking operation would be sold for $2,000. How much straight-line depreciation should be charged on the building each year?

9. Define the following terms as used in accounting for plant assets:

    a. Trade-in value.   c. Book value.   e. Inadequacy.

    b. Market value.   d. Salvage value.   f. Obsolescence.

10. When straight-line depreciation is used, an equal share of the total amount a plant asset is to be depreciated during its life is assigned to each accounting period in that life. Describe a situation in which this may not be a fair basis of allocation. Name a more fair basis for the situation described.

11. What is the sum-of-the-years' digits in the life of a plant asset that will be used for 12 years?

12. Does the recording of depreciation cause a plant asset to appear on the balance sheet at market value? What is accomplished by recording depreciation?

13. What is the essence of the going-concern concept of a business?

14. Explain how a concern that breaks even recovers the cost of its plant assets through the sale of its products? Where are the funds thus recovered?

15. Does the balance of the account, Accumulated Depreciation, Machinery, represent funds accumulated to replace the machinery as it wears out? Tell in your own words what the balance of such an account represents?

16. Why does the taxable income of a business commonly differ from the net income reported on its income statement?

CLASS EXERCISES

Exercise 10–1

A machine was purchased for $3,000, terms 2/10, n/60, FOB shipping point. The invoice was paid within the discount period along with $140 of freight charges. The machine required a special concrete base and power connections costing $345. In moving the machine onto its new concrete base, it was dropped and damaged. The damage cost $65 to repair. After being repaired, $40 of raw materials were consumed in adjusting the machine so that it would produce a satisfactory product. The adjustments were normal for this type of machine and were not the result of its having been damaged. The product produced while the adjustments were being made was not salable. Prepare a calculation to show the cost of the machine for accounting purposes.

Exercise 10–2

Three machines were acquired in a lump-sum purchase for $5,490. The purchaser paid $200 to transport the machines to his factory. Machine No. 1 was twice as big and weighed twice as much as Machine No. 2, and Machines 2 and 3 were approximately equal in size and weight. The machines had the following appraised values and installation costs:

	Machine 1	Machine 2	Machine 3
Appraised values	$2,000	$4,000	$3,000
Installation costs	150	350	200

Determine the cost of each machine for accounting purposes.

Exercise 10–3

A machine was installed at a $3,600 cost. Its useful life was estimated at five years or 5,000 units of product with a $600 trade-in value. During its second year it produced 1,100 units of product. Determine the machine's second-year depreciation under each of the following assumptions. Depreciation was calculated on a *(a)* straight-line basis, *(b)* units-of-production basis, *(c)* declining-balance basis at twice the straight-line rate, and *(d)* sum-of-the-years'-digit basis.

Exercise 10–4

A machine cost $1,600 installed and was estimated to have a four-year life and a $150 trade-in value. Use declining-balance depreciation at twice the straight-line rate to determine the amount of depreciation to be charged against the machine in each of the four years in its life.

Exercise 10–5

A machine was installed on January 4, 19—, at a $3,600 total cost. A full year's depreciation on a straight-line basis was charged against the machine on December 31, at the end of each of the first three years in its life, under the assumption the machine would have a four-year life and no salvage value. The machine was sold at its book value on May 1, during its fourth year. *(a)* Give the entry to record the partial year's depreciation on May 1. *(b)* Give the entry to record the sale.

Exercise 10–6

A company that operates with accounting periods that end on December 31 installed and placed in operation on June 26 a machine that cost $8,000 and was expected to have a four-year life and a $500 salvage value. The machine was to be depreciated on a declining-balance basis at twice the straight-line rate. *(a)* Give the entry to record depreciation on the machine on the first December 31 in its life. *(b)* Give the entry for depreciation on the second December 31 in the machine's life.

PROBLEMS

Problem 10–1

Part 1. A machine costing $20,000 was installed in a factory. Its useful life was estimated at four years, after which it would have a $2,000 trade-in value. It was estimated the machine would produce 60,000 units of product during its life. It actually produced 12,000 units during its first year, 18,000 during the second, 20,000 during the third, and 10,000 during its fourth year.

Required:

1. Prepare a calculation to show the number of dollars of this machine's cost that should be charged to depreciation over its four-year life.
2. Prepare a form with the following column headings:

Year	Straight Line	Units of Production	Declining Balance	Sum-of-the-Years' Digits

Then enter on the form the depreciation for each year and the total depreciation on the machine under each depreciation method. Use twice the straight-line rate for declining-balance depreciation.

Part 2. A secondhand machine was purchased on January 3, 198A, for $1,650. During the next six days it was repaired and repainted at a cost of $265 and was placed in operation on a new specially built concrete base that cost $135. It was estimated the machine would have a three-year life and a $250 salvage value. Depreciation on a straight-line basis was charged against the machine on December 31, 198A; and on August 28, 198B, the machine was sold for its book value.

Required:

Prepare the necessary entries to record these transactions under the assumption the costs of repairing and repainting the machine and its new concrete base were paid for on January 10, 198A.

Problem 10–2

A company purchased four machines during 198A and 198B, and it used four ways to allocate depreciation on them. Information about the machines follows:

Machine number	Placed in use on—	Cost	Estimated life	Salvage value	Depreciation method
1	Oct. 29, 198A	$5,400	8 years	$600	Straight line
2	Nov. 27, 198A	3,650	4 years	650	Sum-of-the-years' digits
3	Mar. 15, 198B	8,310	15,000 units	810	Units of production
4	Aug. 30, 198B	?	8 years	700	Declining balance

Machine No. 3 produced 2,500 units of product during 198B and 3,000 units in 198C. Machine No. 4 had a $5,600 invoice price, 2/10, n/60, FOB shipping point. The invoice was paid on the last day of its discount period, August 31, but the company had to borrow $5,000 in order to do so (90-day, 8% note). The loan was repaid on November 29. Freight charges on Machine No. 4 were $122, and the machine was placed on a special concrete base that cost $190. It was assembled and installed by the company's own employees. Their wages during the installation period were $200. Payment for the freight charges, the concrete base, and the employees' wages were made on August 31.

Required:

1. Prepare a form with the following columnary headings:

Machine Number	Amount to Be Charged to Depreciation	198A Depreciation	198B Depreciation	198C Depreciation

Enter the machine numbers in the first column and complete the information opposite each machine's number. Use twice the straight-line rate in depreciating Machine No. 4. Total all columns.

2. Prepare entries to record all transactions involving the purchase of Machine No. 4, including the note transactions.
3. Prepare an entry to record the 198C depreciation on the machines.

Problem 10-3

Black Rock Company was organized during the first week in January of the current year; and in making the year-end audit of the company's records, you discover that the company's bookkeeper has debited an account called "Land, Buildings, and Equipment" for what he thought was the cost of the company's new factory. The account had a $1,070,500 debit balance made up of the following items:

Cost of the land and an old building on the land purchased as the site of the company's new plant (appraised value of the land, $87,500, and of the old building, $12,500)	$ 90,000
Attorney's fee for a title search to assure clear title	800
Cost of removing the old building from the site	3,000
Cost of grading the plant site	400
Architect's fee for planning the new building	30,000
Cost of new building. (Contract price, $531,600; but in lieu of cash, the contractor accepted $33,500 in cash and 500 bonds the company had purchased as an investment while waiting for the completion of the building. The bonds cost $500,000 and had a $498,100 market value on the day they were given to the contractor.)	533,500
Cost of landscaping the plant site	5,500
Cost of new concrete walks and paving the parking lot	26,000
Cost of installing lights in the parking lot	2,800
Factory machinery and equipment (including the $1,250 cost of a machine dropped and made useless while being installed) ..	332,300
Fine and permit for hauling heavy machinery on the city streets. (The company was cited for hauling the machinery without a permit. The fine was $250 and the cost of the permit was $25.)	275
Cost of installing machinery	44,675
Cost of replacing the dropped and damaged machine	1,250
Total	$1,070,500

An examination of the payroll records showed that an account called "Superintendence" had been debited for the plant superintendent's $18,000 salary for the ten-month period, March 1 through December 31. From March 1 through August 31 the superintendent had supervised construction of the factory building. During September, October, and November he had supervised installation of the factory machinery.

The bookkeeper had set up an account called "Miscellaneous Revenues" and had credited it for the $300 proceeds from the sale of materials salvaged from the old building removed from the plant site and for $50 from the sale of the wrecked machine.

Required:

1. Prepare a form having the following column headings: Land, Land Improvements, Buildings, and Machinery. List the items and sort their amounts to the proper asset columns under the assumption the company's manufacturing operations began on December 1. Show a negative item by enclosing it in parentheses. Total the columns.
2. Under the assumption the company's accounts had not been closed, prepare an entry to remove the item amounts from the accounts in which they were incorrectly recorded and enter them in the proper accounts.
3. Prepare an entry to record the depreciation expense for the partial year. Assume the building and land improvements have an estimated 30-year life and no salvage value and the machinery has a 12-year life and a salvage value equal to 10% of its cost.

Problem 10–4

Essex Company completed these store equipment transactions:

198A

Jan. 4 Purchased on credit from Alpha Equipment Company a Fair scale, serial number 00–123, $200. The scale's service life was estimated at ten years with a $20 trade-in value. It was assigned plant asset number 131–1.

6 Purchased on credit from Alpha Equipment Company an Accurate cash register, serial number XX–1212, $320. The register's life was estimated at eight years with an $80 trade-in value. It was assigned plant asset number 131–2.

Feb. 28 Purchased on credit from Gamma Equipment Sales an Iceair refrigerated display case, serial number MM–777, $2,000. The asset's service life was estimated at 12 years with a $200 trade-in value. It was assigned plant asset number 131–3.

Dec. 31 Recorded the 198A depreciation on the store equipment.

198B

Aug. 24 Sold the Fair scale to Corner Market for its book value.

26 Purchased a new Apex scale from Alpha Equipment Company on credit for $265. Its serial number was BB–321, and it was assigned plant asset number 131–4. The scale's service life was estimated at ten years with a $25 trade-in value.

Dec. 31 Record the 198B depreciation on the store equipment.

Required:

1. Open a Store Equipment account and an Accumulated Depreciation, Store Equipment account plus subsidiary plant asset record cards as needed.
2. Prepare general journal entries to record the transactions. Post to the general ledger accounts and to the plant asset record cards.
3. Prove the December 31, 198B, balances of the Store Equipment and Accumulated Depreciation, Store Equipment accounts by preparing with totals a schedule showing the cost and accumulated depreciation on each plant asset owned on that date.

Problem 10–5

Western Company completed the installation of a new machine in its plant at a $200,000 total cost on January 5, 198A. It was estimated that the machine would have a four-year life, a $20,000 salvage value, and that it would produce $150,000 of income during each of the four years, before depreciation and income taxes. The company allocates income taxes in its reports to stockholders, since it uses straight-line depreciation in its accounting records and sum-of-the-years'-digits depreciation for tax purposes.

Required:

1. Prepare a schedule showing 198A, 198B, 198C, 198D, and total net income for the four years after deducting sum-of-the-years'-digits depreciation and actual taxes. Assume a 50% income tax rate.
2. Prepare a second schedule showing each year's net income and the four-year total after deducting straight-line depreciation and actual taxes.
3. Prepare a third schedule showing income to be reported to stockholders with straight-line depreciation and allocated taxes.
4. Set up a T-account for Deferred Income Taxes and show therein the entries that will result from allocating income taxes.

Problem 10–6

Alpha Sales and Beta Sales are almost identical. Each began operations on January 2 of this year with $22,000 of equipment having an eight-year life and a $2,000 salvage value. Each purchased merchandise during the year as follows:

Jan. 2	100 units @ $200 per unit =	$ 20,000
Mar. 11	200 units @ $230 per unit =	46,000
July 7	200 units @ $250 per unit =	50,000
Oct. 15	100 units @ $260 per unit =	26,000
		$142,000

And now, on December 31 at the end of the first year, each has 110 units of merchandise in its ending inventory. However, Alpha Sales will use straight-line depreciation in arriving at its net income for the year, while Beta Sales will use declining-balance depreciation at twice the straight-line rate. Also, Alpha Sales will use Fifo in costing its ending inventory and Beta Sales will use Lifo. The December 31 trial balances of the two concerns carried these amounts:

	Alpha Sales		Beta Sales	
Cash	$ 1,500		$ 1,500	
Accounts receivable	10,000		10,000	
Equipment	22,000		22,000	
Accounts payable		$ 8,000		$ 8,000
Allen Alpha, capital		32,000		
Bruce Beta, capital				32,000
Sales		170,000		170,000
Purchases	142,000		142,000	
Salaries expense	15,000		15,000	
Rent expense	12,000		12,000	
Other expenses	7,500		7,500	
Totals	$210,000	$210,000	$210,000	$210,000

Required:

Prepare an income statement for each concern and a schedule accounting for the difference in their reported net incomes. Write a short answer to this question: Which, if either, of the concerns is the more profitable and why?

ALTERNATE PROBLEMS

Problem 10–1A

Part 1. A machine costing $13,000 was installed in a factory. Its useful life was estimated at four years, after which it would have a $1,000 trade-in value; and it was estimated the machine would produce 30,000 units of product during its life. It actually produced 6,000 units during its first year, 9,000 during the second, 8,000 during the third, and 7,000 during its last year.

Required:

1. Prepare a calculation to show the number of dollars of this machine's cost that should be charged to depreciation over its four-year life.
2. Prepare a form with the following column headings:

Year	Straight Line	Units of Production	Declining Balance	Sum-of-the-Years' Digits

Then show the depreciation for each year and the total depreciation for the machine under each depreciation method. Use twice the straight-line rate for the declining-balance method.

Part 2. A secondhand delivery truck was purchased for $4,470 on March 5, 198A. The next day it was repainted and the company's name and business were lettered on its sides at a cost of $150. Also, $210 was paid for a new set of tires. The tires were priced at $224, but a $14 trade-in allowance was received on the truck's old tires. Cash was paid in each instance.

At the time of purchase it was estimated the truck would be driven 30,000 miles, after which it would have a $1,830 trade-in value. The truck was driven 12,000 miles in 198A; and between January 1 and November 3, 198B, it was driven an additional 15,000 miles. On the latter date it was sold for its book value.

Required:

Prepare general journal entries to record the transactions.

Problem 10-2A

A company purchased four machines during 198A and 198B. Machine No. 1 was placed in use on September 2, 198A. It cost $13,150, had an estimated eight-year life and a $1,150 salvage value, and was depreciated on a straight-line basis. Machine No. 2 was placed in use on September 29, 198A, and was depreciated on a units-of-production basis. It cost $12,200, and it was estimated that it would produce 50,000 units of product during its five-year life, after which it would have a $2,200 salvage value. It produced 3,000 units during 198A, 11,500 during 198B, and 12,000 during 198C. Machines 3 and 4 were purchased from a bankrupt firm at auction for $17,100 cash on May 17, 198B, and were placed in service on June 25 of that year. Additional information about the machines follow:

Machine number	Appraised value	Salvage value	Estimated life	Installation cost	Depreciation method
3	$ 8,000	$500	6 years	$250	Sum-of-the-years' digits
4	10,000	800	10 years	500	Declining balance

Required:

1. Prepare a form with the following columnar headings:

Machine Number	Amount to Be Charged to Depreciation	198A Depreciation	198B Depreciation	198C Depreciation

Enter the machine numbers in the first column, complete the information opposite each machine number, and total the columns. Assume that twice the straight-line rate was used for the declining-balance depreciation.
2. Prepare entries to record payment for Machines 3 and 4 and for their installation. Assume cash was paid for the installation on the day the machines were placed in use.
3. Prepare an entry to record the 198C depreciation on the four machines.

Problem 10-3A

Assume that you are making the first year-end audit of the records of a manufacturing concern that was organized in January of the current year and you have discovered that the company's bookkeeper has debited an account called "Land, Buildings, and Machinery" for what he thought was the cost of the company's new factory. The account had a $787,750 debit balance made up of the following items:

Cost of land and an old building on the land purchased as the site of the company's new factory (appraised value of the land, $70,000, and of the old building, $10,000)	$ 75,000
Attorney's fee resulting from the purchase of the land	750
Escrow fee resulting from the land purchase	500
Cost of removing old building	2,500
Surveying and grading the plant site	3,800
Cost of retaining wall and drain tile placed on the site	5,900
Cost of new building. (The contract price for the building was $363,700; however, the contractor accepted $60,175 in cash and 30 bonds having a $300,000 par value. The company had purchased the bonds at the beginning of the construction period for $300,000. The bonds had a $303,525 market value on the day they were given to the contractor.)	360,175
Architect's fee for planning the building	23,300
Cost of paving parking lot	21,600
Cost of parking lot lights	1,800
Landscaping	6,600
Machinery (including the $1,150 cost of a machine dropped and made useless while being unloaded from a freight car)	281,875
Fine and permit to haul heavy machinery on the city streets. (The company was cited for hauling machinery without a permit. It then secured the permit. Fine, $275 cost of the permit, $25)	300
Cost of hauling machinery from freight yard to factory	2,500
Cost of replacing the damaged machine	1,150
Total	$787,750

In examining the company's other accounts it was discovered that the bookkeeper had credited the $400 proceeds from the sale of materials salvaged from the old building removed from the plant site to an account called "Miscellaneous Revenues." He had also credited this account for $75 from the sale of the wrecked machine.

An examination of the payroll records showed that an account called "Superintendence" had been debited for the plant superintendent's $16,200 salary for the nine-month period, April 1 through December 31. From April 1 through August 31 the superintendent had supervised construction of the factory building. During September and October he had supervised installation of the factory machinery. The factory began manufacturing operations on November 1.

Required:

1. Prepare a form having the following column headings: Land, Land Improvements, Buildings, and Machinery. List the items and sort their amounts to the proper columns. Show negative amounts in parentheses. Total the columns.
2. Under the assumption the company's accounts had not been closed, prepare an entry to remove any item amounts from the accounts in which they were incorrectly entered and record them in the proper accounts.

3. The company closes its books annually on December 31. Prepare the entry to record the partial year's depreciation on the plant assets. Assume the building and land improvements are estimated to have 30-year lives and no salvage values and that the machinery is estimated to have a 12-year life and a salvage value equal to 10% of its cost.

Problem 10–4A

ABC Company completed these plant asset transactions:

198A

Dec. 28 Purchased on credit from Office Suppliers a Clear copier, serial number WM178, $870. The copier's service life was estimated at eight years with a $150 trade-in value. Assigned plant asset number 131–1 to the machine.

198B

Jan. 3 Purchased on credit from Speedy Typewriter Sales a Speedy typewriter, serial number M0778, $300. The machine's service life was estimated at five years with a $45 trade-in value. Assigned plant asset number 131–2 to the typewriter.

July 7 Purchased on credit from Zippo, Inc., a Zippo calculator, serial number 2X345, $290. The machine's service life was estimated at eight years with a $50 trade-in value. Assigned plant asset number 131–3 to the machine.

Dec. 31 Recorded the 198B straight-line depreciation on the office equipment.

198C

Aug. 23 Sold the Speedy Typewriter to Ted Orr at its book value.

25 Purchased on credit from Office Suppliers an Accurate typewriter, serial number MMM–123, $425. The typewriter's service life was estimated at five years with a $125 trade-in value. Assigned plant asset number 131–4 to the typewriter.

Dec. 31 Recorded the 198C depreciation on the office equipment.

Required:

1. Open Office Equipment and Accumulated Depreciation, Office Equipment accounts plus plant asset record cards as needed.
2. Prepare general journal entries to record the transactions and post to the general ledger accounts and plant asset record cards.
3. Prove the December 31, 198C, balances of the Office Equipment and Accumulated Depreciation, Office Equipment accounts by preparing a schedule showing the cost and accumulated depreciation on each plant asset owned on that date.

Problem 10–5A

Hilltop Company installed a new machine at a $160,000 total cost early in January 198A. It was estimated the machine would have a four-year life, a $12,000 salvage value at the end of that period, and would produce $100,000 of income annually before depreciation and income taxes. The company allocates income taxes in its reports to stockholders since it uses straight-line depreciation in its accounting records but declining-balance depreciation at twice the straight-line rate for tax purposes.

Required:

1. Prepare a schedule showing 198A, 198B, 198C, 198D, and total net income for the four-year period after deducting declining-balance depreciation and actual income taxes. Assume a 50% tax rate.
2. Prepare a second schedule showing each year's net income and the four-year total after deducting straight-line depreciation and actual taxes.
3. Prepare a third schedule showing income to be reported to stockholders with straight-line depreciation and allocated income taxes.
4. Set up a T-account for Deferred Income Taxes and show therein the entries that will result from allocating income taxes.

PROVOCATIVE PROBLEMS

Provocative problem 10–1
First audit

You have graduated from college and are working on your first audit as an employee of a local accounting firm. In examining the plant asset accounts of the concern being audited, you find the following debits and credits in an account called Land and Buildings:

Debits

Jan.	4	Cost of land and buildings acquired for a new plant site	$ 65,000
	5	Attorney's fee for title search before buying land and buildings .	400
	21	Cost of wrecking old building on plant site	5,000
Feb.	1	Six months' liability and fire insurance on new building	1,800
June	30	Payment to building contractor on completion of building	258,500
	30	Architect's fee for new building	15,000
July	10	City assessment for street improvement	4,100
	15	Cost of landscaping new plant site	2,500
			$352,300

Credits

Jan.	22	Proceeds from sale of salvaged materials from old building	$ 2,000
July	3	Refund of one month's insurance on new building	300
Dec.	31	One-half year's depreciation at 2½% per year	4,375
	31	Balance	345,625
			$352,300

In consulting with the senior accountant in charge of the audit, you learn that 40 years is a reasonable life expectancy for a building of the type involved and that it is reasonable to assume that there will be no salvage value at the end of the building's life. He also tells you to prepare a schedule with columns headed Date, Description, Total Amount, Land, Buildings, and Other Accounts, and to enter the items found in the Land and Buildings account on the schedule, distributing the amounts to the proper columns. He suggests that you show credits on your schedule by enclosing them in parentheses; and finally he suggests that since the accounts have not been closed, you draft any required correcting entry or entries. Assume that an account called Depreciation Expense, Land and Buildings was debited in recording the $4,375 of depreciation.

Provocative problem 10–2
Bitton Company

Bitton Company, a manufacturer, is about to invest $120,000 in new machinery to add a new product to its line. The new machinery is expected to have a four-year life and an $8,000 salvage value; and you, the concern's accountant, have prepared the following statement showing the expected results from the sale of the product under the assumption the new machinery will be depreciated on a straight-line basis and that 50% of the income earned will have to be paid out in state and federal income taxes.

BITTON COMPANY

Expected Results from Sale of New Product

	1st year	2d year	3d year	4th year	Total
Sales	$200,000	$200,000	$200,000	$200,000	$800,000
All costs other than depreciation and income taxes	120,000	120,000	120,000	120,000	480,000
Income before depreciation and income taxes..........	$ 80,000	$ 80,000	$ 80,000	$ 80,000	$320,000
Depreciation of machinery ...	28,000	28,000	28,000	28,000	112,000
Income before taxes	$ 52,000	$ 52,000	$ 52,000	52,000	$208,000
Income taxes	26,000	26,000	26,000	26,000	104,000
Net income	$ 26,000	$ 26,000	$ 26,000	$ 26,000	$104,000

When the company president examined your statement, he said that he knew that regardless of how calculated, the company could charge off no more than $112,000 of depreciation on the new machinery during its four-year life. Furthermore, he said, as he could see, this would result in $208,000 of income before taxes for the four years, $104,000 of income taxes, and $104,000 of net income for the period, regardless of how depreciation was calculated. Nevertheless, he continued that he had been talking with a friend on the golf course a few days back and the friend had tried to explain the tax advantage of using declining-balance depreciation. He said he did not understand all the friend had tried to tell him; and as a result he would like for you to prepare an additional statement like the one already prepared, but based on the assumption that declining-balance depreciation at twice the straight-line rate would be used in depreciating the new machinery. He said he would also like a written explanation of the tax advantage gained through the use of declining-balance depreciation, with a dollar estimate of the amount the company would gain in this case. Prepare the information for the president. (In making your estimate, assume the company can invest any deferred tax moneys in its operations and can earn an 8% after-tax return compounded annually on the amounts invested. Also, to simplify the problem, assume that the taxes must be paid on the first day of January in the year following their incurrence.)

After studying Chapter 11, you should be able to:

☐ Prepare entries to record the purchase and sale or discarding of a plant asset.

☐ Prepare entries to record the exchange of plant assets under accounting rules and under income tax rules and tell which rules should be applied in any given exchange.

☐ Make the calculations and prepare the entries to account for revisions in depreciation rates.

☐ Make the calculations and prepare the entries to account for plant asset repairs and betterments.

☐ Prepare entries to account for wasting assets and for intangible assets.

☐ Define or explain the words and phrases listed in the chapter Glossary.

Plant and equipment; intangible assets

■ Some of the problems met in accounting for property, plant, and equipment were discussed in the previous chapter. Additional problems involving plant assets and some of the accounting problems encountered with intangible assets are examined in this chapter.

PLANT ASSET DISPOSALS

Sooner or later a plant asset wears out, becomes obsolete, or becomes inadequate. When this occurs, the asset is discarded, sold, or traded in on a new asset. The entry to record the disposal will vary with its nature.

Discarding a plant asset

When an asset's accumulated depreciation is equal to its cost, the asset is said to be fully depreciated; and if a fully depreciated asset is discarded, the entry to record the disposal is:

Jan.	7	Accumulated Depreciation, Machinery	1,500.00	
		Machinery		1,500.00
		Discarded a fully depreciated machine.		

Although often discarded, sometimes a fully depreciated asset is kept in use. In such situations the asset's cost and accumulated depreciation should not be removed from the accounts but should remain on the books until the asset is sold, traded, or discarded. Otherwise the accounts do not show its continued existence. However, no additional depreciation should be recorded, since the reason for recording depreciation is to charge an asset's cost to depreciation expense. In no case should the expense exceed the asset's cost.

Sometimes an asset is discarded before being fully depreciated. For example, suppose an error was made in estimating the service life of a $1,000 machine and it becomes worthless and is discarded after having only $800 of depreciation recorded against it. In such a situation there is a loss and the entry to record the disposal is:

Jan.	10	Loss on Disposal of Machinery	200.00	
		Accumulated Depreciation, Machinery	800.00	
		Machinery		1,000.00
		Discarded a worthless machine.		

Discarding a damaged plant asset

Occasionally, before the end of its service life, a plant asset is wrecked in an accident or destroyed by fire. For example, a machine that cost $900 and which had been depreciated $400 was totally destroyed in a fire. If the loss was partially covered by insurance and the insurance company paid $350 to settle the loss claim, the entry to record the machine's destruction is:

Jan.	12	Cash	350.00	
		Loss from Fire	150.00	
		Accumulated Depreciation, Machinery	400.00	
		Machinery		900.00
		To record the destruction of machinery and the receipt of insurance compensation.		

If the machine were uninsured, the entry to record its destruction would not have a debit to Cash and the loss from fire would be greater.

Selling a plant asset

When a plant asset is sold, if the selling price exceeds the asset's book value, there is a gain. If the price is less than book value, there is a loss. For example, assume that a machine which cost $5,000 and had been depreciated $4,000 is sold for a price in excess of its book value, say for $1,200. If the machine is sold for $1,200, there is a gain and the entry to record the sale is:

Jan.	4	Cash	1,200.00	
		Accumulated Depreciation, Machinery	4,000.00	
		Machinery		5,000.00
		Gain on the Sale of Plant Assets		200.00
		Sold a machine at a price in excess of book value.		

However, if the machine is sold for $750, there is a $250 loss and the entry to record the sale is:

Jan.	4	Cash	750.00	
		Loss on the Sale of Plant Assets	250.00	
		Accumulated Depreciation, Machinery	4,000.00	
		Machinery		5,000.00
		Sold a machine at a price below book value.		

EXCHANGING PLANT ASSETS

Some plant assets are sold at the ends of their useful lives. Others, such as machinery, automobiles, and office equipment, are commonly exchanged for new up-to-date assets of like purpose. In such exchanges a trade-in allowance is normally received on the old asset, with the balance being paid in cash. The APB ruled that in recording the exchanges a material book loss should be recognized in the accounts but a book gain should not.[1] A book loss is experienced when the trade-in allowance is less than the book value of the traded asset. A book gain results from a trade-in allowance that exceeds the book value of the traded asset.

Recognizing a material book loss

To illustrate recognition of a material book loss on an exchange of plant assets, assume that a machine which cost $18,000 and had been depreciated $15,000 was traded in on a new machine having a $21,000 cash price. A $1,000 trade-in allowance was received, and the $20,000

---

[1] APB, "Accounting for Nonmonetary Transactions," *APB Opinion No. 29* (New York: AICPA, May 1973), par 22. Copyright (1973) by the American Institute of CPAs.

balance was paid in cash. Under these assumptions the book value of the old machine is $3,000, calculated as follows:

```
Cost of old machine ................  $18,000
   Less accumulated depreciation  ....   15,000
Book value ......................  $ 3,000
```

And since the $1,000 trade-in allowance resulted in a $2,000 loss on the exchange, the transaction should be recorded as follows:

Jan.	5	Machinery	21,000.00	
		Loss on Exchange of Machinery	2,000.00	
		Accumulated Depreciation, Machinery	15,000.00	
		Machinery		18,000.00
		Cash		20,000.00
		Exchanged old machine and cash for a new machine of like purpose.		

The $21,000 debit to Machinery puts the new machine in the accounts at its cash price. The debit to Loss on Exchange of Machinery records the loss. The old machine is removed from the accounts with the $15,000 debit to accumulated depreciation and the $18,000 credit to Machinery.

Nonrecognition of a book gain

When there is a book gain on an exchange of plant assets, the APB ruled that the new asset should be taken into the accounts at an amount equal to the book value of the traded-in asset plus the cash given. This results in the nonrecognition of the gain. For example, assume that in acquiring the $21,000 machine of the previous section a $4,500 trade-in allowance, rather than a $1,000 trade-in allowance, was received, and the $16,500 balance was paid in cash. A $4,500 trade-in allowance would result in a $1,500 gain on the exchange. However, in recording the exchange, the book gain should not be recognized in the accounts. Rather, it should be absorbed into the cost of the new machine by taking the new machine into the accounts at an amount equal to the sum of the book value of the old machine plus the cash given. This is $19,500 and is calculated as follows:

```
Book value of old machine ..........  $ 3,000
Cash given in the exchange .........   16,500
Cost basis for the new machine  .....  $19,500
```

And the transaction should be recorded as follows:

Jan.	5	Machinery	19,500.00	
		Accumulated Depreciation, Machinery	15,000.00	
		Machinery		18,000.00
		Cash		16,500.00
		Exchanged old machine and cash for a new machine of like purpose.		

Observe that the $19,500 recorded amount for the new machine is equal to its cash price less the $1,500 book gain on the exchange ($21,000 − $1,500 = $19,500). In other words, the $1,500 book gain was absorbed into the amount at which the new machine was recorded. The $19,500 is called the *cost basis* of the new machine and is the amount used in recording depreciation on the machine or any gain or loss on its sale.

The APB based its ruling that gains on plant asset exchanges should not be recognized on the opinion that ". . . revenue should not be recognized merely because one productive asset is substituted for a similar productive asset but rather should be considered to flow from the production and sale of the goods or services to which the substituted productive asset is committed."[2] In other words, the APB's opinion was that any gain from a plant asset exchange should be taken in the form of increased net income resulting from smaller depreciation charges on the asset acquired. In this case depreciation calculated on the recorded $19,500 cost basis of the new machine is less than if calculated on the machine's $21,000 cash price.

Tax rules and plant asset exchanges

Income tax rules and accounting principles are in agreement on the treatment of gains on plant asset exchanges but do not agree on the treatment of losses. According to the Internal Revenue Service, when an old asset is traded in on a new asset of like purpose, either a gain or a loss on the exchange must be absorbed into the cost of the new asset. This cost basis then becomes for tax purposes the amount that must be used in calculating depreciation on the new asset or any gain or loss on its sale or exchange. Consequently, for tax purposes the cost basis of an asset acquired in an exchange is the sum of the book value of the old asset plus the cash given, and it makes no difference whether there is a gain or a loss on the exchange.

As a result of the difference between accounting principles and tax rules, if a loss on a plant asset exchange is recorded as such, two

---

[2] Ibid., par. 16.

sets of depreciation records must be kept throughout the life of the new asset. One set must be kept for determining net income for accounting purposes, and the other for determining the depreciation deduction for tax purposes. Keeping two sets of records is obviously more costly than keeping one. Yet, when an exchange results in a material loss, the loss should be recorded and the two sets of records kept. On the other hand, when an exchange results in an immaterial loss, it is permissible under the *principle of materiality* to avoid the two sets of records by putting the new asset on the books at its cost basis for tax purposes.

For example, an old typewriter that cost $500 and upon which $420 of depreciation had been recorded was traded in at $50 on a new $600 typewriter, with the $550 difference being paid in cash. In this case the old typewriter's book value is $80; and if it was traded at $50, there was a $30 book loss on the exchange. However, the $30 loss is an immaterial amount, and the following method, called the income tax method, may be used in recording the exchange.

Jan.	7	Office Equipment	630.00	
		Accumulated Depreciation, Office Equipment ...	420.00	
		Office Equipment......................		500.00
		Cash		550.00
		Traded an old typewriter and cash for a new typewriter.		

The $630 at which the new typewriter is taken into the accounts by the income tax method is its cost basis for tax purposes and is calculated as follows:

Book value of old typewriter ($500 less $420)	$ 80
Cash paid ($600 less the $50 trade-in allowance)	550
Income tax basis of the new typewriter	$630

Not recording the loss on this exchange and taking the new typewriter into the accounts at its cost basis for income tax purposes violates the ruling of the APB that a loss on a plant asset exchange should be recorded. However, when there is an immaterial loss on an exchange, as in this case, the violation is permissible under the *principle of materiality*. Under this principle an adherence to any accounting principle, including rulings of the APB and the FASB, is not required when the cost to adhere is proportionally great and the lack of adherence does not materially affect reported periodic net income. In this case failing to record the $30 loss on the exchange would not materially affect the average company's statements. On the other hand, recording the loss and thereafter keeping two sets of depreciation records would be costly.

REVISING DEPRECIATION RATES

An occasional error in estimating the useful life of a plant asset is to be expected. Furthermore, when such an error is discovered, it is corrected by spreading the remaining amount the asset is to be depreciated over its remaining useful life.[3] For example, seven years ago a machine was purchased at a cost of $10,500. At that time the machine was estimated to have a ten-year life with a $500 salvage value. Therefore, it was depreciated at the rate of $1,000 per year [($10,500 − $500) ÷ 10 = $1,000]; and it began its eighth year with a $3,500 book value, calculated as follows:

Cost	$10,500
Less seven years' accumulated depreciation	7,000
Book value	$ 3,500

Assume that at the beginning of its eighth year the estimated number of years remaining in this machine's useful life is changed from three to five years with no change in salvage value. Under this assumption, depreciation for each of the machine's remaining years should be calculated as follows:

$$\frac{\text{Book value} - \text{Salvage value}}{\text{Remaining useful life}} = \frac{\$3,500 - \$500}{5 \text{ years}} = \$600 \text{ per year}$$

And $600 of depreciation should be recorded on the machine at the end of the eighth and each succeeding year in its life.

If depreciation is charged at the rate of $1,000 per year for the first seven years of this machine's life and $600 per year for the next five, depreciation expense is overstated during the first seven years and understated during the next five. However, if a concern has many plant assets, the lives of some will be underestimated and the lives of others will be overestimated at the time of purchase. Consequently, such errors will tend to cancel each other out with little or no effect on the income statement.

ORDINARY AND EXTRAORDINARY REPAIRS

Repairs made to keep an asset in its normal good state of repair are classified as *ordinary repairs*. A building must be repainted and

---

[3] APB, "Accounting Changes," *APB Opinion No. 20* (New York: AICPA, July 1971), par. 31. Copyright (1971) by the American Institute of CPAs.

its roof repaired. A machine must be cleaned, oiled, adjusted, and have any worn small parts replaced. Such repairs and maintenance are necessary, and their costs should appear on the current income statement as an expense.

Extraordinary repairs are major repairs made not to keep an asset in its normal good state of repair but to extend its service life beyond that originally estimated. As a rule, the cost of such repairs should be debited to the repaired asset's accumulated depreciation account under the assumption they make good past depreciation, add to the asset's useful life, and benefit future periods. For example, a machine was purchased for $8,000 and depreciated under the assumption it would last eight years and have no salvage value. As a result, at the end of the machine's sixth year its book value is $2,000, calculated as follows:

Cost of machine	$8,000
Less six years' accumulated depreciation	6,000
Book value.....................................	$2,000

If at the beginning of the machine's seventh year a major overhaul extends its estimated useful life three years beyond the eight originally estimated, the $2,100 cost should be recorded as follows:

Jan.	12	Accumulated Depreciation, Machinery	2,100.00	
		Cash (or Accounts Payable)		2,100.00
		To record extraordinary repairs.		

In addition, depreciation for each of the five years remaining in the machine's life should be calculated as follows:

Book value before extraordinary repairs	$2,000
Extraordinary repairs	2,100
Total	$4,100
Annual depreciation expense for remaining years ($4,100 ÷ 5 years)	$ 820

And, if the machine remains in use for five years after the major overhaul, the five annual $820 depreciation charges will exactly write off its new book value, including the cost of the extraordinary repairs.

BETTERMENTS

A *betterment* may be defined as the replacement of an existing plant asset portion with an improved or superior portion, usually at a cost materially in excess of the replaced item. Replacing the manual controls on a machine with automatic controls is an example. Usually a betterment results in a better, more efficient, or more productive asset, but not necessarily one having a longer life. When a betterment is made, its cost should be debited to the improved asset's account, say, the Machinery account, and depreciated over the remaining service life of the asset. Also, the cost and applicable depreciation of the replaced asset portion should be removed from the accounts.

CAPITAL AND REVENUE EXPENDITURES

A *revenue expenditure* is one that should appear on the current income statement as an expense and a deduction from the period's revenues. Expenditures for ordinary repairs, rent, and salaries are examples. Expenditures for betterments and for extraordinary repairs, on the other hand, are examples of what are called *capital expenditures* or *balance sheet expenditures*. They should appear on the balance sheet as asset increases.

Obviously, care must be exercised to distinguish between capital and revenue expenditures when transactions are recorded. For if errors are made, such errors often affect a number of accounting periods. For instance, an expenditure for a betterment initially recorded in error as an expense overstates expenses in the year of the error and understates net income. Also, since the cost of a betterment should be depreciated over the remaining useful life of the bettered asset, depreciation expense of future periods is understated and net income is overstated.

NATURAL RESOURCES

Natural resources such as standing timber, mineral deposits, and oil reserves are known as wasting assets. In their natural state they represent inventories that will be converted into a product by cutting, mining, or pumping. However, until cut, mined, or pumped they are noncurrent assets and commonly appear on a balance sheet under such captions as "Timberlands," "Mineral deposits," or "Oil reserves."

Natural resources are accounted for at cost, and appear on the balance sheet at cost less accumulated *depletion*. The amount such assets are depleted each year by cutting, mining, or pumping is commonly calculated on a "units-of-production" basis. For example, if a mineral deposit having an estimated 500,000 tons of available ore is purchased for $500,000, the depletion charge per ton of ore mined is $1. Furthermore, if 85,000 tons are mined during the first year, the depletion charge for the year is $85,000 and is recorded as follows:

Dec.	31	Depletion of Mineral Deposit	85,000.00	
		Accumulated Depletion, Mineral Deposit ...		85,000.00
		To record depletion of the mineral deposit.		

On the balance sheet prepared at the end of the first year the mineral deposit should appear at its $500,000 cost less $85,000 accumulated depletion. If the 85,000 tons of ore are sold by the end of the first year, the entire $85,000 depletion charge reaches the income statement as the depletion cost of the ore mined and sold. However, if a portion remains unsold at the year-end, the depletion cost of the unsold ore is carried forward on the balance sheet as part of the cost of the unsold ore inventory, a current asset.

Often machinery must be installed or a building constructed in order to exploit a natural resource. The costs of such assets should be depreciated over the life of the natural resource with annual depreciation charges that are in proportion to the annual depletion charges. For example, if a machine is installed in a mine and one eighth of the mine's ore is removed during a year, one eighth of the amount the machine is to be depreciated should be recorded as a cost of the ore mined.

INTANGIBLE ASSETS

Intangible assets have no physical existence; rather, they represent certain legal rights and economic relationships which are beneficial to the owner. Patents, copyrights, leaseholds, goodwill, trademarks, and organization costs are examples. Notes and accounts receivable are also intangible in nature. However, these appear on the balance sheet as current assets rather than under the intangible assets classification.

Intangible assets are accounted for at cost and should appear on the balance sheet in the intangible asset section at cost or at that portion of cost not previously written off. Normally the intangible asset section follows on the balance sheet immediately after the plant and equipment section. Intangibles should be systematically amortized or written off to expense accounts over their estimated useful lives, which in no case should exceed 40 years. Amortization is a process similar to the recording of depreciation.

Patents

Patents are granted by the federal government to encourage the invention of new machines and mechanical devices. A patent gives its owner the exclusive right to manufacture and sell a patented machine or device for a period of 17 years. When patent rights are purchased, all costs of acquiring the rights may be debited to an account called Patents. Also the costs of a successful lawsuit in defense of a patent may be debited to this account.

A patent gives its owner exclusive rights to the patented device for 17 years. However, its cost should be *amortized* or written off over a shorter period if its useful or economic life is estimated to be less than 17 years. For example, if a patent costing $25,000 has an estimated useful life of only ten years, the following adjusting entry is made at the end of each year in the patent's life to write off one tenth of its cost.

Dec.	31	Patents Written Off	2,500.00	
		Patents		2,500.00
		To write off one tenth of patent costs.		

The entry's debit causes $2,500 of patent costs to appear on the annual income statement as one of the costs of the patented product manufactured. The credit directly reduces the balance of the Patents account. Normally, patents are written off directly to the Patents account as in this entry.

Copyrights

A *copyright* is granted by the federal government and in most cases gives its owner the exclusive right to publish and sell a musical, literary, or artistic work during the life of the composer, author, or artist and for 50 years thereafter. Many copyrights have value for a much shorter time, and their costs should be amortized over the shorter period. Often the only cost of a copyright is the fee paid the Copyright Office. Since this is nominal, it is commonly charged directly to an expense account.

Leaseholds

Property is rented under a contract called a *lease.* The person or company owning the property and granting the lease is called the *lessor.* The person or company securing the right to possess and use the property is called the *lessee.* The rights granted the lessee under the lease are called a *leasehold.*

Some leases require no advance payment from the lessee but do require monthly rent payments. In such cases a Leasehold account is not needed and the monthly payments are debited to a Rent Expense account. Sometimes a long-term lease is so drawn that the last year's rent must be paid in advance at the time the lease is signed. When this occurs, the last year's advance payment is debited to the Leasehold account. It remains there until the last year of the lease, at which time it is transferred to Rent Expense.

Often a long-term lease, one running 20 or 25 years, becomes very valuable after a few years because its required rent payments are much less than current rentals for identical property. In such cases the increase in value of the lease should not be entered on the books since no extra cost was incurred in acquiring it. However, if the property is subleased and a cash payment is made for the rights under the old lease, the new tenant should debit the payment to a Leasehold account and write it off as additional rent expense over the remaining life of the lease.

Leasehold improvements

Long-term leases often require the lessee to pay for any alterations or improvements to the leased property, such as new partitions and store fronts. Normally the costs of *leasehold improvements* are debited to an account called Leasehold Improvements. Also, since the improvements become part of the property and revert to the lessor at the end of the lease, their cost should be amortized over the life of the lease or the life of the improvements, whichever is shorter. The amortization entry commonly has a debit to Rent Expense and a credit to Leasehold Improvements.

Goodwill

The term *goodwill* has a special meaning in accounting. In accounting, *a business is said to have goodwill when its rate of expected future earnings is greater than the rate of earnings normally realized in its industry.* Above-average earnings and the existence of goodwill may be demonstrated as follows with Companies A and B, both of which are in the same industry:

	Company A	Company B
Net assets (other than goodwill)	$100,000	$100,000
Normal rate of return in this industry ...	10%	10%
Normal return on net assets	$ 10,000	$ 10,000
Actual net income earned	10,000	15,000
Earnings above average	$ 0	$ 5,000

Company B has an above-average earnings rate for its industry and is said to have goodwill. Its goodwill may be the result of excellent customer relations, the location of the business, monopolistic privileges, superior management, or a combination of factors. Furthermore, a prospective investor would normally be willing to pay more for Company B than for Company A if the investor felt the extra earnings rate would continue. Thus, goodwill is an asset having value, and it can be sold.

Accountants are in agreement that goodwill should not be recorded unless it is bought or sold. This normally occurs only when a business is purchased and sold in its entirety. When this occurs, the goodwill of the business may be valued in several ways. Examples of three follow:

1. The buyer and seller may place an arbitrary value on the goodwill of a business being sold. For instance, a seller may be willing to sell a business having an above-average earnings rate for $115,000 and a buyer may be willing to pay that amount. If they both agree that the net assets of the business other than its goodwill have a $100,000 value, they are arbitrarily valuing the goodwill at $15,000.
2. Goodwill may be valued at some multiple of that portion of expected earnings which is above average. For example, if a company is expected to have $5,000 each year in above-average earnings, its goodwill may be valued at, say, four times that portion of its earnings which are above average or at $20,000. In this case it may also be said that the goodwill is valued at four years' above-average earnings. However, regardless of how it is said, this too is placing an arbitrary value on the goodwill.
3. The portion of a concern's earnings which is above average may be capitalized in order to place a value on its goodwill. For example, if a business is expected to continue to have $5,000 each year in earnings that are above average and the normal rate of return on invested capital in its industry is 10%, the excess earnings may be capitalized at 10% and a $50,000 value may be placed on its goodwill ($5,000 ÷ 10% = $50,000). Note that this values the goodwill at the amount that must be invested at the normal rate of return in order to earn the extra $5,000 each year ($50,000 × 10% = $5,000). It is a satisfactory method if the extra earnings are expected to continue indefinitely. However, this may not happen. Consequently, extra earnings are often capitalized at a rate higher than the normal rate of the industry, say in this case, at twice the normal rate or at 20%. If the extra earnings are capitalized at 20%, the goodwill is valued at $25,000 ($5,000 ÷ 20% = $25,000).

There are other ways to value goodwill. Nevertheless, in a final analysis goodwill is always valued at the price a seller is willing to take and a buyer is willing to pay.

Trademarks and trade names

Proof of prior use of a trademark or trade name is sufficient under common law to prove ownership and right of use. However, both may be registered at the Patent Office at a nominal cost for the same purpose. The cost of developing a trademark or trade name through, say, advertising should be charged to an expense account in the period or periods incurred. However, if a trademark or trade name is purchased, its cost should be amortized as explained in the next section.

Amortization of intangibles

Some intangibles, such as patents, copyrights, and leaseholds, have determinable lives based on a law, contract, or the nature of the asset. The costs of such assets should be amortized over the shorter of the term of their existence or the period expected to be benefited by their use. Other intangibles, such as goodwill, trademarks, and trade names, have indeterminable lives. However, the APB ruled that the value of any intangible will eventually disappear. As a result, a reasonable estimate of the period of usefulness of such assets should be made. Their costs should then be amortized over the periods estimated to be benefited by their use, which in no case should exceed 40 years.[4]

GLOSSARY

Amortize. To periodically write off as an expense a share of the cost of an asset, usually an intangible asset.

Betterment. The replacement of an existing asset portion with an improved or superior asset portion.

Capital expenditure. An expenditure that increases net assets.

Copyright. An exclusive right granted by the federal government to publish and sell a musical, literary, or artistic work for a period of years.

Depletion. The amount a wasting asset is depleted through cutting, mining, or pumping.

Extraordinary repairs. Major repairs that extend the life of a plant asset beyond the number of years originally estimated.

Goodwill. That portion of the value of a business due to its ability to earn a rate of return greater than the average in its industry.

Income tax rules. Rules governing how income for tax purposes and income taxes are to be calculated.

---

[4] APB, "Intangible Assets," *APB Opinion No. 17* (New York: AICPA, August 1970), par. 29. Copyright (1970) by the American Institute of CPAs.

Intangible asset. An asset having no physical existence but having value due to the rights resulting from its ownership and possession.

Lease. The contractural right to possess and use property under the terms of a lease contract.

Leasehold. Property held under the terms of a lease contract.

Leasehold improvements. Improvements to leased property made by the lessee.

Lessee. An individual granted possession of property under the terms of a lease contract.

Lessor. The individual or enterprise that has granted possession and use of property under the terms of a lease contract.

Ordinary repairs. Repairs made to keep a plant asset in its normal good operating condition.

Patent. An exclusive right granted by the federal government to manufacture and sell a given machine or mechanical device for a period of years.

Revenue expenditure. An expenditure that should be deducted from current revenue on the income statement.

QUESTIONS FOR CLASS DISCUSSION

1. When should a loss on the exchange of a plant asset be recorded? When is it permissible to absorb a loss into the cost basis of the new plant asset? Should a gain on a plant asset exchange be recorded as such?
2. When plant assets of like purpose are exchanged, what determines the cost basis of the newly acquired asset for federal income tax purposes?
3. When the loss on an exchange of plant assets is immaterial in amount, what advantage results from taking the newly acquired asset into the records at the amount of its cost basis for tax purposes?
4. When an old plant asset is traded in at a book loss on a new asset of like purpose, the loss is not recognized for tax purposes. In the end this normally does not work a financial hardship on the taxpayer. Why?
5. What is the essence of the accounting principle of materiality?
6. If at the end of four years it is discovered that a machine that was expected to have a five-year life will actually have an eight-year life, how is the error corrected?
7. Distinguish between ordinary repairs and replacements and extraordinary repairs and replacements.
8. How should ordinary repairs to a machine be recorded? How should extraordinary repairs be recorded?
9. What is a betterment? How should a betterment to a machine be recorded?
10. Distinguish between revenue expenditures and capital expenditures.
11. What are the characteristics of an intangible asset?
12. In general, how are intangible assets accounted for?
13. Define (a) lease, (b) lessor, (c) leasehold, and (d) leasehold improvement.
14. In accounting, when is a business said to have goodwill?

CLASS EXERCISES

Exercise 11–1

A machine that cost $4,000 and that had $2,800 of accumulated depreciation recorded against it was traded in on a new machine of like purpose having a $4,500 cash price. A $1,000 trade-in allowance was received, and the balance was paid in cash. Determine (a) the book value of the old machine, (b) the cash given in making the exchange, (c) the book loss on the exchange, (d) the cost basis of the new machine for income tax purposes, and (e) the annual straight-line depreciation on the new machine for income tax purposes under the assumption it will have an estimated six-year life and a $500 trade-in value.

Exercise 11–2

A machine that cost $3,500 and on which $2,000 of depreciation had been recorded was disposed of on January 2 of the current year. Give without explanations the entries to record the disposal under each of the following unrelated assumptions:

a. The machine was sold for $1,600 cash.
b. The machine was sold for $400 cash.
c. The machine was traded in on a new machine of like purpose having a $4,000 cash price. A $1,600 trade-in allowance was received, and the balance was paid in cash.
d. A $400 trade-in allowance was received for the machine on a new machine of like purpose having a $4,000 cash price. The balance was paid in cash, and the loss was considered material in amount.
e. Transaction (d) was recorded by the income tax method because the loss was considered immaterial.

Exercise 11–3

A machine that cost $8,000 was depreciated on a straight-line basis for 10 years under the assumption it would have a 12-year life and an $800 trade-in value. At that point it was recognized that the machine had four years of remaining useful life, after which it would still have an $800 trade-in value.

a. Determine the machine's book value at the end of its tenth year.
b. Determine the total depreciation to be charged against the machine during its remaining years of life.
c. Give the entry to record depreciation on the machine for its 11th year.

Exercise 11–4

A company's building appeared on its balance sheet at the end of last year at its original $225,000 cost less $165,000 accumulated depreciation. The building had been depreciated on a straight-line basis under the assumption it would have a 30-year life and no salvage value. During the first week in January of the current year, major structural repairs were completed on the building at a $37,500 cost. The repairs did not improve the building's usefulness but they did extend its expected life for seven years beyond the 30 years originally estimated. *(a)* Determine the building's age on last year's balance sheet date. *(b)* Give the entry to record the cost of the repairs. *(c)* Determine the book value of the building after its repairs were recorded. *(d)* Give the entry to record the current year's depreciation.

Exercise 11–5

On January 3, 198A, a company paid $180,000 for an ore body containing an estimated 900,000 tons of ore and it installed machinery costing $240,000, having a 12-year life and capable of removing the entire ore body in 10 years. The company began operations on May 25, and it mined 45,000 tons of ore during the remainder of 198A. Give the entries to record depletion of the ore body and depreciation on the machinery as of December 31, 198A.

Exercise 11–6

Five years ago a company purchased for $500,000 the mineral rights to an ore body containing 500,000 tons of ore. The company invested an additional $500,000 in mining machinery designed to exhaust the mine in ten years. During the first four years the mine produced 200,000 tons of ore that were sold at a profit. During the fifth year 50,000 tons of ore were mined; but due to technological changes in the manufacturing processes of the customers to whom the ore was normally sold, there was little demand for the ore and it was sold at a $1 per ton loss.

Required

Under the assumption that the remaining 250,000 tons of ore can be mined and sold at a $1 per ton loss during the next five years and there is no prospect of ever doing better, recommend whether the mine should be closed and the loss stopped or it should be continued in operation at a loss. Cite figures to back your recommendation.

PROBLEMS

Problem 11–1

Prepare general journal entries to record the following transactions involving the purchase and operation of a secondhand truck:

198A
Jan. 5 Purchased for $4,640 cash a secondhand delivery truck with an estimated three-year remaining useful life and a $1,330 trade-in value.
      6 Paid Service Garage for the following:

Repairs to truck's motor	$ 44
New tires	246
Gas and oil	10
Total	$300

Dec. 31   Recorded straight-line depreciation on the truck.

198B

Jan. 10   Installed a hydraulic loader on the truck at a cost of $570. The loader increased the truck's estimated salvage value to $1,400.

May 25   Paid Service Garage for the following:

Minor repairs to the truck's motor	$35
New battery for the truck	45
Gas and oil	8
Total	$88

Nov. 4   Paid $45 for repairs to the hydraulic loader damaged when the driver backed into a loading dock.

Dec. 31   Recorded straight-line depreciation on the truck.

198C

Jan.   7   Paid Service Garage $400 to overhaul the truck's motor, replacing bearings and rings and extending the truck's life one year beyond the original three-year estimate. However, it was also estimated that the extra year's operation would reduce the truck's trade-in value to $1,050.

Dec. 31   Recorded straight-line depreciation on the truck.

198D

June 29   Traded the old truck on a new one having a $6,100 cash price. Received a $1,700 trade-in allowance and paid cash for the balance. It was estimated the new truck would have a four-year service life and a $1,200 trade-in value.

Dec. 31   Recorded declining-balance depreciation on the new truck at twice the straight-line rate.

Problem 11–2

A company purchased, traded, and sold the following machines:

Machine No. 133–1 was purchased on April 21, 1975, for $5,050. Its useful life was estimated at five years with a $550 trade-in value. Straight-line depreciation was recorded on the machine at the ends of 1975 and 1976; and on January 7, 1977, it was traded in on Machine No. 133–8. A $2,800 trade-in allowance was received.

Machine No. 133–8 was purchased on January 7, 1977, at an installed cost of $6,450 less the trade-in allowance received on Machine No. 133–1. Its life was estimated at five years with a $600 trade-in value. Sum-of-the-years'-digits depreciation was recorded against the machine at the end of each of the five years in its life; and on January 10, 1982, it was sold for $900.

Machine No. 133–9 was purchased on January 11, 1977, at a total cost of $3,200. Its useful life was estimated at four years with a $300 trade-in value. Declining-balance depreciation at twice the straight-line rate was recorded against the machine at the end of each of the four years in its life; and it was traded in on Machine No. 133–15 on January 5, 1981. A $150 trade-in allowance was received.

Machine No. 133–15 was purchased on January 5, 1981, at an installed cost of $3,100 less the trade-in allowance received on Machine No. 133–9. It was estimated the machine would produce 60,000 units of product during its useful life and would then have a $250 trade-in value. It produced 10,200 units in 1981 and an additional 4,000 units before it was sold on March 8, 1982, for $2,500.

Required:

Assume the company's accounting periods end on December 31 and prepare general journal entries to record (1) the purchase of each machine, (2) the depreciation recorded on the first December 31 of each machine's life, and (3) the disposal of each machine. Use the income tax method to record exchanges and treat the entries of the first two machines as one series of transactions and those of the second two machines as an unrelated second series. The exchange of one machine for another should be recorded one time only.

Problem 11–3

Prepare general journal entries to record these transactions:

1977

Jan. 5   Purchased and placed in operation Machine No. 133–52 which was estimated to have an eight-year life and no salvage value. The machine and its special power connections cost $16,000.

Dec. 31   Recorded straight-line depreciation on the machine.

1978

Mar. 17   After a little over a year's operation Machine No. 133–52 was cleaned, oiled, and adjusted by a factory mechanic at a $195 cost.

Dec. 31   Recorded 1978 depreciation on the machine.

1979

July   6   Added a new device to Machine No. 133–52 at a $1,100 cost. The device materially increased the machine's output but did not change its expected life and zero salvage value.

Dec. 31   Recorded depreciation on the machine.

1980

Dec. 31   Recorded depreciation on the machine.

1981

Jan. 10   Completely overhauled Machine No. 133–52 at a $3,000 cost, of which $400 was for ordinary repairs and $2,600 was for extraordinary repairs that extended the service life of the machine an estimated two years beyond the eight originally expected.

Dec. 31   Recorded depreciation on the machine.

1982

June 28   Machine No. 133–52 was destroyed in a fire, and the insurance company settled the loss claim for $7,500.

Problem 11–4

Part 1.   On January 8 of the current year a company paid $720,000 for mineral land containing an estimated 800,000 tons of recoverable ore. It installed machinery costing $192,000, having a 12-year life and no salvage value, and capable of exhausting the mine in 8 years. The machinery was paid for on June 26, three days after mining operations began. During the period June 23 through December 31, the company mined 40,000 tons of ore.

Required:

Prepare entries to record (a) the purchase of the mineral land, (b) payment for the machinery, (c) the depletion of the land during the current year, and (d) depreciation of the machinery.

Part 2. Eight years ago Joe Dean leased a store building for a period of 20 years. His lease contract calls for $9,000 annual rental payments to be paid on January 1 throughout the life of the lease, and it also provides that the leasee must pay for all additions and improvements to the leased property. The recent construction of a new shopping center next door has made the location more valuable, and on January 1 Joe Dean subleased the building to Gary Nash for the remaining 12 years of the lease. Gary Nash paid Joe Dean $24,000 for the privilege of subleasing the property and in addition agreed to assume and pay the building owner the $9,000 annual rental charges. During the first 12 days of January Mr. Nash remodeled the store front on the leased building at a $7,200 cost. The store front is estimated to have a life equal to the remaining life of the building, 30 years, and was paid for on January 14, the day Mr. Nash opened his new store.

Required:

Prepare general journal entries to record: (a) Gary Nash's payment to sublease the building, (b) his payment of the annual rental charge to the building owner, and (c) payment for the new store front. Also, prepare the adjusting entries required at the end of the first year of the sublease to amortize (d) a proper share of the $24,000 cost of the sublease and (e) a proper share of the store front cost.

Problem 11–5

Carl Eble wishes to buy an established business and is considering Companies A and B, both of which have been in business exactly four years, during which time Company A has reported an average annual $16,145 net income and Company B has reported an average annual $16,650 net income. However, the incomes are not comparable because the companies have not used the same accounting procedures. Current balance sheets of the companies show these items:

	Company A	Company B
Assets		
Cash	$ 4,600	$ 5,100
Accounts receivable	42,300	46,600
Allowance for doubtful accounts	-0-	(3,400)
Merchandise inventory	52,400	47,900
Store equipment	23,200	21,600
Accumulated depreciation, store equipment	(11,600)	(15,600)
Total assets	$110,900	$102,200

Liabilities and Owner's Equity

Current liabilities	$ 31,400	$ 25,700
Owner equity................................	79,500	76,500
Total liabilities and owner's equity	$110,900	$102,200

Company A has used the direct write-off method in accounting for bad debts but has been slow to write off bad debts, and an examination of its accounts shows $2,400 of accounts that are probably uncollectible. Company B, on the other hand, has used the allowance method and has added an amount equal to 1% of sales to its allowance for doubtful accounts each year. However, this seems excessive, since an examination shows only $1,600 of its accounts that are probably uncollectible.

During the past four years Company A has priced its inventory on a Fifo basis, and its ending inventory appears at approximately its replacement cost. During the same period Company B has used Lifo with the result that its ending inventory appears on its balance sheet at an amount that is $6,400 below its replacement cost.

Both companies have assumed eight-year lives and no salvage value in depreciating equipment; however, Company A has used straight-line depreciation, while Company B has used sum-of-the-years'-digits depreciation. Mr. Eble is of the opinion that straight-line depreciation has resulted in Company A's equipment appearing on its balance sheet at approximately its fair value, and that fair value would result from the use of the same method for Company B.

Mr. Eble is willing to pay what he considers fair value for the assets of either business, not including cash but including goodwill measured at four times average annual earnings in excess of 20% on the fair value of the net tangible assets. He defines net tangible assets as all assets, including cash and accounts receivable, minus liabilities. He will assume the liabilities of the business purchased, paying its owner the difference between total assets purchased and the liabilities assumed.

Required:

Prepare the following schedules: *(a)* a schedule showing net tangible assets of each company at their fair values according to Mr. Eble, *(b)* a schedule showing the revised net incomes of the companies based on Fifo inventories and straight-line depreciation, *(c)* a schedule showing the calculation of each company's goodwill, and *(d)* a schedule showing the amount Mr. Eble would pay for each business.

ALTERNATE PROBLEMS

Problem 11–1A

A company completed these transactions involving the purchase and operation of a delivery truck:

198A

June 28 Paid cash for a new truck, $6,500 plus $325 state and city sales taxes. The truck's service life was estimated at four years with an $1,800 trade-in value.

June 30 Paid $375 for special racks and shelves installed in the truck. The racks and shelves did not increase the truck's estimated trade-in value.

Dec. 31 Recorded straight-line depreciation on the truck.

198B

July 2 Paid $440 cash to install an air-conditioning unit in the truck. The unit increased the truck's estimated trade-in value $50.

Oct. 11 Paid $60 for repairs to the truck's rear bumper damaged when the driver backed into a loading dock.

Dec. 31 Recorded straight-line depreciation on the truck.

198C

Dec. 31 Recorded straight-line depreciation on the truck.

198D

Dec. 31 Recorded straight-line depreciation on the truck.

198E

Jan. 11 Paid Apex Garage $410 to overhaul the truck's motor, replacing bearings and rings and extending the truck's service life one and one-half years beyond the four originally estimated. However, it was estimated that the extra year and one half of operation would reduce the truck's trade-in value to $1,000.

Oct. 1 Traded the old truck and $5,040 in cash for a new truck. The new truck was estimated to have a three-year life and a $2,790 trade-in value, and the invoice on the exchange showed these items:

Price of the new truck	$6,800
Trade-in allowances granted	2,000
Balance	$4,800
State and city sales taxes	240
Balance paid in cash	$5,040

The loss on the exchange was considered immaterial, and the income tax method was used to record the exchange.

Dec. 31 Recorded straight-line depreciation on the new truck.

Required:

Prepare general journal entries to record the transactions.

Problem 11–2A

A company that has accounting periods which end each December 31 purchased, traded, and sold the following machines:

Machine No. 133–45 was installed on January 5, 1976, at a $9,000 cost. It was estimated the machine would produce 90,000 units of product, after which it would have a $450 salvage value. During its first year it produced 20,000 units; and on July 2, 1979, after producing a total of 80,000 units it was traded on Machine No. 133–81. A $1,200 trade-in allowance was received, and the loss was considered immaterial.

Machine No. 133–81 was purchased on July 2, 1979, at an installed cost of $10,450, less the trade-in allowance received on Machine No. 133–45. It was estimated Machine No. 133–81 would have a four-year life and a $650 salvage value. Straight-line depreciation was recorded on each December 31 of the machine's life; and on January 5, 1983, it was sold for $1,500.

Machine No. 133–58 was purchased on January 7, 1977, for $8,000. Its useful life was estimated at five years, after which it would have a $2,000 trade-in value. Declining-balance depreciation at twice the straight-line rate was used in recording depreciation on this machine at the ends of 1977, 1978, and 1979, after which it was traded on Machine No. 133–87. A $2,400 trade-in allowance was received.

Machine No. 133–87 was purchased on January 5, 1980, at an installed cost of $8,500, less the trade-in allowance received on Machine No. 133–58. It was estimated that Machine No. 133–87 would have a five-year life and a $600 trade-in value. Sum-of-the-years'-digits depreciation was recorded on this machine at the ends of 1980, 1981, and 1982; and on January 11, 1983, it was sold for $2,500.

Required:

Prepare general journal entries to record (1) the purchase of each machine, (2) the depreciation recorded on the first December 31 of each machine's life, and (3) the disposal of each machine. Treat the entries for the first two machines as one series of transactions and those of the next two machines as an unrelated second series. The exchange of machines should be recorded one time only.

Problem 11–3A

On May 4, 1976, a company purchased and placed in operation a machine costing $12,000 and having an estimated eight-year life and no salvage value. The machine was cleaned and inspected; and minor adjustments were made on October 10, 1977, by a factory expert called in for that purpose. This cost $180. On April 27, 1979, a $750 device that increased its hourly output by one fourth was added to the machine. The device did not change the machine's zero salvage value. During the first week in January 1981, the machine was completely overhauled at a $2,900 cost (completed and paid for on January 12). The overhaul increased the machine's remaining useful life to a total of six years beyond the overhaul date but did not change its zero salvage value. On June 25, 1982, the machine was completely destroyed in a fire and the insurance company settled the loss claim for $5,000.

Required:

Under the assumption the machine was depreciated on a straight-line basis, prepare general journal entries to record the purchase, operation, and destruction of the machine.

Problem 11–4A

Part 1. On January 8 of the current year a company paid $1,200,000 for mineral land containing an estimated 500,000 tons of ore. The company installed machinery costing $240,000, having an estimated 12-year life and no salvage value and designed to exhaust the mine in 10 years. The machinery was paid for on August 12, ten days after mining operations began, and during the remainder of the year the company mined 20,000 tons of ore.

Required:

Prepare entries to record *(a)* the purchase of the mineral land, *(b)* payment for the machinery, *(c)* the first partial year's depletion under the assumption the cost of restoring the land to federal standards after exhausting the mineral deposit would equal the resale value of the land, and *(d)* the first partial year's depreciation on the machinery.

Part 2. Five years ago Litton Jewelry Store leased shop space in a building for a period of 15 years. The lease contract calls for a $9,000 annual rental payment on each January 1 throughout the life of the lease, and also provides that the lessee must pay for all additions and improvements to the leased property. Inflation has made the lease valuable, and on December 19 Parkway Opticians subleased the space from Litton Jewelry Store for the remaining ten-year life of the lease. Parkway Opticians paid $25,000 for the privilege of subleasing the property and in addition agreed to pay the $9,000 annual rental charge throughout the life of the lease. During the first ten days after taking possession of the leased space, Parkway Opticians remodeled the shop front at an $8,400 cost. The remodeled shop front was estimated to have a useful life of 14 years and was paid for on January 11.

Required:

Prepare general journal entries for Parkway Opticians to record *(a)* payment to sublease the space, *(b)* payment of the annual rental charge, and *(c)* payment for the new shop front. Also, prepare the adjusting entries required at the end of the first year to amortize *(d)* a proper share of the $25,000 cost to sublease the property and *(e)* a proper share of the cost of the new shop front.

PROVOCATIVE PROBLEMS

Provocative problem 11–1
Second audit

You have graduated from college, taken a job with a public accounting firm, and are working on your second audit; and in helping to verify the records of the firm being audited, you find the following:

1981					
July	12	Cash		10,000.00	
		Loss from Fire		6,000.00	
		Accumulated Depreciation, Machinery ..		12,000.00	
		Machinery			28,000.00
		Received payment of fire loss claim.			
Aug.	15	Cash		18,000.00	
		Factory Land			18,000.00
		Sold unneeded factory land.			

An investigation revealed that the first entry resulted from recording a $10,000 check received from an insurance company in full settlement of a loss claim resulting from the destruction of a machine in a small plant fire on June 30, 1981. The machine had originally cost $24,000, was put in operation on January 7, 1976, and had been depreciated on a straight-line basis at the ends of each of the first five years in its life under the assumption it would have a ten-year life and no salvage value. During the first week in January 1981, the machine had been overhauled at a $4,000 cost. The overhaul did not increase the machine's capacity nor change its zero salvage value. However, it was expected the overhaul would lengthen the machine's service life three years beyond the ten originally estimated.

The second entry resulted from recording a check received from selling a portion of a tract of land. The tract was adjacent to the company's plant and had been purchased on February 22, 1981. It cost $22,000, and $3,000 was paid for clearing and grading it. Both amounts were debited to the Factory Land account. The land was to be used for storing raw materials. However, after the grading was completed, it was obvious the company did not need the entire tract, and it was pleased when it received an offer from a purchaser who was willing to pay $12,000 for the east half or $18,000 for the west half. The company decided to sell the west half, and it recorded the receipt of the purchaser's check with the entry previously given.

Were any errors made in recording the transactions discussed here? If so, describe the errors and in each case give an entry or entries that will correct the account balances under the assumption the 1981 revenue and expense accounts have not been closed.

Provocative problem 11–2
Jane Monroe

Jane Monroe plans to buy an established business, and she has narrowed her list to three choices, Companies A, B, and C. All three have been in business exactly four years. Each employs a manager who is paid $20,000 per year; and they have reported average annual net incomes, after payment of their managers, as follows: Company A, $14,632; Company B, $12,245; and Company C, $22,590. However, since they have used different accounting procedures, their reported incomes are not comparable, nor are their current balance sheets which show these items:

Assets	Company A	Company B	Company C
Cash	$ 10,200	$ 11,400	$ 18,700
Accounts receivable	85,600	94,300	98,200
Allowance for doubtful accounts	(6,200)	(2,100)	-0-
Merchandise inventory	95,800	74,900	93,600
Equipment	30,000	33,000	32,000
Accumulated depreciation, equipment	(17,712)	(20,400)	(12,800)
Building	100,000	96,000	108,000
Accumulated depreciation, building	(10,000)	(9,600)	-0-
Land	21,000	20,000	22,000
Goodwill			2,800
Total assets	$308,688	$297,500	$362,500

Liabilities and Owner's Equity

Current liabilities	$ 80,000	$ 85,000	$ 90,000
Mortgage payable	70,000	75,000	80,000
Owner's equity	158,688	137,500	192,500
Total liabilities and owner's equity ..	$308,688	$297,500	$362,500

Company A has added an amount to its allowance for doubtful accounts each year equal to one half of 1% of sales. These amounts seem to have been excessive, since an analysis shows just $2,000 of the company's accounts receivable that are probably uncollectible. Company B has been more conservative, and its allowance is approximately equal to its uncollectible accounts. Company C has used the direct write-off method in accounting for bad debts; but it has always been slow to recognize a bad debt, and an examination shows accounts totaling $8,600 that are probably uncollectible.

Company B has accounted for its inventories on a Lifo basis; and as a result its current inventory appears on its books as an amount that is $17,000 below replacement cost. Companies A and C have used Fifo, and their inventories are stated at amounts near replacement costs.

The three companies have not added to their plant assets since beginning operations, and all three have assumed ten-year lives and no salvage values in recording depreciation on equipment. However, Company A has used declining-balance depreciation at twice the straight-line rate, Company B has used sum-of-the-years'-digits depreciation, and Company C has used straight line. The buildings of the companies are of concrete construction and are comparable in every respect, excepting as to cost. Companies A and B have recorded straight-line depreciation on their buildings, assuming 40-year lives and no salvage values. However, since its building is of concrete construction and "will last forever," Company C has taken no depreciation on its building. Ms. Monroe is of the opinion that if all three companies had used straight-line depreciation for both buildings and equipment, the resulting book values would approximate market values.

The goodwill on Company C's balance sheet resulted from capitalizing advertising costs during the company's first year in business.

In buying a business, Ms. Monroe will buy its tangible assets, including the accounts receivable, but not including cash, and will pay what she thinks is fair market value. She will assume the liabilities of the business and will pay for goodwill measured at four times average annual earnings in excess of a 10% return on net tangible assets (including accounts receivable) based on first-in, first-out inventories and straight-line depreciation.

Determine the amount Ms. Monroe would be willing to pay for each company. Base the amounts on the following schedules: *(a)* a schedule showing net tangible assets for each company, *(b)* a schedule showing revised and corrected average net incomes, *(c)* a schedule showing the calculation of each company's goodwill, and finally *(d)* a schedule showing the amounts Ms. Monroe should pay for each of the three companies.

PART FOUR
Accounting for equities: Liabilities and partners' equities

After studying Chapter 12, you should be able to:

☐ Prepare entries to record transactions involving short-term notes payable.

☐ Explain the concept of present value.

☐ Calculate the present value of a sum of money to be received a number of periods in the future.

☐ Calculate the present value of a sum of money to be received periodically for a number of periods in the future.

☐ Account for a plant asset purchased with a long-term noninterest-bearing note payable.

☐ Account for a plant asset acquired through leasing.

☐ Prepare entries to record transactions involving a mortgage.

☐ Define and explain the words and phrases listed in the chapter Glossary.

Current and long-term liabilities

■ A liability is a legal obligation requiring the future payment of an asset, the future performance of a service, or the creation of another liability. In accounting for liabilities the *cost principle* applies and each liability is accounted for at the cost of the asset or service received in exchange for the liability.

A business normally has several kinds of liabilities which are classified as either current or long-term liabilities. Current liabilities are debts or other obligations the liquidation of which is reasonably expected to require the use of existing current assets or the creation of other current liabilities.[1] Accounts payable, short-term notes payable, wages payable, payroll and other taxes payable, and unearned revenues are common examples of current liabilities. Long-term liabilities are obligations that will not require the use of existing current assets in their liquidation, generally because they are not to be paid or liquidated within one year.

The current liabilities accounts payable, wages payable, and unearned revenues were discussed in previous chapters. Liabilities resulting from payrolls are discussed in Chapter 13. Consequently, this chapter is devoted to notes payable, liabilities from leasing, and mortgages payable. A discussion of the long-term liability, bonds payable, is deferred to Chapter 18.

---

[1] APB, "Basic Concepts and Accounting Principles Underlying Financial Statements of Business Enterprises," *APB Statement No. 4* (New York: AICPA, October 1970), par. 198. Copyright (1970) by the American Institute of CPAs.

SHORT-TERM NOTES PAYABLE

Short-term notes payable often arise in gaining an extension of time in which to pay an account payable. They frequently arise in borrowing from a bank.

Note given to secure a time extension on an account

A note payable may be given to secure an extension of time in which to pay an account payable. For example, Brock Company cannot pay its past-due, $600 account with Ajax Company, and Ajax Company has agreed to accept Brock Company's 60-day, 8%, $600 note in granting an extension on the due date of the debt. Brock Company will record the issuance of the note as follows:

Aug.	23	Accounts Payable—Ajax Company	600.00	
		Notes Payable		600.00
		Gave a 60-day, 8% note to extend the due date on the amount owed.		

Observe that the note does not pay the debt. It merely changes it from an account payable to a note payable. Ajax Company should prefer the note to the account because in case of default and a lawsuit to collect, the note improves its legal position, since the note is written evidence of the debt and its amount.

When the note becomes due, Brock Company will give Ajax Company a check for $608 and record the payment of the note and its interest with an entry like this:

Oct.	22	Notes Payable	600.00	
		Interest Expense	8.00	
		Cash		608.00
		Paid our note with interest.		

Borrowing from a bank

In lending money, banks distinguish between *loans* and *discounts*. In case of a loan, the bank collects interest when the loan is repaid. In a discount, it deducts interest at the time the loan is made. To illustrate loans and discounts, assume that H. A. Green wishes to borrow approximately $2,000 for 60 days at the prevailing 9% rate of interest.

A loan   In a loan transaction the bank will lend Green $2,000 in exchange for a signed promissory note. The note will read: "Sixty days after date I promise to pay $2,000 with interest at 9%." Green will record the transaction as follows:

Sept.	10	Cash	2,000.00	
		Notes Payable		2,000.00
		Gave the bank a 60-day, 9% note.		

When the note and interest are paid, Green makes this entry:

Nov.	9	Notes Payable	2,000.00	
		Interest Expense	30.00	
		Cash		2,030.00
		Paid our 60-day, 9% note.		

Observe that in a loan transaction the interest is paid at the time the loan is repaid.

A discount   If it is the practice of Green's bank to deduct interest at the time a loan is made, the bank will discount Green's $2,000 note. If it discounts the note at 9% for 60 days, it will deduct from the face amount of the note 60 days' interest at 9%, which is $30, and will give Green the difference, $1,970. The $30 of deducted interest is called *bank discount*, and the $1,970 are the *proceeds* of the discounted note. Green will record the transaction as follows:

Sept.	10	Cash	1,970.00	
		Interest Expense	30.00	
		Notes Payable		2,000.00
		Discounted our $2,000 note payable at 9%.		

When the note matures, Green is required to pay the bank just the face amount of the note, $2,000, and Green will record the transaction like this:

Nov.	9	Notes Payable	2,000.00	
		Cash		2,000.00
		Paid our discounted note payable.		

Since interest is deducted in a discount transaction at the time the loan is made, the note used in such a transaction must state that only the principal amount is to be repaid at maturity. Such a note may read: "Sixty days after date I promise to pay $2,000 with no interest," and is commonly called a noninterest-bearing note. However, banks are not in business to lend money interest free. Interest is paid in a discount transaction. But, since it is deducted at the time the loan is made, the note used must state that no additional interest is to be collected at maturity. Nevertheless, interest is collected in a discount transaction and at a rate slightly higher than in a loan transaction at the same stated interest rate. For example, in this instance Green paid $30 for the use of $1,970 for 60 days, which was at an effective interest rate just a little in excess of 9% on the $1,970 received.

END-OF-THE-PERIOD ADJUSTMENTS

Accrued interest expense

Interest accrues daily on all interest-bearing notes. Consequently, if any notes payable are outstanding at the end of an accounting period, their accrued interest should be recorded. For example, a company gave its bank a $4,000, 60-day, 9% note on December 16 to borrow that amount of money. If the company's accounting period ends on December 31, by then 15 days' or $15 interest has accrued on this note. It may be recorded with this adjusting entry:

Dec.	31	Interest Expense	15.00	
		Interest Payable.........................		15.00
		To record accrued interest on a note payable.		

The adjusting entry causes the $15 accrued interest to appear on the income statement as an expense of the period benefiting from 15 days' use of the money. It also causes the interest payable to appear on the balance sheet as a current liability.

When the note matures in the next accounting period, its payment may be recorded as follows:

Feb.	14	Notes Payable	4,000.00	
		Interest Payable	15.00	
		Interest Expense	45.00	
		Cash		4,060.00
		Paid a $4,000 note and its interest.		

Interest on this note for 60 days is $60. In the illustrated entry the $60 is divided between the interest accrued at the end of the previous period, $15, and interest applicable to the current period, $45. Some accountants avoid the necessity of making this division by reversing the accrued interest adjusting entry as a last step in their end-of-the-period work.

Discount on notes payable

When a note payable is discounted at a bank, interest based on the principal of the note is deducted and the interest is normally recorded as interest expense. Furthermore, since most such notes run for 30, 60, or 90 days, the interest is usually an expense of the period in which it is deducted. However, when the time of a note extends beyond a single accounting period, an adjusting entry is required. For example, on December 11, 198A, a company discounted at 9% its own $6,000, 60-day, noninterest-bearing note payable. It recorded the transaction as follows:

198A				
Dec.	11	Cash	5,910.00	
		Interest Expense	90.00	
		Notes Payable		6,000.00
		Discounted our noninterest-bearing, 60-day note at 9%.		

If this company operates with accounting periods that end each December 31, 20 days' interest on this note, or $30 of the $90 of discount, is an expense of the 198A accounting period and 40 days' interest or $60 is an expense of 198B. Consequently, if revenues and expenses are matched, the company must make the following December 31, 198A, adjusting entry:

198A				
Dec.	31	Discount on Notes Payable	60.00	
		Interest Expense		60.00
		To set up as a contra liability the interest applicable to 198B.		

The adjusting entry removes from the Interest Expense account the $60 of interest that is applicable to 198B. It leaves in the account the $30 that is an expense of 198A. The $30 then appears on the 198A income statement as an expense, and the $60 appears on the

198A balance sheet. If this is the only note the company has outstanding, the $60 is deducted on the balance sheet as follows:

Current liabilities:
  Notes payable $6,000
    Less discount on notes payable 60 $5,940

Putting discount on notes payable on the balance sheet as a contra liability results in showing as a liability on the balance sheet date the amount received in discounting the note plus the accrued interest on the note to the balance sheet date. In this example $5,910 was received in discounting the note and accrued interest on the note is $30. Together they total $5,940, which is the amount actually owed the bank on December 31.

The $60 interest set out as discount on notes payable in the previous paragraphs becomes an expense early in 198B. Consequently, sooner or later it must be taken from the Discount on Notes Payable account and returned to the Interest Expense account. Accountants commonly make this return with a *reversing entry*. The entry is made as the last step in the end-of-the-period work and is dated the first day of the new accounting period. Such a reversing entry appears as follows:

| 198B
Jan. | 1 | Interest Expense ....
   Discount on Notes Payable ....
   To reverse the adjusting entry that set out
   discount on notes payable. | 60.00 | 60.00 |

Observe that the reversing entry is debit for credit and credit for debit the reverse of the adjusting entry it reverses. That is where it gets its name. Also, observe that it returns the $60 interest to the expense account so that it will appear on the 198B income statement as an expense without further ado.

THE CONCEPT OF PRESENT VALUE

The concept of present value enters into many financing and investing decisions and any resulting liabilities. Consequently, an understanding of it is important. The concept is based on the idea that the right to receive, say, $1 a year from today is worth somewhat less than $1 today. Or stated another way, $1 to be received a year hence has a *present value* of somewhat less than $1. How much less depends on how much can be earned on invested funds. If, say, a 10% annual return can be earned, the expectation of receiving $1 a year hence has a present value of $0.909. This can be verified as follows: $0.909 invested today to earn 10% annually will earn $0.0909 in one year, and when the $0.0909 earned is added to the $0.909 invested—

Investment......	$0.909
Earnings........	0.0909
Total	$0.9999

the investment plus the earnings equal $0.9999, which rounds to the $1 expected.

Likewise, the present value of $1 to be received two years hence is $0.826 if a 10% compound annual return is expected. This also can be verified as follows: $0.826 invested to earn 10% compounded annually will earn $0.0826 the first year it is invested, and when the $0.0826 earned is added to the $0.826 invested—

Investment	$0.826
First year earnings	0.0826
End-of-year-one amount	$0.9086

the investment plus the first year's earnings total $0.9086. And during the second year this $0.9086 will earn $0.09086, which when added to the end-of-the-first-year amount—

End-of-year-one amount	$0.9086
Second year earnings	0.09086
End-of-year-two amount	$0.99946

equals $0.99946, which rounds to the $1 expected at the end of the second year.

Present value tables

The present value of $1 to be received any number of years in the future can be calculated by using the formula, $1/(1 + i)^n$. The i is the interest rate, and n is the number of years to the expected receipt. However, the formula need not be used, since tables showing present values computed with the formula at various interest rates are readily available. Table 12–1, with its amounts rounded to either

Present Value of $1 at Compound Interest

Periods hence	3½%	4%	4½%	6%	7%	8%	10%	12%	14%	15%
1	0.9662	0.9615	0.9569	0.943	0.935	0.926	0.909	0.893	0.877	0.870
2	0.9335	0.9246	0.9157	0.890	0.873	0.857	0.826	0.797	0.769	0.756
3	0.9019	0.8890	0.8763	0.840	0.816	0.794	0.751	0.712	0.675	0.658
4	0.8714	0.8548	0.8386	0.792	0.763	0.735	0.683	0.636	0.592	0.572
5	0.8420	0.8219	0.8025	0.747	0.713	0.681	0.621	0.567	0.519	0.497
6	0.8135	0.7903	0.7679	0.705	0.666	0.630	0.565	0.507	0.456	0.432
7	0.7860	0.7599	0.7348	0.665	0.623	0.584	0.513	0.452	0.400	0.376
8	0.7594	0.7307	0.7032	0.627	0.582	0.540	0.467	0.404	0.351	0.327
9	0.7337	0.7026	0.6729	0.592	0.544	0.500	0.424	0.361	0.308	0.284
10	0.7089	0.6756	0.6439	0.558	0.508	0.463	0.386	0.322	0.270	0.247
11	0.6849	0.6496	0.6162	0.527	0.475	0.429	0.351	0.287	0.237	0.215
12	0.6618	0.6246	0.5897	0.497	0.444	0.397	0.319	0.257	0.208	0.187
13	0.6394	0.6006	0.5643	0.469	0.415	0.368	0.290	0.229	0.182	0.163
14	0.6178	0.5775	0.5400	0.442	0.388	0.341	0.263	0.205	0.160	0.141
15	0.5969	0.5553	0.5167	0.417	0.362	0.315	0.239	0.183	0.140	0.123
16	0.5767	0.5339	0.4945	0.394	0.339	0.292	0.218	0.163	0.123	0.107
17	0.5572	0.5134	0.4732	0.371	0.317	0.270	0.198	0.146	0.108	0.093
18	0.5384	0.4936	0.4528	0.350	0.296	0.250	0.180	0.130	0.095	0.081
19	0.5202	0.4746	0.4333	0.331	0.277	0.232	0.164	0.116	0.083	0.070
20	0.5026	0.4564	0.4146	0.312	0.258	0.215	0.149	0.104	0.073	0.061

Table 12–1

three or four decimal places, is such a table. (Three or four decimal places would not be sufficiently accurate for some uses but will suffice here.)

Observe in Table 12–1 that the first amount in the 10% column is the 0.909 used in the previous section to introduce the concept of present value. The 0.909 in the 10% column means that the expectation of receiving $1 a year hence when discounted for one period, in this case one year, at 10%, has a present value of $0.909. Then note that the second amount in the 10% column is the 0.826 previously used, which means that the expectation of receiving $1 two years hence, discounted at 10%, has a present value of $0.826.

Using a present value table

To demonstrate the use of the present value table, Table 12–1, assume that a company has an opportunity to invest $20,000 in a project, the risks of which it feels justify a 12% compound return. The investment will return $10,000 at the end of the first year, $9,000 at the end of the second year, $8,000 at the end of the third year, and nothing thereafter. Will the project return the original investment plus the 12% demanded? The calculations of Illustration 12–1, which use the first three amounts in the 12% column of the Table 12–1, indicate that it will. In Illustration 12–1 the expected returns in the second column are multiplied by the present value amounts in the third column to determine the present values in the last column. Since the total of the present values exceeds the required investment by $1,799, the project will return the $20,000 investment, plus a 12% return thereon, and $1,799 extra.

Years hence	Expected returns	Present value of $1 at 12%	Present value of expected returns
1	$10,000	0.893	$ 8,930
2	9,000	0.797	7,173
3	8,000	0.712	5,696
Total present value of the returns			$21,799
Less investment required			20,000
Excess over 12% demanded			$ 1,799

Illustration 12–1

In Illustration 12–1 the present value of each year's return was separately calculated, after which the present values were added to determine their total. Separately calculating the present value of each of several returns from an investment is necessary when the returns are unequal, as in this example. However, in cases where the periodic returns are equal, there are shorter ways of calculating the sum of their present values. For instance, suppose a $3,500 investment will return $1,000 at the end of each year in its five-year life and an investor wants to know the present value of these returns discounted at 12%. In this case the periodic returns are equal, and a short way to determine their total present value at 12% is to add the present values of $1 at 12% for periods one through five (from Table 12–1), as follows—

```
0.893
0.797
0.712
0.636
0.567
3.605
```

and then to multiply $1,000 by the total. The $3,605 result ($1,000 × 3.605 = $3,605) is the same as would be obtained by calculating the present value of each year's return and adding the present values. However, although the result is the same either way, the method demonstrated here requires four fewer multiplications.

Present value of $1 received periodically for a number of periods

Table 12–2 is based on the idea demonstrated in the previous paragraph, the idea that the present value of a series of equal returns to be received at periodic intervals is nothing more than the sum of the present values of the individual returns. Note the amount on the table's fifth line in the 12% column. It is the same 3.605 amount arrived at in the previous section by adding the first five present values of $1 at 12%. All the amounts shown in Table 12–2 could be arrived at by adding amounts found in Table 12–1. However, there would be some slight variations due to rounding.

When available, Table 12–2 is used to determine the present value of a series of equal amounts to be received at periodic intervals. For example, what is the present value of a series of ten $1,000 amounts, with one $1,000 amount to be received at the end of each of ten successive years, discounted at 8%? To determine the answer, go down

Present Value of $1 Received Periodically for a Number of Periods

Periods hence	3½%	4%	4½%	6%	7%	8%	10%	12%	14%	15%
1	0.966	0.962	0.957	0.943	0.935	0.926	0.909	0.893	0.877	0.870
2	1.900	1.886	1.873	1.833	1.808	1.783	1.736	1.690	1.647	1.626
3	2.802	2.775	2.749	2.673	2.624	2.577	2.487	2.402	2.322	2.283
4	3.672	3.630	3.588	3.465	3.387	3.312	3.170	3.037	2.914	2.855
5	4.515	4.452	4.390	4.212	4.100	3.993	3.791	3.605	3.433	3.352
6	5.329	5.242	5.158	4.917	4.767	4.623	4.355	4.111	3.889	3.784
7	6.115	6.002	5.893	5.582	5.389	5.206	4.868	4.564	4.288	4.160
8	6.874	6.733	6.596	6.210	5.971	5.747	5.335	4.968	4.639	4.487
9	7.608	7.435	7.269	6.802	6.515	6.247	5.759	5.328	4.946	4.772
10	8.317	8.111	7.913	7.360	7.024	6.710	6.145	5.650	5.216	5.019
11	9.002	8.761	8.529	7.887	7.499	7.139	6.495	5.988	5.453	5.234
12	9.663	9.385	9.119	8.384	7.943	7.536	6.814	6.194	5.660	5.421
13	10.303	9.986	9.683	8.853	8.358	7.904	7.103	6.424	5.842	5.583
14	10.921	10.563	10.223	9.295	8.746	8.244	7.367	6.628	6.002	5.724
15	11.517	11.118	10.740	9.712	9.108	8.560	7.606	6.811	6.142	5.847
16	12.094	11.652	11.234	10.106	9.447	8.851	7.824	6.974	6.265	5.954
17	12.651	12.166	11.707	10.477	9.763	9.122	8.022	7.120	6.373	6.047
18	13.190	12.659	12.160	10.828	10.059	9.372	8.201	7.250	6.467	6.128
19	13.710	13.134	12.593	11.158	10.336	9.604	8.365	7.366	6.550	6.198
20	14.212	13.590	13.008	11.470	10.594	9.818	8.514	7.469	6.623	6.259

Table 12–2

the 8% column to the amount opposite ten periods (years in this case). It is 6.710, and $6.71 is the present value of $1 to be received annually at the ends of each of ten years, discounted at 8%. Therefore, the present value of the ten $1,000 amounts is 1,000 times $6.71 or is $6,710.

Discount periods less than a year in length

In the examples thus far the discount periods have been measured in intervals one year in length. Often discount periods are based on intervals shorter than a year. For instance, although interest rates on corporation bonds are usually quoted on an annual basis, the interest on such bonds is normally paid semiannually. As a result, the present value of the interest to be received on such bonds must be based on interest periods six months in length.

To illustrate a calculation based on six-month interest periods, assume an investor wants to know the present value of the interest that will be received over a period of five years on some corporation bonds. The bonds have a $10,000 par value, and interest is paid on them every six months at an 8% annual rate. Interest at an 8% annual rate is at the rate of 4% per six-month interest period. Consequently, the investor will receive $10,000 times 4% or $400 in interest on these bonds at the end of each six-month interest period. In five years there are ten such periods. Therefore, if these ten receipts of $400 each are to be discounted at the interest rate of the bonds, to determine their present value, go down the 4% column of Table 12–2 to the amount opposite ten periods. It is 8.111, and the present value of the ten $400 semiannual receipts is 8.111 times $400 or is $3,244.40.

EXCHANGING A NOTE FOR A PLANT ASSET

When a relatively high-cost plant asset is purchased, particularly if the credit period is long, a note is sometimes given in making the purchase. If the amount of the note is approximately equal to the cash price for the asset and the interest on the note is at approximately the prevailing rate, the transaction is recorded as follows:

Feb.	12	Store Equipment	4,500.00	
		Notes Payable		4,500.00
		Exchanged a $4,500, one-year, 8½% note payable for a refrigerated display case.		

A note given in exchange for a plant asset has two elements, which may or may not be stipulated in the note. They are (1) a dollar amount equivalent to the bargained cash price of the asset and (2) an interest factor to compensate the supplier for the use of the funds that otherwise would have been received in a cash sale. Consequently, when a note is exchanged for a plant asset and the face amount of the note approximately equals the cash price of the asset and the note's interest rate is at or near the prevailing rate, the asset may be recorded at the face amount of the note as in the previous illustration. However, if no interest rate is stated, or the interest rate is unreasonable, or the face amount of the note materially differs from the cash price for the asset, the asset should be recorded at its cash price or at the present value of the note, whichever is more clearly determinable.[2] In such a situation to record the asset at the face amount of the note would cause the asset, the liability, and interest expense to be misstated. Furthermore, the misstatements could be material in case of a long-term note.

To illustrate a situation in which a note having no interest rate stated is exchanged for a plant asset, assume that on January 2, 198A, a noninterest-bearing, five-year, $10,000 note payable is exchanged for a factory machine, the cash price of which is not readily determinable. If the prevailing rate for interest on the day of the exchange is 8%, the present value of the note on that day is $6,810 [based on the fifth amount in the 8% column of Table 12–1 ($10,000 × 0.681 = $6,810)], and the exchange should be recorded as follows:

198A				
Jan.	2	Factory Machinery	6,810.00	
		Discount on Notes Payable	3,190.00	
		Long-Term Notes Payable...............		10,000.00
		Exchanged a five-year, noninterest-bearing note for a machine.		

The $6,810 debit amount in the entry is the present value of the note on the day of the exchange. It is also the cost of the machine and is the amount to be used in calculating depreciation and any future loss or gain on the machine's sale or exchange. The entry's notes payable and discount amounts together measure the liability resulting from the transaction. They should appear on a balance sheet prepared immediately after the exchange as follows:

Long-term liabilities:		
Long-term notes payable	$10,000	
Less unamortized discount based on the 8% interest rate prevailing on the date of issue...................	3,190	$6,810

[2] APB, "Interest on Receivables and Payables," *APB Opinion No. 21* (New York: AICPA, August 1971), pars. 8 and 12. Copyright (1970) by the American Institute of CPAs.

The $3,190 discount is a contra liability and also the interest element of the transaction. Column 3 of Illustration 12–2 shows the portions of the $3,190 that should be amortized and charged to interest expense at the ends of each of the five years in the life of the note.

Year	Beginning-of-the-year carrying amount	Discount to be amortized each year	Unamortized discount at the end of the year	End-of-the-year carrying amount
198A	$6,810	$545	$2,645	$ 7,355
198B	7,355	588	2,057	7,943
198C	7,943	635	1,422	8,578
198D	8,578	686	736	9,264
198E	9,264	736*	–0–	10,000

* Adjusted for rounding.

Illustration 12–2

The first year's amortization entry is:

198A				
Dec.	31	Interest Expense	545.00	
		Discount on Notes Payable		545.00
		To amortize a portion of the discount on our long-term note.		

The $545 amortized is interest at 8% on the note's $6,810 value on the day it was exchanged for the machine. [The $545 is rounded to the nearest full dollar, as are all the Column 3 amounts ($6,810 × 8% = $544.80).]

Posting the amortization entry causes the note to appear on the December 31, 198A, balance sheet as follows:

Long-term liabilities:
Long-term notes payable $10,000
Less unamortized discount based on the 8% interest
rate prevailing on the date of issue 2,645 $7,355

Compare the net amount at which the note is carried on the December 31, 198A, balance sheet with the net amount shown for the note on the balance sheet prepared on its date of issue. Observe that the *carrying amount* increased $545 between the two dates. The $545 is the amount of discount amortized and charged to interest expense at the end of 198A.

At the end of 198B and each succeeding year the remaining amounts of discount shown in Column 3 of Illustration 12–2 should be amortized and charged to interest expense. This will cause the carrying amount of the note to increase each year by the amount of discount amortized that year and to reach $10,000, the note's maturity value, at the end of the fifth year. Payment of the note may then be recorded as follows:

198F				
Jan.	2	Long-Term Notes Payable	10,000.00	
		Cash		10,000.00
		Paid our long-term noninterest-bearing note.		

Now return to Illustration 12–2. Each end-of-the-year carrying amount in the last column is determined by subtracting the end-of-the-year unamortized discount from the $10,000 face amount of the note. For example, $10,000 − $2,645 = $7,355. Each beginning-of-the-year carrying amount is the same as the previous year's end-of-the-year amount. The amount of discount to be amortized each year is determined by multiplying the beginning-of-the-year carrying amount by the 8% interest rate prevailing at the time of the exchange. For example, $7,355 × 8% = $588 (rounded). Each end-of-the-year amount of unamortized discount is the discount remaining after subtracting the discount amortized that year. For example, $3,190 − $545 = $2,645.

LIABILITIES FROM LEASING

The leasing of plant assets, rather than purchasing them, has increased tremendously in recent years, primarily because leasing does not require a large cash outflow at the time the assets are acquired. Leasing has been called "off balance sheet financing" because assets leased under certain conditions do not appear on the balance sheet of the lessee. However, some leases have essentially the same economic consequences as if the lessee secured a loan and purchased the leased asset. Such leases are called *capital leases* or *financing leases.* The FASB ruled that a lease meeting any one of the following criteria is a capital lease.[3]

---

[3] FASB, "Accounting for Leases," *FASB Statement No. 13* (Stamford, Conn., 1976), par. 7. Copyright © by the Financial Accounting Standards Board, High Ridge Park, Stamford, Conn. 06905, U.S.A. Quoted (or excerpted) with permission. Copies of the complete document are available from the FASB.

1. Ownership of the leased asset is transferred to the lessee at the end of the lease period.
2. The lease gives the lessee the option of purchasing the leased asset at less than fair value at some point during or at the end of the lease period.
3. The period of the lease is 75% or more of the estimated service life of the leased asset.
4. The present value of the minimum lease payments is 90% or more of the fair value of the leased asset.

A lease that does not meet any one of the four criteria is classified as an *operating lease*.

To illustrate accounting for leases, assume that Alpha Company plans to produce a product requiring the use of a new machine costing approximately $40,000 and having an estimated ten-year life and no salvage value. It does not have $40,000 in available cash and is planning to lease the machine as of December 31, 198A. It will lease the machine under one of the following contracts, each of which requires Alpha Company to pay maintenance, taxes, and insurance on the machine: (1) Lease the machine for five years, annual payments of $7,500 payable at the end of each of the five years, the machine to be returned to the lessor at the end of the lease period. (2) Lease the machine for five years, annual payments of $10,000 payable at the end of each of the five years, the machine to become the property of Alpha Company at the end of the lease period.

If the prevailing interest rate is 8%, the first lease contract does not meet any of the four criteria of the FASB. Therefore, it is an operating lease. If Alpha Company chooses this contract, it should make no entry to record the lease contract. However, each annual rental payment should be recorded as follows:

198B				
Dec.	31	Machinery Rentals Expense	7,500.00	
		Cash		7,500.00
		Paid the annual rent on a leased machine.		

Alpha Company should also expense the payments for taxes, insurance, and any repairs to the machine, but it should not record depreciation on it. It should also append a footnote to its income statement giving a general description of the leasing arrangements.

The second lease contract meets the first and fourth criteria of the FASB and is a capital lease. It is in effect a purchase transaction with the lessor company financing the purchase of the machine for Alpha Company. To charge each of the $10,000 lease payments to an expense

account would overstate expenses during the first five years of the
machine's life and understate expenses during the last five. It would
also understate the company's assets and liabilities. Consequently, the
FASB ruled that such a lease should be treated as a purchase transaction
and be recorded on the lease date at the present value of the lease
payments.

If Alpha Company chooses the second lease contract and the prevailing interest rate on such contracts is 8% annually, it should (based
on the fifth amount in the 8% column of Table 12–2) multiply $10,000
by 3.993 to arrive at a $39,930 present value for the five lease payments.
It should then make this entry:

198A				
Dec.	31	Machinery	39,930.00	
		Discount on Lease Financing	10,070.00	
		Long-Term Lease Liability		50,000.00
		Purchased a machine through a long-term		
		lease contract.		

The $39,930 is the cost of the machine. As with any plant asset, it
should be charged off to depreciation expense over the machine's expected service life. The $10,070 discount is the interest factor in the
transaction. The long-term lease liability less the amount of the discount
measures the net liability resulting from the purchase. The two items
should appear on a balance sheet prepared immediately after the transaction as follows:

Long-term liabilities:		
Long-term lease liability[4]	$50,000	
Less unamortized discount based on the 8% interest		
rate prevailing on the date of the contract	10,070	$39,930

If Alpha Company plans to depreciate the machine on a straight-
line basis over its ten-year life, it should make the following entries
at the end of the first year in the life of the lease:

198B				
Dec.	31	Depreciation Expense, Machinery	3,993.00	
		Accumulated Depreciation, Machinery		3,993.00
		To record depreciation on the machine.		

---

[4] To simplify the illustration, the fact that the first installment on the lease should
probably be classified as a current liability is ignored here and should be ignored in
the problems at the end of the chapter.

31	Long-Term Lease Liability 10,000.00	
	Cash	10,000.00
	Made the annual payment on the lease.	
31	Interest Expense 3,194.00	
	Discount on Lease Financing	3,194.00
	Amortized a portion of the discount on the lease financing.	

The first two entries need no comment. The $3,194 amortized in the third entry is interest at 8% for one year on the $39,930 beginning-of-the-year carrying amount of the lease liability ($39,930 × 8% = $3,194). The $3,194 is rounded to the nearest full dollar, as are all amounts in Column 5 of Illustration 12–3.

Year	Beginning-of-year lease liability	Beginning-of-year unamortized discount	Beginning-of-year carrying amount	Discount to be amortized	Unamortized discount at the end of the year	End-of-the-year lease liability	End-of-the-year carrying amount
198B	$50,000	$10,070	$39,930	$3,194	$6,876	$40,000	$33,124
198C	40,000	6,876	33,124	2,650	4,226	30,000	25,774
198D	30,000	4,226	25,774	2,062	2,164	20,000	17,836
198E	20,000	2,164	17,836	1,427	737	10,000	9,263
198F	10,000	737	9,263	737*	–0–	–0–	–0–

*Adjusted for rounding.

Illustration 12–3

Posting the entries recording the $10,000 payment and the amortization of the discount causes the lease liability to appear on the December 31, 198B, balance sheet as follows:

Long-term liabilities:		
Long-term lease liability	$40,000	
Less unamortized discount based on the 8% interest rate prevailing on the date of the contract	6,876	$33,124

At the end of 198C and each succeeding year thereafter the remaining amounts in Column 5 of Illustration 12–3 should be amortized. This together with the $10,000 annual payments will reduce the carrying amount of the lease liability to zero by the end of the fifth year.

Return again to Illustration 12–3, Column 5. Each year's amount of discount to be amortized is determined by multiplying the beginning of the year carrying amount of the lease liability by 8%. For example, the 198C amount to be amortized is $2,650 ($33,124 × 8% = $2,650 rounded). Likewise each end-of-the-year carrying amount is determined by subtracting the end-of-the-year unamortized discount from the remaining end-of-the-year lease liability. For example, the December 31, 198C, carrying amount is $30,000 − $4,226 = $25,774.

ISSUING A MORTGAGE TO BORROW MONEY

When a business needs long-term money, it may obtain the money by placing a mortgage on some or all of its plant assets. A mortgage actually involves two legal documents. The first is a kind of promissory note called a *mortgage note,* which is secured by a second legal document called a *mortgage* or a *mortgage contract.* In the mortgage note the mortgagor, the one who mortgages property, promises to repay the money borrowed. The mortgage or mortgage contract commonly requires the mortgagor to keep the mortgaged property in a good state of repair, carry adequate insurance, and pay the interest on the mortgage note. In addition it normally grants the mortgage holder the right to foreclose in case the mortgagor fails in any of the required duties. In a foreclosure a court takes possession of the mortgaged property for the mortgage holder and may order its sale. If the property is sold, the proceeds go first to pay court costs and the claims of the mortgage holder. Any money remaining is then paid to the former owner of the property.

A loan secured by a mortgage is recorded as follows:

Feb.	1	Cash	40,000.00	
		Mortgage Payable		40,000.00
		Borrowed by placing a 20-year, 8½% mortgage on the building.		

In addition to paying interest, a mortgage contract commonly requires the mortgagor to make periodic payments to reduce the mortgage debt. For example, if the foregoing mortgage requires semiannual interest payments plus semiannual $1,000 payments to reduce the mortgage debt, the following entry is used to record the first semiannual payments:

Aug.	1	Mortgage Payable	1,000.00	
		Interest Expense	1,700.00	
		Cash		2,700.00
		Paid the interest and the first semiannual payment on the mortgage principal.		

On a mortgage such as this the balance of the mortgage debt at the beginning of each interest period is normally used in calculating the period's mortgage interest. Likewise, at the end of each year the portion of the mortgage debt to be paid with current assets during the next year becomes a current liability for statement purposes.

GLOSSARY

Bank discount. Interest charged and deducted by a bank in discounting a note.

Capital lease. A lease having essentially the same economic consequences as if the lessee had secured a loan and purchased the leased asset.

Carrying amount of a note. The face amount of a note minus the unamortized discount on the note.

Carrying amount of a lease. The remaining lease liability minus the unamortized discount on the lease financing.

Financing lease. Another name for a capital lease.

Mortgage. A lien or prior claim to an asset or assets given by a borrower to a lender as security for a loan.

Mortgage contract. A document setting forth the terms under which a mortgage loan is made.

Operating lease. A lease not meeting any of the criteria of the FASB that would make it a capital lease.

Present value. The estimated worth today of an amount of money to be received at a future date.

Present value table. A table showing the present value of one amount to be received at various future dates when discounted at various interest rates.

QUESTIONS FOR CLASS DISCUSSION

1. Define *(a)* a current liability and *(b)* a long-term liability.
2. The legal position of a company is improved by its acceptance of a promissory note in exchange for granting a time extension on the due date of a customer's debt. Why?
3. What distinction do banks make between loans and discounts?
4. Which is to the advantage of a bank *(a)* making a loan to a customer in exchange for the customer's $1,000, 60-day, 9% note or *(b)* making a loan to the customer by discounting the customer's $1,000 noninterest-bearing note for 60 days at 9%? Why?
5. Distinguish between bank discount and cash discount.
6. What determines the present value of $1,000 to be received at some future date?

7. If a $5,000, noninterest-bearing, five-year note is exchanged for a machine, what two elements of the transaction are represented in the $5,000 face amount of the note?

8. If the Machinery account is debited for $5,000 and Notes Payable is credited for $5,000 in recording the machine of Question 7, what effects will this have on the financial statements?

9. What is the advantage of leasing a plant asset instead of purchasing it?

10. Distinguish between a capital lease and an operating lease. Which causes an asset and a liability to appear on the balance sheet?

11. At what amount is a machine acquired through a capital lease recorded?

12. What two legal documents are involved when money is borrowed by mortgaging property? What does each document require of the mortgagor?

CLASS EXERCISES

Exercise 12-1

A company borrowed $10,000 from its bank by giving a 9%, 60-day note dated December 11, 198A. Prepare entries to record (a) issuance of the note, (b) the December 31 accrued interest on the note, and (c) the payment of the note under the assumption the company does not make reversing entries. Then under the assumption the company does make reversing entries, prepare (d) the entry to reverse the accrued interest adjusting entry and (e) the entry to record payment of the note under this alternate assumption.

Exercise 12-2

A company borrowed from its bank on December 11, 198A, by discounting its $10,000, noninterest-bearing note for 60 days at 9%. Prepare entries to record (a) the issuance of the note, (b) the December 31 adjusting entry to remove from the Interest Expense account the interest applicable to 198B, (c) the reversing entry, and (d) the payment of the note.

Exercise 12-3

Present calculations to show the following: (a) The present value of $5,000 to be received five years hence, discounted at 8%. (b) The total present value of three payments consisting of $8,000 to be received one year hence, $6,000 to be received two years hence, and $4,000 to be received three years hence, all discounted at 10%. (c) The present value of five payments of $2,000 each, with a payment to be received at the end of each of the next five years, discounted at 8%.

Exercise 12-4

On January 1, 198A, a day when the prevailing interest rate was 8%, a company exchanged a $5,000, noninterest-bearing, four-year note for a machine the cash price of which was not readily determinable. (a) Prepare the entry to record the purchase of the machine. (b) Show how the liability will appear on a balance sheet prepared on the day of the purchase. (c) Prepare the entry to amortize a portion of the discount on the note at the end of its first year.

Exercise 12–5

On January 1, 198A, a day when the prevailing interest rate was 8%, a company had an opportunity to either buy a machine for $16,500 cash or lease it for four years under a contract calling for a $5,000 annual lease payment at the end of each of the next four years, with the machine becoming the property of the lessee company at the end of that period. The company decided to lease the machine. Prepare entries to record (a) the leasing of the machine, (b) the amortization of the discount on the lease financing at the end of the first year, and (c) the first annual payment under the lease.

PROBLEMS

Problem 12–1

Prepare general journal entries to record these transactions:

Mar. 3 Purchased machinery on credit from Litton Company, invoice dated March 1, terms 2/10, n/60, $5,500.

May 4 Borrowed money from Security Bank by discounting our own $6,000 note payable for 60 days at 8%.

      6 Gave Litton Company $1,000 in cash and a $4,500, 60-day, 8% note to secure a time extension on the balance owed on our past-due account.

July 3 Paid the note discounted at Security Bank on May 4.

      5 Paid the note given Litton Company on May 6.

Nov. 1 Borrowed money at Security Bank by discounting our own $8,000 note payable for 90 days at 9%.

Dec. 16 Borrowed money at Guaranty Bank by giving a $6,000, 60-day, 8% note payable.

     31 Made an adjusting entry to remove from the Interest Expense account the interest applicable to next year on the note discounted at Security Bank on November 1.

     31 Made an adjusting entry to record the accrued interest on the note given Guaranty Bank on December 16.

     31 Reversed the adjusting entry applicable to the note given Security Bank on November 1. Dated the entry January 1.

Jan. 30 Paid the note discounted at Security Bank on November 1.

Feb. 13 Paid the note given to Guaranty Bank on December 16.

Problem 12–2

A company completed these transactions involving a factory machine:

198A

Dec. 31 Exchanged an $8,000, three-year, noninterest-bearing note payable for a machine, the cash price of which was not readily determinable.

The prevailing interest rate on the day of the exchange was 8%. The machine's service life was estimated at eight years with no salvage value.

198B

Dec. 31   Amortized a portion of the discount on the note payable. (Round all amounts to the nearest full dollar.)

31   Recorded straight-line depreciation on the machine.

198C

Dec. 31   Amortized a portion of the discount on the note payable.

31   Recorded straight-line depreciation on the machine.

198D

Jan.   5   Added a device onto the machine at a $600 cost. The device increased the machine's output by 25% but did not change its estimated service life or zero salvage value.

Dec. 31   Amortized the remaining amount of discount on the note payable.

31   Paid the noninterest-bearing note payable.

31   Recorded straight-line depreciation on the machine.

198E

Dec. 31   Recorded straight-line depreciation on the machine.

198F

June 28   Traded the old machine on a new machine of like purpose but capable of double the output and having a $10,000 cash price. A $3,500 trade-in allowance was received, and the balance was paid in cash.

Required:

1. Prepare general journal entries to record the transactions, rounding all amounts to the nearest full dollar.
2. Under the assumption that the machine and the note payable were the only machine and note payable of the company on December 31, 198B, show how they would appear on the balance sheet of that date.

Problem 12–3

A company exchanged a $12,000, five-year, noninterest-bearing note payable for a machine, the cash price of which was not readily determinable. The prevailing interest rate on the day of the exchange, January 1, 198A, was 8%. The machine's service life was estimated at nine years with no salvage value, and it was to be depreciated on a straight-line basis.

Required:

1. Prepare a general journal entry to record acquisition of the machine.
2. Prepare a schedule with the columnar headings of Illustration 12–2. Enter the years 198A through 198E in the schedule's first column and complete the schedule by filling in the proper amounts. (Round all amounts to the nearest full dollar and adjust the last year's discount to be amortized for rounding.)
3. Show how the machine and the note should appear on the December 31, 198B, balance sheet.

4. Show how the machine and the note should appear on the December 31, 198C, balance sheet.
5. Prepare entries to record *(a)* the 198D discount to be amortized and *(b)* the 198D depreciation expense. Also, *(c)* prepare the entry to record the payment of the note on January 1, 198F.

Problem 12–4

A company required the use of two machines in its operations. The life of each machine was estimated at ten years with no salvage value. Machine No. 1 would have cost $50,000 and Machine No. 2 $51,750 if purchased for cash. However, the company did not have the required funds, and it leased the machines on December 31, 198A, a day when the prevailing interest rate was 8%. Machine No. 1 was leased for five years under a contract calling for $9,000 annual lease payments and the return of the machine to the lessor at the end of the lease period. Machine No. 2 was leased for eight years under a contract calling for $9,000 annual lease payments, with the machine becoming the property of the lessee company at the end of the lease period. In both cases the payments were to be made at the end of each year in the lives of the leases.

Required:

1. Prepare any required entries to record the lease of *(a)* Machine No. 1 and *(b)* Machine No. 2.
2. Prepare the required entries as of the end of the first year in *(a)* the life of Machine No. 1 and *(b)* the life of Machine No. 2. (Round all amounts to the nearest full dollar and use straight-line depreciation.)
3. Machine No. 1 was returned to the lessor on December 31, 198F, the end of the fifth year. Prepare the required entries as of the end of the fifth year in *(a)* the life of Machine No. 1 and *(b)* the life of Machine No. 2.
4. Show how Machine No. 2 and the lease liability for the machine should appear on the balance sheet as of the end of the fifth year in the life of the lease.

Problem 12–5

A company needed a new machine in its operations. The machine could be purchased for $33,000 cash, or it could be leased for four years under a contract calling for annual payments of $10,000 at the end of each of the four years in the life of the lease, with the machine becoming the property of the lessee after the last lease payment. The machine's service life was estimated at six years with no salvage value. The company decided to lease the machine; and on December 31, 198A, a day when the prevailing interest rate was 8%, it signed the lease contract. The machine was delivered two days later and was placed in operation on January 12, 198B. On April 3, during the sixth year in the life of the machine, it was traded in on a new machine of like purpose having a $40,000 cash price. A $2,000 trade-in allowance was received, and the balance was paid in cash.

Required:

1. Prepare a schedule with the columnar headings of Illustration 12–3. Enter the years 198B through 198E in the first column and complete the schedule by filling in the proper amounts. Round all amounts to the nearest full dollar.
2. Prepare the entry to record the leasing of the machine.
3. Using straight-line depreciation, prepare the required entries as of the end of the first year in the life of the machine and the lease. Show how the machine and the lease liability should appear on the December 31, 198B, balance sheet.
4. Prepare the required entries as of the end of the third year in the life of the lease and the machine. Show how the machine and the lease liability should appear on the December 31, 198D, balance sheet.
5. Prepare the April 3, 198G, entry to record the exchange of the old and new machines, using the income tax method.

ALTERNATE PROBLEMS

Problem 12–1A

Prepare general journal entries to record these transactions:

Mar. 29   Gave $1,200 in cash and a $6,000, 8%, 120-day note to purchase store equipment.

Apr. 12   Borrowed money at the bank by discounting our $5,000 note payable for 60 days at 9%.

June 11   Paid the note discounted at the bank on April 12.

July 27   Paid the $6,000 note of the March 29 transaction and the interest.

Aug. 31   Purchased merchandise on credit from Otto Company, invoice date August 29, terms 2/10, n/60, $4,800.

Nov. 1   Gave Otto Company $300 in cash and a $4,500, 90-day, 8% note dated this day to gain a time extension on the balance owed.

Dec. 1   Borrowed money at Security Bank by discounting our $8,000 note payable for 90 days at 9%.

   31   Made an adjusting entry to record the accrued interest on the note given Otto Company on November 1.

   31   Made an adjusting entry to remove from the Interest Expense account the interest applicable to the next year on the note discounted on December 1.

   31   Reversed the adjusting entry applicable to the note given Security Bank on December 1. Dated the entry January 1.

Jan. 30   Paid the note given Otto Company on November 1.

Mar. 1   Paid the note discounted at Security Bank on December 1.

Problem 12–2A

A company completed these transactions:

198A

Dec. 31   Exchanged a $7,500, three-year, noninterest-bearing note payable for a machine, the cash price of which was not readily determinable.

The machine's service life was estimated at five years with no salvage value. The prevailing interest rate on the day of the exchange was 8%.

198B

Dec. 31   Amortized a portion of the discount on the note payable.
    31   Recorded straight-line depreciation on the machine.

198C

Dec. 31   Amortized a portion of the discount on the note payable.
    31   Recorded straight-line depreciation on the machine.

198D

Jan. 10   Added a $756 device onto the machine, which increased the machine's hourly output by one third but did not change its estimated service life or its zero salvage value.

Dec. 31   Amortized the remaining amount of discount on the note payable.
    31   Paid the noninterest-bearing note payable.
    31   Recorded straight-line depreciation on the machine.

198E

Dec. 31   Recorded straight-line depreciation on the machine.

198F

Apr. 27   Traded the old machine on a new machine having twice the hourly output. The new machine had a $9,000 cash price, and a $1,000 trade-in allowance was received. The balance was paid in cash.

Required:

1. Prepare general journal entries to record the transactions, rounding all amounts to the nearest full dollar.
2. Show how the machine and the note payable should appear on the December 31, 198B, balance sheet.

Problem 12–3A

A company exchanged a $14,000 four-year, noninterest-bearing note payable for a machine, the cash price of which was not readily determinable. The prevailing interest rate on the day of the exchange, January 1, 198A, was 8%. The machine's service life was estimated at six years with no salvage value, and it was to be depreciated on a straight-line basis.

Required:

1. Prepare a general journal entry to record acquisition of the machine.
2. Prepare a schedule with columnar headings like Illustration 12–2. Enter the years 198A through 198D in the schedule's first column and complete the schedule by filling in the proper amounts. (Round all amounts to the nearest full dollar and adjust the last year's discount for rounding.)
3. Show how the machine and the note should appear on the December 31, 198A, balance sheet.
4. Show how the machine and the note should appear on the December 31, 198B, balance sheet.
5. Prepare entries to record (a) the 198C discount to be amortized and (b) the 198C depreciation expense. Also, (c) prepare the entry to record the payment of the note on January 1, 198E.

Problem 12–4A

On December 31, 198A, a day when the prevailing interest rate was 8%, a company leased two machines. Machine No. 1 was leased for six years under a contract calling for an $8,000 lease payment at the end of each year in the life of the lease, with the machine becoming the property of the lessee company after the sixth lease payment. Machine No. 2 was leased for four years under a contract calling for an $8,000 annual lease payment at the end of each year in the life of the lease and the machine to be returned to the lessor at the end of the fourth year. Each machine could have been purchased for $36,950 cash, and each machine was estimated to have no salvage value at the end of an estimated ten-year life.

Required:

1. Prepare any required entries to record the lease of *(a)* Machine No. 1 and *(b)* Machine No. 2.
2. Prepare the required entries as of the end of the first year in *(a)* the life of Machine No. 1 and *(b)* the life of Machine No. 2. (Round all amounts to the nearest full dollar and use straight-line depreciation.)
3. Machine No. 2 was returned to the lessor on December 31, 198E, the end of the fourth year. Prepare the required entries as of the end of the fourth year in *(a)* the life of Machine No. 1 and *(b)* the life of Machine No. 2.
4. Show how Machine No. 1 and the lease liability for the machine should appear on the balance sheet prepared at the end of the fourth year in the life of the lease.

Problem 12–5A

A company leased a machine on December 31, 198A, under a contract calling for annual payments of $12,000 at the end of each of four years, with the machine becoming the property of the lessee company after the fourth $12,000 lease payment. The machine was estimated to have an eight-year life and no salvage value, and the prevailing interest rate on the day the lease was signed was 8%. The machine was delivered on January 3, 198B, and was placed in operation eight days later. During the first week in January, at the beginning of the eighth year in the machine's life, it was overhauled at a $1,200 total cost. The overhaul was paid for on January 10, and it did not increase the machine's efficiency but it did add an additional year to its expected service life. On March 28, during the ninth year in the machine's life, it was traded in on a new machine of like purpose having a $45,000 cash price. A $2,000 trade-in allowance was received and the balance was paid in cash.

Required:

1. Prepare a schedule with the columnar headings of Illustration 12–3. Enter the years 198B through 198E in the first column and complete the schedule by filling in the proper amounts. (Round all amounts to the nearest full dollar.)
2. Prepare the entry to record the leasing of the machine.

3. Using straight-line depreciation, prepare the required entries as of the end of the second year in the life of the lease. Also show how the machine and the lease liability should appear on the December 31, 198C, balance sheet.

4. Prepare the entries to record the machine's overhaul and the depreciation on the machine at the end of its eighth year.

5. Prepare the March 28, 198J, entries to record the exchange of the machines.

After studying Chapter 13, you should be able to:

☐ State which payroll taxes are withheld from employees' wages and which are levied on employers.

☐ Calculate an employee's gross pay and the various deductions from the pay.

☐ Prepare a Payroll Register and make the entries to record its information and to pay the employees.

☐ Explain the operation of a payroll bank account.

☐ Calculate and prepare the entry to record the payroll taxes levied on an employer.

☐ Define or explain the words and phrases listed in the chapter Glossary.

Payroll accounting

■ An employer incurs a number of liabilities as a result of state and federal programs that are financed by payroll taxes. An understanding of these taxes and the resulting liabilities requires some understanding of the laws and programs that affect payrolls. Consequently, the more pertinent of these are discussed in the first portion of this chapter before the subject of payroll records is introduced.

THE FEDERAL SOCIAL SECURITY ACT

The federal Social Security Act provides for a number of programs, two of which materially affect payroll accounting. These are (1) a federal old-age and survivors' benefits program with medical care for the aged and (2) a joint federal-state unemployment insurance program.

Federal old-age and survivors' benefits program

The Social Security Act provides that a qualified worker in a covered industry who reaches the age of 62 and retires shall receive monthly retirement benefits for the remainder of his or her life, and certain medical benefits after reaching 65. It further provides benefits for the family of a worker covered by the act who dies either before or after reaching retirement age and benefits for covered workers who become disabled. The benefits in each case are based upon the earnings of the worker during the years of his or her employment in covered industries.

No attempt will be made here to list or discuss the requirements to be met by a worker or the worker's family to qualify for benefits. In general, any person who works for an employer covered by the act for a sufficient length of time qualifies himself or herself and family. All companies and individuals who employ one or more persons and are not specifically exempted are covered by the law.

Funds for the payment of old-age, survivors', and medical benefits under the Social Security Act come from payroll taxes. These taxes are imposed under a law called the Federal Insurance Contributions Act and are called *FICA taxes*. They are also commonly called "social security taxes." These FICA taxes are imposed in like amounts on covered employers and their employees. At this writing the act imposes a 1980 tax on both employers and their employees amounting to 6.13% of the first $25,900 paid each employee. It also provides for rate increases as follows:

	Tax on employees	Tax on employers	Maximum wages taxed
1981	6.65%	6.65%	$29,700
1982 through 1984	6.70	6.70	29,700
1985	7.05	7.05	29,700
1986 through 1989	7.15	7.15	29,700
1990 and after	7.65	7.65	29,700

The maximum amount of wages subject to FICA taxes is very apt to change; and if history is any indication, Congress will change the rates listed above (probably increasing them) before they become effective. Consequently, since changes are almost certain, you are asked to use an assumed FICA tax rate of 6% on the first $29,700 of wages paid each employee each year in solving the problems at the end of this chapter. The assumed 6% rate is used because it makes calculations easy and because any rate that is correct in, say 1981, may not be correct for the remaining years this text will be used.

The Federal Insurance Contribution Act in addition to setting rates requires that an employer—

1. Withhold from the wages of each employee each payday an amount of FICA tax calculated at the current rate. The withholding to continue each payday during the year until the tax-exempt point is reached.
2. Pay a payroll tax equal to the sum of the FICA taxes withheld from the wages of all employees.

3. Periodically deposit to the credit of the Internal Revenue Service in a bank authorized to receive such deposits (called a *federal depository bank*) both the amounts withheld from the employees' wages and the employer's tax. (A discussion of the required frequency of the deposits follows.)

4. Within one month after the end of each calendar quarter, file a tax information return known as Employer's Quarterly Federal Tax Return, Form 941. (See Illustration 13–1.)

5. Furnish each employee before January 31 following each year a Wage and Tax Statement, Form W–2, which tells the employee the amounts of his wages that were subject to FICA and federal income taxes and the amounts of such taxes withheld. (A W–2 Form is shown in Illustration 13–2.)

6. Send copies of the W–2 Forms to the Social Security Administration, which posts to each employee's social security account the amount of the employee's wages subject to FICA tax and the FICA tax withheld. These posted amounts become the basis for determining the employee's retirement and survivors' benefits. In addition to the posting, the Social Security Administration transmits to the Internal Revenue Service the amount of each employee's wages subject to federal income tax and the amount of such tax withheld.

7. Keep a record for four years for each employee that shows among other things wages subject to FICA taxes and the taxes withheld. (The law does not specify the exact form of the record. However, most employers keep individual employee earnings records similar to the one shown later in this chapter.)

Observe that in addition to reporting its employees' and employer's FICA taxes on Form 941 (Illustration 13–1), an employer also reports the amount of its employees' wages that were subject to federal income taxes and the amount of such taxes that were withheld. (The withholding of employees' federal income taxes is discussed later in this chapter.) Employees' wages subject to federal income tax is shown on Line 2 of Illustration 13–1, and the amount of tax withheld is reported on Lines 3, 4, and 5. The combined amount of the employees' and employer's FICA taxes is reported on Line 6 where it says, "Taxable FICA wages paid . . . $42,615.98 multiplied by 12.26% = Tax, $5,224.72." The 12.26% is the sum of the (1980) 6.13% tax withheld from the employees' wages plus the 6.13% tax levied on the employer.

The frequency with which an employer must deposit to the credit of the Internal Revenue Service the FICA and employees' withheld income taxes depends on the amounts involved. If the sum of the FICA taxes plus the employees' income taxes is less than $200 for a quarter, the taxes may be paid when the employer files his Employer's Quarterly Tax Return, Form 941. This return is due on April 30, July 31, October 31, and January 31 following the end of each calendar

Form **941**
(Rev. July 1979)
Department of the Treasury
Internal Revenue Service

Employer's Quarterly Federal Tax Return

			T	
			FF	
			FD	
			FP	
			I	
			T	

Your name, address, employer identification number, and calendar quarter of return. (If not correct, please change)

Name (as distinguished from trade name)   Date quarter ended

Trade name, if any   Employer identification number

▶ Rockhill Manufacturing Co., Inc.   123-12-1234

Address and ZIP code

5562 West Lane Avenue
Phoenix, Arizona 85012

If address is different from prior return, check here ▶ ☐

1 Number of employees (except household) employed in the pay period that includes March 12th (complete for first quarter only)		12	
2 Total wages and tips subject to withholding, plus other compensation . . . . ——▶		42,615	98
3 Total income tax withheld from wages, tips, annuities, gambling, etc. (see instructions)		4,545	50
4 Adjustment of withheld income tax for preceding quarters of calendar year			
5 Adjusted total of income tax withheld		4,545	50
6 Taxable FICA wages paid . . . . $42,615.98 multiplied by 12.26% = TAX . .		5,224	72
7 Taxable tips reported . . . . $................. multiplied by 6.13% = TAX . .			
8 Total FICA taxes (add lines 6 and 7) . . . . ——▶		5,224	72
9 Adjustment of FICA taxes (see instructions)			
10 Adjusted total of FICA taxes . . . . ——▶		5,224	72
11 Total taxes (add lines 5 and 10)		9,770	22
12 Advance earned income credit (EIC) payments, if any (see instructions)			
13 Net taxes (subtract line 12 from line 11)		9,770	22

Record of Federal Tax Deposits (See instructions on page 4)

Deposit period ending:		I. Tax liability for period	II. Date of deposit	III. Amount deposited
Overpayment from previous quarter				
First month of quarter	1st through 7th day	591.54		
	8th through 15th day	771.94		
	16th through 22d day	759.17	1/25/80	2,122.65
	23d through last day	746.20		
A First month total . . . . [A]		2,868.85		2,122.65
Second month of quarter	1st through 7th day	767.19		
	8th through 15th day	777.34	2/20/80	2,290.73
	16th through 22d day	755.07		
	23d through last day	772.09		
B Second month total . . . . . . [B]		3,071.69		2,290.73
Third month of quarter	1st through 7th day	759.22	3/12/80	2,286.38
	8th through 15th day	774.04		
	16th through 22d day	748.35		
	23d through last day	1,548.07	4/3/80	3,070.46
C Third month total . . . . [C]		3,829.68		5,356.84
D Total for quarter (add items A, B, and C) .		9,770.22		9,770.22
E Final deposit made for quarter. (Enter zero if the final deposit made for the quarter is included in item D)				–0–

14 Total deposits for quarter (including final deposit made for quarter) and overpayment from previous quarter. (See instructions for deposit requirements on page 4)	9,770	22

Note: If undeposited taxes at the end of the quarter are $200 or more, deposit the full amount with an authorized financial institution or a Federal Reserve bank according to the instructions on the back of the Federal Tax Deposit Form 501. Enter this deposit in the Record of Federal Tax Deposits and include it on line 14.

15 Undeposited taxes due (subtract line 14 from line 13—this should be less than $200). Pay to Internal Revenue Service and enter here . . . . ——▶	–0–	

16 If line 14 is more than line 13, enter overpayment here ▶ $ ___ and check if to be: ☐ Applied to next return, or ☐ Refunded.

17 If you are not liable for returns in the future, write "FINAL" (See instructions) ▶ ___ Date final wages paid ▶

Under penalties of perjury, I declare that I have examined this return, including accompanying schedules and statements, and to the best of my knowledge and belief it is true, correct, and complete.

Date ▶ April 28, 1980   Signature ▶ *Walter W. West*   Title ▶ President

Please file this form with your Internal Revenue Service Center (see instructions on "Where to File").   Form **941** (Rev. 7-79)

Illustration 13–1

quarter. A check for the taxes, if less than $200, may be attached to the return or the taxes may be deposited in a federal depository bank at the time the return is filed. The check or the deposit is recorded in the same manner as a check paying any other liability.

If the taxes exceed $200 in a quarter, after each payday the employer must total the amount of his employees' income and FICA taxes withheld since the beginning of the quarter plus his own employer's FICA tax. This total, less any deposits already made during the quarter, is the employer's FICA and income tax liability. Then (1) if on any of the 7th, 15th, 22d, and last day of any month in the quarter this tax liability reaches $2,000 or more, the entire amount must be deposited to the credit of the Internal Revenue Service within three banking days thereafter. (2) If as of the last day of the first or second month of a quarter the tax liability for the quarter is less than $2,000 but more than $200, the amount must be deposited on or before the 15th day of the next month. For the last month in the quarter a deposit of less than $2,000 does not have to be made until the end of the next month, or it may be remitted with the quarterly tax return.

1 Control number							
	22222						
2 Employer's name, address, and ZIP code		3 Employer's identification number			4 Employer's State number		
Rochhill Manufacturing Co., Inc.		123-12-1234			56-5678		
5562 West Lane Avenue		5 Stat. em- De ployee ceased [X]	Pension Legal plan rep. ☐ ☐	942 emp. ☐	Sub- total ☐	Cor- rection ☐	Void ☐
Phoenix, Arizona 85012		6		7 Advance EIC payment			
8 Employee's social security number	9 Federal income tax withheld	10 Wages, tips, other compensation		11 FICA tax withheld			
302-02-0222	1,487.20	14,560.60		892.56			
12 Employee's name, address, and ZIP code		13 FICA wages		14 FICA tips			
Charles Robert Lusk		14,560.60					
1310 East 5th Avenue		16 Employer's use					
Phoenix, Arizona 85005							
		17 State income tax	18 State wages, tips, etc.	19 Name of State			
		728.10	14,560.60	Arizona			
		20 Local income tax	21 Local wages, tips, etc.	22 Name of locality			

Form **W-2 Wage and Tax Statement** 1980 Copy B To be filed with employee's FEDERAL tax return Department of the Treasury
This information is being furnished to the Internal Revenue Service. Internal Revenue Service

Illustration 13–2

A deposit of FICA and withheld employees' income taxes in a federal depository bank pays the taxes. Consequently, if at the time an employer files his Employer's Quarterly Tax Return, Form 941, he has paid the taxes reported on the return by means of deposits, he needs only to mail the return to the Internal Revenue Service, and no accounting entries are required.

In Illustration 13–1 the employer's tax liability reached and exceeded $2,000 once in each of January and February and twice in March. It is assumed in the illustration that the employer deposited the amounts of its tax liability on the third banking day after January 22, February 15, March 7, and March 31. Saturdays and Sundays intervened after February 15 and March 7, and since these are not banking days, this accounts for the more than three days between the ends of these periods and the dates of the deposits.

Joint federal-state unemployment insurance program

The federal government participates with the states in a joint federal-state unemployment insurance program. Within this joint program each state has established and now administers its own unemployment insurance program under which it pays unemployment benefits to its unemployed workers. The federal government approves the state programs and pays a portion of their administrative expenses.

The federal money for administering the state programs is raised by a tax imposed under a law called the Federal Unemployment Tax Act. This act levies a *payroll tax* on employers of one or more people. Note that the tax is imposed on employers only. Employees pay nothing. Also the money from this tax is used for administrative purposes and not to pay benefits.

Historically, in 1935 when the Federal Unemployment Tax Act was first passed, only one state had an unemployment insurance program. Consequently, at that time Congress passed certain sections of the Social Security Act and the Federal Unemployment Tax Act with two purposes in view. The first was to induce the individual states to create satisfactory unemployment insurance programs of their own. The second was to provide funds to be distributed to the states for use in administering the state programs. These acts were successful in accomplishing their first purpose. All states immediately created unemployment programs. Today the acts remain in effect for their second purpose, to provide funds to be distributed to the states, and also to retain a measure of federal control over the state programs.

The Federal Unemployment Tax Act   At this writing the Federal Unemployment Tax Act requires employers of one or more employees to:

1. Pay an excise tax equal to 0.7% of the first $6,000 in wages paid each employee. (Times of payment are discussed later.)
2. On or before January 31 following the end of each year, file a tax return, called an "Employer's Annual Federal Unemployment Tax Return, Form 940," reporting the amount of the tax. (Ten additional days are allowed for filing if all required tax deposits are made on a timely basis and the full amount of the tax is paid on or before January 31.)
3. Keep records to substantiate the information on the tax return. (In general the records required by other payroll laws and the regular accounting records satisfy this requirement.)

An employer's federal unemployment tax for the first three quarters of a year must be deposited in a federal depository bank by the last day of the month following each quarter (i.e., on April 30, July 31, and October 31). However, no deposit is required if the tax for a quarter plus the undeposited tax for previous quarters are $100 or less. The tax for the last quarter of a year plus the undeposited tax for previous quarters must be deposited or paid on or before January 31 following the end of the tax year. If the Employer's Annual Federal Unemployment Tax Return is filed on or before that date, a check for the last quarter's tax and any undeposited tax for previous quarters may be attached to the form.

State unemployment insurance programs   While the various state unemployment insurance programs differ in some respects, all have three common objectives. They are:

1. To pay unemployment compensation for limited periods to unemployed individuals. (To be eligible for benefits, an unemployed individual must have worked for a tax-paying employer covered by the law. In general the state laws cover employers of from one to four or more employees who are not specifically exempted.)
2. To encourage the stabilization of employment by covered employers. (In all states this is accomplished by a so-called *merit-rating plan*. Under a merit-rating plan an employer who provides steady employment for its employees gains a merit rating that substantially reduces its state unemployment tax rate.)
3. To establish and operate employment facilities that assist unemployed individuals in finding suitable employment and assist employers in finding employees.

All states support their unemployment insurance programs by placing a payroll tax on employers. A few states place an additional tax on employees. The basic rate in most states is 2.7% of the first $6,000 paid each employee. However, an employer can gain a merit rating that will reduce this basic rate to as little as 0.5% in some states and to zero in others. An employer gains a merit rating by not laying its employees off during a slack season to draw unemployment benefits. And, to most employers such a rating offers an important tax savings. For example, an employer with just ten employees who each earn $6,000 or more per year can save $1,320 of state unemployment taxes each year by gaining a merit rating that reduces its state unemployment tax rate to 0.5%.

The states vary as to required unemployment tax reports. Nevertheless, in general all require a tax return and payment of the required tax within one month after the end of each calendar quarter. Also, since the benefits paid an eligible unemployed individual are based upon earnings, the tax return must usually name each employee and tell the employee's wages.

In addition to reports and payment of taxes, all states require employers to maintain certain payroll records. These vary but in general require a payroll record for each pay period showing the pay period dates, hours worked, and taxable earnings of each employee. An individual earnings record for each employee is also commonly required.

The earnings record generally must show about the same information required by social security laws. In addition, information is also commonly required as to (1) the date an employee was hired, rehired, or reinstated after a layoff; (2) the date the employee quit, was discharged, or laid off; and (3) the reason for termination.

WITHHOLDING EMPLOYEES' FEDERAL INCOME TAXES

With few exceptions, an employer of one or more persons is required to calculate, withhold, and remit to the Internal Revenue Service the federal income taxes of its employees. The amount of tax to be withheld from each employee's wages is determined by the amount of the wages and the number of the employee's income tax exemptions, which for payroll purposes are called *withholding allowances*. At this writing each exemption or withholding allowance exempts $1,000 of the employee's yearly earnings from income tax. An employee is allowed one exemption for himself or herself, additional exemptions if the employee or the employee's spouse is blind or over 65, and an exemption for each dependent. Every covered employee is required to furnish his or her employer an employee's withholding allowance certificate, called a Form W–4, on which the employee indicates the number of exemptions claimed.

MARRIED Persons — WEEKLY Payroll Period

And the wages are—		And the number of withholding allowances claimed is—										
At least	But less than	0	1	2	3	4	5	6	7	8	9	10 or more
		The amount of income tax to be withheld shall be—										
$200	$210	$26.20	$22.70	$19.20	$15.80	$12.30	$9.40	$6.50	$3.60	$.80	$0	$0
210	220	28.10	24.50	21.00	17.60	14.10	10.90	8.00	5.10	2.30	0	0
220	230	30.20	26.30	22.80	19.40	15.90	12.50	9.50	6.60	3.80	.90	0
230	240	32.30	28.30	24.60	21.20	17.70	14.30	11.00	8.10	5.30	2.40	0
240	250	34.40	30.40	26.40	23.00	19.50	16.10	12.60	9.60	6.80	3.90	1.00
250	260	36.50	32.50	28.50	24.80	21.30	17.90	14.40	11.10	8.30	5.40	2.50
260	270	38.60	34.60	30.60	26.60	23.10	19.70	16.20	12.70	9.80	6.90	4.00
270	280	40.70	36.70	32.70	28.60	24.90	21.50	18.00	14.50	11.30	8.40	5.50
280	290	42.80	38.80	34.80	30.70	26.70	23.30	19.80	16.30	12.90	9.90	7.00
290	300	45.10	40.90	36.90	32.80	28.80	25.10	21.60	18.10	14.70	11.40	8.50
300	310	47.50	43.00	39.00	34.90	30.90	26.90	23.40	19.90	16.50	13.00	10.00
310	320	49.90	45.30	41.10	37.00	33.00	28.90	25.20	21.70	18.30	14.80	11.50
320	330	52.30	47.70	43.20	39.10	35.10	31.00	27.00	23.50	20.10	16.60	13.20
330	340	54.70	50.10	45.50	41.20	37.20	33.10	29.10	25.30	21.90	18.40	15.00
340	350	57.10	52.50	47.90	43.30	39.30	35.20	31.20	27.20	23.70	20.20	16.80
350	360	59.50	54.90	50.30	45.70	41.40	37.30	33.30	29.30	25.50	22.00	18.60
360	370	61.90	57.30	52.70	48.10	43.50	39.40	35.40	31.40	27.30	23.80	20.40
370	380	64.60	59.70	55.10	50.50	45.90	41.50	37.50	33.50	29.40	25.60	22.20
380	390	67.40	62.10	57.50	52.90	48.30	43.70	39.60	35.60	31.50	27.50	24.00
390	400	70.20	64.80	59.90	55.30	50.70	46.10	41.70	37.70	33.60	29.60	25.80
400	410	73.00	67.60	62.30	57.70	53.10	48.50	43.80	39.80	35.70	31.70	27.60
410	420	75.80	70.40	65.00	60.10	55.50	50.90	46.20	41.90	37.80	33.80	29.70

Illustration 13–3

Most employers use a *wage bracket withholding table* similar to the one shown in Illustration 13–3 in determining federal income taxes to be withheld from employees' *gross earnings*. The illustrated table is for married employees and is applicable when a pay period is one week. Different tables are provided for single employees and for biweekly, semimonthly, and monthly pay periods. Somewhat similar tables are also available for determining FICA tax withholdings.

Determining the federal income tax to be withheld from an employee's gross wages is quite easy when a withholding table is used. First the employee's wage bracket is located in the first two columns. Then the amount to be withheld is found on the line of the wage bracket in the column showing the exemption allowances to which the employee is entitled. The column heading numbers refer to the number of exemption allowances claimed by an employee.

In addition to determining and withholding income tax from each employee's wages every payday, employers are required to—

1. Periodically deposit the withheld taxes to the credit of the Internal Revenue Service as was previously explained.
2. Within one month after the end of each calendar quarter, file a report showing the income taxes withheld. This report is the Employer's Quarterly Federal Tax Return, Form 941, discussed previously and shown in Illustration 13–1. It is the same report required for FICA taxes.
3. On or before January 31 following each year, give each employee a Wage and Tax Statement, Form W–2, which tells the employee (1) his or her total wages for the preceding year, (2) wages subject to FICA taxes, (3) income taxes withheld, and (4) FICA taxes withheld. A copy of this statement must also be given to each terminated employee within 30 days after his or her last wage payment.
4. On or before January 31 following the end of each year, send the Social Security Administration copies of all W–2 forms given employees. The Social Security Administration transmits the forms' information as to employees' earnings and withheld taxes to the Internal Revenue Service

CITY AND STATE INCOME TAXES

In addition to deducting employees' federal income taxes, employers in many cities and in three fourths of the states must also deduct employees' city and state income taxes. When levied, the city and state taxes are handled much the same as federal income taxes.

FAIR LABOR STANDARDS ACT

The Fair Labor Standards Act, often called the Wages and Hours Law, sets minimum hourly wages and maximum hours of work per week for employees, with certain exceptions, of employers engaged either directly or indirectly in interstate commerce. The law at this writing sets a $3.10 per hour minimum wage for employees in most occupations and a 40-hour workweek. It also provides that if an employee covered by the act works more than 40 hours in one week, he or she must be paid for the hours in excess of 40 at his or her regular pay rate plus an overtime premium of at least one half the regular rate. This gives an employee an overtime rate of at least one and one half times his or her regular hourly rate. The act also requires employers to maintain records for each covered employee similar to the employee's individual earnings record of Illustration 13–8.

UNION CONTRACTS

Employers commonly operate under contracts with their employees' union that provide even better terms than the Wages and Hours Law. For example, union contracts often provide for time and one half for work in excess of eight hours in any one day, time and one half for work on Saturdays, and double time for Sundays and holidays. When an employer is under such a union contract, since the contract terms are better than those of the Wages and Hours Law, the contract terms take precedence over the law.

In addition to specifying working hours and wage rates, union contracts often provide for the collection of employees' union dues by the employer. Such a requirement commonly provides that the employer shall deduct dues from the wages of each employee and remit the amounts deducted to the union. The employer is usually required to remit once each month and to report the name and amount deducted from each employee's pay.

OTHER PAYROLL DEDUCTIONS

In addition to the payroll deductions discussed thus far, employees may individually authorize additional deductions, such as deductions for the purchase of U.S. savings bonds; to pay health, hospital, or life insurance premiums; to repay loans from the employer or the employees' credit union; and to pay for merchandise purchased from the employer and for donations to charitable organizations.

TIMEKEEPING

Compiling a record of the time worked by each employee is called *timekeeping*. In an individual company the method of compiling such a record depends upon the nature of the business and the number of its employees. In a very small business timekeeping may consist of no more than pencil notations of each employee's working time made in a memorandum book by the manager or owner. On the other hand, in a larger company a time clock or several time clocks are often used to record on *clock cards* each employee's time of arrival and departure. When time clocks are used, they are placed at the entrances to the office, store, or factory. At the beginning of each payroll period a clock card for each employee similar to Illustration 13–4 is placed in a rack at the entrance to be used by the employee. Each day upon arriving at work an employee takes his or her card from the rack and places it in a slot in the time clock. This actuates the clock to stamp the date and arrival time on the card. The employee then returns the card to the rack and proceeds to the employee's place of work. Upon leaving the plant, store, or office at noon or at

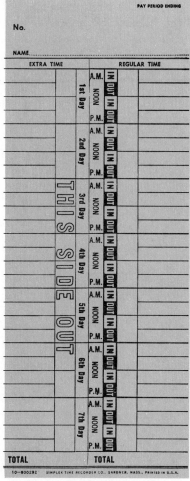

Courtesy Simplex Time Recorder Co.

Illustration 13–4

the end of the day, the procedure is repeated. The employee takes the card from the rack, places it in the clock, and stamps the time of departure. As a result, at the end of a pay period the card shows the hours the employee was on the job.

THE PAYROLL REGISTER

Each pay period the information as to hours worked as compiled on clock cards or otherwise is summarized in a Payroll Register. A pen-and-ink form of such a register is shown in Illustration 13–5. The illustrated register is for a weekly pay period and shows the payroll data for each employee on a separate line. The column headings and the data recorded in the columns are in the main self-explanatory.

The columns under the heading "Daily Time" show hours worked each day by each employee. The total of each employee's hours is entered in the column headed "Total Hours." If hours worked include overtime hours, these are entered in the column headed "O.T. Hours."

The column headed "Reg. Pay Rate" is for the hourly pay rate of each employee. Total hours worked multiplied by the regular pay rate equals regular pay. Overtime hours multiplied by the overtime premium rate equals overtime premium pay. And, regular pay plus overtime premium pay is the gross pay of each employee.

Under the heading "Deductions," the amounts withheld from each employee's gross pay for FICA taxes are shown in the column marked

Payroll
Week ended

| Employees | Clock Card No. | Daily Time | | | | | | | Total Hours | O.T. Hours | Earnings | | | |
		M	T	W	T	F	S	S			Reg. Pay Rate	Regular Pay	O.T. Premium Pay	Gross Pay
Robert Austin	114	8	8	8	8	8			40		5.00	200.00		200.00
Charles Cross	102	8	8	8	8	8			40		7.50	300.00		300.00
John Cruz	108	0	8	8	8	8	8		40		7.00	280.00		280.00
Howard Keife	109	8	8	8	8	8	8		48	8	7.00	336.00	28.00	364.00
Lee Miller	112	8	8	8	8	0			32		7.00	224.00		224.00
Dale Sears	103	8	8	8	8	8	4		44	4	7.50	330.00	15.00	345.00
Totals												1,670.00	43.00	1,713.00

Illustration 13–5

"FICA Taxes." These amounts are determined by multiplying the gross pay of each employee by the FICA tax rate in effect. In this and the remaining illustrations of this chapter it is assumed that the rate is 6% on the first $29,700 paid each employee.

As previously stated, the income tax withheld from each employee depends upon his gross pay and exemptions. This amount is commonly determined by the use of a wage bracket withholding table; and when determined, it is entered in the column headed "Federal Income Taxes."

The column headed "Hosp. Ins." shows the amounts withheld to pay for hospital insurance for the employees and their families. The total withheld from all employees is a current liability of the employer until paid to the insurance company. Likewise the total withheld for employees' union dues is a current liability until paid to the union. The column marked "Union Dues" in the illustrated Payroll Register is for this deduction.

Additional columns may be added to the Payroll Register for any other deductions that occur sufficiently often to warrant special columns. For example, a company that regularly deducts amounts from its employees' pay for U.S. savings bonds may add a special column for this deduction.

An employee's gross pay less total deductions is the employee's *net pay* and is entered in the column headed "Net Pay." The total of this column is the amount to be paid the employees. The numbers

Register
June 26, 19—

	Deductions					Payment		Distribution	
FICA Taxes	Federal Income Taxes	Hosp. Ins.	Union Dues	Total Deduc-tions		Net Pay	Check No.	Sales Salaries	Office Salaries
12.00	33.60	10.00		55.60		144.40	893		200.00
18.00	34.90	18.00	5.00	75.90		224.10	894	300.00	
16.80	30.70	18.00	5.00	70.50		209.50	895	280.00	
21.84	43.50	18.00	5.00	88.34		275.66	896	364.00	
13.44	15.90	18.00	5.00	52.34		171.66	897	224.00	
20.70	39.30	18.00		78.00		267.00	898		345.00
102.78	197.90	100.00	20.00	420.68		1,292.32		1,168.00	545.00

of the checks used in paying the employees are entered in the column headed "Check No."

The two columns under the heading "Distribution" are for sorting the various salaries into kinds of salary expense. Here each employee's gross salary is entered in the proper column according to the type of work. The column totals then tell the amounts to be debited to the salary expense accounts.

RECORDING THE PAYROLL

Generally a Payroll Register such as the one shown is a supplementary memorandum record. As such, its information is not posted directly to the accounts but is first recorded with a general journal entry, which is then posted. The entry to record the payroll shown in Illustration 13–5 is:

June	26	Sales Salaries Expense	1,168.00	
		Office Salaries Expense	545.00	
		FICA Taxes Payable		102.78
		Employees' Income Taxes Payable		197.90
		Employees' Hospital Insurance Payable		100.00
		Employees' Union Dues Payable		20.00
		Accrued Payroll Payable		1,292.32
		To record the June 26 payroll.		

The debits of the entry were taken from the Payroll Register's distribution column totals. They charge the employees' gross earnings to the proper salary expense accounts. The credits to FICA Taxes Payable, Employees' Income Taxes Payable, Employees' Hospital Insurance Payable, and Employees' Union Dues Payable record these amounts as current liabilities. The credit to Accrued Payroll Payable records as a liability the amount to be paid the employees.

PAYING THE EMPLOYEES

Almost every business pays its employees with checks. In a company having but few employees these checks are often drawn on the regular bank account and entered in a Cash Disbursements Journal like the one described in Chapter 6. Each check results in a debit to the Accrued Payroll Payable account. Therefore, posting labor can be saved by adding an Accrued Payroll Payable column in the journal. If such a column is added, entries to pay the employees of the Illustration 13–5 payroll will appear in the journal as in Illustration 13–6.

Although not required by law, most employers furnish each employee an earnings statement each payday. The objective of the state-

Cash Disbursements Journal

Date		Check No.	Payee	Account Debited	P R	Other Accounts Debit	Accts. Pay. Debit	Accr. Payroll Pay Debit	Pur. Dis. Credit	Cash Credit
June	26	893	Robert Austin	Accrued Payroll				144.40		144.40
	26	894	Charles Cross	"				224.10		224.10
	26	895	John Cruz	"				209.50		209.50
	26	896	Howard Keife	"				275.66		275.66
	26	897	Lee Miller	"				171.66		171.66
	26	898	Dale Sears	"				267.00		267.00

Illustration 13–6

ment is to inform the employee and give the employee a record of hours worked, gross pay, deductions, and net pay that may be retained. The statement usually takes the form of a detachable paycheck portion that is removed before the check is cashed. A paycheck with a detachable portion showing deductions is reproduced in Illustration 13–7.

Robert Austin	40		5.00	200.00		200.00	12.00	33.60		10.00	55.60	144.40
Employee	Total Hours	O.T. Hours	Reg. Pay Rate	Regular Pay	O.T. Prem. Pay	Gross Pay	F.I.C.A. Taxes	Income Taxes	Union Dues	Hosp. Ins.	Total Deductions	Net Pay

STATEMENT OF EARNINGS AND DEDUCTIONS FOR EMPLOYEE'S RECORDS—DETACH BEFORE CASHING CHECK

- -

VALLEY SALES COMPANY

2590 Chula Vista Street • Eugene, Oregon

No. 893

PAY TO THE ORDER OF Robert Austin _____ DATE June 26, 19-- $144.40

--One-hundred-forty-four dollars and forty cents_ _ _ _ _ _ _ _ _ _ _ _ _ _ _ _ _

VALLEY SALES COMPANY

Merchants National Bank
Eugene, Oregon

James R. Morris

Illustration 13–7

PAYROLL BANK ACCOUNT

A business with many employees normally makes use of a special *payroll bank account* in paying its employees. When such an account is used, one check for the total of the payroll is drawn on the regular bank account and deposited in the special payroll bank account. Then individual payroll checks are drawn on this special account. Because only one check for the payroll total is drawn on the regular bank account each payday, use of a special payroll bank account simplifies reconciliation of the regular bank account. It may be reconciled without considering the payroll checks outstanding, and there may be many of these.

A company using a special payroll bank account completes the following steps in paying its employees:

1. First, it records the information shown on its Payroll Register in the usual manner with a general journal entry similar to the one previously illustrated. This entry causes the sum of the employees' net pay to be credited to the liability account Accrued Payroll Payable.
2. Next, a single check payable to Payroll Bank Account for the total of the payroll is drawn and entered in the Check Register. This results in a debit to Accrued Payroll Payable and a credit to Cash.
3. The check is then endorsed and deposited in the payroll bank account. This transfers an amount of money equal to the payroll total from the regular bank account to the special payroll bank account.
4. Last, individual payroll checks are drawn on the special payroll bank account and delivered to the employees. These pay the employees and, as soon as all employees cash their checks, exhaust the funds in the special account.

A special Payroll Check Register may be used in connection with a payroll bank account. However, most companies do not use such a register but prefer to enter the payroll check numbers in their Payroll Register, making it act as a Check Register.

EMPLOYEE'S INDIVIDUAL EARNINGS RECORD

An *Employee's Individual Earnings Record,* Illustration 13–8, provides for each employee in one record a full year's summary of the employee's working time, gross earnings, deductions, and net pay. In addition it accumulates information that—

1. Serves as a basis for the employer's state and federal payroll tax returns.
2. Tells when an employee's earnings have reached the tax-exempt points for FICA and state and federal unemployment taxes.
3. Supplies data for the Wage and Tax Statement, Form W–2, which must be given to the employee at the end of the year.

The payroll information on an Employee's Individual Earnings Record is taken from the Payroll Register. The information as to earn-

EMPLOYEE'S INDIVIDUAL EARNINGS RECORD

Employee's Name___Robert Austin_____ S.S. Acct. No.___307-03-2195_____Employee No.____114____

Home
Address_111 South Greenwood_____ Notify in Case
of Emergency__Margaret Austin____ Phone
No.____964-9834____

Employed__June 7, 1980_____ Date of
Termination_____ Reason____

Date of
Birth___June 6, 1962_____ Date
Becomes 65__June 6, 2027__ Male (x)   Married ( )   Number of
Female ( ) Single (x)   Exemptions___1__ Pay
Rate_$5.00____

Occupation___Clerk_____ Place__Office__

Date		Time Lost		Time Wk.		Reg. Pay	O.T. Prem. Pay	Gross Pay	F.I.C.A. Taxes	Federal Income Taxes	Hosp. Ins.	Union Dues	Total Deductions	Net Pay	Check No.	Cumulative Pay
Per. Ends	Paid	Hrs.	Reason	Total	O.T. Hours											
1/5	1/5			40		200.00		200.00	12.00	33.60	10.00		55.60	144.40	173	200.00
1/12	1/12			40		200.00		200.00	12.00	33.60	10.00		55.60	144.40	201	400.00
1/19	1/19			40		200.00		200.00	12.00	33.60	10.00		55.60	144.40	243	600.00
1/26	1/26	4	Sick	36		180.00		180.00	10.80	30.24	10.00		51.04	128.96	295	780.00
2/2	2/2			40		200.00		200.00	12.00	33.60	10.00		55.60	144.40	339	980.00
2/9	2/9			40		200.00		200.00	12.00	33.60	10.00		55.60	144.40	354	1,180.00
2/16	2/16			40		200.00		200.00	12.00	33.60	10.00		55.60	144.40	397	1,380.00
2/23	2/23			40		200.00		200.00	12.00	33.60	10.00		55.60	144.40	446	1,580.00
6/26	6/26			40		200.00		200.00	12.00	33.60	10.00		55.60	144.40	893	5,180.00

Illustration 13–8

ings, deductions, and net pay is first recorded on a single line in the Payroll Register. It is posted each pay period from there to the earnings record. Note the last column of the record. It shows an employee's cumulative earnings and is used to determine when the earnings reach the maximum amounts taxed and are no longer subject to the various payroll taxes.

PAYROLL TAXES LEVIED ON THE EMPLOYER

As previously explained, FICA taxes are levied in equal amounts on both covered employers and their employees. However, only employers are required to pay federal and, usually, state unemployment taxes. The employer's FICA and state and federal unemployment taxes are commonly recorded with a general journal entry made at the time the payroll to which the taxes relate is recorded. For example, the entry to record the employer's payroll taxes on the payroll of Illustration 13–5 is:

June	26	Payroll Taxes Expense	111.28	
		FICA Taxes Payable		102.78
		State Unemployment Taxes Payable		6.75
		Federal Unemployment Taxes Payable		1.75
		To record the employer's payroll taxes.		

The $111.28 debit of the entry records as an expense the sum of the employer's payroll taxes. The $102.78 credit to FICA Taxes Payable is equal to and matches the FICA taxes deducted from the employees' pay and is credited to the same FICA Taxes Payable account. The $6.75 credit to State Unemployment Taxes Payable results from the assumptions that the employer's state unemployment tax rate is 2.7% on the first $6,000 paid each employee and that the employees have cumulative earnings prior to this pay period and earnings subject to the various taxes as shown in Illustration 13–9. Observe in the illustration that four employees have earned more than $6,000 and their pay is assumed, as in most states, to be exempt from state unemployment tax. One employee has previously earned $5,950 and only the first $50 of his pay is subject to tax. The wages of the remaining employee are taxable in full. Consequently, the $6.75 credit to State Unemployment Taxes Payable in the entry recording the employer's payroll taxes resulted from multiplying $250 of wages subject to tax by the assumed 2.7% rate.

As the law is presently amended, an employer's federal unemployment tax is also based on the first $6,000 in wages paid each employee.

Employees' Cumulative Earnings through the Last Pay Period and Earnings Subject to the Various Taxes				
			Earnings Subject to—	
Employees	Earnings through Last Pay Period	Earnings This Pay Period	FICA Taxes	State and Federal Unemployment Taxes
Robert Austin	$5,180.00	$ 200.00	$ 200.00	$200.00
Charles Cross	7,910.00	300.00	300.00	
John Cruz	7,280.00	280.00	280.00	
Howard Keife	7,945.00	364.00	364.00	
Lee Miller	5,950.00	224.00	224.00	50.00
Dale Sears	7,995.00	345.00	345.00	
Totals		$1,713.00	$1,713.00	$250.00

Illustration 13–9

Therefore the $1.75 federal unemployment tax liability in the illustrated journal entry resulted from multiplying $250 by the 0.7% rate.

ACCRUING TAXES ON WAGES

Payroll taxes are levied on wages actually paid; consequently, there is no legal liability for taxes on accrued wages. Nevertheless, if the requirements of the *matching principle* are met, both accrued wages and the accrued taxes on the wages should be recorded at the end of an accounting period. However, since there is no legal liability and the amounts of such taxes vary little from one accounting period to the next, most employers apply the *materiality principle* and do not accrue payroll taxes.

MACHINE METHODS

Manually prepared pen-and-ink records like the ones described in this chapter are found in many small concerns, and very satisfactorily meet their needs. However, concerns having many employees commonly use machines in their payroll work. The machines vary but are usually designed to take advantage of the fact that each pay period much the same information must be entered for each employee in the Payroll Register, on the employee's earnings record, and on the employee's paycheck. The machines take advantage of this and simultaneously print the information in all three places in one operation.

GLOSSARY

Clock card. A card used by an employee to record the time of arrival at his or her place of work and the time of departure.

Employee's Individual Earnings Record. A record of an employee's hours worked, gross pay, deductions, net pay, and certain personal information about the employee.

Federal depository bank. A bank authorized to receive as deposits amounts of money payable to the federal government.

Federal unemployment tax. A tax levied by the federal government and used to pay a portion of the costs of the joint federal-state unemployment programs.

FICA taxes. Federal Insurance Contributions Act taxes, otherwise known as social security taxes.

Gross pay. The amount of an employee's pay before any deductions.

Merit rating. A rating granted an employer by a state, which is based on whether or not the employer's employees have experienced periods of unemployment. A good rating reduces the employer's unemployment tax rate.

Net pay. Gross pay minus deductions.

Payroll bank account. A special bank account into which at the end of each pay period the total amount of an employer's payroll is deposited and on which the employees' payroll checks are drawn.

Payroll tax. A tax levied on the amount of a payroll or on the amount of an employee's gross pay.

State unemployment tax. A tax levied by a state, the proceeds from which are used to pay benefits to unemployed workers.

Timekeeping. Making a record of the time each employee is at his or her place of work.

Withholding allowance. An amount of an employee's annual earnings not subject to income tax.

Wage bracket withholding table. A table showing the amounts to be withheld from employees' wages at various levels of earnings.

QUESTIONS FOR CLASS DISCUSSION

1. What are FICA taxes? Who pays these taxes and for what purposes are the funds from FICA taxes used?

2. Company A has one employee from whose pay it withholds each week $3.75 of federal income tax and $5.76 of FICA tax. Company B has 200 employees from whose pay it withholds each week over $2,000 of employee FICA and federal income taxes. When must each of these companies remit these amounts to the Internal Revenue Service?

3. What benefits are paid to unemployed workers from funds raised by the Federal Unemployment Insurance Act? Why was this act passed?

4. Who pays federal unemployment insurance taxes? What is the tax rate?

5. What are the objectives of state unemployment insurance laws? Who pays state unemployment insurance taxes?

6. What is a state unemployment merit rating? Why are such merit ratings granted?

7. What determines the amount that must be deducted from an employee's wages for federal income taxes?

8. What is a wage bracket withholding table? Use the wage bracket withholding table in Illustration 13–3 to find the income tax to be withheld from the wages of a married employee with three exemptions who earned $245 in a week.

9. What does the Fair Labor Standards Act require of a covered employer?

10. How is a clock card used in recording the time an employee is on the job?

11. How is a special payroll bank account used in paying the wages of employees?

12. At the end of an accounting period a firm's special payroll bank account has a $562.35 balance because the payroll checks of two employees have not cleared the bank. Should this $562.35 appear on the firm's balance sheet? If so, where?

13. What information is accumulated on an employee's individual earnings

record? Why must this information be accumulated? For what purposes
is the information used?

14. What payroll taxes are levied on the employer? What taxes are deducted
from the wages of an employee?

CLASS EXERCISES

Exercise 13–1

An employee of a company subject to the Fair Labor Standards Act worked
44 hours during the week ended January 7. His pay rate is $5 per hour, and
his wages are subject to no deductions other than FICA and federal income
taxes. He claims three income tax exemptions. Calculate his regular pay, overtime premium pay, gross pay, FICA tax deduction at an assumed 6% rate,
income tax deduction (use the wage bracket withholding table of Illustration
13–3), total deductions, and net pay.

Exercise 13–2

On January 6, at the end of its first weekly pay period in the year, the
column totals of a company's Payroll Register showed that its sales employees
had earned $1,200 and its office employees had earned $800. The employees
were to have FICA taxes withheld at an assumed 6% rate plus $210 of federal
income taxes, $40 of union dues, and $80 of hospital insurance premiums.
Calculate the amount of FICA taxes to be withheld and give the general
journal entry to record the Payroll Register.

Exercise 13–3

Prepare a general journal entry to record the employer's payroll taxes resulting from the Exercise 13–3 payroll. Assume the company has a merit rating
that reduces its state unemployment tax rate to 0.75% of the first $6,000
paid each employee.

Exercise 13–4

The following information as to earnings and deductions for the pay period
ended December 20 was taken from a contractor's payroll records:

Employees	Gross Pay	Earnings to End of Previous Week	Federal Income Taxes	Deducted Union Dues
Albert Abbot	$200.00	$ 5,250.00	$ 22.70	
Gary Edwards	500.00	24,650.00	90.70	$10.00
Harold King	500.00	5,900.00	79.40	10.00
Norman Ross	600.00	29,400.00	110.40	10.00
			$303.20	$30.00

Required:

1. Calculate the FICA taxes withheld using an assumed 6% rate on the first $29,700 paid each employee. Then prepare a general journal entry to record the payroll information. Charge Office Salaries Expense for the wages of the first employee and Construction Wages Expense for the wages of the remaining employees.
2. Prepare a general journal entry to record the employer's payroll taxes. The employer does not have a merit rating and its state unemployment tax rate is 2.7% on the first $6,000 paid each employee.

PROBLEMS

Problem 13–1

On January 8, at the end of the first weekly pay period of the year, a company's Payroll Register showed that its employees had earned $3,400 of sales salaries and $600 of office salaries. The employees were to have FICA taxes withheld from their wages at an assumed 6% rate plus $420 of federal income taxes, $140 of hospital insurance, and $50 of union dues.

Required:

1. Calculate the total of the FICA Taxes Payable column in the Payroll Register, and prepare a general journal entry to record the register information.
2. Prepare a general journal entry to record the employer's payroll taxes resulting from the payroll. Assume the company has a merit rating that reduces its state unemployment tax rate to 1.2% of the first $6,000 paid each employee.
3. Under the assumption the company uses a payroll bank account and special payroll checks in paying its employees, give the check register entry (Check No. 815) to transfer funds equal to the payroll from the regular bank account to the payroll bank account.
4. Answer this question: After the check register entry is made and posted, are additional debit and credit entries required to record the payroll checks and pay the employees?

Problem 13–2

The payroll records of A-1 Plumbing Shop provided the following information for the weekly pay period ended December 18:

Employees	Clock Card No.	Daily Time							Pay Rate	Federal Income Taxes	Hospi-tal Insur-ance	Union Dues	Earnings to End of Previous Week
		M	T	W	T	F	S	S					
Roy Andrews ..	11	8	8	8	8	8	4	0	$15.00	$142.30	$15.00	$7.50	$29,850
Jerry Dale	12	8	8	8	8	8	2	0	15.00	130.90	15.00	7.50	29,300
Ray Lewis	13	8	8	8	8	8	0	0	15.00	110.40	15.00	7.50	5,830
John Mohr	14	8	8	8	8	8	0	0	12.00	84.60	10.00	5.00	24,000
Mary Page	15	8	8	8	8	8	4	0	5.00	24.60	15.00		4,670
										$492.80	$70.00	$27.50	

Required:

1. Enter the relevant information in the proper columns of a Payroll Register and complete the register using a FICA tax rate of 6% on the first $29,700 paid each employee. Assume the company is subject to the Fair Labor Standards Act. Charge the wages of Mary Page to Office Salaries Expense and the wages of the remaining employees to Plumbers' Wages Expense.
2. Prepare a general journal entry to record the payroll register information.
3. Make the check register entry (Check No. 234) to transfer funds equal to the payroll from the regular bank account to the payroll bank account under the assumption the company uses special payroll checks and a payroll bank account in paying its employees. Assume the first payroll check is numbered 668 and enter the payroll check numbers in the Payroll Register.
4. Prepare a general journal entry to record the employer's payroll taxes resulting from the payroll. Assume the company has a merit rating that reduces its state unemployment tax rate to 2% of the first $6,000 paid each employee.

Problem 13-3

A company subject to the Fair Labor Standards Act accumulated the following payroll information for the weekly pay period ended December 15:

Employees	Clock Card No.	Daily Time							Pay Rate	Income Tax Exemptions	Medi-cal Insur-ance	Union Dues	Earnings to End of Previous Week
		M	T	W	T	F	S	S					
Paul Baer	22	8	8	8	8	8	0	0	$8.50	3	$17.00	$5.00	$ 9,000
Frank Clift	23	8	8	8	8	8	4	0	8.00	2	17.00	5.00	17,200
Dale Duff	24	8	8	8	8	8	0	0	8.00	4	17.00	5.00	5,908
June Nash	25	8	8	8	9	9	0	0	6.00	2	17.00		3,600

Required:

1. Enter the relevant information in the proper columns of a Payroll Register and complete the register using a 6% FICA tax rate on the wages of each employee, since the wages of none had reached the $29,700 tax exempt point. Use the wage bracket withholding table of Illustration 13-3 to determine the federal income tax to be withheld from the wages of each employee. Assume all employees are married and the first one is a salesperson, the second two work in the shop, and the last one works in the office.
2. Prepare a general journal entry to record the payroll register information.
3. Make the check register entry to transfer funds equal to the payroll from the regular bank account to the payroll bank account (Check No. 567) under the assumption the company uses special payroll checks and a payroll bank account in paying its employees. Assume the first payroll check is numbered 444 and enter the payroll check numbers in the Payroll Register.
4. Prepare a general journal entry to record the employer's payroll taxes resulting from the payroll. Assume the company has a merit rating that reduces its state unemployment tax rate to 1.8% of the first $6,000 paid each employee.

Problem 13-4

A company has four employees to each of whom it pays $850 per month on the last day of each month. On June 1 the following accounts and balances appeared in its ledger:

a. FICA Taxes Payable, $408. (Since the company's FICA and employees' income taxes exceed $200 per month, the balance of this account represents the liability for both the employer and employees' FICA taxes for the May 31 payroll only.)
b. Employees' Federal Income Taxes Payable, $350 (liability for May only).
c. Federal Unemployment Taxes Payable, $119 (liability for first five months of the year).
d. State Unemployment Taxes Payable, $136 (liability for April and May).
e. Employees' Hospital Insurance Payable, $240 (liability for April and May).

During June and July the company completed the following payroll related transactions:

June 12   Issued Check No. 755 payable to Security Bank, a federal depository bank authorized to receive FICA and employee income tax payments from employers. The check was for $758 and was in payment of the May FICA and employee income taxes.

     30   Prepared a general journal entry to record the June Payroll Register which had the following column totals:

FICA Taxes	Federal Income Taxes	Hospital Insurance Deductions	Total Deductions	Net Pay	Office Salaries	Shop Wages
$204	$350	$120	$674	$2,726	$850	$2,550

June 30   Issued Check No. 828 payable to Payroll Bank Account in payment of the June payroll. Endorsed the check, deposited it in the payroll bank account, and issued payroll checks to the employees.

     30   Prepared and posted a general journal entry to record the employer's payroll taxes resulting from the June payroll. The company has a merit rating that reduces its state unemployment tax rate to 2% of the first $6,000 paid each employee.

July 14   Issued Check No. 883 payable to Security Bank. The check was in payment of the June FICA and employee income taxes.

     14   Issued Check No. 884 payable to Apex Insurance Company. The check was for $360 and was in payment of the April, May, and June employees' hospital insurance.

     14   Issued Check No. 885 to the State Tax Commission for the April, May, and June state unemployment taxes. Mailed the check along with the second quarter tax return to the State Tax Commission.

     31   Issued Check No. 915 payable to Security Bank. Since the tax liability exceeded $100, the check was in payment of the employer's federal unemployment taxes for the first two quarters of the year.

     31   Mailed to the Internal Revenue Service the Employer's Quarterly

Tax Return reporting the FICA taxes and the employees' federal income tax deductions for the second quarter of the year.

Required:

Prepare the necessary general journal and check register entries to record the transactions.

ALTERNATE PROBLEMS

Problem 13–1A

On January 7, at the end of the first weekly pay period of the year, the column totals of a company's Payroll Register indicated its sales employees had earned $2,140, its office employees had earned $610, and its delivery employee $250. The employees were to have FICA taxes withheld from their wages at an assumed 6% rate plus $365 federal income taxes, $80 hospital insurance deductions, and $32 of union dues.

Required:

1. Calculate the total of the FICA Taxes Payable column in the Payroll Register, and prepare a general journal entry to record the register information.
2. Prepare a general journal entry to record the employer's payroll taxes resulting from the payroll. Assume the company has a merit rating that reduces its state unemployment tax rate to 2% of the first $6,000 paid each employee.
3. Under the assumption the company uses special payroll checks and a payroll bank account in paying its employees, give the check register entry (Check No. 752) to transfer funds equal to the payroll from the regular bank account to the payroll bank account.
4. Answer this question: After the check register entry is made and posted, are additional debit and credit entries required to record the payroll checks and pay the employees?

Problem 13–2A

The following information was taken from the payroll records of A. Able Plumbing Shop for the weekly pay period ending December 20:

Employees	Clock Card No.	Daily Time							Pay Rate	Federal Income Taxes	Hospital Insurance	Union Dues	Earnings to End of Previous Week
		M	T	W	T	F	S	S					
June Agnew ...	14	8	8	8	8	8	0	0	$ 5.50	$ 22.80	$16.00		$ 4,750
Dale Hall	15	8	8	8	8	8	6	0	14.00	138.60	16.00	$ 8.00	29,850
John Koop.....	16	8	8	8	8	8	0	0	14.00	103.75	16.00	8.00	29,520
Carl Lee	17	8	8	8	8	8	0	0	14.00	91.45	16.00	8.00	28,850
Roy Page......	18	8	8	8	8	8	2	0	12.00	127.84	10.00	6.00	5,820
										$484.44	$74.00	$30.00	

Required:

1. Enter the relevant information in the proper columns of a Payroll Register and complete the register using a 6% FICA tax rate on the first $29,700 paid each employee. Assume the company has a union contract that requires time and a half for work on Saturdays. Charge the wages of June Agnew to Office Salaries Expense and the wages of the remaining employees to Plumbers' Wages Expense.
2. Prepare a general journal entry to record the payroll register information.
3. Assume the company uses special payroll checks drawn on a payroll bank account in paying its employees, and make the check register entry (Check No. 202) to transfer funds equal to the payroll from the regular bank account to the payroll bank account. Also assume the first payroll check is No. 653 and enter the payroll check numbers in the Payroll Register.
4. Prepare a general journal entry to record the employer's payroll taxes resulting from the payroll. Assume the concern has a merit rating that reduces its state unemployment tax rate to 0.8% of the first $6,000 paid each employee.

Problem 13–3A

The following information for the weekly pay period ended December 17 was taken from the records of a company subject to the Fair Labor Standards Act:

Employees	Clock Card No.	Daily Time							Pay Rate	Income Tax Exemp- tions	Medi- cal Insur- ance	Union Dues	Earnings to End of Previous Week
		M	T	W	T	F	S	S					
Mary Alt	21	8	8	8	8	8	4	0	$5.50	2	$16.50		$11,840
Harry Bray	22	8	8	8	8	8	0	0	7.00	3	16.50		3,650
Jerry Hamm ...	23	8	8	8	8	8	8	0	7.50	4	16.50	$4.00	17,380
Alex Hunt	24	8	8	8	8	8	0	0	7.50	2	16.50	4.00	5,830

Required:

1. Enter the relevant information in the proper columns of a Payroll Register and complete the register. Use a 6% FICA tax rate to calculate the FICA tax of each employee. Use the wage bracket withholding table of Illustration 13–3 to determine the federal income taxes to be withheld from the wages of the employees. Assume that all employees are married and that the first employee works in the office, the second is a salesperson, and the last two work in the shop.
2. Prepare a general journal entry to record the payroll register information.
3. Make the check register entry (Check No. 789) to transfer funds equal to the payroll from the regular bank account to the payroll bank account. Assume the first payroll check is numbered 901 and enter the payroll check numbers in the Payroll Register.
4. Prepare a general journal entry to record the employer's payroll taxes result-

ing from the payroll. Assume the company has a merit rating that reduces its state unemployment tax rate to 1.2% of the first $6,000 paid each employee.

Problem 13–4A

Redrock Company has four employees to each of whom it pays $900 per month on the last day of each month. On June 1 the following accounts and balances appeared in its ledger:

FICA taxes payable (liability for the employer's and employees' taxes resulting from the May 31 payroll)	$432.00
Employees' federal income taxes payable (liability for the May 31 payroll deductions)	385.00
Federal unemployment taxes payable (liability for first five months of the year)	126.00
State unemployment taxes payable (liability for April and May)	108.00
Employees' hospital insurance payable (liability for April and May)	84.00

During June and July the company completed the following payroll related transactions:

June 14   Issued Check No. 816 payable to Guaranty Bank, a federal depository bank authorized to accept FICA and employee income tax payments from employers. The check was for $817 and was in payment of the May FICA and employee income taxes.

June 30   Prepared and posted a general journal entry to record the June Payroll Register. The register had the following column totals:

Gross pay	$3,600
Employees' FICA taxes payable	216
Employees' federal income taxes payable	385
Employees' hospital insurance payable	42
Total deductions	643
Net pay	2,957
Sales salaries	2,700
Office salaries	900

  30   Issued Check No. 863 payable to Payroll Bank Account in payment of the June payroll. Endorsed the check, deposited it in the payroll bank account, and issued payroll checks to the employees.

  30   Prepared and posted a general journal entry to record the employer's payroll taxes resulting from the June 30 payroll. Due to a merit rating the company's state unemployment tax rate was 1.5% of the first $6,000 paid each employee, and no employee had earned that amount.

July 15   Issued Check No. 911 payable to Guaranty Bank. The check was in payment of the June FICA and employee income taxes.

  15   Issued Check No. 912 to the State Tax Commission for the April, May, and June state unemployment taxes. Mailed the check along with the second quarter tax return to the State Tax Commission.

20 Issued Check No. 933 payable to Security Insurance Company. The check was for $126 and was in payment of the April, May, and June employees' hospital insurance.

31 Issued Check No. 989 payable to Guaranty Bank. The company's federal unemployment tax for the second quarter plus the undeposited federal unemployment tax for the first quarter exceeded $100; consequently, this check was in payment of the tax for the first two quarters.

31 Mailed the Internal Revenue Service the Employer's Quarterly Tax Return, Form 941, reporting the FICA taxes and the employees' federal income tax deductions for the second quarter.

Required:

Prepare the necessary general journal and check register entries to record the transactions.

PROVOCATIVE PROBLEMS

Provocative problem 13–1
Vale Toy Company

Vale Toy Company has 300 regular employees, all earning in excess of $6,000 per year. The company's plant and office are located in a state in which the maximum state unemployment tax rate is 2.7% on the first $6,000 paid each employee. However, the company has an excellent past unemployment record and a merit rating that reduces its state unemployment tax rate to 0.5% on the first $6,000 paid each employee.

The company has received an order for Christmas toys from a large chain of department stores. The order should be profitable and will probably be repeated each year. In filling the order Vale Toy Company can stamp out the parts for the toys with present machines and employees. However, it will have to add 40 people to its work force for 40 hours per week for 10 weeks to assemble the toys and pack them for shipment.

The company can hire these people and add them to its own payroll or it can secure the services of 40 people through Temporary Help, Inc., a company in the business of supplying temporary help. If the people are secured through Temporary Help, Inc., Vale Toy Company will pay Temporary Help, Inc., $5.50 per hour for each hour worked by each person supplied. The people will be the employees of Temporary Help, Inc., and it will pay their wages and all taxes on the wages. On the other hand, if Vale Toy Company employs the 40 people and places them on its payroll, it will pay them $4 per hour and will pay the following payroll taxes on their wages: FICA tax, 6% (assumed rate); federal unemployment tax, 0.7% on the first $6,000 paid each employee; and state unemployment tax, 2.7% on the first $6,000 paid each employee. The state unemployment tax rate will be 2.7% because if the company hires the temporary people and terminates them each year after ten weeks, it will lose its merit rating.

Should Vale Toy Company place the temporary help on its own payroll or should it secure their services through Temporary Help, Inc.? Justify your answer.

After studying Chapter 14, you should be able to:

☐ List the characteristics of a partnership and explain the importance of understanding mutual agency and unlimited liability by a person about to become a partner.

☐ Explain the nature of partnership earnings and be able to make the calculations to divide partnership earnings *(a)* on a stated fractional basis, *(b)* in the partners' capital ratio, and *(c)* through the use of salary and interest allowances.

☐ Prepare entries for *(a)* the sale of a partnership interest, *(b)* the admission of a new partner by investment, and *(c)* the retirement of a partner by the withdrawal of partnership assets.

☐ Prepare entries required in the liquidation of a partnership.

☐ Define or explain the words and phrases listed in the chapter Glossary.

Partnership accounting

■ A majority of the states have adopted the Uniform Partnership Act to govern the formation and operation of partnerships. This act defines a *partnership* as "an association of two or more persons to carry on as co-owners a business for profit." A partnership has been further defined as "an association of two or more competent persons under a contract to combine some or all their property, labor, and skills in the operation of a business." Both of these definitions tell something of a partnership's legal nature. However, a better understanding of a partnership as a form of business organization may be gained by examining some of its characteristics.

CHARACTERISTICS OF A PARTNERSHIP

A voluntary association

A partnership is a voluntary association into which a person cannot be forced against his or her will. This is because a partner is responsible for the business acts of his or her partners, when the acts are within the scope of the partnership. Too, a partner is unlimitedly liable for the debts of his or her partnership. Consequently, partnership law recognizes it is only fair that a person be permitted to select the people he or she wishes to join in a partnership. Normally a person will select

461

only financially responsible people in whose judgment he or she has respect.

Based on a contract

One advantage of a partnership as a form of business organization is the ease with which it may be begun. All that is required is that two or more legally competent people agree to be partners. Their agreement becomes a *contract*. It should be in writing, with all anticipated points of future disagreement covered. However, it is just as binding if only orally expressed.

Limited life

The life of a partnership is always limited. Death, *bankruptcy*, or anything that takes away the ability of one of the partners to contract automatically ends a partnership. In addition, since a partnership is based on a contract, if the contract is for a definite period, the partnership ends with the period's expiration. If the contract does not specify a time period, the partnership ends when the business for which it was created is completed. Or, if no time is stated and the business cannot be completed but goes on indefinitely, the partnership may be terminated at will by any one of the partners.

Mutual agency

Normally there is *mutual agency* in a partnership. This means that under normal circumstances every partner is an agent of the partnership and can enter into and bind it to any contract within the apparent scope of its business. For example, a partner in a merchandising business can bind the partnership to contracts to buy merchandise, lease a store building, borrow money, or hire employees. These are all within the scope of a merchandising firm. On the other hand, a partner in a law firm, acting alone, cannot bind his or her partners to a contract to buy merchandise for resale or rent a store building. These are not within the normal scope of a law firm's business.

Partners among themselves may agree to limit the right of any one or more of the partners to negotiate certain contracts for the partnership. Such an agreement is binding on the partners and on outsiders who know of the agreement. However, it is not binding on outsiders who are unaware of its existence. Outsiders who are unaware of anything to the contrary have a right to assume that each partner has the normal agency rights of a partner.

Mutual agency offers an important reason for care in the selection of partners. Good partners benefit all; but a poor partner can do great damage. Mutual agency plus unlimited liability are the reasons most partnerships have only a few members.

Unlimited liability

When a partnership business is unable to pay its debts, the creditors may satisfy their claims from the personal assets of the partners. Furthermore, if the property of a partner is insufficient to meet his or her share, the creditors may turn to the assets of the remaining partners who are able to pay. Thus, a partner may be called on to pay all the debts of his or her partnership and is said to have *unlimited liability* for its debts.

Unlimited liability may be illustrated as follows. Ned Albert and Ted Bates each invested $5,000 in a store to be operated as a partnership, under an agreement to share losses and gains equally. Albert has no property other than his $5,000 investment. Bates owns his own home, a farm, and has sizable savings in addition to his investment. The partners rented store space and bought merchandise and fixtures costing $30,000. They paid $10,000 in cash and promised to pay the balance at a later date. However, the night before the store opened the building in which it was located burned and the merchandise and fixtures were totally destroyed. There was no insurance, all the partnership assets were lost, and Albert has no other assets. Consequently, the partnership creditors may collect the full $20,000 of their claims from Bates. However, Bates may look to Albert for payment of half at a later date, if Albert ever becomes able to pay.

ADVANTAGES AND DISADVANTAGES OF A PARTNERSHIP

Limited life, mutual agency, and unlimited liability are disadvantages of a partnership. Yet, a partnership has advantages over both the single proprietorship and corporation forms of organization. A partnership has the advantage of being able to bring together more money and skills than a single proprietorship. It is much easier to organize than a corporation. It does not have the corporation's governmental supervision nor its extra burden of taxation. And, partners may act freely and without the necessity of stockholders' and directors' meetings, as is required in a corporation.

PARTNERSHIP ACCOUNTING

Partnership accounting is exactly like that of a single proprietorship except for transactions that directly affect the partners' equities. Here, because ownership rights are divided between two or more partners, there must be (1) a capital account for each partner, (2) a withdrawals account for each partner, and (3) an accurate measurement and division of earnings.

Each partner's capital account is credited, and asset accounts showing the nature of the assets invested are debited in recording the investment of each partner. A partner's withdrawals are debited to his withdrawals account. And, in the end-of-the-period closing procedure the capital account is credited for a partner's share of the net income. Obviously, these procedures are not new, only the added accounts are new, and they need no further consideration here. However, the matter of dividing earnings among partners does need additional discussion.

NATURE OF PARTNERSHIP EARNINGS

Because, as a member of a partnership, a partner cannot enter into an employer-employee contractural relationship with himself or herself, a partner, like a single proprietor, cannot legally hire himself or herself and pay himself or herself a salary. Law and custom recognize this. Furthermore, law and custom recognize that a partner works for partnership profits and not a salary. Also, law and custom recognize that a partner invests in a partnership for earnings and not for interest. However, it should be recognized that partnership earnings do include a return for services, even though the return is contained within the earnings and is not a salary in a legal sense. Likewise, partnership earnings include a return on invested capital, although the return is not interest in the legal sense of the term. Furthermore, if partnership earnings are to be fairly shared, it is often necessary to recognize this. For example, if one partner contributes five times as much capital as another, it is only fair that this be taken into consideration in the method of sharing. Likewise, if the services of one partner are much more valuable than those of another, it is only fair that some provision be made for the unequal service contributions.

DIVISION OF EARNINGS

The law provides that in the absence of a contrary agreement, all partnership earnings are shared equally. This means that if partners cannot agree as to a method of sharing, each partner receives an equal share. Partners may agree to any method of sharing. If they agree to a method of sharing earnings but say nothing of losses, losses are shared in the same way as earnings.

Several methods of sharing partnership earnings are employed. All attempt in one way or another to recognize differences in service contributions or in investments, when such differences exist. The following three methods are discussed here: (1) on a stated fractional basis, (2) based on the ratio of capital investments, and (3) salary and interest allowances and the remainder in a fixed ratio.

EARNINGS ALLOCATED ON A STATED FRACTIONAL BASIS

The easiest way to divide partnership earnings is to give each partner a stated fraction of the total. A division on a fractional basis may provide for an equal sharing if service and capital contributions are equal. An equal sharing may also be provided when the greater capital contribution of one partner is offset by a greater service contribution of another. Or, if the service and capital contributions are unequal, a fixed ratio may easily provide for an unequal sharing. All that is necessary in any case is for the partners to agree as to the fractional share to be given each.

For example, the partnership agreement of Morse and North may provide that each partner is to receive half the earnings. Or the agreement may provide for two thirds to Morse and one third to North. Or it may provide for three fourths to Morse and one fourth to North. Any fractional basis may be agreed upon as long as the partners feel earnings are thereby fairly shared. For example, assume the agreement of Morse and North provides for a two-thirds and one-third sharing, and earnings for a year are $30,000. After all revenue and expense accounts are closed, if earnings are $30,000, the partnership Income Summary account has a $30,000 credit balance. It is closed, and the earnings are allocated to the partners with the following entry:

Dec.	31	Income Summary	30,000.00	
		A. P. Morse, Capital		20,000.00
		R. G. North, Capital		10,000.00
		To close the Income Summary account and allocate the earnings.		

DIVISION OF EARNINGS BASED ON THE RATIO OF CAPITAL INVESTMENTS

If the business of a partnership is of a nature that earnings are closely related to money invested, a division of earnings based on the ratio of partner's investments offers a fair sharing method. To illustrate this method, assume that Chase, Davis, and Fall have agreed to share earnings in the ratio of their investments. If these are Chase, $50,000, Davis, $30,000, and Fall, $40,000, and if the earnings for the year are $48,000, the respective shares of the partners are calculated as follows:

Step 1:	Chase, capital	$ 50,000
	Davis, capital	30,000
	Fall, capital	40,000
	Total invested	$120,000

Step 2:   Share of earnings to Chase $\dfrac{\$50,000}{\$120,000}$ × $48,000 = $20,000

Share of earnings to Davis $\dfrac{\$30,000}{\$120,000}$ × $48,000 = $12,000

Share of earnings to Fall $\dfrac{\$40,000}{\$120,000}$ × $48,000 = $16,000

The entry to allocate the earnings to the partners is then:

Dec.	31	Income Summary	48,000.00	
		T. S. Chase, Capital		20,000.00
		S. A. Davis, Capital		12,000.00
		R. R. Fall, Capital		16,000.00
		To close the Income Summary account and allocate the earnings.		

SALARIES AND INTEREST AS AIDS IN SHARING

Sometimes partners' capital contributions are unequal. Also, sometimes one partner devotes full time to partnership affairs and the other or others devote only part time. Too, in partnerships in which all partners devote full time, the services of one partner may be more valuable than the services of another. When these situations occur and, for example, the capital contributions are unequal, the partners may allocate a portion of their net income to themselves in the form of interest, so as to compensate for the unequal investments. Or when service contributions are unequal, they may use salary allowances as a means of compensating for unequal service contributions. Or when investment and service contributions are both unequal, they may use a combination of interest and salary allowances in an effort to share earnings fairly.

For example, Hill and Dale began a partnership business of a kind in which Hill has had experience and could command an $18,000 annual salary working for another firm of like nature. Dale is new to the business and could expect to earn not more than $12,000 working elsewhere. Furthermore, Hill invested $15,000 in the business and Dale invested $5,000. Consequently, the partners agreed that in order to compensate for the unequal service and capital contributions, they will share losses and gains as follows:

1. A share of the profits equal to interest at 8% is to be allowed on the partners' initial investments.

2. Annual salary allowances of $18,000 per year to Hill and $12,000 per year to Dale are to be allowed.
3. The remaining balance of income or loss is to be shared equally.

Under this agreement a first year $32,700 net income would be shared as in Illustration 14–1.

	Share to Hill	Share to Dale	Income allocated
Total net income			$32,700
Allocated as interest:			
Hill (8% on $15,000)	$ 1,200		
Dale (8% on $5,000)		$ 400	
Total allocated as interest			1,600
Balance of income after interest allowances			$31,100
Allocated as salary allowances:			
Hill	18,000		
Dale		12,000	
Total allocated as salary allowances			30,000
Balance of income after interest and salary allowances			$ 1,100
Balance allocated equally:			
Hill	550		
Dale		550	
Total allocated equally			1,100
Balance of income			–0–
Shares of the partners	$19,750	$12,950	

Illustration 14–1

After the shares in the net income are determined, the following entry is used to close the Income Summary account. Observe in the entry that the credit amounts may be taken from the first two column totals of the computation of Illustration 14–1.

Dec.	31	Income Summary	32,700.00	
		Robert Hill, Capital		19,750.00
		William Dale, Capital		12,950.00
		To close the Income Summary account and allocate the earnings.		

In a legal sense, partners do not work for salaries, nor do they invest in a partnership to earn interest. They invest and work for earnings. Consequently, when a partnership agreement provides for salaries and interest, the partners should understand that the salaries and interest are not really salaries and interest. They are only a means of sharing losses and gains.

In the illustration just completed the $32,700 net income exceeded the salary and interest allowances of the partners. However, the partners would use the same method to share a net income smaller than their salary and interest allowances, or to share a loss. For example, assume that Hill and Dale earned only $9,600 in a year. A $9,600 net income would be shared by the partners as in Illustration 14–2.

	Share to Hill	Share to Dale	Income allocated
Total net income			$ 9,600
Allocated as interest:			
Hill (8% on $15,000)	$ 1,200		
Dale (8% on $5,000)		$ 400	
Total allocated as interest			1,600
Balance of income after interest allowances			$ 8,000
Allocated as salary allowances:			
Hill	18,000		
Dale		12,000	
Total allocated as salary allowances			30,000
Balance of income after interest and salary allowances (a negative amount)			$(22,000)
Balance allocated equally:			
Hill	(11,000)		
Dale		(11,000)	
Total allocated equally			(22,000)
Balance of income			–0–
Shares of the partners	$ 8,200	$ 1,400	

Illustration 14–2

The Illustration 14–2 items enclosed in parentheses are negative items. It is common practice in accounting to show negative items in red or encircled or to show them enclosed in parentheses as in this illustration.

A net loss would be shared by Hill and Dale in the same manner as the foregoing $9,600 net income. The only difference being that the loss-and-gain-sharing procedure would begin with a negative amount of income, in other words, a net loss. The amount allocated equally would then be a larger negative amount.

PARTNERSHIP FINANCIAL STATEMENTS

In most respects partnership financial statements are like those of a single proprietorship. However, one common difference is that the income allocation is often shown on the income statement following the reported net income. For example, an income statement prepared for Hill and Dale might show the allocation of the $9,600 net income of Illustration 14–2 as in Illustration 14–3.

Hill and Dale
Income Statement for Year Ended December 31, 19—

Sales		$332,400
~~		
~~		
Net income		$ 9,600
Allocation of net income to the partners:		
Robert Hill:		
Interest at 8% on investment	$ 1,200	
Salary allowance	18,000	
Total	$ 19,200	
Less one half the remaining deficit	(11,000)	
Share of the net income		$ 8,200
William Dale:		
Interest at 8% on investment	$ 400	
Salary allowance	12,000	
Total	$ 12,400	
Less one half the remaining deficit	(11,000)	
Share of the net income		1,400
Net income allocated		$ 9,600

Illustration 14–3

ADDITION OR WITHDRAWAL OF A PARTNER

A partnership is based on a contract between specific individuals. Consequently, an existing partnership is ended when a partner withdraws or a new partner is added. A partner may sell his or her partnership interest and withdraw from a partnership. Also, a partner may withdraw his or her equity, taking partnership cash or other assets. Likewise a new partner may join an existing partnership by purchasing an interest from one or more of its partners or by investing cash or other assets in the business.

Sale of a partnership interest

Assume that Abbott, Burns, and Camp are partners in a partnership that has no liabilities and the following assets and equities:

Assets		Equities	
Cash	$ 3,000	Abbott, capital	$ 5,000
Other assets	12,000	Burns, capital	5,000
		Camp, capital	5,000
Total assets	$15,000	Total equities	$15,000

Camp's equity in this partnership is $5,000. If Camp sells this equity to Davis for $7,000, Camp is selling a $5,000 interest in the partnership assets. The entry on the partnership books to transfer the equity is:

Feb.	4	Camp, Capital	5,000.00	
		Davis, Capital		5,000.00
		To transfer Camp's equity in the partner-		
		ship assets to Davis.		

After this entry is posted, the assets and equities of the new partnership are:

Assets		Equities	
Cash	$ 3,000	Abbott, capital	$ 5,000
Other assets	12,000	Burns, capital	5,000
		Davis, capital	5,000
Total assets	$15,000	Total equities	$15,000

Two points should be noted in regard to this transaction. First, the $7,000 Davis paid Camp is not recorded in the partnership books. Camp sold and transferred a $5,000 equity in the partnership assets to Davis. The entry that records the transfer is a debit to Camp, Capital and a credit to Davis, Capital for $5,000. Furthermore, the entry is the same whether Davis pays Camp $7,000 or $70,000. The amount is paid directly to Camp. It is a side transaction between Camp and Davis and does not affect partnership assets.

The second point to be noted is that Abbott and Burns must agree to the sale and transfer if Davis is to become a partner. Abbott and Burns cannot prevent Camp from selling the interest to Davis. On the other hand, Camp cannot force Abbott and Burns to accept Davis as a partner. If Abbott and Burns agree to accept Davis, a new partnership is formed and a new contract with a new loss-and-gain-sharing ratio must be drawn. If Camp sells to Davis and either Abbott or Burns refuses to accept Davis as a partner, under the Uniform Partnership Act Davis gets Camp's share of partnership gains and losses and Camp's share of partnership assets if the firm is liquidated. However, Davis gets no voice in the management of the firm until admitted as a partner.

Investing in an existing partnership

Instead of purchasing the equity of an existing partner, an individual may gain an equity by investing assets in the business, with the invested assets becoming the property of the partnership. For example, assume that the partnership of Evans and Gage has assets and equities as follows:

Assets		Equities	
Cash	$ 3,000	Evans, capital	$20,000
Other assets	37,000	Gage, capital	20,000
Total assets	$40,000	Total equities	$40,000

Also, assume that Evans and Gage have agreed to accept Hart as a partner with a one-half interest in the business upon his investment of $40,000. The entry to record Hart's investment is:

Mar.	2	Cash	40,000.00	
		Hart, Capital		40,000.00
		To record the investment of Hart.		

After the entry is posted the assets and equities of the new partnership appear as follows:

Assets		Equities	
Cash	$43,000	Evans, capital	$20,000
Other assets	37,000	Gage, capital	20,000
		Hart, capital	40,000
Total assets	$80,000	Total equities	$80,000

In this case Hart has a one half equity in the assets of the business. However, he does not necessarily have a right to one half its net income. The sharing of losses and gains is a separate matter on which the partners must agree. Furthermore, the agreed method may bear no relation to their capital ratio.

A bonus to the old partners

Sometimes when a partnership earns an exceptionally high net income year after year, its partners may require an incoming partner to give a bonus for the privilege of joining the firm and sharing in its high earnings. For example, Judd and Kirk operate a partnership business, sharing its exceptionally large earnings equally. Judd has a $38,000 equity in the business, and Kirk has a $32,000 equity. They have agreed to allow Lee a one-third equity and a one-third share of the partnership's earnings upon the investment of $50,000. Lee's equity is determined with a calculation like this:

Equities of the existing partners ($38,000 + $32,000) ..	$ 70,000
Investment of the new partner	50,000
Total equities in the new partnership	$120,000
Equity of Lee (⅓ of total)	$ 40,000

And the entry to record Lee's investment is:

May	15	Cash	50,000.00	
		Lee, Capital		40,000.00
		Judd, Capital		5,000.00
		Kirk, Capital		5,000.00
		To record the investment of Lee.		

The $10,000 difference between the $50,000 invested by Lee and the $40,000 credited to his capital account is a bonus which is shared by Judd and Kirk in their loss and gain sharing ratio. Such a bonus is always shared by the old partners in their loss-and-gain-sharing ratio. Furthermore, this is only fair because the bonus is a form of compensation given for the privilege of receiving a portion of the exceptional profits formally shared exclusively by the old partners.

Recording goodwill   Instead of allowing bonuses to the old partners, goodwill may be recorded in the admission of a new partner, with the amount of the goodwill being used to increase the equities of the old partners. This can be justified only if the old partnership has a sustained earnings rate in excess of the average for its industry. However, in practice, goodwill is seldom recognized upon the admission of a new partner. Instead, the bonus method is used.

Bonus to the new partner

Sometimes the members of an existing partnership may be very anxious to bring a new partner into their firm. The business may need additional cash or the new partner may have exceptional abilities or business contacts that will increase profits. In such a situation the old partners may be willing to give the new partner a larger equity in the business than the amount of his or her investment. For example, Moss and Owen are partners with capital account balances of $30,000 and $18,000, respectively, and sharing losses and gains in a 2 to 1 ratio. The partners are anxious to have Pitt join their partnership and will allow him a one-fourth equity in the firm if he will invest $12,000. If Pitt accepts, his equity in the new firm is calculated as follows:

Equities of the existing partners ($30,000 + $18,000)	$48,000
Investment of the new partner	12,000
Total equities in the new partnership	$60,000
Equity of Pitt (¼ of total)	$15,000

And the entry to record Pitt's investment is:

June	1	Cash	12,000.00	
		Moss, Capital	2,000.00	
		Owen, Capital	1,000.00	
		Pitt, Capital		15,000.00
		To record the investment of Pitt.		

Note that Pitt's bonus is contributed by the old partners in their loss-and-gain-sharing ratio. Also remember that Pitt's one-fourth equity does not necessarily entitle him to one fourth of the earnings of the business, since the sharing of losses and gains is a separate matter for agreement by the partners.

Withdrawal of a partner

The best practice in regard to a partner's withdrawal from a partnership is for the partners to provide in advance in their partnership contract the procedures to be followed. Such procedures commonly provide for an audit of the accounting records and a revaluation of the partnership assets. The revaluation is very desirable since it places the assets on the books at current values. It also causes the retiring partner's capital account to reflect the current value of the partner's equity. Often in such cases the agreement also provides that the retiring partner is to withdraw assets equal to the book amount of the revalued equity.

For example, assume that Blue is retiring from the partnership of Smith, Blue, and Short. The partners have always shared losses and gains in the ratio of Smith, one half; Blue, one fourth; and Short, one fourth. Their partnership agreement provides for an audit and asset revaluation upon the retirement of a partner, and their balance sheet just prior to the audit and revaluation shows the following assets and equities:

Assets			Equities		
Cash		$11,000	Smith, capital		$22,000
Merchandise inventory .		16,000	Blue, capital		10,000
Equipment	$20,000		Short, capital		10,000
Less accum. depr. ...	5,000	15,000			
Total assets		$42,000	Total equities		$42,000

The audit and appraisal indicate the merchandise inventory is overvalued by $4,000. Also, due to market changes the partnership equipment should be valued at $25,000 with accumulated depreciation of $8,000. The entries to record these revaluations are:

Oct.	31	Smith, Capital	2,000.00	
		Blue, Capital	1,000.00	
		Short, Capital	1,000.00	
		Merchandise inventory		4,000.00
		To revalue the inventory.		
	31	Equipment	5,000.00	
		Accumulated Depreciation, Equipment		3,000.00
		Smith, Capital		1,000.00
		Blue, Capital		500.00
		Short, Capital		500.00
		To revalue the equipment.		

Note in the illustrated entries that losses and gains are shared in the partners' loss-and-gain-sharing ratio. Losses and gains from asset revaluations are always so shared. The fairness of this is easy to see when it is remembered that if the partnership did not terminate, such losses and gains would sooner or later be reflected on the income statement.

After the entries revaluing the partnership assets are recorded, a balance sheet will show these revalued assets and equities for Smith, Blue, and Short:

Assets			Equities		
Cash		$11,000	Smith, capital		$21,000
Merchandise inventory .		12,000	Blue, capital		9,500
Equipment	$25,000		Short, capital		9,500
Less accum. depr. ..	8,000	17,000			
Total assets		$40,000	Total equities		$40,000

After the revaluation, if Blue withdraws, taking assets equal to his revalued equity, the entry to record the withdrawal is:

Oct.	31	Blue, Capital	9,500.00	
		Cash		9,500.00
		To record the withdrawal of Blue.		

In withdrawing, Blue does not have to take cash in settlement of his equity. He may take any combination of assets to which the partners agree, or he may take the new partnership's promissory note. Also, the withdrawal of Blue creates a new partnership. Consequently, a new partnership contract and a new loss-and-gain-sharing agreement are required.

Partner withdraws taking assets of less value than his book equity

Sometimes when a partner retires, the remaining partners may not wish to have the assets revalued and the new values recorded. In such cases the partners may agree, for example, that the assets are overvalued. And, due to the overvalued assets, the retiring partner should in settlement of his equity take assets of less value than the book value of his equity. Sometimes, too, when assets are not overvalued, the retiring partner may be so anxious to retire that he is willing to take less than the current value of his equity just to get out of the partnership or out of the business.

When a partner retires taking assets of less value than his equity, he is in effect leaving a portion of his book equity in the business. In such cases, the remaining partners share the unwithdrawn equity portion in their loss-and-gain-sharing ratio. For example, assume that Black, Brown, and Green are partners sharing gains and losses in a 2:2:1 ratio. Their assets and equities are:

Assets		Equities	
Cash	$ 5,000	Black, capital	$ 6,000
Merchandise	9,000	Brown, capital	6,000
Store equipment	4,000	Green, capital	6,000
Total assets	$18,000	Total equities ...	$18,000

Brown is so anxious to withdraw from the partnership that he is willing to retire if permitted to take $4,500 in cash in settlement for his equity. Black and Green agree to the $4,500 withdrawal, and Brown retires. The entry to record the retirement is:

Mar.	4	Brown, Capital	6,000.00	
		Cash		4,500.00
		Black, Capital		1,000.00
		Green, Capital		500.00
		To record the withdrawal of Brown.		

In retiring, Brown did not withdraw $1,500 of his book equity. This is divided between Black and Green in their loss-and-gain-sharing ratio. The loss-and-gain sharing ratio of the original partnership was Black, 2; Brown, 2; and Green, 1. Therefore in the original partnership, Black and Green shared in a 2 to 1 ratio. Consequently, the unwithdrawn book equity of Brown is shared by Black and Green in this ratio.

Partner withdraws taking assets of greater value than his book equity

There are two common reasons for a partner receiving upon retirement assets of greater value than his book equity. First, certain of the partnership assets may be undervalued. Or the partners continuing the business may be so anxious for the retiring partner to withdraw that they are willing for him to take assets of greater value than his book equity.

When assets are undervalued and the partners do not wish to change the recorded values, the partners may agree to permit a retiring member to withdraw assets of greater value than his book equity. In such cases the retiring partner is, in effect, withdrawing his own book equity and a portion of his partners' equities. For example, assume that Jones, Thomas, and Finch are partners sharing gains and losses in a $3:2:1$ ratio. Their assets and equities are:

Assets		Equities	
Cash	$ 5,000	Jones, capital	$ 9,000
Merchandise	10,000	Thomas, capital	6,000
Equipment	3,000	Finch, capital	3,000
Total assets	$18,000	Total equities ...	$18,000

Finch wishes to withdraw from the partnership. Jones and Thomas plan to continue the business. The partners agree that certain of their assets are undervalued, but they do not wish to increase the recorded values. They further agree that if current values were recorded, the asset total would be increased $6,000 and the equity of Finch would be increased $1,000. Therefore, the partners agree that $4,000 is the proper value for Finch's equity and that he may withdraw that amount in cash. The entry to record the withdrawal is:

May	7	Finch, Capital	3,000.00	
		Jones, Capital	600.00	
		Thomas, Capital	400.00	
		Cash		4,000.00
		To record the withdrawal of Finch.		

DEATH OF A PARTNER

A partner's death automatically dissolves and ends a partnership, and the deceased partner's estate is entitled to receive the amount of his or her equity. The partnership contract should contain provisions for settlement in case a partner dies. Included should be provisions for (a) an immediate closing of the books to determine earnings since the end of the previous accounting period and (b) a method for determining and recording current values for the assets. After earnings are shared and the current value of the deceased partner's equity is determined, the remaining partners and the deceased partner's estate must agree to a disposition of the equity. They may agree to its sale to the remaining partners or to an outsider, or they may agree to the withdrawal of assets in settlement. Entries for both of these procedures have already been discussed.

LIQUIDATIONS

When a partnership is liquidated, its business is ended. The assets are converted into cash, and the creditors are paid. The remaining cash is then distributed to the partners, and the partnership is dissolved. Although many combinations of circumstances occur in liquidations, only three are discussed here.

All assets realized before a distribution; assets are sold at a profit

A partnership liquidation under this assumption may be illustrated with the following example. Ottis, Skinner, and Parr have operated a partnership for a number of years, sharing losses and gains in a $3:2:1$ ratio. Due to several unsatisfactory conditions, the partners decide to liquidate as of December 31. On that date the books are closed, the income from operations is transferred to the partners' capital accounts, and a balance sheet showing the following assets and equities is prepared:

Assets		Equities	
Cash	$10,000	Accounts payable	$ 5,000
Merchandise inventory	15,000	Ottis, capital	15,000
Other assets	25,000	Skinner, capital	15,000
		Parr, capital	15,000
Total assets	$50,000	Total equities	$50,000

In a liquidation either a gain or a loss normally results from the sale of each group of assets. These losses and gains are called "losses and gains from realization." They are shared by the partners in their loss-and-gain-sharing ratio. If Otis, Skinner, and Parr sell their inventory for $12,000 and their other assets for $34,000, the sales and the net gain allocation are recorded as follows:

Jan.	12	Cash	12,000.00	
		Loss or Gain from Realization	3,000.00	
		Merchandise inventory		15,000.00
		Sold the inventory at a loss		
	15	Cash	34,000.00	
		Other assets		25,000.00
		Loss or Gain from Realization		9,000.00
		Sold the other assets at a profit		
	15	Loss or Gain from Realization	6,000.00	
		Ottis, Capital		3,000.00
		Skinner, Capital		2,000.00
		Parr, Capital		1,000.00
		To allocate the net gain from realization to the partners in their 3:2:1 loss-and-gain-sharing ratio.		

Careful notice should be taken of the last journal entry. In a partnership termination when assets are sold at a loss or gain, the loss or gain is allocated to the partners in their loss-and-gain-sharing ratio. Often students, in solving liquidation problems, attempt to allocate the assets to the partners in their loss-and-gain-sharing ratio. Obviously this is not correct. It is not assets but losses and gains that are shared in the loss-and-gain-sharing ratio.

After the merchandise and other assets of Ottis, Skinner, and Parr are sold and the net gain allocated, a new balance sheet shows the following assets and equities:

Assets		Equities	
Cash	$56,000	Accounts payable	$ 5,000
		Ottis, capital	18,000
		Skinner, capital	17,000
		Parr, capital	16,000
Total assets	$56,000	Total equities	$56,000

Observe that the one asset, cash, $56,000, exactly equals the sum of the equities of the partners and creditors.

After partnership assets are realized and the gain or loss shared, entries are made to distribute the realized cash to the proper parties. Since creditors have first claim, they are paid first. After the creditors are paid, the remaining cash is divided among the partners. Each partner has the right to cash equal to his equity or, in other words, cash equal to the balance of his capital account. The entries to distribute the cash of Ottis, Skinner, and Parr are:

Jan.	15	Accounts payable	5,000.00	
		Cash		5,000.00
		To pay the claims of the creditors.		
	15	Ottis, Capital	18,000.00	
		Skinner, Capital	17,000.00	
		Parr, Capital	16,000.00	
		Cash		51,000.00
		To distribute the remaining cash to the partners according to their capital account balances.		

Notice that after losses and gains are shared and the creditors are paid, each partner receives liquidation cash equal to the balance remaining in his capital account. The partners receive these amounts because a partner's capital account balance shows his equity in the one partnership asset, cash.

All assets realized before a distribution; assets sold at a loss; each partner's capital account is sufficient to absorb his share of the loss

In a partnership liquidation, the assets are sometimes sold at a net loss. For example, if contrary to the previous assumptions the inventory of Ottis, Skinner, and Parr is sold for $9,000 and the other assets for $13,000, the entries to record the sales and loss allocation are:

Jan.	12	Cash	9,000.00	
		Loss or Gain from Realization	6,000.00	
		Merchandise Inventory		15,000.00
		Sold the inventory at a loss.		
	15	Cash	13,000.00	
		Loss or Gain from Realization	12,000.00	
		Other Assets		25,000.00
		Sold the other assets at a loss.		
	15	Ottis, Capital	9,000.00	
		Skinner, Capital	6,000.00	
		Parr, Capital	3,000.00	
		Loss or Gain from Realization		18,000.00
		To allocate the loss from realization to the partners in their loss-and-gain-sharing ratio.		

In this case also, after the entries are posted a balance sheet shows that the partnership cash exactly equals the combined equities of the partners and creditors, as follows:

Assets		Equities	
Cash	$32,000	Accounts payable	$ 5,000
		Ottis, capital	6,000
		Skinner, capital	9,000
		Parr, capital	12,000
Total assets	$32,000	Total equities	$32,000

The following entries are required to distribute the cash to the proper parties:

Jan.	15	Accounts Payable	5,000.00	
		Cash		5,000.00
		To pay the partnership creditors.		
	15	Ottis, Capital	6,000.00	
		Skinner, Capital	9,000.00	
		Parr, Capital	12,000.00	
		Cash		27,000.00
		To distribute the remaining cash to the partners according to the balances of their capital accounts.		

Notice again that after losses are shared and creditors are paid, each partner receives cash equal to his capital account balance.

All assets realized before a distribution; assets sold at a loss; a partner's capital account is not sufficient to cover his share of the loss

Sometimes a partner's share of realization losses is greater than the balance of his capital account. In such cases the partner must, if he can, cover the deficit by paying cash into the partnership. For example, assume contrary to the previous illustrations that Ottis, Skinner, and Parr sell their merchandise for $3,000 and the other assets for $4,000. The entries to record the sales and the loss allocation are:

Jan.	12	Cash	3,000.00	
		Loss or Gain from Realization	12,000.00	
		Merchandise Inventory		15,000.00
		Sold the inventory at a loss.		
	15	Cash	4,000.00	
		Loss or Gain from Realization	21,000.00	
		Other Assets		25,000.00
		Sold the other assets at a loss.		
	15	Ottis, Capital	16,500.00	
		Skinner, Capital	11,000.00	
		Parr, Capital	5,500.00	
		Loss or Gain from Realization		33,000.00
		To record the allocation of the loss from realization to the partners in their loss-and-gain-sharing ratio.		

After the entry allocating the realization loss is posted, the capital account of Ottis has a $1,500 debit balance and appears as follows:

Ottis, Capital						
Date		Explanation	R	Debit	Credit	Balance
Dec.	31	Balance				15,000.00
Jan.	15	Share of loss from realization		16,500.00		(1,500.00)

The partnership agreement provides that Ottis is to take one half the losses or gains. Consequently, since his capital account balance is not large enough to absorb his loss share in this case, he must, if he can, pay $1,500 into the partnership to cover the *deficit*. If he is able to pay, the following entry is made:

Jan.	15	Cash	1,500.00	
		Ottis, Capital		1,500.00
		To record the additional investment of Ottis to cover his share of realization losses.		

After the $1,500 is received, the partnership has $18,500 in cash. The following entries are then made to distribute the cash to the proper parties:

Jan.	15	Accounts Payable	5,000.00	
		Cash		5,000.00
		To pay the partnership creditors.		
	15	Skinner, Capital	4,000.00	
		Parr, Capital	9,500.00	
		Cash		13,500.00
		To distribute the remaining cash to the partners according to the balances of their capital accounts.		

Often when a partner's share of partnership losses exceeds his capital account balance, he is unable to make up the deficit. In such cases, since each partner has unlimited liability, the deficit must be borne by the remaining partner or partners. For example, assume that Ottis is unable to pay in the $1,500 necessary to cover the deficit in his capital account. If Ottis is unable to pay, his deficit must be shared by Skinner and Parr in their loss-and-gain-sharing ratio. The partners share losses and gains in the ratio of Ottis, 3; Skinner, 2; and Parr, 1. Therefore, Skinner and Parr share in a 2 to 1 ratio. Consequently, the $1,500 that Ottis's share of the losses exceeded his capital account balance is apportioned between them in this ratio. Normally the defaulting partner's deficit is transferred to the capital accounts of the remaining partners. This is accomplished for Ottis, Skinner, and Parr with the following entry:

Jan.	15	Skinner, Capital	1,000.00	
		Parr, Capital	500.00	
		Ottis, Capital		1,500.00
		To transfer the deficit of Ottis to the capital accounts of Skinner and Parr.		

After the deficit is transferred, the capital accounts of the partners appear as in Illustration 14–4.

Ottis, Capital

Date		Explanation	R	Debit	Credit	Balance
Dec.	31	Balance				15,000.00
Jan.	15	Share of loss from realization		16,500.00		(1,500.00)
	15	Deficit to Skinner and Parr			1,500.00	–0–

Skinner, Capital

Date		Explanation	R	Debit	Credit	Balance
Dec.	31	Balance				15,000.00
Jan.	15	Share of loss from realization		11,000.00		4,000.00
	15	Share of Ottis's deficit		1,000.00		3,000.00

Parr, Capital

Date		Explanation	R	Debit	Credit	Balance
Dec.	31	Balance				15,000.00
Jan.	15	Share of loss from realization		5,500.00		9,500.00
	15	Share of Ottis's deficit		500.00		9,000.00

Illustration 14–4

After the deficit is transferred, the $17,000 of liquidation cash is distributed with the following entries:

Jan.	15	Accounts Payable	5,000.00	
		Cash		5,000.00
		To pay the partnership creditors.		
	15	Skinner, Capital	3,000.00	
		Parr, Capital	9,000.00	
		Cash		12,000.00
		To distribute the remaining cash to the partners according to their capital account balances.		

It should be understood that the inability of Ottis to meet his loss share at this time does not relieve him of liability. If at any time in the future he becomes able to pay, Skinner and Parr may collect from him the full $1,500. Skinner may collect $1,000 and Parr, $500.

GLOSSARY

Deficit. A negative amount of an item.

Liquidation. The winding up of a business by converting its assets to cash and distributing the cash to the proper parties.

Mutual agency. The legal situation in a partnership whereby each partner is an agent of the partnership and is able to bind the partnership to contracts within the normal scope of the partnership business.

Partnership. An association of two or more persons to carry on a business as co-owners for profit.

Partnership contract. The document setting forth the agreed terms under which the members of a partnership will conduct the partnership business.

Unlimited liability. The legal situation in a partnership which makes each partner responsible for paying all the debts of the partnership if his or her partners are unable to pay a share.

QUESTIONS FOR CLASS DISCUSSION

1. Hill and Dale are partners. Hill dies and his son claims the right to take his father's place in the partnership. Does he have this right? Why?
2. Ted Hall cannot legally enter into a contract. Can he become a partner?
3. If a partnership contract does not state the period of time the partnership is to exist, when does the partnership end?
4. What is the meaning of the term "mutual agency" as applied to a partnership?
5. Jack and Jill are partners in the operation of a store. Jack without consulting Jill enters into a contract for the purchase of merchandise for resale by the store. Jill contends that she did not authorize the order and refuses to take delivery. The vendor sues the partners for the contract price of the merchandise. Will the firm have to pay? Why?
6. Would your answer to Question 5 differ if Jack and Jill were partners in a public accounting firm?
7. May partners limit the right of a member of their firm to bind their partnership to contracts? Is such an agreement binding (a) on the partners and (b) on outsiders?
8. What is the meaning of the term "unlimited liability" when it is applied to members of a partnership?
9. Kennedy, Porter, and Foulke have been partners for three years. The partnership is dissolving, Kennedy is leaving the firm, and Porter and Foulke plan to carry on the business. In the final settlement Kennedy places a $45,000 salary claim against the partnership. His contention is that since he devoted all of his time for three years to the affairs of the partnership, he has a claim for a salary of $15,000 for each year. Is his claim valid? Why?

10. The partnership agreement of Martin and Tritt provides for a two-thirds, one-third sharing of income but says nothing of losses. The operations for a year result in a loss. Martin claims the loss should be shared equally since the partnership agreement said nothing of sharing losses. Do you agree?

11. A, B, and C are partners with capital account balances of $6,000 each. D gives A $7,500 for his one-third interest in the partnership. The bookkeeper debits A, Capital and credits D, Capital for $6,000. D objects. He wants his capital account to show a $7,500 balance, the amount he paid for his interest. Explain why D's capital account is credited for $6,000.

12. After all partnership assets are converted to cash and all creditor claims paid, the remaining cash should equal the sum of the balances of the partners' capital accounts. Why?

13. J, K, and L are partners. In a liquidation J's share of partnership losses exceeds his capital account balance. He is unable to meet the deficit from his personal assets, and the excess losses are shared by his partners. Does this relieve J of liability?

CLASS EXERCISES

Exercise 14–1

Able and Best began a partnership by investing $18,000 and $12,000, respectively, and during its first year the partnership earned $33,000.

Required:

1. Prepare a schedule with the following columnar headings:

Ways of Sharing	Able's Share	Best's Share

2. List the following ways of sharing income by letter on separate lines in the first column and then opposite each letter show the share of each partner in the $33,000 net income.
   a. The partners could not agree on a method of sharing income.
   b. The partners agreed to share income in their investment ratio.
   c. The partners agreed to share income by granting a $12,000 per year salary allowance to Able, a $15,000 per year salary allowance to Best, 10% interest on their investments, and the balance equally.

Exercise 14–2

Assume the partners of Exercise 14–1 agreed to share losses and gains by allowing salary allowances of $12,000 per year to Able and $15,000 per year to Best, 10% interest on investments, and the balance equally. Determine the partners' shares in (a) a $12,000 net income and (b) a $6,000 net loss.

Exercise 14–3

Cook, Dole, and Eble have equities of $5,000 each in a partnership. With the consent of Dole and Eble, who have agreed to accept Fall as a partner, Cook is selling his equity in the partnership to Fall for $1 in cash and a bag of peanuts. Give the entry to record the sale as of June 10.

Exercise 14–4

Oak and Ash are partners with capital account balances of $70,000 and $60,000 and sharing losses and gains in a 3-to-2 ratio. On October 12 Elm is to invest $50,000 and join the partnership. Give the entry for the admission of Elm under each of these unrelated assumptions: *(a)* Elm is to receive an equity equal to his investment. *(b)* Elm is to receive a one-fourth equity in the partnership. *(c)* Elm is to receive a one-third equity.

Exercise 14–5

Fall is retiring from the partnership of Fall, Ginn, and Hart. The partners have always shared losses and gains in a 2:2:1 ratio; and on the date of Fall's retirement they have the following equities in the partnership: Gary Fall, $8,000; Dale Ginn, $10,000; and Tom Hart, $6,000.

Required:

Using a May 5 date, give entries in general journal form for the retirement of Fall under each of the following unrelated assumptions:

a. Fall retires, taking $8,000 in partnership cash for his equity.
b. Fall retires, taking $9,500 in partnership cash for his partnership rights.
c. Fall retires, taking $7,100 in partnership cash.

Exercise 14–6

Ives, Jones, and Kelly entered into a partnership. Ives invested $4,000, Jones invested $8,000, and Kelly invested $12,000. They agreed to share losses and gains equally. They lost heavily, and at the end of the first year decided to liquidate. After converting all partnership assets to cash and paying all creditor claims, $9,000 in partnership cash remained.

Required:

Under a December 31 date, give the general journal entry to record the distribution of the correct shares of cash to the partners in final liquidation of their business.

PROBLEMS

Problem 14–1

Ted Allen, John Bell, and Gary Cole invested $16,000, $12,000, and $8,000, respectively, in a partnership. During its first year the partnership earned $41,400.

Required:

1. Prepare entries dated December 31 to close the Income Summary account and allocate the net income to the partners under each of the following assumptions:

   a. The partners could not agree on the method of sharing.

   b. The partners agreed to share earnings in the ratio of their beginning investments.

   c. The partners agreed to share income by allowing annual salary allowances of $12,000 each to Allen and Bell and $18,000 to Cole; allowing a share of the income equal to 10% interest on partners' investments; and sharing any remainder equally.

2. Prepare the section of the partners' first year income statement showing the allocation of the income to the partners under assumption *(c).*

Problem 14–2

Mary Clay and Joan Dent are in the process of forming a partnership to which Mary Clay will devote one third of her time and Joan Dent will devote full time. They have discussed the following plans for sharing gains and losses:

a. In the ratio of their investments which they have agreed to maintain at $18,000 for Clay and $12,000 for Dent.

b. In proportion to the time devoted to the business.

c. Salary allowance of $5,000 per year to Clay and $15,000 per year to Dent and the balance in their investment ratio.

d. Salary allowances of $5,000 per year to Clay and $15,000 per year to Dent, 10% interest on their investments, and the balance equally.

Required:

1. Prepare a schedule with the following columnar headings:

Income Sharing Plan	$32,000 Net Income		$18,000 Net Income		$6,000 Net Loss	
	Clay	Dent	Clay	Dent	Clay	Dent

2. List the plans by letter in the first column and show opposite each letter the shares of the partners in a $32,000 net income, an $18,000 net income, and a $6,000 net loss.

Problem 14–3

Part 1. Dodd, Evon, and Falk are partners sharing losses and gains in a 2:1:2 ratio. Dodd plans to withdraw from the partnership, and on the date of his withdrawal the equities of the partners are Ivan Dodd, $12,000; John Evon; $10,000; and Carl Falk, $12,000.

Required:

Under a March 12 date give in general journal form the entries for the withdrawal of Dodd under each of the following unrelated assumptions:

a. Dodd sells his interest to Roy Gill, taking $9,000 in cash and a second-hand car. Evon and Falk agree to accept Gill as a partner.

b. With the agreement of Evon and Falk to accept the son as a partner, Dodd gives his partnership interest to his son, Paul.

c. Dodd withdraws, taking $12,000 of partnership cash for his equity.

d. Dodd withdraws, taking $10,500 of partnership cash for his equity.

e. Dodd withdraws, taking $10,000 in partnership cash and delivery equipment carried on the partnership books at $3,500, less $900 accumulated depreciation.

f. Dodd withdraws, taking $3,000 in partnership cash and a $7,500 note payable of the new partnership for his equity.

Part 2. Bates and Cole are partners with capital account balance of $50,000 and $40,000, respectively, and sharing losses and gains in a 3-to-2 ratio. On October 4 Dory is to invest $60,000 and join the partnership. Give the entry for the admission of Dory under each of these unrelated assumptions: *(a)* Dory is to receive a 40% equity in the partnership. *(b)* Dory is to receive a one-third equity in the partnership. *(c)* Dory is to receive a 45% equity in the partnership.

Problem 14–4

Davis, Eaton, and Farley are about to liquidate their partnership. They have always shared losses and gains in a 3:2:1 ratio, and just prior to the liquidation their balance sheet appeared as follows:

DAVIS, EATON, AND FARLEY
Balance Sheet, October 31, 19—

Assets		*Equities*	
Cash	$ 3,000	Accounts payable	$12,000
Other assets	69,000	Carl Davis, capital	15,000
		Dale Eaton, capital	35,000
		John Farley, capital	10,000
Total assets	$72,000	Total equities	$72,000

Required:

Prepare general journal entries under an October 31 date to record the sale of the other assets, the allocation of the loss or gain, and the distribution of the cash to the proper parties under each of the following unrelated assumptions:

a. The other assets were sold for $72,000.

b. The other assets were sold for $45,000.

c. The other assets were sold for $36,000, and the partner with a deficit was able to pay in the amount of his deficit.

d. The other assets were sold for $21,000, and none of the partners had any personal assets from which to make good a deficit.

Problem 14–5

Until April 3 of the current year Judd, Kern, and Lee were partners sharing losses and gains in a 2:2:1 ratio. On that date Judd suddenly became ill and died. Kern and Lee immediately ended business operations and prepared the following trial balance:

JUDD, KERN, AND LEE
Adjusted Trial Balance April 3, 19—

Cash	$ 5,200	
Accounts receivable	11,800	
Allowance for doubtful accounts		$ 600
Merchandise inventory	30,000	
Store equipment	15,000	
Accumulated depreciation, store equipment		7,500
Land	10,000	
Building	50,000	
Accumulated depreciation, building		10,000
Accounts payable		4,400
Mortgage payable		16,500
Earl Judd, capital		26,000
Ted Kern, capital		28,000
Gary Lee, capital		14,000
Revenues		50,000
Expenses	35,000	
Totals	$157,000	$157,000

Required:

1. Prepare entries to close the revenues, expenses, and income summary accounts of the partnership.
2. Assume that the estate of Judd agreed to accept the land and building and assume the mortgage in full settlement of its claim against the partnership, and that Kern and Lee planned to continue the business and rent the building from the estate. Give under an April 30 date the entry to transfer the land, building, and mortgage and to settle with the estate.
3. Make the contrary assumption that the estate of Judd demanded a cash settlement and the business had to be sold to a competitor who gave $72,200 for the noncash assets and assumed the mortgage but not the accounts payable. Give the entry to transfer the assets and mortgage to the competitor, the entry to allocate the loss to the partners, and the entries to distribute the partnership cash to the proper parties. Date the entries April 30.

ALTERNATE PROBLEMS

Problem 14–1A

During its first year, ended December 31, the partnership of More, Neal, and Orr earned a $42,600 net income.

Required:

1. Prepare entries to close the Income Summary account and to allocate the net income to the partners under each of the following assumptions:
   a. The partners could not agree on a method of sharing earnings.

b. The partners agreed to share earnings in the ratio of their investments, which were Ted More, $12,000; Roy Neal, $16,000; and Ned Orr, $20,000.

c. The partners agreed to share earnings by allowing annual salary allowances of $14,000 to More, $16,000 to Neal, and $12,000 to Orr, plus interest at 10% on investments, and any remainder equally.

2. Prepare the income statement section showing the allocation of the year's net income to the partners under assumption *(c)*.

Problem 14–2A

June Clay and Ann Dent are forming a partnership to which Ms. Clay will devote full time and Ms. Dent will devote one third of her time. They have discussed the following plans for sharing losses and gains.

a. In the ratio of their investments which they have agreed to maintain at $10,000 for Ms. Clay and $20,000 for Ms. Dent.

b. In proportion to the time devoted to the business.

c. Salary allowances of $18,000 per year to Clay and $6,000 per year to Dent and any balance in their investment ratio.

d. Salary allowances of $18,000 per year to Clay and $6,000 per year to Dent, 8% interest on investments, and the balance equally.

Required:

1. Prepare a schedule with the following columnar headings:

Income Sharing Plan	$30,600 Net Income		$20,400 Net Income		$8,400 Net Loss	
	Clay	Dent	Clay	Dent	Clay	Dent

2. List the plans by letter in the first column and show opposite each letter the shares of the partners in a $30,600 net income, a $20,400 net income, and an $8,400 net loss.

Problem 14–3A

Part 1. Doyle and Evans are partners with capital account balances of $60,000 and $30,000, respectively, and sharing losses and gains in a 2-to-1 ratio. On November 12 Field is to invest $45,000 and join the partnership. Give the entry for the admission of Field under each of these unrelated assumptions: *(a)* Field is to receive a one-third equity in the partnership. *(b)* Field is to receive a 40% equity in the partnership. *(c)* Field is to receive a 30% equity in the partnership.

Part 2. As of February 3 Earl Dunn is withdrawing from the partnership of Dunn, Ely, and Farr. The partners have always shared losses and gains in a 2:3:1 ratio; and on the withdrawal date they have these capital account balances: Earl Dunn, $14,000; Alan Ely, $16,000; and Roy Farr, $10,000.

Required:

Prepare general journal entries to record the retirement of Dunn under each of the following unrelated assumptions:

a. Dunn withdraws, taking $14,000 of partnership cash for his equity.
b. Dunn withdraws, taking $15,000 of partnership cash for his equity.
c. Dunn withdraws, taking $10,000 in partnership cash and machinery carried on the partnership books at $3,600, less $1,600 of accumulated depreciation.
d. Dunn withdraws, taking $1,600 of partnership cash and a $12,000 note payable of the new partnership of Ely and Farr.
e. With the consent of Ely and Farr, Dunn sells his interest to Ted Gill, taking from Gill $6,000 in cash and Gill's personal note for $10,000.
f. Dunn transfers his interest to Ely and Farr, taking Ely's $9,000 personal note for 60% of his equity and Farr's $6,000 personal note for 40%.

Problem 14-4A

Mead, Nash, and Owen, who have always shared losses and gains in a 4:2:1 ratio, are liquidating their partnership. Just prior to the first asset sale their balance sheet appeared as follows:

MEAD, NASH, AND OWEN
Balance Sheet, June 30, 19—

Assets		*Equities*	
Cash	$ 2,000	Accounts payable.........	$15,000
Other assets	48,000	John Mead, capital	10,000
		Dale Nash, capital	20,000
		Gary Owen, capital.......	5,000
Total assets	$50,000	Total equities	$50,000

Required:

Under the assumption the other assets are sold and the cash is distributed to the proper parties on July 5, give the entries to record the sale, the loss or gain allocation, and the distribution under each of the following unrelated assumptions:

a. The other assets are sold for $51,500.
b. The other assets are sold for $41,000.
c. The other assets are sold for $27,000, and the partner with a deficit pays in the amount of his deficit.
d. The other assets are sold for $20,000, and the partners have no assets other than those invested in the business.

Problem 14-5A

Long, Macy, and Nunn share partnership losses and gains in a 3:1:1 ratio, since Long devotes full time to partnership affairs and Macy and Nunn give little time to the business. Recently the business has not prospered and the partners plan to liquidate. Just prior to the first asset sale a partnership balance sheet appeared as follows:

LONG, MACY, AND NUNN
Balance Sheet, January 31, 19—

Assets			Equities		
Cash		$ 4,000	Accounts payable...............		$ 8,000
Accounts receivable		12,000	Robert Long, capital		8,000
Merchandise inventory .		24,000	James Macy, capital		20,000
Equipment	$20,000		George Nunn, capital		20,000
Less accumulated					
depreciation	4,000	16,000			
Total assets		$56,000	Total equities		$56,000

The assets were sold, the creditors were paid, and the remaining cash was distributed to the partners on the following dates:

Feb. 2   The accounts receivable were sold for $7,200.
    5   The merchandise inventory was sold for $16,000.
    8   The equipment was sold for $11,800.
    8   The realization loss was allocated to the partners.
    9   The creditors were paid in full.
    9   The remaining cash was distributed to the partners.

Required:

1. Give the entries to record the sale of the assets, the allocation of the losses, and the payment of the creditors.
2. Under the assumption the partner with a deficit pays in the amount of his deficit, give the entries to record the receipt and the payment of cash to the remaining partners.
3. Under the assumption the partner with a deficit cannot pay, give the entry to allocate his deficit to the remaining partners and the entry to pay the partners to whom cash is due.

PROVOCATIVE PROBLEMS

Provocative problem 14–1
Sharing losses and gains

Part 1.   Early this year Lee and Fox formed a partnership to operate a delivery service. Lee invested $7,000 and Fox invested $5,000, and they agreed to share losses and gains equally. Business has been bad; the partners have not been able to make any withdrawals; and now, at the year-end, the partners have decided to end operations and liquidate the business, the assets of which now consist of $4,500 in cash and a truck that both partners agree is worth $4,500. There are no liabilities. In discussing the liquidation, Fox says he is willing to take either the cash or the truck for his partnership rights, and he also says he is willing to flip a coin to see which partner takes the cash and which takes the truck. Lee is unsure who should take what and why, and he has come to you for advice. Advise him, giving reasons for your advice.

Part 2. Macy and Nash formed a partnership in which they agreed to share losses and gains by allowing annual salary allowances of $12,000 to Macy and $14,000 to Nash and sharing any remaining balance equally. At the end of the first year in business, when a work sheet was prepared, it was discovered that the partnership had earned just $10 during the year. As a result, Macy suggested that the $10 be given to the office secretary as a bonus, thereby increasing expenses for the year and causing the partnership to exactly break even. He further suggested that the partnership could then forget the sharing of losses and gains for the year, since there would be none. If Macy's suggestion is followed, who gains most and how much?

Provocative problem 14–2
Coe and Nye

Coe and Nye entered into a partnership a number of years ago in which they agreed to share losses and gains as follows:

a. Annual salary allowances of $12,000 per year to Coe and $14,000 to Nye.
b. Interest at 6% on the excess of his capital account balance over that of his partner is allowed to the partner having the larger capital account balance as of the beginning of the year.
c. Any remainder is divided equally between the partners.

The partnership earned $40,000 last year, and the partners began the year with capital account balances of $50,000 for Coe and $40,000 for Nye.

Although the partners consider last year a successful one. Nye is unhappy with his share of the net income. He feels he should have a larger share, since he spends twice as much time on partnership affairs as Coe. Coe agrees that Nye spends double the time he spends on partnership business and also that Nye is primarily responsible for the 10% compound annual increase in partnership earnings for the past several years. Consequently, he suggests that the partners change their loss-and-gain-sharing plan. He knows that Nye has $30,000 in a savings account on which he earns interest at 5½% annually, so he suggests the following:

a. Nye is to invest an additional $30,000 in the business.
b. Interest at 8% is to be allowed the partners on the full amounts invested, which are to be Coe, $50,000, and Nye, $70,000.
c. Each partner is to get a $5,000 increase in his salary allowance, with the allowances becoming: Coe, $17,000; and Nye, $19,000.
d. Any remaining balance after salary and interest allowances is to be given in full to Nye.

Nye is interested in earning 8% on the $30,000 he now has in the bank, is pleased with the $5,000 increase in his salary allowance, and is impressed with Coe's generosity in giving him any balance over the partners' salary and interest allowances. However, before accepting the offer, he has come to you for advice. Advise Nye, backing your advice with income-sharing schedules where desirable.

PART FIVE
Corporation accounting

After studying Chapter 15, you should be able to:

☐ State the advantages and disadvantages of the corporate form of business organization and explain how a corporation is organized and managed.

☐ Describe the differences in accounting for the owners' equity in a partnership and the stockholders' equity in a corporation.

☐ Record the issuance of par value stock at par or at a premium in exchange for cash or other assets.

☐ Record the issuance of no-par stock with or without a stated value.

☐ Record transactions involving stock subscriptions and explain the effects of subscribed stock on corporation assets and stockholders' equity.

☐ Explain the concept of minimum legal capital and explain why corporation laws governing minimum legal capital were written.

☐ State the differences between common and preferred stocks and explain why preferred stock is issued.

☐ Describe the meaning and significance of par, book, market, and redemption values of corporate stock.

☐ Define or explain the words and phrases listed in the chapter Glossary.

Corporations: Organization and operation

■ The three common types of business organizations are single proprietorships, partnerships, and corporations. Of the three, corporations are fewer in number; yet in dollar volume, they transact more business than do the other two combined. In terms of their economic impact, corporations are clearly the most important form of business organization. Almost every student will at some time either work for or own an interest in a corporation. For these reasons, an understanding of corporations and corporation accounting is important to all students of business.

ADVANTAGES OF THE CORPORATE FORM

Corporations have become the dominant type of business in our country because of the advantages offered by this form of business organization. Among the advantages are the following:

Separate legal entity

A corporation is a separate legal entity, separate and distinct from its stockholders who are its owners. Because it is a separate legal entity, a corporation, through its agents, may conduct its affairs with the rights, duties, and responsibilities of a person.

Lack of stockholders' liability

As a separate legal entity a corporation is responsible for its own acts and its own debts, and its shareholders have no liability for either.

497

From the viewpoint of an investor, this is perhaps the most important advantage of the corporate form.

Ease of transferring ownership rights

Ownership rights in a corporation are represented by shares of stock that generally can be transferred and disposed of any time the owner wishes. Furthermore, the transfer has no effect on the corporation and its operations.

Continuity of life

A corporation's life may continue for the time stated in its charter, which may be of any length permitted by the laws of the state of its incorporation. Furthermore, at the expiration of the stated time, the charter may normally be renewed and the period extended. Thus a perpetual life is possible for a successful corporation.

No mutual agency

Mutual agency does not exist in a corporation. A corporation stockholder, acting as a stockholder, has no power to bind the corporation to contracts. Stockholders' participation in the affairs of the corporation is limited to the right to vote in the stockholders' meetings. Consequently, stockholders need not exercise the care of partners in selecting people with whom they associate themselves in the ownership of a corporation.

Ease of capital assembly

Lack of stockholders' liability, lack of mutual agency, and the ease with which an interest may be transferred make it possible for a corporation to assemble large amounts of capital from the combined investments of many stockholders. Actually, a corporation's capital-raising ability is as a rule limited only by the profitableness with which it can employ the funds. This is very different from a partnership. In a partnership, capital-raising ability is always limited by the number of partners and their individual wealth. The number of partners is in turn usually limited because of mutual agency and unlimited liability.

DISADVANTAGES OF THE CORPORATE FORM

Governmental regulation

Corporations are created by fulfilling the requirements of a state's corporation laws, and the laws subject a corporation to considerable state regulation and control. Single proprietorships and partnerships escape this regulation and also many governmental reports required of corporations.

Taxation

Corporations as business units are subject to all the taxes of single proprietorships and partnerships. In addition, corporations are subject to several taxes not levied on either of the other two. The most burdensome of these are state and federal income taxes which together may take 50% of a corporation's pretax income. However, for the stockholders of a corporation, the burden does not end there. The income of a corporation is taxed twice, first as corporation income and again as personal income when distributed to the stockholders as dividends. This differs from single proprietorships and partnerships, which as business units are not subject to income taxes. Their income is normally taxed only as the personal income of their owners.

ORGANIZING A CORPORATION

As previously stated, a corporation is created by securing a charter from one of the states. The requirements that must be met to secure a charter vary with the states. In general, however, a charter application must be signed by three or more subscribers to the prospective corporation's stock (who are called the incorporators). It must then be filled with the proper state official. If the application complies with the law and all fees are paid, the charter is issued and the corporation comes into existence. The subscribers then purchase the corporation's stock and become stockholders. After this they meet and elect a board of directors who are made responsible for directing the corporation's affairs.

ORGANIZATION COSTS

The *costs* of organizing a corporation, such as legal fees, promoters' fees, and amounts paid the state to secure a charter, are called organization costs and are debited on incurrence to an account called Organization Costs. Theoretically, the sum of these costs represents an intangible asset from which the corporation will benefit throughout its life. However, this is an indeterminable period. Therefore, a corporation should make a reasonable estimate of the benefit period, which in no case should exceed 40 years, and write off its organization costs over the estimated period.[1] Although not necessarily related to the benefit pe-

---

[1] APB, "Intangible Assets," *APB Opinion No. 17* (New York: AICPA, August 1970), par. 29. Copyright (1970) by the American Institute of CPAs.

riod, income tax rules permit a corporation to write off organization costs as a tax-deductible expense over a period of not less than five years. Consequently, many corporations adopt five years as the period over which to write off such costs. There is no theoretical justification for this, but it is generally accepted in practice. Organization costs are usually immaterial in amount, and under the *principle of materiality* the write-off eliminates an unnecessary balance sheet item.

MANAGEMENT OF A CORPORATION

Although ultimate control of a corporation rests with its stockholders, this control is exercised indirectly through the election of the board of directors. The individual stockholder's right to participate in management begins and ends with a vote in the stockholders' meeting, where each stockholder has one vote for each share of stock owned.

Normally a corporation's stockholders meet once each year to elect directors and transact such other business as is provided in the corporation's bylaws. Theoretically, stockholders owning or controlling the votes of 50% plus one share of a corporation's stock can elect the board and control the corporation. Actually, because many stockholders do not attend the annual meeting, a much smaller percentage is frequently sufficient for control. Commonly, stockholders who do not attend the annual meeting delegate to an agent their voting rights. This is done by signing a legal document called a *proxy*, which gives the agent the right to vote the stock.

A corporation's board of directors is responsible and has final authority for the direction of corporation affairs. However, it may act only as a collective body. An individual director, as a director, has no power to transact corporation business. And, as a rule, although it has final authority, a board will limit itself to establishing policy. It will then delegate the day-by-day direction of corporation business to the corporation's administrative officers whom it selects and elects.

A corporation's administrative officers are commonly headed by a president who is directly responsible to the board for supervising the corporation's business. To aid the president, many corporations have one or more vice presidents who are vested with specific managerial powers and duties. In addition, the corporation secretary keeps the minutes of the meetings of the stockholders and directors. In a small corporation the secretary may also be responsible for keeping a record of the stockholders and the changing amounts of their stock interest.

STOCK CERTIFICATES AND THE TRANSFER OF STOCK

When a person invests in a corporation by buying its stock, the person receives a stock certificate as evidence of the shares purchased. Usually in a small corporation only one certificate is issued for each block of stock purchased. The one certificate may be for any number

INCORPORATED UNDER THE LAWS
OF THE
STATE OF ILLINOIS

C9800

-50-

WESTFIELD PUBLISHING COMPANY, LTD.

THIS CERTIFIES that   ROBERT WETZEL   is the owner of

—————— FIFTY ——————

FULLY PAID AND NON-ASSESSABLE SHARES OF COMMON STOCK OF NO PAR OR NOMINAL VALUE
WESTFIELD PUBLISHING COMPANY, LTD. transferable on the books of the Corporation in person or by duly authorized attorney upon surrender of this Certificate properly endorsed. This Certificate is not valid unless countersigned by the Transfer Agent and registered by the Registrar.
    WITNESS the facsimile seal of the Corporation and the facsimile signatures of its duly authorized officers.
Dated: March 10, 1976

SEAL

SECRETARY   PRESIDENT

Illustration 15–1

of shares. For example, the certificate of Illustration 15–1 is for 50 shares. Large corporations commonly use preprinted 100-share denomination certificates in addition to blank certificates that may be made out for any number of shares.

An owner of stock may transfer at will either part or all the shares represented by a stock certificate. To do so the owner fills in and signs the transfer endorsement on the reverse side of the certificate and sends the certificate to the corporation secretary in a small corporation or to the corporation's transfer agent in a large one. The old certificate is canceled and retained, and a new certificate is issued to the new stockholder.

Transfer agent and registrar

A large corporation, one whose stock is sold on a major stock exchange, must have a registrar and a transfer agent who are assigned the responsibilities of transferring the corporation's stock. Also, the registrar is assigned the duty of keeping its stockholder records and preparing the official lists of stockholders for stockholders' meetings and for payment of dividends. Usually registrars and transfer agents are large banks or trust companies.

When the owner of stock in a corporation having a registrar and a transfer agent wishes to transfer the stock to a new owner, he or she completes the transfer endorsement on the back of the stock certificate and, usually through a stockbroker, sends the certificate to the transfer agent. The transfer agent cancels the old certificate and issues one or more new certificates which the agent sends to the registrar. The registrar enters the transfer in the stockholder records and sends the new certificate or certificates to the proper owners.

CORPORATION ACCOUNTING

Corporation accounting was initially discussed in Chapter 4. In that discussion, entries were shown to record several basic transactions. An issue of common stock for cash was recorded. A net income (credit balance) was closed from Income Summary to Retained Earnings. The declaration and later payment of cash dividends were recorded. And, a net loss was closed from Income Summary to Retained Earnings. *At this point, students should review the discussion in Chapter 4 on pages 127 through 130 which explains these entries.* After completing that review, keep in mind that the stockholders' equity accounts of a corporation are divided into (1) contributed capital accounts and (2) retained earnings accounts. Also, remember that when a corporation's board of directors declares a cash dividend on the *date of declaration*, a legal liability of the corporation is incurred. The board of directors declares that on a specific future date, the *date of record*, the stockholders according to the corporation's records will be designated as those to receive the dividend. Finally, on the *date of payment*, the liability for the declared cash dividend is paid by the corporation.

The financial statements of a corporation were first illustrated in Chapter 5. The income statement was shown in Illustration 5–1 on page 158; the balance sheet was shown in Illustration 5–4 on page 164; and the retained earnings statement was shown in Illustration 5–5 on page 165. Reviewing these illustrations, students should note that income taxes were deducted on the income statement as an expense. Recall that a business which is organized as a corporation must pay income taxes, while a proprietorship or partnership usually does not pay income taxes. Also, cash dividends to stockholders are not an expense of the corporation; they are not deducted on the income statement. Instead, dividends are a distribution *of* net income, and are subtracted on the retained earnings statement. Finally, notice that the stockholders' equity in Illustration 5–4 is divided into common stock and retained earnings.

STOCKHOLDERS' EQUITY ACCOUNTS COMPARED TO PARTNERSHIP ACCOUNTS

To demonstrate the use of separate accounts for contributed capital and retained earnings as found in corporation accounting and to contrast their use with the accounts used in partnership accounting, assume the following. On January 5, 198A, a partnership involving two equal partners and a corporation having five stockholders were formed. Assume further that $25,000 was invested in each. In the partnership, J. Olm invested $10,000 and A. Baker invested $15,000; in the corporation, each of the five stockholders bought 500 shares of its $10 par value common stock at $10 per share. Without dates and explanations, general journal entries to record the investments are:

Partnership			Corporation		
Cash 10,000			Cash 25,000		
J. Olm, Capital	10,000		Common Stock	25,000	
Cash 15,000					
A. Baker, Capital	15,000				

After the entries were posted, the owners' equity accounts of the two concerns appeared as follows:

Partnership
J. Olm, Capital

Date	Dr.	Cr.	Bal.
Jan. 5, 198A		10,000	10,000

A. Baker, Capital

Date	Dr.	Cr.	Bal.
Jan. 5, 198A		15,000	15,000

Corporation
Common Stock

Date	Dr.	Cr.	Bal.
Jan. 5, 198A		25,000	25,000

To continue the illustration, assume that during 198A, each concern earned a net income of $8,000 and also distributed $5,000 to its owners. The partners share income equally, and the cash distribution was also divided equally. The corporation declared the dividends on December 20, 198A, and both concerns made the cash payments to owners on December 25, 198A. The entries to record the distribution of cash to partners and the declaration and payment of dividends to stockholders are as follows:

Partnership		Corporation	
J. Olm, Withdrawals 2,500		Retained Earnings 5,000	
A. Baker, Withdrawals 2,500		Dividends Payable	5,000
Cash................	5,000		
		Dividends Payable 5,000	
		Cash................	5,000

At the end of the year, the entries to close the Income Summary account are as follows:

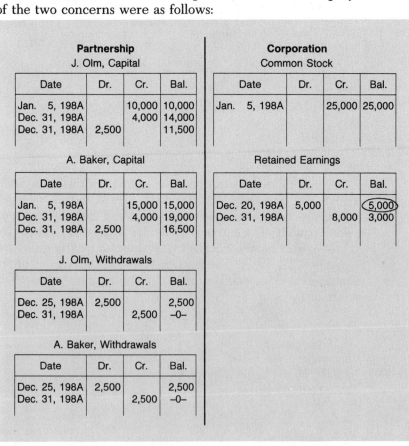

Partnership			Corporation		
Income Summary 8,000			Income Summary 8,000		
J. Olm, Capital	4,000		Retained Earnings	8,000	
A. Baker, Capital	4,000				

Finally, the entry to close the Withdrawals accounts is:

Partnership		Corporation
J. Olm, Capital 2,500		
A. Baker, Capital 2,500		
J. Olm, Withdrawals ...	2,500	
A. Baker, Withdrawals .	2,500	

After the above entries were posted, the owners' equity accounts of the two concerns were as follows:

Partnership
J. Olm, Capital

Date	Dr.	Cr.	Bal.
Jan. 5, 198A		10,000	10,000
Dec. 31, 198A		4,000	14,000
Dec. 31, 198A	2,500		11,500

Corporation
Common Stock

Date	Dr.	Cr.	Bal.
Jan. 5, 198A		25,000	25,000

A. Baker, Capital

Date	Dr.	Cr.	Bal.
Jan. 5, 198A		15,000	15,000
Dec. 31, 198A		4,000	19,000
Dec. 31, 198A	2,500		16,500

Retained Earnings

Date	Dr.	Cr.	Bal.
Dec. 20, 198A	5,000		5,000
Dec. 31, 198A		8,000	3,000

J. Olm, Withdrawals

Date	Dr.	Cr.	Bal.
Dec. 25, 198A	2,500		2,500
Dec. 31, 198A		2,500	–0–

A. Baker, Withdrawals

Date	Dr.	Cr.	Bal.
Dec. 25, 198A	2,500		2,500
Dec. 31, 198A		2,500	–0–

Observe that in the partnership, after all entries have been posted, the $28,000 equity of the owners appears in the capital accounts of the partners:

J. Olm, capital	$11,500
A. Baker, capital	16,500
Total owners' equity	$28,000

By comparison, the stockholders' equity of the corporation is divided between the contributed capital account and the retained earnings account, as follows:

Common stock	$25,000
Retained earnings	3,000
Total stockholders' equity	$28,000

AUTHORIZATION AND ISSUANCE OF STOCK

When a corporation is organized, it is authorized in its charter to issue a certain amount of stock. The stock may be of one kind, *common stock*, or both common and preferred stock may be authorized. (Preferred stock is discussed later in this chapter.) However, regardless of whether one or two kinds of stock are authorized, the corporation may issue no more of each than the amount authorized by its charter.

Often a corporation will secure an authorization to issue more stock than it plans to sell at the time of its organization. This enables it to expand at any time in its future through the sale of the additional stock, and without the need of applying to the state for the right to issue more. When a balance sheet is prepared, both the amount of stock authorized and the amount issued are commonly shown in its equity section as on page 508.

Sale of stock for cash

When stock is sold for cash and immediately issued, an entry in general journal form like the following may be used to record the sale and issuance:

June	5	Cash	300,000.00	
		Common Stock		300,000.00
		Sold and issued 30,000 shares of $10 par value common stock.		

Exchanging stock for noncash assets

A corporation may accept assets other than cash in exchange for its stock. When it does so, the transactions may be recorded like this:

Apr.	3	Machinery	10,000.00	
		Buildings	25,000.00	
		Land	5,000.00	
		Common Stock		40,000.00
		Exchanged 4,000 shares of $10 par value common stock for machinery, buildings, and land.		

A corporation may also give shares of its stock to its promoters in exchange for their services in getting the corporation organized. In such a case the corporation receives the intangible asset of being organized in exchange for its stock. The transaction is recorded as follows:

Apr.	5	Organization Costs	5,000.00	
		Common Stock		5,000.00
		Gave the promoters 500 shares of $10 par value common stock in exchange for their services in getting the corporation organized.		

PAR VALUE AND MINIMUM LEGAL CAPITAL

Many stocks have a *par value*. The par value of a stock is an arbitrary value the issuing corporation chose for the stock at the time it sought authorization of the stock. A corporation may choose to issue stock having a par value of any amount, but par values of $100, $25, $10, $5, and $1 are common.

When a corporation issues par value stock, the par value is printed on each certificate and is used in accounting for the stock. Also, in many states when a corporation issues par value stock, it establishes for itself a *minimum legal capital* equal to the par value of the issued stock. For example, if a corporation issues 1,000 shares of $100 par value stock, it establishes for itself a minimum legal capital of $100,000.

Laws establishing minimum legal capital normally require stockholders in a corporation to invest assets equal in value to minimum legal capital or be liable to the corporation's creditors for the deficiency. In other words, these laws require stockholders to give a corporation par value for its stock or be liable for the deficiency. Minimum legal capital requirements also make illegal any payments to stockholders for dividends or their equivalent when these payments reduce stock-holders' equity below minimum legal capital.

Corporation laws governing minimum legal capital were written in an effort to protect corporation creditors. The authors of these laws reasoned as follows: A corporation's creditors may look only to the assets of the corporation for satisfaction of their claims. Consequently, when a corporation is organized, its stockholders should provide it with a fund of assets equal to its minimum legal capital. Thereafter, this fund of assets should remain with the corporation and should not be returned to the stockholders in any form until all creditor claims are paid.

Par value helps establish minimum legal capital and is used in accounting for par value stock. However, it does not establish a stock's worth nor the price at which a corporation must issue the stock. If purchasers are willing to pay more than par, a corporation may sell and issue its stock at a price above par. Likewise, in some states, if purchasers will not pay par, a corporation may issue its stock at a price below par.

STOCK PREMIUMS AND DISCOUNTS

Premiums

When a corporation sells and issues stock at a price above the stock's par value, the stock is said to be issued at a *premium*. For example, if a corporation sells and issues its $10 par value common stock at $12 per share, the stock is sold at a $2 per share premium. Although a premium is an amount in excess of par paid by purchasers of newly issued stock, it is not considered a profit to the issuing corporation. Rather a premium is part of the investment of stockholders who pay more than par for their stock.

In accounting for stock sold at a premium, the premium is recorded separately from the par value of the stock to which it applies. For example, if a corporation sells and issues 10,000 shares of its $10 par value common stock for cash at $12 per share, the sale is recorded as follows:

Dec.	1	Cash	120,000.00	
		Premium on Common Stock		20,000.00
		Common Stock		100,000.00
		Sold and issued 10,000 shares of $10 par value common stock at $12 per share.		

When stock is issued in exchange for assets other than cash and the fair value of the assets exceeds the par value of the stock, a premium is recorded. If fair value for the assets cannot be determined within reasonable limits, a price established by recent sales of the stock may be used in recording the exchange. This too may require that a premium be recorded.

When a balance sheet is prepared, stock premium is added in the equity section to the par value of the stock to which it applies, as follows:

Stockholders' Equity		
Common stock, $10 par value, 25,000 shares authorized, 20,000 shares issued	$200,000	
Add premium on common stock	30,000	
Total contributed capital		$230,000
Retained earnings		82,400
Total stockholders' equity		$312,400

Discounts

Stock issued at a price below par is said to be issued at a *discount*. Many states prohibit the issuance of stock at a discount because the stockholders invest less than minimum legal capital. Also, in those states in which stock may be issued at a discount, purchasers of the stock usually become contingently liable to the issuing corporation's creditors for the amount of the discount. Consequently, stock is seldom issued at a discount, and a discussion of stock discounts is of little practical importance. However, if stock is issued at less than par, the discount is debited to a discount account and is subtracted on the balance sheet from the par value of the stock to which it applies.

NO-PAR STOCK

At one time all stocks were required to have a par value. Today all jurisdictions permit the issuance of *no-par stocks* or stocks without a par value. The primary advantage claimed for no-par stock is that since it does not have a par value, it may be issued at any price without a *discount liability* attaching. Also, printing a par value, say $100, on a stock certificate may cause a person lacking in knowledge to believe a share of the stock to be worth $100, when it actually may be worthless. Therefore, eliminating the par value helps force such a person to examine the factors which give a stock value, which are earnings, dividends, and future prospects.

In some states the entire proceeds from the sale of no-par stock becomes minimum legal capital and must be credited to a no-par stock account. In these states, if a corporation issues 1,000 shares of no-par stock at $42 per share, the transaction is recorded like this:

Oct.	20	Cash	42,000.00	
		No-Par Common Stock		42,000.00
		Sold and issued 1,000 shares of no-par common stock at $42 per share.		

In other states a corporation may place a *stated value* on its no-par stock. The stated value then becomes minimum legal capital and is credited to the no-par stock account. If the stock is issued at an amount in excess of stated value, the excess is credited to a contributed capital account called, for instance, "Contributed Capital in Excess of Stated Value of No-Par Stock." In these states if a corporation issues at $42 per share 1,000 shares of no-par common stock on which it has placed a $25 per share stated value, the transaction is recorded as follows:

Oct.	20	Cash	42,000.00	
		No-Par Common Stock		25,000.00
		Contributed Capital in Excess of Stated Value, No-Par Common Stock		17,000.00
		Sold at $42 per share 1,000 shares of no-par stock having a $25 per share stated value.		

In still other states a corporation may place a stated value on its no-par stock and record the transaction as in the preceding entry, but the entire proceeds from the sale of the stock are included in minimum legal capital.

SALE OF STOCK THROUGH SUBSCRIPTIONS

Often stock is sold for cash and immediately issued. Often, too, especially in organizing a new corporation, stock is sold by means of *subscriptions*. In the latter instance a person wishing to become a stockholder signs a subscription blank or a subscription list, agreeing to buy a certain number of the shares. When the subscription is accepted by the corporation, it becomes a contract; and the corporation acquires an asset, the right to receive payment from the subscriber. At the same time the subscriber gains an equity in the corporation equal to the amount the subscriber agrees to pay. Payment may be in one amount or in installments.

To illustrate the sale of stock through subscriptions, assume that on June 6 Northgate Corporation accepted subscriptions to 5,000 shares of its $10 par value common stock at $12 per share. The subscription contracts called for a 10% down payment to accompany the subscriptions and the balance in two equal installments due in 30 and 60 days.

The subscriptions were recorded with the following entry:

June	6	Subscriptions Receivable, Common Stock	60,000.00	
		Premium on Common Stock		10,000.00
		Common Stock Subscribed		50,000.00
		Accepted subscriptions to 5,000 shares of $10 par value common stock at $12 per share.		

Notice that the subscriptions receivable account is debited at the time the subscriptions are accepted for the sum of the stock's par value and premium. This is the amount the subscribers agree to pay. Notice, too, that the stock subscribed account is credited for par value and that the premium is credited to a premium account at the time the subscriptions are accepted. The subscriptions receivable and stock subscribed accounts are of temporary nature. The subscriptions receivable will be turned into cash when the subscribers pay for their stock. Likewise, when payment is completed, the subscribed stock will be issued and will become outstanding stock. Normally, subscribed stock is not issued until paid for.

Receipt of the down payments and the two installment payments may be recorded with these entries.

June	6	Cash	6,000.00	
		Subscriptions Receivable, Common Stock ..		6,000.00
		Collected 10% down payments on the common stock subscribed.		
July	6	Cash	27,000.00	
		Subscriptions Receivable, Common Stock ..		27,000.00
		Collected the first installment payments on the common stock subscribed.		
Aug.	5	Cash	27,000.00	
		Subscriptions Receivable, Common Stock ..		27,000.00
		Collected the second installment payments on the common stock subscribed.		

In this case, the down payments accompanied the subscriptions. Consequently, the entry to record the receipt of the subscriptions and the entry to record the down payments may be combined.

When stock is sold through subscriptions, the stock is usually not issued until the subscriptions are paid in full. However, as soon as the subscriptions are paid, the stock is issued. The entry to record the issuance of the Northgate common stock appears as follows:

Aug.	5	Common Stock Subscribed.................	50,000.00	
		Common Stock		50,000.00
		Issued 5,000 shares of common stock sold through subscriptions.		

Most subscriptions are collected in full, although not always. Sometimes a subscriber fails to pay; and when this happens, the subscription contract must be canceled. In such a case, if the subscriber has made a partial payment on the contract, the amount paid may be returned. Or, a smaller amount of stock than that subscribed, an amount equal to the partial payment, may be issued. Or, in some states the subscriber's partial payment may be kept by the corporation to compensate for any damages suffered.

Subscriptions receivable and stock subscribed on the balance sheet

Subscriptions receivable are normally to be collected within a relatively short time. Consequently, they appear on the balance sheet as a current asset. Also, if a corporation prepares a balance sheet after accepting subscriptions to its stock but before the stock is issued, it should show both its issued stock and its subscribed stock on the balance sheet as follows:

Common stock, $10 par value, 25,000 shares authorized, 20,000 shares issued	$200,000
Unissued common stock subscribed, 5,000 shares	50,000
Total common stock issued and subscribed	$250,000
Add premium on common stock......................	40,000
Amount contributed and subscribed by the common stockholders	$290,000

RIGHTS OF COMMON STOCKHOLDERS

When investors buy a corporation's common stock, they acquire all the specific rights granted by the corporation's charter to its common stockholders. They also acquire the general rights granted stockholders by the laws of the state in which the corporation is organized. The laws vary, but in general all common stockholders have the following rights:

1. The right to vote in the stockholders' meetings.
2. The right to sell or otherwise dispose of their stock.
3. The right of first opportunity to purchase any additional shares of common stock issued by the corporation. (This is called the common stockholders' *preemptive right*. It gives common stockholders the opportunity to protect their proportionate interest in the corporation. For example, a stockholder who owns one fourth of a corporation's common stock has the first opportunity to buy one fourth of any new common stock issued. This enables the stockholder to maintain a one-fourth interest.)
4. The right to share pro rata with other common stockholders in any dividends distributed to common stockholders.
5. The right to share in any assets remaining after creditors are paid if the corporation is liquidated.

PREFERRED STOCK

A corporation may issue more than one kind or class of stock. If two classes are issued, one is generally known as common stock and the other as *preferred stock*. Preferred stock is so called because of the preferences granted its owners. These commonly include a preference as to payment of *dividends,* and may include a preference in the distribution of assets in a liquidation.

A preference as to dividends does not give an absolute right to dividends. Rather, if dividends are declared, it gives the preferred stockholders the right to receive their preferred dividend before the common stockholders are paid a dividend. In other words, if dividends are declared, a dividend must be paid the preferred stockholders before a dividend may be paid to the common stockholders. However, if the directors are of the opinion that no dividends should be paid, then neither the preferred nor the common stockholders receive a dividend.

Dividends on the majority of preferred stocks are limited to a fixed maximum amount. For example, a share of $100 par value, 7%, nonparticipating preferred stock has a preference each year to a dividend equal to 7% of its par value, or $7. However, the dividend is limited to that amount. On the other hand, dividends on a corporation's common stock are unlimited, except by the earning power of the corporation and the judgment of its board of directors.

While dividends on most preferred stocks are limited to a fixed basic percentage or amount, some preferred stocks have the right under certain circumstances to dividends in excess of a fixed basic percentage or amount. Such preferred stocks are called *participating preferred stocks.* Participating preferred stocks may be fully participating, or participation may be limited to a fixed amount. If a corporation issues fully participating, 6%, $100 par value, preferred stock and $50 par value common stock, the owners of the preferred stock have a preference to a 6% or $6 per share dividend each year. Then, each year, after the common stockholders have received a 6% or $3 per share dividend, the preferred stockholders have a right to participate with the common stockholders in any additional dividends declared. The participation is usually on the basis of the same additional percent-on-par-value-per-share dividend to each kind of stock. For instance, if in this case the common stockholders are paid an additional 2% or $1 per share dividend, the preferred stockholders should receive an additional 2% or $2 per share dividend.

Often when preferred stock is participating, participation is limited. For example, a $100 par value, 7%, preferred stock may be issued with the right to participate in dividends to 10% of its par value. Such a stock has a preference to dividends of 7% each year. It also has a right after the common stockholders receive a 7% dividend to participate in additional dividends until it has received 10%, or $10, per share. Its participation rights end at this point.

In addition to being participating or nonparticipating, preferred stocks are either *cumulative* or *noncumulative*. A cumulative preferred stock is one on which any undeclared dividends accumulate each year until paid. A noncumulative preferred stock is one on which the right to receive dividends is forfeited in any year in which dividends are not declared.

The accumulation of dividends on cumulative preferred stocks does not guarantee payment. Dividends cannot be guaranteed because earnings from which they are paid cannot be guaranteed. However, when a corporation issues cumulative preferred stock, it does agree to pay its cumulative preferred stockholders both their current dividends and any unpaid back dividends, called *dividends in arrears,* before it pays a dividend to its common stockholders.

In addition to the preferences it receives, preferred stock carries with it all the rights of common stock, unless such rights are specifically denied in the corporation charter. Commonly, preferred stock is denied the right to vote in the stockholders' meetings.

Preferred dividends in arrears on the balance sheet date

A liability for a dividend does not come into existence until the dividend is declared by the board of directors; and unlike interest, dividends do not accrue. Consequently, if on the dividend date a corporation's board fails to declare a dividend on its cumulative preferred stock, the dividend in arrears is not a liability and does not appear on the balance sheet as such. However, if there are preferred dividends in arrears, the *full-disclosure principle* requires that this information appear on the balance sheet, and normally such information is given in a balance sheet footnote. When a balance sheet does not carry such a footnote, a balance sheet reader has the right to assume that there are no dividends in arrears.

WHY PREFERRED STOCK IS ISSUED

Two common reasons why preferred stock is issued can best be shown by means of an example. Suppose that three persons with a total of $100,000 to invest wish to organize a corporation requiring $200,000 capital. If they sell and issue $200,000 of common stock, they will have to share control with other stockholders. However, if they sell and issue $100,000 of common stock to themselves and sell to outsiders $100,000 of 8%, cumulative preferred stock having no voting rights, they can retain control of the corporation for themselves.

Also, suppose the three promoters expect their new corporation to earn an annual after-tax return of $24,000. If they sell and issue $200,000 of common stock, this will mean a 12% return. However, if they sell and issue $100,000 of each kind of stock, retaining the common for themselves, they can increase their own return to 16%, as follows:

Net after-tax income............................	$24,000
Less preferred dividends at 8%	(8,000)
Balance to common stockholders (equal to 16% on their $100,000 investment)	$16,000

In this case the common stockholders earn 16% because the dividends on the preferred stock are less than the amount that can be earned on the preferred stockholders' investment.

STOCK VALUES

In addition to a par value, stocks may have a redemption value, a market value, and a book value.

Redemption value

Redemption values apply to preferred stocks. Often corporations issuing preferred stock reserve the right to redeem the stock by paying the preferred stockholders the par value of their stock plus a premium. The amount a corporation agrees to pay to redeem a share of its preferred stock is called the redemption value of the stock. Normally, a corporation reserves the right to either redeem or permit the stock to remain outstanding, as it chooses.

Market value

The market value of a share of stock is the price at which a share can be bought or sold. Market values are influenced by earnings, dividends, future prospects, and general market conditions.

Book value

The *book value of a share of stock* measures the equity of the owner of one share of the stock in the assets of its issuing corporation. If a corporation has issued only common stock, its book value per share is determined by dividing total stockholders' equity by the number of shares outstanding. For example, if total stockholders' equity is $285,000 and there are 10,000 shares outstanding, the book value per share is $28.50 ($285,000 ÷ 10,000 = $28.50).

To compute book values when both common and preferred stock are outstanding, the preferred stock is assigned a portion of the total stockholders' equity equal to its redemption value plus any cumulative dividends in arrears. The remaining stockholders' equity is then assigned to the common shares outstanding. After this the book value of each class is determined by dividing its share of stockholders' equity by the number of shares of that class outstanding. For instance, assume a corporation has the stockholders' equity shown in Illustration 15–2.

Stockholders' Equity		
Preferred stock, $100 par value, 7% cumulative and nonparticipating, 2,000 shares authorized, 1,000 shares issued and outstanding	$100,000	
Premium on preferred stock	5,000	
Total capital contributed by preferred stockholders		$105,000
Common stock, $25 par value, 12,000 shares authorized, 10,000 shares issued and outstanding	$250,000	
Premium on common stock	10,000	
Total capital contributed by common stockholders		260,000
Total contributed capital		$365,000
Retained earnings		82,000
Total stockholders' equity		$447,000

Illustration 15–2

If the preferred stock is redeemable at $103 per share and two years' of cumulative preferred dividends are in arrears, the book values of the corporation's shares are calculated as follows:

Total stockholders' equity		$ 447,000	
Less equity applicable to preferred shares:			
Redemption value	$103,000		
Cumulative dividends in arrears	14,000	(117,000)	
Equity applicable to common shares			$330,000
Book value of preferred shares ($117,000 ÷ 1,000) $117			
Book value of common shares ($330,000 ÷ 10,000) 33			

Corporations in their annual reports to their shareholders often point out the increase that has occurred in the book value of the corporation's shares during a year. Book value may also be of significance in a contract. For example, a stockholder may enter into a contract to sell shares at their book value at some future date. However, book value should not be confused with *liquidation value* because if a corporation is liquidated, its assets will probably sell at prices quite different from the amounts at which they are carried on the books. Also, book value generally has little bearing upon the market value of stock. Dividends, earning capacity, and future prospects are usually of much more importance. For instance a common stock having a $11 book value may sell for $25 per share if its earnings, dividends, and prospects are good. However, it may sell for $5 per share if these factors are unfavorable.

GLOSSARY

Book value of a share of stock. The equity represented by one share of stock in the issuing corporation's net assets.

Common stock. Stock of a corporation that has only one class of stock; if there is more than one class, the class that has no preferences relative to the corporation's other classes of stock.

Common stock subscribed. Unissued common stock for which the issuing corporation has a subscription contract to issue.

Cumulative preferred stock. Preferred stock on which any undeclared dividends accumulate each year until paid.

Discount on stock. The difference between the par value of stock and the amount below par value contributed by stockholders.

Dividend. A distribution made by a corporation to its stockholders of cash, other assets, or additional shares of the corporation's own stock.

Dividends in arrears. Unpaid back dividends on preferred stock which must be paid before dividends are paid to common stockholders.

Minimum legal capital. An amount that stockholders must invest in a corporation or be contingently liable to its creditors.

Noncumulative preferred stock. A stock for which the right to receive dividends is forfeited in any year in which dividends are not declared.

No par stock. A class of stock having no par value.

Organization costs. Costs of bringing a corporation into existence, such as legal fees, promoters' fees, and amounts paid the state to secure a charter.

Participating preferred stock. Preferred stock that has the right to share in dividends above the fixed basic amount or percentage which is preferred.

Par value. An arbitrary value placed on a share of stock at the time the corporation seeks authorization of the stock.

Preemptive right. The right of a common stockholder to have the first opportunity to purchase additional shares of common stock issued by the corporation.

Preferred stock. Stock other than common stock the owners of which are granted certain preferences such as a preference to payment of dividends or in the distribution of assets in a liquidation.

Premium on stock. The amount of capital contributed by stockholders above the stock's par value.

Proxy. A legal document which gives an agent of a stockholder the right to vote the stockholder's shares.

Redemption value of stock. The amount a corporation must pay for the return of a share of preferred stock previously issued by the corporation.

Stated value of no-par stock. An amount, established by a corporation's board of directors, that is credited to the no-par stock account at the time the stock is issued.

Stock subscription. A contractual commitment to purchase unissued shares of stock and become a stockholder.

QUESTIONS FOR CLASS DISCUSSION

1. What are the advantages and disadvantages of the corporate form of business organization?
2. What is a proxy?
3. What are organization costs? List several.
4. What are the duties and responsibilities of a corporation's registrar and transfer agent?
5. Why is a corporation the stock of which is sold on a stock exchange required to have a registrar and transfer agent? Why is such a corporation required to have both a registrar and a transfer agent?
6. List the general rights of common stockholders.
7. What is the preemptive right of common stockholders?

8. Laws place no limit on the amounts partners may withdraw from a partnership. On the other hand, laws regulating corporations place definite limits on the amounts corporation owners may withdraw from a corporation in dividends. Why is there a difference?

9. What is a stock premium? What is a stock discount?

10. Does a corporation earn a profit by selling its stock at a premium? Does it incur a loss by selling its stock at a discount?

11. Why do corporation laws make purchasers of stock at a discount contingently liable for the discount? To whom are such purchasers contingently liable?

12. What is the main advantage of no-par stock?

13. What are the balance sheet classifications of the accounts: *(a)* Subscriptions Receivable, Common Stock and *(b)* Common Stock Subscribed?

14. What are the meanings of the following when applied to preferred stock: *(a)* preferred, *(b)* participating, *(c)* nonparticipating, *(d)* cumulative, and *(e)* noncumulative?

15. What are the meanings of the following terms when applied to stock: *(a)* par value, *(b)* book value, *(c)* market value, and *(d)* redemption value?

CLASS EXERCISES

Exercise 15–1

A corporation has outstanding 1,000 shares of $100 par value, 7% cumulative and nonparticipating preferred stock and 8,000 shares of $25 par value common stock. During the first four years in its life it paid out the following amounts in dividends: first year, nothing; second year, $8,000; third year, $24,000; and fourth year, $30,000. Determine the total dividends paid to each class of stockholders each year.

Exercise 15–2

Determine the total dividends paid each class of stockholders of the previous exercise under the assumption that rather than being cumulative and nonparticipating, the preferred stock is noncumulative and nonparticipating.

Exercise 15–3

A corporation has outstanding 1,000 shares of $100 par value, 7% cumulative and fully participating preferred stock and 20,000 shares of $10 par value common stock. It has regularly paid all dividends on the preferred stock. This year the board of directors voted to pay out a total of $28,500 in dividends to the two classes of stockholders. Determine the percent on par to be paid each class of stockholders and the dividend per share to be paid each class.

Exercise 15–4

The stockholders' equity section of a corporation's balance sheet appeared as follows:

Stockholders' Equity

Preferred stock, $100 par value, 7% cumulative and nonparticipating, 1,000 shares authorized and outstanding	$100,000	
Premium on preferred stock	6,000	
Total capital contributed by preferred stockholders		$106,000
Common stock, $10 par value, 25,000 shares authorized, 20,000 shares issued and outstanding	$200,000	
Premium on common stock	10,000	
Total capital contributed by common stockholders		210,000
Total contributed capital		$316,000
Retained earnings		64,500
Total stockholders' equity		$380,500

Under the assumption the preferred stock is redeemable at $103.50 per share and one year's preferred dividends are in arrears, determine the book value per share of each class of stock.

Exercise 15–5

On March 3 a corporation accepted subscriptions to 10,000 shares of its $5 par value common stock at $5.50 per share. The subscription contracts called for one fifth of the subscription price to accompany each contract as a down payment and the balance to be paid on April 2. Give the entries to record (a) the subscriptions, (b) the down payments, (c) receipt of the remaining amounts due on the subscriptions on April 2, and (d) issuance of the stock.

Exercise 15–6

A corporation sold and issued 2,000 shares of its no-par common stock for $27,500 on March 6. (a) Give the entry to record the sale under the assumption the board of directors did not place a stated value on the stock. (b) Give the entry to record the sale under the assumption the board placed a $10 per share stated value on the stock.

PROBLEMS

Problem 15–1

Frankfort Corporation received a charter granting the right to issue 1,000 shares of $100 par value, 7% cumulative and nonparticipating preferred stock and 20,000 shares of $10 par value common stock. It then completed these transactions:

Jan. 10 Sold and issued 5,000 shares of common stock at par for cash.
    11 Gave the corporation's attorneys 200 shares of common stock for

their services in securing the corporation's charter. The services were
valued at $2,000.

Jan. 14   Exchanged 1,000 shares of preferred stock for assets having the following fair market values: land, $10,000; buildings, $30,000; and machinery, $60,000.

15   Accepted subscriptions to 8,000 shares of common stock at par. The
subscriptions contracts were accompanied by 20% down payments.

30   Collected the balance due on the stock subscriptions of January 15
and issued the stock.

31   Accepted subscriptions to 2,000 shares of common stock at par. The
subscriptions contracts were accompanied by 20% down payments.

Required:

Prepare general journal entries to record the transactions and prepare a
January 31 classified balance sheet for the corporation.

Problem 15–2

Part 1. The stockholders' equity section from a corporation's balance sheet
appeared as follows:

Stockholders' Equity

Seven percent cumulative and nonparticipating, $100 par value, preferred stock, authorized and issued 1,000 shares	$100,000
Common stock, $25 par value, 10,000 shares authorized and issued	250,000
Retained earnings	18,000
Total stockholders' equity	$368,000

Required:

Prepare a schedule showing the book values per share of the preferred
and common stocks under each of the following assumptions:

1. There are no dividends in arrears on the preferred stock.
2. One year's dividends are in arrears on the preferred stock.
3. Three years' dividends are in arrears on the preferred stock.

Part 2. A corporation has had outstanding since its organization 25,000
shares of $10 par value, 7%, preferred stock and 100,000 shares of $10 par
value common stock. The current year's and two prior years', a total of three
years', dividends are in arrears on the preferred stock. However, the company
has recently prospered and the board of directors wants to know how much
cash will be required for dividends if a $1 per share dividend is paid on the
common stock.

Required:

Prepare a schedule showing the amounts of cash required for dividends
to each class of stockholders under each of the following assumptions:

a. The preferred stock is noncumulative and nonparticipating.

b. The preferred stock is cumulative and nonparticipating.
c. The preferred stock is cumulative and fully participating.
d. The preferred stock is cumulative and participating to 9%.

Problem 15-3

A corporation received a charter granting it the right to issue 2,000 shares of $100 par value, 8% cumulative and nonparticipating, preferred stock and 100,000 shares of $10 par value common stock. It then completed these transactions:

Jan. 27 Accepted subscriptions to 50,000 shares of common stock at $11.50 per share. Down payments equal to 20% of the subscription price accompanied each subscription.

31 Gave the corporation's promoters 1,000 shares of common stock for their services in getting the corporation organized. The board valued the services at $11,500.

Feb. 3 Accepted subscriptions to 1,500 shares of preferred stock at $110 per share. The subscriptions were accompanied by 50% down payments.

26 Collected the balance due on the January 27 common stock subscriptions and issued the stock.

28 Accepted subscriptions to 500 shares of preferred stock at $108 per share. The subscriptions were accompanied by 50% down payments.

Mar. 5 Collected the balance due on the February 3 preferred stock subscriptions and issued the stock.

Required:

1. Prepare general journal entries to record the transactions.
2. Prepare the stockholders' equity section of the corporation's balance sheet as of the close of business on March 5.

Problem 15-4

A corporation received a charter granting the right to issue 50,000 shares of $10 par value common stock. It then completed these transactions:

198A
Feb. 17 Sold and issued 15,000 shares of common stock for cash at $11 per share.

17 Gave the corporation's promoters 1,000 shares of common stock for their services in getting the corporation organized. The board of directors valued the promoters' services at $11,000.

17 Exchanged 25,000 shares of common stock for the following assets at fair values: land, $30,000; buildings, $100,000; and machinery, $145,000.

Dec. 10 Accepted subscriptions to 2,000 shares of common stock at par. Ten percent down payments accompanied the subscriptions.

31 Closed the Income Summary account. A $17,500 loss was incurred.

198B

Jan. 10   Received payment of the balance due on the December 10 subscriptions and issued the stock.

Dec. 31   Closed the Income Summary account. A $34,800 net income was
earned.

198C

Jan. 8   The board of directors declared a $0.20 per share dividend on the
outstanding common stock, payable on February 10 to the January
31 stockholders of record.

Feb. 10   Paid the previously declared dividend.

Required:

1. Prepare general journal entries to record the transactions.
2. Prepare the stockholders' equity section of the corporation's December
31, 198A, balance sheet.

Problem 15–5

A corporation has outstanding 25,000 shares of $10 par value common stock,
all owned by five people who are the corporation's board of directors. The
corporation is in a position to expand; but to do so it needs $250,000 additional
capital which the owners are unable to supply. Consequently, they are considering the issuance at par of 2,500 shares of $100 par value, 8%, cumulative
and nonparticipating preferred stock to gain the needed capital, and they
have asked you to prepare a report showing the return to the two classes of
stockholders from the following amounts of anticipated after-tax earnings:
198A, $25,000; 198B, $35,000; 198C, $55,000; and 198D, $60,000.

Required:

1. Prepare a form with columnar headings as follows:

Year	After-Tax Earnings		Preferred Dividends		Common Dividends	
	Amount	Percent Return on In- vestment	Total Paid to Preferred	Percent Return on In- vestment	Total Paid to Common	Percent Return on In- vestment

2. Enter the years in the first column, each year's anticipated after-tax earnings
in the second column, and each year's rate of return on the total $500,000
investment in the third column. Then complete the form under the assumption that all after-tax earnings are to be paid out in dividends.
3. Explain why at the after-tax levels of $55,000 and $60,000 the after-tax
rate of return of the common stockholders will be greater than the after-
tax rate earned by the corporation as a whole.
4. Prepare a calculation to account for the difference between the rate of
return to the corporation as a whole at the $60,000 level and the rate of
return to the common stockholders at that level.

ALTERNATE PROBLEMS

Problem 15–1A

Twin Lake Corporation received a charter granting the right to issue 1,000 shares of $100 par value, 7% cumulative and nonparticipating preferred stock and 50,000 shares of $5 par value common stock. It then completed these transactions:

Jan. 26   Sold and issued 20,000 shares of common stock for cash.

     29   Accepted subscriptions to the 1,000 shares of preferred stock at par. The subscription contracts were accompanied by 10% down payments.

Feb. 12   Exchanged 15,000 shares of common stock for land having a $25,000 fair market value and a building having a $50,000 fair value.

     15   Gave the corporation's promoters 1,000 shares of common stock for their services in getting the corporation organized. The services were valued by the board of directors at $5,000.

     28   Collected the balance due on the January 29 subscriptions and issued the stock.

     28   Accepted subscriptions to 5,000 shares of common stock at par. Twenty percent down payments accompanied the subscription contracts.

Required:

Prepare general journal entries to record the transactions and prepare a February 28 classified balance sheet for the corporation.

Problem 15–2A

Part 1. Following are the stockholders' equity sections from the balance sheets of three corporations. From the information given prepare a schedule showing the book value per share of the preferred and of the common stock of each corporation.

1. Stockholders' equity:

Seven percent cumulative and nonparticipating, $10 par value, preferred stock, authorized and issued 10,000 shares	$ 100,000
Common stock, $5 par value, authorized and issued 100,000 shares	500,000
Retained earnings	148,000
Total stockholders' equity	$ 748,000

2. Stockholders' equity:

Cumulative and nonparticipating, $100 par value, 6%, preferred stock, 10,000 shares issued and outstanding	$1,000,000*
Common stock, $25 par value, 100,000 shares issued and outstanding	2,500,000
Retained earnings	85,000
Total stockholders' equity	$3,585,000

    * One year's dividends are in arrears on the preferred stock.

3. Stockholders' equity:

Preferred stock, $100 par value, 7% cumulative and nonparticipating, 5,000 shares issued and outstanding ..	$ 500,000*
Common stock, $1 par value, 500,000 shares issued and outstanding.....................................	500,000
Total contributed capital.............................	$1,000,000
Deficit	(40,000)
Total stockholders' equity	$ 960,000

* Two years' dividends are in arrears on the preferred stock.

Part 2. A corporation's common stock is selling on the stock exchange today at $12.50 per share, and a just published balance sheet shows the stockholders' equity in the company as follows:

Stockholders' Equity

Preferred stock, $100 par value, 7% cumulative and non-participating, issued and outstanding 2,500 shares	$250,000
Common stock, $10 par value, issued and outstanding 50,000 shares	500,000
Total contributed capital	$750,000
Retained earnings	63,000
Total stockholders' equity	$813,000

Required:

Answer these questions: (1) What is the market value of the corporation's common stock? (2) What are the par values of its *(a)* preferred stock and *(b)* common stock? (3) If there are no dividends in arrears, what are the book values of the *(a)* preferred stock and *(b)* common stock? (4) If two years' dividends are in arrears on the preferred stock, what are the book values of the *(a)* preferred stock and the *(b)* common stock?

Problem 15–3A

A corporation received a charter which granted it the right to issue 2,000 shares of $100 par value, 8% cumulative and nonparticipating preferred stock and 200,000 shares of $5 par value common stock. It then completed these transactions:

Feb. 3 Exchanged 100,000 shares of common stock for the following assets at fair values: land, $50,000; buildings, $150,000; and machinery, $325,000.

3 Accepted subscriptions to 50,000 shares of common stock at $5.25 per share. The subscription contracts were accompanied by 10% down payments.

5 Accepted subscriptions and $21,000 in down payments on 1,000 shares of preferred stock at $105 per share.

7 Gave the corporation's attorneys $1,000 in cash and 400 shares of common stock for their services in securing the corporation charter. The services were valued by the board of directors at $3,100.

Mar. 5 Collected the balance due on the February 3 common stock subscriptions and issued the stock.

Mar. 7   Collected the balance due on the preferred stock subscriptions and issued the stock.

31   Accepted subscriptions accompanied by 10% down payments to 10,000 shares of common stock at $5.50 per share.

Required:

1. Prepare general journal entries to record the transactions.
2. Prepare the stockholders' equity section of the corporation's balance sheet as of the close of business on March 31.

Problem 15–4A

A corporation received a charter granting it the right to issue 200,000 shares of $5 par value common stock. It then completed these transactions:

198A

Mar. 7   Sold and issued 10,000 shares of common stock at $5.50 per share for cash.

7   Issued 1,000 shares of common stock to the corporation's attorney for services in getting the corporation organized. The board of directors placed a $5,500 value on the services.

8   Exchanged 100,000 shares of common stock for the following assets at fair values: land, $50,000; buildings, $200,000; and machinery, $300,000.

Dec. 20   Accepted subscriptions to 50,000 shares of common stock at $5.25 per share. Down payments of 20% accompanied the subscription contracts.

Dec. 31   Closed the Income Summary account. There was a $11,400 net loss.

198B

Jan. 19   Collected the balance due on the December 20 subscriptions and issued the stock.

Dec. 31   Closed the Income Summary account. There was a $45,800 net income.

198C

Jan. 10   The board of directors declared a $0.10 per share dividend on the outstanding common stock, payable February 10 to the January 31 stockholders of record.

Feb. 10   Paid the dividend previously declared.

Required:

1. Prepare general journal entries to record the transactions.
2. Prepare the stockholders' equity section of the corporation's December 31, 198A, balance sheet.

Problem 15–5A

A corporation has outstanding 10,000 shares of $10 par value, 8%, preferred stock and 20,000 shares of $10 par value common stock. During a five-year period it paid out the following amounts in dividends: 198A, nothing; 198B, $22,000; 198C, $20,000; 198D, $30,000; and 198E, $36,000.

Required:

1. Prepare three schedules with columnar headings as follows:

Year	Amount Distributed in Dividends	Total to Preferred	Balance Due Preferred	Total to Common	Dividend per Share Preferred	Dividend per Share Common

2. Complete a schedule under each of the following assumptions, showing for each year the total dollars paid the preferred stockholders, balance due the preferred stockholders, and so forth. There were no dividends in arrears for the years prior to 198A.

   a. The preferred stock is noncumulative and nonparticipating.

   b. The preferred stock is cumulative and nonparticipating.

   c. The preferred stock is cumulative and fully participating.

PROVOCATIVE PROBLEMS

Provocative problem 15–1
Bill and Bob

Bill Larkin recently received a patent on a gadget on which he had spent his spare time for several years. He is certain the gadget has tremendous market potential, but as a school teacher he has never been able to save much money and does not have the capital to manufacture and sell it. Consequently, last night he approached Bob Walker, a long-time friend who recently inherited several hundred thousand dollars from his father, for a $10,000 loan. Before asking for the loan, Bill demonstrated the gadget to Bob. Bob immediately became excited about its possibilities and agreed to make the loan. However, Bob pointed out that $10,000 would hardly get the item into production, and it would take much more for a marketing campaign.

After discussing production and marketing needs for some time, Bob suggested that instead of a loan he should go into business with Bill. He suggested that he furnish the capital for the business and that Bill transfer his patent rights to the business. Bill accepted the offer, and after more discussion it was agreed that Bill would resign his teaching job at the end of the school year, a month away, and devote full time to organizing and managing the new business. Both men agreed that the marketing campaign should be turned over to professionals, but they did not agree as to the form of business organization for their new business.

Write a report to Bill and Bob outlining the factors they should consider in choosing between a partnership form of organization or a corporate form for their business.

Provocative problem 15–2
Loose Knot Lumber Company

Ed Loose and Ted Knot have operated a building supply firm for a number of years as partners sharing losses and gains in a 3 to 2 ratio. However, they need to increase the inventory of the business but do not have the necessary funds. Consequently, they have entered into an agreement with Lee Nail to reorganize their firm into a corporation, to be called Loose Knot Lumber Company, and they have just received a charter granting their corporation the right to issue 15,000 shares of $10 par value common stock.

On the date of the reorganization, June 8 of the current year, a trial balance of the partnership ledger appears as follows:

LOOSE AND KNOT
Trial Balance, June 8, 19—

Cash	$ 2,800	
Accounts receivable	8,250	
Allowance for doubtful accounts		$ 350
Merchandise inventory	62,700	
Store equipment	16,800	
Accumulated depreciation, store equipment		5,300
Buildings	80,000	
Accumulated depreciation, building		15,000
Land	17,250	
Accounts payable		13,150
Mortgage payable		60,000
Ed Loose, capital		55,000
Ted Knot, capital		39,000
Totals	$187,800	$187,800

The agreement between the partners and Lee Nail carries these provisions:

1. The partnership assets are to be revalued as follows:
   a. The $250 account of Valley Builders is known to be uncollectible and is to be written off as a bad debt, after which (b) the allowance for doubtful accounts is to be increased to 5% of the remaining accounts receivable.
   c. The merchandise inventory is to be written down to $60,000 to provide for damaged and shopworn goods.
   d. Insufficient depreciation has been taken on the store equipment; consequently, its book value is to be decreased to $10,000 by increasing the balance of the accumulated depreciation account.
   e. The building is to be written up to its replacement cost, $100,000, and the balance of the accumulated depreciation account is to be increased to show the building one-fifth depreciated.
2. After the partnership assets are revalued, the assets and liabilities are to be transferred to the corporation in exchange for its stock, with each partner accepting stock at par value for his equity in the partnership.
3. Lee Nail is to buy the remaining stock for cash at par.

After reaching the agreement outlined, the three men hired you as accountant for the new corporation. Your first task is to determine the amount of stock each partner should receive, and to prepare the entry on the corporation's books to record the issuance of stock in exchange for the partnership assets and liabilities. You are then to prepare the entry recording the sale of the remainder of the stock to Lee Nail for cash.

After studying Chapter 16, you should be able to:

☐ **Record purchases and sales of treasury stock and describe their effects on stockholders' equity.**

☐ **Record stock dividends and describe their effects on stockholders' equity.**

☐ **Describe the reasons for appropriations of retained earnings and the disclosure of such appropriations in the financial statements.**

☐ **Prepare consolidated financial statements which include such matters as excess of investment cost over book value and minority interests.**

☐ **Account for the earnings and dividends of an investee corporation by the equity method.**

☐ **Explain the differences between the pooling of interests and purchase methods of accounting for corporate combinations.**

☐ **Define or explain the words and phrases listed in the chapter Glossary.**

Corporations: Additional transactions

■ When a corporation earns a net income, more assets flow into the business from revenues than flow out for expenses. As a result, the net income increases both assets and stockholders' equity. The increase in stockholders' equity appears on the corporation's balance sheet as retained earnings. Once retained earnings were commonly called *earned surplus*. However, since the word "surplus" is subject to misinterpretation, the AICPA's Committee on Terminology recommended that its use be discontinued. Consequently, the term "surplus" has all but disappeared from published balance sheets.

RETAINED EARNINGS AND DIVIDENDS

In most states a corporation must have retained earnings in order to pay a cash dividend. However, the payment of a cash dividend reduces in equal amounts both cash and stockholders' equity. Consequently, in order to pay a cash dividend, a corporation must have not only a credit balance in its Retained Earnings account but also cash with which to pay the dividend. If cash or assets that will shortly become cash are not available, a board may think it wise to forgo the declaration of a dividend, even though retained earnings exist. Often the directors of a corporation having a large amount of retained earnings will not declare a dividend because all current assets are needed in the operation of the business.

In considering the wisdom of a dividend, a board must recognize that earnings are a source of assets. Some assets from earnings should probably be paid out in dividends, but some should be retained for emergencies and for distribution as dividends in years in which earnings are not sufficient to pay normal dividends. Also, some assets from earnings should be retained for use in expanding operations. The last reason is an important one. If a corporation is to expand and grow, it may sell additional stock to secure the assets needed in expansion. However, it may also expand by using assets acquired through earnings.

Entries for the declaration and distribution of a cash dividend were given on page 128 and need not be repeated here.

DISTRIBUTIONS FROM CONTRIBUTED CAPITAL

Some states permit the payment of a "dividend" from amounts received as stock premiums, but others make such distributions illegal. Nevertheless, and regardless of legality, accountants are opposed to calling such a distribution a dividend. It is obviously a return of invested capital and should be labeled clearly as such. Calling it a dividend might lead an uninformed person to believe the payment was from earnings. As to the legality of a dividend, state laws governing the payment of dividends commonly make directors personally liable for repayment to the corporation and its creditors of an illegal dividend.

STOCK DIVIDENDS

A *stock dividend* is a distribution by a corporation of shares of its own common stock to its common stockholders without any consideration being given in return therefor. Usually the distribution is prompted by a desire to give the stockholders some evidence of their interest in retained earnings without distributing cash or other assets which the board of directors thinks it wise to retain in the business. A clear distinction should be made between a cash dividend and a stock dividend. A cash dividend reduces both assets and stockholders' equity. A stock dividend differs in that shares of the corporation's own stock rather than cash are distributed. Such a dividend has no effect on assets, total capital, or the amount of a stockholder's equity.

A stock dividend has no effect on corporation assets, total capital, and the amount of a stockholder's equity because it involves nothing more than a transfer of retained earnings to contributed capital. To illustrate this, assume that Northwest Corporation has the following stockholders' equity:

Stockholders' Equity		
Common stock, $10 par value, authorized 15,000 shares, issued and outstanding 10,000 shares	$100,000	
Premium on common stock	8,000	
Total contributed capital	$108,000	
Retained earnings	35,000	
Total stockholders' equity		$143,000

Assume further that on December 28 the directors of Northwest Corporation declared a 10% or 1,000-share stock dividend distributable on January 20 to the January 15 stockholders of record.

If the market value of Northwest Corporation's stock on December 28 is $15 per share, the following entries may be made to record the dividend declaration and distribution:

Dec.	28	Retained Earnings	15,000.00	
		Common Stock Dividend Distributable		10,000.00
		Premium on Common Stock		5,000.00
		To record the declaration of a 1,000-share common stock dividend.		
Jan.	20	Common Stock Dividend Distributable	10,000.00	
		Common Stock		10,000.00
		To record the distribution of a 1,000-share common stock dividend.		

Note that the entries change $15,000 of the stockholders' equity from retained earnings to contributed capital, or as it is said, $15,000 of retained earnings are *capitalized*. Note also that the retained earnings capitalized are equal to the market value of the 1,000 shares issued ($15 × 1,000 shares = $15,000).

As previously pointed out, a stock dividend does not distribute funds from earnings to the stockholders, nor does it affect in any way the corporation assets. Likewise, it has no effect on total capital and on the individual equities of the stockholders. To illustrate these last points, assume that Johnson owned 100 shares of Northwest Corporation's stock prior to the dividend. The corporation's total contributed and retained capital before the dividend and the book value of Johnson's 100 shares were as follows:

Common stock (10,000 shares)	$100,000
Premium on common stock	8,000
Retained earnings	35,000
Total contributed and retained capital	$143,000

$143,000 ÷ 10,000 shares outstanding = $14.30 per share book value
$14.30 × 100 = $1,430 for the book value of Johnson's 100 shares

A 10% stock dividend gives a stockholder one new share for each ten shares previously held. Consequently, Johnson received ten new shares; and after the dividend, the contributed and retained capital of the corporation and the book value of Johnson's holdings are as follows:

Common stock (11,000 shares) $110,000
Premium on common stock 13,000
Retained earnings 20,000
    Total contributed and retained capital $143,000

$143,000 ÷ 11,000 shares outstanding = $13 per share book value
$13 × 110 = $1,430 for the book value of Johnson's 110 shares

Before the stock dividend, Johnson owned 100/10,000 or 1/100 of the Northwest Corporation stock and his holdings had a $1,430 book value. After the dividend, he owned 110/11,000 or 1/100 of the corporation and his holdings still had a $1,430 book value. In other words, there was no effect on his equity other than that it was repackaged from 100 units into 110. Likewise, the only effect on corporation capital was a permanent transfer to contributed capital of $15,000 of retained earnings. Consequently, insofar as both the corporation and Johnson are concerned, there was no shift in equities or corporation assets.

Why stock dividends are distributed

If a stock dividend has no effect on corporation assets and stockholders' equities other than to repackage the equities into more units, why are such dividends declared and distributed? Insofar as a corporation is concerned, a stock dividend enables it to give its shareholders some evidence of their interest in retained earnings without the necessity of distributing corporation cash or other assets to them. Consequently, stock dividends are often declared by corporations that have used funds from earnings in expanding and, as a result, do not feel they have sufficient cash with which to pay a cash dividend. Also, if a profitable corporation grows by retaining earnings, the price of its common stock also tends to grow. Eventually, the price of a share may become high enough to prevent some investors from considering purchase of the stock. Thus, corporations may declare stock dividends to keep the price of their shares from growing too high. For this reason, some corporations declare small stock dividends each year.

Stockholders may benefit from a stock dividend in another way. Often corporations declaring stock dividends continue to pay the same cash dividend per share after a stock dividend as before, with the result that stockholders receive more cash from each cash dividend.

Amount of retained earnings capitalized

The AICPA Committee on Accounting Procedure recognized that some stockholders incorrectly believe that earnings are distributed in a stock dividend. Consequently, it ruled that the amount of retained earnings capitalized in a small stock dividend and made unavailable for future dividends should equal the market value of the shares to

be distributed.[1] A *small stock dividend* was defined as one of 25%
or less of the previously outstanding shares.

A small stock dividend is likely to have only a small impact on the
price of the stock. On the other hand, a large stock dividend normally
has a pronounced impact, and for this reason is not apt to be perceived
as a distribution of earnings. Consequently, in recording a large stock
dividend (over 25%), the committee ruled that it is only necessary
to capitalize retained earnings to the extent required by law. As a
result, in most states a corporation may record a large stock dividend
by debiting Retained Earnings and crediting the stock account for
the par value of the shares issued.[2]

Stock dividends on the balance sheet

Since a stock dividend is "payable" in stock rather than in assets,
it is not a liability of its issuing corporation. Therefore, if a balance
sheet is prepared between the declaration and distribution dates of
a stock dividend, the amount of the dividend distributable should appear on the balance sheet in the stockholders' equity section as follows:

Common stock, $10 par value, 50,000 shares authorized, 20,000 shares issued	$200,000
Common stock subscribed, 5,000 shares	50,000
Common stock dividend distributable, 1,900 shares	19,000
Total common stock issued and to be issued	$269,000
Capital contributed by common stockholders in excess of the par value of their shares	46,000
Total capital contributed and subscribed by common stockholders	$315,000

In addition to the stock dividend distributable, note in the equity
section the item "Capital contributed by common stockholders in excess of the par value of their shares." The item resulted from common
stock premiums and is probably carried in the ledger in the Premium
on Common Stock account. However, as in this case, items are commonly shown on the balance sheet under more descriptive captions
than the name of the account in which they are recorded.

STOCK SPLITS

Sometimes, when a corporation's stock is selling at a high price,
the corporation will call it in and issue two, three, four, five, or more
new shares in the place of each old share previously outstanding. For
example, a corporation having outstanding $100 par value stock selling

---

[1] Committee on Accounting Procedure, "Accounting Research Bulletin No. 43,"
Accounting Research and Terminology Bulletins, Final Edition (New York: AICPA,
1961), chap. 7, sec. B, pars. 10, 13. Copyright (1961) by the American Institute of CPAs.

[2] Ibid., chap. 7, sec. B, par. 11.

for $375 a share may call in the old shares and issue to the stockholders four shares of $25 par, or ten shares of $10 par, or any number of shares of no-par stock in exchange for each $100 share formerly held. This is known as a *stock split* or a *stock split-up,* and its usual purpose is to cause a reduction in the market price of the stock and, consequently, to facilitate trading in the stock.

A stock split has no effect on total stockholders' equity, the equities of the individual stockholders, or on the balances of any of the contributed or retained capital accounts. Consequently, all that is required in recording a stock split is a memorandum entry in the stock account reciting the facts of the split. For example, such a memorandum might read, "Called in the outstanding $100 par value common stock and issued ten shares of $10 par value common stock for each old share previously outstanding." Also, there would be a change in the description of the stock on the balance sheet.

TREASURY STOCK

Corporations often reacquire shares of their own stock. Sometimes a corporation will purchase its own stock on the open market to be given to employees as a bonus or to be used in acquiring other corporations. Sometimes shares are bought in order to maintain a favorable market for the stock. Regardless, if a corporation reacquires shares of its own stock, such stock is known as *treasury stock.* Treasury stock is a corporation's own stock that has been issued and then reacquired either by purchase or gift. Notice that the stock must be the corporation's own stock. The acquisition of stock of another corporation does not create treasury stock. Furthermore, the stock must have been issued and then reacquired. The last point distinguishes treasury stock from unissued stock. The distinction is important because stock once issued at par or above and then reacquired as treasury stock may be legally reissued at a discount without discount liability. Although treasury stock differs from unissued stock in that it may be sold at a discount without discount liability, in other respects it has the same status as unissued stock. Both are equity items rather than assets. Both are subtracted from authorized stock to determine outstanding stock when such things as book values are calculated. Neither receives cash dividends nor has a vote in the stockholders' meetings.

PURCHASE OF TREASURY STOCK[3]

When a corporation purchases its own stock, it reduces in equal amounts both its assets and its stockholders' equity. To illustrate this,

---

[3] There are several ways of accounting for treasury stock transactions. This text will discuss the so-called cost basis, which seems to be the most widely used, and it will leave a discussion of other methods to a more advanced text.

assume that on May 1 of the current year the condensed balance sheet of Curry Corporation appears as in Illustration 16–1.

Curry Corporation
Balance Sheet, May 1, 19—

Assets		Capital	
Cash	$ 30,000	Common stock, $10 par	
Other assets	95,000	value, authorized and	
		issued 10,000 shares	$100,000
		Retained earnings	25,000
Total assets	$125,000	Total capital	$125,000

Illustration 16–1

If on May 1 Curry Corporation purchases 1,000 shares of its outstanding stock at $11.50 per share, the transaction is recorded as follows:

May	1	Treasury Stock, Common	11,500.00	
		Cash		11,500.00
		Purchased 1,000 shares of treasury stock at $11.50 per share.		

The debit of the entry records a reduction in the equity of the stockholders. The credit records a reduction in assets. Both are equal to the cost of the treasury stock. After the entry is posted, a new balance sheet will show the reductions as in Illustration 16–2.

Curry Corporation
Balance Sheet, May 1, 19—

Assets		Capital	
Cash	$ 18,500	Common stock, $10 par	
Other assets	95,000	value, authorized and issued 10,000 shares of which 1,000 are in the treasury	$100,000
		Retained earnings of which $11,500 is restricted by the purchase of treasury stock	25,000
		Total	$125,000
		Less cost of treasury stock	11,500
Total assets	$113,500	Total capital	$113,500

Illustration 16–2

Notice in the second balance sheet that the cost of the treasury stock appears in the stockholders' equity section as a deduction from common stock and retained earnings. In comparing the two balance sheets, notice that the treasury stock purchase reduces both assets and stockholders' equity by the $11,500 cost of the stock. Also, observe that the dollar amount of issued stock remains at $100,000 and is unchanged from the first balance sheet. The amount of *issued stock* is not changed by the purchase of treasury stock. However, the purchase does reduce *outstanding stock*. In Curry Corporation, the purchase reduced the outstanding stock from 10,000 to 9,000 shares.

There is a distinction between issued stock and outstanding stock. Issued stock may or may not be outstanding. Outstanding stock is stock that has been issued and is currently outstanding. Only outstanding stock is effective stock, receives cash dividends, and is given a vote in the meetings of stockholders.

Restricting retained earnings by the purchase of treasury stock

The purchase of treasury stock by a corporation has the same effect on its assets and stockholders' equity as the payment of a cash dividend. Both transfer corporation assets to stockholders and thereby reduce assets and stockholders' equity. Consequently, in most states a corporation may purchase treasury stock or it may pay cash dividends, but the sum of both cannot exceed the amount of its retained earnings available for dividends.

Unlike the payment of a cash dividend, the purchase of treasury stock does not reduce the balance of the Retained Earnings account. However, the purchase does place a restriction on the amount of retained earnings available for dividends. Note how the restriction is shown in Illustration 16–2. It is also commonly shown by means of a balance sheet footnote. The restriction was once shown in the accounts by transferring an amount of retained earnings from the Retained Earnings account to an account titled Retained Earnings Restricted by the Purchase of Treasury Stock. However, this is seldom done today.

REISSUING TREASURY STOCK

When treasury stock is reissued, it may be reissued at cost, above cost, or below cost. If reissued at cost, the entry to record the transaction is the reverse of the entry used to record the purchase.

Although treasury stock may be sold at cost, it is commonly sold at a price either above or below cost. When sold above cost, the amount received in excess of cost is credited to a contributed capital account called "Contributed Capital, Treasury Stock Transactions." For example, if Curry Corporation sells for $12 per share 500 of the treasury shares purchased at $11.50 per share, the entry to record the transaction appears as follows:

June	3	Cash	6,000.00	
		Contributed Capital, Treasury Stock		
		Transactions		250.00
		Treasury Stock		5,750.00
		Sold at $12 per share 500 treasury shares		
		that cost $11.50 per share.		

When treasury stock is reissued at a price below cost, the entry to record the sale depends upon whether or not there is contributed capital from previous treasury stock transactions. If there is no such contributed capital, the "loss" is debited to Retained Earnings. However, if there is such contributed capital, the "loss" is debited to the account of this contributed capital to the extent of its balance. Any remainder is then debited to Retained Earnings. For example, if Curry Corporation sells its remaining 500 shares of treasury stock at $10 per share, the entry to record the sale is:

July	10	Cash	5,000.00	
		Contributed Capital, Treasury Stock		
		Transactions	250.00	
		Retained Earnings	500.00	
		Treasury Stock		5,750.00
		Sold at $10 per share 500 treasury shares		
		that cost $11.50 per share.		

RETIREMENT OF STOCK

A corporation may purchase shares of its own stock which are not to be held as treasury stock but for immediate retirement, with the shares being permanently canceled upon receipt. Such action is permissible if the interests of creditors and other stockholders are not jeopardized.

When stock is purchased for retirement, all capital items related to the shares being retired are removed from the accounts. If there is a "gain" on the transaction, it should be credited to contributed capital. On the other hand, a loss should be debited to Retained Earnings.

For example, assume a corporation originally issued its $10 par value common stock at $12 per share, with the premium being credited to Premium on Common Stock. If the corporation later purchased for retirement 1,000 shares of this stock at the price for which it was issued, the entry to record the retirement is:

Apr.	12	Common Stock	10,000.00	
		Premium on Common Stock	2,000.00	
		Cash		12,000.00
		Purchased and retired 1,000 shares of common stock at $12 per share.		

If on the other hand the corporation paid $11 per share instead of $12, the entry for the retirement is:

Apr.	12	Common Stock	10,000.00	
		Premium on Common Stock	2,000.00	
		Cash		11,000.00
		Contributed Capital from the Retirement of Common Stock		1,000.00
		Purchased and retired 1,000 shares of common stock at $11 per share.		

Or if the corporation paid $15 per share, the entry for the purchase and retirement is:

Apr.	12	Common Stock	10,000.00	
		Premium on Common Stock	2,000.00	
		Retained Earnings	3,000.00	
		Cash		15,000.00
		Purchased and retired 1,000 shares of common stock at $15 per share.		

CONTRIBUTED CAPITAL AND DIVIDENDS

Generally, contributed capital may not be returned to stockholders as dividends. However, in some states dividends may be debited or charged to certain contributed capital accounts. Seldom may dividends be charged against the par or stated value of the outstanding stock. However, the exact contributed capital accounts to which a corporation may charge dividends depend upon the laws of the state of its incorporation. For this reason it is usually wise for a board of directors to secure competent legal advice before voting to charge dividends to any contributed capital account.

APPROPRIATIONS OF RETAINED EARNINGS

A corporation may *appropriate retained earnings* for some special purpose or purposes and show the amounts appropriated as separate items in the equity section of its balance sheet. The appropriations may be voluntarily made by the board of directors or required by a contract. Such appropriations may be recorded by transferring portions of retained earnings from the Retained Earnings account to accounts such as "Retained Earnings Appropriated for Contingencies" or "Retained Earnings Appropriated for Plant Expansion."

The appropriations do not reduce total retained earnings. Rather, their purpose is to inform balance sheet readers that portions of retained earnings are not available for the declaration of cash dividends. When the contingency or other reason for an appropriation has passed, the appropriation account is eliminated by returning its balance to the Retained Earnings account.

Appropriations of retained earnings were once common, but such appropriations are seldom seen on balance sheets today. Today, the same information is conveyed with less chance of misunderstanding by means of footnotes accompanying the financial statements.

PARENT AND SUBSIDIARY CORPORATIONS

Corporations commonly own and control other corporations. For example, if Corporation A owns more than 50% of the voting stock of Corporation B, Corporation A can elect Corporation B's board of directors and thus control its activities and resources. In such a situation the controlling corporation, Corporation A, is known as the *parent company* and Corporation B is called a *subsidiary.*

When a corporation owns all the outstanding stock of a subsidiary, it can take over the subsidiary's assets, cancel its stock, and fuse the subsidiary into the parent company. However, there are often financial, legal, and tax advantages in operating a large business as a parent company controlling one or more subsidiaries rather than as a single corporation. Actually, most large companies are parent corporations owning one or more subsidiaries.

When a business is operated as a parent company with subsidiaries, separate accounting records are kept for each corporation. Also, from a legal viewpoint the parent and each subsidiary is a separate entity with all the rights, duties, and responsibilities of a separate corporation. However, investors in the parent company depend on the parent to present a set of *consolidated statements* which show the results of all operations under the parent's control, including those of any subsidiaries. In these statements the assets and liabilities of all affiliated companies are combined on a single balance sheet and their revenues and expenses are combined on a single income statement, as though the business were in fact a single company.

CONSOLIDATED BALANCE SHEETS

When parent and subsidiary balance sheets are consolidated, duplications in items are eliminated so that the combined figures do not show more assets and equities than actually exist. For example, a parent's investment in a subsidiary is evidenced by shares of stock which are carried as an asset in the parent company's records. However, these shares actually represent an equity in the subsidiary's assets. Consequently, if the parent's investment in a subsidiary and the subsidiary's assets were both shown on the consolidated balance sheet, the same resources would be counted twice. To prevent this, the parent's investment and the subsidiary's capital accounts are offset and eliminated in preparing a consolidated balance sheet.

Likewise, a single enterprise cannot owe a debt to itself. This would be analogous to a student borrowing $20 for a date from funds saved for next semester's expenses and then preparing a balance sheet showing the $20 as both receivable from himself and payable to himself. To prevent such a double showing, intercompany debts and receivables are also eliminated in preparing a consolidated balance sheet.

Balance sheets consolidated at time of acquisition

When a parent's and a subsidiary's assets are combined in the preparation of a consolidated balance sheet, a work sheet is normally used to effect the consolidation. Illustration 16–3 shows such a work sheet. It was prepared to consolidate the accounts of Parent Company and its subsidiary, called Subsidiary Company, on January 1, 198A, the day Parent Company acquired Subsidiary Company through the purchase for cash of all its outstanding $10 par value common stock. The stock had a book value of $115,000, or $11.50 per share, which in this first illustration is the amount Parent Company is assumed to have paid for it. Explanations of the work sheet's two eliminating entries follow.

Entry (a)   On the day it acquired Subsidiary Company, Parent Company lent Subsidiary Company $10,000 for use in the subsidiary's operations. It took the subsidiary's note as evidence of the transaction. This intercompany debt was in reality a transfer of funds within the organization. Consequently, since it did not increase the total assets and total liabilities of the affiliated companies, it is eliminated by means of Entry *(a)*. To understand this entry, recall that the subsidiary's promissory note is represented by a $10,000 debit in Parent Company's Notes Receivable account. Then observe that the first credit in the Eliminations column exactly offsets and eliminates this item. Next, recall that the subsidiary's note appears as a credit in its Notes Payable account. Then observe that the $10,000 debit in the Eliminations column completes the elimination of this intercompany debt.

Parent Company and Subsidiary Company
Work Sheet for a Consolidated Balance Sheet, January 1, 198A

	Parent Company	Subsidiary Company	Eliminations		Consolidated Amounts
			Debit	Credit	
Assets					
Cash	5,000	15,000			20,000
Notes receivable	10,000			(a) 10,000	
Accounts receivable, net	20,000	13,000			33,000
Inventories	45,000	22,000			67,000
Investment in Subsidiary					
Company	115,000			(b) 115,000	
Buildings and					
equipment, net	100,000	74,000			174,000
Land	25,000	8,000			33,000
	320,000	132,000			327,000
Equities					
Accounts payable	15,000	7,000			22,000
Notes payable		10,000	(a) 10,000		
Common stock	250,000	100,000	(b) 100,000		250,000
Retained earnings	55,000	15,000	(b) 15,000		55,000
	320,000	132,000	125,000	125,000	327,000

Illustration 16–3

Entry (b) When a parent company buys a subsidiary's stock, the investment appears on the parent's balance sheet as an asset, "Investment in Subsidiary." The investment represents an equity in the subsidiary's assets. Consequently, to show both the subsidiary's assets and the investment in the assets on a consolidated balance sheet would be to show more resources than exist. As a result, on the work sheet the amount of the parent's investment (an equity in the subsidiary's assets) is offset against the subsidiary's stockholder equity accounts, which also represent an equity in the assets, and both are eliminated.

After the intercompany items are eliminated on a work sheet like Illustration 16–3, the assets of the parent and the subsidiary and the remaining equities in these assets are combined and carried into the work sheet's last column. The combined amounts are then used to prepare a consolidated balance sheet showing all the assets and equities of the parent and its subsidiary.

Parent company does not buy all of subsidiary's stock and does not pay book value

In the situation just described, Parent Company purchased all of its subsidiary's stock, paying book value for it. Often a parent company purchases less than 100% of a subsidiary's stock, and commonly pays a price either above or below book value. To illustrate such a situation, assume Parent Company purchased for cash only 80% of its subsidiary's stock rather than 100%, and that it paid $13 per share, a price $1.50 above the stock's book value.

These new assumptions result in a more complicated work sheet entry to eliminate the parent's investment and the subsidiary's stockholders' equity accounts. The entry is complicated by (1) the minority interest in the subsidiary and (2) the excess over book value paid by the parent company for the subsidiary's stock.

Minority interest When a parent buys a controlling interest in a subsidiary, the parent company is the subsidiary's majority stockholder. However, when the parent owns less than 100% of the subsidiary's stock, the subsidiary has other stockholders who own a *minority interest* in its assets and share its earnings. Consequently, when there is a minority interest, the minority interest must be set out as on the last line of Illustration 16–4 in making the work sheet entry to eliminate the stockholders' equity accounts of the subsidiary. In this case the minority stockholders have a 20% interest in the subsidiary. Consequently, 20%

Parent Company and Subsidiary Company
Work Sheet for a Consolidated Balance Sheet, January 1, 198A

	Parent Company	Subsidiary Company	Eliminations		Consolidated Amounts
			Debit	Credit	
Assets					
Cash......................	16,000	15,000			31,000
Notes receivable	10,000			(a) 10,000	
Accounts receivable, net	20,000	13,000			33,000
Inventories..................	45,000	22,000			67,000
Investment in Subsidiary Company	104,000			(b) 104,000	
Buildings and equipment, net	100,000	74,000			174,000
Land	25,000	8,000			33,000
Excess of cost over book value			(b) 12,000		12,000
	320,000	132,000			350,000
Equities					
Accounts payable	15,000	7,000			22,000
Notes payable		10,000	(a) 10,000		
Common stock	250,000	100,000	(b) 100,000		250,000
Retained earnings	55,000	15,000	(b) 15,000		55,000
Minority interest				(b) 23,000	23,000
	320,000	132,000	137,000	137,000	350,000

Illustration 16–4

of the subsidiary's common stock and retained earnings accounts [($100,000 + $15,000) × 20% = $23,000] is set out on the work sheet as the minority interest.

Excess of investment cost over book value   Parent Company paid $13 per share for its 8,000 shares of Subsidiary Company's stock. Consequently, the cost of these shares exceeded their book value by $12,000, calculated as follows:

Cost of stock (8,000 shares at $13 per share) $104,000
Book value (8,000 shares at $11.50 per share)   92,000
Excess of cost over book value .... $ 12,000

Now observe how this excess of cost over book value is set out on the work sheet in eliminating the parent's investment in the subsidiary and how it is carried into the Consolidated Amounts column as an asset.

After its completion, the consolidated amounts in the last column of the work sheet of Illustration 16–4 were used to prepare the consolidated balance sheet of Illustration 16–5. Note the treatment of the minority interest in the balance sheet. The minority stockholders have

Parent Company and Subsidiary
Consolidated Balance Sheet, January 1, 198A

Assets

Current assets:		
Cash	$31,000	
Accounts receivable, net	33,000	
Inventories	67,000	
Total current assets		$131,000
Plant and equipment:		
Buildings and equipment, net	$174,000	
Land..	33,000	
Total plant and equipment......................		207,000
Goodwill from consolidation		12,000
Total assets		$350,000

Liabilities and Stockholders' Equity

Liabilities:		
Accounts payable		$ 22,000
Minority interest		23,000
Stockholders' equity:		
Common stock.....................................	$250,000	
Retained earnings	55,000	
Total stockholders' equity		305,000
Total liabilities and stockholders' equity		$350,000

Illustration 16–5

a $23,000 equity in the consolidated assets of the affiliated companies. Many have argued that this item should be disclosed in the stockholders' equity section. Others believe it should be shown in the long-term liabilities section. Both alternatives can be found in published financial statements. However, a more common alternative is to disclose minority interest as a separate item between the liabilities and stockholders' equity sections, as is shown in Illustration 16–5.

Next observe that the $12,000 excess over book value paid by the parent company for the subsidiary's stock appears on the consolidated balance sheet as the asset, "Goodwill from consolidation." When a parent company purchases an interest in a subsidiary, it may pay more than book value for its equity because (1) certain of the subsidiary's assets are carried on the subsidiary's books at less than fair value. It also may pay more because (2) certain of the subsidiary's liabilities are carried at book values which are greater than fair values, or (3) the subsidiary's earnings prospects are good enough to justify paying more than the net fair (market) value of its assets and liabilities. In this illustration, it is assumed that the book values of Subsidiary Company's assets and liabilities are their fair values. However, Subsidiary Company's expected earnings justified paying $104,000 for an 80% equity in the subsidiary's net assets (assets less liabilities).

The APB ruled that where a company pays more than book value because the subsidiary's assets are undervalued or its liabilities are overvalued, the cost in excess of book value should be allocated to those assets and liabilities so that they are restated at fair values. After the subsidiary's assets and liabilities have been restated to reflect fair values, any remaining cost in excess of book value should be reported on the consolidated balance sheet as "Goodwill from consolidation."[4]

Occasionally, a parent company pays less than book value for its interest in a subsidiary. In such a case, since a "bargain" purchase is very unlikely, the logical reason for a price below book value is that certain of the subsidiary's assets are carried on its books at amounts in excess of fair value. In such a situation the APB ruled that the amounts at which the overvalued assets are placed on the consolidated balance sheet should be reduced accordingly.[5]

EARNINGS AND DIVIDENDS OF AN INVESTEE CORPORATION

When one corporation (the investor) buys stock of another (investee) corporation, the investee corporation continues to account for earnings and dividends just as it always did. If the investee corporation's operations are profitable, its net assets and retained earnings increase. Also,

---

[4] APB, "Business Combinations," *APB Opinion No. 16* (New York: AICPA, 1970), par. 87. Copyright (1970) by the American Institute of CPAs.

[5] Ibid., par. 91.

if it pays dividends, the dividends are paid to the investor company and any other stockholders. Furthermore, the investee corporation records the transactions that result in earnings, closes its Income Summary account, and records the declaration and payment of dividends just like any other corporation.

If a corporation acquires 20% or more of another corporation's common stock, the investor is presumed to have a significant financial influence on the investee corporation, and the investment is accounted for according to the *equity method.*[6] Note that this method is also required when the investment is so large (more than 50%) that the investee is classified as a subsidiary. Investments of less than 20% are discussed in Chapter 17.

Under the equity method, it is recognized that an investee's earnings not only increase the investee corporation's net assets but also increase the investor's equity in the assets. Consequently, under this method, when the investee reports the amount of its earnings, the investor company debits its share to its "Investment" account, and credits an account such as Earnings from Investment in XYZ Company (or Subsidiary). For example, if the subsidiary of the previous discussions earned $12,500 during the first year in which 80% of its stock was owned by Parent Company, Parent Company records its share as follows:

Dec.	31	Investment in Subsidiary Company	10,000.00	
		Earnings from Investment in Subsidiary		10,000.00
		To take up 80% of the net income reported		
		by Subsidiary Company.		

The debit of the entry records the increase in Parent Company's equity in the subsidiary. The credit causes 80% of the subsidiary's net income to appear on Parent Company's income statement as earnings from the investment. Parent Company closes the earnings to its Income Summary account and on to its Retained Earnings account just as with earnings from any investment.

In case of a loss the Parent Company debits the loss to an account called Loss from Investment in Subsidiary and credits and reduces the balance of its Investment in Subsidiary account. It then carries the loss to its Income Summary account and on to its Retained Earnings account.

Dividends paid by an investee decrease its net assets and, under the equity method, also decrease the amount of the investor's equity in the investee. For example, if the subsidiary of this discussion paid

---

[6] APB, "The Equity Method of Accounting for Investments in Common Stock," *APB Opinion No. 18* (New York: AICPA, 1971), par. 17. Copyright (1971) by the American Institute of CPAs.

a $7,500 cash dividend at the end of its first year as a subsidiary, the dividend reduced the parent company's equity in the subsidiary by 80% of the $7,500 or by $6,000. Parent Company records receipt of its share of the cash and the reduction in its equity with an entry like this:

Dec.	31	Cash	6,000.00	
		Investment in Subsidiary Company		6,000.00
		To record the receipt of 80% of the $7,500		
		dividend paid by Subsidiary Company.		

From this discussion it can be seen that a subsidiary's earnings and dividends not only affect the balance of its Retained Earnings account but also result in changes in the parent company's account, Investment in Subsidiary Company. As a result, in the years following acquisition, when consolidated balance sheets are prepared, the amounts eliminated from these accounts change as the account balances change.

CONSOLIDATED BALANCE SHEETS AT A DATE AFTER ACQUISITION

If Subsidiary Company earned $12,500 during its first year as a subsidiary and paid out $7,500 in dividends, the balance of its Retained Earnings account increased from $15,000 at the beginning of the year to $20,000 at the year-end. Consequently, $20,000 of retained earnings are eliminated on the year-end work sheet, Illustration 16–6, to consolidate the balance sheets of the companies. (To simplify the illustration, it is assumed that the liabilities of both companies are unchanged and that the subsidiary has not paid the note given Parent Company.)

To continue the explanation, Parent Company paid $104,000 for 80% of Subsidiary Company's stock and debited that amount to its Investment in Subsidiary Company account. During the year Parent Company increased this account $10,000 by taking up 80% of the subsidiary's earnings and decreased it $6,000 upon receipt of its share of the subsidiary's dividend. As a result, the account had a $108,000 year-end balance, which is the amount eliminated on the work sheet.

Two additional items in Illustration 16–6 require explanations. First, the minority interest set out on the year-end work sheet is greater than on the beginning-of-the-year work sheet (Illustration 16–4). The minority stockholders have a 20% equity in Subsidiary Company, and the $24,000 shown on the year-end work sheet is 20% of the year-end balances of the Subsidiary's Common Stock and Retained Earnings accounts. This $24,000 is $1,000 greater than the beginning-of-the-year minority interest because the subsidiary's retained earnings in-

Parent Company and Subsidiary Company
Work Sheet for a Consolidated Balance Sheet, December 31, 198A

	Parent Company	Subsidiary Company	Eliminations		Consolidated Amounts
			Debit	Credit	
Assets					
Cash......................	14,000	10,000			24,000
Notes receivable	10,000			(a) 10,000	
Accounts receivable, net	27,000	14,000			41,000
Inventories.................	50,000	29,000			79,000
Investment in Subsidiary					
Company	108,000			(b) 108,000	
Buildings and					
equipment, net	95,000	76,000			171,000
Land	25,000	8,000			33,000
Excess of cost					
over book value			(b) 12,000		12,000
	329,000	137,000			360,000
Equities					
Accounts payable	15,000	7,000			22,000
Notes payable		10,000	(a) 10,000		
Common stock	250,000	100,000	(b) 100,000		250,000
Retained earnings	64,000	20,000	(b) 20,000		64,000
Minority interest				(b) 24,000	24,000
	329,000	137,000	142,000	142,000	360,000

Illustration 16–6

creased $5,000 during the year and the minority stockholder's share of the increase is 20% or $1,000. Second, the $12,000 amount set out as the excess cost of Parent Company's investment over its book value is, in this illustration, the same on the end-of-the-year work sheet as on the work sheet at the beginning. The APB ruled that such excess cost or "goodwill" should be amortized by systematic charges to income over the accounting periods estimated to be benefited.[7] An explanation of the amortization entries is left to a more advanced text.

OTHER CONSOLIDATED STATEMENTS

Consolidated income statements and consolidated retained earnings statements are also prepared for affiliated companies. However, preparation of these require procedures a discussion of which must be deferred to an advanced accounting course. Knowledge of the procedures is not necessary to a general understanding of such statements. The

---

[7] APB, "Intangible Assets," *APB Opinion No. 17* (New York: AICPA, 1970), pars. 27–31. Copyright (1970) by the American Institute of CPAs.

Betco Corporation
Consolidated Balance Sheet, December 31, 198A

Assets

Current assets:
Cash		$ 15,000
Marketable securities		5,000
Accounts receivable	$ 50,000	
Less allowance for doubtful accounts	1,000	49,000
Merchandise inventory		115,000
Subscriptions receivable, common stock		15,000
Prepaid expenses		1,000
Total current assets		$200,000

Long-term investments:
Bond sinking fund		$ 15,000
Toledo Corporation common stock		5,000
Total long-term investments		20,000

Plant assets:
Land		$ 50,000
Buildings	$285,000	
Less accumulated depreciation	30,000	255,000
Store equipment	$ 85,000	
Less accumulated depreciation	20,000	65,000
Total plant assets		370,000

Intangible assets:
Goodwill from consolidation		10,000
Total assets		$600,000

Liabilities

Current liabilities:
Notes payable	$ 10,000	
Accounts payable	14,000	
State and federal income taxes payable	16,000	
Total current liabilities		$ 40,000

Long-term liabilities:
First 8% real estate mortgage bonds, due in 199E	$100,000	
Less unamortized discount based on the 8¼% market rate for bond interest prevailing on the date of issue...........	2,000	98,000
Total liabilities		$138,000
Minority interest		15,000

Stockholders' Equity

Contributed capital:
Common stock, $10 par value, authorized 50,000 shares, issued 30,000 shares of which 1,000 are in the treasury	$300,000	
Unissued common stock subscribed, 2,500 shares	25,000	
Capital contributed by the stockholders in excess of the par value of their shares	33,000	
Total contributed capital	$358,000	
Retained earnings (Note 1)	105,000	
Total contributed and retained capital	$463,000	
Less cost of treasury stock	16,000	
Total stockholders' equity		447,000
Total liabilities and stockholder's equity		$600,000

Note 1: Retained earnings in the amount of $31,000 is restricted under an agreement with the corporation's bondholders and because of the purchase of treasury stock, leaving $74,000 of retained earnings not so restricted.

Illustration 16–7

reader should recognize that all duplications in items and all profit arising from intercompany transactions are eliminated in their preparation. Also, the amounts of net income and retained earnings which are reported in consolidated statements are equal to the amounts recorded by the parent under the equity method.

PURCHASE VERSUS A POOLING OF INTERESTS

The method of consolidation described thus far is called the *purchase method*. Where a parent company acquired its interest in a subsidiary by paying cash, as here, or by issuing bonds or preferred stock, it is assumed that the subsidiary's shareholders sold their interest in the subsidiary and consolidated statements are prepared by the purchase method.

If a parent company issues common stock to acquire a subsidiary, the transaction may still be regarded as a purchase requiring the preparation of consolidated statements by the purchase method. However, if common stock is issued and certain other criteria are met,[8] consolidated statements are prepared in accordance with the *pooling-of-interests method*. Under this method it is assumed that a sale did not occur and that the stockholders of the parent and subsidiary companies combined or pooled their interests to form the consolidated company.

Time and space do not permit a discussion of pooling-of-interests consolidations. Such a discussion must be deferred to an advanced accounting or finance course.

THE CORPORATION BALANCE SHEET

A number of balance sheet sections have been illustrated in this and previous chapters. To bring together as much of the information from all these sections as space allows, the balance sheet of Betco Corporation is shown in Illustration 16–7.

Betco Corporation's balance sheet is a consolidated balance sheet, as indicated in the title and by the items "Goodwill from consolidation" and "Minority interst." In preparing the balance sheet, Betco Corporation's investment in its subsidiary was eliminated. Consequently, the Toledo Corporation stock shown on the consolidated balance sheet represents an investment in an unconsolidated (outside) company that is not a subsidiary of either Betco or Betco's subsidiary.

GLOSSARY

Appropriated retained earnings. Retained earnings earmarked for a special use as a means of informing stockholders that assets from earnings equal to the appropriations are unavailable for dividends.

---

[8] *APB Opinion No. 16*, pars. 45–49.

Earned surplus. A synonym for retained earnings, no longer in use.

Equity method of accounting for stock investments. The investment is recorded at total cost, investor's equity in subsequent earnings of the investee increases the investment account, and subsequent dividends of the investee reduce the investment account.

Minority interest. Stockholders' equity in a subsidiary not owned by the parent corporation.

Parent company. A corporation that owns a controlling interest (more than 50% of the voting stock is required) in another corporation.

Pooling of interests. A combination between two corporations in which the stockholders of the two companies combine their interests to form the consolidated company without either stockholder group selling its interest.

Purchase method of acquiring a subsidiary. A combination between two corporations where the shareholders of one company sell their interest, taking cash, bonds, and sometimes shares of the parent company's stock in payment.

Small stock dividend. A stock dividend 25% or less of a corporation's previously outstanding shares.

Stock dividend. A distribution by a corporation of shares of its own common stock to its common stockholders without any consideration being received in return therefor.

Stock split. The act of a corporation of calling in its stock and issuing more than one new share in the place of each old share previously outstanding.

Subsidiary. A corporation that is controlled by another (parent) corporation because the parent owns more than 50% of the subsidiary's voting stock.

Treasury stock. Issued stock that has been reacquired by the issuing corporation.

QUESTIONS FOR CLASS DISCUSSION

1. What are the effects in terms of assets and stockholders' equity of the declaration and distribution of (a) a cash dividend and (b) a stock dividend?
2. What is the difference between a stock dividend and a stock split?
3. Courts have held that a dividend in the stock of the distributing corporation is not taxable income to its recipients. Why?
4. If a balance sheet is prepared between the date of declaration and the date of distribution of a dividend, how should the dividend be shown if it is to be distributed in (a) cash and (b) stock?
5. What is treasury stock? How is it like unissued stock? How does it differ from unissued stock? What is the legal significance of this difference?
6. General Plastics Corporation bought 1,000 shares of Capital Steel Corpora-

tion stock and turned it over to its treasurer for safekeeping. Is this treasury stock? Why or why not?

7. What is the effect of a treasury stock purchase in terms of assets and stockholder's equity?
8. Distinguish between issued stock and outstanding stock.
9. Why do state laws place limitations on the purchase of treasury stock?
10. What are consolidated financial statements?
11. What account balances must be eliminated in preparing a consolidated balance sheet? Why are they eliminated?
12. Why would a parent corporation pay more than book value for the stock of a subsidiary?
13. When a parent pays more than book value for the stock of a subsidiary, how should this additional cost be allocated in the consolidated balance sheet?
14. What is meant by "minority interest?" Where is this item disclosed on a consolidated balance sheet?
15. When an investor corporation uses the equity method to account for its investment in an investee, what recognition is given by the investor corporation to the income or loss reported by the investee? What recognition is given to dividends declared by the investee?

CLASS EXERCISES

Exercise 16–1

The stockholders' equity section of a corporation's balance sheet appeared as follows on April 1:

Stockholders' Equity

Common stock, $5 par value, 250,000 shares authorized, 200,000 shares issued	$1,000,000
Premium on common stock	200,000
Total contributed capital	$1,200,000
Retained earnings	270,000
Total stockholders' equity	$1,470,000

On that date, when the stock was selling for $7.50 per share, the corporation's directors voted a 5% stock dividend distributable on May 15 to the May 1 stockholders of record. The dividend's declaration and distribution had no apparent effect on the market price of the shares, since they were still selling at $7.50 per share as of the close of business on May 15.

Required:

1. Give the entries to record the declaration and distribution of the dividend.
2. Under the assumption that Jessie Bork owned 1,000 shares of the stock on April 1 and received the proper number of dividend shares on May 15, prepare a schedule showing the numbers of shares held by this stockholder on April 1 and May 15, with their total book values and total market values.

Exercise 16–2

On February 5 the stockholders' equity section of a corporation's balance sheet appeared as follows:

Stockholders' Equity

Common stock, $10 par value, 25,000 shares		
authorized and issued	$250,000	
Retained earnings	65,000	
Total stockholders' equity		$315,000

On the date of the equity section the corporation purchased 1,000 shares of treasury stock at $13.50 per share. Give the entry to record the purchase and prepare a stockholders' equity section as it would appear immediately after the purchase.

Exercise 16–3

On February 15 the corporation of Exercise 16–2 sold 400 shares of its treasury stock at $14 per share, and on March 10 it sold the remaining treasury shares at $12.75 per share. Give the entries to record the sales.

Exercise 16–4

On January 2 Company B had the following stockholders' equity:

Common stock, $10 par value, 10,000 shares		
authorized and outstanding	$100,000	
Retained earnings	20,000	
Total stockholders' equity		$120,000

a. Under the assumption that Company A purchased all of Company B's stock on January 2, paying $12 per share, and that a work sheet to consolidate the two companies' balance sheets was prepared, give the entry made on this work sheet to eliminate Company A's investment and Company B's stockholders' equity accounts.

b. Make the contrary assumption that Company A purchased only 90% of Company B's stock, paying $14 per share, and give the entry to eliminate Company A's investment and Company B's stockholders' equity accounts.

Exercise 16–5

Assume again that Company A of Exercise 16–4 purchased for cash 90% of Company B's stock, paying $14 per share. Also assume that Company B earned $10,000 during the year following its acquisition, paid out $8,000 of these earnings in dividends, and retained the balance for use in its operations. *(a)* Give the entry made by Company A to take up its share of Company B's earnings. *(b)* Give the entry made by Company A to record its share of the $8,000 in dividends paid by Company B. *(c)* Give the work sheet entry made to eliminate Company A's investment and Company B's stockholders' equity accounts at the end of the year following acquisition.

PROBLEMS

Problem 16-1

On January 1, 198A, stockholders' equity in Hilltop Corporation consisted of the following items:

Common stock, $10 par value, 50,000 shares autho-
rized, 40,000 shares issued and outstanding $400,000
Premium on common stock 60,000
Retained earnings 120,000
　　　　Total stockholders' equity $580,000

During the year the corporation completed these transactions affecting stockholders' equity:

Apr. 4　Purchased 1,000 shares of treasury stock at $14 per share.
June 20　The board of directors voted a $0.25 per share cash dividend payable on July 15 to the July 10 stockholders of record.
July 15　Paid the dividend declared in June.
　　22　Sold 500 of the treasury shares at $17 per share.
Oct. 12　Sold the remaining treasury shares at $13 per share.
Dec. 18　The board of directors voted a $0.25 per share cash dividend and a 5% stock dividend payable on January 15 to the January 10 stockholders of record. The stock was selling at $12.50 per share.
　　31　Closed the Income Summary account and carried the company's $28,000 net income to Retained Earnings.

Required:

1. Prepare general journal entries to record the transactions.
2. Prepare a retained earnings statement for the year and the stockholders' equity section of the company's year-end balance sheet.

Problem 16-2

On October 31, 198A, stockholders' equity in a corporation consisted of the following:

Common stock, $25 par value, 10,000 shares
authorized, 8,000 shares issued $200,000
Premium on common stock 20,000
　　　　Total contributed capital $220,000
Retained earnings 132,000
　　　　Total stockholders' equity $352,000

During the succeeding three months the corporation completed these transactions:

Nov. 1　Declared a $0.25 per share dividend on the common stock, payable on November 28 to the November 20 stockholders of record.
　　28　Paid the dividend declared on November 1.
Dec. 3　Declared a 25% stock dividend, distributable on December 29 to the December 21 stockholders of record. The stock was selling for

$45 per share, and the directors voted to use that amount in recording the dividend.

Dec. 29   Distributed the stock dividend previously declared.

      31   Closed the Income Summary account on a $30,000 after-tax income for the year.

Jan.   5   The board of directors voted to split the corporation's stock 2½ for 1 by calling in the old stock and issuing 25 shares of $10 par value common stock for each 10 of the old $25 par value shares held. The stockholders voted approval of the split and authorization of the required 25,000 new shares; all legal requirements were met, and the split was completed on February 1.

Required:

1. Prepare general journal entries to record the transactions and to close the Income summary account at the year-end.
2. Under the assumption Ted Hall owned 200 of the $25 par value shares on October 31 and neither bought nor sold any shares during the three-month period, prepare a schedule showing in one column the book value per share of the corporation's stock and in a second column the book value of Hall's shares at the close of business on each of October 31, November 1, November 28, December 2, December 29, December 31, and February 1.
3. Prepare the stockholders' equity section of the corporation's balance sheet as of December 31, 198A, and prepare a second stockholders' equity section as of February 1, 198B.

Problem 16–3

A corporation received a charter granting it the right to issue 25,000 shares of $10 par value common stock and 1,000 shares of $100 par value, 7% cumulative and nonparticipating, preferred stock which is redeemable at par and on which a $3.50 dividend is payable semiannually. On May 31 of the year in which the charter was granted, 20,000 shares of the common stock were subscribed at $12 per share. One fourth of that amount accompanied the subscription contracts, and all subscribers paid their remaining balances 30 days thereafter, on which date the stock was issued. The preferred stock was issued at par for cash on the same day. The company prospered from the beginning and paid all dividends on its preferred stock plus dividends on its common stock.

On October 10 of its fourth year when the corporation had a $43,500 balance in its Retained Earnings account and its common stock was selling at $16 per share, the board of directors voted a 5% common stock dividend which was distributed on November 20 to the November 15 stockholders of record.

One year later, on November 20, when the corporation had a $52,000 balance in its Retained Earnings account, the common stock was split two for one by calling in the old $10 par value shares and issuing two $5 par value shares for each old share held.

Near the end of the fifth year, on November 27, the corporation declared the regular $3.50 per share semiannual dividend on its preferred stock and a $0.10 per share dividend on its common stock, payable on December 31 to the December 20 stockholders of record.

Required:

1. Prepare general journal entries to record—
   a. The sale and issuance of the original common stock through subscriptions.
   b. The sale and issuance of the preferred stock.
   c. The declaration and distribution of the common stock dividend.
   d. The declaration and distribution of the fifth-year cash dividends.
2. Dale Nash owned 100 shares of the corporation's common stock on the record date of the fourth-year common stock dividend. Under the assumption the market value of the stock was not affected by the stock dividend and was still $16 per share on the day the dividend was distributed and that Nash neither bought nor sold any shares during the year, prepare a schedule showing the shares held by Nash, their total book value, and their total market value on the day the dividend was declared and on the day it was distributed. (Remember preferred dividends do not accrue.)
3. Prepare the stockholders' equity section of the corporation's balance sheet as of the close of business on the day the $5 par value shares were distributed. (Assume that 50,000 of these shares were authorized.)

Problem 16-4

On May 10 of the current year Alpha Company gained control of Beta Company through the purchase of 85% of Beta Company's outstanding $5 par value common stock at $6.50 per share. On that date Beta Company owed Alpha Company $4,000 for merchandise purchased on credit and $10,000 it had borrowed by giving a promissory note. The condensed May 10 balance sheets of the two companies carried these items:

ALPHA AND BETA COMPANIES
Balance Sheets, May 10, 19—

Assets	*Alpha Company*	*Beta Company*
Cash	$ 6,500	$ 10,500
Note receivable, Beta Company	10,000	
Accounts receivable, net	29,000	24,500
Inventories	42,000	35,000
Investment in Beta Company	110,500	
Equipment, net	80,000	70,000
Buildings, net	85,000	
Land	20,000	
Total assets	$383,000	$140,000

Equities		
Note payable, Alpha Company		$ 10,000
Accounts payable	$ 20,000	10,000
Common stock	250,000	100,000
Retained earnings	113,000	20,000
Total equities	$383,000	$140,000

Prepare a consolidated balance sheet for Alpha Company and its subsidiary, and write a short explanation of why consolidated statements are prepared and explain the principles of consolidation.

Problem 16–5

The following items appeared in the first two columns of a work sheet prepared to consolidate the balance sheets of Company X and Company Y on the day Company X gained control of Company Y by purchasing for cash 8,000 shares of its $10 par value common stock at $12 per share.

Assets	Company X	Company Y
Cash	$ 7,000	$ 12,000
Note receivable, Company Y	5,000	
Accounts receivable, net	32,000	28,000
Inventories	45,000	30,000
Investment in Company Y	96,000	
Equipment, net	75,000	60,000
Buildings, net	80,000	
Land	20,000	
Total assets	$360,000	$130,000

Equities		
Accounts payable	$ 28,000	$ 10,000
Note payable, Company X		5,000
Common stock	250,000	100,000
Retained earnings	82,000	15,000
Total equities	$360,000	$130,000

At the time Company X acquired control of Company Y it took Company Y's note in exchange for $5,000 in cash and it sold and delivered to it $3,000 of equipment at cost on open account (account receivable). Both transactions are reflected in the foregoing accounts. Management of Company X believed that Company Y's earnings prospects justified the $12 per share paid for its stock.

Required:

1. Prepare a work sheet for consolidating the balance sheets of the two companies and prepare a consolidated balance sheet.
2. Under the assumption Company Y earned $11,000 during the first year after it was acquired by Company X, paid out $6,000 of the earnings in dividends, and retained the balance in its operations, give in general journal form the entries made by Company X (a) to take up its share of Company Y's earnings and (b) to record the receipt of its share of the dividends paid by Company Y. Also (c) give the entry to eliminate Company X's investment in Company Y and Company Y's stockholders' equity accounts on the end-of-the-first-year work sheet to consolidate the balance sheets of the two companies.

ALTERNATE PROBLEMS

Problem 16–1A

The stockholders' equity in Phoenix Corporation consisted of the following items on January 1, 198A:

Common stock, $25 par value, 10,000 shares autho-
 rized, 8,000 shares issued and outstanding $200,000
Premium on common stock 40,000
Retained earnings 85,000
  Total stockholders' equity $325,000

During 198A the company completed these transactions affecting its stock-holders' equity:

Apr. 10 The directors voted a $0.50 per share cash dividend payable on May 15 to its May 10 stockholders of record.

May 15 Paid the previously declared cash dividend.

Aug. 21 Purchased 500 shares of treasury stock at $40 per share.

Oct. 11 The directors voted a $0.50 per share cash dividend payable on November 15 to the November 10 stockholders of record.

Nov. 15 Paid the previously declared cash dividend.

  25 Sold the 500 treasury shares at $45 per share.

Dec. 12 The directors voted a 5% stock dividend distributable on January 15 to the January 10 stockholders of record. The stock was selling at $45 per share.

  31 Closed the Income Summary account and carried the company's $32,000 net income to Retained Earnings.

Required:

1. Prepare general journal entries to record the transactions.
2. Prepare a retained earnings statement for the year and the stockholders' equity section of the corporation's year-end balance sheet.

Problem 16–2A

On September 30, 198A, stockholders' equity in a corporation consisted of the following:

Common stock, $10 par value, 50,000 shares
 authorized, 40,000 shares issued $400,000
Premium on common stock 20,000
  Total contributed capital $420,000
Retained earnings 192,000
  Total stockholders' equity $612,000

On October 1, 198A, the corporation's board of directors declared a $0.10 per share cash dividend payable on October 25 to the October 20 stockholders of record. On November 1 the board declared a 25% stock dividend distributable on November 25 to the November 20 stockholders of record. The stock was selling at $16 per share on the day of the declaration, and the board voted to use that price in recording the dividend. The corporation earned $40,000, after taxes, during 198A; and on January 2, 198B, the board voted to split the stock two for one by calling in the old shares and issuing each stockholder two shares of $5 par value common stock for each $10 share previously held. The stockholders voted to approve the split and the authorization of the necessary 100,000 new shares; all legal requirements were fulfilled, and the split was completed on January 30.

Required:

1. Prepare general journal entries to record the transactions and to close the Income Summary account.
2. Under the assumption that Ted Gage owned 400 shares of the corporation's stock on September 30 and neither bought nor sold any shares during the next six months, prepare a schedule showing the book value per share of the corporation's stock in one column and the book value of all of Gage's shares in a second column at the close of business on September 30, October 1, October 25, October 31, November 25, January 1, and January 30.
3. Prepare the stockholders' equity section of the corporation's balance sheet as of the close of business on December 31, and prepare another equity section as of the close of business on January 30.

Problem 16–3A

Stockholders' equity in Potter Corporation on October 25 consisted of the following:

Common stock, $5 par value, 500,000 shares authorized, 400,000 shares issued	$2,000,000	
Premium on common stock	200,000	
Retained earnings	2,024,000	
Total stockholders' equity		$4,224,000

On the equity section date, when the stock was selling at $12 per share, the corporation's directors voted a 20% stock dividend, distributable on November 30 to the November 20 stockholders of record. The directors also voted a $0.45 per share annual cash dividend payable on December 15 to the December 1 stockholders of record. The amount of the latter dividend was a disappointment to some stockholders, since the company had paid a $0.50 per share annual cash dividend for a number of years.

Walter Nash owned 1,000 shares of the corporation's stock on October 25, which he had purchased a number of years previously, and as a result he received his dividend shares. He continued to hold all of his shares until after he received the December 15 cash dividend. However, he did note that his stock had a $12 per share market value on October 25, a market value it held until the close of business on November 20, when the market value declined to $10.50 per share.

Required:

Give the entries to record the declaration and payment of the dividends involved here, and answer these questions:

a. What was the book value of Nash's total shares on October 25, and what was the book value on November 30, after he received his dividend shares?
b. What fraction of the corporation did Nash own on October 25, and what fraction did he own on November 30?
c. What was the market value of Nash's total shares on October 25, and what was the market value at the close of business on November 20?
d. What did Nash gain from the stock dividend?

Problem 16–4A

The following items appeared in the first two columns of a work sheet prepared to consolidate the balance sheets of Company S and Company T on the day Company S gained control of Company T by purchasing 3,600 shares of its $25 par value common stock at $35 per share:

Assets	Company S	Company T
Cash	$ 8,000	$ 12,000
Note receivable, Company T	5,000	
Accounts receivable, net	37,000	22,000
Inventories	35,000	32,000
Investment in Company T ....,......	126,000	
Equipment, net	75,000	70,000
Buildings, net	100,000	
Land	25,000	
Total assets	$411,000	$136,000

Equities		
Note payable, Company S		$ 5,000
Accounts payable	$ 24,000	11,000
Common stock	300,000	100,000
Premium on common stock	30,000	5,000
Retained earnings	57,000	15,000
Total equities	$411,000	$136,000

At the time Company S gained control of Company T it took Company T's note in exchange for equipment that cost Company S $5,000 and it also sold and delivered $2,000 of inventory at cost to Company T on credit. Both transactions are reflected in the foregoing accounts.

Required:

Prepare a consolidated balance sheet for Company S and its subsidiary. Then write a short explanation of why consolidated statements are prepared and the principles of consolidation.

Problem 16–5A

The following assets and equities appeared on the balance sheets of Company A and Company B on the day Company A acquired control of Company B by purchasing 8,500 shares of its $10 par value common stock for cash at $13 per share:

Assets	Company A	Company B
Cash	$ 9,500	$ 9,000
Accounts receivable	39,000	21,000
Allowance for doubtful accounts	(3,000)	(2,000)
Inventories	40,000	32,000
Investment in Company B	110,500	
Equipment	85,000	80,000
Accumulated depreciation, equipment	(14,000)	(5,000)
Buildings	90,000	
Accumulated depreciation, buildings	(12,000)	
Land	15,000	
Total assets	$360,000	$135,000

Equities

Accounts payable	$ 27,000	$ 15,000
Note payable	10,000	
Common stock	250,000	100,000
Retained earnings	73,000	20,000
Total equities	$360,000	$135,000

Included in the items is a $5,000 debt of Company B to Company A for the sale and delivery of some equipment at cost on the day Company A acquired control of Company B. The sale was an open account (account receivable). Management of Company A believed Company B's earnings prospects justified the $13 per share paid for its stock.

Required:

1. Enter the items on a work sheet and consolidate them for preparation of a consolidated balance sheet.
2. Prepare a consolidated balance sheet for Company A and its subsidiary.
3. Under the assumption that Company B earned $10,000 during the first year after it was acquired by Company A, paid out $6,000 of the earnings in dividends, and retained the balance in its operations, give in general journal form the entries made by Company A *(a)* to take up its share of Company B's earnings and *(b)* to record receipt of its share of the dividends paid by Company B. Also *(c)* give the entry to eliminate Company A's investment in Company B and Company B's stockholders' equity accounts on the end-of-the-first-year work sheet to consolidate the balance sheets of the two companies.

PROVOCATIVE PROBLEMS

Provocative problem 16–1
Holloway Corporation

The equity sections of Holloway Corporation's 198A and 198B balance sheets carried the shareholders' equity items shown below.

On March 15, June 12, September 17, and again on December 14, 198B, the corporation's board of directors declared $0.20 per share dividends on the outstanding stock. The treasury stock was purchased on July 20. On September 17, when the stock was selling at $21 per share, the corporation declared a 5% stock dividend on its outstanding shares. The new shares were issued on October 20.

Shareholders' Equity
As of December 31, 198A

Common stock, $10 par value, 150,000 shares		
authorized, 100,000 shares issued	$1,000,000	
Premium on common stock	150,000	
Total contributed capital	$1,150,000	
Retained earnings	655,500	
Total shareholders' equity		$1,805,500

Shareholders' Equity
As of December 31, 198B

Common stock, $10 par value, 150,000 shares
   authorized, 104,900 shares issued of which
   2,000 are in the treasury $1,049,000
Premium on common stock   203,900
       Total contributed capital $1,252,900
Retained earnings of which $41,000 is restricted
   by the purchase of treasury stock   665,820
       Total $1,918,720
Less cost of treasury stock   41,000
       Total shareholders' equity $1,877,720

Under the assumption there were no transactions affecting retained earnings other than the ones given, determine the corporation's net income. Present calculations to prove your net income figure.

Provocative problem 16–2
Detrick Stores, Inc.

Detrick Stores, Inc., operates six hardware stores in a western city and its suburbs. Stockholders' equity in the corporation consists of 50,000 shares of $10 par value common stock, all owned by Carlos Detrick, his wife, and only son, and approximately $800,000 of retained earnings. Mr. Detrick began the business 32 years ago with one store, and the business has grown to its present size primarily from the retention of assets from earnings. The company has no long-term debt and only normal amounts of accounts payable, short-term bank loans, and accrued payables. It has an excellent reputation with its creditors and has always paid its debts on time.

An opportunity to expand the number of the company's stores from six to eight has recently arisen, but the expansion will make it necessary to borrow $300,000 by issuing a ten-year mortgage note. The company has never before borrowed to an extent that made the issuance of financial statements to outsiders necessary. Actually, since all the company's stock is owned by the three members of the Detrick family and Carlos Detrick has always been most secretive about his business affairs, the only people who have ever seen the company's financial statements are the family members, a very few employees, and some internal revenue service people. Consequently, when Carlos Detrick was told by the company's bank that it could not consider the loan unless it was provided with detailed financial statements for the past five years and audited statements for the most recent year, he was ready to call off the expansion. However, after additional consideration he changed his position to a willingness to have the audit and to provide the balance sheets for the most recent five years, but he was unwilling to provide income statements or retained earnings statements.

If the balance sheets are detailed and the last one is audited, what information will they give the bank? Will this information be sufficient to justify the loan? If you were the bank's loan officer and sought to compromise with Mr. Detrick in order to secure more financial information without receiving summarized or complete income statements and retained earnings statements, what information would you seek?

After studying Chapter 17, you should be able to:

☐ State the criteria for classifying stock investments as current assets or as long-term investments and the criteria for using the cost method of accounting versus the equity method.

☐ Record and maintain the accounts for stock investments according to the cost method and explain the application of the lower of cost or market rule.

☐ State the difference between a share of stock and a bond and the advantages and disadvantages of securing capital by issuing bonds.

☐ Use present value tables to calculate the premium or discount on a bond issue.

☐ Prepare entries to account for bonds issued between interest dates at par.

☐ Prepare entries to account for bonds sold on their date of issue at par, at a discount, and at a premium.

☐ Explain the purpose and operation of a bond sinking fund and prepare entries to account for the operation of such a fund.

☐ Define or explain the words and phrases listed in the chapter Glossary.

Corporations: Stock investments and bonds payable

■ The previous chapter included discussions of the equity method of accounting and of consolidated statements. As was explained, the equity method is used only when the investor can significantly influence the investee; this usually means that the investor owns 20% or more of the investee's common stock. Consolidated statements are only prepared if the investor has a controlling interest in the investee; this requires the investor to own more than 50% of the investee. In the present chapter, investments are considered where the investor does not have a significant influence on the investee. Generally, this means that the investor owns less than 20% of the investee's outstanding common stock. The issuance of bonds payable by a corporation is also examined in this chapter.

STOCKS AS INVESTMENTS

Most of the stock transactions discussed in previous chapters have been transactions in which a corporation issued or repurchased its own stock. However, such transactions represent only a very small portion of the daily transactions in stocks. The great daily volume of security sales are transactions between investors, some selling and some buying. The transactions take place through brokers who charge a commission for their services.

Brokers, acting as agents for their customers, buy and sell stocks and bonds on stock exchanges such as the New York Stock Exchange. Each day the prices at which sales occurred are published on the financial pages of many newspapers. Stock prices are quoted on the basis of dollars and ⅛ dollars per share. For example, a stock quoted at 46⅛ sold for $46.125 per share, and a stock quoted at 25½ sold for $25.50 per share.

Some securities are not traded in large enough quantities to warrant being listed on an organized stock exchange, and brokers act for their customers to buy and sell such securities in the "over-the-counter" market. Each security in this market is handled by one or more brokers who receive from other brokers offers to buy or sell the security at specific "bid" or "ask" prices. The broker essentially provides a market place for the security, arranging for trades between customers who "bid" and "ask" prices are consistent.

CLASSIFYING INVESTMENTS

Equity securities generally include common, preferred, or other capital stock. Many equity securities are actively traded so that "sales prices or bid and ask prices are currently available on a national securities exchange or in the over-the-counter market." Such securities are classified as *"marketable equity securities."*[1] If, in addition to being marketable, a stock investment is held as "an investment of cash available for current operations,"[2] it is classified as a current asset, and appears on the balance sheet immediately following cash. The stock may be held for a number of years; this is not important. The important point is that in case of need it may quickly be turned into cash without interfering with the normal operations of the business.

Investments that are not intended as a ready source of cash in case of need are classified as *long-term investments*. They include funds earmarked for a special purpose, such as bond sinking funds, as well as land or other assets owned but not employed in the regular operations of the business. They also include investments in stocks which are not marketable or which, although marketable, are not intended to serve as a ready source of cash. Long-term investments appear on the balance sheet in a classification of their own entitled "Long-term investments," which is placed immediately following the current asset section.

---

[1] FASB, "Accounting for Certain Marketable Securities," *Statement of Financial Accounting Standards No. 12* (Stamford, Conn., 1975), par. 7. Copyright © by the Financial Accounting Standards Board, High Ridge Park, Stamford, Conn. 06905, U.S.A. Quoted (or excerpted) with permission. Copies of the complete document are available from the FASB.

[2] Committee on Accounting Procedure, "Accounting Research Bulletin No. 43," *Accounting Research and Terminology Bulletins, Final Edition* (New York, AICPA, 1961), chap. 3, sec. A, par. 4. Copyright (1961) by the American Institute of CPAs.

THE COST METHOD OF ACCOUNTING FOR STOCK INVESTMENTS

Most investments in a corporation's stock represent a small percentage of the total amount of stock outstanding. As a consequence, the investor does not exercise a significant influence over the operating and financial policies of the corporation. In such cases, whether the stock is purchased as a short- or long-term investment, the investor accounts for the investment according to the *cost method*. That method is described in the following paragraphs.

Assume that an investor corporation purchased 1,000 (10%) of American Sales Corporation's 10,000 outstanding common shares at 23¼ plus a $300 broker's commission. The entry to record the investment is:

Sept.	10	Investment in American Sales Corporation Stock	23,550.00	
		Cash		23,550.00
		Purchased 1,000 shares of stock for $23,250 plus a $300 broker's commission.		

Observe that nothing is said about a premium or a discount on the American Sales Corporation stock. Premiums and discounts apply only when stock is first issued. They do not apply to sales and purchases between investors. Thus, premiums and discounts are normally recorded only by the corporation which issues the stock. Even if the investor acquires newly issued stock, a premium or discount on the stock is not usually recorded in a separate account.

When the cost method of accounting is being used and a dividend is received on the stock, an entry similar to the following is made:

Oct.	5	Cash	1,000.00	
		Dividends Earned		1,000.00
		Received a $1 per share dividend on the American Sales Corporation stock.		

Dividends on stocks do not accrue; consequently, an end-of-the-accounting-period entry to record accrued dividends is never made. However, if a balance sheet is prepared after a dividend is declared but before it is paid, an entry debiting Dividends Receivable and crediting Dividends Earned may be made. Nevertheless, since dividend earnings are often immaterial and not taxable until received in cash, most companies do not record such dividends until received. While this is not theoretically correct, it does keep reported and taxable dividends the same.

A dividend in shares of stock is not income, and a debit and credit entry recording it should not be made. However, a memorandum entry or a notation as to the additional shares should be made in the investment account. Also, receipt of the stock does affect the per share cost basis of the old shares. For example, if a 20-share dividend is received on 100 shares originally purchased for $1,500 or at $15 per share, the cost of all 120 shares is $1,500 and the cost per share is $12.50 ($1,500 ÷ 120 shares = $12.50 per share).

Using the cost method, when an investment in stock is sold, normally a gain or a loss is incurred. If the amount received is greater than the original cost of the investment plus the commission on the sale and other costs, there is a gain. For example, assume the 1,000 shares of American Sales Corporation common stock are sold at 25¾ less a commission and taxes on the sale amounting to $315. Since the previously recorded cost of the shares was $23,550, the sale resulted in a gain of $1,885. The entry to record the sale is as follows:

Jan.	7	Cash	25,435.00	
		Investment in American Sales Corporation		
		Stock		23,550.00
		Gain on the Sale of Investments		1,885.00
		Sold 1,000 shares of stock for $25,750 less a		
		$315 commission and other costs.		

If the net amount received for these shares had been less than their $23,550 cost, there would have been a loss on the transaction.

LOWER OF COST OR MARKET

For balance sheet presentation, an investment in stock that is not marketable is accounted for at cost. However, investments in marketable equity securities are divided into two portfolios: (1) those to be shown as current assets and (2) those to be shown as long-term investments. Then the total current market value of each portfolio is calculated and compared to the total cost of each portfolio. Each portfolio is reported at the lower of cost or market.[3]

In the case of the current asset portfolio, a decline in total market value below the previous balance sheet valuation (or cost) is reported in the income statement as a loss. Subsequent recoveries of market

---

[3] FASB, "Accounting for Certain Marketable Securities," par. 8.

value are reported in the income statement as gains, but market value increases above original cost are not recorded.[4]

In the case of long-term investment portfolios of marketable equity securities, market value declines are reported in the income statement *only* if they appear to be permanent. More often they are not assumed to be permanent, in which case the market value decline is disclosed as a separate item in the stockholders' equity section of the balance sheet.[5]

DIFFERENCE BETWEEN STOCKS AND BONDS

Before beginning a study of bonds, the difference between a share of stock and a bond should be clearly understood. A share of stock represents an equity or ownership right in a corporation. By comparison, a bond is a type of long-term note payable. For example, if a person owns 1,000 of the 10,000 shares of common stock a corporation has outstanding, the person has an equity in the corporation measured at $\frac{1}{10}$ of the corporation's total stockholders' equity and has a right to $\frac{1}{10}$ of the corporation's earnings. If on the other hand a person owns a $1,000, 10%, 20-year bond issued by a corporation,[6] the *bond* represents a debt or a liability of the corporation. Its owner has two rights: (1) the right to receive 10% or $100 interest each year the bond is outstanding and (2) the right to be paid $1,000 when the bond matures 20 years after its date of issue.

WHY BONDS ARE ISSUED

A corporation in need of long-term funds may secure the funds by issuing additional shares of stock or by selling bonds. Each has its advantages and disadvantages. Stockholders are owners, and issuing additional stock spreads ownership, control of management, and earnings over more shares. Bondholders, on the other hand, are creditors and do not share in either management or earnings. However, bond interest must be paid whether there are any earnings or not. Otherwise the bondholders may foreclose and take the assets pledged for their security.

Nevertheless, issuing bonds, rather than additional stock, will commonly result in increased earnings for the owners (the common stockholders) of the issuing corporation. For example, assume a corporation with 200,000 shares of common stock outstanding needs $1,000,000

---

[4] Ibid., par. 11.

[5] Ibid., pars. 11, 21.

[6] The federal government and other governmental units, such as cities, states, and school districts also issue bonds. However, the discussions in this chapter are limited to the bonds of corporations.

to expand its operations. The corporation's management estimates that after the expansion the company can earn $600,000 annually before bond interest, if any, and corporation income taxes; and it has proposed two plans for securing the needed funds. Plan No. 1 calls for issuing 100,000 additional shares of the corporation's common stock at $10 per share. This will increase the total outstanding shares to 300,000. Plan No. 2 calls for the sale at par of $1,000,000 of 8% bonds. Illustration 17–1 shows how the plans will affect the corporation's earnings.

	Plan 1	Plan 2
Earnings before bond interest and income taxes	$600,000	$600,000
Deduct bond interest expense		(80,000)
Income before corporation income taxes	$600,000	$520,000
Deduct income taxes (assumed 50% rate)	(300,000)	(260,000)
Net income	$300,000	$260,000
Plan 1 income per share (300,000 shares)	$1.00	
Plan 2 income per share (200,000 shares)		$1.30

Illustration 17–1

Corporations are subject to state and federal income taxes, which together may take as much as 50% of the corporation's before-tax income. However, bond interest expense is a deductible expense in arriving at income subject to taxes. Consequently, when the combined state and federal tax rate is 50%, as in Illustration 17–1, the tax reduction from issuing bonds equals one half the annual interest on the bonds. In other words, the tax savings in effect pays one half the interest cost of the bonds.

BORROWING BY ISSUING BONDS

When a large corporation wishes to borrow several millions of dollars, it will normally borrow by issuing bonds. Bonds are issued because few banks or insurance companies are able or willing to make a loan of such size. Also, bonds enable the corporation to divide the loan among many lenders.

Borrowing by issuing bonds is in many ways similar to borrowing by giving a *mortgage*. Actually, the real difference is that a number of bonds, often in denominations of $1,000, are issued in the place of a single mortgage note. For all practical purposes each bond is a promissory note, promising to pay a definite sum of money to its holder, or owner of record, at a fixed future date. Like promissory notes, bonds bear interest; and like a mortgage note, they are often secured by a mortgage. However, since bonds may be owned and transferred during their lives by a number of people, they differ from promissory notes in that they do not name the lender.

When a company issues bonds secured by a mortgage, it normally sells the bonds to an investment firm, known as the *underwriter*. The underwriter in turn resells the bonds to the public. In addition to the underwriter, the company issuing bonds selects a trustee to represent the bondholders. In most cases the trustee is a large bank or trust company to which the company issuing the bonds executes and delivers the mortgage contract that acts as security for the bonds. It is the duty of the trustee to see that the company fulfills all the pledged responsibilities of the *mortgage contract*, or as it is often called the *deed of trust*. It is also the duty of the trustee to foreclose if any pledges are not fulfilled.

CHARACTERISTICS OF BONDS

Over the years corporation lawyers and financiers have created a wide variety of bonds, each with different combinations of characteristics. For example, bonds may be *serial bonds* or *sinking fund bonds*. When serial or term bonds are issued, portions of the issue become due and are paid in installments over a period of years. Sinking fund bonds differ in that they are paid at maturity in one lump sum from a sinking fund created for that purpose. Sinking funds are discussed later in this chapter.

Bonds may also be either *registered bonds* or *coupon bonds*. Ownership of registered bonds is registered or recorded with the issuing corporation. This offers some protection from loss or theft. Interest payments on such bonds are usually made by checks mailed to the registered owners. Coupon bonds secure their name from the interest coupons attached to each bond. Each coupon calls for payment on the interest payment date of the interest due on the bond to which it is attached. The coupons are detached as they become due and are deposited with a bank for collection. Often ownership of a coupon bond is not registered. Such unregistered bonds are payable to bearer or are bearer paper, and ownership is transferred by delivery. Sometimes bonds are registered as to principal with interest payments by coupons.

Bonds also may be secured or unsecured. Unsecured bonds are called *debentures* and depend upon the general credit standing of their issuing corporation for security. Only financially strong companies are able to sell unsecured bonds or bonds that are not secured by a mortgage.

ISSUING BONDS

When a corporation issues bonds, the bonds are printed and the deed of trust is drawn and deposited with the trustee of the bondholders. At that point a memorandum describing the bond issue is commonly entered in the Bonds Payable account. Such a memorandum might read, "Authorized to issue $8,000,000 of 9%, 20-year bonds dated January 1, 19—, and with interest payable semiannually on each July 1 and January 1." As in this case, bond interest is usually payable semiannually.

After the deed of trust is deposited with the trustee of the bondholders, all or a portion of the bonds may be sold. If all are sold at their *par value*, also called their *face amount*, an entry like this is made to record the sale:

Jan.	1	Cash	8,000,000.00	
		Bonds Payable		8,000,000.00
		Sold bonds at par on their interest date.		

When the semiannual interest is paid on these bonds, the transaction is recorded as follows:

July	1	Bond Interest Expense	360,000.00	
		Cash		360,000.00
		Paid the semiannual interest on the bonds.		

And when the bonds are paid at maturity, an entry like this is made:

Jan.	1	Bonds Payable	8,000,000.00	
		Cash		8,000,000.00
		Paid bonds at maturity.		

BONDS SOLD BETWEEN INTEREST DATES

Sometimes bonds are sold on their date of issue, which is also their interest date, as in the previous illustration. More often they are sold after their date of issue and between interest dates. In such cases, it is customary to charge and collect from the purchasers the interest that has accrued on the bonds since the previous interest payment and to return this accrued interest to the purchasers on the next interest date. For example, assume that on March 1, a corporation sold at par $100,000 of 9% bonds on which interest is payable semiannually on each January 1 and July 1. (Small dollar amounts are used in order to conserve space.) The entry to record the sale between interest dates is:

Mar.	1	Cash	101,500.00	
		Bond Interest Expense		1,500.00
		Bonds Payable		100,000.00
		Sold $100,000 of bonds on which two months' interest has accrued.		

At the end of four months, on the July 1 semiannual interest date, the purchasers of these bonds are paid a full six months' interest. This payment includes four months' interest earned by the bondholders after March 1 and the two months' accrued interest collected from them at the time the bonds were sold. The entry to record the payment is:

July	1	Bond Interest Expense	4,500.00	
		Cash		4,500.00
		Paid the semiannual interest on the bonds.		

After both of these entries are posted, the Bond Interest Expense account has a $3,000 debit balance and appears as follows:

Bond Interest Expense			
July 1 (Payment)	4,500.00	Mar. 1 (Accrued interest)	1,500.00

The $3,000 debit balance is the interest on the $100,000 of bonds at 9% for the four months from March 1 to July 1.

Students often think it strange to charge bond purchasers for accrued interest when bonds are sold between interest dates, and to return this accrued interest in the next interest payment. However, this is the custom. All bond transactions are "plus accrued interest"; and there is a good reason for the practice. For instance, if a corporation sells portions of a bond issue on different dates during an interest period without collecting the accrued interest, it must keep records of the purchasers and the dates on which they bought bonds. Otherwise it cannot pay the correct amount of interest to each. However, if it charges each buyer for accrued interest at the time of the purchase, it need not keep records of the purchasers and their purchase dates. It can pay a full period's interest to all purchasers for the period in which they bought their bonds and each receives the interest he or she has earned and gets back the accrued interest paid at the time of the purchase.

BOND INTEREST RATES

At this point students who are not sure of their understanding of the concept of present value should turn back to Chapter 12, pages 408–413, and review this concept before going further into this chapter.

A corporation issuing bonds specifies in the deed of trust and on each bond the interest rate it will pay. This rate is called the *contract rate*. It is usually stated on an annual basis, although bond interest is normally paid semiannually. Also, it is applied to the par value of the bonds to determine the dollars of interest the corporation will pay. For example, a corporation will pay $80 each year in two semiannual installments of $40 each on a $1,000, 8% bond on which interest is paid semiannually.

Although the contract rate establishes the interest a corporation will pay, it is not necessarily the interest the corporation will incur in issuing bonds. The interest it will incur depends upon what lenders consider their risks to be in lending to the corporation and upon the current *market rate for bond interest.* The market rate for bond interest is the rate borrowers are willing to pay and lenders are willing to take for the use of money at the level of risk involved. It fluctuates from day to day at any level of risk as the supply and demand for loanable funds fluctuate. It goes up when the demand for bond money increases and the supply decreases, and it goes down when the supply increases and the demand decreases.

A corporation issuing bonds usually offers a contract rate of interest equal to what it estimates the market will demand on the day the bonds are to be issued. If its estimate is correct, and the contract rate and market rate coincide on the day the bonds are issued, the bonds will sell at par, their face amount. However, when bonds are sold, their contract rate seldom coincides with the market rate. As a result, bonds usually sell either at a premium or at a discount.

BONDS SOLD AT A DISCOUNT

When a corporation offers to sell bonds carrying a contract rate below the prevailing market rate, the bonds will sell at a *discount*. Investors can get the market rate of interest elsewhere for the use of their money, so they will buy the bonds only at a price that will yield the prevailing market rate on the investment. What price will they pay and how is it determined? The price they will pay is the *present value* of the expected returns from the investment. It is determined by discounting the returns at the current market rate for bond interest.

To illustrate how bond prices are determined, assume that on a day when the market rate for bond interest is 9%, a corporation offers to sell and issue bonds having a $100,000 par value, a ten-year life, and on which interest is to be paid semiannually at an 8% annual rate.[7] In exchange for current dollars a buyer of these bonds will gain two monetary rights.

1. The right to receive $100,000 at the end of the bond issue's ten-year life.
2. The right to receive $4,000 in interest at the end of each six-month interest period throughout the ten-year life of the bonds.

Since both are rights to receive money in the future, to determine their present value, the amounts to be received are discounted at the prevailing market rate of interest. If the prevailing market rate is 9% annually, it is 4½% semiannually; and in ten years there are 20 semiannual periods. Consequently, using the last number in the 4½% column of Table 12–1, page 410, to discount the first amount and the last number in the 4½% column of Table 12–2, page 412, to discount the series of $4,000 amounts, the present value of the rights and the price an informed buyer will offer for the bonds is:

Present value of $100,000 to be received 20 periods hence, discounted at 4½% per period ($100,000 × 0.4146) $41,460
Present value of $4,000 to be received periodically for 20 periods, discounted at 4½% ($4,000 × 13.008) 52,032
Present value of the bonds $93,492

If the corporation accepts the $93,492 offer for its bonds and sells them on their date of issue, it will record the sale with an entry like this:

Jan.	1	Cash	93,492.00	
		Discount on Bonds Payable	6,508.00	
		Bonds Payable		100,000.00
		Sold bonds at a discount on their date of issue.		

---

[7] The spread between the contract rate and the market rate of interest on a new bond issue is seldom more than a fraction of a percent. However, a spread of a full percent is used here to simplify the illustrations.

If the corporation prepares a balance sheet on the day the bonds are sold, it may show the bonds in the long-term liability section as follows:

Long-term liabilities:		
First mortgage, 8% bonds payable, due January 1, 199A	$100,000	
Less unamortized discount based on the 9% market rate for bond interest prevailing on the date of issue	6,508	$93,492

On a balance sheet any unamortized discount on a bond issue is deducted from the par value of the bonds to show the amount at which the bonds are carried on the books, called the *carrying amount.*

Amortizing the discount

The corporation of this discussion received $93,492 for its bonds, but in ten years it must pay the bondholders $100,000. The difference, the $6,508 discount, is a cost of using the $93,492 that was incurred because the contract rate of interest on the bonds was below the prevailing market rate. It is a cost that must be paid when the bonds mature. However, each semiannual interest period in the life of the bond issue benefits from the use of the $93,492. Consequently, it is only fair that each should bear a fair share of this cost.

The procedure for dividing a discount and charging a share to each period in the life of the applicable bond issue is called *amortizing* a discount. A simple method of amortizing a discount is the *straight-line method,* a method in which an equal portion of the discount is amortized each interest period. If this method is used to amortize the $6,508 discount of this discussion, the $6,508 is divided by 20, the number of interest periods in the life of the bond issue, and $325.40 ($6,508 ÷ 20 = $325.40) of discount is amortized at the end of each interest period with an entry like this:

July	1	Bond Interest Expense	4,325.40	
		Discount on Bonds Payable		325.40
		Cash		4,000.00
		To record payment of six months' interest and amortization of ½₀ of the discount.		

The amortization of $325.40 of discount each six months will completely write off the $6,508 of discount by the end of the issue's ten-year life. It also increases the amount of bond interest expense recorded each six months to the sum of the $4,000 paid the bondholders plus the discount amortized.

Straight-line amortization is easy to understand and once was commonly used. However, the APB ruled that it may now be used only in situations where the results do not materially differ from those obtained through use of the so-called interest method.[8] The APB favored the interest method because it results in a constant rate of interest on the carrying amount of a bond issue. The straight-line method results in a decreasing rate when a discount is amortized and an increasing rate when a premium is amortized.

When the interest method is used, the interest expense to be recorded each period is determined by applying a constant rate of interest to the beginning-of-the-period carrying amount of the bonds. The constant rate applied is the market rate prevailing at the time the bonds were issued. The discount amortized each period is then determined by subtracting the interest to be paid the bondholders from the interest expense to be recorded. Illustration 17–2, with amounts

Period	Beginning-of-period carrying amount	Interest expense to be recorded	Interest to be paid the bond-holders	Discount to be amortized	Un-amortized discount at end of period	End-of-period carrying amount
1	$93,492	$4,207	$4,000	$207	$6,301	$ 93,699
2	93,699	4,216	4,000	216	6,085	93,915
3	93,915	4,226	4,000	226	5,859	94,141
4	94,141	4,236	4,000	236	5,623	94,377
5	94,377	4,247	4,000	247	5,376	94,624
6	94,624	4,258	4,000	258	5,118	94,882
7	94,882	4,270	4,000	270	4,848	95,152
8	95,152	4,282	4,000	282	4,566	95,434
9	95,434	4,295	4,000	295	4,271	95,729
10	95,729	4,308	4,000	308	3,963	96,037
11	96,037	4,322	4,000	322	3,641	96,359
12	96,359	4,336	4,000	336	3,305	96,695
13	96,695	4,351	4,000	351	2,954	97,046
14	97,046	4,367	4,000	367	2,587	97,413
15	97,413	4,384	4,000	384	2,203	97,797
16	97,797	4,401	4,000	401	1,802	98,198
17	98,198	4,419	4,000	419	1,383	98,617
18	98,617	4,438	4,000	438	945	99,055
19	99,055	4,457	4,000	457	488	99,512
20	99,512	4,488*	4,000	488	–0–	100,000

* Adjusted to compensate for accumulated rounding of amounts.

Illustration 17–2

[8] APB, "Interest on Receivables and Payables," *APB Opinion No. 21* (New York: AICPA, August 1971), par. 15. Copyright (1970) by the American Institute of CPAs.

rounded to full dollars, shows the interest expense to be recorded, the discount to be amortized, and so forth, when the interest method of amortizing a discount is applied to the bond issue of this discussion. In examining Illustration 17–2, note these points:

1. The bonds were sold at a $6,508 discount, which when subtracted from their face amount gives a beginning of period 1 carrying amount of $93,492.
2. The interest expense amounts result from multiplying each beginning-of-the-period carrying amount by the 4½% semiannual market rate prevailing when the bonds were issued. For example, $93,-492 × 4½% = $4,207 and $93,699 × 4½% = $4,216.
3. Interest to be paid bondholders each period is determined by multiplying the par value of the bonds by the contract rate of interest.
4. The discount to be amortized each period is determined by subtracting the amount of interest to be paid the bondholders from the amount of interest expense.
5. The unamortized discount at the end of each period is determined by subtracting the discount amortized that period from the unamortized discount at the beginning of the period.
6. The end-of-the-period carrying amount for the bonds is determined by subtracting the end-of-the-period amount of unamortized discount from the face amount of the bonds. For example, at the end of period 1: $100,000 − $6,301 = $93,699.

When the interest method is used in amortizing a discount, the periodic amortizing entries are like the entries used with the straight-line method, excepting as to the amounts. For example, the entry to pay the bondholders and amortize a portion of the discount at the end of the first semiannual interest period of the issue of Illustration 17–2 is:

July	1	Bond Interest Expense	4,207.00	
		Discount on Bonds Payable		207.00
		Cash		4,000.00
		To record payment of the bondholders and amortization of a portion of the discount.		

Similar entries, differing only in the amounts of interest expense recorded and discount amortized, are made at the end of each semiannual interest period in the life of the bond issue.

BONDS SOLD AT A PREMIUM

When a corporation offers to sell bonds carrying a contract rate of interest above the prevailing market rate for the risks involved, the bonds will sell at a *premium*. Buyers will bid up the price of the bonds, going as high but no higher than a price that will return the current market rate of interest on the investment. What price will they pay? They will pay the present value of the expected returns from the investment, determined by discounting these returns at the prevailing market rate for bond interest. For example, assume that on a day the current market rate for bond interest is 7%, a corporation offers to sell bonds having a $100,000 par value and a ten-year life with interest to be paid semiannually at an 8% annual rate. An informed buyer of these bonds will discount the expectation of receiving $100,000 in ten years and the expectation of receiving $4,000 semiannually for 20 periods at the current 7% market rate as follows:

Present value of $100,000 to be received 20 periods hence, discounted at 3½% per period ($100,000 × 0.5026)	$ 50,260
Present value of $4,000 to be received periodically for 20 periods, discounted at 3½% ($4,000 × 14.212)	56,848
Present value of the bonds	$107,108

And the informed investor will offer the corporation $107,108 for its bonds. If the corporation accepts and sells the bonds on their date of issue, say, May 1, 198A, it will record the sale as follows:

198A					
May	1	Cash	107,108.00		
		Premium on Bonds Payable		7,108.00	
		Bonds Payable		100,000.00	
		Sold bonds at a premium on their date of issue.			

It may then show the bonds on a balance sheet prepared on the day of the sale as follows:

Long-term liabilities:		
First mortgage, 8% bonds payable, due May 1, 199A ...	$100,000	
Add unamortized premium based on the 7% market rate for bond interest prevailing on the date of issue	7,108	$107,108

On a balance sheet any unamortized premium on bonds payable is added to the par value of the bonds to show the carrying amount of the bonds, as illustrated.

Amortizing the premium

Although the corporation discussed here received $107,108 for its bonds, it will have to repay only $100,000 to the bondholders at maturity. The difference, the $7,108 premium, represents a reduction in the cost of using the $107,108. It should be amortized over the life of the bond issue in such a manner as to lower the recorded bond interest expense. If the $7,108 premium is amortized by the interest method, Illustration 17–3 shows the amounts of interest expense to be recorded each period, the premium to be amortized, and so forth.

Observe in Illustration 17–3 that the premium to be amortized each period is determined by subtracting the interest to be recorded from the interest to be paid the bondholders.

Based on Illustration 17–3 the entry to record the first semiannual interest payment and premium amortization is:

198A				
Nov.	1	Bond Interest Expense	3,749.00	
		Premium on Bonds Payable	251.00	
		Cash		4,000.00
		To record payment of the bondholders and amortization of a portion of the premium.		

Period	Beginning-of-period carrying amount	Interest expense to be recorded	Interest to be paid the bond-holders	Premium to be amortized	Un-amortized premium at end of period	End-of-period carrying amount
1	$107,108	$3,749	$4,000	$251	$6,857	$106,857
2	106,857	3,740	4,000	260	6,597	106,597
3	106,597	3,731	4,000	269	6,328	106,328
4	106,328	3,721	4,000	279	6,049	106,049
5	106,049	3,712	4,000	288	5,761	105,761
6	105,761	3,702	4,000	298	5,463	105,463
7	105,463	3,691	4,000	309	5,154	105,154
8	105,154	3,680	4,000	320	4,834	104,834
9	104,834	3,669	4,000	331	4,503	104,503
10	104,503	3,658	4,000	342	4,161	104,161
11	104,161	3,646	4,000	354	3,807	103,807
12	103,807	3,633	4,000	367	3,440	103,440
13	103,440	3,620	4,000	380	3,060	103,060
14	103,060	3,607	4,000	393	2,667	102,667
15	102,667	3,593	4,000	407	2,260	102,260
16	102,260	3,579	4,000	421	1,839	101,839
17	101,839	3,564	4,000	436	1,403	101,403
18	101,403	3,549	4,000	451	952	100,952
19	100,952	3,533	4,000	467	485	100,485
20	100,485	3,515*	4,000	485	–0–	100,000

* Adjusted to compensate for accumulated rounding of amounts.

Illustration 17–3

Note how the amortization of the premium results in a reduction in the amount of interest expense recorded. Similar entries having decreasing amounts of interest expense and increasing amounts of premium amortization are made at the ends of the remaining periods in the life of the bond issue.

ACCRUED BOND INTEREST EXPENSE

Often when bonds are sold the bond interest periods do not coincide with the issuing company's accounting periods. In such cases it is necessary at the end of each accounting period to make an adjustment for accrued interest. For example, it was assumed that the bonds of Illustration 17–3 were issued on May 1, 198A, and interest was paid on these bonds on November 1 of that year. If the accounting periods of the corporation end each December 31, on December 31, 198A, two months' interest has accrued on these bonds, and the following adjusting entry is required:

198A				
Dec.	31	Bond Interest Expense	1,246.67	
		Premium on Bonds Payable	86.66	
		Bond Interest Payable		1,333.33
		To record two months' accrued interest and amortize one third of the premium applicable to the interest period.		

Two months are one third of a semiannual interest period. Consequently, the amounts in the entry are one third of the amounts applicable to the second interest period in the life of the bond issue. Similar entries will be made on each December 31 throughout the life of the issue. However, the amounts will differ, since in each case they will apply to a different interest period.

When the interest is paid on these bonds on May 1, 198B, an entry like this is required:

198B				
May	1	Bond Interest Expense	2,493.33	
		Bond Interest Payable	1,333.33	
		Premium on Bonds Payable	173.34	
		Cash		4,000.00
		Paid the interest on the bonds, a portion of which was previously accrued, and amortized four months' premium.		

SALE OF BONDS BY INVESTORS

A purchaser of a bond may not hold it to maturity but may sell it after a period of months or years to a new investor at a price determined by the market rate for bond interest on the day of the sale. The market rate for bond interest on the day of the sale determines the price because the new investor can get this current rate elsewhere. Therefore, the investor will discount the right to receive the bond's face amount at maturity and the right to receive its interest for the remaining periods in its life at the current market rate to determine the price to pay for the bond. As a result, since bond interest rates may vary greatly over a period of months or years, a bond that originally sold at a premium may later sell at a discount, and vice versa.

REDEMPTION OF BONDS

Bonds are commonly issued with the provision that they may be redeemed at the issuing corporation's option, usually upon the payment of a redemption premium. Such bonds are known as *callable bonds.* Corporations commonly insert redemption clauses in deeds of trust because if interest rates decline, it may be advantageous to call and redeem outstanding bonds and issue in their place new bonds paying a lower interest rate.

Not all bonds have a provision giving their issuing company the right to call. However, even though the right is not provided, a company may secure the same effect by purchasing its bonds on the open market and retiring them. Often such action is wise when a company has funds available and its bonds are selling at a price below their carrying amount. For example, a company has outstanding on their interest date $1,000,000 of bonds on which there is $12,000 unamortized premium. The bonds are selling at 98½ (98½% of par value), and the company decides to buy and retire one tenth of the issue. The entry to record the purchase and retirement is:

April	1	Bonds Payable	100,000.00	
		Premium on Bonds Payable	1,200.00	
		Gain on the Retirement of Bonds		2,700.00
		Cash		98,500.00
		To record the retirement of bonds.		

The retirement resulted in a $2,700 gain in this instance because the bonds were purchased at a price $2,700 below their carrying amount.

In the previous paragraph the statement was made that the bonds were selling at 98½. Bond quotations are commonly made in this manner. For example, a bond may be quoted for sale at 101¼. This means the bond is for sale at 101¼% of its par value, plus accrued interest, of course, if applicable.

CONVERTIBLE BONDS

To make an issue more attractive, bond owners may be given the right to exchange their bonds for a fixed number of shares of the issuing company's common stock. Such bonds are known as *convertible bonds.* They offer investors initial investment security, and if the issuing company prospers and the market value of its stock goes up, an opportunity to share in the prosperity by converting their bonds to stock. Conversion is always at the bondholders' option and is not exercised except when to do so is to their advantage.

When bonds are converted into stock, the conversion changes creditor equity into ownership equity. The generally accepted rule for measuring the contribution for the issued shares is that the carrying amount of the converted bonds becomes the book value of the capital contributed for the new shares. For example, assume the following: (1) A company has outstanding $1,000,000 of bonds upon which there is $8,000 unamortized discount. (2) The bonds are convertible at the rate of a $1,000 bond for 90 shares of the company's $10 par value common stock. And (3) $100,000 in bonds have been presented on their interest date for conversion. The entry to record the conversion is:

May	1	Bonds Payable	100,000.00	
		Discount on Bonds Payable		800.00
		Common Stock		90,000.00
		Premium on Common Stock		9,200.00
		To record the conversion of bonds.		

Note in this entry that the bonds' $99,200 carrying amount sets the accounting value for the capital contributed. Usually when bonds have a conversion privilege, it is not exercised until the stock's market value and normal dividend payments are sufficiently high to make the conversion profitable to the bondholders.

BOND SINKING FUND

Because of their fixed return and greater security, bonds appeal to a portion of the investing public. A corporation issuing bonds may offer investors a measure of security by placing a mortgage on certain of its assets. Often it will give additional security by agreeing in its deed of trust to create a *bond sinking fund.* This is a fund of assets accumulated to pay the bondholders at maturity.

When a corporation issuing bonds agrees to create a bond sinking fund, it normally agrees to create the fund by making periodic cash deposits with a sinking fund trustee. It is the duty of the trustee to safeguard the cash, to invest it in good sound securities, and to add the interest or dividends earned to the sinking fund. Generally, when the bonds become due, it is also the duty of the sinking fund trustee to sell the sinking fund securities and to use the proceeds to pay the bondholders.

When a *sinking fund* is created, the amount that must be deposited periodically in order to provide enough money to retire a bond issue at maturity will depend upon the net rate of compound interest that can be earned on the invested funds. The rate is a compound rate because earnings are continually reinvested by the sinking fund trustee to earn an additional return. It is a net rate because the trustee commonly deducts the fee for its services from the earnings.

To illustrate the operation of a sinking fund, assume a corporation issues $1,000,000 of ten-year bonds and agrees to deposit with a sinking fund trustee at the end of each year in the issue's life sufficient cash to create a fund large enough to retire the bonds at maturity. If the trustee is able to invest the funds in such a manner as to earn a 7% net return, $72,378 must be deposited each year and the fund will grow to maturity (in rounded dollars) as shown in Illustration 17–4.

When a sinking fund is created by periodic deposits, the entry to record the amount deposited each year appears as follows:

Dec.	31	Bond Sinking Fund	72,378.00	
		Cash		72,378.00
		To record the annual sinking fund deposit.		

Each year the sinking fund trustee invests the amount deposited, and each year it collects and reports the earnings on the investments. The earnings report results in an entry to record the sinking fund income. For example, if $72,378 is deposited at the end of the first year in the sinking fund, the accumulation of which is shown in Illustration 17–4, and 7% is earned, the entry to record the sinking fund earnings of the second year is:

Dec.	31	Bond Sinking Fund	5,066.00	
		Sinking Fund Earnings		5,066.00
		To record the sinking fund earnings.		

End of year	Amount deposited	Interest earned on fund balance	Balance in fund after deposit and interest
1	$72,378	$ -0-	$ 72,378
2	72,378	5,066	149,822
3	72,378	10,488	232,688
4	72,378	16,288	321,354
5	72,378	22,495	416,227
6	72,378	29,136	517,741
7	72,378	36,242	626,361
8	72,378	43,845	742,584
9	72,378	51,981	866,943
10	72,378	60,679*	1,000,000

* Adjusted for rounding.

Illustration 17–4

Sinking fund earnings appear on the income statement as financial revenue in a section entitled "Other revenues and expenses." A sinking fund is the property of the company creating the fund and should appear on its balance sheet in the long-term investments section.

When bonds mature, it is usually the duty of the sinking fund trustee to convert the fund's investments into cash and pay the bondholders. Normally the sinking fund securities, when sold, produce either a little more or a little less cash than is needed to pay the bondholders. If more cash than is needed is produced, the extra cash is returned to the corporation; and if less cash is produced than is needed, the corporation must make up the deficiency. For example, if the securities in the sinking fund of a $1,000,000 bond issue produce $1,001,325 when converted to cash, the trustee will use $1,000,000 to pay the bondholders and will return the extra $1,325 to the corporation. The corporation will then record the payment of its bonds and the return of the extra cash with an entry like this:

Jan.	3	Cash	1,325.00	
		Bonds Payable........................	1,000,000.00	
		Bond Sinking Fund		1,001,325.00
		To record payment of our bonds and the return of extra cash from the sinking fund		

RESTRICTION ON DIVIDENDS DUE TO OUTSTANDING BONDS

To protect a corporation's financial position and the interests of its bondholders, a deed of trust may restrict the dividends the corporation may pay while its bonds are outstanding. Commonly the restriction provides that the corporation may pay dividends in any year only to the extent that the year's earnings exceed sinking fund requirements.

LONG-TERM NOTES

When bond interest rates are temporarily unfavorable and funds are available from several large banks or insurance companies, often long-term notes maturing in two, three, or more years are issued with the intention of refinancing the debt at maturity by issuing bonds. Also, in some instances, in order to avoid the costs of issuing bonds and dealing with several thousand bondholders, long-term notes maturing in 10, 20, or more years are issued instead of bonds.

Long-term notes are often secured by mortgages, and those maturing in ten or more years may provide for periodic payments to reduce the amounts owed. Consequently, long-term notes take on the characteristics of both mortgages and bonds. Ordinarily they differ only in that they may be placed with several lenders, normally at the current market rate of interest. This causes their present value at issuance to equal their maturity value. As a result, they are normally issued at par and receive the same accounting treatment as mortgages or bonds issued at par.

GLOSSARY

Bond. A type of long-term note payable issued by a corporation or a political subdivision.

Bond discount. The difference between the par value of a bond and the price at which it is issued when issued at a price below par.

Bond premium. The difference between the par value of a bond and the price at which it is issued when issued at a price above par.

Bond sinking fund. A fund of assets accumulated to pay a bond issue at maturity.

Callable bond. A bond that may be called in and redeemed at the option of the corporation or political subdivision that issued it.

Carrying amount of a bond issue. The par value of a bond issue less any unamortized discount or plus any unamortized premium.

Contract rate of bond interest. The rate of interest to be paid the bondholders.

Convertible bond. A bond that may be converted into shares of its issuing corporation's stock at the option of the bondholder.

Cost method of accounting for stock investments. The investment is recorded at total cost and maintained at that amount; subsequent investee earnings and dividends do not affect the investment account.

Coupon bond. A bond having coupons that are detached by the bondholder to collect interest on the bond.

Debenture bond. An unsecured bond.

Deed of trust. The contract between a corporation and its bondholders governing the duties of the corporation in relation to the bonds.

Face amount of a bond. The bond's par value.

Marketable equity securities. Equity securities that are actively traded so that sales prices or bid and ask prices are currently available on a national securites exchange or in the over-the-counter market.

Market rate of bond interest. The current bond interest rate that borrowers are willing to pay and lenders are willing to take for the use of their money.

Mortgage. A lien or prior claim to an asset or assets given by a borrower to a lender as security for a loan.

Mortgage contract. A document setting forth the terms under which a mortgage loan is made.

Par value of a bond. The face amount of the bond, which is the amount the borrower agrees to repay at maturity and the amount on which interest is based.

Registered bond. A bond the ownership of which is registered with the issuing corporation or political subdivision.

Serial bonds. An issue of bonds that will be repaid in installments over a period of years.

Sinking fund. A fund of assets accumulated for some purpose.

Sinking fund bonds. Bonds which are to be paid at maturity from funds accumulated in a sinking fund.

QUESTIONS FOR CLASS DISCUSSION

1. What is meant by "marketable securities?"
2. In accounting for common stock investments, when should the cost method be used? When should the equity method be used?
3. Do stock dividends provide income to the investor? How should stock dividends be recorded by the investor?
4. Explain how a stock dividend affects the cost per share owned by the investor.
5. What two legal documents are involved when a company borrows by giving a mortgage? What is the purpose of each?
6. What is the primary difference between a share of stock and a bond?
7. What is a deed of trust? What are some of the provisions commonly contained in a deed of trust?
8. Define or describe (a) registered bonds, (b) coupon bonds, (c) serial bonds,

(d) sinking fund bonds, (e) callable bonds, (f) convertible bonds, and (g) debenture bonds.

9. Why does a corporation issuing bonds between interest dates charge and collect accrued interest from the purchasers of the bonds?

10. As it relates to a bond issue, what is the meaning of "contract rate of interest"? What is the meaning of "market rate for bond interest"?

11. What determines bond interest rates?

12. Convertible bonds are very popular with investors. Why?

13. If a $1,000 bond is sold at 98¼, at what price is it sold? If a $1,000 bond is sold at 101½, at what price is it sold?

14. If the quoted price for a bond is 97¾, does this include accrued interest?

15. What purpose is served by creating a bond sinking fund?

16. How are bond sinking funds classified for balance sheet purposes?

CLASS EXERCISES

Exercise 17–1

Give entries in general journal form to record the following events on the books of A Company:

198A
Jan. 10   Purchased 10,000 shares of B Company common stock for $125,000 plus broker's fee of $3,500. B Company has 100,000 shares of common stock outstanding.

Apr. 15   B Company declared and paid a cash dividend of $0.50 per share.

Dec. 31   B Company announced that net income for the year amounted to $140,000.

198B
Apr. 14   B Company declared and paid a cash dividend of $0.40 per share.

July 9   B Company declared and issued a stock dividend of one additional share for each ten shares already outstanding.

Dec. 26   A Company sold 5,500 shares of B Company for $70,000.

31   B Company announced that net income for the year amounted to $75,000.

Exercise 17–2

On May 1 of the current year a corporation sold at par plus accrued interest $1,000,000 of its 8.4% bonds. The bonds were dated January 1 of the current year, with interest payable on each July 1 and January 1. (a) Give the entry to record the sale. (b) Give the entry to record the first interest payment. (c) Set up a T-account for Bond Interest Expense and post the portions of the entries that affect the account. Answer these questions: (d) How many months' interest were accrued on these bonds when they were sold? (e) How many months' interest were paid on July 1? (f) What is the balance of the Bond Interest Expense account after the entry recording the first interest payment is posted? (g) How many months' interest does this balance represent? (h) How many months' interest did the bondholders earn during the first interest period?

Exercise 17–3

On December 31, 198A, a corporation sold $100,000 of its own 7.8%, eight-year bonds. The bonds were dated December 31, 198A, with interest payable on each June 30 and December 31, and were sold to yield the buyers an 8% annual return. *(a)* Prepare a calculation to show the price at which the bonds sold and *(b)* prepare an entry in general journal form to record the sale. (Use the present value tables, Tables 12–1 and 12–2, pages 410 and 412.)

Exercise 17–4

Prepare a form with the columnar heading of Illustration 17–3, and under the assumption the corporation of Exercise 17–3 sold its bonds for $98,833, determine and fill in the amounts for the first two interest periods on the form. Round all amounts to the nearest full dollar. In general journal form, present the entries to record the first and second annual payments of interest to the bondholders.

Exercise 17–5

On October 1, 198A, a corporation sold $100,000 of its own 8.2%, ten-year bonds. The bonds were dated October 1, 198A, with interest payable on each April 1 and October 1. The bonds were sold to yield the buyers an 8% annual return. *(a)* Prepare a calculation to show the price at which the bonds sold and *(b)* prepare an entry in general journal form to record the sale. (Use the present value tables, Tables 12–1 and 12–2, pages 410 and 412.)

Exercise 17–6

Assume the bonds of Exercise 17–5 sold for $101,350 and that the annual accounting periods of the corporation selling the bonds end on December 31. Then prepare entries to record *(a)* the accrued interest on the bonds on the first December 31 they were outstanding and *(b)* the payment of the bondholders on the following April 1. *(c)* Assume that on April 1 the corporation repurchased the bonds on the open market for $101,000. In general journal form, record the entry to retire the bonds.

Exercise 17–7

A corporation has outstanding $1,000,000 of 9%, 20-year bonds on which there is $25,000 of unamortized bond premium. The bonds are convertible into the corporation's $10 par value common stock at the rate of one $1,000 bond for 95 shares of the stock, and $100,000 of the bonds have been presented for conversion. Give the entry to record the conversion as of May 1.

PROBLEMS

Problem 17–1

A corporation sold $1,000,000 of its own 8.8%, ten-year bonds on their date of issue, January 1, 198A. Interest was payable on the bonds on each

June 30 and December 31, and they were sold at a price to yield the buyers a 9% annual return.

Required:

1. Prepare a calculation to show the price at which the bonds were sold. (Use the present value tables, Tables 12–1 and 12–2, pages 410 and 412.)
2. Prepare a form with the columnar headings of Illustration 17–2 and fill in the amounts for the first two interest periods of the bond issue. Round all amounts to the nearest full dollar.
3. Prepare entries in general journal form to record the sale of the bonds and the payment of interest at the ends of the first two interest periods.

Problem 17–2

On January 1, 198A, a corporation sold $1,000,000 of its own 9.2%, ten-year bonds. The bonds were dated January 1, 198A, with interest payable on each June 30 and December 31, and were sold to yield the buyers a 9% annual return.

Required:

1. Prepare a calculation to show the price at which the bonds were sold. (Use the present value tables, Tables 12–1 and 12–2, pages 410 and 412.)
2. Prepare a form with the columnar headings of Illustration 17–3 and fill in the amounts for the first two interest periods of the bond issue. Round all amounts to the nearest full dollar.
3. Prepare entries in general journal form to record the sale of the bonds and the payment of interest at the ends of the first two interest periods.

Problem 17–3

Part 1. A corporation completed these bond transactions:

198A

Jan. 1 Sold $1,000,000 of its own 8.7%, ten-year bonds dated January 1, 198A, with interest payable each June 30 and December 31. The bonds sold for $980,448, a price to yield the buyers a 9% annual return on their investment.

June 30 Paid the semiannual interest on the bonds and amortized a portion of the discount calculated by the interest method.

Dec. 31 Paid the semiannual interest on the bonds and amortized a portion of the discount calculated by the interest method.

Required:

Prepare general journal entries to record the transactions. Round the amounts of discount amortized each period to the nearest full dollar.

Part 2. A corporation completed these bond transactions:

198A

May 1 Sold $1,000,000 of its own 9.3%, ten-year bonds dated May 1, 198A, with interest payable each November 1 and May 1. The bonds were sold for $1,019,472, a price to yield the buyers a 9% annual return.

Nov.   1   Paid the semiannual interest on the bonds and amortized a portion of the premium calculated by the interest method.

Dec. 31   Made an adjusting entry to record the accrued interest on the bonds and amortize one third of the amount of premium applicable to the second interest period of the bond issue.

198B

May   1   Paid the semiannual interest on the bonds and amortized the remainder of the premium applicable to the second interest period of the issue.

Required:

Prepare general journal entries to record the transactions. Round all amounts of premium amortized to the nearest whole dollar.

Problem 17–4

Part 1. A corporation completed these transactions.

198A

Jan.   1   Sold $1,000,000 par value of its own 8.9%, ten-year bonds at a price to yield the buyers a 9% annual return. The bonds were dated January 1, 198A, with interest payable each June 30 and December 31.

June 30   Paid the semiannual interest on the bonds and amortized a portion of the discount calculated by the interest method.

Dec. 31   Paid the semiannual interest on the bonds and amortized a portion of the discount calculated by the interest method.

Required:

Prepare general journal entries to record the transactions. Round all dollar amounts to the nearest whole dollar.

Part 2. A corporation completed these transactions:

198A

Apr.   1   Sold $1,000,000 par value of its 9.1%, ten-year bonds at a price to yield the buyers a 9% annual return. The bonds were dated April 1, 198A, with interest payable each October 1 and April 1.

Oct.   1   Paid the semiannual interest on the bonds and amortized a portion of the premium calculated by the interest method.

Dec. 31   Made an adjusting entry to record the accrued interest on the bonds and to amortize one half of the premium applicable to the second interest period of the bond issue.

198B

Apr.   1   Paid the semiannual interest on the bonds and amortized the remainder of the premium applicable to the second interest period of the issue.

Required:

Prepare general journal entries to record the transactions. Round the amounts of premium amortized each period to the nearest full dollar.

Problem 17–5

Prepare general journal entries to record the following bond transactions of a corporation. Round all dollar amounts to the nearest full dollar.

198A

Nov. 1 Sold $2,000,000 par value of its own 9.2%, ten-year bonds at a price to yield the buyers a 9% annual return. The bonds were dated November 1, 198A, with interest payable on each May 1 and November 1.

Dec. 31 Made an adjusting entry to record the accrued interest on the bonds and amortize one third of the premium applicable to the first interest period of the issue. (Use the interest method in calculating the premium to be amortized.)

198B

May 1 Paid the semiannual interest on the bonds and amortized the remainder of the premium applicable to the first interest period.

Nov. 1 Paid the semiannual interest on the bonds and amortized the premium applicable to the second interest period of the issue.

198F

Nov. 1 After recording the semiannual interest payment and amortizing the applicable premium, the carrying amount of the bonds on the corporation's books was $2,015,500, and the corporation purchased one tenth of the bonds at 99¼ and retired them.

ALTERNATE PROBLEMS

Problem 17–1A

A corporation sold $1,000,000 of its own 8.6%, ten-year bonds on their date of issue, January 1, 198A. Interest was payable on the bonds on each June 30 and December 31, and they were sold at a price to yield the buyers a 9% annual return.

Required:

1. Prepare a calculation to show the price at which the bonds were sold. (Use the present value tables, Tables 12–1 and 12–2, pages 410 and 412.)
2. Prepare a form with the columnar headings of Illustration 17–2 and fill in the amounts for the first two interest periods of the bond issue. Round amounts to the nearest full dollar.
3. Prepare general journal entries to record the sale of the bonds and the payment of interest at the ends of the first two interest periods.

Problem 17–2A

On January 1, 198A, a corporation sold $1,000,000 of its own 9.4%, ten-year bonds. The bonds were dated January 1, 198A, with interest payable on each June 30 and December 31, and were sold to yield the buyers a 9% annual return.

Required:

1. Prepare a calculation to show the price at which the bonds were sold. (Use the present value tables, Tables 12–1 and 12–2, pages 410 and 412.)
2. Prepare a form with the columnar headings of Illustration 17–3 and fill in the amounts for the first two interest periods of the bond issue. Round all amounts to the nearest full dollar.
3. Prepare entries in general journal form to record the sale of the bonds and the payment of interest at the ends of the first two interest periods.

Problem 17–3A

Part 1. A corporation completed these bond transactions:

198A
Jan. 1 Sold $2,000,000 of its own 8.9%, ten-year bonds dated January 1, 198A, with interest payable each June 30 and December 31. The bonds sold for $1,986,912, a price to yield the buyers a 9% annual return on their investment.

June 30 Paid the semiannual interest on the bonds and amortized a portion of the discount calculated by the interest method.

Dec. 31 Paid the semiannual interest on the bonds and amortized a portion of the discount calculated by the interest method.

Required:

Prepare general journal entries to record the transactions. Round the amounts of discount amortized each period to the nearest full dollar.

Part 2. A corporation completed these bond transactions:

198A
Nov. 1 Sold $2,000,000 of its own 9.1%, ten-year bonds dated November 1, 198A, with interest payable each May 1 and November 1. The bonds were sold for $2,012,928, a price to yield the buyers a 9% annual return.

Dec. 31 Made an adjusting entry to record the accrued interest on the bonds and to amortize one third of the premium applicable to the first interest period of the issue calculated by the interest method.

198B
May 1 Paid the semiannual interest on the bonds and amortized the remainder of the premium applicable to the first interest period of the issue.

Nov. 1 Paid the semiannual interest on the bonds and amortized the premium applicable to the second interest period of the issue.

Required:

Prepare general journal entries to record the transactions. Round all amounts of premium amortized to the nearest full dollar.

Problem 17–4A

Part 1. Prepare general journal entries to record the following transactions of a corporation. Round dollar amounts of interest expense and discount amortized to the nearest full dollar.

198A

Jan.   1   Sold $2,000,000 par value of its own 8.8%, ten-year bonds at a price to yield the buyers a 9% annual return. The bonds were dated January 1, 198A, with interest payable each June 30 and December 31.

June 30   Paid the semiannual interest on the bonds and amortized a portion of the discount calculated by the interest method.

Dec. 31   Paid the semiannual interest on the bonds and amortized a portion of the discount calculated by the interest method.

Part 2. Prepare general journal entries to record the following bond transactions of a corporation. Round all dollar amounts to the nearest full dollar.

198A

Sept. 1   Sold $2,000,000 par value of its 9.3%, ten-year bonds at a price to yield the buyers a 9% annual return. The bonds were dated September 1, 198A, with interest payable each March 1 and September 1.

Dec. 31   Made an adjusting entry to record the accrued interest on the bonds, calculated by the interest method, and to amortize two thirds of the premium applicable to the first interest period of the issue.

198B

Mar.   1   Paid the semiannual interest on the bonds and amortized the remainder of the premium applicable to the first interest period of the issue.

Sept. 1   Paid the semiannual interest on the bonds and amortized the premium applicable to the second interest period.

Problem 17–5A

Prepare general journal entries to record the following bond transactions of a corporation. Round the interest expense of each interest period to the nearest whole dollar.

198A

Oct.   1   Sold $2,000,000 par value of its own 8.7%, ten-year bonds at a price to yield the buyers a 9% annual return. The bonds were dated October 1, 198A, with interest payable each April 1 and October 1.

Dec. 31   Made an adjusting entry to record the accrued interest on the bonds, calculated by the interest method, and to amortize one half the discount applicable to the first interest period of the issue.

198B

Apr.   1   Paid the semiannual interest on the bonds and amortized the remainder of the discount applicable to the first interest period.

Oct.   1   Paid the semiannual interest on the bonds and amortized the discount applicable to the second interest period.

198F

Oct. 1 After recording the semiannual interest payment and amortizing the applicable amount of discount, the carrying amount of the bonds on the corporation's books was $1,975,000, and the corporation bought one tenth of the issue at 97½ and retired the bonds.

PROVOCATIVE PROBLEMS

Provocative problem 17–1
Rockhill, Inc.

Stockholders' equity in Rockhill, Inc., is represented by 200,000 shares of outstanding common stock on which the corporation has earned an unsatisfactory average of $0.60 per share during each of the last three years. And, as a result of the unsatisfactory earnings, management of the corporation is planning an expansion that will require the investment of an additional $1,000,000 in the business. The $1,000,000 is to be acquired either by selling an additional 100,000 shares of the company's common stock at $10 per share or selling at par $1,000,000 of 9%, 20-year bonds. Management estimates that the expansion will double the company's before-tax earnings in the years following completion of the expansion.

The company's management wants to finance the expansion in the manner that will best serve the interests of present stockholders, and they have asked you to determine this. In your report express an opinion as to the relative merits and disadvantages of each proposed way of securing the funds needed for the expansion. Attach to your report a schedule showing expected earnings per common share under each method of financing. Assume the company presently pays out in state and federal income taxes 50% of its before-tax earnings and that it will continue to pay out the same share after the expansion.

Provocative problem 17–2
Fan Corporation

Fan Corporation was organized on January 1, 198A, for the purpose of investing in the shares of other companies. Fan Corporation immediately issued 1,000 shares of $100 par, common stock for which it received $100,000 cash. On January 2, 198A, Fan Corporation purchased 5,000 shares (20%) of Breeze Company's outstanding stock at a cost of $100,000. The following transactions and events subsequently occurred:

198A

May 17 Breeze Company declared and paid a cash dividend of $1 per share.

Dec. 31 Breeze Company announced that its net income for the year was $40,000.

198B

June 1 Breeze Company declared and issued a stock dividend of one share for each two shares already outstanding.

Oct. 7 Breeze Company declared and paid a cash dividend of $0.75 per share.

Dec. 31   Breeze Company announced that its net income for the year was
          $48,000.

198C

Jan.   3 Fan Corporation sold all of its investment in Breeze Company for
          $112,000 cash.

Part 1. Because Fan Corporation owns 20% of Breeze Company's outstanding stock, Fan Corporation is presumed to have a significant financial influence
over Breeze Company.

Required:

1. Give the entries on the books of Fan Corporation to record the above
   events regarding its investment in Breeze Company.
2. Calculate the cost per share of Fan Corporation's investment, as reflected
   in the investment account on January 1, 198C.
3. Calculate Fan Corporation's retained earnings balance on January 5, 198C,
   after a closing of the books.

Part 2. Although Fan Corporation owns 20% of Breeze Company's outstanding stock, a thorough investigation of the surrounding circumstances indicates that Fan Corporation does not have a significant financial influence over
Breeze Company, and the cost method is the appropriate method of accounting
for the investment.

Required:

1. Give the entries on the books of Fan Corporation to record the above
   events regarding its investment in Breeze Company.
2. Calculate the cost per share of Fan Corporation's investment, as reflected
   in the investment account on January 1, 198C.
3. Calculate Fan Corporation's retained earnings balance on January 5, 198C,
   after a closing of the books.

PART SIX
Financial statements, interpretation and modifications

After studying Chapter 18, you should be able to:

☐ Tell of what working capital consists and explain why an adequate amount of working capital is important in the operation of a business.

☐ List a number of sources and uses of working capital.

☐ Explain why the net income reported on an income statement is not the amount of working capital generated by operations.

☐ Tell the adjustments that must be made to the reported net income figure in order to determine the amount of working capital generated by operations.

☐ Prepare a statement of changes in financial position.

☐ Prepare an analysis of changes in working capital items.

☐ Explain why cash generated by operations differs from net income from operations.

☐ Prepare a simple cash flow statement.

☐ Define or explain the words and phrases listed in the glossary.

Statement of changes in financial position

■ When financial statements are prepared for a business, the income statement shows the income earned or the loss incurred during the accounting period. The retained earnings statement summarizes the changes in retained earnings, and the balance sheet shows the end-of-the-period financial position. However, for a better understanding of the financing and investing activities of the business, more information is needed. This information is supplied by a *statement of changes in financial position*. Such a statement summarizes the changes that occurred in the financial position of the business by showing where it acquired resources during the period and where it applied or used resources. Usually the statement is also designed to emphasize and account for the change in the *working capital* of the business.

WORKING CAPITAL

The working capital of a business is the excess of its current assets over its current liabilities. Sometimes, working capital is called *net working capital*. The more important of a concern's current assets are usually its cash, accounts receivable, and merchandise. The merchandise is normally acquired through the use of short-term credit, primarily accounts payable. It is sold and turned into accounts receivable, which are collected and turned into cash. The cash is then used to pay bills so that short-term credit can be used again to buy more merchandise. As a result, it can be said that a concern's current assets and current liabilities circulate. Furthermore, in the circulation it is important for the current assets to exceed the current liabilities by an adequate amount.

An adequate excess of current assets over current liabilities, in other words, an adequate amount of working capital, enables a business to meet current debts, carry sufficient inventory, take advantage of cash discounts, and offer favorable credit terms to customers. A company that is deficient in working capital and unable to do these things is in a poor competitive position. Its survival may even be threatened unless its working capital position can be improved. Inadequacy of working capital has ended the business lives of many companies in which the assets far exceeded the liabilities.

Funds

The general public uses the word *funds* to mean cash, but business people apply a broader meaning. They commonly use the word as a synonym for working capital. This is understandable. Since working capital items circulate, it is only normal to think of that portion of the current assets not immediately needed to pay current debts as liquid resources or available funds. However, business people recognize that only a portion of the funds can be drawn off at any one time to pay dividends, buy plant assets, pay long-term debt, or for other like purposes. Only a portion can be used because a large share must remain in circulation.

SOURCES AND USES OF WORKING CAPITAL

Transactions that increase working capital are called *sources of working capital,* and transactions that decrease working capital are called *uses of working capital.* If the working capital of a business increased during an accounting period, more working capital was generated by its transactions than was used. On the other hand, if working capital decreased, more working capital was used than was generated.

Sources of working capital

Some of the more common sources of working capital are as follows:

Current operations   Funds in the form of cash and accounts receivable flow into a business from sales; and most expenses and goods sold result in outflows of funds. Consequently, working capital is increased by normal operations if the inflow of funds from sales exceeds the outflows for goods sold and expenses. However, the net income figure appearing on an income statement generally does not represent the amount of working capital generated by operations, because some expenses listed on the income statement do not cause working capital outflows in the period of the statement.

For example, Rexel Sales Company of Illustration 18–1 experienced a $50,000 funds inflow from sales during the year. It also experienced outflows of $30,000 for goods sold, $8,000 for salaries, and $1,200 for rent. However, there was no outflow of working capital for depreciation expense. Consequently, during the period the company gained working capital from operations equal to the sum of its reported net income plus the recorded depreciation, or it gained $9,800 plus $1,000 or $10,800 of working capital from operations.

Business executives often speak of depreciation as a source of funds, but it is not. Look again at Illustration 18–1. Sales are the source of working capital on this statement. No funds flowed into this company from recording depreciation. In this case, as with every business, the revenues are the source of working capital from operations. However, since depreciation, unlike most expenses, did not and does not cause a funds outflow in the current period, it must be added to the net income to determine working capital from operations.

Rexel Sales Company
Income Statement for Year Ended December 31, 19—

Sales		$50,000
Cost of goods sold		30,000
Gross profit from sales		$20,000
Operating expenses:		
Sales salaries expense	$8,000	
Rent expense	1,200	
Depreciation expense, equipment....	1,000	10,200
Net income		$ 9,800

Illustration 18–1

Long-term liabilities   Transactions that increase long-term liabilities increase working capital or are so treated. Therefore, they are sources of working capital regardless of whether long-term notes, mortgages, or bonds are involved. On the other hand, short-term credit, whether obtained from banks or other creditors, is not a source of working capital because short-term credit does not increase working capital. For example, if $10,000 is borrowed for, say, six months, both current assets and current liabilities are increased. However, since both are increased the same amount, total working capital is unchanged.

Sale of noncurrent assets   When a plant asset, long-term investment, or other noncurrent asset is sold for cash or receivables, working capital is increased by the amount of the sale. Therefore, such sales are sources of working capital.

Sale of capital stock   The issuance of stock for cash or current receivables increases current assets; and as a result, such sales are sources of funds. Likewise, an additional investment of current assets by a single proprietor or partner is also a source of working capital.

Uses of working capital

Common uses of working capital are the following:

Purchase of noncurrent assets   When noncurrent assets such as plant and equipment or long-term investments are purchased, working capital is reduced. Consequently, such purchases are uses of working capital.

Payment of noncurrent liabilities   Payment of a long-term debt such as a mortgage reduces working capital and is a use of working capital. Likewise, a contribution to a debt retirement fund, bond sinking fund, or other special noncurrent fund is also a use of working capital.

Capital reductions   The withdrawals of cash or other current assets by a proprietor, the purchase of treasury stock, or the purchase of stock for retirement reduce working capital and are uses of working capital.

Declaration of a dividend   The declaration of a dividend which is to be paid in cash or other current assets reduces working capital and is a use of working capital. Note that it is the declaration that is the use. The declaration creates a current liability, dividends payable, and therefore reduces working capital as soon as it is voted by the board of directors. The final payment of a dividend previously declared does not affect working capital because it reduces current assets and current liabilities in equal amounts.

STATEMENT OF CHANGES IN FINANCIAL POSITION

As previously stated, a statement of changes in financial position summarizes and discloses the financing and investing activities of the business for which it was prepared. The statement covers a period of time and is commonly designed to account for the change in the concern's working capital during the period. Such a statement is shown in Illustration 18–2.

The ability of an enterprise to generate working capital in its operations is an important factor in evaluating its ability to pay dividends, to finance new investment opportunities, and to grow. Consequently, the amount of working capital generated by operations is commonly summarized first on a statement of changes in financial position. Normally, the summary begins with the amount of the net income reported on the income statement. To this are added any expenses deducted on the income statement that did not decrease working capital, such as depreciation, depletion, and bond discount. (Bond premium is deducted from the income figure on the statement.) The resulting amount is then described as, for example, "Working capital provided by opera-

Delta Company
Statement of Changes in Financial Position
For Year Ended December 31, 198B

Sources of working capital:		
Current operations:		
Net income	$12,200	
Add expenses not requiring outlays of working		
capital in the current period:		
Depreciation of buildings and equipment	4,500	
Working capital provided by operations	$16,700	
Other sources:		
Sale of common stock...............................	12,500	
Total sources of working capital		$29,200
Uses of working capital:		
Purchase of office equipment	$ 500	
Purchase of store equipment	6,000	
Addition to building..	15,000	
Reduction of mortgage debt............................	2,500	
Declaration of dividends	3,100	
Total uses of working capital		27,100
Net increase in working capital		$ 2,100

Illustration 18–2

tions." (If the summary begins with a net loss, rather than a net income, and the net loss exceeds the expenses that did not decrease working capital, the resulting amount may be described as "Working capital used in operations.")

Working capital is commonly secured from sources other than operations. These are shown next on the statement of changes in financial position. The uses of working capital are then listed, after which the net increase or decrease in working capital is shown.

PREPARING A STATEMENT OF CHANGES IN FINANCIAL POSITION

A statement of changes in financial position could be prepared by searching through a concern's current asset and current liability accounts for the transactions that increased or decreased its working capital. However, this would be time consuming because almost every transaction completed by a concern affected these accounts and only a very few of the transactions either increased or decreased its working capital. Therefore, in preparing a statement of changes in financial position, it is not the current asset and current liability accounts that are examined for working capital changes but rather the *noncurrent accounts*. (The noncurrent accounts are the accounts other than the current asset and current liability accounts.) The noncurrent accounts are examined because (1) only a few transactions affected these accounts and (2) almost every one either increased or decreased working capital.

Normally, in making an audit of a company's noncurrent accounts, the auditor makes a list of the transactions that affected these accounts during the period under review. This list is then used along with the company's balance sheets as of the beginning and end of the period to prepare the statement of changes in financial position. The comparative balance sheet of Illustration 18–3 and the following list of transactions that affected the noncurrent accounts of Delta Company were used in preparing the Illustration 18–2 statement of changes in financial position.

Delta Company
Comparative Balance Sheet
December 31, 198B, and December 31, 198A

Assets	198B	198A
Current assets:		
Cash	$ 7,500	$ 4,800
Accounts receivable, net	8,000	9,500
Merchandise inventory	31,500	32,000
Prepaid expenses	1,000	1,200
Total current assets	$ 48,000	$ 47,500
Plant and equipment:		
Office equipment	$ 3,500	$ 3,000
Accumulated depreciation, office equipment	(900)	(600)
Store equipment	26,200	21,000
Accumulated depreciation, store equipment	(5,200)	(4,200)
Buildings	95,000	80,000
Accumulated depreciation, buildings	(10,600)	(8,200)
Land	25,000	25,000
Total plant and equipment	$133,000	$116,000
Total assets	$181,000	$163,500
Liabilities		
Current liabilities:		
Notes payable	$ 2,500	$ 1,500
Accounts payable	16,700	19,600
Dividends payable	1,000	700
Total current liabilities	$ 20,200	$ 21,800
Long-term liabilities:		
Mortgage payable	$ 17,500	$ 20,000
Total liabilities	$ 37,700	$ 41,800
Stockholders' Equity		
Common stock, $10 par value	$115,000	$100,000
Premium on common stock	8,500	5,000
Retained earnings	19,800	16,700
Total stockholders' equity	$143,300	$121,700
Total liabilities and stockholders' equity	$181,000	$163,500

Illustration 18–3

a. Purchased office equipment costing $500 during the year.
b. Purchased store equipment that cost $6,000.
c. Discarded and junked fully depreciated store equipment that cost $800 when new.
d. Added a new addition to the building that cost $15,000.
e. Earned a $12,200 net income during the year.
f. Delta Company deducted on its 198B income statement $300 of depreciation on office equipment, (g) $1,800 on its store equipment, and (h) $2,400 on its building.
i. Made a $2,500 payment on the mortgage.
j. Declared a 5% stock dividend at a time when the company's stock was selling for $12 per share.
k. Sold and issued 1,000 shares of common stock at $12.50 per share.
l. Declared cash dividends totaling $3,100 during the year.

Steps in preparing a statement of changes in financial position

Three steps are involved in preparing a statement of changes in financial position. They are the following:

1. Determine the increase or decrease in working capital for the period of the statement.
2. Prepare a working paper to account for the changes in the company's noncurrent accounts and in the process set out on the working paper the period's sources and uses of working capital.
3. Use the working paper to prepare the formal statement of changes in financial position.

DETERMINING THE CHANGE IN WORKING CAPITAL

The 198B change in Delta Company's working capital is calculated in Illustration 18–4. The calculation is a simple one requiring nothing more than a determination of the amounts of working capital at the beginning and at the end of the period and a subtraction to arrive at the increase or decrease in working capital.

Working capital, December 31, 198B:		
Current assets	$ 48,000	
Current liabilities	(20,200)	
Working capital		$ 27,800
Working capital, December 31, 198A:		
Current assets	$ 47,500	
Current liabilities	(21,800)	
Working capital		(25,700)
Increase in working capital		$ 2,100

Illustration 18–4

PREPARING THE WORKING PAPER

Delta Company's sources and uses of working capital resulted from simple transactions, and a statement of changes in financial position could be prepared for the company without a working paper. However, the working paper helps to organize the information needed for the statement and also offers a proof of the accuracy of the work.

The working paper for Delta Company's statement of changes in

Delta Company
Working Paper for Statement of Changes in Financial Position
For Year Ended December 31, 198B

	Account Balances 12/31/8A	Analyzing Entries Debit	Analyzing Entries Credit	Account Balances 12/31/8B
Debits				
Working capital	25,700			27,800
Office equipment..........................	3,000	(a) 500		3,500
Store equipment	21,000	(b) 6,000	(c) 800	26,200
Buildings	80,000	(d) 15,000		95,000
Land	25,000			25,000
Totals	154,700			177,500
Credits				
Accumulated depreciation, office equipment	600		(f) 300	900
Accumulated depreciation, store equipment	4,200	(c) 800	(g) 1,800	5,200
Accumulated depreciation, buildings	8,200		(h) 2,400	10,600
Mortgage payable	20,000	(i) 2,500		17,500
Common stock	100,000		(j) 5,000 (k) 10,000	115,000
Premium on common stock	5,000		(j) 1,000 (k) 2,500	8,500
Retained earnings.........................	16,700	(j) 6,000 (l) 3,100	(e) 12,200	19,800
Totals	154,700			177,500
Sources of working capital:				
Current operations:				
Net income............................		(e) 12,200		
Depreciation of office equipment		(f) 300		
Depreciation of store equipment		(g) 1,800		
Depreciation of buildings		(h) 2,400		
Other sources:				
Sale of stock		(k) 12,500		
Uses of working capital:				
Purchase of office equipment			(a) 500	
Purchase of store equipment			(b) 6,000	
Addition to building			(d) 15,000	
Reduction of mortgage			(i) 2,500	
Declaration of dividends			(l) 3,100	
Totals		63,100	63,100	

Illustration 18–5

financial position is shown in Illustration 18–5. Such a working paper is prepared as follows:

1. First, the amount of working capital at the beginning of the period under review is entered on the first line in the first money column and the amount of working capital at the end is entered in the last column.
2. Next, the noncurrent balance sheet amounts are entered on the working paper. The amounts or account balances as of the beginning of the period are entered in the first money column and those of the end in the last. Observe that debit items are listed first and are followed by credit items. This is a convenience that places the accumulated depreciation items with the liability and capital amounts.
3. After the noncurrent account balances are entered, the working capital amount and debit items in each column are added. Next, the credit items are added to be certain that debits equal credits.
4. After the items are added to see that debits equal credits, the phrase "Sources of working capital:" is written on the line following the total of the credit items. Sufficient lines are then skipped to allow for listing all possible sources and then the phrase "Uses of working capital:" is written.
5. Next, analyzing entries are entered in the second and third money columns. These entries do two things: (1) they account for or explain the amount of change in each noncurrent account and (2) they set out the sources and uses of working capital. (The analyzing entries on the illustrated working paper are discussed later in this chapter.)
6. After the last analyzing entry is entered, the working paper is completed by adding the Analyzing Entries columns to determine their equality. The information on the paper as to sources and uses of working capital is then used to prepare the formal statement of changes in financial position.

In passing it should be observed that the working paper is prepared solely for the purpose of bringing together information as to sources and uses of working capital. Its analyzing entries are never entered in the accounts.

Analyzing entries

As previously stated, in addition to setting out sources and uses of working capital, the analyzing entries on the working paper also account for or explain the amount of change in each noncurrent account. The change in each noncurrent account is explained with one or more analyzing entries because every transaction that caused an increase or decrease in working capital also increased or decreased a noncurrent account. Consequently, when all increases and decreases in noncurrent accounts are explained by means of analyzing entries, all sources and uses of working capital are set out on the working paper.

The analyzing entries on the working paper of Illustration 18–5 account for the changes in Delta Company's noncurrent accounts and set out its sources and uses of working capital. Explanations of the entries follow:

a. During the year Delta Company purchased new office equipment that cost $500. This required the use of working capital and also caused a $500 increase in the balance of its Office Equipment account. Consequently, analyzing entry (a) has a $500 debit to Office Equipment and a like credit to "Uses of working capital: Purchase of office equipment." The debit accounts for the change in the Office Equipment account, and the credit sets out the use of working capital.

b. Delta Company purchased $6,000 of new store equipment during the period. This required the use of $6,000 of working capital, and the use is set out with analyzing entry (b). However, the $6,000 debit of the entry does not fully account for the change in the balance of the Store Equipment account. Analyzing entry (c) is also needed.

c. During the period under review Delta Company discarded and junked fully depreciated store equipment. The equipment when new had cost $800, and the entry made to record the disposal decreased the company's Store Equipment and related accumulated depreciation accounts by $800. However, the disposal had no effect on the company's working capital. Nevertheless, analyzing entry (c) must be made to account for the changes in the accounts. Otherwise all changes in the company's noncurrent accounts will not be explained. Unless all changes are explained, the person preparing the working paper cannot be certain that all sources and uses of working capital have been set out on the working paper.

d. Delta Company used $15,000 to increase the size of its building. The cost of the addition was debited to the Buildings account, and analyzing entry (d) sets out this use of working capital.

e. Delta Company reported a $12,200 net income for 198B, and the income was a source of working capital. In the end-of-the-year closing procedures the amount of this net income was transferred from the company's Income Summary account to its Retained Earnings account. It helped change the balance of the latter account from $16,700 at the beginning of the year to $19,800 at the year-end. Observe the analyzing entry that sets out this source of working capital. The entry's debit sets out the net income as a source of working capital, and the credit helps explain the change in the Retained Earnings account.

f. *(g)*, and *(h)*. On its 198B income statement Delta Company deducted $300 of depreciation expense on its office equipment, $1,800 on its store equipment, and $2,400 on its building. As previously explained, although depreciation is a rightful deduction from revenues in arriving at net income, any depreciation so deducted must be added to net income in determining working capital from operations. The debits of entries *(f)*, *(g)*, and *(h)* show the depreciation taken by the company as part of the working capital generated by operations. The credits of the entries either account for or help account for the changes in the accumulated depreciation accounts.

i. On June 10 Delta Company made a $2,500 payment on the mortgage on its plant and equipment. The payment required the use of working capital, and it reduced the balance of the Mortgage Payable account by $2,500. Entry *(i)* sets out this use of working capital and accounts for the change in the Mortgage Payable account.

j. At the September board meeting the directors of the company declared a 5% or 500-share stock dividend on a day the company's stock was selling at $12 per share. The declaration and later distribution of this dividend had no effect on the company's working capital. However, it did decrease Retained Earnings $6,000 and increase the Common Stock account $5,000 and Premium on Common Stock $1,000. Entry *(j)* accounts for the changes in the accounts resulting from the dividend.

k. In October the company sold and issued 1,000 shares of its common stock for cash at $12.50 per share. The sale was a source of working capital that increased the balance of the company's Common Stock account $10,000 and the balance of its Premium on Common Stock account $2,500. Entry *(k)* sets out this source of working capital and completes the explanation of the changes in the stock and premium accounts.

l. At the end of each of the first three quarters in the year the company delcared a $700 quarterly cash dividend. Then, on December 22 it declared a $1,000 dividend, payable on the following January 15. The fourth dividend brought the total cash dividends declared during the year to $3,100. Each declaration required the use of working capital, and each reduced the balance of the Retained Earnings account. On the working paper the four dividends are combined and one analyzing entry is made for the $3,100 use of working capital. The entry's debit helps account for the change in the balance of the Retained Earnings account, and its credit sets out the use of working capital.

After the last analyzing entry is entered on the working paper, an examination is made to be certain that all changes in the noncurrent accounts listed on the paper have been explained with analyzing entries. To make this examination, the debits and credits in the Analyzing

Entries columns opposite each beginning account balance are added to or are subtracted from the beginning balance. The result must equal the ending balance. For example, the $3,000 beginning debit balance of office equipment plus the $500 debit of analyzing entry *(a)* equals the $3,500 ending amount of office equipment. Likewise, the $21,000 beginning balance of store equipment plus the $6,000 debit and minus the $800 credit equals the $26,200 ending balance for this asset, and so on down the working paper until all changes are accounted for. Then, after all sources and uses of working capital have been set out on the working paper, it is completed by adding the amounts in its Analyzing Entries columns.

Preparing the statement of changes in financial position from the working paper

After the working paper is completed, the sources and uses of working capital set out on the bottom of the paper are used to prepare the formal statement of changes in financial position. This is a simple task that requires little more than a relisting of the sources and uses of working capital on the formal statement. A comparison of the items appearing on the statement of Illustration 18–2 with the items at the bottom of the working paper of Illustration 18–5 will show this.

A net loss on the working paper

When a concern incurs a net loss, the amount of the loss is debited to its Retained Earnings account in the end-of-the-period closing procedures. Then, when the working paper for a statement of changes in financial position is prepared, the words "Net loss" are substituted for "Net income" in its sources of working capital section. The amount of the loss is then debited to Retained Earnings and credited to "Net loss" on the working paper. After this the loss is placed on the formal statement of changes in financial position as the first monetary item and the expenses not requiring outlays of working capital are deducted therefrom. If the net loss is less than these expenses, the resulting amount is working capital provided by operations. If the net loss exceeds these expenses, the result is working capital used in operations.

BROAD CONCEPT OF FINANCING AND INVESTING ACTIVITIES

The APB held that a statement of changes in financial position should be based on a broad concept of the financing and investing activities of a business. Also, it should disclose all important aspects of such activities even though elements of working capital are not directly affected.[1]

---

[1] APB, "Reporting Changes in Financial Position," *APB Opinion No. 19* (New York: AICPA, 1971), par. 8. Copyright (1971) by the American Institute of CPAs.

For example, the acquisition of a building in exchange for a mortgage or the conversion of bonds to stock are transactions that do not directly affect elements of working capital. However, the Board has held that such transactions should be disclosed on the statement of changes in financial position even though working capital is not directly involved. For example, if a building is acquired by issuing a mortgage, the issuance of the mortgage should be disclosed on the statement as a source of working capital, "Mortgage issued to acquire building." Likewise the acquisition of the building should appear as a use of working capital, "Building acquired by issuing a mortgage."

ANALYSIS OF WORKING CAPITAL CHANGES

The APB ruled that where a statement of changes in financial position accounts for the change in working capital, the usefulness of the statement is enhanced if it is accompanied by a report on which the changes in the various elements of working capital are analyzed in appropriate detail.[2] Such a report for Delta Company is shown in Illustration 18–6. Note how the report's final figure ties back to the final figure in Illustration 18–2.

Information for preparing the analysis of changes in working capital is taken from balance sheets as of the beginning and end of the period

Delta Company
Analysis of Changes in Working Capital Items
For Year Ended December 31, 198B

	Dec. 31, 198B	Dec. 31, 198A	Working Capital Increases	Working Capital Decreases
Current assets:				
Cash	$ 7,500	$ 4,800	$2,700	
Accounts receivable, net	8,000	9,500		$1,500
Merchandise inventory	31,500	32,000		500
Prepaid expenses	1,000	1,200		200
Total current assets	$48,000	$47,500		
Current liabilities:				
Notes payable	$ 2,500	$ 1,500		1,000
Accounts payable	16,700	19,600	2,900	
Dividends payable	1,000	700		300
Total current liabilities	$20,200	$21,800		
Working capital	$27,800	$25,700		
			$5,600	$3,500
Net increase in working capital				2,100
			$5,600	$5,600

Illustration 18–6

---

[2] Ibid., par. 12.

under review. (Compare the information in Illustration 18–6 with that in Illustration 18–3). The current asset and current liability items in the analysis and the preparation of the analysis need little discussion. However, students sometimes have difficulty understanding how, for example, an increase in a current liability results in a decrease in working capital. They should not, for when a current liability increases, a larger amount is subtracted from current assets in determining working capital.

STATEMENT OF CHANGES IN FINANCIAL POSITION, CASH BASIS

The primary purpose of a statement of changes in financial position is to show where a company acquired resources and where it applied or used resources. Most such statements are also designed to account for the change in working capital. However, the statement may instead be designed to account for the change in cash. If it is, the terminology used should clearly indicate this. For example, terminology such as "Cash provided by operations" should be used rather than "Working capital provided by operations."

The procedures for preparing a statement of changes in financial position that show the change in cash are similar to the ones used when the statement is to show change in working capital. However, a discussion of these procedures and the APB requirements that must be met if the statement is to be published are left to a more advanced book.

CASH FLOW STATEMENT

An important phase of management's work is the management of cash so that adequate cash is available to meet current debts, pay dividends, and so on, with any temporarily unneeded cash being invested to earn interest or dividends. To assist management in planning and controlling cash, a statement called a *cash flow statement* is commonly prepared. Such a statement is prepared for internal use, is not to be published, and commonly does not meet the APB requirements for a published statement of changes in financial position, cash basis.

A cash flow statement covers a period of time and accounts for the increase or decrease in a company's cash by showing where the company got cash and the uses it made of cash during the period. For example, Royal Supply Company of Illustration 18–7 began the period of the statement with $2,200 of cash. This beginning balance was increased $22,000 by cash from operations and $4,500 by cash from the sale of investments. It was decreased $12,000 by the withdrawals of the business owner and $6,500 by the purchase of plant

Royal Supply Company
Cash Flow Statement
For Year Ended December 31, 19—

Cash balance, January 1, 19—		$ 2,200
Sources of cash:		
Cash generated by operations $22,000		
Sale of investments 4,500		
Total sources of cash	$26,500	
Uses of cash:		
Withdrawals of owner $12,000		
Purchase of plant assets 6,500		
Total uses of cash	18,500	
Increase in cash		8,000
Cash balance, December 31, 19—		$10,200

Illustration 18–7

assets. All of this resulted in an $8,000 net increase in cash during the period.

A work sheet is commonly used to bring together the data needed to prepare a cash flow statement. A discussion of this work sheet is deferred to a more advanced text, and a simple analysis based on the difference between the cash basis and the accrual basis of accounting is used here to introduce the subject of cash flow. However, before beginning the analysis, a review of the difference between the cash and the accrual bases of accounting is in order.

Under the cash basis of accounting a revenue appears on the income statement of the period in which it is collected in cash, regardless of when earned. For example, if a sale of merchandise is made in November 198A but the customer does not pay for the goods until January 198B, under the cash basis of accounting the revenue from the sale appears on the 198B income statement. Likewise, under the cash basis an expense appears on the income statement of the period in which cash is disbursed in its payment, regardless of which accounting period benefited from its incurrence. Consequently, under the cash basis the gain or loss reported for an accounting period is the difference between cash received from revenues and cash disbursed for expenses. The difference is also the amount of cash generated by operations during the period.

Under the accrual basis of accounting all of this differs. Under the accrual basis, revenues are credited to the period in which they are earned regardless of when cash is received and expenses are matched with revenues regardless of when cash is disbursed. As a result, under the accrual basis the profit or loss of an accounting period is the difference between revenues earned and the expenses incurred in earning the revenues. Most enterprises use the accrual basis of accounting, and all accounting demonstrated thus far in this text has been accrual basis accounting.

PREPARING A CASH FLOW STATEMENT

Reexamine the cash flow statement of Illustration 18–7. The cash inflow shown thereon from the sale of investments and the outflow for withdrawals and to buy plant assets need no explanations. However, the inflow of cash from operations does.

Cash flows into a company from sales, and it flows out for goods sold and expenses. However, although cost of goods sold and expenses are deducted from sales on an accrual basis income statement, the resulting net income figure does not show the amount of cash generated by operations. To determine cash from operations, it is necessary to convert the item amounts on a company's income statement from an accrual basis to a cash basis.

Royal Supply Company's accrual basis income statement appears in Illustration 18–8, and its amounts are converted from an accrual

Royal Supply Company
Income Statement for Year Ended December 31, 19—

Sales, net		$90,000
Cost of goods sold:		
Inventory, January 1, 19—	$10,000	
Purchases, net	55,000	
Goods for sale	$65,000	
Inventory, December 31, 19—	11,000	
Cost of goods sold		54,000
Gross profit from sales		$36,000
Operating expenses:		
Depreciation expense	$ 3,400	
Bad debts expense	300	
Salaries and wages expense	12,500	
Other expenses	3,300	
Total operating expenses		19,500
Net income		$16,500

Illustration 18–8

basis to a cash basis in Illustration 18–10. The conversion is based on the information in the company's condensed Cash account which is shown in Illustration 18–9. Explanations of the conversion follow.

a. Cash flowed into Royal Supply Company from sales. However, the $90,000 sales figure on the company's income statement was not the amount. Rather, cash from goods sold consisted of cash sales,

$40,000, plus collections from customers, $50,500, a total of $90,500, as shown in the condensed Cash account of Illustration 18–9. Consequently, since cash from goods sold was $500 greater than the income statement sales figure, $500 is added to convert the sales figure from an accrual basis to a cash basis.

b. Likewise, the $54,000 cost of goods sold figure on the income statement is not the amount of money that flowed out to pay for goods sold. Rather, the actual cash outflow for merchandise amounted to $53,000, $200 for cash purchases plus $52,800 paid to creditors for merchandise, as shown in the condensed Cash account. Since the cash outflow for the purchase of merchandise was $1,000 less

Condensation of Royal Supply Company's Cash Account

(Debits)		(Credits)	
Balance, January 1	2,200	Cash purchases of merchandise	200
Cash sales	40,000	Payments to creditors for	
Accounts receivable		merchandise purchased	52,800
collections	50,500	Salary and wage payments	12,100
Sale of investments	4,500	Payments for other expenses	3,400
		Plant asset purchases	6,500
		Withdrawals by owner	12,000
		Balance, December 31	10,200
Total	97,200	Total	97,200

Illustration 18–9

Royal Supply Company
Conversion of Income Statement Amounts from an Accrual to a Cash Basis for Year Ended December 31, 19—

	Accrual basis amounts	Add (deduct)	Cash basis amounts
Sales, net	$90,000	$ 500	$90,500
Cost of goods sold	54,000	(1,000)	53,000
Gross profit from sales	$36,000		$37,500
Operating expenses:			
Depreciation expense	$ 3,400	(3,400)	$ –0–
Bad debts expense	300	(300)	–0–
Salaries and wages expense	12,500	(400)	12,100
Other expenses	3,300	100	3,400
Total operating expenses	$19,500		$15,500
Net income	$16,500		
Cash generated by operations			$22,000

Illustration 18–10

than the accrual basis cost of goods sold figure, $1,000 is subtracted in converting cost of goods sold from an accrual to a cash basis.

c. Since depreciation and bad debts expense did not take cash, the amounts for these items are deducted in converting the income statement amounts to a cash basis.

d. And since the cash paid by Royal Supply Company for salaries and wages was $400 less than the accrual basis income statement amount for this expense and cash disbursed for "other expenses" was $100 more, $400 is deducted and $100 is added in converting these expenses to a cash basis.

The last figure in Illustration 18–10, the $22,000 of cash generated by operations, is the amount Royal Supply Company would have reported as net income had it kept its books on a cash basis rather than an accrual basis. The $22,000 is also the amount of cash the company got from its operations and the amount that appears on its Illustration 18–7 cash flow statement as cash from this source.

GLOSSARY

Cash flow statement. A financial statement that accounts for the increase or decrease in a company's cash during a period by showing where the company got cash and the uses it made of cash.

Funds. Cash to the general public; working capital to business people.

Net working capital. A synonym for working capital.

Source of working capital. A transaction that increases working capital.

Statement of changes in financial position. A statement that reports the financing and investing activities of a business during a period, generally indicating their effects on working capital.

Use of working capital. A transaction that decreases working capital.

Working capital. The excess of a company's current assets over its current liabilities.

QUESTIONS FOR CLASS DISCUSSION

1. Tell two different meanings of the word "funds."
2. List several sources of working capital and several uses of working capital.
3. Explain why such expenses as depreciation, amortization of patents, and amortization of bond discount are added to the net income in order to determine working capital provided by operations.
4. Some people of depreciation as a source of funds. Is depreciation a source of funds?
5. On May 14 a company borrowed $30,000 by giving its bank a 60-day, interest-bearing note. Was this transaction a source of working capital?

6. A company began an accounting period with a $90,000 merchandise inventory and ended it with a $50,000 inventory. Was the decrease in inventory a source of working capital?
7. What is shown on a statement of changes in financial position?
8. Why are the noncurrent accounts examined to discover changes in working capital?
9. When a working paper for the preparation of a statement of changes in financial position is prepared, all changes in noncurrent balance sheet accounts are accounted for on the working paper. Why?
10. A company discarded and wrote off fully depreciated store equipment. What account balances appearing on the statement of changes in financial position working paper were affected by the write-off? What analyzing entry was made on the working paper to account for the write-off? If the write-off did not affect working capital, why was the analyzing entry made on the working paper?
11. Explain why a decrease in a current liability represents an increase in working capital.
12. How is the amount of cash generated by a company's operations determined?

CLASS EXERCISES

Exercise 18–1

From the following income statement, list and total the amounts of working capital the company gained from current operations.

ROCKHILL, INC.
Income Statement for Year Ended December 31, 19—

Sales		$750,000
Cost of goods sold		525,000
Gross profit from sales		$225,000
Operating expenses:		
Salaries and wages	$115,000	
Depreciation expense	20,000	
Advertising expense	5,000	
Patent costs written off	2,000	
Bad debts expense	3,000	145,000
Operating income		$ 80,000
Bond interest expense (including $6,000 accrued interest and $500 of bond discount amortized)		12,500
Net income		$ 67,500

Exercise 18–2

The 198A and 198B balance sheets of Blue Haze, Inc., carried these debit and credit amounts:

Debits	*198B*	*198A*
Cash	$ 4,000	$ 3,000
Accounts receivable, net	8,000	10,000
Merchandise inventory	22,000	20,000
Equipment..........................	19,000	15,000
Totals.........................	$53,000	$48,000

Credits		
Accumulated depreciation, equipment	$ 5,000	$ 4,000
Accounts payable	4,000	6,000
Taxes payable	2,000	1,000
Common stock, $10 par value	27,000	25,000
Premium on common stock	1,000	
Retained earnings	14,000	12,000
Totals.........................	$53,000	$48,000

Required:

Prepare a working paper for a 198B statement of changes in financial position, using the following information from the company's 198B income statement and accounts:

a. The company's income statement showed an $8,000 net income for 198B.
b. The company's equipment was depreciated $2,000 during the year.
c. Equipment costing $5,000 was purchased.
d. Fully depreciated equipment that cost $1,000 was discarded, and its cost and accumulated depreciation were removed from the accounts.
e. Two hundred shares of the company's common stock were sold and issued at $15 per share.
f. Dividends totaling $6,000 were declared and paid during the year.

Exercise 18–3

From the working paper prepared for Exercise 18–2, prepare a statement of changes in financial position for Blue Haze, Inc.

Exercise 18–4

From the information supplied in Exercise 18–2, prepare an analysis of changes in the corporation's working capital items for the year ended December 31, 198B.

Exercise 18–5

Following is the 198A income statement of Olive Company and an analysis of the items in its Cash account.

OLIVE COMPANY
Income Statement for Year Ended December 31, 198A

Sales, net		$80,000
Cost of goods sold:		
Merchandise inventory, January 1, 198A	$10,000	
Purchases, net	52,000	
Goods for sale	$62,000	
Merchandise inventory, December 31, 198A	12,000	
Cost of goods sold		50,000
Gross profit on sales		$30,000
Operating expenses:		
Salaries and wages expense	$10,000	
Rent expense	6,000	
Depreciation expense, equipment	3,000	
Bad debts expense	1,000	20,000
Net income		$10,000

Cash Account Analysis

Cash balance, January 1, 198A		$ 5,000
Debits:		
Cash sales	$25,000	
Accounts receivable collections	50,000	
Bank loan	3,000	78,000
Total		$83,000
Credits:		
Payments to creditors for merchandise	$51,000	
Salary and wage payments	9,700	
Rent payments	6,000	
Payment for new equipment purchased	3,800	
Personal withdrawals of proprietor	8,000	78,500
Cash balance, December 31, 198A		$ 4,500

Required:

1. Prepare a statement converting the company's income statement amounts from an accrual basis to a cash basis.
2. Prepare a cash flow statement for the company.

PROBLEMS

Problem 18–1

The December 31, 198A, and 198B, balance sheets of Mesa, Inc., carried the following items:

Assets	198B	198A
Cash	$ 7,000	$ 4,800
Accounts receivable, net	8,500	9,500
Merchandise inventory	31,500	32,000
Prepaid expenses	1,000	1,200
Equipment............................	30,100	24,000
Accumulated depreciation, equipment	(6,100)	(4,800)
Total assets	$72,000	$66,700

Equities		
Notes payable	$ 2,500	$ 1,500
Accounts payable	14,300	17,900
Mortgage payable	6,000	10,000
Common stock, $10 par value	30,000	25,000
Premium on common stock	2,500	
Retained earnings	16,700	12,300
Total equities....................	$72,000	$66,700

The company's 198B income statement and accounts revealed the following:

a. Net income for the year, $7,400.
b. The equipment depreciated $2,100 during the year.
c. Fully depreciated equipment that cost $800 was discarded, and its cost and accumulated depreciation were removed from the accounts.
d. Equipment costing $6,900 was purchased.
e. The mortgage was reduced by a $4,000 payment.
f. Five hundred shares of common stock were issued at $15 per share.
g. Cash dividends totaling $3,000 were declared and paid.

Required:

Prepare a working paper for a statement of changes in financial position, a formal statement of changes in financial position, and an analysis of changes in working capital items.

Problem 18–2

Ed Mills operates Racquet Shop as a single proprietorship, and the shop's 198A and 198B balance sheets carried these items:

Assets	198B	198A
Cash	$ 5,200	$ 4,400
Accounts receivable, net	15,100	15,600
Merchandise inventory	30,300	31,200
Prepaid expenses	1,100	900
Office equipment	2,800	2,600
Accumulated depreciation, office equipment	(900)	(800)
Store equipment	14,900	12,500
Accumulated depreciation, store equipment	(4,700)	(3,800)
Total assets	$63,800	$62,600

Liabilities and Owner's Equity	198B	198A
Notes payable	$ 4,000	$ 5,000
Accounts payable	16,000	14,500
Ed Mills, capital	43,800	43,100
Total liabilities and owner's equity	$63,800	$62,600

The store's 198B balance sheet summarized the change in owner's equity as follows:

Ed Mills, capital, January 1, 198B		$43,100
Net income for the year	$10,300	
Less withdrawals	9,600	
Excess of income over withdrawals		700
Ed Mills, capital, December 31, 198B		$43,800

The accounts showed that the following occurred during 198B: (1) Office equipment that cost $400 and had been depreciated $200 was traded on office equipment having a $500 cash price. A $100 trade-in allowance was received, and the income tax method was used to record the transaction. (2) Store equipment costing $3,000 was purchased. (3) Fully depreciated store equipment that cost $600 when new was discarded. (4) The 198B income statement showed depreciation expense on office equipment, $300; and on store equipment, $1,500.

Required:

Prepare a working paper for a statement of changes in financial position, a formal statement of changes in financial position, and an analysis of changes in working capital items.

Problem 18–3

Greentree Corporation's December 31, 198A, and 198B balance sheets carried the following items:

Assets	198B	198A
Cash	$ 19,100	$ 22,300
Accounts receivable, net	16,200	15,600
Merchandise inventory	50,200	51,400
Prepaid expenses	1,300	1,100
Investment in bonds	–0–	15,000
Office equipment	4,400	4,200
Accumulated depreciation, office equipment	(1,400)	(1,300)
Store equipment	26,000	24,300
Accumulated depreciation, store equipment	(5,200)	(3,600)
Store building	100,000	–0–
Accumulated depreciation, store building	(1,200)	–0–
Land	20,000	–0–
Total assets	$229,400	$129,000

Equities	198B	198A
Accounts payable	$ 20,300	$ 21,700
Income taxes payable	1,400	1,100
Mortgage payable	65,000	–0–
Common stock, $10 par value	100,000	80,000
Premium on common stock	4,000	–0–
Retained earnings	38,700	26,200
Total equities	$229,400	$129,000

The company's 198B income statement and accounting records showed:

a. The company had earned a $18,500 net income during the year.

b. It sold a long-term investment in bonds for cash at cost.

c. It then purchased for $120,000 the land and building it had occupied as a rental for a number of years, giving $55,000 in cash and issuing a mortgage for the balance.

d. Office equipment that cost $500 and had been depreciated $300 was traded in on new office equipment priced at $800. A $300 trade-in allowance was received.

e. Store equipment that cost $2,500 was purchased during the year.

f. Fully depreciated store equipment that cost $800 was discarded, and its cost and accumulated depreciation were removed from the accounts.

g. The office equipment was depreciated $400, the store equipment $2,400, and the building $1,200 during the year.

h. Two thousand shares of common stock were sold and issued at $12 per share.

i. Cash dividends totaling $6,000 were declared and paid during the year.

Required

Prepare a working paper for a statement of changes in financial position, a formal statement of changes in financial position, and an analysis of changes in the company's working capital items.

Problem 18–4

The December 31, 198A, and 198B balance sheets of Hardrock, Inc., carried the following items:

Assets	198B	198A
Cash	$ 20,200	$ 15,400
Accounts receivable, net	33,200	32,100
Inventories	60,700	56,400
Prepaid expenses	2,000	1,700
Bond sinking fund	8,000	–0–
Long-term investment, bonds.................	–0–	10,000
Machinery	126,600	92,800
Accumulated depreciation, machinery	(39,700)	(33,700)
Buildings	194,500	112,500
Accumulated depreciation, buildings	(25,000)	(20,200)
Factory land	30,000	30,000
Total assets	$410,500	$297,000

Equities	198B	198A
Accounts payable	$ 24,400	$ 26,600
Wages payable	2,900	2,800
Federal income taxes payable	2,100	1,200
Bonds payable	100,000	–0–
Discount on bonds payable	(1,800)	–0–
Common stock, $10 par value	210,000	200,000
Premium on common stock	22,500	20,000
Retained earnings	50,400	46,400
Total equities	$410,500	$297,000

At the end of 198B the company's noncurrent accounts showed these amounts:

Bond Sinking Fund

Date		Explanation	Debit	Credit	Balance
198B					
Dec.	31	First annual deposit	8,000		8,000

Long-Term Investment, Bonds

Date		Explanation	Debit	Credit	Balance
198B					
Jan.	1	Balance			10,000
May	7	Sold		10,000	–0–

Machinery

Date		Explanation	Debit	Credit	Balance
198B					
Jan.	1	Balance			92,800
	23	Purchase	38,100		130,900
July	8	Discarded machinery		4,300	126,600

Accumulated Depreciation, Machinery

Date		Explanation	Debit	Credit	Balance
198B					
Jan.	1	Balance			33,700
July	8	Discarded Machinery	4,300		29,400
Dec.	31	Year's depreciation		10,300	39,700

Buildings

Date		Explanation	Debit	Credit	Balance
198B					
Jan.	1	Balance			112,500
	8	Building addition	82,000		194,500

Accumulated Depreciation, Buildings

Date		Explanation	Debit	Credit	Balance
198B					
Jan.	1	Balance			20,200
Dec.	31	Year's depreciation		4,800	25,000

Factory Land

Date		Explanation	Debit	Credit	Balance
198B					
Jan.	1	Balance			30,000

Bonds Payable

Date		Explanation	Debit	Credit	Balance
198B					
Jan.	1	Issued 8½%, ten-year bonds		100,000	100,000

Bond Discount

Date		Explanation	Debit	Credit	Balance
198B					
Jan.	1	Discount on issuance	2,000		2,000
June	30	Amortization		100	1,900
Dec.	31	Amortization		100	1,800

Common Stock, $10 Par Value

Date		Explanation	Debit	Credit	Balance
198B					
Jan.	1	Balance			200,000
Dec.	1	Stock dividend		10,000	210,000

Premium on Common Stock

Date		Explanation	Debit	Credit	Balance
198B					
Jan.	1	Balance			20,000
Dec.	1	Stock dividend		2,500	22,500

Retained Earnings

Date		Explanation	Debit	Credit	Balance
198B					
Jan.	1	Balance			46,400
June	9	Cash dividend	16,000		30,400
Dec.	1	Stock dividend	12,500		17,900
	31	Net income		32,500	50,400

The bonds held as a long-term investment were sold for cash at cost, and the proceeds were used to help finance the plant expansion. The company reported a 198B net income of $32,500.

Required:

Use the information supplied to prepare a working paper for a statement of changes in financial position, a formal statement of changes in financial position, and an analysis of changes in working capital items.

Problem 18–5

The income statement of Pro Shop and an analysis of the entries in its Cash account for the year of the income statement follow:

PRO SHOP

Income Statement for Year Ended December 31, 19—

Sales, net		$121,400
Cost of goods sold:		
Merchandise inventory, January 1, 19—	$22,400	
Purchases, net	77,100	
Goods for sale..............................	$99,500	
Merchandise inventory, December 31, 19—	21,300	
Cost of goods sold		78,200
Gross profit on sales		$ 43,200
Operating expenses:		
Salaries and wages expense....................	$30,300	
Rent expense	9,000	
Depreciation expense........................	2,400	
Bad debts expense	600	
Store supplies expense	1,200	
Total operating expenses		43,500
Operating loss		$ (300)
Interest expense		200
Net loss		$ (500)

Analysis of Cash Account

Cash balance, January 1, 19—		$ 6,200
Debits:		
Cash sales	$26,400	
Accounts receivable collections	97,100	
Sale of unneeded equipment at book value	200	
Bank loan	5,000	128,700
Total		$134,900
Credits:		
Payments to creditors for merchandise	$78,400	
Payments for store supplies	1,400	
Salary and wage payments	30,200	
Rent payments	8,250	
Purchase of equipment	1,500	
Personal withdrawals of proprietor	7,200	126,950
Cash balance, December 31, 19—		$ 7,950

Required:

Prepare a statement converting the shop's income statement amounts from an accrual basis to a cash basis and prepare a cash flow statement for the shop

---

ALTERNATE PROBLEMS

Problem 18–1A

The 198A and 198B balance sheets of Hilltop, Inc., carried these items:

Assets	*198B*	*198A*
Current assets:		
Cash	$ 12,700	$ 11,800
Accounts receivable, net	34,900	33,400
Merchandise inventory	85,900	86,700
Prepaid expenses	2,000	1,800
Total current assets	$135,500	$133,700
Plant and equipment:		
Office equipment	$ 5,400	$ 6,100
Accumulated depreciation, office equipment ...	(2,500)	(2,400)
Store equipment	31,700	27,800
Accumulated depreciation, store equipment ...	(7,400)	(6,500)
Total plant and equipment	$ 27,200	$ 25,000
Total assets	$162,700	$158,700

Equities	198B	198A
Current liabilities:		
Accounts payable	$ 22,500	$ 23,200
Notes payable	4,500	5,000
Income taxes payable	500	300
Total liabilities	$ 27,500	$ 28,500
Stockholders' equity:		
Common stock, $5 par value	$105,000	$100,000
Premium on common stock	8,500	5,500
Retained earnings	21,700	24,700
Total stockholders' equity	$135,200	$130,200
Total equities	$162,700	$158,700

An examination of the company's 198B income statement and accounting records revealed this additional information:

a. A $15,000 net income was earned in 198B.
b. Depreciation charged on office equipment, $600; and on store equipment, $1,500.
c. Office equipment that cost $700 and had been depreciated $500 was sold to an employee for its book value.
d. Store equipment that cost $4,500 was purchased during 198B.
e. Fully depreciated store equipment that cost $600 was discarded, and its cost and accumulated depreciation were removed from the accounts.
f. Cash dividends totaling $10,000 were declared during the year.
g. A 5% stock dividend was declared and distributed during the year at a time when the company's stock was selling at $8 per share.

Required:

Prepare a working paper for a statement of changes in financial position, a formal statement of changes in financial position, and an analysis of the changes in working capital items.

Problem 18–2A

The December 31, 198A, and 198B, balance sheets of Seaside, Inc. carried these items:

Assets	198B	198A
Cash	$ 10,400	$ 11,500
Accounts receivable, net	26,600	27,300
Merchandise inventory........................	68,700	64,200
Prepaid expenses	1,100	800
Office equipment	6,100	6,200
Accumulated depreciation, office equipment	(2,100)	(1,900)
Store equipment	39,900	39,800
Accumulated depreciation, store equipment	(10,900)	(7,600)
Total assets	$139,800	$140,300

Liabilities and Stockholders' Equity	198B	198A
Notes payable	$ 5,000	$ 2,500
Accounts payable	17,300	17,600
Common stock, $5 par value	105,000	100,000
Premium on common stock	5,500	4,000
Retained earnings	7,000	16,200
Total liabilities and stockholders' equity ...	$139,800	$140,300

The company's 198B income statement and accounting records revealed the following:

a. A $700 net loss was incurred in 198B.

b. Depreciation on office equipment, $600; and on store equipment, $3,800.

c. Office equipment costing $300 was purchased during the year.

d. Fully depreciated office equipment that cost $400 was discarded, and its cost and accumulated depreciation were removed from the accounts.

e. Store equipment that cost $800 and had been depreciated $500 was traded in on new equipment having a $1,000 cash price. A $400 trade-in allowance was received.

f. A 1,000-share stock dividend was declared and distributed while the stock was selling at $6.50 per share.

g. Cash dividends totaling $2,000 were declared and paid during the year.

Required:

Prepare a working paper for a statement of changes in financial position, a formal statement of changes in financial position, and an analysis of changes in working capital items.

Problem 18–3A

Dale Corporation's 198A and 198B balance sheets carried these items:

	December 31,	
Assets	*198B*	*198A*
Cash	$ 14,800	$ 18,600
Accounts receivable, net	15,800	16,200
Merchandise inventory	73,500	72,400
Other current assets	1,100	1,400
Office equipment	4,500	4,700
Accumulated depreciation, office equipment ..	(1,900)	(1,600)
Store equipment	22,000	15,500
Accumulated depreciation, store equipment ...	(4,600)	(4,200)
Building	85,000	–0–
Accumulated depreciation, building	(2,000)	–0–
Land	20,000	–0–
Total assets	$228,200	$123,000

| | December 31, | |
Equities	198B	198A
Notes payable	$ 7,500	$ –0–
Accounts payable	29,200	28,400
Other current liabilities	1,800	2,100
Mortgage payable	60,000	–0–
Common stock, $25 par value	100,000	75,000
Premium on common stock	5,000	–0–
Retained earnings	24,700	17,500
Total equities	$228,200	$123,000

The company's 198B income statement and accounting records showed the following:

a. A 198B net income of $13,200.

b. Depreciation on office equipment, $500; on store equipment, $1,600; and on the building, $2,000.

c. Fully depreciated office equipment that cost $200 was discarded, and its cost and accumulated depreciation were removed from the accounts.

d. Store equipment that cost $8,000 was purchased during the year.

e. Store equipment that cost $1,500 and had been depreciated $1,200 was sold to an employee for its book value.

f. The mortgage was incurred in purchasing for $105,000 the land and building previously rented by the company.

g. One thousand shares of common stock were sold and issued at $30 per share.

h. Cash dividends totaling $6,000 were declared and paid during the year.

Required:

Prepare a working paper for a statement of changes in financial position and a formal statement of changes in financial position. Also prepare an analysis of changes in working capital items.

Problem 18–5A

The income statement of Westgate Shop and an analysis of its Cash account for the year of the income statement follow:

WESTGATE SHOP
Income Statement for Year Ended December 31, 19—

Sales, net		$258,400
Cost of goods sold:		
Merchandise inventory, January 1, 19—	$ 52,200	
Purchases, net	174,500	
Goods for sale	$226,700	
Merchandise inventory, December 31, 19—	53,800	
Cost of goods sold		172,900
Gross profit on sales		$ 85,500

Operating expenses:

Salaries and wages expense	$ 48,600	
Rent expense	15,000	
Depreciation expense	3,200	
Bad debts expense	1,200	
Store supplies expense	1,000	
Other operating expenses	1,800	
Total operating expenses		70,800
Operating income		$ 14,700
Interest expense		100
Net income		$ 14,600

Analysis of Cash Account

Cash balance, January 1, 19—		$ 10,200
Debits:		
Cash sales	$ 62,500	
Accounts receivable collections	196,500	
Bank loan	5,000	
Sale of unneeded equipment at book value	300	264,300
Total		$274,500
Credits:		
Creditor payments for merchandise purchased	$175,300	
Rent payments	16,250	
Creditor payments for store supplies bought	800	
Salary and wage payments	48,100	
Other operating expense payments	1,700	
New equipment purchased	10,000	
Personal withdrawals by proprietor	12,000	264,150
Cash balance, December 31, 19—		$ 10,350

Required:

Prepare a statement converting the shop's income statement amounts from an accrual basis to a cash basis and prepare a cash flow statement for the shop.

PROVOCATIVE PROBLEMS

Provocative problem 18–1
Alpha Company

The presidents of Alpha Company and Beta Company are goods friends and often play golf together. Today on the golf course the president of Alpha Company bragged that his company had purchased $2,500,000 of new plant and equipment during the past two years without incurring any long-term debt or issuing any additional stock. The president of Beta Company wondered how this was done, but he did not ask. However, on returning to his office he got out the published year-end financial statements of Alpha Company, which provided the following information:

	In thousands of dollars		
Assets	*198C*	*198B*	*198A*
Cash	$ 790	$ 660	$ 510
Temporary investments	–0–	1,150	1,550
Accounts receivable, net	840	790	820
Inventories	960	1,020	930
Plant and equipment	7,000	5,300	4,500
Accumulated depreciation, plant and equipment	(1,990)	(1,570)	(1,210)
Total assets	$7,600	$7,350	$7,100

Equities			
Accounts payable	$ 960	$ 970	$ 940
Other short-term payables	830	810	800
Common stock	3,000	3,000	3,000
Premium on common stock	500	500	500
Retained earnings	2,310	2,070	1,860
Total equities	$7,600	$7,350	$7,100
Net income after taxes	$ 390	$ 360	$ 320
Depreciation expense, plant and equipment ...	420	360	300
Dividends declared and paid	150	150	150

Explain how Alpha Company was able to purchase $2,500,000 of new plant and equipment during 198B and 198C. Back your explanation with figures and a statement of changes in financial position.

Provocative problem 18–2
Sports Center

Ed Mann owns Sports Center, a sporting goods store. During 198B he remodeled and replaced $18,000 of the store's fully depreciated equipment with new equipment costing $22,000. However, by the year-end he was having trouble meeting the store's current expenses and had to borrow $5,000 from the bank on a short-term note payable. As a result, he asked his accountant to prepare some sort of a report showing what had happened to the store's funds during the year. The accountant analyzed the changes in the store's accounts and produced the following statement of changes in financial position, which he called a statement of sources and uses of funds.

SPORTS CENTER
Statement of Sources and Uses of Funds
Year Ended December 31, 198B

Sources of funds:
  Current operations:
    Net income earned in 198B $17,200
    Add expenses not requiring the use of funds:
      Depreciation of store equipment   4,500
        Total funds from operations $21,700
  Other sources:
    Mortgage on new store equipment 15,000
        Total new funds $36,700

Uses of funds:
  Purchase of new equipment $22,000
  Personal withdrawals of proprietor 12,000
      Total uses of funds   34,000
Net increase in funds .... $ 2,700

On reading the report, Mr. Mann was dumbfounded by the $2,700 increase in funds in a year he knew his store's bank balance had decreased by $8,500. Also, he could not understand how depreciation was a source of funds, but the $5,000 bank loan was not. Explain these points to Mr. Mann, and use the following post-closing trial balances from the store's ledger to prepare a different statement from that prepared by the accountant to help make your explanation clear.

SPORTS CENTER
Post-Closing Trial Balances

	Dec. 31, 198B		Dec. 31, 198A	
Cash	$ 2,900		$11,400	
Accounts receivable	17,900		13,900	
Allowance for doubtful accounts		$ 500		$ 400
Merchandise inventory	27,400		17,200	
Prepaid expenses	800		500	
Store equipment	39,000		35,000	
Accumulated depreciation, store equipment		10,500		24,000
Notes payable		5,000		
Accounts payable		8,800		10,400
Accrued payables		500		700
Mortgage payable		15,000		
Ed Mann, capital		47,700		42,500
Totals	$88,000	$88,000	$78,000	$78,000

After studying Chapter 19, you should be able to:

☐ Describe comparative financial statements, how they are prepared, and the limitations associated with interpeting them.

☐ Prepare common-size comparative statements and interpret them.

☐ Explain the importance of working capital in the analysis of financial statements and list the typical ratios used to analyze working capital.

☐ Calculate the common ratios used in analyzing the balance sheet and income statement and state what each ratio purports to measure.

☐ State the limitations associated with using financial statement ratios and the sources from which standards for comparison may be obtained.

☐ Define or explain the words and phrases listed in the chapter Glossary.

Analyzing financial statements

■ The financial statements of a business are analyzed to determine its overall position and to find out about certain aspects of that position, such as earnings prospects and debt-paying ability. In making the analysis, individual statement items are in themselves generally not too significant. However, relationships between items and groups of items plus changes that have occurred are significant. As a result, financial statement analysis requires that relationships between items and groups of items and changes in items and groups be seen.

COMPARATIVE STATEMENTS

Changes in statement items can usually best be seen when item amounts for two or more successive years are placed side by side in columns on a single statement. Such a statement is called a *comparative statement*. Each of the financial statements, or portions thereof, may be presented in the form of a comparative statement.

In its most simple form a comparative balance sheet consists of the item amounts from two or more of a company's successive balance sheets arranged side by side, so that changes in amounts may be seen. However, such a statement can be improved by also showing in both dollar amounts and in percentages the changes that have occurred. When this is done, as in Illustration 19–1, large dollar and large percentage changes become more readily apparent.

A comparative income statement is prepared in the same manner as a comparative balance sheet. Income statement amounts for two

Anchor Supply Company
Comparative Balance Sheet
December 31, 1981, and December 31, 198B

	Years Ended December 31		Amount of Increase or (Decrease) during 198B	Percent of Increase or (Decrease) during 198B
	198B	198A		
Assets				
Current assets:				
Cash..................................	$ 18,000	$ 90,500	$ (72,500)	(80.1)
Accounts receivable, net	68,000	64,000	4,000	6.3
Merchandise inventory	90,000	84,000	6,000	7.1
Prepaid expenses	5,800	6,000	(200)	(3.3)
Total current assets	$181,800	$244,500	$ (62,700)	(25.6)
Long-term investments:				
Real estate	–0–	$ 30,000	$ (30,000)	(100.0)
Apex Company common stock	–0–	50,000	(50,000)	(100.0)
Total long-term investments	–0–	$ 80,000	$ (80,000)	(100.0)
Plant and equipment:				
Office equipment, net	$ 3,500	$ 3,700	$ (200)	(5.4)
Store equipment, net	17,900	6,800	11,100	163.2
Buildings, net	176,800	28,000	148,800	531.4
Land................................	50,000	20,000	30,000	150.0
Total plant and equipment	$248,200	$ 58,500	$189,700	324.3
Total assets	$430,000	$383,000	$ 47,000	12.3
Liabilities				
Current liabilities:				
Notes payable	$ 5,000	–0–	$ 5,000	
Accounts payable	43,600	$ 55,000	(11,400)	(20.7)
Taxes payable	4,800	5,000	(200)	(4.0)
Wages payable	800	1,200	(400)	(33.3)
Total current liabilities	$ 54,200	$ 61,200	$ (7,000)	(11.4)
Long-term liabilities:				
Mortgage payable	$ 60,000	$ 10,000	$ 50,000	500.0
Total liabilities	$114,200	$ 71,200	$ 43,000	60.4
Capital				
Common stock, $10 par value	$250,000	$250,000	–0–	–0–
Retained earnings	65,800	61,800	$ 4,000	6.5
Total capital	$315,800	$311,800	$ 4,000	1.3
Total liabilities and capital	$430,000	$383,000	$ 47,000	12.3

Illustration 19–1

or more successive periods are placed side by side, with dollar and percentage changes in additional columns. Such a statement is shown in Illustration 19–2.

Analyzing and interpreting comparative statements

In analyzing and interpreting comparative data, it is necessary for the analyst to select for study any items showing significant dollar or percentage changes. The analyst then tries to determine the reasons for each change and if possible whether they are favorable or unfavorable. For example, in Illustration 19–1, the first item, "Cash," shows a large decrease. At first glance this appears unfavorable. However, when the decrease in "Cash" is considered with the decrease in "Investments" and the increases in "Store equipment," "Buildings," and "Land," plus the increase in "Mortgage payable," it becomes apparent the company has materially increased its plant assets between the two balance sheet dates. Further study reveals the company has apparently constructed a new building on land it has held as an investment until needed in this expansion. Also, it seems the company paid for its new plant assets by reducing cash, selling its Apex Company Common stock, and issuing a $50,000 mortgage.

As an aid in controlling operations, a comparative income statement is usually more valuable than a comparative balance sheet. For example, in Illustration 19–2, "Gross sales" increased 14.1% and "Net sales" increased 13.9%. At the same time, "Sales returns" increased 32.4%, or at a rate more than twice that of gross sales. Returned sales represent wasted sales effort and indicate dissatisfied customers. Consequently, such an increase in returns should be investigated, and the reason therefor determined if at all possible. Also, in addition to the large increase in the "Sales returns," it is significant that the rate of increase in "Cost of goods sold" is greater than that of "Net sales." This is an unfavorable trend and should be remedied if at all possible.

In attempting to account for Anchor Supply Company's increase in sales, the increases in advertising and in plant assets merit attention. It is reasonable to expect an increase in advertising to increase sales. It is also reasonable to expect an increase in plant assets to result in a sales increase.

Calculating percentage increases and decreases

When percentage increases and decreases are calculated for comparative statements, the increase or decrease in an item is divided by the amount shown for the item in the base year. No problems arise in these calculations when positive amounts are shown in the base year. However, when no amount is shown or a negative amount is shown in the base year, a percentage increase or decrease cannot be

Anchor Supply Company
Comparative Income Statement
Years Ended December 31, 198A, and 198B

	Years Ended December 31		Amount of Increase or (Decrease) during 198B	Percent of Increase or (Decrease) during 198B
	198B	198A		
Gross sales	$973,500	$853,000	$120,500	14.1
Sales returns and allowances	13,500	10,200	3,300	32.4
Net sales	$960,000	$842,800	$117,200	13.9
Cost of goods sold	715,000	622,500	92,500	14.9
Gross profit from sales	$245,000	$220,300	$ 24,700	11.2
Operating expenses:				
Selling expenses:				
Advertising expense	$ 7,500	$ 5,000	$ 2,500	50.0
Sales salaries expense	113,500	98,000	15,500	15.8
Store supplies expense	3,200	2,800	400	14.3
Depreciation expense, store equipment	2,400	1,700	700	41.2
Delivery expense	14,800	14,000	800	5.7
Total selling expenses	$141,400	$121,500	$ 19,900	16.4
General and administrative expenses:				
Office salaries expense	$ 41,000	$ 40,050	$ 950	2.4
Office supplies expense	1,300	1,250	50	4.0
Insurance expense	1,600	1,200	400	33.3
Depreciation expense, office equipment	300	300	–0–	–0–
Depreciation expense, buildings	2,850	1,500	1,350	90.0
Bad debts expense	2,250	2,200	50	2.3
Total general and admin. expenses	$ 49,300	$ 46,500	$ 2,800	6.0
Total operating expenses	$190,700	$168,000	$ 22,700	13.5
Operating income	$ 54,300	$ 52,300	$ 2,000	3.8
Less interest expense	2,300	1,000	1,300	130.0
Income before taxes	$ 52,000	$ 51,300	$ 700	1.4
Income taxes	19,000	18,700	300	1.6
Net income	$ 33,000	$ 32,600	$ 400	1.2

Illustration 19–2

calculated. For example, in Illustration 19–1 there were no notes payable at the end of 198A and a percentage change for this item cannot be calculated.

In this text, percentages and ratios are typically rounded to one or two decimal places. However, there is no uniform agreement on this matter. In general, percentages should be carried out to the point of assuring that meaningful information is conveyed. However, they should not be carried so far that the significance of relationships tend to become "lost" in the length of the numbers.

Trend percentages

Trend percentages or index numbers are useful in comparing data covering a number of years, since they emphasize changes that have occurred during the period. They are calculated as follows:

1. A base year is selected, and each item amount on the base year statement is assigned a weight of 100%.
2. Then each item from the statements for the years after the base year is expressed as a percentage of its base year amount. To determine these percentages, the item amounts in the years after the base year are divided by the amount of the item in the base year.

For example, if 198A is made the base year for the following data, the trend percentages for "Sales" are calculated by dividing by $210,000, the amount shown for "Sales" in each year after the first. The trend percentages for "Cost of goods sold" are found by dividing by $145,000 the amount shown for "Cost of goods sold" in each year after the first. And, the trend percentages for "Gross profit" are found by dividing the amounts shown for "Gross profit" by $65,000.

	198A	198B	198C	198D	198E	198F
Sales	$210,000	$204,000	$292,000	$284,000	$310,000	$324,000
Cost of goods sold	145,000	139,000	204,000	198,000	218,000	229,000
Gross profit	$ 65,000	$ 65,000	$ 88,000	$ 86,000	$ 92,000	$ 95,000

When these divisions are made, the trends for these three items appear as follows:

	198A	198B	198C	198D	198E	198F
Sales	100	97	139	135	148	154
Cost of goods sold	100	96	141	137	150	158
Gross profit	100	100	135	132	142	146

It is interesting to note in the illustrated trends that while after the second year the sales trend is upward, the cost of goods sold trend is upward at a slightly more rapid rate. This indicates a contracting gross profit rate and should receive attention.

It should be pointed out in a discussion of trends that the trend for a single balance sheet or income statement item is seldom very informative. However, a comparison of trends for related items often tells the analyst a great deal. For example, a downward sales trend with an upward trend for merchandise inventory, accounts receivable, and loss on bad debts would generally indicate an unfavorable situation. On the other hand, an upward sales trend with a downward trend or a slower upward trend for accounts receivable, merchandise inventory, and selling expenses would indicate an increase in operating efficiency.

Anchor Supply Company
Common-Size Comparative Balance Sheet
December 31, 198A, and December 31, 198B

	Years Ended December 31		Common-Size Percentages	
	198B	198A	198B	198A
Assets				
Current assets:				
Cash	$ 18,000	$ 90,500	4.19	23.63
Accounts receivable, net	68,000	64,000	15.81	16.71
Merchandise inventory	90,000	84,000	20.93	21.93
Prepaid expenses	5,800	6,000	1.35	1.57
Total current assets	$181,800	$244,500	42.28	63.84
Long-term investments:				
Real estate	–0–	$ 30,000		7.83
Apex Company common stock	–0–	50,000		13.05
Total long-term investments	–0–	$ 80,000		20.88
Plant and equipment:				
Office equipment, net	$ 3,500	$ 3,700	0.81	0.97
Store equipment, net	17,900	6,800	4.16	1.78
Buildings, net	176,800	28,000	41.12	7.31
Land	50,000	20,000	11.63	5.22
Total plant and equipment	$248,200	$ 58,500	57.72	15.28
Total assets	$430,000	$383,000	100.00	100.00
Liabilities				
Current liabilities:				
Notes payable	$ 5,000	–0–	1.16	
Accounts payable	43,600	$ 55,000	10.14	14.36
Taxes payable	4,800	5,000	1.12	1.31
Wages payable	800	1,200	0.19	0.31
Total current liabilities	$ 54,200	$ 61,200	12.61	15.98
Long-term liabilities:				
Mortgage payable	$ 60,000	$ 10,000	13.95	2.61
Total liabilities	$114,200	$ 71,200	26.56	18.59
Capital				
Common stock, $10 par value	$250,000	$250,000	58.14	65.27
Retained earnings	65,800	61,800	15.30	16.14
Total capital	$315,800	$311,800	73.44	81.44
Total liabilities and capital	$430,000	$383,000	100.00	100.00

Illustration 19–3

Common-size comparative statements

The comparative statements illustrated thus far do not show proportional changes in items except in a general way. Changes in proportions are often shown and emphasized by *common-size comparative statements*.

A common-size statement is so called because its items are shown in common-size figures, figures that are fractions of 100%. For example, on a common-size balance sheet (1) the asset total is assigned a value of 100%. (2) The total of the liabilities and owners' equity is also assigned a value of 100%. Then (3), each asset, liability, and owners' equity item is shown as a fraction of one of the 100% totals. When a

Anchor Supply Company
Common-Size Comparative Income Statement
Year Ended December 31, 198A, and 198B

	Years Ended December 31		Common-Size Percentages	
	198B	198A	198B	198A
Gross sales	$973,500	$853,000	101.41	101.21
Sales returns and allowances	13,500	10,200	1.41	1.21
Net sales	$960,000	$842,800	100.00	100.00
Cost of goods sold	715,000	622,500	74.48	73.86
Gross profit from sales	$245,000	$220,300	25.52	26.14
Operating expenses:				
Selling expenses:				
Advertising expense	$ 7,500	$ 5,000	0.78	0.59
Sales salaries expense	113,500	98,000	11.82	11.63
Stores supplies expense	3,200	2,800	0.33	0.33
Depreciation expense, store equipment	2,400	1,700	0.25	0.20
Delivery expense	14,800	14,000	1.54	1.66
Total selling expenses	$141,400	$121,500	14.72	14.41
General and administrative expenses:				
Office salaries expense	$ 41,000	$ 40,050	4.27	4.75
Office supplies expense	1,300	1,250	0.14	0.15
Insurance expense	1,600	1,200	0.17	0.14
Depreciation expense, office equipment	300	300	0.03	0.04
Depreciation expense, buildings	2,850	1,500	0.30	0.18
Bad debts expense	2,250	2,200	0.23	0.26
Total general and administrative expenses	$ 49,300	$ 46,500	5.14	5.52
Total operating expenses	$190,700	$168,000	19.86	19.93
Operating income	$ 54,300	$ 52,300	5.66	6.21
Less interest expense	2,300	1,000	0.24	0.12
Income before taxes	$ 52,000	$ 51,300	5.42	6.09
Income taxes	19,000	18,700	1.98	2.22
Net income	$ 33,000	$ 32,600	3.44	3.87

Illustration 19–4

company's successive balance sheets are shown in this manner (see Illustration 19–3), proportional changes are emphasized.

A common-size income statement is prepared by assigning net sales a 100% value and then expressing each statement item as a percent of net sales. Such a statement is an informative and useful tool. If the 100% sales amount on the statement is assumed to represent one sales dollar, then the remaining items show how each sales dollar was distributed to costs, expenses, and profit. For example, on the comparative income statement shown in Illustration 19–4, the 198A cost of goods sold consumed 73.86 cents of each sales dollar. In 198B cost of goods sold consumed 74.48 cents of each sales dollar. While this increase is small, if in 198B the proportion of cost of goods sold had remained at the 198A level, almost $6,000 additional net income would have been earned.

Common-size percentages point out efficiencies and inefficiencies that are otherwise difficult to see. For this reason they are a valuable management tool. To illustrate, sales salaries of Anchor Supply Company took a higher percentage of each sales dollar in 198B than in 198A. On the other hand, office salaries took a smaller percentage. Furthermore, although the loss from bad debts was greater in 198B than in 198A, loss from bad debts took a smaller proportion of each sales dollar in 198B than in 198A.

ANALYSIS OF WORKING CAPITAL

When balance sheets are analyzed, working capital always receives close attention because an adequate amount of working capital enables a company to meet current debts, carry sufficient inventories, and take advantage of cash discounts. However, the *amount* of working capital a company has is not a measure of these abilities. This may be demonstrated as follows with Companies A and B:

	Company A	Company B
Current assets	$100,000	$20,000
Current liabilities	90,000	10,000
Working capital	$ 10,000	$10,000

Companies A and B have the same amounts of working capital. However, Company A's current liabilities are nine times its working capital, while Company B's current liabilities and working capital are equal. As a result, if liabilities are to be paid on time, Company A must experience much less shrinkage and delay in converting its current assets to cash than Company B. Thus, the amount of a company's working capital is not a measure of its working capital position. However, the relation of its current assets to its current liabilities is such a measure.

Current ratio

The relation of a company's current assets to its current liabilities is known as its *current ratio*. A current ratio is calculated by dividing current assets by current liabilities. The current ratio of the foregoing Company B is calculated as follows:

$$\frac{\text{Current assets, \$20,000}}{\text{Current liabilities, \$10,000}} = 2$$

After the division is made, the relation is expressed as, for example, Company B's current assets are two times its current liabilities or simply Company B's current ratio is 2 to 1.

The current ratio is the relation of current assets and current liabilities expressed mathematically. A high current ratio indicates a large proportion of current assets to current liabilities. The higher the ratio, the better is a company's current position, and normally the better it can meet current obligations.

For years bankers and other credit grantors measured a credit-seeking company's debt-paying ability by whether or not it had a 2-to-1 current ratio. Today, most credit grantors realize that the 2-to-1 rule of thumb is not an adequate test of debt-paying ability. They realize that whether or not a company's current ratio is good or bad depends upon at least three factors:

1. The nature of the company's business.
2. The composition of its current assets.
3. The turnover of certain of its current assets.

The nature of a company's business has much to do with whether or not its current ratio is adequate. A public utility which has no inventories other than supplies and grants little or no credit can operate on a current ratio less than 1 to 1. On the other hand, because a misjudgment of style can make an inventory of goods for sale almost worthless, a company in which style is the important sales factor may find a current ratio of much more than 2 to 1 to be inadequate. Consequently, when the adequacy of working capital is studied, consideration must be given to the type of business under review.

Also, in an analysis of a company's working capital, the composition of its current assets should be considered. Normally a company with a high proportion of cash to accounts receivable and merchandise is in a better position to meet quickly its current obligations than is a company with most of its current assets tied up in accounts receivable and merchandise. The company with cash can pay its current debts at once. The company with accounts receivable and merchandise must often turn these items into cash before it can pay.

Acid-test ratio

An easily calculated check on current asset composition is the *acid-test ratio,* also called the *quick ratio* because it is the ratio of "quick assets" to current liabilities. "Quick assets" are cash, notes receivable, accounts receivable, and marketable securities. They are the current assets that can quickly be turned into cash. An acid-test ratio of 1 to 1 is normally considered satisfactory. However, this is a rule of thumb and should be applied with care. The acid-test ratio of Anchor Supply Company as of the end of 198B is calculated as follows:

Quick assets:		Current liabilities:	
Cash	$18,000	Notes payable	$ 5,000
Accounts receivable	68,000	Accounts payable	43,600
		Taxes payable	4,800
		Wages payable	800
Total	$86,000	Total	$54,200

Acid-test ratio is $86,000 ÷ $54,200 = 1.59 or is 1.6 to 1

Accounts receivable turnover

Certain current asset turnovers affect working capital requirements. For example, assume Companies A and B sell the same amounts of merchandise on credit each month. However, Company A grants 30-day terms to its customers, while Company B grants 60 days. Both collect their accounts at the end of the credit periods granted. But as a result of the difference in terms, Company A turns over or collects its accounts twice as rapidly as does Company B. Also, as a result of the more rapid turnover, Company A requires only one half the investment in accounts receivable that is required of Company B and can operate with a smaller current ratio.

Accounts receivable turnover is calculated by dividing net sales for a year by the year-end accounts receivable. Anchor Supply Company's turnovers for 198A and 198B are calculated as follows:

	198B	198A
a. Net sales for year	$960,000	$842,800
b. Year-end accounts receivable	68,000	64,000
Times accounts receivable were turned over (a ÷ b)	14.1	13.2

The turnover of 14.1 times in 198B in comparison to 13.2 in 198A indicates the company's accounts receivable were collected more rapidly in 198B.

The year-end amount of accounts receivable is commonly used in calculating accounts receivable turnover. However, if year-end accounts receivable are not representative, an average of the year's accounts receivable by months should be used. Also, credit sales, rather than the sum of cash and credit sales, and accounts receivable before subtracting the allowance for doubtful accounts should be used. However, information as to credit sales is seldom available in a published balance sheet. Likewise, many published balance sheets report accounts receivable at their net amount. Consequently, total sales and net accounts receivable must often be used.

Days' sales uncollected

Accounts receivable turnover is one indication of the speed with which a company collects its accounts. *Days' sales uncollected* is another indication of the same thing. To illustrate the calculation of days' sales uncollected, assume a company had charge sales during a year of $250,000 and that it has $25,000 of accounts receivable at the year-end. In other words, one tenth of its charge sales, or the charge sales made during one tenth of a year, or the charge sales of 36.5 days ($\frac{1}{10} \times$ 365 days in a year = 36.5 days) are uncollected. This calculation of days' sales uncollected in equation form appears as follows:

$$\frac{\text{Accounts receivable, \$25,000}}{\text{Charge sales, \$250,000}} \times 365 = 36.5 \text{ days' sales uncollected}$$

Days' sales uncollected takes on more meaning when credit terms are known. According to a rule of thumb, a company's days' sales uncollected should not exceed one and one-third times the days in its credit period when it does not offer discounts and one and one-third times the days in its discount period when it does. If the company, whose days' sales uncollected is calculated in the illustration just given, offers 30-day terms, then 36.5 days is within the rule-of-thumb amount. However, if its terms are 2/10, n/30, its days' sales uncollected seem excessive.

Turnover of merchandise inventory

A company's *merchandise turnover* is the number of times its average inventory is sold during an accounting period. A high turnover is considered an indication of good merchandising. Also, from a working capital point of view, a company with a high turnover requires a smaller investment in inventory than one producing the same sales with a low turnover. Merchandise turnover is calculated by dividing cost of goods sold by average inventory. Cost of goods sold is the amount of merchandise at cost that was sold during an accounting period. Average inventory is the average amount of merchandise, at cost on hand during the period. The 198B merchandise turnover of Anchor Supply Company is calculated as follows:

$$\frac{\text{Cost of goods sold, \$715,000}}{\text{Average merchandise inventory, \$87,000}} = \frac{\text{Merchandise turnover of}}{\text{8.2 times}}$$

The cost of goods sold is taken from the company's 198B income statement. The average inventory is found by dividing by two the sum of the $84,000, January 1, 198B, inventory and the $90,000, December 31, 198B, inventory. In a company in which beginning and ending inventories are not representative of the inventory normally on hand, a more accurate turnover may be secured by using the average of all the 12 month-end inventories.

STANDARDS OF COMPARISON

When financial statements are analyzed by computing ratios and turnovers, the analyst must determine whether the ratios and turnovers obtained are good, bad, or just average. Furthermore, in making the decision the analyst must have some basis for comparison. The following are available:

1. A trained analyst may compare the ratios and turnovers of the company under review with mental standards acquired from past experiences.
2. An analyst may calculate for purposes of comparison the ratios and turnovers of a selected group of competitive companies in the same industry as the one whose statements are under review.
3. Published ratios and turnovers such as those put out by Dun & Bradstreet may be secured for comparison.
4. Some local and national trade associations gather data from their members and publish standard or average ratios for their trade or industry. These offer the analyst a very good basis of comparison when available.
5. Rule-of-thumb standards may be used as a basis for comparison.

Of these five standards, the ratios and turnovers of a selected group of competitive companies normally offer the best basis for comparison. Rule-of-thumb standards should be applied with care if erroneous conclusions are to be avoided.

OTHER BALANCE SHEET AND INCOME STATEMENT RELATIONS

Several balance sheet and income statement relations in addition to those having to do with working capital are important to the analyst. Some of the more important are discussed below.

Capital contributions of owners and creditors

The share of a company's assets contributed by its owners and the share contributed by creditors are always of interest to the analyst. The owners' and creditors' contributions of Anchor Supply Company are calculated as follows:

		198B	198A
a.	Total liabilities	$114,200	$ 71,200
b.	Total owners' equity	315,800	311,800
c.	Total liabilities and owners' equity	$430,000	$383,000
	Creditors' equity (a ÷ c)	26.6%	18.6%
	Owners' equity (b ÷ c)	73.4	81.4

Creditors like to see a high proportion of owners' equity because owners' equity acts as a cushion in absorbing losses. The greater the equity of the owners in relation to liabilities, the greater the losses that can be absorbed by the owners before the creditors begin to lose.

From the creditors' standpoint a high percentage of owners' equity is desirable. However, if an enterprise can earn a return on borrowed capital that is in excess of the capital's cost, then a reasonable amount of creditors' equity is desirable from the owners' viewpoint.

Pledged plant assets to long-term liabilities

Companies commonly borrow by issuing a note or bonds secured by a mortgage on certain of their plant assets. The ratio of pledged plant assets to long-term debt is often calculated to measure the security granted to mortgage or bondholders by the pledged assets. This ratio is calculated by dividing the pledged assets' book value by the liabilities for which the assets are pledged. It is calculated for Anchor Supply Company as of the ends of 198A and 198B as follows:

		198B	198A
	Buildings, net	$176,800	$28,000
	Land...................................	50,000	20,000
a.	Book value of pledged plant assets	$226,800	$48,000
b.	Mortgage payable	$ 60,000	$10,000
	Ratio of pledged assets to secured liabilities (a ÷ b)	3.8 to 1	4.8 to 1

The usual rule-of-thumb minimum for this ratio is 2 to 1. However, the ratio needs careful interpretation because it is based on the *book value* of the pledged assets. Often book values bear little or no relation to the amount that would be received for the assets in a foreclosure or a liquidation. As a result, estimated liquidation values or foreclosure values are normally a better measure of the protection offered bond or mortgage holders by pledged assets. Also, the long-term earning ability of the company whose assets are pledged is usually more important to long-term creditors than the pledged assets' book value.

Times fixed interest charges earned

The number of times fixed interest charges were earned is often calculated to measure the security of the return offered to bondholders or a mortgage holder. The amount of income before the deduction of fixed interest charges and income taxes is available to pay the fixed interest charges. Consequently, the calculation is made by dividing income before fixed interest charges and income taxes by fixed interest charges. The result is the number of times fixed interest charges were earned. Often, fixed interest charges are considered secure if the company consistently earns its fixed interest charges two or more times each year.

Rate of return on total assets employed

The *rate of return on total assets employed* is a measure of management's performance. Assets are used to earn a profit, and management is responsible for the way in which they are used. Consequently, the return on assets employed is a measure of management's performance.

The return figure used in this calculation should be after-tax income plus interest expense. Interest expense is included because it is a return paid creditors for assets they have supplied. Likewise, if the amount of assets has fluctuated during the year, an average of the beginning- and end-of-the-year assets employed should be used.

The rates of return earned on the average total assets employed by Anchor Supply Company during 198A and 198B are calculated as follows:

	198B	198A
Net income after taxes	$ 33,000	$ 32,600
Add interest expense	2,300	1,000
a. Net income plus interest expense......	$ 35,300	$ 33,600
b. Average total assets employed	$406,500	$380,000
Rate of return on total assets employed *(a ÷ b)*	8.7%	8.8%

In the case of Anchor Supply Company the change in the rates is not too significant. It is also impossible to tell whether the returns are good or bad without some basis of comparison. The best comparison would be the returns earned by similar-size companies engaged in the same kind of business. A comparison could also be made with the returns earned by this company in previous years. Neither of these is available in this case.

Rate of return on common stockholders' equity

A primary reason for the operation of a corporation is to earn a net income for its common stockholders. The *rate of return on the common stockholder's equity* is a measure of the success achieved in this area. Usually an average of the beginning- and end-of-the-year equities is used in calculating the return. For Anchor Supply Company the 198A and 198B calculations are as follows:

		198B	198A
a.	Net income after taxes	$ 33,000	$ 32,600
b.	Average stockholders' equity	313,800	309,000
	Rate of return on stockholders' equity *(a ÷ b)*	10.5%	10.6%

Compare Anchor Supply Company's returns on stockholders' equity with its returns on total assets employed and note that the return on the stockholders' equity is greater in both years. The greater returns resulted from using borrowed money.

When there is preferred stock outstanding, the preferred dividend requirements must be subtracted from net income to arrive at the common stockholders' share of income to be used in this calculation.

Earnings per common share

Earnings per common share data are among the most commonly quoted figures on the financial pages of daily newspapers. Such data are used by investors in evaluating the past performance of a business, in projecting its future earnings, and in weighing investment opportunities. Because of the significance attached to earnings per share data by investors and others, the APB concluded that earnings per common share or net loss per common share data should be shown on the face of a published income statement.[1]

For corporations having only common stock outstanding, the amount of earnings per share is determined by dividing net income by the number of common shares outstanding. For example, Anchor Supply Company of previous illustrations earned $33,000 in 198B and it had 25,000 common shares outstanding. Consequently, the amount of its earnings per common share is calculated:

---

[1] APB, "Earnings per Share," *APB Opinion No. 15* (New York: AICPA, 1969), par. 12. Copyright (1970) by the American Institute of CPAs.

$$\frac{\text{Net income, \$33,000}}{\text{25,000 common shares}} = \$1.32 \text{ per share}$$

Where there are also nonconvertible preferred shares outstanding, the year's preferred dividend requirement must be deducted from net income before dividing by the number of outstanding common shares. Also, if the number of common shares changed during the year, a weighted-average number of shares (weighted by the length of time each share was outstanding) is used in the calculation.

Many corporations, like Anchor Supply Company, have simple capital structures consisting only of common stock and, perhaps, preferred stock that is not convertible into common stock. Other corporations have more complex capital structures which include preferred stocks and bonds that are convertible into common stock at the option of the owners. In the latter corporations, if conversion should occur earnings per share would undoubtedly change due solely to the conversion. Recognizing this, the APB provided specific requirements in *Opinion No. 15* for calculating and reporting earnings per share for corporations with complex capital structures. However, these requirements are so lengthy and involved that a discussion must be left to an advanced course.

Price-earnings ratio

Price-earnings ratios are commonly used in comparing investment opportunities. A price-earnings ratio is calculated by dividing market price per share by earnings per share. For example, if Anchor Supply Company's common stock sold at $12 per share at the end of 198B, the stock's end-of-the-year price-earnings ratio is calculated:

$$\frac{\text{Market price per share, \$12}}{\text{Earnings per share, \$1.32}} = 9.09$$

After the calculation is made, it may be said that the stock had a 9.1 price-earnings ratio at the end of 198B, or it may be said that approximately $9.10 was required at that time to buy $1 of the company's 198B earnings.

In comparing price-earnings ratios it must be remembered that such ratios vary from industry to industry. For example, in the steel industry a 9 or 10 price-earnings ratio is normal, while in a growth industry, such as electronics, 20 or 25 price-earnings ratios are common.

GLOSSARY

Accounts receivable turnover. An indication of how long it takes a company to collect its accounts, calculated by dividing net sales or credit sales by ending or average accounts receivable.

Acid-test ratio. The relation of quick assets, such as cash, notes receivable, accounts receivable, and marketable securities to current liabilities, calculated as quick assets divided by current liabilities.

Common-size comparative statements. Comparative financial statements in which each amount is expressed as a percentage of a base amount. In the balance sheet, total assets is usually selected as the base amount and is expressed as 100%. In the income statement, net sales is usually selected as the base amount.

Comparative statement. A financial statement with data for two or more successive years placed in columns side by side in order to better illustrate changes in the data.

Current ratio. The relation of a company's current assets to its current liabilities; that is, current assets divided by current liabilities.

Merchandise turnover. The number of times a company's average inventory is sold during an accounting period, calculated by dividing cost of goods sold by average merchandise inventory.

Price-earnings ratio. Market price per share of common stock divided by earnings per share.

Quick ratio. A synonym for acid-test ratio.

Rate of return on common stockholders' equity. Net income after taxes and dividends on preferred stock divided by average common stockholders' equity.

Rate of return on total assets employed. Net income after taxes, plus interest expense, expressed as a percentage of total assets employed during the period.

Times fixed charges earned. An indicator of a company's ability to satisfy fixed charges, calculated as net income before fixed charges and income taxes divided by fixed charges (e.g., interest).

QUESTIONS FOR CLASS DISCUSSION

1. Comparative balance sheets often have columns showing increases and decreases in both dollar amounts and percentages. Why is this so?
2. When trends are calculated and compared, what item trends should be compared with the trend of sales?
3. What is meant by "common size" financial statements?
4. What items are assigned a value of 100% *(a)* on a common-size balance sheet and *(b)* on a common-size income statement?
5. Why is working capital given special attention in the process of analyzing balance sheets?
6. For the following transactions tell which increase working capital, which decrease working capital, and which have no effect on working capital:
   a. Collected accounts receivable.
   b. Borrowed money by giving a 90-day interest-bearing note.
   c. Declared a cash dividend.

  d. Paid a cash dividend previously declared.
  e. Sold plant assets at their book value.
  f. Sold merchandise at a profit.

7. List several factors that have an effect on working capital requirements.
8. A company has a 2-to-1 current ratio. List several reasons why this ratio may not be adequate.
9. State the significance of each of the following ratios and turnovers and tell how each is calculated:

  a. Current ratio.
  b. Acid-test ratio.
  c. Turnover of accounts receivable.
  d. Turnover of mer- chandise inventory.

  e. Rate of return on common stock- holders' equity.
  f. Ratio of pledged plant assets to long-term liabilities.

10. How are days' sales uncollected calculated? What is the significance of the number of days' sales uncollected?
11. Why do creditors like to see a high proportion of owners' equity?
12. What is the ratio of pledged plant assets to long-term liabilities supposed to measure? Why must this ratio be interpreted with care?
13. What does the rate of return on assets employed tell about management?
14. How are earnings per share calculated in a corporation having outstanding only common stock and preferred stock not convertible into common stock?
15. How is a price-earnings ratio calculated?

CLASS EXERCISES

Exercise 19–1

Where possible, calculate percentages of increase and decrease for the following unrelated items. The parentheses indicate deficit items.

	198B	198A
Buildings, net	$75,000	$60,000
Investments	–0–	20,000
Notes payable	5,000	–0–
Retained earnings	(4,500)	15,000
Cash	12,000	(1,500)

Exercise 19–2

Calculate trend percentages for the following items and tell whether the situation shown by the trends is favorable or unfavorable.

	198A	198B	198C
Sales	$150,000	$169,500	$178,500
Merchandise inventory	30,000	36,000	39,600
Accounts receivable	18,000	23,040	24,300

Exercise 19–3

Express the following income statement information in common-size percentages and tell whether the situation shown is favorable or unfavorable.

MAPLE SALES, INC.
Comparative Income Statement
Years Ended June 30, 198A, and 198B

	198B	198A
Sales	$100,000	$90,000
Cost of goods sold	67,500	60,390
Gross profit from sales	$ 32,500	$29,610
Operating expenses...........	25,300	22,860
Net income	$ 7,200	$ 6,750

Exercise 19–4

The 198A statements of Agate, Inc., follow:

AGATE, INC.
Income Statement for Year Ended December 31, 198A

Sales		$365,000
Cost of goods sold:		
Merchandise inventory, January 1, 198A	$ 29,400	
Purchases	241,200	
Goods for sale	$270,600	
Merchandise inventory, December 31, 198A	30,600	
Cost of goods sold		240,000
Gross profit on sales		$125,000
Operating expenses.............................		106,200
Operating income		$ 18,800
Interest expense................................		3,000
Income before taxes		$ 15,800
Income taxes...................................		3,300
Net income		$ 12,500

AGATE, INC.
Balance Sheet, December 31, 198A

Assets		Equities	
Cash	$ 6,500	Accounts payable	$ 20,000
Accounts receivable, net	22,500	Mortgate payable secured by	
Merchandise inventory	30,600	a lien on the plant assets ...	50,000
Prepaid expenses	400	Common stock $10 par value .	100,000
Plant assets, net	140,000	Retained earnings	30,000
Total assets	$200,000	Total equities	$200,000

Required:

Calculate the following: *(a)* current ratio, *(b)* acid-test ratio, *(c)* days' sales uncollected, *(d)* merchandise turnover, *(e)* capital contribution of the owners expressed as a percent, *(f)* ratio of pledged plant assets to long-term liabilities, *(g)* return on total assets employed, *(h)* return on stockholders' equity, and *(i)* earnings per share. (Assume all sales were on credit, the stockholders' equity was $120,000 on January 1, 198A, and total assets has not fluctuated during the year.)

Exercise 19–5

Common-size and trend percentages for a company's sales, cost of goods sold, and expenses follow:

COMMON-SIZE PERCENTAGES	198A	198B	198C		TREND PERCENTAGES	198A	198B	198C
Sales	100	100	100		Sales	100	110	120
Cost of goods sold	68	67	65		Cost of goods sold	100	108	115
Expenses	22	24	27		Expenses	100	120	147

Required:

Present statistics to prove whether the company's net income increased, decreased, or remained unchanged during the three-year period.

PROBLEMS

Problem 19–1

The condensed statements of Apple Corporation follow. Calculate the following ratios and turnovers for 198B: (1) current ratio, (2) acid-test ratio, (3) days' sales uncollected, (4) accounts receivable turnover, (5) merchandise turnover, (6) earnings per share, (7) rate of return on total assets employed, (8) rate of return on stockholders' equity, (9) percent of capital contributed by owners, and (10) ratio of pledged plant assets to long-term liabilities (assume both building and equipment are mortgaged).

APPLE CORPORATION
Comparative Balance Sheets
December 31, 198A, and 198B

Assets	*198B*	*198A*
Cash	$ 6,000	$ 8,000
Accounts receivable, net	16,000	14,000
Merchandise inventory	32,000	28,000
Building and equipment, net	186,000	180,000
Total assets	$240,000	$230,000

Equities

Current liabilities	$ 20,000	$ 15,000
Mortgage payable	80,000	85,000
Common stock, $10 par value	100,000	100,000
Retained earnings	40,000	30,000
Total equities	$240,000	$230,000

APPLE CORPORATION
Comparative Income Statements
Years Ended December 31, 198A, and 198B

	198B	*198A*
Sales, all on credit	$200,000	$180,000
Cost of goods sold	120,000	109,000
Gross profit on sales	$ 80,000	$ 71,000
Operating expenses	49,000	45,000
Operating income	$ 31,000	$ 26,000
Interest expense	5,000	5,500
Income before taxes	$ 26,000	$ 20,500
Income taxes	6,000	5,500
Net income	$ 20,000	$ 15,000

Problem 19–2

The 198B and 198C statements of Oxbow Corporation follow:

OXBOW CORPORATION
Comparative Income Statements
Years Ended December 31, 198B, and 198C

	198C	*198B*
Sales	$900,000	$800,000
Cost of goods sold	559,200	488,500
Gross profit from sales	$340,800	$311,500
Operating expenses	247,000	226,000
Income before taxes	$ 93,800	$ 85,500
Income taxes	46,900	42,750
Net income	$ 46,900	$ 42,750

OXBOW CORPORATION
Comparative Balance Sheets
December 31, 198B, and 198C

Assets	*198C*	*198B*
Cash	$ 24,000	$ 24,000
Accounts receivable	50,000	56,000
Merchandise inventory	84,000	64,000
Plant assets, net	167,000	168,000
Total assets	$325,000	$312,000

Liabilities and Capital

Current liabilities	$ 50,000	$ 50,000
Long-term liabilities	60,000	60,000
Common stock	150,000	150,000
Retained earnings	65,000	52,000
Total liabilities and capital	$325,000	$312,000

Required:

1. Express the income statement data in common-size percentages and calculate the current ratio, acid-test ratio, merchandise turnover, and days' sales uncollected for each year. Assume the January 1, 198A, inventory was $58,000.
2. Comment on the situation shown by your calculations.

Problem 19–3

The condensed 198A, 198B, and 198C statements of Doric, Inc., follow:

DORIC, INC.
Comparative Income Statements
Years Ended December 31, 198A, 198B, and 198C
(in $000)

	198C	198B	198A
Sales	$13,000	$12,000	$10,000
Cost of goods sold	8,995	8,260	6,800
Gross profit on sales	$ 4,005	$ 3,740	$ 3,200
Selling expenses	$ 2,120	$ 1,970	$ 1,600
Administrative expenses	1,120	1,110	1,000
Interest expense	25		
Total expenses	$ 3,265	$ 3,080	$ 2,600
Income before taxes	$ 740	$ 660	$ 600
Income taxes	370	330	$ 300
Net income...................	$ 370	$ 330	$ 300

DORIC, INC.
Comparative Balance Sheets
December 31, 198A, 198B, and 198C
(in $000)

Assets	198C	198B	198A
Current assets	$ 750	$ 600	$ 800
Plant assets, net	4,000	3,520	3,200
Total assets	$4,750	$4,120	$4,000

Liabilities and Capital			
Current liabilities	$ 250	$ 295	$ 250
Long-term liabilities.....................	500		
Common stock, $10 par value.............	2,500	2,500	2,500
Retained earnings......................	1,500	1,325	1,250
Total liabilities and capital	$4,750	$4,120	$4,000

Required:

1. Express the income statement items in common-size percentages.
2. Express the balance sheet items in trend percentages, using 198A as the base year.
3. Comment on the trends and relations shown by your calculations.

Problem 19–4

The condensed comparative statements of Zoom Corporation follow:

ZOOM CORPORATION
Comparative Income Statements
Years Ended December 31, 198A–8F
(in $000)

	198F	198E	198D	198C	198B	198A
Sales	$975	$930	$890	$735	$625	$500
Cost of goods sold	714	672	637	511	411	350
Gross profit from sales	$216	$258	$253	$224	$184	$150
Operating expenses	202	190	181	146	124	100
Income before taxes	$ 59	$ 68	$ 72	$ 78	$ 60	$ 50

ZOOM CORPORATION
Comparative Balance Sheets
December 31, 198A–8F
(in $000)

Assets	198F	198E	198D	198C	198B	198A
Cash	$ 9	$ 11	$ 13	$ 19	$ 21	$ 20
Accounts receivable, net	99	97	92	56	58	50
Merchandise inventory	204	194	186	112	106	100
Long-term investments				30	30	30
Plant and equipment, net	462	468	465	306	297	300
Total assets	$774	$770	$756	$523	$512	$500
Liabilities and Capital						
Current liabilities	$114	$107	$ 96	$ 58	$ 53	$ 50
Long-term liabilities	165	165	165	60	60	60
Common stock	300	300	300	250	250	250
Premium on common stock	45	45	45	20	20	20
Retained earnings	150	153	150	135	129	120
Total liabilities and capital	$774	$770	$756	$523	$512	$500

Required:

1. Express the data of the statements in trend percentages.
2. Analyze and comment on any situation shown in the statements.

Problem 19–5

A company had $250,000 of current assets, a 2½ to 1 current ratio, and a 1¼ to 1 acid-test ratio. It then completed these transactions:

a. Collected a $1,500 account receivable.

b. Sold for $35,000 a short-term investment carried on the books at its $25,000 cost.

c. Wrote off a $500 bad debt against the allowance for doubtful accounts.

d. Declared a $0.10 per share cash dividend on the 100,000 shares of $10 par value common stock.

e. Paid the cash dividend declared in transaction (d).

f. Borrowed $10,000 by issuing a 60-day, 6% note payable.

g. Declared a 5,000-share stock dividend. The stock was selling for $12 per share on the day of the declaration.

h. Distributed the stock dividend of transaction (g).

i. Sold for $15,000 merchandise that cost $10,000.

j. Purchased $10,000 of merchandise on credit. The company uses a perpetual inventory system.

Required:

Prepare a three-column schedule showing the company's current ratio, acid-test ratio, and working capital after each transaction.

ALTERNATE PROBLEMS

Problem 19–1A

The condensed 198A financial statements of Castle, Inc., follow:

CASTLE, INC.
Balance Sheet, December 31, 198A

Assets		Equities	
Cash	$ 7,750	Accounts payable	$ 17,500
Accounts receivable, net	18,250	Federal income taxes payable	2,500
Merchandise inventory	38,500	Mortgage payable, secured by	
Prepaid expenses	1,500	a lien on land and building	40,000
Equipment, net	78,000	Common stock, $10 par value	125,000
Building, net	84,000	Retained earnings	55,000
Land	12,000		
Total assets	$240,000	Total equities	$240,000

CASTLE, INC.
Income Statement for Year Ended December 31, 198A

Sales		$365,000
Cost of goods sold:		
Merchandise inventory, January 1, 198A	$ 41,500	
Purchases, net	257,000	
Goods for sale	$298,500	
Merchandise inventory, December 31, 198A	38,500	

Cost of goods sold	260,000
Gross profit on sales	$105,000
Operating expenses	75,500
Operating income	$ 29,500
Interest expense............................	2,500
Income before taxes	$ 27,000
Federal income taxes	6,000
Net income	$ 21,000

Problem 19–3A

The 198A, 198B, and 198C income statements of Webster Corporation carried the following information (in $000):

	198C	198B	198A
Sales	$14,000	$12,000	$10,000
Cost of goods sold	10,150	8,580	7,000
Gross profit from sales	$ 3,850	$ 3,420	$ 3,000
Operating expenses	3,190	2,810	2,450
Income before taxes	$ 660	$ 610	$ 550
Income taxes	330	305	275
Net income	$ 330	$ 305	$ 275

Its balance sheets for the same period carried this information (in $000):

Assets	198C	198B	198A
Current assets	$ 900	$ 700	$1,000
Plant and equipment	4,600	4,400	4,000
Total assets	$5,500	$5,100	$5,000

Liabilities and Capital	198C	198B	198A
Current liabilities	$ 360	$ 410	$ 400
Long-term liabilities.......................	1,000	1,000	1,000
Common stock, $25 par value..............	2,800	2,500	2,500
Other contributed capital	260	200	200
Retained earnings.........................	1,080	990	900
Total liabilities and capital	$5,500	$5,100	$5,000

Required:

1. Express the income statement items in common-size percentages.
2. Express the balance sheet items in trend percentages, using 198A as the base year.
3. Comment on the trends and relations shown by your calculations.

Problem 19–5A

A company had $120,000 of current assets, a 2.4 to 1 current ratio, and a 1.2 to 1 acid-test ratio before completing the following transactions:

a. Wrote off against the allowance for doubtful accounts an $800 uncollectible account receivable.

b. Sold for $5,000 a plant asset having a $6,000 book value.

c. Sold for $10,000 temporary investments that cost $15,000.

d. Sold for $15,000 merchandise that cost $10,000.

e. Borrowed $10,000 by giving the bank a 60-day note payable.

f. Declared a $0.50 per share dividend on the 10,000 outstanding shares of $10 par value common stock.

g. Paid the dividend declared in transaction *(f).*

h. Borrowed $20,000 by placing a 6%, 20-year mortgage on the plant.

i. Declared a 1,000-share common stock dividend on a day when the stock was selling at $12.50 per share.

j. Distributed the stock of the dividend declared in transaction *(i).*

Required:

Prepare a three-column schedule showing in columns the company's current ratio, acid-test ratio, and working capital after each of the transactions.

PROVOCATIVE PROBLEMS

Provocative problem 19–1
Companies A and B

Company A and Company B are competitors; both were organized ten years ago; and both have seen their sales increase tenfold during the ten-year period. However, the tenfold increase is not as good as it sounds because both companies' costs and selling prices have doubled during the same period. Nevertheless, the sales of both companies have and are increasing. Both offer the same credit terms, age their accounts receivable to allow for bad debts, and collect their accounts in about the same length of time. Actually, about the only real difference in their accounting procedures is that Company A since its organization has used Fifo in costing its goods sold and Company B has used Lifo.

The current ratios of the two companies for the past four years were as follows:

	Company A	Company B
December 31, 198A	5.2 to 1	3.3 to 1
December 31, 198B	5.6 to 1	3.1 to 1
December 31, 198C	5.9 to 1	2.8 to 1
December 31, 198D	6.0 to 1	3.0 to 1

You are the loan officer of a bank, and both companies have come to your bank for 90-day loans. In addition to the current ratios, you note that Company B has turned its inventory more than two and one half times as fast as Company A in each of the last four years. You also discover that for each $10,000 of current liabilities the companies have the following amounts of inventory:

	Company A	Company B
December 31, 198A	$41,000	$21,000
December 31, 198B	47,000	20,000
December 31, 198C	50,000	18,000
December 31, 198D	52,000	18,000

Which company do you think is the better short-term credit risk? Back your opinion with computations showing why. Are the inventory turnovers of the two companies comparable? Explain. Which company seems to have the better inventory turnover?

Provocative problem 19–2
Jane Howe

Jane Howe is considering an investment in either Company O or Company P. Either company's stock can be purchased at book value, and she is undecided as to which is the better managed company and the better investment. Following are data from the financial statements of the two companies:

Data from the Current Year-End Balance Sheets

Assets	Company O	Company P
Cash	$ 12,000	$ 14,500
Accounts receivable, net	30,000	40,000
Merchandise inventory	44,000	54,800
Prepaid expenses	1,200	1,200
Plant and equipment, net	165,800	174,500
Total assets	$253,000	$285,000

Liabilities and Capital		
Current liabilities	$ 40,000	$ 50,000
Mortgage payable	50,000	50,000
Common stock, $10 par value	100,000	100,000
Retained earnings	63,000	85,000
Total liabilities and capital	$253,000	$285,000

Data from the Current Year's Income Statements

	Company O	Company P
Sales	$597,000	$696,000
Cost of goods sold	430,500	502,200
Gross profit on sales	$166,500	$193,800
Operating expenses	142,000	167,000
Operating income	$ 24,500	$ 26,800
Interest expense	3,000	3,500
Income before taxes	$ 21,500	$ 23,300
Income taxes	4,700	5,200
Net income	$ 16,800	$ 18,100

Beginning-of-the-Year Data

	Company O	Company P
Merchandise inventory	$ 38,000	$ 53,200
Total assets	247,000	277,000
Stockholders' equity	157,000	177,000

Prepare a report to Jane Howe stating which company you think is the better managed and which company's stock you think is the better investment. Back your report with any ratios, turnovers, and other analyses you think pertinent.

After studying Chapter 20, you should be able to:

☐ Describe the effects of inflation on historical financial statements.

☐ Explain how price-level changes are measured.

☐ Tell how to construct both general and specific price-level indexes.

☐ Describe the use of price indexes in constant dollar accounting.

☐ Restate unit-of-money financial statements for general price-level changes.

☐ Explain how purchasing power gains and losses arise and how they are computed and integrated into constant dollar financial statements.

☐ State the differences between general price-level-adjusted costs and current values such as exit prices and current costs.

☐ Explain what current costs measure and the use of recoverable amounts in current cost accounting.

☐ Describe the reporting requirements of *FASB Statement No. 33.*

☐ Define or explain the words and phrases listed in the chapter Glossary.

Accounting for price-level changes

■ Perhaps all accountants agree that conventional financial statements provide useful information for making economic decisions. However, many accountants also agree that conventional financial statements fail to adequately account for the impact of price-level changes. Usually, this means a failure to adequately account for the impact of inflation. Indeed, this failure of conventional financial statements may sometimes even make the statements misleading. That is, the statements may imply certain facts that are inconsistent with the real state of affairs. As a result, decision makers may be inclined to make decisions that are inconsistent with their objectives.

In what ways do conventional financial statements fail to account for inflation? The general problem is that transactions are recorded in terms of the historical number of dollars received or paid. These amounts are not adjusted even though subsequent price changes may dramatically change the purchasing power of the dollars received or paid. For example, Old Company purchased ten acres of land for $25,000. At the end of each accounting period thereafter, Old Company presented a balance sheet showing "Land, $25,000." Six years later, after inflation of 97% (12% per year, compounded for six years), New Company purchased ten acres of land that was adjacent and nearly identical to Old Company's land. New Company paid $49,250 for the land. In comparing the conventional balance sheets of the two companies, which own identical pieces of property, the following balances are observed:

Balance Sheets		
	Old company	New company
Land	$25,000	$49,250

Without knowing the details that underlie these balances, a statement reader is likely to conclude that New Company either has more land than does Old Company or that New Company's land is more valuable than is Old Company's. But, both companies own ten acres, which are identical in value. The entire difference between the prices paid by the two companies is explained by the 97% inflation between the two purchase dates. That is, $25,000 \times 1.97 = $49,250.

The failure of conventional financial statements to adequately account for inflation also shows up in the income statement. For example, assume that in the previous example, machinery was purchased instead of land. Also, assume that the machinery of Old Company and New Company is identical except for age; it is being depreciated on a straight-line basis over a ten-year period, with no salvage value. As a result, the annual income statements of the two companies show the following:

Income Statements		
	Old company	New company
Depreciation expense, machinery	$2,500	$4,925

Although assets of equal value are being depreciated, the income statements show that New Company's depreciation expense is 97% higher than is Old Company's. And, if all other revenue and expense items are the same, Old Company will appear more profitable than New Company. This is inconsistent with the fact that both companies own the same machines that are subject to the same depreciation factors. Furthermore, although Old Company will appear more profitable, it must pay more income taxes due to the apparent extra profits. Old Company also may not recover the full replacement cost of its machinery through the sale of its product.

Some of the procedures used in conventional accounting tend to reduce the impact of price-level changes on the income statement. Lifo inventory pricing and accelerated depreciation are examples. However, these are only partial solutions, since they do not offset the impact on both the income statement and the balance sheet.

Because of these deficiencies in conventional accounting practices, accountants have devoted increasing attention to alternatives that make comprehensive adjustments for the effects of price-level changes. This chapter discusses the two that have received the greatest attention. The first alternative involves adjusting conventional financial statements for changes in the general level of prices. This is called *constant dollar accounting,* or *general price-level adjusted accounting,* or sometimes *GPLA accounting.* Later, consideration is given to another alternative, *current cost accounting.* This makes adjustments for changes in the specific prices of the specific assets owned by the company.

UNDERSTANDING PRICE-LEVEL CHANGES

In one way or another, all readers of this book have experienced the effects of inflation, which is a general increase in the prices paid for goods and services. Of course, the prices of specific items do not all change at the same rate. Even when most prices are rising, the prices of some goods or services may be falling. For example, consider the following prices of four different items:

Item	Price/unit in 1980	Price/unit in 1981	Percent change
A	$1.00	$1.30	+30
B	2.00	2.20	+10
C	1.50	1.80	+20
D	3.00	2.70	−10
Totals	$7.50	$8.00	

What can be said to describe these price changes? One possibility is to state the percentage change in the price per unit of each item (see above). This information is very useful for some purposes. But, it does not show the average effect or impact of the price changes that occurred. A better indication of the average effect would be to determine the average increase in the per unit prices of the four items. Thus: $8.00/$7.50 − 1.00 = 6.7%[1] average increase in per unit prices. However, even this average may fail to indicate the impact of the price changes on most individuals or businesses. It is a good indicator only if the typical individual or business purchased an equal number of units of each item. But what if these items are typically purchased in the following ratio? For each unit of A purchased, 2 units of B, 5 units of C, and 1 unit of D are purchased. With a different number of each item being purchased, the impact of changing prices

---

[1] Throughout this chapter amounts are rounded to the nearest $\frac{1}{10}$ percent or to the nearest full dollar.

must take into account the typical quantity of each item purchased. Hence, the average change in the price of the A, B, C, D "market basket" would be calculated as follows:

Item	Units purchased	1980 prices			Units purchased	1981 prices		
A	1 unit	× $1.00	=	$ 1.00	1 unit	× $1.30	=	$ 1.30
B	2 units	× $2.00	=	4.00	2 units	× $2.20	=	4.40
C	5 units	× $1.50	=	7.50	5 units	× $1.80	=	9.00
D	1 unit	× $3.00	=	3.00	1 unit	× $2.70	=	2.70
Totals				$15.50				$17.40

Weighted-average price change = $17.40/$15.50 − 1.00 = 12%

It may now be said that the annual rate of inflation in the prices of these four items was 12%. Of course, not every individual and business will purchase these four items in exactly the same proportion of 1 unit of A, 2 units of B, 5 units of C, and 1 unit of D. As a consequence, the stated 12% inflation rate is only an approximation of the impact of price changes on each buyer. But if these proportions represent the typical buying pattern, the stated 12% inflation rate fairly reflects the inflationary impact on the average buyer.

CONSTRUCTION OF A PRICE INDEX

When the cost of purchasing a given market basket is determined for each of several periods, the results can be expressed as a *price index*. In constructing a price index, one year is arbitrarily selected as the "base" year. The cost of purchasing the market basket in that year is then assigned a value of 100. For example, suppose the cost of purchasing the A, B, C, D market basket in each year is:

1975......	$ 9.00
1976......	11.00
1977......	10.25
1978......	12.00
1979......	13.00
1980......	15.50
1981......	17.40

If 1978 is selected as the base year, then the $12 cost for 1978 is assigned a value of 100. The index number for each of the other years is then calculated and expressed as a percent of the base year's cost. For example, the index number for 1977 is 85, or ($10.25/$12.00 ×

$100 = 85$). The index numbers for the remaining years are calculated in the same way. The entire price index for the years 1975 through 1981 is presented in Illustration 20–1.

Year	Calculations of price level	Price index
1975......	($9.00/$12.00) × 100 =	75
1976......	($11.00/$12.00) × 100 =	92
1977......	($10.25/$12.00) × 100 =	85
1978......	($12.00/$12.00) × 100 =	100
1979......	($13.00/$12.00) × 100 =	108
1980......	($15.50/$12.00) × 100 =	129
1981......	($17.40/$12.00) × 100 =	145

Illustration 20–1

Having constructed a price index for the A, B, C, D market basket, it is possible to make comparative statements about the cost of purchasing these items in various years. For example, it may be said that the price level in 1981 was 45% (145/100) higher than it was in 1978, the price level in 1981 was 34% (145/108) higher than it was in 1979, and 12% (145/129) higher than it was in 1980. Stated another way, it may be said that $1 in 1981 would purchase the same amount of A, B, C, D as would $0.69 in 1978 (100/145 = 0.69). Also, $1 in 1981 would purchase the same amount of A, B, C, D as would $0.52 in 1975 (75/145 = 0.52).

USING PRICE INDEX NUMBERS

In accounting, the most important use of a price index is to restate dollar amounts of cost that were paid in earlier years into the current price level. In other words, a specific dollar amount of cost in a previous year can be restated in terms of the comparable number of dollars that would be incurred if the cost were paid with dollars of the current amount of purchasing power. For example, suppose that $1,000 were paid in 1977 to purchase items A, B, C, D. Stated in terms of 1981 prices, that 1977 cost is $1,000 × (145/85) = $1,706. As another example, if $1,500 were paid for A, B, C, D in 1978, that 1978 cost, restated in terms of 1981 prices, is $1,500 × (145/100) = $2,175.

Note that the 1978 cost of $1,500 correctly states the number of monetary units (dollars) expended for items A, B, C, D in 1978. Also, the 1977 cost of $1,000 correctly states the units of money expended in 1977. And, these two costs can be added together to determine the cost for the two years, stated in terms of the historical number of monetary units (units of money) expended. However, in a very important way, the 1977 monetary units do not mean the same thing as do the 1978 monetary units. A dollar (one monetary unit) in 1977 represented a different amount of purchasing power than did a dollar in 1978. Both of these dollars represent different amounts of purchasing power than a dollar in 1981. If one intends to communicate the amount of purchasing power expended or incurred, the historical number of monetary units must be adjusted so that they are stated in terms of dollars with the same amount of purchasing power. For example, the total amount of cost incurred during 1977 and 1978 could be stated in terms of the purchasing power of 1978 dollars, or stated in terms of the purchasing power of 1981 dollars. These calculations are presented in Illustration 20–2.

Year cost was incurred	Monetary units expended	Adjustment to 1978 dollars	Historical cost stated in 1978 dollars	Adjustment to 1981 dollars	Historical cost stated in 1981 dollars
1977	$1,000	1,000 × (100/85)	$1,176	1,176 × (145/100)	$1,706*
1978	1,500	—	1,500	1,500 × (145/100)	2,175
Total cost	$2,500		$2,676		$3,881

* Raised $1 to correct for rounding. An alternative calculation is $1,000 × (145/85) = $1,706.

Illustration 20–2

SPECIFIC VERSUS GENERAL PRICE-LEVEL INDEXES

Price changes and price-level indexes can be calculated for narrow groups of commodities or services, such as housing construction material costs; or for broader groups of items, such as all construction costs; or for very broad groups of items, such as all items produced in the economy. A *specific price-level index*, as for housing construction materials, indicates the changing purchasing power of a dollar spent for items in that specific category, that is, to pay for housing construction materials. A *general price-level index*, as for all items produced in the economy, indicates the changing purchasing power of a dollar, in general. Two general price-level indexes are the Consumer Price Index for all urban consumers (prepared by the Bureau of Labor Statistics) and the Gross National Product (GNP) Implicit Price Deflator (prepared by the U.S. Department of Commerce).

USING PRICE INDEXES IN ACCOUNTING

There are at least two important accounting systems that use price indexes to develop comprehensive financial statements. Both are major alternatives to the conventional accounting system in general use in the United States. One alternative, called current cost accounting, uses specific price-level indexes (along with appraisals and other means) to develop statements that report assets and expenses in terms of the current costs to acquire those assets or services. Additional consideration is given to this alternative later in this chapter.

The other alternative is called general price-level-adjusted (GPLA) accounting or constant dollar accounting. It uses general price-level indexes to restate the conventional, unit-of-money financial statements into dollar amounts that represent current, general purchasing power. Most of the proposals for making constant dollar (GPLA) financial statements have suggested using the GNP Implicit Price Deflator because it is the broadest index of general price-level changes.[2] However, the FASB's recent *Statement No. 33* requires use of the Consumers' Price Index for all urban consumers. (CPI).[3] The following sections of this chapter explain how a general price index, such as the CPI, is used to prepare general price-level-adjusted (GPLA) financial statements.

CONSTANT DOLLAR (GPLA) ACCOUNTING

Conventional financial statements disclose revenues, expenses, assets, liabilities, and owners' equity in terms of the historical monetary units exchanged when the transactions occurred. As such, they are sometimes referred to as *unit-of-money* or *nominal dollar financial statements.* This is intended to emphasize the difference between conventional statements and constant dollar or general price-level-adjusted (GPLA) statements. In the latter, the dollar amounts shown are adjusted for changes in the general purchasing power of the dollar.

Students should understand clearly that the same principles for determining depreciation expense, cost of goods sold, accruals of revenue, and so forth, apply to both unit-of-money statements and GPLA statements. The same generally accepted accounting principles apply to both. The only difference between the two is that GPLA statements reflect adjustments for general price-level changes; unit-of-money statements do not. As a matter of fact, GPLA financial statements are

---

[2] See, for example, APB "Financial Statements Restated for General Price Level Changes," *APB Statement No. 3* (New York: AICPA, 1969), par. 30. Copyright (1969) by the American Institute of CPAs. Also see FASB, "Financial Reporting in Units of General Purchasing Power," *Proposed Statement of Financial Accounting Standards, Exposure Draft* (Stamford, Conn., 1974), par. 35. Copyright © by the Financial Accounting Standards Board, High Ridge Park, Stamford, Conn. 06905, U.S.A. Quoted (or excerpted) with permission. Copies of the complete document are available from the FASB.

[3] FASB, "Financial Reporting and Changing Prices," *Statement of Financial Accounting Standards No. 33* (Stamford, Conn., 1979), par. 39. Copyright © by the Financial Accounting Standards Board, High Ridge Park, Stamford, Conn. 06905, U.S.A. Quoted (or excerpted) with permission. Copies of the complete document are available from the FASB.

prepared by adjusting the amounts appearing on the unit-of-money financial statements.

CONSTANT DOLLAR (GPLA) ACCOUNTING FOR ASSETS

The effect of general price-level changes on investments in assets depends on the nature of the assets involved. Some assets, called *monetary assets,* represent money or claims to receive a fixed amount of money. The number of dollars owned or to be received is fixed in amount, regardless of changes that may occur in the purchasing power of the dollar. Examples of monetary assets are cash, accounts receivable, notes receivable, and investments in bonds.

Because the amount of money owned or to be received from a monetary asset does not change with price-level changes, the (GPLA) balance sheet amount of a monetary asset is not adjusted for general price-level changes. For example, if $200 in cash was owned at the end of 1980 and was held throughout 1981, during which time the general price-level index increased from 150 to 168,[4] the cash reported on both the December 31, 1980, and 1981, general price-level-adjusted (GPLA) balance sheets is $200. However, although no balance sheet adjustment is made, it is important to note that the investment in such a monetary asset held during a period of inflation does result in a loss of purchasing power. The $200 would buy less at the end of 1981 than it would have at the end of 1980. This reduction in purchasing power constitutes a loss. The amount of the loss is calculated as follows:

Monetary asset balance on December 31, 1980	$ 200
Adjustment to reflect an equal amount of purchasing power on December 31, 1981: $200 × 168/150	$ 224
Amount of monetary asset balance on December 31, 1981	(200)
General purchasing power loss	$ 24

Nonmonetary assets are defined as all assets other than monetary assets. The prices at which nonmonetary assets may be bought and sold tend to increase or decrease over time as the general price level increases or decreases. Consequently, as the general price level changes, investments in nonmonetary assets tend to retain the amounts

---

[4] Observe that these index numbers, and those used in the remaining sections of the chapter, are different from those that were calculated on page 665. Since the earlier calculations were based on only four items (A, B, C, D), that index would not be appropriate to illustrate a general price index, which must reflect the prices of many, many items.

of purchasing power originally invested. As a result, the reported amounts of nonmonetary assets on GPLA balance sheets are adjusted to reflect changes in the price level that have occurred since the nonmonetary assets were acquired.

For example, say $200 was invested in land (a nonmonetary asset) at the end of 1980 and the investment was held throughout 1981. During this time the general price index increased from 150 to 168. The GPLA balance sheets would disclose the following amounts:

Asset	December 31, 1980, GPLA balance sheet	Adjustment to December 31, 1981 price level	December 31, 1981, GPLA balance sheet
Land	$200	$200 × (168/150)	$224

The $224 shown as the investment in land at the end of 1981 has the same amount of general purchasing power as did $200 at the end of 1980. Thus, no change in general purchasing power was recognized from holding the land.

CONSTANT DOLLAR (GPLA) ACCOUNTING FOR LIABILITIES AND STOCKHOLDERS' EQUITY

The effect of general price-level changes on liabilities depends on the nature of the liability. Most liabilities are monetary items, but stockholders' equity and a few liabilities are nonmonetary items.[5] *Monetary liabilities* represent fixed amounts that are owed, with the number of dollars to be paid not changing regardless of changes in the general price level.

Since monetary liabilities are unchanged in amounts owed even when price levels change, monetary liabilities are not adjusted for price-level changes. However, a company with monetary liabilities outstanding during a period of general price-level change will experience a general purchasing power gain or loss. Assume, for example, that a note payable for $300 was outstanding on December 31, 1980, and remained outstanding throughout 1981. During that time the general price index increased from 150 to 168. On the GPLA balance sheets for December 31, 1980, and 1981, the note payable would be reported at $300. The general purchasing power gain or loss is calculated as follows:

---

[5] Depending on its nature, preferred stock may be treated as a monetary item. If so, it is an exception to the general rule that stockholders' equity items are nonmonetary items.

Monetary liability balance on December 31, 1980 . . . . $ 300

Adjustment to reflect an equal amount of purchasing power on
December 31, 1981: $300 × (168/150) . . . . $ 336
Amount of monetary liability balance on December 31, 1981 . . . . . .   (300)
General purchasing power gain . . . . $ 36

The $336 at the end of 1981 has the same amount of general purchasing power as $300 had at the end of 1980. Since the company can pay the note with $300, the $36 difference is a gain in general purchasing power realized by the firm. Alternatively, if the general price index had decreased during 1981, the monetary liability would have resulted in a general purchasing power loss.

Nonmonetary liabilities are obligations that are not fixed in amount. They therefore tend to change with changes in the general price level. For example, product warranties may require that a manufacturer pay for repairs and replacements for a specified period of time after the product is sold. The amount of money required to make the repairs or replacements tends to change with changes in the general price level. Consequently, there is no purchasing power gain or loss associated with such warranties. Further, the balance sheet amount of such a nonmonetary liability must be adjusted to reflect changes in the general price index which occur after the liability comes into existence. Stockholders' equity items, with the possible exception of preferred stock, are also nonmonetary items. Hence, they also must be adjusted for changes in the general price index.

Illustration 20–3 summarizes the impact of general price-level changes on monetary items and nonmonetary items. The illustration

Financial statement item	When the general price level rises (inflation)		When the general price level falls (deflation)	
	Balance sheet adjustment required	Income statement gain or loss	Balance sheet adjustment required	Income statement gain or loss
Monetary assets	No	Loss	No	Gain
Nonmonetary assets	Yes	None	Yes	None
Monetary liabilities	No	Gain	No	Loss
Nonmonetary equities and liabilities*	Yes	None	Yes	None

* However, a nonmonetary liability may require an additional adjustment to assure that the balance sheet shows the current estimated amount to satisfy the liability.

Illustration 20–3

indicates what adjustments must be made in preparing a GPLA balance sheet and what purchasing power gains and losses must be recognized on a GPLA income statement.

PREPARING COMPREHENSIVE, CONSTANT DOLLAR (GPLA) FINANCIAL STATEMENTS

The previous discussion of price indexes and of GPLA accounting for assets, liabilities, and stockholders' equity provides a basis for understanding the procedures used in preparing comprehensive GPLA financial statements. In the following discussion, examples of these procedures are based on the unit-of-money (nominal dollar) financial statements for Delivery Service Company (Illustration 20–4).

Delivery Service Company
Balance Sheets
For Years Ended December 31, 1980, and 1981

Assets	1980	1981
Cash	$ 8,000	$30,000
Land (acquired December 31, 1980)	12,000	12,000
Delivery equipment (acquired January 1, 1980)	25,000	25,000
Less accumulated depreciation	(4,000)	(8,000)
Total assets	$41,000	$59,000

Equities		
Note payable (issued July 1, 1980)	$ 5,000	$ 5,000
Capital stock (issued January 1, 1980)	30,000	30,000
Retained earnings	6,000	24,000
Total equities	$41,000	$59,000

Delivery Service Company
Income Statement
For Year Ended December 31, 1981

Delivery revenues	$100,000
Depreciation expense	(4,000)
Other expenses	(78,000)
Net income	$ 18,000

Illustration 20–4

Delivery Service Company was organized on January 1, 1980. Of the original $30,000 invested in the company, $25,000 was used to buy delivery trucks. The trucks are being depreciated over five years on a straight-line basis. They have a $5,000 salvage value. Since the company was organized, the general price index has changed as follows:

Date	Price index
December 1979	130
June 1980 (also average for 1980)	140
December 1980	150
Average for 1981	160
December 1981	168

Delivery Service Company's cash balance increased from $8,000 to $30,000 during 1981 and is explained as follows:

Beginning cash balance	$ 8,000
Revenues, earned uniformly throughout the year	100,000
Expenses, paid uniformly throughout the year	(78,000)
Ending cash balance	$ 30,000

Restatement of the balance sheet

In preparing a GPLA balance sheet, the account balances are first classified as being monetary items or nonmonetary items. Since monetary items do not change regardless of changes in the price level, each monetary item is placed on the GPLA balance sheet without adjustment. Each nonmonetary item, on the other hand, must be adjusted for the price-level changes occurring since the original transactions that gave rise to the item.

The restatement of Delivery Service Company's balance sheet is presented in Illustration 20–5. Observe that the monetary items "Cash" and "Note payable" are transferred without adjustment from the unit-of-money column to the price-level-adjusted column. All of the remaining items are nonmonetary and are adjusted. The land was purchased on December 31, 1980, when the price level was 150.[6] Thus, the historical cost of the land is restated from December 1980 dollars to December 1981 dollars (price index 168) as follows: $12,000 × (168/150) = $13,440. The delivery equipment was purchased on January 1, 1980, at the same time the capital stock was issued. Therefore, "Delivery equipment," "Accumulated depreciation," and "Capital stock" are restated from January 1980 prices (index number 130) to December 1981 prices by applying the restatement factor of 168/130.

The retained earnings balance of $24,000 cannot be adjusted in a

---

[6] Normally, price index numbers are determined for a period of time, such as one quarter or one month, and are not determined for a specific point in time, such as December 31. For example, the CPI for all urban consumers is prepared for each month. Thus, the index number for December is used to approximate the price level on December 31.

Delivery Service Company
Restatement of Balance Sheet
December 31, 1981

Assets	Unit-of-money balances	Restatement factor from price index	GPLA Amounts
Cash	$30,000	—	$ 30,000
Land	12,000	168/150	13,440
Delivery equipment	25,000	168/130	32,308
Less accumulated depreciation	(8,000)	168/130	(10,338)
Total assets	$59,000		$ 65,410
Equities			
Note payable	$ 5,000	—	$ 5,000
Capital stock	30,000	168/130	38,769
Retained earnings	24,000	(See discussion)	21,641
Total equities	$59,000		$ 65,410

Illustration 20–5

single step because this balance resulted from more than one transaction. However, the correct, adjusted amount of retained earnings can be determined simply by "plugging" the necessary amount to make the balance sheet balance, as follows:

Total assets, adjusted		$ 65,410
Less: Note payable	$ 5,000	
Capital stock	38,769	(43,769)
Necessary retained earnings		$ 21,641

The process of confirming this restated retained earnings amount is explained later in the chapter.

Students should recognize that Delivery Service Company is a simplified illustration; only two of its balance sheet amounts (cash and retained earnings) resulted from more than one transaction. In a more complex case, most account balances would reflect several past transactions that took place at different points in time. In such a situation, the adjustment procedures are more detailed. For example, suppose that the $12,000 balance in the Land account resulted from three different purchases of land, as follows:

January 1, 1980, purchased land for	$ 3,000
July 1, 1980, purchased land for	4,000
December 31, 1980, purchased land for	5,000
Total	$12,000

Under this assumption the following adjustments would be required to prepare the GPLA balance sheet, as of December 31, 1981:

	Unit-of-money balances	Adjustment factor from price index	Restated to December 31, 1981, general price level
Land purchased on:			
January 1, 1980	$ 3,000	168/130	$ 3,877
July 1, 1980	4,000	168/140	4,800
December 31, 1980	5,000	168/150	5,600
Total	$12,000		$14,277

Restatement of the income statement

The general procedure followed in preparing a GPLA income statement is that every individual revenue and expense transaction must be restated from the price index level on the date of the transaction to the price index level at the end of the year. The restated amounts are then entered on the GPLA income statement along with the purchasing power gain or loss that resulted from holding or owing monetary items.

The calculations to restate the 1981 income statement of Delivery Service Company from units of money to the price-level-adjusted amounts are presented in Illustration 20–6.

As previously mentioned, Delivery Service Company's revenues were received and its other expenses were incurred in many transactions that occurred throughout the year. To be completely precise, each of these individual transactions would have to be separately re-

Delivery Service Company
Restatement of Income Statement
For Year Ended December 31, 1981

	Unit-of-money amounts	Restatement factor from price index	GPLA amounts
Delivery service revenues	$100,000	168/160	$105,000
Depreciation expense	(4,000)	168/130	(5,169)
Other expenses	(78,000)	168/160	(81,900)
	$ 18,000		$ 17,931
Purchasing power loss (from Illustration 20–7)			(1,460)
Net income	$ 18,000		$ 16,471

Illustration 20–6

stated. However, these revenues and expenses occurred in a nearly uniform pattern throughout the year. Restating the total revenue and the total other expenses from the average price level during the year (160) to the end-of-the-year price level (168) is therefore an acceptable approximation procedure.

The unit-of-money amount of depreciation expense on delivery trucks ($4,000) was determined by taking 20% of the $25,000 − $5,000 cost to be depreciated. Since this cost was incurred on January 1, 1980, the restatement of depreciation expense must be based on the price index for that date (130) and on the index number for the end of 1981 (168).

Purchasing power gain or loss

As was explained, the purchasing power gain or loss experienced by Delivery Service Company (shown in Illustration 20–6) stems from the amount of monetary assets held and monetary liabilities owed by the company during the year. During 1981, cash was the only monetary asset held by the company; the only monetary liability was a $5,000 note payable. The purchasing power gain or loss for these items is calculated in Illustration 20–7.

Note in Illustration 20–7 that the purchasing power loss from holding cash must take into account the changes in the cash balance that occurred during the year. First, the beginning cash balance of $8,000 is restated as an equivalent amount of general purchasing power at the end of the year. Since the December 1981 price index was 168

Delivery Service Company
Calculation of Purchasing Power Gain or Loss
For Year Ended December 31, 1981

	Unit-of-money amounts	Restatement factor from price index	Restated to December 31, 1981	Gain or loss
Cash				
Beginning balance	$ 8,000	168/150	$ 8,960	
Delivery revenue receipts .	100,000	168/160	105,000	
Payments for expenses ..	(78,000)	168/160	(81,900)	
Ending balance, adjusted ..			$ 32,060	
Ending balance, actual	$ 30,000		(30,000)	
Purchasing power loss				$2,060
Note payable: beginning				
balance	$ 5,000	168/150	$ 5,600	
Ending balance, actual	$ 5,000		(5,000)	
Purchasing power gain				(600)
Net purchasing power loss .				$1,460

Illustration 20–7

and the December 1980 price index was 150, the balance is restated as follows: $8,000 × 168/150 = $8,960. Next, each cash change is adjusted from the price level at the time the change occurred to the price level at the end of the year. In the example, cash receipts from revenues occurred uniformly throughout the year. Therefore, the average price index number for the year (160) is used to approximate the price level in effect when the revenues were received. The $100,000 cash received from revenues during the year is restated to the equivalent general purchasing power at the year's end, as follows: $100,000 × 168/160 = $105,000. Cash payments for expenses were also made uniformly throughout the year, so they are restated using the same index numbers. In other words, the $78,000 of cash expenses are restated as follows: $78,000 × 168/160 = $81,900. With the initial cash balance and the cash changes restated into end-of-the-year purchasing power, the adjusted end-of-the-year purchasing power for cash is $32,060. Since the actual ending cash balance is only $30,000, the $2,060 difference represents a loss of general purchasing power.

The $5,000 note payable was issued on July 1, 1980, when the price index was 140. Nevertheless, the purchasing power gain associated with this monetary liability is calculated by adjusting the $5,000 from the beginning-of-1981 price level (index number 168). Since the calculation is being made for the purpose of preparing a 1981 GPLA income statement, only the purchasing power gain arising from inflation during 1981 should be included. The gain associated with the price index change from 140 to 150 occurred during 1980, and would have been included in the GPLA income statement for 1980.

Adjusting the retained earnings balance

The December 31, 1981, adjusted retained earnings balance was previously determined by "plugging" the amount necessary to make liabilities plus stockholders' equity equal to total assets (page 673). Alternatively, if a GPLA balance sheet for December 31, 1980, was available, the adjusted retained earnings balance on that date could be restated to the December 31, 1981, price level. Then the GPLA net income for 1981 could be added to determine GPLA retained earnings at December 31, 1981. For example, had GPLA financial statements been prepared for 1980, the $6,000 retained earnings balance in units of money (see Illustration 20–4) would have been adjusted to a December 31, 1980, general price-level-adjusted amount of $4,616.[7] With this additional information, the adjusted retained earnings balance for December 31, 1981, is calculated as follows:

---

[7] Notice that the $4,616 price-level-adjusted retained earnings on December 31, 1980, is smaller than the $6,000 units-of-money amount. This decrease was caused by the same factors that caused the adjusted net income for 1981 to be less than the units-of-money net income (see Illustration 20–6).

	Restated to December 31, 1980, general price level	Factor from price index	Restated to December 31, 1981, general price level
Retained earnings, December 31, 1980	$4,616	168/150	$ 5,170
GPLA net income for 1981 (see Illustration 20–6)			16,471
Dividends declared during 1981			–0–
Retained earnings, December 31, 1981 ..			$21,641

CONSTANT DOLLAR (GPLA) ACCOUNTING AND CURRENT VALUES

Early in this chapter, the fact that prices do not all change at the same rate was discussed. Indeed, when the general price level is rising, some specific prices may be falling. If this were not so, if prices all changed at the same rate, then constant dollar accounting would report current values on the financial statements. For example, suppose that a company purchased land for $50,000 on January 1, 1980, when the general price index was 130. Then the price level increased until December 1981, when the price index was 168. A GPLA balance sheet for this company on December 31, 1981, would report the land at $50,000 × 168/130 = $64,615. If all prices increased at the same rate during that period, the price of the land would have increased from $50,000 to $64,615, and the company's GPLA balance sheet would coincidentally disclose the land at its current value.

However, since all prices do not change at the same rate, the current value of the land may differ substantially from the GPLA amount of $64,615. For example, assume that the company obtained an appraisal of the land and determined that its current value on December 31, 1981, was $80,000. The difference between the original purchase price of $50,000 and the current value of $80,000 can be explained as follows:

Unrealized holding gain	$80,000 −	$64,615 =	$15,385
Adjustment for general price-level increase	$64,615 −	$50,000 =	14,615
			$30,000

In that case, the GPLA balance sheet would report land at $64,615, which is $15,385 ($80,000 − $64,615) less than its current value. This illustrates a very important fact concerning constant dollar (GPLA) accounting; it is not a form of current value accounting. Rather, GPLA accounting restates original transaction prices into equivalent amounts of current, *general* purchasing power. Only if current, *specific* purchasing power were the basis of valuation would the balance sheet display current values.

CURRENT VALUE ACCOUNTING

Constant dollar (GPLA) accounting often has been proposed as a way of improving accounting information. Proponents of GPLA accounting argue that conventional, unit-of-money financial statements have questionable relevance to decision makers. Conventional statements may even be misleading in a world of persistent, long-run inflation. Since GPLA accounting adjusts for general price-level changes, its proponents believe that GPLA financial statements provide a more meaningful portrayal of a company's past operations and financial position. And, they argue, GPLA accounting is sufficiently objective to allow its practical application without damaging the credibility of financial statements.

Other accountants argue that even GPLA accounting fails to communicate to statement readers the economic values of most relevance. They would design financial statements so that each item in the statements is measured in terms of current value.

Some arguments for current value accounting conclude that the current liquidation price or "exit value" of an item is the most appropriate basis of valuation for financial statements. However, other arguments, which appear to be more widely supported, conclude that the price to replace an item, its *current cost*, is the best basis of financial statement valuation.

CURRENT COST ACCOUNTING

Current costs on the income statement

In the current cost approach to accounting, the reported amount of each expense should be the number of dollars that would be required, at the time the expense is incurred, to acquire the resources consumed. For example, assume that the annual sales of a company included an item that was sold in May for $1,500 and the item had been acquired on January 1 for $500. Also, suppose that in May, at the time of the sale, the cost to replace this item was $700. Then the annual current cost income statement would show sales of $1,500 less cost of goods sold of $700. To state this idea more generally, when an asset is acquired and then held for a time before it expires, the historical cost of the asset likely will differ from its current cost at the time it expires. *Current cost accounting* requires that the reported amount of expense be measured at the time the asset expires.

The result of measuring expenses in terms of current costs is that revenue is matched with the current (at the time of the sale) cost of the resources that were used to earn the revenue. Thus, operating profit is not positive unless revenues are sufficient to replace all of the resources that were consumed in the process of producing those revenues. The operating profit figure is therefore thought to be an important (and improved) basis for evaluating the effectiveness of operating activities.

Current costs on the balance sheet

On the balance sheet, *current cost accounting* requires that assets be reported at the amounts that would have to be paid to purchase them as of the balance sheet date. Similarly, liabilities should be reported at the amounts that would have to be paid to satisfy the liabilities as of the balance sheet date. Note that this valuation basis is similar to GPLA accounting in that a distinction exists between monetary and nonmonetary assets and liabilities. Monetary assets and liabilities are fixed in amount regardless of price-level changes. Therefore, monetary assets need not be adjusted in amount. But all of the nonmonetary items must be evaluated at each balance sheet date to determine the best approximation of current cost.

A little reflection on the variety of assets reported on balance sheets will confirm the presence of many difficulties in obtaining reliable estimates of current costs. In some cases, specific price indexes may provide the most reliable source of current cost information. In other cases, where an asset is not new and has been partially depreciated, its current cost may be estimated by determining the cost to acquire a new asset of like nature. Depreciation on the old asset is then based on the current cost of the new asset. Clearly, the accountant's professional judgment is an important factor in developing current cost data.

FASB REQUIREMENTS FOR CONSTANT DOLLAR AND CURRENT COST INFORMATION

In October 1979, the FASB issued *Statement No. 33*, which contains reporting requirements for both constant dollar and current cost information. These requirements were effective for financial statements issued after December 24, 1979, but with a one-year delay of the current cost requirements if a reporting company had difficulty implementing the requirements more quickly.[8] The requirements apply only to large companies with assets of more than $1 billion or inventories

---

[8] *FASB Statement No. 33*, pars. 67–69.

plus property, plant, and equipment (before deducting depreciation) of more than $125 million.[9]

Statement No. 33 does not affect the conventional financial statements; only supplemental information is required. The supplemental information to be presented includes:[10]

  a. Income from continuing operations adjusted for general price-level changes.[11]
  b. The general purchasing power gain or loss.
  c. Income from continuing operations on a current cost basis.
  d. Current cost of inventory at the end of the year.
  e. Current cost of property, plant, and equipment at the end of the year.
  f. The increase or decrease in the current cost of inventory, property, plant, and equipment, net of general price-level changes.
  g. A five-year summary of selected financial data.

Examples of the required disclosures are presented in Illustrations 20–8 and 20–9. Compare the requirements listed as items *a* through *f* (above) with the information shown in Illustration 20–8. Each of the required items is disclosed.

Observe in Illustration 20–8 that the only restated income statement items are Cost of goods sold and Depreciation and amortization expense. These are the only income statement items (plus depletion expense, if any) which must be restated to meet the minimum FASB requirements. Net sales, Other operating expense, Interest expense, and Provision for income taxes do not have to be restated. These latter items may well have been affected by inflation. And the FASB would *permit* companies to adjust such items. But the Board does not require it.

Note that the general purchasing power gain or loss is called "gain from decline in purchasing power of net amounts owed." The FASB decided not to include this item in the calculation of income (loss) from continuing operations; instead, it is shown separately.

The five-year summary of financial data is shown in Illustration 20–9. Observe that the constant cost and current cost information is shown for the years 1979 and 1980 only. This is because the requirements of *FASB Statement No. 33* apply only to financial statements issued after December 24, 1979.

---

  [9] Ibid., par. 23.

  [10] Ibid., pars. 29–37.

  [11] Income from continuing operations excludes the effects of accounting changes, extraordinary items, and income or loss from operations that are being discontinued. Detailed discussions of these items are left to a more advanced accounting course.

**Statement of Income from Continuing Operations
Adjusted for Changing Prices
For the Year Ended December 31, 1980
(in $000s)**

	As reported in the primary statements	Adjusted for general inflation	Adjusted for changes in specific prices (current costs)
Net sales and other operating revenues	$253,000	$253,000	$253,000
Cost of goods sold	$197,000	$204,384	$205,408
Depreciation and amortization expense	10,000	14,130	19,500
Other operating expense	20,835	20,835	20,835
Interest expense	7,165	7,165	7,165
Provision for income taxes	9,000	9,000	9,000
	$244,000	$255,514	$261,908
Income (loss) from continuing operations	$ 9,000	$ (2,514)	$ (8,908)
Gain from decline in purchasing power of net amounts owed		$ 7,729	$ 7,729
Increase in specific prices (current cost) of inventories and property, plant, and equipment held during the year*			$ 24,608
Effect of increase in general price level			18,959
Excess of increase in specific prices over increase in the general price level			$ 5,649

* At December 31, 1980, current cost of inventory was $65,700 and current cost of property, plant, and equipment, net of accumulated depreciation was $85,100.
Source: *FASB Statement No. 33*, Appendix A, Schedule B, p. 33.

Illustration 20–8

Using recoverable amounts that are lower than current cost

In general, "current cost" is the cost that would be required to currently acquire (or replace) an asset or service. Current cost accounting involves reporting assets and expenses in terms of their current costs. However, the FASB recognizes an important exception to this general description of current cost accounting. That exception involves the use of recoverable amounts.

In the case of an asset about to be sold, the recoverable amount is its net realizable value. In other words, recoverable amount is the asset's expected sales price less related costs to sell. If an asset is to be used rather than sold, recoverable amount is the present value of future cash flows expected from using the asset. A recoverable amount is reported instead of current cost whenever the recoverable amount appears to be materially and permanently lower than current cost. Both the asset and the expense associated with using it (or selling it) should be measured in terms of the recoverable amount.[12]

[12] *FASB Statement No. 33*, pars. 62–63.

Five-Year Comparison of Selected
Supplementary Financial Data Adjusted for Effects of Changing Prices
(in 000s of average 1980 dollars)

	Years ended December 31,				
	1976	1977	1978	1979	1980
Net sales and other operating revenues.........................	$265,000	$235,000	$240,000	$237,063	$253,000
Historical cost information adjusted for general inflation					
Income (loss) from continuing operations				(2,761)	(2,514)
Income (loss) from continuing operations per common share				(1.91)	(1.68)
Net assets at year-end				55,518	57,733
Current cost information					
Income (loss from continuing operations				(4,125)	(8,908)
Income (loss) from continuing operations per common share				(2.75)	(5.94)
Excess of increase in specific prices over increase in the general price level				2,292	5,649
Net assets at year-end				79,996	81,466
Gain from decline in purchasing power of net amounts owed....................				7,027	7,729
Cash dividends declared per common share	2.59	2.43	2.26	2.16	2.00
Market price per common share at year-end	32	31	43	39	35
Average consumer price index	170.5	181.5	195.4	205.0	220.9

Source: *FASB Statement No. 33*, Appendix A, Schedule B, p. 34.

Illustration 20–9

The reason for using recoverable amounts emphasizes the value of an asset to its owner. The idea is that an asset should not be reported at an amount that is larger than its value to its owner. If the recoverable amount of an asset is less than its current cost, a business is not likely to replace it. A business would not be willing to pay more for an asset than it could expect to recover from using or selling the asset. Hence, the value of the asset to the business can be no higher than the recoverable amount. When value to the business is less than current cost, it is believed that current cost is not relevant to an analysis of the business. Following this line of reasoning, *Statement No. 33* calls for reporting current cost or recoverable amount, if lower.

Using recoverable amounts lower than historical cost in constant dollars

In constant dollar accounting, assets and their associated expenses are generally reported in terms of historical cost, adjusted for general price-level changes. However, the FASB requirements for constant dollar accounting involve the same "recoverable amount" exception as is applied in the case of current cost accounting. In other words, recoverable amounts must be substituted for historical costs in constant dollars if the recoverable amounts are lower. The Board argues that using recoverable amounts in such cases avoids overstating the "worth" of assets.[13]

THE MOMENTUM TOWARD MORE COMPREHENSIVE PRICE-LEVEL ACCOUNTING

The question of whether procedures of accounting for price-level changes should be implemented has been debated and discussed for many years. Granted, inflation (and taxes) has caused the expanded use of certain procedures such as Lifo. But the first significant require-ments to report inflation-adjusted information were not imposed until 1976. At that time, the Securities and Exchange Commission (SEC) began to require certain large companies to report supplemental in-formation on a replacement cost basis. They were required to estimate the

. . . current replacement cost of inventories and productive capacity at the end of each fiscal year for which a balance sheet is required and the approxi-mate amount of cost of sales and depreciation based on replacement cost for the two most recent full fiscal years.[14]

To see an actual example of the disclosures required by the SEC, turn to the Appendix after Chapter 28 which contains the 1979 financial statements of Masonite Corporation. Footnote 15 to those statements (pages 961 and 962) contains the replacement cost disclosures.

The SEC's replacement cost disclosure requirements generated many complaints and public statements of opposition by corporate managements. Time will tell whether the FASB's requirements are more or less acceptable. The SEC has withdrawn its 1976 requirements and supports those specified by the FASB.

The SEC's requirements were limited to large companies, and the required information was obviously much less than a complete set of financial statements prepared on a replacement cost basis. Neverthe-

---

[13] Ibid., pars. 62, 195.

[14] Securities and Exchange Commission, *Accounting Series Release No. 190* (Washing-ton, D.C., 1976).

less, the SEC requirements represented a major break with the U.S. tradition of relying totally on unit-of-money financial statements.

The recent FASB requirements constitute another major step toward improved accounting for price-level changes. While still limited to large companies and still substantially less than complete financial statements, they involve both constant dollar and current cost information, with important inclusions of income statement information. Whether or not current cost accounting and/or constant dollar accounting will eventually be required in most financial statements remains to be seen. No doubt, conventional, unit-of-money financial statements will continue to represent the primary basis of U.S. accounting in the near future. But a basic shift to one or the other inflation accounting alternative is a distinct possibility. Both constant dollar accounting and current cost accounting are being used in some countries. The strength of the calls for expanded usage of them in the United States will probably depend on how much future inflation as well as specific price changes undermine the perceived relevance of existing reporting methods.

GLOSSARY

Constant dollar accounting. Synonym for *general price-level adjusted accounting.*

Current cost. On the income statement, the number of dollars that would be required, at the time the expense is incurred, to acquire the resources consumed. On the balance sheet, the amounts that would have to be paid to replace the assets or satisfy the liabilities as of the balance sheet date.

Current cost accounting. An accounting system that uses specific price-level indexes (and other means) to develop financial statements that report items such as assets and expenses in terms of the current costs to acquire or replace those assets or services.

Current value accounting. An accounting system that provides financial statements in which current values are reported; different versions of current value are possible, for example, current replacement costs or current exit values.

General price-level-adjusted (GPLA) accounting. An accounting system that adjusts unit-of-money financial statements for changes in the general purchasing power of the dollar. Also called *constant dollar accounting.*

General price-level index. A measure of the changing purchasing power of a dollar in general; measures the price changes for a broad market basket that includes a large variety of goods and services, for example, the Gross National Product Implicit Price Deflator or the Consumers Price Index for all urban consumers.

General purchasing power gain or loss. The gain or loss that results from holding monetary assets and/or owing monetary liabilities during a period in which the general price level changes.

Monetary assets. Money or claims to receive a fixed amount of money.

Monetary liabilities. Fixed amounts which are owed, with the number of dollars to be paid fixed in amount and not changing regardless of changes in the general price level.

Nonmonetary assets. All assets other than monetary assets.

Nonmonetary liabilities. Obligations that are not fixed in amount and therefore tend to change with changes in the general price level.

Price index. A measure of the changes in prices of a particular market basket of goods and/or services.

Specific price-level index. An indicator of the changing purchasing power of a dollar spent for items in a specific category; includes a much more narrow range of goods and services than does a general price index.

Unit-of-money financial statements. Conventional financial statements which disclose revenues, expenses, assets, liabilities, and owners' equity in terms of the historical monetary units exchanged at the time the transactions occurred.

QUESTIONS FOR CLASS DISCUSSION

1. Some people argue that conventional financial statements fail to adequately account for inflation. What is the general problem with conventional financial statements that generates this argument?
2. Are there any procedures used in conventional accounting that offset the effects of inflation on financial statements? Give some examples.
3. What is the fundamental difference in the price-level adjustments made under current cost accounting and under constant dollar accounting?
4. Explain the difference between an "average change in per unit prices" and a "weighted-average change in per unit prices."
5. What is the significance of the "base" year in constructing a price index? How is the base year chosen?
6. For accounting purposes, what is the most important use of a price index?
7. What is the difference between a specific price-level index and a general price-level index?
8. What is meant by "unit-of-money" financial statements?
9. Define "monetary assets."
10. Explain the meaning of "nonmonetary assets."
11. Define "monetary liabilities" and "nonmonetary liabilities." Give examples of both.
12. If the monetary assets held by a firm exceed its monetary liabilities throughout a period in which prices are rising, which should be recorded on a GPLA income statement—a purchasing power gain or loss? What if mone-

tary liabilities exceed monetary assets during a period in which prices are falling?

13. If accountants preferred to display current values in the financial statements, would they use constant dollar accounting or current cost accounting? Are there any other alternatives?

14. Describe the meaning of "operating profit" under a current cost accounting system.

15. "The distinction between monetary assets and nonmonetary assets is just as important for current cost accounting as it is for general price-level-adjusted accounting." Is this statement true? Why?

16. *FASB Statement No. 33* requires several specific disclosures of constant dollar items and current cost items. List the general disclosure requirements of *FASB Statement No. 33*.

CLASS EXERCISES

Exercise 20–1

Market basket No. 1 consists of 2 units of A, 5 units of B, and 3 units of D. Market basket No. 2 consists of 3 units of A, 2 units of B, and 4 units of C. The per unit prices of each item during 198A and during 198B are as follows:

Item	198A price per unit	198B price per unit
A	$1.50	$2.00
B	3.00	3.30
C	2.00	1.88
D	4.00	4.60

Required:

Compute the annual rate of inflation for market basket No. 1 and for market basket No. 2.

Exercise 20–2

The following total prices of a specified market basket were calculated for each of the years 198A through 198F:

Year	Total price
198A	$250
198B	400
198C	320
198D	480
198E	600
198F	640

Required:

1. Using 198D as the base year, prepare a price index for the six-year period.
2. Convert the index from a 198D base year to a 198F base year.

Exercise 20–3

Franklin Company's plant and equipment consisted of equipment purchased during 198A for $100,000, land purchased during 198C for $30,000, and a building purchased during 198D for $215,000. The general price index during these and later years was as follows:

198A	80
198B	95
198C	112
198D	125
198E	140
198F	154
198G	168

Required:

1. Assuming the above price index adequately represents end-of-the-year price levels, calculate the amount of each cost that would be shown on a GPLA balance sheet for *(a)* December 31, 198E, and *(b)* December 31, 198G. Ignore any accumulated depreciation.
2. Would the GPLA income statement for 198G disclose any purchasing power gain or loss as a consequence of holding the above assets? If so, how much?

Exercise 20–4

Classify the following items as monetary or nonmonetary.

1. Cash.
2. Investment in U.S. Government bonds.
3. Retained earnings.
4. Product warranties liability.
5. Accounts receivable.
6. Goodwill.
7. Salaries payable.
8. Common stock.
9. Prepaid fire insurance.
10. Common stock subscribed.
11. Delivery equipment.
12. Merchandise.
13. Accounts payable.
14. Patents.
15. Trademarks.
16. Unearned subscriptions revenue.

Exercise 20–5

The monetary items owned and owed by the J. Fields Company include cash, accounts payable, and a note payable. Calculate the general purchasing power gain or loss incurred by the company in 198B, given the following information:

Time period	Price index
December 198A	116
Average during 198B	125
December 198B	145

a. The balance in the Cash account on December 31, 198A, was $4,400. Cash sales were made uniformly throughout the year and amounted to $13,000. Payments on accounts payable were also made uniformly during the year and amounted to $6,400. Other expenses amounting to $3,000 were paid in cash and were evenly distributed during the year.

b. Accounts payable amounted to $800 on December 31, 198A. Credit purchases of merchandise amounting to $8,000 were spread evenly throughout the year, and $6,400 in cash was paid to accounts payable creditors.

c. A note payable of $5,000 was issued in June 198A when the price index was 110.

PROBLEMS

Problem 20–1

The costs of purchasing a common market basket in each of several years are as follows:

Year	Cost of market basket
198A	$18,000
198B	15,000
198C	21,000
198D	25,500
198E	27,000
198F	30,000
198G	33,000
198H	36,000

Required:

1. Construct a price index using 198F as the base year.
2. Using the index constructed in Requirement 1, what was the percent increase in prices from 198F to 198H?
3. Using the index constructed in Requirement 1, how many dollars in 198H does it take to have the same purchasing power as $1 in 198B?
4. Using the index constructed in Requirement 1, if $10,000 were invested in land during 198A and $15,000 were invested in land during 198B, what would be reported as the total land investment on a GPLA balance sheet

prepared in 198E? What would your answer be if the investments were in U.S. long-term bonds rather than in land?

Problem 20-2

Western Produce Company purchased equipment for $480,000 on January 4, 198B. The equipment was expected to last six years and have no salvage value; straight-line depreciation was to be used. The equipment was sold on December 31, 198D, for $340,000. End-of-the-year general price index numbers during this period of time were as follows:

198A 100
198B 125
198C 150
198D 175

Required:

1. What should be presented for the equipment and accumulated depreciation on a GPLA balance sheet dated December 31, 198B?
2. How much depreciation expense should be shown on the GPLA income statement for 198C?
3. How much depreciation expense should be shown on the GPLA income statement for 198D?
4. How much gain on the sale of equipment would be reported on the conventional, unit-of-money income statement for 198D?
5. After adjusting the equipment's cost and accumulated depreciation to the end-of-198D price level, how much gain in (loss of) general purchasing power was realized by the sale of the equipment?

Problem 20-3

The Laurleen Transit Company's only monetary asset or liability during 198D was cash, which changed during the year as follows:

Beginning balance .... $ 3,500
Revenues received evenly throughout the year ... 25,000
Payments of expenses (spread evenly
  throughout the year) .... (10,000)
Dividends declared and paid early in
  January 198D............................... (1,500)
Dividends declared and paid late in
  December 198D .... (4,500)
Ending balance .... $ 12,500

The unit-of-money income statement for 198D appeared as follows:

Sales		$ 25,000
Cash expenses	$10,000	
Depreciation expense, equipment	4,000	
Amortization expense, patents.........	3,000	
Total expenses		(17,000)
Net income		$ 8,000

The depreciation expense refers to equipment purchased in December 198A, and the amortization expense refers to patents acquired in December 198B. General price index numbers covering the periods of time mentioned above are as follows:

December 198A 120.0
December 198B 135.0
December 198C 150.0
December 198D 180.0
Average for 198D 160.0

Required:

1. Calculate the general purchasing power gain or loss experienced by Laurleen Transit Company in 198D.
2. Prepare a schedule that restates the income statement for 198D from units of money to GPLA amounts.

Problem 20–4

DeShazo Company's unit-of-money income statement for 198B and balance sheets for December 31, 198A, and December 31, 198B, are given below:

DESHAZO COMPANY
Income Statement for Year Ended December 31, 198B

Sales revenue		$250,000
Depreciation expense	$ 20,000	
Other expenses	200,000	220,000
Net income		$ 30,000

DESHAZO COMPANY
Comparative Balance Sheets
December 31, 198A, and 198B

Assets	198A	198B
Cash	$ 60,000	$ 90,000
Accounts receivable	40,000	70,000
Equipment (net of depreciation)	95,000	75,000
Total assets	$195,000	$235,000

Liabilities and Stockholders' Equity		
Notes payable	$ 40,000	$ 50,000
Capital stock	100,000	100,000
Retained earnings	55,000	85,000
Total liabilities and stockholders' equity	$195,000	$235,000

Selected numbers from a general price-level index are as follows:

December 198A 75
Average during 198B 78
August 198B 80
December 198B 84

The increase in notes payable during 198B occurred on August 20, and the funds derived from the increase in notes payable were used to increase the cash balance. DeShazo Company purchased the equipment at a time when the general price index was 60. Revenue from sales was earned evenly throughout the year and was debited to Accounts Receivable. Cash receipts from receivables ($220,000) were also distributed evenly throughout the year, and expenses other than depreciation were paid in cash evenly throughout the year.

Required:

1. Calculate the purchasing power gain or loss incurred by DeShazo Company during 198B.
2. Prepare a general price-level-adjusted income statement for 198B.

Problem 20–5

Assume the same facts as were presented in Problem 20–4. In addition, DeShazo Company was organized at a time when the price index was 60. All of the capital stock ($100,000) was issued at that time.

Required:

1. Based on the above information and the data provided in Problem 20–4, prepare a GPLA balance sheet for DeShazo Company on December 31, 198B. (The retained earnings balance may be determined simply by "plugging" in the amount that is necessary to make the balance sheet balance.)
2. On DeShazo Company's GPLA balance sheet on December 31, 198A, retained earnings was $53,750. Also, assume that DeShazo Company reported a GPLA net income for 198B of $14,800. Present a calculation that confirms the retained earnings balance as it is reported on the GPLA balance sheet for December 31, 198B.

Problem 20–6

The December 31, 198B, and December 31, 198C, comparative balance sheets of Frost Company and its 198C income statement are presented below:

FROST COMPANY
Comparative Balance Sheets
December 31, 198B, and 198C

Assets	198B	198C
Cash	$15,000	$ 27,000
Accounts receivable	20,000	30,000
Inventory	7,000	9,000
Machinery	35,000	35,000
Accumulated depreciation	(5,000)	(10,000)
Investment in bonds of ABC Company	25,000	25,000
Total assets	$97,000	$116,000

Liabilities and Stockholders' Equity

Accounts payable	$ 8,000	$ 10,000
Notes payable	5,000	5,000
Common stock	65,000	65,000
Retained earnings	19,000	36,000
Total liabilities and stockholders' equity	$97,000	$116,000

FROST COMPANY

Income Statement for Year Ended December 31, 198C

Sales		$80,000
Cost of goods sold:		
Beginning inventory	$ 7,000	
Purchases	40,000	
Total available merchandise	$47,000	
Ending inventory	9,000	38,000
Gross profit		$42,000
Depreciation expense	$ 5,000	
Other expenses	18,000	23,000
Net income		$19,000

Additional information about Frost Company:

1. All sales are on credit and recorded to Accounts Receivable. Cash collections of Accounts Receivable occurred evenly throughout the year.
2. All merchandise purchases were credited to Accounts Payable, and cash payments of Accounts Payable occurred evenly throughout the year. The beginning inventory was acquired when the price index was 112.
3. Other expenses ($18,000) were paid in cash evenly throughout the year.
4. Dividends of $2,000 were paid to stockholders in June 198C.
5. The machinery was acquired in January 198A. The Investment in Bonds of ABC Company was acquired on January 1, 198B. The outstanding stock was issued on January 1, 198A.
6. Sales and purchases of merchandise occurred evenly throughout the year.
7. The changes during the year in Cash, Accounts Payable, and Accounts Receivable accounts are as follows:

Cash

Beginning balance	15,000	Payments of accounts	38,000
Receipts from customers	70,000	Other expenses	18,000
		Dividend payments	2,000

Accounts Payable

Cash payments	38,000	Beginning balance	8,000
		Merchandise purchases	40,000

Accounts Receivable

Beginning balance	20,000	Cash receipts	70,000
Credit sales	80,000		

Selected index numbers from a general price-level index are the following:

	General price index
January 198A	80
December 198A	100
December 198B	112
June 198C (also average for 198C)	125
December 198C	140

Required:

1. Calculate the purchasing power gain or loss to be reported on the GPLA income statement for 198C.
2. Prepare the GPLA income statement for 198C.
3. Prepare a GPLA balance sheet as of December 31, 198C. (Retained earnings may be determined by "plugging" in the amount necessary to make the balance sheet balance.)

ALTERNATE PROBLEMS

Problem 20–1A

The costs of purchasing a common market basket in each of several years are as follows:

Year	Cost of market basket
198A	$36,000
198B	31,500
198C	42,750
198D	45,000
198E	54,000
198F	58,500
198G	63,000
198H	60,750

Required:

1. Construct a price index using 198D as the base year.
2. Using the index constructed in Requirement 1, what was the percent increase in prices from 198E to 198H?
3. Using the index constructed in Requirement 1, how many dollars in 198G does it take to have the same purchasing power as $1 in 198D?
4. Using the index constructed in Requirement 1, if $16,000 were invested in land during 198A and $20,000 were invested in land during 198D, what would be reported as the total land investment on a GPLA balance sheet

prepared in 198G? What would your answer be if the investments were in corporate bonds (purchased at par) rather than in land?

Problem 20–2A

Clendinning Company purchased machinery for $300,000 on January 2, 198B. The machinery was expected to last five years and have no salvage value; straight-line depreciation was to be used. The machinery was sold on December 30, 198E, for $125,000. End-of-the-year general price index numbers during this period of time were the following:

198A   80
198B.............   96
198C   120
198D   112
198E   132

Required:

1. What should be presented for the machinery and accumulated depreciation on a GPLA balance sheet dated December 31, 198C?
2. How much depreciation expense should be shown on the GPLA income statement for 198D?
3. How much depreciation expense should be shown on the GPLA income statement for 198E?
4. How much gain on the sale of machinery would be reported on the conventional, unit-of-money income statement for 198E?
5. After adjusting the machinery's cost and accumulated depreciation to the end-of-198E price level, how much gain in (loss of) general purchasing power was realized by the sale of the machinery?

Problem 20–3A

The conventional, unit-of-money income statement of Jerry Hunt Enterprises for 198F appears as follows:

Sales		$ 40,000
Cash expenses	$18,000	
Depreciation expense, building	7,000	
Amortization expense, trademark	6,000	
Total expenses		(31,000)
Net income		$ 9,000

Cash was the only monetary item held by the company during 198F, and the changes that occurred in the Cash account during the year were as follows:

Beginning balance	$ 10,000
Revenues received uniformly during the year	40,000
Payment of dividend on January 3, 198F	(5,000)
Payment of expenses evenly throughout the year ..	(18,000)
Purchase of land on December 28, 198F	(20,000)
Ending balance	$ 7,000

The only depreciable asset belonging to Jerry Hunt Enterprises is a building that was purchased early in January 198B. The trademark owned by the company was purchased in late December 198C. General price index numbers covering the periods of time mentioned above are as follows:

December 198A 80.0
December 198B 95.0
December 198C 105.0
December 198D 110.0
December 198E 108.0
December 198F 120.0
Average for 198F 112.0

Required:

1. Calculate the general purchasing power gain or loss experienced by Jerry Hunt Enterprises in 198F.
2. Prepare a schedule that restates the income statement for 198F from units of money to GPLA amounts.

Problem 20–4A

The directors of Cooke Company have expressed an interest in general price-level-adjusted financial statements and the concepts of purchasing power gains and losses. The price index in December 198A was 135, and in December 198B it was 146. The average price index during 198B was 140.

The unit-of-money financial statements for Cooke Company are presented below. The increase in notes payable during 198B occurred on May 15, at which time the reported price index was 138. The funds derived from the increase in notes payable were used to increase the cash balance. Cooke Company purchased the machinery several years ago when the price index was 100.

COOKE COMPANY
Comparative Balance Sheets
December 31, 198A, and 198B

Assets	198A	198B
Cash	$ 40,000	$100,000
Accounts receivable	75,000	75,000
Machinery (net of depreciation)....................	60,000	54,000
Total assets	$175,000	$229,000

Liabilities and Stockholders' Equity		
Notes payable	$ 25,000	$ 35,000
Capital stock	100,000	100,000
Retained earnings	50,000	94,000
Total liabilities and stockholders' equity	$175,000	$229,000

COOKE COMPANY
Income Statement for Year Ended December 31, 198B

Sales revenue		$150,000
Depreciation expense	$ 6,000	
Other expenses	100,000	106,000
Net income....................		$ 44,000

Required:

1. Calculate the purchasing power gain or loss incurred by Cooke Company during 198B. You should assume that sales revenues were received in cash evenly throughout the year and that expenses other than depreciation were paid in cash evenly throughout the year.
2. Prepare a general price-level-adjusted income statement for 198B.

Problem 20–5A

Cooke Company, for which data were presented in Problem 20–4A, was organized at a time when the general price index was 100. All of the $100,000 capital stock was issued at that time.

Required:

1. Based on the above information and the data provided in Problem 20–4A, prepare a GPLA balance sheet for Cooke Company as of December 31, 198B. (The retained earnings balance may be determined simply by "plugging" in the amount that is necessary to make the balance sheet balance.)
2. On Cooke Company's GPLA balance sheet on December 31, 198A, retained earnings was reported as $36,000. Assume also that GPLA net income for 198B was $33,907. Present a calculation that confirms the retained earnings balance as it is reported on the GPLA balance sheet for December 31, 198B.

PROVOCATIVE PROBLEMS

Provocative problem 20–1
Sutter Company

Sutter Company has often been willing to consider new, innovative ways of reporting to its stockholders. For example, it has presented supplemental GPLA financial statements in its annual reports. The GPLA balance sheets of Sutter Company for December 31, 198A, and 198B, were as follows:

SUTTER COMPANY
GPLA Balance Sheets

Assets	As presented on December 31, 198B	As presented on December 31, 198A
Cash	$ 12,000	$ 5,000
Accounts receivable	20,000	10,000
Notes receivable	5,000	—
Inventory	6,429	3,250
Equipment	47,727	41,364
Accumulated depreciation	(13,636)	(5,909)
Land	37,987	23,636
Total assets	$115,507	$77,341

Liabilities and Stockholders' Equity

Accounts payable...........................	$ 17,000	$ 3,500
Notes payable..............................	9,000	2,500
Common stock	68,182	59,091
Retained earnings	21,325	12,250
Total liabilities and stockholders' equity	$115,507	$77,341

A new member of Sutter Company's board of directors has expressed interest in the relationship between GPLA statements and unit-of-money statements. The board member understands that GPLA statements are derived from unit-of-money statements, but wonders if this process can be reversed. Specifically, you are asked to show how the GPLA balance sheets for December 31, 198A, and 198B could be restated back into unit-of-money statements.

Additional information:

1. The outstanding stock was issued in January 198A, and the company's equipment was purchased at that time. The equipment has no salvage value and is being depreciated over seven years.
2. The note receivable was acquired on June 30, 198B.
3. Notes payable consists of two notes, one for $2,500 which was issued on January 1, 198A, and the other for $6,500 which was issued on January 1, 198B.
4. The land account includes two parcels, one of which was acquired for $20,000 on January 1, 198A. The remaining parcel was acquired in June 198B.
5. Selected numbers from a general price-level index are:

January 198A	110
June 198A (also average for 198A)	120
December 198A	130
June 198B (also average for 198B)........	140
December 198B	150

6. The inventory at the end of each year was acquired evenly throughout that year.

Provocative problem 20–2
Wilkins Development Company

Wilkins Development Company purchased a plot of land in 198A when the general price index was 98. The land cost $350,000 and was zoned for commercial use. In 198E the general price index is 128. However, a specific price index for commercial property in the general area of the land in question has risen from 90 in 198A to 138 in 198E.

Wilkins Development Company has no intention of building on the property. It is being held only as an investment and will eventually be sold. Some of the employees of Wilkins Development Company have been arguing over the matter of how the land should be presented in the balance sheet at the close of 198E and also over the amount of real economic benefit the company will have obtained from the investment if the land were to be sold immediately. Prepare an analysis which recognizes the alternative balance sheet valuation possibilities and which will help resolve the dispute.

PART SEVEN
Managerial accounting for costs

After studying Chapter 21, you should be able to:

☐ State the reasons for departmentalization of businesses.

☐ Describe the differences between manufacturing and merchandising firms and how each records its departmental costs.

☐ Describe the types of expenses that should be allocated among departments, the bases for allocating such expenses, and the procedures involved in the allocation process.

☐ Explain the bases for determining profitability of a department and evaluating the department managers.

☐ Describe the problems associated with allocation of joint costs between departments.

☐ Define or explain the words and phrases listed in the chapter Glossary.

Departmental accounting; responsibility accounting

■ In previous chapters, attention was focused on understanding financial statements and related accounting information for a *whole* business. This chapter shifts the attention to accounting information which is primarily meant to be useful in managing the internal affairs of a business. Financial statements for a whole business, of course, provide important information to the business' managers. But, managers need a large variety of additional accounting information if they are to effectively run the business. Accounting that is designed to provide information to the managers of the business is called *managerial accounting*. The remaining chapters of the book are devoted to this general topic.

The present chapter deals with the matter of accounting for the "parts" or subunits of a business; this is normally called *departmental accounting*. The chapter's discussion shows that in departmental accounting, a primary goal is to assign costs and expenses to the particular managers who are responsible for controlling those costs and expenses. In this way, the performance of managers can be evaluated in terms of their responsibilities. Thus, departmental accounting is closely related to what is called *responsibility accounting*.

WHY BUSINESSES ARE DEPARTMENTALIZED

A business is divided into subunits or departments when it becomes too large to be effectively managed as a single unit. When a business is departmentalized, a manager is usually placed in charge of each department. If the business grows even larger, each department may be further divided into smaller segments. Thus, a particular manager can be assigned responsibilities over the activities of a unit that is not too large for the manager to effectively oversee and control. Also, departments can be organized so that the specialized skills of each manager can be used most effectively.

BASIS FOR DEPARTMENTALIZATION

In a departmentalized business there are two basic kinds of departments, *productive departments* and *service departments*. In a factory, the productive departments are those engaged directly in manufacturing operations. In a store, they are the departments making sales. Departmental divisions in a factory are commonly based on manufacturing processes employed or products or components manufactured. The divisions in a store are usually based on kinds of goods sold, with each selling or productive department being assigned the sale of one or more kinds of merchandise. In either type of business the service departments, such as the general office, advertising, purchasing, payroll, and personnel departments, assist or perform services for the productive departments.

INFORMATION TO EVALUATE DEPARTMENTS

When a business is divided into departments, management must be able to find out how well each department is performing. Thus, it is necessary for the accounting system to supply information by departments as to resources expended and outputs achieved. This requires that revenue and expense information be measured and accumulated by departments. However, before going further it should be observed that such information is generally not made public, since it might be of considerable benefit to competitors. Rather, it is for the use of management in controlling operations, appraising performances, allocating resources, and in taking remedial actions. For example, if one of several departments is particularly profitable, perhaps it should be expanded. Or, if a department is showing poor results, information as to its revenues, costs, and expenses may point to a proper remedial action.

The information used to evaluate a department depends on whether the department is a *cost center* or a *profit center*. A cost center is a unit of the business that incurs costs (or expenses) but does not directly generate revenues. The productive departments of a factory and such service departments as the general office, advertising, and purchasing departments are cost centers. A profit center differs from a cost center in that it not only incurs costs but also generates revenues. The selling departments of a store are profit centers. In judging departmental efficiencies in the two kinds of centers, managers of cost centers are judged on their ability to control costs and keep costs within a satisfactory range. Managers of profit centers, on the other hand, are judged on their ability to generate earnings, which are the excess of revenues over costs.

SECURING DEPARTMENTAL INFORMATION

Modern cash registers enable a merchandising concern to accumulate information as to sales and sales returns by departments. In large stores the registers commonly enter the information directly into the store's computer; and the registers and the computer are capable of much more than accumulating sales information by departments. The cash registers will print all pertinent information on the sales ticket given to the customer, total the ticket, and initiate entries to record credit sales in the customer's account. Also, if the required information as to type of goods sold is keyed into the registers by means of code numbers, the computer will at the end of the day print out detailed departmental summaries of goods sold and item inventories of unsold goods.

Cash registers also enable a small store to determine daily totals for sales and sales returns by departments. However, since the registers are normally not connected to a computer, their totals must be accumulated in some other way. Two ways are common. A small store may provide separate Sales and Sales Returns accounts in its ledger for each of its departments or it may use analysis sheets. Either method may also be used to accumulate information as to purchases and purchases returns by departments.

If a store chooses to provide separate Sales, Sales Returns, Purchases, and Purchases Returns accounts in its ledger for each of its departments, it may also provide columns in its journals to record transactions by departments. Illustration 21–1 shows such a journal for recording sales by departments. The amounts to be debited to the customers' accounts are entered in the Accounts Receivable debit column and

						Departmental Sales		
Date	Account Debited	Invoice Number	P R	Accounts Receivable Debit		Dept. 1 Credit	Dept. 2 Credit	Dept. 3 Credit
Oct. 1	Walter Marshfield	737		145.00		90.00	55.00	.....
1	Thomas Higgins	738		85.00		.....	40.00	45.00

Sales Journal

Illustration 21–1

are posted to these accounts each day. The column's total is debited to the Accounts Receivable controlling account at the end of the month. The departmental sales are entered in the last three columns and are posted as column totals at the end of the month.

Separate departmental accounts are practical only for a store having a limited number of departments. In a store having more than a few departments, a more practical procedure is to use departmental sales analysis sheets.

When a store uses departmental sales analysis sheets, it provides only one undepartmentalized general ledger account for sales, another account for sales returns, another for purchases, and another for purchases returns; and it records its transactions and posts to these accounts as though it were not departmentalized. But, in addition to this, each day it also summarizes its transactions by departments and enters the summarized amounts on analysis sheets. For example, a concern using analysis sheets, in addition to recording sales in its usual manner, will total each day's sales by departments and enter the daily totals on a sales analysis sheet like Illustration 21–2. As a result, at the end of a month or other period, the column totals of the analysis sheet show sales by departments, and the grand total of all the columns should equal the balance of the Sales account.

Departmental Sales Analysis Sheet

Date		Men's Wear Dept.	Boys' Wear Dept.	Shoe Dept.	Leather Goods Dept.	Women's Wear Dept.
May	1	$357.15	$175.06	$115.00	$ 75.25	$427.18
	2	298.55	136.27	145.80	110.20	387.27

Illustration 21–2

When a store uses departmental analysis sheets, it uses one analysis sheet to accumulate sales figures, another for sales returns, another for purchases, and still another for purchases returns; and at the end of the period the several analysis sheets show the store's sales, sales returns, purchases, and purchases returns by departments. If the store then takes inventories by departments, it can calculate gross profits by departments.

Accumulating information and arriving at a gross profit figure for each selling department in a departmentalized business is not too difficult, as the discussion thus far reveals. However, to go beyond this and arrive at useful departmental net income figures is not so easy; consequently, many concerns make no effort to calculate more than gross profits by departments.

ALLOCATING EXPENSES

If a business attempts to measure not only departmental gross profit but also departmental net income, special problems are confronted. They involve dividing the expenses of the business among the selling departments of the business. Some expenses, called *direct expenses,* are easily traced to specific departments. The direct expenses of a department are easily traced to the department because they are incurred for the sole benefit of that department. For example, the salary of an employee who works in only one department is a direct expense of that department.

The expenses of a business include both direct expenses and *indirect expenses.* Indirect expenses are incurred for the joint benefit of more than one department. For example, where two or more departments share a single building, the expenses of renting, heating, and lighting the building jointly benefit all of the departments in the building. Although such indirect expenses cannot be easily traced to a specific department, they must be allocated among the departments which benefited from the expenses. Each indirect expense should be allocated on a basis that fairly approximates the relative benefit received by each department. But, measuring the benefit each department receives from an indirect expense is often difficult. Thus, even after a reasonable allocation basis is chosen, considerable doubt often exists regarding the proper share to be charged to each department.

To illustrate the allocation of an indirect expense, assume that a jewelry store purchases janitorial services from an outside firm. The jewelry store then allocates the cost among its three departments according to the floor space occupied. The cost of janitorial services for a short period is $280, and the amounts of floor space occupied are:

Jewelry department	250 sq. ft.
Watch repair department	125
China and silver department	500
Total	875 sq. ft.

The calculations to allocate janitorial expense to the departments are:

$$\text{Jewelry department:} \quad \frac{250}{875} \times \$280 = \$80$$

$$\text{Watch repair department:} \quad \frac{125}{875} \times \$280 = \$40$$

$$\text{China and silver department:} \frac{500}{875} \times \$280 = \$160$$

Students should note that the concepts of "direct" costs or expenses and "indirect" costs or expenses can be usefully applied in a variety of situations in addition to departmental accounting. In general, direct costs are easily traced to or associated with a "cost object." In this chapter, the cost object of significance is the department. However, other cost objects may also be of interest. For example, in manufacturing units of products, the cost object may be a unit of product (see Chapter 22). In that case, costs that can be easily identified with a unit of product may be called direct costs. Other costs which are essential to the manufacturing process but which cannot be easily traced to specific units of product would be called indirect costs.

BASES FOR ALLOCATING EXPENSES

In the following paragraphs, bases for allocating some common indirect expenses are discussed. In the discussions, no hard-and-fast rules are given because several factors are often involved in an expense allocation and the importance of the factors varies from situation to situation. As previously stated, indirect expenses are, by definition, subject to doubt as to how they should be allocated between departments. Judgment rather than hard-and-fast rules is required, and different accountants often will not agree on the proper basis for allocating an indirect expense.

Wages and salaries

An employee's wages may be either a direct or an indirect expense. If an employee's time is spent all in one department, the employee's wages are a direct expense of the benefited department; but if an employee works in more than one department, the wages become an indirect expense to be allocated between or among the benefited departments. Normally, working time spent in each department is a fair basis for allocating wages.

A supervisory employee at times supervises more than one department, and in such cases the time spent in each department is usually a fair basis for allocating his or her salary. However, since a supervisory employee is frequently on the move from department to department, the time spent in each is often difficult to measure. Consequently, some companies allocate the salary of such an employee to his or her departments on the basis of the number of employees in each department, while others make the allocation on the basis of the supervised departments' sales. When a supervisor's salary is allocated on the basis of employees, it is assumed that he or she is supervising people and the time spent in each department is related to the number of employees in each. When the salary is allocated on the basis of sales, it is assumed that the time devoted to each department is related to the department's production.

Rent or depreciation and related expenses of buildings

Rent expense is normally allocated to benefited departments on the basis of the amount and value of the floor space occupied by each. Furthermore, since all customers who enter a store must pass the departments by the entrance and only a fraction of these people go beyond the first floor, ground floor space is more valuable for retail purposes than is basement or upper floor space, and space near the entrance is more valuable than is space in an out-of-the-way corner. Yet, since there is no exact measure of floor space values, all such values and the allocations of rent based on such values must depend on judgment. Nevertheless, if good judgment, statistics as to customer traffic, and the opinions of experts who are familiar with current rental values are used, fair allocations can be made. When a building is owned instead of being rented, expenses such as depreciation, taxes, and insurance on the building are allocated like rent expense.

Advertising

When a store advertises a department's products, if the advertising is effective, people come into the store to buy the products. However, at the same time they also often buy other unadvertised products. Consequently, advertising benefits all departments, even those the products of which are not advertised. Thus, many stores treat advertising as an indirect expense and allocate it on the basis of sales. When advertising costs are allocated on a sales basis, a department producing one tenth of the total sales is charged with one tenth of the advertising cost; a department producing one sixth of the sales is charged with one sixth.

Although in many stores advertising costs are allocated to departments on the basis of sales, in others each advertisement is analyzed and the cost of the column inches of newspaper space or minutes of TV or radio time devoted to the products of a department is charged to the department.

Depreciation of equipment

Depreciation on equipment used solely in one department is a direct expense of that department; and if detailed plant asset records are kept, the depreciation applicable to each department may be determined by examining the records. Where adequate records are not maintained, depreciation must be treated as an indirect expense and allocated to the departments on the basis of the value of the equipment in each. Where items of equipment are used by more than one department, the relative number of hours used is usually a fair basis of allocating depreciation costs to the departments.

Heating and lighting expense

Heating and lighting expense is usually allocated on the basis of floor space occupied under the assumption that the amount of heat and the number of lights, their wattage, and the extent of their use are uniform throughout the store. Should there be a material variation in lighting, however, further analysis and a separate allocation may be advisable.

Service departments

In order to make sales, selling departments must have the services supplied by departments such as the general office, personnel, payroll, advertising, and purchasing departments. Such departments are called *service departments*. Since service departments do not produce revenues, they are evaluated as cost centers rather than as profit centers. Although each service department should be separately evaluated, the costs it incurs must also be allocated among the departments it services. Thus, the costs of service departments are, in effect, indirect expenses of the selling departments; and the allocation of service department costs to selling departments is required if net incomes of the selling departments are to be calculated. The following list shows commonly used bases for these allocations:

Departments	Expense Allocation Bases
General office department	Number of employees in each department or sales.
Personnel department	Number of employees in each department.
Payroll department	Number of employees in each department.
Advertising department	Sales or amounts of advertising charged directly to each department.
Purchasing department	Dollar amounts of purchases or number of purchase invoices processed.
Cleaning and maintenance department	Square feet of floor space occupied.

MECHANICS OF ALLOCATING EXPENSES

It would be difficult or impossible to analyze each indirect expense incurred and to allocate and charge portions to several departmental expense accounts at the time of incurrence or payment. Consequently, expense amounts paid or incurred, both direct and indirect, are commonly accumulated in undepartmentalized expense accounts until the end of a period, when a *departmental expense allocation sheet* (see Illustration 21–3) is used to allocate and charge each expense to the benefited departments.

Beta Hardware Store
Departmental Expense Allocation Sheet
Year Ended December 31, 19—

Undepartmentalized Expense Accounts and Service Departments	Bases of Allocation	Expense Account Balance	Allocation of Expenses to Departments				
			General Office Dept.	Purchasing Dept.	Hardware Dept.	Housewares Dept.	Appliances Dept.
Salaries expense	Direct, payroll records	51,900	13,300	8,200	15,600	7,000	7,800
Rent expense	Amount and value of space	12,000	500	500	6,000	1,400	3,600
Heating and lighting	Floor space	2,000	100	100	1,000	200	600
Advertising expense	Sales	1,000	.....	.....	500	300	200
Depreciation, equipment	Direct, depreciation records	1,500	500	300	400	100	200
Supplies expense	Direct, requisitions	900	200	100	300	200	100
Insurance expense	Value of assets insured	2,500	400	200	900	600	400
Total expenses by departments		71,800	15,000	9,400	24,700	9,800	12,900
Allocation of service department expenses:							
General office department	Sales		15,000		7,500	4,500	3,000
Purchasing department	Purchase requisitions			9,400	3,900	3,400	2,100
Total expenses applicable to selling departments		71,800			36,100	17,700	18,000

Illustration 21-3

To prepare an expense allocation sheet, the names of the to-be-allocated expenses are entered in the sheet's first column along with the names of the service departments. Next, the bases of allocation are entered in the second column, and the expense amounts are entered in the third. Then, each expense is allocated according to the basis shown, and the allocated portions are entered in the departmental columns. After this the departmental columns are totaled and the service department column totals are allocated in turn to the selling departments. Upon completion, the amounts in the departmental columns are available for preparing income statements showing net income by departments, as in Illustration 21–4.

Beta Hardware Store
Departmental Income Statement
Year Ended December 31, 19—

	Hardware department	Housewares department	Appliances department	Combined
Sales	$119,500	$71,700	$47,800	$239,000
Cost of goods sold	73,800	43,800	30,200	147,800
Gross profit on sales	$ 45,700	$27,900	$17,600	$ 91,200
Gross profit percentages	38.2%	38.9%	36.8%	.2%
Operating expenses:				
Salaries expense	$ 15,600	$ 7,000	$ 7,800	$ 30,400
Rent expense	6,000	1,400	3,600	11,000
Heating and lighting expense	1,000	200	600	1,800
Advertising expense	500	300	200	1,000
Depreciation expense, equipment	400	100	200	700
Supplies expense	300	200	100	600
Insurance expense	900	600	400	1,900
Share of office dept. expenses	7,500	4,500	3,000	15,000
Share of purchasing dept. expenses	3,900	3,400	2,100	9,400
Total operating expenses	$ 36,100	$17,700	$18,000	$ 71,800
Net income (loss)	$ 9,600	$10,200	$ (400)	$ 19,400

Illustration 21–4

DEPARTMENTAL CONTRIBUTIONS TO OVERHEAD

Some people argue that departmental net incomes do not provide a fair basis for evaluating departmental performance. This is because all of the assumptions and somewhat arbitrary decisions involved in allocating the indirect expenses impact on the net income figures. The criticism of departmental net incomes is most likely heard in companies where indirect expenses represent a large portion of total expenses. Those who criticize departmental net income numbers usually suggest the substitution of what are known as *departmental contributions to overhead*. A department's contribution to overhead is the amount its revenues exceed its direct costs and expenses. Illustration 21–5 shows the departmental contributions to overhead for Beta Company.

Compare the performance of the appliance department as it is shown in Illustrations 21–4 and 21–5. Illustration 21–4 shows an absolute loss of $400 resulting from the department's operations. On the other hand, Illustration 21–5 shows a positive contribution to overhead

Beta Hardware Store
Income Statement Showing Departmental Contributions to Overhead
Year Ended December 31, 19—

	Hardware department	Housewares department	Appliances department	Combined
Sales	$119,500	$71,700	$47,800	$239,000
Cost of goods sold	73,800	43,800	30,200	147,800
Gross profit on sales	$ 45,700	$27,900	$17,600	$ 91,200
Direct expenses:				
Salaries expense	$ 15,600	$ 7,000	$ 7,800	$ 30,400
Depreciation expense, equipment	400	100	200	700
Supplies expense	300	200	100	600
Total direct expenses	$ 16,300	$ 7,300	$ 8,100	$ 31,700
Departmental contributions to overhead	$ 29,400	$20,600	$ 9,500	$ 59,500
Contribution percentages	24.6%	28.7%	19.9%	24.9%
Indirect expenses:				
Rent expense				$ 11,000
Heating and lighting expense				1,800
Advertising expense				1,000
Insurance expense				1,900
General office department expense				15,000
Purchasing department expense				9,400
Total indirect expenses				$ 40,100
Net income				$ 19,400

Illustration 21–5

of $9,500, which is 19.9% of sales. While this contribution is not as good as for the other departments, it appears much better than the $400 loss. Which is the better basis of evaluation? To resolve the matter, one must critically review the bases used for allocating the indirect expenses to departments. In the final analysis, answering the question is a matter of judgment.

ELIMINATING THE UNPROFITABLE DEPARTMENT

When a department's net income shows a loss or when its contribution to overhead appears very poor, management may consider the extreme action of eliminating the department. However, in considering this extreme action, neither the net income figure nor the contribution to overhead provides the best information on which to base a decision. Instead, consideration should be given to the department's *escapable expenses* and *inescapable expenses*. Escapable expenses are those that would end with the elimination of the department; inescapable expenses are those that would continue even though the department were eliminated. For example, the management of Beta Company is considering whether to eliminate its appliances department. An evaluation of the inescapable expenses and escapable expenses of the appliances department reveals the following:

	Escapable expenses	Inescapable expenses
Salaries expense	$ 7,800	
Rent expense		$3,600
Heating and lighting expense		600
Advertising expense	200	
Depreciation expense, equipment		200
Supplies expense	100	
Insurance expense (merchandise and equipment)	300	100
Share of office department expenses	2,200	800
Share of purchasing department expenses	1,000	1,100
Totals	$11,600	$6,400

If the appliances department is discontinued, its $6,400 of inescapable expenses will have to be borne by the remaining departments; thus, until the appliances department's annual loss exceeds $6,400, Beta Company is better off continuing the unprofitable department. In addition, another factor must be weighed when considering the elimination of an unprofitable department. Often, the existence of a department, even though unprofitable, contributes to the sales and profits of the other departments. In such a case, a department might be continued even when its losses exceed its inescapable expenses.

CONTROLLABLE COSTS AND EXPENSES

Net income figures and contributions to overhead are used in judging departmental efficiencies, but is either a good index of how well a department manager has performed? Many people hold that neither is. These people say that since many expenses entering into the calculation of a department's net income or into its contribution to overhead are beyond the control of the department's manager, neither net income nor contribution to overhead should be used in judging how well the manager has performed. These people are of the opinion that only a department's *controllable costs and expenses* should be used in judging a manager's performance.

A department's controllable costs and expenses are those over which the department's manager has control as to the amounts expended. They are not the same as direct costs and expenses. Direct costs and expenses are easily traced and therefore chargeable to a specific department, but the amounts expended may or may not be under the control of the department's manager. For example, a manager often has little or no control over the amount of equipment assigned to his department and the resulting depreciation expense, but he commonly has some control over the employees and the amount of work they do. Also, he normally has some control over supplies used in his department, but no control over the amount of his own salary.

When controllable costs and expenses are used in judging a manager's efficiency, statistics are prepared showing the department's output and its controllable costs and expenses. The statistics of the current period are then compared with prior periods and with planned levels, and the manager's performance is judged.

The concepts of *controllable costs* and *uncontrollable costs* must be defined with reference to a particular manager and within a definite time period. Without these two reference points, all costs are controllable; that is, all costs are controllable at some level of management if the time period is long enough. For example, a cost such as property insurance may not be controllable at the level of a department manager, but it is subject to control by the executive who is responsible for obtaining insurance coverage for the concern. Likewise the executive responsible for obtaining insurance coverage may not have any control over insurance expense resulting from insurance contracts presently in force; but when a contract expires, the executive is free to renegotiate and thus has control over the long run. Thus, it is recognized that all costs are subject to the control of some manager at some point in time. Revenues are likewise subject to the control of some manager.

RESPONSIBILITY ACCOUNTING

The concept of controllable costs and expenses leads naturally to the idea of responsibility accounting. In responsibility accounting—

a. A determination is made of the person responsible for each activity carried on by the business, and the controllable costs and expenses of each activity are assigned to the person responsible for the activity. Responsibility assignments are normally made at the lowest possible managerial level, under the assumption that the manager nearest the action is in the best position to control its costs. For example, a factory foreman is made responsible for the raw materials and supplies used in his department.

b. The accounting system is then designed to accumulate costs and expenses so that timely reports can be made to each manager of the costs for which the manager is responsible. The ability to control costs and keep them within a budgeted range is then used as the basis for judging performance; and managers are not held responsible for costs over which they have no control. Furthermore, prorations and arbitrary allocations of costs are not made because it is recognized that responsibilities cannot be allocated.

At the lowest levels of management, responsibilities and costs over which control is exercised are limited. Consequently, cost reports to this management level cover only a few costs, usually just those costs over which a manager exercises control. Moving up the management hierarchy, responsibilities and control broaden, and reports to higher level managers are broader and cover a wider range of costs. However, reports to higher level managers normally do not contain the details reported to their subordinates. Rather, the details reported to lower level managers are normally summarized on the reports to their superiors. The details are summarized for two reasons: (1) lower level managers are primarily responsible and (2) too many details can confuse. If the reports to higher level managers contain too much detail, they may have difficulty "seeing the forest for the trees."

In conclusion, it should be said that our ability to produce vast amounts of raw figures mechanically and electronically has far outstripped our ability to use the figures. What is needed is the ability to select those figures that are meaningful for planning and control. This is recognized in responsibility accounting, and every effort is made to get the right figure to the right person at the right time, and the right person is the person who can control the cost or revenue.

JOINT COSTS

Joint costs are encountered in some manufacturing concerns and are introduced here because they have much in common with indirect expenses. A *joint cost* is a cost incurred to secure two or more essentially different products. For example, a meat-packing company incurs a joint cost when it buys a pig from which it will get bacon, hams, shoulders, liver, heart, hide, pig feet, and a variety of other products. Likewise, a sawmill incurs joint costs when it buys a log and saws it into portions of Clears, Select Structurals, No. 1 Common, No. 2 Common, and other grades of lumber. In both cases, as with all joint costs, the problem is one of allocating the costs to the several joint products.

A joint cost may be, but is not commonly, allocated on some physical basis, such as the ratio of pounds, square feet, or gallons of each joint product to total pounds, square feet, or gallons of all joint products flowing from the cost. The reason this method is not commonly used is that the resulting cost allocations may be completely out of keeping with the market values of the joint products, and thus may cause certain of the products to sell at a profit while other products always show a loss. For example, a sawmill bought for $30,000 a number of logs which when sawed produced a million board feet of lumber in the grades and amounts shown in Illustration 21–6.

Observe in Illustration 21–6 that the logs produced 200,000 board feet of No. 3 Common lumber and that this is two tenths of the total lumber produced from the logs. If the No. 3 lumber is assigned two tenths of the $30,000 cost of the logs, it will be assigned $6,000 of the cost ($30,000 × $\%_{10}$ = $6,000); and since this lumber can be sold for only $4,000, the assignment will cause this grade to show a loss. As a result, as in this situation, to avoid always showing a loss on one or more of the products flowing from a joint cost, such costs are commonly allocated to the joint products *in the ratio of the market values of the joint products at the point of separation.*

Grade of Lumber	Production in Board Feet	Market Price per 1,000 Board Feet	Market Value of Production of Each Grade	Ratio of Market Value of Each Grade to Total
Structural	100,000	$120	$12,000	12/50
No. 1 Common	300,000	60	18,000	18/50
No. 2 Common	400,000	40	16,000	16/50
No. 3 Common	200,000	20	4,000	4/50
	1,000,000		$50,000	

Illustration 21–6

The ratios of the market values of the joint products flowing from the $30,000 of log cost are shown in the last column of Illustration 21–6. If these ratios are used to allocate the $30,000 cost, the cost will be apportioned between the grades as follows:

```
Structural:      $30,000 × 12/50 = $ 7,200
No. 1 Common: $30,000 × 18/50 =   10,800
No. 2 Common: $30,000 × 16/50 =    9,600
No. 3 Common: $30,000 ×  4/50 =    2,400
                                 $30,000
```

Observe that if the No. 3 Common is allocated a share of the $30,000 joint cost based on market values by grades, it is allocated $2,400 of the $30,000. Furthermore, when the $2,400 is subtracted from the grade's $4,000 market value, $1,600 remains to cover other after-separation costs and provide a profit.

GLOSSARY

Controllable costs or expenses. Costs over which the manager has control as to the amounts incurred.

Cost center. A unit of a business that incurs costs or expenses but does not directly generate revenues.

Departmental accounting. Accounting for the "parts" or subunits of a business.

Departmental contribution to overhead. The amount by which a department's revenues exceed its direct costs and expenses.

Direct costs or expenses. Costs that are easily traced to or associated with a cost object, for example, costs incurred by a department for the sole benefit of the department.

Escapable expenses. Costs that would end with an unprofitable department's elimination.

Indirect costs or expenses. Costs that are not easily traced to a cost object, for example, costs incurred for the joint benefit of more than one department.

Inescapable expenses. Expenses that would continue even though the department were eliminated.

Joint cost. A single cost incurred to secure two or more essentially different products.

Managerial accounting. Accounting that is designed to provide information for the managers of a business.

Productive departments. In a factory, those departments engaged directly in manufacturing operations, and in a store, those departments making sales.

Profit center. A unit of a business that incurs costs and generates revenues.

Responsibility accounting. An accounting system designed to accumulate controllable costs in timely reports to be given to each manager determined responsible for the costs, and also to be used in judging the performance of each manager.

Service departments. Departments that do not produce revenue but which supply other departments with essential services.

Uncontrollable cost. A cost the amount of which a specific manager cannot control within a given period of time.

QUESTIONS FOR CLASS DISCUSSION

1. Explain the general difference between departmental accounting and managerial accounting.
2. Why is a business divided into departments?

3. Differentiate between productive departments and service departments. What are the productive departments of *(a)* a factory and *(b)* a store?

4. Name several examples of service departments.

5. Are service departments analyzed as cost centers or as profit centers? Why?

6. How is a departmental sales analysis sheet used in determining sales by departments?

7. Differentiate between direct and indirect expenses.

8. Suggest a basis for allocating each of the following expenses to departments: *(a)* salary of a supervisory employee, *(b)* rent, *(c)* heat, *(d)* electricity used in lighting, *(e)* janitorial services, *(f)* advertising, *(g)* expired insurance, and *(h)* taxes.

9. How is a departmental expense allocation sheet used in allocating expenses to departments?

10. How reliable are the amounts shown as net incomes for the various departments of a store when expenses are allocated to the departments?

11. How is a department's contribution to overhead measured?

12. As the terms are used in departmental accounting, what are *(a)* escapable expenses and *(b)* inescapable expenses?

13. What are controllable costs and expenses?

14. In responsibility accounting, who is the right person to be given timely reports and statistics on a given cost?

15. What is a joint cost? How are joint costs normally allocated?

CLASS EXERCISES

Exercise 21–1

A company rents for $30,000 per year all the space in a building, which is assigned to its departments as follows:

Department	Location	Floor space
A	Basement	1,500 sq. ft.
B	Basement	1,500 sq. ft.
C	1st floor	600 sq. ft.
D	1st floor	800 sq. ft.
E	1st floor	1,600 sq. ft.
F	2d floor	2,000 sq. ft.
G	2d floor	1,000 sq. ft.

The company allocates 20% of the total rent to the basement, 50% to the first floor, and 30% to the second floor; and it then allocates the rent of each floor to the departments on that floor. Determine the rent expense to be allocated to each department.

Exercise 21–2

Dack Company rents for $20,000 per year all the space in a small building, and it occupies the space as follows:

Department A: 1,000 sq. ft. of first-floor space
Department B: 3,000 sq. ft. of first-floor space
Department C: 4,000 sq. ft. of second-floor space

Determine the rent expense to be allocated to each department under the assumption that in the city in which this building is located, second-floor space rents on an average for two thirds as much as first-floor space.

Exercise 21-3

Afton Company has a general office department, a purchasing department, and two sales departments, A and B. During the past year the departments had the following direct expenses: general office, $15,000; purchasing department, $11,600; Department A, $48,000; and Department B, $36,000. The departments occupy the following square feet of floor space: office, 600; purchasing, 300; A, 1,500; and B, 1,200. Department A had twice as many dollars of sales during the year as did Department B. During the year the purchasing department processed three purchase orders for Department A for every two processed for Department B.

Required:

Prepare an expense allocation sheet for Afton Company on which the direct expenses are entered by departments, the year's $14,400 of rent expense is allocated to the departments on the basis of floor space occupied, office department expenses are allocated to the sales departments on the basis of dollars of sales, and purchasing department expenses are allocated on the basis of purchase orders processed.

Exercise 21-4

Sport Shop is departmentalized, and Ted Lee works as a salesclerk in both the men's shoe department and the men's clothing department. His work consists of waiting on customers in turn as they enter either department, and also of straightening and rearranging merchandise in either department as needed after the merchandise has been shown to customers.

The shop divides Lee's $6,000 annual salary between the two selling departments in which he works, and last year the division was based on a sample of the time Lee spent working in the two departments. To gain the sample, observations were made on several days throughout the year of the manner in which he spent his time while at work. Following are the results of these observations:

Observed manner in which employee spent his time	*Elapsed time in minutes*
Selling in men's clothing department	2,100
Straightening and rearranging merchandise in men's clothing department	300
Selling in shoe department	1,450
Straightening and rearranging merchandise in shoe department	150
Doing nothing while waiting for a customer to enter one or the other of the selling departments	400

Required:

Prepare a calculation showing the shares of the employee's salary to be allocated to the selling departments.

Exercise 21–5

A real estate agent bought four acres of hilly land at $5,000 per acre, spent $36,000 putting in a street and sidewalks, and divided the land into 12 lots of equal size. However, since some of the lots sloped downhill and some sloped uphill and some had trees and some did not, the lots were not of equal value. Therefore, two lots were marked for sale at $5,000 each, five at $6,000 each, and five at $8,000 each.

Required:

Under the assumption that land and development costs are assigned to the lots as joint costs, determine the share of costs to be assigned to a lot in each price class.

PROBLEMS

Problem 21–1

Yellow Department Store occupies all the space in a building having two floors with 10,000 square feet of usable floor space on each floor. The store maintains an account in its ledger called Building Occupancy Expenses, and it debited the following to the account last year:

Building depreciation	$10,200
Mortgage interest, building	25,300
Taxes, building and land	8,500
Heating and cooling expenses	4,500
Lighting expense	2,800
Cleaning and maintenance expenses	12,600
Total	$63,900

At the end of the year the company divided the $63,900 by the number of square feet of space in the building, 20,000, and charged each of its departments with building occupancy expenses at the rate of $3.195 per square foot occupied.

Joe Kelly manages a department for the company that occupies 3,000 square feet of second-floor space, and he feels his department was charged with an unfair share of the building occupancy expenses. Furthermore, in a discussion with a friend in the real estate business he learned that first-floor space comparable to that occupied by Yellow Department Store is renting for an average of $3 per square foot and that like second-floor space is renting for $2 per square foot, including heating and cooling.

Required:

Prepare a computation showing the amount of building occupancy expenses you think should be charged to Joe Kelly's department for the year.

Problem 21–2

Dipprey Department Store has three selling departments, A, B, and C, and two supporting departments, general office and purchasing. For an annual accounting period that ended on December 31, its accountant brought together the following information for use in allocating expenses to the departments.

Direct departmental expenses:

The store's payroll, requisition, and plant asset records showed the following amounts of direct expenses by departments:

	Salaries expense	Supplies expense	Depr. of equipment	Equipment insurance
General office	$18,550	$ 235	$ 625	$ 250
Purchasing department	12,620	195	375	150
Department A	17,460	385	850	300
Department B	11,250	215	450	175
Department C	15,960	295	500	200
Totals	$75,840	$1,325	$2,800	$1,075

Indirect expenses:

The store incurred the following amounts of indirect expenses:

Rent expense	$13,200
Advertising expense	5,500
Heating and lighting expense	3,500
Janitorial expense	8,400

The store allocates its indirect expenses to its departments as follows:

a. Rent expense on the basis of the amount and value of floor space occupied. The general office and purchasing departments occupy space in the rear of the store which is not as valuable as space in the front; consequently, $1,200 of the total rent is allocated to these two departments in proportion to the space occupied by each. The remainder of the rent is divided between the selling departments in proportion to the space occupied. The five departments occupy these amounts of space: general office, 600 square feet; purchasing department, 400 square feet; Department A, 3,000 square feet; Department B, 1,500 square feet; and Department C, 1,500 square feet.
b. Advertising expense on the basis of sales which were Department A, $165,500; Department B, $99,300; and Department C, $66,200.
c. Heating and lighting and janitorial expenses on the basis of floor space occupied.

Supporting department expenses:

The store allocates its general office department expenses to its selling departments on the basis of sales, and it allocates purchasing department expenses on the basis of purchases. Purchases were Department A, $98,000; Department B, $60,000; and Department C, $42,000.

Required:

Prepare a departmental expense allocation sheet for the store.

Problem 21–3

Pine Company began operations one year ago with two selling departments and an office department. The year's results appear below.

The company plans to open a third selling department, Department C, which it estimates will produce $80,000 in sales with a 35% gross profit margin and will require the following direct expenses: sales salaries, $10,000; store supplies, $800; and depreciation of equipment, $1,000.

When the company began business, it had to rent store space in excess of its requirements. The extra space was assigned to and used by Departments A and B; but when the new department, Department C, is open, it will take one third of the space presently assigned to Department A and one sixth of the space assigned to Department B.

The company allocates its general office department expenses to its selling departments on the basis of sales, and it expects the new department to cause a $1,900 increase in these expenses.

The company expects Department C to bring new customers into the store who in addition to buying goods in the new department will also buy sufficient merchandise in the two old departments to increase the sales of Department A by 4% and Department B by 5%. And although the old departments' sales are expected to increase, their gross profit percentages are not expected to change. Likewise, their direct expenses, other than supplies, are not expected to change. The supplies used will increase in proportion to sales.

PINE COMPANY

Income Statement for Year Ended December 31, 19—

	Dept. A	*Dept. B*	*Combined*
Sales	$150,000	$120,000	$270,000
Cost of goods sold	90,000	78,000	168,000
Gross profit on sales	$ 60,000	$ 42,000	$102,000
Direct expenses:			
Sales salaries	$ 19,200	$ 15,000	$ 34,200
Store supplies expense	1,500	1,000	2,500
Depreciation expense, equipment	2,600	1,200	3,800
Total direct expenses	$ 23,300	$ 17,200	$ 40,500
Indirect expenses:			
Rent expense	$ 12,000	$ 6,000	$ 18,000
Heating and lighting expenses	1,200	600	1,800
Share of the office department			
expenses	9,000	7,200	16,200
Total indirect expenses	$ 22,200	$ 13,800	$ 36,000
Total expenses	$ 45,500	$ 31,000	$ 76,500
Net income	$ 14,500	$ 11,000	$ 25,500

Required:

Prepare a departmental income statement showing the company's expected operations with three selling departments.

Problem 21–4

Tom Citrus marketed a million pounds of grapefruit from his citrus grove last year, and he prepared the following statement to show the results:

Tom Citrus

Income from the Sale of Grapefruit

For Year Ended March 31, 19—

	Results by grades			Combined
	No. 1	No. 2	No. 3	
Sales by grades:				
No. 1, 400,000 lbs. @ $0.055 per lb	$22,000			
No. 2, 400,000 lbs. @ $0.045 per lb		$18,000		
No. 3, 200,000 lbs. @ $0.01 per lb			$ 2,000	
Combined sales				$42,000
Costs:				
Tree pruning and grove care @ $0.00756 per lb	$ 3,024	$ 3,024	$ 1,512	$ 7,560
Fruit picking, grading, and sorting @ $0.0126 per lb	5,040	5,040	2,520	12,600
Marketing @ $0.0034 per lb	1,360	1,360	680	3,400
Total costs	$ 9,424	$ 9,424	$ 4,712	$23,560
Net income or (loss)	$12,576	$ 8,576	$(2,712)	$18,440

Upon completing the statement, Mr. Citrus thought a wise course of action might be to leave the small No. 3 grapefruit on the trees to fall off and be plowed under when he cultivated between the trees, and thus avoid the loss from their sale. However, before doing so he consulted you.

When you examined the statement, you recognized the grove care, picking, grading, and sorting costs as joint costs that Mr. Citrus had allocated on a per pound basis. You asked about the marketing costs and learned that $3,200 of the $3,400 was incurred in placing the No. 1 and No. 2 fruit in boxes and delivering it to the warehouse of the fruit buyer. The cost per pound for this was the same for both grades. You also learned that the remaining $200 was for loading the No. 3 fruit on the trucks of a soft drink bottler who bought this grade in bulk at the citrus grove for use in making a soft drink.

Required:

Prepare an income statement that will reflect better the results of producing and marketing the grapefruit.

Problem 21–5

The income statement at the bottom of this page reflects last year's results for High Tide Sales.

As a result of its loss, the concern's management is considering the elimination of its Department B, and it has an offer from a noncompeting business to sublease the department's space and half of its equipment for $3,500 per year on a long-term lease.

An analysis of the operating expenses indicates the following:

a. If Department B is discontinued, its advertising, store supplies, and bad debts expenses will be eliminated. Also, the two sales employees assigned to the department may be terminated and their $13,260 salaries eliminated.

b. The Department B equipment that will be leased along with its space accounts for one half the depreciation presently charged to the department. As to the remainder of Department B's equipment, Department A will have to make whatever use it can of it, since it has little or no resale value.

c. Two thirds of the insurance expense presently charged to Department B, the portion on its inventory, will be eliminated when Department B is discontinued.

d. Eliminating Department B will reduce total office expenses by 30%.

HIGH TIDE SALES

Income Statement for Year Ended December 31, 19—

	Dept. A	Dept. B	Combined
Sales	$152,000	$93,000	$245,000
Cost of goods sold	93,500	69,600	163,100
Gross profit on sales	$ 58,500	$23,400	$ 81,900
Operating expenses:			
Direct expenses:			
Advertising expense	$ 2,350	$ 1,770	$ 4,120
Store supplies expense	650	425	1,075
Depreciation expense,			
equipment	1,800	1,000	2,800
Total direct expenses	$ 4,800	$ 3,195	$ 7,995
Indirect expenses:			
Sales salaries expense	$ 22,100	$13,260	$ 35,360
Rent expense	5,400	3,000	8,400
Bad debts expense	760	465	1,225
Insurance expense	400	300	700
Share of office expenses	6,080	3,720	9,800
Total indirect expenses	$ 34,740	$20,745	$ 55,485
Total expenses	$ 39,540	$23,940	$ 63,480
Net income (loss)	$ 18,960	$ (540)	$ 18,420

Required:

1. List in separate columns and total the amounts of Department B's escapable and inescapable expenses.

2. Under the assumption that Department A's sales will not be affected by the elimination of Department B, prepare an income statement showing what the concern can expect to earn from the operation of Department A after the elimination of Department B and with the subleasing of its equipment and space.

ALTERNATE PROBLEMS

Problem 21-1A

Broadway Department Store occupies all of a building having selling space on three floors, basement, street floor, and second floor; and it has in its ledger an account called Building Occupancy to which it debited the following last year:

Building depreciation	$ 6,000
Mortgage interest, building	18,000
Taxes and insurance, building	6,500
Heating and cooling expenses	1,900
Lighting expense	1,500
Cleaning and maintenance expenses	10,500
Total	$44,400

The building has 4,000 square feet of floor space on each of its three floors, a total of 12,000 feet; and the bookkeeper divided the $44,400 of building occupancy costs by 12,000 and charged the selling departments on each floor with $3.70 of building occupancy costs for each square foot of space occupied.

When the manager of a basement department saw the $3.70 per square foot of building occupancy costs charged to his department, he complained and cited a recent study by the local real estate board which showed average rental charges for like space, not including lights and janitorial service, but including heating and cooling, as follows:

Basement level space	$2 per sq. ft.
Street level space	$4 per sq. ft.
Second-floor level space	$3 per sq. ft.

Required:

Prepare a computation to show the amount of building occupancy costs per square foot you think should be charged on each floor to the selling departments.

Problem 21-2A

Playbox Sales has three selling departments, X, Y, and Z, and two supporting departments, the general office and the purchasing department. Its accountant brought together the following information for use in allocating expenses to the departments:

Direct departmental expenses:

The store's direct departmental expenses for its annual accounting period which ended December 31, 19—, as shown by its payroll, requisition, and plant asset records were:

	Salaries expense	Supplies expense	Depr. of equipment	Equipment insurance
General office	$16,665	$ 195	$ 565	$185
Purchasing department	11,710	160	345	115
Department X	15,240	275	780	260
Department Y	10,860	210	395	130
Department Z	12,440	230	460	155
Totals	$66,915	$1,070	$2,545	$845

Indirect expenses:

The store incurred these indirect expenses:

Rent expense	$11,200
Advertising expense	4,500
Heating and lighting expense	3,900
Janitorial expense	7,800

The store allocates its indirect expenses to its departments as follows:

a. Rent expense on the basis of the amount and value of the floor space occupied. The general office and purchasing departments occupy space on a balcony at the rear of the store which is not as valuable as the space occupied by the selling departments; consequently, $1,200 of the total rent is allocated to these two departments in proportion to the space occupied. The remainder of the rent is divided between the selling departments in proportion to the space they occupy. The departments occupy the following amounts of space: general office, 600 square feet; purchasing department, 400 square feet; Department X, 2,500 square feet; Department Y, 1,000 square feet; and Department Z, 1,500 square feet.

b. Advertising expense on the basis of sales which were Department X, $180,000; Department Y, $84,000; and Department Z, $136,000.

c. Heating and lighting and janitorial expenses on the basis of square feet of space occupied.

Supporting department expenses:

The store allocates its general office department expenses to its selling departments on the basis of sales, and it allocates purchasing department expenses on the basis of purchases. Purchases were Department X, $124,400; Department Y, $62,200; and Department Z, $93,300.

Required:

Prepare a departmental expense allocation sheet for the concern.

Problem 21–4A

Ted Orchard marketed a half million pounds of apples last year, and he prepared the following income statement to show the results:

TED ORCHARD
Income from the Sale of Apples
Year Ended December 31, 19—

	Results by Grades			Combined
	No. 1	No. 2	No. 3	
Sales by grades:				
No. 1, 200,000 lbs. @ $0.10 per lb	$20,000			
No. 2, 200,000 lbs. @ $0.06 per lb		$12,000		
No. 3, 100,000 lbs. @ $0.03 per lb			$3,000	
Combined sales				$35,000
Costs:				
Tree pruning and orchard care @ $0.0147				
per lb	$ 2,940	$ 2,940	$1,470	$ 7,350
Fruit picking, grading, and sorting @ $0.0175 .	3,500	3,500	1,750	8,750
Marketing @ $0.0064 per lb	1,280	1,280	640	3,200
Total costs	$ 7,720	$ 7,720	$3,860	$19,300
Net income or (loss)	$12,280	$ 4,280	$ (860)	$15,700

Upon completing the statement, Mr. Orchard thought a wise course of future action might be to leave the No. 3 apples on the trees to fall off and be plowed under when he cultivated between the trees, and thus avoid the loss from their sale. However, before doing so he consulted you.

When you examined the statement, you recognized that Mr. Orchard had divided all his costs by 500,000 and allocated them on a per pound basis. You asked him about the marketing costs and learned that $3,040 of the $3,200 was incurred in placing the No. 1 and No. 2 fruit in boxes and delivering them to the warehouse of the fruit buyer. The cost for this was the same for both grades. You also learned that the remaining $160 was for loading the No. 3 fruit on the trucks of a cider manufacturer who bought this grade of fruit in bulk at the orchard for use in making apple cider.

Required:

Prepare an income statement that will reflect better the results of producing and marketing the apples.

Problem 21–5A

Zephyr Sales is considering the elimination of its unprofitable Department 1, which lost $405 last year as the income statement at the top of page 727 shows.

If Department 1 is eliminated—

1. Its advertising, store supplies, and bad debts expenses will be eliminated. Also, two thirds of its insurance expense, the portion on its merchandise,

ZEPHYR SALES
Income Statement for Year Ended December 31,19—

	Dept. 1	Dept. 2	Combined
Sales	$58,500	$97,600	$156,100
Cost of goods sold	43,800	59,100	102,900
Gross profit on sales	$14,700	$38,500	$ 53,200
Operating expenses:			
Direct expenses:			
Advertising expense	$ 1,225	$ 1,650	$ 2,875
Store supplies expense	350	425	775
Depreciation expense, equipment	950	1,200	2,150
Total direct expenses	$ 2,525	$ 3,275	$ 5,800
Indirect expenses:			
Sales salaries expense	$ 7,800	$13,000	$ 20,800
Rent expense	2,000	2,800	4,800
Bad debts expense	250	375	625
Office salaries expense	2,080	3,120	5,200
Insurance expense	150	225	375
Miscellaneous office expenses	300	450	750
Total indirect expenses	$12,580	$19,970	$ 32,550
Total operating expenses	$15,105	$23,245	$ 38,350
Net income (loss)	$ (405)	$15,255	$ 14,850

and 20% of the miscellaneous office expenses presently allocated to Department 1 will be eliminated.

2. The company has one office clerk and four salesclerks who each earn $100 per week or $5,200 per year. At present the salaries of two and one-half salesclerks are allocated to Department 2 and one and one-half salesclerks to Department 1. Management feels that two salesclerks may be dismissed if Department 1 is eliminated, leaving two full-time salesclerks in Department 2, and making up the difference by assigning the office clerk to part-time sales work in the department. Management feels that if the office clerk devotes the same amount of time to selling in Department 2 as she has to the office work of Department 1, this will be sufficient to carry the load.

3. The lease on the store is long term and cannot be changed; therefore, the space presently occupied by Department 1 will have to be used by and charged to Department 2.

4. One half of Department 1's store equipment can be sold at its book value, and this will eliminate one half of the department's depreciation expense. However, Department 2 will have to make whatever use it can of the other half of the department's equipment and be charged with the depreciation, since it has little or no sale value.

Required:

1. List in separate columns and total the amounts of Department 1's escapable and inescapable expenses.

2. Under the assumption that Department 2's sales and gross profit will not be affected by the elimination of Department 1, prepare an income statement showing what the company can expect to earn from the operation of Department 2 after the elimination of Department 1.

PROVOCATIVE PROBLEMS

Provocative problem 21–1
Awn, May, and Nash

Fran Awn inherited a small plot of land; and to develop it, she entered into a partnership with Roy May, an investor, and Sue Nash, a real estate operator. Awn invested land in the partnership at its $45,000 fair value, May invested $45,000 in cash, and Nash invested $6,000 cash; and the partners agreed to share losses and gains equally. The partnership installed streets and water mains costing $51,000 and divided the land into 14 building lots. They priced Lots 1, 2, 3, and 4 for sale at $9,000 each; Lots 5, 6, 7, 8, 9, 10, 11, and 12 at $10,500 each; and Lots 13 and 14 at $12,000 each. The partners agreed that Nash could take Lot 14 at cost for her personal use. The remaining lots were sold, and the partnership dissolved. Determine the amount of partnership cash each partner should receive in the dissolution.

Provocative problem 21–2
Tick-Tack Sales

Dale Hall asked his new bookkeeper to prepare a departmental income statement for his company, Tick-Tack Sales. Following is the statement the bookkeeper prepared:

TICK-TACK SALES
Departmental Income Statement
Year Ended December 31, 19—

	Tick Department	Tack Department	Combined
Sales	$80,000	$120,000	$200,000
Cost of goods sold	54,560	81,840	136,400
Gross profit on sales	$25,440	$ 38,160	$ 63,600
Warehousing expenses	$ 5,900	$ 5,900	$ 11,800
Selling expenses	10,200	11,200	21,400
General and administrative expenses	3,300	3,300	6,600
Total expenses	$19,400	$ 20,400	$ 39,800
Net income	$ 6,040	$ 17,760	$ 23,800

Mr. Hall does not think the bookkeeper's statement reflects the profit situation in the company's two selling departments and he has asked you to redraft it with any supporting schedules or comments you think appropriate. Your investigation reveals the following:

1. The company sold 400 Ticks and 350 Tacks during the year. A Tack costs twice as much as a Tick, but the bookkeeper ignored all of this and apportioned cost of goods sold between the two departments on the basis of sales.
2. A Tick and a Tack are approximately the same weight and bulk. However, because there are two styles of Ticks and three styles of Tacks, the company must carry a 50% greater number of Tacks than Ticks in its inventory.
3. The company occupies the building on the following basis:

	Area of space	Value of space
Warehouse	80%	60%
Tick sales office space	5	10
Tack sales office space	5	10
General office space	10	20

4. Warehousing expenses consisted of the following:

Wages expense	$ 6,200
Depreciation of building	4,000
Heating and lighting expenses	1,000
Depreciation of warehouse equipment	600
Total	$11,800

The bookkeeper charged all the building's depreciation plus all of the heating and lighting expenses to warehousing expenses.

5. Selling expenses as apportioned by the bookkeeper consisted of the following:

	Tick Department	Tack Department
Sales salaries	$ 8,000	$ 9,000
Advertising	2,000	2,000
Depreciation of office equipment	200	200
Totals	$10,200	$11,200

Sales salaries and depreciation of office equipment were charged to the two departments on the basis of actual amounts incurred. Advertising was apportioned equally by the bookkeeper. The company had an established advertising budget based on dollars of sales which it followed closely during the year.

6. General and administrative expenses consisted of the following:

Office salaries	$6,000
Depreciation of office equipment	400
Miscellaneous office expenses	200
Total	$6,600

Provocative problem 21–3
Motor Sales Company

Motor Sales Company sells a standard model and a deluxe model of a motor that is manufactured for it. Statistics on last year's sales of the two models were as follows:

	Standard	Deluxe
Units sold	800	400
Selling price per unit	$200	$300
Cost per unit	110	155
Sales commission per unit	20	30
Indirect selling and administrative expenses	50	75

Indirect selling and administrative expenses totaled $70,000 and were allocated on a "joint cost" basis. In other words, the standard model produced $160,000 of revenue and the deluxe model produced $120,000; consequently, the standard model was assigned $\frac{4}{7}$ of the $70,000 of indirect expenses and the deluxe model was assigned $\frac{3}{7}$. The shares assigned to the models were in each case divided by the units sold to get the $50 and $75 per unit for each model.

Management of Motor Sales Company is not certain which of three courses of action it should take. It can (1) through advertising push the sales of the standard model, (2) through advertising push the sales of the deluxe model, or (3) do no additional advertising, in which case sales of each model will continue at present levels. The demand for the motor is fairly stable, and an increase in the number of units of one model sold will cause a proportionate decrease in the sales of the other model. However, through the expenditure of $5,000 for advertising, the company can shift the sale of 200 units of the standard model to the deluxe model, or vice versa, depending upon which model receives the advertising attention.

Should the company advertise; and if so, should it advertise the standard model or the deluxe model? Back your position with income statements.

After studying Chapter 22, you should be able to:

☐ Describe the basic differences in the financial statements of manufacturing companies and merchandising companies.

☐ Describe the procedures inherent in a general accounting system for a manufacturing company.

☐ List the different accounts which appear on a manufacturing company's books and state what the accounts represent.

☐ Explain the purpose of a manufacturing statement, how one is composed, and how the statement is integrated with the primary financial statements.

☐ Prepare financial statements for a manufacturing company from a work sheet.

☐ Prepare the adjusting and closing entries for a manufacturing company.

☐ Explain the procedures for assigning costs to the different manufacturing inventories.

☐ Define or explain the words and phrases listed in the chapter Glossary.

Manufacturing accounting

■ In previous chapters consideration has been given to the accounting problems of service-type and merchandising concerns. In this chapter some problems of manufacturing enterprises are examined.

Manufacturing and merchandising concerns are alike in that both depend for revenue upon the sale of one or more commodities or products. However, they differ in one important way. A merchandising company buys the goods it sells in the finished state in which they are sold. On the other hand, a manufacturing concern buys raw materials which it manufactures into the finished products it sells. For example, a shoe store buys shoes and sells them in the same form in which they are purchased; but a manufacturer of shoes buys leather, cloth, glue, nails, and dye and turns these items into salable shoes.

BASIC DIFFERENCE IN ACCOUNTING

The basic difference in accounting for manufacturing and merchandising concerns grows from the idea in the preceding paragraph. That is, the idea that a merchandising company buys the goods it sells in their finished ready-for-sale state. A manufacturer must create what it sells from raw materials. As a result the merchandising company can easily determine the cost of the goods it has bought for sale by examining the debit balance of its Purchases account; but the manufacturer must combine the balances of a number of material, labor, and overhead accounts to determine the cost of the goods it has manufactured for sale.

733

To emphasize this difference, the cost of goods sold section from a merchandising concern's income statement is condensed and presented below along side the cost of goods sold section of a manufacturing company.

Merchandising Company		Manufacturing Company	
Cost of goods sold:		Cost of goods sold:	
Beginning merchandise		Beginning finished goods	
inventory	$14,200	inventory	$ 11,200
Cost of goods purchased	34,150	Cost of goods manufactured (see	
Goods available for sale	$48,350	Manufacturing Statement)	170,500
Ending merchandise inventory	12,100	Goods available for sale	$181,700
Cost of goods sold	$36,250	Ending finished goods inventory	10,300
		Cost of goods sold	$171,400

Notice in the costs of goods sold section from the manufacturing company's income statement that the inventories of goods for sale are called *finished goods inventories* rather than merchandise inventories. Notice too that the "Cost of goods purchased" element of the merchandising company becomes "Cost of goods manufactured (see Manufacturing Statement)" on the manufacturer's income statement. These differences result because the merchandising company buys its goods ready for sale, while the manufacturer creates its salable products from raw materials.

The words "see Manufacturing Statement" refer the income statement reader to a separate schedule called a manufacturing statement (see page 740) which shows the costs of manufacturing the products produced by a manufacturing company. The records and techniques used in accounting for these costs are the distinguishing characteristics of manufacturing accounting.

SYSTEMS OF ACCOUNTING IN MANUFACTURING CONCERNS

The accounting system used by a manufacturing concern may be either a so-called general accounting system like the one described in this chapter or a cost accounting system. A general accounting system uses periodic physical inventories of raw materials, goods in process, and finished goods; and it has as its goal the determination of the total cost of all goods manufactured during each accounting period. Cost accounting systems differ in that they use perpetual inventories and have as their goal the determination of the unit cost of manufacturing a product or performing a service. Such systems are discussed in Chapter 23.

ELEMENTS OF MANUFACTURING COSTS

A manufacturer takes *raw materials* and by applying *direct labor* and *factory overhead* converts these materials into finished products. Raw materials, direct labor, and factory overhead are the "elements of manufacturing costs."

Raw materials

Raw materials are the commodities that enter into and become a part of a finished product. Such items as leather, dye, cloth, nails, and glue are raw materials of a shoe manufacturer. Raw materials are often called *direct materials*. Since direct materials physically become part of the finished product, the cost of direct materials is easily traced to units of product or batches of production, and the direct materials cost of production can be directly charged to units of product or batches of production without the use of arbitrary or highly judgmental cost allocation procedures.

Direct materials are distinguished from *indirect materials* or factory supplies which are such items as grease and oil for machinery, cleaning fluids, and so on. Indirect materials are not easily traced to specific units or batches of production and are accounted for as factory overhead.

The materials of a manufacturer are called "raw materials," even though they may not necessarily be in their natural raw state. For example, leather is manufactured from hides, nails from steel, and cloth from cotton. Nevertheless, leather, nails, and cloth are the raw materials of a shoe manufacturer even though they are the finished products of previous manufacturers.

Direct labor

Direct labor is often described as the labor of those people who work, either with machines or hand tools, specifically on the materials converted into finished products. The cost of direct labor can therefore be easily associated with and charged to the units or batches of production to which the labor was applied. In manufacturing, direct labor is distinguished from *indirect labor*. Indirect labor is the labor of superintendents, foremen, millwrights, engineers, janitors, and others who do not work specifically on the manufactured products. Indirect labor aids in production; often it makes production possible but it does not enter directly into the finished product. Indirect labor is accounted for as a factory overhead cost.

In a general accounting system, an account called *Direct Labor* is debited each payday for the wages of those workers who work directly on the product. Likewise, each payday, the wages of indirect workers are debited to one or more indirect labor accounts. Also, at the end of each period, the amounts of accrued direct and indirect labor are recorded in the direct and indirect labor accounts by means of adjusting entries. From this it can be seen that a manufacturing company's payroll accounting is similar to that of a merchandising concern. When a cost accounting system is not involved, no new techniques are required and only the new direct and indirect labor accounts distinguish the payroll accounting of a manufacturer from that of a merchant.

Factory overhead

Factory overhead, often called *manufacturing overhead* or *factory burden,* includes all manufacturing costs other than for direct materials and direct labor. Factory overhead may include:

Indirect labor.	Heat, lights, and power.
Factory supplies.	Depreciation of plant and equipment.
Repairs to buildings and equipment.	Patents written off.
Insurance on plant and equipment.	Small tools written off.
Taxes on plant and equipment.	Workmen's compensation insurance.
Taxes on raw materials and work in process.	Payroll taxes on the wages of the factory workers.

Factory overhead does not include selling and administrative expenses. Selling and administrative expenses are not factory overhead because they are not incurred in order to produce the manufactured products. They could be called selling and administrative overhead, but not factory overhead.

All factory overhead costs are accumulated in overhead cost accounts which vary from company to company. The exact accounts depend in each case upon the nature of the company and the information desired. For example, one account called "Expired Insurance on Plant Equipment" may be maintained, or an expired insurance account each for buildings and the different kinds of equipment may be used. But regardless of accounts, overhead costs are recorded in the same ways as are selling and administrative expenses. Some, such as indirect labor and light and power, are recorded in registers or journals as they are paid and are then posted to the accounts. Others, such as depreciation and expired insurance, reach the accounts through adjusting entries.

ACCOUNTS UNIQUE TO A MANUFACTURING COMPANY

Because of the nature of its operations, a manufacturing concern's ledger normally contains more accounts than that of a merchandising concern. However, some of the same accounts are found in the ledgers of both, for example, Cash, Accounts Receivable, Sales, and many selling and administrative expenses. Nevertheless, many accounts are unique to a manufacturing company. For instance, accounts such as Machinery and Equipment, Accumulated Depreciation of Machinery and Equipment, Factory Supplies, Factory Supplies Used, Raw Materials Inventory, Raw Material Purchases, Goods in Process Inventory, Finished Goods Inventory, and Manufacturing Summary are normally found only in the ledgers of manufacturing concerns. Some of these accounts merit special attention.

Raw Material Purchases account

When a general accounting system is in use, the cost of all raw materials purchased is debited to an account called Raw Material Purchases. Often a special column is provided in the Voucher Register or other special journal for the debits of the individual purchases. Thus, it is possible to periodically post these debits in one amount, the column total.

Raw Materials Inventory account

When a general accounting system is in use, the raw materials on hand at the end of each accounting period are determined by a physical inventory count; and through an adjusting entry the cost of this inventory is debited to Raw Materials Inventory. That account becomes a record of the materials on hand at the end of one period and the beginning of the next.

Goods in Process Inventory account

Most manufacturing concerns have on hand at any time partially processed products called *goods in process* or *work in process*. These are products in the process of being manufactured, products that have received a portion or all of their materials and have had some labor and overhead applied but that are not completed.

When a general manufacturing accounting system is used, the amount of goods in process at the end of each accounting period is determined by a physical inventory count; and through an adjusting entry the cost of this inventory is debited to Goods in Process Inventory. That account becomes a record of the goods in process at the end of one period and the beginning of the next.

Finished Goods Inventory account

The finished goods of a manufacturer are the equivalent of a store's merchandise; they are products in their completed state ready for sale. Actually, the only difference is that a manufacturing concern creates its finished goods from raw materials, while a store buys its merchandise in a finished, ready-for-sale state.

In a general accounting system the amount of finished goods on hand at the end of each period is determined by a physical inventory; and through an adjusting entry the cost of this inventory is debited to Finished Goods Inventory. That account provides a record of the finished goods at the end of one period and the beginning of the next.

The three inventories—raw materials, goods in process, and finished goods—are current assets for balance sheet purposes. Factory supplies is also a current asset.

INCOME STATEMENT OF A MANUFACTURING COMPANY

The income statement of a manufacturing company is similar to that of a merchandising concern. To see this, compare the income statement of Kona Sales Incorporated, Illustration 5–1 on page 158, with that of Excel Manufacturing Company, Illustration 22–1 on page 739. Notice that the revenue, selling, and general and administrative expense sections are very similar. However, when the cost of goods sold sections are compared, a difference is apparent. Here the item "Cost of goods manufactured" replaces the "purchases" element, and finished goods inventories take the place of merchandise inventories.

Observe the cost of goods sold section of Excel Manufacturing Company's income statement. Only the *total* cost of goods manufactured is shown. It would be possible to expand this section to show the detailed costs of the materials, direct labor, and overhead entering into the cost of goods manufactured. However, this would make the income statement long and unwieldy. Consequently, the common practice is to show only the total cost of goods manufactured on the income statement and to attach a supporting schedule showing the details. This supporting schedule is called a *schedule of the cost of goods manufactured* or a *manufacturing statement.*

MANUFACTURING STATEMENT

The cost elements of manufacturing are raw materials, direct labor, and factory overhead; and a manufacturing statement is normally constructed in such a manner as to emphasize these elements. Notice in Illustration 22–2 that the first section of the statement shows the cost of raw materials used. Also observe the manner of presentation is the same as that used on the income statement of a merchandising company to show cost of goods purchased and sold.

The second "section" shows the cost of direct labor used in production, and the third section shows factory overhead costs. If overhead

The Excell Manufacturing Company
Income Statement for Year Ended December 31, 19—

Revenue:			
Sales			$310,000
Cost of goods sold:			
Finished goods inventory, January 1, 19— ...		$ 11,200	
Cost of goods manufactured (see Manufacturing Statement)		170,500	
Goods available for sale		$181,700	
Finished goods inventory, December 31, 19—		10,300	
Cost of goods sold			171,400
Gross profit			$138,600
Operating expenses:			
Selling expenses:			
Sales salaries expense	$18,000		
Advertising expense	5,500		
Delivery wages expense	12,000		
Shipping supplies expense	250		
Delivery equipment insurance expense	300		
Depreciation expense, delivery equipment .	2,100		
Total selling expenses		$ 38,150	
General and administrative expenses:			
Office salaries expense..................	$15,700		
Miscellaneous general expense	200		
Bad debts expense	1,550		
Office supplies expense	100		
Depreciation expense, office equipment ...	200		
Total general and administrative expenses		17,750	
Total operating expenses			55,900
Operating income			$ 82,700
Financial expense:			
Mortgage interest expense................			4,000
Income before state and federal income taxes .			$ 78,700
Less state and federal income taxes			32,600
Net income			$ 46,100
Net income per common share (20,000 shares outstanding)			$2.31

Illustration 22–1

accounts are not too numerous, the balance of each is often listed in this third section, as in Illustration 22–2. However, if overhead accounts are numerous, only the total of all may be shown; and in such cases the total is supported by a separate attached schedule showing each cost.

In the fourth section the calculation of costs of goods manufactured is completed. Here the cost of the beginning goods in process inventory is added to the sum of the manufacturing costs to show the cost of all goods in process during the period. Then, the cost of the goods

Excel Manufacturing Company
Manufacturing Statement for Year Ended December 31, 19—

1	Raw materials:		
	Raw materials inventory, January 1, 19—........		$ 8,000
	Raw materials purchased	$85,000	
	Freight on raw materials purchased	1,500	
	Delivered cost of raw materials purchased		86,500
	Raw materials available for use		$94,500
	Raw materials inventory, December 31, 19— ...		9,000
	Raw materials used		$ 85,500
2	Direct labor		60,000
3	Factory overhead costs:		
	Indirect labor	$ 9,000	
	Supervision	6,000	
	Power.......................................	2,600	
	Repairs and maintenance	2,500	
	Factory taxes	1,900	
	Factory supplies used	500	
	Factory insurance expired	1,200	
	Small tools written off	200	
	Depreciation of machinery and equipment	3,500	
	Depreciation of building	1,800	
	Patents written off	800	
4	Total factory overhead costs		30,000
	Total manufacturing costs		$175,500
	Add goods in process inventory, January 1, 19—		2,500
	Total goods in process during the year .		$178,000
	Deduct goods in process inventory,		
	December 31, 19—		7,500
	Cost of goods manufactured		$170,500

Illustration 22–2

still in process at the end is subtracted to show cost of the goods manufactured.

The manufacturing statement is prepared from the Manufacturing Statement columns of a work sheet. The items that appear on the statement are summarized in these columns, and all that is required in constructing the statement is a rearrangement of the items into the proper statement order. Illustration 22–3 shows the manufacturing work sheet.

WORK SHEET FOR A MANUFACTURING COMPANY

In examining Illustration 22–3, note first that there are no Adjusted Trial Balance columns. The experienced accountant commonly omits such columns to save time and effort. How a work sheet without Adjusted Trial Balance columns is prepared and how this saves time and effort were explained in Chapter 5.

To understand the work sheet of Illustration 22–3, recall that a work sheet is a tool with which the accountant—

1. Achieves the effect of adjusting the accounts before entering the adjustments in a journal and posting them to the accounts.
2. Sorts the adjusted account balances into columns according to the financial statement upon which they appear.
3. Calculates and proves the mathematical accuracy of the net income.

With the foregoing in mind, a primary difference between the work sheet of a manufacturing company and that of a merchandising company is an additional set of columns. Also, the work sheet for a manufacturing company includes special adjustments regarding the Raw Materials Inventory and Goods in Process Inventory accounts. Otherwise, the adjustments are made in the same way on both kinds of work sheets. Also, the mathematical accuracy of the net income is proved in the same way. However, since an additional accounting statement, the manufacturing statement, is prepared for a manufacturing company, the work sheet of such a company has an additional set of columns, the Manufacturing Statement columns, into which are sorted the items appearing on the manufacturing statement.

PREPARING A MANUFACTURING COMPANY'S WORK SHEET

A manufacturing company's work sheet is prepared in the same manner as that of a merchandising concern. First a trial balance of the ledger is entered in the Trial Balance columns. Next, information for the adjustments is assembled, and the adjustments are entered in the Adjustments columns. The adjustments information for the work sheet shown in Illustration 22–3 is as follows:

a. The beginning-of-period Raw Materials Inventory balance was $8,000.
b. The end-of-period physical inventory count of raw materials totaled $9,000.
c. The beginning-of-period Goods in Process Inventory balance was $2,500.
d. The end-of-period physical inventory count of goods in process totaled $7,500.
e. The beginning-of-period Finished Goods Inventory balance was $11,200.
f. The end-of-period physical inventory count of finished goods totaled $10,300.
g. Estimated bad debt losses ½% of sales, or $1,550.
h. Office supplies used, $100.
i. Shipping supplies used, $250.
j. Factory supplies used, $500.

The Excel Manufacturing Company
Manufacturing Work Sheet for Year Ended December 31, 19—

Account Titles	Trial Balance Dr.	Trial Balance Cr.	Adjustments Dr.	Adjustments Cr.	Mfg. Statement Dr.	Mfg. Statement Cr.	Income Statement Dr.	Income Statement Cr.	Balance Sheet Dr.	Balance Sheet Cr.
Cash	11,000								11,000	
Accounts receivable	32,000								32,000	
Allowance for doubtful accounts		300		(g) 1,550						1,850
Raw materials inventory	8,000		(b) 9,000	(a) 8,000					9,000	
Goods in process inventory	2,500		(d) 7,500	(c) 2,500					7,500	
Finished goods inventory	11,200		(f) 10,300	(e) 11,200					10,300	
Office supplies	150			(h) 100					50	
Shipping supplies	300			(i) 250					50	
Factory supplies	750			(j) 500					250	
Prepaid insurance	1,800			(k) 1,500					300	
Small tools	1,300			(l) 200					1,100	
Delivery equipment	9,000								9,000	
Accumulated depreciation of delivery equipment		1,900		(m) 2,100						4,000
Office equipment	1,700								1,700	
Accumulated depreciation of office equipment		200		(n) 200						400
Machinery and equipment	72,000								72,000	
Accumulated depr. of machinery and equipment		3,000		(o) 3,500						6,500
Factory building	90,000								90,000	
Accumulated depreciation of factory building		1,500		(p) 1,800						3,300
Land	9,500								9,500	
Patents	12,000			(q) 800					11,200	
Accounts payable		14,000								14,000
Mortgage payable		50,000								50,000
Common stock, $5 par value		100,000								100,000
Retained earnings		3,660								3,660
Manufacturing summary			(a) 8,000 (c) 2,500 (e) 11,200	(b) 9,000 (d) 7,500 (f) 10,300	8,000 2,500	9,000 7,500	11,200	10,300		
Income summary										
Sales		310,000						310,000		
Raw material purchases	85,000				85,000					
Freight on raw materials	1,500				1,500					
Direct labor	59,600		(r) 400		60,000					
Indirect labor	8,940		(r) 60		9,000					

Account	Trial Balance Dr	Trial Balance Cr	Adjustments Dr	Adjustments Cr	Cost of Goods Mfd. Dr	Cost of Goods Mfd. Cr	Income Statement Dr	Income Statement Cr	Balance Sheet Dr	Balance Sheet Cr
Supervision	6,000				6,000					
Power expense	2,600				2,600					
Repairs and maintenance	2,500				2,500					
Factory taxes	1,900				1,900					
Sales salaries expense	18,000						18,000			
Advertising expense	5,500						5,500			
Delivery wages expense	11,920		(r) 80				12,000			
Office salaries expense	15,700						15,700			
Miscellaneous general expense	200						200			
Mortgage interest expense	2,000		(s) 2,000				4,000			
	484,560	484,560								
Bad debts expense			(g) 1,550				1,550			
Office supplies expense			(h) 100				100			
Shipping supplies expense			(i) 250				250			
Factory supplies used			(j) 500		500					
Factory insurance expired			(k) 1,200		1,200					
Delivery equipment insurance expense			(k) 300				300			
Small tools written off			(l) 200		200					
Depreciation expense, delivery equipment			(m) 2,100				2,100			
Depreciation expense, office equipment			(n) 200				200			
Depreciation of machinery and equipment			(o) 3,500		3,500					
Depreciation of building			(p) 1,800		1,800					
Patents written off			(q) 800		800					
Accrued wages payable				(r) 540						540
Mortgage interest payable				(s) 2,000						2,000
State and federal income taxes expense			(t) 32,600				32,600			
State and federal income taxes payable				(t) 32,600						32,600
			96,140	96,140						
					187,000	16,500			264,950	218,850
Cost of goods manufactured to Income Statement columns						170,500	170,500			
					187,000	187,000	274,200	320,300		
Net income							46,100			46,100
							320,300	320,300	264,950	264,950

Illustration 22-3

k. Expired insurance on factory, $1,200; and expired insurance on the delivery equipment, $300.

l. The small tools inventory shows $1,100 of usable small tools on hand. As is frequently done, small hand tools are in this case accounted for in the same manner as are supplies.

m. Depreciation of delivery equipment, $2,100.

n. Depreciation of office equipment, $200.

o. Depreciation of factory machinery and equipment, $3,500.

p. Depreciation of factory building, $1,800.

q. Yearly write-off of one seventeenth of the cost of patents, $800.

r. Accrued wages: direct labor, $400; indirect labor, $60; delivery wages, $80. All other employees paid monthly on the last day of each month.

s. One-half year's interest accrued on the mortgage, $2,000.

t. State and federal income taxes expense, $32,600.

Observe the adjustments labeled (a), (b), (c), and (d) in Illustration 22–3. These four adjustments are unique to manufacturing companies. The adjustment labeled (a) transfers the beginning-of-period balance in the Raw Materials Inventory account to the Manufacturing Summary account. Similarly, adjustment (c) transfers the beginning-of-period balance in the Goods in Process Inventory account to the Manufacturing Summary account. Adjustment (b) withdraws the end-of-period amount of raw materials from the Manufacturing Summary account and establishes that amount in the Raw Materials Inventory account. Adjustment (d) withdraws the end-of-period amount of goods in process from Manufacturing Summary and establishes that amount in the Goods in Process Inventory account. Later discussion of the adjusting and closing entries for a manufacturing company shows that the Manufacturing Summary account is used to accumulate all of the cost of goods manufactured.

After the adjustments are completed, the amounts in the Trial Balance columns are combined with the amounts in the Adjustments columns and are sorted to the proper Manufacturing Statement, Income Statement, or Balance Sheet columns, according to the statement on which they appear.

In the sorting process, just two decisions are required for each item. First, does the item have a debit balance or a credit balance? Second, on which statement does it appear? The first decision is necessary because a debit must be sorted to a Debit column and a credit item to a Credit column. As for the second, a work sheet is a tool for sorting items according to their statement appearance. Asset, liability, and owners' equity items appear on the balance sheet and are sorted to the Balance Sheet columns.

The Income Summary account plus the revenue and selling, general and administrative, and financial expense items go on the income statement and are sorted to the Income Statement columns. And finally, the Manufacturing Summary account plus direct labor and factory overhead items appear on the manufacturing statement and are sorted to the Manufacturing Statement columns. Note that the adjustments to the Manufacturing Summary account are sorted to the Manufacturing Statement columns without netting debits against credits. As a consequence, the Manufacturing Statement columns show amounts for both the beginning and ending raw materials and goods in process inventories. This retains all of the information necessary to prepare the manufacturing statement. In a similar fashion, both the debit and credit adjustments to the Income Summary account are sorted to the Income Statement columns without netting one against the other. Thus, the Income Statement columns show both the beginning and ending finished goods inventories. This retains all of the information necessary to calculate cost of goods sold on the income statement.

After the trial balance items with their adjustments are sorted to the proper statement columns, the Manufacturing Statement columns are added and their difference determined. This difference is the cost of the goods manufactured; and it is entered in the Manufacturing Statement credit column to make the two columns equal. Also, it is entered in the Income Statement debit column, the same column in which the balance of the Purchases account of a merchant is entered. After this the work sheet is completed in the usual manner.

PREPARING STATEMENTS

After completion, the manufacturing work sheet is used in preparing the statements and in making adjusting and closing entries. The manufacturing statement is prepared from the information in the work sheet's Manufacturing Statement columns, the income statement from the information in the Income Statement columns, and the balance sheet from information in the Balance Sheet columns. After this the adjusting and closing entries are entered in the journal and posted.

ADJUSTING ENTRIES

The adjusting entries of a manufacturing company are prepared in the same way as those of a merchandising concern. An adjusting entry is entered in the General Journal for each adjustment appearing in the work sheet Adjustments columns. The only adjusting entries that are unique to a manufacturing company are those related to raw materials and goods in process inventories. Adjusting entries are used to transfer the beginning-of-period balances of these two inventory accounts to the Manufacturing Summary account. Also, adjusting entries are required to set up the end-of-period amount of each inventory in the appropriate asset account and to remove these balances from the Manufacturing Summary account. Regarding the inventory of finished goods, the adjusting entry for a manufacturing company is just like that for a merchandising company; the beginning balance is transferred to the Income Summary account, and the ending balance is removed from Income Summary and set up as an asset.

Excel Manufacturing Company's adjusting entries for raw materials, goods in process, and finished goods are as follows:

Dec.	31	Manufacturing Summary	8,000	
		Raw Materials Inventory		8,000
		To transfer the beginning-of-period balance of raw materials to Manufacturing Summary.		
	31	Raw Materials Inventory	9,000	
		Manufacturing Summary		9,000
		To set up the ending raw materials inventory and to remove its balance from the Manufacturing Summary account.		
	31	Manufacturing Summary	2,500	
		Goods in Process Inventory		2,500
		To transfer the beginning-of-period balance of goods in process to Manufacturing Summary.		
	31	Goods in Process Inventory	7,500	
		Manufacturing Summary		7,500
		To set up the ending goods in process inventory and to remove its balance from the Manufacturing Summary account.		
	31	Income Summary	11,200	
		Finished Goods Inventory		11,200
		To transfer the beginning-of-period balance of finished goods to Income Summary.		
	31	Finished Goods Inventory	10,300	
		Income Summary		10,300
		To set up the ending finished goods inventory and to remove its balance from the Income Summary account.		

CLOSING ENTRIES

After the Manufacturing Summary account is adjusted for the beginning and ending balances of raw materials and goods in process, the remaining accounts which enter into the calculation of cost of goods manufactured must be closed. Excel Company's entry to close these accounts to Manufacturing Summary is as follows:

Dec	31	Manufacturing Summary	176,500.00	
		Raw Material Purchases		85,000.00
		Freight on Raw Materials		1,500.00
		Direct Labor		60,000.00
		Indirect Labor		9,000.00
		Supervision		6,000.00
		Power Expense		2,600.00
		Repairs and Maintenance		2,500.00
		Factory Taxes		1,900.00
		Factory Supplies Used		500.00
		Factory Insurance Expired		1,200.00
		Small Tools Written Off		200.00
		Depr. of Machinery and Equipment		3,500.00
		Depreciation of Building		1,800.00
		Patents Written Off		800.00
		To close manufacturing accounts to the Manufacturing Summary account.		

After the adjusting entries and the above closing entry are posted, the Manufacturing Summary account appears as follows:

Manufacturing Summary					
Date	Explanation	P.R.	Debit	Credit	Balance
Dec 31	Beginning raw materials		8,000		8,000
31	Beginning goods in process		2,500		10,500
31	Ending raw materials			9,000	1,500
31	Ending goods in process			7,500	(6,000)
31	Other manufacturing costs		176,500		170,500

The balance in the Manufacturing Summary account is then closed to Income Summary along with all other cost and expense accounts having balances in the Income Statement debit column of the work sheet. Next, the income statement items with credit balances are closed to Income Summary. And finally, the Income Summary balance is closed to Retained Earnings. These entries for Excel Company are as follows:

Dec	31	Income Summary	263,000.00	
		Sales Salaries Expense		18,000.00
		Advertising Expense		5,500.00
		Delivery Wages Expense		12,000.00
		Office Salaries Expense		15,700.00
		Miscellaneous General Expense		200.00
		Mortgage Interest Expense		4,000.00
		Bad Debts Expense		1,550.00
		Office Supplies Expense		100.00
		Shipping Supplies Expense		250.00
		Delivery Equipment Insurance Expense		300.00
		Depreciation Expense, Delivery Equipment		2,100.00
		Depreciation Expense, Office Equipment		200.00
		State and Federal Income Taxes Expense		32,600.00
		Manufacturing Summary		170,500.00
		To close the income statement accounts having debit balances.		
	31	Sales	310,000.00	
		Income Summary		310,000.00
		To close the Sales account.		
	31	Income Summary	46,100.00	
		Retained Earnings		46,100.00
		To close the Income Summary account.		

INVENTORY VALUATION PROBLEMS OF A MANUFACTURER

In a manufacturing company using a general accounting system, at the end of each period, an accounting value must be placed on the inventories of raw materials, goods in process, and finished goods. No particular problems are encountered in valuing raw materials because the items are in the same form in which they were purchased and a cost or market price may be applied. However, placing a valuation on goods in process and finished goods is generally not so easy. They consist of raw materials to which certain amounts of labor and overhead have been added. They are not in the same form in which they were purchased. Consequently, a price paid a previous producer cannot be used to measure their inventory amount. Instead, their inventory amount must be built up by adding together estimates of the raw materials, direct labor, and overhead costs applicable to each item.

Estimating raw material costs applicable to a goods in process or finished goods item is usually not too difficult. Likewise, from its percentage of completion, a responsible plant official can normally make a reasonably accurate estimate of the direct labor applicable to an item. However, estimating factory overhead costs presents more of a problem, which is often solved by assuming that factory overhead costs are closely related to direct labor costs. This is often a fair assumption.

Frequently there is a close relation between direct labor costs and such things as supervision, power, repairs, and so forth. Furthermore, when this relation is used to apply overhead costs, it is assumed that the relation of overhead costs to the direct labor costs in each goods in process and finished goods item is the same as the relation between total factory overhead costs and total direct labor costs for the accounting period.

For example, an examination of the manufacturing statement in Illustration 22–2 shows that Excel Manufacturing Company's total direct labor costs were $60,000 and its overhead costs were $30,000. Or, in other words, during the year the company incurred in the production of all its products $2 of direct labor for each $1 of factory overhead costs; overhead costs were 50% of direct labor cost.

Overhead costs, $30,000 ÷ Direct labor, $60,000 = 50%

Consequently, in estimating the overhead applicable to a goods in process or finished goods item, Excel Manufacturing Company may assume that this 50% overhead rate is applicable. It may assume that if in all its production the overhead costs were 50% of the direct labor costs, then in each goods in process and finished goods item this relationship also exists.

If Excel Manufacturing Company makes this assumption and its goods in process inventory consists of 1,000 units of Item X with each unit containing $3.75 of raw material and having $2.50 of applicable direct labor, then the goods in process inventory is valued as shown in Illustration 22–4.

Product	Estimated Raw Material Cost	Estimated Direct Labor Applicable	Overhead (50% of Direct Labor)	Estimated Total Unit Cost	No. of Units	Estimated Inventory Cost
Item X	$3.75	$2.50	$1.25	$7.50	1,000	$7,500.00

Illustration 22–4

Excel Manufacturing Company may use the same procedure in placing an accounting value on the items of its finished goods inventory.

GLOSSARY

Direct labor. The labor of those people who work specifically on materials converted into finished products; in other words, with units of product designated as the cost object, labor that can be easily associated with units of product.

Direct materials. A synonym for raw materials.

Factory overhead. All manufacturing costs other than for direct materials and direct labor.

Finished goods. Products in their completed state, ready for sale; equivalent to a store's merchandise.

Indirect labor. The labor of superintendents, foremen, millwrights, engineers, janitors, and others who do not work specifically on the manufactured products, and whose labor therefore cannot be easily associated with specific units of product.

Indirect materials. Commodities that are used in production but that do not enter into and become a part of the finished product, for example, grease and oil for machinery, or cleaning fluid.

Manufacturing overhead. A synonym for factory overhead. Also called manufacturing burden.

Manufacturing statement. A financial report showing the costs incurred to manufacture a product or products during a period. Also called schedule of the cost of goods manufactured.

Raw materials. Commodities that enter into and become a part of a finished product; therefore, commodities that are easily associated with specific units of product.

Work in process. Products in the process of being manufactured that have received a portion or all of their materials and have had some labor and overhead applied but that are not completed. Also called goods in process.

QUESTIONS FOR CLASS DISCUSSION

1. Manufacturing costs consist of three elements. What are they?
2. Explain how the income statement of a manufacturing company differs from the income statement of a merchandising company.
3. What are (a) direct labor, (b) indirect labor, (c) direct material, (d) indirect material, and (e) factory overhead costs?
4. Factory overhead costs include a variety of items. List several examples of factory overhead costs.
5. Name several accounts that are often found in the ledgers of both manufacturing and merchandising companies. Name several accounts that are found only in the ledgers of manufacturing companies.
6. What three new inventory accounts appear in the ledger of a manufacturing company?
7. How are the raw material inventories handled on the work sheet of a manufacturing company? How are the goods in process inventories handled? How are the finished goods inventories handled?
8. Which inventories of a manufacturing company receive the same work sheet treatment as the merchandise inventories of a merchandising company?
9. Which inventories of a manufacturing company appear on its manufacturing statement? Which appear on the income statement?

10. What accounts are summarized in the Manufacturing Summary account? What accounts are summarized in the Income Summary account?

11. What are the three manufacturing cost elements emphasized on the manufacturing statement?

12. What account balances are carried into the Manufacturing Statement columns of the manufacturing work sheet? What account balances are carried into the Income Statement columns? What account balances are carried into the Balance Sheet columns?

13. Why is the cost of goods manufactured entered in the Manufacturing Statement credit column of a work sheet and again in the Income Statement debit columns?

14. May prices paid a previous manufacturer for items of raw materials determine the balance sheet value of the items of the raw material inventory? Why? May such prices also determine the balance sheet values of the goods in process and finished goods inventories? Why?

15. Standard Company used an overhead rate of 70% of direct labor cost to apply overhead to the items of its goods in process inventory. If the manufacturing statement of the company showed total overhead costs of $84,700, how much direct labor did it show?

CLASS EXERCISES

The following items appeared in the Manufacturing Statement and Income Statement columns of Toto Company's year-end work sheet:

	Manufacturing Statement		Income Statement	
	Debit	Credit	Debit	Credit
Manufacturing summary (*)	11,000	12,000	....	....
(†)	14,000	10,000	....	....
Income summary	....	....	15,000	16,000
Sales	....	....	....	225,000
Raw material purchases.........................	45,000	....	....	....
Direct labor	50,000	....	....	....
Indirect labor	11,000	....	....	....
Power	6,000	....	....	....
Machinery repairs...........................	1,000	....	....	....
Rent of factory building	9,000	....	....	....
Selling expenses controlling	....	....	42,000	....
Administrative expenses controlling..............	....	....	25,000	....
Income taxes expense	....	....	9,000	....
	147,000	22,000	....	....
Cost of goods manufactured.....................		125,000	125,000	....
	147,000	147,000	216,000	241,000
Net income.....................................			25,000	....
			241,000	241,000

(*) Raw materials adjustments.
(†) Goods in process adjustments.

Exercise 22–1

From the information just given prepare a manufacturing statement for Toto Company.

Exercise 22–2

Under the assumption Toto Company has outstanding 20,000 shares of $10 par value common stock and no preferred stock, prepare an income statement for the company.

Exercise 22–3

Prepare Toto Company's adjusting entries which relate to its raw materials inventory, goods in process inventory, and finished goods inventory. Also, prepare closing entries for Toto Company.

Exercise 22–4

A company that uses the relation between its overhead and direct labor costs to apply overhead to its goods in process and finished goods inventories incurred the following costs during a year: materials, $75,000; direct labor, $60,000; and factory overhead costs, $90,000. (a) Determine the company's overhead rate. (b) Under the assumption the company's $10,000 ending goods in process inventory had $3,000 of direct labor costs, determine the inventory's material costs. (c) Under the assumption the company's $15,000 finished goods inventory had $5,000 of material costs, determine the inventory's labor costs and its overhead costs.

Exercise 22–5

The trial balance of Balloon Company follows on the next page. To save time the trial balance amounts are in numbers of one or two digits.

Required:

Prepare a work sheet form on ordinary notebook paper, copy the trial balance on the work sheet form, and complete the work sheet using the following information:

a. Ending inventories: raw materials, $2; goods in process, $4; finished goods, $3; and factory supplies, $2.
b. Allowance for doubtful accounts, an additional $1. (Debit Administrative Expenses Controlling.)
c. Factory insurance expired, $2.

d. Depreciation of machinery, $3.

e. Accrued payroll payable: direct labor, $4; and indirect labor, $2.

BALLOON COMPANY

Trial Balance, December 31, 19—

Cash	$ 2	
Accounts receivable	4	
Allowance for doubtful accounts		$ 1
Raw materials inventory	3	
Goods in process inventory	2	
Finished goods inventory	4	
Factory supplies	3	
Prepaid factory insurance	4	
Machinery	20	
Accumulated depreciation, machinery		6
Common stock		15
Retained earnings		8
Sales		76
Raw material purchases	17	
Direct labor	14	
Indirect labor	3	
Power	4	
Machinery repairs	2	
Rent of factory building	9	
Selling expenses controlling	8	
Administrative expenses controlling	7	
Totals	$106	$106

PROBLEMS

Problem 22–1

The items on the next page appeared in the Manufacturing Statement and Income Statement columns of a work sheet prepared for Algoe Products Company on December 31, 19—, the end of its annual accounting period.

Required:

1. Prepare a manufacturing statement and an income statement for Algoe Products Company. Assume the company has 15,000 shares of $10 par value common stock and no preferred stock outstanding.
2. Prepare the adjusting entries which relate to raw materials inventory, goods in process inventory, and finished goods inventory.
3. Prepare closing entries.

	Manufacturing Statement		Income Statement	
	Debit	Credit	Debit	Credit
Manufacturing summary (*)	18,500	17,600	....	....
(†)	12,200	15,400	....	....
Income summary	....	....	22,400	21,500
Sales	....	....	....	282,200
Raw material purchases.........................	94,400	....	....	....
Direct labor	53,900	....	....	....
Indirect labor	9,600	....	....	....
Factory rent	6,000	....	....	....
Supervision	12,000	....	....	....
Power	4,800	....	....	....
Repairs to machinery	3,200	....	....	....
Selling expenses controlling	....	....	28,700	....
Administrative expenses controlling..............	....	....	29,900	....
Factory supplies used.........................	2,400	....	....	....
Factory insurance expired	1,200	....	....	....
Small tools written off	600	....	....	....
Depreciation of machinery....................	7,100	....	....	....
Patents written off	800	....	....	....
State and federal income taxes expense	....	....	6,200	....
	226,700	33,000	....	....
Cost of goods manufactured.....................	....	193,700	193,700	....
	226,700	226,700	280,900	303,700
Net income.....................................			22,800	....
			303,700	303,700

(*) Raw materials adjustments.
(†) Goods in process adjustments.

Problem 22–2

The Manufacturing Statement columns from the work sheet prepared by Highway Products Company at the end of last year follow. The item amounts shown are after all adjustments were completed except for the ending goods in process inventory.

Highway Products Company produces a single product. On December 31, its goods in process inventory consisted of 4,000 units of the product with each unit containing an estimated $1.40 of materials and having an estimated $1 of direct labor applied.

	Manufacturing Statement	
	Debit	Credit
Manufacturing summary (*)	14,200	12,800
(†)	15,300	?
Raw material purchases	59,900	
Direct labor	90,000	
Indirect labor	13,800	
Factory supervision	12,000	
Heat, light, and power	17,900	
Machinery repairs	4,400	
Rent of factory	7,200	
Property taxes, machinery	800	
Factory insurance expense........................	2,200	
Factory supplies used	6,300	
Depreciation of factory machinery	9,900	
Small tools written off	700	
Patents written off	1,300	
	255,900	?
Cost of goods manufactured		?
	255,900	255,900

(*) Raw materials adjustments.
(†) Work in process adjustments.

Required:

1. Calculate the relation between direct labor and factory overhead costs and use this relation to determine a cost for the ending goods in process inventory. Prepare the adjusting entry for the ending goods in process inventory.
2. Prepare a manufacturing statement for Highway Products Company.
3. Prepare entries to close the remaining manufacturing cost accounts to Manufacturing Summary and to close the Manufacturing Summary account.

Problem 22–3

The December 31, 19—, trial balance of Plasti-Box Company appeared as shown on the next page.

The following inventory and adjustments information was available at the year-end:

a. Allowance for doubtful accounts to be increased to $1,200. (Debit General Expenses Controlling.)
b. An examination of policies showed $3,100 of factory insurance expired.
c. An inventory of factory supplies showed $3,400 of unused supplies on hand.
d. Estimated depreciation on factory machinery, $31,300.
e. Accrued direct labor, $500; and accrued indirect labor, $300.
f. State and federal income taxes expense, $14,800.
g. Year-end inventories:
    (1) Raw materials, $16,700.

PLASTI-BOX COMPANY
Trial Balance, December 31, 19—

Cash	$ 12,300	
Accounts receivable	16,200	
Allowance for doubtful accounts		$ 200
Raw materials inventory	17,100	
Goods in process inventory	24,400	
Finished goods inventory	28,700	
Prepaid factory insurance	4,100	
Factory supplies	13,100	
Machinery	287,500	
Accumulated depreciation, machinery		78,400
Accounts payable		15,300
Common stock, $10 par value		150,000
Retained earnings		64,900
Sales		572,500
Raw material purchases	185,100	
Direct labor	79,500	
Indirect labor	36,600	
Heat, light, and power	13,600	
Machinery repairs	9,400	
Selling expenses controlling	81,200	
General expenses controlling	72,500	
Totals	$881,300	$881,300

(2) Goods in process consisted of 3,000 units of product with each unit containing an estimated $3.85 of materials and having $1.50 of direct labor applied.

(3) Finished goods inventory consisted of 2,000 units of product with each unit containing an estimated $6.20 of materials and having an estimated $3 of direct labor applied.

Required:

1. Enter the trial balance on a work sheet form and make the adjustments from the information given. In preparing the adjustments for the ending work in process inventory and the ending finished goods inventory, the amount of each inventory includes materials, direct labor, and overhead. Determine the amount of overhead costs by calculating an overhead rate based on direct labor costs; then, apply the overhead rate to the direct labor costs in each inventory.

2. Sort the adjusted amounts to the proper Manufacturing Statement, Income Statement, and Balance Sheet columns, and complete the work sheet.

3. From the work sheet prepare a manufacturing statement and an income statement.

4. Prepare adjusting entries.

5. Prepare closing entries.

Problem 22–4

The December 31, 198A, trial balance of San Marcus Products Company and related year-end adjustment information are as follows:

SAN MARCUS PRODUCTS COMPANY
Trial Balance, December 31, 19—

Cash	$ 6,700	
Raw materials inventory	14,200	
Goods in process inventory	15,100	
Finished goods inventory	13,800	
Prepaid factory insurance	4,100	
Factory supplies	8,600	
Machinery	172,700	
Accumulated depreciation, machinery		$ 38,400
Small tools	3,800	
Patents	9,200	
Common stock, $5 par value		100,000
Retained earnings		28,700
Sales		355,600
Raw material purchases	62,400	
Discounts on raw material purchases		1,200
Direct labor	79,200	
Indirect labor	19,500	
Factory supervision	14,800	
Heat, light, and power	17,600	
Machinery repairs	5,500	
Rent of factory	12,000	
Property taxes, machinery	3,800	
Selling expenses controlling	32,100	
Administrative expenses controlling	28,800	
Totals.............................	$523,900	$523,900

a. Expired factory insurance, $2,800.
b. Factory supplies used, $7,400.
c. Depreciation of factory machinery, $20,900.
d. Small tools written off, $700.
e. Patents written off, $2,500.
f. Accrued wages payable: (1) direct labor, $800; (2) indirect labor, $300; and (3) factory supervision, $200.
g. State and federal income taxes expense, $14,500.
h. Ending inventories: (1) raw materials, $13,500; (2) goods in process consists of 4,000 units of product with each unit containing an estimated $1.25 of materials and having had an estimated $1 of direct labor applied; and (3) finished goods consists of 2,500 units of product with each unit containing an estimated $1.37 of raw materials and having had an estimated $1.80 of direct labor applied.

Required:

1. Enter the trial balance on a work sheet form and make the adjustments from the information given. The ending balances of work in process and finished goods should include materials, direct labor, and overhead costs. Determine the amount of overhead costs by calculating an overhead rate based on direct labor costs; then, apply the overhead rate to the direct labor costs in each inventory.
2. Sort the adjusted amounts to the proper columns and complete the work sheet.
3. Prepare an income statement and a manufacturing statement.
4. Journalize the adjusting entries.
5. Journalize the closing entries.

Problem 22–5

The following information was taken from the records of a manufacturing concern:

Inventories	*Beginning*	*Ending*
Raw materials..........................	$10,900	$11,400
Goods in process	14,800	12,900
Finished goods	16,100	19,300
Cost of goods sold	$226,900	
Direct labor	90,000	
Factory overhead costs	79,500	

Required:

On the basis of the information given determine for the accounting period:

1. Cost of goods manufactured.
2. Total manufacturing costs.
3. Cost of raw materials used.
4. Cost of raw materials purchased.
   (Hint: It may be helpful to set up the manufacturing statement and the cost of goods sold section of the income statement.)

ALTERNATE PROBLEMS

Problem 22–1A

The following items appeared in the Manufacturing Statement and Income Statement columns of a work sheet prepared for Oslo Manufacturing Company on December 31, 19—, the end of its annual accounting period.

	Manufacturing Statement		Income Statement	
	Debit	Credit	Debit	Credit
Manufacturing summary: (*)	14,000	17,500	....	....
(†)	6,500	5,000	....	....
Income summary	....	....	18,500	17,600
Sales	....	....	....	308,500
Raw material purchases........................	102,500	....	....	....
Discounts on raw material purchases............	....	5,500	....	....
Freight on raw materials	1,600	....	....	....
Direct labor	47,900	....	....	....
Indirect labor	7,500	....	....	....
Superintendence	10,400	....	....	....
Heat, lights, and power	4,300	....	....	....
Maintenance and repairs.......................	3,000	....	....	....
Factory taxes expense	4,800	....	....	....
Miscellaneous factory expenses	2,700	....	....	....
Selling expenses controlling	....	....	58,700	....
Administrative expenses controlling.............	....	....	37,200	....
State and federal income taxes expense	....	....	6,800	....
Depreciation of factory building	1,200	....	....	....
Depreciation of machinery and equipment	4,800	....	....	....
	211,200	28,000	....	....
Cost of goods manufactured	....	183,200	183,200	....
	211,200	211,200	304,400	326,100
Net income			21,700	
			326,100	326,100

(*) Raw materials adjustments.
(†) Goods in process adjustments.

Required:

1. From the information in the columns prepare an income statement and a manufacturing statement. Assume the company has outstanding 10,000 shares of $10 par value common stock and no preferred stock.
2. Prepare Oslo Manufacturing Company's adjusting entries which relate to raw materials inventory, goods in process inventory, and finished goods inventory.
3. Prepare closing entries.

Problem 22–2A

The work sheet prepared for Andersen Manufacturing Company at the end of last year had the following items in its Manufacturing Statement columns:

	Manufacturing Statement	
	Debit	Credit
Manufacturing summary (*)	12,500	11,900
(†)	14,800	?
Raw materials purchases	58,200	
Direct labor	100,000	
Indirect labor	14,300	
Factory supervision	12,000	
Heat, light, and power	18,400	
Machinery repairs	4,500	
Rent of factory	7,800	
Property taxes, machinery	1,100	
Factory insurance expense.....................	2,400	
Factory supplies used	6,100	
Depreciation expense, machinery	10,500	
Small tools written off........................	400	
Patents written off	2,500	
	265,500	?
Cost of goods manufactured		?
	265,500	265,500

(*) Raw materials adjustments.
(†) Work in process adjustments.

The columns do not show the amount of the ending goods in process inventory and the cost of the goods manufactured. However, the company makes a single product; and on December 31, at the end of last year, there were 3,000 units of this product in the goods in process inventory, with each unit containing an estimated $1.40 of materials and having an estimated $2 of direct labor applied.

Required:

1. Calculate the relation between direct labor and factory overhead costs and use this relation to place an accounting value on the ending goods in process inventory. Prepare the adjusting entries related to raw materials and to goods in process.
2. Prepare a manufacturing statement for the company.
3. Prepare entries to close all remaining manufacturing costs to the Manufacturing Summary account and to close the Manufacturing Summary account.

Problem 22–4A

The year-end trial balance of the Utah Manufacturing Company carried the following items:

UTAH MANUFACTURING COMPANY
Trial Balance, December 31, 19—

Cash	$ 10,800	
Raw materials inventory	12,300	
Goods in process inventory	14,700	
Finished goods inventory	13,200	
Prepaid factory insurance	3,400	
Factory supplies	7,200	
Machinery	165,700	
Accumulated depreciation, machinery		$ 48,400
Small tools	3,100	
Patents	7,300	
Common stock, $5 par value		100,000
Retained earnings		27,400
Sales		338,500
Raw material purchases	55,400	
Discounts on raw material purchases		1,100
Direct labor	89,400	
Indirect labor	16,900	
Factory supervision	18,500	
Heat, light, and power	16,700	
Machinery repairs	5,400	
Rent of factory	12,000	
Property taxes, machinery	3,200	
Selling expenses controlling	30,800	
Administrative expenses controlling	29,400	
Totals	$515,400	$515,400

Additional information:

a. Expired factory insurance, $2,600.
b. Factory supplies used, $6,100.
c. Depreciation of factory machinery, $15,300.
d. Small tools written off, $600.
e. Patents written off, $1,500.
f. Accrued wages payable: (1) direct labor, $600; and (2) indirect labor, $200.
g. State and federal income taxes expense, $10,500.
h. Ending inventories: (1) raw materials, $13,500; (2) goods in process consisted of 3,000 units of product with each unit containing an estimated $1.05 of materials and having had $1.50 of direct labor applied; and (3) finished goods consisted of 2,000 units of product with each unit containing an estimated $1.64 of materials and having had an estimated $2.60 of direct labor applied.

Required:

1. Calculate the amount of the ending work in process inventory and the ending finished goods inventory. In so doing, the amount of overhead costs in each inventory should be determined by calculating an overhead rate based on direct labor cost and applying that rate to the direct labor cost in each inventory.

2. Enter the trial balance on a work sheet form and make the adjustments from the information given. Then sort the items to the proper columns and complete the work sheet.
3. Use the information in the work sheet to prepare an income statement and a manufacturing statement.
4. Journalize the adjusting entries.
5. Journalize closing entries.

Problem 22–5A

Baker Tools Company uses the relation between its overhead and direct labor costs to apply overhead to its goods in process and finished goods inventories. Last December 31, at the end of its annual accounting period, the concern's ending goods in process and finished goods inventories were assigned these costs:

	Goods in process	Finished goods
Materials	$ 2,200	$ 3,600
Labor	3,000	4,500
Overhead	?	5,400
Totals	$?	$13,500

This additional information was available from the concern's records:

Ending raw materials inventory	$ 8,400
Cost of goods manufactured during the year	181,300
Factory overhead costs for the year	71,400
Beginning of the year inventories:	
Raw materials	8,700
Goods in process	9,400

Required:

On the basis of the information given and any data that can be derived from it, prepare the concern's manufacturing statement for the past year.

PROVOCATIVE PROBLEMS

Provocative problem 22–1
Decker Boat Shop

Several years ago Danny Decker took over the operation of his family's cabinet shop from his father. Once the shop specialized in manufacturing cabinets for homes, but of late years it has turned more and more to building boats to the specifications of its customers. However, this business is seasonal in nature, since few people order boats in October, November, December, and January. As a result, things are rather slow around the shop during these months.

Danny has tried to increase business during the slow months. However, most prospective customers who come into the shop during these months are shoppers; and when Danny quotes a price for a new boat, they commonly decide the price is too high and walk out. Danny thinks the trouble arises from his application of a rule established by his father when he ran the shop. The rule is that in pricing a job to a customer, "always set the price so as to make a 10% profit over and above all costs, and be sure that all costs are included."

Danny says that in pricing a job, the material and labor costs are easy to figure, but that overhead is another thing. His overhead consists of depreciation of building and machinery, heat, lights, power, taxes, and so on, which in total run to $600 per month whether he builds any boats or not. Furthermore, when he follows his father's rule, he has to charge more for a boat built during the slow months because the overhead is spread over fewer jobs. He readily admits that this seems to drive away business during the months he needs business most, but he finds it difficult to break his father's rule, for as he says, "Dad did alright in this business for many years."

Explain with assumed figures to illustrate your point why Danny charges more for a boat made in December than for one built in May, a very busy month. Suggest how Danny might solve his pricing problem and still follow his father's rule.

Provocative problem 22–2
Track Manufacturing Company

On January 1, 198A, Track Manufacturing Company had outstanding 4,000 shares of $10 par value common stock, issued at par, and it had the following assets and liabilities:

Cash	$ 4,000
Accounts receivable	10,000
Raw materials inventory	4,000
Goods in process inventory	2,000
Finished goods inventory	3,000
Plant and equipment, net	32,000
Accounts payable	5,000

During 198A the company paid no dividends, although it earned a 198A net income (ignore income taxes) that increased its retained earnings by 50%. At the year-end the amounts of the company's accounts receivable, accounts payable, and common stock outstanding were the same as of the beginning of the year. However, its cash increased $5,000, its raw materials and goods in process inventories each increased 50%, and its finished goods inventory increased by one third during the year. The net amount of its plant and equipment decreased $4,000 due to depreciation, chargeable three fourths to factory overhead costs and one fourth to general and administrative expenses. The year's direct labor costs were $12,000 and factory overhead costs were 75% of that amount. Cost of finished goods sold was $40,000, and all sales were made at prices 50% above cost. Selling expenses were 10%, and general and administrative expenses were 15% of sales.

Based on the information given and on amounts you can derive therefrom, prepare a manufacturing work sheet for the company.

Provocative problem 22–3
DeShazo Wrench Company

DeShazo Wrench Company has been in business for three years, manufacturing a single product, a wrench, which is sold to mail-order companies. Sales have increased substantially each year, but net income has not, and the company president has asked you to analyze the situation and tell him why.

The company's condensed income statements for the past three years show the following:

	1st year	2d year	3d year
Sales	$228,000	$306,000	$366,000
Cost of goods sold:			
Finished goods inventory, January 1 ...	$ 0	$ 6,000	$ 18,000
Cost of goods manufactured	128,000	187,000	216,000
Goods for sale	$128,000	$193,000	$234,000
Finished goods inventory, December 31	6,000	18,000	15,000
Cost of goods sold	$122,000	$175,000	$219,000
Gross profit from sales	$106,000	$131,000	$147,000
Selling and administrative expenses	83,600	107,100	122,000
Net income	$ 22,400	$ 23,900	$ 25,000

Investigation disclosed the following additional information:

a. The company sold 7,600 units of its product during the first year in business, 10,200 during the second year, and 12,200 during the third year. All sales were at $30 per unit, and no discounts were granted.

b. There were 400 units in the finished goods inventory at the end of the first year, 1,200 at the end of the second year, and 1,000 at the end of the third year.

c. The units in the finished goods inventory were priced each year at 50% of their selling price, or at $15 per unit.

Prepare a report to the president which shows: (1) the number of units of product manufactured each year, (2) the cost each year to manufacture a unit of product, and (3) the selling and administrative expenses per unit of product sold each year. Also, (4) prepare an income statement showing the correct net income each year, using a first-in, first-out basis for pricing the finished goods inventory. And finally, (5) express an opinion as to why net income has not kept pace with the rising sales volume.

After studying Chapter 23, you should be able to:

☐ State the conditions under which job order cost accounting should be used and those under which process cost accounting should be used.

☐ Describe how costs for individual jobs are accumulated on job cost sheets and how control accounts are charged with the total costs of all jobs.

☐ Allocate overhead to jobs and distribute any over- or underapplied overhead.

☐ Describe how costs are accumulated by departments under process costing.

☐ Explain what an equivalent finished unit is and how equivalent finished units are used in calculating unit costs.

☐ Prepare a process cost summary.

☐ Define or explain the words and phrases listed in the chapter Glossary.

Cost accounting, job order, and process

■ In a general manufacturing accounting system such as that described in the previous chapter, physical counts of inventories are required at the end of each accounting period in order to determine cost of goods manufactured. Furthermore, cost of goods manufactured as determined under such a system is the cost of all goods that were manufactured during the period; usually, no effort is made to determine unit costs. A *cost accounting system* differs in that it is based on perpetual inventories and its emphasis is on unit costs and the control of costs.

There are two common types of cost accounting systems: (1) job order cost systems and (2) process cost systems. However, of the two there are an infinite number of variations and combinations. A job order system is described first.

JOB ORDER COST ACCOUNTING

In job order cost accounting a *job* is a turbine, machine, or other product manufactured especially for and to the specifications of a customer. A job may also be a single construction project of a contractor. A *job lot* is a quantity of identical items, such as 500 typewriters, manufactured in one lot as a job or single order; and a *job order cost system* is one in which costs are assembled in terms of jobs or job lots of product.

As previously stated, a job cost system differs from a general accounting system in that its primary objective is the determination of the cost of producing each job or job lot. A job cost system also differs in that all inventory accounts used in such a system are perpetual inventory accounts which control subsidiary ledgers. For example, in a job cost system the purchase and use of all materials are recorded in a perpetual inventory account called Materials. The Materials account controls a subsidiary ledger having a separate ledger card (Illustration 23–1) for each different kind of material used. Likewise, in a job cost system the Goods in Process and Finished Goods accounts are also perpetual inventory accounts controlling subsidiary ledgers.

MATERIALS LEDGER CARD

Item _whatsit clip_   Stock No. _C-347_   Location in Storeroom _Bin 137_

Maximum _400_   Minimum _150_   Number to Reorder _200_

	Received				Issued				Balance		
Date	Receiving Report No.	Units	Unit Price	Total Price	Requi- sition No.	Units	Unit Price	Total Price	Units	Unit Price	Total Price
3/1									180	1.00	180.00
3/5					4345	20	1.00	20.00	160	1.00	160.00
3/11					4416	10	1.00	10.00	150	1.00	150.00
3/12	C-114	200	1.00	200.00					350	1.00	350.00
3/25					4713	21	1.00	21.00	329	1.00	329.00

Illustration 23–1

In addition to perpetual inventory controlling accounts, job cost accounting is also distinguished by the flow of manufacturing costs through the accounts. Costs flow from the Materials, Factory Payroll, and Overhead Costs accounts into and through the Goods in Process and Finished Goods accounts and on to the Cost of Goods Sold account. The flow is diagrammed in Illustration 23–2 on the next page. An examination of the diagram will show that costs flow through the accounts in the same way materials, labor, and overhead are placed in production in the factory, are combined to become finished goods, and finally are sold.

JOB COST SHEETS

The heart of a job cost system is a subsidiary ledger of *job cost sheets* called a *Job Cost Ledger*. The cost sheets are used to accumulate costs by jobs. A separate cost sheet is used for each job.

Observe in Illustration 23–3 how a job cost sheet is designed to accumulate costs. Although this accumulation is discussed in more de-

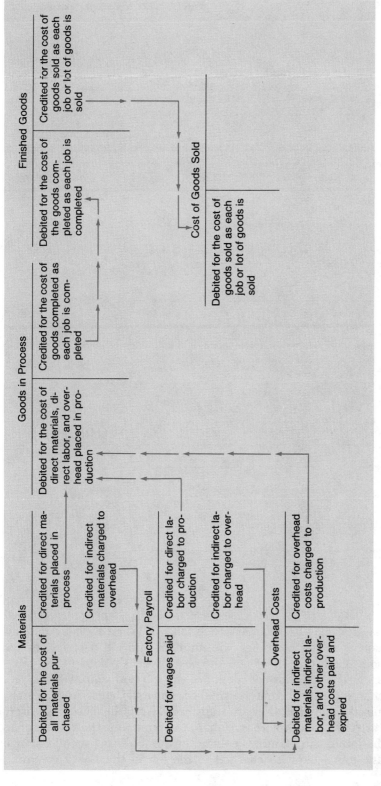

Illustration 23–2
Diagram showing
the flow of costs in
a job cost system

JOB COST SHEET

Customer's Name _Cone Lumber Company_   Job No. _7452_
Address _Eugene, Oregon_
Job Description _10 H.P. electric motor to customer's specifications_

Date Promised _4/1_   Date Started _3/23_   Date Completed _3/29_

Date	Materials		Labor		Overhead Costs Applied		
	Requisition No.	Amount	Time Ticket No.	Amount	Date	Rate	Amount
19-- Mar. 23	4698	53.00	C-3422	6.00	3/29	150 per-cent of the direct labor	$123.00
24			C-3478 C-3479	16.00 6.00			
25	4713	21.00	C-4002	16.00			
26			C-4015	16.00	Summary of Costs		
27			C-4032	12.00	Materials		$ 74.00
28			C-4044	10.00	Labor		82.00
					Overhead		123.00
					Total Cost of the job		279.00
	Total	74.00	Total	82.00	Remarks: Completed and shipped 3/29		

Illustration 23–3

tail later, it may be summarized as follows. When a job is begun, information as to the customer, job number, and job description is filled in on a blank cost sheet and the cost sheet is placed in the Job Cost Ledger. The job number identifies the job and simplifies the process of charging it with materials, labor, and overhead. As materials are required for the job, they are transferred from the materials storeroom and are used to complete the job. At the same time their cost is charged to the job in the Materials column of the job's cost sheet. Labor used on the job is likewise charged to the job in the Labor column; and when the job is finished, the amount of overhead applicable is entered in the Overhead Costs Applied column. After this, the cost totals are summarized to determine the job's total cost.

THE GOODS IN PROCESS ACCOUNT

The job cost sheets in the Job Cost Ledger are controlled by the Goods in Process account, which is kept in the General Ledger. And, the Goods in Process account and its subsidiary ledger of cost sheets operate in the usual manner of controlling accounts and subsidiary ledgers. The material, labor, and overhead costs debited to each individual job on its cost sheet must be debited to the Goods in Process account either as individual amounts or in totals. Likewise all credits to jobs on their cost sheets must be credited individually or in totals to the Goods in Process account.

In addition to being a controlling account, the Goods in Process account is a perpetual inventory account operating somewhat as follows: At the beginning of a cost period the cost of any unfinished jobs in process is shown by its debit balance. Throughout the cost period materials, labor, and overhead are placed in production in the factory; and periodically their costs are debited to the account (note the last three debits in the Goods in Process account that follows). Also, throughout the period the cost of each job completed (the sum of the job's material, labor, and overhead costs) is credited to the account as each job is finished. As a result, the account is a perpetual inventory account. After all entries are posted, the debit balance shows the cost of the unfinished jobs still in process. This current balance is obtained and maintained without having to take a physical count of inventory, except as an occasional means of confirming the account balance. For example, the following Goods in Process account shows a $12,785 March 31 ending inventory of unfinished jobs in process.

Goods in Process					
Date		Explanation	Debit	Credit	Balance
Mar.	1	Balance, beginning inventory			2,850
	10	Job 7449 completed		7,920	(5,070)
	18	Job 7448 completed		9,655	(14,725)
	24	Job 7450 completed		8,316	(23,041)
	29	Job 7452 completed		279	(23,320)
	29	Job 7451 completed		6,295	(29,615)
	31	Materials used	17,150		(12,465)
	31	Labor applied	10,100		(2,365)
	31	Overhead applied	15,150		12,785

ACCOUNTING FOR MATERIALS UNDER A JOB COST SYSTEM

Under a job cost system all materials purchased are placed in a materials storeroom under the care of a storeroom keeper, and are issued to the factory only in exchange for properly prepared material *requisitions* (Illustration 23–4). The storeroom provides physical control over materials. The requisitions enhance the control and also provide a means of charging material costs to jobs or, in the case of indirect materials, to factory overhead costs. The use of requisitions is described in the next paragraphs.

When a material is needed in the factory, a material requisition is prepared and signed by a foreman, superintendent, or other responsible person. The requisition identifies the material and shows the number of the job or overhead account to which it is to be charged, and is given to the storeroom keeper in exchange for the material. The storeroom keeper collects the requisitions, and then forwards them, in batches, to the accounting department.

Issuing units of material to the factory reduces the amount of that particular material in the storeroom. Consequently, when a material requisition reaches the accounting department, it is first recorded in the Issued column of the materials ledger card of the material issued. This reduces the number of units of that material shown to be on hand. Note the last entry in Illustration 23–1, which records the requisition of Illustration 23–4.

Materials issued to the factory may be used on jobs or for some overhead task, such as machinery repairs. Consequently, after being entered in the Issued columns of the proper materials ledger cards, a batch of requisitions is sorted by jobs and overhead accounts and charged to the proper jobs and overhead accounts. Materials used on jobs are charged to the jobs in the Materials columns of the job cost sheets. (Note the last entry in the Materials column on the cost sheet of Illustration 23–3 where the requisition of Illustration 23–4 is recorded.) Materials used for overhead tasks are charged to the proper

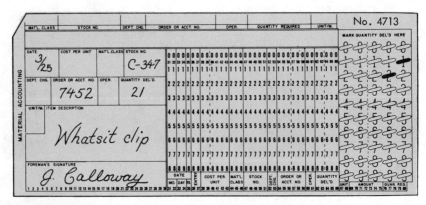

Illustration 23–4

overhead accounts in the Overhead Costs Ledger. A company using a job cost system commonly has an Overhead Costs, controlling account in its General Ledger which controls a subsidiary Overhead Costs Ledger having an account for each overhead cost, such as Heating and Lighting or Machinery Repairs. Consequently, a requisition for light bulbs, for example, is charged to the Heating and Lighting account in the subsidiary Overhead Costs Ledger.

Material ledger cards, job cost sheets, and overhead cost accounts are all subsidiary ledger accounts controlled by accounts in the General Ledger. Consequently, in addition to the entries just described, entries must also be made in the controlling accounts. To make these entries, the requisitions charged to jobs and the requisitions charged to overhead accounts are accumulated until the end of a month or other cost period when they are separately totaled. If, for example, the requisitions charged to jobs during the month total $17,150 and those charged to overhead accounts total $320, an entry like the following is made:

Mar.	31	Goods in Process	17,150.00	
		Overhead Costs	320.00	
		Materials		17,470.00
		To record the materials used during March.		

The debit to Goods in Process in the illustrated entry is equal to the sum of the requisitions charged to jobs on the job cost sheets during March. The debit to Overhead Costs is equal to the sum of the requisitions charged to overhead accounts, and the credit to Materials is equal to the sum of all requisitions entered in the Issued columns of the material ledger cards during the month.

ACCOUNTING FOR LABOR IN A JOB COST SYSTEM

Time clocks, clock cards, and a Payroll Register similar to those described in an earlier chapter are commonly used in a factory to record the hours and cost of the work of each direct and indirect labor employee. Furthermore, without the complications of payroll taxes, income taxes, and other deductions, the entry to pay the employees is as follows:

Mar.	7	Factory Payroll	2,900.00	
		Cash		2,900.00
		To record the factory payroll and pay the employees.		

This entry is repeated at the end of each pay period. Thus, at the end of a month or other cost period the Factory Payroll account has a series of debits (see Illustration 23–6) like the debit of this entry, and the sum of these debits is the total amount paid the direct and indirect labor employees during the month.

The clock cards just mentioned are a record of hours worked each day by each employee, but they do not show how the employees spent their time or the specific jobs and overhead tasks on which they worked. Consequently, if the hours worked by each employee are to be charged to specific jobs and overhead accounts, another record called a *labor time ticket* must be prepared. Labor time tickets like the one shown in Illustration 23–5 tell how each employee's time was spent while at work.

The time ticket of Illustration 23–5 is a "pen-and-ink" ticket and is suitable for use in a plant in which only a small number of such tickets are prepared and recorded each day. In a plant in which many tickets are prepared, a time ticket that can be made into a punched card similar to Illustration 23–4 would be more suitable.

Labor time tickets serve as a basis for charging jobs and overhead accounts for an employee's wages. Throughout each day a labor time ticket is prepared each time an employee is changed from one job or overhead task to another. The tickets may be prepared by the worker, the worker's supervisor, or a clerk called a timekeeper. If

TIME TICKET _____ C-3422

EMPLOYEE
name_____ *George Jones*
clock number ___ 342 ___
JOB
number ___ 7452 ___
description ___ *Armature winding* ___

OVERHEAD ACCOUNT NUMBER _____
TIME/RATE

started	stopped	elapsed	rate	pay
8:00	10:00	2	3.00	6.00

Date: *George Jones*
                        employee
3/23   *J. Calloway*
                        foreman

Illustration 23–5
A labor time ticket

Factory Payroll				
Date	Explanation	Debit	Credit	Balance
Mar. 7	Weekly payroll payment	2,900		2,900
14	Weekly payroll payment	2,950		5,850
21	Weekly payroll payment	3,105		8,955
28	Weekly payroll payment	3,040		11,995
31	Labor cost summary		12,600	(605)

Illustration 23-6

the employee works on only one job all day, only one ticket is prepared. If more than one job is worked on, a separate ticket is made for each. At the end of the day all the tickets of that day are sent to the accounting department.

In the accounting department the direct labor time tickets are charged to jobs on the job cost sheets (see the first entry in the Labor column of Illustration 23–3 where the ticket of Illustration 23–5 is recorded); and the indirect labor tickets are charged to overhead accounts in the Overhead Costs Ledger. The tickets are then accumulated until the end of the cost period when they are separately totaled. If, for example, the direct labor tickets total $10,100 and the indirect labor tickets total $2,500, the following entry is made:

Mar. 31	Goods in Process	10,100.00	
	Overhead Costs	2,500.00	
	Factory Payroll..........................		12,600.00
	To record the March time tickets.		

The first debit in the illustrated entry is the sum of all direct labor time tickets charged to jobs on the job cost sheets, and the second debit is the sum of all tickets charged to overhead accounts. The credit is the total of the month's labor time tickets, both direct and indirect. Notice in Illustration 23–6 that after this credit is posted, the Factory Payroll account has a $605 credit balance. This $605 is the accrued factory payroll payable at the month's end, and it is also the dollar amount of time tickets prepared and recorded during the days following the end of the March 28 pay period.

ACCOUNTING FOR OVERHEAD IN A JOB COST SYSTEM

In a job cost system, if the cost of each job is to be determined at the time it is finished, it is necessary to associate with each job the cost of its materials, labor, and overhead. Requisitions and time tickets make possible a direct association of material and labor costs with jobs. However, overhead costs are incurred for the benefit of all jobs and cannot be related directly to any one. Consequently, to associate overhead with jobs it is necessary to relate overhead to, for example, direct labor costs and to apply overhead to jobs by means of a *predetermined overhead application rate.*

A predetermined overhead application rate based on direct labor cost is established by (1) estimating before a cost period begins the total overhead that will be incurred during the period; (2) estimating the cost of the direct labor that will be incurred during the period; then (3) calculating the ratio, expressed as a percentage, of the estimated overhead to the estimated direct labor cost. For example, if a cost accountant estimates that a factory will incur $180,000 of overhead during the year about to begin and that $120,000 of direct labor will be applied to production during the period, and these estimates are used to establish an overhead application rate, the rate is 150% and is calculated as follows:

$$\frac{\textbf{Next year's estimated overhead costs, \$180,000}}{\textbf{Next year's estimated direct labor costs, \$120,000}} = \textbf{150\%}$$

After a predetermined overhead application rate is established, it is used throughout the year to apply overhead to jobs as they are finished. Overhead is assigned to each job, and its cost is calculated as follows: (1) As each job is completed, the cost of its materials is determined by adding the amounts in the Materials column of its cost sheet. Then (2) the cost of its labor is determined by adding the amounts in the Labor column. Next (3) the applicable overhead is calculated by multiplying the job's total labor cost by the predetermined overhead application rate and is entered in the Overhead Costs Applied column. Finally (4) the job's material, labor, and overhead costs are entered in the summary section of the cost sheet and totaled to determine the cost of the job.

The predetermined overhead application rate is also used to assign overhead to any jobs still in process at the cost period end. Then, the total overhead assigned to all jobs during the period is recorded in the accounts with an entry like this:

Mar.	31	Goods in Process	15,150.00	
		Overhead Costs........................		15,150.00
		To record the overhead applied to jobs during March.		

The illustrated entry assumes that the overhead applied to all jobs during March totaled $15,150. After it is posted, the Overhead Costs account appears as in Illustration 23–7.

Overhead Costs					
Date	Explanation	P R	Debit	Credit	Balance
Mar. 31	Indirect materials	G24	320		320
31	Indirect labor	G24	2,500		2,820
31	Miscellaneous payments	D89	3,306		6,126
31	Accrued and prepaid items	G24	9,056		15,182
31	Applied			15,150	32

Illustration 23–7

In the Overhead Costs account of Illustration 23–7 the actual overhead costs incurred during March are represented by four debits. The first two need no explanation; the third represents the many payments for such things as water, telephone, and so on; the fourth represents such things as depreciation, expired insurance, taxes, and so forth.

When overhead is applied to jobs on the basis of a predetermined overhead rate based upon direct labor costs, it is assumed that the overhead applicable to a particular job bears the same relation to the job's direct labor cost as the total estimated overhead of the factory bears to the total estimated direct labor costs. This assumption may not be proper in every case. However, when the ratio of overhead to direct labor cost is approximately the same for all jobs, an overhead rate based upon direct labor cost offers an easily calculated and fair basis for assigning overhead to jobs. In those cases in which the ratio of overhead to direct labor cost does not remain the same for all jobs, some other relationship must be used. Often overhead rates based upon the ratio of overhead to direct labor hours or overhead to machine-hours are used. However, a discussion of these is reserved for a course in cost accounting.

OVERAPPLIED AND UNDERAPPLIED OVERHEAD

When overhead is applied to jobs by means of an overhead application rate based on estimates, the Overhead Costs account seldom, if ever, has a zero balance. At times actual overhead incurred exceeds overhead applied, and at other times overhead applied exceeds actual overhead incurred. When the account has a debit balance (overhead incurred in excess of overhead applied), the balance is known as *underapplied overhead* (see Illustration 23–7); and when it has a credit balance (overhead applied in excess of overhead incurred), the balance is called *overapplied overhead*. Usually the balance is small and fluctuates from debit to credit throughout a year. However, any balance in the account must be disposed of at the end of each year before a new accounting period begins.

If the year-end balance of the Overhead Costs account is material in amount, it is reasonable that it be disposed of by apportioning it among the goods still in process, the finished goods inventory, and cost of goods sold. This has the effect of restating the inventories and goods sold at "actual" cost. For example, assume that at the end of an accounting period, (1) a company's Overhead Costs account has a $1,000 debit balance (underapplied overhead), and (2) the company had charged the following amounts of overhead to jobs during the period: jobs still in process, $10,000; jobs finished but unsold, $20,000; and jobs finished and sold, $70,000. In such a situation the following entry apportions fairly the underapplied overhead among the jobs worked on during the period:

Dec.	31	Goods in Process	100.00	
		Finished Goods	200.00	
		Cost of Goods Sold	700.00	
		Overhead Costs........................		1,000.00
		To clear the Overhead Costs account and charge the underapplied overhead to the work of the accounting period.		

Sometimes when the amount of over- or underapplied overhead is immaterial, all of it is closed to Cost of Goods Sold under the assumption that the major share would be charged there anyway and any extra exactness gained from prorating would not be worth the extra record keeping involved.

RECORDING THE COMPLETION OF A JOB

When a job is completed, its cost is transferred from the Goods in Process account to the Finished Goods account. For example, the following entry transfers the cost of the job the cost sheet of which appears on page 770.

Mar.	29	Finished Goods	279.00	
		Goods in Process		279.00
		To transfer the cost of Job No. 7452 to Finished Goods		

At the same time the entry is made, the completed job's cost sheet is removed from the Job Cost Ledger, marked "completed," and filed. This is in effect the equivalent of posting a credit to the Job Cost Ledger equal to the credit to the Goods in Process controlling account.

RECORDING COST OF GOODS SOLD

When a cost system is in use, the cost to manufacture a job or job lot of product is known as soon as the goods are finished. Consequently, when goods are sold, since their cost is known, the cost can be recorded at the time of sale. For example, if goods costing $279 are sold for $450, the cost of the goods sold may be recorded with the sale as follows:

Mar.	29	Accounts Receivable—Cone Lumber Co.	450.00	
		Cost of Goods Sold	279.00	
		Sales		450.00
		Finished Goods		279.00
		Sold for $450 goods costing $279.		

When cost of goods sold is recorded at the time of each sale, the balance of the Cost of Goods Sold account shows at the end of an accounting period the cost of goods sold during the period.

PROCESS COST ACCOUNTING

A *process* is a step in manufacturing a product, and a *process cost system* is one in which costs are assembled in terms of processes or manufacturing steps.

Process cost systems are found in companies producing cement, flour, or other products the production of which is characterized by a large volume of standardized units manufactured on a more or less continuous basis. In such companies responsibility for completing each step in the production of a product is assigned to a department. Costs are then assembled by departments, and the efficiency of each department is measured by the processing costs incurred in processing the units of product that flow through the department.

ASSEMBLING COSTS BY DEPARTMENTS

When costs are assembled by departments in a process cost system, a separate goods in process account is used for the costs of each department. For example, assume a company makes a product from metal that is cut to size in a cutting department, sent to a bending department to be bent into shape, and then on to a painting department to be painted. Such a concern would collect costs in three goods in process accounts, one for each department, and costs would flow through the accounts as in Illustration 23–8.

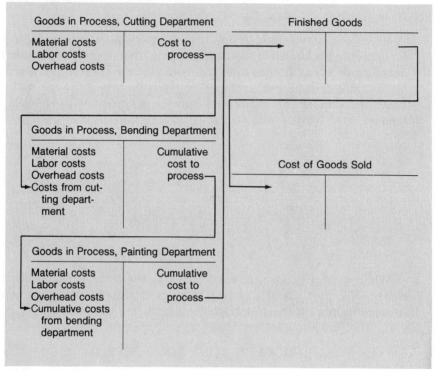

Illustration 23–8

Observe in Illustration 23–8 that each department's material, labor, and overhead costs are charged to the department's goods in process account. (It is assumed there were additional materials charged directly to the bending department.) Observe too how costs are transferred from department to department, just as the product is transferred in the manufacturing procedure. The cost to cut the product in the cutting department is transferred to the bending department; and the sum of the costs in the first two departments is transferred to the third department; and finally the sum of the processing costs in all three departments, which is the cost to make the product, is transferred to finished goods.

CHARGING COSTS TO DEPARTMENTS

Since there are no jobs in a process cost system, accounting for material and labor costs in such a system is much simplified. Material requisitions may be used. However, a consumption report kept by the storeroom keeper and showing the materials issued to each department during a cost period is often substituted. Likewise, labor time tickets may be used; but since most employees spend all their working time in the same department, an end-of-the-period summary of the payroll records is usually all that is required in charging labor to the departments. And since there are no jobs, there is no need to distinguish between direct and indirect materials and direct and indirect labor. All that is required is that material and labor costs, both direct and indirect, be charged to the proper departments.

The lack of jobs also simplifies accounting for overhead in a process cost system. Since there are no jobs to charge with overhead on completion, predetermined overhead application rates are not required and actual overhead incurred may be charged directly to the goods in process accounts of the departments.

EQUIVALENT FINISHED UNITS

A basic objective of a process cost system is the determination of unit processing costs for material, labor, and overhead in each processing department. This requires that (1) material, labor, and overhead costs be accumulated for each department for a cost period of, say, a month; (2) a record be kept of the number of units processed in each department during the period; and then (3) that costs be divided by units processed to determine unit costs. However, it should be observed that when a department begins and ends a cost period with partially processed units of product, the units completed in the department are not an accurate measure of the department's production. When the production of the period includes completing units which were partially finished at the beginning of the period, and also includes working on units which remain partially finished at the end of the period, the following question arises: How many units did the department produce during the period? In other words, how many units would have been produced if all activity in the department had been concentrated on units which were started this period and finished this period? The answer is the number of *equivalent finished units* produced by the department during the period. Thus, when a department's beginning and ending inventories include partially finished units, the department's production for the period must be measured in terms of *equivalent finished units* and unit costs become *equivalent finished unit costs.*

The idea of an equivalent finished unit is based on the assumption that it takes the same amount of labor, for instance, to one-half finish each of two units of product as it takes to fully complete one, or it takes the same amount of labor to one-third finish each of three units as to complete one. Also, since a department may add materials to production at a different rate than it adds labor and overhead, separate measures of production are often required for materials and for labor and overhead. For example, a department may have added enough materials to produce 1,000 equivalent finished units, and during the same period, the department may have added enough labor and overhead to produce 900 equivalent finished units. The concept of equivalent finished units and the related calculations are discussed further in the Delta Processing Company illustration that follows.

PROCESS COST ACCOUNTING ILLUSTRATED

The process cost system of Delta Processing Company, a company manufacturing a patented home remedy called Noxall, is used to illustrate process cost accounting.

The procedure for manufacturing Noxall is as follows: Material A is finely ground in Delta Processing Company's grinding department. Then, it is transferred to the mixing department where Material B is added, and the two materials are thoroughly mixed. The mixing process results in finished product, Noxall, which is transferred on completion to finished goods. All Material A placed in process in the grinding department is placed in process when the grinding process is first begun; but the Material B added in the mixing department is added evenly throughout its process. In other words, a product one-third mixed in the latter department has received one third of its Material B and a product three-fourths mixed has received three fourths. Labor and overhead are applied evenly throughout each department's process.

At the end of the April cost period, after entries recording materials, labor, and overhead were posted, the company's two goods in process accounts appeared as follows:

Goods in Process, Grinding Department

Date		Explanation	Debit	Credit	Balance
Apr.	1	Beginning inventory			4,250
	30	Materials	9,900		14,150
	30	Labor	5,700		19,850
	30	Overhead	4,275		24,125

Goods in Process, Mixing Department

Date		Explanation	Debit	Credit	Balance
Apr.	1	Beginning inventory			3,785
	30	Materials	2,040		5,825
	30	Labor	3,570		9,395
	30	Overhead	1,020		10,415

The production reports prepared by the company's two department foremen give the following information about inventories and goods started and finished in each department during the month:

	Grinding department	Mixing department
Units in the beginning inventories of goods in process	30,000	16,000
April 1 stage of completion of the beginning inventories of goods in process	⅓	¼
Units started in process and finished during period........................	70,000	85,000
Total units finished and transferred to next department or to finished goods...	100,000	101,000
Units in the ending inventories of goods in process	20,000	15,000
Stage of completion of ending inventories of goods in process	¼	⅓

After receiving the production reports, the company's cost accountant prepared a process cost summary, Illustration 23–9, for the grinding department. A process cost summary is a report peculiar to a processing company. A separate report is prepared for each processing department and shows (1) the costs charged to the department, (2) the department's equivalent unit processing costs, and (3) the costs applicable to the department's goods in process inventories and its goods started and finished.

Observe in Illustration 23–9 that a process cost summary has three sections. In the first, headed Costs Charged to the Department, are summarized the costs charged to the department. Information for this section comes from the department's goods in process account. Compare the first section of Illustration 23–9 with the goods in process account of the grinding department shown on page 782.

The second section of a process cost summary shows the calculation of equivalent unit costs. The information for this section as to units involved and fractional units applicable to the inventories comes from the production report of the department foreman. Information as to material, labor, and overhead costs comes from the first section of the summary.

Notice in the second section of Illustration 23–9 that there are two separate equivalent unit calculations. Two calculations are required because material added to the product and labor and overhead added are not added in the same proportions and at the same stages in the processing procedure of this department. As previously stated, all material is added at the beginning of this department's process, and labor and overhead are added evenly throughout the process. Consequently, the number of equivalent units of material added is not the same as the number of equivalent units of labor and overhead added.

Delta Processing Company
Process Cost Summary, Grinding Department
For Month Ended April 30, 19—

COSTS CHARGED TO THE DEPARTMENT:

Material requisitioned	$ 9,900
Labor charged	5,700
Overhead costs incurred	4,275
Total processing costs	$19,875
Goods in process at the beginning of the month	4,250
Total costs to be accounted for	$24,125

EQUIVALENT UNIT PROCESSING COSTS:

	Units involved	Fraction of a unit added	Equivalent units added
Material:			
Beginning inventory	30,000	–0–	–0–
Units started and finished	70,000	One	70,000
Ending inventory	20,000	One	20,000
			90,000

Equivalent unit processing cost for material: $9,900 ÷ 90,000 = $0.11

	Units involved	Fraction of a unit added	Equivalent units added
Labor and overhead:			
Beginning inventory	30,000	⅔	20,000
Units started and finished	70,000	One	70,000
Ending inventory	20,000	¼	5,000
			95,000

Equivalent unit processing cost for labor: $5,700 ÷ 95,000 = $0.06
Equivalent unit processing cost for overhead: $4,275 ÷ 95,000 = $0.045

COSTS APPLICABLE TO THE WORK OF THE DEPARTMENT:

Goods in process, one-third processed at the beginning of April:

Costs charged to the beginning inventory of goods in process during previous month	$4,250	
Material added (all added during March)................................	–0–	
Labor applied (20,000 × $0.06)	1,200	
Overhead applied (20,000 × $0.045)	900	
Cost to process		$ 6,350

Goods started and finished in the department during April:

Material added (70,000 × $0.11)..	$7,700	
Labor applied (70,000 × $0.06)	4,200	
Overhead applied (70,000 × $0.045)	3,150	
Cost to process		15,050
Total cost of the goods processed in the department and transferred to the mixing department (100,000 units at $0.214 each)*		$21,400

Goods in process, one-fourth processed at the end of April:

Material added (20,000 × $0.11)..	$2,200	
Labor applied (5,000 × $0.06)	300	
Overhead applied (5,000 × $0.045)	225	
Cost to one-fourth process		2,725
Total costs accounted for..		$24,125

* Note that the $0.214 is an average unit cost based on all 100,000 units finished. Other alternatives such as Fifo and Lifo are deferred to a more advanced course.

Illustration 23–9

Observe in the calculation of equivalent finished units for materials that the beginning-of-the-month inventory is assigned no additional material. In the grinding department all material placed in process is placed there at the beginning of the process. The 30,000 beginning inventory units were begun during March and were one-third completed at the beginning of April. Consequently, these units received all their material during March when their processing was first begun.

Note also how the $9,900 cost of the material charged to the department in April is divided by 90,000 equivalent units of material to arrive at an $0.11 per equivalent unit cost for material consumed in this department.

Now move on to the calculation of equivalent finished units for labor and overhead and note that the beginning inventory units were each assigned two thirds of a unit of labor and overhead. If these units were one-third completed on April 1, then two thirds of the work done on these units was done in April. Beginning students often have difficulty at this point. In a situation such as this they are apt to assign only an additional one-third unit of labor and overhead when two thirds is required.

Before going further observe that the essence of the equivalent unit calculation for labor and overhead is that to do two thirds of the work on 30,000 units, all the work on 70,000 units, and one fourth the work on 20,000 units is the equivalent of doing all the work on 95,000 units. Consequently, the $5,700 of labor cost and $4,275 of overhead cost charged to the department are each divided by 95,000 to determine equivalent unit costs for labor and overhead.

When a department begins and ends a cost period with partially processed units of product, it is necessary to apportion the department's costs between the units that were in process in the department at the beginning of the period, the units started and finished during the period, and the ending inventory units. This division is necessary to determine the cost of the units completed in the department during the period; and the division and assignment of costs are shown in the third section of the process cost summary.

Notice in the third section of Illustration 23–9 how costs are assigned to the beginning inventory. The first amount assigned is the $4,250 beginning inventory costs. This amount represents the material, labor, and overhead costs used to one-third complete the inventory during March, the previous cost period. Normally, the second charge to a beginning inventory is for additional material assigned to it. However, in the grinding department no additional material costs are assigned the beginning inventory because these units received all of their material when their processing was first begun during the previous month. The second charge to the beginning inventory is for labor. The $1,200 portion of applicable labor costs is calculated by multiplying the number of equivalent finished units of labor used in completing the beginning inventory by the cost of an equivalent finished unit of labor (20,000 equivalent finished units at $0.06 each). The third charge to the beginning inventory is for overhead. The applicable $900 portion is determined by multiplying the equivalent finished units of overhead used in completing the beginning inventory by the cost of an equivalent finished unit of overhead (20,000 × $0.45).

After costs are assigned to the beginning inventory, the procedures used in their assignment are repeated for the units started and finished. Then the cost of the units completed and transferred to finished goods, in this case the cost of the 30,000 beginning inventory units plus the cost of the 70,000 units started and finished, is determined by adding the costs assigned to the two groups. In this situation the total is $21,400 or $0.214 per unit ($21,400 ÷ 100,000 units = $0.214 per unit).

Before going further, notice in the second section of the grinding department's process cost summary that the equivalent finished unit cost for materials is $0.11, for labor is $0.06, and for overhead is $0.045, a total of $0.215. Notice, however, in the third section of the summary that the unit cost of the 100,000 units finished and transferred is $0.214, which is less than $0.215. It is less because costs were less in the department during the previous month and the 30,000 beginning units were one-third processed at these lower costs.

The grinding department's process cost summary is completed by assigning costs to the ending inventory, and after it was completed the accountant prepared the following entry to transfer from the grinding department to the mixing department the cost of the 100,000 units processed in the department and transferred during April. Information for the entry as to the cost of the units transferred was taken from the third section of Illustration 23–9.

Apr.	30	Goods in Process, Mixing Department	21,400.00	
		Goods in Process, Grinding Department ...		21,400.00
		To transfer the cost of the 100,000 units of product transferred to the mixing department.		

Posting the entry had the effect on the accounts shown in Illustration 23–10. Observe that the effect is one of transferring and advancing costs from one department to the next just as the product is transferred and advanced in the manufacturing procedure.

After posting the entry transferring to the mixing department the grinding department costs of the units transferred, the cost accountant prepared a process cost summary for the mixing department. Information required in its preparation was taken from the mixing department's goods in process account and production report. The summary appeared as in Illustration 23–11.

Goods in Process, Grinding Department

Date		Explanation	Debit	Credit	Balance
Apr.	1	Beginning inventory			4,250
	30	Materials	9,900		14,150
	30	Labor	5,700		19,850
	30	Overhead	4,275		24,125
	30	Units to mixing department		21,400	2,725

Goods in Process, Mixing Department

Date		Explanation	Debit	Credit	Balance
Apr.	1	Beginning inventory			3,785
	30	Materials	2,040		5,825
	30	Labor	3,570		9,395
	30	Overhead	1,020		10,415
	30	Units from grinding department	21,400		31,815

Illustration 23–10

Two points in Illustration 23–11 require special attention. The first is the calculation of equivalent finished units. Since the materials, labor, and overhead added in the mixing department are all added evenly throughout the process of this department, only a single equivalent unit calculation is required. This differs from the grinding department, the previous department, where two equivalent unit calculations were required. Two were required because material was not placed in process at the same stage in the processing procedure as were the labor and overhead.

The second point needing special attention in the mixing department cost summary is the method of handling the grinding department costs transferred to this department. During April, 100,000 units of product, with accumulated grinding department costs of $21,400, were transferred to the mixing department. Of these 100,000 units, 85,000 were started in process in the department, finished, and transferred to finished goods. The remaining 15,000 were still in process in the department at the end of the cost period.

Notice in the first section of Illustration 23–11 how the $21,400 of grinding department costs transferred to the mixing department are added to the other costs charged to the department. Compare the information in this first section with the mixing department's goods in process account as it is shown on page 782 and again in Illustration 23–10.

Notice again in the third section of the mixing department's process cost summary how the $21,400 of grinding department costs are apportioned between the 85,000 units started and finished and the 15,000

Delta Processing Company
Process Cost Summary, Mixing Department
For Month Ended April 30, 19—

COSTS CHARGED TO THE DEPARTMENT:

Materials requisitioned	$ 2,040
Labor charged	3,570
Overhead costs incurred	1,020
Total processing costs	$ 6,630
Goods in process at the beginning of the month	3,785
Cost transferred from the grinding department (100,000 units at $0.214 each)	21,400
Total costs to be accounted for	$31,815

EQUIVALENT UNIT PROCESSING COSTS:

	Units involved	Fraction of a unit added	Equivalent units added
Materials, labor, and overhead:			
Beginning inventory	16,000	¾	12,000
Units started and finished........................	85,000	One	85,000
Ending inventory	15,000	⅓	5,000
Total equivalent units			102,000

Equivalent unit processing cost for materials: $2,040 ÷ 102,000 = $0.02
Equivalent unit processing cost for labor: $3,570 ÷ 102,000 = $0.035
Equivalent unit processing cost for overhead: $1,020 ÷ 102,000 = $0.01

COSTS APPLICABLE TO THE WORK OF THE DEPARTMENT:

Goods in process, one-fourth completed at the beginning of April:		
Costs charged to the beginning inventory of goods in process during previous month...	$ 3,785	
Materials added (12,000 × $0.02)...................................	240	
Labor applied (12,000 × $0.035)....................................	420	
Overhead applied (12,000 × $0.01).................................	120	
Cost to process		$ 4,565
Goods started and finished in the department during April:		
Costs in the grinding department (85,000 × $0.214)...................	$18,190	
Materials added (85,000 × $0.02)...................................	1,700	
Labor applied (85,000 × $0.035)....................................	2,975	
Overhead applied (85,000 × $0.01).................................	850	
Cost to process		23,715
Total accumulated cost of goods transferred to finished goods (101,000 units at $0.28)		$28,280
Goods in process, one-third processed at the end of April:		
Costs in the grinding department (15,000 × $0.214)...................	$ 3,210	
Materials added (5,000 × $0.02)...................................	100	
Labor applied (5,000 × $0.035)....................................	175	
Overhead applied (5,000 × $0.01).................................	50	
Cost to one-third process..		3,535
Total costs accounted for......................................		$31,815

Illustration 23–11

units still in process in the department. The 16,000 beginning goods in process units received none of this $21,400 charge because they were transferred from the grinding department during the previous month. Their grinding department costs are included in the $3,785 beginning inventory costs.

The third section of the mixing department's process cost summary shows that 101,000 units of product (16,000 beginning inventory units plus 85,000 started and finished) with accumulated costs of $28,280 were completed in the department during April and transferred to finished goods. The cost accountant used the entry below to transfer the accumulated cost of these 101,000 units from the mixing department's goods in process account to the finished goods account. Posting the entry had the effect shown in Illustration 23–12.

Apr.	30	Finished Goods	28,280.00	
		Goods in Process, Mixing Department		28,280.00
		To transfer the accumulated grinding department and mixing department costs of the 101,000 units transferred to Finished Goods.		

Goods in Process, Mixing Department

Date		Explanation	Debit	Credit	Balance
Apr.	1	Beginning inventory			3,785
	30	Materials	2,040		5,825
	30	Labor	3,570		9,395
	30	Overhead	1,020		10,415
	30	Units from grinding department	21,400		31,815
	30	Units to finished goods		28,280	3,535

Finished Goods

Date		Explanation	Debit	Credit	Balance
Apr.	30	Units from mixing department	28,280		28,280

Illustration 23–12

GLOSSARY

Cost accounting system. An accounting system based on perpetual inventory records that is designed to emphasize the determination of unit costs and the control of costs.

Equivalent finished units. A measure of production with respect to materials or labor, expressed as the number of units that could have been manufactured from start to finish during a period given the amount of materials or labor used during the period.

Job. A special production order to meet customers' specifications.

Job Cost Ledger. A subsidiary ledger to the Goods in Process account in which are kept the job cost sheets of unfinished jobs.

Job cost sheet. A record of the costs incurred on a single job.

Job lot. A quantity of identical items manufactured in one lot or single order.

Job order cost system. A cost accounting system in which costs are assembled in terms of jobs or job lots.

Labor time ticket. A record of how an employee's time was spent on the job that serves as the basis for charging jobs and overhead accounts for the employee's wages.

Overapplied overhead. The amount by which overhead applied on the basis of a predetermined overhead application rate exceeds overhead actually incurred.

Predetermined overhead application rate. A rate that is used to charge overhead cost to production; calculated by relating estimated overhead cost for a period to another variable such as estimated direct labor cost.

Process cost system. A cost accounting system in which costs are assembled in terms of steps in manufacturing a product.

Requisition. A document that identifies the materials needed for a certain job and the account to which the materials cost should be charged, and that is given to a storeroom keeper in exchange for the materials.

Underapplied overhead. The amount by which actual overhead incurred exceeds the overhead applied to production, based on a predetermined application rate and evidenced by a debit balance in the overhead account.

QUESTIONS FOR CLASS DISCUSSION

1. What are the two primary types of cost accounting systems? Indicate which of the two would best fit the needs of a manufacturer who (a) produces special-purpose machines designed to fit the particular needs of each customer, (b) produces electric generators in lots of 10, and (c) manufactures copper tubing.

2. Define the following terms in the context of cost accounting:
   a. Job order cost system.
   b. Process cost system.
   c. Job.
   d. Job lot.

e. Job cost sheet. g. Materials requisition.

f. Labor time ticket. h. Process cost summary.

3. The Materials account and the Goods in Process account each serves as a control account for a subsidiary ledger. What subsidiary ledgers do these accounts control?

4. How is the inventory of goods in process determined in a general accounting system like that described in Chapter 22? How may this inventory be determined in a job cost system?

5. What is the purpose of a job cost sheet? What is the name of the ledger containing the job cost sheets of the unfinished jobs in process? What account controls this ledger?

6. What business papers are the bases for the job cost sheet entries for (a) materials and (b) labor?

7. Refer to the job cost sheet of Illustration 23–3. How was the amount of overhead costs charged to this job determined?

8. How is a predetermined overhead application rate established? Why is such a predetermined rate used to charge overhead to jobs?

9. Why does a company using a job cost system normally have either overapplied or underapplied overhead at the end of each accounting period?

10. At the end of a cost period the Overhead Costs controlling account has a debit balance. Does this represent overapplied or underapplied overhead?

11. What are the basic differences in the products and in the manufacturing procedures of a company to which a job cost system is applicable as opposed to a company to which a process cost system is applicable?

12. What is an equivalent finished unit of labor? Of materials?

13. What is the assumption on which the idea of an equivalent finished unit of, for instance, labor is based?

14. What is the production of a department measured in equivalent finished units if it began an accounting period with 8,000 units of product that were one-fourth completed at the beginning of the period, started and finished 50,000 units during the period, and ended the period with 6,000 units that were one-third processed at the period end?

15. The process cost summary of a department commonly has three sections. What is shown in each section?

CLASS EXERCISES

Exercise 23–1

Part 1. In December 198A, Fardo Company's cost accountant established the company's 198B overhead application rate based on direct labor cost. In setting the rate, the cost accountant estimated Fardo Company would incur $240,000 of overhead costs during 198B and it would apply $160,000 of direct labor to the products that would be manufactured during 198B. Determine the rate.

Part 2. During February, 198B, Fardo Company began and completed Job No. 874. Determine the job's cost under the assumption that on its completion the job's cost sheet showed the following materials and labor charged to it:

JOB COST SHEET

Customer's Name   Shafer Motors   Job No.   874

Job Description   No. 3 Pump

Date	Materials		Labor		Overhead Costs Applied		
	Requisition Number	Amount	Time Ticket Number	Amount	Date	Rate	Amount
Feb. 2	1524	68.00	2116	12.00			
3	1527	47.00	2117	20.00			
4	1531	10.00	2122	16.00			

Exercise 23–2

In December 198A, a company's cost accountant established the following overhead application rate for applying overhead to the jobs that would be completed by the company during 198B:

$$\frac{\text{Estimated overhead costs, \$152,000}}{\text{Estimated direct labor costs, \$95,000}} = 160\%$$

At the end of 198B the company's accounting records showed that $158,000 of overhead costs had actually been incurred during 198B and $100,000 of direct labor, distributed as follows, had been applied to jobs during the year.

Direct labor on jobs completed and sold	$ 80,000
Direct labor on jobs completed and in the finished goods inventory	15,000
Direct labor on jobs still in process	5,000
Total	$100,000

Required:

1. Set up an Overhead Costs T-account and enter on the proper sides the amounts of overhead costs incurred and applied. State whether overhead was overapplied or underapplied during the year.
2. Give the entry to close the Overhead Costs account and allocate its balance between jobs sold, jobs finished but unsold, and jobs in process.

Exercise 23–3

Buzzer Company uses a job cost system in which overhead is charged to jobs on the basis of direct labor cost, and at the end of a year the company's Goods in Process account showed the following:

Goods in Process

Materials	175,00	To finished goods	391,000
Labor	75,000		
Overhead	150,000		

Required:

1. Determine the overhead application rate used by the company.
2. Determine the cost of the labor and the cost of the overhead charged to the one job in process at the year-end under the assumption it had $4,000 of materials charged to it.

Exercise 23–4

During a cost period a department finished and transferred 25,000 units of product to finished goods, of which 5,000 units were in process in the department at the beginning of the cost period and 20,000 were begun and completed during the period. The 5,000 beginning inventory units were three-fifths completed when the period began. In addition to the transferred units, 6,000 additional units were in process in the department, one-third completed when the period ended.

Required:

1. Calculate the equivalent units of product completed in the department during the cost period.
2. Under the assumption that $12,000 of labor was used in processing the units worked on in the department during the period, and that labor is applied evenly throughout the process of the department, determine the cost of an equivalent unit of labor.
3. Determine the shares of the $12,000 of labor cost that should be charged to each of the inventories and to the units begun and completed during the period.

Exercise 23–5

A department completed 56,000 units of product during a cost period, of which 16,000 units were in process at the beginning of the period and 40,000 units were begun and completed during the period. The beginning inventory units were one-fourth processed when the period began. In addition to the completed units, 9,000 more units were in process in the department and were two-thirds processed when the period ended.

Required:

Calculate the equivalent units of material added to the product of the department under each of the following unrelated assumptions: *(a)* All the material added to the product of the department is added when its process is first begun. *(b)* The material added to the product of the department is added evenly throughout the process. *(c)* One half the material added in the department is added when the product is first begun, and the other half is added when the product is three-fifths completed.

PROBLEMS

Problem 23–1

During December 198A, a company's cost accountant established the 198B overhead application rate by estimating the company would assign four persons to direct labor tasks in 198B and that each person would work 2,000 hours at $8.50 per hour during the year. At the same time the accountant estimated the company would incur the following amounts of overhead costs during 198B:

Indirect labor	$34,500
Depreciation of factory building	10,300
Depreciation of machinery	18,000
Machinery repairs	3,200
Heat, lights, and power	6,900
Property taxes, factory	6,800
Factory supplies expense	1,900
Total	$81,600

At the end of 198B the accounting records showed the company had actually incurred $78,200 of overhead costs during the year while completing five jobs and beginning the sixth. The completed jobs were assigned overhead on completion, and the in-process job was assigned overhead at the year-end. The jobs had the following direct labor costs:

Job 207 (sold and delivered)	$11,900
Job 208 (sold and delivered)	12,100
Job 209 (sold and delivered)	13,300
Job 210 (sold and delivered)	12,200
Job 211 (in finished goods inventory)	13,200
Job 212 (in process, unfinished)	3,300
Total	$66,000

Required:

1. Determine the overhead application rate established by the cost accountant under the assumption it was based on direct labor cost.
2. Determine the total overhead applied to jobs during the year and the amount of over- or underapplied overhead at the year-end.
3. Prepare the general journal entry to dispose of the over- or underapplied overhead by prorating it between goods in process, finished goods, and goods sold.

Problem 23–2

Soaper Manufacturing Company completed the following external and internal transactions during its first cost period:

a. Purchased materials on account, $21,000.
b. Paid the wages of factory employees, $18,650.

c. Paid miscellaneous overhead costs, $2,600.

d. Material requisitions were used during the cost period to charge materials to jobs. The requisitions were then accumulated until the end of the cost period when they were totaled and recorded with a general journal entry. (Instructions for the entry are given in item j.) An abstract of the requisitions showed the following amounts of materials charged to jobs. (Charge the materials to the jobs by making entries directly in the job T-accounts in the subsidiary Job Cost Ledger.)

Job No. 1	$ 3,950
Job No. 2	1,950
Job No. 3	4;200
Job No. 4	4,450
Job No. 5	850
Total	$15,400

e. Labor time tickets were used to charge jobs with direct labor. The time tickets were then accumulated until the end of the cost period when they were totaled and recorded with a general journal entry. (Instructions for the entry are given in item k.) An abstract of the tickets showed the following amounts of labor charged to the several jobs. (Charge the labor to the several jobs by making entries directly in the job T-accounts in the Job Cost Ledger.)

Job No. 1	$ 3,600
Job No. 2	2,100
Job No. 3	3,900
Job No. 4	4,200
Job No. 5	450
Total	$14,250

f. Job Nos. 1, 3, and 4 were completed and transferred to finished goods. A predetermined overhead application rate of 160% of direct labor cost was used to apply overhead to each job upon its completion. (Enter the overhead in the job T-accounts; mark the jobs "completed"; and make a general journal entry to transfer their costs to the Finished Goods account.)

g. Job Nos. 1 and 3 were sold on account for a total of $38,000.

h. At the end of the cost period, charged overhead to the uncompleted jobs at the rate of 160% of direct labor cost. (Enter the overhead in the job T-accounts.)

i. At the end of the cost period made an adjusting entry to record:

Depreciation of factory building	$ 3,500
Depreciation of machinery	6,300
Expired factory insurance	1,000
Accrued factory taxes payable	1,800
Total	$12,600

j. Separated the material requisitions into direct material requisitions and indirect material requisitions, totaled each kind, and made a general journal entry to record them. The requisition totals were:

Direct materials	$15,400
Indirect materials	3,000
Total	$18,400

k. Separated the labor time tickets into direct labor time tickets and indirect labor time tickets, totaled each kind, and made a general journal entry to record them. The ticket totals were:

Direct labor	$14,250
Indirect labor	4,650
Total	$18,900

l. Determined the total overhead assigned to all jobs and made a general journal entry to record it.

Required:

1. Open the following general ledger T-account: Materials, Goods in Process, Finished Goods, Factory Payroll, Overhead Costs, and Cost of Goods Sold.
2. Open an additional T-account for each of the five jobs. Assume that each job's T-account is a job cost sheet in a subsidiary Job Cost Ledger.
3. Prepare general journal entries to record the applicable information of items a, b, c, f, g, i, j, k, and l. Post the portions of the entries affecting the general ledger accounts.
4. Enter the applicable information of items d, e, f, and h directly in the T-accounts that represent job cost sheets.
5. Present statistics to prove the balances of the Goods in Process and Finished Goods accounts.
6. List the general ledger accounts and tell what is represented by the balance of each.

Problem 23–3

(If the working papers that accompany this text are not being used, omit this problem.)

Top Job Shop manufactures to the special order of its customers a machine called a tiptop. On April 1 the company had a $4,090 materials inventory but no inventories of goods in process or finished goods. However, on that date it began Job No. 1, a tiptop for Big Company, and Job No. 2, a tiptop for Little Company. It then completed the following summarized internal and external transactions:

1. Recorded invoices for the purchase of 350 units of Material X and 260 units of Material Y on credit. The invoices and receiving reports carried this information.

Receiving Report No. 1, Material X, 350 units at $5 each.
Receiving Report No. 2, Material Y, 260 units at $10 each.

(Record the invoices with a single journal entry and post to the general ledger T-accounts, using the transaction numbers to identify the amounts in the accounts. Enter the receiving report information on the proper materials ledger cards.)

2. Requisitioned materials as follows:

Requisition No. 1, for Job 1 . . . . 200 units of Material X
Requisition No. 2, for Job 1 . . . . 230 units of Material Y
Requisition No. 3, for Job 2 . . . . 90 units of Material X
Requisition No. 4, for Job 2 . . . . 200 units of Material Y
Requisition No. 5, for ten units of machinery lubricant.
(Enter the requisition amounts for direct materials on the materials ledger cards and on the job cost sheets. Enter the indirect material amount on the proper materials ledger card and debit it to the Indirect Materials account in the subsidiary Overhead Costs Ledger. Assume the requisitions are accumulated until the end of the month and will be recorded with a general journal entry. Instructions for the entry follow in the problem.)

3. Received time tickets from the timekeeping department as follows:
Time tickets Nos. 1 through 50 for direct labor on Job No. 1, $1,200.
Time tickets Nos. 51 through 90 for direct labor on Job No. 2, $1,000.
Time tickets Nos. 91 through 100 for machinery repairs, $375.
(Charge the direct labor time tickets to the proper jobs; charge the indirect labor time tickets to the Indirect Labor account in the Subsidiary Overhead Costs Ledger. Assume the tickets are accumulated until the end of the month for recording with a general journal entry.)

4. Made the following cash disbursements during the month:
Paid factory payrolls totaling $2,350 during the April cost period.
Paid for miscellaneous overhead items totaling $1,200.
(Record the payments with general journal entries and post to the ledger accounts. Enter the charge for miscellaneous overhead items in the Subsidiary Overhead Costs Ledger.)

5. Finished Job No. 1 and transferred it to the finished goods warehouse.
(Top Job Shop charges overhead to each job on completion by means of a predetermined overhead application rate based on direct labor costs. The rate is 70%. Enter the overhead charge (1) on the cost sheet of Job No. 1. (2) Complete the cost summary section of the cost sheet. (3) Mark "Finished" on the cost sheet. (4) Prepare and post a general journal entry to record completion of the job and its transfer to finished goods.)

6. Prepared and posted a general journal entry to record the sale on credit of Job No. 1 to Big Company for $8,500.

7. At the end of the April cost period, charged overhead to Job. No. 2 based on the direct labor applied to the job in April. *(Enter the applicable amount of overhead on the job's cost sheet.)*

8. Totaled the requisitions for direct materials, totaled the requisitions for indirect materials, and made and posted a general journal entry to record them.

9. Totaled the direct labor time tickets, totaled the indirect labor time tickets, and made and posted a general journal entry to record them.

10. Determined the amount of overhead applied to jobs and made and posted a general journal entry to record it.

Required:

a. Record the transactions as instructed in the narrative.

b. Complete the statements in the book of working papers by filling in the blanks.

Problem 23-4

A department that produces a product on a continuous basis incurred $9,520 of labor cost during the cost period just ended. During the period the department completed and transferred 27,500 units of its product to finished goods. Of these 27,500 units, 4,500 were in process in the department when the period began and 23,000 were begun and completed during the period. The 4,500 beginning inventory units were one-third finished when the period began. In addition to the transferred units, 8,000 other units were in process in the department and were one-fourth finished when the period ended.

Required:

Calculate (1) the equivalent units of labor applied to the product of the department during the cost period, (2) the cost of an equivalent unit of labor, and (3) the shares of the $9,520 of labor cost applicable to the beginning inventory, the units started and finished, and the ending inventory. Assume that labor is added to the product of the department evenly throughout its process.

Problem 23-5

Crafter Processing Company manufactures a simple product on a continuous basis in a single department. All materials are added in the manufacturing process when the process is first begun. Labor and overhead are added evenly throughout the process.

During the current April cost period the company completed and transferred to finished goods a total of 50,000 units of product. These consisted of 15,000 units that were in process at the beginning of the cost period and 35,000 units that were begun and finished during the period. The 15,000 beginning goods in process units were complete as to materials and one-fifth complete as to labor and overhead when the period began.

In addition to the completed units, 9,000 other units were in process at the end of the period, complete as to materials and one-third complete as to labor and overhead.

Since the company has but one processing department, it has only one Goods in Process account in its ledger. At the end of the period, after entries recording materials, labor, and overhead had been posted, the account appeared as follows:

Goods in Process

Date		Explanation	Debit	Credit	Balance
Apr.	1	Balance			6,474.00
	30	Materials	14,564.00		21,038.00
	30	Labor	13,800.00		34,838.00
	30	Overhead	10,850.00		45,688.00

Required:

Prepare a process cost summary and a general journal entry to transfer to finished goods the cost of the product completed by the company during April.

Problem 23–6

Iron Products Company manufactures a product that is processed in two departments, the casting department and the polishing department. The product is begun in the casting department and completed in the polishing department. All materials used in the product are added in the casting department, and labor and overhead are applied. The product is then complete insofar as the casting department is concerned and is transferred to the polishing department where more labor and overhead, but no additional materials, are added to complete the product, which is then transferred to finished goods.

At the end of the April cost period, after entries charging the polishing department with labor and overhead costs and the cost of the units transferred to it from the casting department were posted, the goods in process account of the polishing department appeared as follows:

Goods in Process, Polishing Department

Date	Explanation	Debit	Credit	Balance
Apr. 1	Balance (3,900 units, one-third processed)			7,325.00
30	Labor	4,650.00		11,975.00
30	Overhead	12,450.00		24,425.00
30	Cost of 14,400 units transferred from casting department	21,600.00		46,025.00

There were no units lost or spoiled in the polishing department during April, and 15,900 units were completed in the department during the month and were transferred to finished goods, leaving 2,400 units in the department that were one-sixth processed at the month end.

Required:

1. Prepare a process cost summary for the department under the assumption that labor and overhead are added evenly throughout the department's process.
2. Prepare the entry to transfer to finished goods the cost of the 15,900 units finished in the department during April.

ALTERNATE PROBLEMS

Problem 23–1A

A company's cost accountant estimated before a year began that the company would incur during the ensuing year the direct labor of 6 persons working 2,000 hours each at an average rate of $10.50 per hour. The accountant also estimated the concern would incur the following overhead costs during the year.

Indirect labor	$ 28,800
Depreciation of factory building	18,500
Depreciation of machinery..................	32,600
Machinery repairs	5,400
Heat, lights, and power	12,700
Property taxes, factory.....................	10,800
Factory supplies	4,600
Total	$113,400

At the end of the year for which the cost estimates were made the company's records showed that it had actually incurred $114,500 of overhead costs during the year and that it had completed five jobs and had begun the sixth. The completed jobs were assigned overhead on completion, and the in-process job was assigned overhead at the year-end. The jobs had the following direct labor costs:

Job No. 203 (sold and delivered)	$ 24,450
Job No. 204 (sold and delivered)	26,800
Job No. 205 (sold and delivered)	20,100
Job No. 206 (sold and delivered)	28,650
Job No. 207 (in finished goods inventory)	18,750
Job No. 208 (in process, unfinished)	6,250
Total	$125,000

Required:

Under the assumption the concern used a predetermined overhead application rate based on the cost accountant's estimates of overhead and direct labor costs in applying overhead to the six jobs, determine: (1) the predetermined overhead application rate used, (2) the total overhead applied to jobs during the year, and (3) the over- or underapplied overhead at the year-end. (4) Prepare a general journal entry to close the Overhead Costs account and to prorate its balance between goods in process, finished goods, and goods sold.

Problem 23–2A

Hydrex Company completed the following transactions, among others, during a cost period:

a. Purchased materials on credit, $12,200.
b. Paid factory wages, $11,800.
c. Paid miscellaneous factory overhead costs, $800.
d. Material requisitions were used during the cost period to charge materials to jobs. The requisitions were then accumulated until the end of the cost period when they were totaled and recorded with a general journal entry. (Instructions for the entry are given in item *j.*) An abstract of the requisitions showed the following materials charged to jobs. (Charge the materials to the jobs by making entries directly in the job T-accounts in the subsidiary Job Cost Ledger.)

Job No. 1	$2,500
Job No. 2	2,000
Job No. 3	2,400
Job No. 4	2,100
Job No. 5	800
Total	$9,800

e. Labor time tickets were used to charge jobs with direct labor. The time tickets were then accumulated until the end of the cost period when they were totaled and recorded with a general journal entry. (Instructions for the entry are given in item *k*.) An abstract of the tickets showed the following labor charged to the several jobs. (Charge the labor to the jobs by making entries directly in the job T-accounts in the Job Cost Ledger.)

Job No. 1	$2,200
Job No. 2	1,600
Job No. 3	2,100
Job No. 4	1,900
Job No. 5	600
Total	$8,400

f. Job Nos. 1, 3, and 4 were completed and transferred to finished goods. A predetermined overhead application rate of 140% of direct labor cost was used to apply overhead to each job upon its completion. (Enter the overhead in the job T-accounts; mark the jobs "completed"; and make a general journal entry to transfer their cost to the Finished Goods account.)

g. Job Nos. 1 and 3 were sold on credit for a total of $22,500.

h. At the end of the cost period, charged overhead to the uncompleted jobs at the rate of 140% of direct labor cost. (Enter the overhead in the job T-accounts.)

i. At the end of the cost period, made an entry to record depreciation on the factory building, $1,500; depreciation on the machinery, $3,300; expired factory insurance, $400; and accrued factory taxes payable, $300.

j. Separated the material requisitions into direct material requisitions and indirect material requisitions, totaled each kind, and made a general journal entry to record them. The requisition totals were:

Direct materials	$ 9,800
Indirect materials	1,800
Total	$11,600

k. Separated the labor time tickets into direct labor time tickets and indirect labor time tickets, totaled each kind, and made a general journal entry to record them. The ticket totals were:

Direct labor	$ 8,400
Indirect labor	3,500
Total	$11,900

l. Determined the total overhead charged to all jobs and made a general journal entry to record it.

Required:

1. Open the following general ledger T-accounts: Materials, Goods in Process, Finished Goods, Factory Payroll, Overhead Costs, and Costs of Goods Sold.
2. Open an additional T-account for each of the five jobs. Assume that each job's T-account is a job cost sheet in a subsidiary Job Cost Ledger.
3. Prepare general journal entries to record the applicable information of items *a, b, c, f, g, i, j, k,* and *l.* Post the portions of the entries affecting the general ledger accounts.
4. Enter the applicable information of items *d, e, f,* and *h* directly in the T-accounts that represent job cost sheets.
5. Present statistics to prove the balances of the Goods in Process and Finished Goods accounts.
6. List the general ledger accounts and tell what is represented by the balance of each.

Problem 23–3A

(If the working papers that accompany this text are not being used, omit this problem.)

Valley Company manufactures to the special order of its customers a machine called a dripdrop. On April 1 of the current year the company had a $4,090 materials inventory but no inventories of goods in process or finished goods. However, on that date it began Job No. 1, a dripdrop for Big Company, and Job No. 2, a dripdrop for Little Company; and during April it completed the following summarized internal and external transactions:

1. Recorded invoices for the purchase on credit of 450 units of Material X and 50 units of Material Y. The invoices and receiving reports carried this information:

    Receiving Report No. 1, Raw Material X, 450 units at $5 each
    Receiving Report No. 2, Raw Material Y, 50 units at $10 each

    (Record the invoices with a single journal entry and post to the general ledger T-accounts, using the transaction numbers to identify the amounts in the accounts. Enter the receiving report information on the proper materials ledger cards.)
2. Requisitioned materials as follows:

    Requisition No. 1, for Job No. 1 .... 220 units of Material X
    Requisition No. 2, for Job No. 1 .... 60 units of Material Y
    Requisition No. 3, for Job No. 2 .... 176 units of Material X
    Requisition No. 4, for Job No. 2 .... 50 units of Material Y
    Requisition No. 5, for 20 units of machinery lubricant.

    (Enter the requisition amounts for direct materials on the materials ledger cards and on the job cost sheets. Enter the indirect material amount on the proper materials ledger card and debit it to the Indirect Materials account in the subsidiary Overhead Costs Ledger. Assume the requisitions are accumulated until the end of the month and will be recorded with a general journal entry. Instructions for this entry follow in the problem.)
3. Received time tickets from the timekeeping department as follows:

    Time tickets Nos. 1 through 60 for direct labor on Job No. 1, $1,000.

Time tickets Nos. 61 through 100 for direct labor on Job No. 2, $800.
Time tickets Nos. 101 through 120 for machinery repairs, $350.

(Charge the direct labor tickets to the proper jobs and charge the indirect labor time tickets to the Indirect Labor account in the Subsidiary Overhead Costs Ledger. Assume the time tickets are accumulated until the end of the month for recording with a general journal entry.)

4. Made the following cash disbursements during the month:

Paid factory payrolls totaling $2,000.

Paid for miscellaneous overhead items totaling $950.

(Record the payments with general journal entries and post to the general ledger accounts. Enter the charge for miscellaneous overhead items in the Subsidiary Overhead Costs Ledger.)

5. Finished Job No. 1 and transferred it to the finished goods warehouse. *(The company charges overhead to each job by means of a predetermined overhead application rate based on direct labor costs. The rate is 75%. (1) Enter the overhead charge on the cost sheet of Job No. 1. (2) Complete the cost summary section of the cost sheet. (3) Mark "Finished" on the cost sheet. (4) Prepare and post a general journal entry to record completion of the job and its transfer to finished goods.)*

6. Prepared and posted a general journal entry to record both the cost of goods sold and the sale of Job No. 1 to Big Company for $4,700.

7. At the end of the cost period, charged overhead to Job No. 2 based on the amount of direct labor applied to the job thus far. *(Enter the applicable amount of overhead on the job's cost sheet.)*

8. Totaled the requisitions for direct materials, totaled the requisitions for indirect materials, and made and posted a general journal entry to record them.

9. Totaled the direct labor time tickets, totaled the indirect labor time tickets, and made and posted a general journal entry to record them.

10. Determined the amount of overhead applied to jobs and made and posted a general journal entry to record it.

Required:

a. Record the transactions as instructed in the narrative.

b. Complete the statements in the book of working papers by filling in the blanks.

Problem 23–4A

A department in which labor is added evenly throughout its process incurred $18,500 of labor cost during a period in which it completed 52,000 units of product. Of these 52,000 units, 8,000 were in process in the department, three-fourths processed when the period began and 44,000 were begun and completed during the period. In addition to the completed units, 10,000 other units were in process in the department and were two-fifths processed at the period end.

Required:

Determine (1) the equivalent units of labor applied to the product of the department during the period, (2) the cost of an equivalent unit of labor, and (3) the shares of the $18,500 of labor cost that should be charged to the beginning inventory, the units started and finished, and the ending inventory.

Problem 23–5A

Ferro-Box Company manufactures a product that is processed in two departments, the mixing department and the drying department. At the end of the May cost period the mixing department reported the following: beginning goods in process inventory, 5,000 units, three-fifths completed at the beginning of the period; units started and finished during the cost period, 13,000; and ending inventory of goods in process, 4,000 units, one-fourth completed.

The company assumes that all materials, labor, and overhead applied to the product in the mixing department are applied evenly throughout the department's process; and after all material, labor, and overhead costs had been charged to the department, its goods in process account appeared as follows:

Goods in Process, Mixing Department

Date		Explanation	Debit	Credit	Balance
May	1	Balance			1,878.00
	31	Materials	3,520.00		5,398.00
	31	Labor	4,000.00		9,398.00
	31	Overhead	2,400.00		11,798.00

Required:

Prepare a process summary for the mixing department and draft the general journal entry to transfer to the drying department the cost of the product finished in the mixing department and transferred.

PROVOCATIVE PROBLEMS

Provocative problem 23–1
Abner Manufacturing Company

Abner Manufacturing Company uses a job cost system in accounting for manufacturing costs, and following are a number of its general ledger accounts with the January 1 balances and some January postings shown. The postings are incomplete. Commonly only the debit or credit of a journal entry appears in the accounts, with the offsetting debits and credits being omitted. Also, the amounts shown represent total postings for the month and no date appears. However, this additional information is available: (1) The company charges jobs with overhead on the basis of direct labor cost, using a 75% overhead application rate. (2) The $13,000 debit in the Overhead Costs account represents the sum of all overhead costs for January other than indirect materials and indirect labor. (3) The accrued factory payroll on January 31 was $2,000.

Materials		
Jan. 1 bal. 9,000	11,000	
14,000		

Factory Payroll		
21,000	Jan. 1 bal. 1,000	

Goods in Process		
Jan. 1 bal. 5,000	44,000	
Materials 10,000		
Labor 20,000		

Cost of Goods Sold	

Finished Goods		
Jan. 1 bal. 8,000	45,000	

Factory Overhead Costs	
13,000	

Copy the accounts on a sheet of paper, supply the missing debits and credits, and use key letters to tie together the debits and credits of the entries. Answer these questions: (1) What was the January 31 balance of the Finished Goods account? (2) How many dollars of factory payroll were paid during January? (3) What was the cost of goods sold during January? (4) How much overhead was actually incurred during the month? (5) How much overhead was charged to jobs during the month? (6) Was overhead overapplied or underapplied during the month?

Provocative problem 23–2
Dunsmoor Company

On May 17, 198B, a fire destroyed the plant, the inventories, and some of the accounting records of the Dunsmoor Company, and you have been asked to determine for insurance purposes the amounts of raw materials, goods in process, and finished goods destroyed. The company used a job order cost system, and you were able to obtain this additional information:

a. The company's December 31, 198A, balance sheet showed the following inventory amounts: materials, $12,000; goods in process, $15,000; and finished goods, $18,000. The balance sheet also showed a $2,000 liability for accrued factory wages payable.

b. The company's predetermined overhead application rate was 80% of direct labor cost.

c. Goods costing $75,000 were sold and delivered to customers between January 1 and May 17, 198B.

d. Materials costing $26,000 were purchased between January 1 and May 17, and $24,000 of direct and indirect materials were issued to the factory.

e. Factory wages totaling $29,000 were paid between January 1 and May 17, and on the latter date there were $1,000 of accrued factory wages payable.

f. The debits to the Overhead Costs account during the period before the fire totaled $19,000 of which $2,000 was for indirect materials and $3,000 was for indirect labor.

g. Goods costing $72,000 were finished and transferred to finished goods between January 1 and May 17.

h. It was decided that the May 17 balance of the Overhead Costs account should be apportioned between goods in process, finished goods, and cost of goods sold. Between January 1 and May 17 the company had charged the following amounts of overhead to jobs: to jobs sold, $14,000; to jobs finished but unsold, $4,000; and to jobs still in process on May 17, $2,000.

Determine the May 17 inventories of materials, goods in process, and finished goods. (T-accounts may be helpful in organizing the data.)

PART EIGHT
Planning and controlling business operations

After studying Chapter 24, you should be able to:

- ☐ Explain the importance of budgeting.
- ☐ Describe the specific benefits to be derived from budgeting.
- ☐ List the sequence of steps involved in preparing a master budget.
- ☐ Prepare each budget in a master budget and explain the importance of each budget to the overall budgeting process.
- ☐ Integrate the individual budgets into planned financial statements.
- ☐ Define or explain the words and phrases listed in the chapter Glossary.

The master budget: A formal plan for the business

■ The process of managing a business consists of two basic elements: planning and control. If a business is to accomplish the variety of objectives expected of it, management must first carefully plan the activities and events the business should enter and accomplish during future weeks, months, and years. Then, as the activities take place, they must be monitored and controlled so that actual events conform as closely as possible to the plan.

The management functions of planning and control are perhaps equally important to ensure the long-run success of a business. Nevertheless, most business failures are said to result from inadequate planning. Countless pitfalls can be avoided if management carefully anticipates the future conditions within which the business will operate and prepares a detailed plan of the activities the business should pursue. Furthermore, the plans for future business activities should be formally organized and preserved. This process of planning future business actions and expressing those plans in a formal manner is called *budgeting*. Correspondingly, a *budget* is a formal statement of future plans. Since the economic or financial aspects of the business are the primary matters of consideration, a budget is usually expressed in monetary terms.

THE MASTER BUDGET

When the plan to be formalized is a comprehensive or overall plan for the business, the resulting budget is called a *master budget*. As an overall plan, the master budget should include specific plans for expected sales, the units of product to be produced, the materials or merchandise to be purchased, the expense payments to be made, the long-term assets to be purchased, and the amount of cash to be borrowed, if any. The planned activities of each subunit of the business should be separately organized and presented within the master budget. Thus, the master budget for a business consists of several sub-budgets, all of which articulate or join with each other to form the overall, coordinated plan for the business. As finally presented, the master budget typically includes sales, expense, production, equipment, and cash budgets. Also, the expected impact of the planned future activities may be expressed in terms of a planned income statement for the budget period and a planned balance sheet for the end of the budget period.

BENEFITS FROM BUDGETING

All business managements engage in planning; some planning is absolutely necessary if business activities are to continue. However, a typical characteristic of poor management is sloppy or incomplete planning. But, if management plans carefully and formalizes its plans completely enough, that is, if management engages in a thorough budgeting process, it may expect to obtain the following benefits.

Study, research, and a focus on the future

When a concern plans with sufficient care and detail to prepare a budget, the planning process usually involves thorough study and research. Not only should this result in the best conceivable plans but it should also instill in executives the habit of doing a reasonable amount of research and study before decisions are made. In short, budgeting tends to promote good decision-making processes. In addition, the items of interest to a budgetary investigation lie in the future. Thus, the attention of management is focused on future events and the associated opportunities available to the business. The pressures of daily operating problems naturally tend to take precedence over planning, thereby leaving the business without carefully thoughtout objectives. Budgeting counteracts this tendency by formalizing the planning process; it makes planning an explicit responsibility of management.

The basis for evaluating performance

The control function of management requires that performance be evaluated in light of some norms or objectives. On the basis of this evaluation, appropriate corrective actions can be implemented. In evaluating performance, there are two alternative norms or objectives against which actual performance can be compared: (1) past performance or (2) expected (budgeted) performance. Although past performance is sometimes used as the basis of comparison, budgeted performance is generally superior for determining whether actual performance is acceptable or in need of corrective action. Past performance fails to take into account all of the environmental changes that may impact on the performance level. For example, in the evaluation of sales performance, past sales may have occurred under economic conditions that were dramatically different from those that apply to the current sales effort. Economy-wide fluctuations, competitive shifts within the industry, new product line developments, increased or decreased advertizing commitments, and so forth, all tend to invalidate comparisons between past performance and present performance. On the other hand, budgeted (anticipated) performance levels are developed after a research and study process which attempts to take such environmental factors into account. Thus, budgeting provides the benefit of a superior basis for evaluating performance and a more effective control mechanism.

Coordination

Coordination requires that a business be operated as a whole rather than as a group of separate departments. When a budget plan is prepared, each department's objectives are determined in advance, and these objectives are coordinated. For example, the production department is budgeted to produce approximately the number of units the selling department can sell. The purchasing department is budgeted to buy raw materials on the basis of budgeted production; and the hiring activities of the personnel department are budgeted to take into account budgeted production levels. Obviously, the departments and activities of a business must be closely coordinated if the business operations are to be efficient and profitable. Budgeting provides this coordination.

Communication

In a very small business, adequate communication of business plans might be accomplished by direct contact between the employees. Frequent conversations could perhaps serve as the means of communicating management's plans for the business. However, oral conversations often leave ambiguities and potential confusion if not backed up by documents that clearly state the content of the plans. Further, businesses need not be very large before informal conversations become obviously inadequate. When a budget is prepared, the budget becomes a means of informing the organization not only of plans that have been approved by management but also of budgeted actions management wishes the organization to take during the budget period.

A source of motivation

As previously mentioned, budgets provide the standards against which actual performance is evaluated. Because of this, the budget and the manner in which it is used can significantly effect the attitudes of those who are to be evaluated. If management is not careful, the whole budgeting process may have a negative impact on the attitudes of the employees. Budgeted levels of performance must be realistic. Also, the personnel who will be evaluated in terms of a budget should be consulted and involved in preparing the budget. Finally, the subsequent evaluations of performance must not be given critically, without offering the affected employees an opportunity to explain the reasons for performance failures. These three factors are important: (1) If the affected employees are consulted when the budget is prepared, (2) if obtainable objectives are budgeted, and (3) if the subsequent evaluations of performance are made fairly with opportunities provided to explain performance deficiencies, budgeting can be a strongly positive, motivating force in the organization. Budgeted performance levels can provide goals that individuals will attempt to attain or even exceed as they fulfill their responsibilities to the organization.

THE BUDGET COMMITTEE

The task of preparing a budget should not be made the responsibility of any one department; and the budget definitely should not be handed down from above as the "final word." Rather, budget figures and budget estimates should be developed from "the bottom up." For example, the sales department should have a hand in preparing sales estimates. Similarly, the production department should have initial responsibility for preparing its own expense budget. Otherwise, production and salespeople may say the budget figures are meaningless, as they were prepared by front office personnel who know nothing of sales and production problems.

Although budget figures should be developed from "the bottom up," the preparation of a budget needs central guidance. This is commonly supplied by a budget committee of department heads or other high-level executives who are responsible for seeing that budget figures are realistic and coordinated. If a department submits budget figures that do not reflect proper performance, the figures should be returned to the department with the budget committee's comments. The originating department then either adjusts the figures or defends them. It should not change the figures just to please the committee, since it is important that all parties agree that the figures are reasonable and attainable.

THE BUDGET PERIOD

Budget periods normally coincide with accounting periods. This means that in most companies the budget period is one year in length. However, in addition to their annual budgets, many companies prepare long-range budgets setting forth major objectives for from three to five or ten years in advance. These long-range budgets are particularly important in planning for major expenditures of capital to buy plant and equipment. Additionally, the financing of major capital projects, for example, by issuing bonds, by issuing stock, by retaining earnings, and so forth, can be anticipated and planned as a part of preparing long-range budgets.

Long-range budgets of two, three, five, and ten years should reflect the planned accomplishment of long-range objectives. Within this context, the annual master budget for a business reflects the objectives that have been adopted for the next year. The annual budget, however, is commonly broken down into quarterly or monthly budgets. Short-term budgets of a quarter or a month are useful yardsticks that allow management to evaluate actual performance and take corrective actions promptly. After the quarterly or monthly results are known, the actual performance is compared to the budgeted amounts in a report similar to that disclosed in Illustration 24–1.

Consolidated Stores, Inc.
Income Statement with Variations from Budget for Month Ended April 30, 19—

	Actual	Budget	Variations
Sales	$63,500	$60,000	$+3,500
Less: Sales returns and allowances	1,800	1,700	+100
Sales discounts	1,200	1,150	+50
Net sales	$60,500	$57,150	$+3,350
Cost of goods sold:			
Merchandise inventory, April 1, 19—	$42,000	$44,000	$−2,000
Purchases, net	39,100	38,000	+1,100
Freight-in	1,250	1,200	+50
Goods for sale	$82,350	$83,200	$ −850
Merchandise inventory, April 30, 19—	41,000	44,100	−3,100
Cost of goods sold	$41,350	$39,100	$+2,250
Gross profit	$19,150	$18,050	$+1,100
Operating expenses:			
Selling expenses:			
Sales salaries	$ 6,250	$ 6,000	$ +250
Advertising expense	900	800	+100
Store supplies used	550	500	+50
Depreciation of store equipment	1,600	1,600	
Total selling expenses	$ 9,300	$ 8,900	$ +400
General and administrative expenses:			
Office salaries	$ 2,000	$ 2,000	
Office supplies used	165	150	$ +15
Rent	1,100	1,100	
Expired insurance	200	200	
Depreciation of office equipment	100	100	
Total general and administrative expenses	$ 3,565	$ 3,550	$ +15
Total operating expenses	$12,865	$12,450	$ +415
Income from operations	$ 6,285	$ 5,600	$ +685

Illustration 24–1

Many businesses follow the practice of "continuous" budgeting, and are said to prepare *rolling budgets*. As each monthly or quarterly budget period goes by, these firms revise their entire set of budgets, adding new monthly or quarterly sales, production, expense, equipment, and cash budgets to replace the ones that have elapsed. Thus, at any point in time, monthly or quarterly budgets are available for a full year in advance.

PREPARING THE MASTER BUDGET

As indicated in the previous discussion, the master budget consists of a number of budgets that collectively express the planned activities of the business. The number and arrangement of the budgets included in the master budget depend on the size and complexity of the business. However, a master budget typically includes:

1. Operating budgets.
   a. Sales budget.
   b. For merchandising companies: Merchandise purchases budget.
   c. For manufacturing companies:
      (1) Production budget (stating the number of units to be produced).
      (2) Manufacturing budget.
   d. Selling expense budget.
   e. General and administrative expense budget.
2. Capital expenditures budget, which includes the budgeted expenditures for new plant and equipment.
3. Financial budgets.
   a. Budgeted statement of cash receipts and disbursements, called the cash budget.
   b. Budgeted income statement.
   c. Budgeted balance sheet.

In addition to these budgets, numerous calculations or schedules may be required to support the information disclosed in these budgets.

Some of the budgets listed above cannot be prepared until other budgets on the list are first completed. For example, the merchandise purchases budget cannot be prepared until the sales budget is available, since the number of units to be purchased depends upon how many units are to be sold. As a consequence, preparation of the budgets within the master budget must follow a definite sequence, as follows:

First: The sales budget must be prepared first because the operating and financial budgets depend upon information provided by the sales budget.

Second: The remaining operating budgets are prepared next. For manufacturing companies, the production budget must be prepared prior to the manufacturing budget, since the number of units to be manufactured obviously affects the amounts of materials, direct labor, and overhead to be budgeted. Other than this, the budgets for manufacturing costs or merchandise costs, general and administrative expenses, and selling expenses may be prepared in any sequence.

Third: If capital expenditures are anticipated during the budget period, the capital expenditures budget is prepared next. This budget usually depends upon long-range sales forecasts more than it does upon the sales budget for the next year.

Fourth: Based upon the information provided in the above budgets, the budgeted statement of cash receipts and disbursements is prepared. If this budget discloses unrealistic disbursements compared to planned receipts, the previous plans may have to be revised.

Fifth: The budgeted income statement is prepared next. If the plans contained in the master budget result in unsatisfactory profits, the entire master budget may be revised to incorporate any corrective measures available to the firm.

Sixth: The budgeted balance sheet for the end of the budget period is prepared last. An analysis of this statement may also lead to revisions in the previous budgets. For example, the budgeted balance sheet may disclose too much debt resulting from an overly ambitious capital expenditures budget, and revised plans may be necessary.

PREPARATION OF THE MASTER BUDGET ILLUSTRATED

The following sections explain the procedures involved in preparing the budgets that comprise the master budget. Northern Company, a wholesaler of a single product, provides an illustrative basis for the discussion. The September 30, 198A, balance sheet for Northern Company is presented in Illustration 24–2. The master budget for Northern Company is prepared on a monthly basis, with a budgeted balance

Northern Company
Balance Sheet, September 30, 198A

Cash	$ 20,000	Accounts payable	$ 58,200
Accounts receivable	42,000	Loan from bank	10,000
Inventory (9,000 units @ $6)	54,000	Accrued income taxes payable	
Equipment*	200,000	(due October 15, 198A)	20,000
Less accumulated depreciation	(36,000)	Common stock	150,000
		Retained earnings	41,800
Total	$280,000	Total	$280,000

* The equipment is being depreciated on a straight-line basis over ten years. Estimated salvage value is $20,000.

Illustration 24–2

sheet prepared for the end of each quarter. Also, a budgeted income statement is prepared for each quarter. In the following sections, Northern Company budgets are prepared for October, November, and December 198A.

Sales budget

The *sales budget,* an estimate of goods to be sold and revenue to be derived from sales, is the starting point in the budgeting procedure, since the plans of all departments are related to sales and expected revenue. The sales budget commonly grows from a reconciliation of forecasted business conditions, plant capacity, proposed selling expenses such as advertising, and estimates of sales. As to sales estimates, since people normally feel a greater responsibility for reaching goals they have had a hand in setting, the sales personnel of a concern is often asked to submit, through the sales manager, estimates of sales for each territory and department. The final sales budget is then based on these estimates as reconciled for forecasted business conditions, selling expenses, and so forth.

During September 198A, Northern Company sold 7,000 units of product at a price of $10 per unit. After obtaining the estimates of sales personnel and considering the economic conditions affecting the market for Northern Company's product, the sales budget (Illustration 24–3) is established for October, November, and December 198A. Since the purchasing department must base December 198A purchases on estimated sales for January 198B, the sales budget is expanded to include January 198B.

Northern Company
Monthly Sales Budget
October 198A–January 198B

	Budgeted unit sales		Budgeted unit price		Budgeted total sales
September 198A (actual)	7,000	×	$10	=	$ 70,000
October 198A	10,000	×	10	=	100,000
November 198A	8,000	×	10	=	80,000
December 198A	14,000	×	10	=	140,000
January 198B	9,000	×	10	=	90,000

Illustration 24–3

Observe in Illustration 24–3 that the sales budget is more detailed than simple projections of total sales; both unit sales and unit prices are forecasted. Some budgeting procedures are less detailed, expressing the budget only in terms of total sales volume. Also, many sales budgets are far more detailed than the one illustrated. The more detailed sales budgets may show units and unit prices for each of many different products, classified by salesperson and by territory or by department.

Merchandise purchases budget

A variety of sophisticated techniques have been developed to assist management in making inventory purchase decisions. All of these techniques recognize that the number of units to be added to inventory depends upon the budgeted sales volume. Whether a company manufactures or purchases the product it sells, budgeted future sales volume is the primary factor to be considered in most inventory management situations.

The amount of merchandise or materials to be purchased each month is determined as follows:

Budgeted sales for the month	XXX
Add the budgeted end-of-the-month inventory	XXX
Required amount of available merchandise	XXX
Deduct the beginning-of-the-month inventory	(XXX)
Inventory to be purchased	XXX

The calculation may be made in either dollars or in units. If the calculation is in units and only one product is involved, the number of dollars of inventory to be purchased may be determined by multiplying units to be purchased by the cost per unit.

After considering the cost of maintaining an investment in inventory and the potential cost associated with a temporary inventory shortage, Northern Company has decided that the number of units in its inventory at the end of each month should equal 90% of the next month's sales. In other words, the inventory at the end of October should equal 90% of the budgeted November sales, the November ending inventory should equal 90% of the expected December sales, and so on. Also, the company's suppliers have indicated that the September 198A per unit cost of $6 can be expected to remain unchanged through January 198B. Based on these factors the company prepared the merchandise purchases budget of Illustration 24–4.

The calculations in Northern Company's merchandise purchases budget differ slightly from the basic calculation previously given in that the first lines are devoted to determining the desired end-of-each-month inventory. Also, budgeted sales are added to the desired end-of-each-month inventory instead of vice versa, and on the last lines the number of dollars of inventory to be purchased is determined by multiplying units to be purchased by the cost per unit.

Northern Company
Merchandise Purchases Budget
October, November, and December 198A

	October	November	December
Next month's budgeted sales (in units)	8,000	14,000	9,000
Ratio of inventory to future sales	×90%	×90%	×90%
Desired end-of-the-month inventory	7,200	12,600	8,100
Budgeted sales for the month (in units)	10,000	8,000	14,000
Required units of available merchandise	17,200	20,600	22,100
Deduct beginning-of-the-month inventory	(9,000)	(7,200)	(12,600)
Number of units to be purchased	8,200	13,400	9,500
Budgeted cost per unit	×$6	×$6	×$6
Budgeted cost of merchandise purchases......	$49,200	$80,400	$57,000

Illustration 24–4

It was previously mentioned that some budgeting procedures are designed to provide only the total dollars of budgeted sales. Likewise, the merchandise purchases budget may not state the number of units to be purchased, and may be expressed only in terms of the total cost of merchandise to be purchased. In such situations, it is assumed that there is a constant relationship between sales and cost of goods sold. For example, Northern Company expects that cost of goods sold will equal 60% of sales. (Note that the budgeted sales price is $10 and the budgeted unit cost is $6.) Thus, its cost of purchases can be budgeted in dollars on the basis of budgeted sales without requiring information on the number of units involved.

Production budgets and manufacturing budgets

Since Northern Company does not manufacture the product it sells, its budget for acquiring goods to be sold is a merchandise purchases budget (Illustration 24–4). If Northern Company had been a manufacturing company, a production budget rather than a merchandise purchases budget would be required. In a *production budget* the number of units to be produced each month is shown. For Northern Company such a budget would be very similar to a merchandise purchases budget. It would differ in that the number of units to be purchased each month (see Illustration 24–4) would be described as the number of units to be manufactured each month. Also, it would not show costs, since a production budget is always expressed entirely in terms of units of product and does not include budgeted production costs. Such costs are shown in the manufacturing budget, which is based on the production volume shown in the production budget.

A *manufacturing budget* shows the budgeted costs for raw materials, direct labor, and manufacturing overhead. In many manufacturing companies, the manufacturing budget is actually prepared in the form of three subbudgets: a raw materials purchases budget, a direct labor budget, and a manufacturing overhead budget. These budgets show the total budgeted cost of goods to be manufactured during the budget period.

Selling expense budget

The responsibility for preparing a budget of selling expenses typically falls on the vice president of marketing or the equivalent sales manager. Although budgeted selling expenses should affect the expected amount of sales, the typical procedure is to prepare a sales budget first and then to budget selling expenses. Estimates of selling expenses are based on the tentative sales budget and upon the experience of previous periods adjusted for known changes. After the entire master budget is prepared on a tentative basis, it may be decided that the projected sales volume is inadequate. If so, subsequent adjustments in the sales budget would generally require that corresponding adjustments be made in the selling expense budget.

Northern Company's selling expenses consist of commissions paid to sales personnel and a $24,000 per year salary, paid on a monthly basis to the sales manager. Sales commissions amount to 10% of total sales and are paid during the month the sales are made. The selling expense budget for Northern Company is presented in Illustration 24–5.

General and administrative expenses

General and administrative expenses usually are the responsibility of the office manager, who should therefore be charged with the task of preparing the budget for these items. The amounts of some general

Northern Company
Selling Expense Budget
October, November, and December 198A

	October	November	December	Total
Budgeted sales	$100,000	$80,000	$140,000	$320,000
Sales commission percentage	×10%	×10%	×10%	×10%
Sales commissions	$ 10,000	$ 8,000	$ 14,000	$ 32,000
Salary for sales manager ($24,000/12 = $2,000 per month)	2,000	2,000	2,000	6,000
Total selling expenses	$ 12,000	$10,000	$ 16,000	$ 38,000

Illustration 24–5

and administrative expenses may depend upon budgeted sales volume. However, most of these expenses depend more upon other factors such as management policies, inflationary influences, and so forth, than they do upon monthly fluctuations in sales volume. Although interest expense and income tax expense are frequently classified as general and administrative expenses, they generally cannot be budgeted at this point in the budgeting sequence. Interest expense must await preparation of the cash budget, which determines the need for loans, if any. Income tax expense must await preparation of the budgeted income statement, at which time taxable income and income tax expense can be estimated.

General and administrative expenses for Northern Company include administrative salaries amounting to $54,000 per year and depreciation of $18,000 per year on equipment (see Illustration 24–2). The salaries are paid each month as they are earned. Illustration 24–6 shows the budget for these expenses.

Northern Company
General and Administrative Expense Budget
October, November, and December 198A

	October	November	December	Total
Administrative salaries				
($54,000/12 = $4,500)	$4,500	4,500	$4,500	$13,500
Depreciation of equipment				
($18,000/12 = $1,500)	1,500	1,500	1,500	4,500
	$6,000	$6,000	$6,000	$18,000

Illustration 24–6

Capital expenditures budget

The capital expenditures or plant and equipment budget lists equipment to be scrapped and additional equipment to be purchased if the proposed production program is carried out. The purchase of additional equipment requires funds; and anticipating equipment additions in advance normally makes it easier to provide the funds. Also, at times, estimated production may exceed plant capacity. Budgeting makes it possible to anticipate this and either revise the production schedule or increase plant capacity. Planning plant and equipment purchases is called capital budgeting, and this is discussed in more detail in Chapter 27.

Northern Company does not anticipate any sales or retirements of equipment through December 198A. However, management plans to acquire additional equipment for $25,000 cash near the end of December 198A.

Cash budget

After tentative sales, merchandise purchases, expenses, and capital expenditures budgets have been set, the *cash budget* is prepared. This budget is important because a company should have at all times enough cash to meet needs, but it should not hold too much cash. Too much cash is undesirable because it often cannot be profitably invested. A cash budget requires management to forecast cash receipts and disbursements, and usually results in better cash management. Also, it enables management to arrange well in advance for loans to cover any anticipated cash shortages.

In preparing the cash budget, anticipated receipts are added to the beginning cash balance and anticipated expenditures are deducted. If the resulting cash balance is inadequate, the required additional cash is provided in the budget through planned increases in loans.

Much of the information that is needed to prepare the cash budget can be obtained directly from the previously prepared operating and capital expenditures budgets. However, further investigation and additional calculations may be necessary to determine the amounts to be included.

Illustration 24–7 shows the cash budget for Northern Company. October's beginning cash balance was obtained from the September 30, 198A, balance sheet (Illustration 24–2).

Budgeted sales of Northern Company are shown in Illustration 24–3. An investigation of previous sales records indicates that 40% of Northern Company's sales are for cash. The remaining 60% are credit sales, and customers can be expected to pay for these sales in the month after the sales are made. Thus, the budgeted cash receipts from customers are calculated as follows:

	September	October	November	December
Sales	$70,000	$100,000	$80,000	$140,000
Credit sales percentage	×60%	×60%	×60%	×60%
Accounts receivable, end of month	$42,000	$ 60,000	$48,000	$ 84,000
Cash sales percentage		×40%	×40%	×40%
Cash sales		$ 40,000	$32,000	$ 56,000
Collections of accounts receivable		42,000	60,000	48,000
Total cash receipts		$ 82,000	$92,000	$104,000

Observe in the calculation that the October cash receipts consist of $40,000 from cash sales ($100,000 × 40%) plus the collection of $42,000 of accounts receivable as calculated in the previous column. Also, note that each month's total cash receipts are listed on the second line of Illustration 24–7.

Northern Company's purchases of merchandise are entirely on ac-

Northern Company
Cash Budget
October, November, and December 198A

	October	November	December
Beginning cash balance	$ 20,000	$ 20,000	$ 22,272
Cash receipts from customers	82,000	92,000	104,000
Total	$102,000	$112,000	$126,272
Cash disbursements:			
Payments for merchandise	$ 58,200	$ 49,200	$ 80,400
Sales commissions (Illustration 24–5)	10,000	8,000	14,000
Salaries: Sales (Illustration 24–5)	2,000	2,000	2,000
Administrative (Illustration 24–6)	4,500	4,500	4,500
Accrued income taxes payable	20,000		
Dividends ($150,000 × 0.02 = $3,000)		3,000	
Interest on loan from bank:			
$10,000 × 0.01 = $100	100		
$22,800 × 0.01 = $228		228	
Purchase of equipment			25,000
Total cash disbursements	$ 94,800	$ 66,928	$125,900
Balance	$ 7,200	$ 45,072	$ 372
Additional loan from bank	12,800		19,628
Repayment of loan from bank		(22,800)	
Ending cash balance	$ 20,000	$ 22,272	$ 20,000
Loan balance, end of month	$ 22,800	$ -0-	$ 19,628

Illustration 24–7

count, and full payments are made regularly in the month following purchase. Thus, in Illustration 24–7, the cash disbursements for purchases are obtained from the September 30, 198A, balance sheet (Illustration 24–2) and from the merchandise purchases budget (Illustration 24–4), as follows:

September 30, accounts payable equal October payments	$58,200
October purchases equal November payments	49,200
November purchases equal December payments	80,400

Sales commissions and all salaries are paid monthly, and the budgeted cash disbursements for these items are obtained from the selling expense budget (Illustration 24–5) and the general and administrative expense budget (Illustration 24–6).

As indicated in the September 30, 198A, balance sheet (Illustration 24–2), accrued income taxes are paid in October. Estimated income tax expense for the quarter ending December 31 is 40% of net income and is due in January 198B.

Northern Company pays 2% quarterly cash dividends, and the November payment of $3,000 is the planned disbursement for this item.

Also, Northern Company has an agreement with the bank whereby additional loans are granted at the end of each month if they are necessary to maintain a minimum cash balance of $20,000 at the end of the month. Interest is paid at the end of each month at the rate of 1% per month; and if the cash balance at the end of a month exceeds $20,000, the excess is used to repay the loans to the bank. Illustration 24–7 indicates that the $10,000 loan from the bank at the end of September was not sufficient to provide a $20,000 cash balance at the end of October and, as a result, the loan was increased by $12,800 at the end of October. The entire loan was repaid at the end of November, and $19,628 was again borrowed at the end of December.

Budgeted income statement

One of the final steps in preparing a master budget is to summarize the effects of the various budgetary plans on the income statement. The necessary information to prepare a budgeted income statement is drawn primarily from the previously prepared budgets or from the investigations that were made in the process of preparing those budgets.

For many companies, the volume of information that must be summarized in the budgeted income statement and the budgeted balance sheet is so large that a work sheet must be used to accumulate all of the budgeted transactions and to classify them in terms of their impact on the income statement and/or on the balance sheet. However, the transactions and account balances of Northern Company are few in number, and the budgeted income statement (and balance sheet) can be prepared simply by inspecting the previously discussed budgets and recalling the information that was provided in the related discussions. Northern Company's budgeted income statement is shown in Illustration 24–8.

Northern Company
Budgeted Income Statement for Three Months Ended December 31, 198A

Sales (Illustration 24–3, 32,000 units @ $10)		$320,000
Cost of goods sold (32,000 units @ $6)		192,000
Gross profit		$128,000
Operating expenses:		
Sales commissions (Illustration 24–5)	$32,000	
Sales salaries (Illustration 24–5)	6,000	
Administrative salaries (Illustration 24–6)	13,500	
Depreciation on equipment (Illustration 24–6)	4,500	
Interest expense (Illustration 24–7)	328	(56,328)
Net income before income taxes		$ 71,672
Income tax expense ($71,672 × 40%)		(28,669)
Net income		$ 43,003

Illustration 24–8

Budgeted balance sheet

If a work sheet is used to prepare the budgeted income statement and balance sheet, the first two columns of the work sheet are used to list the estimated post-closing trial balance of the period prior to the budget period. Next the budgeted transactions and adjustments are entered in the second pair of work sheet columns in the same manner as end-of-period adjustments are entered on an ordinary work sheet. For example, if the budget calls for sales on account of $250,000, the name of the Sales account is entered on the work sheet in the Account Titles column below the names of the post-closing trial balance accounts; and then Sales is credited and Accounts Receivable is debited for $250,000 in the second pair of money columns. After all budgeted transactions and adjustments are entered on the work sheet, the estimated post-closing trial balance amounts in the first pair of money columns are combined with the budget amounts in the second pair of columns and are sorted to the proper Income Statement and Balance Sheet columns of the work sheet. Finally, the information in these columns is used to prepare the budgeted income statement and budgeted balance sheet.

As previously mentioned, the transactions and account balances of Northern Company are few in number, and its budgeted balance sheet, shown in Illustration 24–9 (below), can be prepared simply by inspecting the previously prepared budgets and recalling the related discussions of those budgets.

Northern Company
Budgeted Balance Sheet, December 31, 198A

Assets

Cash (Illustration 24–7)		$ 20,000
Accounts receivable (page 821)		84,000
Inventory (Illustration 24–4, 8,100 units @ $6)		48,600
Equipment (Illustrations 24–2 and 24–7)	$225,000	
Less accumulated depreciation (Illustrations 24–2 and 24–6)	40,500	184,500
Total assets		$337,100

Liabilities and Stockholders' Equity

Liabilities:		
Accounts payable (Illustration 24–4)	$ 57,000	
Accrued income taxes payable (Illustration 24–8)	28,669	
Bank loan payable (Illustration 24–7)	19,628	$105,297
Stockholders' equity:		
Common stock (Illustration 24–2)	$150,000	
Retained earnings (see discussion)	81,803	231,803
Total liabilities and stockholders' equity		$337,100

Illustration 24–9

Observe that the retained earnings balance in Illustration 24–9 is $81,803. This amount was determined as follows:

Retained earnings, September 30, 198A (Illustration 24–2)	$41,800
Net income for three months ended December 31, 198A (Illustration 24–8)	43,003
Total	$84,803
Dividends declared in November, 198A (Illustration 24–7)	(3,000)
Retained earnings, December 31, 198A	$81,803

GLOSSARY

Budget. A formal statement of future plans, usually expressed in monetary terms.

Budgeting. The process of planning future business actions and expressing those plans in a formal manner.

Capital expenditures budget. A listing of the plant and equipment to be purchased if the proposed production program is carried out. Also called the plant and equipment budget.

Cash budget. A forecast of cash receipts and disbursements.

Manufacturing budget. A statement of the estimated costs for raw materials, direct labor, and manufacturing overhead associated with producing the number of units estimated in the production budget.

Master budget. A comprehensive or overall plan for the business that typically includes budgets for sales, expenses, production, equipment, cash, and also a planned income statement and balance sheet.

Merchandise purchases budget. An estimate of the units (or cost) of merchandise to be purchased by a merchandising company.

Production budget. An estimate of the number of units to be produced during a budget period.

Rolling budgets. A sequence of revised budgets that are prepared in the practice of continuous budgeting.

Sales budget. An estimate of goods to be sold and revenue to be derived from sales; serves as the usual starting point in the budgeting procedure.

QUESTIONS FOR CLASS DISCUSSION

1. What is a budget? What is a master budget?
2. What are the benefits from budgeting?

3. How does the process of budgeting tend to promote good decision making?
4. What are the two alternative norms or objectives against which actual performance is sometimes compared and evaluated? Which of the two is generally superior?
5. Why should each department be asked to prepare or at least to participate in the preparation of its own budget estimates?
6. What are the duties of the budget committee?
7. What is the normal length of a master budget period? How far in advance are long-range budgets generally prepared?
8. What is meant by the terms "continuous" budgeting and "rolling" budgets?
9. What are the three primary types of budgets that make up the master budget?
10. In comparing merchandising companies and manufacturing companies, what differences show up in the operating budgets?
11. What is the sequence that is followed in preparing the set of budgets that collectively make up the master budget?
12. What is a sales budget? A selling expense budget? A capital expenditures budget?
13. What is the difference between a production budget and a manufacturing budget?
14. What is a cash budget? Why must it be prepared after the operating budgets and the capital expenditures budget?

CLASS EXERCISES

Exercise 24–1

The Hardware Department of the Hatfield Department Store has prepared a sales budget for the month of June which calls for a sales volume of $12,000. The department expects to begin June with a $7,100 inventory and end the month with a $9,000 inventory. Its cost of goods sold averages 70% of sales.

Required:

Prepare a merchandise purchases budget for the hardware department showing the amount of goods to be purchased during June.

Exercise 24–2

The Devine Company manufactures a product called Telecats. The company's management estimates there will be 6,000 units of Telecats in the December 31, 198A, finished goods inventory, that 16,300 units will be sold during the first quarter of 198B, that 20,000 units will be sold during the second quarter, and that 25,000 units will be sold during the third quarter. Management also believes the concern should attempt to begin each quarter with units in the finished goods inventory equal to 25% of the next quarter's budgeted sales.

Required:

Prepare a production budget showing the units of Telecats to be manufactured during the first quarter and the second quarter of 198B.

Exercise 24–3

Socco Company has budgeted the following cash receipts and cash disbursements from operations during the second quarter of 198A:

	Receipts	Disbursements
April	$220,000	$155,000
May	85,000	160,000
June	194,000	155,000

According to a credit agreement with the bank, the company promises to maintain a minimum, end-of-month cash balance of $25,000. In return, the bank has agreed to provide the company the right to receive loans up to $130,000 with interest of 14% per year, paid monthly on the last day of the month. (Interest payments should be rounded to the nearest dollar.) If the loan must be increased during the last ten days of a month to provide enough cash to pay bills, interest will not begin to be charged until the end of the month.

The company is expected to have a cash balance of $25,000 and a loan balance of $30,000 on March 31, 198A.

Required:

Prepare a monthly cash budget for the second quarter of 198A.

Exercise 24–4

Your investigation of Hall Company discloses the following information which should be used to prepare a cash budget for the month of October.

1. Beginning cash balance on October 1, $52,000.
2. Budgeted sales for October, $400,000; 30% is collected in the month of sale, 55% in the next month, 10% in the following month, and 5% is uncollectible.
3. Sales for September, $450,000.
4. Sales for August, $300,000.
5. Budgeted merchandise purchases for October, $260,000; 60% is paid in the month of purchase, 40% is paid in the month following purchase.
6. Merchandise purchased in September, $240,000.
7. Budgeted cash disbursements for salaries in October, $92,000.
8. Depreciation expense in October, $16,000.
9. Other cash expenses budgeted for October, $29,000.
10. Budgeted taxes payable in October, $21,000.
11. Budgeted interest payable on bank loan in October, $2,050.

Exercise 24–5

Use the information in Exercise 24–4 and the additional information which follows to prepare a budgeted income statement for the month of October and a budgeted balance sheet for October 31.

1. Cost of goods sold is 56% of sales.
2. The inventory at the end of September was $63,000.

3. Salaries payable on September 30 was $19,000 and is expected to be $11,000 on October 31.

4. The Equipment account shows a balance of $472,000 on September 30; Accumulated Depreciation had a balance of $118,000.

5. The $2,050 cash payment of interest represents the 1% monthly expense on a bank loan of $205,000.

6. Income taxes payable on September 30 amounted to $21,000, and the income tax rate applicable to the company is 40%.

7. The 5% of sales which prove to be uncollectible is debited to Bad Debts Expense and credited to Allowance for Doubtful Accounts during the year of sale. However, specific accounts that prove to be uncollectible are not written off until the second month after the sale, at which time all accounts not yet collected are so written off.

8. The only balance sheet accounts other than those implied by the previous discussion are Common Stock, which shows a balance of $250,000, and Retained Earnings, which shows a balance of $200,500.

PROBLEMS

Problem 24-1

The Sapp Production Company manufactures a wooden product called an "autofeed." Each "autofeed" requires 110 board feet of lumber. The management of Sapp Production Company estimates there will be 150 units of the product and 20,000 board feet of lumber on hand on June 30 of the current year, and that 1,000 units of the product will be sold during the year's third quarter. Management also believes that due to the possibility of a shipping strike affecting the lumber industry, the company should begin the fourth quarter with a lumber inventory of 50,000 board feet and a finished goods inventory of 300 autofeeds. Lumber can be purchased for approximately $1.20 per board foot.

Required:

Prepare a third-quarter production budget and a third-quarter lumber purchases budget for the company.

Problem 24-2

In the last week of June, the owner of Columbus General Store approached the company's bank for a $30,000 loan to be made on August 1 and repaid 60 days later with interest at 12%. The owner planned to increase the store's inventory by $30,000 during July and needed the loan to pay for the merchandise during August. The bank's loan officer was interested in Columbus General Store's ability to repay the loan and asked the owner to forecast the store's September 30 cash position.

On July 1, Columbus General Store was expected to have a $10,000 cash balance, $89,000 of accounts receivable, and $38,000 of accounts payable. Its budgeted sales, purchases, and cash expenditures for the following three months are as follows:

	July	August	September
Sales	$72,000	$80,000	$90,000
Merchandise purchases	80,000	45,000	40,000
Payroll	10,500	10,500	10,500
Rent	4,000	4,000	4,000
Other cash expenses	2,600	5,000	3,100
Repayment of bank loan			30,600

The budgeted July purchases include the inventory increase. All sales are on account; and past experience indicates 70% is collected in the month following the sale, 24% in the next month, 4% in the next, and the remainder is not collected. Application of this experience to the July 1 accounts receivable balance indicates $60,000 of the $89,000 will be collected during July, $22,000 during August, and $3,000 during September. All merchandise is paid for in the month following its purchase.

Required:

Prepare cash budgets for July, August, and September for Columbus General Store under the assumption the bank loan will be paid on September 29.

Problem 24–3

Hammerhill Company has a cash balance of $18,000 on August 1, 198A. The product sold by the company sells for $40 per unit. Actual and projected sales are as follows:

June, actual	$300,000
July, actual	180,000
August, estimated	200,000
September, estimated	260,000
October, estimated	210,000

Experience has shown that 40% of the billings is collected in the month of sale, 45% in the second month, 12% in the third month, and 3% will prove to be uncollectible.

Approximately 60% of the purchases in a month is due and payable in the month of purchase; the remainder is due the following month. The unit purchase cost is $25. Hammerhill Company's management has established a policy of maintaining an end-of-month inventory of 200 units plus 30% of the next month's unit sales, and the August 1 inventory is consistent with this policy.

Selling and general administrative expenses (excluding depreciation) for the year amount to $450,000 and are distributed evenly throughout the year.

Required:

Prepare a monthly cash budget for August and September, with supporting schedules showing cash receipts from collections of receivables and cash payments for merchandise purchases.

Problem 24–4

Near the end of 198A, Atwell Company's management prepared a budgeted balance sheet for December 31, 198A, as follows:

ATWELL COMPANY
Balance Sheet, December 31, 198A

Assets		Equities	
Cash	$ 13,000	Accounts payable	$ 19,000
Accounts receivable	35,520	Loan from bank	7,200
Inventory	39,600	Taxes payable (due	
Equipment	72,000	March 15, 198B)	13,500
Accumulated deprecia-		Common stock	80,000
tion	(9,000)	Retained earnings	31,420
Total assets	$151,120	Total equities	$151,120

The following information pertains to the preparation of a master budget for January, February, and March 198B:

1. Atwell Company's sales are of one product, which is purchased for $18 per unit and sold for $24 per unit. Although the inventory level of 2,200 units on December 31, 198A, is smaller than desired, management has established a new inventory policy for 198B whereby the end-of-month inventory should be 75% of the next month's expected sales (in units). Budgeted unit sales are January, 8,000; February, 9,000; March, 13,000; and April, 11,000.

2. Total sales each month are 40% for cash and 60% on account. Of the credit sales, 70% is collected in the first month after the sale and 30% in the second month after the sale. Similarly, 70% of the Accounts Receivable balance on December 31, 198A, should be collected during January and 30% should be collected in February.

3. The company pays for 80% of its merchandise purchases in the month after purchase; the remaining 20% is paid for in the second month after purchase. Similarly, 80% of the Accounts Payable balance on December 31, 198A, will be paid during January and 20% will be paid during February.

4. Sales commissions amounting to 9% of sales are paid each month. Also, the salary of the sales manager is $27,000 per year.

5. General administrative salaries amount to $96,000 per year, and repair expenses amount to $600 per month and are paid in cash.

6. The equipment shown in the December 31, 198A, balance sheet was purchased one year ago. It is being depreciated over eight years according to the straight-line method. Regarding new purchases of equipment, management has decided to take a full month's depreciation (rounded to the nearest dollar) during the month the equipment is purchased, and to use straight-line depreciation over eight years, assuming no salvage value. The company plans to purchase additional equipment worth $12,000 in January, $4,000 in February, and $16,000 in March.

7. The company plans to acquire some land in March at a cost of $30,000. The land will not require a cash outlay until the last day of March. Thus, if a bank loan is necessary, the first payment of interest will be due at the end of April.

8. Atwell Company has an arrangement with the bank whereby additional loans are available as they are needed at a rate of 12% per year, paid monthly. If part or all of a loan is repaid during a month, the payment

will be made on the last day of the month, along with any interest that is due. Atwell Company has agreed to maintain an end-of-month cash balance of at least $10,000.

9. The income tax rate applicable to the company is 40%. However, tax on the income for the first quarter of 198B will not be paid until April.

Required:

Prepare a master budget for the first quarter of 198B, with the operating budgets, capital expenditures budget, and the cash budget prepared on a monthly basis. The budgeted income statement should show operations for the first quarter, and the budgeted balance sheet should be prepared as of March 31, 198B. The operating budgets included in the master budget should include a sales budget (showing both budgeted unit sales and dollar sales), a merchandise purchases budget, a selling expense budget, and a general and administrative expense budget. Round all amounts to the nearest dollar.

ALTERNATE PROBLEMS

Problem 24–1A

Columbia Sales Company sells three products that it purchases in their finished ready-for-sale state. The products' July 1 inventories are Product A, 4,000 units; Product B, 3,600 units; and Product C, 7,000 units. The company's manager is disturbed because each product's July 1 inventory is excessive in relation to immediately expected sales. Consequently, a new goal has been set for each product's month-end inventory; the inventory is to equal one half the following month's expected sales. Expected sales in units for July, August, September, and October are as follows:

	Expected sales in units			
	July	*August*	*September*	*October*
Product A	6,000	8,200	5,000	6,300
Product B........	2,100	1,800	2,400	2,800
Product C	9,000	9,500	8,000	8,200

Required:

Prepare purchases budgets in units for the three products for each of July, August, and September.

Problem 24–2A

Clipper Company expects to have a $7,100 cash balance on March 30 of the current year. It also expects to have a $32,000 balance of accounts receivable and $22,300 of accounts payable. Its budgeted sales, purchases, and cash expenditures for the following three months are as follows:

	April	*May*	*June*
Sales	$30,000	$24,000	$28,000
Purchases	17,000	16,000	18,000
Payroll	3,600	3,600	3,600
Rent	2,000	2,000	2,000
Other cash expenses	600	800	1,000
Purchase of store equipment	—	3,000	—
Payment of quarterly dividend	—	—	2,000

All sales are on account; and past experience indicates that 75% will be collected in the month following the sale, 15% in the next month, and 6% in the third month. Notwithstanding these expectations for future sales, an analysis of the March 30 accounts receivable balance indicates that $25,000 of the $32,000 balance will be collected in April, $4,500 in May, and $1,200 in June.

Purchases of merchandise on account are paid in the month following each purchase; likewise, the store equipment will be paid for in the month following its purchase.

Required:

Prepare cash budgets for the months of April, May, and June.

Problem 24–3A

The actual and projected monthly sales of the Webster Company are as follows:

March 198A, actual	$60,000
April 198A, actual	50,000
May 198A, estimated	55,000
June 198A, estimated	65,000
July 198A, estimated	56,000

Experience has shown that 45% of the sales is collected in the month of sale, 35% is collected in the first month after the sale, 16% in the second month after the sale, and 4% prove to be uncollectible.

Merchandise purchased by the Webster Company is paid for 15 days after the date of purchase. Thus, approximately one half of the purchases in a month are due and paid for in the next month. Webster Company pays $20 per unit of merchandise and subsequently sells the merchandise for $40 per unit. Webster Company always plans to maintain an end-of-month inventory of 100 units plus 40% of the next month's unit sales, and the April 30, 198A, inventory is consistent with the policy.

In addition to cost of goods sold, Webster Company incurs other operating expenses (excluding depreciation) of $240,000 per year, and they are distributed evenly throughout the year. On April 30, 198A, the company has a cash balance of $12,000.

Required:

Prepare a monthly cash budget for May and June, with supporting schedules showing cash receipts from collections of receivables and cash payments for merchandise purchases. Round all amounts to the nearest dollar.

Problem 24–4A

Shortly before the end of 198A, XYZ Company's management prepared a budgeted balance sheet for December 31, 198A, as follows:

XYZ COMPANY

Balance Sheet, December 31, 198A

Assets		Equities	
Cash	$ 5,000	Accounts payable	$ 8,000
Accounts receivable	15,000	Loan from bank	5,000
Inventory	25,000	Taxes payable (due March	
Equipment	60,000	15, 198B)	12,000
Accumulated deprecia-		Common stock	50,000
tion	(6,000)	Retained earnings	24,000
Total assets	$99,000	Total equities	$99,000

In the process of preparing a master budget for January, February, and March 198B, the following information has been obtained:

1. The product sold by XYZ Company is purchased for $10 per unit and resold for $15 per unit. Although the inventory level on December 31, 198A (2,500 units), is smaller than desired, management has established a new inventory policy for 198B whereby the end-of-month inventory should be 80% of the next month's expected sales (in units). Budgeted unit sales are January, 10,000; February, 9,000; March, 12,000; and April, 12,000.

2. Total sales each month are 50% for cash and 50% on account. Of the credit sales, 80% is collected in the first month after the sale and 20% in the second month after the sale. Similarly, 80% of the Accounts Receivable balance on December 31, 198A, should be collected during January and 20% should be collected in February.

3. Merchandise purchased by the company is paid for as follows: 70% in the month after purchase and 30% in the second month after purchase. Similarly, 70% of the Accounts Payable balance on December 31, 198A, will be paid during January and 30% will be paid during February.

4. Sales commissions amounting to 10% of sales are paid each month. Additionally, the salary of the sales manager is $12,000 per year.

5. Repair expenses amount to $500 per month and are paid in cash. General administrative salaries amount to $108,000 per year.

6. The equipment shown in the December 31, 198A, balance sheet was purchased one year ago. It is being depreciated over ten years according to the straight-line method. Regarding new purchases of equipment, management has decided to take a full month's depreciation (rounded to the nearest dollar) during the month the equipment is purchased and to use straight-line depreciation over ten years, assuming no salvage value. The company plans to purchase additional equipment worth $10,000 in January, $5,000 in February, and $15,000 in March.

7. The company plans to acquire some land in March at a cost of $100,000. The land will not require a cash outlay until the last day of March. Thus, if a bank loan is necessary, the first payment of interest will be due at the end of April.

8. XYZ Company has an arrangement with the bank whereby additional loans are available as they are needed at a rate of 10% per year, paid monthly.

If part or all of a loan is repaid during a month, the payment will be made on the last day of the month, along with any interest that is due. XYZ Company has agreed to maintain an end-of-month cash balance of at least $5,000.

9. The income tax rate applicable to the company is 48%. However, tax on the income for the first quarter of 198B will not be paid until April.

Required:

Prepare a master budget for the first quarter of 198B, with the operating budgets, capital expenditures budget, and the cash budget prepared on a monthly basis. The budgeted income statement should show operations for the first quarter, and the budgeted balance sheet should be prepared as of March 31, 198B. The operating budgets included in the master budget should include a sales budget (showing both budgeted unit sales and dollar sales), a merchandise purchases budget, a selling expense budget, and a general and administrative expense budget. Round all amounts to the nearest dollar.

PROVOCATIVE PROBLEMS

Provocative problem 24–1
Hardsnap Corporation

Hardsnap Corporation produces winches for sailboats. Each winch requires 16 pounds of brass. The management of Hardsnap Corporation is in the process of negotiating with the bank for the approval to make loans as they are needed by the company. One of the important items in their discussion has been the question of how much cash will be needed to pay for purchases of brass. Hardsnap Corporation purchases brass on account, and the resulting payables are paid in cash as follows: 70% during the month after purchase and 30% during the second month after purchase. The company plans to manufacture enough winches to maintain an end-of-month inventory of finished units equal to 60% of the next month's sales, and enough brass is purchased each month to maintain an end-of-month inventory equal to 50% of the next month's production requirements. Budgeted sales (in units) are as follows: February, 180; March, 190; April, 240; and May, 260. On January 31, 198A, the following data are available: finished winches on hand, 100; pounds of brass on hand, 1,000; Accounts Payable, $144,000 due in February plus $54,000 due in March.

In recent months the price of brass has varied substantially, and the management estimates that during the next few months the price could range from $180 to $240 per pound. You are asked to assist management by estimating the cash payments to be made in February, in March, and in April. In preparing your answer, you should prepare separate estimates based on a $180 price and a $240 price.

Provocative problem 24–2
Dipprey-Dow Company

The Dipprey-Dow Company has budgeted the following monthly sales volumes: April, 60,000 units; May, 35,000 units; June, 50,000 units; and July, 70,000 units. The company policy is to maintain an end-of-month finished goods inventory equal to 10,000 units plus 30% of the next month's budgeted sales in units. Consistent with this policy, the April 1 inventory was 28,000 units.

An analysis of Dipprey-Dow Company's manufacturing costs show the following:

Material cost per unit $1.60
Direct labor cost per unit 2.00
Manufacturing overhead costs which remain constant
    each month regardless of how many units are
    manufactured .... $14,000 per month
Manufacturing overhead costs the total amount of which
    depends on how many units are manufactured ..... $1.50 per unit
                                    manufactured

Required:

Prepare production budgets and manufacturing budgets for the months of April, May, and June.

After studying Chapter 25, you should be able to:

☐ Describe the different types of cost behavior experienced by a typical company.

☐ State the assumptions that underlie cost-volume-profit analysis and explain how these assumptions restrict the usefulness of the information obtained from the analysis.

☐ Calculate a break-even point for a single product company and plot the costs and revenues of a company on a graph.

☐ Describe some extensions that may be added to the basic cost-volume-profit analysis of break-even point.

☐ Calculate a composite sales unit for a multiproduct company and a break-even point for such a company.

☐ Define or explain the words and phrases listed in the chapter Glossary.

Cost-volume-profit analysis

■ Cost-volume-profit analysis is a means of predicting the effect of changes in costs and sales levels on the income of a business. In its simplest form it involves the determination of the sales level at which a company neither earns a profit nor incurs a loss; in other words, the point at which it breaks even. For this reason it is often called break-even analysis. However, the technique can be expanded to answer additional questions, such as: What sales volume is necessary to earn a desired net income? What net income will be earned if unit selling prices are reduced in order to increase sales volume? What net income will be earned if a new machine that will reduce unit labor costs is installed? What net income will be earned if we change the sales mix? When the technique is expanded to answer such additional questions, the descriptive phrase, "cost-volume-profit analysis," is more appropriate than "break-even analysis."

COST BEHAVIOR

Conventional cost-volume-profit analyses require that costs be classified as either fixed or variable. Some costs are definitely fixed in nature. Others are strictly variable. But, when costs are examined, some are observed to be neither completely fixed nor completely variable.

Fixed costs

A *fixed cost* remains unchanged in total amount over a wide range of production levels. For example, if the factory building is rented for, say, $1,000 per month, this cost remains the same whether the factory operates on a one-shift, two-shift, or an around-the-clock basis. Likewise, the cost is the same whether one hundred units of product are produced in a month, a thousand units are produced, or any other number up to the full capacity of the plant. Note, however, that while the total amount of a fixed cost remains constant as the level of production changes, fixed costs per unit of product decrease as volume increases. For example, if rent is $1,000 per month and two units of product are produced in a month, the rent cost per unit is $500; but if production is increased to ten units per month, rent cost per unit decreases to $100. Likewise it decreases to $2 per unit if production is increased to 500 units per month.

When production volume is plotted on a graph, units of product are shown on the horizontal axis and dollars of cost are shown on the vertical axis. Fixed costs are then expressed as a horizontal line, since the total amount of fixed costs remains constant at all levels of production. This is shown in the Illustration 25–1 graph where the

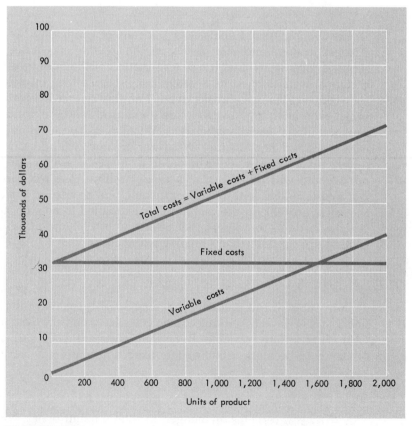

Illustration 25–1

fixed costs remain at $32,000 at all production levels up to 2,000 units of product.

Variable costs

A *variable cost* changes in total amount as production volume changes. For example, the cost of the material that enters into a product is a variable cost. If material costing $20 is required in the production of one unit of product, total material costs are $20 if one unit of product is manufactured, $40 if two units are manufactured, $60 if three units are manufactured, and so on up for any number of units. In other words, the variable cost per unit of production remains constant while the total amount of variable cost changes in direct proportion to changes in the level of production. Variable costs appear on a graph as a straight line that climbs up the graph as the production volume increases, as in Illustration 25–1.

Semivariable costs and stair-step costs

All costs are not necessarily either fixed or variable. For example, some costs go up in steps. Consider the salaries of production supervisors. Supervisory salaries may be more or less fixed for any production volume from zero to the maximum that can be completed on a one-shift basis. Then, if an additional shift must be added to increase production, a whole new group of supervisors must be hired and supervisory salaries go up by a lump-sum amount. They then remain fixed at this level until a third shift is added when they go up another lump sum. Costs such as these are called *stair-step costs* and are shown graphically in Illustration 25–2 on the next page.

In addition to stair-step costs, some costs may be semivariable or curvilinear in nature. *Semivariable costs* go up with volume increases, but when plotted on a graph, they must be plotted as a curved line (see Illustration 25–2). They change with production-level changes, but not proportionately.

For example, at low levels of production, the addition of more laborers may allow each laborer to specialize so that the whole crew becomes more efficient. Each new laborer increases the total cost, but the increased production more than compensates for the increased cost so that the cost per unit is reduced. Eventually, however, the addition of more laborers in a given plant may cause inefficiencies; laborers may begin to waste time bumping into each other. Thus, the addition of a new laborer adds some production but the cost per unit increases.

Cost assumptions

Conventional *cost-volume-profit analysis* is based on relationships that can be expressed as straight lines. Costs are assumed to be either

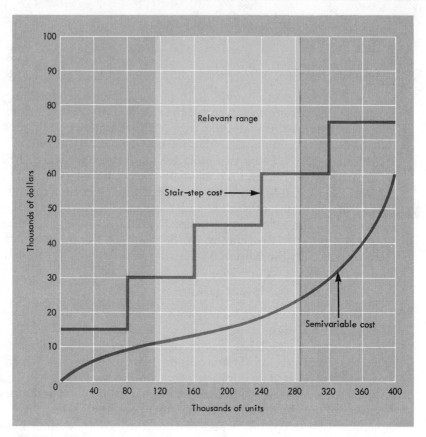

Illustration 25–2

fixed or variable. With the costs expressed as straight lines, the lines are then compared in order to answer a variety of questions. Consequently, the reliability of the answers secured through application of the technique rests on three basic assumptions, which for any one analysis are the following:

1. The per unit selling price is constant. (The selling price per unit will remain the same regardless of production level.)
2. The costs that are classified as "variable" do, in fact, behave as variable costs; that is, the actual (variable) cost per unit of production remains constant.
3. The costs that are classified as "fixed" do, in fact, remain constant over wide changes in the level of production.

When these assumptions are met, costs and revenues may be correctly represented by straight lines. However, the actual behavior of costs and revenues often is not completely consistent with these assumptions, and if the assumptions are violated by significant amounts, the results of cost-volume-profit analysis will not be reliable. Yet, there are at least two reasons why these assumptions tend to provide reliable analyses. First, while individual variable costs may not act in a truly variable manner, the process of adding such costs together may offset such violations of the assumption. In other words, the assumption of variable behavior may be satisfied in respect to total variable costs even though it is violated in respect to individual variable costs.

Second, the assumptions that revenues, variable costs, and fixed costs can be resonably represented as straight lines are only intended to apply over the *relevant range of operations*. The relevant range of operations, as plotted in Illustration 25–2, is the normal operating range for the business. It excludes the extremely high and low levels that are not apt to be encountered. Thus, a specific fixed cost is expected to be truly fixed only within the relevant range. It may be that beyond the limits of the relevant range, the fixed cost would not remain constant.

The previous discussion defined variable costs and fixed costs in terms of levels of production activity. However, in cost-volume-profit analysis, the level of activity is usually measured in terms of sales volume, whether stated as sales dollars or number of units sold. Thus, an additional assumption is frequently made that the level of production is the same as the level of sales, or if they are not the same, that the difference will not be enough to materially damage the reliability of the analysis.

It must also be recognized that cost-volume-profit analysis yields approximate answers to questions concerning the interrelations of costs, volume, and profits. So long as management understands that the answers provided are approximations, cost-volume-profit analysis can be a useful managerial tool.

BREAK-EVEN POINT

A company's *break-even point* is the sales level at which it neither earns a profit nor incurs a loss. It may be expressed either in units of product or in dollars of sales. To illustrate, assume that Alpha Company sells a single product for $100 per unit and incurs $70 of variable costs per unit sold. If the fixed costs involved in selling the product are $24,000, the company breaks even on the product as soon as it sells 800 units or as soon as its sales volume reaches $80,000. This break-even point may be determined as follows:

1. Each unit sold at $100 recovers its $70 variable costs and contributes $30 toward the fixed costs.
2. The fixed costs are $24,000; consequently, 800 units ($24,000 ÷ $30 = 800) must be sold to pay the fixed costs.
3. And 800 units at $100 each produce an $80,000 sales volume.

The $30 amount that the sales price of this product exceeds variable costs per unit is its *contribution margin per unit*. In other words, the contribution margin per unit is the amount that the sale of one unit contributes toward recovery of the fixed costs and then toward a profit.

Also, the contribution margin of a product expressed as a percentage of its sales price is its *contribution rate*. For instance, the contribution rate of the $100 product of this illustration is 30% ($30 ÷ $100 = 30%).

With contribution margin and contribution rate defined, it is possible to set up the following formulas for calculating a break-even point in units and in dollars:

$$\text{Break-even point in units} = \frac{\text{Fixed costs}}{\text{Contribution margin}}$$

$$\text{Break-even point in dollars} = \frac{\text{Fixed costs}}{\text{Contribution rate}}$$

Application of the second formula to figures for the product of this illustration gives this result:

$$\text{Break-even point in dollars} = \frac{\$24,000}{30\%} = \frac{\$24,000}{0.30} = \$80,000$$

Although the present example comes out evenly, a contribution rate may have to be carried out several decimal places to avoid minor rounding errors when calculating the break-even point in dollars. In solving the exercises and problems at the end of this chapter, for example, calculations of contribution rate should be carried to six decimal places unless the requirements state otherwise. Calculated either way, Alpha Company's break-even point may be proved with an income statement, as in Illustration 25–3. Observe in the illustration that reve-

---

Alpha Company
Income Statement at the Break-Even Point

Sales (800 units @ $100 each)		$80,000
Costs:		
Fixed costs	$24,000	
Variable costs (800 units @ $70 each)....	56,000	80,000
Net income		$ –0–

Illustration 25–3

---

nue from sales exactly equals the sum of the fixed and variable costs at the break-even point. Recognizing this will prove helpful in understanding the material that follows in this chapter.

BREAK-EVEN GRAPH

A cost-volume-profit analysis may be shown graphically as in Illustration 25–4. When presented in this form, the graph is commonly called a break-even graph or break-even chart. On such a graph the horizontal axis shows units sold, the vertical axis shows both dollars of sales and dollars of costs, and costs and revenues are plotted as straight lines.

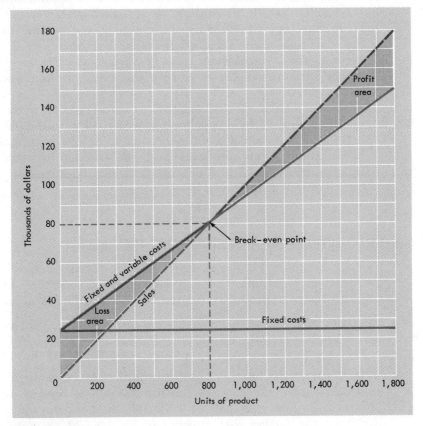

Illustration 25–4

The illustrated graph shows the break-even point of Alpha Company. A break-even graph is prepared as follows:

1. The line representing fixed costs is plotted at the fixed cost level. Note that it is a horizontal line, since the fixed costs are the same at all sales levels. Actually, the fixed costs line is not essential to the analysis; however, it contributes important information and is commonly plotted on a break-even chart.
2. Next the sales line is projected from the point of zero units and

zero dollars of sales to the point of maximum sales shown on the graph. In choosing the maximum number of units to be shown, a better graph results if the number chosen is such that it will cause the break-even point to fall near the center of the graph.

3. Next the variable cost plus fixed cost line is plotted. Note that it begins at the fixed cost level and, as a result, shows total costs at all production levels. At the zero sales level there are no variable costs, only fixed costs. However, at any level above zero sales all the fixed costs are present and so are the variable costs for that level. Also observe that the variable cost plus fixed cost line intersects the sales line at the break-even point. It intersects at this point because at the break-even point the revenue from sales exactly equals the sum of the fixed and variable costs, in other words, the total costs.

In reading a break-even chart, the vertical distance between the sales line and the total cost line represents a loss to the left of the breakeven point and a profit to the right of it. The amount of profit or loss at any given sales level can be determined from the graph by measuring the vertical distance between the sales line and the total cost line at the given level.

SALES REQUIRED FOR A DESIRED NET INCOME

A slight extension of the concept behind the break-even calculation will produce a formula that may be used in determining the sales level necessary to produce a desired net income. The formula is:

$$\text{Sales at desired income level} = \frac{\text{Fixed costs} + \text{Net Income} + \text{Income taxes}}{\text{Contribution rate}}$$

To illustrate the formula's use, assume that Alpha company of the previous section, the company having $24,000 of fixed costs and a 30% contribution rate, has set a $20,000 after-tax income goal for itself. Assume further that in order to have a $20,000 net income, the company must earn $28,500 and pay $8,500 in income taxes. Under these assumptions, $175,000 of sales are necessary to produce a $20,000 net income. This is calculated as follows:

$$\text{Sales at desired income level} = \frac{\text{Fixed costs} + \text{Net income} + \text{Income taxes}}{\text{Contribution rate}}$$

$$\text{Sales at desired income level} = \frac{\$24,000 + \$20,000 + \$8,500}{30\%}$$

$$\text{Sales at desired income level} = \frac{\$52,500}{30\%} = \$175,000$$

In the formula just given, the contribution rate was used as the divisor and the resulting answer was in dollars of sales. The contribution margin can also be used as the divisor; when it is, the resulting answer is in units of product.

MARGIN OF SAFETY

The difference between a company's current sales and sales at its break-even point, when sales are above the break-even point, is known as its margin of safety. The *margin of safety* is the amount sales may decrease before a loss is incurred. It may be expressed in units of product, dollars, or as a percentage of sales. For example, if current sales are $100,000 and the break-even point is $80,000, the margin of safety is $20,000 or 20% of sales, calculated as follows:

$$\frac{\text{Sales} - \text{Break-even sales}}{\text{Sales}} = \text{Margin of safety}$$

or

$$\frac{\$100,000 - \$80,000}{\$100,000} = 20\% \text{ margin of safety}$$

INCOME FROM A GIVEN SALES LEVEL

Cost-volume-profit analysis goes beyond break-even analysis and can be used to answer other questions. For example, what income will result from a given sales level? To understand the analysis used in answering this question, recall the factors that enter into the calculation of income. When expressed in equation form, they are:

$$\text{Sales} - (\text{Fixed costs} + \text{Variable costs}) = \text{Income}$$

Or:

$$\text{Income} = \text{Sales} - (\text{Fixed costs} + \text{Variable costs})$$

This equation may be used to calculate the income that will result at a given sales level. For example, assume that Alpha Company of the previous illustrations wishes to know what income will result if its sales level can be increased to $200,000. That would be 2,000 units of its product at $100 per unit. To determine the answer, recall that the variable costs per unit of this product are $70 and note that the $70 is 0.7 of the product's selling price. Consequently, variable costs for 2,000 units of the product are 0.7 of the selling price of these units, or (0.7 × $200,000) = $140,000. Alpha Company's fixed costs are $24,000. Therefore, if these known factors are substituted in the equation for determining income, the equation will read:

Income = $200,000 − [$24,000 + (0.7 × $200,000)]
Income = $200,000 − $164,000
Income = $36,000

The $36,000 is "before-tax" income; and as a result, if Alpha Company wishes to learn its after-tax income from the sale of 2,000 units of its product, it will have to apply the appropriate tax rates to the $36,000.

OTHER QUESTIONS

A company may wish to know what would happen to its break-even point if it reduced the selling price of its product in order to increase sales. Or it might wish to know what would happen if it installed a new machine that would increase its fixed costs but which would reduce variable costs. These are two of several possible questions involving changes in selling prices and costs. At first glance such changes seem to violate the basic assumptions on which cost-volume-profit analysis is based. But this is not true. A constant selling price, truly variable costs, and truly fixed costs are assumed to hold for any analysis involving the assumed price and costs. However, changes may be made, and if made, the new price and new costs are assumed to remain constant for the analyses involving that price and those costs. The fact that changes can be made in the factors makes it possible to predict the effect of changes before the changes are actually made.

To illustrate the effect of changes, assume that Alpha Company is considering the installation of a new machine that will increase the fixed costs of producing and selling its product from $24,000 to $30,000. However, the machine will reduce the variable costs from $70 per unit of product to $60. The selling price of the product will remain unchanged at $100, and the company wishes to know its break-even point if the machine is installed. Examination of the costs shows that the installation will not only increase the company's fixed costs but it will also change the contribution margin and contribution rate of the company's product. The new contribution margin will be $40, that is, ($100 − $60) = $40, and the new contribution rate will be 40%, that is, ($40 ÷ $100) = 0.4 or 40%. Consequently, if the machine is installed, the company's new break-even point will be:

$$\text{Break-even point in dollars} = \frac{\$30,000}{0.4} = \$75,000$$

In addition to their use in determining Alpha Company's break-even point, the new fixed costs and the new contribution rate may be used to determine the sales level needed to earn a desired net income. They may also be used to determine the expected income at a given sales level, or to answer other questions the company will want to answer before installing the new machine.

MULTIPRODUCT BREAK-EVEN POINT

The break-even point for a company selling a number of products can be determined by using a hypothetical unit made up of units of each of the company's products in their expected *sales mix*. Such a hypothetical unit is really a composite unit and is treated in all analyses as though it were a single product. To illustrate the use of such a hypothetical unit, assume that Beta Company sells three products, A, B, and C, and it wishes to calculate its break-even point. Unit selling prices for the three products are Product A, $5; Product B, $8; and Product C, $4. The sales mix or ratio in which the products are sold is 4:2:1, and the company's fixed costs are $48,000. Under these assumptions a composite unit selling price for the three products can be calculated as follows:

```
4 units of Product A @ $5 per unit  =  $20
2 units of Product B @ $8 per unit  =   16
1 unit  of Product C @ $4 per unit  =    4
Selling price of a composite unit .....  $40
```

Also, if the variable costs of selling the three products are Product A, $3.25; Product B, $4.50; and Product C, $2, the variable costs of a composite unit of the products are:

```
4 units of Product A @ $3.25 per unit  =  $13
2 units of Product B @ $4.50 per unit  =    9
1 unit  of Product C @ $2.00 per unit  =    2
Variable costs of a composite unit ......  $24
```

With the variable costs and selling price of a composite unit of the company's products calculated, the contribution margin for a composite unit may be determined by subtracting the variable costs of a composite unit from the selling price of such a unit, as follows:

$$\$40 - \$24 = \$16 \text{ contribution margin per composite unit}$$

The $16 contribution margin may then be used to determine the company's break-even point in composite units. The break-even point is:

$$\text{Break-even point in composite units} = \frac{\text{Fixed costs}}{\text{Composite contribution margin}}$$

$$\text{Break-even point in composite units} = \frac{\$48,000}{\$16}$$

$$\text{Break-even point} = 3,000 \text{ composite units}$$

The company breaks even when it sells 3,000 composite units of its products. However, to determine the number of units of each product it must sell to break even, the number of units of each product in the composite unit must be multiplied by the number of composite units needed to break even, as follows:

```
Product A:  4 × 3,000 = 12,000 units
Product B:  2 × 3,000 =  6,000 units
Product C:  1 × 3,000 =  3,000 units
```

The accuracy of all these computations can be proved by preparing an income statement showing the company's revenues and costs at the break-even point. Such a statement is shown in Illustration 25–5.

Beta Company
Income Statement at the Break-Even Point

Sales:		
Product A (12,000 units @ $5)		$ 60,000
Product B (6,000 units @ $8)		48,000
Product C (3,000 units @ $4)		12,000
Total revenues		$120,000
Costs:		
Fixed costs	$48,000	
Variable costs:		
Product A (12,000 units @ $3.25)..........	$39,000	
Product B (6,000 units @ $4.50)	27,000	
Product C (3,000 units @ $2.00)	6,000	
Total variable costs		72,000
Total costs		120,000
Net income		–0–

Illustration 25–5

A composite unit made up of units of each of a company's products in their expected sales mix may be used in answering a variety of cost-volume-profit questions. In making all such analyses it is assumed that the product mix remains constant at all sales levels just as the other factors entering into an analysis are assumed to be constant. Nevertheless, this does not prevent changes in the assumed sales mix in order to learn what would happen if the mix were changed. However, problems involving changes in the sales mix require a recomputation of the composite unit selling price and composite unit variable costs for each change in the mix.

EVALUATING THE RESULTS

Cost-volume-profit analyses have their greatest use in predicting what will happen when changes are made in selling prices, product mix, and the various cost factors. However, in evaluating the results of such analyses, several points should be borne in mind. First, the analyses are used to predict future results. Therefore, the data put into the formulas and on the graphs are assumed or forecasted data. Consequently, the results of the analyses are no more reliable than the data used. Second, cost-volume-profit analyses as presented here are based on the assumptions that in any one analysis selling price will remain constant, fixed costs are truly fixed, and variable costs are truly variable. These assumptions do not always reflect reality. Therefore, at best the answers obtained through cost-volume-profit analyses are approximations. However, if this is recognized, cost-volume-profit analyses can be useful to management in making decisions.

The cost-volume-profit analyses presented in this chapter are based on the assumption that revenues and costs may be expressed as straight lines; and as pointed out, such an assumption does not always hold. Therefore, it should be noted that cost-volume-profit analyses based on curvilinear relationships are also possible. However, the use of curvilinear relationships takes some rather sophisticated mathematics, and a discussion is deferred to a more advanced text.

GLOSSARY

Break-even point. The sales level at which a company neither earns a profit nor incurs a loss.

Contribution margin per unit. The dollar amount that the sale of one unit contributes toward recovery of fixed costs and then toward a profit.

Contribution rate. The contribution margin per unit expressed as a percentage of sales price.

Cost-volume-profit analysis. A method of predicting the effects of changes in costs and sales level on the income of a business.

Fixed cost. A cost that remains unchanged in total amount over a wide range of production levels.

Margin of safety. The difference between a company's current sales and sales at its break-even point, when sales are above the break-even point.

Relevant range of operations. The normal operating range for the business, which excludes extremely high and low levels of production that are not apt to be encountered.

Sales mix. The ratio in which a company's different products are sold.

Semivariable cost. A cost that changes with production volume but not in the same proportion.

Stair-step cost. A cost that remains constant over a range of production, then increases by a lump sum if production is expanded further, then remains constant over another range of production increases, and so forth.

Variable cost. A cost that changes in total amount proportionately with production-level changes.

QUESTIONS FOR CLASS DISCUSSION

1. For what is cost-volume-profit analysis used?
2. What is a fixed cost? Name two fixed costs.
3. When there are fixed costs in manufacturing a product and the number of units manufactured is increased, do fixed costs per unit increase or decrease? Why?
4. What is a variable cost? Name two variable costs.
5. What is a semivariable cost?
6. The reliability of cost-volume-profit analysis rests upon three basic assumptions. What are they?
7. What two factors tend to make it possible to classify costs as either fixed or variable.
8. What is the break-even point in the sale of a product?
9. A company sells a product for $90 per unit. The variable costs of producing and selling the product are $54 per unit. What is the product's contribution margin per unit? What is its contribution rate?
10. If a straight line is begun at the fixed cost level on a break-even graph and the line rises at the variable cost rate, what does the line show?
11. When a break-even graph is prepared, why are the fixed costs plotted as a horizontal line?
12. What is a company's margin of safety?
13. When we speak of a company's sales mix, what is meant by sales mix?
14. If a company produces and sells more than one product, the reliability of cost-volume-profit analysis depends on an additional assumption in regard to sales mix. What is that assumption?

CLASS EXERCISES

Exercise 25–1

Bracken Company manufactures Product X which it sells for $75 per unit. The variable costs of manufacturing the product are $60 per unit, and the annual fixed costs incurred in manufacturing it are $35,640. Calculate (1) the product's contribution margin, (2) its contribution rate, (3) the break-even point for the product in units, and (4) the break-even point in dollars of sales.

Exercise 25–2

Prepare an income statement for Bracken Company's Product X (Exercise 25–1), showing sales, fixed costs, and variable costs at the break-even point.

Exercise 25–3

Assume that Bracken Company of Exercise 25–1 wishes to earn a $30,000 annual after-tax income from the sale of its Product X and that it must pay 50% of its income in state and federal income taxes. Calculate (1) the number of units of its Product X it must sell to earn a $30,000 after-tax income from the sale of the product. (2) Calculate the number of dollars of sales of Product X that are needed to earn a $30,000 after-tax income.

Exercise 25–4

The sales manager of Bracken Company (Exercise 25–1) thinks that within two years annual sales of the company's Product X will reach 8,000 units at $75 each. Calculate the company's (1) before-tax income from the sale of these units and (2) calculate its after-tax income from the sale of the units.

Exercise 25–5

Astor Company markets Products A and B which it sells in the ratio of five units of Product A at $2 each to each three units of Product B at $6 each. The variable costs of marketing Product A are $1.68 per unit, and the variable costs for Product B are $4.20 per unit. The annual fixed costs for marketing both products are $14,000. Calculate (1) the selling price of a composite unit of these products, (2) the variable costs per composite unit, (3) the break-even point in composite units, and (4) the number of units of each product that will be sold at the break-even point.

PROBLEMS

Problem 25–1

Capper Company manufactures a number of products, one of which, Product Z, sells for $400 per unit. The fixed costs of manufacturing Product Z are $62,400, and the variable costs are $280 per unit.

Required:

1. Calculate the company's break-even point in the sale of Product Z *(a)* in units and *(b)* in dollars of sales.
2. Prepare a break-even graph for Product Z. Use 1,000 as the maximum number of units on your graph.
3. Prepare an income statement showing sales, fixed costs, and variable costs for Product Z at the break-even point.

4. Determine the sales volume in dollars that the company must achieve to earn a $45,000 after-tax (50% rate) income from the sale of Product Z.
5. Determine the after-tax income the company will earn from a $600,000 sales level for Product Z.

Problem 25–2

Caster Company buys its only product, Rolleralls, in bulk and packages them for resale. Last year the company earned an unsatisfactory after-tax return from the sale of 20,000 packages of Rolleralls at $5 per package. Last year's costs for the product were:

Fixed costs	$38,500
Variable costs:	
Bulk Rolleralls (sufficient for 20,000 packages)	55,000
Packaging materials and other variable packaging costs	5,000
Income tax rate	50%

The sales manager believes that if the selling price of the product is reduced 10% and a slight change is made in its packaging, the number of units sold will double. The packaging change will increase variable packaging costs 25% per unit, but doubling the units sold will gain a 5% reduction in the product's bulk price. The packaging and volume changes will not affect fixed costs.

Required:

1. Calculate the dollar break-even points for the product at the $5 sales price and at the $4.50 sales price.
2. Prepare a break-even graph for the sale of the product at each price. Use 40,000 as the maximum number of units on both graphs.
3. Prepare a condensed comparative income statement showing the results of selling the product at $5 per unit and the estimated results of selling it at $4.50 per unit.

Problem 25–3

Last year Tappit Company earned an unsatisfactory $2,610 after-tax income from the sale of 25,000 packages of its Product S at $4 each. The company buys Product S in bulk and packages it for resale. Following is condensed income statement information showing last year's results from the sale of the product:

Sales		$100,000
Bulk cost of Product S	$50,000	
Packaging material and other variable packaging costs .	10,000	
Fixed costs	34,780	94,780
Income before taxes		$ 5,220
Income taxes (50% rate)		2,610
Net income from sale of Product S		$ 2,610

It has been suggested that if the company will invest $5,000 in advertising and make a small change in the packaging of Product S, sales will increase 60%. The packaging change will increase variable packaging costs 10% per unit but will not affect other fixed and variable costs.

Required:

1. Calculate last year's break-even point for Product S in dollars.
2. Calculate the break-even point in dollars under the assumption the $5,000 is spent for advertising and the packaging change is made.
3. Prepare a break-even graph under the assumptions of Requirement 2. Use 50,000 as the maximum number of units on the graph.
4. Prepare an income statement showing the expected results under the assumption the $5,000 is spent for advertising, the packaging change is made, and sales increase by 60%.
5. Assume that instead of increasing 60% with the advertising and packaging change, sales increased to 50,000 units at $4 per unit. *(a)* Present calculations that show the amount of after-tax income that will be earned at this level. *(b)* Prepare an income statement showing sales, costs, and net income at this $200,000 sales level.

Problem 25–5

Lighter Company sells a number of products, among which are Products X and Y. Last year the company sold 10,000 units of each of these products at $100 per unit, earning $100,000 from the sale of each as the following condensed income statement shows:

	Product X	Product Y
Sales	$1,000,000	$1,000,000
Costs:		
Fixed costs	$ 200,000	$ 600,000
Variable costs	600,000	200,000
Total costs	$ 800,000	$ 800,000
Income before taxes	$ 200,000	$ 200,000
Income taxes (50% rate)	100,000	100,000
Net income	$ 100,000	$ 100,000

Required:

1. Calculate the break-even point for each product in dollars.
2. Prepare a break-even graph for each product. Use 10,000 as the maximum number of units on each graph.
3. Prepare a condensed income statement showing in separate columns the net income the company will earn from the sale of each product under the assumption that without a change in selling prices, the number of units of each product sold declines 25%.
4. Prepare a second condensed income statement showing in separate columns the net income the company will earn if the number of units of each product sold increases 25% without a change in selling prices.

Problem 25–5

Best Company manufactures and sells three products, A, B, and C. Product A sells for $15 per unit, Product B sells for $10 per unit, and Product C sells for $8 per unit. Their sales mix is in the ratio of 4:2:5, and the variable costs of manufacturing and selling the products have been Product A, $10;

Product B, $6.50; and Product C, $5. The fixed costs of manufacturing and selling the three products are $151,200. Material X has been used in manufacturing both Products A and C; however, a new material has just come on the market, and if it is substituted for Material X, it will reduce the variable cost of manufacturing Product A by $1 and Product C by $0.40.

Required:

1. Determine the company's break-even point in dollars and the number of units of each product sold at the break-even point under the assumption Material X is used in manufacturing Products A and C. Show all pertinent calculations.
2. Determine the company's break-even point in dollars and the number of units of each product sold at the break-even point under the assumption the new material is used in manufacturing products A and C. Show all pertinent calculations.

ALTERNATE PROBLEMS

Problem 25-1A

Among the products sold by Damen Company is Product N, which sells for $450 per unit. The fixed costs of selling Product N are $85,500, and the variable costs are $270 per unit.

Required:

1. Calculate the company's break-even point in the sale of Product N *(a)* in units and *(b)* in dollars of sales.
2. Prepare a break-even graph for Product N, using 1,000 as the maximum number of units on the graph.
3. Prepare an income statement showing sales, fixed costs, and variable costs for Product N at the break-even point.
4. Determine the sales volume in dollars required to achieve a $40,000 after-tax (50% rate) income from the sale of Product N.
5. Determine the after-tax income the company will earn from a $500,000 sales level for Product N.

Problem 25-2A

Last year Gale Company sold 40,000 units of its product at $5 per unit with the following results:

Sales		$200,000
Costs:		
Fixed	$60,000	
Variable:		
Material X (40,000 lbs. @ $2 per lb.)	80,000	
Other variable	40,000	180,000
Income before taxes		$ 20,000

A new material, Material Y, has recently come on the market; and if substituted for the Material X presently used in the product, material costs can be reduced from $2 per unit to $1 pr unit. The substitution will have no effect on the product's quality; but it will give Gale Company a choice in pricing the product. (1) The company can maintain the present per unit price, sell the same number of units, and make a $1 per unit greater profit. Or (2) it can reduce the product's price $1 per unit, an amount equal to the material savings, and because of the lower price, increase the units sold by 40%. If the latter choice is made, the $60,000 of fixed costs will remain fixed and the "other variable" costs will vary with volume.

Required:
1. Calculate the break-even point in dollars for each alternative.
2. Prepare a break-even graph for each alternative. The company's capacity is 60,000 units, and this should be used as the upper limit on the graphs.
3. Prepare a comparative income statement showing sales, fixed costs, variable costs, and after-tax (50% rate) net income for each alternative.

Problem 25–3A

Zest Company manufactured and sold 5,000 units of its Product Z last year with the following unsatisfactory results:

Sales		$100,000
Costs:		
Fixed	$22,000	
Variable	80,000	102,000
Loss from the sale of Product Z		$ (2,000)

An investigation shows that if the company will install a new machine it can save sufficient piece-rate labor and spoiled materials to reduce the variable costs of manufacturing Product Z by 15%. The new machine will increase fixed costs $2,320 annually.

Required:
1. Calculate last year's break-even point for Product Z in dollars and in units.
2. Calculate the break-even point in dollars and in units under the assumption the new machine is installed.
3. Prepare a break-even graph for Product Z under the assumption the new machine is installed. Use 8,000 as the maximum number of units on your graph.
4. Prepare an income statement showing expected annual results from the sale of Product Z with the new machine installed, no change in selling price, and no change in the number of units sold. Assume a 50% income tax rate.
5. Calculate the sales level required to earn a $12,000 annual after-tax income from the sale of Product Z with no change in its selling price and the new machine installed. Prepare an income statement showing the results from the sale of Product Z at this level.

Problem 25–5A

West Company manufactures and sells Products X, Y, and Z in the ratio of three units of Product X to two units of Product Y to four units of Product Z. Product X sells for $10 per unit, Product Y sells for $6 per unit, and Product Z sells for $2 per unit. The variable costs of manufacturing and selling the products have been Product X, $6; Product Y, $4; and Product Z, $1.50; and the fixed costs incurred in manufacturing and selling the three products are $126,000.

Material M has been used in manufacturing Products Y and Z; however, a new material has just come on the market, and if substituted for Material M, it will reduce the variable costs of Product Y by $0.50 per unit and Product Z by $0.25 per unit.

Required:

1. Determine the company's break-even point in dollars and the number of units of each product sold at the break-even point when Material M is used in manufacturing Products Y and Z. Show all pertinent calculations.
2. Determine the company's break-even point in dollars and the number of units of each product sold at the break-even point under the assumption the new material is substituted in manufacturing Products Y and Z. Show all pertinent calculations.

PROVOCATIVE PROBLEMS

Provocative problem 25–1
Eastern Company

Eastern Company manufactures and sells Products A, B, and C. Last year's sales mix for the three products was in the ratio of 5:4:1, with combined sales totaling 10,000 units. Product A sells for $100 per unit and has a 20% contribution rate, Product B sells for $80 per unit and has a 30% contribution rate, and Product C sells for $60 per unit and has a 40% contribution rate. The fixed costs of manufacturing and selling the products total $139,000. The company estimates that sales of the three products will continue at the 10,000 unit level next year. However, the sales manager is of the opinion that if the company's advertising and sales efforts are slanted further toward Products B and C during the coming year, with no increases in the amounts of money expended, the sales mix of the three products can be changed to the ratio of 3:5:2.

Should the company change its sales mix through advertising and sales efforts? What effect will the change have on the composite contribution rate of the three products? What effect will it have on the company's break-even point? Back your answers with figures.

Provocative problem 25–2
Ft. Dodge Company

Ft. Dodge Company earned $75,000 before taxes in 198A, and its income statement provided the following summarized information.

Sales		$600,000
Costs:		
Variable costs	$300,000	
Fixed costs	225,000	525,000
Income before taxes		$ 75,000

The company operated at near capacity during 198A, and a 10% annual increase in the demand for its product is expected. As a result the company's management is trying to decide how to meet this demand. Two alternatives are being considered. The first calls for changes that will increase variable costs to 55% of the selling price of the company's product but will not change fixed costs. The second calls for a capital investment that will increase fixed costs 10% but will not affect variable costs.

Which alternative do you recommend? Back your recommendation with income statement information and any other data you consider relevant.

Provocative problem 25–3
Astor Company

Astor Company operated at near capacity last year, producing and selling 200,000 gallons of its product with the following results:

Sales			$500,000
Manufacturing costs:			
Fixed	$100,000		
Variable	200,000	$300,000	
Selling and general expenses:			
Fixed	$ 70,000		
Variable	50,000	120,000	420,000
Income before taxes			$ 80,000

The company has an opportunity to enter into a five-year contract for the annual sale of 150,000 gallons of the product in the export market at $1.90 per gallon, FOB factory. Delivery on the contract would require a plant addition that would increase fixed manufacturing costs by 75% annually. The contract would not increase the totals of present fixed and variable selling and general expenses. Variable manufacturing costs would vary with volume.

Management is not certain it should enter into the contract, and it has asked you for your opinion, including the following:

1. An estimated income statement for the first year following the plant addition, assuming no change in domestic sales.
2. A comparison of break-even sales levels before the plant addition and after the contract expiration. Assume after-contract sales and expense levels, other than fixed manufacturing costs, will be at the same levels as last year.
3. A statement showing net income after the contract expiration but at sales and expense levels of last year, other than fixed manufacturing costs.

After studying Chapter 26, you should be able to:

☐ State the deficiencies of fixed budgets.

☐ Prepare flexible budgets and state their advantages.

☐ State what standard costs represent, how they are determined, and how they are used in the evaluation process.

☐ Calculate material, labor, and overhead variances, and state what each variance indicates about the performance of a company.

☐ Explain the relevance of standard cost accounting to the management philosophy known as "management by exception."

☐ Define or explain the words and phrases listed in the chapter Glossary.

Flexible budgets; standard costs

■ The development of a master plan for the business was discussed in Chapter 24; consideration was also given to the importance of controlling subsequent operations. This function of control was recognized as one of the two basic functions of management. In order to control business operations, management must obtain information or feedback regarding how closely actual operations conform to the plans. To the extent possible, the comparison of actual performance with planned performance should direct management's attention toward the reasons why actual performance differs from planned performance. Flexible budgets and standard costs are important techniques that are used to help management determine why actual performance differs from the plan.

FIXED BUDGETS AND PERFORMANCE REPORTS

In preparing a master budget as discussed in Chapter 24, the initial step is to determine the expected sales volume for the budget period. All of the subsequent budget procedures are based on this specific estimate of sales volume. The amount of each budgeted cost is based on the assumption that a specific or fixed amount of sales will take place. When a budget is based on a single estimate of sales or production volume, the budget is called a *fixed* or *static budget*. In budgeting the total amount of each cost, a fixed budget gives no consideration to the possibility that the actual sales or production volume may be different from the fixed or budgeted amount.

If a company uses only fixed budgets, the comparison of actual performance with the budgeted performance is presented in a performance report such as that shown in Illustration 26–1.

Tampa Manufacturing Company
Fixed Budget Performance Report
For Month Ended November 30, 19—

	Fixed budget	Actual performance	Variances
Sales: In units	10,000	12,000	
In dollars	$100,000	$125,000	$25,000 F
Cost of goods sold:			
Raw materials	$ 10,000	$ 13,000	$ 3,000 U
Direct labor	15,000	20,000	5,000 U
Overhead:			
Factory supplies	2,000	2,100	100 U
Utilities	3,000	4,000	1,000 U
Depreciation of machinery	8,000	8,000	—
Supervisory salaries	11,000	11,000	—
Selling expenses:			
Sales commissions	9,000	10,800	1,800 U
Shipping expenses	4,000	4,300	300 U
General and administrative expenses:			
Office supplies	5,000	5,200	200 U
Insurance expense	1,000	1,200	200 U
Depreciation of office equipment	7,000	7,000	—
Administrative salaries	13,000	13,000	—
Total expenses	$ 88,000	$ 99,600	$11,600 U
Income from operations	$ 12,000	$ 25,400	$13,400 F

F = favorable variance, that is, compared to the budget, the actual cost or revenue contributes to a higher income.
U = unfavorable variance, that is, compared to the budget, the actual cost or revenue contributes to a lower income.

Illustration 26–1

The budgeted sales volume of Tampa Manufacturing Company is 10,000 units (see Illustration 26–1). Also, to simplify the discussion, production volume is assumed to equal sales volume; and no beginning or ending inventory is maintained by the company. In evaluating Tampa Manufacturing Company's operations, management should be interested in answering such questions as: Why is the actual income from operations $13,400 higher than the budgeted amount? Are the prices being paid for each expense item too high? Is the manufacturing department using too much raw material? Is it using too much direct labor? The performance report shown in Illustration 26–1 provides little help in answering questions such as these. Since the actual sales volume was 2,000 units higher than the budgeted amount, it may be assumed that this increase caused total dollar sales and many of the expenses to be higher. But other factors may have influenced the amount of income, and the fixed budget performance report fails to provide management much information beyond the fact that the sales volume was higher than budgeted.

FLEXIBLE BUDGETS

To help answer questions such as those mentioned above, many companies prepare *flexible* or *variable budgets.* In contrast to fixed budgets, which are based on one, fixed amount of budgeted sales or production, flexible budgets recognize that different levels of activity should produce different amounts of cost.

PREPARING A FLEXIBLE BUDGET

To prepare a flexible budget, each type of cost is examined to determine whether it should be classified as a variable cost or as a fixed cost. Recall from Chapter 25 that the total amount of a variable cost changes in direct proportion to a change in the level of activity. Thus, variable cost per unit of activity remains constant. On the other hand, the total amount of a fixed cost remains unchanged regardless of changes in the level of activity (within the relevant or normal operating range of activity).[1]

After each cost item is classified as variable or fixed, each variable cost is expressed as a constant amount of cost per unit of sales (or per sales dollar). Fixed costs are, of course, budgeted in terms of the total amount of each fixed cost that is expected regardless of the sales volume that may occur within the relevant range.

Illustration 26–2 shows how the fixed budget of Tampa Manufacturing Company is reformulated as a flexible budget. Compare the first column of Illustration 26–2 with the first column of Illustration 26–1. Notice that seven of the expenses have been reclassified as variable costs; the remaining five expanses have been reclassified as fixed costs. This classification results from an investigation of each expense incurred by Tampa Manufacturing Company, and the classification should not be misunderstood. It does not mean that these particular expenses are always variable costs in every company. For example, Office Supplies Expense may frequently be a fixed cost, depending upon the nature of the company's operations. Nevertheless, Tampa Manufacturing Company's accountant investigated this item and concluded that the Office Supplies cost behaves as a variable cost.

Observe in Illustration 26–2 that the variable costs of Tampa Manufacturing Company are listed together, totaled, and subtracted from

---

[1] In Chapter 25, it was recognized that some costs are neither strictly variable nor strictly fixed. However, in the present discussion, it is assumed that all costs can be reasonably classified as being either variable or fixed.

Tampa Manufacturing Company
Flexible Budget
For Month Ending November 30, 19—

	Fixed budget	Flexible budget Variable cost per unit	Flexible budget Total fixed cost	Flexible budget for unit sales of 12,000	Flexible budget for unit sales of 14,000
Sales: In units	10,000			12,000	14,000
In dollars	$100,000	$10.00		$120,000	$140,000
Variable costs:					
Raw materials	$ 10,000	$ 1.00		$ 12,000	$ 14,000
Direct labor	15,000	1.50		18,000	21,000
Factory supplies	2,000	0.20		2,400	2,800
Utilities	3,000	0.30		3,600	4,200
Sales commissions	9,000	0.90		10,800	12,600
Shipping expenses	4,000	0.40		4,800	5,600
Office supplies	5,000	0.50		6,000	7,000
Total variable costs	$ 48,000	$ 4.80		$ 57,600	$ 67,200
Contribution margin	$ 52,000	$ 5.20		$ 62,400	$ 72,800
Fixed costs:					
Depreciation of machinery ..	$ 8,000		$ 8,000	$ 8,000	$ 8,000
Supervisory salaries	11,000		11,000	11,000	11,000
Insurance expense	1,000		1,000	1,000	1,000
Depreciation of office equipment	7,000		7,000	7,000	7,000
Administrative salaries	13,000		13,000	13,000	13,000
Total fixed costs	$ 40,000		$40,000	$ 40,000	$ 40,000
Income from operations	$ 12,000			$ 22,400	$ 32,800

Illustration 26–2

sales. As explained in Chapter 25, the difference between sales and variable costs is identified as the contribution margin. The budgeted amounts of fixed costs are then listed and totaled.

In Illustration 26–2, columns 2 and 3 show the flexible budget amounts which may be applied to any volume of sales that occurs. The last two columns merely illustrate what form the flexible budget takes when the budget amounts are applied to particular sales volumes.

Recall from Illustration 26–1 that Tampa Manufacturing Company's actual sales volume for November 19—, was 12,000 units. This was 2,000 units more than the 10,000 units originally forecasted in the master budget. The effect of this sales increase on the income from operations can be determined by comparing the budget for 10,000 units with the budget for 12,000 units (see Illustration 26–2). At a sales volume of 12,000 units, the budgeted income from operations is $22,400, whereas the budget for sales of 10,000 units shows income from operations of $12,000. Thus, if sales volume is 12,000 rather than

10,000 units, management should expect income from operations to be higher by $10,400 ($22,400 − $12,000). In other words, the difference between the $25,400 actual income from operations (see Illustration 26–1) and the $12,000 income from operations shown on the master budget can be analyzed, as follows:

Actual income from operations (12,000 units)		$25,400
Income from operations on master budget (10,000 units)		12,000
Difference to be explained		$13,400
Income from operations:		
On the flexible budget for 12,000 units	$22,400	
On the budget for 10,000 units	12,000	
Additional income caused by increase in sales volume		(10,400)
Unexplained difference		$ 3,000

This $3,000 unexplained difference is the amount by which the actual income from operations exceeds budgeted income from operations as shown on the flexible budget for a sales volume of 12,000 units. As management seeks to determine what steps should be taken to control Tampa Manufacturing Company's operations, the next step is to determine what caused this $3,000 unexplained difference. Information to help answer this question is provided by a flexible budget performance report.

FLEXIBLE BUDGET PERFORMANCE REPORT

A *flexible budget performance report* is designed to analyze the difference between actual performance and budgeted performance, where the budgeted amounts are based on the actual sales volume or level of activity. The report should direct management's attention toward those particular costs or revenues where actual performance has differed substantially from the budgeted amount.

The flexible budget performance report for Tampa Manufacturing Company is presented in Illustration 26–3.

Observe in Illustration 26–3 the $5,000 favorable variance in total dollar sales. Since the actual number of units sold amounted to 12,000 and the budget was also based on unit sales of 12,000, the $5,000 variance must have resulted entirely from a difference between the average price per unit and the budgeted price per unit. Further analysis of the $5,000 variance is as follows:

Average price per unit, actual	$125,000/12,000	= $10.42
Budgeted price per unit	$120,000/12,000	= 10.00
Favorable variance in price per unit..............	$5,000/12,000	= $ 0.42

Tampa Manufacturing Company
Flexible Budget Performance Report
For Month Ended November 30, 19—

	Flexible budget	Actual performance	Variances
Sales (12,000 units)	$120,000	$125,000	$5,000 F
Variable costs:			
Raw materials	$ 12,000	$ 13,000	$1,000 U
Direct labor	18,000	20,000	2,000 U
Factory supplies	2,400	2,100	300 F
Utilities	3,600	4,000	400 U
Sales commissions	10,800	10,800	
Shipping expenses	4,800	4,300	500 F
Office supplies	6,000	5,200	800 F
Total variable costs	$ 57,600	$ 59,400	$1,800 U
Contribution margin	$ 62,400	$ 65,600	$3,200 F
Fixed costs:			
Depreciation of machinery	$ 8,000	$ 8,000	
Supervisory salaries	11,000	11,000	
Insurance expense	1,000	1,200	$ 200 U
Depreciation of office equipment	7,000	7,000	
Administrative salaries	13,000	13,000	
Total fixed costs	$ 40,000	$ 40,200	$ 200 U
Income from operations	$ 22,400	$ 25,400	$3,000 F

F = favorable variance, that is, compared to the budget, the actual cost or revenue contributes to a higher income.

U = unfavorable variance, that is, compared to the budget, the actual cost or revenue contributes to a lower income.

Illustration 26–3

The variances in Illustration 26–3 direct management's attention toward the areas in which corrective action may be necessary in controlling Tampa Manufacturing Company's operations. In addition, students should recognize that each of the cost variances can be analyzed in a manner similar to the above discussion of sales. Each of the expenses can be thought of as involving the use of a given number of units of the expense item, and paying a specific price per unit. Following this approach, each of the cost variances shown in Illustration 26–3 might result in part from a difference between the actual price per unit and the budgeted price per unit (a price variance); and they may also result in part from a difference between the actual number of units used and the budgeted number of units to be used (a quantity variance). This line of reasoning, called variance analysis, is discussed more completely in the following section on standard costs.

STANDARD COSTS

In Chapter 23 it was said that there are two basic types of cost systems, job order and process, but a large number of variations of the two. A *standard cost system,* one based on *standard* or *budgeted costs,* is such a variation.

The costs of a job or a process as discussed in Chapter 23 were historical costs, historical in the sense that they had been incurred and were history by the time they were recorded. Such costs are useful; but to judge whether or not they are reasonable or what they should be, management needs a basis of comparison. Standard costs offer such a basis.

Standard costs are the costs that should be incurred under normal conditions in producing a given product or part or in performing a particular service. They are established by means of engineering and accounting studies made before the product is manufactured or the service performed. Once established, they are used to judge the reasonableness of the actual costs incurred when the product or service is produced. Standard costs are also used to place responsibilities when actual costs vary from standard.

Accountants speak of *standard material cost, standard labor cost,* and *standard overhead cost;* and this terminology is used in this chapter. However, it should be observed that standard material, labor, and overhead costs are really budgeted material, labor, and overhead costs.

ESTABLISHING STANDARD COSTS

Great care and the combined efforts of people in accounting, engineering, personnel administration, and other management areas are required in establishing standard costs. Time and motion studies are made of each labor operation in a product's production or in performing a service. From these studies, management learns the best way to perform the operation and the standard labor time required under normal conditions for performance. Exhaustive investigations are also made of the quantity, grade, and cost of each material required; and machines and other productive equipment are subject to detailed studies in an effort to achieve maximum efficiencies and to learn what costs should be.

However, regardless of care exercised in establishing standard costs and in revising them as conditions change, actual costs incurred in producing a given product or service are apt to vary from standard costs. When this occurs, the difference in total cost is likely to be a composite of several cost differences. For example, the quantity and/or the price of the material used may have varied from standard. Also, the labor time and/or the labor price may have varied. Likewise, overhead costs may have varied.

VARIANCES

When actual costs vary from standard costs, the differences are called *variances.* Variances may be favorable or unfavorable. A favorable variance is one in which actual cost is below standard cost, and an unfavorable variance is one in which actual cost is above standard.

When variances occur, they are isolated and studied for possible remedial action and to place responsibilities. For example, assume the standard material cost for producing 2,000 units of Product A is $800 but material costing $840 was used in producing the units. The $40 variance may have resulted from paying a price higher than standard for the material. Or a greater quantity of material than standard may have been used. Or there may have been some combination of these causes. The price paid for a material is a purchasing department responsibility; consequently, if the variance was caused by a price greater than standard, responsibility rests with the purchasing department. On the other hand, since the production department is usually responsible for the amount of material used, if a quantity greater than standard was used, responsibility normally rests with the production department. However, if more than a standard amount of material was used because the material was of a grade below standard, causing more than a normal waste, responsibility is back on the purchasing department for buying a substandard grade.

ISOLATING MATERIAL AND LABOR VARIANCES

As previously stated, when variances occur, they are isolated and studied for possible remedial action and to place responsibilities. For example, assume that XL Company has established the following standard costs per unit for its Product Z:

```
Material (1 lb. per unit at $1 per lb.) ........... $1.00
Direct labor (1 hr. per unit at $3 per hr.) ........  3.00
Overhead ($2 per standard direct labor hour) ...  2.00
            Total standard cost per unit ............ $6.00
```

Material variances

Assume further that during May, XL Company completed 3,500 units of Product Z, using 3,600 pounds of material costing $1.05 per pound, or $3,780. Under these assumptions the actual and standard material costs for the 3,500 units are:

```
Actual cost:    3,600 lbs @ $1.05 per lb. ............ $3,780
Standard cost: 3,500 lbs. @ $1 per lb. ..............  3,500
             Material cost variance (unfavorable)  ......... $  280
```

Observe that the actual material cost for these units is $280 above their standard cost. This unfavorable material cost variance may be isolated as to causes in the following manner:

QUANTITY VARIANCE:
Actual units at the standard price ..... 3,600 lbs. @ $1.00 = $3,600
Standard units at the standard price ... 3,500 lbs. @ $1.00 — 3,500
    Variance (unfavorable) .... 100 lbs. @ $1.00 = $100

PRICE VARIANCE:
Actual units at the actual price .... 3,600 lbs. @ $1.05 = $3,780
Actual units at the standard price ..... 3,600 lbs. @ $1.00 = 3,600
    Variance (unfavorable) .... 3,600 lbs. @ $0.05 = 180
    Material cost variance
    (unfavorable) $280

The analysis shows that $100 of the excess material cost resulted from using 100 more pounds than standard, and $180 resulted from a unit price $0.05 above standard. With this information management can go to the responsible individuals for explanations.

Labor variances

Labor cost in manufacturing a given part or in performing a service depends on a composite of the number of hours worked (quantity) and the wage rate paid (price). Therefore, when the labor cost for a task varies from standard, it too may be analyzed into a *quantity variance* and a *price variance*.

For example, the direct labor standard for the 3,500 units of Product Z is one hour per unit, or 3,500 hours at $3 per hour. If 3,400 hours costing $3.10 per hour were used in completing the units, the actual and standard labor costs for these units are:

Actual Cost: 3,400 hrs. @ $3.10 per hr. $10,540
Standard cost: 3,500 hrs. @ $3.00 per hr............. 10,500
    Direct labor cost variance (unfavorable) .... $ 40

In this case actual cost is only $40 over standard, but isolating the quantity and price variances involved reveals the following:

QUANTITY VARIANCE:
Standard hours at standard price .... 3,500 hrs. @ $3.00 = $10,500
Actual hours at standard price .... 3,400 hrs. @ $3.00 = 10,200
    Variance (favorable) .... 100 hrs. @ $3.00 = $300

PRICE VARIANCE:
Actual hours at actual price .... 3,400 hrs. @ $3.10 = $10,540
Actual hours at standard price .... 3,400 hrs. @ $3.00 = 10,200
    Variance (unfavorable) .... 3,400 hrs. @ $0.10 = 340
    Direct labor cost variance
    (unfavorable) .... $ 40

The analysis shows a favorable quantity variance of $300, which resulted from using 100 fewer direct labor hours than standard for the units produced. However, this favorable variance was more than offset by a wage rate that was $0.10 above standard.

When a factory or department has workers of various skill levels, it is the responsibility of the foreman or other supervisor to assign to each task a worker or workers of no higher skill level than is required to accomplish the task. In this case an investigation could reveal that workers of a higher skill level were used in producing the 3,500 units of Product Z; hence, fewer labor hours were required for the work. However, because the workers were of higher grade, the wage rate paid them was higher than standard.

CHARGING OVERHEAD TO PRODUCTION

When standard costs are used, factory overhead is charged to production by means of a predetermined standard overhead rate. The rate may be based on the relation of overhead to standard labor cost, standard labor hours, standard machine-hours, or some other measure of production. For example, XL Company charges its Product Z with $2 of overhead per standard direct labor hour; and since the direct labor standard for Product Z is one hour per unit, the 3,500 units manufactured in May were charged with $7,000 of overhead.

Before going on, recall that only 3,400 actual direct labor hours were used in producing these units. Then note again that overhead is charged to the units, not on the basis of actual labor hours but on the basis of standard labor hours. Standard labor hours are used because the amount of overhead charged to these units should not be less than standard simply because less than the standard (normal) amount of labor was used in their production. In other words, overhead should not vary from normal simply because labor varied from normal.

ESTABLISHING OVERHEAD STANDARDS

A variable or flexible factory overhead budget is the starting point in establishing reasonable standards for overhead costs. A flexible budget is necessary because the actual production level may vary from the expected level; and when this happens, certain costs vary with production, but others remain fixed. This may be seen by examining XL Company's flexible budget shown in Illustration 26–4.

Observe in Illustration 26–4 that XL Company's flexible budget has been used to establish standard costs for four production levels ranging from 70% to 100% of capacity. When actual costs are known, they should be compared with the standards for the level actually achieved and not with the standards at some other level. For example, if the plant actually operated at 70% capacity during May, actual costs incurred should be compared with standard costs for the 70% level.

XL Company
Flexible Overhead Costs Budget For Month Ended May 31, 19—

	Budget amounts	Production levels			
		70%	80%	90%	100%
Production in units	1 unit	3,500	4,000	4,500	5,000
Standard direct labor hours		3,500	4,000	4,500	5,000
Budgeted factory overhead:					
Fixed costs:					
Building rent	$1,000	$1,000	$1,000	$1,000	$1,000
Depreciation, machinery	1,200	1,200	1,200	1,200	1,200
Supervisory salaries	1,800	1,800	1,800	1,800	1,800
Totals	$4,000	$4,000	$4,000	$4,000	$4,000
Variable costs:					
Indirect labor	$0.40	$1,400	$1,600	$1,800	$2,000
Indirect materials	0.30	1,050	1,200	1,350	1,500
Power and lights	0.20	700	800	900	1,000
Maintenance	0.10	350	400	450	500
Totals	$1.00	$3,500	$4,000	$4,500	$5,000
Total factory overhead		$7,500	$8,000	$8,500	$9,000

Illustration 26–4

Actual costs should not be compared with costs established for the 80% or 90% levels.

In setting overhead standards, after the flexible overhead budget is prepared, management must determine the expected operating level for the plant. This can be 100% of capacity but it seldom is. Errors in scheduling work, breakdowns, and, perhaps, the inability of the sales force to sell all the product produced are factors that commonly reduce the operating level to some point below full capacity.

After the flexible budget is set up and the expected operating level is determined, overhead costs at the expected level are related to, for example, labor hours at this level to establish the standard overhead rate. The rate thus established is then used to charge overhead to production. For example, assume XL Company decided that 80% of capacity is the expected operating level for its plant. The company then arrived at its $2 per direct labor hour overhead rate by dividing the budgeted $8,000 of overhead costs at the 80% level by the 4,000 standard direct labor hours required to produce the product manufactured at this level.

OVERHEAD VARIANCES

As previously stated, when standard costs are used, overhead is applied to production on the basis of a predetermined overhead rate. Then, at the end of a cost period the difference between overhead applied and overhead actually incurred is analyzed and variances are calculated to set out responsibilities for the difference.

Overhead variances are computed in several ways. A common way divides the difference between overhead applied and overhead incurred into (1) the *volume variance* and (2) the *controllable variance*.

Volume variance

The *volume variance* is the difference between (1) *the amount of overhead budgeted at the actual operating level achieved during the period* and (2) *the standard amount of overhead charged to production during the period*. For example, assume that during May, XL Company actually operated at 70% of capacity. It produced 3,500 units of Product Z, which were charged with overhead at the standard rate. Under this assumption the company's volume variance for May is:

VOLUME VARIANCE:
Budgeted overhead at 70% of capacity $7,500
Standard overhead charged to production (3,500 standard
    labor hours at the $2 per hour standard rate) 7,000
          Variance (unfavorable) .... $ 500

To understand why this volume variance occurred, reexamine the flexible budget of Illustration 26–4. Observe that at the 80% level the $2 per hour overhead rate may be subdivided into $1 per hour for fixed overhead and $1 per hour for variable overhead. Furthermore, at the 80% (normal) level, the $1 for fixed overhead exactly covers the fixed overhead. However, when this $2 rate is used for the 70% level, and again subdivided, the $1 for fixed overhead will not cover all the fixed overhead because $4,000 is required for fixed overhead and 3,500 hours at $1 per hour equals only $3,500. In other words, at this 70% level the $2 per hour standard overhead rate did not absorb all the overhead incurred; it lacked $500, the amount of the volume variance. Or again, the volume variance resulted simply because the plant did not reach the expected operating level.

An unfavorable volume variance tells management that the plant did not reach its normal operating level; and when such a variance is large, management should investigate the cause or causes. Machine breakdowns, failure to schedule an even flow of work, and a lack of sales orders are common causes. The first two may be corrected in the factory, but the third requires either more orders from the sales force or a downward adjustment of the operating level considered to be normal.

Controllable variance

Tho *controllable variance* is the difference between (1) *overhead actually incurred and* (2) *the overhead budgeted at the operating level achieved.* For example, assume that XL Company incurred $7,650 of overhead during May. Since its plant operated at 70% of capacity during the month, its controllable overhead variance for May is:

```
CONTROLLABLE VARIANCE:
  Actual overhead incurred ....................... $7,650
  Overhead budgeted at operating level achieved ....  7,500
      Variance (unfavorable) ..................... $  150
```

The controllable overhead variance measures management's efficiency in adjusting controllable overhead costs (normally variable overhead) to the operating level achieved. In this case management failed by $150 to get overhead down to the amount budgeted for the 70% level.

The controllable overhead variance measures management's efficiency in adjusting overhead costs to the operating level achieved. However, an overhead variance report is a more effective means for showing just where management achieved or failed to achieve the budgeted expectations. Such a report for XL Company appears in Illustration 26–5 on the next page.

Combining the volume and controllable variances

The volume and controllable variances may be combined to account for the difference between overhead actually incurred and overhead charged to production. For example, XL Company incurred $7,650 of overhead during May and charged $7,000 to production. Its overhead variances may be combined as follows to account for the difference:

```
VOLUME VARIANCE:
  Overhead budgeted at operating level achieved ............. $7,500
  Standard overhead charged to production (3,500 standard
    hours at $2 per hour) ...................................  7,000
      Variance (unfavorable) .................................          $500
CONTROLLABLE VARIANCE:
  Actual overhead incurred ................................. $7,650
  Overhead budgeted at operating level achieved ............  7,500
      Variance (unfavorable) .................................           150
  Excess of overhead incurred over overhead charged to
    production ............................................          $650
```

CONTROLLING A BUSINESS THROUGH STANDARD COSTS

Business operations are carried on by people, and control of a business is gained by controlling the actions of the people responsible for its revenues, costs, and expenses. When a budget is prepared and standard costs established, control is maintained by taking appropriate action when actual costs vary from standard or from the budget.

Reports like the ones shown in this chapter are a means of calling management's attention to these variations, and a review of the reports is essential to the successful operation of a budget program. However, in making the review, management should practice the control technique known as *management by exception*. Under this technique, management gives its attention only to the variances in which actual costs are significantly different from standard; it ignores the cost situations in which performance is satisfactory. In other words, management concentrates its attention on the exceptional or irregular situations and pays little or no attention to the normal.

Many companies develop standard costs and apply variance analysis only when dealing with manufacturing costs. In these companies, the master budget includes selling, general, and administrative expenses, but the subsequent process of controlling these expenses is not based

---

XL Company
Factory Overhead Variance Report
For Month Ended May 31, 19—

VOLUME VARIANCE:

Normal production level	80%	of capacity.
Production level achieved	70%	of capacity.
Volume variance	$ 500 (unfavorable)	

CONTROLLABLE VARIANCE:

	Budget	Actual	Favorable	Unfavorable
Fixed overhead costs:				
Building rent	$1,000	$1,000		
Depreciation, machinery	1,200	1,200		
Supervisory salaries	1,800	1,800		
Total fixed	$4,000	$4,000		
Variable overhead costs:				
Indirect labor	$1,400	$1,525		$125
Indirect materials	1,050	1,025	$ 25	
Power and lights	700	750		50
Maintenance	350	350		
Total variable	$3,500	$3,650		
Total controllable variances...................			$ 25	$175
Net controllable variance (unfavorable)................			150	
			$175	$175

Illustration 26–5

upon the establishment of standard costs and variance analysis. However, other companies have recognized that standard costs and variance analysis may help control selling, general, and administrative expenses just as well as manufacturing costs. Students should understand that the previous discussions of material and labor cost variances can easily be adapted to many selling, general, and administrative expenses.

STANDARD COSTS IN THE ACCOUNTS

Standard costs can be used solely in the preparation of management reports and need not be taken into the accounts. However, in most standard cost systems such costs are taken into the accounts to facilitate both the record keeping and the preparation of reports.

No effort will be made here to go into the record-keeping details of a standard cost system. This is reserved for a course in cost accounting. Nevertheless, when standard costs are taken into the accounts, entries like the following (the data for which are taken from the discussion of material variances on pages 866–67) may be used to take the standard costs into the Goods in Process account and to set out in variance accounts any variances:

May	31	Goods in Process	3,500.00	
		Material Quantity Variance	100.00	
		Material Price Variance	180.00	
		Materials		3,780.00
		To charge production with 3,600 pounds of material @ $1.05 per pound.		

Variances taken into the accounts are allowed to accumulate in the variance accounts until the end of an accounting period. If at that time the variance amounts are immaterial, they are closed to Cost of Goods Sold as an adjustment of the cost of goods sold. However, if the amounts are large, they may be prorated between Goods in Process, Finished Goods, and Cost of Goods Sold.

GLOSSARY

Controllable variance. The difference between overhead actually incurred and the overhead budgeted at the operating level achieved.

Fixed budget. A budget based on a single estimate of sales or production volume that gives no consideration to the possibility that the actual sales or production volume may be different from the assumed amount.

Flexible budget. A budget that provides budgeted amounts for all levels of production within the relevant range.

Flexible budget performance report. A report designed to analyze the difference between actual performance and budget performance, where the budgeted amounts are based on the actual sales volume or level of activity.

Performance report. A financial report that compares actual cost and/or revenue performance with budgeted amounts and designates the differences between them as favorable or unfavorable variances.

Price variance. A difference between actual and budgeted revenue or cost caused by the actual price per unit being different from the budgeted price per unit.

Quantity variance. The difference between actual cost and budgeted cost caused by the actual number of units used being different from the budgeted number of units.

Standard costs. The costs that should be incurred under normal conditions in producing a given product or part or in performing a particular service.

Static budget. A synonym for fixed budget.

Variable budget. A synonym for flexible budget.

Volume variance. The difference between the amount of overhead budgeted at the actual operating level achieved during the period and the standard amount of overhead charged to production during the period.

QUESTIONS FOR CLASS DISCUSSION

1. What is a "fixed" or "static" budget?
2. What limits the usefulness of fixed budget performance reports?
3. What is the essential difference between a fixed budget and a flexible budget?
4. What is the initial step in preparing a flexible budget?
5. Is there any sense in which a variable cost may be thought of as being constant in amount? Explain.
6. A particular type of cost may be classified as variable by one company and fixed by another company. Why might this be appropriate?
7. What is meant by contribution margin?
8. What is a flexible budget performance report designed to analyze?
9. In cost accounting, what is meant by a "variance?"
10. A cost variance can be analyzed so as to show that it consists of a price variance and a quantity variance. What is a price variance? What is a quantity variance?

11. What is the purpose of a "standard cost?"
12. Who is usually responsible for a material price variance? Who is generally responsible for a material quantity variance?
13. What is a "predetermined standard overhead rate?"
14. In analyzing the overhead variance, explain what is meant by a "volume variance?"
15. In analyzing the overhead variance, explain what is meant by a "controllable variance?"
16. What is the relationship between standard costs, variance analysis, and "management by exception?"

CLASS EXERCISES

Exercise 26–1

A manufacturing company produces and sells aluminum hulls for fishing boats. The company's plant normally operates eight hours a day, five days per week. The basic production process involves cutting aluminum sheeting, punching a number of holes, riveting the pieces together, and painting the assembled hull. Given this general information, classify the following costs as fixed or variable. In those instances where further investigation might reverse your classification, comment on the possible reasons for treating the item in the opposite manner.

a. Aluminum sheets.
b. Direct labor.
c. Rivets.
d. Paint.
e. Electricity to run shears, punching machines, and rivet guns.
f. Manager's salary.
g. Repair expense on machines.
h. Utilities (gas and water).
i. Depreciation expense on production machines.
j. Fire and theft insurance on property.
k. Office supplies expense.
l. Shipping expense for forwarding finished hulls to customers.
m. Sales commissions.

Exercise 26–2

Dawes Company's fixed budget for the third quarter of 198A is presented below. Recast the budget as a flexible budget and show the budgeted amounts for 7,000 units and 8,000 units of production.

Sales (8,500 units)		$178,500
Cost of goods sold:		
Materials	$33,150	
Direct labor	36,975	
Production supplies	5,100	
Depreciation	7,500	
Plant manager's salary	4,000	(86,725)
Gross profit		$ 91,775

Selling expenses:

Sales commissions	$14,790	
Packaging expense	3,825	(18,615)

Administrative expenses:

Administrative salaries	$18,000	
Insurance expense	1,800	
Office rent expense	27,000	(46,800)
Income from operations		$ 26,360

Exercise 26–3

A furniture manufacturer has just completed 1,000 identical tables using 9,800 board feet of lumber costing $3,626. The company's material standards for one unit of this table are 10 board feet of lumber at $0.35 per board foot.

Required:

Isolate the material price and material quantity variances in manufacturing the 1,000 tables.

Exercise 26–4

The manufacturer of Exercise 26–3 takes standard costs into its accounts. As a result, in charging material costs to Goods in Process, it also takes any variances into its accounts.

Required:

1. Under the assumption that the materials used in manufacturing the tables of Exercise 26–3 were charged to Goods in Process on April 7, give the entry to charge the materials and to take the variances into the accounts.
2. Under the further assumption that the variances of Exercise 26–3 were the only variances of the year and were considered immaterial, give the year-end entry to close the variance accounts.

Exercise 26–5

Following are the standard costs for one unit of a company's product:

Material (1 unit @ $5 per unit)	$ 5
Direct labor (1 hr. @ $3 per hr.)	3
Factory overhead (1 hr. @ $2 per hr.)	2
Standard cost	$10

The $2 per direct labor hour overhead rate is based on a normal, 85% of capacity operating level and the following monthly flexible budget information:

	Operating levels	
	80%	85%
Budgeted production in units	8,000	8,500
Budgeted overhead:		
Fixed overhead	$8,500	$8,500
Variable overhead	8,000	8,500

During the past month the company operated at 80% of capacity and produced 8,000 units of product with the following overhead costs:

Fixed overhead costs	$ 8,500
Variable overhead costs	8,100
Total overhead costs	$16,600

Required:

Isolate the overhead variance into a volume variance and a controllable variance.

PROBLEMS

Problem 26–1

The accountant for Thompkins Company prepared a master budget for 198A, based on an assumed sales and production volume of 20,000 units. The resulting budgeted income statement included the following items that comprise income from operations:

THOMPKINS COMPANY
Master Budget
For the Year Ended December 31, 198A

Sales		$ 350,000
Cost of goods sold:		
Raw materials................................	$80,000	
Direct labor	45,560	
Factory supplies	4,660	
Depreciation of plant	7,800	
Utilities (of which $6,000 is a fixed cost)	12,440	
Salary of plant manager	18,000	(168,460)
Gross profit		$ 181,540
Selling expenses:		
Packaging	$42,220	
Sales commissions	28,000	
Shipping...................................	15,780	
Salary of vice president–marketing	24,000	
Promotion (variable cost)	17,500	(127,500)

General and administrative expenses:

Depreciation	$ 7,000	
Consultant's fees (annual retainer)	4,500	
Administrative salaries	32,500	(44,000)
Income from operations		$ 10,040

Required:

1. Prepare a flexible budget for Thompkins Company, showing specific budget columns for sales and production volumes of 18,000 units and 22,000 units.
2. What would be the expected increase in income from operations if sales and production volume were 21,000 units rather than 20,000 units?
3. The management of Thompkins Company has approved the master budget and believes that 20,000 units is the best estimate of sales volume. Nevertheless, management recognizes a possibility that sales and production volume could fall to 17,000 units. What would be the effect on income from operations if this occurs?

Problem 26–2

Refer to the discussion of Thompkins Company in Problem 26–1. The actual statement of income from 198A operations of Thompkins Company is as follows:

THOMPKINS COMPANY
Statement of Income from Operations
For the Year Ended December 31, 198A

Sales (22,000 units)		$ 363,000
Cost of goods sold:		
Raw materials	$85,000	
Direct labor	49,100	
Factory supplies	5,050	
Depreciation of plant	7,800	
Utilities (of which $6,500 is a fixed cost)	13,800	
Salary of plant manager	22,000	(182,750)
Gross profit		$ 180,250
Selling expenses:		
Packaging	$44,600	
Sales commissions	31,100	
Shipping	19,000	
Salary of vice president–marketing	25,000	
Promotion (a variable cost)	18,200	(137,900)
General and administrative expenses:		
Depreciation	$ 7,000	
Consultant's fees	4,500	
Administrative salaries	35,000	(46,500)
Income (loss) from operations		$ (4,150)

Required:

1. Using the flexible budget you prepared for Problem 26–1, present a flexible budget performance report for 198A.
2. Explain the sales variance.

Problem 26–3

A company has established the following standard costs for one unit of its product:

Material (3 gals. @ $5 per gal.)	$15.00
Direct labor (3 hrs. @ $3.50 per hr.)	10.50
Overhead (3 hrs. @ $3 per hr.)	9.00
Total standard cost	$34.50

The $3 per direct labor hour overhead rate is based on a normal, 80% of capacity, operating level for the company's plant and the following flexible budget information for April:

	Operating levels	
	80%	*90%*
Production in units	800	900
Direct labor hours	2,400	2,700
Fixed factory overhead	$4,000	$4,000
Variable factory overhead	3,200	3,600

During April the company operated at 90% of capacity, producing 900 units of product having the following actual costs:

Material (2,650 gals. @ $5.10 per gal.)	$13,515
Direct labor (2,800 hrs. @ $3.40 per hr.)	9,520
Fixed factory overhead	4,000
Variable overhead	3,425

Required:

Isolate the material and labor variances into price and quantity variances and isolate the overhead variance into the volume and the controllable variances.

Problem 26–4

Calco Company makes a single product for which it has established the following standard costs per unit:

Materials (20 lbs. @ $0.50 per lb.)	$10
Direct labor (4 hrs. @ $3 per hr.)	12
Factory overhead (4 hrs. @ $3.25 per hr.)	13
Total standard cost	$35

The $3.25 per direct labor hour overhead rate is based on a normal, 90% of capacity, operating level for the plant. The company's monthly flexible factory overhead budget shows the following:

	Operating levels		
	80%	*90%*	*100%*
Production in units	400	450	500
Standard direct labor hours	1,600	1,800	2,000
Budgeted factory overhead:			
Fixed costs:			
Rent	$ 800	$ 800	$ 800
Depreciation, machinery	1,400	1,400	1,400
Insurance and taxes	200	200	200
Supervisory salaries	1,200	1,200	1,200
Variable costs:			
Indirect materials	600	675	750
Indirect labor	800	900	1,000
Power and lights	400	450	500
Maintenance	200	225	250

During April the company operated at 80% of capacity and completed 400 units of its product, which were charged with the following standard costs:

Materials (8,000 lbs. @ $0.50 per lb.)	$ 4,000
Direct labor (1,600 hrs. @ $3 per hr.)	4,800
Factory overhead (1,600 hrs. @ $3.25 per hr.)	5,200
Total	$14,000

The actual April costs were:

Materials (8,100 lbs.)	$ 3,969
Direct labor (1,550 hrs.)	4,805
Rent	800
Depreciation, machinery	1,400
Insurance and taxes	200
Supervisory salaries	1,200
Indirect materials	650
Indirect labor	775
Power and lights	380
Maintenance	210
Total	$14,389

Required:

1. Isolate the material and labor variances into price and quantity variances.
2. Prepare a factory overhead variance report showing the volume and controllable variances.

Problem 26–5

Dodger Company has established the following standard costs for one unit of its product:

```
Material (5 lbs. @ $0.75 per lb.) ....................  $3.75
Direct labor (1 hr. @ $3 per hr.) ..................    3.00
Overhead (1 hr. @ $2.50 per hr.) ..................    2.50
     Total standard cost .........................  $9.25
```

The $2.50 per direct labor hour overhead rate is based on a normal, 80% of capacity operating level, and at this level the company's monthly output is 2,000 units. However, production does vary slightly, and each 1% variation results in a 20-unit increase or decrease in the production level. Following are the company's budgeted overhead costs at the 80% level for one month:

DODGER COMPANY
Budgeted Monthly Factory Overhead at 80% Level

```
Fixed costs:
    Depreciation expense, building ........  $  800
    Depreciation expense, machinery ......   1,000
    Taxes and insurance ..................     200
    Supervision ..........................   1,000
        Total fixed costs ................             $3,000

Variable costs:
    Indirect materials ...................  $  800
    Indirect labor .......................     500
    Power.................................     400
    Repairs and maintenance ..............     300
        Total variable costs .............             2,000
Total overhead costs.....................              $5,000
```

During April of the current year the company operated at 75% of capacity, produced 1,900 units of product, and incurred the following actual costs:

```
Material (9,800 lbs.) ........................  $ 7,252
Direct labor (1,850 hrs.) ....................    5,920
Depreciation expense, building ...............      800
Depreciation expense, machinery ..............    1,000
Taxes and insurance ..........................      200
Supervision ..................................    1,000
Indirect materials ...........................      725
Indirect labor ...............................      500
Power.........................................      385
Repairs and maintenance ......................      260
        Total ................................  $18,042
```

Required:

1. Prepare a flexible overhead budget for the company showing the amount of each fixed and variable cost at the 75%, 80%, and 85% levels.
2. Isolate the material and labor variances into quantity and price variances and isolate the overhead variance into the volume variance and the controllable variance.
3. Prepare a factory overhead variance report showing the volume and controllable variances.

ALTERNATE PROBLEMS

Problem 26–1A

Haskel Company's master (fixed) budget for 198A was based on an expected production and sales volume of 8,400 units, and included the following operating items:

HASKEL COMPANY
Fixed Budget
For Year Ended December 31, 198A

Sales		$168,000
Cost of goods sold:		
Materials	$42,000	
Direct labor	25,200	
Machinery repairs (variable cost)	1,260	
Depreciation of plant	5,000	
Utilities ($3,360 of which is a variable cost)	8,880	
Supervisory salaries	12,000	(94,340)
Gross profit		$ 73,660
Selling expenses:		
Packaging	$ 4,200	
Shipping	6,300	
Sales salary (an agreed-upon, annual salary)	14,000	(24,500)
General and administrative expenses:		
Insurance expense	$ 3,000	
Salaries	21,000	
Rent expense	16,000	(40,000)
Income from operations		$ 9,160

Required:

1. Prepare a flexible budget for the company and show detailed budgets for sales and production volumes of 9,200 units and 10,000 units.
2. A consultant to the company has suggested that developing business conditions in the area are reaching a crossroads, and that the impact of these events on the company could result in a sales volume of approximately 10,800 units. The president of Haskel Company is confident that this is within the relevant range of existing production capacity but is hesitant to estimate the impact of such a change on operating income. What would be the expected increase in operating income?
3. In the consultant's report, the possibility of unfavorable business events was also mentioned, in which case production and sales volume for 198A would likely fall to 7,000 units. What amount of income from operations should the president expect if these unfavorable events occur?

Problem 26–2A

Refer to the discussion of Haskel Company in Problem 26–1A. Haskel Company's actual statement of income from 198A operations is as follows:

HASKEL COMPANY
Statement of Income from Operations
For Year Ended December 31, 198A

Sales (9,200 units)			$ 179,400
Cost of goods sold:			
Materials		$42,000	
Direct labor		30,000	
Machinery repairs		1,000	
Depreciation of plant		5,000	
Utilities (40% of which was a variable cost)		10,500	
Supervisory salaries		11,500	(100,000)
Gross profit			$ 79,400
Selling expenses:			
Packaging		$ 4,100	
Shipping		8,200	
Sales salary		14,000	(26,300)
General and administrative expenses:			
Insurance expense		$ 3,500	
Salaries		21,500	
Rent expense		18,000	(43,000)
Income from operations			$ 10,100

Required:

1. Using the flexible budget you prepared for Problem 26–1A, present a flexible budget performance report for 198A.
2. Explain the sales variance.

Problem 26–3A

Mork Company has established the following standard costs for one unit of its product:

Materials (2 units @ $1.60 per unit)	$ 3.20
Direct labor (3 hrs. @ $3.25 per hr.)	9.75
Factory overhead (3 hrs. @ $1.50 per hr.)	4.50
Total standard cost per unit	$17.45

The $1.50 per direct labor hour overhead rate is based on a normal, 90% of capacity operating level for the company's plant and the following flexible budget information for April:

	Operating levels	
	80%	*90%*
Production in units	5,000	6,000
Direct labor hours	15,000	18,000
Fixed factory overhead	$ 9,000	$ 9,000
Variable factory overhead	15,000	18,000

During April the company operated at 80% of capacity and produced 5,000 units of product having the following actual costs:

Materials (10,500 units @ $1.55 per unit)......... $16,275
Direct labor (14,800 hrs. @ $3.40 per hr.) 50,320
Fixed factory overhead   9,000
Variable factory overhead ....: 15,500

Required:

Isolate the material and labor variances into price and quantity variances and isolate the overhead variance into the volume variance and the controllable variance.

Problem 26–4A

Hydra Company manufactures a product for which it has established the following standard costs per unit:

Material (6 lbs. @ $2.50 per lb.) $15.00
Direct labor (3 hrs. @ $3.50 per hr.) 10.50
Overhead (3 hrs. @ $3 per hr.) 9.00
       Total standard cost $34.50

The $3 per direct labor hour overhead rate is based on a normal, 90% of capacity, operating level for the company's plant and the following flexible budget information for one month's operations.

	Operating levels		
	80%	*90%*	*100%*
Production in units...............	800	900	1,000
Standard direct labor hours	2,400	2,700	3,000
Budgeted factory overhead:			
Fixed costs:			
Depreciation, building........	$1,200	$1,200	$1,200
Depreciation, machinery	1,500	1,500	1,500
Taxes and insurance	200	200	200
Supervisory salaries	1,600	1,600	1,600
Total fixed costs..........	$4,500	$4,500	$4,500
Variable costs:			
Indirect materials	$1,280	$1,440	$1,600
Indirect labor...............	1,200	1,350	1,500
Power	400	450	500
Maintenance	320	360	400
Total variable costs	$3,200	$3,600	$4,000
Total factory overhead .	$7,700	$8,100	$8,500

During April the company operated at 80% of capacity and incurred the following actual costs in producing 800 units of its product:

Materials (4,700 lbs. @ $2.55 per lb.)		$11,985
Direct labor (2,500 hrs. @ $3.40 per hr.) .		8,500
Overhead costs:		
Depreciation expense, building	$1,200	
Depreciation expense, machinery	1,500	
Taxes and insurance	200	
Supervisory salaries	1,600	
Indirect materials	1,250	
Indirect labor	1,300	
Power	425	
Maintenance	300	7,775
Total		$28,260

Required:

1. Isolate the material and labor variances into price and quantity variances.
2. Prepare a factory overhead variance report showing the volume and controllable variances.

Problem 26–5A

Anders Company manufactures a product for which it has established the following standard costs per unit:

Material (2 lbs. @ $1.25 per lb.)	$2.50
Direct labor (½ hr. @ $3.40 per hr.)	1.70
Overhead (½ hr. @ $3 per hr.)	1.50
Total standard cost	$5.70

The $3 per direct labor hour overhead rate is based on a normal, 80% of capacity operating level, and at this level the company's monthly output is 4,000 units. However, production does vary slightly, and each 1% variation results in a 40-unit increase or decrease in the production level. Following are the company's budgeted overhead costs at the 80% level for one month.

ANDERS COMPANY

Budgeted Monthly Factory Overhead at 80% Level

Fixed overhead costs:		
Depreciation expense, building	$1,100	
Depreciation expense, machinery . . .	1,000	
Taxes and insurance	200	
Supervision	1,500	
Total fixed overhead costs		$3,800
Variable overhead costs:		
Indirect materials	$ 840	
Indirect labor	600	
Power	360	
Repairs and maintenance	400	
Total variable overhead costs . . .		2,200
Total overhead costs		$6,000

During March of the current year the company operated at 90% of capacity, produced 4,400 units of product, and incurred the following actual costs:

Materials (8,600 lbs.)	$10,922
Direct labor (2,300 hrs.)	7,705
Depreciation expense, building	1,100
Depreciation expense, machinery	1,000
Taxes and insurance	200
Supervision	1,500
Indirect materials	950
Indirect labor	650
Power	385
Repairs and maintenance	475
	$24,887

Required:

1. Prepare a flexible overhead budget for the company showing the amount of each fixed and variable cost at the 70%, 80%, and 90% levels.
2. Isolate the material and labor variances into quantity and price variances and isolate the overhead variance into the volume variance and the controllable variance.
3. Prepare a factory overhead variance report showing the volume and controllable variances.

PROVOCATIVE PROBLEMS

Provocative problem 26–1
Guide Mark Company

Karen Kirby has been an employee of Guide Mark Company for the past five years, the last four of which she has worked in the assembly department. Eight months ago she was made supervisor of the department, and since then has been able to end a long period of internal dissention, high employee turnover, and inefficient operation in the department. Under Karen's supervision the department's production has increased, employee morale has improved, absenteeism has dropped, and for the past three months the department has been beating its standard for the first time in years.

However, a few days ago Lee Wilkins, an employee in the department, suggested to Karen that the company install a new kind of controls on the department's machines similar to those developed by a competitor. The controls would cost $19,000 installed and would have an eight-year life and no salvage value. They should increase production 5%, reduce maintenance costs $500 per year, and do away with the labor of one worker.

Karen's answer to Lee was, "Forget it. We are doing OK now; we don't need the extra production; and I don't want to be faced with the problem of letting one worker go."

Might standard costs have had anything to do with Karen's answer to Lee? Explain. Do you agree with Karen's answer? Should Karen be the person to make a decision such as this?

Provocative problem 26–2
Ottawa Company

Ottawa Company manufactures Product A for which the demand is seasonal and which cannot be stored for long periods; consequently, the number of units manufactured varies with the season. In accounting for costs, the company charges actual costs incurred to a goods in process account maintained for the product, which it closes at the end of each quarter to Finished Goods. At the end of last year, which was an average year, the following cost report was prepared for the company manager:

OTTAWA COMPANY
Quarterly Report of Costs for Product A
Year Ended December 31, 19—

	1st quarter	2d quarter	3d quarter	4th quarter
Materials	$ 46,800	$ 54,250	$ 31,400	$ 23,700
Direct labor...................	140,100	162,400	94,000	70,800
Fixed factory overhead costs....	70,000	70,000	70,000	70,000
Variable factory overhead costs .	76,800	89,250	51,800	39,000
Total manufacturing costs	$333,700	$375,900	$247,200	$203,500
Production in units	60,000	70,000	40,000	30,000
Cost per unit.................	$5.56	$5.37	$6.18	$6.78

The manager asked you to explain why unit costs for the product varied from a low of $5.37 in the second quarter to a high of $6.78 in the last quarter, and he asked you to suggest a better way to accumulate or allocate costs. He feels he must have quarterly reports for purposes of control, so attach to your explanation a schedule showing what last year's material, labor, and overhead costs per unit would have been had your suggestion or suggestions been followed for the year.

Provocative problem 26–3
Toolbox Company

Toolbox Company manufactures and sells a specially designed toolbox at a price of $16 each. A toolbox requires 6 pounds of a particular metal which the company expects to purchase for $1 per pound. Management believes that two toolboxes should be produced per direct labor hour, and workers should be available at $8 per hour. Each toolbox will be packaged in a pasteboard container which weighs 1.5 pounds, and the company will attempt to buy the pasteboard for $0.30 per pound.

If sales and production volume of toolboxes range from 20,000 to 40,000 units, overhead costs should be as follows:

Administrative salaries	$40,000
Depreciation expense	12,000
Insurance expense	1,500
Utilities expenses	14,000

During 198A, Toolbox Company actually produced and sold 21,000 toolboxes at an average price of $15.50. It used 117,600 pounds of metal, which were purchased at $1.125 per pound. Laborers were paid $8.20 per hour and worked 10,100 hours to produce the toolboxes. Pasteboard was purchased for $0.27 per pound, and 32,400 pounds were purchased and used. All other expenses were consistent with the planned amounts.

The owners of Toolbox Company are aware of all the facts provided above. However, they are uncertain about their evaluation of the company's operating performance. Income from operations was clearly different from their expectations, but the causes of the difference are not yet clear. The owners have come to you asking for help in understanding the impact of the various prices paid and received by the company as well as any other factors that effected performance.

After studying Chapter 27, you should be able to:

☐ Describe the impact of capital budgeting on the operations of a company.

☐ Calculate a payback period on an investment and state the inherent limitations of this method.

☐ Calculate a rate of return on an investment and state the assumptions on which this method is based.

☐ Describe the information obtained by using the discounted cash flow method, the procedures involved in using this method, and the problems associated with its use.

☐ Explain the effects of incremental costs on a decision to accept or reject additional business and on a decision whether to make or buy a given product.

☐ State the meaning of sunk costs, out-of-pocket costs, and opportunity costs, and describe the importance of each type of cost to capital budgeting decisions such as to scrap or rebuild defective units or to sell a product as is or process it further.

☐ Define or explain the words and phrases listed in the chapter Glossary.

Capital budgeting;
managerial decisions

■ A business decision involves choosing between two or more courses of action, and the best choice normally offers the highest return on the investment or the greatest cost savings. Business managers at times make decisions intuitively, without trying to measure systematically the advantages and disadvantages of each possible choice. Often they make intuitive decisions because they are unaware of any other way to choose; but sometimes the available information is so sketchy or unreliable that systematic measurement is useless. Also, intangible factors such as convenience, prestige, and public opinion are at times more important than the factors that can be reduced to a quantitative basis. Nevertheless, in many situations it is possible to reduce the anticipated consequences of alternative choices to a quantitative basis and measure them systematically. This chapter will examine several.

CAPITAL BUDGETING

Planning plant asset investments is called *capital budgeting*. The plans may involve new buildings, new machinery, or whole new projects; but in every case the objective is to earn a satisfactory return on the invested funds. Capital budgeting often requires some of the most crucial and difficult decisions faced by management. The decisions are difficult because they are commonly based on estimates projected well into a future that is at best uncertain; and they are crucial because (1) large sums of money are often involved; (2) funds are committed for long periods of time; and (3) once a decision is made and a project is begun, it may be difficult or impossible to reverse the effects of a poor decision.

Capital budgeting involves the preparation of cost and revenue estimates for all proposed projects, an examination of the merits of each, and a choice of those worthy of investment. It is a broad field, and this text must limit its discussion to three ways of comparing investment opportunities. They are the *payback period,* the *return on average investment,* and *discounted cash flows.*

Payback period

Generally an investment in a machine or other plant asset will produce a *net cash flow,* and the *payback period* for the investment is the time required to recover the investment through this net cash flow. For example, assume that Murray Company is considering several capital investments. One investment involves the purchase of a machine to be used in manufacturing a new product. The machine will cost $16,000, have an eight-year service life, and no salvage value. The company estimates that 10,000 units of the machine's product will be sold each year, and the sales will result in $1,500 of after-tax net income, calculated as follows:

Annual sales of new product		$30,000
Deduct:		
Cost of materials, labor, and overhead other than depreciation on the new machine	$15,500	
Depreciation on the new machine	2,000	
Additional selling and administrative expenses	9,500	27,000
Annual before-tax income		$ 3,000
Income tax (assumed rate, 50%)		1,500
Annual after-tax net income from new product sales		$ 1,500

Through annual sales of 10,000 units of the new product, Murray Company expects to gain $30,000 of revenue and $1,500 of net income. The net income will be available to pay back the new machine's cost; but in addition, since none of the funds that flow in from sales flow out for depreciation, so will the amount of the annual depreciation charge. The $1,500 of net income plus the $2,000 depreciation charge total $3,500, and together are the *annual net cash flow* expected from the investment. Furthermore, this annual net cash flow will pay back the investment in the new machine in 4.6 years, calculated as follows:

$$\frac{\text{Cost of new machine, \$16,000}}{\text{Annual net cash flow, \$3,500}} = \text{4.6 years to recover investment}$$

The answer just given is 4.6 years. Actually, when $16,000 is divided by $3,500, the result is just a little over 4.57; but 4.6 years is close enough for a decision. Remember that the calculation is based on estimated net income and estimated depreciation; consequently, it is pointless to carry the answer to several decimal places.

In choosing investment opportunities, a short payback period is desirable because (1) the sooner an investment is recovered the sooner the funds are available for other uses and (2) a short payback period also means a short "bail-out period" if conditions should change. However, the payback period should never be the only factor considered because it ignores the length of time revenue will continue to be earned after the end of the payback period. For example, one investment may pay back its cost in three years and cease to produce revenue at that point, while a second investment may require five years to pay back its cost but will continue to produce income for another 15 years.

Rate of return on average investment

The *rate of return on the average investment* in a machine is calculated by dividing the after-tax net income from the sale of the machine's product by the average investment in the machine. For example, Murray Company estimates it will earn a $1,500 after-tax net income from selling the product of the $16,000 machine it proposes to buy. As to average investment, each year depreciation will reduce the book value of the machine $2,000, and the company will recover this amount of its investment through the sale of the machine's product. Consequently, the company may assume it will have $16,000 invested in the machine during its first year, $14,000 during the second, $12,000 during the third, and so on for the machine's eight-year life. Or, in other words, the company may assume it will have an amount equal to the machine's book value invested each year. If it makes this assumption, then the average amount it will have invested during the eight-year life is the average of the machine's book values. This is $9,000 and may be calculated as follows:

Year	Beginning of the year book value	
1	$16,000	
2	14,000	
3	12,000	$\dfrac{\$72,000}{8} = \$9,000$ average book value and average investment
4	10,000	
5	8,000	
6	6,000	
7	4,000	
8	2,000	
Total	$72,000	

In the illustrated calculation the eight yearly book values were averaged to determine average investment. A shorter way to the same answer is to average the book values of the machine's first and last years in this manner:

$$\frac{\$16,000 + \$2,000}{2} = \$9,000$$

After average investment is determined, the rate of return on average investment is calculated. As previously stated, this involves dividing the estimated annual after-tax net income from the sale of the machine's product by average investment, as follows:

$$\$1,500 \div \$9,000 = 16\tfrac{2}{3}\% \text{ return on average investment}$$

At this point students commonly want to know if $16\tfrac{2}{3}\%$ is a good investment return. The answer is that it is better than, say, 12%, but not as good as 18%. In other words, a return is good or bad only when related to other returns. Also, factors other than return, such as risk, are always involved in investment decisions. However, when average investment returns are used in comparing and deciding between capital investments, the one having the least risk, the shortest payback period, and the highest return for the longest time is usually the best.

Rate of return on average investment is easy to calculate and understand, and as a result has long been used in selecting investment opportunities. Furthermore, when the opportunities produce uniform cash flows, it offers a fair basis for selection. However, a comparison of *discounted cash flows* with amounts to be invested offers a better means of selection.

An understanding of discounted cash flows requires an understanding of the concept of present value. This concept was explained in Chapter 12, beginning on page 408. That explanation should be reviewed at this point by any student who does not fully understand it. The present value tables in Chapter 12, on pages 410 and 412, must be used to solve some of the problems which follow the present chapter.

Discounted cash flows

When a business invests in a new plant asset, it expects to secure from the investment a stream of future cash flows. Normally it will not invest unless the flows are sufficient to return the amount of the investment plus a satisfactory return on the investment. For example, will the cash flows from Murray Company's investment in the machine return the amount of the investment plus a satisfactory return? If Murray Company considers a 10% compound annual return a satisfactory return on its capital investments, it can answer this question with the calculations of Illustration 27–1.

Analysis of Proposed Investment in Machine

Years Hence	Net Cash Flows	Present Value of $1 at 10%	Present Value of Net Cash Flows
1	$3,500	0.909	$ 3,181.50
2	3,500	0.826	2,891.00
3	3,500	0.751	2,628.50
4	3,500	0.683	2,390.50
5	3,500	0.621	2,173.50
6	3,500	0.565	1,977.50
7	3,500	0.513	1,795.50
8	3,500	0.467	1,634.50
Total present value			$18,672.50
Amount to be invested			16,000.00
Positive net present value			$ 2,672.50

Illustration 27–1

To secure the machine of Illustration 27–1, Murray Company must invest $16,000. However, from the sale of the machine's product it will recapture $2,000 of its investment each year in the form of depreciation; in addition, it will earn a $1,500 annual net income. In other words, the company will receive a $3,500 net cash flow from the investment each year for eight years. The first column of Illustration 27–1 indicates that the net cash flows of the first year are received one year hence, and so forth for subsequent years. This means that the net cash flows are received at the end of the year. To simplify the discussion of this chapter and the problems at the end of the chapter, the net cash flows of a company's operations are generally assumed to occur at the end of the year. More refined calculations are left for consideration in an advanced course.

The annual net cash flows, shown in the second column of Illustration 27–1, are multiplied by the amounts in the third column to determine their present values, which are shown in the last column. Observe that the total of these present values exceeds the amount of the required investment by $2,672.50. Consequently, if Murray Company considers a 10% compound return satisfactory, this machine will recover its required investment, plus a 10% compound return, and $2,672.50 in addition.

Generally, when the cash flows from an investment are discounted at a satisfactory rate and have a present value in excess of the investment, the investment is worthy of acceptance. Also, when several investment opportunities are being compared, and each requires the same investment and has the same risk, the one having the highest positive net present value is the best.

Shortening the calculation

In Illustration 27-1 the present values of $1 at 10% for each of the eight years involved are shown. Each year's cash flow is multiplied by the present value of $1 at 10% for that year to determine its present value. Then, the present values of the eight cash flows are added to determine their total. This is one way to determine total present value. However, since in this case the cash flows are uniform, there are two shorter ways. One shorter way is to add the eight yearly present values of $1 at 10% and to multiply $3,500 by the total. Another even shorter way is based on Table 12-2 on page 412. Table 12-2 shows the present value of $1 to be received periodically for a number of periods. In the case of the Murray Company machine, $3,500 is to be received annually for eight years. Consequently, to determine the present value of these annual receipts discounted at 10%, go down the 10% column of Table 12-2 to the amount opposite eight periods. It is 5.335. Therefore, the present value of the eight annual $3,500 receipts is $3,500 multiplied by 5.335, or is $18,672.50.

Cash flows not uniform

Present value analysis has its greatest usefulness when cash flows are not uniform. For example, assume a company can choose one capital investment from among Projects A, B, and C. Each requires a $12,000 investment and will produce cash flows as follows:

Years Hence	Annual Cash Flows		
	Project A	Project B	Project C
1	$ 5,000	$ 8,000	$ 1,000
2	5,000	5,000	5,000
3	5,000	2,000	9,000
	$15,000	$15,000	$15,000

Note that all three projects produce the same total cash flow. However, the flows of Project A are uniform, those of Project B are greater in the earlier years, while those of Project C are greater in the later years. Consequently, when present values of the cash flows, discounted at 10%, are compared with the required investments, the statistics of Illustration 27-2 result.

Note that an investment in Project A has a $430 positive net present value; an investment in Project B has a $904 positive net present value; and an investment in Project C has a $202 negative net present value. Therefore, if a 10% return is required, an investment in Project

	Years Hence	Present Values of Cash Flows Discounted at 10%		
		Project A	Project B	Project C
	1	$ 4,545	$ 7,272	$ 909
	2	4,130	4,130	4,130
	3	3,755	1,502	6,759
Total present values		$12,430	$12,904	$11,798
Required investments		12,000	12,000	12,000
Net present values		+$ 430	+$ 904	−$ 202

Illustration 27–2

C should be rejected, since the investment's net present value indicates it will not earn such a return. Furthermore, as between Projects A and B, other things being equal, Project B is the better investment, since its cash flows have the higher net present value.

Salvage value and accelerated depreciation

The $16,000 machine of the Murray Company example was assumed to have no salvage value at the end of its useful life. Often a machine is expected to have a salvage value, and in such cases the expected salvage value is treated as an additional cash flow to be received in the last year of the machine's life.

Also, in the Murray Company example, depreciation was deducted on a straight-line basis; but in actual practice, an accelerated depreciation method, such as the sum-of-the-years'-digits method, is commonly used for tax purposes. Accelerated depreciation results in larger depreciation deductions in the early years of an asset's life and smaller deductions in the later years. This results in smaller income tax liabilities in the early years and larger ones in later years. However, this does not change the basic nature of a present value analysis. It only results in larger cash flows in the early years and smaller ones in later years, which normally make an investment more desirable.

Selecting the earnings rate

The selection of a satisfactory earnings rate for capital investments is always a matter for top-management decision. Formulas have been devised to aid management. But, in many companies the choice of a satisfactory or required rate of return is largely subjective. Management simply decides that enough investment opportunities can be found that will earn, say, a 10% compound return; and this becomes the minimum below which the company refuses to make an investment of average risk.

Whatever the required rate, it is always higher than the rate at which money can be borrowed, since the return on a capital investment must include not only interest but also an additional allowance for risks involved. Therefore, when the rate at which money can be borrowed is around 10%, a required after-tax return of 15% may be acceptable in industrial companies, with a lower rate for public utilities and a higher rate for companies in which investment opportunities are unusually good or the risks are high.

Replacing plant assets

In a dynamic economy, new and better machines are constantly coming on the market. As a result, the decision to replace an existing machine with a new and better machine is common. Often the existing machine is in good condition and will produce the required product; but the new machine will do the job with a large savings in operating costs. In such a situation management must decide whether the after-tax savings in operating costs justifies the investment.

The amount of after-tax savings from the replacement of an existing machine with a new machine is complicated by the fact that depreciation on the new machine for tax purposes is based on the book value of the old machine plus the cash given in the exchange. There can be other complications too. Consequently, a discussion of the replacement of plant assets is deferred to a more advanced course.

ACCEPTING ADDITIONAL BUSINESS

Costs obtained from a cost accounting system are average costs and also historical costs. They are useful in product pricing and in controlling operations. But, in a decision to accept an additional volume of business they are not necessarily the relevant costs. In such a decision the relevant costs are the additional costs, commonly called the *incremental* or *differential costs*.

For example, a concern operating at its normal capacity, which is 80% of full capacity, has annually produced and sold approximately 100,000 units of product with the following results:

Sales (100,000 units @ $10)		$1,000,000
Materials (100,000 units @ $3.50)	$350,000	
Labor (100,000 units @ $2.20)	220,000	
Overhead (100,000 units @ $1.10)	110,000	
Selling expenses (100,000 units @ $1.40)	140,000	
Administrative expenses (100,000 units @ $0.80)	80,000	900,000
Operating income		$ 100,000

The concern's sales department reports it has an exporter who has offered to buy 10,000 units of product at $8.50 per unit. The sale to the exporter is several times larger than any previous sale made by the company; and since the units are being exported, the new business will have no effect on present business. Therefore, in order to determine whether the order should be accepted or rejected, management of the company asks that statistics be prepared to show the estimated net income or loss that would result from accepting the offer. It received the following figures based on the average costs previously given:

Sales (10,000 units @ $8.50)		$85,000
Materials (10,000 units @ $3.50)	$35,000	
Labor (10,000 units @ $2.20)	22,000	
Overhead (10,000 units @ $1.10)	11,000	
Selling expenses (10,000 units @ $1.40)	14,000	
Administrative expenses (10,000 units @ $0.80)	8,000	90,000
Operating loss		$ (5,000)

If a decision were based on these average costs, the new business would likely be rejected. However, in this situation average costs are not relevant. The relevant costs are the added costs of accepting the new business. Consequently, before rejecting the order, the costs of the new business were examined more closely and the following additional information obtained: (1) Manufacturing 10,000 additional units of product would require materials and labor at $3.50 and $2.20 per unit just as with normal production. (2) However, the 10,000 units could be manufactured with overhead costs, in addition to those already incurred, of only $5,000 for power, packing, and handling labor. (3) Commissions and other selling expenses resulting from the sale would amount to $2,000 in addition to the selling expenses already incurred. And (4) $1,000 additional administrative expenses in the form of clerical work would be required if the order were accepted. Based on this added information, the statement of Illustration 27–3 showing the effect of the additional business on the company's normal business was prepared.

Illustration 27–3 shows that the additional business should be accepted. Present business should be charged with all present costs, and the additional business should be charged only with its incremental or differential costs. When this is done, accepting the additional business at $8.50 per unit will apparently result in $20,000 additional income before taxes.

Incremental or differential costs always apply to a particular situation at a particular time. For example, adding units to a given production volume may or may not increase depreciation expense. If the additional units require the purchase of more machines, depreciation expense

	Present business		Additional business		Present plus the additional business	
Sales		$1,000,000		$85,000		$1,085,000
Materials	$350,000		$35,000		$385,000	
Labor	220,000		22,000		242,000	
Overhead	110,000		5,000		115,000	
Selling expenses	140,000		2,000		142,000	
Administrative expense	80,000		1,000		81,000	
Total		900,000		65,000		965,000
Operating income		$ 100,000		$20,000		$ 120,000

Illustration 27–3

is increased. Likewise, if present machines are used but the additional units shorten their life, more depreciation expense results. However, if present machines are used and their depreciation depends more on the passage of time or obsolescence rather than on use, additional depreciation expense might not result from the added units of product.

BUY OR MAKE

Incremental or differential costs are often a factor in a decision as to whether a given part or product should be bought or made. For example, a manufacturer has idle machines upon which he can make Part 417 of his product. This part is presently purchased at a $1.20 delivered cost per unit. The manufacturer estimates that to make Part 417 would cost $0.45 for materials, $0.50 for labor, and an amount of overhead. At this point a question arises as to how much overhead should be charged. If the normal overhead rate of the department in which the part would be manufactured is 100% of direct labor cost, and this amount is charged against Part 417, then the unit costs of making Part 417 would be $0.45 for materials, $0.50 for labor, and $0.50 for overhead, a total of $1.45. At this cost, the manufacturer would be better off to buy the part at $1.20 each.

However, on a short-run basis the manufacturer might be justified in ignoring the normal overhead rate and in charging Part 417 for only the additional overhead costs resulting from its manufacture. Among these additional overhead costs might be, for example, power to operate the machines that would otherwise be idle, depreciation on the machines if the part's manufacture resulted in additional depreciation, and any other overhead that would be added to that already incurred. Furthermore, if these added overhead items total less than

$0.25 per unit, the manufacturer might be justified on a short-run basis in manufacturing the part. However, on a long-term basis, Part 417 should be charged a full share of all overhead.

Any amount of overhead less than $0.25 per unit results in a total cost for Part 417 that is less than the $1.20 per unit purchase price. Nevertheless, in making a final decision as to whether the part should be bought or made, the manufacturer should consider in addition to costs such things as quality, the reactions of customers and suppliers, and other intangible factors. When these additional factors are considered, small cost differences may become a minor factor.

OTHER COST CONCEPTS

Sunk costs, out-of-pocket costs, and *opportunity costs* are additional concepts that may be encountered in managerial decisions.

A sunk cost is a cost resulting from a past irrevocable decision, and is sunk in the sense that it cannot be avoided. As a result, sunk costs are irrelevant in decisions affecting the future.

An out-of-pocket cost is a cost requiring a current outlay of funds. Material costs, supplies, heat, and power are examples. Generally, out-of-pocket costs can be avoided; consequently, they are relevant in decisions affecting the future.

Costs as discussed thus far have been outlays or expenditures made to obtain some benefit, usually goods or services. However, the concept of costs can be expanded to include *sacrifices made to gain some benefit.* For example, if a job that will pay a student $1,200 for working during the summer must be rejected in order to attend summer school, the $1,200 is an opportunity cost of attending summer school.

Obviously, opportunity costs are not entered in the accounting records; but they may be relevant in a decision involving rejected opportunities. For example, decisions to scrap or rebuild defective units of product commonly involve situations which evidence both sunk costs and opportunity costs.

SCRAP OR REBUILD DEFECTIVE UNITS

Any costs incurred in manufacturing units of product that do not pass inspection are sunk costs and as such should not enter into a decision as to whether the units should be sold for scrap or be rebuilt to pass inspection. For example, a concern has 10,000 defective units of product that cost $1 per unit to manufacture. The units can be sold as they are for $0.40 each, or they can be rebuilt for $0.80 per unit, after which they can be sold for their full price of $1.50 per unit. Should the company rebuild the units or should it sell them in their present form? The original manufacturing costs of $1 per unit are sunk costs and are irrelevant in the decision; so, based on the information given, the comparative returns from scrapping or rebuilding are:

	As scrap	Rebuilt
Sales of defective units	$4,000	$15,000
Less cost to rebuild		(8,000)
Net return	$4,000	$ 7,000

From the information given, it appears that rebuilding is the better decision. This is true if the rebuilding does not interfere with normal operations. However, suppose that to rebuild the defective units the company must forgo manufacturing 10,000 new units that will cost $1 per unit to manufacture and can be sold for $1.50 per unit. In this situation the comparative returns may be analyzed as follows:

	As scrap	Rebuilt
Sale of defective units	$ 4,000	$15,000
Less cost to rebuild the defective units		(8,000)
Sale of new units	15,000	
Less cost to manufacture the new units	(10,000)	
Net return	$ 9,000	$ 7,000

If the defective units are sold without rebuilding, then the new units can also be manufactured and sold, with a $9,000 return from the sale of both the new and old units, as shown in the first column of the analysis. Obviously, this is better than forgoing the manufacture of the new units and rebuilding the defective units for a $7,000 net return.

The situation described here also may be analyzed on an opportunity cost basis as follows: If to rebuild the defective units the company must forgo manufacturing the new units, then the return on the sale of the new units is an opportunity cost of rebuilding the defective units. This opportunity cost is measured at $5,000 (revenue from sale of new units, $15,000, less their manufacturing costs, $10,000 equals the $5,000 benefit that will be sacrificed if the old units are rebuilt); and an opportunity cost analysis of the situation is as follows:

	As scrap	Rebuilt
Sale of defective units......................................	$4,000	$15,000
Less cost to rebuild the defective units		(8,000)
Less opportunity cost (return sacrificed by not manufacturing the new units)		(5,000)
Net return	$4,000	$ 2,000

Observe that it does not matter whether this or the previous analysis is made. Either way there is a $2,000 difference in favor of scrapping the defective units.

PROCESS OR SELL

Sunk costs, out-of-pocket costs, and opportunity costs are also encountered in a decision as to whether it is best to sell an intermediate product as it is or process it further and sell the product or products that result from the additional processing. For example, a company has 40,000 units of Product A that cost $0.75 per unit or a total of $30,000 to manufacture. The 40,000 units can be sold as they are for $50,000 or they can be processed further into Products X, Y, and Z at a cost of $2 per original Product A unit. The additional processing will produce the following numbers of each product, which can be sold at the unit prices indicated:

Product X	10,000 units @ $3
Product Y	22,000 units @ $5
Product Z	6,000 units @ $1
Lost through spoilage	2,000 units (no salvage value)
Total	40,000 units

The net advantage of processing the product further is $16,000, as shown in Illustration 27–4.

Note that the revenue available through the sale of the Product A units is an opportunity cost of further processing these units. Also notice that the $30,000 cost of manufacturing the 40,000 units of Product A does not appear in the Illustration 27–4 analysis. This cost is present regardless of which alternative is chosen; therefore, it is irrelevant to the decision. However, the $30,000 does enter into a calculation

Revenue from further processing:		
Product X, 10,000 units @ $3	$ 30,000	
Product Y, 22,000 units @ $5	110,000	
Product Z, 6,000 units @ $1	6,000	
Total revenue		$146,000
Less:		
Additional processing costs, 40,000 units @ $2	$ 80,000	
Opportunity cost (revenue sacrificed by not		
selling the Product A units)	50,000	
Total		130,000
Net advantage of further processing		$ 16,000

Illustration 27–4

of the net income from the alternatives. For example, if the company chooses to further process the Product A units, the gross return from the sale of Products X, Y, and Z may be calculated as follows:

Revenue from the sale of Products X, Y, and Z		$146,000
Less:		
Cost to manufacture the Product A units	$30,000	
Cost to further process the Product A units	80,000	110,000
Gross return from the sale of Products X, Y, and Z		$ 36,000

DECIDING THE SALES MIX

When a company sells a combination of products, ordinarily some of the products are more profitable than others, and normally management should concentrate its sales efforts on the more profitable products. However, if production facilities or other factors are limited, an increase in the production and sale of one product may require a reduction in the production and sale of another. In such a situation management's job is to determine the most profitable combination or sales mix for the products and concentrate on selling the products in this combination.

To determine the best sales mix for its products, management must have information as to the contribution margin of each product, the facilities required to produce and sell each product, and any limitations on these facilities. For example, assume that a company produces and sells two products, A and B. The same machines are used to produce both products, and the products have the following selling prices and variable costs per units:

	Product A	Product B
Selling price	$5.00	$7.50
Variable costs	3.50	5.50
Contribution margin	$1.50	$2.00

If the amount of production facilities required to produce each product is the same and there is an unlimited market for Product B, the company should devote all its facilities to Product B because of its larger contribution margin. However, the answer differs if the company's facilities are limited to, say, 100,000 machine-hours of production per month and one machine-hour is required to produce each unit of Product A but two machine-hours are required for each unit of

Product B. Under these circumstances, if the market for Product A is unlimited, the company should devote all its production to this product because it produces $1.50 of contribution margin per machine-hour, while Product B produces only $1 per machine-hour.

Actually, when there are no market or other limitations, a company should devote all its efforts to its most profitable product. It is only when there is a market or other limitation on the sale of the most profitable product that a need for a sales mix arises. For example, if in this instance one machine-hour of production facilities are needed to produce each unit of Product A and 100,000 machine-hours are available, 100,000 units of the product can be produced. However, if only 80,000 units can be sold, the company has 20,000 machine-hours that can be devoted to the production of Product B, and 20,000 machine-hours will produce 10,000 units of Product B. Consequently, the company's most profitable sales mix under these assumptions is 80,000 units of Product A and 10,000 units of Product B.

The assumptions in this section have been kept simple. More complicated factors and combinations of factors exist. However, a discussion of these is deferred to a more advanced course.

GLOSSARY

Capital budgeting. Planning plant asset investments; involves the preparation of cost and revenue estimates for all proposed projects, an examination of the merits of each, and a choice of those worthy of investment.

Discounted cash flows. The present value of a stream of future cash flows from an investment, based on an interest rate that gives a satisfactory return on investment.

Incremental cost. An additional cost resulting from a particular course of action.

Opportunity cost. A sacrifice made to gain some benefits; that is, in choosing one course of action, the lost benefit associated with an alternative course of action.

Out-of-pocket cost. A cost requiring a current outlay of funds.

Payback period. The time required to recover the original cost of an investment through net cash flows from the investment.

Rate of return on average investment. The annual, after-tax income from the sale of an asset's product divided by the average investment in the asset.

Sunk cost. A cost incurred as a consequence of a past irrevocable decision and that, therefore, cannot be avoided; hence, irrelevant to decisions affecting the future.

QUESTIONS FOR CLASS DISCUSSION

1. What is capital budgeting? Why are capital budgeting decisions crucial to the business concern making the decisions?
2. A successful investment in a machine will produce a net cash flow. Of what does this consist?
3. If depreciation is an expense, explain why, when the sale of a machine's product produces a net income, the portion of the machine's cost recovered each year through the sale of its product includes both the net income from the product's sale and the year's depreciation on the machine.
4. Why is a short payback period on an investment desirable?
5. What is the average amount invested in a machine during its life if the machine cost $28,000, has an estimated five-year life, and an estimated $3,000 salvage value?
6. Is a 15% return on the average investment in a machine a good return?
7. Why is the present value of the expectation of receiving $100 a year hence less than $100? What is the present value of the expectation of receiving $100 one year hence, discounted at 12%?
8. What is indicated when the present value of the net cash flows from an investment in a machine, discounted at 12%, exceeds the amount of the investment? What is indicated when the present value of the net cash flows, discounted at 12%, is less than the amount of the investment?
9. What are the incremental costs of accepting an additional volume of business?
10. A company manufactures and sells 250,000 units of product in this country at $5 per unit. The product costs $3 per unit to manufacture. Can you describe a situation under which the company may be willing to sell an additional 25,000 units of the product abroad at $2.75 per unit?
11. What is a sunk cost? An out-of-pocket cost? An opportunity cost? Is an opportunity cost a cost in the accounting sense of the term?
12. Any costs that have been incurred in manufacturing a product are sunk costs. Why are such costs irrelevant in deciding whether to sell the product in its present condition or to make it into a new product through additional processing?

CLASS EXERCISES

Exercise 27–1

Machine A cost $12,000 and has an estimated five-year life and no salvage value. Machine B cost $12,000 and has an estimated five-year life and a $2,000 salvage value. Under the assumption that the average investment in each machine is the average of its yearly book values, calculate the average investment in each machine.

Exercise 27–2

A company is planning to buy a new machine and produce a new product. The machine will cost $16,000, have a four-year life, and no salvage value, and will be depreciated on a straight-line basis. The company expects to sell 2,000 units of the machine's product each year with these results:

Sales		$60,000
Costs:		
Materials, labor, and overhead excluding		
depreciation on the new machine	$32,000	
Depreciation on the new machine	4,000	
Selling and administrative expenses	20,000	56,000
Income before taxes		$ 4,000
Income taxes		2,000
Net income		$ 2,000

Required:

Calculate (1) the payback period and (2) the return on the average investment in this machine.

Exercise 27–3

Under the assumption that due to the high risk involved, the company of Exercise 27–2 demands a 14% compound return from capital investments such as that described in Exercise 27–2, determine the total present value and net present value of the net cash flows, discounted at 14%, from the machine it plans to buy.

Exercise 27–4

A company can invest in each of three projects, A, B, and C. Each project requires a $10,000 investment and will produce cash flows as follows:

Years Hence	Annual Cash Flows		
	Project A	Project B	Project C
1	$ 4,000	$ 6,000	$ 2,000
2	4,000	4,000	4,000
3	4,000	2,000	6,000
	$12,000	$12,000	$12,000

Required:

Under the assumption the company requires a 10% compound return from its investments, determine in which of the projects it should invest.

Exercise 27–5

A company has 7,000 units of Product B that cost $2 per unit to manufacture. The 7,000 units can be sold for $22,000, or they can be further processed at a cost of $11,000 into Products C and D. The additional processing will produce

3,400 units of Product C that can be sold for $4 each and 2,100 units of Product D that can be sold for $8 each.

Required:

Prepare an analysis to show whether the Product B units should be further processed.

PROBLEMS

Problem 27–1

A company that sells a number of products is planning to add a new one to its line. It estimates it can sell 40,000 units of the new product annually at $5 per unit, but to manufacture the product will require new machinery costing $50,000 and having a five-year life and no salvage value. The new product will have a $2 per unit direct material cost and a $1 per unit direct labor cost. Manufacturing overhead chargeable to the new product, other than for depreciation on the new machinery, will be $25,000 annually; and $35,000 of additional selling and administrative expenses will be incurred annually in selling the product. The company's combined state and federal income tax rate is 50%.

Required:

Using straight-line depreciation, calculate (1) the payback period on the investment in new machinery, (2) the rate of return on the average investment, and (3) the net present value of the net cash flows discounted at 14%.

Problem 27–2

A company can invest in either of two projects, A or B. With straight-line depreciation, the projects will produce the following estimated annual results:

	Project A		*Project B*	
Sales		$140,000		$150,000
Costs:				
Materials	$35,000		$38,000	
Labor	28,000		32,000	
Manufacturing overhead including depreciation on new machinery	40,000		42,000	
Selling and administrative expenses	29,000	132,000	30,000	142,000
Income before taxes		$ 8,000		$ 8,000
Income taxes		4,000		4,000
Net income		$ 4,000		$ 4,000

Project A will require a $50,000 investment in new machinery that will have a six-year life and a $2,000 salvage value. Project B will require a $50,000 investment in new machinery that will have a five-year life and no salvage value.

Required:

Calculate the payback period, the return on average investment, and the net present value of the net cash flows from each project discounted at 12%. State which project you think is the better investment and why.

Problem 27-3

A company is considering a $90,000 investment in machinery to produce a new product. The machinery is expected to have a five-year life and no salvage value, and sales of its product are expected to produce $34,000 of income before depreciation and income taxes. Since state and federal income taxes take 50% of the company's income, with depreciation calculated on a straight-line basis, this means an $8,000 annual after-tax income, calculated as follows:

Income before depreciation and income taxes	$34,000
Depreciation ($90,000 ÷ 5 years)	18,000
Income before taxes	$16,000
Income taxes	8,000
Net income from sale of product	$ 8,000

The company demands a 12% compound return on such investments, and its controller has calculated that the $90,000 investment will earn such a return. However, in presenting his figures to the company president, he pointed out that the desirability of the investment could be increased by depreciating the machinery on a sum-of-the-years'-digits basis. The president wanted to know why an accounting method would improve the desirability of an investment in machinery.

Required:

1. Calculate the company's net income from the sale of the new product for each of the five years with depreciation calculated by the sum-of-the-years'-digits method.
2. With the machinery depreciated on a straight-line basis, calculate the net present value of the net cash flows discounted at 12%.
3. With the machinery depreciated on a sum-of-the-years'-digits basis, calculate the net present value of the net cash flows discounted at 12%.
4. Explain why sum-of-the-years'-digits depreciation improves the desirability of this investment.

Problem 27-4

Prather Company annually manufactures and sells 10,000 units of one of its products at $25 per unit. The units cost $22.50 each to manufacture and sell, and in producing and selling the 10,000 units the company has the following costs and expenses:

Fixed costs and expenses:

Manufacturing overhead	$60,000
Selling expenses	15,000
Administrative expenses................	25,000

Variable costs and expenses:

Materials ($3 per unit)	30,000
Direct labor ($5 per unit)	50,000
Manufacturing overhead ($2 per unit)	20,000
Selling expenses ($1.50 per unit)	15,000
Administrative expenses ($1 per unit)	10,000

An exporter has offered to buy 2,000 units of the product at $17.50 each to be sold abroad. The new business will not affect the company's present sales, its fixed costs and expenses, nor any of its per unit variable costs and expenses.

Required:

Prepare an income statement showing (1) in one set of columns the revenue, costs, expenses, and income before taxes from present business; (2) in a second set of columns the revenue, costs, expenses, and income before taxes from the sales to the exporter; and (3) in a third set of columns the combined results of both kinds of sales.

Problem 27–5

Last year St. Charles Company manufactured and sold 1,000 units of a machine called a pin-puller with the following results:

Sales (1,000 units @ $200).................		$200,000
Costs and expenses:		
Variable:		
Materials	$40,000	
Labor	50,000	
Factory overhead......................	30,000	
Selling and administrative expenses	10,000	
Fixed:		
Factory overhead......................	30,000	
Selling and administrative expenses	20,000	180,000
Income before taxes		$ 20,000

A federal agency has asked for bids on 100 pin-pullers almost identical to St. Charles Company's machine, the only difference being an extra part not presently installed on the St. Charles Company's pin-puller. To install the extra part would require the purchase of a new machine costing $1,000, plus $1 per unit for additional material and $2 per unit for additional labor. The new machine would have no further use after the completion of the government contract, but it could be sold for $300. Sale of the additional units would not affect the company's fixed costs and expenses, but all variable costs and expenses, including variable selling and administrative expenses, would vary with volume.

Required:

1. List with their total the unit costs of the material, labor, and et cetera that would enter into the lowest unit price the company could bid on the special order without causing a reduction in income from normal business.
2. Under the assumption the company bid $170 per unit and was awarded the contract for the 100 special units, prepare an income statement showing (1) in one set of columns the revenues, costs, expenses, and income before taxes from present business; (2) in a second set of columns the revenue, costs, expenses, and income before taxes from the new business; and (3) in a third set of columns the combined results of both the old and new business.

ALTERNATE PROBLEMS

Problem 27–1A

Airslide Company is considering a $60,000 investment in new machinery to produce a new product. The machinery will have a five-year life and no salvage value, and this additional information is available:

Estimated sales of new product	$140,000
Estimated costs:	
Materials	25,000
Labor	40,000
Overhead excluding depreciation on new machinery	33,000
Selling and administrative expenses	20,000
Income taxes	50%

Required:

Using straight-line depreciation, calculate (1) the payback period on the investment in new machinery, (2) the rate of return on the average investment, and (3) the net present value of the net cash flows discounted at 12%.

Problem 27–2A

Becker Company is considering an investment in one of two projects. Project One requires a $72,000 investment in new machinery having a six-year life and no salvage value. Project Two requires a $74,000 investment in new machinery having a five-year life and a $4,000 salvage value. The products of the projects differ; however, each will produce an estimated $6,000 after-tax net income for the life of the project.

Required:

Calculate the payback period, the return on average investment, and the net present value of the net cash flows from each project discounted at 12%. State which project you think is the better investment and why.

Problem 27–3A

Travis Company is considering a project that requires a $65,000 investment in machinery having a five-year life and a $5,000 salvage value. The project will annually produce $24,000 of income before depreciation on the new machinery and income taxes. The company's state and federal income taxes take 50% of its before-tax income; consequently, with depreciation calculated on a straight-line basis, the project will produce a $6,000 annual after-tax income calculated as follows:

Income before depreciation and income taxes	$24,000
Depreciation [($65,000 − $5,000) ÷ 5]	12,000
Income before taxes	$12,000
Income taxes	6,000
Net income from the project	$ 6,000

The company refuses to invest in a project that will not earn at least a 12% compound return, and it has been determined that this project will earn such a return. However, it has been pointed out that if the company will depreciate the machinery of the project on a sum-of-the-years'-digits basis, the compound return from the investment can be materially increased.

Required:

1. Calculate the company's net income from the project for each of the five years with depreciation calculated on a sum-of-the-years'-digits basis.
2. With the machinery depreciated on a straight-line basis, calculate the net present value of the net cash flows discounted at 12%.
3. With the machinery depreciated on a sum-of-the-years'-digits basis, calculate the net present value of the net cash flows discounted at 12%.
4. Explain why sum-of-the-years'-digits depreciation increases the desirability of this investment.

Problem 27–4A

Bobstay Company manufactures and sells in this country a number of products, one of which is a machine that sells for $15 per unit. During a normal year the company manufactures and sells 10,000 units of this machine with these results:

Sales		$150,000
Costs:		
Materials	$28,000	
Direct labor	30,000	
Manufacturing overhead	20,000	
Selling expenses	22,000	
Administrative expenses	25,000	125,000
Income before taxes		$ 25,000

An exporter has offered to buy 1,000 of the machines at $11.50 each for sale abroad, but since the price is below normal cost, the company president does not think the offer should be accepted. However, an examination of a normal year's costs and their relation to the new business shows: (1) Material costs are 100% variable. (2) One third of the direct labor on the additional machines could be done during regular hours with additional employees at regular wage rates, but two thirds would have to be done at overtime rates 50% above regular rates. (3) Of a normal year's manufacturing overhead, one half remains fixed at any production level from zero to 12,000 units and one half varies with volume. (4) There would be no additional selling expenses resulting from the new business. (5) Accepting the new business would increase administrative expenses $1,200.

Required:

Prepare a comparative income statement showing in one set of columns the sales, costs, and income before taxes from normal business, in a second set of columns the sales, costs, and income from the new business, and in the third set of columns the combined results of both the old and new business.

Problem 27–5A

Duo Company's sales and costs for its two products last year were:

	Product A	*Product B*
Unit selling price	$20	$10
Variable costs per unit	$5	$5
Fixed costs	$100,000	$50,000
Units sold	10,000	20,000

Through sales effort the company can change its sales mix. However, sales of the two products are so interrelated that a percentage increase in the sales of one product causes an equal percentage decrease in the sales of the other, and vice versa.

Required:

1. State which of its products the company should push, and why.
2. Prepare a columnar statement showing last year's sales, fixed costs, variable costs, and income before taxes for Product A in the first pair of columns, the results for Product B in the second set of columns, and the combined results for both products in the third set of columns.
3. Prepare a like statement for the two products under the assumption that the sales of Product A are increased 20%, with a resulting 20% decrease in the sales of Product B.
4. Prepare a third statement under the assumption that the sales of Product A are decreased 20%, with a resulting 20% increase in the sales of Product B.

PROVOCATIVE PROBLEMS

Provocative problem 27–1
L. A. Paper Company

L. A. Paper Company operates a number of paper mills, one of which is in Sudbury. The Sudbury mill was once a profitable operation, but its plant and equipment are getting old and the immediate area no longer produces sufficient pulp logs to supply the mill's needs. Consequently, logs are being hauled from greater and greater distances, with a resulting increase in their cost, and the mill is now just breaking even.

Construction of a new mill is under consideration, to be located in an area with an ample supply of pulp, good water, and low-cost hydroelectric power. However, demand for the company's product is not sufficient to keep both the old and new mills in operation; therefore, if the new mill is built, the old mill will have to be abandoned.

The company's directors have asked you to analyze the situation and recommend whether or not the old mill should be abandoned and the new mill built. The following information is available:

LOSS FROM ABANDONING THE SUDBURY MILL. The land, buildings, and machinery of the Sudbury mill have a $3,700,000 book value. Very little of the machinery can be moved to the new mill. Most will have to be scrapped. Therefore, if the mill is abandoned, it is estimated that only $500,000 of the investment in the mill can be recovered through the sale of its land and buildings, the sale of scrap, and by moving some of its machinery to the new mill. The remaining $3,200,000 will be lost.

COST OF THE NEW MILL. The new mill will cost $10,000,000 and will have an estimated 20-year life. It will double the present 100,000-ton capacity of the Sudbury mill, and it is estimated the 200,000 tons of product produced in the new mill can be sold without a price reduction.

COMPARATIVE PRODUCTION COSTS. A comparison of the production costs per ton at the old mill with the estimated costs at the new mill shows the following:

	Old Mill	New Mill
Raw materials, labor, and plant expenses (exclusive of depreciation)	$65.00	$55.50
Depreciation	4.00	2.50
Total costs per ton	$69.00	$58.00

The higher per ton depreciation charge at the old mill results primarily from depreciation being allocated to fewer units of product.

Prepare a report analyzing the advantages and disadvantages of the move, including your recommendations. You may assume that sufficient pulp logs are available for the Sudbury mill to continue in operation long enough to recover the mill's full cost. However, due to the mill's high costs, operation will be at the break-even point. Present any pertinent analyses based on the data given.

Provocative problem 27–2
Casner

Casner Company sells an average of 50,000 units of its Product BAC each year and earns a $1 per unit after-tax (50% rate) net income on each unit sold. The company assembles the product from components, some of which it buys and some of which it manufactures. One of the components is a gage that the company manufactures on special equipment that has a $25,000 book value, a five-year remaining life, and is depreciated at the rate of $5,000 per year. The variable costs of manufacturing the gage are:

Direct materials $1.15
Direct labor 1.00
Variable overhead 0.25
     Total variable costs $2.40

The gage can be purchased from a supplier at a $2.66 per unit delivered cost. If it is purchased, the special equipment used to manufacture it can be sold for cash at its book value (no profit or loss) and the cash can be invested in other projects that will pay a 10% compound after-tax return, which is the return the company demands on all its capital investments.

Should the company continue to manufacture the gage, or should it sell the special equipment and buy the gage? Back your answer with explanations and computations.

Provocative problem 27-3
Vang

Vang Company has operated for a number of years selling an average of 50,000 units of its product annually at $15 per unit. Its costs at this sales level are:

Direct materials $250,000
Direct labor   150,000
Manufacturing overhead:
    Variable   60,000
    Fixed................................   40,000
Selling and administrative expenses:
    Variable   50,000
    Fixed................................   110,000
Income taxes...........................   50%

At a 50,000-unit level the company does not utilize all of its plant capacity, but management thinks that by further processing the product, it can do so. If the product is further processed, it can be sold for $16.50 per unit. Further processing will increase fixed manufacturing overhead by $5,000 annually, and it will increase variable manufacturing costs per unit as follows:

Materials $0.30
Direct labor 0.40
Variable manufacturing overhead 0.20
    Total........................... $0.90

Selling the further processed product will not affect fixed selling and administrative expenses, but it will increase variable selling and administrative expenses 10%. Further processing is not expected to either increase or decrease the number of units sold.

Should the company further process the product? Back your opinion with a simple calculation and also a comparative income statement showing present results and the estimated results with the product further processed.

After studying Chapter 28, you should be able to:

☐ Explain the importance of tax planning.

☐ Describe the steps an individual must go through to calculate his tax liability, and explain the difference between deductions to arrive at adjusted gross income, deductions from adjusted gross income, and tax credits.

☐ Calculate the taxable income and net tax liability for an individual.

☐ State the procedures used to determine the tax associated with capital gains and losses.

☐ Describe the differences between the calculations of taxable income and tax liability for corporations and for individuals.

☐ Explain why income tax expenses shown in financial statements may differ from taxes actually payable.

☐ Define or explain the terms and phrases listed in the chapter Glossary.

Tax considerations in business decisions

■ Years ago, when income tax rates were low, management could afford to ignore or dismiss as of minor importance the tax effects of a business decision; but today, when nearly half the income of a business must commonly be paid out in income taxes, this is no longer wise. Today, a successful management must constantly be alert to every possible tax savings, recognizing that it is often necessary to earn two "pretax dollars" in order to keep one "after-tax dollar," or that a dollar of income tax saved is commonly worth a two-dollar reduction in any other expense.

TAX PLANNING

When taxpayers plan their affairs in such a way as to incur the smallest possible tax liability, they are engaged in *tax planning*. Many business deals can be designed in more than one alternative way. For example, equipment might be purchased for cash, purchased through borrowed money, or perhaps even leased from the owner. Tax planning involves an evaluation of each alternative in terms of its tax consequences, and selecting the one alternative that will result in the smallest tax liability.

Normally tax planning requires that a tax-saving opportunity be recognized prior to the occurrence of the transaction. Although it is sometimes possible to take advantage of a previously overlooked tax saving, the common result of an overlooked opportunity is a lost opportunity, since the Internal Revenue Service usually deems the original action in a tax situation the final action for tax purposes.

Since effective tax planning requires an extensive knowledge of both tax laws and business procedures, it is not the purpose of this chapter to make expert tax planners of elementary accounting students. Rather, the purpose is to make students aware of the merits of effective tax planning, recognizing that for complete and effective planning, the average student, business executive, or citizen should seek the advice of a certified public accountant, tax attorney, or other person qualified in tax matters.

TAX EVASION AND TAX AVOIDANCE

In any discussion of taxes a clear distinction should be drawn between tax evasion and tax avoidance. *Tax evasion* is illegal and may result in heavy penalties, including prison sentences in some instances; but *tax avoidance* is a perfectly legal and profitable activity.

Taxes are avoided by preventing a tax liability from coming into existence. This may be accomplished by any legal means, for example, by the way in which a transaction is completed, or the manner in which a business is organized, or by a wise selection from among the options provided in the tax laws. It makes no difference how, so long as the means is legal and it prevents a tax liability from arising.

In contrast, tax evasion involves the fraudulent denial and concealment of an existing tax liability. For example, taxes are evaded when taxable income, such as interest, dividends, tips, fees, or profits from the sale of stocks, bonds, and other assets, is unreported. Taxes are also evaded when items not legally deductible from income are deducted. For example, taxes are evaded when the costs of operating the family automobile are deducted as a business expense, or when charitable contributions not allowed or not made are deducted. Tax evasion is illegal and should be scrupulously avoided.

STATE AND MUNICIPAL INCOME TAXES

Most states and a number of cities levy income taxes, in most cases modeling their laws after the federal laws. However, other than noting the existence of such laws and that they increase the total tax burden and make tax planning even more important, the following discussion is limited to the federal income tax.

HISTORY AND OBJECTIVES OF THE FEDERAL INCOME TAX

Although the federal government first used an income tax during the War between the States, the history of today's federal income tax dates from the 1913 ratification of the Sixteenth Amendment, which cleared away all questions as to the constitutionality of such a tax. Since its ratification, Congress has passed more than 50 revenue acts and other laws implementing the tax, placing the responsibility for their enforcement in the hands of the Treasury Department acting through the Internal Revenue Service. Collectively, the statutes dealing with taxation that have been adopted by Congress are called the *Internal Revenue Code.*

The original purpose of the federal income tax was to raise revenue, but over the years this original goal has been expanded to include the following and other nonrevenue objectives:

1. To assist small businesses.
2. To encourage foreign trade.
3. To encourage exploration for oil and minerals.
4. To redistribute the national income.
5. To control inflation and deflation.
6. To stimulate business.
7. To attain full employment.
8. To support social objectives.

Also, just as the objectives have expanded over the years, so have the rates and the number of people required to pay taxes. In 1913 the minimum rate was 1% and the maximum for individuals was 7%. This contrasts with today's minimum 14% rate for individuals and maximum of 70%. Likewise, the total number of tax returns filed each year has grown from a few thousand in 1913 to well over 100,000,000 in recent years.

SYNOPSIS OF THE FEDERAL INCOME TAX

The following brief synopsis of the federal income tax is given at this point because it is necessary to know something about the federal income tax in order to appreciate its effect on business decisions.

Classes of taxpayers

Federal income tax law recognizes three classes of taxpayers: individuals, corporations, and estates and trusts. Members of each class must file returns and pay taxes on taxable income.

A business operated as a single proprietorship or partnership is not treated as a separate taxable entity under the law. Rather, single proprietors must include the income from their businesses on their individual tax returns; and although a partnership must file an information return showing its net income and the distributive shares of the partners, the partners are required to include their shares on their individual returns. In other words, the income of a single proprietorship or partnership, whether withdrawn from the business or not, is taxed as the individual income of the single proprietor or partners.

The treatment given corporations under the law is different, however. A business operated as a corporation must file a return and pay taxes on its taxable income. Also, if a corporation pays out in dividends some or all of its "after-tax income," its stockholders must report these dividends as income on their individual returns. Because of this, it is commonly claimed that corporation income is taxed twice, once to the corporation and again to its stockholders.

A discussion of the federal income tax as applied to estates and trusts is not necessary at this point and is deferred to a more advanced course.

The individual income tax

The amount of federal income tax individuals must pay each year depends upon their gross income, deductions, exemptions, and tax credits. For those individuals who do not qualify to use the simplified Tax Tables, the typical calculation of the tax liability involves the sequence shown in Illustration 28–1.

To determine the federal income tax liability of an individual, the amounts of gross income, deductions, exemptions, tax credits (if any), and prepayments are listed on forms supplied by the federal government. (For many individuals, simplified Tax Tables automatically incorporate *some* of the deductions, exemptions, and credits so that fewer of these items must be separately listed.) Then the appropriate calculations (additions, subtractions, and so forth) are performed in accordance with the instructions. The listing of the items on the forms is not precisely the same for all classes of taxpayers and does not always follow

Gross income			$xx,xxx
Less: Deductions to arrive at adjusted gross income			(xx,xxx)
Adjusted gross income			$xx,xxx
Less: Itemized deductions	$x,xxx		
Less: Zero bracket amount (formerly called "standard deduction")	(x,xxx)		
Itemized deductions in excess of zero bracket amount		$x,xxx	
Deduction for exemptions		x,xxx	(x,xxx)
Taxable income			$xx,xxx
Gross tax liability from tax rate schedule			$xx,xxx
Less: Tax credits and prepayments			(xx,xxx)
Net tax payable (or refund)			$ xxx

Illustration 28–1

the general pattern shown in Illustration 28–1; however, the illustration does show the relation of the items and the basic mathematics required in completing the tax forms.

The items that appear on a tax return as gross income, adjusted gross income, deductions, exemptions, tax credits, and prepayments require additional description and explanation.

Gross income Income tax law defines *gross income* as *all income from whatever source derived, unless expressly excluded from taxation by law.* Gross income therefore includes income from operating a business, gains from property sales, dividends, interest, rents, royalties, and compensation for services, such as salaries, wages, fees, commissions, bonuses, and tips. Actually, the answers to two questions are all that is required to determine whether an item should be included or excluded. The two questions are: (1) Is the item income? (2) Is it expressly excluded by law? If an item is income and not specifically excluded, it must be included.

Certain items are specifically excluded from gross income, for example, gifts, inheritances, scholarships, social security benefits, veterans' benefits, workmen's compensation insurance, and in most cases the proceeds of life insurance policies paid upon the death of the insured. Because these items are excluded from gross income, they are nontaxable.

Another item that is specifically excluded from gross income is interest on the obligations of the states and their subdivisions. The Supreme Court has held that a federal income tax on such items would, in effect, amount to having the power to destroy these governmental units. Thus, a federal income tax on the interest from bonds or other obligations of states or their subdivisions would violate constitutional guarantees. With a few exceptions, interest from such items is therefore nontaxable.

For many years, the law has also allowed individuals to exclude a limited amount of dividend income. One reason for this exclusion (among others) is to partially recognize the fact that corporation income is taxed twice, first as income earned by the corporation and second as dividends received by stockholders. However, beginning in 1981 and continuing through 1982, this exclusion has been expanded to include interest income from investments such as savings accounts. For these years, an individual may exclude a total of $200 of dividend income received from a qualifying domestic corporation and interest income. (On a joint return of a husband and wife, each may exclude $200 for a total of $400. However, to do so husbands and wives who do not live in states with community property laws must each have received $200 in dividends or interest, and neither may exclude dividends or interest from investments owned by the other.) According to present law, this exclusion is effective only for 1981 and 1982. After those years, the exclusion will apply only to dividends (not interest) and will be limited to $100 for an individual taxpayer and $200 total for husbands and wives filing a joint return.

Deductions to arrive at adjusted gross income   These are generally deductions of a business nature. For example, all ordinary and necessary expenses of carrying on a business, trade, or profession are deductions to arrive at adjusted gross income. To understand this, recognize that under income tax law gross profit from sales (sales less cost of goods sold) is gross income to a merchant, that gross legal fees earned are gross income to a lawyer, and gross rentals from a building are gross income to a landlord. Consequently, the merchant, the lawyer, and the landlord may each deduct all ordinary and necessary expenses of carrying on the business or profession, such as salaries, wages, rent, depreciation, supplies used, repairs, maintenance, insurance, taxes, interest, and so on.

Also, as with the business executive, employees may deduct from gross income certain expenses incurred in connection with their employment if paid by the employees. These include transportation and travel expenses, expenses of an outside salesperson, and moving expenses. Employees who work in more than one place during a day may deduct transportation costs incurred in moving from one place of employment to another during the day. However, as a general rule they may not deduct the cost of commuting from home to the first place of employment or from the last place of employment to home. Travel expenses include in addition to transportation expenses, the costs of meals and lodging while away from home overnight on employment connected business. Expenses of outside salespersons are expenses incurred in soliciting orders for an employer while away from the employer's place of business. They include such things as transportation, telephone, stationery, and postage. Moving expenses are expenses incurred by employees (or self-employed individuals) in moving their place of residence upon being transferred by their employer or to take a new job. Certain minimum requirements as to the distance moved and the length of employment in the new location must be met. Commonly an employer reimburses employees for the foregoing expenses. In such cases employees may deduct only that portion of their expenses not reimbursed by the employer; and if the reimbursement exceeds the expenses, employees must include the excess in their gross income.

In addition to the foregoing business expenses, from a tax management point of view, a very important deduction from gross income is the long-term capital gain deduction. This permits (under certain circumstances) the deduction from gross income of 60% of the net long-term gains from capital asset sales and exchanges. More detailed discussion is given to the long-term capital gain deduction later in this chapter.

Deductions from adjusted gross income

By legislative grace an individual taxpayer is permitted certain deductions from adjusted gross income. These are of two kinds: (1) the zero bracket amount or deduction of itemized personal expenses and (2) the deduction for exemptions.

The first type consists of certain personal expenses which the taxpayer is allowed to itemize and deduct, or alternatively, it consists of a *zero bracket amount*. The taxpayer chooses between these two. Regarding the zero bracket amount, all individual taxpayers are entitled to have a certain minimum amount of taxable income before owing any income taxes. This amount is known as the zero bracket amount; formerly it was referred to as the *standard deduction*. In other words, if the taxpayer reports taxable income not in excess of the zero bracket amount, the schedules of tax rates will show that zero tax is levied against this amount. The zero bracket amount is a flat amount that depends upon the taxpayer's filing status. For a single taxpayer, the zero bracket amount is $2,300; for married taxpayers filing a joint return or for a surviving spouse, it is $3,400; and for a married taxpayer filing a separate return, the zero bracket amount is $1,700.

Instead of choosing the zero bracket amount, taxpayers may itemize their allowable deductions and deduct the amount by which the itemized deductions are in excess of the zero bracket amount. Obviously, taxpayers tend to elect whichever alternative results in the largest deduction. Itemized deductions commonly consist of the taxpayer's personal interest expense, state and local taxes, charitable contributions, casualty losses over $100 for each loss, one half the cost of medical and hospital insurance (but not more than $150 per year), and a medical expense deduction. The medical expense deduction consists of that portion of medical, dental, and hospital expenses in excess of 3% of the taxpayer's adjusted gross income, including the cost of medicines and drugs in excess of 1% of adjusted gross income and including the excess over $150 of the cost of medical and hospital insurance.

In addition to itemized deductions or the zero bracket amount, a taxpayer is allowed a second kind of deduction, called the deduction for exemptions. For each exemption, the taxpayer may deduct $1,000 from adjusted gross income, and a taxpayer is allowed one exemption for himself and one for each dependent. Additional exemptions are allowed if the taxpayer is 65 or over or is blind. If a husband and wife file a joint return, each is a taxpayer and they may combine their exemptions.

To qualify as a dependent for whom an exemption may be claimed, the person must meet these tests: (1) be closely related to the taxpayer or have been a member of the taxpayer's household for the entire year; (2) have received over half his or her support from the taxpayer during the year; (3) if married, has not and will not file a joint return with his or her spouse; and (4) had less than $1,000 of gross income during the year. An exception to the gross income test is granted if the person claimed as a dependent is a child of the taxpayer and under 19 years of age at the end of the tax year or was a full-time student in an educational institution during each of five months of the year. This exception is always of interest to college students because it commonly results in two exemptions for such students, if they qualify in all other respects as a dependent. One exemption may be taken by the parent who claims the student as a dependent and the other exemption may be taken on the student's own tax return.

Observe in the discussion thus far that there are *deductions to arrive at adjusted gross income* and also *deductions from adjusted gross income*. Furthermore, it is important that each kind be subtracted at the proper point in the tax calculation, because the allowable amounts of some deductions from adjusted gross income are determined by the amount of adjusted gross income.

Federal income tax rates   Federal income tax rates are progressive in nature. By this is meant that each additional segment or bracket of taxable income is subject to a higher rate than the preceding segment or bracket. This may be seen by examining Illustration 28–2 which shows the rates for an unmarried person not qualifying as a head of household and for married persons filing a joint return or qualifying widows or widowers.

The Tax Rate Schedules shown in Illustration 28–2 are used by taxpayers who do not qualify to use simplified Tax Tables, which are discussed later in the chapter. To use the rate schedules of Illustration 28–2, a taxpayer reads down the first two columns of the appropriate schedule until he comes to the bracket of his taxable income. For example, if an unmarried taxpayer's taxable income is $29,000, the taxpayer reads down the proper columns to the bracket "over $28,800 but not over $34,100." The remaining columns then tell him that the tax on $29,000 is $7,434 plus 44% of the excess over $28,800, or is $7,434 + (44% × $200), or is $7,522.

A husband and wife have a choice. They may combine their incomes and use the rate schedule shown for married individuals (Schedule Y) or they may each file a separate return using a rate schedule (not shown) that results in a tax for each somewhat in excess of that shown in Illustration 28–2 for single taxpayers. The phrase "qualified widows and widowers" in the title of Schedule Y refers to surviving spouses who, if they are not remarried and if they have a dependent child, may continue to use Schedule Y for two tax years after the year of their spouse's death.

Also, a person who can qualify as a *head of household* may use a rate schedule (not shown) in which the rates fall between those for

Schedule X—Single Taxpayers					Schedule Y—Married Filing Joint Returns and Qualifying Widows and Widowers				
TAXABLE INCOME			**TAX**		**TAXABLE INCOME**			**TAX**	
Not over $2,300			-0-		Not over $3,400			-0-	
Over—	But not over—			Of the amount over—	Over—	But not over—			Of the amount over—
$ 2,300	$ 3,400		14%	$ 2,300	$ 3,400	$ 5,500		14%	$ 3,400
$ 3,400	$ 4,400	$ 154 +	16%	$ 3,400	$ 5,500	$ 7,600	$ 294 +	16%	$ 5,500
$ 4,400	$ 6,500	$ 314 +	18%	$ 4,400	$ 7,600	$ 11,900	$ 630 +	18%	$ 7,600
$ 6,500	$ 8,500	$ 692 +	19%	$ 6,500	$ 11,900	$ 16,000	$ 1,404 +	21%	$ 11,900
$ 8,500	$ 10,800	$ 1,072 +	21%	$ 8,500	$ 16,000	$ 20,200	$ 2,265 +	24%	$ 16,000
$ 10,800	$ 12,900	$ 1,555 +	24%	$ 10,800	$ 20,200	$ 24,600	$ 3,273 +	28%	$ 20,200
$ 12,900	$ 15,000	$ 2,059 +	26%	$ 12,900	$ 24,600	$ 29,900	$ 4,505 +	32%	$ 24,600
$ 15,000	$ 18,200	$ 2,605 +	30%	$ 15,000	$ 29,900	$ 35,200	$ 6,201 +	37%	$ 29,900
$ 18,200	$ 23,500	$ 3,565 +	34%	$ 18,200	$ 35,200	$ 45,800	$ 8,162 +	43%	$ 35,200
$ 23,500	$ 28,800	$ 5,367 +	39%	$ 23,500	$ 45,800	$ 60,000	$ 12,720 +	49%	$ 45,800
$ 28,800	$ 34,100	$ 7,434 +	44%	$ 28,800	$ 60,000	$ 85,600	$ 19,678 +	54%	$ 60,000
$ 34,100	$ 41,500	$ 9,766 +	49%	$ 34,100	$ 85,600	$109,400	$ 33,502 +	59%	$ 85,600
$ 41,500	$ 55,300	$13,392 +	55%	$ 41,500	$109,400	$162,400	$ 47,544 +	64%	$109,400
$ 55,300	$ 81,800	$20,982 +	63%	$ 55,300	$162,400	$215,400	$ 81,464 +	68%	$162,400
$ 81,800	$108,300	$37,677 +	68%	$ 81,800	$215,400	....	$117,504 +	70%	$215,400
$108,300	....	$55,697 +	70%	$108,300					

Illustration 28–2

unmarried individuals and those for married couples filing jointly. Generally a head of household is an unmarried or legally separated person who maintains a home in which lives his or her unmarried child or a qualifying dependent.

Regardless of the rate schedule used, it is generally recognized that our federal income tax rates are steeply progressive. Proponents claim that this is only fair, since the taxpayers most able to pay, those with higher incomes, are subject to higher rates. Opponents, on the other hand, claim the high rates stifle initiative. For example, a young unmarried executive with $34,100 of taxable income per year, upon being offered a new job carrying additional responsibilities and a $6,000 salary increase, might turn the new job down, feeling the after-tax increase in pay insufficient to compensate for the extra responsibilities. In this case the executive could keep after federal income taxes just $3,060 or 51% of the increase.

In a situation like that described here, a decision as to whether another dollar of income is desirable or worth the effort depends on the *marginal tax rate* that applies to that dollar. The marginal tax rate is the rate that applies to the next dollar of income to be earned. For example, the highest rate that is applicable to the young executive before taking the new job is 44% on the taxable dollars between $28,800 and $34,100 (see Illustration 28–2). However, if the new job is taken, the marginal rate on the next $7,400 of taxable income goes up to 49%.

Whether or not our progressive income tax rates stifle initiative is probably open to debate. Notwithstanding the progression of marginal tax rates up to 70%, as shown in Illustration 28–2, it should be noted that certain types of income are subject to lesser tax rates. For example, an individual's "personal service income" includes wages, salaries, other compensation for personal services, and certain pensions, annuities, and deferred compensation. Importantly, the maximum tax rate on personal service income is 50%. In terms of Illustration 28–2, this means that for single taxpayers, all personal service income in excess of $41,500 (taxable income) is taxed at a 50% rate. For married taxpayers filing a joint return and certain widows and widowers, all personal service income in excess of $60,000 (taxable income) is taxed at a 50% rate. However, there is no question that the progressive nature of the tax rates causes high-income taxpayers to search for tax-saving opportunities.

Tax credits and prepayments　After an individual's gross income tax liability is computed from the appropriate tax rate schedule, his tax credits, if any, and prepayments are deducted to determine his net tax liability. *Tax credits* represent direct, dollar for dollar, reductions in the amount of tax liability, that is, a $100 tax credit reduces the tax liability by $100. By comparison, deductions (as discussed earlier) reduce the amount of taxable income, against which is applied the appropriate tax rates to determine the gross tax liability. Thus, a tax credit of $100 is more valuable to the taxpayer than would be a tax deduction of $100. Assuming a marginal tax rate of 30%, an additional tax deduction of $100 effectively reduces the tax liability by $30 ($100 × 30%), whereas a tax credit of $100 reduces the tax liability by $100.

Examples of tax credits include the following. A retired taxpayer with retirement income may receive a "credit for the elderly." A taxpayer who has paid income taxes to a foreign government may be eligible for a "foreign tax credit." A taxpayer who has contributed to a political candidate or party may be eligible for a "political contribution credit." The latter credit is limited to one half the donation with a maximum of $50 on a separate return and $100 on a joint return.

An "investment tax credit" equal to 10% of the purchase price of certain qualified property is also available to taxpayers. And taxpayers may also qualify for an "earned income credit" equal to 10% of "earned income up to $5,000," or (10% × $5,000 = $500). "Earned income" consists of wages, professional fees, and certain compensation for personal services. But, as earned income or adjusted gross income, whichever is larger, increases from $6,000 to $10,000, the amount of the earned income credit gradually declines from $500 to $0. The earned income credit, unlike the other tax credits, can generate a tax refund. Thus, it is similar to a negative income tax.

In addition to tax credits, any prepayments of tax are also deducted in order to determine the net tax liability. Most taxpayers have income taxes withheld from their salaries and wages. Other taxpayers have income that is not subject to withholding and on which they are required to estimate the tax, file an estimated tax return, and pay the estimated amount of the tax on the income in advance installments. Both the income tax withholdings and the estimated tax paid in advance are examples of tax prepayments that are deducted in determining a taxpayer's net tax liability.

Special tax treatment of capital gains and losses

From a tax-saving point of view, one of the most important features of our federal income tax laws is the special treatment given long-term gains from *capital asset* sales and exchanges. For individuals, the usual effect of this special treatment is a tax on net long-term capital gains that is only 40% as high as the tax on an equal amount of income from some other source, commonly called "ordinary income." For this reason, whenever possible, tax planners try to cause income to emerge in the form of long-term capital gains rather than as ordinary income.

The Internal Revenue Code defines a capital asset as any item of property except *(a)* inventories; *(b)* trade notes and accounts receivable; *(c)* real property and depreciable property used in a trade or business; *(d)* copyrights, letters, and similar property in the hands of the creator of the copyrighted works or his donee and certain other transferees; and *(e)* any government obligation due within one year and issued at a discount. Common examples of capital assets held by individuals and subject to sale or exchange are stocks, bonds, and a personal residence.

A gain on the sale of a capital asset occurs when the proceeds of the sale exceed the *basis* of the asset sold, and a loss occurs when the asset's basis exceeds the proceeds. The basis of a purchased asset is generally its cost less any depreciation previously allowed or allowable for tax purposes. Not all capital assets are acquired by purchase; but rules for determining the basis of an asset acquired other than by purchase are at times complicated and need not be discussed here.

For tax purposes, a distinction is made between short- and long-term *capital gains and losses.* Short-term gains and losses result when capital assets are held 12 months or less before being sold or exchanged, and long-term gains and losses result when such assets are held more than 12 months. Furthermore, under the law, net short-term gains must be reported in full and are taxed as ordinary income; but only 40% of the amount of any excess net long-term capital gains over net short-term capital losses, if any, must be included in adjusted gross income.

For example, if an individual taxpayer has $1,000 of long-term gains, no losses, and other income that places these gains in a 36% bracket, he is required to include only $400 of the gains in adjusted gross income and to pay only a $144 ($400 × 36% = $144) tax thereon. Consequently, his effective tax rate on the gains is 14.4% ($144 ÷ $1,000 = 14.4%), and is only 40% of what it would be if the $1,000 were ordinary income.

In the preceding paragraphs, the terms "net long-term gains" and "net short-term gains" appear. When long-term gains exceed long-term losses, a net long-term gain results. Likewise, when long-term losses exceed long-term gains, a net long-term loss occurs. Short-term gains and losses are combined in a like manner to arrive at either a net short-term gain or loss.

When an individual's net short-term capital losses exceed his net long-term capital gains, he may deduct up to $3,000 of the excess losses ($1,500 for a married taxpayer filing a separate return) from ordinary income in the year of the loss. However, when net long-term capital losses exceed net short-term capital gains, he may in any one year deduct from ordinary income only one half of the excess losses up to $3,000 ($1,500 for a married taxpayer filing a separate return). A carry-over provision is available to allow deduction in subsequent years of amounts which exceeded the $3,000 or $1,500 limitations.

One last point in regard to real property and depreciable property used in a taxpayer's trade or business (see definition of capital assets in a previous paragraph). Such properties are legally not capital assets; consequently, when sold or exchanged, the excess of losses over gains is fully deductible in arriving at taxable income. However, if such properties are held over 12 months, the excess of gains over losses is eligible for capital gain treatment, except to the extent of certain amounts of depreciation taken after 1961. As to depreciation taken after 1961, there may be a share of the gain equal to a portion or all of this depreciation, depending on the nature of the property and the method of depreciation, which must be treated as ordinary income.

Tax Tables   As previously mentioned, not all taxpayers are required to use the Tax Rate Schedules such as those shown in Illustration 28–2. Instead, most individual taxpayers use simplified Tax Tables. The Tax Tables are constructed from the Tax Rate Schedules, and both of them incorporate the zero bracket amount. In addition, the Tax Tables incorporate the number of exemptions claimed by the taxpayer. Thus, individuals who use the Tax Tables do not have to calculate the deduction for exemptions. The taxpayer simply has to calculate his *tax table income* and then search through the appropriate Tax Table to determine the gross income tax liability. Depending upon whether the taxpayer has itemized deductions in excess of the zero bracket amount, tax table income is calculated as is shown in Illustration 28–3.

For taxpayers without itemized deductions in excess of the zero bracket amount:		
Gross income		$x,xxx
Less: Deductions to arrive at adjusted gross income		(x,xxx)
Tax table income		$x,xxx
For taxpayers with itemized deductions in excess of the zero bracket amount:		
Gross income		$x,xxx
Less: Deductions to arrive at adjusted gross income		(x,xxx)
Adjusted gross income		$x,xxx
Less: Itemized deductions	$x,xxx	
Less: Zero bracket amount	(x,xxx)	
Itemized deductions in excess of zero bracket amount		(xxx)
Tax table income		$x,xxx

Illustration 28–3

The corporation income tax

For federal tax purposes, the taxable income of a corporation organized for profit is calculated in much the same way as the taxable income of an individual. However, there are important differences, five of which follow:

a. Instead of the $200 ($100 after 1982) dividend exclusion of an individual, a corporation may deduct from gross income the first 85% of dividends received from stock it owns in other domestic corporations. This in effect means that only 15% of such dividends are taxed. However, if two corporations qualify as affiliated corporations, which essentially means that one owns 80% or more of the other's stock, then 100% of the dividends received by the investor corporation from the investee corporation may be excluded.

b. The capital gains of a corporation are also treated differently. Recall that the taxable income of individuals must include only 40% of their long-term capital gains in excess of short-term capital losses. Corporations must include 100% of such gains in income. However, a 28% alternative tax rate is available on all such gains accruing to a corporation.

c. A corporation may only offset capital losses against capital gains; and if in any year the offset results in a net capital loss, the loss may not be deducted from other income, but it may be carried back to the three preceding years and forward to the next five years and deducted from any capital gains of those years.

d. The zero bracket amount and the deduction for exemptions do not apply to a corporation, and a corporation does not have certain other deductions of an individual, such as that for personal medical expenses.

e. In addition, the big difference between the corporation and the individual income tax is that the corporation tax is progressive in just five steps. The corporate income tax rates are as follows:

Amount of taxable income	Tax rate
Portion from $0 to $25,000	17%
Portion from $25,000 to $50,000	20
Portion from $50,000 to $75,000	30
Portion from $75,000 to $100,000	40
Portion in excess of $100,000	46

Thus, for a corporation with $110,000 of taxable income, its tax liability is $31,350; that is, [(17% × $25,000) + (20% × $25,000) + (30% × $25,000) + (40% × $25,000) + (46% × $10,000)].

TAX EFFECTS OF BUSINESS ALTERNATIVES

Alternative decisions commonly have different tax effects. Following are several examples illustrating this.

Form of business organization

The difference between individual and corporation tax rates commonly affects one of the basic decisions a business executive must make, which is to select the legal form the business should take. Should it be a single proprietorship, partnership, or corporation? The following factors influence the decision:

a. As previously stated, a corporation is a taxable entity. Its income is taxed at corporation rates, and any portion distributed in dividends is taxed again as individual income to its stockholders. On the other hand, the income of a single proprietorship or partnership, whether withdrawn or left in the business, is taxed as individual income of the proprietor or partners.

b. In addition, a corporation may pay reasonable amounts in salaries to stockholders who work for the corporation, and the sum of these salaries is a tax-deductible expense in arriving at the corporation's taxable income. In a partnership or a single proprietorship on the other hand, salaries of the partners or the proprietor are nothing more than allocations of income.

In arriving at a decision as to the legal form a business should take, a business executive, with the foregoing points in mind, must estimate how he will fare taxwise under each form, and select the best. For example, assume that a business executive is choosing between the single proprietorship and corporate forms, and that he estimates his business will have annual gross sales of $250,000, with cost of goods sold and operating expenses, other than his own salary as manager, of $185,000. Assume further than $45,000 per year is a fair salary for managing such a business and the owner plans to withdraw all profits from the business. Under these assumptions, the business executive will fare taxwise as shown in Illustration 28–4.

Under the assumptions of Illustration 28–4, the business executive will incur the smaller tax and have the larger after-tax income under the single proprietorship form. However, this may not be true in every case. For instance, if he has large amounts of income from other sources, he may find he would incur less tax if the business were organized as a corporation.

Furthermore, in the example just given it is assumed that all profits are withdrawn and none are left in the business for growth. This happens. However, growth is commonly financed through the retention of earnings; and when it is, the relative desirability of the two forms may change. This is because income retained in a business organized as a corporation is not taxed as individual income to its stockholders,

	Proprietorship		Corporation	
Operating results under each form:				
Estimated sales.....................................		$250,000		$250,000
Cost of goods sold and operating expenses				
other than owner-manager's salary............	$185,000		$185,000	
Salary of owner-manager	–0–	185,000	45,000	230,000
Before-tax income		$ 65,000		$ 20,000
Corporation income tax at 17%		–0–		3,400
Net income		$ 65,000		$ 16,600
Owner's after-tax income under each form:				
Single proprietorship net income		$ 65,000		
Corporation salary..............................				$ 45,000
Dividends				16,600
Total individual income		$ 65,000		$ 61,600
Individual income tax (assuming a joint return with itemized deductions of $9,100 (less the zero bracket amount of $3,400) and a deduction for exemptions of $2,000 under both forms plus a $200 dividend exclusion under the corporation form)		18,355		16,591
Owner's after-tax income		$ 46,645		$ 45,009

Illustration 28–4

but the income of a single proprietorship or partnership is so taxed, whether retained in the business or withdrawn.

For instance, if the business of Illustration 28–4 is organized as a single proprietorship, the tax burden of the owner remains the same whether he withdraws any of his profits or not. But, in case of the corporation, if all $16,600 of the earnings are retained in the business, the owner is required to pay individual income taxes on his $45,000 salary only. This would reduce his annual individual income tax from the $16,591 shown in Illustration 28–4 to $9,065, and would reduce the total tax burden with the corporation form to $12,465 ($3,400 + $9,065), which is $5,890 less than the tax burden under the single proprietorship form.

The foregoing is by no means all of the picture. Other tax factors may be involved. For example, a corporation may incur an extra tax if it accumulates more than $150,000 of retained earnings and such accumulations are beyond the reasonable needs of the business. Also, under present laws a corporation may elect to be taxed somewhat like a single proprietorship, thus eliminating the corporate tax. Furthermore, in a decision as to the legal form a business should take, factors other than taxes are often important, for example, lack of stockholder liability in a corporation.

Dividends and growth

It was pointed out earlier in this chapter that it is normally to a taxpayer's advantage to have income emerge in the form of long-term capital gains rather than as ordinary income. Furthermore, earnings paid out in dividends result in ordinary income to stockholders, but earnings retained in an incorporated business commonly result in its growth and an increase in the value of its stock, which may be turned into long-term capital gains through a later sale of the stock. For this reason it is often to the advantage of the owner of an incorporated business to forego dividends and at a later date, through the sale of the business, to take the profits of his business in the form of long-term gains resulting from growth.

Method of financing

When a business organized as a corporation is in need of additional financing, the owners may supply the corporation whatever funds are needed by purchasing its stock. However, an overall tax advantage may often be gained if instead of purchasing stock, they supply the funds through long-term loans. Insofar as the owners are concerned, beyond the allowable dividend exclusion, it makes no difference on their individual returns whether they report interest or dividends from the funds supplied. However, whether the corporation issues stock or floats a loan usually makes a big difference on its return. Interest on borrowed funds is a tax-deductible expense, but dividends are a distribution of earnings and have no effect on the corporation's taxes. Consequently, if owners lend the corporation funds rather than buy its stock, the total tax liability (their own plus their corporation's) will be reduced. In addition, the repayment of long-term debt always is considered to be a return of capital transaction. The redemption of stock, however, may result in the proceeds being treated as dividend income to the shareholders.

In making financial arrangements such as these, owners must be careful not to overreach themselves in attempting to maximize the interest deduction of their corporation. If they do so and thereby create what is called a "thin corporation," one in which the owners have supplied an unreasonably "thin" portion of capital, the Internal Revenue Service may disallow the interest deductions and require that such deductions be treated as dividends. Furthermore, repayments of "principal" may also be held to be taxable dividends.

Timing transactions

The timing of transactions can be of major importance in tax planning. For example, securities may be held a little longer in order to make the gain on their sale subject to treatment as a long-term capital gain. Or as another example, if a company has several items of real or depreciable property to be sold and some of the sales will result in losses and others in gains, the losses should be taken in one year and the gains in another. The losses and gains should be taken this way because if the losses and gains are both incurred in the same year, they must be offset. However, if the losses are taken in one year and the gains in another, the losses may be deducted in full from other ordinary income, while the gains become eligible in their year for long-term capital gain treatment, at least to the extent they exceed depreciation taken after 1961.

Forms in which related transactions are completed

The tax consequences of related transactions are often dependent upon the forms in which they are completed. For example, the sale of one property at a profit and the immediate purchase of another like property normally results in a taxable gain on the property sold, but an exchange of these properties may result in a tax-free exchange.

A tax-free exchange occurs when like kinds of property are exchanged for each other, or when one or more persons transfer property to a corporation and immediately thereafter are in control of the corporation. Control in such cases is interpreted as meaning that after the transfer the transferring persons (or person) must own at least 80%

of the corporation's voting stock plus at least 80% of the total number of shares of all other classes of stock.

At first glance it seems that it should be to anyone's advantage to take a tax-free exchange rather than to pay taxes, but this may not be so. For example, ten years ago a corporation acquired, for $50,000, land then at the edge of the city. Today, due to booming growth, the land is well within the city and has a fair market value of $250,000. Aside from a fully depreciated fence, the land is without improvements, having been used over the years for storage of idle equipment and excess inventory. The corporation plans to move part of its operations to a suburb and has an opportunity to trade the city property for vacant suburban acreage on which it would build a factory. Should it make the trade? From a tax viewpoint, since the new land is not depreciable, the answer is probably, yes, the company should make the tax-free exchange.

However, if the suburban property rather than being vacant consisted of land having a fair market value of $25,000 with a suitable factory building thereon valued at $225,000, the corporation would probably be better off if it sold the city property, paid the tax on its gain, and purchased the suburban factory and its site. The corporation would probably be better off because the gain on the city land would be taxable as a long-term capital gain on which the tax would not exceed $56,000 (28% of [$250,000 − $50,000] = $56,000). However, by purchasing the new factory, the corporation gains the right to deduct the building's $225,000 cost (over its life) in the form of depreciation, an expense deductible in full in arriving at taxable income.

Accounting basis and procedures

With certain exceptions, the accounting basis and procedures used by a taxpayer in keeping his records must also be used in computing his taxable income. Generally, a taxpayer keeps his records on either a cash or accrual basis (see pages 88–89); but regardless of which he uses, the basis and any procedures used must clearly reflect income and be consistently followed.

When inventories are a material factor in calculating income, a taxpayer is required to use the accrual basis in calculating gross profit from sales. Also, plant assets cannot be expensed in the year of purchase but must be depreciated over their useful lives. However, other than for gross profit from sales and depreciation, a taxpayer may use the cash basis in accounting for income and expenses. Furthermore, this is often an advantage, since under the cash basis, a taxpayer can often shift expense payments and the receipt of items of revenue other than from the sale of merchandise from one accounting period to the next and thus increase or decrease his taxable income.

An accrual-basis taxpayer cannot shift income from year to year by timing receipts and payments; however, somewhat of the same thing may be accomplished through a choice of accounting procedures. For example, recognition of income on a cash collection basis (see Chapter 1) commonly shifts income from one year to another. Likewise, a contractor may use the percentage-of-completion basis (Chapter 1) to shift construction income from one year to another and to level taxable income over a period of years.

Furthermore, any taxpayer may shift taxable income to future years through a choice of inventory and depreciation procedures. For example, during periods of rising prices the Lifo inventory method results in charging higher costs for goods sold against current revenues, and thus reduces taxable income and taxes. It may be argued that this only postpones taxes since in periods of declining prices the use of Lifo results in lower costs and higher taxes. However, the history of recent years has been one of constantly rising prices; therefore, it may also be argued that Lifo will postpone taxes indefinitely.

Depreciation methods that result in higher depreciation charges in an asset's early years and lower charges in later years, such as the sum-of-the-years'-digits or declining-balance methods, also postpone taxes. And while tax postponement is not as desirable as tax avoidance, postponement does give the taxpayer interest-free use of tax dollars until these dollars must be paid to the government.

Before turning to a new topic, it should be pointed out that the opportunities for tax planning described in these pages are only illustrative of those available. The wise business executive will seek help from a tax consultant in order to take advantage of every tax-saving opportunity.

NET INCOME AND TAXABLE INCOME

The taxable income of a business commonly differs from its reported net income. In regard to corporations, one reason for this difference is that net income as reported on the income statement is calculated after subtracting income tax expense, whereas taxable income obviously does not include a deduction for federal income taxes. Taxable income and net income also differ because net income is determined by the application of generally accepted accounting principles, while tax rules are used in determining taxable income, and the rules differ from generally accepted accounting principles on some points. For example:

  a. The application of accounting principles requires that dividend income be fully included in the reported net income or, where appropriate, the investment be accounted for according to the equity method. But, for tax purposes, some of the dividends received are excluded from taxable income, and the equity method is not used.

b. For accounting purposes, interest received on state and municipal bonds must be included in net income, but such interest is usually not taxable income.

c. As a rule, unearned income, such as rent collected in advance, is taxable in the year of receipt; however, under an accrual basis of accounting such items are taken into income in the year earned regardless of when received.

d. Accounting principles require an estimate of future costs, such as, for example, costs of making good on guarantees; and accounting principles require a deduction of such costs from revenue in the year the guaranteed goods are sold. However, tax rules do not permit the deduction of such costs until after the guarantor has to make good on his guarantee.

In addition, reported net income commonly differs from taxable income because the taxpayer is permitted by law in some cases to use one method or procedure for tax purposes and a different method or procedure in keeping his accounting records. For example, a taxpayer may elect to use declining-balance depreciation for tax purposes but to use straight-line depreciation in his accounting records.

Some accountants believe the interests of government, business, and the public would better be served if there were more uniformity between taxable income and reported net income. However, since the federal income tax is designed to serve other purposes than raising revenue, it is apt to be some time before this is achieved.

TAXES AND THE DISTORTION OF NET INCOME

The remaining topics in this chapter were covered in Chapter 10. They are repeated here to reinforce the importance of accounting for timing differences in the recognition of revenues and expenses.

Sometimes one procedure is elected for tax purposes and an alternative procedure is used in the accounting records, and the two procedures differ only in respect to their timing of expense recognition or revenue recognition. When this occurs, pretax net income for the year differs from taxable income, and a problem arises as to how much income tax expense should be deducted each year on the income statement. If the tax liability for each year were deducted as tax expense, the amount of the reported tax expense would not appear to have a meaningful relationship to the amount of pretax net income, and the final net income figures might be misleading. Consequently, in cases such as this, the Accounting principles Board concluded that income taxes should be allocated so that the distortion caused by timing differences between tax accounting procedures and financial accounting procedures will be avoided.

To appreciate the problem involved here, assume that a corporation has installed a $100,000 machine, the product of which will produce a half million dollars of revenue in each of the succeeding four years and $80,000 of income before depreciation and taxes. Assume further that the company must pay income taxes at a 40% rate (round number assumed for easy calculation) and that it plans to use straight-line depreciation in its records but the declining-balance method for tax purposes. If the machine has a four-year life and an $8,000 salvage value, annual depreciation calculated by each method will be as follows:

Year	Straight line	Declining balance
1	$23,000	$50,000
2	23,000	25,000
3	23,000	12,500
4	23,000	4,500
Totals	$92,000	$92,000

And since the company has elected declining-balance depreciation for tax purposes, it will be liable for $12,000 of income tax on the first year's income, $22,000 on the second, $27,000 on the third, and $30,200 on the fourth. The calculation of these taxes is shown in Illustration 28–5.

Furthermore, if the company were to deduct its actual tax liability each year in arriving at income to be reported to its stockholders, it would report the amounts shown in Illustration 28–6.

Observe in Illustrations 28–5 and 28–6 that total depreciation, $92,000, is the same whether calculated by the straight-line or the declining-balance method. Also note that the total tax liability for the four years, $91,200, is the same in each case. Then note the distortion of the final income figures in Illustration 28–6 due to the postponement of taxes.

Annual income taxes	Year 1	Year 2	Year 3	Year 4	Total
Income before depreciation and income taxes	$80,000	$80,000	$80,000	$80,000	$320,000
Depreciation for tax purposes (declining balance)	50,000	25,000	12,500	4,500	92,000
Taxable income	$30,000	$55,000	$67,500	$75,500	$228,000
Annual income taxes (40% of taxable income)	$12,000	$22,000	$27,000	$30,200	$ 91,200

Illustration 28–5

Income after deducting actual tax liabilities	Year 1	Year 2	Year 3	Year 4	Total
Income before depreciation and income taxes	$80,000	$80,000	$80,000	$80,000	$320,000
Depreciation per books (straight line)	23,000	23,000	23,000	23,000	92,000
Income before taxes	$57,000	$57,000	$57,000	$57,000	$228,000
Income taxes (actual liability of each year)	12,000	22,000	27,000	30,200	91,200
Remaining income	$45,000	$35,000	$30,000	$26,800	$136,800

Illustration 28–6

If this company should report successive annual income figures of $45,000, $35,000, $30,000, and then $26,800, some of its stockholders might be misled as to the company's earnings trend. Consequently, in cases such as this the Accounting Principles Board requires that income taxes be allocated so that the distortion caused by the postponement of taxes is removed from the income statement. In essence, *APB Opinion No. 11* requires that—

When a procedure used in the accounting records and an alternative procedure used for tax purposes differ in respect to their timing of expense recognition or revenue recognition, the tax expense deducted on the income statement should not be the actual tax incurred, but the amount that would have resulted if the procedure used in the records had also been used in calculating the tax.

If the foregoing is applied in this case, the corporation will report to its stockholders in each of the four years the amounts of income shown in Illustration 28–7.

Net income that should be reported to stockholders	Year 1	Year 2	Year 3	Year 4	Total
Income before depreciation and income taxes	$80,000	$80,000	$80,000	$80,000	$320,000
Depreciation per books (straight line)	23,000	23,000	23,000	23,000	92,000
Income before taxes	$57,000	$57,000	$57,000	$57,000	$228,000
Income taxes (amounts based on straight-line depreciation)	22,800	22,800	22,800	22,800	91,200
Net income	$34,200	$34,200	$34,200	$34,200	$136,800

Illustration 28–7

In examining Illustration 28–7, recall that the company's tax liabilities are actually $12,000 in the first year, $22,000 in the second, $27,000 in the third, and $30,200 in the fourth, a total of $91,200. Then observe that when this $91,200 liability is allocated evenly over the four years, the distortion of the annual net incomes due to the postponement of taxes is removed from the published income statements.

ENTRIES FOR THE ALLOCATION OF TAXES

When income taxes are allocated as in Illustration 28–7, the tax liability of each year and the deferred taxes are recorded with an adjusting entry. The adjusting entries for the four years of Illustration 28–7 and the entries in general journal form for the payment of the taxes (without explanations) are as follows:*

Year 1	Income Taxes Expense	22,800.00	
	Income Taxes Payable		12,000.00
	Deferred Income Taxes		10,800.00
Year 1	Income Taxes Payable	12,000.00	
	Cash		12,000.00
Year 2	Income Taxes Expense	22,800.00	
	Income Taxes Payable		22,000.00
	Deferred Income Taxes		800.00
Year 2	Income Taxes Payable	22,000.00	
	Cash		22,000.00
Year 3	Income Taxes Expense	22,800.00	
	Deferred Income Taxes	4,200.00	
	Income Taxes Payable		27,000.00
Year 3	Income Taxes Payable	27,000.00	
	Cash		27,000.00
Year 4	Income Taxes Expense	22,800.00	
	Deferred Income Taxes	7,400.00	
	Income Taxes Payable		30,200.00
Year 4	Income Taxes Payable	30,200.00	
	Cash		30,200.00

* To simplify the illustration, it is assumed here that the entire year's tax liability is paid at one time. However, corporations are usually required to pay estimated taxes on a quarterly basis.

In the entries the $22,800.00 debited to Income Taxes Expense each year is the amount that is deducted on the income statement in reporting annual net income. Also, the amount credited to Income Taxes Payable each year is the actual tax liability of that year.

Observe in the entries that since the actual tax liability in each of the first two years is less than the amount debited to Income Taxes Expense, the difference is credited to *Deferred Income Taxes*. Then note that in the last two years, since the actual liability each year is greater than the debit to Income Taxes Expense, the difference is debited to Deferred Income Taxes. Now observe in the following illustration of the company's Deferred Income Taxes account that the debits and credits exactly balance each other out over the four-year period:

Deferred Income Taxes

Year	Explanation	Debit	Credit	Balance
1			10,800.00	10,800.00
2			800.00	11,600.00
3		4,200.00		7,400.00
4		7,400.00		–0–

GLOSSARY

Adjusted gross income. Gross income minus ordinary and necessary expenses of carrying on a business, trade, or profession, or in the case of an employee, gross income minus expenses incurred in connection with his employment if paid by the employee.

Basis. In general, the cost of a purchased asset less any depreciation previously allowed or allowable for tax purposes.

Capital asset. Any item of property except (1) inventories, (2) trade notes and accounts receivable, (3) real property and depreciable property used in a trade or business, (4) copyrights or similar property, and (5) any government obligation due within one year and issued at a discount.

Capital gain or loss. The difference between the proceeds from the sale of a capital asset and the basis of the asset.

Deferred income taxes. The difference between the income tax expense in the financial statements and the income taxes payable according to tax law, resulting from financial accounting and tax accounting timing differences with respect to expense or revenue recognition.

Gross income. All income from whatever source derived, unless expressly excluded from taxation by law.

Head of household. An unmarried or legally separated person who maintains a home in which lives his or her unmarried child or a qualifying dependent.

Internal Revenue Code. Collectively, the statutes dealing with taxation that have been adopted by Congress.

Marginal tax rate. The rate that applies to the next dollar of income to be earned.

Standard deduction. The name formerly used in reference to the zero bracket amount.

Tax avoidance. A legal means of preventing a tax liability from coming into existence.

Tax credit. A direct, dollar for dollar, reduction in the amount of tax liability.

Tax evasion. The fraudulent denial and concealment of an existing liability.

Tax planning. Planning the affairs of a taxpayer in such a way as to incur the smallest possible tax liability.

Tax table income. Adjusted gross income for those taxpayers without itemized deductions in excess of the zero bracket amount; adjusted gross income less itemized deductions in excess of the zero bracket amount for those taxpayers with itemized deductions in excess of the zero bracket amount.

Zero bracket amount. The amount of income, after subtracting all allowable deductions, that is not subject to tax; for married taxpayers filing jointly and qualifying widows and widowers, $3,400; for married taxpayers filing separately, $1,700; and for an unmarried taxpayer, $2,300.

QUESTIONS FOR CLASS DISCUSSION

1. Jackson expects to have $500 of income in a 50% bracket; consequently, which should be more desirable to him: *(a)* a transaction that will reduce his income tax by $100 or *(b)* a transaction that will reduce an expense of his business by $150?
2. Why must a taxpayer normally take advantage of a tax-saving opportunity at the time it arises?
3. Distinguish between tax avoidance and tax evasion. Which is legal and desirable?
4. What are some of the nonrevenue objectives of the federal income tax?
5. What questions must be answered in determining whether an item should be included or excluded from gross income for tax purposes?
6. Name several items that are not included in gross income for tax purposes.
7. What justification is given for permitting an individual to exclude a limited amount of dividends from domestic corporations from his gross income for tax purposes?

8. For tax purposes, define a capital asset.

9. What is a short-term capital gain? A long-term capital gain?

10. An individual had capital asset transactions that resulted in nothing but long-term capital gains. What special tax treatment may be given these gains?

11. For tax purposes, what is "ordinary income"?

12. Why do tax planners try to have income emerge as a long-term capital gain?

13. It is often a wise tax decision for the owner of an incorporated business to forgo the payment of dividends from the earnings of his business. Why?

14. Why does the taxable income of a business commonly differ from its net income?

CLASS EXERCISES

In some of the Exercises and Problems which follow, the taxpayers would qualify to use the simplified Tax Tables (not provided in the book) rather than the Tax Rate Schedules. However, to restrict the length of the chapter and to facilitate student understanding of the underlying concepts, calculations of individual tax liability should be based on the Tax Rate Schedules shown in Illustration 28–2 on page 925.

Exercise 28–1

List the letters of the following items and write after each either the word *included* or *excluded* to tell whether the item should be included in or excluded from gross income for federal income tax purposes.

a. A stereo radio having a $200 fair market value which was received as a door prize.

b. Tips received while working as a waiter.

c. Cash inherited from a deceased parent.

d. Scholarship received from a state university.

e. Social security benefits.

f. Workmen's compensation insurance received as the result of an accident while working on a part-time job.

g. Gain on the sale of a personal automobile bought and rebuilt.

h. Dividends amounting to $75 from stock in domestic corporations received by an individual.

i. Interest in excess of $400 on a savings account.

Exercise 28–2

Susan Power earned $30,000 during 1981 as an employee of a CPA firm. She is unmarried, and furnishes more than half the support of her brother, a college student living in a dormitory. Susan had $6,500 of federal income tax and $1,975 of FICA tax withheld from her paychecks. She received $240 interest on a savings account and $50 in dividends from a domestic corporation in which she owned stock. During the year she paid $900 state income tax, $750 interest on the balance owed on a car she purchased, and gave her church $1,200. Show the calculation of Susan's taxable income in the manner outlined in Illustration 28–1. Then, using the rate schedule of Illustration 28–2, show the calculation of the net federal income tax payable or refund due Susan.

Exercise 28–3

In 1981, a married taxpayer who files a joint return and had no other capital gains, sold for $7,500 a number of shares of stock he had purchased for $5,500. Use the rate schedule of Illustration 28–2 and determine the amount of federal income tax the taxpayer will have to pay on the gain from this transaction under each of the following unrelated assumptions:

a. The taxpayer had $41,000 of taxable income from other sources and had held the shares four months.
b. The taxpayer had $41,000 of taxable income from other sources and had held the shares for 14 months.
c. The taxpayer had $46,000 of taxable income from other sources and had held the shares six months.
d. The taxpayer had $46,000 of taxable income from other sources and had held the shares for 12 months and one day.
e. The taxpayer had $86,000 of taxable income from other sources (which was not subject to the 50% maximum tax provision) and had held the shares for two months.
f. The taxpayer had $86,000 of taxable income from other sources (which was not subject to the 50% maximum tax provision) and had held the shares for 15 months.

Exercise 28–4

Luke Dow, Darcy DeShazo, and Scott Winters are unmarried and have three income tax exemptions each. Last year their adjusted gross incomes were Dow, $20,500; DeShazo, $21,500; and Winters, $19,800. Their itemized deductions were Dow, $2,800; DeShazo, $2,400; and Winters, $2,000. Prepare calculations to show the taxable income of each person.

Exercise 28–5

Ron and Jean Bringol had $25,000 of adjusted gross income last year. They are 35 and 38 years old, respectively, and have two children, ages 9 and 14. Last year their automobile having a fair value of $1,350 was stolen and their insurance did not cover the loss. They donated $360 to the college from which they had both graduated, and incurred the following expenses during the year: local property taxes, $700; interest on home mortgage, $940; hospital insurance, $290; and uninsured doctor and dentist bills, $810. Prepare a calculation to show their taxable income on a joint return.

PROBLEMS

Problem 28-1

Clay and Marion Wilkins are married and are also partners in Western Prints, a profitable business which averages $350,000 annually in sales, with a 40% gross profit and $100,000 of operating expenses. The Wilkins file a joint tax return, have no dependents, but each year have $3,000 of itemized deductions and two exemptions. In the past, the Wilkins have withdrawn $12,000 annually from the business for personal living expenses plus sufficient additional cash to pay the income tax on their joint return.

Clay and Marion think that they can save taxes by reorganizing their business into a corporation beginning with the 1981 tax year. If the corporation is organized, it will issue 1,000 shares of no-par stock, 300 to Clay and 700 to Marion. Also, $15,000 per year is a fair salary for managing such a business, and the corporation will pay that amount to Clay.

Required:

1. Prepare a comparative income statement for the business showing its net income as a partnership and as a corporation.
2. Use the rate schedule of Illustration 28–2 and determine the amount of federal income taxes the Wilkins will pay for themselves on a joint return and for the business under each of the following assumptions: (1) the business remains a partnership; (2) the business is incorporated, pays Clay Wilkins a $15,000 salary, but pays no dividends; and (3) the business is incorporated, pays Clay Wilkins a $15,000 salary, and pays $16,000 in dividends, $4,800 to Clay and $11,200 to Marion. (Each may exclude the first $200 of dividends.)

Problem 28-2

Joe and Kay Madden, husband and wife who file a joint return, own all the outstanding stock of Madden Corporation. The corporation has an opportunity to expand, but to do so it will need $50,000 additional capital. The Maddens have the $50,000 and can either lend this amount to the corporation at 9% interest or they can invest the $50,000 in the corporation, taking its presently unissued stock in exchange for the money.

They calculate that with the additional $50,000 the corporation will earn a total of $30,000 annually after paying Joe $15,000 per year as president and manager but before interest on the loan, if made, and before income taxes. They require $23,000 for personal living expenses and their own income taxes. Consequently, if they invest the additional $50,000 in the corporation, they will pay $8,000 per year to themselves in dividends in addition to Joe's salary. But if they lend the corporation the $50,000, they will use the interest on the loan, plus $3,500 in dividends and Joe's salary, for their personal expenses.

Required:

Determine whether the loan to the corporation or an investment in its stock is to the best interest of the Maddens. Assume that the decision is being made in 1981.

Problem 28–3

Paul Grudnitski owns all the outstanding stock of Candit Company. The corporation is a small manufacturing concern; however, over the years it has purchased and owns stocks costing $85,000 (present market value much higher) which it holds as long-term investments. The corporation has seldom paid a dividend, but it does pay Mr. Grudnitski a $12,000 annual salary as president and manager. In 1981 the corporation earned $28,000, after its president's salary but before income taxes, consisting of $20,000 in manufacturing income and $8,000 in dividends on its long-term investments.

Mr. Grudnitski has no dependents, but he had $3,300 of itemized deductions during 1981 plus a single $1,000 exemption deduction. He had no income other than his corporation salary and $1,000 in interest from a real estate loan.

Required:

1. Prepare a comparative statement showing for 1981 the operating income, investment income, total income, share of the dividend income deducted, taxable income, and income tax of the corporation under the *(a)* and *(b)* assumptions which follow. *(a)* The corporation owns the investment stocks and had the operating income just described. *(b)* The corporation had the operating income described; but instead of owning the investment stocks, over the years it paid dividends (none in 1981) and Mr. Grudnitski used them to buy the stocks in his own name rather than in the corporation name.
2. Calculate the amounts of individual income tax and corporation income tax incurred by Mr. Grudnitski and the corporation under the *(a)* assumptions, and the amounts that would have been incurred under the *(b)* assumptions. Also calculate the amount of individual income tax Mr. Grudnitski would have incurred with the business organized as a single proprietorship and the stocks registered in Mr. Grudnitski's name. Under this last assumption remember that the corporation's operating income plus its president's salary equal the operating income of the single proprietorship. Use the rate schedule of Illustration 28–2 in all individual income tax calculations.

Problem 28–4

Tackle Corporation installed a new machine at a $160,000 total cost early in January, 198A. It was estimated the machine would have a four-year life, a $12,000 salvage value at the end of that period, and would produce $100,000 of income annually before depreciation and income taxes. The company allocates income taxes in its reports to stockholders since it uses straight-line depreciation in its accounting records but declining balance depreciation at twice the straight-line rate for tax purposes. In this problem, disregard the investment tax credit.

Required:

1. Prepare a schedule showing 198A, 198B, 198C, 198D, and total net income for the four years after deducting declining balance depreciation and actual income taxes. Assume a 50% tax rate.

2. Prepare a second schedule showing each year's net income and the four-year total after deducting straight-line depreciation and actual taxes.
3. Prepare a third schedule showing income to be reported to stockholders with straight-line depreciation and allocated income taxes.
4. Set up a T-account for Deferred Income Tax and show therein the entries that will result from allocating income taxes.

Problem 28–5

Mr. and Mrs. Robert Algoe are both 43 years old and file a joint income tax return. They have two children, Cindy and Bill. Cindy is a student in high school, lives at home, and earned $550 for baby sitting jobs in 1981. Bill is 20 years old and a sophomore in college. He was a full-time student for two semesters in 1981; however, he did not go to summer school but drove a delivery truck and earned $1,400 during the summer, which was less than half what his parents paid during the year for his tuition, books, and other items of support. Mr. and Mrs. Algoe had the following cash receipts and disbursements during 1981:

CASH RECEIPTS

Mr. Algoe:

Salary as manager of Marsh Harbor Marina ($38,000 gross pay less $7,860 federal income taxes, $1,975 FICA taxes, and $450 hospital and medical insurance withheld)	$27,715
Dividends from stocks in domestic corporations	325
Interest on bonds of the city of Denver	450

Mrs. Algoe:

Rentals from a small house purchased some years ago (the house cost $15,000 and is depreciated on a straight-line basis under the assumption that it had 25 years of remaining life with no salvage value when purchased)	3,740
Interest from bonds of a corporation	265
Proceeds of insurance received on the death of an aunt	5,000

CASH DISBURSEMENTS

Charitable contributions	1,300
Interest on mortgage on family residence	1,385
Property taxes on family residence	1,615
Property taxes on Mrs. Algoe's rental house	285
Interest on mortgage on rental house	420
Plumbing repairs at rental house	280
Insurance (one year) on rental house	165
Uninsured doctor and dental bills	427
Medicines and drugs	250
Advance payments of estimated federal income tax on income not subject to withholding	1,000

Also, Mr. Algoe had a $1,150 capital gain on shares of stock held 15 months and a $610 capital gain on shares held 7 months.

Required:

Follow the form of Illustration 28–1 and use the rate schedule of Illustration 28–2 to calculate the net federal income tax payable or refund for Mr. and Mrs. Algoe.

Problem 28–1A

Hank Carson has operated the Lonestar Store for a number of years with the following average annual results:

LONESTAR STORE
Income Statement for an Average Year

Sales		$280,000
Cost of goods sold	$155,000	
Operating expenses	85,000	240,000
Net income		$ 40,000

Mr. Carson is unmarried and without dependents and has been operating Lonestar Store as a single proprietorship. He has been withdrawing $32,000 each year to pay his personal living expenses, including $4,300 of charitable contributions, state and local taxes, and other itemized deductions. He has no income other than from Lonestar Store.

Required:

1. Assume that Mr. Carson is considering the incorporation of his business beginning with the 1981 tax year and prepare a comparative income statement for the business showing its net income as a single proprietorship and as a corporation. Assume that if he incorporates, Mr. Carson will pay $32,000 per year to himself as a salary, which is a fair amount.
2. Use the rate schedule of Illustration 28–2 and determine the amount of federal income tax Mr. Carson will have to pay for himself and for his business under each of the following assumptions; *(a)* the business is not incorporated; *(b)* the business is incorporated, pays Mr. Carson a $32,000 annual salary as manager, and also pays him $5,000 per year in dividends; and *(c)* the business is incorporated, pays Mr. Carson a $32,000 salary, but does not pay any dividends.

Problem 28–2A

Baffet Corporation needs additional capital for a new investment that will cost $100,000 and will increase its earnings $20,000 annually before interest on the money used in the expansion, if borrowed, and before income taxes. The Froh family owns all the outstanding stock of Baffet Corporation, and will supply the money to finance the investment, either investing an additional $100,000 in the corporation by purchasing its unissued stock or lending it $100,000 at 11% interest.

The corporation presently earns well in excess of $100,000 annually and pays $20,000 per year to the family in dividends. If the loan is made, the dividends will be reduced by an amount equal to the interest on the loan.

Required:

Prepare an analysis showing whether it would be advantageous for the family to make the loan or to purchase the corporation's stock.

Problem 28–3A

Norm Olson, Jr., recently inherited the business of his father. The business, Tacket, Inc., is a small manufacturing corporation; however, a share of its assets, $75,000 at cost, consists of blue-chip investment stocks purchased over the years by the corporation from earnings. The father was the sole owner of the corporation at his death, and before his death he had paid himself a $15,000 annual salary for a number of years as president and manager. Over the years the corporation seldom paid a dividend but instead had invested any earnings not needed in the business in the blue-chip stocks previously mentioned. At the father's death the market value of these stocks far exceeded their cost.

Norm's mother is dead, and after Norm graduated from college, the father had no dependents. The father's tax return for the year before his death (1981) showed $16,500 of gross income, consisting of his $15,000 corporation salary plus $1,500 interest (net of the $200 exclusion) from real estate loans. It also showed $3,300 of itemized deductions plus a single $1,000 exemption deduction. The corporation had earned during the year before the father's death $23,000 from its manufacturing operations plus $10,000 in dividends from its investments, a total of $33,000 after the president's salary but before income taxes.

Required:

1. Prepare a comparative statement showing for the year before the father's death the corporation's operating income, dividend income, total income, share of the dividend income deducted, taxable income, and income tax under the following *(a)* and *(b)* assumptions. *(a)* The corporation owns the investment stocks and had the operating income just described. *(b)* The corporation had the operating income described; but instead of owning the investment stocks, over the years it paid dividends (none last year) and Norm Olson, Sr., used the dividends to buy the stocks in his own name rather than in the corporation name.
2. Calculate the amounts of individual income tax and corporation income tax incurred by Mr. Olson, Sr., and the corporation for the year before Mr. Olson's death under the foregoing *(a)* assumptions, and the amounts that would have been incurred under the *(b)* assumptions. Also calculate the amount of individual income tax Mr. Olson would have incurred with the business organized as a single proprietorship and the stocks registered in his own name. Under this last assumption remember that the corporation's operating income plus the salary paid its president equal the operating income of the single proprietorship. Use the rate schedule of Illustration 28–2 in the individual income tax calculations.

Problem 28–4A

On January 8, 198A, Arizona Company completed the installation of a new machine in its plant at a $200,000 total cost. It was estimated the machine would have a four-year life, a $20,000 salvage value, and that it would produce $150,000 of income during each of the four years, before depreciation and income taxes. The company allocates income taxes in its reports to stockholders, since it uses straight-line depreciation in its accounting records and sum-of-the-years'-digits depreciation for tax purposes.

Required:

1. Prepare a schedule showing 198A, 198B, 198C, 198D, and total net income for the four years after deducting sum-of-the-years'-digits depreciation and actual taxes. Assume a 50% income tax rate.
2. Prepare a second schedule showing each year's net income and the four-year total after deducting straight-line depreciation and actual taxes.
3. Prepare a third schedule showing income to be reported to stockholders with straight-line depreciation and allocated income taxes.
4. Set up a T-account for Deferred Income Tax and show therein the entries that will result from allocating the income taxes.

PROVOCATIVE PROBLEMS

Provocative problem 28–1
Sailbag Corporation

Jerry Hern and his wife own all the outstanding stock of Sailbag Corporation, a company Jerry organized several years ago and which is growing rapidly and needs additional capital. Ted Cole, a friend of the family, examined the following comparative income statement, which shows the corporation's net income for the past three years and which was prepared by its bookkeeper. Ted expressed a tentative willingness to invest the required capital by purchasing a portion of the corporation's unissued stock.

SAILBAG CORPORATION
Comparative Income Statement, 198A, 198B, 198C

	198A	198B	198C
Sales	$750,000	$825,000	$890,000
Costs and expenses other than depreciation and federal income taxes	$465,000	$500,000	$540,000
Depreciation expense	105,000	115,000	120,000
Federal income taxes	75,000	80,000	90,000
Total costs and expenses	$645,000	$695,000	$750,000
Net income	$105,000	$130,000	$140,000

However, before making a final decision, Ted Cole asked permission for his own accountant to examine the accounting records of the corporation. Permission was granted, the examination was made, and the accountant prepared the following comparative income statement covering the same period of time.

SAILBAG CORPORATION
Comparative Income Statement, 198A, 198B, and 198C

	198A	198B	198C
Sales	$750,000	$825,000	$890,000
Costs and expenses other than depreciation	$465,000	$500,000	$540,000
Depreciation expense*	105,000	115,000	120,000
Total costs and expenses...........	$570,000	$615,000	$660,000
Income before federal income taxes	$180,000	$210,000	$230,000
Applicable federal income taxes	90,000	105,000	115,000
Net income	$ 90,000	$105,000	$115,000

* The corporation deducted $135,000 of depreciation expense on its 198A tax return, $165,000 on its 198B return, and $170,000 on its 198C return.

Jerry Hern was surprised at the difference in annual net incomes reported on the two statements and immediately called for an explanation from the public accountant who set up the corporation's accounting system and who prepares the annual tax returns of the corporation and the Herns.

Explain why there is a difference between the net income figures on the two statements, and account for the difference in the net incomes. Prepare a statement that will explain the amounts shown on the corporation bookkeeper's statement. Assume a 50% federal income tax rate.

appendix
Masonite Corporation
1979 Financial Statements

Report of Independent Public Accountants

To the Shareholders and Board of Directors of MASONITE CORPORATION:

We have examined the consolidated balance sheets of Masonite Corporation (a Delaware Corporation) and subsidiaries as of August 31, 1979, and 1978, and the consolidated statements of income, retained earnings and changes in financial position for the years then ended. Our examinations were made in accordance with generally accepted auditing standards and, accordingly, included such tests of the accounting records and such other auditing procedures as we considered necessary in the circumstances.

In our opinion, the financial statements referred to above present fairly the financial position of Masonite Corporation and subsidiaries as of August 31, 1979, and 1978, and the results of their operations and the changes in their financial position for the years then ended, in conformity with generally accepted accounting principles applied on a consistent basis.

ARTHUR ANDERSEN & CO.

Chicago, Illinois,
October 9, 1979.

Consolidated Statements of Income and Retained Earnings

MASONITE CORPORATION and subsidiary companies

	Year Ended August 31	
	1979	1978
STATEMENT OF INCOME		
Net sales	$542,467,000	$529,024,000
Cost of sales (Note 2)	421,430,000	406,224,000
Selling, administrative, and research expenses	53,881,000	49,295,000
Income from operations	$ 67,156,000	$ 73,505,000
Other income (expense):		
Income from sale of timber	$ 3,717,000	$ 4,703,000
Income from oil operations, net	1,617,000	1,692,000
Income from foreign affiliates (Note 7)	1,250,000	879,000
Interest, net	1,844,000	1,443,000
Other, net	3,516,000	(1,333,000)
Income before income taxes	$ 79,100,000	$ 80,889,000
Provision for income taxes:		
Federal		
Current	$ 20,881,000	$ 29,219,000
Deferred	2,119,000	2,448,000
State	4,000,000	4,500,000
Deferred investment credit, net	600,000	233,000
Total income taxes (Note 13)	$ 27,600,000	$ 36,400,000
Net income	$ 51,500,000	$ 44,489,000
Per share	$ 3.49	$ 2.73
STATEMENT OF RETAINED EARNINGS		
Balance at beginning of year	$209,701,000	$176,701,000
Net income	51,500,000	44,489,000
Cash dividends declared ($1.10 per share in 1979 and $.71 in 1978)	(15,983,000)	(11,489,000)
Retirement of treasury stock (Note 11)	(35,606,000)	—
Balance at end of year (includes $8,659,000 and $7,613,000 of undistributed retained earnings of unconsolidated foreign affiliates at August 31, 1979 and 1978, respectively)	$209,612,000	$209,701,000

The accompanying notes are an integral part of these financial statements.

Consolidated Balance Sheets

MASONITE CORPORATION and subsidiary companies

	August 31	
	1979	1978
ASSETS		
Current Assets:		
Cash (Note 8)	$ 1,009,000	$ 5,713,000
Marketable securities, at cost (substantially market)	26,535,000	29,134,000
Receivables, less allowances of $1,944,000 in 1979 and $1,665,000 in 1978 (Note 12)	71,425,000	70,272,000
Inventories (Note 2)	56,927,000	50,966,000
Prepaid expenses, principally prepayments on timber contracts	8,354,000	6,094,000
Total current assets	$164,250,000	$162,179,000
Property, Plant, and Equipment, at cost (Notes 3, 9 and 10):		
Land, timber, and roadways	$ 47,376,000	$ 44,345,000
Buildings	58,036,000	58,091,000
Machinery and equipment	308,255,000	287,473,000
	$413,667,000	$389,909,000
Less-Accumulated depreciation and depletion	217,854,000	203,404,000
	$195,813,000	$186,505,000
Investment in Foreign Affiliates (Note 7)	$ 11,674,000	$ 10,628,000
Other Assets	$ 5,624,000	$ 3,582,000
	$377,361,000	$362,894,000
LIABILITIES AND SHAREHOLDERS' EQUITY		
Current Liabilities:		
Current maturities of long-term debt (Notes 9 and 10)	$ 2,593,000	$ 1,871,000
Payable to banks resulting from checks in transit	6,990,000	—
Accounts payable	16,985,000	9,023,000
Payable on treasury stock purchases	4,032,000	1,949,000
Cash dividend payable	4,294,000	3,133,000
Accrued liabilities—		
Payrolls	7,557,000	7,812,000
Taxes, other than Federal and state income taxes	3,571,000	8,333,000
Miscellaneous	6,994,000	8,307,000
Federal and state income taxes (Note 13)	6,375,000	17,678,000
Total current liabilities	$ 59,391,000	$ 58,106,000
Long-Term Debt (Note 9)	$ 5,493,000	$ 2,869,000
Obligations Under Capital Leases (Note 10)	$ 5,619,000	$ 3,931,000
Deferred Federal Income Taxes (Note 13)	$ 32,734,000	$ 30,615,000
Deferred Compensation (Note 6)	$ 897,000	$ 422,000
Commitments and Contingent Liabilities (Notes 10 and 18)		
Shareholders' Equity (Notes 6 and 11)		
Preferred stock, without par value, authorized 1,000,000 shares; none issued		
Common stock, without par value, authorized 24,000,000 shares; issued 14,313,621 shares in 1979 and 16,756,763 in 1978	$ 63,615,000	$ 76,387,000
Retained earnings	209,612,000	209,701,000
Less—Treasury stock—1,091,300 shares at cost in 1978	—	(19,137,000)
	$273,227,000	$266,951,000
	$377,361,000	$362,894,000

The accompanying notes are an integral part of these financial statements.

Consolidated Statements of Changes in Financial Position

MASONITE CORPORATION and subsidiary companies

	Year Ended August 31	
	1979	1978
SOURCE OF FUNDS:		
Net income	$51,500,000	$44,489,000
Expenses (income) not affecting working capital:		
Depreciation	22,764,000	21,954,000
Investment tax credits amortized	(1,654,000)	(1,504,000)
Depletion	1,201,000	1,138,000
Foreign equity (income)	(1,250,000)	(879,000)
Provision for deferred Federal income taxes	2,119,000	2,448,000
Provision for deferred compensation	475,000	422,000
Working capital provided from operations	$75,155,000	$68,068,000
Long-term financing, including capital leases	7,092,000	665,000
Disposition of property, plant, and equipment	3,202,000	12,085,000
Investment tax credits deferred	2,254,000	1,737,000
Common stock issued under stock incentive program	198,000	—
Dividends from foreign affiliates	204,000	—
	$88,105,000	$82,555,000
DISPOSITION OF FUNDS:		
Property, plant, and equipment additions	$37,075,000	$31,289,000
Cash dividends	15,983,000	11,489,000
Long-term debt and capital lease maturities	2,780,000	3,869,000
Purchase of treasury stock	29,439,000	19,137,000
Other	2,042,000	(865,000)
	$87,319,000	$64,919,000
INCREASE IN WORKING CAPITAL	$ 786,000	$17,636,000
ANALYSIS OF INCREASE IN WORKING CAPITAL:		
Increase (decrease) in current assets:		
Cash and marketable securities	$(7,303,000)	$23,404,000
Receivables	1,153,000	5,472,000
Inventories	5,961,000	(2,581,000)
Prepaid expenses	2,260,000	1,622,000
Decrease (increase) in current liabilities:		
Current maturities of long-term debt	(722,000)	1,538,000
Payable to banks resulting from checks in transit	(6,990,000)	—
Accounts payable and accrued liabilities	(4,876,000)	711,000
Federal and state income taxes	11,303,000	(12,530,000)
	$ 786,000	$17,636,000

The accompanying notes are an integral part of these financial statements.

Notes to Consolidated Financial Statements

1. STATEMENT OF ACCOUNTING POLICIES

Principles of Consolidation. The consolidated financial statements include the accounts of all domestic subsidiaries. All intercompany balances and transactions have been eliminated.

Investments in Foreign Affiliates. The investment in Masonite Canada Ltd. (50% owned) and Masonite (Africa) Limited (65% owned) is carried at cost, adjusted for equity in earnings net of estimated taxes on remittance and dividends received.

Depreciation and Depletion. Provision for depreciation is made on a straight-line basis on the estimated service lives of the various classes of property. Buildings are depreciated over a 10 to 50 year period, and machinery and equipment are depreciated over a 3 to 20 year period.

Major replacements which extend the useful lives of units of equipment are capitalized and depreciated over the estimated remaining useful lives of the property. All other maintenance and repairs are expensed as incurred.

Costs of property retired or otherwise disposed of, and the related accumulated depreciation, are removed from the accounts; the net gain or loss on retirements is credited or charged to earnings.

Depletion of timberlands and roadways is computed on the cost of timberlands and roadways (less an allowance for land values) divided by the estimated recoverable timber to obtain overall average depletion rates.

Income Taxes. Investment tax credits on eligible property are amortized to earnings over the useful lives of the related assets. The unamortized amounts of investment tax credits are included in "Accumulated Depreciation and Depletion."

Accelerated depreciation is used for tax purposes. Deferred taxes are provided on the difference between book and tax depreciation.

Inventories. Substantially all inventories are valued on the last-in, first-out cost basis. Other inventories are valued at the lower of first-in, first-out cost or market. Market is the lower of current replacement cost or net realizable value (sales price less cost to convert, sell and deliver). Appropriate allowances are made for overaged and obsolete inventory items. Quantities reflect physical counts at or near year end.

Retirement Plans. The company's policy is to fund retirement costs accrued under several retirement plans covering a majority of its employees, including unfunded past-service costs which are funded over a maximum of 30 years.

2. INVENTORIES

If the first-in, first-out method of inventory accounting had been used by the company, inventories would have been $21,639,000 and $19,369,000 higher than reported at August 31, 1979 and 1978, respectively.

Inventories used in the determination of cost of sales are summarized as follows:

(000 omitted)	August 31, 1979	August 31, 1978	August 31, 1977
Finished stock	$28,784	$26,605	$28,320
Raw materials and supplies	28,143	24,361	25,227
Total	$56,927	$50,966	$53,547

3. PROPERTY, PLANT AND EQUIPMENT

Property, plant and equipment are stated at cost less accumulated depreciation and depletion, as follows:

(000 omitted)	Land	Timberlands & Roadways	Buildings	Machinery & Equipment	Construction in Progress	Investment Credit	Total
1978							
Cost basis, 9/1/77	$5,189	$36,979	$58,360	$277,657	$ 4,831		$383,016
Additions	160	4,894		1,496	24,739		31,289
Retirements or sales	(169)	(2,540)	(2,609)	(18,709)	(138)		(24,165)
Construction in progress transfers			2,443	17,808	(20,251)		—
Miscellaneous	(70)	(98)	(103)	40			(231)
Total	5,110	39,235	58,091	278,292	9,181		389,909
Less:							
Accumulated depreciation*, 9/1/77		11,173	24,077	147,407		$ 9,733	192,390
Depreciation* expensed during year		1,138	1,504	20,450			23,092
Adjustment for retirements, etc.			(665)	(11,393)			(12,058)
Investment credit deferred						1,737	1,737
Investment credit amortized						(1,504)	(1,504)
Miscellaneous			(36)	(217)			(253)
Total deductions		12,311	24,880	156,247		9,966	203,404
Balance, August 31, 1978	$5,110	$26,924	$33,211	$122,045	$ 9,181	$ (9,966)	$186,505
1979							
Cost basis, 9/1/78	$5,110	$39,235	$58,091	$278,292	$ 9,181		$389,909
Additions	140	4,460	393	5,993	26,089		37,075
Retirements or sales	(126)	(1,399)	(1,950)	(10,087)	(25)		(13,587)
Construction in progress transfers			2,170	22,342	(24,512)		—
Miscellaneous	(156)	112	(668)	982			270
Total	4,968	42,408	58,036	297,522	10,733		413,667
Less:							
Accumulated depreciation*, 9/1/78		12,311	24,880	156,247		$ 9,966	203,404
Depreciation* expensed during year		1,201	1,994	20,770			23,965
Adjustment for retirements, etc.		(612)	(571)	(9,144)			(10,327)
Investment credit deferred						2,254	2,254
Investment credit amortized						(1,654)	(1,654)
Miscellaneous			(749)	961			212
Total deductions		12,900	25,554	168,834		10,566	217,854
Balance, August 31, 1979	$4,968	$29,508	$32,482	$128,688	$ 10,733	$(10,566)	$195,813

*Includes depletion and amortization

4. RETIREMENT PLANS

The total retirement plans expenses for 1979 and 1978 were approximately $4,800,000 and $4,600,000, respectively. The actuarially computed value of vested benefits for four of the plans exceeded the total of the assets of their retirement funds and balance sheet accruals as of August 31, 1979, by approximately $10,586,000. Unfunded past-service costs under the plans at August 31, 1979, approximated $10,996,000.

5. PROFIT SHARING PLAN

The Masonite Profit Sharing Stock Plan provides that each fiscal year the company contribute 2% of that part of the consolidated income before income taxes, as defined, of the divisions participating in the Plan, which is in excess of 6% of consolidated net worth of said divisions at the beginning of the fiscal year. To be eligible for participation, an employee must be a full-time salaried employee, permanently and continuously in the employ of the company for one year. The company's contributions for 1979 and 1978 were $1,276,000 and $1,315,000, respectively.

6. STOCK INCENTIVE PROGRAMS

The company's 1971 Incentive Plan for officers and key employees provides that options are granted at a price per share which is not less than 100% of market value on the date the options are granted. Qualified options expire five years after date of grant and non-qualified options expire ten years after date of grant. Terms of the options vary; but, in all cases for all options granted to date, a minimum service requirement of three years must be fulfilled before an option becomes exercisable.

At August 31, 1979 options for 107,610 shares were outstanding. By fiscal year of grant these outstanding options were 97,610 in 1976 and 10,000 in 1977.

At August 31, 1979 and 1978, respectively, options for 107,610 shares and 147,440 were outstanding with market values at date of grant totaling $2,264,000 and $3,129,000. Prices of outstanding options ranged from $19.56 to $21.25 at August 31, 1979 and from $19.56 to $33.75 at August 31, 1978.

Options became exercisable as follows:

	1979	1978
Number of Shares	None	3,180
Option price—Per share	—	$21.25
Total	—	$68,000
Market value at date exercisable—Per share	—	$15.75-$15.88
Total	—	$50,000

During 1979, options for 6,900 shares, having an aggregate option price of $146,625, were exercised at a price per share of $21.25. At the dates exercised, the aggregate market value was $178,881 and the market price per share ranged from $24.13 to $27.50. No options were exercised during 1978.

In addition, the company's 1971 Incentive Plan provides for Performance Share Awards to officers and key employees. Awards of 25,390 common shares granted September 19, 1978 were earned based on fiscal 1979 results and 23,580 common shares granted October 13, 1977 were earned based on fiscal 1978 results. These awards will be paid in five annual installments providing the recipients are still employees of the company. During 1979, 2,358 common shares were paid as Performance Share Awards. No Performance Share Awards were paid during 1978.

At August 31, 1979 and 1978, 249,802 and 240,532 shares, respectively, were reserved for future issuance under employee stock incentive programs.

The option price on options exercised has been credited to common stock. No charges or credits have been made to income for stock options.

The amount charged to income for Performance Share Awards, based upon the year-end market value of the shares, was $695,000 and $528,000 for 1979 and 1978, respectively.

7. KEY DATA, UNCONSOLIDATED FOREIGN AFFILIATES (unaudited)

(000 omitted)	Masonite Canada		Masonite (Africa)	
	1979	1978	1979	1978
Current assets	$19,807	$22,077	$ 6,641	$ 4,851
Noncurrent assets	27,301	27,314	13,492	13,959
Current liabilities	9,349	11,126	4,194	4,191
Long-term debt	17,203	19,020	1,200	1,873
Other noncurrent liabilities	5,688	4,565	1,261	593
Shareholders' equity	14,868	14,680	13,478	12,153
Masonite Corporation's investment	5,914	5,632	5,760	4,996
Net sales	$59,071	$56,071	$17,099	$14,157
Net earnings	564	1,232	1,490	407
Masonite Corporation's equity in earnings	282	616	968	263

8. SHORT-TERM BORROWINGS

The company had no short-term borrowings during 1979 and 1978. The company maintains compensating balances of approximately 10% of its lines of credit pursuant to informal agreements with the lending banks. Normal daily deposits in the banks are sufficient to cover this arrangement, and none of the cash balances are legally restricted as to withdrawal. Lines of credit with banks for short-term borrowings are available to support commercial paper borrowings when bank borrowings are not being utilized. Unused lines of credit for short-term borrowings aggregated $14,000,000 at August 31, 1979 and 1978. Such lines are not subject to contractual arrangements and can be withdrawn by the banks at anytime.

9. LONG-TERM DEBT

Property, plant and equipment with a cost of approximately $8,756,000 are pledged for notes, mortgages, and timberland purchase contracts outstanding at August 31, 1979. The obligations become due November 1, 1979 to March 31, 1994, and have interest rates ranging from .875% to 8.5%. Aggregate maturities on long-term debt are $1,830,000 (included in current liabilities), $1,015,000, $547,000, $441,000, and $298,000 for the years ending August 31, 1980 through August 31, 1984, respectively.

10. LEASE COMMITMENTS

The company has various lease agreements relating primarily to office space and transportation, data processing and office equipment that extend through 2015. The terms of the leases vary from one month to 40 years. Some of the leases also include renewal options for various terms and some require the company to pay contingent rentals based primarily on usage for data processing and office equipment, and mileage for transportation equipment.

Capital Leases—The following is an analysis of the leased property under capital leases by major classes, as recorded in the financial statements:

	August 31	
	1979	**1978**
Buildings	$ 1,823,000	$ 2,390,000
Machinery and equipment	8,680,000	7,119,000
	$10,503,000	$ 9,509,000
Less: Accumulated amortization	4,535,000	5,407,000
	$ 5,968,000	$ 4,102,000

Amortization of assets recorded under capital leases is included with depreciation expense.

The following is a schedule by years of future minimum lease payments under capital leases together with the present value of the net minimum lease payments as of August 31, 1979:

Fiscal Periods	
1980	$ 1,586,000
1981	1,583,000
1982	1,581,000
1983	1,502,000
1984	1,059,000
Later Years	4,878,000
Total minimum lease payments	$12,189,000
Less amounts representing—Interest	2,432,000
—Estimated lessor executory costs	3,395,000
Present value of net minimum lease payments ($743,000 current and $5,619,000 long-term)	$ 6,362,000

Operating Leases — The following is a schedule by years of future minimum rental payments required under operating leases that have initial or remaining noncancellable lease terms in excess of one year as of August 31, 1979:

Fiscal Periods

1980	$ 1,473,000
1981	1,078,000
1982	723,000
1983	101,000
1984	58,000
Later Years	177,000
Total minimum payments required	$ 3,610,000

Rental Expense for 1979 and 1978 consisted of:

	1979	1978
Minimum rentals	$ 4,230,000	$ 4,038,000
Contingent rentals	90,000	1,142,000
Less: Sublease rentals	(336,000)	(165,000)
Total	$ 3,984,000	$ 5,015,000

11. CAPITAL STOCK TRANSACTIONS

Transactions in the common stock account for the two years ended August 31, 1979, are summarized as follows:

	Common Stock		Treasury Stock	
	Shares	Amount	Shares	Amount
Balance at August 31, 1977	16,756,763	$76,387,000		
Purchase of treasury stock			1,091,300	$19,137,000
Balance at August 31, 1978	16,756,763	$76,387,000	1,091,300	$19,137,000
Exercise of stock options	6,900	147,000		
Issuance of performance share awards	2,358	51,000		
Purchase of treasury stock			1,361,100	29,439,000
Retirement of treasury stock	(2,452,400)	(12,970,000)	(2,452,400)	(48,576,000)
Balance at August 31, 1979	14,313,621	$63,615,000	—	$ —

The cost of treasury shares retired was prorated between common stock and retained earnings on the basis of the respective balances in these accounts as of August 31, 1978.

12. ACCOUNTS RECEIVABLE ALLOWANCES

Allowances for doubtful accounts, cash discounts and claims amounted to $1,944,000 at August 31, 1979 compared to $1,665,000 at August 31, 1978. The increase of $279,000 was charged to expense in 1979, as were bad debt write-offs, net of recoveries, amounting to $194,000, compared to $170,000 in 1978.

13. INCOME TAXES

The provision for deferred Federal income taxes results primarily from timing differences in the recognition of depreciation expense for book and tax purposes.

The difference between the statutory Federal income tax rate and the company's effective income tax rate is summarized as follows:

	1979	1978
Federal income tax rate	46.7%	48.0%
Increase (decrease) as a result of—		
Value of timber appreciation taxed at capital gains rates	(10.2)	(5.7)
Tax effect of road donation	(2.7)	—
State income taxes, net of Federal tax benefit	2.7	2.9
Other, including amortization of investment credit	(1.6)	(0.2)
Effective tax rate	34.9%	45.0%

14. SUPPLEMENTARY INCOME STATEMENT INFORMATION

Charged to expense during 1979 and 1978 were amounts shown in the table below for the indicated categories:

	1979	1978
Maintenance and repairs	$35,252,000	$32,606,000
Provision for:		
Depreciation of buildings and equipment	22,764,000	21,954,000
Depletion of timberlands and roadways	1,201,000	1,138,000
Taxes (other than Federal and state taxes on income):		
Real estate and personal property	2,781,000	4,084,000
Unemployment and old age benefit	8,903,000	8,209,000
Franchise, privilege, sales and use	1,536,000	1,406,000
Advertising costs	5,170,000	5,972,000
Research and development costs*	6,749,000	4,754,000

*Research and development costs include depreciation of $352,000 in 1979 and $331,000 in 1978.

15. REPLACEMENT COST DATA (unaudited)

General. The information presented herein does not necessarily represent the current value of existing assets or future costs of replacing them; nor should it be interpreted that the company presently has plans to replace its productive capacity or that replacement, if and when made, would occur in the form and manner assumed for purposes of developing the information. In reality, such replacement will take place over an extended period of time during which technology, price levels and competitive factors most likely will change. Additionally, the replacement cost information should not be used to impute the effects of inflation on the company's net income without considering such other factors as the impact of general price level changes, methods of financing and statutory taxing policies. Finally, the replacement cost information standing alone does not recognize customary relationships between changes in costs and changes in selling prices. Over the years, the company has attempted to adjust selling prices to maintain margins and, competitive conditions permitting, expects to do so in the future.

SUMMARY OF REPLACEMENT COST AMOUNTS AND RELATED HISTORICAL AMOUNTS

(000 omitted)	Historical Amounts Included in Financial Statements (a)	Less: Items For Which Replacement Cost Information Is Not Provided			Historical Amounts For Which Replacement Cost Information Is Provided	Replacement Cost Amounts (a)
		Land	Construction In Progress	Assets Which Will Not Be Replaced		
For the Year Ended August 31, 1979:						
Inventories	$ 56,927			$ —	$ 56,927	$ 80,873
Property, Plant and Equipment	$371,259	$4,968	$10,733	$ 3,008	$352,550	$705,677
Less:						
Accumulated Depreciation	194,388			1,698	192,690	377,330
	$176,871	$4,968	$10,733	$ 1,310	$159,860	$328,347
Cost of Sales Excluding Depreciation	$397,060			$ 3,764	$393,296	$393,296
Depreciation	$ 22,764			$ 216	$ 22,548(b)	$ 42,955(b)
For the Year Ended August 31, 1978:						
Inventories	$ 50,966			$ 2,351	$ 48,615	$ 69,206
Property, Plant and Equipment	$350,674	$5,110	$9,181	$ 5,149	$331,234	$639,096
Less:						
Accumulated Depreciation	181,127			3,399	177,728	319,375
	$169,547	$5,110	$9,181	$ 1,750	$153,506	$319,721
Cost of Sales Excluding Depreciation	$383,290			$18,831	$364,459	$369,833
Depreciation	$ 21,954			$ 699	$ 21,255(c)	$ 38,338(c)

(a) Historical and replacement cost information for timber and roadways and related depletion and forest management expenditures is excluded from this summary and discussed in the section captioned "Timberlands and Roadways."
(b) $19,397 historical cost and $37,759 replacement cost depreciation applicable to cost of sales.
(c) $18,197 historical cost and $33,670 replacement cost depreciation applicable to cost of sales.

METHODS USED TO DETERMINE 1979 AND 1978 REPLACEMENT COST

Inventories and Cost of Sales Excluding Depreciation. The replacement cost of inventories was estimated by applying the first-in, first-out (FIFO) method of inventory valuation. Inventories under the FIFO method reasonably approximate the most current production and purchase costs. Depreciation included as an element of inventory costs was adjusted to give effect to the replacement cost values of productive capacity.

In its financial statements, the company values substantially all of its inventories on the last-in, first-out (LIFO) method. Cost of sales under this method reasonably approximates cost of sales on a replacement cost basis. Also, the turnover rate of non-LIFO inventories is sufficiently rapid to approximate replacement cost. Accordingly, replacement cost of sales was estimated by using reported cost of sales, adjusted for the effect of the liquidation of prior years' LIFO layers, which was not material.

The estimated replacement cost amounts for inventory and cost of sales do not consider any cost savings that would result from replacing productive capacity.

Productive Capacity. Generally, replacement cost of productive capacity at August 31, 1979 and 1978 was determined by indexing forward the prior year replacement cost estimate and adjusting for additions and retirements made during the year.

The replacement cost estimate to which indexes were applied was determined as follows: (1) For buildings, by applying either internally developed construction costs on a per square foot basis to the applicable square footage or published construction cost indexes to the applicable historical cost or recent appraisal amounts; (2) For a significant portion of the company's machinery and equipment, using engineering estimates, vendor quotations or installation cost data, indexed forward if necessary; and (3) For the remaining machinery and equipment, by applying published indexes to historical costs or recent appraisal data.

Depreciation and Accumulated Depreciation. Estimated replacement cost depreciation was determined by applying historical cost composite depreciation rates on a straight-line basis to the estimated average replacement cost of composite asset groups. Estimated accumulated replacement cost depreciation was based upon the weighted-average historical lives of the composite asset groups. No adjustment was made for additional asset life that might result from technological improvements.

Operating Efficiencies. If the company's productive capacity were replaced in the manner assumed, costs other than depreciation (such as direct labor, repairs and maintenance, energy and certain other indirect costs) would be altered. Although these expected cost changes cannot be quantified with any precision, in the opinion of management the current level of operating costs other than depreciation would be reduced as a result of the technological improvements assumed in the hypothetical replacement, and would substantially offset the additional depreciation on a replacement cost basis.

Timberlands and Roadways. The replacement cost of the company's fee timber was determined as reforestation costs plus forest management expenditures that would be required to bring timber holdings from a theoretically harvested state to a state of maturity equal to that existing at August 31, 1979 and 1978. Accordingly, the total estimated replacement cost of the company's fee timber at August 31, 1979 and 1978 was calculated to be $101,451,000 and $94,534,000, respectively, of which $26,130,000 (1979) and $23,843,000 (1978) represent reforestation costs and $75,321,000 (1979) and $70,691,000 (1978) represent forest management expenditures. Timber replacement cost excludes replacement amounts for the land component of timberlands, minor amounts of acreage that will not be replaced and roadways. Estimated replacement cost amounts for timber harvested during 1979 and 1978, based on the replacement cost of fee timber and the amount of timber cut, were $3,515,000 and $2,696,000, respectively.

The above estimates are not comparable with the financial statement amounts for timberlands and roadways ($29,508,000 and $26,924,000 at August 31, 1979 and 1978, respectively) and depletion ($1,201,000 and $1,138,000 in 1979 and 1978, respectively). This is attributable primarily to the fact that forest management expenditures, amounting to $4,013,000 in 1979 and $3,235,000 in 1978, are charged to cost of sales as incurred for financial statement purposes.

Index

*This book has been set in 10 and 9 point Gael,
leaded 2 points. Part and chapter numbers are
Friz Quadrata Bold. Part and chapter titles
are Friz Quadrata regular. The size of the overall type page area is 30 by 48 picas.*